Industrial Law

Industrial Law

Eighth edition

I T Smith MA, LLB (CANTAB)
of Gray's Inn and Devereux Chambers, Barrister
Clifford Chance Professor of Employment Law
at the University of East Anglia
Member of the ACAS Panel of Industrial Arbitrators

Gareth Thomas LLB (WALES), BCL (OXON)
Director, Centre for Employment Law and
Senior Lecturer in Law at the University of East Anglia

Human Rights at Work section contributed by

David Mead BA (CANTAB), LLM (LOND)
Lecturer in Law at the University of East Anglia

LexisNexis™ UK

Members of the LexisNexis Group worldwide

United Kingdom	LexisNexis UK, a Division of Reed Elsevier (UK) Ltd, Halsbury House, 35 Chancery Lane, LONDON, WC2A 1EL, and 4 Hill Street, EDINBURGH EH2 3JZ
Argentina	LexisNexis Argentina, BUENOS AIRES
Australia	LexisNexis Butterworths, CHATSWOOD, New South Wales
Austria	LexisNexis Verlag ARD Orac GmbH & Co KG, VIENNA
Canada	LexisNexis Butterworths, MARKHAM, Ontario
Chile	LexisNexis Chile Ltda, SANTIAGO DE CHILE
Czech Republic	Nakladatelství Orac sro, PRAGUE
France	Editions du Juris-Classeur SA, PARIS
Germany	LexisNexis Deutschland GmbH, FRANKFURT, MUNSTER
Hong Kong	LexisNexis Butterworths, HONG KONG
Hungary	HVG-Orac, BUDAPEST
India	LexisNexis Butterworths, NEW DELHI
Ireland	LexisNexis, DUBLIN
Italy	Giuffrè Editore, MILAN
Malaysia	Malayan Law Journal Sdn Bhd, KUALA LUMPUR
New Zealand	LexisNexis Butterworths, WELLINGTON
Poland	Wydawnictwo Prawnicze LexisNexis, WARSAW
Singapore	LexisNexis Butterworths, SINGAPORE
South Africa	LexisNexis Butterworths, DURBAN
Switzerland	Stämpfli Verlag AG, BERNE
USA	LexisNexis, DAYTON, Ohio

© Reed Elsevier (UK) Ltd 2003

A CIP Catalogue record for this book is available from the British Library.

1st edn	1980
2nd edn	1983
3rd edn	1986
4th edn	1989
5th edn	1993
6th edn	1996
7th edn	2000

ISBN 0 406 96381 9

Typeset by Doyle & Co, Colchester
Printed and bound in Great Britain by Clays Ltd, Bungay, Suffolk

Visit LexisNexis UK at www.lexisnexis.co.uk

Preface

This has been a particularly difficult time in which to produce a new edition, but such an edition (on its desired three-year cycle) has certainly been necessary. The difficulty has arisen from the quite amazing pace of change that we have seen recently. The swan of state may seem to glide effortlessly along, but beneath the surface the webbed feet of legislation-producers such as the DTI have been paddling furiously. The output of consultation documents, draft regulations and their eventual forms has been unremitting. The Employment Act 2002 was a major event and is a mixture of truly primary legislation and power-giving provisions which will require considerable fleshing-out by the now inevitable raft of orders and regulations. We have seen one Big Bang in April 2003 in relation to new and amended family-friendly policies and, at the time of writing, it is likely that we will have another in October 2004 in relation to the new laws on disciplinary and grievance procedures. EU-inspired changes to discrimination laws (including the innovative coverage of religion/belief and sexual orientation) are to be largely in place by the end of 2003, with amendments to disability discrimination due in 2004 and (most difficult of all in its potential width and unforeseeable reach) age discrimination to be left until 2006.

Even without going to the case law (which has been significant since the last edition, even in areas long thought to be stable, such as vicarious liability for an employee's acts) the currency of this edition will see vital developments in the subject. Given the timescale of producing the new edition, we have stated the law as at May 2003, though it has sometimes been possible to allude to later developments, in particular the flurry of consultation documents in mid-2003. In fact, this has turned out to be not too bad a time for the new edition because most of these myriad developments, if not actually in force, have been at a relatively certain stage of development. The reader will, of course, have to ensure that he or she chases up where necessary the final form of any development referred to here as being in draft or at consultation stage at the time of writing.

ITS
GHT

Norwich
July 2003

Contents

Chapter 4

Wages and hours 214

Chapter 5

Discrimination in employment 267

Chapter 6

Maternity and parental rights 403

Table of statutes

References in this Table to *Statutes*, are to Halsbury's Statutes of England, Fourth
Edition, showing the page at which the annotated text may be found.
References printed in **bold** type indicate where the Act is set out in part or in full.

Table of statutory instruments

References in the right-hand column are to page number. Page references printed in **bold** type indicate where the Statutory Instrument is set out in part or in full.

Table of European legislation

References in the right-hand column are to page. Page references printed in **bold** type
indicate where the provision is set out in part or in full.

Table of cases

PAGE

PAGE

PAGE

PAGE

PAGE

PAGE

PAGE

PAGE

PAGE

PAGE

PAGE

PAGE

G

PAGE

H

PAGE

PAGE

PAGE

J

PAGE

PAGE

Kwik-Fit (GB) Ltd v Lineham [1992] ICR 183, [1992] IRLR 156, [1992] 4 LS
Gaz R 31, EAT 545, 551

L

PAGE

M

PAGE

PAGE

PAGE

PAGE

PAGE

PAGE

PAGE

PAGE

PAGE

V

PAGE

Decisions of the European Court of Justice are listed below numerically. These decisions are also included in the preceding alphabetical list.

PAGE

Table of decisions of the National Insurance and Social Security Commissioners

Chapter I

Introduction

I GENERAL

Industrial law has been the subject of as rapid a transformation as can have happened to any legal subject in recent times, and is certainly one of the most difficult areas of law in which to keep up to date. In some ways it is a curious mixture of ancient and modern, for much old law lies behind or at the basis of new statutory law and in some cases the old law continues to exist alongside the new (eg the continued existence of the separate actions for wrongful dismissal and unfair dismissal, the former being a common law action and the latter entirely a creation of statute). To take one small example, as late as 1969 it could still be seriously debated before the Court of Appeal[1] whether a general hiring of an employee (ie one not subject to any express time limitation) was a hiring only for a year, under the old 'presumption of a yearly hiring' which used to apply in the nineteenth century and before, principally in order to guarantee year-round employment for agricultural labourers, but which is now totally irrelevant to modern employment law. Ghosts can still clank their chains, particularly in the law relating to contracts of employment where a strictly contractual approach may not always lead to a realistic result. However, the subject is unrecognisable from what it was only forty years ago with the enormous increase in statute law and the ever increasing volume of case law on the modern statutes. Thus, the intending student must be able to exercise the lawyer's skill in dealing both with extensive case law and with major statutes, sometimes of astounding complexity. Moreover, he or she must be able to deal with this mass of law with a certain amount of intelligence and discernment, for example being able to tell when a line of old cases, authoritative in themselves, may be so out of line with the modern approach to employment or industrial relations that they are unlikely to be applied in practice, or to tell when a case on a modern statutory provision is merely *illustrative* (however interesting) rather than setting a definite precedent on a point of interpretation, for if this distinction is not borne in mind the student will soon find himself or herself buried alive under the case law, particularly in an area such as unfair dismissal where so much is vested in the discretion of the tribunal and, furthermore, where any actual point of law which does arise should normally be approached primarily by reference to the wording of the statute; the student will soon realise when reading this book (particularly chapter 8) that now, more than ever, this desire to escape from over-legalism in decision making on industrial matters is one of the dominant themes of modern industrial law. Case law of course remains important, but equally clearly some cases are more equal than others. While the approach of this book is avowedly legal, treating the subject as it now has to be treated as an important area of substantive law which leads in practice to a very considerable amount of litigation, at the same time it must be realised that in certain ways this is law with a difference; this must be reflected in the approach of the student, and it is hoped that it is reflected in this book, which in turn reflects the love-hate relationship to the law adopted by so many industrial relations practitioners.

As well as a whole new body of law, industrial law is also subject to a separate jurisdiction exercised by employment tribunals (with appeal to the Employment Appeal Tribunal (EAT), and only then into the ordinary court structure, with appeal to the Court of Appeal and then to the House of Lords). Even though tribunals gained some common law jurisdiction (on termination of employment) in 1994, not all matters may go to a tribunal, for many common law actions must still go to the ordinary courts (eg an action for breach of the contract of employment during employment, or the sort of action by a union member against his union for unconstitutional action that was so prevalent and so important during the course of the miners' strike of 1984/5). However, the large majority of cases which are brought do in fact go before the tribunals, and in the last few years the numbers of such cases have increased alarmingly.

This has led to a mushrooming in specialised sources and materials in industrial law, many ephemeral, but some of major practical use to the industrial lawyer. The two main series of law reports are the Industrial Cases Reports (ICR)[2] and the Industrial Relations Law Reports (IRLR)[3]; preference will be given to citation of these reports throughout this book. The Industrial Tribunal Reports (ITR) commenced publication in 1966 and have now ceased, to avoid further duplication. The leading academic journal is the Industrial Law Journal[4], and the principal up-dating aids, so vital in this rapidly developing subject, are:

(i)   The IDS Brief[5] – published twice per month; IDS also publish occasional supplements with the brief, covering recent developments in one particular topic, and the more substantial IDS Handbooks which aim to up-date the reader on the major areas of the subject.

(ii) The Industrial Relations Review and Report (IR-RR)[6] – also published twice a month; it covers industrial relations matters generally, but also includes a Legal Bulletin (IR-LB – separately numbered from the IR-RR itself) covering recent case law and 'guidance notes' on particular topics, and a Health and Safety Information Bulletin (HSIB – also separately numbered).

(iii) Various websites – some are of course private, subscripton sites, but of particular use as open public services are the websites of the Department of Trade and Industry: Employment Relations branch, the Stationery Office

1   *Richardson v Koefod* [1969] 3 All ER 1264, [1969] 1 WLR 1812, CA.
2   These are the official reports, published by the Incorporated Council of Law Reporting for England and Wales; until 1974 they were called the Industrial Court Reports.
3   Published by LexisNexis UK.
4   Published for the Industrial Law Society by Oxford University Press.
5   Published by Incomes Data Services, 140 Great Portland Street, London W1.
6   Published by Industrial Relations Services, through LexisNexis, n 3 above.

(particularly for new statutory instruments) and the Information Comissioner (for developments relation to data protection issues)[7].

The leading practitioner work is *Harvey on Industrial Relations and Employment Law*[8], a six-volume looseleaf work (updated six times per year, with a monthly Bulletin) which is used extensively by practitioners, advisers and tribunals, and is frequently cited in court judgments (especially in the EAT).

Codes of Practice are of ever increasing importance in industrial law, allowing the statute to lay down merely the general principle on a topic and then amplifying that principle in a way that is likely to be of more use to the people concerned; so far, they have been used in the fields of unfair dismissal, employment protection, union rights, picketing, the closed shop, health and safety at work and disability discrimination, and they should be consulted whenever appropriate. Also, much useful information can be obtained from the Annual Reports of ACAS. In the collective sphere the Donovan Report[9] should still be consulted, for it formed the analytical background to many of the reforms (successful or unsuccessful) in this area. Finally, many of the bodies connected with industrial relations in the widest sense publish from time to time reports or studies with important impacts upon the legal framework[10].

2 THE SCOPE OF THE SUBJECT AND THE LEGISLATIVE FRAMEWORK

The subject of industrial law may be split, for convenience if not for accuracy, into three principal areas – industrial safety law, employment law and the law relating to industrial relations. Each has a different legal and social background, and until recently the level (and type) of legal involvement was markedly different in each. Industrial safety law has a history of statutory intervention dating back to the beginning of the nineteenth century, with a formidable volume of case law on the statutes and on the actions which could be brought by an injured employee. Employment law, however, was based almost entirely upon the common law concept of the contract of employment; it attracted little statutory intervention and even much of the common law, though extensive in theory, was a dead letter in practice, principally due to the inadequacies of the remedies for breach of the employment contract by the employer. Industrial relations law was characterised by the voluntary principle and the abstention of the law (once legislation had been used in the latter part of the nineteenth century and the first part of the twentieth to legalise the operations and purposes of trade unions and to protect them and their members from tortious liability for industrial action); it is true that wage negotiation in certain industries was encouraged by Wages Councils which were the creation of statute, but even here the law merely provided a minimum framework and did not attempt to impose legal rights and duties on the substance of the negotiation itself.

---

7   These are at, respectively, www.dti.gov.uk/er; www.legislation.hmso.gov.uk; and www.dataprotection.gov.uk. In more specialised contexts, the websites of the discrimination bodies (EOC, CRE, DRC) and the Health and Safety Exectutive may be of use.
8   Published by Butterworths. Cross-references are made to *Harvey* in certain parts of this book, especially in the chapter on tribunals and unfair dismissal.
9   Report of the Royal Commission on Trade Unions and Employers' Associations Cmnd 3623 (1968) .
10 The annual reports of, the CAC, the Certification Officer, the EOC, the CRE and the Health and Safety Commission are particularly useful sources of information.

Major developments have occurred in the last three decades which have changed this previous picture, in some areas out of all recognition. In the industrial safety sphere, the major development has been the Health and Safety at Work etc. Act 1974 which creates administrative machinery, provides for more effective enforcement procedures and widens the general duties owed by employers (and others). One possible major development (in the area of compensation for industrial injuries) did not come about in the end, for the Pearson Commission on Civil Liability did *not* recommend the institution of a no-fault system of liability in place of our present tort system which depends essentially upon the ability to prove fault or breach of statutory duty. However, the substance of our safety laws has now been subject to major reform from a different source, namely the EU, with increased emphasis on attempting to harmonise laws on major safety matters throughout the Community[11].

Employment law has been the subject of major revision by the provision of new statutory rights for those in employment (and, in the area of sex, race and disability discrimination, for those seeking employment); moreover, these rights (which usually have little or no dependence upon the theoretical contractual basis of employment) are now the subject of *realistic* enforcement procedures through the tribunal system and so are doubly preferable to most common law rights. These rights are many and various, from what is now a relatively minor matter such as minimum periods of notice according to length of service, to the more important employment protection rights; clearly the most important is the right not to be unfairly dismissed, and these cases have always constituted a major part of the tribunals' case load.

Industrial relations law suffered a great upheaval with the Industrial Relations Act 1971, which unsuccessfully attempted to impose an overall legislative framework on industrial relations, giving rights and imposing duties by law as is done in some other jurisdictions. The Act was repealed in toto in 1974 (except for the unfair dismissal provisions, which were re-enacted), but ironically we then saw under the same Labour government the enactment of significant new legal rights for trade unions which were capable of having an effect on some of the most fundamental aspects of collective labour relations, such as recognition, bargaining information, standardisation of terms and conditions throughout an industry, prior consultation on impending redundancies and direct union involvement in safety procedures. Certainly, where industrial relations remain on a collective level (and there has been a significant decline in collective bargaining over the past two decades), such relations are still on a voluntary basis and voluntary procedures remain paramount; however, this field is no longer devoid of legal intervention, and the modern legislation has also played an important part in setting up machinery for the settlement of certain industrial disputes (in particular, the Advisory, Conciliation and Arbitration Service and the Central Arbitration Committee) and subsequently in placing stringent limitations on what the previous Conservative government saw as unacceptable forms of industrial action or unacceptable purposes behind such industrial action, while at the same time they sought ever greater deregulation of the labour market itself.

The whole subject is thus heavily overlaid with modern statutes[12]. In the employment law area, this process started with the Contracts of Employment Act 1963 (consolidated in 1972) which introduced new rules on notice periods,

---

11   See, in particular the six new sets of regulations ('The Six Pack') which came into force on 1 January 1993 and revolutionised our workplace legislation, ch. 13, below.
12   The statutes currently in force are set out, with annotations, in *Harvey*, Division Q.

required an employer to give his employee a written statement of terms of employment, and laid down for the first time the statutory rules on 'continuity of employment' which were to take on much greater significance when more extensive employee rights were later enacted which depended on the concept of continuity (either for qualification for rights or computation of benefits, or both). The first of these rights was the right to a redundancy payment under the Redundancy Payments Act 1965. As well as attempting to introduce a new, but politically unacceptable, framework for industrial relations, the Industrial Relations Act 1971 was notable for introducing the new law on unfair dismissal, and this was re-enacted by the Trade Union and Labour Relations Act 1974 which repealed the 1971 Act and (a) restored the essentially voluntary nature of industrial relations (abolishing, in the process, the National Industrial Relations Court which had adjudicated cases arising under the 1971 Act) and (b) consolidated the law relating to trade union immunities and internal affairs; the 1974 Act was itself amended by the Trade Union and Labour Relations (Amendment) Act 1976 which made the immunities more watertight, abolished the statutory action against a union for unfair expulsion or exclusion, and tightened up the law on the closed shop.

The Employment Protection Act 1975 made significant steps forward in many directions. On the collective side, it gave statutory backing to ACAS, set up the CAC and introduced the important new trade union rights mentioned above; it also set up the Employment Appeal Tribunal (to take the place of the NIRC) and modernised the provisions relating to wages councils. On the individual employment side, it introduced new employment protection rights (eg guarantee payments, time off work for union purposes, a right not to be discriminated against on trade union grounds, and the rights relating to maternity pay and leave) and it made significant alterations to the law on unfair dismissal (particularly as regards the available remedies). By this time, the statute law was something of a jungle and indeed was on one occasion castigated in the House of Lords as a bad example of legislation by reference, in that it was frequently the case that a point of law could only be discovered by referring to separate but complementary provisions in two or more Acts. The *individual* aspects were therefore consolidated into the Employment Protection (Consolidation) Act 1978 which covered particulars of terms of employment, employment protection rights, termination of employment, unfair dismissal, redundancy payments, and industrial tribunals and the EAT, and was for years the principal statute.

The Employment Act 1980 marked a major change of direction after the election in 1979 of a Conservative government. Although it adopted, at the very beginning of that government, a 'softly, softly' approach, avoiding a rerun of the Industrial Relations Act 1971, it started the remarkable transformation of industrial law that marked the 1980s. On the collective side, it affected statutory trade union rights by repealing the provisions of the Employment Protection Act 1975 relating to the statutory recognition procedure and the extension of terms and conditions of employment by the CAC ('Schedule 11 claims'). It also affected the internal government of trade unions by allowing financial support for union elections and by reinstating a statutory right of complaint to a tribunal for people unreasonably expelled or excluded from a union where there is a closed shop in operation. The law relating to picketing was altered, and new curbs introduced on secondary industrial action. On the individual side, the Act altered certain aspects of unfair dismissal law (principally those relating to the burden of proof, the closed shop and compensation) and made changes in the rules governing maternity rights and guarantee pay.

The Employment Act 1982, an altogether 'drier' statute by a more established government, contained some new provisions (eg altering the law of unfair dismissal in cases where the persons dismissed were on strike) and a host of minor amendments. However, it was principally designed to tighten up the 1980 Act in two areas – the closed shop and the law on industrial disputes. With regard to the former, it imposed more stringent procedural requirements of balloting, radically increased the compensation payable to an employee unfairly dismissed because of a closed shop, and made it more likely that in such a case compensation will in fact be paid by the union rather than the employer. Also, new provisions were introduced to discourage the inclusion of union-labour-only requirements in contracts and tenders. In the area of industrial disputes, the Act basically left alone the restrictions introduced by the 1980 Act (though with a tightening-up of the definition of 'trade dispute' on which the statutory immunities are based); however, the radical change in the 1982 Act was the removal of the union's complete immunity from suit in tort (which the unions had had, with the exception of the years of the Industrial Relations Act 1971, since the Trade Disputes Act 1906), so that now the union itself may be sued (subject to statutory maxima on the damages recoverable) if it contravenes the strengthened laws on industrial disputes.

The Trade Union Act 1984 (following the 1983 election when 'giving unions back to their members' was a prominent Conservative theme) was the third major statute passed by the previous government, but in large part marked a significant departure. While Part II can be seen as following on from the Employment Acts 1980 and 1982 by allowing an employer to sue a union (for damages or an injunction) if the union takes strike or other industrial action without the now obligatory strike ballot, Parts I and III were different in that the causes of action contained within them are vested in the union *members*. Part I obliged a union to hold secret ballots for high union offices and Part III introduced compulsory periodic reballoting on whether a union should continue to operate a political fund. This Act was therefore aimed at the *internal* affairs of a trade union particularly as the events surrounding the miners' strike and certain other major industrial disputes tended to show a greater degree of readiness on the part of union members (or of whole sections of a union) to resort to legal action in order to secure compliance with the union's rules. This process was taken a stage further by the Employment Act 1988 (following the 1987 election and the experiences of the miners' strike), which tightened up some of the provisions of the 1984 Act (in relation to balloting) and introduced certain new statutory rights for union members (eg rights to ballots before industrial action, to inspect union accounts, to restrain unlawful expenditure by the union and not to be unjustifiably disciplined); to assist in the enforcement of rights against a union, the Act also established the office of Commissioner for the Rights of Trade Union Members. In one respect, the Act harked back to the early legislation of that government, for it took the changes to the law on the closed shop to their logical conclusion by removing *all* legal protection from it as an institution, so that it is now no longer possible for a union to establish or maintain a legally effective, post-entry closed shop.

While the Employment Act 1989 was largely a tinkering measure, the Employment Act 1990 in several ways set the seal on a decade of change[13], taking

13   Highly recommended reading to set this series of statutes into their political context is Auerbach *Legislating for Conflict* (1990), commented on in Foch et al 'Politics, pragmatism and ideology: the wellsprings of Conservative union legislation' (1993) 22 ILJ 14; and Davies and Freedland *Labour Legislation and Public Policy* (1993). The political progress of the three governments of Mrs Thatcher is set out in excellent and highly readable form in Young *One of Us* (1990).

several themes first developed in 1980 to their logical conclusions. In particular, it rendered illegal the *pre*-entry closed shop, made illegal *all* secondary action and attacked *un*official industrial action. Thus, by 1990 laws were in place which many Conservatives would have liked to have seen in 1980, had they been able to wave a magic wand. Crucially, of course, by that time there had also been a significant decrease in union membership, a radical decrease in union influence and a very noticeable move away, in many areas, from collectively negotiated terms and conditions of employment, towards more individual contracting, flexibility in employment and more use of what used to be called atypical employments. Indeed, by the early 1990s the encouragement of such moves had been adopted as government policy[14], along with continuing deregulation.

After the fourth Conservative election victory in 1992, another Bill was expected, though possibly of a tinkering nature again, meant politically to show that the government had not run out of steam in the hitherto politically profitable area of industrial relations. However, the Trade Union Reform and Employment Rights Act 1993 turned out to be far more than that. It again addressed union elections and ballots, and the financial affairs of unions; it recast members' rights on disciplining and expulsion; further restrictions were introduced on industrial action (including strike notice and a Citizen's Charter right for individuals to challenge industrial action in the public sector). In the individual field, it altered the laws on maternity, employment particulars, redundancy consultation and transfers of undertakings in response to changes in EC law, and introduced two new heads of unfair dismissal. As a logical, but much criticised, further measure to deregulate the labour market, it finally abolished wages councils.

Outside the above mainstream legislation, the 1980s also saw very significant changes in social security laws relevant to industrial law (especially payment through the employer, through statutory sick pay and statutory maternity pay), and the Wages Act 1986 introduced new laws on deductions from wages that saw quite remarkable development in the early 1990s. In the field of discrimination law there were, again, consistent developments, but this time largely through the intervention of EC law rather than changes in domestic legislation. If all of this does not provide the reader with enough excitement in life, there are always the Transfer of Undertakings Regulations ...

Given this quite remarkable series of statutes (and, often, their supporting regulations and orders) we have at least been fortunate in having five major consolidations in the period 1992–1996, bringing some order to the chaos. The Trade Union and Labour Relations (Consolidation) Act 1992 consolidated the morass of laws (ancient and modern) on collective labour law, replacing in particular the Trade Union and Labour Relations Act 1974 and most of the Conservative Employment Acts 1980–1993. Social security law was consolidated into the Social Security Contributions and Benefits Act 1992 and the Social Security Administration Act 1992; it took a particularly strong river to clean out those Augean stables, and shortly after it was done major changes were then made by the Social Security (Incapacity for Work) Act 1994 and the Jobseekers Act 1995 (though largely by amending the two Consolidation Acts, which therefore remain the primary source). The law relating to individual employment matters was finally consolidated in the Employment Rights Act 1996 which replaced the Employment Protection (Consolidation) Act 1978 (as, by then, heavily amended) and the Wages Act 1986, with the law relating to tribunals and the EAT being

14 Employment for the 1990s (Cm 540, 1988); People, Jobs and Opportunity (Cm 1810, 1992).

consolidated at the same time in the Industrial Tribunals Act 1996 (since renamed the Employment Tribunals Act 1996). Outside that framework lay the Equal Pay Act 1970, the Sex Discrimination Act 1975, the Race Relations Act 1976, the Disability Discrimination Act 1995 and the Pensions Act 1995.

The 1997 General Election saw the end of a period of eighteen years of Conservative administrations and a landslide victory for New Labour. Dramatic though this political reversal of fortunes was, it was far removed from the previous return of a Labour government in 1974, when the Trade Union and Labour Relations Act 1974 (sweeping away the previous Conservative government's employment laws) was the first statute passed by that incoming government. Instead, New Labour seemed to put a relatively low priority on employment law changes (reflecting the equally low priority of the subject at the election), and it had been made clear for some time by the 'modernisers' within the party that there were to be no wholesale repeals of the reforms of the Thatcher administration[15]. Indeed, the first statute passed was the Employment Rights (Dispute Resolution) Act 1998 (reforming tribunal procedures and establishing the ACAS arbitration alternative to tribunals for unfair dismissal cases) which was inherited at Green Paper stage from the previous government. The National Minimum Wage Act 1998 enacted one of New Labour's relatively few election commitments on employment law, and the Working Time Regulations 1998 were an obligation under EC law (the previous government's challenge to the legality of the backing Directive having failed in the ECJ); the Public Interest Disclosure (or 'Whistleblowers') Act 1998 was also in many ways relatively uncontroversial and commanded widespread support. It was only with the publication of the White Paper 'Fairness at Work'[16] that a clear idea could be obtained of the likely direction of the new government in this area. Again, however, in spite of some reforms important in themselves, this was hardly a major sea-change, and even then the government were accused of some back-sliding by the unions on the eventual form of the resulting statute, the Employment Relations Act 1999, especially in relation to the union recognition procedure and the mere lifting of the limit on the unfair dismissal compensatory award (from £12,000 to £15,000), rather than its abolition as had been mooted in the White Paper. The introduction to the White Paper said that this Act was not to be seen as merely a first step in reforms, because it 'seeks to draw a line under the issue of industrial relations law' and this was largely the case in the first Labour government, at least in relation to purely domestic legislation (though with amendments to discrimination law – the Disability Rights Commission Act 1999 and the Race Relations (Amendment) Act 2000). However, the second Labour government (after their emphatic re-election in 2001) has seen a renewed increase in the pace of domestic legislation with the enactment of the Employment Act 2002, a bad example of 'Henry VIII' drafting, ie requiring supplementation by a huge raft of statutory instruments over a prolonged period (possibly stretching into 2004). The two main themes of this Act were the extension of family-friendly

---

15 'The abolition of the closed shop was one of the many employment law reforms of the 1980s that were justified and will remain . . . Other measures which will remain include those on picketing, secondary action, ballots and notice before strikes, unofficial action, elections for certain trade union offices and rights to join the trade union of one's choice and not to be unjustifiably disciplined': Fairness at Work (Cm. 3968, May 1998), p 22. For the background political changes, especially in relations with the trade unions, see McIlroy 'The enduring alliance? Trade unions and the making of the New Labour 1994–1997' (1998) 36 BJIR 537.

16 See n 15, above. See generally Taylor 'Annual review article 1997' (1998) 36 BJIR 293.

policies (longer maternity leave; paternity and adoption leave; the right to request flexible working) and fairly desperate attempts to halt the inexorable rise in tribunal applications by further reforms to tribunal procedures and the enactment of basic procedures for dismissal and grievances, which are to become, in effect, compulsory. At the same time as these developments, EC law was becoming more active. Prior to the 2001 election there had been the transposition of one Directive in the Part-time Workers (Prevention of Less Favourable Treatment) Regulations 2000, SI 2000/1551, and not long after it the transposition of another in the Fixed-term Employees (Prevention of Less Favourable Treatment) Regulations 2002, SI 2002/2034. Waiting in the wings (at the time of writing) are the new Equal Treatment Directive 2000/78/EC (requiring laws on sexual orientation and religious discrimination by 2003 and on disability and age discrimination by 2006), the Information and Consultation Directive 2002/14/EC (requiring mechanisms for consulting and informing the workforce in large firms of 150 or more employees by 2005, firms of 100 or more by 2007 and finally firms of 50 or more by 2008) and the possibility of a Directive on temporary/agency workers, to complete the trilogy with part-timers and fixed-termers.

From this review it will be clear that statute law now dominates much of this subject, but at the same time it must be recognised that there are certain areas where the common law is still very much alive. Further, much of the statute law in both the individual and collective spheres rests on two non-statutory foundations – first the status of a person in question as an *employee* and secondly the voluntary principle which still governs the substance of most industrial relations. It is to these two, fundamental, non-statutory foundations that we must now turn, following that by introductory consideration of two other major influences on the subject, namely the existing and longer-term influence of Europe and the potential influence of the Human Rights Act 1998.

3 THE RELATIONSHIP OF EMPLOYER AND EMPLOYEE

The fact that someone is an employee of someone else is a major jurisdictional factor in several areas of law, for example in tort law on the question of vicarious liability, and in the fields of taxation and social security on the questions of assessment, payment and contributions. In industrial law, both ancient and modern, it is often of fundamental importance; most of the common law on employment only applies to employees, and it has hitherto been the same with the important statutory rights which usually require the applicant to be an employee and to have served a certain qualifying period as such[17]. As the only definition of 'employee' in the Employment Rights Act 1996 and the Trade Union and Labour Relations (Consolidation) Act 1992[18] is 'an individual who has entered into or works under (or, where the employment has ceased, worked under) a contract of employment', the question of what constitutes a contract of employment is left to the courts and tribunals. The major divide here is between

---

17 For the arguments in favour of freeing statutory employment rights from their present basis on the contract of employment, see Hepple 'Restructuring Employment Rights' (1986) 15 ILJ 69; for a criticism that court tend still to lean too strongly on contractual principles when interpreting employement statutes, see Anderman 'The interpretation of protective employement statutes and contracts of employment' (2000) 29 ILJ 223.

18 Ss 230(1) and 295 respectively.

employment and self-employment, between a contract of employment and a contract for services (although other relationships such as agency or partnership could perhaps be used to avoid the relationship of employer and employee and the concept of the 'office holders' has occasionally caused problems for such individuals trying to enforce statutory rights[19]). A person with a contract for services is usually referred to as an 'independent contractor' and there may be several reasons why an individual may wish to be classed as such; the prime one is usually taxation, for there may well be tax advantages in being self-employed, of a legal nature (ie tax avoidance through being assessed under Schedule D with its payment at least partly in arrears and more generous allowances) or an illegal nature (ie tax evasion through part- or non-disclosure of income, not being under the PAYE system for Schedule E taxation of employees). From the employer's point of view it may be desirable to hire independent contractors, for this relieves him of the administrative tasks involved in deducting PAYE deductions and national insurance contributions from wages, and may relieve him of certain other administrative burdens (eg statutory sick pay and statutory maternity pay); further, it may have certain VAT advantages and help to avoid the need to negotiate with unions (indeed in an area of large-scale self-employment such as the building industry it may be a long-standing cause of weak unionism generally)[20].

Advantages to the individual, however, tend to be of a short-term nature, and categorisation as 'independent' may have certain serious longer-term disadvantages, for most of the industrial safety legislation, some of the most important social security rights (particularly disablement benefit and jobseeker's allowance) and much of the modern employment protection legislation only applies to employed persons – to put it shortly, the independent contractor may be in a better monetary position while working, but at a grave disadvantage if he falls off a ladder or is sacked. Moreover, categorisation as independent may indirectly affect the rights of third parties too, for example a passer-by injured by the acts of that person, for the action then lies only against that independent contractor and *not* against the employer who may in the realities of the case be the only person worth suing[21].

(i) Definition of the relationship

In spite of the obvious importance of the distinction between an employee and an independent contractor, the tests to be applied are vague and may, in a

---

19 In *Lincolnshire County Council v Hopper* [2002] ICR 1301 a registrar of birth, deaths and marriages was unable to claim unfair dismissal. See generally the discussion of different kinds of office holding by Morison P in *Johnson v Ryan* [2000] IRLR 236 where, on the facts, it was held that a rent officer could so claim.

20 Bird 'The self employed: small entrepreneurs or disguised wage labourers?' in Pollert (ed) *Farewell to Flexibility* (1991). In the winter of 1997/98 3.3m people were self-employed in their main job, which was 13% of all those in work; of these, 74% were men and 26% women: Moralee 'Self employment in the 1990s' [1998] Labour Market Trends 121.

21 There are certain exemptions to this general rule, where an employer can be liable for the acts of his independent contractor, but they are narrow and, in some cases, uncertain: see *Clerk and Lindsell on Torts* (2000) paras 3–36ff and Grugg (ed) *The Law of Tort* (2002) pp 115–117.

22 The tests to be applied are a matter of law, but the *application* of those tests is a question of fact; where it arises in a statutory action, this means that the decision on categorisation lies almost entirely with the employment tribunal with little chance of a successful appeal from their decision: *O'Kelly v Trusthouse Forte plc* [1983] ICR 728, [1983] IRLR 369, CA; *Lee v Chung* [1990] ICR 409, [1990] IRLR 236, PC; see p 501, below, and Leighton (1984) 13 ILJ 62.

borderline case, be difficult to apply.[22] Historically, the solution lay in applying the 'control' test, ie could the employer control not just what the person was to do, but also the manner of his doing it – if so, that person was his employee[23]. In the context in which it mainly arose in the nineteenth century, of domestic, agricultural and manual workers, this test had much to commend it, but with the increased sophistication of industrial processes and the greater numbers of professional and skilled people being in salaried employment, it soon became obvious that the test was insufficient[24] (for example in the case of a doctor, architect, skilled engineer, pilot, etc.) and so, despite certain attempts to modernise it[25], it is now accepted that in itself control is no longer the sole test, though it does remain a factor and perhaps, in some cases, a decisive one[26]. In the search for a substitute test, ideas have been put forward of an 'integration' test, ie whether the person was fully integrated into the employer's concern, or remained apart from and independent of it[27]. Once again, this is not now viewed as a sufficient test in itself, but rather as a potential factor (which may be useful in allowing a court to take a wider and more realistic view). The modern approach has been to abandon the search for a single test, and instead to take a multiple or 'pragmatic' approach, weighing up all the factors for and against a contract of employment and determining on which side the scales eventually settle[28]. As Cook J put it, in his much-cited judgment in *Market Investigations Ltd v Minister of Social Security*[29] the question ultimately is whether the person in question is performing the services as 'a person in business on his own account'; factors which are usually of importance are as follows – the power to select and dismiss, the direct payment of some form of remuneration, deduction of PAYE and national insurance contributions[30], the organisation of the workplace, the supply of tools and materials (though there can still be a labour-only sub-contract) and the economic realities (in particular who bears the risk of loss and has the chance of profit); however, even this is not an exhaustive check list, and a court or tribunal

---

23 See, eg, *Performing Right Society Ltd v Mitchell and Booker (Palais de Danse) Ltd* [1924] 1 KB 762; *Mersey Docks and Harbour Board v Coggins and Griffiths (Liverpool) Ltd* [1947] AC 1, [1946] 2 All ER 345, HL.

24 *Cassidy v Ministry of Health* [1951] 2 KB 343, [1951] 1 All ER 574, CA (a surgeon).

25 See, eg, *Zuijs v Wirth Bros Ltd* (1955) 93 CLR 561 (concerning the control which could be exercised over a circus acrobat).

26 Particularly where the control demonstrates the reality of the relationship (eg in a case where there is more than one possible employer): *Clifford v Union of Democratic Mineworkers* [1991] IRLR 518, CA.

27 *Stevenson Jordan & Harrison Ltd v McDonald and Evans* [1952] 1 TLR 101, CA, per Denning LJ.

28 *Ready Mixed Concrete (South East) Ltd v Minister of Pensions and National Insurance* [1968] 2 QB 497, [1968] 1 All ER 433; *Construction Industry Training Board v Labour Force Ltd* [1970] 3 All ER 220; *Global Plant Ltd v Secretary of State for Health and Social Security* [1972] 1 QB 139, [1971] 3 All ER 385; *Hitchcock v Post Office* [1980] ICR 100; *Andrews v King* [1991] ICR 846, [1991] STC 481 (a fascinating tax case on the legal position of the archaic system of agricultural gang labour).

29 [1969] 2 QB 173, [1968] 3 All ER 732, approved and applied by the Privy Council in *Lee v Chung* [1990] ICR 409, [1990] IRLR 236.

30 Though perhaps a potent factor, this is not decisive (being primarily a matter between the person and the tax and insurance authorities) and so the non-deduction of these sums does *not* inevitably point to an independent contract if the other factors are against it: *Davis v New England College of Arundel* [1977] ICR 6; *Airfix Footwear Ltd v Cope* [1978] ICR 1210, [1978] IRLR 396; *Thames Television Ltd v Wallis* [1979] IRLR 136; conversely, deduction of these amounts does not per se mean that the relationship is one of employment: *O'Kelly v Trusthouse Forte plc*, n 22 above.

31 *Hall (Inspector of Taxes) v Lorimer* [1994] ICR 218, [1994] IRLR 171, CA.

must still look at the overall picture in the particular case[31]. A further development in the modern case law (particularly concerning atypical employments) has been the idea of 'mutuality of obligations' as a possible factor, ie whether the course of dealings between the parties demonstrates sufficient such mutuality for there to be an overall employment relationship. It is true that such an approach can be disadvantageous to certain particularly irregular workers, making it more difficult to establish that they are employees[32], but on the other hand it has the positive aspect that it is capable of extending employed status to groups of atypical workers (especially of an external or part-time nature) if the relationship with the employer is sufficiently longstanding and stable; thus in *Nethermere (St Neots) Ltd v Gardiner*[33] outworkers making garments at home on a piecework basis were held to be employees of the garment manufacturer, largely because of the regular, longstanding arrangement which showed the necessary mutuality of obligations (to do and to be provided with the work) in practice, even though the outworkers were not covered by a formal contractual obligation to undertake a particular quantity of work; this is an important development, capable of extending employee status (and thereby employment rights) to workers employed otherwise than on a nine-to-five basis on the employer's premises. On the other hand, 'mutuality' was used as an argument *against* employee status for 'casual, as required' power station guides in the rather regressive decision of the House of Lords in *Carmichael v National Power plc*[34], where it was seen as an irreducible minimum for the existence of a contract of employment. This idea of an 'irreducible minimum' is rather worrying because it could cut across the usual approach of weighing all the factors (all factors are equal, but some are more equal than others) and could be seen as the higher courts searching for a philosopher's stone in this area. It was seen again in *Express & Echo Publications Ltd v Tanton*[35] where the Court of Appeal viewed personal service as an irreducible minimum (so that a power to delegate by the individual was fatal to employment status). While it is true that *Tanton* was 'explained' and restrictively interpreted by the EAT in later cases[36], the Court of Appeal showed a similar approach again in *Montgomery v Johnson Underwood Ltd*[37] in relation to a necessary amount of control by the employer. We have therefore seen qualifications on the pure 'balancing of factors' approach in the higher courts, but reluctance to go down such a route in the (specialist) EAT.

Finally, given the vagueness of the tests, there is considerable scope for an 'instinctive' approach in this area, ie that the judge knows a contract of employment when he sees one. In *Cassidy v Ministry of Health*[38], Somervell LJ said:

> 'One perhaps cannot get too much beyond this, "Was the contract a contract of [employment] within the meaning which an ordinary person would give under the words?"'

32   *O'Kelley v Trusthouse Forte plc* [1983] ICR 728, [1983] IRLR 369, CA; *Wickens v Champion Employment* [1984] ICR 365.
33   [1984] ICR 612, [1984] IRLR 240, CA.
34   [1999] ICR 1226, [2000] IRLR 43, HL, applied in *Stevedoring Haulage Services Ltd v Fuller* [2001] IRLR 627, CA, where the employer had set this argument up in advance by saying in the hiring contract that there were to be *no* mutual obligations between the parties.
35   [1999] ICR 693, [1999] IRLR 367, CA.
36   *MacFarlane v Glasgow City Council* [2001] IRLR 7; *Byrne Bros Ltd v Baird* [2002] ICR 667, [2002] IRLR 96.
37   [2001] IRLR 269, CA.
38   [1951] 2 KB 343, [1951] 1 All ER 574, CA at 352 and 579 respectively; see also McKenna J's third condition for a contract of employment in the *Ready Mixed Concrete* case, n 28 above. *Withers v Flackwell Heath Football Supporters' Club* [1981] IRLR 307.

This may be unsatisfactory from an analytical point of view, but it probably reflects the practical position and indeed may not be as unsatisfactory as it first seems when considered in the context of the modern statutory rights where it falls to be applied by employment tribunals where the lay members may be expected to apply their industrial experience in its resolution[39]. The real problem with a vague test or tests is, however, that it can make advising in advance very difficult; not only is this a problem for the lawyer, but also it concerns an area of fundamental importance for both employer and employee who need to be certain as to the legal basis of their relationship. The parties' primary contact on this matter is likely to be, not with lawyers or tribunals, but with government departments and agencies, in particular the Inland Revenue[40] and the DSS; given the practical importance of such contacts, there has unfortunately been evidence in the past of different departments and agencies giving different advice and using different criteria on a person's employment status[41]. The previous government acknowledged that this can cause problems for employers and undertook to make internal changes to lessen the possibility of it happening[42]. In the context of taxation, the Inland Revenue has published a leaflet 'Tax: Employed or Self-Employed'[43] which attempts to clarify the distinction between employment and self-employment, using the criteria set out above. While stressing that no one factor is a conclusive test, it suggests that you are an employee if you can answer 'yes' to the following questions[44]: Do you have to do the work that you have agreed to undertake yourself? Can someone tell you what to do, and when and how to do it? Are you paid so much an hour, a week or a month? Can you get overtime pay? Are you expected to work set hours, or a given number of hours a week or month? Are you expected to work at the premises of the person you are working for, or at a place or places they decide? It is then suggested that you are self-employed if you can answer 'yes' to the following questions: Are you ultimately responsible for how the business is run? Do you risk your own capital? Are you responsible for bearing losses as well as taking profits? Do you provide the major items of equipment you need to do your job? Are you free to hire other people, on terms of your own choice, to do the work that you have agreed to undertake? Do you have to correct unsatisfactory work in your own time and at your own expense? While these are not authoritative statements of law, and ultimately the decision on a person's status may have to be taken by a court or tribunal, it is to be welcomed that at least an attempt is being made to standardise the rules of the game (in the most important context in which in practice the issue initially

---

39   *Challinor v Taylor* [1972] ICR 129; *Thames Television Ltd v Wallis* [1979] IRLR 136.
40   In many cases, the parties will in practice consider that they have successfully created the relationship of self-employment if the Inland Revenue have accepted it and not required the employer to operate the PAYE system. As stated above, however, this is not legally conclusive and the Inland Revenue can later decide to reconsider, the second principle of tax law being that the Revenue cannot be estopped (the first principle being that they always win eventually).
41   See Leighton 'Observing Employment Contracts' (1984) 13 ILJ 86.
42   'Lifting the Burden' (Cmnd 9571, 1985) paras 4.13, 4.14.
43   IR56. See also IR53 'Thinking of taking someone on?'.
44   The leaflet does not, however, explain what is the position if you answer 'yes' to half of these questions and to half of the next set of questions!

arises, ie tax and NI contributions), though one might be cynical and say that in marginal cases a game is precisely what it remains[45].

In addition to the general uncertainties here, one particular problem has caused some disagreement in the cases; it concerns the emphasis (or lack of it) which can be placed upon the statements and intentions of the parties themselves. They may stipulate (orally or in writing) that their contract shall be viewed one way (usually as an independent contract) – how is the court or tribunal to treat that?[46] In the past the usual approach has been to ignore the statements of the parties and apply an objective test[47], and this can be seen in the decision of the Court of Appeal in *Ferguson v John Dawson & Partners (Contractors) Ltd*[48] where a man taken on at a building site with no written contract but on an oral understanding that he was on the 'lump', ie a labour-only sub-contractor, who was later injured, was held to have been in fact an employee (and so able to rely on certain industrial safety provisions in order to bring his action). The majority, Megaw and Brown LJJ, took a clearly objective approach and said that a declaration by the parties, even if incorporated into the contract, should be *disregarded entirely* if the remainder of the contractual terms pointed to the opposite conclusion (though for the purpose of their decision, they were prepared to adopt the less stringent approach that such a declaration or statement can be a relevant, but certainly not conclusive, factor). Lawton LJ dissented strongly, stating[49]:

'… I can see no reason why in law a man cannot sell his labour without becoming another man's servant even though he is willing to accept control as to how, when and where he shall work. If he makes his intention not to be a servant sufficiently clear, the implications which would normally arise from implied terms do not override the prime object of the bargain. In my judgment, this is just such a case.'

In a subsequent Court of Appeal case, *Massey v Crown Life Insurance Co*[50] however, a different approach was taken. In that case a branch manager who was an ordinary employee asked to change the basis of his contract to self-employment (for tax purposes); the employer consented to this and negotiated a new agreement. When the agreement was subsequently terminated, the manager tried to claim

---

45 With the Inland Revenue permanently having the service, through their ability to raise an assessment on the basis that they have decided upon (usually employment and Schedule E), leaving it up to the employer and/or 'employee' to appeal and challenge the correctness of that basis. In the light of this, the National Federation of the Self-Employed argued for a registration system for self-employment, with registration under it being conclusive of a person's status, and the Institute of Directors put forward the most radical proposal, that people should simply be able to *elect* to be self-employed. Neither of these suggestions has been taken up officially.

46 There may be the added complication that the employee is now trying to *change* the basis of the contract, eg where he initially agreed to be self-employed, but has now been injured or dismissed and so needs to show that he was in fact an employee in order to claim the appropriate remedy.

47 For examples, see *Davis v New England College of Arundel* [1977] ICR 6; *Tyne and Clyde Warehouses Ltd v Hamerton* [1978] ICR 661; *Thames Television Ltd v Wallis* [1979] IRLR 136.

48 [1976] 3 All ER 817, [1976] IRLR 346, CA.

49 [1976] 3 All ER 817 at 828, [1976] IRLR 346 and 351.

50 [1978] ICR 590, [1978] IRLR 31, CA, applied in *BSM (1257) Ltd v Secretary of State for Social Services* [1978] ICR 894 and *Calder v H Kitson Vickers & Sons (Engineers) Ltd* [1988] ICR 232, CA.

unfair dismissal on the basis that he was in fact an employee all along, but the Court of Appeal held unanimously that he could not do so, since the new agreement had effectively altered the basis of his engagement so that he was no longer an employee. It must be said at the outset that the desire to avoid a position whereby a person could claim various tax advantages, and then argue exactly to the contrary to obtain unfair dismissal benefits at a later stage, obviously played a part in this decision[51] but, in spite of that, the approach to the problem was different from that of the previous Court of Appeal. Lord Denning MR said[52]:

'It seems to me on the authorities that, when it is a situation which is in doubt or which is ambiguous, so that it can be brought under one relationship or the other, it is open to the parties by agreement to stipulate what the legal situation between them shall be. ... So the way in which the parties draw up their agreement and express it can be a very important factor in defining what the true relation was between them. If they declare that one party is self-employed, that may be decisive.'

His Lordship distinguished the *Ferguson* case quite simply 'on its facts' and Lawton LJ did likewise (pointing primarily to the lack of a written agreement or, indeed of any particularly reliable evidence as to the relationship in that case), adding[53]:

'*Ferguson* clearly established that the parties cannot change a status merely by putting a new label on it. But if in all the circumstances of the case, including the terms of the agreement, it is manifest that there was an intention to change status, then, in my judgment, there is no reason why the parties should not be allowed to make the change.'

However, this wider approach in *Massey* was called into question in the further Court of Appeal case of *Young & Woods Ltd v West*[54] where a sheet metal worker who had been engaged on a self-employed basis (and had been treated as such by the Inland Revenue) was held to have in fact been an employee so that after his dismissal he could claim unfair dismissal. The court did not indicate that *Massey's* case was wrong, and did not take as purely an objective approach as the majority in *Ferguson's* case would have liked to do. They did, however, seek to narrow the effect of *Massey's* case; in particular they did not accept that if the parties deliberately set out to create a relationship of self-employment, that intention should normally be put into effect by a court or tribunal. A further contribution to this question was made by Lord Hoffmann in *Carmichael v National Power plc*[55] , where 'casual, as required' power station guides were held not to be employees; pointing out that in reality many employment relationships will not be contained purely in written form, but will also need to be discerned from correspondence and conduct, he envisaged a significant role for the parties' intentions, at least as a factor:

'The evidence of a party as to what terms he understood to have been agreed is some evidence tending to show that those terms, in an objective

51 See also the dissenting judgment of Lawton LJ in *Ferguson v John Dawson & Partners (Contractors) Ltd*, n 5 above.
52 *Massey v Crown Life Insurance Co* [1978] ICR 590 at 595, [1978] IRLR 31 at 33.
53 [1978] ICR 590 at 597, [1978] IRLR 31 at 34.
54 [1980] IRLR 201, CA.
55 [1999] ICR 1226, [2000] IRLR 43, HL.

sense, were agreed. Of course, the tribunal may reject such evidence and conclude the party misunderstood the effect of what was being said and done. But when both parties are agreed about what they understood their mutual obligations (or lack of them) to be, it is a strong thing to exclude their evidence from consideration.'[56]

Thus, the position now seems to be that, as a matter of practice, the declared intention of the parties may be more important if (a) there has been a deliberate *change* in the basis of employment, (b) the work in question was of an unusual nature so that an ambiguity as to its true nature might be found more easily[57], or (c) the arrangement has been entered into in a relatively informal manner and has to be construed in the light of several factors and circumstances, as in *Carmichael*. On the question of the policy behind the earlier decisions, the court in *Young & Woods Ltd v West* thought that the danger of allowing employers to avoid the employment protection legislation simply by labelling people as self-employed was an important consideration. They recognised the fears expressed (particularly in *Massey's* case) of injustice being caused by allowing a person to claim to be self-employed for tax purposes during employment, but then to claim on dismissal to have been an employee all along in order to claim unfair dismissal, but suggested that this could be overcome by a court or tribunal finding that the person was employed (thereby permitting the unfair dismissal action) but then informing the Inland Revenue of that fact, thereby inviting a reassessment of his tax liability for the past years of his employment under Schedule E[58]; knowledge that this is a possibility could be a considerable disincentive to the person who is thinking of trying to alter his status at this late stage.

(ii) Three particular applications

In addition to these general principles relating to the existence of a contract of employment, three specific points are worthy of mention. The first is that, although some of the cases cited on this problem are tort cases concerning vicarious liability,

---

56 [1999] ICR 1226 at 1235, [2000] IRLR 43 at 47. Lord Hoffmann disapproved the view of the majority of the Court of Appeal that the relationship had to be considered purely objectively, disregarding the parties' understandings.

57 Both (a) and (b) were considered by Stephenson LJ in *Young & Woods Ltd v West* to have been important aspects of *Massey's* case; on the latter factor, Mr Massey's position as a manager with a separate agency agreement was more unusual employment than Mr West's job of sheet metal worker (working alongside other people doing exactly the same work, but as employees). The Court of Appeal found that Mr West's circumstances did not raise the sort of ambiguity necessary if the label of self-employment was to be decisive. Likewise in *Dacas v Brooke Street Bureau* [2003] IRLR 190 (p 22 below) there was no such ambiguity in the relationship beteen agency worker and agency, and so an employment relationship was found in spite of a clear statement in the agency's contract of hiring that no employment contract was to arise.

58 Thus it could be that the ex-employee would end up owing more to the Inland Revenue than he gained in compensation for unfair dismissal. In *Young's* case, Ackner LJ said that Mr West had probably won a 'hollow, indeed an expensive, victory'. The problem from the employer's point of view is that if this happens he will end up liable to pay the employer's NI contributions that should have been paid over the course of the employment; moreover, if the employee is unable to pay the back tax, the Inland Revenue could seek to recover it from the employer on the basis that he should have been operating the PAYE system all along.

some care may be needed, for the test for vicarious liability is not necessarily identical to that for the existence of an employment relationship in industrial law. It is true that it *looks* the same – was there a contract of employment? – but the factors behind it may be different, for in tort (for example, in a 'borrowed servant' case[59], where employer A lends B a crane plus driver and, while acting under B's orders the driver injures C – should A or B be liable to C?) the court is essentially looking at the liability question at one moment in time, whereas in an industrial case (eg on redundancy rights or unfair dismissal) the tribunal may have to assess the legal consequences of a potentially long-term relationship; it may be, therefore, that 'static' ideas of control may be more important in a tort case than in an industrial case where more factors may need to be taken into account to achieve a realistic result. Thus, in the borrowed servant example, it may be that, on the facts, B is liable to C[60], whereas it is clear that for unfair dismissal or employment protection purposes, A remains his employer. Thus, tort precedents may have to be used with care in other contexts[61].

The second point is that various practical problems may arise over the use of independent contracting, particularly in a system of labour-only sub-contracting as on the 'lump' in the building industry[62]. The Court of Appeal showed some hostility to this in *Ferguson's* case, particularly as there was clear suspicion in that case of unlawful tax evasion; as it stood, that case could perhaps have been developed by subsequent courts as a way of curbing the over-use of sub-contracting by placing stringent limits upon its legal recognition, but even the majority did not feel that they could go as far as to strike down such an agreement as an illegal contract and, in the light of the subsequent case law discussed above, a major judicial assault on the lump and other such practices is unlikely[63]. Legislative reforms have been suggested in order to rule out all but bona fide contractors but, except in the area of income tax where provisions have been introduced to extend the PAYE system and counter unlawful tax evasion[64], little has been done.

The third point concerns the position of company directors. An ordinary director will not normally be under a contract of employment, even when in receipt of directors' fees. However, there is nothing to prevent a director from being 'employed' (even by his own one-man company[65]) if the relationship is in fact over and above that of ordinary director, as in the case of an executive or

---

59 *Mersey Docks and Harbour Board v Coggins and Griffiths (Liverpool) Ltd* [1947] AC 1, [1946] 2 All ER 345, HL.

60 *Donovan v Laing, Wharton and Down Construction Syndicate Ltd* [1893] 1 QB 629, CA; *Sime v Sutcliffe Catering Scotland Ltd* [1990] IRLR 228, Ct of Sess. For variations on this, see *McDermid v Nash Dredging and Reclamation Co Ltd* [1987] ICR 917, [1987] IRLR 334, HL and *Interlink Express Parcels Ltd v Night Trunkers Ltd* [2001] EWCA Civ 360, [2001] RTR 338, [2001] 20 LS Gaz R 43, CA.

61 For a clear indication of this, see Denning LJ's judgment in *Denham v Midland Employers' Mutual Assurance Ltd* [1955] 2 QB 437, [1955] 2 All ER 561, CA and more recently, the decision of the Court of Appeal in *Morris v Breaveglen Ltd* [1993] ICR 766, [1993] IRLR 350, CA.

62 Clark 'Industrial law and the labour-only sub-contract' (1967) 30 MLR 6; Drake 'Wage slave or entrepreneur?' (1968) 31 MLR 408; Mordesley 'Some problems of the "lump"' (1975) 38 MLR 504.

63 In *Costain Building and Civil Engineering Ltd v Smith* [2000] ICR 215 an agency-suppled building engineer was held not to have been lawfuly appointed by her union or a safety representative because he was not an 'employee' as required by the relevant regulations (see p 886 below).

64 Finance Act 1971, ss 29–31; Finance (No 2) Act 1975, ss 68–71; Finance (No 2) Act 1979, s 15.

managing director. However, the mere fact that a director performs some duties for the company may not be enough[66] and if he wishes to establish a contract of employment (for example to be able to claim unfair dismissal when his services are dispensed with) he must show further factors. Thus in *Parsons v Albert J Parsons & Sons Ltd*[67] the Court of Appeal held that a director was not 'employed', in spite of working full time for the company, since the company records did not contain a written contract of employment for him or memorandum setting out the terms of an oral contract[68], his sole remuneration was that categorised in the accounts as 'directors' fees' and he had been treated as self-employed for tax and national insurance purposes. Moreover, it may be possible to argue that a director should not be classed as an 'employee' because to do so would be inconsistent with the employment right that that person is trying to claim; the area in which this has arisen to date is the state guarantee for moneys outstanding to employees on a company's insolvency[69], where it had been held by the EAT that it would be improper to allow the de facto owner of a one-man company to claim from the state on his company's insolvency[70]. However, the Court of Appeal later reaffirmed strongly that there was no such rule of law, and that in each case it remains a question of fact – the person's status as a controlling director may well be a *factor* against employment status, but must be balanced against other factors such as the bona fides of the contract, the degree of control exercised by the company, the position of any other directors and the conduct of the parties[71].

(iii) Atypical workers – domestic law

It has become increasingly clear that atypical workers such as 'outworkers' (ie people who perform work for another at home rather than in a factory) may have their employment protection, etc, rights jeopardised by a finding that they are independent contractors[72]. Part-time workers in factories may have had problems in the past with the old '16 hours per week' rule for computing continuity of employment until its repeal in 1995[73], but at least there was usually no question that they were in fact 'employed', whereas in the case of an outworker even that might be in doubt, for if on the facts it appears that the work is brought to them, and accepted, purely on an ad hoc basis, the tribunal might take the view that the

---

65 *Lee v Lee's Air Farming Ltd* [1961] AC 12, [1960] 3 All ER 420, PC.
66 *Stanbury v Overmass and Chapple Ltd* (1976) 11 ITR 7, IT. However, there may be a presumption of employed status if the director is required to work full time for the company in return for a salary: *Folami v Nigerline (UK) Ltd* [1978] ICR 277.
67 [1979] ICR 271, [1979] IRLR 117, CA; *Morley v C T Morley Ltd* [1985] ICR 499; *Eaton v Robert Eaton Ltd* [1988] ICR 302, [1988] IRLR 83.
68 As required by the Companies Act 1985, s 318.
69 See p 264 below.
70 *Buchan v Secretary of State for Employment* [1997] IRLR 80.
71 *Secretary of State for Trade and Industry v Botterill* [1999] ICR 592, [1999] IRLR 326, CA (director held to be an employee for insolvency guarantee purposes; reasoning in *Buchan* disapproved).
72 Collins 'Independent contractors and the challenge of vertical disintegration to employment protection laws' (1990) 10 OJLS 353. To take another example, youth trainees are not employees (being in fact in limbo, since they are not self-employed either); for this reason, training agreements have to contain contractual rights akin to those they would have had if they had been employees, and regulations and orders have had to be made in order to extend health and safety legislation and the laws on sex and race discrimination to them specifically.
73 See p 189 below.

outworker was not in fact 'employed'[74]. Where, however, the outworker works on a regular basis the EAT held in *Airfix Footwear Ltd v Cope*[75] that there is no reason why there should not be a finding of a contract of employment, even though the work is done elsewhere than on the employer's premises, if there is sufficient mutuality of obligations; as seen above, this approach was approved by the Court of Appeal in *Nethermere (St Neots) Ltd v Gardiner*[76]. While an arrangement such as homeworking is still generally considered 'atypical', it is increasingly recognised that nine-to-five employment throughout the year in a manufacturing factory is becoming *less* typical, and so increasingly the law will have to consider the position of those working under more diverse and less full-time conditions. In particular, much of the recent job creation in the economy has been in forms hitherto thought to be atypical, but fast becoming the norm in many sectors of the labour market[77]. At the same time, with the decline of traditional manufacturing industries and the expansion of the service and IT sectors, the nature of the employing concern has been changing, with larger numbers of people now being employed by what hitherto would have been considered 'small firms'[78].

Part-time and temporary work is now more prevalent[79] and in some areas teleworking (the modern form of more traditional homeworking) is being increasingly considered[80]. Generally, the workforce has become more flexible[81]

---

74 *Mailway (Southern) Ltd v Willsher* [1978] ICR 511, [1978] IRLR 322; there is also a possible argument, adverted to in the *Airfix* case (n 75 below) that there could be a *separate* contract of employment for each job where it is only on a sporadic basis, but no overall contract.

75 [1978] ICR 1210, [1978] IRLR 396. See generally Ewing 'Homeworking, a framework for reform' (1982) 11 ILJ 94; and Hakim 'Homeworking in Britain' [1987] Employment Gazette 92.

76 [1984] ICR 612, [1984] IRLR 240, CA.

77 See, eg, Fredman 'Labour law in flux: the changing composition of the workforce' (1997) 26 ILJ 337.

78 This was strikingly demonstrated by research undertaken when considering whether to decrease the exemption for small firms from the Disability Discrimination Act 1995. This showed that 1m employers in the private sector (95% of the total number of employers in the UK) employing 4.5m workers were firms employing fewer than twenty people: *Disability Discrimination Act 1995: Employment Provisions and Small Employers* (DFEE, 1998).

79 In 1998, there were 6.6m part-time workers, comprising 1.3m men and 5.3m women, or 8% of the male workforce and 44% of the female workforce; of those aged between 25 and 49, 47% of men said they worked part time because they could not find full time work and 34% did not want full-time work, whereas 8% of women said they worked part-time because they could not find full-time work and 90% did not want full-time work: [1998] Labour Market Trends 600. According to the same survey, in 1998 there were 1.8m in temporary jobs (8% of the workforce), comprising 880,000 men and 967,000 women: [1998] Labour Market Trends at 598. The literature on this is voluminous. See eg Millward et al *Workplace Industrial Relations in Transition* (1992), pp 337ff; Dickens 'Working time and employment equality' (1992) 21 ILJ 146; views can vary, however, as to how to define 'part-time work' and therefore how prevalent it is: see Hakim 'Employment rights: a comparison of part-time and full-time employees' (1989) 18 ILJ 69 and the reply by Disney and Szyszczak (1989) 18 ILJ 223.

80 For the extent of this, see Hotopp 'Teleworking in the UK' (2002) Labour Market Trends 311.

81 ACAS Annual Report 1987, pp 14, 18; Hakim 'Trends in the flexible workforce' [1987] Employment Gazette 549; Labour Flexibility in Britain, the 1987 ACAS Survey (ACAS Occasional Paper No 41, 1988); Wareing 'Working arrangements and patterns of working hours in Britain' [1992] Employment Gazette 88; McGregor and Sproull 'Employers and the flexible workforce' [1992] Employment Gazette 225; Dickens *Whose Flexibility?* (1992); Beatson 'Progress towards a flexible labour market' (1995) Employment Gazette 55; Nolan and Walsh 'The structure of the economy and labour market' in Edwards (ed) *Industrial Relations, Theory and Practice in Britain* (1995); Collins 'Regulating the employment relation for competitiveness (2001) 30 ILJ 17.

82 See Employment for the 1990s (Cm 540, 1988) and People, Jobs and Opportunity (Cm 1810, 1992) for the previous government's policy; Fairness at Work (Cm 3968, 1998) for the present government's policy.

and indeed encouraging such flexibility is government policy[82], since it is seen as a way of encouraging more use of individual contracting, flexible pay and payment by results, the antithesis of the collective approach to wage determination. However, this development may cause strains in applying laws evolved basically against the background of full-time, 'normal' employment. While it is important to remember that, for better or for worse, the juristic basis here remains the traditional contract of employment, it is also important to ensure that there is not too much scope for employers to use devices such as temporary or part-time work in order to evade statutory obligations[83]. It been argued for some time now that in Britain we are in danger of evolving a two-tier labour force – those in traditional full-time employment with a fair degree of job security and statutory protection, and those (increasingly) in part-time, temporary or otherwise atypical employment with little security, and hitherto generally excluded from statutory protection[84]. In fact, the principal moves towards protection of part-time employees have come through EC law. Initially, this was under EC sex equality laws which apply because of the disparate effect on women of rules prejudicing part-timers; the most notable success lay in the enforced removal (first by court action and then by amending regulations) of the requirement of working 16 hours per week in order to gain continuity of employment (for the purposes of qualifying for the major statutory rights)[85]. This approach is now largely being superseded by EC law directives aimed at giving protection *directly* to specific forms of atypical employees, relieving them of the necessity of going through the hoops of a discrimination action; this development is considered separately below.

One legal device that has shown some signs of evolving as a possible remedy in cases where part-time or sporadic work (for example, on a series of short-term contracts) appears to be being misused is that of the 'umbrella or global contract', ie a finding that although the employee was only actually working for certain periods (possibly on an irregular basis), there was sufficient mutuality between the parties to justify a finding that in law there was one overall contract governing the whole period in question. However, this argument failed in one of the leading cases, *Hellyer Bros Ltd v McLeod*[86], where trawlermen who had sailed exclusively for

83 *Lewis v Surrey County Council* [1987] ICR 982 at 998, [1987] IRLR 509 and 516, HL, per Lord Ackner. One employer's ace wheeze, to avoid employment responsibilities (such as SSP), of putting an employee or to 'daily contracts' (sic) for a total period of nine months was kicked into touch by the Court of Appeal who applied the Employment Rights Act 1996, s 86(4) which states that any contract for less than a month which in fact lasts for more than three months is deemed to be for an indefinite period (thus requiring notice to end it): *Brown v Chief Adjudication Officer* [1997] ICR 266, [1997] IRLR 110, CA.

84 Dickens 'Falling through the net: employment change and worker protection' (1988) 19 IRJ 139. A current view is that this movement has been a pragmatic reaction to market conditions and business uncertainties rather than deliberate and widespread managerial policy: Sisson and Marguison 'Management: systems, structures and strategy' in Edwards (ed) *Industrial Relations, Theory and Practice in Britain* (1995) p 113.

85 See p 189, below. See also the enforced extension to part-timers of rights under occupational pension schemes, p 352, below.

86 [1987] ICR 526, [1987] IRLR 232, CA. The possibility of such a finding was, however, considered to be an important possibility (for countering the abuse of short-term contracts by an employer) by Lord Ackner in *Lewis v Surrey County Council*, n 83, above. Continuity of employment was preserved by the Court of Appeal in *Flack v Kodak Ltd* [1986] ICR 775, [1986] IRLR 255 in a case of irregular, sporadic contracts by the alternative device of resorting to the ERA 1996, s 212(3)(b) ('temporary cessation of work'), see p 194, below.

one company for many years were held unable to claim redundancy payments when dispensed with, since the facts only established a series (albeit a long series) of separate contracts for each voyage. In an appropriate case, however, this could be a useful device, though it is clear that it is no panacea, and that if it does not apply an applicant may be in severe difficulties, for example in establishing the necessary continuity of employment for claiming the statutory right in question.[87]

Casual work has always caused problems legally, especially as there is a persistent folk myth among many employers that *because* a person is termed 'casual', *therefore* they cannot have any employment rights. It is important to realise, however, that 'casual' is not a legal term of art, that the word appears nowhere in the Employment Rights Act 1996, that the only legal distinction is between those who do and those who do not qualify for employment rights, and that a casual worker may or may not so qualify, depending on the facts. On the other hand, it has to be accepted that casual workers can have more problems than most in meeting qualification conditions, obviously in relation to continuity of employment, and more fundamentally in relation to employee status. Although the general trend in the past in the case law has been towards extension of legal rights to casuals, the signs are now that this may no longer be the case. In *Clarke v Oxfordshire Health Authority*[88] a 'bank' nurse (being offered and accepting work or as when it was available at any of the authority's hospitals) who was paid at standard rates and charged to PAYE and NI contributions, but who was not guaranteed any regular work, was held by the Court of Appeal *not* to be an employee (after three years working in the authority's hospitals, with only four breaks totalling fourteen weeks) and so unable to claim unfair dismissal[89]. In *Carmichael v National Power plc*[90] a question was raised as to the employment status of two power station guides employed on a 'casual, as required' basis to show parties around when the need arose, given uniforms and charged to PAYE and NI contributions. The Court of Appeal split, with the majority finding that they were employees, in a thoughtful decision in favour of extending employment status, perfecting the potentially informal relationship by finding implied terms that (a) the employer would offer each guide a reasonable amount of the work available and (b) each guide would accept a reasonable amount of the work offered. However, on further appeal the House of Lords disapproved this completely and held that the guides were not employees, largely due to lack of a level of mutuality of obligations which Lord Irvine LC said was an irreducible minimum for any contract of employment. This was taken one step further in *Stevedoring and Haulage Services ltd v Fuller*[91], where the employer in effect achieved this result in advance by

---

87 For a good example, see *Letheby & Christopher Ltd v Bond* [1988] ICR 480.
88 [1998] IRLR 125, CA.
89 There was, however, a major qualification in the judgment. In the tribunal this issue had arguably been confused by considering not just whether there was an employment contract, but whether there was an umbrella contract covering the whole period (above). What had not been considered was whether there was a series of *individual* contracts (for each stint at one of the hospitals), possibly *linked* by the rules on continuity of employment; the result of the decision was a remission to the tribunal to consider this possibility.
90 [1999] ICR 1226, [2000] IRLR 43, HL. The principal speech is by Lord Irvine LC; the other speech by Lord Hoffmann is of interest on the fact/law distinction as applied to the existence of a contract of employment, holding that the Court of Appeal had been wrong to interfere with the tribunal's decision for the employer *at all*.
91 [2001] EWCA Civ 651, [2001] IRLR 627. Dockers who had been made redundant as full-time employees and retired on a casualised basis, could not claim statutory rights, even though in fact working consistently for the same employer, because of the clause in the contract. How much of a sham would such a clause have to be in practice before a tribunal would feel able to ignore it?

putting a clause into the hiring contract that no mutual duties (to offer work or to turn up for it) were to arise under it. This is a serious blow to any prospect of further extension of employment status by judicial action, and indeed might even be used to attack existing case law granting such status to certain atypical workers (for example, homeworkers). In the light of this any further moves towards extending employment status and ensuring that employment protection laws continue to apply widely to an ever more diverse workforce are for the moment having to come from legislation, which is considered below.

One other form of engagement currently causing problems at common law of a surprisingly fundamental nature is agency working. This has traditionally been seen by employers as *the* way to keep staff out of employment status and to achieve a high level of flexibility. Although the relationship legally between the agency and the worker has been far from straightforward[92], it was thought to be clear that the worker could *not* be the employee of the client. This made particular sense (and continues to do so) when the nature of the work is such that the identity of the worker is unimportant, there is a high level of rotation of staff to the particular client and the standards are fluctuating (ie classic 'temping'). The situation is, however, now being made more difficult by the evolution of a very different form of agency working, where the work is specialised, the worker's own skills are a key point, labour is in short supply, and when the client discovers a good worker it will want to *keep* him or her. In such a case, the agency in practice is little more than a recruiter; from that stage on, the client takes over 'running' the worker as the agency soon recedes into the background (remaining technically the conduit for payment). That individual worker then works nine-to-five, fifty-two weeks a year, for that one client for a significant period of time, by the end of which he or she is virtually indistinguishable from the client's permanent employees doing similar work[93]. It is well known that in similar circumstances a self-employed 'consultant' who ends up working permanently for the one 'client' can transmute over time into an employee. Could that happen with an agency worker? In *Montgomery v Johnson Underwood Ltd*[94] an agency worker was held not to be the employee (for unfair dismissal purposes) of the agency because once supplied to the client, she worked for that one client for two years, subject to little or no control, supervision or direction by the agency. A case such as this suggests that, if the worker is not to be cast into the outer darkness with no rights against anyone, a sympathetic tribunal might be tempted to look for another candidate for 'employer' and there is only one – the client. This was generally thought to be legally impossible (without the deliberate, separate hiring of a good temp on to the permanent staff) until the bombshell case of *Motorola Ltd v Davidson*[95],

92   The leading case is *McMeechan v Secretary of State for Employment* [1997] ICR 549, [1997] IRLR 353, CA, where it was held that the relationship is a question of fact (ie, no rules of law either way) and that there could be two distinct employments with the agency – a general one (to be on the books) and an individual one covering a particular assignment. In *Dacas v Brook Street Bureau* [2003] IRLR 190 an agency was held to have sufficient control over the worker (with sufficient mutuality between them) to found an employment contract, in spite of express wording in their initial agreement to the contrary – again on general principles (there being no rule of law either way). One reason for the lack of wider case law here is that temps are taxed under special provisions, whatever their past employment law status, and so the issue has not been forced in the taxation context. Moreover, discrimination statutes cover 'contract' or 'agency' workers separately.

93   Particularly as good HR practice tends to be to treat 'outsiders' as much like your own as possible; legally, this is exactly what the client should not do.

94   [2001] EWCA Civ 318, [2001] IRLR 269, [2001] ICR 819.

95   [2001] IRLR 4.

where the EAT held that it was a possibility. The worker in question was a skilled telephone repairer who was recruited by an agency to the client's own specifications. He then worked wholly for the client for two years, entirely under its control and with no further contact with the agency. When he gave cause for concern, he was disciplined under the client's own disciplinary procedures (though termination was effected through the agency). On his complaint of unfair dismissal, the tribunal held that on these facts there was a contract of employment with the *client*, against whom the action lay. The client's appeal against this finding was dismissed by the EAT. What effect does *Motorola* have? It certainly caused a renewal of interest in this area. However, its future is uncertain for two reasons: first, it is a fragile authority because of the peculiarity that when the appeal came before the EAT the client (for partly tactical reasons) restricted the appeal to the question whether there could be enough *control* to enable it to be the employer and so, when the EAT (carefully restricting themselves to that ground of appeal) held that there could, that was an end of the matter and none of the other normal indicia of employment were considered. Secondly, two reported cases since the decision took a much more traditional view and held the agency worker not to be the client's employee – in *Hewlett Packard Ltd v O'Murphy*[96] the worker had hired himself to the agency through his own service company and it was held that this remained a commercial arrangement, not a employment one with the eventual client; more fundamentally, in *Esso Petroleum Co v Jarvis*[97] (where the two workers had worked for the one client for nine and eleven years) the EAT, overturning findings of employment by the tribunal, seized on part of the tribunal's reasoning that there was 'no contract' between worker and client, and said simply that if there was no contract there could be no contract of employment[98]. On the other hand, in *Franks v Reuters Ltd*[99] when this matter reached the Court of Appeal they upheld a tribunal decision on the facts that an agency-provided worker who had worked for the same employer for six years (on a series of jobs and eventually becoming indistinguishable from permanent staff) *did* transmute into an employee of the client. Two points of particular significance in this decision (arguably going beyond the partial authority of *Motorola*) were that (a) the court picked up on the point argued above to be missing in *Esso Petroleum* that what may be relevant is the growth of an *implied* contract to supersede the original agreement, and (b) Mummery LJ expressly said that, although long service with the one client cannot of itself establish such an implied contract, it may well be an important *factor* when applying the general fact-based tests for employment. Put at its most basic, the decision in *Motorola* and *Franks* breach the principle that the agency worker cannot be the client's employee. We are in need of further case law on this important point, especially as statutory reforms to employment agencies (expected during the currency of this edition) are limited to the operation of such businesses and will not resolve this fundamental issue of employment status.

---

96 [2002] IRLR 4.
97 [2002] All ER(D) 112 (Jan).
98 The EAT disapproved the idea that, even if there was no contract, there could be an employment *relationship*. One worrying point was that what the tribunal might have meant is that there was no *express* contract with the client; however, an employment contract may in law be wholly implied.
99 [2003] EWCA Civ 417, [2003] IRLR 423.

(iv) Atypical workers – EU intervention on part-time, fixed-term and agency work

The principal developments extending legal protection to certain types of employment are now coming from the EU. One original idea was for a single, overarching Directive covering all atypical workers, but this was always found politically unacceptable, and so the successful approach has been to propose individual Directives on specific categories of work, primarily through the medium of 'Framework Directives' which are agreed between the social partners (ETUC, UNICE and CEEP) and then merely promulgated by the relevant EU bodies[100].

(a) Part-time workers

The Part-time Workers Directive[101] is transposed into domestic law in the Part-time Workers (Prevention of Less Favourable Treatment) Regulations 2000[102] in relation to its primary requirement of a regime of non-discrimination. Thus, a part-time worker has a right not to be treated less favourably than a comparable full-time worker, as regards the terms of his contract or by being subjected to any other detriment by any act, or deliberate failure to act, of his employer, unless the treatment in question is objectively justified[103]. In assessing whether treatment has been less favourable the pro rata principle may be applied[104] (for example, half pay for half time, not one-third pay) which could make less than pro-rata 'part-timer rates' unlawful and may cause technical problems with terms of employment other than pay (for example, in trying to pro-rata holidays or bank holiday entitlements, or a firm's car). There may be some scope here for the objective justification defence, but at a more general level it may be difficult to argue for any widespread use for that defence, given the aim of the Directive to enhance the position of part-time work generally – why should part-timers be treated any less favourably than on a pro-rata by time basis? A part-timer is defined quite simply as any worker who 'having regard to the custom and practice of his employer in relation to workers employed by the worker's employer under the same type of contract is not identifiable as a full-time worker'[105]. This covers anyone working fewer hours than full-time and so is not confined to those working, for example, half time. There must normally be a comparison with a comparable full-time worker, except where a worker changes from full-time to part-time or

---

100 This has two main effects in employment law. The first is that the drafting may be vague and aspirational (being more like a supranational collective agreement than a statute) which causes problems for transposition into UK law with its literalist tradition. The second is that this vagueness means that it is unlikely that many parts of such Directives will be precise enough to support direct effect (see *Gibson v East Riding of Yorkshire Council* [2000] ICR 890, [2000] IRLR 598, CA where even the relatively precise provisions of the holiday entitlement in the Working Time Directive were held to be insufficient).

101 Directive 97/81/EC, applied to the UK by Directive 98/23/EC. For a strong critique of its minimalist approach, see Jeffrey 'Not really going to work?' (1998) 27 ILJ 193.

102 SI 2000/1551, *Harvey* R [1288]. One immediate point to note is that these Regulations apply to 'workers', not just 'employees'; for the significance of the wider 'worker' definition, see p 32 below.

103 Reg 5(1), (2).

104 Reg 5(3). It is specifically provided that a part-timer does not qualify for overtime rates until he has completed normal full-time hours, ie he cannot claim such rates at the expiry of his own part-time hours: reg 5(4).

105 Reg 2(2). Reg 2(3) sets out categories of persons not to be considered as being under the same type of contract.

has a period of absence for full-time work and returns part-time, in which case the comparison may be with their own previous full-time terms.[106] A worker may present a complaint to an employment tribunal that his or her employer has infringed the Regulations; in such a case the burden of proof is on the employer and if the tribunal finds the complaint established it may make a declaration to that effect, award compensation and/or recommend action to be taken by the employer within a specified time to obviate or reduce the adverse effect on the complainaint.[107]

As seen above, less favourable treatment of part-timers because of their status has already been under attack from existing law for many years, on the basis that it constitutes indirect sex discrimination which would be difficult to justify objectively. This has been known to good employers for a long time, and so it is arguable that these Regulations are largely pushing at an already opened door. They should get rid of any lingering attachment of the less-than-good employer to ideas of 'part-timer rates' for these 'peripheral' staff and their major advantage legally is that a worker still faced by such antediluvian treatment now has a *direct* cause of action before a tribunal, rather than having to go through the hoops of a sex discrimination action. The Directive does, however, have a secondary aim, much more difficult to transpose into UK law. As is clear from the recitals to the Directive and its second half, it aims generally to increase the value placed on part-time work within organisations and to encourage the facilitation of movement between full-time and part-time working, which may include 'timely information' on such job opportunities and 'access by part-time workers to vocational training to enhance career opportunities and occupational mobility'. Moreover, it is made clear that part-time working is to be viewed as a realistic and valued option not just for hewers of wood and drawers of water (or even stackers of shelves), but 'at all levels of the enterprise, including skilled and managerial positions'. This sentiment sits easily alongside the present government's family-friendly and work/life balance policies, but is difficult to put into the usual format of black letter law. The original idea was to produce a Code of Practice but this was dropped and the eventual solution was DTI Best Practice Guidance[108]. This covers matters such as widening access to part-time work, making more jobs available on that basis, jobsharing, taking requests to change to and from part-time seriously, providing information to staff, training and other measures to facilitate part-time working. Some of this advice is potentially far-reaching and in places could be seen as placing an informal onus on an employer to *justify* any refusal of part-time working. Moreover, it pre-empted legislative moves towards the new right to request a contract variation in the Employment Act 2002[109] and

106 Regs 2(4), 3, 4. A worker who considers that the employer may have treated him or her less favourably on the ground of being part-time has a right to a written statement by the employer of the reasons for the treatment in question: reg 6.
107 Reg 8(1), (6), (7). The complaint must be presented within three months, with the usual discrimination law 'just and equitable' ground for extension of the period: reg 8(2)–(5). Compensation is such as is just and equitable having regard to the infringement and the worker's loss; it is not capped, but may not include injury to feelings and is subject to mitigation and compensatory fault (as in the case of unfair dismissal): reg 8(9)–(13). If an employer fails without reasonable justification to comply with a recommendation, compensation may be increased: reg 8(14).
108 'Part-time work: the law and best practice', available at www.dti.gov.uk/er/pt-detail. The first half contains guidance on the Regulations; the second half contains best practice guidance on the second part of the Directive. *Quaere* whether there could be an issue under EC law as to whether this format is sufficient to transpose the Directive properly.
109 Employment Act 2002, s 47; see p 437 below.

remains available to those not covered by that new right, ie those without a child under 6. Of course, the lawyer might be tempted to dismiss this all as non-legalistic wishful thinking, but it is possible that in the future employment lawyers will have to take this form of 'soft law' more seriously, especially as it comes from a Directive. It is true that the guidance has no direct form of enforcement, but increasingly in areas such as this employment lawyers are having to think laterally and try to envisage how soft law might be *used* in other contexts. Two are mentioned here: (i) a refusal of part-time working might be attacked as indirect sex discrimination which would require the employer to justify the refusal, at which point the guidance could be powerful evidence (particularly if it suggested that part-time working should be possible in those circumstances); (ii) the guidance might be relevant as evidence of reasonable or unreasonable employer action in a case where the refusal was made in such circumstances as to result in the employee leaving and claiming constructive dismissal. Thus, to write the guidance off as 'only' soft law might be a very short-sighted view.

(b) Fixed-term employees

The Fixed-term Worker Directive[110] has two principal objectives, to establish a regime of non-discrimination and to require member states to have laws to prevent the perceived abuse of keeping individuals on successive fixed-term contracts for unreasonable periods. The first objective is thus very similar to that in the Part-time Worker Directive but the second is legally much more precise. Both of these objectives are transposed into domestic law in the Fixed-term Employees (Prevention of Less Favourable Treatment) Regulations 2002[111]. With regard to the first, a fixed-term employee has a right not to be treated less favourably than the employer treats a comparable permanent employee as regards the terms of his or her contract or by being subjected to any other detriment by any act, or deliberate failure to act, of his employer, unless the treatment in question is objectively justified[112]. As with the part-time provisions, the pro rata principle may be applied in determining whether there has been less favourable treatment[113]. The Regulations define a fixed-term contract by adopting the Directive's definition which extends that hitherto used by domestic law – in the latter a contract was only for a fixed-term if it was time limited (ie until an expressed or ascertainable date) but the Regulations cover contracts terminating (a) on the expiry of a specific term, (b) on the completion of a particular task or (c) on the occurrence or non-occurrence of any other specific event (other than reaching retirement age)[114]; heads (b) and (c) extend the definition to what have usually

---

110 Directive 99/70/EC.
111 SI 2002/2034, *Harvey* R [1551]. These are explained in the DTI 'Fixed-term Work: a guide to the regulations', available at www.dti.gov.uk/er/fixed/fixed-pl512. Unlike the Part-time Worker Regulations (above) these Regulations are deliberately restricted to applying only to 'employees', not to 'workers'.
112 Reg 3(1), (3). Reg 3(2) particularises the right not to be less favourably treated in relation to any period of service qualification for a condition of service, the opportunity to receive training and the opportunity to secure any permanent position in the establishment. With regard to the last, the employee has a right to be informed by the employer of available vacancies in the establishment, by advertisement or other reasonable form of notification: reg 3(6), (7).
113 Reg 3(5).
114 Reg 1(2). The Regulations in fact went much further and applied this wider definition to fixed-term contracts generally in the Employment Rights Act 1996, see p 454 below.

been referred to as 'purpose' or 'task' contracts (eg employment 'until this building is demolished'). There must be a comparison with a comparable permanent employee[115]. An employee may present a complaint to an employment tribunal that his or her employer has breached this part of the Regulations.[116]

It is likely that a key issue under these Regulations will be justification for continuing disparity of treatment (especially in relation to terms and conditions other than pay), for at least two reasons – (i) there is less likelihood of a straight pro rata solution than there is with part-timers, and (ii) there are known problems of mismatch between those on *short* fixed-term contracts and major, long-term benefits primarily intended for long-term permanent employees (for example, generous sickness benefits and pension entitlements). Thus, justification is likely to be a much more live issue here than under the part-time provisions. It may be affected by three particular points under the Regulations:

(i) There is a specific provision (inserted at a late stage) that, in determining whether a fixed-termer has been less favourably treated than a permanent employee without justification, one can look at whether the terms of the fixed-termer's employment *taken as a whole* are at least as favourable as those of the comparator. This allows the employer to rely on a 'package' approach, rather than a term-by-term approach[117]. This may be particularly useful where the employer pays the fixed-termer *more* (eg a higher hourly rate) to reflect the fact that he or she does not qualify for longer-term benefits.

(ii) Employees on short-term contracts may lawfully be excluded from particular benefits by attaching qualifying periods to those benefits, *provided* that the period in question does not discriminate between fixed-term and permanent employees[118].

(iii) Ultimately an employer could rely on straightforward objective justification for the disparity in treatment. The DTI Guide to the Regulations suggests a general three-stage test for justification (which must be considered on a case-by-case basis), namely whether the employer can show that the less favourable treatment is to achieve a legitimate objective, is necessary to achieve that objective and is an appropriate way to achieve it. Specific guidance is given on when it may be justifiable to exclude those on short-term contracts from pension schemes (where the benefit to the employee may be marginal and the administrative problems for the employer great) and from contractual redundancy/assurance schemes (which may be argued to be constructed to compensate permanent employees for the *unexpected* loss of their jobs, this being inappropriate at the end of a deliberately defined period of a fixed-term contract).

One final point to note on this first objective of removing discrimination is that one piece of institutionalised discrimination had to be removed. Prior to

---

115 Reg 2. An employee who considers that the employer may have treated him or her less favourably on the ground of being fixed-term has a right to a written statement by the employer of the reasons for the treatment in question: reg 5.

116 Reg 8. Such a complaint as to procedure and remedies is subject to the same rules as those applying to a complaint under the Part-time Worker Regulations 2000, see above.

117 Reg 4. This package approach is unusual – there is no mention of it in the Part-time Worker Regulations and it is *not* permitted in equal pay law, where the applicant can demand equality on a term-by-term approach (see p 329 below). There is guidance in the DTI Guide (n 111 above) on applying the package approach; one problem may be how to quantify the monetary worth of the benefit foregone.

118 Reg 3(2)(a); Directive 99/63/EC, cl 4(4) (which rather Delphiclly adds 'except where different length-of-service qualifications are justified on objective grounds').

October 2002 when the Regulations came into force it was possible for the employer of an employee on a fixed-term contract of two years or more to get the employee to sign away his or her rights to a statutory redundancy payment at the end of it. This has now been repealed[119], so a fixed-term contract can no longer be used for this purpose (common though it was in the past).

Moving on to the second objective of the Directive, the placing of limits on the unfair use of successive fixed-term contracts, the government adopted a hybrid of two of the three approaches permitted by the Directive. As from October 2002 a worker kept on successive fixed-term contracts for four years or more is deemed in law to be a permanent employee, unless the employer can objectively justify keeping that person on a fixed-term basis[120]. Justification is not defined, the DTI Guide contenting itself with repeating the general three-fold test (above) here too. It would clearly need a strong business case which, after four years, may well be wearing thin. One possible candidate would be where the post is paid for by 'hot money funding', ie where it is supported by some outside source providing the money on, for example, a one or two-year basis only, with no guarantee that it will continue into the future. Otherwise, case law on this point is anticipated with interest. One exception provided by the Regulations is that these provisions generally can be disapplied by a collective or workforce agreement and replaced by other controls on abuse, in the form of one or more of the following: (i) a different maximum period for successive contracts; (ii) a maximum number of successive contracts; or (iii) the laying down of what are to be objective grounds for renewal of fixed-term contracts[121]. An employee who considers that he or she has become a permanent employee under these provisions is entitled to a written statement from the employer acknowledging this or giving reasons why the employer contends that the contract remains fixed-term. If a dispute arises, the employee may present an application to an employment tribunal for a declaration of permanent status.

What is likely to be the effect of the Regulations? It is possible that they will have a greater effect than the Part-time Worker Regulations because, while part-time working had for some time been exposed to scrutiny under the law of indirect sex discrimination, this had not happened in relation to fixed-term working and so the possibilities for disparate treatment have remained greater, particularly as in managerial folklore such working has tended to be viewed as a prime way of keeping workers at arm's length legally, and of providing a reservoir

119 Sch 2, Pt I, repealing the Employment Rights Act 1996, s 197(3)–(5). Existing clauses on 1 October 2002 were allowed to run their course, but no new clause is permitted either in a new or extended/renewed contract. Also abolished was exclusions of those on fixed-term contracts of three months or less from statutory sick pay, guarantee payments, medical suspension and minimum notice.

120 Reg 8. There have to have been *successive* contracts and so an initial contract of five years would not be converted on the fourth anniversary. Where there have been successive contracts, the conversion occurs on that anniversary. Major uncertainty here is caused by the fact that 'successive' contracts are defined simply by adopting the normal statutory rules on continuity of employment (see pp 188ff below), under which quite substantial gaps between contracts can be 'forgiven', especially where the contract themselves are for relatively long periods. A key point for employers historically using this form of employment was that reg 8 is *not* retrospective. By virtue of reg 8(4) the employee cannot count towards the four years any service before 10 July 2002 (the due date for implementation for the Directive, which the government missed slightly).

121 Reg 8(5). A 'workforce agreement' is an agreement between an employer and his employees or their representatives, satisfying the conditions (as to form, duration and the election of representatives) in Sch 1 to the Regulations.

of flexible staff with few or no legal rights. Ironically, shortly before the Regulations were drafted there arose the first reported case of a successful attack on disparate treatment of fixed-termers based on sex discrimination. In *Whiffen v Milham Ford Girl's School*[122] a school faced with making compulsory redundancies adopted the hitherto common policy of not renewing fixed-term contracts first, and then (and only then) applying fair selection criteria to the permanent staff in order to make the last few redundancies. This was held to be unjustified indirect sex discrimination. As with the Part-time Worker Regulations, a major advantage now is that an employee in that position would no longer have to go through the complexities of a sex discrimination action, but could instead complain directly under the Fixed-term Employees Regulations that this was unjustified discrimination against fixed-termers. The Regulations do *not* ban the use of fixed-term contracts, and bona fide use may continue. What they may, however, do is to alter the economic balance of advantage in using them – if they can no longer be used to lower labour costs, increase flexibility, make redundancies easier and cheaper and keep those advantages for year after year by keeping individuals on them, what are their remaining advantages? It may be that in many circumstances employees are to be advised to give them up in most instances (possibly sharpening up probation and redundancy procedures instead), reserving them for where the real need arises and objective justification could if necessary be shown. Doubtless it will be a long time before this sea change percolates down to line manager level, where assumptions about the continued desirability of fixed-term engagements may persist that are now either totally inaccurate or, at least, greatly exaggerated. It may now be that, if a manager indicates that he or she wishes a new or replacement post to be on a fixed-term basis, an advising lawyer or HR professional will need to start the advice by asking one key question – 'Why?'.

(c) Agency workers

At the time of writing there was considerable controversy over EU proposals for an agency worker Directive, extending to such workers a regime of equality with the permanent staff of the client for the time being, akin to that applying to part-timers and fixed-termers. UK employers' association were strongly opposed, on grounds of cost and administrative inconvenience, pointing out that the UK is by far the heaviest user of agency labour in the EU. One particular flashpoint has been how long a worker should have to be with the one client before the proposed Directive should apply; UK employers wanted a period of months (to exclude all short-term hirings) whereas the EU authorities have tended to want a short qualifying period (weeks only), if any. It seems that such a Directive is now almost certain to come eventually. Legal problems of comparability with permanent staff may be, if anything, greater than in the case of part-timers and fixed-termers, and a 'package approach' to overall terms and conditions may be an essential element, given that certain long-term terms and conditions of employment may well be quite inappropriate for agency staff. Moreover, a directive is most unlikely to resolve the key problem legally at the moment, namely deciding who if anyone *employs* the agency worker. On the other hand, a Directive here would be the logical final step towards coverage of atypical workers, as pointed out at the beginning of this section.

---

122 [2001] EWCA Civ 385, [2001] ICR 1023, [2001] IRLR 468.

(v) Associated employers

When considering the relationship of employer and employee, 'the employer' will normally be readily identifiable. If an employee decides voluntarily to change employer (eg to further their career), it is accepted that he or she will in doing so lose the rights he or she has accrued already and have to start again with the new employer. However, in the realities of modern business, the employer is likely to be a body corporate and here it may be more difficult to identify 'the employer' in that the particular company for which the employee works may itself be merely one part of a larger organisation. Such an organisation may be split down into smaller units for reasons (usually financial) which have little to do with employment law. It is, therefore, important that there should be provisions ensuring that employees do not lose their rights as a result of the composition of the employing concern and that an excessively technical view should not be taken of who or what constitutes the employer. Such provisions also serve as an anti-avoidance device, ensuring that employers cannot gain by dividing undertakings artificially into small units.

The provisions in question are those relating to 'associated employers', whereby two or more units (such as companies within one group) can be treated as one employer. The most important application of the concept of associated employers is in the context of continuity of employment (a vital factor in modern employment rights, both as to qualification to claim the right in question, such as unfair dismissal or a redundancy payment, and quantification of the employee's entitlement under that right). Thus, if an employee transfers (or is transferred) from the employment of one employer to the employment of an associated employer, their continuity of employment is *preserved*, and time spent with the first employer can count as time with the second employer[123]. The concept goes further, however, and can be found throughout the employment legislation. Thus for example, when deciding whether an employer can claim to be a 'small employer' (and so entitled to certain exceptions), any employees employed by an associated employer are usually counted in when computing the total number of employees[124]. Also, offers of 'suitable alternative employment' (important in redundancy law and in relation to maternity leave) may be made by the employer or an associated employer[125].

From these examples, it is easy to see the importance of the concept of associated employers. The definition is contained in the Employment Rights Act 1996, section 231:

'... any two employers are to be treated as associated if one is a company of which the other (directly or indirectly) has control, or if both are companies of which a third person (directly or indirectly) has control ...'[126].

---

123 See p 200, below. To be an 'associated employer', it is not essential that the company in question was already employing labour when the employee in question transferred to it: *Lucas v Henry Johnson (Packers and Shippers) Ltd* [1986] ICR 384.

124 See eg the maternity leave exemption for small firms. Strangely, the concept does not apply (for comparison purposes) in either the Part-time Worker Regulations or the Fixed-Term Employee Regulations (above).

125 See pp 641 and 420 below.

126 This definition, introduced by the Employment Protection Act 1975, is wider than that originally in the Contracts of Employment Acts, which required all parties to be companies, so did not apply to two companies under the control of one person: *Price v Syd Long (Stockton) Ltd* [1976] IRLR 41, IT.

'Control' is thus crucial, and there must be voting control in some form, not just de facto influence, however strong.[127] An extension to this narrow approach was suggested by the EAT in *Zarb and Samuels v British and Brazilian Produce Co (Sales) Ltd*[128] where it was held that control by a third person could include control by third *persons*, so that if two or more persons between them own more than 50% of the voting shares of the two companies *and* in practice act together, that may satisfy the definition. However, this approach has caused considerable difficulties, since the Court of Appeal in *South West Launderettes Ltd v Laidler*[129] questioned the correctness of *Zarb* and declined to apply it where on the facts it may have been possible to do so. The position is not absolutely clear because it was not necessary for the court to decide the matter and in the subsequent case of *Harford v Swiftrim Ltd*[130] the EAT applied *Zarb* (on the basis that it has been consistently followed) and expressly refused to apply the criticisms of it in *Laidler*. A different division of the EAT under Wood P then declined to follow *Harford* in *Strudwick v Iszatt Bros Ltd*[131], stating obiter that if necessary they would have followed the criticisms in *Laidler* and held against any concept of plural control (largely because of the major problems of discovery, evidence and proof that are capable of arising under such a concept). On the other hand, *Zarb* was applied again by a later EAT in *Tice v Cartwright*[132], which perhaps showed that the present position (until we have a definitive ruling of the Court of Appeal) is that *Zarb* remains there to be used where common sense and justice demand that two organisations be deemed to be one, especially where (or in this case) the facts concern a very restricted shareholding in a family concern, where the necessary de facto control and common action can be shown.

One significant problem which arose under this definition was that it only refers to *companies* as being associated employers. What was to be the position where the two employers in question were *not* companies (eg in the public sector, bodies such as health trusts, local authorities or universities) or if *one* of the employers was not a company (eg where one farmer runs two farms, one constituted as a company and the other as a partnership)? There were conflicting EAT decisions on this point. One view was that the definition was not exhaustive (only governing the position where the two employers in fact are companies) so that other bodies can be 'associated' if that is the practical position[133]. The other view was that the definition *was* exhaustive, so that only companies can be associated[134].

---

127 *Secretary of State for Employment v Newbold* [1981] IRLR 305; *Umar v Pliastar Ltd* [1981] ICR 727. This even applies when the person in question owns 50% of the shares in one of the companies, for that is *not* a voting majority and so the companies are not associated: *Hair Colour Consultants Ltd v Mena* [1984] ICR 671, [1984] IRLR 386; *South West Launderettes Ltd v Laidler* [1986] ICR 455, [1986] IRLR 305, CA; cf, however, *Payne v Secretary of State for Employment* [1989] IRLR 352, CA, where one person held 50% as a nominee of the other person.

128 [1978] IRLR 78. For this principle to apply, it must be the same group of persons exercising control in the case of each company claimed to be associated: *Poparm Ltd v Weekes* [1984] IRLR 388, approved by the Court of Appeal in *South West Launderettes Ltd v Laidler*, n 127, below.

129 [1986] ICR 455, [1986] IRLR 305, CA.

130 [1987] ICR 439, [1987] IRLR 360.

131 [1988] ICR 796, [1988] IRLR 457; *Russell v Elmdon Freight Terminal Ltd* [1989] ICR 629, EAT.

132 [1999] ICR 769.

133 *Hillingdon Area Health Authority v Kauders* [1979] ICR 472, [1979] IRLR 197.

134 *Southwood Hostel Management Committee v Taylor* [1979] ICR 813, [1979] IRLR 397.

This conflict was resolved in *Merton London Borough Council v Gardiner*[135] where the Court of Appeal held that the definition is exhaustive, so that an employee who was unfairly dismissed by a local authority could only claim to have his compensation calculated by reference to the two years he had worked with that authority, not by reference to the ten years he had previously served with three other local authorities. Thus, except under the first part of the definition ('vertical' associated employers) where one of the employers can be any sort of person provided that he, she or it has control of the company which is the other employer, the bodies claimed to be associated must be companies, which is a significant limitation on the definition (in the absence of any special statutory exception; the most important such exception now is that employees in local government service are covered by Regulations which deem their employment to be continuous, for redundancy rights purposes, when they move from one local government body to another[136]).

(vi) 'Worker' and the wider definition of employment

It can be argued that the traditional legal dichotomy between 'employee' and 'independent contractor' is now too simplistic to fit our diverse workforce, and leaves too many people potentially in a hole in the middle. One way to avoid (or at least mitigate) this, would be to move the goal posts and extend the definition of 'employee'.

This is not a new idea, and it has in the past been done in one of two ways, namely to use the term 'worker' instead (with a correspondingly wider definition) or to retain the term 'employee' but add to the normal definition (ie as a person under a contract of employment). Trade union legislation has always used the term 'worker', defining it as 'an individual who works ... (a) under a contract of employment or (b) under any other contract whereby he undertakes to do or perform personally any work or services for another party to the contract who is not a professional client of his'[137]. The extension in (b) is highly significant. Discrimination legislation uses the term 'employment' but applies it to employment under a contract of service or apprenticeship or a contract personally to execute any work or labour[138]. The Transfer of Undertakings (Protection of Employment) Regulations 1981 use the term 'employee' but define it as working 'for another person whether under a contract of service or apprenticeship or otherwise but does not include anyone who provides services under a contract

---

135 [1981] ICR 186, [1980] IRLR 472, CA.
136 Redundancy Payments (Continuity of Employment in Local Government, etc) (Modification) Order 1999, SI 1999/2277; *Harvey* R [1186]. See also the Redundancy Payments (National Health Service) (Modification) Order 1993, SI 1993/3167; *Harvey* R[755] which performs a similar function in the now-fragmented structure of the NHS, and the ERA 1996, s 218(7) which preserves continuity through the movement by teachers between schools maintained by a local education authority and that authority.
137 Trade Union and Labour Relations (Consolidation) Act 1992, s 296; the 'Wages Act' provisions or deductions from wages use a similar term and definition, see now the ERA 1996, s 230(3) and the recovery of commission by a self-employed investment consultant in *Robertson v Blackstone Franks Investment Management Ltd* [1998] IRLR 376, CA.
138 Equal Pay Act 1970, s 1(6)(a); Sex Discrimination Act 1975, s 82(1); Race Relations Act 1976, s 78(1); Disability Discrimination Act 1995, s 68(1). These definitions do not contain the express exclusion of a professional client.
139 SI 1981/1794, reg 2(1).

for services'[139]. While these definitions contain subtle differences (with the TUPE definition being arguably narrowest, with its exclusion of *anyone* under a contract for services), they do show a deliberate extension of statutory coverage. Perhaps surprisingly, the case law on them has been relatively scarce, though the leading authority of *Mirror Group Newspapers Ltd v Gunning*[140] emphasises the element of 'personal service', and states that that must be the dominant purpose of the contract in question.

This whole matter has, however, become topical again for two reasons. The first is that similar expanded definitions have been used by the present government in the Public Interest Disclosure Act 1998[141], the National Minimum Wage Act 1998[142] and the regulations on working time and part-time workers[143]. The second is that the government have expressed interest in making a similar extension to more mainstream employment legislation, in particular the Employment Rights Act 1996. This was raised in the White Paper 'Fairness at Work'[144] as a possible solution to the problem of the increased use by some employers of unfair forms of contracting such as 'nil hours contracts', which would be difficult to control or ban specifically, but might effectively be negated by wider coverage for employment protection laws. To that end, there is now a power in the Employment Relations Act 1999, section 23 for the Secretary of State by order to extend any right under the 1996 Act, the trade union legislation or any instrument made under the European Communities Act 1972 to individuals of a specified description. What use is to be made of this? Unfortunately, few clues were given in the Parliamentary debates (which got enmeshed on the question of the employment status of vicars!), and so it all remains to be determined. On the one hand, the power could be used sparingly to extend coverage to distinct groups of employees currently excluded. On the other hand, there could be a major extension of rights such as unfair dismissal and maternity/parental leave to cover those currently in the hole between employment and self-employment. At the time of writing, the government has started to consult on this issue but only at a very preliminary stage, canvassing the options[145]. Arguably, legislative action is now necessary here, since the regressive decision of the House of Lords on casual workers in *Carmichael v National Power plc*[146]. A major, across-the-board extension would have the effect of replacing the present, essentially exclusive definition of 'employee' with a wider, essentially *inclusive* definition

---

140 [1986] ICR 145, [1986] IRLR 27, CA, applied by the EAT in *Sheehan v Post Office Counters* [1999] ICR 734 in holding that a sub-postmaster was not covered by the disability legislation. The provision on legal services was held by the House of Lords to be capable of coming within the similar definition in the Northern Ireland fair employment legislation in *Kelly and Laughran v Northern Ireland Housing Executive* [1998] ICR 828, [1998] IRLR 593.
141 This is because the Act puts new sections into the ERA 1996 and adopts the latter's definition of 'worker'.
142 S 54.
143 SI 1998/1833, reg 2(1); SI 2000/1551, reg 1(2). the wider definition is, however, not used in the Fixed-Term Employees (Prevention of Less Favourable Treatment) Regulations 2002.
144 Cm 3968, para 3.18.
145 DTI 'Discussion document on employment status in relation to statutory employment rights' (2002) URN 02.1058.
146 [1999] 4 All ER 897, [2000] IRLR 43, HL; see p 21 above, and also *Clark v Oxfordshire Health Authority* [1998] IRLR 125, CA where a PAYE and NI-paying bank nurse working for only one authority was held not to be an employee.

capable of covering much of the present middle ground that causes so much difficulty[147]. The way that this is put in the DTI Guides on the national minimum wage and working time may be significant – they both state that it is only the '*genuinely* self employed' who will not be covered by these laws. Clearly, there will be as many problems defining this as there are currently in defining a person under a contract of employment; however, it does give a flavour of the intent of the legislation which can be seen graphically from the case of *Byrne Brothers (Farmwork) Ltd v Baird*[148]. In this case self-employed building workers (under a sub-contracting contract which stated that no holiday pay was due) were effectively laid off by a Christmas/New Year closure by the one firm that they worked for. Even though they were clearly not employees (being Schedule D labour-only sub-contractors in the longstanding tradition of the building industry) they successfully sued the firm for paid annual holiday for the period in question under the Working Time Regulations 1998; they were under *a* contract, performing work personally for that firm, and in practical terms were subordinate workers (dependent for work on that firm) and so not genuinely in business on their own account. This is a cautionary tale, particularly at the dodgier end of the self-employment spectrum; it backs the argument that if the section 23 power is eventually used widely, that could well turn out to be the most radical single change by the present government.

4 GENERAL PRINCIPLES OF INDUSTRIAL RELATIONS

Of all the 'legal' subjects it is truest of labour law that it does not belong fully to lawyers. A great deal of the background takes its principles from other disciplines – from politics, from economics and from social psychology. Each has its own literature and it is inevitable, though unfortunate, that there is still little synthesis. Tensions inevitably arise. Indeed it is not unknown for the slogan 'keep the law out of industrial relations' to be raised. The reader of this book, aware of the number of pages that follow, must know that those words have a special meaning.

They reflect the belief that British industrial relations are informal rather than formal; collective rather than individual. The best starting point for an understanding of this view is still the Donovan Report[149], already mentioned. That report was a comprehensive overview of our system of industrial relations. In the various notes of dissent and in the vigorous Note of Reservation by Andrew Schonfield the areas where views can sharply diverge are indicated.

Before looking at this central theme it is necessary to point to two trends which may be pulling in the opposite direction. Since 1963[150] great emphasis has been put upon the legal regulation binding employer and employee. Although prior to the Contracts of Employment Act 1963 it was clear that the law of contract governed what was archaically referred to by lawyers as the relationship between master and servant, recourse to the law was relatively rare. Indeed the subsidiary

147 It was held under equivalent provisions of the Industrial Relations Act 1971 that the extended definition can cover some self-employed workers, provided they are giving personal service: *Writers' Guild of Great Britain v BBC* [1974] 1 All ER 574, [1974] ICR 234, NIRC; *Broadbent v Crisp* [1974] 1 All ER 1052, [1974] ICR 248 NIRC.
148 [2002] ICR 667, [2002] IRLR 96.
149 Royal Commission on Trade Unions and Employers' Associations (Cmnd 3623, 1968).
150 Contracts of Employment Act 1963.

terms of the average contract of employment, that is to say features other than wages, hours and holidays, were rarely specified and at best could be determined from recourse to the vague concept of 'custom and practice'. Few knew, or had ready access to, the full terms of their employment contract.

Two factors have changed this. Since 1963 a series of statutes[151] have laid down a considerable number of basic individual rights. There are, as a result, an increasing number of standard terms that apply except where something better is expressly provided. These will be discussed in due course[152]. In addition the provision that each employee should be given a note of the principal terms of his contract stressed the centrality of the legal aspect of the relationship. The change is remarkable – before 1960, for example, it was exceptionally difficult to answer simple questions such as what the law allowed an employer to do when his employee was regularly absent as a result of ill health.

That difficulty was compounded by the paucity of reported cases. Few cases were litigated, very few indeed found a place in the reports[153]. Those that did tended naturally to concern highly paid employees[154]. This meant that the rules that evolved were by no means of general application. The sparsity of rules also meant that old cases, long since made questionable by a change in social circumstances and attitudes, retained at least the appearance of being good law[155]. It will not be necessary to read far into this book to realise how greatly this has changed. The danger now is that the law is groaning under a surfeit of reported cases.

The reason for the change is not just the swing of attention back to the legal aspect of the employment contract, just described. It arises too because an accessible, cheap forum for disputes has been provided by the establishment and use of the system of employment tribunals. They began in 1964 and the growth in their workload is amazing[156]. This jurisdiction has syphoned off a great deal of decision making that would have traditionally been the business of the employer and his recognised trade unions. It is somewhat surprising that almost no use has been made of the provision that in some areas there can be approved private arrangements[157].

The second development is the closer regulation of collective relationships by statute. Again these will form important topics elsewhere in this book[158]. It is only necessary to pause here to stress that they flow from a different general approach than that traditionally held by industrial relations specialists, by trade

---

151 See pp 3–9, above.
152 See particularly chs 3 and 4.
153 The Law Reports Index 1951–60 did not have a heading 'Employment'. There are not more than 30 cases reported during that period – and this Index includes the Weekly Law Reports from 1953.
154 *Laws v London Chronicle (Indicator Newspapers) Ltd* [1959] 2 All ER 285, [1959] 1 WLR 698, CA.
155 The law on obedience of orders is a marked example. Textbooks after World War II were still including cases such as *Spain v Arnott* (1817) 2 Stark 256 and *Hallward v Snell* (1886) 2 TLR 836.
156 ACAS has applications referred to it for conciliation. Its statistics show that from 1972 (before ACAS was instituted) there were 200 per week. By 1975 this had risen to 400 per week – see Annual Report 1975. By 1980 the figure was 800 per week – see Annual Report 1980. Having remained stable throughout the 1980s, the figures doubled again in the mid-1990s, promoting proposals for reform of the system: see p 508 below.
157 See ERA 1996, s 110. Only the electrical contracting industry took advantage of this provision, and that was terminated in 2001.
158 See particularly chs 10 and 11.

unions almost as a whole, and by a considerable number of employers. A continuing spate of statutes since the Employment Act 1980 have attempted to bring the regulation of collective disputes firmly within a legal framework. Of course the law has always been, and must always be, there to define the limits of permitted behaviour. It is the underlying assumption of those statutes that there can be advantage gained by framing the law so that it gives the courts a significant regulating role that is so important, and different.

It has also been the aim of this legislation, taken as a whole, to reduce considerably the disruptive power of trade unions. An earlier debate[159], addressing the question whether trade unions should be protected by positive rights rather than by the current system of immunities has faded, leaving the traditional immunities system with its considerable complexity and continuing uncertainty, tending to inhibit trade union actions. It cannot be doubted that a change to a rights system would give the trade unions sounder foundations, with less chance of surprise attacks by the courts and what they see as continuing limitations on their powers.

Despite the legislative changes the basic thinking that underpins the approach of many industrial relations practitioners, though difficult to summarise, is still based upon some form of collective bargaining. Indeed this was the first principle set out in the Industrial Relations Act 1971, despite its different philosophy, and section 1(1)(a) formulated 'the principle of collective bargaining freely conducted on behalf of workers and employers and with due regard to the general interests of the community'. That idea reappeared in the Employment Protection Act 1975, where ACAS was charged in section 1(2) with 'the general duty of promoting the improvement of industrial relations, and in particular of encouraging the extension of collective bargaining and the development and, where necessary, reform of collective bargaining machinery'. We shall see, however, that this formulation was significantly changed in 1993, to drop from 'in particular' onwards, significant in showing at least the desired direction of the previous government. The formulation was changed again in 1999 by the present government, but without reinstating the reference to collective bargaining.

Collective bargaining by its very nature requires the organisation of workers into trade unions. This had increased steadily over the years. It has been estimated that in 1901 12.6% of the workforce were unionised, a figure that had risen to 52.6% in 1976. Those crude figures hid big variations and changing patterns. That process was largely without legislative assistance, although in the Industrial Relations Act 1971[160] and again in the Employment Protection Act 1975[161] statutory recognition procedures were set out. These suffered mixed fortunes and indicate the industrial relations difficulties that prevented the smooth use of a statutory procedure. Indeed ACAS took the view that because of the attitude taken by the courts[162] it found it impossible to work the procedure as it considered it should be worked and the whole procedure was repealed by the Employment Act 1980. There were serious underlying difficulties, eg the bad feelings that

---

159 Cmnd 8128, January 1981.
160 Ss 44–60.
161 Ss 11–16, repealed by the Employment Act 1980.
162 Especially in *Grunwick Processing Laboratories Ltd v ACAS* [1978] 1 All ER 338, [1978] ICR 231, HL; *UKAPE v ACAS* [1979] ICR 303, [1979] IRLR 68, CA; *National Employers Life Assurance Co v ACAS* [1979] ICR 620, [1979] IRLR 282; and *EMA v ACAS (No 2)* [1979] ICR 637, [1979] IRLR 246, CA. The decisions of the Court of Appeal in *UKAPE v ACAS* and *EMA v ACAS* were eventually reversed by the House of Lords.

existed between those trade unions affiliated to the TUC and those that were not, and dilemmas, eg where the workers wanted to be represented by a trade union that did not fit into the accepted industrial relations pattern. In the light of all of this, it is perhaps initially surprising that the present government have reintroduced a statutory recognition procedure (under a revamped Central Arbitration Committee). This was, however, an important undertaking to the trade unions, and it was enacted by the Employment Relations Act 1999. However, lessons have certainly been learned and, showing an almost paranoid desire to avoid judicial review (on grounds of perversity), the drafting seeks to define and delineate as much as possible, leaving very little indeed to discretion. The legislation is remarkably long and detailed; its effectiveness remains to be gauged in the longer term, in the sense of the extent to which it may reverse the hitherto consistent decline in recognition, in economic conditions very different from those in the 1970s.

Along with levels of union recognition, the coverage of collective bargaining declined steeply through the 1980s and 1990s, due partly to deep structural changes in the economy and partly to government policies (privatisation and contracting out having played significant roles). It now appears that for the first time since the twentieth century, only a minority of employees are covered by it.[163] However, again the picture is patchy; reports of its death may be greatly exaggerated, and in the significant areas where it still exists it remains well established (though, like everything else, subject to change and modification). It too has a distinctive flavour. Although some agreements (eg those in the engineering industry) look like a properly drawn contract, a great many such agreements are extremely sketchy and it is difficult to separate rules from expressions of intent or to determine exactly what the agreement covers. This is made more confusing to a lawyer by the extensive reliance upon custom and practice. In these circumstances it was no surprise that the attempt in the Industrial Relations Act 1971 to make these agreements legally binding failed, neither trade unions nor employers being willing to adopt a more rigorous legal approach[164].

We shall see that the substantive aspects of a collective bargain (ie the wage rates and other terms of employment) do gain legal effect by incorporation into the individual contract of the employee covered, but those aspects that bind employer and trade union (eg procedures or length of time to elapse before re-negotiation) do so only informally, for the collective bargain itself is *not* legally binding[165].

---

163 Millward et al *Workplace Industrial Relations in Transition* (1992); Millward *The New Industrial Relations?* (1994); Brown et al 'Management: pay determination and collective bargaining' in Edwards (ed) *Industrial Relations, Theory and Practice in Britain* (1995). In 1997 8.1m (36% of all employees) were covered by collective bargains over pay and conditions: Culley and Woodland 'Trade union membership and recognition in 1997' [1998] Labour Market Trends 353. In 1998 unions were recognised in 45% of workplaces (down from 66% in 1984 and 53% in 1990); 47% of workplaces had no trade union members at all (up from 36% in 1990): DTI/ACAS/ESRC/PSI 1998 Workplace Employee Relations Survey – the First Findings (URN/98/934).

164 See the Industrial Relations Act 1971, ss 34–36 which give birth to the 'TINA LEA' clause – 'This is not a legally enforceable agreement'.

165 Trade Union and Labour Relations (Consolidation) Act 1992, s 179. *Monterosso Shipping Co v ITWF* [1982] ICR 675, [1982] IRLR 468, CA. For the (similar) position at common law, see *Ford Motor Co Ltd v AUEW* [1969] 2 QB 303, [1969] 2 All ER 481; Lewis 'Collective agreements: the Kahn-Freund legacy' (1979) 42 MLR 613.

The same approach colours the areas of dispute regulation. ACAS is an independent, tripartite body[166]. It seeks to persuade the parties to a dispute to settle it by means of conciliation or, less frequently, mediation. In addition it provides facilities for arbitration. All three processes are subject to voluntary co-operation – they are offered, not enforced upon either party. The Grunwick dispute will remain for a long time an example of the clash of two principles. The employer's view was that he need only do what he was required to do by law. That of the trade union (and ACAS when it was called in) followed the traditional course and sought voluntary agreement by compromise. The Scarman Report[167] is an excellent study of these two approaches and its conclusion lends support to the industrial relations rather than the legalistic view.

The law has made little systematic attempt to encourage the use of collective bargaining or influence the form of collective agreements. The initiative has been generally left to the parties. This is somewhat surprising in view of the emphasis laid upon this aspect of industrial relations by the Donovan Commission[168]. Paragraph 182 summarises the Commission's thinking by indicating that 'orderly and effective' industrial relations would be promoted by the development of 'comprehensive and authoritative' bargaining machinery set up with the trade unions; by the development of grievance and dismissal procedures; by the development of redundancy procedures; and by measures to promote health and safety[169].

Several of these aims have been underlined by statutes and will be discussed elsewhere. There are provisions leading to the setting up of grievance and dismissal procedures[170]; the Health and Safety at Work Act etc 1974 has dealt with several aspects of employer-employee relationships in that sphere[171]. But little has been done to further the general objective of developing collective bargaining or other forms of determination of terms and conditions; government policy has for years now indicated a deregulated labour market and the previous government opposed legally enforceable works councils (though they stated that in principle they were in favour of better communication and participation, but as a matter for the *parties*, not the state). The present government have so far not shown a markedly different approach, in particular where it could lead to compulsion on employers, or lead to them being accused of placing more bureaucratic burdens on businesses[172].

Indeed, one of the uncertainties in the current practical background to much of the law here is the *form* that future industrial relations should take. The old system of collective negotiation through recognised trade unions has declined or changed and in many areas newly pervasive ideas of 'human resource management' techniques may be seen cynically as a way of avoiding collective

---

166 TUC and CBI representatives and independent members: three of each plus the Chairman.
167 Cmnd 6922 (1977).
168 Royal Commission on Trade Unions and Employers' Associations, 1965–1968 Cmnd 3623.
169 Cmnd 3623, p 45.
170 See p 530 below. These are subject to further reform, with a view to their stengthening, in the Employment Act 2002.
171 See p 885 below.
172 Fairness at Work (CM. 3968, 1998), para 1.13.
173 See the conclusion in Millward *The New Industrial Relations?* (1994) at p 133: 'British industry and commerce appear to be moving towards a situation in which non-managerial employees are treated as a "factor of production". Britain is approaching the position where few employees have any mechanism through which they can contribute to the operation of their workplace in a broader context than that of their own job. There is no sign that the shrinkage in the extent of trade union representation is being offset by a

negotiation and replacing it, not with new forms of communication, but in fact with very little[173]. This all gives particular significance to four legal developments to be seen in this book. The first is the movement (through the pressure of EC law) towards requirements of forms of consultation with employees through the direct election of employee representatives, even where there are no recognised unions[174]. This now affects collective redundancies, transfers of undertaking and health and safety; it could provide a model for future developments on a more general basis, particularly in relation to the Information and Consultation Directive[175], which is due for implementation in the UK between 2005 and 2008 and, although inaccurately referred to as the 'Works Council Directive', may move this country towards such a system. Depending on the eventual form of implementation, this could be a challenge to the unions, not just to management, because it would be significantly different from the old model of the unions being the sole or even the principal channels of communications. The second development, already seen in this chapter, is the increased involvement of EC law in governing certain *types* of employment, quite independently of any collective bargaining or lack thereof covering individuals within those categories. Already enacted are the new, across-the-board laws on part-time and fixed-term working, with agency working in the wings. The third development, partly flowing from the second, is the increasing importance of 'soft law', which is often taking the form of 'best practice guidance' (usually from the DTI), either explaining these new laws or (more fundamentally) actually constituting a form of implementation of EU Directives, especially ones which are drafted in a vague and aspirational way[176]. This trend is likely to continue, and soft law is likely to have an increasing practical effect in laying down the ground rules, especially as it is taken seriously by the non-lawyers involved in employment relations. It would be very short-sighted for an employment lawyer to dismiss such developments as 'not real law'. Indeed, this increase in reliance on soft law could be seen as a modern version of the very old ideas discussed above that industrial or employment relations are *not* to be governed primarily by the law – frameworks are increasingly being set out legally (and the growth recently in the sheer size of the legislation is frightening) but ultimately the aim is to have matters settled consensually and pragmatically at the sharp end[177]. The fourth development, if increased individualism is to

---

growth in other methods of representing non-managerial employees' interests or views . . . Nor is there much of the legal regulation that is so extensive in other developed countries to provide a basic floor of employment rights and minimum labour standards'. In 1998 (taking workplaces with twenty five or more employees) of workplaces with no union presence, only 11% had some form of non-union workforce representation, and 89% had no workforce representation at all: the 1998 Workplace Employee Relations Survey – the First Findings (DTI/ACAS/ESRC/PSI, URN/98/934), p 17.

174 Collective Redundancies and Transfer of Undertakings (Protection of Employment) (Amendment) Regulations 1995, SI 1995/2587 (see pp 84–94); Health and Safety (Consultation with Employees) Regulations 1996, SI 1996/1513 (see p 888). See also the novel concept of the workforce agreement in the Working Time Regulations 1998, SI 1998/1833 (see p 244), the Maternity and Parental Leave etc Regulations 1999, SI 1999/3312 (see p 434) and the Fixed-term Employee Regulations 2002, SI 2002/2034 (see p 28).

175 Directive 2002/14/EC; see p 97 below.

176 See particularly the second half of the Part-time Worker Directive, p 25 above.

177 Considering the problem of too much employment law and its effects on businesses, the first recommendation made by the Better Regulation Task Force was that governmental bodies should always consider initially whether there are better ways of achieving a policy objective *without* resort to state regulation: 'Employment regulation: striking a balance' (May 2002).

remain dominant in the political and economic fields, is the renewed interest in protection for employees through the medium of the contract of employment and court decisions thereon, this being increasingly seen as one of the reasons for the dramatic rise in the number of tribunal applications in the last fifteen years.

Given this diversity of legal involvement, it is essential to appreciate the tension that can arise between the different approaches of the industrial relations specialist (the company personnel or HR officer or trade union official) on the one hand and the lawyer on the other. The lawyer's virtues – the search for clarity, the anticipation of future difficulty, the demand for good records and the concept of relevance which narrows the area of dispute – all present difficulty when applied to the fluid, amorphous, interlinked problems of industrial relations and/or human resource management.

5 EUROPE

The expectation on the part of the trade unions that they would continue to play a part as one of the partners with the employers and government began to wane in the 1980s. The growth of individual rights for workers had progressed well – the Industrial Relations Act 1971 had introduced the concept of unfair dismissal, and equality legislation was making progress, albeit rather slowly, on the basis of the Equal Pay Act 1970 and the Sex Discrimination Act 1975. But the central concept of joint regulation, envisaging the trade unions as playing a major part in the regulation of industry and work did not develop well. The final years of the Labour government of 1974–79 were stormy and the advent of Conservative power, in the event to last until 1997, meant the inevitable reconstruction along lines less favourable to the trade unions. What in the early statutes, such as the Employment Act 1980, the Employment Act 1982 and the Trade Union Act 1984 – which showed greater hostility to the enlarged trade union role – might have been regarded as a realignment later showed itself to be a 'step by step' reduction of trade union power and rejection of their aspirations as far as joint regulation was concerned.

Faced with this hostility, one of the consequences was that the trade unions looked to the increasing impact that membership of the EC was having. The UK had, by a Treaty of Accession, along with the Republic of Ireland and Denmark joined the community[178].

This had effects on several areas of the law of employment. For example, Article 48 governed the free movement of workers within the community. But the most immediately fruitful area was that of sex equality. Article 119 provided for equal pay for equal work and a number of later Directives expand this – notably Directive 75/117 which introduced the concept of work of equal value, Directive 76/207 which provides more generally for equal treatment and Directive 79/7 which extended the concept of equality to social security and Directive 2000/78 which will require new equality laws relating to sexual orientation, religion, disability and age.

---

178 The treaties were incorporated into the law by the European Communities Act 1972, which (crucially here) provides for Directives to be implemented by Regulations (not necessarily by Act of Parliament), even where that requires the amendment of such an Act.

A difference in statutory interpretation between the English and the European Court soon became obvious. This was clearly demonstrated in early cases such as *Garland v British Rail Engineering Ltd*[179] and *Worringham v Lloyds Bank Ltd*[180] in the ECJ in the initial phase of the application of EC equality laws, and the need for the domestic courts to state a novel approach to the interpretation of domestic legislation in order to comply with a backing Directive was made equally clear by the House of Lords in *Litster v Forth Dry Dock and Engineering Co Ltd*[181]. Even more revolutionary was the decision of that court in *R v Secretary of State for Employment, ex p Equal Opportunities Commission*[182] that the statutory requirement of sixteen hours per week minimum employment in order to qualify for the major statutory rights was indirectly discriminatory (and *not* justified by the British government's political/economic arguments in its favour) and contrary to EC law, with the result that (pending legislative amendment several months later) it had to be 'disapplied' by tribunals, even though it continued to be present in the UK Act of Parliament. When these matters are discussed below at greater length the impact of the European approach will be clear.

Even so, progress from this source has in the past been both patchy and slow. Perhaps the most important impact is in the sphere of health and safety, where underlying political attitudes to trade unions are of minimal importance[183]. Even there it is only since 1990 that rapid strides are being made. Other candidates for increasing coverage have been consultation requirements and specific forms of atypical work (part-time, fixed-term and agency working).

The central feature of the EU, as far as employment relations are concerned, has been the so-called Social Charter – The Community Charter of Fundamental Social Rights. This was adopted in December 1990 at the Strasbourg Summit. Its aim was stated as being 'the completion of the internal market, with the free movement of goods, people, capital and services by 1992'. Its effect was undoubtedly to increase the pace of action.

The Charter has twelve chapters dealing with matters such as uniformity of employment conditions, remuneration, training, living and working conditions, information, consultation, participation and industrial democracy, and protection for children, the elderly and the disabled.

It was at Maastricht in 1992 that a Treaty of European Union was signed. This represented 'a new stage in the process of creating an even closer union among the people of Europe'. The Treaty was adopted by all the countries, but the UK did not sign the Protocol on Social Policy (the 'Social Chapter'). This was the part of the Treaty dealing with the matters which are very much the concern of this book, as the list of topics set out in the last paragraph above clearly indicates.

This much-vaunted 'opt out' from the Social Chapter by the previous government was starting to look of dubious longevity even before the 1997 election[184], but it did provoke one of the relatively few disagreements between

---

179 [1982] ICR 420, [1982] IRLR 111, ECJ.
180 [1981] ICR 558, [1981] IRLR 178, ECJ.
181 [1989] ICR 341, [1989] IRLR 161, HL.
182 [1994] ICR 317, [1994] IRLR 176, HL.
183 See ch 13 below.
184 This was particularly so in the case of the Working Time Directive which was passed against the will of the previous government, by the device of classifying it as a health and safety measure (majority voting), not as an employment law measure (unanimity required); the government's challenge to the legality of this was rejected by the ECJ: *United Kingdom v EU Council* C-84/94 [1997] ICR 443, [1997] IRLR 30, ECJ.

the parties over employment policy by that time, since the Labour party were in favour of a social dimension to Europe and shortly after their election victory they indicated their intention to sign up to the Social Chapter and end the UK's opt out. This was to be done through the mechanism of the redrafting of the EC Treaty as a result of the 1997 Amsterdam Treaty[185]; although the effect immediately was in fact very limited because so little had been done by the signatories to the 1992 Protocol[186], the importance of course lay in the *future* participation by the UK in the negotiation and implementation of social policy initiatives. This is simply one further reason why the interplay between domestic employment law and the EU remains at the centre of the stage.

6 HUMAN RIGHTS AT WORK[187]

This section considers the ever-increasing importance on the workplace of the European Convention on Human Rights (ECHR) as a result of the Human Rights Act (HRA) 1998. It assumes some familiarity with both the ECHR and the HRA but highlights certain crucial aspects[188]. Mainly, it evaluates the extent to which the ECHR, mediated by the HRA, alters the domestic legal relationship between employee and the employer and assesses how this will be done. Might an employee now be able to claim against an employer an enforceable right of privacy (under Article 8 ECHR) or religious freedom under Article 9? If so, what is the effect on an employer who wishes to monitor employees' phone calls and email or who wishes the business to be open on Sundays?

(i) The ECHR and the HRA

The ECHR is legally distinct from the EC and EU and so its system should never be confused with or equated to EC law[189]. Employment lawyers reading the ECHR for the first time will be struck by the near-absence of express protection for rights in and surrounding the workplace. There are no rights, for example, to strike, to work, to a fair wage, to social security or to protection against arbitrary (or unfair) dismissal. Probably the only rights directly and obviously relevant to employment law are those to freedom from slavery, servitude and forced labour, of association and from discrimination (Articles 4, 11 and 14). However, merely reading the words of any article may belie a true picture of the extent of its

185 Barnard 'The UK, the "social chapter" and the Amsterdam Treaty' (1997) 26 ILJ 275. The treaty renumbers the relevant Articles, a source of some confusion.

186 The immediate effect was to commit the UK only to the European Works Council Directive 94/95 and the Parental Leave Directive 96/34. To these have now been added directives on the burden of proof in discrimination cases, part-time workers, posted workers, fixed-term workers, race discrimination, discrimination on the grounds of sexual orientation, religion, disability and age, and informing or consulting the workforce.

187 Despite its seeming broad scope, this section focuses exclusively on the ECHR. There are various other instruments – international and regional – which guarantee to employees certain human rights. These include Conventions made under the auspices of the tri-partite International Labour Organization, the system of state reports (and claims) made under the Council of Europe's Social Charter 1961 and human rights protection at EC level such as the Fundamental Charter agreed in Nice in 2000.

188 Readers unfamiliar with the ECHR and the HRA might consider Wadham and Mountfield *Blackstones Guide to the Human Rights Act 1998* (2003).

189 Although membership overlaps; it is a precondition of EC membership that a state joins the Council of Europe and signs up to the ECHR.

coverage; the European Court of Human Rights at Strasbourg (ECtHR) has actively developed and moulded rights jurisprudentially over the past fifty years. A pertinent example would be *Young, James and Webster v United Kingdom*[190] where the ECtHR implied into Article 11 (the right to associate) a right not to associate, although not necessarily of equal value. The effect was to give workers the right not to be forced to join a union under a closed-shop arrangement[191].

Some familiarity with the underpinning jurisprudence of the ECtHR may prove helpful. The ECtHR has developed the concept of *positive* obligations so instead of a 'mere' requirement to refrain from depriving someone of a guaranteed right, states may also in some cases be required to act in order to prevent breaches by other state actors or even other private parties. For example, in *Sibson v United Kingdom*[192] the case was argued that the failure was not the state's direct violation of the right to disassociate in Article 11 but that the UK had failed properly to regulate 'closed shop' dismissals of private sector employees. The ECtHR is also guided in its interpretative task by certain underlying principles[193] and, rightly or wrongly, is increasingly coming to view proportionality as a fundamental principle of the whole structure of the ECHR. This is despite the word never appearing in its text. In *Soering v UK*[194], the ECtHR said that 'inherent in the whole of the Convention is a search for a fair balance between the demands of the general interest of the community and the requirements of the protection of the individual's fundamental rights'.

Most important for present purposes is reiterating the fact that very few of the rights in the ECHR are absolute; most can be restricted, removed or otherwise lawfully qualified in some way for some purpose[195]. The main method is the 'clawback' from what would otherwise be expansive unlimited rights in Articles 8(2)–11(2), each of which is in broadly the same standard form. For example, whether or not there has been an unlawful invasion of privacy (Article 8) requires resolution of a three-stage analysis:

(i)   Is the restriction in accordance with law?[196]
(ii) Can the restriction achieve one of the listed legitimate aims in Article 8(2) such as the wide-ranging scope of the catch-all 'protection of the rights and freedoms of others'?
(iii) In any event, is the restriction 'necessary in a democratic society', sometimes shortened to asking whether or not there is a 'pressing social neeed'[197]. In

190 (1982) 4 EHRR 38.
191 See p 590 below.
192 (1993) 17 EHRR 193. Although it was ultimately unsuccessful, it was not on this point.
193 These include taking a purposive or teleological approach so as to protect individual human rights by giving effect to the ECHR as a 'living instrument' in the light of present day conditions; maintaining democratic values of pluralism, broadmindedness and tolerance; and requiring that the protection of rights should be practical and effective not theoretical and illusory.
194 (1989) 11 EHRR 439, para 89.
195 The only two absolute articles are Arts 3 (torture, inhuman or degrading treatment or punishment) and 4(1) (slavery and servitude). Art 15 for example permits a temporary opt-out (a 'derogation') from almost all the articles but only to the extent proportionately necessary to deal with an emergency or the threat of war.
196 As well as there being an actual domestic law, the phrase also requires that the law is adequately accessible and sufficiently precisely formulated: *Sunday Times v United Kingdom* (1979) 2 EHRR 245.
197 *Handyside v Unitd Kingdom* (1976) 1 EHRR 737. Within the resolution of this, states have what is referred to as a 'margin of appreciation'. This is an element of discretion for determining, first, whether there is any need for a restriction at all and, second, what measure is necessary to combat the perceived problem.

other words, is the restriction a proportionate response to the perceived problem?

The HRA marks a legal watershed by introducing enforceable positive rights in stark contrast to the negative, remedy-based system of residual liberties that existed before 4 October 2000[198]. To assess the HRA's impact on employment law it is crucial to understand what it does not do. The HRA does *not* incorporate the ECHR into domestic law[199]; instead it 'brings home' what it calls 'Convention rights'[200]. Convention rights are therefore very different from rights created by EC law which latter become part of English law and are directly enforceable with direct effect. In promoting the HRA, the government wrestled with two conflicting desires. It wished to give effective protection for human rights but wished too to maintain Parliamentary sovereignty, with Parliament alone being constitutionally capable of altering the law.

The main means by which human rights are given greater protection under the HRA are:

(i)   A new duty of interpretation (section 3) imposed on judges. All courts and tribunals are required to read and to give effect to all legislation whenever passed 'so far as is possible to do so' in a way that is compatible with Convention rights. If that is impossible, judges may not 'strike down' offending primary legislation (although they can for secondary legislation) but may[201] grant a declaration of incompatibility under section 4. This affords no relief to claimants and is neither new nor particularly extensive. If we compare it to judicial developments in EC law, we can see that not only have declarations of incompatibility been granted against primary Acts[202] but injunctions too, thus preventing the effective operation of otherwise valid primary legislation[203].

The crux will be the extent of the formula 'so far as possible' – there must be some limit to a court's interpretative power since section 3 expressly reserves to Parliament the power to legislate in conflict with the ECHR; why else have section 4 declarations?[204] Does it extend to permitting judges to read words into Acts so as to ensure their compatibility[205] or to narrow statutory phrases by 'reading down' legislative words and phrases or even to take a strained meaning rather than any other to ensure compatibility?

(ii) The duty of Convention compliance on public authorities under section 6. This makes it unlawful for a public authority to act in a way that is incompatible with a Convention right and so the HRA now requires courts to do that

---

198 The date on which the HRA came into force in England and Wales. Remedy-based because to protect 'rights' successfully, claimants would need to ground an action in an existing wrong with an existing remedy.

199 Of all the major works setting out the operation of the HRA, the most complete and most detailed is Clayton and Tomlinson *The Law of Human Rights* (2000).

200 In fact, it does not bring home all rights in the ECHR in any event; it specifically excludes as 'Convention rights' Arts 1 and 13. Claims for breaches of these cannot be litigated at all before domestic courts.

201 Judges in superior courts only.

202 *R v Secretary of State for Employment, ex p Equal Opportunities Commission* [1994] IRLR 176 HL.

203 *R v Secretary of State for Transport, ex p Factortame (No 2)* [1991] 1 AC 603.

204 There has been little consistent articulation of s 3 so far even at the highest level. Contrast *R v A* [2001] UKHL 25, [2002] 1 AC 45, especially Lord Steyn with *Re S (Care Plan)* [2002] UKHL 10, [2002] 2 AC 91 (Lord Nicholls).

205 This seems to have the implicit support of Lord Irvine [1998] PL 221 and, as importantly, the House of Lords in the EC context at least: see *Litster v Forth Dry Dock Engineering* [1989] IRLR 161 discussed at p 207 below.

which they previously forswore: using the ECHR as a greater constraint on the discretionary decisions of public bodies[206] . In brief[207], we can identify standard or pure public authorities, which are always under a duty to be Convention complaint whether acting publicly or privately, and functional public authorities (or quasi-public bodies or hybrids) which are bound by section 6 only when exercising functions of a public nature. Purely private bodies are not governed directly by the section 6 duty but since courts and tribunals are expressly included as 'public authorities' in section 6, this raises the possibility of private individuals claiming the benefit of Convention rights against other private individuals through the indirect horizontal effect of the HRA. This is duscussed below. Although there is no list, it is fairly clear that pure public authorities will include both central and local government, the police and prison service together with, it is imagined, bodies such as schools, universities, the military and medical institutions. Whether the test for functional authorities will be the same as the public law test determining amenability to judicial review has not yet been decided[208] but some assistance has been given in a series of cases all involving the section 6 status of housing associations[209]. An example of a functional authority given by the government was Railtrack (now Network Rail). It would have public functions when acting as a safety regulator but would be acting privately in relation to the sale of land, for example[210]. We know it is generally not a violation of a Convention right to deprive an employee of their freedom of speech or to impose a measure which restricts their enjoyment of family life *per se* but will be so if the restriction is not necessary. Does it meet a 'pressing social need' or is it disproportionate? Courts[211] are likely to inquire retrospectively as to whether the measure is actually able to achieve its aim (suitability) and can be achieved by a measure which is demonstrably less restrictive of individual rights (necessity) and whether in any event the measure still had a disproportionate effect (balance)?[212]

(iii) The moulding and developing of private law as between purely private parties. Although only public authorities are directly bound by section 6, purely private sector employers will still be bound by and subject to the ECHR indirectly. First, where the relationship with employees has been put onto a statutory footing or is in some way is governed by legislation, the section 3 duty discussed above becomes relevant. Secondly, even where the

206 Thus, pre-HRA, the three traditional heads of judicial review – irrationality, illegality and procedural impropriety – were not expanded to include challenges to decisions based on their effect being a (disproportionate) breach of a Convention right: *R v Secretary of State for the Home Department, ex p Brind* [1991] 1 AC 696, [1990] 1 All ER 469.
207 See also Clayton and Tomlinson, n 199 above, para 5.08 and *Poplar Housing Association v Donoghue* [2001] EWCA Civ 595, [2002] QB 48 at [63].
208 Cases such as *R v Panel on Takeovers and Mergers, ex p Datafin* [1987] QB 815, [1987] 1 All ER 564.
209 *Poplar Housing Association* (n 207 above), *R (Heather) v Leonard Cheshire Foundation* [2002] EWCA Civ 366, [2002] 2 All ER 936 (on appeal to the House of Lords) and *R (A) v Partnerships in Care* [2002] EWHC 529 (Admin), [2001] 1 WLR 261. The House of Lords has provided some general guidance on s 6 in the ecclesiastical case *Aston Cantlow and Wilmcote with Billesley Parochial Church Council v Wallbank* [2003] UKHL 37, [2003] 3 WLR 283.
210 *Hansard*, HL Committee 24 November 1997, col 784. Similarly, it was accepted that doctors might be a public authority in dealing with NHS patients but not if dealing with private patients: see col 811.
211 Following *R (on the application of Daly) v Secretary of State for the Home Department* [2001] UKHL 26, [2001] 2 AC 532 and *Gough v Chief Constable of Derbyshire Constabulary* [2002] EWCA Civ 351, [2002] QB 1213, [2002] 2 All ER 985.
212 Supperstone and Coppel [1999] EHRLR 301, 313.

relationship is governed by common law *simpliciter* (including the contractual employment relationship and tortuous duties owed to each other) or equitable rules, then the ECHR may still have an indirect horizontal effect[213]. In short, whenever the judicial process is engaged by private litigants in dispute, judges should decide cases or exercise their discretion in a way that accords with and gives effect to Convention rights albeit that[214] they are not able to confer new causes of action. In other words, there is no actionable wrong for breach of the Convention by another private individual. But, even though private individuals have no independent Convention rights *inter se,* if employee A decides to sue employer B in tort, contract or in equity (or any claim not based on a statutory right[215]) under an *existing* head of claim and/or damage, then once the case is being heard the court must decide its outcome in accordance with the relevant Convention rights of the parties. This would include any Convention rights of B.

(iv) Enabling victims[216] to use Convention arguments under section 7(1) as a sword or a shield in legal proceedings. Section 7(1)(a) allows proceedings to be brought while section 7(1)(b) allows reliance 'on the Convention right ... concerned in any legal proceedings'. In practice employees might be able to:

- seek judicial review of a decision by a public authority (employer or perhaps the DfEE or DTI) alleging a (disproportionate) restriction on Convention rights;

- sue a public authority employer in tort for damages for breach of its section 6 statutory duty[217],

- institute proceedings against any employer using an existing common law or statutory claim and rely on the indirect horizontal effect or the court's new interpretation duty under section 3; and

- use the Convention collaterally as a defence in (existing) proceedings brought by any employer. For example, if an employer seeks an injunction restraining an employee from whistle blowing, contrary to a contractual term, employees might argue that all they were doing was exercising their right to free expression. Of course, this does not mean that the employee will win; the court may hold such a restriction to be justified and proportionate[218].

(ii) The impact of the HRA on employment law

Rather than outlining the impact of the HRA on discrete areas of employment law, this section provides a more detailed overview showing how Convention

---

213 A summary of the views of various commentators can be found in Clayton and Tomlinson, n 199 above, paras 5.74–5.99.

214 *Venables and Thompson v News Group Newspapers* [2001] 1 All ER 908 at [108]–[109] and [126] (Butler Sloss P).

215 Where of course the s 3 duty of statutory interpretation will apply in any event.

216 The victim test is based on the Strasbourg case law under Art 34 and requires a direct and actual effect; it is therefore likelier to be narrower than under (old) RSC Ord 53 for judicial review since it will exclude NGOs bringing public interest claims: *R v Foreign Secretary, ex p World Development Movement* [1995] 1 All ER 611, [1995] 1 WLR 386.

217 Although query what this adds to existing tortious claims.

218 Equally, an employee might argue that judicial discretion should be exercised in a manner that least interferes with a Convention right, eg when deciding to award a remedy, such as injunctive relief or an award of damages.

rights will 'bite' upon the employment relationship generally[219]. It considers the areas in which the HRA might affect workplace relations and employment law, whether or not all employers are bound by the HRA to the same extent and the means by which this is done. Crucially important is whether or not employees can enforce their Convention rights against their employer directly, as a result of the section 6 duty on public authority employers, or only indirectly by virtue of section 3 and indirect horizontal effect.

(a) In what areas might the HRA affect workplace relations and employment law?

- Could employees who have been harassed or discriminated[220] against at work or who have been subjected to compulsory drugs testing or to hostile criticism in front of colleagues argue these are forms of degradation, sufficient to found a possible claim under Article 3? Could being asked to work extremely long hours be a form of inhuman treatment?
- Could employees who are required to perform services additional to those in their contracts, such as a *pro bono* requirement, argue that this is forced or compulsory labour under Article 4[221]?
- Clearly external dispute resolution mechanisms, such as the tribunal system itself, must comply with the right to a fair trial contained in Article 6(1) with its additional express or implicit rights[222]. These include independence and impartiality of the decision-maker and 'equality of arms' (that neither side should be in an advantageous position) in terms of evidence and calling witnesses. Current ECtHR case law holds that dismissal from public sector jobs falls outside the protection of Article 6[223] but if it can be said that private employers' own internal disciplinary or dismissal processes *determine* employees' and employers' 'civil rights and obligations', then Article 6 would be relevant there too. Professional disciplinary hearings which affect not just employment but the right to practice a profession will attract Article 6 protection[224].
- The various rights in Article 8 raise a series of employment issues. The right to private life might well extend to decisions to start drug testing or searches at work (as aspects of employees' personal and bodily integrity); to making promotion or dismissal decisions based on employees' sexuality, sexual choice and sexual behaviour[225]; to keep records or to conduct surveillance on employees' activities (as aspects of informational privacy);

219 Texts include O'Dempsey et al *Employment Law and the Human Rights Act* (1998); Allen et al *Employment Law and the Human Rights Act 1998* (2001); Baker *The Human Rights Act A Practitioner's Guide* (1998) ch 13; and Collins, Ewing and McColgan *Labour Law Text and Materials* (2001) ch 6. Articles include Palmer (2000) 59 CLJ 168, Ewing (1998) 27 ILJ 275, Bowers and Lightman [1998] EHRLR 560 and Morris (1998) 27 ILJ 293, [1999] EHRLR 496 and (2001) 30 ILJ 49.
220 *East African Asians v United Kingdom* (1973) 3 EHRR 76.
221 In *Van der Musselle v Belgium* (1983) 6 EHRR 163, such a claim failed as the ECtHR concluded that he had offered himself voluntarily for such work, knowing that free legal advice would be required of him.
222 *Smith v Secretary of State for Trade and Industry* (2000) ICR 69 and, more recently, *Lowal v Northern Spirit* [2003] UKHL 35.
223 See, eg, *Huber v France* (1998) 26 EHRR 457. Following *Vogt v Germany* (1995) 21 EHRR 205, the dismissal of a civil servant teacher from a state teaching post might be thought to attract the protection of Article 6 but the additional factor there was Art 10 as the dismissal was because of the teacher's political views.
224 *X v United Kingdom* (1998) 26 EHRR 480.
225 Including the right to recognition of the 'new' sex for post-operative transsexuals: *Goodwin v United Kingdom* (2002) 35 EHRR 18, [2002] IRLR 664.

or to discipline or otherwise take action against employees for activities outside of and unconnected with work[226] (since that interferes with an employee's autonomy and personal choice). The other limbs of Article 8(1) will give some protection for employees where employers' actions affect or restrict their ability to enjoy family life – such as insisting on weekend working – and protection against employer monitoring of communications such as phone calls, email or Internet traffic.

- Absent domestic legislation outlawing religion-based discrimination, by guaranteeing the right freely to hold and manifest religious beliefs, Article 9 may well be the only means by which purely religious minorities[227] may obtain legal protection. This might be relevant where employees are required to work on days when they would normally observe religious practices. It also covers freedom of conscience and thought. For example, it might give employees at aeronautical firms limited rights to refuse to work, on ethical grounds, if their employer decides to move from purely civilian operations into producing military aircraft[228].

- Expressive activity by employees under Article 10 might include objecting to dress codes[229]; seeking to publicise possible health hazards by broadcasting secret company information (whistleblowing)[230]; or membership of political parties or active participation within the political framework[231]. As there is no right to force disclosure of information[232], it is unlikely that employees could require a greater opening up of company accounts for collective bargaining purposes.

- Article 11 is one of the few articles that is clearly of direct relevance in the employment sphere. It first guarantees freedom of peaceful assembly so as to give a measure of protection to collective action such as picketing. Secondly, it guarantees the right to associate and by doing so gives the right to form and join a trade union. Until recently much of the case law was concerned with the negative associational right – the right not to join an association – whereas trade unionists did not generally enjoy great success[233], This must now be viewed in the light of *Wilson and Palmer v UK*[234]. Article 11(2) specifically empowers lawful restrictions on the associational rights of certain groups such as police, armed forces and members of the 'administration of the state'[235].

226 Two examples might assist: the first is where an employer seeks to punish an employee for (publicly viewed) football hooliganism: see the unreported case *Liddiard v Post Office* [2001] EWCA Civ 940. The other might include claims such as the one brought by a female employee (Fleur Maidment) dismissed after nude photographs of her appeared in *Escort*, a soft porn magazine (*Guardian* Society section, 13 August 2001).

227 Rather than those religions which also constitute a race, such as Jews and Sikhs but not Moslems.

228 Cf *Cresswell v Inland Revenue* [1984] ICR 508, [1984] IRLR 190, see p 170 below.

229 *Kara v United Kingdom* Case 36528/97 [1999] EHRLR 232, declared inadmissible on 22 October 1998. Available via http://hudoc.echr.coe.int. Most of these cases have been fought domestically on the basis of discrimination, ie men and women are subject to different rules. See the report of the tribunal victory by civil servant Matthew Thompson (*Guardian*, 12 March 2003).

230 *Bobo v Spain* (2001) 31 EHRR 50; see now the Public Interest Disclosure Act 1998 contained in ss 43A–43L; Employment Rights Act 1996, p 181 below.

231 *Rekvenyi v Hungary* (1999) 30 EHRR 519; *Vogt v Germany*, n 223 above. Several cases have been brought, with varying success, by members of the British National Party after they have been expelled from their union for brining it into disrepute as a result of their extreme views. See *Guardian*, 31 May 2003 (ASLEF) and 19 June 2003 (UNISON).

232 *Leander v Sweden* (1987) 9 EHRR 433.

233 See eg *Young James and Webster* n 190 above and *Sigurjonsson v Iceland* (1993) 16 EHRR 462.

234 (2002) 35 EHRR 20, discussed further at p 569 below.

235 The *GCHQ* case was declared inadmissible as 'manifestly unfounded' on this basis: *Council of Civil Service Unions v United Kingdom* (1987) 50 DR 228.

• Employees who feel they have been discriminated against may be given greater protection by Article 14 than domestic law currently provides. Article 14 expressly extends the potentially discriminatory categories to include language, religion, political or other opinion, social origins, association with a national minority, property, birth or 'other status'. That last non-exhaustive category has led to the ECtHR holding that discrimination can take place for differential treatment of children born within and outwith wedlock[236]; between those of different sexual orientations[237]; and between trade unionist and non-unionist[238]. However, Article 14 is also significantly limited by being a parasitic claim; it does not permit free standing non-discrimination claims[239]. It only outlaws the discriminatory provision of other rights in the ECHR. So, if an employer conducted surveillance of only one group or allowed certain employees to remain members of one political party but not others, that might constitute a claim based on discriminatory protection of rights of privacy or expression whereas discriminatory access to employment will most likely fail given there is no ECHR 'right to a job'. If a prima facie case of discrimination is made out, the ECtHR has read in a permitted justification of proportionality.

• Article 1 of the First Protocol guarantees to all natural or legal persons the peaceful enjoyment of possessions and is likely to be of use in employment law only for claims revolving around social security payments, especially those paid on an allegedly discriminatory basis[240]. Case law[241] has established that generally restrictions on using property must be proportionate.

The term 'Convention protected behaviour' is used hereafter to encapsulate all employee activities and behaviour that are guaranteed and permitted as a right under any of the articles of the ECHR. We can also see that in many ways the HRA will not alter the law greatly – it may merely add another avenue by which a challenge can be made or extend slightly its scope. For example, employees are already given some indirect protection against the Article 3 claims set out above[242].

(b) The position of 'public' sector employees

The government's view was that employees of pure public authorities (such as all local and central government) would be able to enforce all Convention rights directly against that employer even if they related to the body's 'private' functions, such as employment of its workers. If so, that would be a significant change from pre-HRA case law. It would mean that pure public authority employees could claim a breach of privacy at work by bringing a public law judicial review application within (new) CPR Part 54 seeking the remedies of mandatory and quashing orders, as well as 'private' law remedies of damages, declaring and injunction. Previously, the employment relationship, unless sufficiently infused with public

236 *Marckx v Belgium* (1979) 2 EHRR 330.
237 *Smith and Grady v UK* (1999) 29 EHRR 493.
238 *Rekvenyi*, n 231 above.
239 Anti-discrimination under the ECHR has been strengthened by a recently concluded free standing protocol addition (Protocol 12) but which the UK has not yet signed or ratified.
240 See *Gaygusuz v Austria* (1996) 23 EHRR 365. Case law indicates that claims to a pension (against either the employer or the state) may succeed provided it is a contributory rather than a non-contributory scheme and thus is dependent on a legal right rather than on the exercise of discretion.
241 *Sporrong v Sweden* (1982) 5 EHRR 35.
242 See *Bracebridge Engineering v Darby* [1990] IRLR 3; *Bliss v South East Thames Regional Health Authority* [1987] ICR 700; and *Palmanor v Cedron* [1978] ICR 1008, [1978] IRLR 303.

law elements (such as statutory underpinning) retained its essentially private law nature and remained outside the scope of judicial review.[243] Since unions, even if representing members, would not be the 'victim' within section 7 of the HRA, any new section 6 claims will be by individual employees rather than collective union legal action. This may decrease its impact.

Of greater moment is whether or not employees of hybrid public authorities can enforce their Convention rights directly against their quasi public sector employer?[244] Section 6 clearly states that these bodies need only be Convention complaint when 'performing a function of a public nature'. Does employing someone constitute performing a public function? Employing someone to undertake a hybrid authority's purely private functions (such as owning land or administering payroll) is probably not covered by section 6[245] but what about employing someone to undertake the public regulatory functions of that body? We can discern two differing viewpoints. First, employment relationships are quintessentially private, as much as entering any other contractual relationship, no matter what the underlying purpose of the relationship. Thus, employing someone even to undertake a hybrid body's public functions is private in nature.[246] Gillian Morris takes the opposite view[247]. Such employment can still be seen as sufficiently public in nature as to be included within the section 6 duty. There are several reasons for this expansive approach. Logically, employees are only employed as a result of a public law duty which requires the authority to employ staff to perform it. On principle, taking such a position means that the protection of employees' Convention rights does not depend on the vagaries of political choice as to the vehicle to carry out government policy. Holding otherwise would mean that prison officers employed by the Prison Service to escort those in custody to court can claim the direct benefit of Convention rights (if for example, they are subjected to harassment from prisoners[248]) whereas officers employed by Group 4 to do the same task are not able to do so. Morris cites ECtHR case law in support[249] of her conclusion that the state has no different responsibility for the employment practices of a body to whom it has delegated its functions when they are engaged in performance of those functions and that this is irrespective of the level of control or supervision which the state retains or assumes. It would also be consistent with EC law jurisprudence on the meaning of an 'organ of the state'. Once a body is performing a public function, there is no scope to argue that employment is private act[250].

243 *R v East Berkshire Health Authority, ex p Walsh* [1984] ICR 743, [1984] IRLR 278; see p 478 below.
244 And, of course, private employers.
245 This does not leave these employees without a remedy but puts them in the same position as purely private sector employees (see below) leading to a fracturing of status within any one employer.
246 Although by no means clear, the government's view was that non-public acts, even incidental to public functions are not within the ambit of the HRA so that whenever a hybrid body is engaging in *any* private act, it ceases to be liable for convention breaches even if the act is one made pursuant to a public function: Lord Irvine, *Hansard* HL Deb, 24 November 1997, col 812. Contrast this with Lord Irvine's view on pure public authority employers, cols 810–811.
247 Morris (1998) 27 ILJ 293.
248 On the basis of a positive duty owed by employers under Article 3.
249 *Costello-Roberts v United Kingdom* (1993) 19 EHRR 112 (a state cannot evade responsibility by contracting out its functions) and *Swedish Engine Drivers v Sweden* (1976) 1 EHRR 617 (that there is no difference between the state as employer and the state as holder of public power).
250 *Foster v British Gas* [1990] ECR-I 3313.

(c) How are employers bound by the HRA?

Having established that employees may enforce their Convention rights directly against employers as result of the public nature of that employer and its business does not mean that merely because an employer company is in private hands, whether corner shop or a multi-million pound conglomerate, it can disregard its employees' Convention rights.

The HRA creates no new remedies or rights in the private sphere. Section 7(1)(a) talks of victims 'bringing proceedings' only against public authorities and must therefore exclude *direct* claims by employees against private bodies. Private employers are not absolved from proceedings since private sector employees may 'rely on their Convention rights in any legal proceedings' under section 7(1)(b). This does of course require some extant legal proceedings on which Convention rights may 'bite'. As we saw above, there are essentially two main means by which the HRA will bind a private body[251]. The first is when, during an action, a court or tribunal is asked to interpret legislation in a Convention compatible manner, according to section 3 of the HRA. The other is where the court or tribunal, as a section 6 public authority itself, is asked to adjudicate on the Convention rights of competing private claimants. This so-called indirect horizontal effect is inextricably linked to the contractual nexus between employees and employers.

The absence of new rights or remedies for private employees means, as Keith Ewing points out, that some seemingly meritorious claims may still fail. For example, to those who are not given employment, perhaps as a result of their political beliefs, the HRA still grants no ground to challenge decisions of a future employer that are arbitrary or which violate their rights. There is no known free-standing, pre-HRA claim upon which such a parasitic challenge would be allowed to rest. There is, by definition, no contractual relations upon which the HRA could 'bite' and no statutory regulation for such decisions, save for those based on discrimination[252]. In fact, even potential public employees could not challenge such a refusal to employ. The ECtHR has long held that a refusal to offer public sector employment does not constitute an interference with, for example, freedom of expression. This logically insupportable position is one of the ECHR's drawbacks – a major limitation to the extent of workplace protection under the HRA[253].

A. Statutory interpretation

Section 3 will 'bite' upon any and all statutory employment legislation, individual or collective: rights guaranteeing the fairness of dismissal or to redundancy pay; non-discrimination rights; rights relating to the life–work balance; and trade union rights – formation, membership, union activities and industrial action. All statutory terms, words and phrases must now be read and given effect to so as

---

251 Of course both of theses would be available to public-sector employees, in addition to more direct challenges, under s 7(1)(a), based on their employer's s 6 duty to them.

252 Sex Discrimination Act 1975, s 6(1)(c) and Race Relations Act 1976, s 4(1)(c); Disability Discrimination Act 1995, s 4(1)(c).

253 See Ewing (1998) 27 ILJ 275 and Morris [1999] EHRLR 496, 497–501 and, eg, *Vogt v Germany,* n 223 above. The court's conclusions have been based on the intention of the framers of the ECHR deliberately to exclude a right of access to public service. But even if that were so, why should it exclude those who seek private employment?

to ensure so far as possible that they are compatible with an employee's (and employer's) Convention rights. This will be so whether the legislation that calls for a section 3 interpretation is the main or only a collateral issue in the case. There is as yet surprisingly little case law, making it difficult to assess whether or not re-visiting settled interpretation will lead to a wholesale re-balancing of the employment relationship and the managerial prerogative.

Might employees who are dismissed for Convention-protected behaviour now argue that those dismissals were unfair within the Employment Rights Act 1996? For example[254] could the dismissals of lesbian employees for wearing badges at work indicating their sexuality or support for other lesbians now be seen as unfair as disproportionate denial of Convention rights under Articles 8, 10 and 14?[255] Wide wording such as 'some other substantial reason' for dismissal is ripe for narrowing, by reading down or reading in, so as to exclude reasons not related to workplace competence or ability. Further, might section 3 require:

- reading 'sex' in the Sex Discrimination Act 1975 as meaning sexual orientation or transsexualism;[256]
- reading 'conduct' in s 98(2) as '. . . excluding conduct that relates to an employee's private life[257]' so as to render unfair any dismissals of employees for extra-curricular activity of which the employer disapproves such as football hooliganism[257a] or posing for pornographic photos;
- reading all legislation that is in issue when peaceful picketing takes place as subject to the proviso that, no matter its express wording, no offence is committed 'where the act in question is no more than a lawful exercise of the right of peaceful assembly contained in Article 11'?[258]

Keith Ewing has argued[259] that Convention-based claims could be maintained in one of two ways when an employee is dismissed. First, dismissals for Convention-protected behaviour can never be treated as a valid reason within Part X of the Employment Rights Act 1996. Secondly that an employer can never be held to be acting reasonably within section 98 in treating the Convention-protected behaviour as the reason for dismissal[259a]. If an employee has not been dismissed or the issue is more one of the extent of statutory protection per se, the question is more complicated. Could employees excluded from the protection of the

---

254 Much of this is based on Ewing, n 253 above, which, although it predates the coming into force of the HRA, has much still to commend it.

255 Cf *Boychuk v HJ Symons Holdings* [1977] IRLR 395. Those rights are to express herself as she wants at work; to autonomy in sexual relations; and the right to be free from discrimination based on sexuality. See too *Saunders v Scottish National Camps* [1980] IRLR 174.

256 And with it a rewriting of the 'less favourable treatment' test which has proved the stumbling block in pre-HRA cases such as *Pearce v Governors of Mayfield School* [2003] UKHL 34. This would be independently of moves to cover such discrimination specifically by new legislation.

257 This itself could be qualified by adding '. . . purely' or less so by adding '. . . mainly' after '. . . relates'.

257a See *Liddiard*, n 226 above.

258 Examples include Trade Union and Labour Relations (Consolidation) Act 1992, s 241 or Highways Act 1980, s 137; see p 630 below.

259 N 253 above. Employees could also argue at common law (see below) that contractual dismissal provisions be read subject to their Convention rights. Could an employee who has been dismissed, either summarily or with notice, argue that a ground for dismissal can never be lawful if it would mean that an employer had breached the Convention rights of the employee? If so, it would be an automatically wrongful dismissal.

259a Cf the obiter view of Tuckey LJ in *Liddiard* (n 226 above) was that he could 'see nothing which requires s 98 to be construed and applied in any way differently from the way it was before the Human Rights Act came into force'.

Working Time Regulations seek a declaration that the wording be interpreted so as to include them and, failing that, that the regulations should be struck down as ultra vires the Article 4 prohibition on forced labour?[260] Alternatively, they could wait for the statutory section to be applied to them and set their Convention rights up as a collateral defence to any action.

B. The common law, contract and Convention rights

As no new rights or remedies are created by the HRA, private employees cannot claim directly against their employers for breach of Convention rights. However, if they can bring their claim under a pre-existing head, the court that hears the case may be required to decide the issues before it so as best to preserve the Convention rights of employees (and employers). The most likely, given the pre-eminence of the employment contract, is to claim that an employer has in some way breached an employee's contract by failing to permit employees to exercise their Convention rights. This area raises two discrete issues. The first is whether or not Convention rights become part of employees' contracts with employers either as an independent implied term or as part of the general duty of mutual trust and confidence. Secondly, what is the relationship between Convention rights and express terms – can an employee contract out of Convention rights or otherwise waive them? Some examples might assist: contractual terms requiring Sunday work might mean that employees cannot attend a religious service and so are prevented from exercising their Article 9 rights; a company policy permitting an employer to monitor all email traffic might constitute a potential infringement of an employee's rights under Article 8; a wide mobility clause or a clause permitting the employer to call for working anti-social hours might restrict the ability of an employee to spend time with their family under Article 8; an employer who exercises a contractual right to dismiss a doctor summarily for taking part in a TV broadcast which is critical of the NHS might be seen as restricting the doctor's Article 10 rights.

A court could[261] hold all Convention rights to be implied terms of the employment contract[262]. This might be either on public policy grounds[263] or because it is implicit in the now well-established duty of mutual trust and confidence that employers will accord to their employees the Convention rights that Parliament has given them *qua* citizens. Whichever of these two approaches is followed, it does not mean that an employee will always be able to claim rights of privacy, expression or religion. Since these are not absolute, it will only be a violation of the Convention if the employer's decision has the effect of *disproportionately* interfering with an employee's rights.

The main problem created but not resolved by either approach is the clash between the implied term to Convention rights and an express contractual term which defeats its exercise. This might result from either contractual waiver (which permits, for example, a restriction on religious freedom) or the effect of other

---

260 Of course, since the Regulations are not contained within primary legislation, they could be struck down.
261 And query *must*, as part of its s 6 duty to an employee litigant before it.
262 Of course, an employer might grant Convention rights expressly in the contract.
263 The ECHR has been held to be a fundamental tenet of public policy (*Balthwayte v Cawley* [1976] AC 397) but this means only that a contractual term which is in breach of the ECHR will be void for breaching public policy. Thus, terms in an employment contract which can be viewed as being in breach of Convention rights would be given no effect by a court but it does not positively grant rights.

express terms entered into. A broad waiver – 'I agree to waive all my Convention rights' – might be seen as insufficiently precise to be 'prescribed by/in accordance with law' under Articles 8–11[264]. Thus restrictions on religion or expression under the guise of broad 'contracting out' provisions would be unlawful since they would be restrictions that had not been effected lawfully.[265] Would a court uphold narrower or more targeted waivers such as 'I agree to waive any claims to privacy and allow my employer to monitor all my phone calls, email and Internet use while I am at work'? Extra-curially, Lindsey J has argued that the answer might depend on the relative bargaining power of the parties with Convention rights incapable of waiver individually but not incapable by collective agreement[266]. We might view obiter in cases such as *Malik*[267] and *Scally*[268] as indicative of moves towards the employment relationship as derivative of status rather than purely a function of agreed-to terms. If some terms are seen as judicially imposed necessary incidents of a particular contractual relationship, this may make it harder to contract out of them[269].

Strangely, Strasbourg has treated very differently cases where compliance by an employee with one express contractual provision will mean denying themselves the exercise of a Convention right. In those latter cases, Strasbourg has held against employees. In both *Stedman v United Kingdom*[270] and *Ahmed v United Kingdom*[271], neither was seen as a breach broadly because whatever restrictions occurred were the result of other contractual obligations freely entered into. Strasbourg expressly acknowledged that the employee's choice was limited to resigning or to declining the job in the first place, rather than accepting the contract with its consequent restrictions, but did not seem to put any great store on this being a 'restriction' on freedom. As Gillian Morris notes, this reasoning ignores the practical reality of labour markets and jurisprudentially it fails properly to explain the distinction between these situations and express waiver clauses where justification of the need for a conflicting contractual provision is sought[272].

264 Nn 195–197 above.
265 Equally, we know from *Johnstone v Bloomsbury* [1991] IRLR 118, CA and certainly the judgment of Stuart-Smith LJ that it is by no means certain that express contractual terms will per se 'trump' implied terms, however heretical in non-employment contracts that seems to be: see p 142 below.
266 (2001) 30 ILJ 1, 10.
267 *Malik v Bank of Credit and Commerce International SA (in liquidation)* [1997] ICR 606, [1997] IRLR 462 HL.
268 *Scally v Southern Health and Social Services Board* [1991] ICR 771, [1991] IRLR 522, HL.
269 In analysing ECHR cases, Gillian Morris (2001) 30 ILJ 49, 53–55 has identified four questions that should determine the validity of a contractual waivers. (1) Is this unequivocal and freely obtained, without constraint? (2) Is this a non-waivable or, in Convention parlance, non-derogable right such as Article 3? (3) Is there a wider public policy issue which should deem this Convention right non-waivable at the instance of an individual? (4) In any event, it is necessary or proportionate to uphold the waiver? In other words, at both the time when the employer asked the employee to waive Convention rights and when the employer sought to rely upon the waiver, did the waiver meet a 'pressing social need' of the employer's or was there an alternative means open to the employer to protect his own (or another's) rights? Thus, under (2), a waiver, 'I agree to humiliating and degrading treatment if my employer subjects me to body searches in public', would be invalid.
270 1997 23 EHRR CD 168.
271 *X v United Kingdom* (1981) 22 DR 27.
272 See *Rommelfanger v FRG* (1989) DR 151.

Chapter 2

The law relating to industrial relations

I MACHINERY

As seen in chapter 1 above, the voluntary and non-legal nature of British industrial relations has been its dominant characteristic, and there is not an overall statutory framework for compulsory conciliation and arbitration leading to enforceable awards and agreements as may be found in certain other countries. Moreover, we do not formally distinguish between what are conceptually two different types of industrial dispute – those about the negotiation of new and improved terms of employment (disputes of interest) and those about the interpretation, application and enforcement of existing terms (disputes of right)[1]; arguably there should be separate procedures for dealing with them, particularly as the second type is inherently more amenable to legal adjudication, but in this country any such differentiation will be the exception rather than the rule, and so both kinds of dispute tend (in areas where collective bargaining is still the norm) to be subject to voluntarily negotiated procedures of varying quality (or ad hoc arrangements), leading as has been seen to non-enforceable collective agreements. However, although the law has been non-interventionist (except for the period covered by the Industrial Relations Act 1971) it has not abstained totally, and has attempted in various ways at various times to provide certain residual machinery to facilitate industrial relations and minimise industrial conflict. Wages Councils were historically used (prior to their abolition in 1993) to aid collective bargaining in under-unionised trades, and since the Conciliation Act 1896 there has existed machinery (in various forms, but before 1975 principally under the Department of Employment and its predecessors) for industrial conciliation. Since the Industrial Courts Act 1919[2] there has also existed machinery for

---

1   Report of the Royal Commission on Trade Unions and Employers' Associations (Cmnd. 3623, 1968) para 60.
2   Now the Trade Union and Labour Relations (Consolidation) Act 1992, ss 215–216, in relation to courts of inquiry.

industrial arbitration, previously under the Industrial Court (a tri-partite arbitral body, not to be confused with the NIRC, set up by the Industrial Relations Act 1971) which was renamed the Industrial Arbitration Board between 1971 and 1974, under the 1971 Act; once again, however, the arbitration has always[3] been basically voluntary, ie by the consent of the parties. Since 1975, these conciliation and arbitration services have been largely provided by the Advisory, Conciliation and Arbitration Service (ACAS), and are considered below. In addition to such general provisions, it used to be common to find in statutes establishing or governing major employers in the public sector a standard clause placing them under a duty to seek consultations with appropriate trade unions with a view to concluding agreements for establishing joint industrial negotiating machinery. However, such provisions do not apply in the private sector where the establishment of negotiating machinery normally remains a voluntary matter; this has, of course, increasingly been the case because of the previous government's widespread policy of privatisation of bodies or industries previously in the public sector (and, indeed, the mandatory contracting-out of services by bodies still in the public sector). In far more areas, it is now the case therefore that legal intervention is restricted to the provision of outside agencies which the parties may, or may not, decide to call upon in the event of a dispute.

In the resolution of industrial disputes by the intervention of an outside agency there is an important conceptual distinction. On the one hand there is conciliation which is where the conciliator attempts to bring the parties together in the hope that a common discussion will reveal a means of settlement acceptable to both parties; one variation of this is 'mediation' where the mediator takes a more active role in putting forward detailed solutions, though still with a view to settlement by agreement[4]. These functions are now within the jurisdiction of ACAS, which was originally established by the Employment Protection Act 1975 and is the successor to the conciliatory functions of the Department of Employment (and the Commission on Industrial Relations which functioned under the 1971 Act). On the other hand there is arbitration, which is where the arbitrator fulfils a quasi-judicial role in that the parties have agreed to submit their dispute to that person for his *decision* on what should be the result; he or she therefore has to look into the relevant facts and law, and it is clearly understood that the parties will abide by the decision. This function is now within the jurisdiction of both ACAS and the Central Arbitration Committee (CAC), which also was established by the Employment Protection Act 1975 and is the successor to the Industrial Court and the Industrial Arbitration Board; as we shall see, it may conduct voluntary arbitrations, but also has certain powers of unilateral arbitration under statute and has now been given important new jurisdictions in relation to the statutory recognition procedure and European Works Councils.

3   Except for the period 1940–59 when, initially as a result of wartime measures aimed at avoiding industrial disruptions, some arbitration was compulsory. In 1951 Order 1376 replaced Order 1305 of 1940; some 1,270 cases were heard before its revocation in 1959: see Cooper's *Outlines of Industrial Law* (6th edn, 1972), pp 446–451; Kahn-Freund *Labour and the Law* (1983) pp 151–153.

4   Mediation may be used particularly (a) where issues cannot be presented in a sufficiently clear-cut manner for arbitration (eg major changes of work, linked to a pay settlement) or (b) where one or both of the parties is or are unwilling to submit the matter formally to arbitration (on the principle that a party who agrees to arbitration must ultimately be able to afford to lose). Either way, mediation must be properly understood by the parties – it does not result in an 'award' by the mediator, though there may be considerable moral pressure to comply with the mediator's suggestions.

(i) The Advisory Conciliation and Arbitration Service

The composition of ACAS is governed primarily by Part VI of the Trade Union and Labour Relations (Consolidation) Act 1992. It is directed by a Council consisting of a chairman and between nine and fifteen members (three or four representing employers, three or four representing unions and the rest 'independents'). ACAS itself is set up as a body independent of the government, in particular independent of the Department of Trade and Industry, and appoints its own staff[5]. It maintains a central office in London and regional offices in Scotland, Wales and in eight regions in England, and must produce an annual report for the Secretary of State for Trade and Industry to lay before Parliament.

Amongst its staff, it maintains 'conciliation officers'[6] who have particular responsibility for conciliating in statutory actions brought by individual employees.

The functions of ACAS are set out in Part IV of the 1992 Act; in addition to the detailed functions considered below, there is a statement of its general duty in section 209, as follows:

'It is the general duty of ACAS to promote the improvement of industrial relations.'

This apparently simple formulation has in fact gone through three phases, with considerable symbolic significance (if little practical effect). From 1975 to 1993 the section continued '... and in particular to encourage the extension of collective bargaining and the development and, where necessary, reform of collective bargaining machinery'. That may well have been the ethos of the 1970s, but after a decade in the 1980s of overt government hostility to any such aims it was hardly surprising that the previous government took the opportunity in the Trade Union Reform and Employment Rights Act 1993 to repeal that wording. They substituted '... in particular by exercising its functions in relation to the settlement of trade disputes under sections 210 and 212 [ie by conciliation and arbitration]'. ACAS had certainly proved useful to the previous government in certain disputes (a measure of that use being that they were never seriously threatened with abolition, unlike most tri-partite bodies of the 1970s), and this formulation reflected that. However, it arguably placed too much emphasis on reactive, problem-solving work ('fire fighting' in IR jargon), and too little on long-term advice work ('fire prevention') which ACAS wanted to enhance. With the change of government in 1997, an increased emphasis on fire prevention could be seen to be consistent with the present government's 'partnership' ideas in the White Paper 'Fairness at Work'. As a result, the Employment Relations Act 1999 removed the 1993 wording and left ACAS with the widest possible general duty as set out above. Of course, the cynic could argue that the extent to which ACAS can increase their pro-active work will depend not on a change to their statutory remit but on the resources they are to be given over the next few years.

---

5   In 2001 there were 798 staff in ACAS, the majority being located in the regional offices: ACAS Annual Report 2000–01.

6   Trade Union and Labour Relations (Consolidation) Act 1992, s 211; they are known as Conciliation Officers Tribunals (COTS) to distinguish them from those specialising in collective conciliation.

The specific statutory functions[7] of ACAS are as follows.

(a) Collective conciliation

Where a trade dispute[8] exists or seems imminent ACAS may, at the request of one or more of the parties or on its own initiative, offer its assistance for the purposes of conciliation or mediation. In doing so, it may also refer the parties to a third person for conciliation, and it must where possible encourage the parties to use any existing negotiation or disputes procedures[9]. The traditional form of conciliation is carried out by an individual ACAS officer working directly with the parties, but in recent years there has been an increase in the use of a hybrid form, referred to as 'advisory mediation', aimed at encouraging a co-operative and problem-solving approach by the parties themselves, possibly on a longer-term basis; this tends to be done by the setting up of a joint workshop or joint working party, chaired by the ACAS officer, and may be particularly appropriate for resolving disputes over matters such as handling organisational change[10]. In addition to these forms of voluntary conciliation, ACAS also has statutory conciliation functions at certain stages in union claims for disclosure of bargaining information or under the statutory recognition procedure, both of which are considered below.

One area of potential difficulty for ACAS in the context of collective conciliation may arise if it transpires in a particular dispute that the employer is seeking to bring a legal action against the union, initially for an injunction to restrain the industrial action or threat of it and then possibly in a suit for damages (both more feasible since the reforms in the Employment Acts 1980 and 1982 and the balloting provisions in the Trade Union Act 1984; see chapter 10 below). In such a case, any ACAS intervention would have to be more circumspect. However, there is another side to it, since such ACAS intervention might in practice be more likely to resolve an impasse than legal proceedings, and at one stage the suggestion was made tentatively that the law should be amended to include provision for a judge to stay proceedings in any action arising from an industrial dispute in order for ACAS to attempt conciliation[11] which, if successful, might well make considerable savings in cost, time, acrimony and accusations against the courts of partiality in industrial disputes; however, this interesting

---

7   These services have in the past been free to the parties, but s 251A of the 1992 Act (inserted by the Trade Union Reform and Employment Rights Act 1993) gives a power to charge fees *and* a power for the Secretary of State to require the charging of fees for some or all services. This change was not wanted by ACAS itself.

8   The wide definition as originally contained in the Trade Union and Labour Relations Act 1974, s 29 (and now in the Trade Union and Labour Relations (Consolidation) Act 1992, s 218) continues to apply for this purpose; the narrowed definition for the purpose of immunity from tort action in industrial disputes enacted by the Employment Act 1982 and now in the 1992 Act, s 244 does not apply here. Perhaps an example of governmental propensity to have cake and consume same.

9   Trade Union and Labour Relations (Consolidation) Act 1992, s 210. In 2001/02, 1,270 collective conciliation cases were completed, 92% ending in settlement or progress towards it. Of these cases, 44% concerned pay and terms of employment, 27% recognition, 5% changed working practices, 5% other trade union matters, 8% redundancy and 8% discipline and dismissal: ACAS Annual Report 2001/02. Independent research carried out in 1985 and published in 1988 showed a high level of satisfaction with the service provided, by both unions and employers: ACAS Annual Report 1987, p 26.

10   See Kessler and Purcell 'Joint problem solving' (ACAS Occasional Paper No 55).

11   ACAS Annual Report 1983, para 1.16.

suggestion has never been taken up. It can be further noted that where the parties engage lawyers the lines of communication may be lengthened and the process of conciliation made more difficult.

(b) Individual conciliation

ACAS, through its conciliation officers, has a statutory duty to attempt to conciliate in cases brought before tribunals by individuals claiming unfair dismissal or denial of employment protection rights; this also applies to cases of sex, race and disability discrimination and to the various rights enacted by the legislation for the protection of trade union members, including the statutory redundancy handling procedures[12]. The ACAS regional offices receive copies of originating applications to the tribunals and a conciliation officer must attempt to settle a case without reference to a tribunal if requested to do so by the parties or if, in the absence of a request, he thinks there may be a reasonable prospect of success[13]. In all cases, the conciliation officer must consider encouraging the use of established grievance procedures within the firm. In unfair dismissal cases, the officer must in theory seek to promote a settlement primarily by way of reinstatement or re-engagement, and only attempt a monetary settlement if that is impracticable, or not wanted by the ex-employee[14]. The conciliation process is confidential, in that anything said to the officer during it is not admissible evidence in subsequent tribunal proceedings without the consent of the person who said it. It must be emphasised that if the conciliation is successful in leading to an agreed settlement as a consequence of action taken by a conciliation officer under his statutory duties, that will bar any future tribunal proceedings in the matter[15], so that the claimant should be certain that he or she is happy with the terms of the proposed settlement before irrevocably agreeing with it. For this reason alone, it is vital that ACAS should behave, and be seen to behave, entirely

12 Employment Tribunals Act 1996, s 18. See ACAS *Individual Employment Rights – ACAS Conciliation between Individuals and Employers.*

13 For many years the total number of such cases received by ACAS was stable at about 35,000 pa. However, they started to climb alarmingly in the 1990s, reaching 79,332 cases received in 1994. This was at a time of some decrease in numbers of staff and placed a severe strain on other ACAS functions. The figures took another lurch upwards in 1995 to 91,568, topped 100,000 in 1996 and stood at 165,093 in 2001/02. This has been the background to attempts by successive governments to lessen reliance on the tribunal system, first in the Employment Rights (Dispute Resolution) Act 1998 and now in the Employment Act 2002.

Of the cases received in 2001/2002, 31% were for unfair dismissal, 1.6% for equal pay, 4.5% for sex discrimination, 2.3% for race discrimination, 3% for disability discrimination, 21.5% for protection of wages and 17.5% for breach of contract: ACAS Annual Report 2001/2002. The combination of 39% for the latter two shows where much of the growth has been in recent years. Note that the ACAS statistics (unlike those used by the employment tribunals) count applications, not applicants, so that one applicant claiming under several headings gives rise to that number of 'cases received'.

Of the total cases in 2001/02, 42% resulted in a conciliated settlement, 33% were withdrawn and only 25% proceeded to a tribunal.

14 Employment Tribunals Act 1996, s 18(4). This is wholly ineffective in practice, as can be seen from the consistently low rate of re-employment (whether by order or by agreement): see p 604 below; Williams and Lewis *The aftermath of tribunal reinstatement and re-engagement* (DE Research Paper No 23) pp 31 and 39.

15 ERA 1996, s 203(2); Sex Discrimination Act 1975, s 77(4)(a); Race Relations Act 1976, s 72(4)(a); Trade Union and Labour Relations (Consolidation) Act 1992, s 288(2); Disability Discrimination Act 1995, s 9(2). Because of the form on which they are recorded, these are known as 'COT3 settlements'.

impartially as between the claimant and the employer when conducting negotiations.

In this respect, a serious problem arose for ACAS through the rise throughout the 1980s of the number of cases submitted to them *without* any formal application having been made to a tribunal. In these cases (referred to as 'non-IT 1' cases in the jargon) the employer would often be wanting ACAS to record an agreement already reached, in order to achieve legal finality, but doubts could arise as to whether the employee had really understood the terms of the agreement. A conflict arose between law and practice. Legally, it was clear from the cases that there was no statutory obligation on an ACAS officer to ensure that it was a *fair* settlement and so an employee could not later challenge the binding nature of the settlement on the grounds that ACAS had not explained his rights to him properly or given him independent advice[16]. On the other hand, it was the established ACAS view that their officers should not simply act as rubber stamps for possibly inequitable settlements and should at least enquire whether the employee understood his position and his rights[17]. Eventually, however, the considerable rise in non-IT 1 cases placed such a strain on resources that ACAS had to reconsider its policy. This was done with effect from July 1990 and the current position is that: (a) officers will only act in non-IT 1 cases where the employee claims infringement of specified employment rights; (b) they will decline to conciliate where any qualifying period is clearly not satisfied; (c) they will not become involved where employment ended voluntarily or where a redundancy occurred under fairly applied customary arrangements or agreed procedures; and (d) (most importantly) they will not have any role to play in *any* case (whether or not a non-IT 1 case) where a firm agreement has already been reached independently, *unless* the terms of the agreement are capable of being changed as a result of conciliation[18].

(c) Arranging arbitration

Under section 212 of the Trade Union and Labour Relations (Consolidation) Act 1992, ACAS may arrange arbitration for an actual or anticipated trade dispute if one or more of the parties request it *and* all parties consent to it[19]. This is clearly voluntary arbitration, and the resulting decision will not be legally enforceable per se[20], though in practice the arbitrator's decision is invariably

---

16   In *Moore v Duport Furniture Products Ltd* [1982] ICR 84, [1982] IRLR 31, HL, it was held (1) that the action of the conciliation officer in recording an agreement to accept compensation of £300 on the standard form COT3 was sufficient to bar further proceedings, and (2) that where an officer is presented with such an agreement already worked out by the parties, his duty is only to verify the fact of agreement and record it – he is not under a further duty to enquire into the 'fairness' of the agreement or to give the applicant any further advice. Likewise, an ACAS official is under no legal duty to explain the law to the applicant and is not bound to adopt any particular formula or approach: *Slack v Greenham (Plant Hire) Ltd* [1983] ICR 617, [1983] IRLR 271. See further p 518 below.

17   ACAS Annual Report 1984, p 63.

18   ACAS Annual Report 1991, p 45. As a result of this change, the non-IT 1 caseload declined from 17,724 in 1989 to only 2,431 in 1992.

19   Mumford 'Arbitration and ACAS in Britain: a historical perspective' (1996) 34 BJIR 287.

20   Pt I of the Arbitration Act 1996 does not apply to this form of arbitration: s 212(5). One rare example of binding arbitration on terms and conditions of employment was contained in the Pilotage Act 1987, s 5 and the Terms of Employment of Pilots (Arbitration) Regulations 1988, SI 1988/1089, but it was meant to be a temporary expedient; see Smith 'The pilots' compensation scheme: a study in arbitration, interpretation and causation' (1994) 32 BJIR 379.

complied with. ACAS does not automatically have to arrange arbitration; as well as being satisfied that all parties consent, it must also consider whether conciliation might be successful instead, and should not arrange arbitration unless satisfied that existing negotiation and disputes procedures have been exhausted (unless there are special reasons why arbitration should be used *instead* of such procedures). The conciliation stage is important – if successful it removes the need for an arbitration; if unsuccessful the ACAS conciliation officer then has the task of determining with the parties the precise terms of reference for the arbitrator, for it is important in an arbitration that the terms are not themselves a subject for dispute; in fact, the terms of reference are usually kept as simple as possible and, further, nothing of what has happened or been said at the conciliation stage is made known to the arbitrator, who approaches the issue afresh. The usual practice is for ACAS to appoint one person to conduct the arbitration (from the panel of approximately eighty appropriate people whom they use), though occasionally a board of arbitration may be convened; officials and employees of ACAS are *not* used, though ACAS do of course provide the necessary secretarial and administrative services[21]. It is also possible for a voluntary arbitration to be referred to the CAC, though there are only a few such cases each year. Legal representation at an arbitration is unusual (and indeed usually discouraged if suggested) and although the proceedings may be conducted in a relatively structured manner (aimed at giving both sides a full opportunity to expand upon their written submissions and to query the other side's case), matters of procedure are largely for the arbitrator to determine and will not normally include legalistic forms, such as prolonged cross-examination.

Certain particular aspects in arbitration might be noted here briefly. First, references may come from *standing* arbitration agreements, usually taking the form of a clause in the disputes procedure section of a collective bargain stating that in the absence of agreement on a disputed point through internal procedures, the matter shall be referred to ACAS for conciliation and/or arbitration. This may be a general reference, or the clause itself may cover the procedure that is to be adopted. Second, it is possible for parties to a dispute to approach ACAS to ask them simply to *nominate* an arbitrator to conduct an arbitration which has already been agreed upon, without going through the normal conciliation procedures; such arbitrations do not figure in the annual ACAS statistics[22]. Third, at times there has been considerable interest in and publicity about the form of arbitration variously known as 'pendulum', 'flip-flop', 'straight choice' or 'final offer', where the arbitrator is constrained to choose

---

21 In 2001/02 the number of references to arbitration was on 68; of these, 24% concerned annual pay, 32% other pay and conditions of employment, 32% dismissal and discipline and 7% grading: ACAS Annual Report 2001/2002. Requests to ACAS simply to nominate an arbitrator for a purely internal arbitration are not included in these figures; on the use of third-party intervention, see Millward et al *Workplace Industrial Relations in Transition* (1992), pp 194–196 and 208–211.

22 This, however, can lead to a problem: the resulting arbitration is *not* an ACAS arbitration within the Act and so the exclusion of the Arbitration Act 1996 by s 212(5) (n 20 above) does not apply. Thus the 1996 Act could be applicable (if the agreement to arbitrate is in writing) and so the resulting decision could be legally binding (and any recourse to the courts excluded) under that Act, possibly without the parties realising it at the time.

between acceptance in full of one side's case or that of the other[23]. The aim of this is said to be to narrow the field of dispute and ensure that each side puts forward a realistic (rather than a bargaining) case, capable of being accepted in full. While this may be a natural form of adjudication in disputes of right, ACAS is by no means convinced that it is a panacea in disputes of interest such as pay determinations where flexibility in the arbitration may be just as important. Although ACAS will arrange such an arbitration if the parties desire it, it does *not* adopt it as its policy, preferring to encourage responsible bargaining in other ways and pointing out consistently that the fact that an arbitrator is normally given full discretion in coming to his award does *not* mean in practice that all he does is to split the disputed area down the middle, with half a baby to each.

(d) Arbitration in unfair dismissal and flexible working cases

Although voluntary arbitration has always been available to the parties to a dismissal dispute, it has in the past worked on an informal basis (with a disappointed complainant employee still able to go to a tribunal for a further hearing), and in recent years has declined in numbers along with arbitration generally. Faced with the steep rise in tribunal applications, the previous government explored the possibility of a re-vamped ACAS-run arbitration scheme to act as an *alternative* to tribunal proceedings[24]. This idea was taken up by the present government, and made possible by the Employment Rights (Dispute Resolution) Act 1998, section 7 (inserting the Trade Union and Labour Relations (Consolidation) Act 1992, section 212A) which gives ACAS the power to produce a scheme for promulgation by the Secretary of State by order. Although this power has existed since August 1998, progress has been slow because of delays in approval at the DTI level. The outlines of the scheme are set out in chapter 8 on unfair dismissal (see p 529 below). The major problem for ACAS has been in anticipating the likely level of usage and therefore how many arbitrators to recruit and train. In 2001/2002 there were only thirteen cases referred to the scheme. In spite of this, the scheme was extended in April 2003 when the new right came into force to request flexible working and not be unreasonably refused[25]. It will be interesting to see if this is found to be a more appropriate and acceptable area for arbitration than dismissal cases.

23 See the CAC Annual Report 1984, ch 3 for a discussion of this development. This form of arbitration was particularly controversial within the union movement in the mid-1980s, especially where it was combined with a 'no-strike' clause, as in certain innovatory collective agreements negotiated by the EETPU with foreign companies in 'high-tech' industries. For the incorporation of 'no strike' agreements into individual contracts of employment, see p 146 below. The aim is to avoid the damage arbitration is said to do to conciliation. Parties in negotiation anticipating arbitration tend to 'stand off' leaving a wide band of discretion for the arbitrator. Final offer arbitration encourages them to adopt a more realistic position, even perhaps to reach agreement. While this is a natural process in disputes of right, where the arbitrator has usually two positions to choose from, it is less certain in its application to disputes of interest. There is considerable North American experience in public sector arbitration. This shows that difficulties arise where there are several issues in the same arbitration: it is difficult to be absolutely clear on the exact form of last positions and it prevents flexibility at the hearing of the dispute. Several devices have been adopted, eg issue splitting, to meet these difficulties.
24 Resolving employment rights disputes: options for reform (Cm 2707, 1994).
25 See p 437 below.

(e) Advice

The statutory power to give advice, contained in the Trade Union and Labour Relations (Consolidation) Act 1992, section 213, was altered by the Trade Union Reform and Employment Rights Act 1993. It used to contain eleven particular categories of relevant areas, including matters affecting collective bargaining, worker organisation and recognition of unions. It now reads more simply:

> 'ACAS may, on request or otherwise, give employers, employers' associations, workers and trade unions such advice as it thinks appropriate on matters concerned with or affecting or likely to affect industrial relations.'

As with the change at that time (considered above) to the general duty of ACAS, this alteration was likely to have little practical effect, but could be seen (in its removal of express references to collective means of resolving industrial problems) to be symbolic. Again, references to such matters have not been reinstated by the present government.

The power to advise remains wide and will doubtless continue to be heavily used[26]. It covers general advice, specific replies to queries (for example on the meaning of modern employment laws), in-depth surveys and projects, giving conferences or seminars and the publishing of advisory booklets[27]. Diagnostic work within a company on a longer-term basis may in fact be the result of one particular problem which arose and was settled through ACAS conciliation – the approach may have been made for the ACAS officer to attempt to find a settlement for the immediate problem on the understanding that the whole area in dispute would be looked at, either by the officer himself or, increasingly, by the setting up of a joint working party or workshop under the aegis of ACAS. This latter approach (more recently known as 'advisory mediation', see above) has expanded and largely replaced the older ideas of externally conducted 'IR audits' for two reasons – (1) it fits the current industrial relations realities better, reflecting their more diverse nature with less chance of one desirable model being appropriate, but (2) at the same time it enables ACAS still to make a distinctive contribution towards ideas of *joint* resolution of problems and employee involvement, even in areas where formal bargaining with unions is no longer the norm[28].

(f) Powers of inquiry

ACAS may on its own initiative hold an inquiry into aspects of industrial relations generally or in any particular industry or firm[29]. It may add its advice to its eventual

---

26 This advice function is of great importance in practice: Armstrong 'Evaluating the work of ACAS' [1985] Employment Gazette 143 and 'Asking ACAS' (ACAS Occasional Paper No 56; Dix, Hawes and Pinkstone). In 2001/02 the ACAS Helpline received 755,449 calls and 1.896 advisory meetings were held: ACAS Annual Report 2001/2002.

27 See ACAS Advisory Booklets – No 1, Job Evaluation; No 2, Introduction to payment systems; No 3, Personnel records; No 4, Labour turnover; No 5, Absence; No 6, Recruitment and selection; No 7, Induction of new employees; No 8, Workplace communications; No 9, The company handbook; No 10, Employment policies; No 11, Employee appraisal; No 12, Redundancy handling; No 13, Hours of Work; No 14, Appraisal-related Pay; No 15, Health and Employment; No 16, Effective Organisations; No 17, Supervision; No 18, Teamwork. Advisory Handbooks have also been published on employing people in small firms, and discipline at work, along with the general Employment Handbook.

28 Kessler and Purcell 'Joint problem solving – does it work? An evaluation of ACAS in-depth advisory mediation' (ACAS Occasional Paper No 55).

29 Trade Union and Labour Relations (Consolidation) Act 1992, s 214.

findings, and is empowered to publish both if it thinks publication desirable (after hearing any representations on the question by those involved). In cases of greater public interest, however, the Secretary of State may decide to appoint a Court of Inquiry under the Trade Union and Labour Relations (Consolidation) Act 1992, section 215 (originally the Industrial Courts Act 1919). This is a more formal procedure than that adopted by ACAS and results in the laying before Parliament and publication of a formal report[30]. In appointing such a court, the Secretary of State lays down rules regulating its procedure, which may include powers to compel witnesses to provide information or give evidence on oath.

(g) Codes of practice

Pursuant to its powers of inquiry and advice, ACAS is empowered by the Trade Union and Labour Relations (Consolidation) Act 1992, section 199 to issue Codes of Practice. The procedure is that a draft Code will be drawn up with a view to comment by interested parties. The final draft is then submitted to the Secretary of State, who, if he approves, may lay it before Parliament. If no objection is taken to it, the Secretary of State may then bring it into force by order. Codes of Practice are of increasing importance in modern industrial law, to attempt to fill out the bare bones of the legislation and give practical advice on how to put that legislation (often of considerable legal complexity) into effect. A Code of Practice is not law in itself, so a person will not be liable for its breach; like the Highway Code in motoring cases, however, breach of its terms may be used as evidence against an employer in any proceedings before a tribunal or the CAC[31]. The first three Codes of Practice issued by ACAS covered disciplinary practices and procedures in employment, disclosure of bargaining information and time off work for trade union duties and activities. In 1987 ACAS submitted the draft of a revised and greatly expanded Code of Practice on discipline and dismissals, but unfortunately the then Secretary of State for Employment refused to approve it (see p 508 below); it was subsequently published (in part) as the ACAS Handbook 'Discipline at Work', which did not need ministerial approval and has been in wide demand. The three original Codes of Practice were reissued in 1998, but only in order to bring them up to date with current legislation, and not to make any substantive changes. The Code of Practice No 1 on discipline and dismissal was then reissued in 2000, in an expanded form also covering grievance procedures and the statutory right to be accompanied at a disciplinary or grievance hearing.

(ii) The Central Arbitration Committee

The CAC, successor to the Industrial Court and the Industrial Arbitration Board, was established by the Employment Protection Act 1975 and its procedure is now

---

30   Use of this device is relatively rare; a notable example was the Report of the Court of Inquiry under Scarman LJ into the dispute between Grunwick Processing Laboratories Ltd and APEX, (Cmnd 6922, 1977).

31   Trade Union and Labour Relations (Consolidation) Act 1992, s 207(2). Under s 203 the Secretary of State for Employment may himself issue codes of practice (after consultation with ACAS) and any such COP may replace part or all of one already issued by ACAS. This power has been used to issue the COP's in the politically contentious areas of picketing and the closed shop; it was extended to cover Codes of Practice on union ballots and elections.

governed by Part VI of the Trade Union and Labour Relations (Consolidation) Act 1992. It is a permanent arbitration body, independent of both ACAS and the sponsoring department and sitting centrally in London and elsewhere as the need arises. It consists of a chairman and deputy chairmen and a panel of persons appointed from both sides of industry. It will normally sit with a chairman or deputy chairman and two 'wingmen', though if it cannot reach a unanimous decision, the power of decision lies with the chairman or deputy chairman, acting as an umpire. It may sit in public or in private, and its decisions made in the exercise of its statutory functions (but not its consensual arbitrations) must be published; these decisions are given in the form of arbitral awards, with the emphasis upon a statement of 'general consideration' and then the terms of the award, rather than in the form of a closely reasoned legal judgment. If a question arises as to the interpretation of one of its awards, any party to it may refer the matter back to the CAC for decision. The functions of the CAC were progressively lessened by the previous government (which had a general distaste for third party intervention in industrial disputes) and were restricted to the following:

(a) to arbitrate on matters voluntarily submitted to it by the parties through (ACAS[32]; the CAC may thus be an alternative to the (more usual) single arbitrator and such a reference may be ad hoc or may be because reference to the CAC is formally built into the relevant procedure agreement between employer and union;

(b) to enforce the disclosure of certain bargaining information – see below.

The workload of the CAC was therefore drastically reduced[33]. Under the Labour governments of the 1970s not only was the CAC involved in enforcing the then statutory recognition procedure, but also it had as its major function the determination of claims for the extension of terms and conditions of employment under Schedule 11 to the Employment Protection Act 1975. This form of statutory adjudication over wages was viewed with disfavour by the previous government (having been used extensively in the late 1970s during periods of wage restraint, to which awards under Schedule 11 were not subject) and so Schedule 11 was repealed completely by the Employment Act 1980 (along with the statutory recognition procedure). This decreased the CAC's workload, and this process was taken further when the government revoked the Fair Wages Resolution in September 1983[34]. Moreover, there was no compensating increase in voluntary arbitrations, which in practice have not arisen in recent years.

The CAC has, however, seen a revival in its use under the present government, being involved in two major developments. The first, and most high-profile, is the new statutory recognition procedure under the Employment Relations Act 1999 (see p 74, below); jurisdiction to adjudicate on disputes arising from this

32   Trade Union and Labour Relations (Consolidation) Act 1992, s 212(1)(b).

33   In 2001/02 the CAC received only eight references under these jurisdictions, all concerning disclosure of information; these case are usually disposed of by Recommendations and ACAS assistance. The comparable figures at its busiest period in the 1970s were: 1977 – 1,030 references and 308 awards; 1978 – 1,065 references and 836 awards; 1979 – 617 references and 594 awards.

34   In addition to the Fair Wages Resolution, the CAC also had jurisdiction under several particular statutes which imposed requirements analogous to those in the Resolution. However, some of these were repealed (particularly the Road Haulage Wages Act 1938, the Civil Aviation Act 1949, s 15 and the Broadcasting Act 1981, s 25) and the remainder (in the Housing Act 1957, s 92, the Films Act 1960, s 42 and the Public Passenger Vehicles Act 1981, s 28) no longer had effect since they were so framed that they only applied while the Resolution itself was in force.

procedure is given to the CAC[35]. The second development is the enactment of the European Works Councils Directive 94/45/EC (see p 95, below); here, the CAC is given jurisdiction to adjudicate on certain specified issues concerning employee members, applicability of the new Regulations to a particular company, constituencies and confidentiality of information (with other matters going to a tribunal or the EAT). These important new functions are likely to be sensitive and contentious, as can be seen from three further developments. The first is that when the CAC is operating the recognition procedure, it now has separate procedural requirements as to appointment, composition and decision taking[36], aimed at increasing openness and minimising challenges to its decisions. The second is that its decisions in relation to disputes over European works councils are subject to appeal on a point of law to the EAT[37]. The third is that, in expanding its membership to cope with the likely increase in its case law, the government were keen to stress (again) openness and adhesion to the 'Nolan principles' on open competition for public appointments. Moreover, the possible legal complexity of these new jurisdictions was reflected in the choice as the new Chairman (to replace the long-serving previous Chairman, Professor Sir John Wood, on his retirement) of not just another eminent employment lawyer, but a High Court judge, Burton J.

(iii) The Certification Officer

In addition to ACAS and the CAC the other principal institution which the reader is likely to encounter in the areas of industrial relations and trade union law is the Certification Officer (CO). The office was established by the Employment Protection Act 1975 and is now governed by Part VI of the Trade Union and Labour Relations (Consolidation) Act 1992, though with major changes made by the Employment Relations Act 1999. It takes its name from the major function at that time of certifying trade unions as 'independent', such certification being the key to enjoyment of the new statutory rights given to unions and their members by that Act; the procedure of certification is considered in head 2 below. However, it becomes immediately obvious that in fact this official is, if not misnamed, at least inadequately named, since his functions now extend far beyond certification (which is now of course quantitatively far less important). In fact, he resembles more the old institution of the Registrar of Trade Unions, with a wide supervisory jurisdiction which may be generally split into two functions – administrative and judicial. The administrative functions include the listing of trade unions, dealing with the mechanics of union amalgamations, and receiving the audited annual returns and actuarial reports on members' superannuation schemes that are required of trade unions under the Trade Union and Labour

35 In exercising these functions, the CAC 'must have regard to the object of encouraging and promoting fair and efficient practices and arrangements in the workplace': Trade Union and Labour Relations (Consolidation) Act 1992, Sch A1, para 171. In 2001/02 there were 119 references under this jurisdiction; 90 were completed or withdrawn; CAC Annual Report 2001/2002.

36 Trade Union and Labour Relations (Consolidation) Act 1992, s 263A. In particular, there *must* be a side member for each side of industry; where there is a split of opinion, but a majority have the same opinion, that is to be the decision (and so the chairman only has the power of umpire to decide the case if there is no majority opinion).

37 Transnational Information and Consultation of Employees Regulations 1999, SI 1999/3323, reg 38(8).

Relations (Consolidation) Act 1992[38]. In addition, however, the CO has judicial functions, in that he has the power to adjudicate on complaints brought by individuals of infringements of the laws relating to (a) political expenditure by a union, the running of a political fund and the necessary balloting thereon; (b) the balloting required for a union amalgamation; and (c) the balloting required for the appointment of union officers. Although the CO is funded and provided with staff through ACAS, he operates independently of it (and of the Department of Trade and Industry). He is expressly empowered to regulate his own procedure on any application or complaint to him, and he produces an Annual Report on his activities, which is an important source of up-to-date information and statistics on trade unions and their operations.

The powers of the CO were markedly increased by the Employment Relations Act 1999. The previous Conservative government had created two politically contentious posts of Commissioners for the Rights of Trade Union Members and Commissioners for Protection Against Unlawful Industrial Action, charged with the duties of assisting union members to assert their rights and members of the public to challenge unlawful strike action. When the present government decided to abolish them they offered the quid pro quo of increasing the CO's powers in most areas previously covered by the Commissioners[39], the idea being to provide an easier and more accessible forum than the ordinary courts. The CO's jurisdiction was extended by the 1999 Act to cover breach of a member's rights to see union accounts and breach of the statutory rules on the use of funds for political objects. In addition, the CO's existing powers in relation to registers of members, disqualification for union office, union office ballots and political resolution ballots were strengthened, largely by allowing him to issue enforcement orders akin to those available in court proceedings[40]. However the most fundamental change was to give him powers to hear complaints by a member of breach of a trade union's own rules (relating to union office, disciplinary proceedings, balloting of members on any issue other than industrial action, the constitution or proceedings of the executive committee or similar body and such other matters as may be prescribed by order, which has not yet been done). Here, as in the other areas affected by the changes, the CO is in effect made into a full alternative to the courts; because of this, the Act also laid down new procedural requirements on the CO when operating in these areas, with an appeal to the EAT on a point of law.

2 THE INDEPENDENCE OF TRADE UNIONS

(i) The importance of independence

For the purposes of the present legislation, the concept of the 'independence' of trade unions was first to be found in the Trade Union and Labour Relations

---

38 These matters are dealt with in ch 10, below.
39 Areas previously covered by the Commissioners which are *not* covered by the CO's increased powers are the statutory power of an individual to sue on behalf of the union, the right to restrain trustees from unlawful use of union property, the right of a member to restrain union industrial action without a ballot and the member's common law right to challenge breach of the union's rules relating to industrial action.
40 Employment Relations Act 1999, Sch 6.

Act 1974, where it was important in the definition of a union membership agreement (closed shop). However, with the advent of the new statutory trade union rights in the Employment Protection Act 1975 (and in other related legislation), the concept took on far greater significance, for the general scheme is that these new rights may only be exercised by *independent* trade unions, not by any bodies which are liable in any way to be under the influence or control of the employer. Thus, only an independent trade union may receive certain bargaining information as of right, demand to be consulted on pending redundancies or a planned transfer of the employer's undertaking, and appoint safety representatives under the Health and Safety at Work etc. Act 1974[41]; likewise, only a member of an independent trade union has a right to certain time off work, a right not to have detrimental action taken against him or be dismissed because of his union activities, and, in the case of dismissal, a right to apply for interim relief pending the hearing of an unfair dismissal action. The availability of these rights to such a union and its members may be a significant help in recruiting members and, perhaps more to the point, lack of them could be very damaging to any nascent organisation wishing to establish itself as a viable union. In the past this has been particularly important in an area of disputed or growing unionisation, for example in the white collar area, where there is competition for members between a larger, established union and a smaller body such as a staff association, for if that smaller body fails to obtain a certificate of independence it may stand little chance of competing effectively. Staff associations (or 'house' unions) have been particularly at risk in this certification procedure, since they may have evolved from little more than social clubs, and as they only operate with one employer they may be inherently more susceptible to interference (although this is by no means conclusive – the NUM and RMT could be said to be one-employer unions). Also at risk would be non-TUC affiliated bodies and breakaway groups from larger unions[42], where again they may face opposition from established affiliated unions.

(ii) The machinery of certification

A listed[43] trade union may apply to the CO[44] for a certificate of independence, under the Trade Union and Labour Relations (Consolidation) Act 1992, section 6. He must decide whether the union is in fact 'independent' within the statutory definition; if his decision is favourable he must grant the certificate, and if unfavourable he must give his reasons for refusal. In coming to his decision he is at liberty to make such inquiries as he thinks fit and 'shall take into account any

---

41   This refers to the position where a trade union of some sort is involved; as will be seen below, the consultation requirements or redundancies and business transfers were extended in 1995 to elected worker representatives, in cases where no trade union is being involved, and similar reforms were made in the case of health and safety representatives in 1996.

42   Non-affiliated bodies would not be able to use, or be bound by, the TUC's internal disputes procedure for the settlement of inter-union rivalries – see p 738 below. A particularly newsworthy example of a breakaway group was the Union of Democratic Mineworkers which split from the NUM after the miners' strike, and was granted a certificate of independence.

43   Ie listed under the Trade Union and Labour Relations (Consolidation) Act 1992, s 2 – see p 559 below.

44   See p 66, above.

relevant information submitted to him by any person', which will of course include any other union which has an interest in the area in question and may wish to oppose the application for a certificate. If an applicant union is refused a certificate, it may appeal against that decision to the EAT. Unlike most other appeals to that body, this is an appeal of law *and fact,* so that the EAT may reconsider the decision completely[45] It should be noted, however, that the right to appeal is so worded that only a refused applicant union may appeal; if a certificate is in fact granted, there is no appeal against that decision by another union which may have opposed the application[46]. Finally, an application can be made more than once so that if a union is at first refused a certificate (whether after an appeal or not) it may reconsider its organisation etc. (possibly in the light of the reasons given for refusal), make any necessary changes and then apply again[47]. In practice, however, where there is rivalry with an established union this delay might give the latter a considerable tactical advantage.

(iii) The tests to be applied

An independent trade union is defined in the Trade Union and Labour Relations (Consolidation) Act 1992, section 5 as one which (a) is not under the domination or control of an employer or a group of employers or of one or more employers' associations, and (b) is not liable to interference by an employer or any such group or association (arising out of the provision of financial or material support or by any other means whatsoever) tending towards such control. The CO has evolved certain criteria, particularly on limb (a), and these were approved by the EAT in the first case to come before it on certification, *Blue Circle Staff Association v Certification Officer*[48]. These criteria are the financing of the union (any direct subsidy from the employer being potentially fatal); any other material support from the employer, such as free premises, time off work for officials or office facilities[49]; any interference in the running of the union by the employer; the history of the union, particularly if it started off as the creation of the employer; the union's rules, particularly if they allow intervention by the employer or give much control to senior members of the management; whether the union only operates within a single company (not a fixed criterion, but of course a more broadly based union would be more difficult to influence); the organisation of the union (its structure, financial position, recruiting ability); and its general attitude towards the employer in negotiating, for while it would be going too far to expect industrial chaos as a necessary sign of independence, the nascent union may be expected to have evolved far enough to show some 'robustness' in its negotiations. In the *Blue Circle* case the EAT approved the CO's refusal of a certificate on the basis that the staff association in question had originated as 'little more than a sophisticated instrument of personnel control' and had not evolved far enough to qualify as independent, in spite of certain changes to its rules and procedures which had, however, not gone far enough:

45   Trade Union and Labour Relations (Consolidation) Act 1992, s 9.
46   *GMWU v Certification Officer* [1977] 1 All ER 771, [1977] ICR 183.
47   *Blue Circle Staff Association v Certification Officer* [1977] ICR 224, [1977] IRLR 20; *HSD (Hatfield) Employees Association v Certification Officer* [1978] ICR 21, [1977] IRLR 261.
48   See n 47, above.
49   After certification, of course, the union might well bargain for such facilities, and indeed in the case of time off demand it as of right, but before certification it would be wiser not to accept them.

'... we are not satisfied that the Association has yet attained that freedom from domination which it has been pursuing since it first decided to reorganise its constitution last year. When the matrix of the new constitution is regarded, it is found to be an organisation whereby the association of the salaried staff members was penetrated at every point by the interference and control of the management. There must be a heavy onus on such a body to show that it has shaken off the paternal control which brought it into existence and fostered its growth, and which finally joined in drafting the very rules by which the control appears to be relaxed[50].'

In order to qualify as independent, the union must satisfy limb (b) of the definition too, for it could be the case that limb (a) is satisfied as things stand, but the union might still in some way be liable to interference, perhaps indirectly[51]. This second stage of the test requires a certain amount of speculation and foresight, and raised a question of interpretation – what was meant by 'liable' to interference? The wider view (ie more indulgent to the applicant union) was that 'liable' meant 'likely to suffer in practice', so that even if there were some provisions in the union's rules which might in theory permit interference by the management they should be ignored if in practice that was unlikely to happen. The narrower view was that 'liable' meant 'vulnerable to' or 'exposed to the risk of' interference, so that any factors raising a possibility of interference should disentitle the union to a certificate of independence even if, as things stood at the time of the application, there was little likelihood in practice of it happening. In *Squibb UK Staff Association v Certification Officer*, the applicant association had a proportionally large membership of the employees involved and was recognised by the employer for bargaining purposes; however, it was dependent upon the employer for material support such as accommodation and communications and was in a weak financial position, though there was found to be little likelihood of withdrawal of the employer's support. The EAT gave 'liable' the wider meaning and held that the union was independent[52] but, on the CO's appeal, the Court of Appeal reversed that decision, holding that the correct interpretation was the narrower view so that on the facts the CO's decision to refuse the certificate was correct[53]. Thus, the overall test for independence is more stringent than it might have been, in the light of the practical significance of the certificate of independence, and an applicant union or staff association should be quite sure before applying that none of its rules or procedures leave open a way for interference by an employer, so that it can claim to pass limb (b) as well as limb (a) – it is not enough to say that, although interference may be a theoretical possibility it is not likely to happen because of the present attitude of the employer:

---

50 [1977] ICR 224 at 233, [1977] IRLR 20 at 24, per Cumming-Bruce J.
51 *HSD (Hatfield) Employees Association v Certification Officer* [1978] ICR 21, [1977] IRLR 261.
52 [1978] ICR 115, [1977] IRLR 355; see also the *HSD (Hatfield)* case, n 51, above.
53 [1979] ICR 235, [1979] IRLR 75, CA. For an application of these principles, see *A Monk & Co Staff Association v Certification Officer* [1980] IRLR 431, EAT. More recently, the staff association formed at GCHQ, Cheltenham (after the government's decision in 1984 to ban unions there on the grounds of national security) was refused a certificate of independence on this second limb of the test and that refusal was upheld by the EAT: *Government Communications Staff Federation v Certification Officer* [1993] ICR 163, [1993] IRLR 260.

'One has to envisage the possibility that there may be a difference of opinion in the future between the employers and the staff association. It does not matter whether it is likely or not. ... It may be a mere possibility. But when it arises the questions have to be asked. What is the strength of the employers? What pressures could they bring to bear against the staff association? What facilities could they withdraw?[54]'

Beneath the legal challenges lies an important principle. The TUC and its affiliated trade unions resist the establishment and growth of non-affiliated unions – often within the one company (the house union). It is difficult for such trade unions to satisfy the criteria of independence and they will rarely, in the early stages of development, be 'effective'[55].

3 RECOGNITION FOR COLLECTIVE BARGAINING PURPOSES

The question of recognition of unions for collective bargaining purposes is not normally a matter for statute; usually it is a question of practical industrial relations and most practical consequences of recognition are extra-legal, particularly in the light of the non-enforceability of collective bargains. The same applies to the withdrawal of recognition, which saw a considerable increase in the 1980s and 1990s. Recognition is expressly covered as a proper subject for a 'trade dispute'[56], and in an appropriate case the parties to such a dispute over recognition may decide to seek the conciliatory help of ACAS in the ordinary way[57]. Other than that, the law has tended to keep out of questions of recognition. However, under the modern legislation, recognition has arisen as a matter of law in two ways. The first, and most obvious, concerns the question whether there should be a residual statutory procedure for a union to claim recognition by an employer (once it has a certain level of membership). Under the Industrial Relations Act 1971 and, more important, during the period from 1976 to 1980 under the Employment Protection Act 1975 there was an attempt to use legal machinery for resolving disputes about union recognition; this was ultimately unsuccessful and the machinery was abolished in the Employment Act 1980, but not before being the source of notable case law going to the root of the problem of how far the courts should control the exercise of its functions by a body such as ACAS when those functions relate to difficult questions of industrial relations[58]. The incoming

54 [1979] ICR 235 at 245, [1979] IRLR 75 at 78, per Lord Denning MR. The staff association was eventually granted a certificate by the Certification Officer (Employment News No 62 (May/June 1979)).
55 The Certification Officer's Annual Report for 1987 showed a cumulative total of 52 refusals of applications in the first ten years of operation – a large proportion of these were staff associations; 231 certificates had been issued and were still in force at the end of 1987; 140 had been issued and subsequently cancelled (largely due to union amalgamation). Needless to say, the rate of application slowed dramatically; in 1992 six certificates were granted, and by 1995 none: Annual Reports 1992, 1995.
56 Trade Union and Labour Relations (Consolidation) Act 1992, ss 218(1)(g), 244(1)(g).
57 Trade Union and Labour Relations (Consolidation) Act 1992, s 210; see p 58 above; in 2001/02 it accounted for 27% of collective conciliation cases.
58 *Grunwick Processing Laboratories Ltd v Advisory Conciliation and Arbitration Service* [1978] 1 All ER 338, [1978] ICR 231, HL; *United Kingdom Association of Professional Engineers v Advisory Conciliation and Arbitration Service* [1980] ICR 201, [1980] IRLR 124, HL; *EMA v ACAS (No 2)* [1980] ICR 215, [1980] IRLR 164, HL. For details of the repealed procedure, see the previous editions of this book; particularly interesting is ch 8 of the ACAS Annual Report 1980, giving their own assessment of the operation of the procedure from 1976 until its demise in 1980.

New Labour government in 1997 were committed to reintroducing a statutory scheme for obtaining recognition, and this featured largely in the 'Fairness at Work' White Paper[59] and the resulting legislation in the Employment Relations Act 1999, which obviously tries to avoid the fatal shortcomings of the pre-1980 legislation.

The second form of legal involvement (always existing independently of the statutory recognition procedures and therefore unaffected by their presence or absence) is that under many provisions of the modern statutes it is necessary to be able to *define* recognition. This is because the key to some of the basic rights is not just that a union is 'independent'[60], but also that it is 'recognised' by the employer in question. Thus, a recognised independent trade union has rights to receive bargaining information[61], to be consulted on impending redundancies[62], to appoint safety representatives[63], to receive information and be consulted about an impending transfer of the employer's undertaking[64], and to be notified about certain matters relating to company pension schemes[65]. Further, the status of a union as recognised also figures in the rights of officers and members to time off work[66]. The definition of recognition must therefore be considered first, then the new statutory recognition procedure and, after that, some incidental aspects of the involvement of the law.

(i) The definition of recognition

As seen above, the question of whether a union can claim to be 'recognised' in law is an important point of jurisdiction for claiming significant legal rights. The clearest case is where there is an express recognition agreement between employer and union. However, the lack of a written recognition agreement (or disputes procedure involving the union) will not be conclusive, for recognition may also be implied if it exists in practice, no matter what the employer might call it[67].

The starting point is the statutory definition, which states that a recognised trade union is one which is recognised by an employer, or two or more associated employers[68], to any extent for the purposes of collective bargaining[69]. The phrase

59 Cm 3968, 1998, paras 4.11–4.20 and Annex 1.
60 See pp 61–71 above.
61 See pp 80–83 below. The right to receive the information is drafted in such a way that, if recognition is less than total, the *extent* of the recognition can determine not only whether a particular union may make a claim but also what information must actually be disclosed: *R v Central Arbitration Committee, ex p BTP Tioxide Ltd* [1981] ICR 843, [1982] IRLR 60. The question is therefore doubly important.
62 See pp 84–91 below. Most of the case law on the definition of recognition has arisen under this head. As will be seen below, in this area and in that of transfers of undertakings, equivalent rights have now been extended to directly elected worker representatives.
63 Health and Safety at Work etc. Act 1974, s 2, as amended by the Employment Protection Act 1975, s 116. Again, there has been an extension to directly elected worker representatives.
64 Transfer of Undertakings (Protection of Employment) Regulations 1981, SI 1981/1794, reg 10; see pp 91–94 below.
65 Pension Schemes Act 1993, s 113; Occupational Pension Schemes (Disclosure of Information) Regulations 1996, SI 1996/1655.
66 See p 582 below.
67 *Joshua Wilson & Bros Ltd v Union of Shop, Distributive and Allied Workers* [1978] ICR 614, [1978] IRLR 120.
68 For associated employers, see pp 30–32 above.
69 Trade Union and Labour Relations (Consolidation) Act 1992, s 178(3); collective bargaining is itself defined in s 178(1), (2).

'to any extent' could have been ambiguous, meaning either (a) that there must be full agreement to recognise the union, though possibly only with regard to certain matters, or (b) that the agreement to recognise might itself only be equivocal or sporadic. However, it has been held that it means the former[70] and so, although the recognition may only be partial in coverage, there must still be clear evidence of agreement to recognise.

Further than this, the statutes give little guidance in the sort of case where a problem of definition might arise, for example where a union with no express recognition agreement claims for the first time to be recognised in order to insist on one of the statutory rights (usually in the past, in a case such as this, the right to be consulted about threatened collective redundancies). The task of definition has therefore fallen principally on the courts, and the decisions of the Court of Appeal in *National Union of Gold, Silver and Allied Trades v Albury Bros Ltd*[71] and the EAT in *Union of Shop, Distributive and Allied Workers v Sketchley Ltd*[72] are particularly instructive. In the former, the Court of Appeal held that the concept of recognition is so important and so fundamental to the statutory union rights that, in the absence of an express agreement, it should not be held to be established unless there was clear and unequivocal evidence of conduct (probably over a period of time) from which recognition could be inferred; on the facts of the case, evidence of recruitment of a few employees by the union followed shortly after by a letter to the employer raising the question of rates of pay, leading to one inconclusive meeting, was held to be too insubstantial to establish the recognition that would have obliged the employer to consult the union over subsequent redundancies. In addition to this general point, the case established a further point of considerable importance in any case where the employer observes terms and conditions negotiated at a higher level – the employer in the case was in fact a member of an employers' association which *did* conduct collective bargaining with the union in question but it was held that that could not of itself be construed as recognition by that employer; this reinforces the point that recognition is ultimately a matter of agreement between a union and an individual employer, which could cause problems for unions in industries which are composed of many small firms, even if there is established bargaining at a higher level, for example nationally[73].

So far, discussion has been as to whether a union is recognised or not, and in many industries it is obvious which unions are recognised and that that recognition will cover all foreseeable industrial relations contexts. However, it must be remembered that the statutory definition talks of recognition 'to any extent' and this means that the definition may be satisfied even if the employer has agreed to

70 *Transport and General Workers' Union v Dyer* [1977] IRLR 93; *National Union of Gold, Silver and Allied Trades v Albury Bros Ltd* [1978] ICR 62, [1977] IRLR 173 (upheld on appeal by the Court of Appeal – n 71, below).
71 [1979] ICR 84, [1978] IRLR 504, CA; *National Union of Tailors and Garment Workers v Charles Ingram & Co Ltd* [1977] ICR 530, [1977] IRLR 147. The *NUGSAT* case was applied in *Cleveland County Council v Springett* [1985] IRLR 131, EAT (concerning health and safety representatives) where it was held that the addition of the union to the Burnham Committee by the Secretary of State did *not* per se mean that the union became recognised by one of the employers represented on that committee.
72 [1981] ICR 644, [1981] IRLR 291.
73 A prime example of this is the agriculture industry, where terms and conditions are worked out centrally each year before the Agricultural Wages Board in negotiations between the agricultural section of the TGWU and the NFU, but where any question of union recognition would have to be determined on a farm-by-farm basis. This diversity had long been a cause of weakness of the NUAAW and was one of the reasons for its amalgamation in 1982 with the TGWU.

bargain and negotiate with the union only on certain topics. As long as the necessary level of agreement can be shown, this form of partial recognition will be sufficient in law[74]. However, an important distinction must be drawn here, for there also exists in practice a form of 'recognition' involving only the right of a union to represent its members in individual matters, for example under a grievance or discipline procedure[75]. This may perhaps be granted while a union recruits a sufficient number of members to warrant full recognition, or may be all that is left after an employer has derecognised the union for most purposes; however it arises, it falls short of an agreement to negotiate and bargain and so does *not* qualify as recognition in law. This can clearly be seen in *USDAW v Sketchley Ltd*[76], where an agreement between the employer and the union in 1978 granting recognition for representation purposes was held by the EAT to be insufficient in itself to entitle the union to be consulted in 1980 about impending redundancies, particularly as the 1978 agreement expressly stated that it did not confer recognition on USDAW for negotiation of terms and conditions. However, the case also shows that recognition is not a static concept, because the evidence showed that in February 1980, when the employer began to select candidates for redundancy, the union threatened strike action if they were not given information about this, as a consequence of which a meeting took place at which it was agreed that, in return for the union calling off the strike threat, the employer would give the union certain advance information on redundancies, adopt a procedure involving the union and in certain cases make redundancy payments above the legal minimum. While the 1978 agreement could not constitute recognition, the EAT thought it possible that the subsequent events in February 1980 were capable of showing that the union had indeed become accepted as having sufficient negotiating rights (at least in the area of redundancy) to satisfy the definition of recognition, and so they remitted the case to the tribunal for determination of that question.

(ii) The statutory recognition procedure

In its manifesto for the 1997 election, the Labour Party stated its intention to reintroduce a statutory recognition procedure. On coming into power, the new government in typical fashion sought to achieve agreement among the 'social partners' (TUC and CBI) on such a procedure, but consultations merely reinforced existing deep divisions. Thus, the government themselves had to take the initiative in the White Paper Fairness at Work and propose a scheme. The failure to discern an agreed version had two principal effects: (i) in an attempt to steer a middle path, the government introduced certain limitations or qualifications to which strong objection was taken by the unions (leading to arguments that there had been resiling from the manifesto pledge of recognition

74   It will be sufficient to claim to be consulted about impending redundancies or transfer and to claim to appoint safety representatives; however, to claim bargaining information the union must be able to go further and show that the information requested is relevant to one of the purposes for which the union is recognised: (*R v Central Arbitration Committee, ex p BTP Tioxide Ltd* [1981] ICR 843, [1982] IRLR 60) and this now also applies to the right to time off for union duties (Trade Union and Labour Relations (Consolidation) Act 1992, s 168(1)(a)).

75   This is now backed by the employee's statutory right to be accompanied by a trade union official (or fellow worker) before a disciplinary or grievance procedure: Employment Relations Act 1999, ss 10–15; see p 538 below.

76   N 72 above; this distinction can also be seen in the *BTP Tioxide* case.

where a simple majority of the workforce voted for it); (ii) the prospect of legal enforcement (raising spectres of the failed 1970s version) meant that there had to be a satisfactory forum, eventually meaning a revamped CAC[77]. In relation to (i), the White Paper introduced the qualifications that the procedure should not apply to employers of fewer then twenty and that in a ballot those voting in favour of recognition should comprise not just over 50% of those taking part, but also at least 40% of those *eligible* to vote. There was added later the further qualification that, even where there is already a majority union membership the CAC may still insist on a ballot if it considers it necessary to gauge 'real' support.

The new statutory recognition procedure was introduced by the Employment Relations Act 1999, which adds a new Schedule A1 to the Trade Union and Labour Relations (Consolidation) Act 1992[78]. The level of detail is stunning; the Schedule entered Parliament 88 paragraphs long and left 172. The intention to avoid the fatal pitfall of its 1970s predecessor (based on broad discretions) is obvious, and was made express by the government minister steering the Bill. He described the main features of the Bill as follows: (a) the legislation would provide the greatest scope for voluntary arrangements to be reached, with compulsion only as a last resort; (b) the threshold for frivolous complaints would be set at 10% of the relevant workforce; (c) the crucial test when determining the appropriate bargaining unit would be effective management, with fragmentation to be avoided; (d) if more than 50% of the workforce were already members of the relevant union, there would be a simplified procedure; (e) if no voluntary arrangement was reached, the dispute would be determined by the CAC; (f) the CAC's determination would be binding *but* would only relate to procedural matters[79]; (g) existing arrangements should, where possible, be left untouched[80]. For most purposes, these statements of principle were adhered to (though with many technical amendments), as was the point that statutory recognition per se would only cover pay, hours and holidays, unless widened by agreement[81].

Part 1 of the Schedule contains the principal provision on statutory recognition, which may be requested by one or more independent trade unions. In keeping with the voluntarist approach, the request is made in the first instance to the employer[82]. If there is agreement (possibly involving ACAS help), that is the end of the procedure[83]. If, however, the employer rejects the request or negotiations fail, the union(s) may apply to the CAC to decide (a) what is to be the appropriate bargaining

---

77 See p 65 above.
78 For a critical and comparative analysis of these provisions, see Wood and Goddard 'The statutory union recognition procedure in the Employment Relations Bill: a comparative analysis' (1999) 37 BJIR 203; see also Simpson (1998) 27 ILJ 253 and Wedderburn 'Collective bargaining or legal enactment' (2000) 29 ILJ 1 at 33 ff. FOr detailed consideration of the CAC case law, see *Harvey* Div N7F.
79 The government strongly resisted amendments aimed at going further and providing for either a legal duty to bargain in good faith or some form of binding arbitration on substantive claims: HL Committee, 7 June 1999, cols 1276–1280.
80 See the ministerial statements at HC SC E, 16 March 1999, cols 344–410.
81 Sch A1, para 3(4). 'Pay' can include employer contributions to company pension schemes: *UNIFI v Union Bank of Nigeria* [2001] IRLR 712, CAC. Questions of industrial training were originally mooted too, but are now dealt with separately by the Employment Relations Act 1999, s 5.
82 Para 4. The exclusion of employers with 20 or fewer employees is contained in para 7, which contains a calculation method; employees of any associated employer are included.
83 Para 10. The CAC may, however be subsequently involved in any dispute over operating the agreement; also, such an agreement may not be unilaterally terminated by the employer for three years: paras 52–63.

unit for these purposes and (b) whether the union has the support of the majority of workers in the appropriate bargaining unit[84]. In order to proceed, the CAC must be satisfied that at least 10% of the workers in the bargaining unit are union members[85].

Determination of the bargaining unit may clearly be a crucial factor. Once again, the initial emphasis is on encouraging the parties to agree it, but in default of that the CAC must determine it, taking into consideration the need for effective management, the views of the parties, existing national and local arrangements, the need to avoid fragmentation, the characteristics of the relevant workers and their location[86]. Once this is determined, the CAC is to proceed to the main question, namely whether there is the necessary support for collective bargaining to make an order for recognition. This can be determined in two ways. The short method is that if the CAC is satisfied that a majority of workers in the unit are union members, it may make the order, *unless* it considers that (a) it would still be in the interests of good industrial relations to hold a ballot, (b) a significant number of members in the unit inform the CAC that they do not want collective bargaining, or (c) there are doubts about the membership evidence[87]. The longer method (where membership numbers are insufficient to trigger the first method) is for the CAC to go straight to a ballot[88]. If the ballot shows that a majority of those voting support the union *and* that those voting in favour constitute at least 40% of the workers in the bargaining unit, the CAC must issue a declaration that the union is entitled to recognition; if not, the application is dismissed[89].

On the making of a declaration, the parties are given a period of thirty working days (or longer by agreement) to negotiate a method by which they will conduct collective bargaining. If no agreement is reached, either side may apply to the CAC for assistance[90]. A further period is determined for CAC-assisted negotiations, but then the CAC is to specify a method[91], which has effect as if in

---

84   Paras 11, 12. The term used here is 'worker', as defined in the Trade Union and Labour Relations (Consolidation) Act 1992, s 296(1) (see p 32 above); for an example on marginal facts, see *R (on the application of the BBC) v CAC* [2003] IRLR 460.
85   Para 14.
86   Paras 18, 19. The CAC's function at this stage is to determine whether the unit sought by the union is 'appropriate'; while it must consider the employer's representations (including any alternative unit proposed), it is not to consider whether such an alternative is *more* appropriate: *R v CAC, ex p Kwik-Fit (GB) Ltd* [2003] IRLR 395, CA. The doctrine of associated employers does *not* apply at this stage, so that there cannot be a bargaining unit spanning more than one employer unless (per the CAC in an inventive judgment) there are 'exceptional' circumstances showing that in reality two or more employers are one: *Graphical Paper and Media Union v Derry Print Ltd* [2002] IRLR 380, CAC.
87   Para 22. The CAC discretion here, as elsewhere in the Schedule, is wide and difficult to challenge; as there is no obligation to give reasons there can be no challenge on the basis of inadequacy of reasons, only on the basis that any reasons that are given are erroneous in law or perverse: *Fullarton Computer Industries Ltd v Central Arbitration Committee* [2001] IRLR 752. In fact, the incidence of judicial review applications has been low, causing few problems for the CAC (see the CAC Annual Report 2001/02 at p 3 and the Annual Report 2002/03 at p 2).
88   Para 23. Procedure for the ballot is set out in paras 24–28; it must be conducted by an appointed independent person, and may be either workplace or postal. The employer must co-operate, in particular by allowing access to the workforce; this is backed by a DTI Code of Practice.
89   Para 29.
90   Para 30.
91   Para 30. Obviously the hope must be that this power would rarely have to be operated, because compulsion at this stage is an odd concept (analogous to the ancient family law order for restitution of conjugal rights!). To ease the situation in such a case, the Secretary of State has exercised his power under para 168 to issue a model form of collective bargaining, to be taken into account by the CAC. By March 2003 this power had only had to be exercised in six cases: CAC Annual Report 2002/03.

a legally enforceable agreement between the parties, subject to specific performance.

Two further significant matters are covered by the Schedule (in addition to a plethora of highly detailed subsidiary and explanatory provisions). The first concerns subsequent changes in the bargaining unit. Part III (paragraphs 64–95) sets out complex procedures for dealing with circumstances which necessitate changes to the established collective bargaining structure. The second matter is, of course, derecognition. Normally, this is simply a question of industrial realities, but where recognition has been obtained under the statutory scheme there are special procedures for its removed. These fall into six main categories: (i) where voluntary agreement has been reached under the procedure (where derecognition is not permitted in the first three years); (ii) where the relevant employees fall below the threshold of twenty-one; (iii) where the employer applies for derecognition even though the threshold requirement is still met[92]; (iv) where the request comes from employees; (v) where recognition was originally granted under the short method (ie more than 50% membership)[93]; (vi) where the union is not independent[94].

As stated above, the complexity of these provisions is remarkable. At the time of implementation, views varied as to the significance of this new procedure. A restrictive view was that this innovation was more important politically than industrially, and was principally aimed at a restricted number of firms which did not recognise unions (or, indeed, may have positively derecognised them in the last decade or more) but where union membership remained quite high. A more expansive view was that the very existence of the procedure may have a normative effect on the renewed acceptability of union involvement more generally. As evidence for this, the TUC stated that in the last three quarters of 1999 (with the statutory procedure imminent) their members negotiated voluntarily over seventy recognition agreements. While this may be significant (though subject to the cynical view that such agreements may have been in order to stave off the inevitable, in a way not involving the complexities of Schedule A1, and thus basically defensive), the question still arose whether this return to formal union recognition would be of major practical significance. Even now there are still two main views on their likely impact. The wider view is that they could stem and reverse the decline of union membership and representation that had marked the 1980s and 1990s. The narrower, more cynical, view was that these provisions remain largely explicable on political grounds, as a debt owed by the government to the trade unions which has been honoured in a restricted way and not with a view to any across-the-board reversion to a collective bargaining system.

The figures at the time of writing could give support to either view. By March 2003 there had been 255 applications; of these, 57 were in the first year of operation

---

92 This is the most significant category; the procedure to be adopted is set out in paras 104–111, and requires a secret ballot.
93 Pt V (paras 122–133); this again requires a secret ballot. As with voluntary recognition, a request by an employer may not be made until the expiry of three years.
94 Pt VI (paras 134–148). Part VII (paras 149–155) applies where a union loses its certificate of independence.

(2000/01), 118 in 2001/02 and 80 in 2002/03. Thus, an intial hump can be seen, in line with the narrower view, but on the other hand, the absolute numbers are probably higher than the cynic might have expected. The figures show the importance of agreement and compromise throughout the procedure. Of the 255 applications to March 2003, 150 were accepted and of these the bargaining unit was agred in 56 cases, with only 59 having to go to the CAC for decision. Of these 115 cases proceeding, recognition was granted without a ballot in 23 cases and a ballot held in 58 cases. Of those ballots the union won 35 and lost 23. In the 58 cases in which recognition was ordered, the method of bargaining was agreed in 35 cases and only had to be adjuciated on in six cases. The figures for the next couple of years will be of particular interest, to see whether the 38% decrease in 2002/03 from the peak in 2001/02 continues. Will the statutory procedure eventually be seen as an integral part of the industrial relations system, or as a short-term solution to a level of imbalance in union recognition as a legacy of the 1980s and 1990s?

Two final points are offered in relation to the future of the procedure. The first is that it has now been subject to review by the government as part of their commitment to the unions to review the working of the Employment Relations Act 1999. The principal finding of this review (published by the DTI in February 2003) was that 'the Act has been a resounding success'; one result of this wholly objective opinion was that very few changes were suggested, those that were being of a technical nature. Thus anyone wanting to see serious changes in the recognition procedure to rectify what they saw as its limitations when introduced will have been disappointed. In particular, there were no proposals to drop the small firm exemption, extend the areas for negotiation beyond pay, hours and holidays, or to abandon the 'super majority' (ie the requirement not just of a majority of those voting, but also of 40% of those *entitled* to vote being in favour of union representation). The second point is that, if the procedure does turn out to be more than of short-term significance, a question may arise whether a return to formal unon recognition is really the government's preferred route towards 'partnership' (a key feature of the White Paper 'Fairness at Work'), rather than the arguably more modern and 'Third Way' concept of EU-inspired consultation with and involvement of the workforce *as such*, with more emphasis on the direct election of representatives. This potential conflict may well be seen in the debates on implementing the Information and Consultation Directive (see below), which is not limited to the involvement of recognised unions and where, indeed, one of the key issues is likely to be whether (and if so how) to introduce the new machinery required by the Directive into organisations which already have a level of union recognition (with the possibility of more under the statutory procedure). Further tensions between these two models of employee representation may be expected.

(iii) Further legal provisions

In addition to the legal definition of recognition and the new statutory recognition procedure, three other areas of legal involvement should be noted at this point – one of general importance and two specific points, one supporting the concept of recognition and the other possibly restricting it.

The general point is that the abolition of the previous statutory recognition procedure in 1980 did not mean the end of all ACAS involvement in such matters. This is because a recognition dispute can of course still be a valid subject for voluntary conciliation by ACAS. This should not be underestimated, and it is interesting to note that according to ACAS during the period 1976–80 (when the previous statutory procedure was in force) collective bargaining was extended to more workers through voluntary conciliation than by the use of that statutory procedure[95].

The second point is that by virtue of the Transfer of Undertakings (Protection of Employment) Regulations 1981, where an undertaking or part of one is transferred by the original employer to a new employer and it retains an identity distinct from the rest of the transferee employer's business, then if the original employer recognised a particular union, that recognition continues through the transfer and the new employer is deemed to recognise the union to the same extent[96]. This was not the case before, for a recognition agreement was viewed as personal to the employer and was not protected on a transfer[97].

The third, restrictive, point is that by virtue of the Trade Union and Labour Relations (Consolidation) Act 1992, sections 186 and 187 it is unlawful to insert into a contract for the supply of goods or services a condition that a party to that contract must recognise a particular union or unions in relation to persons employed by him; any such clause is declared to be void. Likewise it is unlawful to refuse to contract with or accept tenders from an employer on the ground that he does not recognise a particular trade union. This is to be read along with the wider provisions in sections 144 and 145 aimed at outlawing union-labour-only contracts and tenders[98] and is presumably included to prevent much the same result being reached, not by a direct requirement that contractors or tenderers must employ members of a particular union, but instead by making recognition of the union in question a condition of obtaining the contract. These provisions do not create criminal offences, but the imposition of such a condition or the refusal to contract or accept tenders on the ground of non-recognition is made tortious as a breach of statutory duty (actionable at the suit of the contracting party against whom it is aimed, or 'any other person who may be adversely affected' by it) and section 225 removes the statutory immunities from actions aimed at inducing the incorporation of such a condition or such refusal and from industrial action aimed at disrupting the supply of goods and services because of non-recognition of a particular trade union by the supplier. Thus, not only did the previous government remove the possibility of obtaining recognition through a legal procedure, they also attempted to place legal limits on the ways in which a union may try to obtain it as a matter of practical industrial relations. In practice, these provisions have not had much direct effect – as in the case of industrial dispute cases generally, all that the new legislation does is to remove bars to legal action, but that legal action must be taken, if at all, by individual claimants and therefore must be seen by them to be worthwhile; perhaps it was thought that this may be the case more often with disappointed commercial tenderers (particularly

---

95 During that period, 2,292 recognition cases were completed through voluntary conciliation leading to full recognition in 726 cases (concerning 55,500 employees) and partial recognition in 255 cases (concerning 22,000 employees); this total figure of 77,000 employees exceeds the figure of 64,000 employees to whom collective bargaining was extended by virtue of the statutory procedure: ACAS Annual Report 1980. In 2001/02, 337 recognition disputes were dealt with by ACAS on a voluntary basis (comprising 27% of collective concilation cases in that year): ACAS Annual Report 2001/2002.

96 SI 1981/1794, reg 9. For the Regulations to apply at all, the transfer must be a 'relevant transfer'; see p 201 below. Of course, there is nothing to stop the transferee employer later rescinding the deemed recognition agreement.

97 *UCATT v Burrage* [1978] ICR 314.

98 See p 785 below.

for local government contracts) than in the more usual case of an employer simply being affected generally by industrial action which under the legislation is now illegal (for example as being unlawful secondary action or without the necessary ballot – see chapter 11 below), where actual litigation still remains relatively uncommon or, at most, confined to notable exceptions.

4 DISCLOSURE OF BARGAINING INFORMATION

One vestige of earlier times when the law actively encouraged rational collective bargaining is the imposition upon an employer of a duty to disclose certain information to an independent trade union which is recognised by him, for the purpose of facilitating the conduct of collective bargaining by that union. This duty was first enacted in the Industrial Relations Act 1971, and is now contained in the Trade Union and Labour Relations (Consolidation) Act 1992, sections 181–185 and the Code of Practice No 2 'Disclosure of information to trade unions for collective bargaining purposes', produced by ACAS pursuant to section 181(4)[99].

(i) The duty to disclose

Section 181 lays upon an employer the general duty to disclose information which is in his possession and relates to his undertaking or that of an associated employer, if it is (a) information without which the union would be impeded to a material extent in carrying out collective bargaining with him, *and* (b) information which he ought to disclose in the interests of good industrial relations. This formulation by itself is so vague as to be meaningless, indeed head (a) tends to ignore the fact that effective bargaining is possible (some would say easier) with virtually no information. The scheme is to explain it further in the Code of Practice, which states that the detail, form and depth of information in any given case will vary with the level of bargaining to which it may be relevant, and goes on in paragraph 11 to give particular examples of information which may be amenable to compulsory disclosure. These are under the headings of 'pay and benefits' (including pay systems, job evaluation and grading schemes; total pay bill, fringe benefits and the way that the overall pay bill is analysed); 'conditions of service' (recruitment, training, promotion and redundancy policies; appraisal systems; health and safety matters); 'man-power' (analysis of workforce, manpower and investment plans, any planned changes); 'performance' (productivity, efficiency and their savings; return on capital; state of order book); and 'financial' (cost structures, gross and net profits, sources of earnings, assets, liabilities, allocation of profits, government aid, transfer prices, loans within the group and interest charged). The aim of the Code is to show the *sort* of information within the ambit of section 181; it is at pains to point out that

---

99   See Kahn-Freund *Labour and the Law* (3rd edn, 1983), pp 106–118; Gospel 'Disclosure of information to trade unions' (1976) 5 ILJ 223; Gospel and Williams 'Disclosure of information: the CAC approach' (1981) 10 ILJ 10; Gospel and Lockwood 'Disclosure of Information for Collective Bargaining: the CAC Approach revisited' (1999) 28 ILJ 233.

these examples are not an exhaustive check list[100]. Further, the Code stresses the desirability of reaching joint agreement on what should be disclosed, possibly including an agreement to disclose certain information on a regular basis. Where a union wishes to resort to the statutory duty, it must make its request in writing if the employer so wishes, and any information disclosed must also be in writing if the union so wishes.

There is one possible limitation on the right to bargaining information which is inherent in the wording of section 181. As seen above, the union must be 'recognised' in order to make a claim, but that recognition might only be partial (for example restricted to negotiating rights only in respect of certain matters). If that is the case, section 181(1) applies to restrict the disclosure of information to matters 'in respect of which the trade union is recognised by him' and so, although the partial recognition is sufficient to qualify the union as 'recognised', the union will not be able to claim information relating to matters outside the scope of that partial recognition. Thus, in *R v CAC, ex p BTP Tioxide Ltd*[101] the union, ASTMS, had bargaining rights in respect of certain terms and conditions of employment, but in respect of a particular job evaluation scheme it only had the right to make representations on behalf of its members seeking re-evaluation of their job[102], not the right to negotiate over the scheme itself. Because of this, the Divisional Court held that the CAC had exceeded its jurisdiction in ordering disclosure by the employer of information relating to the scheme.

(ii) Exceptions to the duty to disclose

The duty is not an absolute one, for it is subject to certain exceptions which are contained in section 182, and which should be known to the prudent employer. Three obvious exceptions are where disclosure would be against the interests of national security or in contravention of other legislation, and where the information was obtained by the employer for the purpose of bringing or defending legal proceedings (for example resisting an unfair dismissal action). The most important exceptions are likely to be:
(a) Information which has been communicated to the employer in confidence, or in some way in consequence of a confidence; this is not further defined, either in the Act or the Code, and could lead to litigation[103].

---

100 One marginal area of interest is redundancy selection; in *Rolls Royce plc and AEEU* (CAC Award 94/1) the CAC upheld a union request for further information on how a points-based selection system had been applied, accepting that this process fell within the sphere of collective bargaining. In the individual context, this question has caused severe difficulties to the tribunals and courts (see p 590, below); see the CAC Annual Report 1994 for a contrasting of the CAC and the tribunal approach.
101 [1981] ICR 843, [1982] IRLR 60. In his judgment, Forbes J said that there were three categories of case where a union would not be entitled to information, on the wording of s 181 – (i) where the bargaining between employer and union does not meet the statutory definition of 'collective bargaining' because it does not relate to matters referred to in the Trade Union and Labour Relations (Consolidation) Act 1992, s 178(2); (ii) where dealings between employer and union do not amount to 'collective bargaining' because they cannot properly be described as 'negotiations' (s 78(2)); (iii) where there is 'collective bargaining' but it does not relate to matters in respect of which the union is recognised. For a good example, see *Babtie Shaw & Morton and UKAPE* (CAC Award 82/4).
102 This form of recognition for representation is not sufficient to qualify as 'recognition' for the purpose of claiming statutory union rights; see p 74 above.
103 This exception was held to apply to information included in a commercial tender submitted to the employer in confidence: *Civil Service Union v CAC* [1980] IRLR 274.

(b) Information relating specifically to an individual (unless he has consented to its disclosure); thus, while the union may be able to require disclosure of the wages bill for a whole department, the employer may resist a request for details of each individual's salary. This exception has caused some difficulties in areas where the trend has been towards individual contracting and performance-related pay[104].

(c) Information the disclosure of which could cause 'substantial injury' to the employer's undertaking for reasons other than its effect on collective bargaining.

This last category is perhaps the most contentious – what is likely to be substantial injury? Clearly an employer cannot rely on this on the ground simply that he has hitherto as a matter of policy kept the information secret, but on the other hand there will be cases where the employer's genuine interest in preserving secrecy will outweigh the benefits to the union of disclosure. The Code gives some further guidance in paragraphs 14 and 15. It gives as examples of information possibly under this exception – cost information on individual products, detailed analysis of proposed investment, marketing or pricing policies and price quotas or tender prices. It further states:

> 'Substantial injury may occur if, for example, certain customers would be lost to competitors, or suppliers would refuse to supply necessary materials, or the ability to raise funds to finance the company would be seriously impaired as a result of disclosing certain information. The burden of establishing that disclosure of certain information would cause substantial injury lies with the employer.'

Section 182(2) gives some practical protection to an employer by providing that he need not produce original documentation (so that an abstract or precis will suffice) and that he need not compile or assemble information where to do so would involve work or expenditure 'out of reasonable proportion to the value of the information in the conduct of collective bargaining' (a positive invitation to litigation).

One final point concerns the use made of the information by the union. Even if an employer has to divulge information which he would rather have kept secret, the statute only obliges disclosure to the union officials concerned, and then only for the purposes of conducting collective bargaining with that employer; it is thus an open question whether an employer could restrain further use (or, from his point of view, misuse) of that information by the union by the threat of an action for breach of confidence.

(iii) Enforcement provisions

If a union considers that an employer is refusing to disclose information which he ought by law to disclose, it may complain to the CAC under section 183. If the CAC thinks that a solution may be reached by conciliation, it must, and most often does, refer the matter to ACAS for that purpose. This is the opposite of the normal ACAS system of conciliation *first*, with arbitration only if that fails; it has

---

104 CAC Annual Report 1991, p 3.
105 In 2001/02 there were eight references to the CAC under these provisions and only one award had to be issued: CAC Annual Report 2001/2002.

been argued that this approach is more effective, with the initial approach to the CAC concentrating the parties' minds on possibilities for conciliation, and this view certainly appears to be supported by the figures, though the statistical basis is small since use of the procedure remains generally low[105]. If the matter is not referred to conciliation (or if it is but no settlement is reached), the CAC must hear and determine the complaint, giving the reasons for its decision. If it upholds the complaint, its declaration to that effect must specify the material which ought to be divulged, the date on which the employer failed to do so, and a period during which the employer should comply by disclosure. If at the expiry of this period the employer has still failed to disclose the specified information, the union may make a further complaint to the CAC under section 184, and this time may attach a substantive claim on behalf of some or all of the employees in question (for higher pay, better benefits, etc). It is this substantive claim which gives the teeth to this enforcement procedure, for if the CAC finds the union's further complaint well founded (in whole or in part) it may make a declaration to that effect *and* award all or part of the attached claim. Any terms and conditions granted in the CAC's award are automatically incorporated into the contracts of employment of the employees concerned, and are then enforceable in the ordinary courts.

One unfortunate limitation upon the power of the CAC under this procedure is that, as it is drafted, the committee is limited to deciding upon information which has in fact already been refused by the employer; this means that it cannot go on to give guidance on information which should be divulged in the future, even if to do so might avoid future litigation on linked matters where it is foreseeable that disputes may well arise[106].

(iv) Other obligatory disclosure

The employer must also disclose information to a recognised trade union concerning pending redundancies, under the statutory provisions covering the procedure for handling redundancies[107]. This covers the reasons for the proposed redundancies, the numbers and descriptions of employees involved, the total number affected at each establishment, the proposed method of selection, timing, and the proposed method of calculating any redundancy payments. Further, the employer must publish to his employees a statement of his health and safety policies[108] and divulge certain information relating to such matters to the Health and Safety Commission upon request[109] and to safety representatives appointed under Regulations[110]. Also, in a more specialised but linked context, an employer who intends to establish a contracted-out

---

106 *R v CAC, ex p BTP Tioxide Ltd* [1981] ICR 843, [1982] IRLR 60.
107 Trade Union and Labour Relations (Consolidation) Act 1992, ss 188–192; this has also been extended to elected worker representatives.
108 Health and Safety at Work etc. Act 1974, s 2(3).
109 Health and Safety at Work etc. Act 1974, ss 2(3), 27; note that s 28 imposes statutory restrictions on further publication of this information by the recipient officials.
110 Safety Representatives and Safety Committees Regulations 1977, SI 1977/500, reg 7; this contains grounds upon which an employer may refuse to disclose similar to those in the Trade Union and Labour Relations (Consolidation) Act 1992, s 182, above. See also the Health and Safety Commission's Code of Practice on Safety Representatives (1978), para 6. Again, there has been an extension to elected worker representatives: Health and Safety (Consultation with Employees) Regulations 1996, SI 1996/1513.

occupational pensions scheme must issue notices to that effect to earners who are to be covered by the scheme, giving certain basic information, and must also convey this information to 'all independent trade unions recognised to any extent for the purpose of collective bargaining in relation to the earners concerned', with whom the employer is then under a statutory obligation to consult on the proposed scheme[111]. Likewise, there are regulations providing for the disclosure of more information generally about the running of occupational pension schemes; in the first instance, such disclosure is envisaged as being to the members themselves, but the relevant provisions also mention disclosure to independent trade unions recognised to any extent for the purposes of collective bargaining in relation to members and prospective members of the scheme in question[112].

A further category of compulsory disclosure was enacted in the case of transfers of business by the Transfers of Undertakings (Protection of Employment) Regulations 1981, considered separately in head 6, below, and of course there are to be major developments on information that must be given to the workforce on economic matters generally when the Information and Consultation Directive 2002/14/EC is transposed into domestic law between 2005 and 2006, see head 7 below.

5 SPECIAL REDUNDANCY PROCEDURES

The redundancy payments legislation gives to individuals rights to payments upon redundancy, but does not itself lay down any particular procedures for handling redundancies. However, pursuant to two European Directives on collective redundancies[113], procedural requirements were established and are to be found in the Trade Union and Labour Relations (Consolidation) Act 1992, sections 188–198, as amended by the Trade Union Reform and Employment Rights Act 1993, the Collective Redundancies and Transfer of Undertakings (Protection of Employment) (Amendment) Regulations 1995 and 1999[114]. In many industries, it appears that these provisions have had little effect due to more sophisticated approaches to necessary reductions in manpower, such as voluntary redundancies, redeployment and natural wastage[115]; in some 'problem' industries of greater labour fluctuations, such as the construction industry, the provisions are more relevant. There are two obligations laid upon the employer who is about to make employees redundant – first, to consult employee or trade union representatives and, second, to notify the Secretary of State.

111 Occupational Pension Schemes (Contracting-Out) Regulations 1996, SI 1996/1172.
112 Occupational Pension Schemes (Disclosure of Information) Regulations 1996, SI 1996/1655. The Pensions Act 1995, passed in reaction to the Maxwell scandal, has provisions for obligatory member trustees, but not surprisingly this is cast in terms of individual appointment, *not* in terms of any formal involvement of recognised trade unions.
113 Directives 75/129/EEC and 92/56/EEC, consolidated in Directive 98/59/EC. The 1975 Directive was held not to be directly applicable in *Griffin v South West Water Services Ltd* [1995] IRLR 15, and so cannot be used as the basis of a separate legal action.
114 SI 1995/2587 and SI 1999/1925. On the latter, see Hall and Edwards 'Reforming the statutory redundancy consultation procedure' (1999) 28 ILJ 299.
115 Daniel and Stilgoe *The Impact of Employment Protection Laws* (Policy Studies Institute No 577, June 1978), summarised [1978] Employment Gazette 658; Millward et al. *Workplace Industrial Relations in Transition* (1992) pp 320–329. One interesting finding in the latter was that in 1990 compulsory redundancies were reported in 46% of workplaces without recognised unions that had made workforce reductions, compared with 17% where recognised unions were present: p 324.

(i) Consultation with employee or trade union representatives

It was enacted in the Employment Protection Act 1975 that where an employer proposes to dismiss as redundant[116] an employee of a class in respect of which he recognises an independent trade union, he must consult officials of that union, with a set time framework in the case of collective redundancies; these provisions are now contained in the Trade Union and Labour Relations (Consolidation) Act 1992, section 188. They were updated by the 1993 Act to take into account the 1992 amending Directive, but the whole basis of their enactment of the original 1975 Directive was severely shaken in enforcement proceedings brought by the EC Commission in *EC Commission v United Kingdom*[117]. The problem was the restriction of the consultation requirement to cases where there was a recognised union, whereas the Directive was held in that case to require far more general consultation with 'the workers' representatives'[118] Given that this country does not have any mandatory system of works councils, this caused a problem as to *whom* to consult where there is no recognised union. The previous government's response came in the 1995 Regulations, which retained the possibility of consultation with a recognised union, but added the alternative route of consultation with elected employee representatives[119]. This system was subject to further refinement by the present government in the 1999 Regulations. As a combined result of the 1993 Act and the 1995 and 1999 Regulations, section 188 now requires the following.

Where an employer is proposing to dismiss as redundant twenty or more employees at one establishment within a period of ninety days or less, he must consult about the dismissals all the persons who are appropriate representatives of any of the employees who may be affected by the dismissals or measures taken in relation to them. Appropriate representatives are defined as (a) if the employees are of a description in respect of which an independent trade union is recognised by their employer, representatives of that union; or (b) in any other case employee representatives already appointed or elected who have authority

---

116 The definition of redundancy for these purposes in s 195(1) was substituted by the Trade Union Reform and Employment Rights Act 1993, and now refers more simply and widely to 'dismissal for a reason not related to the individual concerned or for a number of reasons all of which are not so related'; under s 195(2) there is a rebuttable presumption that a dismissal or proposed dismissal is for redundancy. It was because of this wider definition in s 195(1) that an employer tactic (for forcing through changes in terms) of dismissing all employees and hiring them on the new terms was held to be a collective redundancy; as (not surprisingly!) there had not been the obligatory consultation, the employer was liable for hefty protective awards: *GMB v Man Truck and Bus UK Ltd* [2000] ICR 1101, [2000] IRLR 636.

117 C-383/92: [1994] ECR I-2479, [1995] 1 CMLR 345, ECJ. Other infringements by the UK were found, but these had been dealt with by the 1993 Act, as well as taking the new Directive into account.

118 There is a political irony here, because the Conservative government ended up defending the result of a Labour Government's pro-union policies; the aim of the restriction to recognised unions in 1975 was to concentrate industrial power in the latter's hands (see also the health and safety and pension legislation of that period). This of course backfired when the membership and influence of the unions declined dramatically, along with union recognition, so that the consultation requirements applied to fewer and fewer employees.

119 This was not purely defensive on the previous government's part, as they also viewed the need to change as an opportunity for some deregulation. Thus, the cut-off number was raised from 10 to 20 employees and the requirement still to consult under that number was dropped. These changes have not been reversed by the present government.

from the affected employees in relation to the proposed dismissals, or such representatives elected specifically for these purposes[120]. It is specifically provided that existing elected representatives can be used if 'it is appropriate (having regard to the purposes for which they were elected) for the employer to consult them about dismissals proposed by him'[121]; taken together with other consultation requirements (especially on TUPE) and increasing advantages to be gained from workforce agreements (for example in relation to the Working Time Regulations and the law on parental leave), this may argue strongly in favour of the employer having *standing* elected machinery for all of these purposes, even where no union is recognised.

The consultation must begin in good time[122], and in any event 90 days before the first dismissal takes effect (if the employer is proposing to dismiss 100 or more within the 90 days), or at least 30 days beforehand otherwise. According to the statute, the consultation must include ways of avoiding the dismissals, reducing the numbers and mitigating the consequences; these three requirements are to be construed disjunctively (ie the employer must consult on each of them[123]) and this must be undertaken by the employer with a view to reaching agreement with the appropriate representatives. The case law also establishes that as a matter of general principle 'consultation' requires (a) consultation while the proposals are still at a formative stage, (b) adequate information, (c) adequate time in which to respond and (d) conscientious consideration of the responses to the consultation[124].

With regard to information, section 188(4) specifies that an employer must disclose in writing to the appropriate representatives (a) the reason for the proposals, (b) the numbers and descriptions of employees proposed to be dismissed, (c) the total number of such employees at the establishment, (d) the proposed method of selection, (e) the proposed method of carrying out the dismissals and (f) the proposed method of calculating any non-statutory redundancy payments to be made to those selected.

Four problems of definition have arisen under this section. The first is when it can be said that the employer is 'proposing' to make an employee redundant (as it is this that sets the wheels in motion); under the existing law, it appears that the word 'proposing' requires a certain amount of planning and resolution on the part of the employer, not just speculation:

---

120 Trade Union and Labour Relations (Consolidation) Act 1992, s 188 (1B), as substituted in 1999. The previous government's provisions had allowed the employer to choose to use directly elected representatives even if there was a recognised union, to allow the employer if desired to sideline the union; that has now been stopped by the current wording. Where elections are held specifically for this purpose, they must comply with rules ensuring fair elections, laid down in s 188A.

121 S 196(1). They must be employed by the employer at the time when they are elected or appointed: s 196(2).

122 Where an ad hoc election is being carried out, 'in good time' means as soon as reasonably practicable after the representatives are elected: s 188(7A). If the employees fail to elect representatives within a reasonable time, the employer can give each affected employee the information required by law, but is absolved from the requirement to consult collectively: s 188 (7B).

123 *Middlesbrough Borough Council v TGWU* [2002] IRLR 324.

124 *R v British Coal Corpn and Secretary of State for Trade and Industry, ex p Price* [1994] IRLR 72, Div Ct (one of the 'pit closure' cases). Even if time limits are technically met, it may still be argued that in substance the whole exercise was a sham: *Transport and General Workers' Union v Ledbury Preserves (1928) Ltd* [1985] IRLR 412.

'... a proposal to make redundant within the meaning of [section 188] connotes a state of mind directed to a planned or proposed course of events. The employer must have formed some view as to how many are to be dismissed, when this is to take place and how it is to be arranged. This goes beyond the mere contemplation of a possible event.[125]'

However, this use of the word 'proposing' has led to the argument that the UK provisions do not enact the original 1975 EC Directive properly. The latter states that an employer should begin consultation when 'contemplating' collective redundancies, which may be construed as meaning *before* the employer has formed any definite views on the need for redundancies, whereas the domestic provision appears to apply only once that decision has been taken and therefore to apply principally to the question of *how* to deal with the proposed redundancies. This argument was accepted by Glidewell LJ in the Divisional Court in *R v British Coal Corpn and Secretary of State for Trade, ex p Vardy*[126] (the highly publicised decision declaring the previous government's original coal-mine closure programme to be unlawful), which was ironic because at the very time that the 1993 Act was being enacted with provisions stated to be bringing the UK legislation into line with the new 1992 Directive, that legislation was considered to be out of line in this fundamental way with the original 1975 Directive all along[127]. Subsequently Blackburne J in *Griffin v South West Water Services Ltd*[128] was unimpressed with this argument but when the matter was considered by the EAT in *MSF v Refuge Assurance plc*[129] (a case where it was directly relevant because the union was trying to get domestic law changed to reflect the Directive's approach) it was held (approving *Ex p Vardy*) that there is indeed a conflict but it was not possible to resolve it by re-construing section 188 (and, moreover, there could not be reliance on any arguments for direct effect because the employer was in the private sector).

The second problem of definition is whether, in a case where a union is involved, it is 'recognised' in respect of the employees to be made redundant; this is considered in head 3, above.

The third problem concerns the nature of an 'establishment', for the purpose of applying the statutory time limits. The word appears in the Collective Redundancies Directive, but once again there is no statutory definition, even though the width of its construction could have an important effect on section 188 in cases where the employer operates at several locations; if each location is a separate 'establishment' and there are less than twenty redundancies at each, the requirements of the section will not apply, even if the overall number of

---

125 *Association of Pattern Makers and Allied Craftsmen v Kirvin Ltd* [1978] IRLR 318 at 320 per Lord McDonald. *Union of Shop, Distributive and Allied Workers v Leancut Bacon Ltd* [1981] IRLR 295; *Hough v Leyland DAF Ltd* [1991] ICR 696, [1991] IRLR 194. It may be enough to trigger these provisions if the employer has decided *either* to go down the redundancy route *or* to adopt some other solution (eg sale of the busines): *Scotch Premier Meat Ltd v Burns* [2000] IRLR 639.

126 [1993] IRLR 104; the issue had been previously (understandably!) ducked in *Re Hartlebury Printers Ltd* [1992] ICR 559, [1992] IRLR 516. Another interesting facet of *ex p Vardy* is that it shows that a collective redundancy might be subject to challenge, not just under the employment legislation, but also by way of judicial review if there is a sufficient element of public law involved.

127 This had long been argued in *Harvey*, see E[2431]ff. The amendments in the 1993 Act requiring consultation as to ways of avoiding or minimising dismissals may now go some way towards mitigating this divergence between domestic and EC law, but are unlikely to be a complete answer, since they do not directly address the question of timing.

128 [1995] IRLR 15.

129 [2002] ICR 1365, [2002] IRLR 324.

redundancies is high. In *Barratt Developments (Bradford) Ltd v Union of Construction, Allied Trades and Technicians*[130] the EAT said that what constitutes an 'establishment' is a question for the employment tribunal to decide, as an industrial jury using its common sense, on the particular facts of the case and upheld the tribunal's decision that fourteen housebuilding sites administered from one central base in fact constituted one establishment. A similar decision was reached by the tribunal in *Baker's Union v Clarks of Hove Ltd* [131] where a firm employing 368 employees in their factory, bakery and 28 retail shops was held to constitute one establishment. It might be different, however, where one organisation is split into smaller parts which in fact have considerable autonomy, as for example in the case of one education authority in overall control of many different schools. However, the ECJ have stated that in interpreting the term the protective intent of the Directive must be kept in mind, and not frustrated by the technicalities of corporate structure[132].

The fourth problem is the converse of the third. Even where the 'establishment' has been discerned, it may still be necessary to decide who is the 'employer' and here there may be a problem because the concept of 'associated employers', so important elsewhere in employment law[133], is surprisingly *not* adopted by section 188 and the EAT has held that it will not unilaterally lift the veil of incorporation in this context. Thus, in *E Green & Son (Castings) Ltd v Association of Scientific, Technical and Managerial Staffs*[134] three companies were making redundancies of 97, 36 and 24 employees respectively but the relevant consultation period was 30 days (not 90) since they were each separate employers even though (a) they were all subsidiaries of one holding company (and so would be associated employers in other contexts) and (b) they all operated from the same physical 'establishment'.

The sanction for failure to consult is a special device, the 'protective award'. This may be sought by employee representatives, the trade union or in any other case (including where no machinery at all has been set up) by any of the employees affected or dismissed. The matter is referred to a tribunal which, if it finds the complaint established, must make a declaration to that effect and may make a protective award, which is an order that the employer shall continue to pay wages to the employees concerned for a 'protected period'[135]. This period is within the tribunal's discretion, subject to a maximum of 90 days. The employee is entitled to a 'week's pay'[136] for each week of the protected period; if the employer fails to make any or all of the payments due for this period, the individual employee may complain within three months to a tribunal which may order payment. The

---

130 [1978] ICR 319, [1977] IRLR 403.
131 [1977] IRLR 167. The tribunal's decision was later affirmed by the Court of Appeal: [1978] ICR 1076, [1978] IRLR 366, CA.
132 *Rockfon A/S v Nielsen* Case C-449/93 [1996] ICR 673, [1996] IRLR 168, ECJ. In particular, they held that a company in a group can still be an 'establishment' even if the power to make redundancies as a matter of policy lies elsewhere in the group. On the other hand (applying *Rockfon*), central management is not enough in itself to constitute one establishment where the organisation emphasis remains at the branch level: *MSFU Refuge Assurance plc*, n 129 above.
133 See pp 30–32, above.
134 [1984] ICR 352, [1984] IRLR 135.
135 Trade Union and Labour Relations (Consolidation) Act 1992, ss 189, 190. The period starts with the *proposed* date of the first dismissal, whether or not the *actual* date is different: *E Green & Son (Castings) Ltd v Association of Scientific, Technical and Managerial Staffs* [1984] ICR 352, [1984] IRLR 135, applied in *Transport and General Workers' Union v Ledbury Preserves (1928) Ltd* [1986] ICR 855, [1986] IRLR 492.
136 As defined in the Employment Rights Act 1996, Pt XIV, Ch II.

employee may be disqualified from claiming under the protective award if he is fairly dismissed for a reason other than redundancy, unreasonably resigns during the period or unreasonably refuses suitable alternative employment[137].

The only guidance given to the tribunals by the statute on the way to apply a protective award is that it should be 'just and equitable in all the circumstances having regard to the seriousness of the employer's default'; this however could mean either a compensatory approach (looking at the employee's actual loss) or a punitive one (looking at the seriousness of the employer's default and its effect on industrial relations). In *Talke Fashions v Amalgamated Society of Textile Workers and Kindred Trades*[138] the EAT clearly preferred the compensatory approach, so that the tribunal should start by assessing the period of employment which the employee has lost through the employer not applying the statutory consultation time before dismissing, and then deduct any contractual payments referring to that time (for example any wages in lieu) and certain other payments such as accrued holiday money. This gives the minimum award, and any amount added on top because of the 'employer's default' should be because of the effect of that default in increasing hardship to the employee, not just as a punishment for an act of bad industrial relations. However, this distinction could be too subtle to apply in practice, as one tribunal pointed out[139], as well as arguably being a wrongful limitation on the wording of the subsection, and the EAT subsequently resiled from it, so that tribunals can take into account more general matters such as the potential disruption caused by unnotified redundancies[140] and the 'moral' responsibility of the employer, eg where he was acting upon wrong advice given by the Department of Employment[141]. Certainly increases or reductions in the protected period in some subsequent cases have fairly clearly been on a punitive basis, as has been recognised by the EAT in Scotland[142], so the position appears to be that the figure calculated on a compensatory basis is prima facie the period to be specified by the tribunal, but it is subject to variation (up to the statutory maxima) in the light of the seriousness of the employer's default. As a result, there may still be a protective award based upon the employer's default, even if the employees in question have suffered no pecuniary loss (for example through being found immediate alternative employment)[143].

(ii) Notification to the Secretary of State

Where an employer proposes to dismiss as redundant 20 or more employees at one establishment within 30 days, he must give the Secretary of State written notice of the proposal at least 30 days before the first dismissal takes effect; where

---

137 Trade Union and Labour Relations (Consolidation) Act 1992, s 191; where there is an offer of alternative employment, the 'trial period' provisions are specially applied (see p 643 below).
138 [1977] ICR 833, [1977] IRLR 309; *Barratt Developments (Bradford) Ltd v UCATT* [1978] ICR 319, [1977] IRLR 403.
139 *TGWU v Nationwide Haulage Ltd* [1978] IRLR 143, IT.
140 *TGWU v Gainsborough Distributors (UK) Ltd* [1978] IRLR 460.
141 *UCATT v H Rooke & Son Ltd* [1978] ICR 818, [1978] IRLR 204.
142 *APAC v Kirvin Ltd* [1978] IRLR 318.
143 *Spillers-French (Holdings) Ltd v USDAW* [1980] ICR 31, [1979] IRLR 339, applied in *GKN Sankey Ltd v NSMM* [1980] ICR 148, [1980] IRLR 8.
144 Trade Union and Labour Relations (Consolidation) Act 1992, s 193; the requirement of notice does not apply where less than 20 are dismissed.

he proposes to dismiss 100 or more within 90 days, he must give 90 days' notice[144]. A copy of the notice must be sent to the appropriate representatives. If the employer fails to give this notice, the Secretary of State may prosecute the employer summarily (the maximum fine being level 5 on the standard scale)[145].

(iii) The 'special circumstances' defence

It is expressly provided, in the case of both consultation and notification, that if there are special circumstances rendering it not reasonably practicable for an employer to comply with the statutory requirements, he need only take such steps towards compliance as are reasonably practicable[146]. The burden of proof is upon the employer to establish special circumstances, but if he can do so, and can show that he did what was reasonably practicable (which may in some cases be nothing), he has a good case that there should be *no* protective award, not just a reduction in it. The meaning of 'special circumstances' has been left to the tribunals and courts, and will be a question of fact in each case. The Court of Appeal in *Clarks of Hove Ltd v Bakers' Union*[147] held that the employer's insolvency and collapse were not in themselves special circumstances:

'... insolvency is, on its own, neither here nor there. It may be a special circumstance, it may not be a special circumstance. It will depend entirely on the cause of the insolvency whether the circumstance can be described as special or not. If, for example, a sudden disaster strikes a company, making it necessary to close the concern, then plainly that would be a matter which was capable of being a special circumstance; and that is so whether the disaster is physical or financial. If the insolvency however were merely due to a gradual run-down of the company, as it was in this case, then those are facts on which the industrial tribunal can come to the conclusion that the circumstances were not special. In other words, to be special the event must be something out of the ordinary, something uncommon ...[148]'

Thus, although insolvency itself may not be special, the employer has been held to have a good defence where he carried on trading in the face of insolvency in the genuine hope that he would be able to sell the company as a going concern and so prevent redundancies, but had to appoint a receiver (without any consultation) when the last prospective purchaser disappeared[149]. In such a case, extensive consultation could be fatal to delicate negotiations, but on the other hand it may still be reasonable to expect *some* consultation and if that is the case the employer will not have shown that he did all that was reasonably practicable and so will remain liable[150]. The requirement of doing all that is reasonable puts

---

145 S 194.
146 Ss 188(7) and 193(7).
147 [1978] ICR 1076, [1978] IRLR 366, CA.
148 [1978] ICR 1076 at 1085, [1978] IRLR 366 at 369, per Geoffrey Lane LJ. Sudden financial deterioration following collapse of negotiations to sell the firm's shares to a third party was held to constitute a special circumstance in *USDAW v Leancut Bacon Ltd* [1981] IRLR 295; the shedding of labour normal on an insolvency was held not to in *GMB v Rankin and Harrison* [1992] IRLR 514.
149 *APAC v Kirvin Ltd* [1978] IRLR 318.
150 *Hamish Armour v ASTMS* [1979] IRLR 24; cf *USDAW v Leancut Bacon Ltd*, n 148 above.

a considerable onus on the employer to know and understand these legal requirements, so that in general a mistaken view of the law and its application to him will not be a 'special circumstance' unless it was a reasonable mistake[151], even if he was acting upon wrong advice, though in such a case the facts may support an argument for reduction of the protective award if the 'employer's default' is considered less[152].

The 1992 Directive sought to increase the protection for employees of transnational concerns who may be made redundant by decisions taken at higher levels than their immediate employer; this was put into effect in domestic law by the Trade Union Reform and Employment Rights Act 1993, which added to the 'special circumstances' defences a provision declaring that where the decision leading to the proposed dismissals is that of a person controlling the employer, a failure on the part of that person to provide information to the employer does *not* constitute special circumstances.

(iv) Protection of representatives

Where the 'appropriate representatives' are officials of a recognised trade union, then they will have the ordinary protection for such offices when taking part in union activities, and the ordinary right to time off work for these duties[153]. However, these provisions would not apply to the new category of elected employee representatives, and so the 1995 and 1999 Regulations enacted parallel provisions for them. Thus, an elected representative (or candidate for that office) has a statutory right not to be victimised (short of dismissal), dismissed or later selected for redundancy on the grounds of having performed or proposed to perform such duties, and similar protection is extended to employees participating in the election of representatives[154]. A representative or candidate also has the right to paid time off work in order to perform such duties or to undergo training[155].

6 CONSULTATION ON TRANSFERS OF UNDERTAKING

As in the case of obligatory consultation on redundancies considered in the previous head, the legal obligations to inform and consult trade unions in advance of certain transfers of business were enacted pursuant to an EEC Directive, generally known as the Acquired Rights Directive[156]; this time, however, the enactment was done in the form of regulations, the Transfer of Undertakings

---

151 *Joshua Wilson & Bros Ltd v USDAW* [1978] ICR 614, [1978] IRLR 120.
152 *UCATT v Rooke & Son Ltd* [1978] ICR 818, [1978] IRLR 204, applied in *Secretary of State for Employment v Helitron Ltd* [1980] ICR 523.
153 See ch 10.
154 Employment Rights Act 1996, ss 47, 103, 105(6).
155 S 61.
156 EEC Directive 77/187; see Hepple (1976) 5 ILJ 197 and (1977) 6 ILJ 106; the original draft of the Directive was issued in 1974. Draft regulations were produced by the Labour government in 1978 but not proceeded with; the present regulations were introduced by the Conservative government, under pressure from the EEC Commission, with a declared lack of enthusiasm. The 1977 Directive has now been replaced by Directive 2001/23/EC.
157 SI 1981/1794. See Hepple (1982) 11 ILJ 29; McMullen *Business Transfers and Employee Rights* and *Harvey*, Division F.

(Protection of Employment) Regulations 1981[157], rather than by Act of Parliament. This caused some controversy at the time, inside and outside Parliament, and may not be the best way in which to introduce important new labour law provisions, particularly as the Regulations make little attempt to integrate the new provisions with certain existing ones and do not amend the existing statutes, thus leading to some duplication, though that is not the case in the present context since these consultation obligations were novel. At the time of writing, proposals were expected for new TUPE Regulations (see p 212 below, though it was not anticipated that they would make major changes to those provisions on information and consultation.

The existing regulations have caused major problems in interpretation, and in particular as to whether they enact the EC Directive properly. As problems of application have arisen primarily in the context of continuity of employment and the statutory novation of contracts of employment, the question of the applicability of the regulations is considered in that context, below[158]. What is said there also applies here. For present purposes, it may be noted that, for the regulations to apply, there must be 'a relevant transfer', which may be affected by sale, or some other disposition as by operation of law[159]. This gives rise to their principal limitation in the context of union consultation, which is that they do *not* apply to the takeover of a business by the purchase of its shares, a limitation which does also appear in the Directive[160]. Also, there may be problems with the always-troublesome distinction between the sale of an 'undertaking' and a mere sale of assets.

If a projected transfer of undertakings does qualify as a 'relevant transfer', regulation 10 imposes duties to inform and consult and regulation 11 contains enforcement provisions similar in part to those applying to redundancy consultation (head 5, above), but in one crucial respect falling far short of them. However, it was the basic obligation to consult and inform that fell foul of EC law in *EC Commission v United Kingdom*[161], in the same way as the obligation to consult and inform on collective redundancies (above), through being confined to cases where there was a recognised trade union, whereas the Directive refers to workers or their representatives. Again, this has to be rectified by the Collective Redundancies and Transfer of Undertakings (Protection of Employment) (Amendment) Regulations 1995 and 1999[162]; the amended provisions largely mirror those that now apply to collective redundancies.

---

158 See p 201 below.
159 Reg 3(2). *Robert Seligman Corpn v Baker* [1983] ICR 770.
160 Art 1.1 which applies the Directive to the transfer of an undertaking, business or part of a business to another employer as a result of a legal transfer or merger. The original draft Directive of 1974 did apply to share takeovers. It is the case that the exclusion of such takeovers is not quite so drastic in the context of preservation of continuity of employment, since the corporate employer still exists unchanged (albeit under different control which may, in the longer term, have effects on the company's economic prospects, for better or for worse); in the present context, however, it is a serious limit on union rights to consultation.
161 Case C-382/92: [1994] ECR I-2435, [1995] 1 CMLR 345, ECJ.
162 SI 1995/2587 and SI 1999/1925.

(i) The duty to inform and consult

Long enough before a relevant transfer to enable the employer of any affected employees[163] to consult all their appropriate representatives, the employer must give those representatives information of (a) the fact that the relevant transfer is to take place, when, and the reasons for it, (b) the legal, economic and social implications for the affected employees, (c) the measures which he envisages he will take in relation to those employees in connection with the transfer and, (d) if the employer is the transferor, the measures which the transferee envisages he will be taking[164]. As with collective redundancies, the concept of appropriate representatives was materially widened by the 1995 Regulations to cover not just the officials of a recognised trade union, but also employee representatives directly elected, either ad hoc for this purpose[165] or having been elected for other purposes but being appropriate for this purpose too; as with collective redundancies, the 1999 Regulations removed the employer's choice of route, by providing that where a union is recognised in respect of affected employees, that is the proper channel. One possible problem relates to the timing. The Regulation says that the information must be given 'long enough before a relevant transfer to enable consultations to take place', which is not further defined or qualified (contrast this with the provisions on collective redundancies); moreover, as has been pointed out[166], head (a) of the information to be given concerns the *fact* that the transfer is to take place, ie there need be no information or consultation at the stage of *proposals* for a transfer[167].

Where an employer of affected employees envisages that he will be 'taking measures' in relation to them in connection with the transfer, he must enter into consultations with the appropriate representatives with a view to seeking their agreement to measures to be taken, and in doing so must (a) consider any representations and (b) reply to them, giving reasons for any rejections[168]. If

163 An affected employee is defined as an employee of either the transferor or transferee who may be affected by the transfer or may be affected by measures taken in connection with it: reg 10(1). This is a very wide definition, particularly as it also says that the employee does not have to be employed in the undertaking or part thereof to be transferred. As such, it seems open-ended, given that a transfer 'may' affect practically anyone in the two businesses in some way, which could cause problems of line drawing in businesses which recognise several unions (particularly if they know their Donne: no man is an island; any man's transfer diminishes me).

164 Reg 10(2). In order to fulfil the transferor's obligation under (d) the transferee must give him the necessary information: reg 10(3).

165 If elected ad hoc, the election must satisfy the requirements for a fair election set out in reg 10A, as to numbers, constituencies, tenure of office, candidature, voting rights, secret voting and accurate counting.

166 Hepple (1982) 11 ILJ at 38.

167 Again this may be contrasted with the provisions on collective redundancies where the Trade Union and Labour Relations (Consolidation) Act 1992, s 188 requires an employer 'proposing' to make redundancies to consult recognised unions; see p 87 above. Reg10(8) provides that where the employer is going through the process of electing representatives, the employer complies with the time requirement if he acts as soon as reasonably practicable after the representatives are elected. If the employees fail to elect representatives within a reasonable time, the employer may give individual affected employees the information required by law, and is then absolved from collective consultation: reg 10(8A).

168 Regs. 10(5) and (6). In *Institution of Professional Civil Servants v Secretary of State for Defence* [1987] IRLR 373 (decided under the Dockyard Services Act 1986 which adopted and applied the provisions of reg 10), Millett J emphasised that although the obligation to give information applied to all four heads above, the obligation to consult only applies to head (c), the measures which are envisaged; his judgment gives guidance on the meaning of 'measures', which is not defined in the regulations.

there are special circumstances making it not reasonably practicable for an employer to inform or consult as required, he must take all steps as are reasonably practicable in the circumstances to comply; this means that an employer cannot say that, merely because full compliance was impossible, he did not need to do anything at all[169].

As in the case of consultation on impending collective redundancies (above), special legal protection is given to employee representatives from victimisation, dismissal and subsequent selection for redundancy, on the grounds of having fulfilled those functions; there is also a statutory right to time off work with pay for fulfilling them or for training.

(ii) Enforcement provision

As in the case of a failure to consult on impending redundancies, a complaint of failure to comply with regulation 10 may be presented to a tribunal by the employee representatives, or the recognised trade union or, in any other case, by any affected employee[170]. The employer may raise the 'special circumstances' defence (ie that there were such circumstances making performance of the obligations not reasonably practicable *and* that he did all that was reasonably practicable in the circumstances), in which case the burden of proof is upon him[171]. If the tribunal finds the complaint well founded it must make a declaration to that effect and award compensation to affected employees[172]. The maximum amount was raised from four to thirteen weeks' pay by the 1999 Regulations[173].

7 FURTHER DEVELOPMENTS – TOWARDS WORKS COUNCILS?

As seen in this chapter and the preceding one, British industrial relations have been subject to major changes in the last two decades, and that has been reflected in some of the legal changes discussed above. The inception of the new statutory recognition laws may see the return of a level of collective negotiation in certain well-unionised industries which has been missing for some time. However, large

---

169 Reg 10(7). This establishes a 'special circumstances' defence in similar terms to that applying to collective redundancies; see p 90 above. Presumably the case law which has arisen in that context will be applied here.

170 Reg 11(1). The complaint must be brought within three months of the date on which the transfer was completed (undefined): reg 11(8); it may be brought *before* the transfer is effected: *Banking Insurance and Finance Union v Barclays Bank plc* [1987] ICR 495; *South Durham Health Authority v UNISON* [1995] ICR 495, [1995] IRLR 407.

171 Reg 11(2). If the complaint is against the transferor and he maintains that his reason for default was that the transferee had not provided him with the necessary information (see n 164 above), he cannot raise the special circumstances defence unless he joins the transferee as a party to the proceedings: reg 11(3).

172 Reg 11(3). If it is not paid, the employee himself may complain to the tribunal within three months of the date of the order: reg 11(5)–(8). Appeal on a point of law lies to the EAT: reg 11(10).

173 Reg 11(11). 'Week's pay' is calculated in accordance with the Employment Rights Act 1996, Pt XIV, Ch II. Reg 11(11) actually says that the award is of such sum 'as the tribunal considers just and equitable having regard to the seriousness of the failure of the employer to comply with his duty', so that the precedents on the similar wording governing protective awards under the Trade Union and Labour Relations (Consolidation) Act 1992, s 189 (p 88 above) should apply.

parts of the economy are likely to remain untouched by it, but it may be that we are seeing the emergence of an alternative form of, at least, employee *involvement* in decision taking which, while falling significantly short of the old model of co-determination with recognised unions, could at least start to fill the void left in many areas by the demise of that old model and its replacement by ideas of 'human resource management', which a cynic might argue can be a euphemism for managerial discretion. The question is – are we seeing the beginnings of movements towards a consultation regime not dissimilar to the works council system that is common in much of the rest of the EU (to the extent that its existence is often implicitly assumed in certain employment-related EU Directives)?

We have seen the advent of consultation requirements (and their extension more recently to firms not recognising unions, through the concept of directly elected employee representatives), largely driven by EU law requirements, which suggest a *via media* (or even Third Way?) of treating the workforce as possessing legal expectations of involvement, not just as a managerial resource[174]. Moreover, to these sticks (requiring consultation with elected representatives where there is no union recognition, in relation to collective redundancies, TUPE and health and safety) we have now seen added certain legal carrots. Thus, the Working Time Regulations 1998 lay down prima facie relatively strict rules on hours, night work and breaks, but then allow very major 'derogations' from them, in ways that can be highly advantageous to the employer[175]. In the case of most of them, the safeguard is that the derogation in question must be agreed; in the case of a non-unionised workplace, the mechanism established for this is the 'workforce agreement', ie a written agreement with elected employee representatives. A similar regime can be seen in relation to parental leave under the Maternity and Parental Leave etc Regulations 1999[176], where the 'default rules' on some of the principal administrative requirements for parental leave are to apply unless supplemented by a collective agreement or workforce agreement[177]. Moreover, a collective or workforce agreement can be used under the Fixed-term Employees Regulations 2002[178] to amend the rules relating to the use of successive fixed-term contracts[179].

Does this mean that we are moving towards a works council system? The negative approach to this is that there are currently no legal requirements for them at domestic level. The only such requirements currently are at transnational level, under the European Works Council Directive[180]. This applies to a 'community scale undertaking', meaning one with at least 1,000 employees within the EU and at least 150 employees in each of at least two member states. Initially, the Directive did not apply in this country because of the previous government's opt-out, but the incoming New Labour government stated their intention to

---

174 Current ideas of 'partnership at work' and the involvement of the workforce suffused the White Paper 'Fairness at Work' (Cm 3968, 1998), especially ch 2 'Modern business at work'. See generally Hyman 'The future of employee representation' (1997) 35 BJIR 309.

175 See p 244, below.

176 SI 1999/3312.

177 See p 434 below.

178 SI 2002/2034.

179 See p 28 above.

180 Council Directive 94/45; *Harvey* P [488]. See Bercusson *European Labour Law* (1996), ch 19; Barnard *EC Employment Law* (1996), p 422; Wedderburn 'Consultation and collective bargaining in Europe: success or ideology' (1997) 26 ILJ 1 at 21.

adopt it. Thus, a further Directive extended it to this country, and it was implemented as from January 2000 by the Transnational Information and Consultation of Employees Regulations 1999[181]. These complex Regulations largely follow the Directive and provide for an undertaking covered by them to set up a Special Negotiating Body, either of its own motion, or in response to a written request from at least 100 employees or their representatives in at least two member states. The purpose of this body is to negotiate on the establishment of a European Works Council (EWC) or, as a lesser form, an 'information and consultation procedure'[182]. It is primarily for the parties to agree the composition and procedure of the relevant body. If, however, the central management refuse to commence negotiations within six months of a request, or if negotiations are still fruitless after three years, the 'default' provision of Schedule 1 to the Regulations apply, ie there will be imposed a 'statutory EWC'[183]. These provisions lay down the basic rules for composition (between three and 30 members, with minimum numbers for each member state involved), appointment or election of UK members, conduct of ballots, the competence of the EWC[184], yearly information and consultation meetings on the progress of the business[185], exceptional information and consultation meetings[186] (where exceptional circumstances affect the employers' interests to a considerable extent, particularly in the event of relocations, closure of establishments or undertakings, or collective redundancies) and procedures. Provision is made for certain information not to be divulged by the central management where it would cause serious harm to the undertaking[187], and any disclosure by an individual representative of information given to him by the central management on the basis that it is to be held in confidence is declared to be a breach of statutory duty[188]. The usual series of employment protection laws (paid time off and protection from detriment or dismissal) are extended to members of the body in question. Disputes over procedural matters in setting up an EWC are heard by the CAC; complaints of failure to establish a EWC (or information and consultation procedure), or of failure to operate the

---

181 SI 1999/3323.
182 The central management and the special negotiating body are under a duty to 'negotiate in a spirit of co-operation with a view to reaching a written agreement': reg 17(1). There is then a further statutory obligation to *work* in such a spirit once the relevant body is set up: reg 19.
183 Reg 18.
184 This is 'limited to information and consultation on the matters which concern the Community-scale undertaking or Community-scale group of undertakings as a whole or at least two of its establishments or group undertakings in different Member States: Sch 1, para 6(1).
185 This relates particularly to 'the structure, economic and financial situation, the probable development of the business and of production and sales, the situation and probable trend of employment, investments, and substantial changes concerning organisation, introduction of new working methods or production processes, transfers of production, mergers, cut-backs or closures of undertakings, establishments or important parts thereof, and collective redundancies': para 7(2).
186 This may be done through a 'select committee' of the EWC, comprising no more than three members acting on its behalf: para 2(6).
187 Reg 24; the operation of this exception may be challenged before the CAC (this matter being similar to its longstanding jurisdiction over the disclosure of bargaining information, see above).
188 Reg 23. Again, a declaration by the management that information is confidential may be challenged before the CAC. Further, the normal provisions of the Public Interest Disclosure Act 1998 on 'protected disclosures' apply.

system properly once it is set up are heard by the EAT[189]; employment protection disputes go to an employment tribunal in the ordinary way.

The likely impact of these Regulations has been a matter of some speculation. Their use may be limited by two factors. The first is that many UK supranationals have already been covered by the original Directive for some time because of their activities elsewhere in the EU; they could have set up an EWC only in relation to employees in other member states but in practice they have strongly tended to include UK employees as a matter of good practice, and so have pre-empted the Regulations. The second is that in any event the Directive extending the EWC Directive to the UK allowed undertakings here (not already covered) until December 1999 to reach voluntary agreements on transnational information and consultation, in which case the Regulations do not apply; again, a significant number of these 'Article 13' agreements have been entered. TUC estimates of undertakings in the UK likely to be covered by the Regulations for the first time were 111 UK-based undertakings and between 35 and 140 non-UK-based[190].

Not surprisingly, there have been moves within the European Commission to build on these transnational provisions and move towards a European obligation to have consultative machinery at the member state level, ie to have a *domestic* works council requirement. This has resulted in the Information and Consultation Directive[191] which, though stopping short of any institutional requirement of works councils as such, will have the effect of widening the level of consultation with the workforce (in some form or other) well beyond that currently required in the individual areas of collective redundancies, TUPE transfers and health and safety. When the Directive was negotiated, the UK government were successful in having it drafted in such a way as to leave most questions of detail and implementation to the member states (the much-vaunted 'subsidiary'). Thus, its final form in the UK remains to be determined, as at the time of writing[192]. It is due to be bought into force in relation to undertakings[193] of 150 employees or more in 2005, 100 or more in 2007 and 150 or more in 2008; there are currently no plans for it to apply to smaller firms.

The basic obligation on the member state is to determine the practical arrangements for exercising the right to:

(a) information[194] on the recent and probable development of the undertaking's activities and economic situation;

---

189 Regs 20, 21. The EAT may declare what steps are to be taken to remedy the default and issue a penalty notice on the employer, to pay a penalty up to £75,000 to the Secretary of State: reg 22.

190 TUC General Council Report 1998, p 94, cited in the DTI Consultation Document 'Implementation in the UK of the EWC Directive' (URN 99/926, July 1999), Appendix 2.

191 Directive 2002/14/EC; Bercusson, 'The European social model comes to Britain' (2002) 31 ILJ 209; Young, 'Common sense or nonsense' [2002] NLJ 794.

192 Initial consultation at a very general level, started in July 2002 with 'High performance workplaces: the role of employee involvement in a modern economy' (DTI). One interesting point is that the document seeks at this early stage to disprove one objection to enlarged consultation requirements, ie that in a merger or take-over case there would be a conflict with Stock Exchange rules on a releasing price-sensitive information (see Annex B to the document).

193 Member states may choose to apply these provisions to 'undertakings' (in which case 50 employees will be the minimum size) or 'establishments' (in which case 20 employees will be the minimum size). The British government are going down the 'undertaking' route.

194 Information is to be given at such time, in such fashion, and with such content as are appropriate to enable employees' representatives to conduct an adequate study and, where necessary, prepare for consultation: Art 4(3).

(b) information and consultation[195] on the situation, structure and probable development of employment within the undertaking and on any anticipatory measures envisaged, in particular where there is a threat to employment;

(c) information and consultation on decisions likely to lead to substantial changes in work organisation or in contractual relations.[196]

There are (typically by now) provisions for derogation by agreements between management and labour and requirements for the protection of employee representatives and for 'adequate administrative or judicial procedures . . . to enable the obligations deriving for this Directive to be enforced'[197]. The Directive also addresses an obvious source of concern to employers, namely that some of the information may be sensitive; member states must provide that employee representative are not authorised to reveal to employees or third parties any information expressly provided in confidence, and that in specified categories the employer is not obliged to inform or consult where to do so would 'seriously harm the functioning of the undertaking . . . or would be prejudicial to it'.[198] Clearly, how this exception is eventually drafted will be of considerable importance.

These requirements are in addition to the existing, specific information and consultation provisions on collective redundancies, TUPE transfers and European Worker Councils[199] . They clearly go much further, in particular into coverage of the economic affairs of the undertaking generally. While this could be of considerable significance in relation to the whole ethos of employee relations (particularly in areas which either departed from the traditional collective bargaining model or were never subject to it), from a more purely legal point of view it may be that it is the references in heads (b) and (c) to 'anticipatory measures, in particular where there is a threat to employment' and 'substantial changes in work organisation or is contractual relations' that are the most significant. The former reference could be important in redundancy situations – we have already seen above (on collective redundancies) that hitherto the economic decision as to the *need* for redundancies has been an area of managerial discretion, with consultation only necessary on *methods*, once the initial decision has been taken. It is fairly clear (and accepted in the government consultation exercise) that this could change radically under the new Directive which may extend the consultation requirement backwards into the area of the economic need for the redundancies. The latter reference could be used even more widely to counter certain employer tactics to force through changes in terms and conditions, for example by suddenly 'proposing' changes on a 'take-it-or-leave-

---

195 Consultation is to take place (a) while ensuing that the timing, method and content are appropriate; (b) at the relevant level of management and representation, depending on the subject under discussion: (c) on the basis of the information supplied by the employer, and of the opinion which the employees' representatives are entitled to formulate (a rather pen-of-my-aunt formulation whose meaning is unclear); (d) in such a way as to enable employees' representatives to meet the employer and obtain a response, and the reasons for that response, to any opinion they might formulate; (e) with a view to reaching an agreement on decisions within the scope of the employer's powers over work organisation or contractual relations: Art 4(4).

196 Art 4(1), (2).

197 Arts 5, 7, 8. A possible precedent for enforcement might be the protective award for failure to consult on collective redundancies, see p 88 above.

198 Art 6. A possible precedent here might be the exemptions for the duty to disclose bargaining information, see p 81 above.

199 Art 9.

it' basis, putting the onus on to the employees to object, or face the prospect of having consented by acquiescence[200]. While the contractual propriety of this have always been open to doubt, and there has been one recent attack on it under the existing law on collective redundancies (requiring rather a 'stretch' in its interpretation)[201], it may be that the language of head (c) will cover such a case *directly* and diminish significantly the scope for change by employer ambush[202]. Of course, the effectiveness of this will depend largely on the nature of the penalties eventually imposed for failure to consult; at the time of writing, this remained unclear. Also, it must be remembered that even when wholly in force for 2008 the Directive will not apply to employers of fewer than fifty employees.

200 See p 119 below.
201 *GMB v Man Truck and Bus UK Ltd* [2000] ICR 1101, [2000] IRLR 636 (see p 85 above) which concerned the tactic of dismissing all employees and re-engaging them on the new terms. This was held to be a 'redundancy' (under the wider EC law definition employed in the law on collective redundancies); as by definition the employer had not consulted the staff as required by law, it was liable for large protective awards.
202 One possible further extension here may be important. For 'contractual relations' changes existing contract law requires consent of some form or other, but traditionally this has always been contrasted with non-contractual matters (eg works rules or employment practices/policies) which remained within the employer prerogative. However, head (c) requires information and consultation on changes in 'work organisation *or* in contractual relations'. If this 'or' is disjunctive, head (c) applies not just to contractual changes requiring employee consent but also to changes in *non*-contractual changes, hitherto in the employer's power to make. Of course, consultation ultimately does not mean agreement (on the old model of co-determination), but one complicating factor here might be the requirement of art 4(4)(e) (n 195 above) that the consultation must be undertaken 'with a view to agreement', whatever this is ultimately held to mean.

Chapter 3

Contracts of employment (1): formation and content

1 FORMATION

(i) The contractual basis of employment

We have already seen that the relationship of employer and employee arises out of a contract. This however was not always so, for before the latter half of the nineteenth century the relationship was viewed more as one arising out of the 'status' of being a servant. Blackstone refers to master and servant as being one of the three great relationships in private life, along with husband and wife and parent and child[1], and the extensive legislation governing supply and conditions of employment, dating back to the Statute of Labourers 1351, was not finally abolished until 1875[2]. The movement towards contract proceeded throughout the nineteenth and twentieth centuries, becoming firmly established. In *Laws v London Chronicle*[3] Lord Evershed MR said:

> 'A contract of service is but an example of contracts in general, so that the general law of contract will be applicable.'

No sooner was this established beyond real doubt than the trend was arguably reversed. Since 1963, and particularly since the concept of unfair dismissal was introduced in 1971, the employment relationship has been increasingly overlaid with statutory criteria, rights and duties, to such an extent that it is certainly open to doubt whether we should still accept that contract law alone provides the underlying structure of employment law, or whether we should talk instead of a modern 'status' relationship of some sort or, at the least, of a sui generis Law of Employment which of necessity looks to contractual theories for guidance in

1   1 Bl Com 422.
2   See Wedderburn *The Worker and the Law* (3rd edn, 1986), p 141.
3   [1959] 2 All ER 285 at 287, [1959] 1 WLR 698 at 287, CA. This case demonstrates the purely contractual approach to summary dismissal, which can also be seen in the more colourful case of *Pepper v Webb* [1969] 2 All ER 216, [1969] 1 WLR 514, CA.

given areas[4]. Against that, it must be stressed that employment remains for the most part a voluntary relationship, and the content of most of the terms of employment remains to be negotiated by the parties, either individually or through the medium of collective industrial relations. The contract theory remains paramount and, if anything, of renewed importance, given the moves over the last two decades in many areas away from a collective model of wage and conditions determination, towards an emphasis on individual contracting; we therefore now have to consider the character of the contract, its formation and its content.

A contract is an agreement by which two or more persons agree to regulate their legal relationships recognised and, generally speaking, enforced by the law. Before the law will recognise an agreement as a contract certain essential conditions must be fulfilled. They are as follows:

(i)   One party must agree expressly or implicitly to perform an undertaking and the other party must agree to accept such performance, that is to say, there must be offer and acceptance.

(ii) The agreement must be supported by consideration or entered into according to certain prescribed forms.

(iii) Both parties must be persons whom the law acknowledges as competent to enter contracts; they must have capacity.

(iv) The objects of the contracts must be legal.

(v)   Both parties must intend that the agreement shall give rise to a legally recognised obligation.

The first two principles serve to ensure that a contract is bilateral in nature, as opposed, for example, to a gift. The employment relationship is by its very nature bilateral, at its simplest work for wages[5], so much of the case law on this aspect of contract is of little practical importance. It is extensively dealt with in the contract textbooks which should be consulted as required. Form used to be of supreme importance in apprenticeship contracts whose impact has greatly declined and still is in the particular case of merchant seamen, but it will be noted later that one of the major features of the modern legislation is a revived interest in form generally. Capacity needs brief consideration and legality in the field of employment law concerns principally the doctrine of restraint of trade, a relatively rare oasis where the courts over many decades have adopted an important stance based on public policy. It merits detailed treatment below, along with the way in which the general doctrine of illegality has been imported into unfair dismissal law, occasionally doing it considerable violence. The question of 'intent to create legal relations' plays a major part in the sphere of collective agreements, where it

---

4   For general discussion, see Rideout 'The contract of employment' [1966] CLP 111; Khan-Freund 'A note on status and contract in British labour law' (1967) 30 MLR 635; Smith 'Is employment properly analysed in terms of a contract?' (1975) 6 NZULR 341; Napier 'Judicial attitudes towards the employment relationship' (1977) 6 ILJ 1; Kerr 'Contract doesn't live here any more?' (1984) 47 MLR 30; Honeyball 'Employment law and the primacy of contract' (1989) 18 ILJ 97; Anderman 'The interpretation of protective employment statutes and contracts of employment' (2000) 29 ILJ 223. In particular, Professor Hepple argues that the statutory rights should be freed from their existing contractual basis, in order to avoid 'a multitude of common law snares': 'Restructuring employment rights' (1986) 15 ILJ 69.

5   Even here, however, complications can arise in cases of partial performance by an employee, eg when taking part in industrial action short of a strike (such as a go-slow or refusal to perform certain duties) – is he still entitled to payment, and if so how much? See pp 217–219 below.

is discussed, being largely responsible for the longstanding rule that collective agreements are not legally binding.

One further significance of the contractual base is that certain tenets of contractual interpretation or modification (common law or statutory) may be argued by one party or the other to good effect. Thus, for example, in *Levett v Biotrace International plc*[6] a managing director benefiting from valuable share options was wrongfully dismissed and then told by the company that those options had lapsed under a clause in his employment contract providing for such lapse on termination of employment. However, the Court of Appeal interpreted the clause as only applying to *lawful* termination (thus preserving their benefit for him), relying on the general contractual rule of construction that a party should not be able to take advantage of his own breach of contract. Similarly, the general contract law rules on penalty clauses could apply to a provision in a contract of employment stating that a set amount must be paid by the employee to the employer in the case of some particular act or default by that employee, for example a failure to give notice when leaving; under ordinary contract principles, such a clause would be void unless the employer could show that it was a genuine pre-estimate of loss to the employer, which in the employment context could be difficult[7]. Further, two uncertainties arise in the area of statutory coverage of ordinary contract law. The first is whether the Unfair Contract Terms Act 1977 could be relied on in an employment case. At first this was thought unlikely, but in *Brigden v American Express Bank Ltd*[8] Morland J held that the Act can apply, though he went on to find that a clause stating that an employee could be dismissed within the first two years without implementation of the disciplinary procedure was *not* an exclusion clause within section 3 of the Act (with its requirement of reasonableness). Such a finding (that the Act applies) involves the rather artificial reasoning that the employee deals with the employer 'as consumer', but the answer to this is that that phrase is not a term of art, and that in fact the definition of it in section 12 is satisfied because the employee does not contract in the 'course of a business', whereas the employer does. It may be, however, that (even though applicable) the Act will have little effect for the reason that the claim actually failed in *Brigden* – the Act renders subject to the reasonabless test *exclusion* clauses, not ones merely thought to be 'unfair' in some sense; the clause in *Bigden* was held not to be an exclusion clause because it was in fact a basic provision in the contract *defining* the relationship between employer and employee in the first place. It is likely that most clauses in a contract of employment would also come within that category and so *not* be subject to the Act. The second uncertainty is whether the Contracts (Rights of Third Parties) Act 1999 could apply. Employment contracts were of course not primarily the contemplation of its framers, but it does provide that third party rights can be established against employers or ex-employers (but not employees). As such rights can generally be excluded or modified by agreement, the lawyer drafting an employment contract may wish to cover this point in any case where a third party right might arise, especially where one of the benefits in the contract might apply to a spouse or dependant of the employee, for example use of a company car or coverage by medical insurance, life insurance or pensions.[9]

6   [1999] ICR 818, [1999] IRLR 375, CA.
7   *Giraud (UK) Ltd v Smith* [2000] IRLR 763.
8   [2000] IRLR 94, relying on Watson 'Employees and the Unfair Contract Terms Act' (1985) 14 ILJ 323.
9   Smith and Randall *Contracts Actions in Modern Employment Law – Development and Issues* (2002) p 244; Milgate 'Third party rights' [2000] Employment Law Journal 5.

(ii) Recruitment issues

The recruitment of staff has traditionally been an area of little legal involvement, being largely left as a matter for employer discretion, with few rights at common law for job applicants.[10]   Given that the common law basis for employment is contractual, the refused applicant has by definition no contract on which to sue and so even the implied term of trust and respect (so important in safeguarding the legal rights of persons once employed) could not be relied on at this inchoate stage[11].   This common law abstentionism is now subject to four particular qualifications, three by statute and the fourth arising from separate developments in relation to employment references.   Important though these are in their contexts, we still do not have any overarching 'law of recruitment'.

The first and most important institution of the law is, of course, through the discrimination statutes.   Recruitment is a vital area in which to counter discrimination and it has always been clear that it is covered by the laws on sex, race and disability discrimination, which are considered below in detail in chapter 5. Under the new Equal Treatment Directive 2000/78/EC, to these existing categories are to be added sexual orientation and religion or belief in 2003 and (of particular practical importance to recruitment) age by 2006.

The second, and very different, form of statutory intervention has come under the Data Protection Act 1998.   This Act, materially increasing the coverage of previous legislation ostensibly does not affect the process of recruitment but can apply to documentation produced and/or stored as part of that process.   However, the guardian of the Act, now renamed the Information Commissioner, has tended to take a wide view of this remit and has issued guidance which arguably strays significantly into the process itself.   This guidance is in the form of the 'Employment Practices Data Protection Code Part I: Recruitment and Selection'[12].   It covers advertising, handling applications, verification of details, short-listing, interviews, pre-employment vetting and retention of treatment records.   It should be consulted in detail on any of these matters, and is likely to have considerable practical significance for HR practitioners.   Among its key recommendations (showing its overall approach) are to (a) make a staff member responsible for compliance, (b) make serious data protection breaches by employees handling their information a disciplinary offence, (c) only request data about an applicant that is relevant to recruitment, (d) ensure that job applicants sign a consent form if documents are needed from a third party, (e) inform applicants if automated short-listing is the sole basis of decision, (f) retain

---

10   See the well-known quote from Lord Allen in the foundation case on common law liabilities, *Allen v Flood* [1898] AC 1, HL (set out at p 267 below), asserting the employer's right to refuse employment for any reason or none.

11   One of the stranger cases on direct enforcement of contracts of employment was *Giles & Co Ltd v Morris* [1972] 1 All ER 960, [1972] 1 WLR 307 where specific performance of the execution of an offered job was ordered, largely so that the individual would then, as an employee (technically, if not actually), have common law rights on his 'dismissal'. On the other hand, in *Wishart v National Association of Citizens Advice Bureaux Ltd* [1990] ICR 794, [1990] IRLR 393, CA the Court of Appeal refused to enforce a job offer which was withdrawn in the light of references; there was no subsisting employment relationship to which any argument of trust and confidence could attach; 'instead there is a stillborn relationship to which one party strongly objects' (per Mustill LJ).

12   This is available on www.dataprotection.gov.uk. The other three parts of the Code are on employee records, monitoring of employees and medical records. The Code, though physically large, is aimed to be user-friendly with each chapter taking a 'benchmarking' format of key questions to be asked, followed by detailed notes.

interview notes[13], (g) establish a retention period for recruitment records[14], (h) dispose of salary information from previous employers and (i) only ask for sensitive personal data for successful applicants[15]. This part of the Code has a slightly ambiguous position in employment law. Unlike Part 3 on employee monitoring (which could well be relevant in an unfair dismissal action, eg by an employee dismissed for Internet abuse)[16], Part I is unlikely to link indirectly into mainstream employment law, at least in the case of unsuccessful applicants because they have no subsisting contract on which to sue (and successful applicants are less likely to have a grievance, though it is not impossible). Its effect will therefore be primarily within its own context of enforcement under the Data Protection Act itself; here, the Code states that (while it is not law per se and does not *have* to be followed) an employer who does follow it knows that there has been compliance with the Act.

The third form of statutory intervention, dating back much further though with some topicality, is under the Rehabilitation of Offenders Act 1974 whereby a person whose conviction or convictions is or are 'spent' is to be treated as not having been convicted. The key point here is of course that a spent conviction does *not* have to be disclosed on a job application form, even in response to a direct question[17]. This is of importance because if the Act does not apply any false answer at the recruitment stage is likely to be considered fraudulent, leading if necessary to a later lawful dismissal (even if the individual thought at the time that he or she had good reason to be sparing with the actualité)[18]. Also of major importance here, however, is the Rehabilitation of Offenders Act 1974 (Exceptions) Order 1975[19] which sets out certain professions, offices, employments and occupations which are *not* subject to the Act, so that in these

13 This would be advised by a lawyer anyway, in case of a later complaint of discrimination by a disappointed applicant (the time limit normally being three months). As these notes may now be obtainable under the Data Protection Act (there being some evidence that this is now being used as a novel and possibly wider form of discovery, in advance of commencing proceedings) those conducting interviews must be advised to be careful what appears in them, including 'pen portraits' of the applicant in the margin.

14 Together with point (c) this shows an application of the general data protection tenet that a data controller should only gather and retain information that is necessary for the purpose; a variant of that here is that not all information relevant at the recruitment stage will be relevant later – any that is not should not automatically be transferred into the successful applicant's personnel file (see also point (h)).

15 Sensitive personal data, subject to special rules in the Act, covers racial origins, political opinions, religious beliefs, union membership, physical or mental health, sexual life, commission of offences and court proceedings or sentences: Data Protection Act 1998, s 2. Of particular relevance here is health. The employer will probably want a health check on the applicant, but in a possibly important change of practice the Code suggests asking for this only from the *successful* applicant (ie after his or her prima facie selection) rather than from all those shortlisted in advance of selection. The aim here is clearly to minimise the amount of sensitive data collected by the employer. It does mean, however, that the employer will need to make any letter of appointment heavily conditional on meeting health criteria.

16 See pp 165 and 581 below.

17 Rehabilitation of Offenders Act 1974, s 4. The rehabilitation periods necessary for a conviction to become spent are set out in s 5.

18 This general rule is strongly set out in *City of Birmingham District Council v Beyer* [1978] 1 All ER 910, [1977] IRLR 211. It was applied to concealment of a non-spent conviction in *Torr v British Railways Board* [1977] ICR 785, [1977] IRLR 184. On the other hand, dismissal because of discovery of a spent conviction is likely to be unfair: *Property Guards Ltd v Taylor* [1982] IRLR 175.

19 SI 1975/1023.

cases a conviction can never become spent and must always be disclosed when asked. This has always covered areas such as the legal profession, medical profession and law enforcement agencies. More recently, however, there was a significant extension of the exempted categories in 2001 in the light of contemporary concerns about cases of sexual or physical abuse; the Order now also covers wide categories of those employed to care for children and vulnerable adults. This necessary change in the law for this purpose was accompanied by administrative changes, in particular the establishment of the Criminal Records Bureau[20] which is aimed at putting the disclosure of individual's criminal histories on a statutory footing and subject to safeguards about the handling of such information. Disclosure at the request of a potential employer only applies to posts exempted from the 1974 Act[21]. An individual may request what is termed a 'basic disclosure' on himself or herself which may be used when applying for a job; however, there is no legal obligation to supply it and the Data Protection Code, Part 1 (see above) cautions that an employer should not seek to obtain information about criminal convictions by enforced subject access or from sources other than the Criminal Records Bureau or the applicant, or this is likely to breach data protection law[22].

The fourth intervention of the law has been in relation to employment references. Hitherto this involvement of the law has been primarily in relation to possible tortious liability for negligent misstatement. Ever since the foundation case of *Hedley Byrne & Co Ltd v Heller & Partners Ltd*[23] it has been arguable that the referee owed a duty of care to the potential employer requesting the reference, but there was no development of this in the employment context, probably because the tradition in the UK was that the applicant for the job did *not* see the referee at any stage. The resurgence of interest here of late has been for two reasons – first, it was held in *Spring v Guardian Assurance plc*[24] that the referee owes a duty of care to the *applicant* for the job who, if turned down because of a negligently bad reference may be more likely to contemplate legal action

---

20 This operates in England and Wales; in Scotland similar rules are operated by the Disclosure Bureau.

21 'Standard disclosure' may be sought by the employer directly from the Bureau in such a case, this will disclose spent and unspent convictions, cautions, reprimands and final warnings held on the Police National Computer. The highest level is 'Enhanced disclosure' which is similar to standard disclosure but also contains other information from local police records if thought relevant to the position applied for; it applies to posts involving greater contact with children or vulnerable adults, particularly caring or being in sole charge. The Bureau has published a code of practice on the use of information obtained through standard or enhanced disclosure, which could be used in any proceedings under the Data Protection Act.

22 Data Protection Code Part I: Recruitment and Selection, Section 3. It is a criminal offence for an employer or prospective employer to require an employee or applicant to supply him with information about convictions obtained by that individual's own right of subject access ('enforced subject access'): Data Protection Act 1998 s 56. The Code suggests generally that any information sought should be kept to a minimum and kept only for as long as necessary after the employment decision has been made (with a limit of 6 months); the information so obtained should not be shared with other employers. Outside the exempted areas, the Code generally recommends 'only request information about the applicant's criminal convictions if that information is justified in terms of the role offered'; thus, a policy of doing so simply as a matter of course might now breach data protection law.

23 [1964] AC 465, [1963] 2 All ER 575, HL; the case in fact concerned a reference, but as to commercial creditworthiness, not individual employability.

24 [1994] ICR 596, [1994] IRLR 460, HL

(especially in the financial services sector which has spawned most of the case law) particularly as, secondly, under the Data Protection Act 1998 an employment reference can now be seen by an individual. We have thus seen serious changes here (both in the law and the likelihood of it being used), though wholly in relation to the rights of the *subject* of the reference, not its recipient. These matters are considered below under head 5, the employer's duty to exercise care, along with the difficult question whether the law now imposes any positive duty on an employer or ex-employer to *give* a reference (the common law position in the past having been that there is no such duty at all).[25] Apart from tortious liability, there has been little law on references in the purely employment contract context, except for one important point of definition. When an employer makes an appointment 'subject to satisfactory references' this simply operates in the law of contract as a condition precedent. However, the question could arise as to what is meant by 'satisfactory'. In *Wishart v National Association of Citizens Advice Bureaux Ltd*[26] the Court of Appeal held that this only meant satisfactory *to the employer*, ie a subjective test; it is not open to a refused applicant (already pushing a rock uphill in trying to enforce employment) to argue that the reference *ought* to have been satisfactory to a reasonable employer. Finally, there has recently been one other form of legal involvement in references, but again in the slightly separate context of data protection law. The Employment Practices Data Protection Code Part 2: Employment Records contains advice (in Section 2, part 10) on the handling of reference-giving. It suggests that an organisation should have a policy on who can give references and in what circumstances[27]. Moreover, an employer should not provide confidential information about an individual unless sure that that is their wish, and when employment ends should establish whether the departing employee wishes references to be provided in the future. Breach of this guidance could mean a breach of the Data Protection Act, but it is possible that the Code could also be used as evidence for collateral purposes more specifically within employment law. Apart from tortious liability for negligent misstatement (above), one interesting cross-over can be seen in *TSB Bank Ltd v Harris*[28] where an employee who left employment when they discovered that highly unfair references were being sent to potential future employers successfully claimed constructive dismissal (for the purposes of an unfair dismissal action); in such circumstances it is possible that any breach of the Code could now be evidence in such an action.

2 CAPACITY

Although principles of law are designed to operate in normal circumstances on persons who are not subject to legal disabilities, there must be provisions relating to those who, because of their status or condition, require exceptional treatment.

---

25   See p 157 below.
26   [1990] ICR 794, [1990] IRLR 393, CA.
27   *Spring's* case (n 24 above) is a prime example of how corporate references should not be given – inaccurate, unchecked statements were made (highly prejudicial to the subject) in an ad hoc exercise by a manager just collecting others' opinions. While there is no law against a bad reference, this could be a recipe for a *negligently* bad reference. Some organisations (especially in the public sector) have policies as to the only information they will give, and the only form in which they will give it, regardless of what the requesting organisation may ask.
28   [2000] IRLR 157.

The principles of contract law which evolved to cover questions of capacity will apply to contracts of employment so that, for example, employment by a foreign sovereign, a diplomatic agent or an enemy alien may be subject to special common law and statutory rules. Such cases, however, will be rare and are best dealt with elsewhere. It is of more importance to note that companies and partnerships do not lack capacity to enter into contract of employment, and to consider in more detail two classes of employee who are subject to special rules – Crown employees and minors.

(i) Crown employees

Historically the Crown occupied a position of privilege in the law of contract in that it could not be sued in its own courts. This position has now been substantially amended[29], but the law relating to Crown employment is still distinct from ordinary employment law.

A contract of employment with the Crown is terminable without notice at the Crown's pleasure[30], and any term to the contrary is invalid[31] (unless there is some statutory restriction on the Crown's power to dismiss[32]). This proposition shows how far away from reality the law can stray, for civil servants are in practice renowned for the security of their employment. However, the theory is otherwise, and indeed was taken further at common law, for the earlier view was that the Crown employee in fact has no contract of employment *at all* (a point which was important in certain cases where the payment of arrears of remuneration was in issue)[33]. Other cases, however, have tended to assume that there *is* a contract of employment (albeit terminable at pleasure), and certainly the balance of authority is now in favour of the view[34]. This has been affirmed more recently in cases exploring the borderline between private and public law remedies for Crown employees, the point being that if there is a contract of employment it is less likely (though not impossible) that the employee will be able to obtain a judicial review of an employment-related grievance. In *McClaren v Home Office*[35] it was held by the Court of Appeal that a prison officer was under a contract of employment and so could pursue private law remedies for an alleged breach of

---

29 Crown Proceedings Act 1947. Fredman and Morris 'The state as employer: is it unique?' (1990) 19 ILJ 142.
30 *Dunn v R* [1896] 1 QB 116, CA.
31 *Denning v Secretary of State for India* (1920) 37 TLR 138; *Riordan v War Office* [1959] 3 All ER 552, [1959] 1 WLR 1046 (affd by the Court of Appeal: [1960] 3 All ER 774n, [1961] 1 WLR 210); cf *Reilly v R* [1934] AC 176, PC.
32 *Gould v Stuart* [1896] AC 575, PC.
33 *Mulvenna v Admiralty* 1926 SC 842; *Lucas v Lucas* [1943] P 68, [1943] 2 All ER 110.
34 *Owners of SS Raphael v Brandy* [1911] AC 413, HL; *Sutton v A-G* (1923) 39 TLR 295; *Reilly v R* [1934] AC 176, PC; *A-G for Guyana v Nobrega* [1969] 3 All ER 1604, PC, *Kodeeswaran v A-G of Ceylon* [1970] AC 1111, PC.
35 [1990] ICR 824, [1990] IRLR 338, CA. In this case, a finding of a contract of employment was in the employee's favour since he was seeking contractual remedies, not judicial review. In the judgment of Woolf LJ there is a valuable summary of grounds on which a public employee can obtain judicial review (see p 479, below); in *R v Secretary of State for the Home Department, ex p Benwell* [1984] ICR 723, [1985] IRLR 6 a prison officer was granted judicial review, but this was explained by Woolf LJ as a case where even though the relationship was contractual, there *still* arose a matter of public law.

his contractual rights, and in *R v Lord Chancellor's Department, ex p Nangle*[36] the Divisional Court held that a civil servant's appointment was intended to, and did, create a contract of employment. However, even though there is a contract, its terms have always been variable unilaterally by the Minister of the Civil Service (in relation to the Home Civil Service) by virtue of the Civil Service Orders in Council, a point which came to the fore in 1984 when the government altered the terms of employment of employees at GCHQ to exclude union membership[37]. Moreover, the basis of civil service employment was subject to radical change in 1996, with each department or agency becoming responsible for setting its own terms and conditions of employment, which further emphasises the movement towards a more normal, contract-based model of employment.

Turning to the far more important question of the application of the modern statutory rights to Crown employees, the first point to notice is that the controversy over whether there is a contract of employment in existence is a sterile one in this context, for by virtue of the Employment Rights Act 1996, section 191 persons in Crown employment are to be treated as if in ordinary employment for the purpose of applying the statutory provisions to them. The important question is *which* statutory provisions are to apply to them. As the general rule is that an Act of Parliament does not bind the Crown unless it says so, this is a matter for the statute which provides[38] that all the major employment protection rights (including unfair dismissal) apply to Crown employees, except those relating to minimum notice periods and redundancy payments; in the case of the last right, civil servants are covered by more generous internal schemes[39]. The Trade Union Reform and Employment Rights Act 1993 extended most of the major employment protection rights to members of the armed forces, but the police are ineligible (except for those relating to written statements of terms of employment, minimum notice periods and redundancy payments)[40]. One general limitation is that a Minister of the Crown may issue a certificate that a certain type of work is required to be outside the scope of the statutory rights for reasons of national security[41];

---

36 [1991] ICR 743, [1991] IRLR 343. Here, ironically, it was the Crown arguing that there *was* a contract, in order to defeat the civil servant's claim for judicial review. This was successful. In the earlier case of *R v Civil Service Appeal Board, ex p Bruce* [1988] 3 All ER 686, [1988] ICR 649 the Divisional Court has said that there was nothing to *prevent* the Crown from entering a contract of employment, but *ex p Nangle* is a much stronger case, holding that it had.

37 Such orders are made under prerogative powers and are not contained in a statutory instrument. The fact that an order or decision is made under the prerogative does not mean that it is not subject to judicial review; however, it will only be so subject if the substance of the issue in question is 'justiciable', which was not so in the GCHQ case which concerned national security: *Council of Civil Service Unions v Minister for the Civil Service* [1985] ICR 14, [1985] IRLR 28, HL.

38 Employment Rights Act 1996, s 191(2). The Sex Discrimination Act 1975 and the Equal Pay Act 1970 apply to Crown employees, ss 85 and 1(8) respectively; see *Department of the Environment v Fox* [1980] 1 All ER 58, [1979] ICR 736. See also the Race Relations Act 1976, s 75; the Disability Discrimination Act 1995, s 64; the National Minimum Wage Act 1998, s 36; the Working Time Regulations 1998, SI 1998/1833, reg 37, the Part-time Worker Regulations 2000, SI 2000/1551, reg 12 and the Fixed-term Employees Regulations 2002, SI 2002/2034, reg 13. At the collective level, the provisions relating to enforcement of disclosure of information and the rules on union contributions, and procedures for handling redundancies do not apply to Crown employment: Trade Union and Labour Relations (Consolidation) Act 1992; s 273.

39 Employment Rights Act 1996, s 159.

40 S 200. The statutory exclusion also applies to prison officers: *Home Office v Robinson* [1982] ICR 31, [1981] IRLR 524.

41 S 193. Trade Union and Labour Relations (Consolidation) Act 1992, s 275.

this power was used in 1984 to support the instructions given by the government altering the terms of employment of civil servants at GCHQ to exclude union membership (referred to above), thus depriving anyone objecting to the ban of the right to complain to a tribunal.

Finally, there has been one further recent legislative development in a specialised area of Crown employment. The argument that Crown employees have no contract of employment might have been used to evade liability for unlawful industrial action since certain of the applicable torts presuppose the existence of such contracts (particularly the tort of inducement of breach of contract[42]); to cover this, there is now deemed to be a contract of employment between the Crown and a Crown employee for the purposes of the economic torts[43].

(ii) Minors

The contractual capacity of a minor[44] rests upon a common law basis. It used to be modified and, in some directions, restricted by the Infants Relief Act 1874, but that statute was repealed by the Minors' Contracts Act 1987[45] and so the common law rules now apply to all contracts, including those with which we are concerned, namely contracts of employment and apprenticeship. These are prima facie binding[46] and if they are, on the whole, for the minor's benefit at the time they are entered into, they will bind him. As Fry LJ said[47]:

'The question is this – is the contract for the benefit of the [minor]? Not, is any one particular stipulation for the benefit of the [minor] ... the court must look at the whole contract having regard to the circumstances of the case.'

The principle involved is not difficult to state or to understand, but its application has not been without difficulty[48]. It was laid down with great clarity by Lord Esher MR in *Corn v Matthews*[49]:

'It is impossible to frame a deed as between a master and apprentice in which some of the stipulations are not in favour of one and some in favour of the other. But if we find a stipulation in the deed which is of such a kind that it makes the whole contract an unfair one, then that makes the whole contract void.'

---

42 See p 763 below.
43 This was introduced by the Employment Act 1988 and is now contained in the Trade Union and Labour Relations (Consolidation) Act 1992, s 245.
44 See the Family Law Reform Act 1969, ss 1 and 9, which reduced the age from 21 to 18.
45 The statute was based upon 'Law of Contract; Minors' Contracts' (Law Com No 134).
46 *Wood v Fenwick* (1842) 10 M & W 195; *De Francesco v Barnum* (1890) 45 Ch D 430.
47 *De Francesco v Barnum* 1890) 45 Ch D 430 at 439.
48 Contrast *Doyle v White City Stadium* [1935] 1 KB 110, CA with *Olsen v Corry and Gravesend Aviation Ltd* [1936] 3 All ER 241; see also *Chaplin v Leslie Frewin (Publishers) Ltd* [1966] Ch 71, [1965] 3 All ER 764, CA.
49 [1893] 1 QB 310 at 314, CA. This dictum applies to minors generally, not just to apprentices: *Clements v London and North Western Rly Co* [1894] 2 QB 482, CA at 495 per A. L. Smith, LJ.

However, where a stipulation, though repugnant, does not make the whole contract unfair, and is severable from the rest, it may in fact be severed and the remainder of the contract, being for the minor's benefit, will bind him[50].

In assessing whether a contract is for the minor's benefit, courts have sometimes posed the question as to what would be the position if the offending clause were not in the contract at all – would the minor be able to enter into a contract of equal or greater benefit?[51] Another way of asking this would be – is the clause usual in contracts with minors of this particular type? Thus, although trade usage is only of evidential importance, a clause which is usual in a particular trade or industry will not generally be against the minor's benefit.

3 FORM

(i) Form generally

According to a doctrine peculiar to English law a contract must be under seal or based upon consideration. A promise gratuitously to perform services will not be actionable unless it is by deed. Subject to this, however, a contract of employment may be entered into orally at common law, and statute has not intervened to alter this general position. However, some particular contracts of employment or contracts relating to employment may have to be in writing. Thus, under Part II of the Employment Rights Act 1996, an employer and employee may agree for the former to make deductions from the latter's wages, provided that the agreement is either contained in a written contract (or in a contract whose effect has been notified to the employee in writing) or otherwise evidenced in writing signed by the employee prior to the making of the deductions[52]. Certain other provisions of the 1996 Act also require writing; thus under section 71 and the Maternity and Parental Leave etc Regulations 1999 a woman claiming to exercise her right to take maternity leave must inform her employer of her intention in writing if so requested by the employer. Similarly, an employee may consent in writing to work beyond the maximum 48 hours per week under the Working Time Regulations 1998.

(ii) Notice of terms of employment

Although English law is basically informal about the form of a contract of employment, Part I of the Employment Rights Act 1996 (first passed in 1963 as the Contracts of Employment Act) provides that an employee to whom the Act applies must be given written particulars of the salient terms of his employment. These provisions were amended and extended by the Trade Union Reform and Employment Rights Act 1993, in order to comply with an EC Directive on information concerning employment conditions[53], which the previous

---

50 *Bromley v Smith* [1909] 2 KB 235.
51 *Bromley v Smith* [1909] 2 KB 235; *Doyle v White City Stadium* [1935] 1 KB 110, CA.
52 S 13 see p 260, below. There are exceptions in s 14 and obviously certain statutory deductions (such as income tax under PAYE) do not need written consent.
53 Directive 91/533/EEC; see Clark and Hall 'The Cinderella Directive' (1992) 21 ILJ 106 and Kenner 'Statement or contract? – Some reflections on the EC Employee Information (Contract or Employment Relationship) Directive' (1999) 28 ILJ 205.

government were ready to agree to, for two reasons – (1) the existing law was already largely in compliance and (2) the extensions necessary (which stressed the need to give these written statements on an individual basis) were in line with their policy of encouraging more individual contracting, at the expense of collective negotiation of terms.

(a) The status of the written statement

The incontrovertible starting point is that the written ('section 1') statement is *not* per se the contract of employment; it is, however, evidence of the terms of the contract. This may seem a technical distinction (especially in a case where a longstanding statement appears to be the *only* tangible evidence), but it has the important consequence in law that it leaves the door open for an employee to argue in later proceedings that the statement was inaccurate as to the real terms on a given matter. The question then becomes how compelling the statement is to be as evidence. It is certainly not conclusive[54], but it is possible to point to earlier cases where courts showed themselves ready to incorporate terms from the written statement into the individual contract of employment, particularly where the statement appeared to have been accepted without protest for a reasonable period of time[55]. Later cases have, however, shown a tendency to treat the statement with more circumspection in circumstances where a major dispute has arisen as to the accuracy of a particular term, especially where 'acceptance without protest' is relied upon by the employer as showing the correctness of the statement. In *System Floors (UK) Ltd v Daniel*[56] Browne-Wilkinson J put the position thus:

> 'It seems to us, therefore, that in general the status of the statutory statement is this. It provides very strong prima facie evidence of what were the terms of the contract between the parties, but does not constitute a written contract between the parties. Nor are the statements of the terms finally conclusive: at most, they place a heavy burden on the employer to show that the actual terms of contract are different from those which he has set out in the statutory statement.'

This case concerned the less typical situation of the *employer* arguing that the statement did not properly reflect the contract; the burden is less heavy in the more typical case where it is the employee contesting the correctness of the statement, for as against him the statement will be (in Browne-Wilkinson J's words) 'no more than persuasive, though not conclusive, evidence'. It is therefore open for him to adduce hopefully more persuasive evidence that the real term was other than that contained in the employer's statement (for example evidence of what was said at the job interview, in letters of appointment, or even what was accepted in practice from the beginning of the employment). This can be seen

---

54   *Turriff Construction Ltd v Bryant* (1967) 2 ITR 292; *Parkes Classic Confectionery v Ashcroft* (1973) 8 ITR 43; see Dumville and Leighton 'From Statement to Contract' (1977) 6 ILJ 133.

55   *Camden Exhibition and Display Ltd v Lynott* [1966] 1 QB 555, [1965] 3 All ER 28, CA.

56   [1982] ICR 54, [1981] IRLR 475. This approach can also be seen in *Jones v Associated Tunnelling Co Ltd* [1981] IRLR 477 in the context of alterations to contractual terms, considered below.

from the subsequent decision of the Court of Appeal in *Robertson and Jackson v British Gas Corpn*[57] in which the above dicta by Browne-Wilkinson J were approved and the employee successfully challenged the accuracy of the section 1 statement on the basis that it did not reflect what was agreed at the commencement of employment on the bonus that was to be paid. At one stage, Ackner LJ seems to go further and say that the statement was not *even* evidence of the terms, but that must be taken in the light of the facts of the case, particularly the fact that the statement was not given until seven years after the commencement of the employment. In the more usual case, where the statement has been given at the time of or shortly after the commencement of employment and not dissented from, it certainly will be evidence, possibly compelling, for in practice these statements assume considerable importance in many employments.

One case that has caused some difficulty in this area is *Gascol Conversions Ltd v Mercer*[58] where the employer had sent written terms of employment to the employee who had signed them and a receipt which was attached; the Court of Appeal held that this constituted a written contract, governing inter alia the question of hours which was in dispute. The result of such a decision is that the written term in question is binding and not to be supplanted by evidence of extraneous matters or implied terms. However, this decision does not compromise the principles set out above, since it appears that the employee actually signed the written instrument as the new terms of his contract of employment, not just the attached receipt. It is common for section 1 statements to be signed for, but merely signing for receipt will *not* constitute a binding written contract, unlike in *Mercer's* case where the crucial extra step of signing *as the contract* was present. This view of *Mercer's* case (and the distinction between signing a contract and signing a receipt) has been accepted in the later cases[59]. It is thus possible for what would normally be a section 1 statement to be transformed into a formal written contract by the parties signing it as such, but if they are to do so it is doubly important that they should ensure that the terms are correct.

(b) Requirements of the written statement

The obligation on an employer to give the section 1 statement arises whenever a person is taken on as an 'employee', thus excluding (as usual in statutory employment laws) the self-employed. Certain categories of employee are excluded; thus, this part of the Act does not apply to certain types of mariners,[60] employees working wholly outside Great Britain[61], or those employed for less than one month[62].

Wherever this part of the Act applies, the employer is given the period of two months from the beginning of the employment in question in which to deliver to

---

57   [1983] ICR 351, [1983] IRLR 302, CA; note Leighton (1983) 12 ILJ 115. The case is also of particular interest on the incorporation of terms from collective agreements; see p 145, below.
58   [1974] ICR 420, [1974] IRLR 155, CA; cf. *Hawker Siddeley Power Engineering Ltd v Rump* [1979] IRLR 425. See Hepple (1974) 3 ILJ 164.
59   *System Floors (UK) Ltd v Daniel*, n 56, above; *Robertson and Jackson v British Gas Corpn*, n 57, above.
60   S 199.
61   This appears to be the case on general principles, in spite of the repeal of the Employment Rights Act 1996, s 196 (by the Employment Relations Act 1999).
62   S 198.

his employee the necessary written statement[63], though in practice many employers will have the statement ready at the beginning, often as part of a 'starter pack' for new employees (along with other documents, such as a health and safety statement, disciplinary rules and company handbook). Where there is, subsequent to the giving of notice of particulars, a change in them the employer has one month in which to issue a statement of the change[64].

The initial notice must identify the parties and specify the date of commencement of employment and whether any employment with a previous employer is to count as part of the employee's continuous employment[65]. Section 1(4) then provides that certain particulars of the terms of employment must be stated (and if there are no agreed particulars under any of the heads that fact must be stated too)[66]. These particulars are – the scale or rate of remuneration; the intervals at which remuneration is to be paid; terms and conditions relating to hours of work (and possibly 'normal working hours'); any terms and conditions relating to holidays (including public holidays and holiday pay) with sufficient information to enable the entitlement to be calculated precisely, incapacity for work due to sickness or injury, and pensions and pension schemes; the length of notice which the employee is obliged to give and entitled to receive to determine the contract; the title of the job which the employee is employed to do[67]; how long the employment is to last if it is not permanent; the place of work; any collective agreements affecting terms and conditions; and, where the employee is to work outside the UK for more than a month, the period abroad, currency for remuneration, any additional remuneration or benefits, and any terms and conditions relating to his return to the UK. In addition section 3 provides that the employer must include a note specifying any disciplinary rules and procedures, how and to whom the employee may apply if dissatisfied with a disciplinary decision relating to him or if seeking redress of any grievance relating to his employment, and any further steps in the employer's grievance procedure, though these requirements do not apply to any rules, procedures, etc, relating to health and safety at work. Also under section 3 the note must state whether a contracting-out certificate is in force for the employment, for the purposes of the Pension Schemes Act 1993.

---

63 S 1(2), as substituted by the 1993 Act.
64 S 4; see below on changing the terms of employment.
65 This should now be viewed with caution by an employee, for a simple assurance of continuity of employment by a new employer (where such continuity is not preserved by a provision in the relevant statute) is not enough to safeguard continuity for the purpose of a later claim for a statutory right (especially a redundancy payment); *Secretary of State for Employment v Globe Elastic Thread Co Ltd* [1979] ICR 706, [1979] IRLR 327, HL, overruling *Evenden v Guildford City AFC Ltd* [1975] 3 All ER 269, [1975] ICR 367, CA; see p 638 below.
66 Thus, the obligation is to notify terms that exist, not to have a particular term in the first place: *Morley v Heritage plc* [1993] IRLR 400, CA (no term on accrued holiday pay).
67 This is not necessarily a full 'job description', but the employer should approach it with care, because the more specific the title is the less the employer will be able lawfully to demand flexibility on the part of the employee, a factor which could be of importance in a redundancy or unfair dismissal case; conversely, the wider the title, the more difficult it may be to establish that a dismissal is for redundancy. This one example of the job title (in addition to other clear examples such as job location clauses) shows how important it is for both employers and employees to treat contracts and/or written statements not as tedious bureaucracy, but rather as documents which may be decisive in actions before tribunals for modern statutory rights.

Two changes were made by the Trade Union Reform and Employment Rights Act 1993 and the Employment Act 2002 relating not to what has to be specified, but how it is to be notified to the employee. Prior to 1993, the employer was given a wide power to refer in the section 1 statement to other documentation, provided it was reasonably available to the employee. Thus, even on major terms such as pay, the statement could refer, for example, to a collective agreement. Increasingly, this technique was used where the firm produced a company handbook, to which frequent reference could be made[68]. However, that power of reference was restricted in 1993 and now only applies to (a) any particulars relating to sickness, sick pay or pensions, when reference may be made to some other document reasonably available, and (b) the length of notice, when reference may be made to the general law[69] or any relevant collective agreement[70]. Other than that (and the note on disciplinary and grievance procedures), the new rule is that the particulars required must be specifically included in a 'single document'[71]. Similarly, any changes must be notified specifically in a written statement, subject to the same exceptions. As stated above, this change was consistent with the previous government's stated policy to encourage the extension of individual contracting and flexibility in the setting of terms and conditions but it could lead to an unrealistic requirement being imposed (at least technically) when employment is entered as process rather than a single transaction[72]; moreoever (whether by design or oversight) this change also removed the previous provision stating that a full contract can fulfil the function of the written statement. Some tidying up on this was done by the Employment Act 2002, which adds a new section 7A, stating that where the employer gives the employee a document in the form of a contract of employment or a letter of appointment, that document contains all the information required by section 1 and it is given within the normal two-month period, that discharges the requirement of giving the written statement. This goes some way towards rationalising the position, but does not go back to the pre-1993 right to refer to any other documents. It may still be necessary, for example, to consider whether a letter of appointment referring to a company handbook could be construed as 'one document'.

(c) Enforcement

Contractual rights may of course be enforced by an ordinary common law action and so, for example, a claim that the employer should be paying more in wages under the contract may be tested by bringing an action for those wages in the county court (or in a tribunal, under the guise of the underpayment being a

---

68 Company handbooks became increasingly popular with employers and ACAS have published advice on producing them (Advisory Booklet No 9). However, there can be difficulties with the contractual status of different parts of such a handbook (see p 150 below) and the new rules on written statements may make them less useful.

69 The legal minima are set out in the Employment Rights Act 1996, s 86, see p 460 below.

70 S 2(2), (3).

71 S 2(4). There is a peculiarity in the new drafting. The old s 5 used to state specifically that the need to give a statement did not apply if the employer instead gave a full written contract covering the relevant matters; no such provision now appears, so it must be assumed to be implied that such a written contract constitutes a 'written statement to the employee' under s 1(1).

72 Particularly as Lord Hoffmann emphasised in *Carmichael v National Power plc* [1999] ICR 1226, [2000] IRLR 43, HL, that at common law it may be necessary to look at several sources to determine and continue a contract of employment.

'deduction for wages'), which may involve a determination by the court or tribunal of the correct contractual term on wages, which in turn may involve a determination of the accuracy of the written statement on the question of wages. In addition to this, however, the Act provides for the *direct* enforcement of the requirement to give the written statement.

Under section 11 the method of direct enforcement of these provisions is by reference of the issue to a tribunal. Where either no statement has been given under sections 1 or 4 or a statement does not comply with those sections the employee may refer the matter, and where a statement has been given but a dispute has arisen as to the particulars which ought to have been included or referred to in it so as to comply with the statutory provisions, either the employer or the employee may refer the matter. By section 12 the tribunal is given wide powers to determine what particulars ought to have been included, or whether any particulars which were included are to be confirmed, amended or substituted. These powers of the tribunal should be a considerable incentive for the employer to comply with the requirements of section 1 in the first place; if he does not do so, and a dispute later arises with his workforce over a particular term of employment (for example overtime arrangements) it would be possible for them to take him to a tribunal under section 11 and invite the tribunal to write into their statements the version of the term on overtime that *they* say they originally agreed – if they were successful that would in practice end the dispute in their favour[73].

However, two problems have arisen as to the construction of these powers. The first arises from the fact that they are declared to be only for the purpose of deciding what 'ought to have been included or referred to in the statement *so as to comply with the requirements of [these provisions]*'. This means that in a section 11 claim the tribunal may only declare what ought to have been included in the sense of what was agreed on these various enumerated matters between the parties; it cannot therefore go further and *interpret* any terms expressed in the written statement, for that would be to usurp the functions of the ordinary civil courts to whom traditionally the employee had to turn for interpretation and enforcement of his contractual rights[74]. Thus, in *Cuthbertson v AML Distributors*[75] the employee had not had any written statement of the terms of his notice and when he was dismissed the question arose as to what the length of his notice should have been. The tribunal could find no evidence of express or implied agreement between the parties on this matter, and therefore held that the term which ought to have been included on the question of notice was that it should have been governed by the residual common law requirement of 'reasonable notice'. The applicant employee had claimed that three months would have been reasonable, but the tribunal refused to quantify 'reasonable' as that would

---

73 Note, however, that it is essential that there should be a dispute between the parties; it is an abuse of procedure to bring a s 11 claim where there is no dispute, merely the parties wanting a ruling on a particular matter for some extrinsic purpose: *Baker v Superite Tools Ltd* [1986] ICR 189 (parties wanting a ruling as to whether the workers involved were employed or self-employed, for use in dealings with the Inland Revenue).

74 Unless the matter has arisen on termination of the employment, in which case a tribunal may have jurisdiction to determine a contract claim (see p 528 below) or the case may be brought before a tribunal during employment under Pt II of the Employment Rights Act 1996, concerning deductions from pay. This would now cover the case of *Cuthbertson* (see n 75 below).

75 [1975] IRLR 228, IT.

have been to interpret the contract, which was the province of the ordinary courts to which the employee would have to apply. The case of *Owens v Multilux Ltd*[76] in the NIRC may seem to go against this restricted view of the tribunal's jurisdiction, for there the court not only declared that the parties had agreed upon a salary of '£2500 net deductions' but also declared that this meant that the employer should pay the deductions other than those for income tax. The line here is of course a fine one, but the EAT clearly decided in favour of the restricted view in *Construction Industry Training Board v Leighton*[77] where the written statement had set out the salary terms for the employee but a dispute had arisen as to whether a salary increment mentioned in the terms was in fact payable to the employee. The tribunal decided that it was and so declared, but the EAT allowed the appeal. Kilner Brown J said:

> '... the industrial tribunal allocated to themselves a jurisdiction which they did not have. They acted upon [s. 12(2)] which undoubtedly gives wide powers of amendment and substitution without giving proper consideration to the limitations imposed by [s. 11(2)]. An industrial tribunal can only embark upon an exercise of amendment or substitution of particulars where there is an omission to include or refer to a statutory requirement when setting out the terms of a contract of employment. Here the salary was set out in the contract. All that was unclear was whether the supplementary bonus for one year was already included in the expressed figure. In effect the industrial tribunal was exercising the power of the civil courts to declare what a contract meant or to rectify an error manifest in an otherwise binding contract. We are unanimously of the opinion that the words of the statute do not mean ... that the industrial tribunal could re-write or amend a binding contract which has one small area of misunderstanding between the parties'.

The second problem was potentially more far-reaching, for while it was clear on the wording of section 12 that a tribunal could determine a case where there was a partial or total *failure* by the employer to include the necessary terms in the statement, it was argued that it did not have jurisdiction where the employer had indeed given terms but the employee claimed that they were *inaccurate* (ie that they did not reflect what had actually been agreed)[78]. This very narrow view was supported by the ambiguous third sentence in the above dictum by Kilner Brown J in *Leighton's* case, and could be seen in the judgment of the EAT in *Brown v Stuart, Scott & Co Ltd*[79], though in each case the pronouncements were obiter. It is true that the wording of section 12 was not explicit on the point (though the use of words such as 'amend' and 'substitute' surely points in the direction of including claims that particulars are inaccurate) however it certainly seemed that the narrow view was contrary to Parliament's intention and an unnecessary restriction on the tribunals' jurisdiction. As originally drafted, the Employment Bill 1982 contained a provision which would have stated expressly that tribunals could hear complaints

---

76   [1974] IRLR 113; likewise, there are dubious dicta by Parker LJ in *Eagland v British Telecommunications plc* [1993] ICR 644, [1992] IRLR 323, CA that a tribunal would have power to *quantify* a 'reasonable notice' term.

77   [1978] IRLR 60. The decision in this case, and the rule that tribunals may not interpret statements, were approved by Stephenson LJ in *Mears v Safecar Security Ltd* [1982] IRLR 183, CA at 188, though certain dicta in the case no longer stand (see below).

78   See Mogridge 'Giving written particulars of employment – a valueless exercise' [1981] NLJ 1250.

79   [1981] ICR 166.

about particulars which had been included or referred to in statements, but this provision was removed as unnecessary when the position was rectified by the decision of the Court of Appeal in the important case of *Mears v Safecar Security Ltd*[80]. It is made clear in this case that a tribunal *does* have jurisdiction to hear complaints of inaccurate particulars. However, on its facts the case concerned the *failure* to give particulars[81] and in this context too the case is important for its clarification and extension of existing principles. Here, Stephenson LJ said that the complaint could be either (a) a complaint that the statement does not contain a term which had actually been agreed, or (b) a complaint that a term had not been included where in fact there had been no express agreement. In the latter case, a tribunal must consider all the facts to determine what term should be implied[82], and normally there will be sufficient evidence for them to be able to do so (in particular, evidence of general working practices which are obvious at the latest by the end of the two-month period that the employer has in which to give the written statement). However, a further problem arose because the court went further and said obiter that the obligation upon the tribunal to declare the relevant particulars (on a complaint of failure to give them) applied even in the untypical case where there is no clear evidence at all, in which case the tribunal might ultimately be left to 'invent' them, on the basis of what would be reasonable and sensible terms in all the circumstances. However, the Court of Appeal subsequently disapproved strongly of that extreme position in *Eagland v British Telecommunications plc*[83], where it was reaffirmed that the tribunal's function is only to declare what has already been agreed in some way, not to impose upon the parties terms which have not been agreed. They adopted the distinction drawn by Wood P in the EAT in the case between 'mandatory' and 'non-mandatory' particulars[84]. In the case of the latter, if there is no evidence at all of any agreement, the tribunal should simply state that there is no term on the matter[85]. Mandatory terms cause more difficulty. They said that it is most unlikely that this problem will arise (an employment relationship with *nothing* ever said about pay?), but if it did a tribunal would have to look at what the law would normally include as the ordinary requirements of an employment relationship (the obvious example being the implication of a term of reasonable notice if there was no evidence of any agreement). However, Leggatt LJ in a short, concurring judgment stated what must eventually be the bottom line if no power of invention is allowed:

---

80 [1982] 2 All ER 865, [1982] IRLR 183, CA. The case includes a detailed explanation by Stephenson LJ of the original drafting of ss 11 and 12.

81 The particulars in question related to the payment (or non-payment) of sick pay; this aspect of the case is considered on p 221 below.

82 The case is also important on this general question of the implication of terms into contracts of employment (see p 139 below), for the approach of the Court of Appeal was not constrained by old contract law notions of the intent of the parties or business efficacy.

83 [1993] ICR 644, [1992] IRLR 323, CA.

84 [1990] ICR 248, [1990] IRLR 328. According to Parker LJ, giving the leading judgment in the Court of Appeal, mandatory terms (as the section stood pre-1993) are those relating to the parties, date of commencement, continuity of employment, rate of pay, intervals for payment, notice and job title; non-mandatory terms are those relating to hours of work, holidays, sickness/sick pay and pensions. Of the particulars added in 1993, those relating to termination of non-permanent employment, place of work and applicable collective agreements appear to be mandatory; the extra particulars relating to employment abroad appear to be split.

85 *Morley v Heritage plc* [1993] IRLR 400, CA.

'If an essential term, such as a written statement must contain, has not been agreed, there will be no agreement.'

The question of the enforcement of the section 1 statement arose in the present government's deliberations on new methods of dispute resolution in order to lessen recourse to tribunals. They took the view that too many essentially contractual disputes are taken to tribunals, a view borne out by the statistics[86], and that one reason for this was that it is still the case that in too many such disputes the empoyee had not been given either a contract or a written statement of terms (the giving of which might have settled the issue in dispute at the beginning). This view was backed by research showing that, in a survey of 2,700 completed tribunal cases, 82% of employers but only 60% of employees said that terms had been given in writing, and that only 51% of employers and 28% of employees said that there were written procedures at the workplace for dealing with the issue or issues that had led to the tribunal application[87]. One obvious problem was that under existing law a section 1 statement could only be enforced by the individual employee (in section 11 proceedings); these remained rare. The Employment Act 2002 addressed this issue of insufficient enforcement in a novel way. Under section 38, where a tribunal hearing a case finds in favour of the employee and discovers that the employer was in a breach of the duty to give written particulars it must award extra compensation of between two and four weeks' pay (unless there are exceptional circumstances making that unjust or inequitable). The important point here is that there is *no* causative element, ie it need not be shown that the employee won the substantive claim *because* there was no section 1 statement; thus, this new provision simply gives a new responsibility to tribunals to police the giving of these statements.

(d) Changing the terms of employment

We have already seen that section 4 states that changes in the relevant terms and conditions must be notified to the employee within one month. However, it is important to realise that section 4 only adds a procedural requirement – it does *not* give the employer any substantive right to alter the terms of employment simply by issuing an amending notice. Any such variation must first be lawful and effective under the ordinary law of employment contracts. There may be certain, untypical, cases where the employment contract itself is drafted to give the employer a right of unilateral variation[88]. Less drastically, it may be that a particular

---

86   The ACAS Annual Report 2001/2002 shows that, of 165,093 cases brought before tribunals, 38,591 were for unlawful deductions from wages and 28,804 were for breach of contract on termination of employment.

87   Findings of the 1998 Survey of Employment Tribunal Applications (Employment Relations Research Services No 13, 2002; available on the DTI website).

88   The terms and conditions of employment of senior civil servants may be varied unilaterally by the government under the Civil Service Orders in Council; see p 108 above. In an ordinary contract of employment, it would be an interesting question as to whether a term allowing unrestricted unilateral variation ('You are employed to do what I say, on any terms I may decide upon') could be held to be void for uncertainty; the Court of Appeal in *Wandsworth London Borough Council v D'Silva* [1998] IRLR 193 (obiter) recognised the possible contractual validity of such a clause, but stated that particularly clear language would be necessary to reserve such an unusual power to the employer, and courts should seek to avoid any unreasonable results of such a power; se also *Securities and Facilities Division v Hayes* [2001] IRLR 81, CA and Smith and Randall, *Contract Actions in Modern Employment Law - Developments and Issues* (2002) p 42.

'variation' in fact falls within the managerial discretion to order changes[89], either because it is within an area of flexibility envisaged by the contract or because it falls within the scope of an implied term that the employee will adapt to necessary changes in what remains essentially the same job[90]. However, both of these possibilities show the basic problem here, that contracts are essentially static whereas work and work methods may change (sometimes rapidly), and the possibility may equally arise that the employer may wish to effect changes which are *not* envisaged by the contract. In such a case there has to be a legally effective variation; if this does not happen, an employee may insist upon adhering to the original contract and may bring a common law action to underline that adherence (for example by bringing an action in the county court for his wages, which are due by virtue of his being willing and able to continue performing his duties under the original, unamended contract)[91] or (in the case of a pay cut) proceedings before a tribunal on the basis that the change constitutes an unlawful 'deduction' from wages. In such a case, an employer who is insistent upon forcing through changes may have to grasp the nettle, dismiss those who still refuse to accept changes and take his chances before an employment tribunal by seeking to show that the dismissals were fair because of the business's need to alter working patterns[92].

From the employer's point of view, these uncertainties can be avoided if it can be shown that the employee in question in fact agreed to the proposed variation in the contract. How is that to be shown? Obviously the clearest case is where the employee has expressly agreed to the variation, either individually or collectively (through negotiations with his union). However, there remains a middle ground (especially where union representation is not involved), which is where the employer 'proposes' a variation simply by announcing it (possibly by reissuing an amended section 1 statement), thus putting the onus on the employee to *object*. If the employee does not object, that gives rise to the argument that he has impliedly assented to the variation. If such an argument were easily accepted, the contractual rights of an employee would mean little and so it was held in *Jones v Associated Tunnelling Co Ltd*[93] that the question of the correct interpretation to be placed on a lack of objection following a unilateral change in terms by the employer must be approached realistically; if the term in question is of immediate practical importance (for example a reduction in wages or alteration of working

89 As in the case of the introduction of a no-smoking policy in *Dryden v Greater Glasgow Health Board* [1992] IRLR 469, which was held not to be a breach of contract, so that the employee who left was not constructively dismissed.
90 This was the case with the computerisation of Inland Revenue procedures; this was held to be merely an updated version of the plaintiff tax officers' existing jobs (with which they were expected to cope), *not* a substantive variation of their terms of employment: *Cresswell v Board of Inland Revenue* [1984] ICR 508, [1984] IRLR 190; see p 170 below.
91 As in *Burdett-Coutts v Hertfordshire County Council* [1984] IRLR 91 where dinner ladies who had refused to accept a unilateral decrease in their hours of work successfully sued their employer for arrears of wages due under their original contract.
92 This is one of the most difficult areas of unfair dismissal, for it is well established that dismissal because of refusal to accept a necessary business reorganisation can constitute dismissal for 'some other substantial reason' within the Employment Rights Act 1996, s 98 (see p 599 below and, again concerning dinner ladies and cost-cutting councils, *Gilham v Kent County Council (No 2)* [1985] ICR 233, [1985] IRLR 18, CA) but to take the final step and hold that that dismissal was *fair* is to give priority to the employer's business considerations over what the employee would normally expect to be his contractual rights (particularly the right not to have his contract altered except by agreement).
93 [1981] IRLR 477.

hours) and the employee fails to object, that may show implied assent on his part, but in the case of other terms of little immediate importance (for example as to sick pay or possible future changes in workplace) it may be expecting too much of an employee to make immediate objection (even if he understands the full significance of the changes) and so a tribunal in such a case should be slow to infer assent merely from lack of objection.

Finally, there is one other tactic that has featured largely in employer mythology in the past, but which has always been legally more complex than employers have assumed. This is to dismiss all the employees in question (by giving lawful notice) and then re-engage them all on the new terms. Purely as a matter of contract law, this can work, but there are two reasons under statute law why it is now legally dangerous – (1) it is possible that the employees could claim unfair dismissal from the old contract and seek compensation to reflect the net loss of value to them of the new contract[94]; (ii) this tactic has been held to constitute a 'redundancy' under the wider EC law definition used in the law on collective redundancies and so if (as will usually be the case, given that the employer is looking to force the change through) there has not been the obligatory period of consultation with trade union or workforce representatives (where twenty or more employees are involved), the employer may lay himself open to protective awards which could total a significant amount if large numbers of employees have been subject to this tactic[95]. Moreover, when the Information and Consultation Directive comes into force (between 2005 and 2008) an employer using this tactic (or the previous one of simply announcing changes, leaving it to employees to object) as an alternative to discussions with the employees involved may fall foul of the requirement of informing and consulting worker representatives on 'decisions likely to lead to substantial changes in work organisation or in contractual relations[96].

4 LEGALITY AND RESTRAINT OF TRADE

(i) The doctrine of illegality generally

All contracts having objects contrary to statute or common law, or which entail the passing of an illegal consideration, are void. So an agreement by which an employee purports to permit his employer to make deductions from his remuneration will be void unless there is compliance with the provisions of Part II of the Employment Rights Act 1996[97]. So too will a purported agreement to waive a breach of duty imposed by statute on an employer[98]. Sundry other forms

---

94   This is because of the rule in *Hogg v Dover College* [1990] ICR 39 that an employee can be 'dismissed' from a particular contract and so can claim unfair dismissal even if still in that employer's employment but under a different contract; see *Alcan Extrusions v Yates* [1996] IRLR 327.

95   *GMB v Man Truck and Bus UK Ltd* [2000] ICR 1101, [2000] IRLR 636. For the law on collective redundancies (including the wider EC law definition and liability for protective awards), see p 84 above.

96   Directive 2002/14/EC art 4(2)(c); see p 97 above. Even when fully in force in 2008, this will not apply to employers of less than 50 employees.

97   *Kearney v Whitehaven Colliery Co* [1893] 1 QB 700, CA (case on the now-repealed Truck Acts); see p 259 below.

98   *Baddeley v Earl of Granville* (1887) 19 QBD 423; for a strong case, see *Wheeler v New Merton Board Mills Ltd* [1933] 2 KB 669, CA.

of illegality may theoretically apply to contracts of employment as well as to contracts generally even if in practice they are less likely to do so. One which could arise directly in the context of employment is the rule that a contract of employment must not contain 'servile incidents', which may best be described as harsh terms showing a lack of mutuality, as where a cinema company obtained sole use of an actor's stage name[99] or where the defendant borrowed money from a money-lender on terms which made it impossible for him to change employment, deal with his possessions, change address, etc, without prior permission[100].

One particular application of notions of illegality has caused problems in the field of employment law. These problems arise when one of the parties (usually the employer) to a tribunal action concerning modern statutory rights such as redundancy payments or unfair dismissal argues that the contract of employment in question was in some sense illegal, usually because it contained some element of unlawful tax evasion (for example under-declaration of income payable under it, or the payment of non-declared extra amounts of income). If this is proved, it can lead to a decision that the contract itself is void and, as such a contract is necessary before an applicant can show that he was an 'employee' for the purpose of claiming his statutory rights, that the applicant's claim must be struck out[101]. The doctrine of illegality in the law of contract is a complicated subject at the best of times[102], but in the sphere of employment law can have particularly drastic effects by depriving tribunals of jurisdiction, even where the element of illegality might be incidental and (in the case of tax evasion) where the amount of money concerned is small. Moreover, it can lead to the problem, which arises generally under the doctrine of illegality in contract law, of one party to the contract (here usually the employer) benefiting from his own illegality, eg in a case where the evasion scheme was in fact initiated by the employer who later used it to try to defeat an employee's claim for unfair dismissal. The starting point here is that the general argument that the doctrine of illegality should not apply to contracts of employment (either at all, or at least to the extent of prejudicing statutory actions) on the grounds of employment law policy has clearly been disapproved by the EAT[103]. Thus, the doctrine is applicable and in a series of cases the tribunals have had to work out its effects. It may of course apply to forms of illegality other than tax evasion, for example in *Coral Leisure Group Ltd v Barnett*[104] where it was

---

99 *Hepworth Manufacturing Co v Ryott* [1920] 1 Ch 1, CA; however, some cinema contracts have validly imposed highly personal restraints on employees' diets, health, personal life etc, probably on the ground that they were in the interests of both parties; *Gaumont-British Picture Corpn v Alexander* [1936] 2 All ER 1686. A tie to pay back the cost of training is not illegal (*Strathclyde Regional Council v Neil* [1984] IRLR 11); indeed, the previous government expressed interest in extending such a system of self-financed training, backed by 'stay or pay' clauses: People, Jobs and Opportunity (Cm 1810, 1992), see (1992) NLJ 358.

100 *Horwood v Millar's Timber and Trading Co Ltd* [1917] 1 KB 305, CA.

101 *Napier v National Business Agency Ltd* [1951] 2 All ER 264, CA; *Jennings v Westwood Engineering Ltd* [1975] IRLR 245; *Tomlinson v Dick Evans U Drive Ltd* [1978] ICR 639, [1978] IRLR 77.

102 Especially as the purely contract law cases tend to be on abstruse facts.

103 *Newland v Simons and Willer (Hairdressers) Ltd* [1981] ICR 521, [1981] IRLR 359. It is of course possible for a statute to state expressly that contravention of its terms shall *not* make any resulting contract void for illegality (see, for example, the Company Securities (Insider Dealing) Act 1985, s 8(3) and, in particular, the Social Security Contributions and Benefits Act 1992, s 97 which covers industrial accidents in the course of illegal employments); it is unfortunate that the Employment Rights Act does not have such an exclusory provision.

104 [1981] ICR 503, [1981] IRLR 204.

claimed that an ex-employee could not maintain an action for unfair dismissal because part of his job had entailed hiring prostitutes for the employer's clients, thus falling foul of the law on immoral contracts. In this sort of case it is easier to apply the basic common law distinction that contracts illegal in inception are void, but contracts which are legal in inception but later performed in an illegal manner may not be[105]. However, that distinction may be more difficult to apply to the more usual cases of tax evasion. The tendency has fortunately been to treat them as illegal only in performance, with the result that 'innocence' is a defence, and so in practice the determining factor has been whether the employee *knew* of the evasion being practised by the employer – if not, he can still claim his statutory rights[106]; moreover, it is clear that knowledge here means actual, subjective knowledge, so that it is an error of law for a tribunal to consider whether the employee ought to have realised what was happening[107]. The most difficult case here is *Corby v Morrison* where the primary ground for ruling out a claim for unfair dismissal by an ex-employee who had received £5 per week without deduction of income tax was that the contract of employment was illegal *in inception*, which renders the knowledge or otherwise of the employee irrelevant; the EAT did give as a secondary ground of judgment that, even if it was only illegal in performance, she knew what was going on and so was ruled out anyway. This second ground of judgment was emphasised in the explanation of the case subsequently in *Newland v Simons and Willer (Hairdressers) Ltd*[108], but the first ground was not disapproved. However, in *Hewcastle Catering Ltd v Ahmed*[109] the Court of Appeal clearly leaned towards treating tax evasion cases as illegality in performance, to which the doctrine should be applied sparingly. Beldam LJ stated that the modern law is that it applies only if in all the circumstances it would be an affront to the public conscience to allow the claim to proceed; further, the defence will not be allowed if the defendant employer's conduct in participating in the illegal contract is so much more reprehensible than the employee's conduct that it would be wrong to allow the employer to rely on it. This is an important case because of the facts – the employees were waiters at the employers' club who were involved in operating the employers' VAT fraud, *but* they did *not* derive any personal benefit from it. After the employers were caught (and the employees gave evidence against them), the employees were dismissed

---

105 In this case, the EAT held that the tribunal had jurisdiction to hear the claim. The ex-employee had not been taken on to hire prostitutes, and it was not part of his contract to do so (merely one of the ways in practice of discharging his functions); the contract was therefore not illegal in inception. Dicta in the case suggest that, because it was only illegal in performance, *therefore* it was not void, but it is submitted that the better view is that that means that it *may* not be void, and that the ground for the decision is that, given that the illegality was only in performance, that particular form of illegality (hiring prostitutes) was not sufficiently grave to justify invalidating the whole contract.

106 *Tomlinson v Dick Evans 'U' Drive Ltd*, n 101 above; *Davidson v Pillay* [1979] IRLR 275; *McConnell v Bolik* [1979] IRLR 422 has an interesting twist in the story in that the case concerned non-declaration of income by the employee, so that the crucial question was the state of the *employer's* knowledge. The knowledge in question is as to the facts; lack of knowledge of the illegality of the transaction (ie a mistake of law) will not help the party: *Salvesen v Simons* [1994] ICR 409, [1994] IRLR 52.

107 *Corby v Morrison* [1980] ICR 564, [1980] IRLR 218; *Newland v Simons and Willer (Hairdressers) Ltd* [1981] IRLR 359.

108 See n 107 above; the same judge presided over the EAT in both cases. *Newland's* case was clearly viewed as one of illegality in performance, and was remitted to the tribunal to make more precise findings of fact on the employee's knowledge of the evasion.

109 [1992] ICR 626, [1991] IRLR 473, CA.

and the employers raised illegality as a defence. Had the court simply applied the existing test (did they *know* of it?) the defence would have succeeded, but on the two wider principles above the court was able to disallow it since (a) public policy did not demand its application and (b) the employers were clearly the more guilty. While this decision does not go as far as to say that an employee with knowledge (though possibly only an unwilling minion) *cannot* be debarred from an action if he made no personal gain, it did allow a decision to be taken much along those lines on the facts. Moreover, it may permit further developments towards what, it is submitted, would be the best solution (given that the doctrine has to apply at all), namely that any incidental tax evasion should only ever make the contract illegal in performance and that for the illegality then to make the contract void the employee must have known of *and benefited from* the evasion to such an *extent* (in comparison with the gain to the employer) that the court or tribunal has no option but to declare the whole contract void.

Finally, three points might be noted. The first is that on general principles it is not every form of illegality that can render a contract void – the illegality must be sufficiently grave or of such a nature as to show (in the case of illegality through contravention of a statute) that the intention of the legislation is to affect contracts if necessary, not just to penalise the conduct in question in other ways[110]. It is this principle that prevents, for example, a lorry driver's contract of employment being totally void as soon as he exceeds a speed limit. However, it cannot help an applicant before a tribunal in a case involving tax evasion, for it has so far been the approach of the courts (subject to any possible new emphasis on the respective moral blameworthiness of employee and employer, see above) that *any* element of tax evasion (even if concerning only small amounts, or only extra remuneration[111] on top of basic wages on which full tax may have been paid) is grave enough to activate the rules on illegality; likewise the tribunals have not accepted the argument that protection of tax revenue can be adequately left to the tax authorities and legislation and does not need to be reinforced by the striking down of contracts, though it has been accepted that employers may be deterred from making illegal payments and then trying to rely on them to defeat statutory claims by the power of a tribunal at the end of the day to transmit the evidence that they have received to the Inland Revenue[112]. The second point is that a slightly different approach to illegality was taken in the case of *Hyland v J H Barker (North West) Ltd*[113]. In this case the employee had taken illegal payments for a period of only four weeks (out of a total period of employment of sixteen years);

---

110 The authority usually cited for this is the judgment of Devlin J in *St John Shipping Corpn v Joseph Rank Ltd* [1957] 1 QB 267, [1956] 3 All ER 683. One potentially controversial question now may be whether a contract to work hours in excess of the maxima in the Working Time Regulations could be argued to be illegal; this is probably *not* the intent of the Regulations (except to the extent of the excess?), and the results of so holding could be harsh and unpredictable for the employee.

111 If, however, the tax evasion applies only to extraneous payments (eg gifts) which are *not* part of contractual remuneration, the validity of the contract is not affected: *Annandale Engineering v Samson* [1994] IRLR 59.

112 A course advocated in *Corby v Morrison* and put into effect in *Newland v Simons and Willer (Hairdressers) Ltd* (n 103 above). A similar device has been suggested to deter a person from claiming to be self-employed for tax purposes while working, but then turning round and claiming to have been in reality an employee all along when later dismissed and wanting to bring an action for unfair dismissal – he may end up with a tribunal finding in his favour outweighed by the hefty tax demand: *Young & Woods Ltd v West* [1980] IRLR 201, CA (see p 16 above).

113 [1985] ICR 861, [1985] IRLR 403.

it was accepted that this did not render the whole contract void *but* that did not help the employee much since it transpired that those four weeks fell during his final year before dismissal and thus (as the contract was void for those four weeks) he could not show the year's continuous employment ending with the date of dismissal that was required in order to bring proceedings for unfair dismissal. The case shows a possibly unfortunate combination of the restrictive rules on illegality and continuity of employment and also, more generally, the harsh effects of the doctrine of illegality in this field; it also leaves open the question as to how major and/or longstanding the illegality has to be to render the *whole* contract void (not just part of it, the timing of which could be entirely fortuitous). The third point is that, as a matter of statutory construction and policy, it has been held that the doctrine of illegality cannot be used to defeat a sex discrimination claim[114]; this would also apply to a racial discrimination claim and, presumably, to an equal pay claim and a disability discrimination claim.

In addition to these general applications of the doctrine of illegality, much case law has been produced by one particular area of it, the area of restraint of trade. Indeed now that this has been held to apply to harsh and one-sided contractual conditions during employment as well as after it[115], it has probably made much of the law on servile incidents redundant. The classic restraint of trade clause in a contract of employment is where the employee agrees not to work in the same trade or not to solicit his employer's customers in a certain area for a certain period, after the termination of his employment with that employer. It is to the doctrine of restraint of trade, and the validity or otherwise of such an agreement, that we now turn.

(ii) The doctrine of restraint of trade

The doctrine of restraint of trade is a legal device to attempt to hold the balance between two competing factors – an employee's freedom to take employment as and when he wishes, and an employer's interest in preserving certain aspects of his business from disclosure or exploitation by an employee or, more usually, an ex-employee[116]. Both factors are important, and indeed the law will protect the employer if necessary by the implication of a term of fidelity in the contract of employment thereby restraining the employee inter alia from divulging confidential information[117]. However, the employer may wish to go further and extract an express promise from the employee (a) not to disclose certain information and, more important, (b) not to place himself in a position in which he may do so, for example by not working for a competitor for a certain period of time within a certain area after leaving the employment.

---

114 *Leighton v Michael* [1995] ICR 1091, [1996] IRLR 67, [2001] ICR 99. This was approved by the Court of Appeal in *Hall v Woolston Hall Leisure Ltd* [2000] IRLR 578, both as a matter of domestic law and in the light of the Equal Treatment Directive 76/207/EEC.

115 *Schroeder Music Publishing Co v Macaulay* [1974] 3 All ER 616, [1974] 1 WLR 1308, HL; *Clifford Davis Management Ltd v WEA Records Ltd* [1975] 1 All ER 237, [1975] 1 WLR 61, CA.

116 The leading work on this area is Brearley and Bloch *Employment Covenants and Confidential Information: Law, Practice and Technique* (2nd edn, 1999) which gives an excellent exposition of the law and practice.

117 This topic is discussed later in this chapter, under head 5.

'It is thus established that an employer can stipulate for protection against having his confidential information passed on to a rival in trade. But experience has shown that it is not satisfactory to have simply a covenant against disclosing confidential information. The reason is because it is so difficult to draw the line between information which is confidential and information which is not; and it is very difficult to prove a breach when the information is of such a character that a servant can carry it away in his head. The difficulties are such that the only practicable solution is to take a covenant from the servant by which he is not to go to work for a rival in trade. Such a covenant may well be held to be reasonable ...'[118]

The question then arises whether any given restraint clause is valid and enforceable against the ex-employee, or void. The modern law on restraint of trade is to be found in *Nordenfelt v Maxim Nordenfelt Guns and Ammunition Co*[119] and *Esso Petroleum Co Ltd v Harper's Garage (Stourport) Ltd*[120], a case on 'solus' agreements in the garage trade, in which the House of Lords reconsidered the whole doctrine. In the *Nordenfelt* case it was established that a restraint clause is to be considered void unless the party alleging its validity can prove that it is (a) reasonable as between the parties and (b) in the public interest. The two principal forms of agreement which have been subject to the doctrine are agreements by the vendor of a business not to compete with the purchaser of it, as in the *Nordenfelt* case, and by an employee not to act in a certain way after finishing the employment, and it has been clearly stated that it will be more difficult to establish the validity of a restraint clause in the latter case, with which we are primarily concerned here, for it concerns not a commercial transaction at arm's length, but rather a transaction, potentially between parties of different bargaining strengths, which could have a major effect on an individual's livelihood (future and present) to the disadvantage of himself and the public interest[121]. For present purposes, the decision in the *Esso Petroleum* case clarified the law in two major ways. The first was to confirm that not all agreements which restrain a person's freedom of action are subject to the doctrine, for some are so accepted as normal incidents of particular businesses or transactions that they are not subject to challenge[122]. The test for deciding what is subject to the doctrine and what is not subject is not entirely clear, but what is important for present purposes is that the House of Lords said clearly that restraint clauses by employees in favour of employers are definitely subject to the doctrine. The second major effect of the case was to revive the ailing second limb of the rule in *Nordenfelt's* case, ie public interest. This had been so neglected as to have been virtually ignored[123], but this can no

---

118 *Littlewoods Organisation Ltd v Harris* [1978] 1 All ER 1026 at 1033, CA, per Lord Denning MR.

119 [1894] AC 535, HL, as explained by a subsequent House of Lords in *Mason v Provident Clothing and Supply Co Ltd* [1913] AC 724, HL.

120 [1968] AC 269, [1967] 1 All ER 699, HL.

121 See particularly *Herbert Morris Ltd v Saxelby* [1916] 1 AC 688, HL, per Lord Parker at 710 and Lord Shaw at 714.

122 Tied houses in the brewery trade are valid, whereas 'solus' agreements in the garage trade, not being so widely accepted, have been the subject of several legal cases.

123 'Their Lordships are not aware of any case in which a restraint, though reasonable in the interests of the parties, has been held unenforceable because it involved some injury to the public,' *A-G of Commonwealth of Australia v Adelaide Steamship Co Ltd* [1913] AC 781, PC, at 795 per Lord Parker. One exceptional case was *Wyatt v Kreglinger and Fernau* [1933] 1 KB 793, CA, followed by *Bull v Pitney-Bowes* [1966] 3 All ER 384, [1967] 1 WLR 273.

longer be so and indeed Lord Reid and Lord Hodson intimated[124] that certain past cases which were decided on the first limb, reasonableness as between the parties, might well have been better decided on the second limb. In the employment context this could be of some importance, as there might be certain forms of agreement as we shall see below, such as labour stabilisation agreements between employer and employer, which might be eminently reasonable as between the parties, but would now be subject to challenge on the wider ground of the public interest.

Thus, an employee might validly bind himself in a contract of employment as to his future activities, usually when he enters the contract, but also possibly during its currency[125] or at its termination, provided in the latter case that the agreement is genuinely referable to the contract of employment, and not just an after-thought 'in gross'[126]. Moreover, it is now established that a clause restraining certain activities by the employee *during* employment may be subject to challenge as well as one restricting activities upon termination of the employment; in *Schroeder Music Publishing Co v Macaulay*[127] an agreement whereby the plaintiff, a young and unknown songwriter, gave his exclusive services to the defendants for five years without any obligation on the latter to publish his works or provide him with any livelihood, and whereby the defendants could terminate or extend the contract at their election but the plaintiff could not, was held to be void as in restraint of trade. That was, however, an unusual case, and any more normal restraints during employment, for example not to work for competitors or not to disclose information, might well be held to be so common as to require no justification, under the *Esso Petroleum* case, and indeed certain standard ones would possibly be implied by operation of law even if not expressed[128].

Given that restraint clauses in contracts of employment are amenable to challenge, the next relevant questions are: what interests warrant protection, how extensive can the restraint be if it is to be valid, and what remedies are available to the parties.

(iii) Protectable interests

The clearest starting point is that an employer cannot simply restrain an ex-employee from competing with him in an ordinary manner; it must go far beyond that, and in the employment context this in practice means that the restraint must be necessary to protect either (a) trade secrets or (b) customer connections.

'I cannot find any case in which a covenant against competition by a servant or apprentice has as such ever been upheld by the court. Wherever such covenants have been upheld it has been on the grounds, not that the servant or apprentice would, by reason of his employment or training, obtain the skill or knowledge necessary to equip him as a possible competitor in the

---

124 [1968] AC 269 at 300 and 319, [1967] 1 All ER 699 at 709 and 721.
125 *RS Components Ltd v Irwin* [1974] 1 All ER 41, [1973] ICR 535.
126 *Stenhouse Australia Ltd v Phillips* [1974] AC 391, [1974] 1 All ER 117, PC.
127 [1974] 3 All ER 616, [1974] 1 WLR 1308, HL, followed in *Clifford Davis Management Ltd v WEA Records Ltd* [1975] 1 All ER 237, [1975] 1 WLR 61, CA.
128 See head 5 of this chapter, under the duty of fidelity.

trade, *but* that he might obtain such personal knowledge of, and influence over, the customers of his employers, or such an acquaintance with his employer's trade secrets as would enable him, if competition were allowed, to take advantage of his employer's trade connection or utilise information confidentially obtained.[129]'

From this basic principle, certain important points arise. The first is that although 'trade secret' is difficult to define, it is an important concept and must be distinguished from the employee's own skill and general knowledge of the trade (albeit gained in the employer's service)[130], knowledge of general business methods and organisations[131], and information which lacks confidentiality (for example through having been published)[132], none of which merit lawful protection. The subject matter must be something more in the nature of a secret process or formula or the detailed design of a machine (albeit from parts the individual specifications of which are generally known)[133] and in modern circumstances may also cover highly confidential information of a non-technical or non-scientific nature (disclosure of which to a competitor could cause significant harm)[134] or detailed knowledge of the workings of a specialised business[135]. Particularly difficult questions may now arise in the computer and information technology industries, in deciding what remains confidential at the cutting edge and what is merely the (expert) employee's own knowledge, or indeed general knowledge in such a rapidly developing field.[136] The second point is that the phrase 'customer connections' is even more intangible; naturally, an employee in constant touch with customers may in certain circumstances attract a personal following, be they a solicitor's clerk[137], estate agent[138], bookmaker's assistant[139], or milkman[140]; sales representatives and canvassers might well be subject to valid restraints. Every case will depend heavily upon the facts, and in essence what must be shown is that there is a *real* possibility of *misuse* of the employee's knowledge of customers; if this is missing, for example because the employee's contact with the customers was insufficiently direct or influential, the restraint will be void[141]. However, once this elusive element is established, it may well be reasonable to restrain the ex-employee from soliciting not only his

---

129 *Herbert Morris Ltd v Saxelby* [1916] 1 AC 688 at 709, HL, per Lord Parker. For a modern reaffirmation of this principle, see *Faccenda Chicken Ltd v Fowler* [1986] ICR 297, [1986] IRLR 69, CA.

130 *Herbert Morris Ltd v Saxelby*, n 129 above; *Mason v Provident Clothing and Supply Co Ltd* [1913] AC 724, HL; *Faccenda Chicken Ltd v Fowler*, n 8 above.

131 *Commercial Plastics Ltd v Vincent* [1965] 1 QB 623, [1964] 3 All ER 546, CA.

132 *Mustad v Dosen* [1963] 3 All ER 416, [1964] 1 WLR 109n, HL (though in fact decided in 1928).

133 *Haynes v Doman* [1899] 2 Ch 13, CA; *Forster & Sons Ltd v Suggett* (1918) 35 TLR 87; and see the detailed knowledge of current research carried on by the plaintiffs in *Commercial Plastics Ltd v Vincent* [1965] 1 QB 623, [1964] 3 All ER 546, CA.

134 *Lansing Linde Ltd v Kerr* [1991] ICR 428, [1991] IRLR 80, CA.

135 *Littlewoods Organisation Ltd v Harris* [1978] 1 All ER 1026, [1977] 1 WLR 1472, CA.

136 *FSS Travel and Leisure Systems Ltd v Johnson* [1998] IRLR 382, CA.

137 *Fitch v Dewes* [1921] 2 AC 158, HL.

138 *Scorer v Seymour-Johns* [1966] 3 All ER 347, [1966] 1 WLR 1419, CA.

139 *SW Strange Ltd v Mann* [1965] 1 All ER 1069, [1965] 1 WLR 629.

140 *Home Counties Dairies Ltd v Skilton* [1970] 1 All ER 1227, [1970] 1 WLR 526, CA; *Dairy Crest Ltd v Pigott* [1989] ICR 92, CA.

141 *Bowler v Lovegrove* [1921] 1 Ch 642; *SW Strange Ltd v Mann* [1965] 1 All ER 1069, [1965] 1 WLR 629.

particular customers at the date of termination of employment, but also any other persons who were the employer's customers at any other time during the period of employment or some specified part thereof[142], though it will not generally be reasonable to restrain solicitation of persons who might become the employer's customers at some time after termination[143], as for example by a clause restraining a commercial traveller from soliciting anyone in the relevant trade in the area in which he used to travel for the employer, not limiting it to those who were the employer's customers, or from whom he had attempted to solicit custom for the employer[144].

The third point is that if the restraint clause cannot fairly be said to protect a trade secret or customer connection, the longstanding view has been that it should be void on the basis that it concerns no protectable interest known to the law, unless the court is to establish a new one. In *Kores Manufacturing Co v Kolok Manufacturing Co*[145], two neighbouring employers producing similar goods agreed that neither would employ anyone who had been employed by the other within the previous five years. As this mainly concerned labourers there was no question of trade secrets or customer connections, and the sole purpose of the agreement was to encourage a stable labour supply. The Court of Appeal held it to be void on the ground that it was, on its facts, unreasonable as between the parties[146], but it is submitted that conceptually the prime reason for invalidity should have been that it concerned no known protectable interest, and there are dicta in the judgment in support of this. This has, however, caused recent controversy and a change in the law, at least partially, because of moves by employers to prevent solicitation by leaving employees of *other employees*, especially in highly competitive areas such as the City and/or in the case of highly marketable executives. At first, the traditional view was taken that such anti-solicitation clauses were not permitted. In *Hanover Insurance Bros Ltd v Schapiro*[147] certain standard clauses preventing solicitation of customers were enforced against the company's departing chairman and managing director, but a clause stating that they would not, within one year of leaving, solicit any *employees* to join them in their new venture was held to be unenforceable, the court giving its opinion that staff preservation was not a protectable interest. However, that was swiftly followed by an unreported Court of Appeal case, *Ingham v ABC Contract Services Ltd*[148] in which it was held that an employer does have a 'legitimate interest in maintaining a stable trained workforce in what is acknowledged to be a highly competitive business'. In the light of this, an injunction was granted in *Alliance Paper Group Ltd v Prestwich*[149] by a Chancery judge to enforce a covenant not to entice away certain employees, on the basis that the remarks on protectable interests in *Hanover* were obiter (the actual decision

---

142 *G W Plowman & Son Ltd v Ash* [1964] 2 All ER 10, [1964] 1 WLR 568, CA, applied in *Home Counties Dairies Ltd v Skilton* [1970] 1 All ER 1227, [1970] 1 WLR 526, CA; *John Michael Design plc v Cooke* [1987] 2 All ER 332, [1987] ICR 445, CA.

143 *Konski v Peet* [1915] 1 Ch 530.

144 *Gledhow Autoparts Ltd v Delaney* [1965] 3 All ER 288, [1965] 1 WLR 1366, CA.

145 [1959] Ch 108, [1958] 2 All ER 65, CA.

146 This case is expressly mentioned by Lord Reid and Lord Hodson in *Esso Petroleum Ltd v Harper's Garage (Stourport) Ltd* [1968] AC 269, [1967] 1 All ER 699, HL as one which should have been decided on the other limb of the *Nordenfelt* test, public interest. It is interesting to note that the agreement was between employers; the existence of such contracts is difficult to discover.

147 [1994] IRLR 82, CA.

148 (1994) unreported.

149 [1996] IRLR 25.

having been that the clause was too wide in any event), and that it was *Ingham* that was to be followed on this point. Likewise, when it went before the Court of Appeal again in *Dawnay, Day & Co Ltd v De Braconier d'Alphen*[150], where three Eurobond dealers broke away from their employer to join a similar competing venture, the court upheld the decision of Walker J to enforce (inter alia) covenants prohibiting for one year solicitation of certain other employees, again expressly on the basis of the employer's interest in maintaining a stable, trained workforce, within the bounds of reasonableness. Thus, this form of staff retention may now be seen as joining trade secrets and customer connections as a third protectable interest *but* with limits. It does not necessarily mean that *Kores v Kolok* is wrong, and simple attempts to stabilise non-key and non-specialist staff (ie just for administrative convenience) may still not be valid. The cases so far have concerned the solicitation of *senior* staff, in highly competitive industries subject to high turnover and 'head-hunting' of people with instantly marketable skills and knowledge[151]. It is possible that this legal development is confined to such cases, though with two caveats – there could also be arguments for a valid protectable interest in relation to a more junior employee if (i) that person, though junior, is a key employee in terms of skills, for example in computer technology[152], or (ii) that person is a member of a whole *team* being enticed away by the departing employee.

(iv) The extent of the restraint

Once there is a legally protectable interest, the question which then arises concerns the extent to which the employer can bind the employee's future conduct in order to protect that interest. Cases on this are as infinitely variable as are the facts upon which they are based, but certain important factors can be discerned. The terms of the restraint must be no more than is reasonably necessary to give the employer adequate protection[153], and in approaching this the court might first look at the type of business concerned to see how much protection it warrants[154]; in this context it might be significant if the business is either

---

150 [1998] ICR 1068, [1997] IRLR 442, CA. This case was also notable for deciding that a joint venture had sufficient interest to protect. For extensive discussion of these cases, see *TSC Europe (UK) Ltd v Massey* [1999] IRLR 22.

151 In *Alliance Paper Group* the restraint related to company employees 'in a senior capacity' and in *Dawnay, Day* to directors or senior employees; in each case the court held that such phrasing was sufficiently precise to be enforceable, on the elephant principle, ie that you cannot define it but you know one when you see it. By contrast, in *Hanover* a non-solicitation clause applying to 'any employees' was too wide.

152 Readers of Joseph Heller's *Catch 22* will know that the whole Mediterranean theatre of war was in fact run by Ex-PFC Wintergreen, not the general staff.

153 *Herbert Morris Ltd v Saxelby* [1916] 1 AC 688, HL; the longstanding test was reaffirmed by Millett J in *Allied Dunbar (Frank Weisinger) Ltd v Weisinger* [1988] IRLR 60, where he disapproved an attempt to replace it with a more flexible concept of 'proportionality' between the extent of the restraint and the benefit of the employer. For a good factual example, see *Scully UK Ltd v Lee* [1998] IRLR 259, CA.

154 The business in question must be that in which the employer is actually engaged, and not one in which it might be interested at some future date: *Bromley v Smith* [1909] 2 KB 235; however, it may be valid for the employer to protect the business carried out by its subsidiaries, provided the restraint does not go wider than that and apply to activities not covered by the group: *Stenhouse Australia Ltd v Phillips* [1974] AC 391 at 404, [1974] 1 All ER 117 at 125, PC.

specialised in its product or service or localised in its area of operation. The position of the employee is also a matter for consideration. The closer his contacts with customers or prospective customers the easier it will be to justify a restraint[155]. Similarly the higher the employee is in the hierarchy of employees the easier it will be. Thus in *M and S Drapers v Reynolds*[156] where the restraint was imposed on a collector salesman, the court rejected the analogy with a managing director based on *Gilford Motor Co v Horne*[157] and held that in the light of its particular circumstances the restraint was unreasonable. It is nothing more than a question of fact for again, in *G W Plowman & Son Ltd v Ash*[158], a restraint on a sales representative was accepted as valid.

Given that the business merits some protection from an employee such as the one in question, the major factual problem is how wide the terms of the restraint may be in terms of geographical area and duration of time. There are no rules of law here; a 25-year worldwide restraint was valid in the context of the international armaments trade in the *Nordenfelt* case[159]; but a one-year restraint was held to be void in the context of the plastics industry in *Commercial Plastics Ltd v Vincent*[160] partly on the ground that it was unlimited in area. The only general rule is that the two factors of geographical area and duration of time tend to be complementary, in that the wider the geographical area, the shorter the period of time that might be considered reasonable, and vice versa as in *Fitch v Dewes*[161] where a restraint that a solicitor's clerk in Tamworth would *never* practice as such within seven miles of Tamworth Town Hall upon ceasing the employment was held to be valid in the light of the restricted area. Further than this, all that can be said is that the drafting of a restraint clause may require a delicate balance in order to protect the lawful interests of the employer whilst at the same time achieving no more protection than is reasonably necessary for that purpose in all the circumstances. After warning of the dangers of 'home-made' restraint clauses, Pearson LJ said in *Commercial Plastics v Vincent*[162]:

'It would seem that a good deal of legal "know-how" is required for the successful drafting of a restraint clause.'

---

155 It was felt in *SW Strange Ltd v Mann* [1965] 1 All ER 1069, [1965] 1 WLR 629, that a bookmaker's clerk built up no real contact with clients as business was largely conducted on the telephone.
156 [1956] 3 All ER 814, [1957] 1 WLR 9, CA.
157 [1933] Ch 935, CA.
158 [1964] 2 All ER 10, [1964] 1 WLR 568, CA.
159 See also the permanent, worldwide restraint on a servant of the royal household, preventing disclosure of any personal information on the royal family in *A-G v Barker* [1990] 3 All ER 257, CA.
160 [1965] 1 QB 623, [1964] 3 All ER 546, CA; other grounds of invalidity were that the clause covered work in the whole field of PVC not just that part which was secret, and it applied to any employment not just research. On the importance of geographical area, see also *Greer v Sketchley Ltd* [1979] IRLR 445, CA; and *Marley Tile Co Ltd v Johnson* [1982] IRLR 75, CA. A longer period is more likely to be reasonable in the case of a non-solicitation of customers' clause than a non-competition clause: *Dentmaster (UK) Ltd v Kent* [1997] IRLR 636, CA (citing *Office Angels Ltd v Rainer-Thomas and O'Connor* [1991] IRLR 214, CA). The judgment of Slade LJ in *Office Angels* is now often cited as a good summary of the basic law.
161 [1921] 2 AC 158, HL.
162 [1965] 1 QB 623 at 647, [1964] 3 All ER 546 at 555; though cf. the possible qualification in section (v) below.

(v) Enforcement

In looking to see if a restraint agreement is valid and enforceable, the court is entitled to look at the realities and effect of any stipulation so that, for example, an employer may not disguise a restraint clause by providing that the employee is at liberty to solicit any customers but must pay a premium or commission for any of the employer's customers solicited[163]. Moreover, this point is reinforced by the fact that restraint of trade as a doctrine is not confined to bilateral contracts involving the party concerned[164], and for present purposes the significance of this is that two or more employers cannot evade the doctrine by agreeing between themselves to do that which if done between each one of them and his employees would be void. The facts of *Kores v Kolok*[165] are set out above under head (iii); the indirect restraint there, which would clearly have been invalid if put directly into the contracts of employment of the individual employees affected, was held to be void, thus increasing the legal protection given to the employee. However, the question then arose whether the employee could himself challenge such an agreement, for the agreement in *Kores v Kolok* had in fact lasted for 23 years and was only finally challenged because one of the parties became dissatisfied with it. In *Eastham v Newcastle United Football Club Ltd*[166], a case concerning the 'retain and transfer' system whereby the restrictive agreement between the club and the Football Association and League could have a major effect on the livelihood of the individual players, Wilberforce J held that the individual does in fact have the right to challenge such an agreement even though he is not a party to it, and this was accepted as correct by Lord Upjohn in *Pharmaceutical Society of Great Britain v Dickson*[167].

If the restraint clause is void, it cannot be enforced by the employer, but there are two ways in which a court might be able to save a clause even if it is prima facie void. The first is that, although such a clause must normally be construed strictly, it may be the case that the potential invalidity arises from an ambiguity in the wording which, read one way, could mean that the restraint is too wide; if however, it is possible to read the clause realistically in the sense in which the parties obviously meant it, and in that sense it is valid, the court may feel able so to validate it. In *Home Counties Dairies Ltd v Skilton*[168] the agreement was not to 'serve or sell milk or dairy products' and it was pointed out that taken literally this could stop the ex-employee from working in a grocer's shop as well as in the capacity of milkman, and was therefore void for being too wide, but the Court of Appeal held that the true meaning, in the light of the intention of the parties at the time of entering the agreement, was only to restrain future employment as a milkman, and as such the clause was valid. Likewise in *Marion White Ltd v Francis*[169] it was held that a clause restraining employment in the hairdressing business 'in any way' which could conceivably have prevented the ex-hairdresser from working as, for example, a receptionist or book-keeper, in fact was intended by the parties to

---

163 *Stenhouse Australia Ltd v Phillips* [1974] AC 391, [1974] 1 All ER 117, PC.
164 See, eg, *Nagle v Feilden* [1966] 2 QB 633, [1966] 1 All ER 689, CA, and *Edwards v Society of Graphical and Allied Trades* [1971] Ch 354, [1970] 3 All ER 689, CA.
165 [1959] Ch 108, [1958] 2 All ER 65, CA; see also *Mineral Water Bottle Exchange and Trade Protection Society v Booth* (1887) 36 Ch D 465, CA.
166 [1964] Ch 413, [1963] 3 All ER 139, HC of A.
167 [1970] AC 403 at 433, [1968] 2 All ER 686 at 701, HL.
168 [1970] 1 All ER 1227, [1970] 1 WLR 526, CA.
169 [1972] 3 All ER 857, [1972] 1 WLR 1423, CA.

refer only to actual hairdressing and as such was narrow enough to be valid. This power of construction was applied quite liberally by the majority of the Court of Appeal in *Littlewoods Organisation Ltd v Harris*[170] (in which Lord Denning MR suggested that the restraint clause in *Commercial Plastics Ltd v Vincent*[171] which the court had regretfully held to be too wide might have been validated in this way), but was treated much more circumspectly by a subsequent Court of Appeal in *J A Mont (UK) Ltd v Mills*[172] on the grounds that otherwise an employer would have little incentive to phrase covenants in appropriately restricted terms in the first place; clearly the matter is one of balance.

The second possible way to validate a potentially void clause is if the offending part may be severed, leaving the valid remainder capable of enforcement. The concept of severance is a difficult one best dealt with in detail elsewhere[173]. Suffice it to say that where a contract in restraint of trade contains some stipulations which are void and some which by themselves would be valid, it may be possible to sever the void ones and enforce the valid ones. However, the court will not rewrite the contract, and may only be prepared to sever where each stipulation is distinct in itself. In *Mason v Provident Clothing and Supply Co Ltd*[174] Lord Moulton said:

> 'It would in my opinion be pessimi exempli if when an employer had exacted a covenant deliberately framed in unreasonably wide terms, the courts were to come to his assistance and by applying their ingenuity and knowledge of the law, carve out of this void covenant the maximum of what he might validly have required.'

From this it has been argued that the courts should be less willing to sever in an employer-employee restraint case, but any such general principle was disapproved by the Court of Appeal in *T Lucas & Co Ltd v Mitchell*[175] where severance of words within a clause was allowed and the valid part of the restraint enforced.

If the restraint clause is held to be valid (either generally or via one of the above validation methods) it may be enforced against the employee, subject to the caveat that if the employer is in fact in breach of the contract of employment, for example by wrongfully dismissing the employee, he loses the benefit of any

---

170 [1978] 1 All ER 1026, CA.
171 [1965] 1 QB 623, [1964] 3 All ER 546, CA.
172 [1993] IRLR 172, CA.
173 Contrast *Attwood v Lamont* [1920] 3 KB 571, CA with *Goldsoll v Goldman* [1915] 1 Ch 292, CA.
174 [1913] AC 724 at 745, HL.
175 [1974] Ch 129, [1972] 3 All ER 689, CA; see also *Sadler v Imperial Life Assurance Co of Canada Ltd* [1988] IRLR 388 and *Scully UK Ltd v Lee* [1998] IRLR 259, CA. Severance was allowed with little difficulty in *Stenhouse Australia Ltd v Phillips* [1974] AC 391, [1974] 1 All ER 117, PC, where the relevant stipulations were not only separate in content but also expressed in separate clauses in the agreement, and in *Hinton & Higgs (UK) Ltd v Murphy* [1989] IRLR 519, Ct of Sess, where the contract itself contained a clause inviting severance if any particular restriction was held to be too wide, though the validity of the latter point was later doubted in *Living Design (Home Improvements) Ltd v Davidson* [1994] IRLR 69, Ct of Sess. In *Marshall v NM Financial Management Ltd* [1997] ICR 1065, [1997] IRLR 449, CA severance was allowed at the request of the *employee* in order for him to rely on a linked clause in his favour.

restraint clauses contained in it[176]. Provided this is not so, the employer may sue the employee for damages (and indeed either party may seek a declaration on the validity of the clause in question)[177]; in practice, however, the real importance of the action to the employer is that he may seek an injunction to restrain the employee from acting in breach of the clause, and in an urgent case may be granted an interlocutory injunction (provided he can show that he will suffer immediate loss, so that the 'balance of advantage' lies in his favour, within the principles in *American Cyanamid Co v Ethicon Ltd*[178]). Normally, the court will not grant an injunction to enforce a contract of employment on the basis that it is a personal contract not amenable to such enforcement[179]; one longstanding exception to this, however, is the rule in *Lumley v Wagner*[180] that the courts will enforce a valid negative restraint clause, provided that to do so will not have the effect of specifically enforcing the actual contract. This will normally mean that an injunction *will* lie for breach of a restraint clause[181], but in an untypical case an

176 *General Billposting Co v Atkinson* [1909] AC 118, HL; *Spafax Ltd v Harrison* [1980] IRLR 442, CA; *Rex Stewart Jeffries Parker Ginsberg Ltd v Parker* [1988] IRLR 483, CA; *Briggs v Oates* [1990] ICR 473, [1990] IRLR 472; *Cantor Fitzgerald International v Bird* [2002] IRLR 867 (where it was reaffirmed that repudiatory breach of the term of trust and respect short of dismisal could justify the employee in leaving and claiming to be free of the restraint clause). In *Rock Refrigeration Ltd v Jones* [1997] 1 All ER 1, [1997] ICR 938, the Court of Appeal held that this still applies even if the employer has stated that the clause is to apply on termination 'however caused'; possibly significantly there are dicta in the case that they only so held because bound by *General Billposting*, not because they agreed with the principle. For an argument that *General Billposting* is too sweeping and that decisions here should be more responsive to the justice of the case, see Freedland (2003) 32 ILJ 48. One open question is whether it would apply to a dismissal which was not a breach of contract by the employer (ie with proper notice, therefore not wrongful) but which was later held to have been *unfair* by an employment tribunal; from a strictly contractual view, unfairness under the statute would have no effect on the restrictive covenants which would remain enforceable by the employer against the unfairly dismissed employee. It might be thought equally unjust that a (probably fair) dismissal for *redundancy* does not terminate a restraint clause, for here by definition the employer has no further need for the employee's skills, but the latter could still be restrained from using them to earn his living.
177 Even if the period of restraint is already over, provided the applicant can prove that he still has a worthwhile interest in pursuing it (eg where an employer has other employees who are subject to the same clause): *Marion White Ltd v Francis* [1972] 3 All ER 857, [1972] 1 WLR 1423, CA.
178 [1975] AC 396, [1975] 1 All ER 504, HL; there was disagreement in the Court of Appeal as to whether these principles apply to a restraint of trade case in *Fellowes & Son v Fisher* [1976] QB 122, [1975] 2 All ER 829, CA, the majority applying the 'balance of convenience' principle and Lord Denning MR declaring that the case came within an exception to the new rules, whereby the court could apply the old principles and look at the relative strength of each party's case; in *Lawrence David Ltd v Ashton* [1991] 1 All ER 385, [1989] ICR 123 the Court of Appeal affirmed that *American Cyanamid* normally does apply to restraint cases, but in *Lansing Linde Ltd v Kerr* [1991] ICR 428, [1991] IRLR 80, CA, an exception was established where full trial is not likely to occur quickly enough. The requirement of showing real harm (not just breach of a reasonable restraint) where the application is interlocutory was stressed by Lord Johnston in *Jack Allen (Sales & Service) Ltd v Smith* [1999] IRLR 19, OH.
179 *Whitwood Chemical Co v Hardman* [1891] 2 Ch 416; CA; cf *Hill v CA Parsons & Co Ltd* [1972] Ch 305, [1971] 3 All ER 1345, CA. S 236 of the Trade Union and Labour Relations (Consolidation) Act 1992 provides that no injunction may be granted compelling an employee to work. See ch 7 below on remedies for wrongful dismissal.
180 (1852) 1 De GM & G 604, 42 ER 687; see also *Warner Bros Pictures Inc v Nelson* [1937] 1 KB 209.
181 Normally, damages will not be considered a sufficient remedy instead; likewise, an injunction should not normally be refused on the ground that the defendant is willing to undertake not to use the trade secrets, etc until final judgment: *Johnson & Bloy (Holdings) Ltd v Wolstenholme Rink plc* [1987] IRLR 499, CA (a case on the duty of confidentiality generally, but the principles should apply to a restraint of trade clause case).

injunction could be refused as in *Page One Records Ltd v Britton*[182] where the dismissed manager of a pop group, The Troggs, sought to enforce a clause in their agreement that they would not engage any other person or firm as manager during a five-year period and would not act as such themselves; Stamp J held that, as they had to have a manager in order to operate, to enforce the clause would be to force them to employ him, and so no injunction could be granted.

It can be seen from this discussion that restraint clauses are not simple, either in their framing or in their enforcement, especially as they tend to operate on an 'all or nothing' basis. It is probably this that has led to the search for other, more reliable, ways to safeguard the employer's confidences when an employee leaves the employment. One way that has attracted interest is the 'garden leave' clause, which operates on the basis of a very long notice requirement, during which the employee is paid in full (even though not actually working), but with an express obligation on the employee not to work for anyone else during the notice period. Such clauses may be more certain (though more expensive) than restraint clauses and are considered at p 464, below.

5 TERMS OF THE CONTRACT OF EMPLOYMENT

(i) Express terms

While the employer and employee are generally free to determine the content of the terms of employment, there are now legislative provisions in Part I of the Employment Rights Act 1996 requiring the employer to give written notice of certain basic terms. These provisions were considered above in head 3 of this chapter, where it was seen that while this notice does not itself constitute the contract it will be strong evidence as to its terms and indeed if it is signed as such by the employee it may be construed as the written contract, according to *Gascol Conversions Ltd v Mercer*[183]. For present purposes, the importance of these provisions is that they require that major terms be put down in writing and probably encourage the employer to give the employee an individual written contract of employment; as with all contracts, written terms are generally to be preferred for the certainty that they bring[184], and the legislation attempts to minimise the incidence of 'factory gate employment' where an employee was taken on without having the relevant terms settled, leaving potentially important matters to later decision by the courts. Certainty, however, can work both ways, and if the parties set something down in writing they should ensure that it is accurate, for once it is expressed there is less room for further extrinsic evidence as to their intentions. As an example of this, in *Nelson v BBC*[185] the contract stated that the employee could be

---

182 [1967] 3 All ER 822, [1968] 1 WLR 157; *Warren v Mendy* [1989] ICR 525, [1989] IRLR 210, CA.
183 [1974] ICR 420, [1974] IRLR 155, CA; see p 112 above.
184 For a particularly salutary example, see *Stubbes v Trower, Still & Keeling* [1987] IRLR 321, CA where solicitors, in offering articles, omitted to state expressly that the applicant had to pass the requisite examinations before beginning, and the Court of Appeal refused to find that there was an implied term to that effect on the facts; in the words of one commentator, you cannot always rely on common sense and implied terms to rectify a contractual oversight.
185 [1977] ICR 649, [1977] IRLR 148, CA; see the discussion of this case in *Cowen v Haden Ltd* [1983] ICR 1, [1982] IRLR 314, CA which shows the importance of the proper construction to be placed upon the express term in question.

required to work when and where the corporation demanded, but when the corporation closed down the Caribbean service in which he worked, they claimed that it was to be implied that he was only employed for the purposes of that one service and therefore that he was redundant; the tribunal and the EAT accepted this, but the Court of Appeal rejected it, since the express term was in unrestricted language, and as a basic principle of contract law it was impossible to imply a restriction of the kind that the tribunal had found. On the other hand, even in contract law there are exceptions to the rule against extrinsic evidence, particularly where a written contract does not completely cover all the matters upon which the parties had previously agreed. Thus, in *Tayside Regional Council v McIntosh*[186] a job advertisement for a vehicle mechanic stated that a clean driving licence was essential and this was restated at interview. When later the employee lost his licence and was dismissed, he pointed to the fact the written terms which he had been given upon appointment made no mention of a driving licence, but the Scottish EAT refused to accept that that meant there was no express term as to a licence. The basic distinction between these two case examples (out of many) is that in the latter extrinsic evidence was being properly used to amplify a written agreement which was incomplete, whereas in the former it was being used improperly to alter the meaning of an existing written term.

Three current uncertainties relating to express terms of contracts of employment are worth mentioning at this stage. The first is whether there is any requirement that an express contractual right for an employer (however clearly expressed) must be *exercised* reasonably. The traditional view is that there can be no such requirement; a contract is a contract, and if the employee agrees a term he must abide by it, even if its application by the employer seems harsh (eg where an employer activates an unrestricted mobility clause to require an employee to move hundreds of miles with little or no warning)[187]. However, recent case law has suggested a significant modification of that position and this is considered below at p 141; if this trend continues, it will be of major importance and marks another departure of contracts of employment from orthodox contract law.

The second uncertainty is whether an employer can, in effect, try to pre-empt any attempts by the employee to add to the written terms by casting the employment contract in terms of an 'entire contract'.[188] In the leading case on this developing area of contract law generally, Lightman J put it thus:

'The purpose of an entire agreement clause is to preclude a party to a written agreement from threshing through the undergrowth and finding, in the course of negotiations, some (chance) remark or statement (often long-forgotten or difficult to recall or explain) upon which to found a claim, such as the present, to the existence of a collateral warranty. The entire agreement clause obviates the occasion for any such search . . . For such a clause constitutes a binding agreement between the parties that the full contractual terms are to be found in the document containing the

---

186 [1982] IRLR 272. This is consistent with the view expressed by Lord Hoffmann in *Carmichael v National Power plc* [1999] ICR 1226, [2000] IRLR 43, HL that it may be necessary to look to several sources to discern the whole contract of employment.

187 *Rank Xerox Ltd v Churchill* [1988] IRLR 280.

188 One form of this would be a clause stating to the effect that 'This agreement constitutes the entire agreement between us with regard to its subject matter, and supersedes any previous agreement (whether verbal or written) made between us at any time'.

clause and not elsewhere, and that, accordingly, any promises or assurances made in the course of the negotiations (which, in the absence of such a clause, might have effect as a collateral warranty) shall have no contractual force, save in so far as they are reflected and given effect in the document'.[189]

Should this development in commercial contracts law apply equally to employment contracts? There is an argument that it should not; commercial contracts are *expected* to be certain and preferably reduced to clear written terms (hence the general dislike of implied terms in ordinary contract law, see below) whereas an employment relationship is likely to be far more amorphous, easily entered and possibly rapidly evolving. An entire contract clause could lead in practice to an even greater danger of the contract terms and employment realities diverging radically than is already inherent in our present contract-based law on employment. However, the little authority that currently exists does not support this argument. In *White v Bristol Rugby Club Ltd*[190] a professional rugby player signed up by a club under a contract which provided for an advance on earnings tried to avoid going through with the engagement by arguing that if he returned the advance he was free to go elsewhere. His primary argument was that there was an oral express term to that effect, arising from discussions that he had had before signing the contract with the club's chief executive. The contract, however, contained an entire agreement clause, stating that the contract contained the whole agreement and that the parties had not relied on any oral or written representations made by other persons[191]. The judge held that this clause was applicable and, as a matter purely of construction, covered the circumstances here, so that no oral term could arise. This forced the employee back on to arguments relating to the terms of the contract *as they stood*, and whether under these he had a right not to go through with the engagement; it was held that he did not. In *Fontana (GB) Ltd v Fabio*[192] a general manager's contract made no reference to any right to pension contributions (in fact it contained a clause stating that there were to be none) but the manager said that there had been on oral agreement to such a right. When later dismissed, he claimed arrears of pension contributions alongside an unfair dismissal claim. The contract contained a clause stating that it *substituted* previous agreements and arrangements, whether written, oral or implied. Did this preclude his claim? The EAT held that it did not; they accepted that an entire contract clause can apply to an employment contract but, applying *White v Bristol Rugby Club Ltd*, held that as a matter of construction this particular clause was not strong enough to preclude this claim because it did not expressly claim that the contract contained all the terms[193]. The result therefore seems to be that a court or tribunal will have to apply an *unambiguous* entire contract clause which clearly covers the facts in

---

189 *Intrepreneur Pub Co v East Crown Ltd* [2000] 3 EGLR 31 at 33.
190 [2002] IRLR 204, QBD.
191 There is some discussion in the judgment (at paras 30–35) as to whether the latter half of the clause (no reliance) could be subject to the Misrepresentation Act 1967, s 3 which subjects a clause of a contract excluding or restricting liability for misrepresentation to the reasonableness test that applies under the Unfair Contract Terms Act 1977. The relationship between s 3 and an entire agreement clause remains subject to conflicting authority, as the judge here did not have to decide the issue because the first half of the clause was effective anyway.
192 (July 2002, unreported), EAT; see Employment Lawyer No 94 (September 2002).
193 In fact the claimant employee still lost because, although a collateral warranty was in law possible, on the facts the alleged agreement was too vague to constitute one.

question. Presumably, such a clause is to be construed strictly; indeed as a matter of policy it should be construed particularly strictly in an employment case. Where one applies, it would have a strongly dampening effect on any later arguments based on custom and practice, and instead of using collateral warranty arguments the party trying to 'add' to the written contract would be forced back on to other arguments, such as that the representations claimed to have been made are relevant to construing written clauses in the contract (difficult in *Fontana* because the written clause said there was *no* entitlement to pension contributions) or that there had been a legally-valid *variation* of the original agreement (difficult in a case where it is a *pre*-contractual representation that is being relied upon). Clearly, both parties will have to be careful what they sign if the agreement contains one of these clauses[194]. To the extent that they are used in specifically negotiated contracts for the engagement of higher and/or key employees, this may be fair enough, but if it were ever to be the case that they were being put into many, far more standard, contracts as a matter of course (where they could cause many more difficulties and potential injustices) the employment-related courts and tribunals might have to look at them afresh in this context, with a more critical eye[195].

The third uncertainty concerns the extent to which an employer may use express terms to reserve to himself a right of unilateral variation. Flexibility in employment has been a nostrum of modern managerialism for some time now, and there will certainly be cases where an employer can lawfully claim to have carefully built in flexibility and an ability to change a particular term or, alternatively, that the matter has been so drafted as to remain non-contractual (so that change remains in the employer's discretion[196]). The question is whether a point could be reached where such phrasing became so unconscionable and vague as to be unenforceable; the contractual doctrine of uncertainty would be inappropriate in an employment context because it would render the whole contract void (to the employee's disadvantage), and so far this point has not had to be explored by the courts. The nearest that they have come is in *Wandsworth London Borough Council v D'Silva*[197] where, after upholding the employer's contention that a sickness absence policy in a code of practice remained non-contractual and so within the employer's power to change, Lord Woolf MR said obiter that, although a party to the contract could reserve a right of unilateral variation, it would take clear language to do it and a court should, in construing the contract, try to avoid a construction allowing a power of unilateral variation of significant employee rights which could produce an unreasonable result. Whether a court could go further in the case of an absolutely clearly drafted power of unilateral variation that was equally clearly inequitable in its result remains to be seen.

---

194 Normally, it will be the employee who stands to lose, but it could be the employer – on the facts of *Tayside Regional Council v McIntosh*, n 186 above, if there had been an entire agreement clause the employer would have had difficulty relying on the requirement of a clean driving licence which had only been mentioned in the job advertisement.

195 If the effect of such a clause was ever to threaten an employee's *statutory* rights, it might be attacked as an attempt to contract out of the protection of the statute, which might be void; see particularly the Employment Rights Act 1996, s 203(1).

196 *Airlie v City of Edinburgh District Council* [1996] IRLR 516, EAT (terms of a bonus scheme expressly subject to variation by employer after consultation with the workforce; no requirement of agreement before revision, provided consultation carried out).

197 [1998] IRLR 193, CA. See Smith and Randall *Contract Actions in Modern Employment Law – Developments and Issues* (2002) pp 41–43.

(ii) The implication of terms

(a) The process of implication

Even when the statutory provisions for written particulars are complied with, there will be areas left in a contract of employment where no terms are expressed, so that if a dispute arises in one of these areas the court or tribunal may have to have recourse to implied terms. The implication of terms is a concept of application to the whole law of contract, but in the context of employment it has evolved along more specialised lines. Starting from orthodox contract theory1, the basis of implication is subjective, in that the court or tribunal should look at the likely intention of the parties at the time of contracting, and should not imply terms simply because they appear (objectively) reasonable when the case is viewed in hindsight[198]. The two classic tests for an implied term are (i) that it is necessary to give 'business efficacy' to the transaction as must have been intended by both parties[199], or (ii) that it is so obvious that it goes without saying, so that if an officious bystander had suggested that it be expressed the parties would have testily suppressed him with a common 'Oh, of course!'[200]. Moreover, it has been clearly stated that the presumption is against the adding to contracts of terms which the parties have not expressed, particularly if the term in question is of a novel nature[201]. This traditional view of implied terms has, however, been considerably modified in the case of contracts of employment where, particularly before the Contracts of Employment Act 1963, so many terms (often the basic ones) were not expressed and where the process of implication has been much used to fill in the details once it was clear that an employment relationship existed[202]. It has been modified in three main ways:

(1) Inferred terms

Although cases will of course arise where courts find implied terms on the above traditional grounds[203], there are also cases where they appear to have been more willing to imply terms because they appear reasonable in all the circumstances, rather than because of the supposed subjective intention of the parties, which, in

---

198 *Reigate v Union Manufacturing Co (Ramsbottom) Ltd* [1918] 1 KB 592 at 605, CA, per Scrutton LJ.

199 *The Moorcock* (1889) 14 PD 64 at 68, CA per Bowen LJ.

200 *Shirlaw v Southern Foundries Ltd* [1939] 2 KB 206 at 227, CA, per McKinnon LJ; see *Spring v National Amalgamated Stevedores and Dockers Society* [1956] 2 All ER 221, [1956] 1 WLR 585.

201 *Luxor (Eastbourne) Ltd v Cooper* [1941] AC 108 at 137, HL per Lord Wright.

202 Certainty of terms is classically a prerequisite for a binding contract, but this too has been qualified almost to the point of extinction in contracts of employment: see *Powell v Braun* [1954] 1 All ER 484, [1954] 1 WLR 401, CA; and *National Coal Board v Galley* [1958] 1 All ER 91, [1958] 1 WLR 16, CA. The problem is that the result of applying it could be to make the whole contract of employment void (regardless of how long the employee had actually been working for the employer), which is simply not an option in employment law. On the other hand, the doctrine of certainty might apply to one particular aspect or term of the contract, where the rest of the agreement is not in issue: see *Fontana (GB) Ltd v Fabio*, nn 192 and 193 above.

203 See eg *Ali v Christian Salvesen Food Services Ltd* [1997] ICR 25, [1997] IRLR 17, CA, where the question was whether it was possible to imply a term into an 'annualised hours' contract as to what was to happen to an employee leaving part of the way through the year, the parties having failed to cover the point expressly. The EAT thought it was, but the Court of Appeal held to the contrary and the loss lay where it fell.

the reality of a vague hiring, may have been non-existent. There is still a large role for the genuine factual implied term but in this context the court or tribunal may feel more ready to imply, or, more accurately perhaps, infer, a term because it seems reasonable in all the circumstances. This more objective approach can clearly be seen in the reasoning of the Court of Appeal in *Mears v Safecar Security Ltd*[204]. The case primarily concerned a complaint of failure to give the obligatory written statement of terms of employment, and the question of whether wages are to be paid during sickness[205], but (although certain rather extreme dicta that ultimately a tribunal may have to 'invent' a term were later disapproved[206]) it also contains important guidance on the implication of terms into contracts of employment, showing that in the case of such contracts the normal concepts of implied intention of the parties and business efficacy may have little part to play. Instead, a tribunal may have to take a broader approach and be ready to insert a reasonable term based on all the evidence of the relationship between the parties *and* what had happened in practice *since* the employment began (particularly where it is important that *some* term be included, eg whether or not such pay is payable, or where the employee could be made to work[207]). It is true that this case arose under the Employment Rights Act 1996, s 11, and much of what is said about implying terms is inextricably linked to the court's approach to the tribunal's powers to declare or amend terms of employment under that section, but it is submitted that their approach to the implication of terms should be applicable to a common law action as well as a statutory one – it would be ridiculous if different principles were to apply depending on which forum the employee happened to choose; after all, on the facts of the case, the employee could just as easily have gone to the county court and *claimed* sick pay. The same approach can be seen in the later decision of the Court of Appeal in *Courtaulds Northern Spinning Ltd v Sibson*[208] where, in the context of the necessary implication into a contract of employment of a location/mobility clause (where the contract was silent on the matter, but the question was vital for deciding a point on constructive dismissal) Slade LJ said:

> '… [I]n cases such as the present where it is essential to imply some term into the contract of employment as to place of work, the court does not have to be satisfied that the parties, if asked, would in fact have agreed the term before entering into the contract. The court merely has to be satisfied that the implied term is one which the parties would probably have agreed *if they were being reasonable*'. (emphasis added)

(2) Imposed terms

The contract of employment has long been surrounded not only by terms implied or inferred from the facts of any given employment, but also by a quite distinct form of 'implied term', namely the term which will be imposed by the law on to most or all contracts of employment simply because the relationship of employment exists (except in so far as the parties are free to exclude it expressly and do so), which once again has little to do with any supposed intention of the parties. In *Lister v Romford Ice and Cold Storage Co Ltd*[209] Viscount Simonds said that the question

---

204 [1982] 2 All ER 865, [1982] IRLR 183, CA.
205 See p 117 above and p 221 below.
206 *Eagland v British Telecommunications plc* [1993] ICR 644, [1992] IRLR 323, CA.
207 See the facts of *Jones v Associated Tunnelling Co Ltd* [1981] IRLR 477.
208 [1988] ICR 451, [1988] IRLR 305, CA; the dictum cited is at 460 and 309, respectively.
209 [1957] AC 555, [1957] 1 All ER 125, HL.

whether there was an implied term that the employer would ensure that the employee was insured had little to do with the facts of a particular contract or any question of business efficacy, but depended instead on more general considerations relating to the very nature of contracts of employment. This approach is clearly seen in the following two dicta. In *Sterling Engineering Co Ltd v Patchett*[210] Lord Reid said:

> 'There are cases in which it has been said that the employer's right to inventions made by an employee in the course of his employment arises from an implied term in the contract of employment. Strictly speaking, I think that an implied term is something which, in the circumstances of a particular case, the law may read into the contract if the parties are silent, and it would be reasonable to do so; it is something over and above the ordinary incidents of the particular type of contract. If it were necessary in this case to find an implied term in that sense I should be in some difficulty. But the phrase "implied term" can be used to denote a term inherent in the nature of the contract which the Law will imply in every case unless the parties agree to vary or exclude it.'

In *Scally v Southern Health and Social Services Board*[211] Lord Bridge referred to the clear distinction between

> '... the search for an implied term necessary to give business efficacy to a particular contract and the search, based on wider considerations, for a term which the law will imply as a necessary incident of a definable category of contractual relationship'.

In *Malik v BCCI SA (in liquidation)*[212] Lord Steyn referred to such terms as 'default rules' which are standardised terms which are incidents of all contracts of employment.

It is this form of 'implied term' that will be discussed below under the headings of Employer's Duties and Employee's Duties, and it could well be argued that the phrase 'implied term' should be discarded, and these duties viewed simply as incidents of the Law of Employment.

(3) Overriding terms

One of the most interesting recent developments in this area is the possible development of the concept of 'overriding terms' in a contract of employment, ie that certain terms may be so important that they will be applied by the courts irrespective of the parties' intentions[213]. This would have the radical effect that

---

210 [1955] AC 534 at 547, [1955] 1 All ER 369 at 376, HL.
211 [1991] ICR 771, [1991] IRLR 522, HL; the decision in this case is considered at p 163 below.
212 [1997] ICR 606, [1997] IRLR 462, HL; the decision in this case is considered at p 160 below.
213 This would mark them off from the above discussion of imposed terms, since the latter (as in the above dictum from Lord Reid) are conceived of applying 'unless the parties agree to vary or exclude them'; see also per Lord Steyn in *Malik v BCCI*, n 212 above. For an interesting argument that the courts should go even further and hold that the employment relationship gives rise to *fiduciary* duties (which could not be excluded), see Clarke 'Mutual trust and confidence, fiduciary relationships and the duty of disclosure' (1999) 28 ILJ 348. The current judicial approach, however, is entirely to the contrary, finding no fiduciary duties in an ordinary employment relationship: *Nottingham University v Fishel* [2000] ICR 1462, [2000] IRLR 471: see Sims (2001) 30 ILJ 101.

they could even be used to qualify or attack clear express terms of the contract, something that in orthodox contract law no 'implied' term should be able to do. The prime candidate for beatification as an overriding term is the implied term of trust and respect[214] which, if applied widely, could be seen as having the effect that even where an employer has the contractual right to insist on something, he must do so *reasonably*. If not, the employee would be able to leave and claim constructive dismissal, through the employer's breach of that implied term. Perhaps the clearest example is an unrestricted mobility clause. Can the employer simply insist on the literal wording and require the employee to move his place of work from Norwich to Carlisle over a weekend and with no prior warning, or can the employee claim that that insistence (though technically within the employer's contractual power) is in breach of the term of trust and respect on the facts? Orthodox contract law is, of course, on the employer's side[215], but there have been developments. Where there is no express mobility clause and a court is having to imply one, there may be less problem in attaching implied conditions such as reasonable notice[216]. However, what may eventually prove to have been the crucial step was taken by the EAT in *United Bank Ltd v Akhtar*[217], where there was an express clause allowing the employer to move the employee to any branch in the UK. In spite of that, the EAT held that the employee could claim constructive dismissal when the employer ordered him to move from Leeds to Birmingham on only six days' notice and refused to grant his request for more time because of his personal circumstances. As well as finding an implied term of reasonable notice, the EAT held even more fundamentally that the employers' conduct in exercising their contractual rights was a fundamental breach of the implied term of trust and respect:

'... we take it as inherent that there may well be conduct which is either calculated or likely to destroy or seriously damage the relationship of trust and respect between employer and employee which a literal interpretation of the written words of the contract might appear to justify, and it is in this sense that we consider that in the field of employment law it is proper to imply an *overriding obligation* [of trust and respect] which is independent of, and in addition to, the literal interpretation of the actions which are permitted to the employer under the terms of the contract'[218]. (emphasis added)

At first sight, the subsequent EAT decision in *White v Reflecting Roadstuds Ltd*[219] may appear to resile from *Akhtar*, for it was held that an employee who resigned

---

214 See p 158 below.
215 This straightforward approach was applied as late as *Rank Xerox Ltd v Churchill* [1988] IRLR 280.
216 *Prestwick Circuits Ltd v McAndrew* [1990] IRLR 191, Ct of Sess; however, the Court of Appeal had earlier declined to add any 'reasonable exercise' conditions to an implied mobility clause in *Courtaulds Northern Spinning Ltd v Sibson* [1988] IRLR 305, CA.
217 [1989] IRLR 507. See also *French v Barclays Bank plc* [1998] IRLR 646, CA where the termination of an interest-free bridging loan to a relocated employee when it became too onerous was held to be in breach of the term of trust and respect, even though the granting of such a loan was clearly expressed to be discretionary.
218 At 512, per Knox J. There was an unreported tribunal decision in Cambridge in 1990 where an employee was dismissed for refusing to work 12 hours per day, seven days per week, for nine weeks; the employer had the power to require this under the strict terms of the contract, but the tribunal held that to do so was unreasonable, and the dismissal was unfair, on similar reasoning: see Earnshaw [1992] NLJ 1011.
219 [1991] ICR 733, [1991] IRLR 331.

after a transfer on to a lower-paid job which was permitted by the contract could not claim constructive dismissal. However, it is suggested that that was because the employee argued simply that a contractual right such as this must always be exercised reasonably; this was too much to accept and Wood P said that *Akhtar* does not establish any such sweeping principle. However, at the end of his judgment, he recognised that there was a problem with unconscionable action by an employer and offered the following solutions:

> 'As Knox J emphasised in *Akhtar* a purely "capricious" decision would not be within the express mobility clause. Likewise, in the present case if there were no reasonable or sufficient grounds for the view that Mr White required to be moved ... then there would be a breach of the clause. Secondly, it must be emphasised that as a result of the *Woods* decision[220] there is the *overriding implied term* as to the relationship of trust and respect between employer and employee and this is where communication is so important.'[221] (emphasis added)

The implication must therefore be that in a case such as this the employee may have a good argument if it is couched properly (in terms of the term of trust and respect, *not* simply as a general allegation of unreasonableness), and that *White* does not negate *Akhtar*.[222]

In addition to mobility and flexibility clauses, similar ideas of the use of the overriding term of trust and respect to qualify or restrain reliance by an employer on his strict contractual rights have been seen in relation to the imposition of disciplinary measures[223], the exercise of a power to suspend an employee[224] and (most strikingly of all) in the administration of employee pension funds[225].

The other principal candidate so far for an overriding term is the employer's obligation to take care for the employee's health and safety. The leading case, *Johnstone v Bloomsbury Health Authority*[226], shows very different approaches to the matter, which in turn shows well the conceptual difficulties yet to be addressed. This was the highly publicised case of the legal challenge to excessive hours by

---

220 Ie *Woods v WM Car Services (Peterborough) Ltd* [1981] ICR 666, [1981] IRLR 347, the leading decision of Browne-Wilkinson P in the EAT on trust and respect; see p 159 below.

221 [1991] ICR 733 at 742, [1991] IRLR 331 at 335.

222 In the unreported decision in *St Budeaux Royal British Legion Club v Cropper* (EAT 39/94) *Akhtar* was applied to hold that a flexibility clause applied in a 'high-handed and irresponsible manner' by the employer (when cutting hours) was a breach of the term of trust and respect.

223 The idea being that the exercise by an employer of his discretion under a disciplinary procedure must be subject to requirements of reasonableness and proportionality: *BBC v Beckett* [1983] IRLR 43; *Cawley v South Wales Electricity Board* [1985] IRLR 89; *Stanley Cole (Wainfleet) Ltd v Sheridan* [2003] ICR 297, [2003] IRLR 52.

224 *McClory v Post Office* [1992] ICR 758, [1993] IRLR 159. Previously, an express lay-off clause had been held to be subject to an implied limitation to a reasonable period in *Dakri & Co Ltd v Tiffen* [1981] ICR 256, [1981] IRLR 57, but a subsequent EAT had refused to follow this in *Kenneth MacRae Ltd v Dawson* [1984] IRLR 5.

225 *Imperial Group Pension Trust Ltd v Imperial Tobacco Ltd* [1991] ICR 524, [1991] IRLR 66 where Browne-Wilkinson V-C (applying his own previous decision in *Woods v WM Car Services (Peterborough) Ltd* [1981] ICR 666, [1981] IRLR 347) held that the black and white of pension fund deeds and rules should be impliedly subject to the limitation that they must be exercised in good faith and so as not to undermine the employees' trust and respect: see Nobles (1991) 20 ILJ 137.

226 [1991] ICR 269, [1991] IRLR 118, CA; see Dolding and Fawlk (1992) 55 MLR 562.

junior hospital doctors. The doctor plaintiff's contract stated a standard working week of 40 hours, but a further 48 hours on call, which was regularly required, sometimes up to 100 hours per week. He argued that this had a detrimental effect on his health[227] and was a breach of the employer's duty to take reasonable care for his health and safety. The proceedings in fact concerned an interlocutory application by the employers to have the claim struck out, as disclosing no cause of action. By a majority, the Court of Appeal allowed it to proceed. Leggett LJ, dissenting, applied orthodox contract law, stating that reliance on a clear express power could not make the employer in breach of an implied term (ie the traditional primacy of express terms; the doctor had signed the contract and must abide by its clear terms). The problem and fascination of the case is that the two majority judges differed in their reasoning. Browne-Wilkinson V-C took a middle path; he said that the extra 48 hours in question were an 'optional right' for the employers, not an absolute right and, while there must be no blatant conflict between an express term and an implied term, it was not improper to read in a term that, in exercising their *discretion* to call for further hours, the employers had to have regard to the employee's health and safety. However, possibly the more significant judgment for the future is that of Stuart-Smith LJ who held more simply that, although the contract gave the power to require work of up to 88 hours on average, that power had to be exercised subject to other contractual terms, in particular that relating to health and safety. The difference between the two majority judgments would be shown if a contract required a mandatory 88 hours, for Browne-Wilkinson V-C accepted that in that case that express term would have to be allowed to stand, whereas Stuart-Smith LJ would still have been prepared to make it subject to the requirement of health and safety[228].

(b) Particular sources of terms

(1) Collective bargains

Although its use as the primary form of setting terms and conditions of employment has declined markedly in recent years[229], collective bargaining in the past was of central importance, and still is in areas retaining such coverage and yet the precise legal effect of a collective bargain on the contracts of employment of employees potentially affected by it has always been a topic of some difficulty. The bargain is often classified as performing two functions – regulating the relationship between the bargainers, ie employers' association or

---

227 Let alone the prospects for a patient (treated in the hundredth hour) of a long and prosperous life.
228 The judge makes the significant point that even where the contract stipulates high hours, that still only gives the employer a *power* to call for them: 'There is no obligation to require the men to [work] for 88 hours in the week, and if by so doing he exposes him to foreseeable risk of injury he will be liable': [1991] ICR 269 at 277, [1991] IRLR 118 at 121, CA.
229 'The decline in the extent of union recognition naturally fed through into a fall in the proportion of employees covered by collective bargaining. This had shrunk to 54 per cent in 1990 from 71 per cent six years earlier. As most employees outside the scope of the survey [ie those employed by small firms] are almost certainly not covered, it is clear that only a minority of employees in the economy as a whole had their pay jointly determined by management and trade unions': Millward et al 'Workplace industrial relations in transition' (the ED/ESRC/PSI/ACAS Survey) (1992), p 102.

employer and trade union, and settling provisions (for example wage rates and hours) intended for the individual contracts of the employees who are covered. The collective bargain itself is generally not enforceable by the union or employer[230], and, as the individual is a third party not privy to the agreement, it will not generally be directly enforceable by an employee, particularly as the union is not viewed as acting as the employee's agent during negotiations[231]; in *Burton Group Ltd v Smith*[232] the EAT considered that any agency relationship must be capable of inference from the particular facts of the case and does not arise merely from the relationship of union and member. Thus, the employee will only be legally entitled to any parts of a collective bargain which in some way became terms of his individual contract of employment[233].

A term may be incorporated into a contract of employment from a collective bargain either expressly or impliedly. Express implication may come through the parties agreeing in writing that all or part of a particular collective bargain shall be binding upon them, as in *National Coal Board v Galley*[234]. In the past, this fitted in with the statutory requirements for written particulars in Part I of the Employment Rights Act 1996 (see above, under 'Form') which allowed the employer to refer the employee to some other document which the employee has reasonable opportunities of reading, and this 'other document' could well be the relevant parts of the current collective bargain. There may now be less scope for this approach, because the amendments to Part I by the Trade Union Reform and Employment Rights Act 1993 restrict the employer's right to refer to other documents (except in relation to sickness, pensions, and disciplinary notice guidance procedures); on the other hand, there is added to the list of matters to be notified in writing 'any collective agreements which directly affect the terms and conditions of the employment', which could be significant in any argument for the incorporation of terms other than those which now have to be given individually.

In *Marley v Forward Trust Group Ltd*[235] the EAT caused a considerable stir by holding that where a collective bargain was expressed to be binding in honour only, a contractual term purporting to incorporate a provision from the bargain was itself therefore of no legal effect; fortunately, this startling decision was quickly reversed by the Court of Appeal and orthodoxy re-established. However, some care may be needed with this form of incorporation (where it is still viable), for reference to a particular aspect of a collective bargain (for example sickness) does not necessarily incorporate other aspects of it (for example the right to lay off employees) which may need specific incorporation[236], and indeed the parties must be clear which particular collective agreement they are wishing to incorporate, which may not be as simple as it sounds where either there has been

---

230 *Ford Motor Co Ltd v Amalgamated Union of Engineering and Foundry Workers* [1969] 2 QB 303, [1969] 2 All ER 481 (see Selwyn (1969) 32 MLR 377); Trade Union and Labour Relations (Consolidation) Act 1992, s 179; see ch 1 above; *National Coal Board v National Union of Mineworkers* [1986] ICR 736, [1986] IRLR 439.

231 *Holland v London Society of Compositors* (1924) 40 TLR 440; cf *Edwards v Skyways Ltd* [1964] 1 All ER 494, [1964] 1 WLR 349.

232 [1977] IRLR 351.

233 *Hulland v William Sanders & Sons* [1945] KB 78, [1944] 2 All ER 568, CA.

234 [1958] 1 All ER 91, [1958] 1 WLR 16, CA.

235 [1986] ICR 115, [1986] IRLR 43, EAT; revsd [1986] ICR 891, [1986] IRLR 369, CA, applying *Robertson and Jackson v British Gas Corpn* [1983] ICR 351, [1983] IRLR 302, CA.

236 *Jewell v Neptune Concrete Ltd* [1975] IRLR 147, IT; *Cadoux v Central Regional Council* [1986] IRLR 131, Ct of Sess; *Alexander v Standard Telephones and Cables Ltd (No 2)* [1991] IRLR 286.

a series of agreements over a period of time or where there is, at any one time, more than one agreement possibly applicable; the latter possibility could well arise where there is both national and local bargaining within an industry, or where there has been a tendency over time to move the emphasis from national to local bargaining[237]. Moreover, in *Burroughs Machines Ltd v Timmoney*[238] the Court of Session, reversing the EAT, treated a contractual reference to a particular clause in a collective bargain as an independent term of the contract which merely relied on the clause for its exposition and definition, so that the employees continue to be bound by part of the clause that allowed the employer to lay them off in certain relevant circumstances, even though the employer had in fact left the employers' federation which was a party to the collective bargain. In this case the principle of the independent effect of a collective bargain term once incorporated worked to the employee's disadvantage. However, it is equally likely (if not more so) to work to the employer's disadvantage as can be seen from *Robertson and Jackson v British Gas Corpn*[239] where the Court of Appeal held that employees could still claim a bonus which had been incorporated into their contracts even though the collective agreement whence it had originally come had been unilaterally abrogated by the employer. The lesson is clear for an employer wishing to resile from the terms of a collective agreement – it may not be enough just to abrogate the agreement if in fact some of its provisions have been incorporated into individual contracts of employment; he may have to go further and show that those contracts have themselves also been varied (which will principally mean by consent, see p 118, above) to exclude or amend the terms in question.

In the absence of express reference, a tribunal or court may be asked to incorporate a term of a collective bargain by implication, and this may raise difficulties, for if one thing is certain it is that implication is by no means automatic. On a structural level, it cannot be argued that an agreement is incorporated simply because the employer belongs to an employers' association that bargained for that agreement[240]. Further, it must be remembered that vague reliance upon implied terms from collective bargains (whether national or local) cannot oust or qualify clear express terms of a contract of employment covering the matters in question[241]. In *Young v Canadian Northern Rly Co*[242] an employee sued the company for wrongful dismissal on the basis that his dismissal for redundancy was not in accordance with the agreed seniority provisions in a collective bargain; he was not a member of the union, but claimed that the company's practice was to observe the terms of the agreement and apply them to all employees, whether or not

---

237 This problem can be seen on the facts of *Gascol Conversions Ltd v Mercer* [1974] ICR 420, [1974] IRLR 155, CA (see p 112, above). Site level bargaining was taken into account by the EAT in holding a site bonus to be contractually binding in *Donelan v Kerrby Constructions Ltd* [1983] ICR 237, [1983] IRLR 191, noted Freedland (1983) 12 ILJ 256.

238 [1977] IRLR 404.

239 [1983] ICR 351, [1983] IRLR 302, CA. See, to like effect, *Gibbons v Associated British Ports* [1985] IRLR 376. This was taken one stage further in *Whent v T Cartledge Ltd* [1997] IRLR 153 where employees could still claim a wage increase under a local authority collective agreement incorporated into their terms, even after their work was contracted out and they became employed by the private contractor (their incorporated term having been preserved because it was a TUPE transfer).

240 *Hamilton v Futura Floors Ltd* [1990] IRLR 478, OH. There is a similar rule in the law relating to recognition, see p 73 above.

241 *Gascol Conversions Ltd v Mercer*, n 237 above.

242 [1931] AC 83, PC; *Land v West Yorkshire Metropolitan County Council* [1979] ICR 452, [1979] IRLR 174; revsd on other grounds [1981] ICR 334, [1981] IRLR 87, CA.

members of the union. The Privy Council held for the company, refusing to incorporate the necessary collective terms into his contract of employment. They said that he had not shown that the company's implementation of the collective bargain was due to contractual liability, that it was equally explicable on grounds of company policy, and that any remedy for breach, as in this case, was industrial and not legal. It may be argued that this is too strict an approach, making it too difficult to incorporate a collective bargain even in cases where there are no other clear, obvious terms in the contract of employment itself. All that can be said is that each case will depend on its own facts, and that one of the factors that may sway a court or tribunal is whether the clause of the bargain in question is really relevant to the individual circumstances of the employee claiming the benefit of it; if it concerns larger questions relating primarily to industrial relations, such as recognition of one or more unions[243], machinery for resolving collective disputes[244], or longer term policy planning on matters such as retraining or redundancy[245], the court or tribunal might decide that the clause is not to be incorporated into the contracts of the individuals concerned. On the other hand, if the correct inference is that it was envisaged that those conducting the bargaining would be binding those concerned in some relevant matters, the resulting clause might well be incorporated into the individual contracts and so binding, as with the 'no-strike' clause in *Rookes v Barnard*[246]. One of the strongest arguments in favour of incorporation would be custom and practice, evidenced by previous changes in the individual's contract in line with changes in the collective bargain; likewise, the collective bargain may itself be used as evidence of custom and practice within an industry where for some reason it becomes necessary to decide on such matters[247]. In *Henry v London General Transport Services Ltd*[248] (a relatively rare recent case on this point) a management buy-out involved negotiations with a recognised trade union leading to a 'framework agreement' worsening certain terms and conditions as a cost of retaining jobs. In the past, the company had negotiated annually with the union and changes in terms (beneficial or not) had always ensued from this, though the contracts were silent on the matter. When, two years later, 94 of the employees brought claims for unlawful deductions for wages on the basis that the new terms had never been incorporated into their contracts the Court of Appeal held that there was a custom

---

243 *Gallagher v Post Office* [1970] 3 All ER 712. Though cf *City and Hackney Health Authority v National Union of Public Employees* [1985] IRLR 252, CA where it was thought arguable (on an interlocutory application) that a clause from a Whitley Council agreement concerning shop stewards *was* incorporated into a steward's individual contract of employment.
244 *National Coal Board v National Union of Mineworkers* [1986] ICR 736, [1986] IRLR 439; the judgment of Scott J is a useful affirmation of the principle.
245 *British Leyland UK Ltd v McQuilken* [1978] IRLR 245. In *Alexander v Standard Telephones and Cables Ltd (No 2)* [1991] IRLR 286 the court refused to incorporate a term in a collective bargain covering seniority in the redundancy procedure, though in *Anderson v Pringle of Scotland Ltd* [1998] IRLR 64 the Court of Session thought that it was at least arguable (in interlocutory proceedings) that a redundancy handling clause in a collective government had been incorporated (*Alexander* not cited). *Quaere* whether a term quantifying individuals' severance payments might be appropriate for incorporation.
246 [1964] AC 1129, [1964] 1 All ER 367, HL. No-strike clauses may now only be incorporated into individual contracts in restricted circumstances: Trade Union and Labour Relations (Consolidation) Act 1992, s 180; they took on renewed topicality with the conclusion of 'single union' agreements by, in particular, the EETPU with employers in the so-called 'sunrise' industries, including inter alia no-strike agreements and pendulum arbitration.
247 *Howman & Son v Blyth* [1983] ICR 416, [1983] IRLR 139.
248 [2002] EWCA Civ 488, [2002] ICR 910, [2002] IRLR 472.

or practice of change coming through dealings with that union; that custom was 'reasonable, certain and notorious' (see below) and so incorporation was proved and the claims failed[249]. This form of incorporation may thus defeat objection by dissidents who are union members; it has always been a known problem in the case of the non-unionist within a union shop. Ostensibly a similar principle should apply (especially if the non-member had taken the benefit in the past of union-negotiated increases in pay), but what little scrap of authority that exists on the point suggests a different approach.

In *Singh v British Steel Corpn*[250] the employee resigned from the union which subsequently negotiated a new shift system which the employee did not want to work; he refused to work it and was dismissed. One of the questions in the case was whether the new union agreement could be considered to have been incorporated into his contract which would have thereby been modified and would have obliged him to work the new shift system. The tribunal held that it was not incorporated so he remained subject to his original contractual terms. The fact that he was no longer a member of the union obviously weighed heavily with the tribunal, and it will be recalled that in *Young v Canadian Northern Rly Co*, above, the employee was also a non-member and the fact that the employer in practice treated all employees alike was to little avail. To deny a non-unionist the rights (or, as in *Singh's* case, the obligations) under a collective bargain by not incorporating terms may perhaps seem just, but on the other hand, to say that *because* he was a non-member, therefore the term will not be incorporated would appear to be based principally on an agency theory (that the union always acts as agent of its members), which as seen above has been rejected in other contexts.

One final point to note is that the fact that incorporation of collective agreement terms is accomplished contractually may affect not just the incorporation itself, but also the *interpretation* of such terms. Although they may in practice have their origins in a loosely-drafted collective agreement, probably the result of compromise and horse-trading, once they are incorporated into a contract they take effect as contractual terms and are to be interpreted as such. In *Hooper v British Railways Board*[251] a sick pay term was incorporated into an employee's contract from an agreement of the Railway Staff Joint Council; the problem was that it was (according to the employers) badly drafted, did not reflect what the employers considered to be the actual basis of agreement and (when applied literally) produced arguably a bizarre result. The employers argued that the fact that the term came from a collective agreement should be taken into account when interpreting and applying it, and that the court should also look at the real intent of the employers at the time, and at how it had subsequently been applied in practice. The Court of Appeal, however, disagreed and held that it must be construed in the normal contractual way, ie objectively as it stood, and *not* by reference to any subsequent behaviour of the parties. The case, with its relatively strict contractual approach, shows that even though collective agreements are not themselves legally binding, the drafting of any clauses within them that may

---

249 One complication was that in the past any new terms negotiated by the union had been put to a ballot of members; in the difficult circumstances of the buy-out this had not been done. Was it an essential part of the custom and practice? This point was remitted to the tribunal. However, as an alternative the tribunal had held that the two-year delay meant that the employees had acquiesced to the new terms anyway and so lost their right to object; the Court of Appeal indicated that this was probably correct.
250 [1974] IRLR 131, IT.
251 [1988] IRLR 517, CA.

be incorporated into individual contracts (either expressly or by implication) should be approached with care.

(2) Custom

Trade usage or custom may have a role to play in filling a gap in the expressed terms of a contract of employment[252], or perhaps in the interpretation of a particular term (for example an incorporated clause in a collective bargain, as above[253]), as in the cases of *Sager v H Ridehalgh & Son Ltd*[254] (custom that the employer might deduct sums from weavers' wages for bad work held to be part of the individual weaver's contract) and *Marshall v English Electric Co Ltd*[255] (established practice of using suspension as a disciplinary measure held to be incorporated). To be thus accepted, a custom must be certain, general (eg in a trade or a particular area) and reasonable, but the legal basis for its incorporation into a contract of employment is not certain – is it automatically incorporated once it is certain, general and reasonable? Or does it have to be known to and, perhaps freely accepted by the employee? In *Marshall v English Electric Co Ltd* there was a division of opinion, Lord Goddard accepting automatic incorporation, but du Parcq LJ (dissenting) considering that mere operation is not enough, there being some further element of acceptance necessary. *Meek v Port of London Authority*[256] is some authority in favour of a requirement of knowledge, but is a rather unusual case since it involved a change of employer and a custom (the payment by the employer of the employee's income tax if payable) which did not affect the employee when he commenced employment and had in fact been discontinued by the time the employee might be affected by it. It appears therefore that, although evidence of knowledge and acceptance might be most useful in establishing a binding custom, in some cases a custom might be applied without proof of them, and in particular in three instances:

(i) Where the custom is so notorious that the court or tribunal may take judicial notice of it[257].

(ii) Where it is so well established that the employee must be said to have accepted employment subject to it. In *Sagar v H Ridehalgh & Son Ltd* the practice of deductions from pay for bad work was widespread in Lancashire factories, and Lawrence LJ said[258]:

---

252 Where this is the case, the Court of Appeal in *Mears v Safecar Security Ltd* [1982] ICR 626, [1982] IRLR 183, CA took a broad approach to the evidence that can be taken into account to imply the necessary term, in particular allowing evidence of actual working practices adopted or continued after the employment had commenced (following *Liverpool City Council v Irwin* [1977] AC 239, [1976] 2 All ER 39, HL and *Wilson v Maynard Shipbuilding Consultants AB* [1978] ICR 376, [1977] IRLR 491, CA); this involves stretching ordinary contract law, where terms are not normally to be construed by later conduct, but this may be essential in employment law: *Stevedoring and Haulage Services Ltd v Fuller* [2001] IRLR 627 at 628, CA, per Tuckey LJ

253 *Parry v Holst & Co Ltd* (1968) 3 ITR 317; *Dunlop Tyres Ltd v Blows* [2001] IRLR 629, CA, where it was said that later conduct could be used as a guide to interpreting an ambiguous collective agreement.

254 [1931] 1 Ch 310, CA.

255 [1945] 1 All ER 653, CA.

256 [1918] 1 Ch 415. The decsion in *Henry v London Transport Services Ltd* [2002] EWCA 488, [2002] ICR 910, [2002] IRLR 472 reaffirmed the 'certain, general and reasonable' formulation but did not address this point of knowledge because it concerned whether the custom existed at all.

257 *George v Davies* [1911] 2 KB 445.

258 [1931] 1 Ch 310 at 336, CA.

'I think that it is clear that the plaintiff accepted employment in the defendant's mill on the same terms as the other weavers employed at that mill ... Although I entirely agree with the [first instance judge] in finding it difficult to believe that the plaintiff did not know of the existence of the practice at the mill, I think that it is immaterial whether he knew or not, as I am satisfied that he accepted his employment on the same terms as to deductions for bad work as the other weavers at the mill.'

Much here may depend upon the certainty and generality of the custom, so that the mere fact that it has happened before in one firm may be insufficient[259]. Also there is the 'reasonableness' limb of the test which might be important[260].

(iii) Where a practice grew up while the employee was in that employment and he impliedly accepted it (eg by accepting benefits under it). This might be a less certain area, for it should not cover unilateral practices, and might be subject to du Parcq LJ's caveat in *Marshall v English Electric Co Ltd* that mere continuance at work may not be enough for acceptance, for it might be caused by other factors such as fear of dismissal.

One particular application of custom and practice merits special mention. This concerns the question whether payments ostensibly made by the employer on an ex gratia (ie non-contractual) basis, if made frequently or consistently, can be argued to become contractual through custom and practice, so that in future they can be *demanded* by the employees. In *Quinn v Calder Industrial Materials Ltd*[261] the employers had paid enhanced redundancy terms on four occasions between 1987 and 1994, pursuant to a management policy document but in each case as a result of an individual decision by senior managers. When redundancies were made in 1994 no such enhanced terms were offered and the employees claimed them as a contractual right by virtue of custom and practice. The EAT rejected this argument, on the basis of insufficient evidence that the employers intended the policy to have contractual effect. A similar result was reached in *Warman International v Wilson*[262], and in *Hagen v ICI Chemicals and Polymers Ltd*[263] the court refused to incorporate a security of employment policy statement into individual contracts. However, these are ultimately decisions on the facts, and incorporation is legally possible. In *Albion Automotive Ltd v Walker*[264] the employers' predecessor (Volvo) had carried out six redundancy exercises between 1990 and 1994. Enhanced terms had been agreed with the union for the first, but in fact they were then given on each occasion. In 1995 the current employers took over the business and in 1999 made the applicant employees redundant, offering only the statutory redundancy payments. The applicants claimed the enhanced terms in a breach of contract action and won. Upholding the tribunal decision in

---

259 *Spencer Jones v Timmens Freeman* [1974] IRLR 325, IT; *Samways v Swan Hunter Shipbuilders Ltd* [1975] IRLR 190, IT.

260 *Hardwick v Leeds Area Health Authority* [1975] IRLR 319, IT.

261 [1996] IRLR 126. The EAT relied on the statement of Browne-Wilkinson P in *Duke v Reliance Systems* [1982] IRLR 347 that a unilaterally adopted management policy cannot become contractual on the grounds of custom and practice unless it is at least shown that the policy had been drawn to the attention of the employees or had been followed without exception for a substantial period.

262 [2002] All ER (D) 94 (Mar).

263 [2002] IRLR 31 at 42.

264 [2002] IRLB 702 at para 9. There is the interesting twist that Albion were liable for their *predecessor's* custom and practice; this may be a salutary lesson for lawyers advising on a TUPE transfer

their favour, the Court of Appeal pointed particularly to the facts that the policy was known to the employees; it had originally been adopted by agreement and reduced to writing; it had been applied frequently, and automatically on each occasion; the employees had a reasonable expectation of benefiting from it; and the manner in which it was communicated implied contractual intent. Future cases on this important point will depend heavily on their facts, and mining the difficult middle ground between *Quinn* and *Albion*.

In the light of this uncertain legal position it is perhaps fortunate that the scope for custom in establishing terms of contracts of employment is much diminished in modern conditions, particularly in the light of the growing number of areas which are covered by statutory provisions or compulsory written terms, bearing in mind that the orthodox approach is that a 'custom' could not be used to overturn or alter a clear express term[265].

(3) Works rules, company handbooks and policy statements

An employer may lay down works or company rules, and it is possible that these may become, in whole or in part, terms of the contract of employment particularly if the employee expressly agrees to abide by them or have some particular aspect of his employment governed by them, or if they are sufficiently brought to his notice when entering the employment. Also, some matters covered in a rule book may now be matters of which written notice must be given by statute, and so they may be strong evidence of the terms of employment by virtue of that (see above, under 'Form'). However, it is clear from *Secretary of State for Employment v Associated Society of Locomotive Engineers and Firemen (No 2)*[266] that not all such rules will have contractual effect. Lord Denning MR said:

> 'Each man signs a form saying that he will abide by the rules, but these rules are in no way terms of the contract of employment. They are only instructions to a man as to how he is to do his work.'

The distinction between contractual and non-contractual rules is significant because if a rule is contractual, (a) it cannot be altered unilaterally by the employer, for that would require consensual variation in some form, and (b) the employee could, in the absence of such variation, insist upon continuing to work that rule and refuse to operate some other rule; if the rule is non-contractual, (a) it can be changed unilaterally by the employer for, being non-contractual, it remains in the sphere of managerial prerogative[267], and (b) if an employee refuses to operate the rule, or an alteration to it, he is refusing to obey a proper order and so at common law could be dismissed and under the statutes would quite possibly be fairly dismissed. Thus, the more the rules are considered to be contractual, the more restraints are placed upon the manager's prerogative, and where a rule is not expressly made contractual in some way a court or tribunal may have to make a difficult decision whether it is to be considered contractual by implication. A particularly good example (in an area which has plagued personnel managers

---

265 Although the dividing line between unacceptable alteration and acceptable interpretation may be a thin one, see *McColl v Norman Insurance Co Ltd* (1969) 4 ITR 285.
266 [1972] 2 QB 455, [1972] 2 All ER 949, CA.
267 See, eg, *Wandsworth London Borough Council v D'Silva* [1998] IRLR 193, CA where it was held that the council's sickness absence procedures were non-contractual and so could be lawfully altered by the council.

in recent years) is *Dryden v Greater Glasgow Health Board*[268] where the employers introduced a no-smoking policy into the hospital and the employee, a heavy smoker, left and claimed constructive dismissal. Her claim failed because the EAT held that the no-smoking policy was in the realm of working rules and employer discretion, and so there was no breach of contract on which to base constructive dismissal:

> 'There can, in our view, be no doubt that an employer is entitled to make rules for the conduct of employees in their place of work, as he is entitled to give lawful orders, within the scope of the contract.[269]'

This long-standing law on 'works rules', itself rather an old-fashioned phrase, thus retains substantive significance and may be seen in two more current developments in managerial practice. The first is the modern tendency in medium and large firms to produce company handbooks; while these are in many ways a Good Thing (being readily available, relatively informal and much more of a guide to new employees) and are encouraged by ACAS[270], they could cause problems in that they may well mix together some matters that are formal contractual terms and others that are mere guidance or rules made within the managerial discretion, without any clear differentiation. The second development has been the increased use by employers of 'policies' of various kinds[271]. Again, these may or may not have contractual effect, though the cases so far have not accorded them great legal significance. In *Secretary of State for Scotland v Taylor*[272] prison officers tried to oppose a unilateral decrease in their retirement age by arguing that it was a breach of contract because it contravened their employer's equal opportunities policy which included a reference to age discrimination; the Scottish EAT held that the policy was part of the contract (largely because the employer was hoist by its own petard by having introduced it in a way consistent with contractual intent), but as a matter of construction further held that the parties could not have intended it to outlaw an otherwise lawful retirement provision in the contract. Perhaps more significantly, when in *Grant v South-West Trains Ltd*[273] an attempt was made to establish sexual orientation discrimination as a breach of contract (again because it appeared in the firm's equal opportunities

---

268 [1992] IRLR 469.
269 [1992] IRLR 469 at 471, per Lord Coulsfield. The employee's second argument (if, as found, there was no contractual entitlement to smoke) was that the introduction of the policy was in breach of the implied term of trust and respect, but this failed on the facts since the employer had adopted a reasonable procedure for introducing it. One might be tempted, however, to the mischievous thought that formal approval for such a blatant exercise in managerial prerogative might have been more controversial had the case not concerned the politically correct matter of the current Jihad against smokers.
270 See p 63 above.
271 See the Code of Practice on sickness absence in *Wandsworth London Borough Council v D'Silva*, n 267 above. One variation of this problem is where a policy is initially non-contractual but is applied so frequently and/or consistently that it is later argued to have become incorporated into contracts by custom and practice: see p 149 above.
272 [1997] IRLR 608, EAT, upheld by the House of Lords (where the incorporation point was not argued): [2000] IRLR 502.
273 [1998] IRLR 206, ECJ. One distinction with *Taylor* was that in the latter the employer's circular introducing the new equal opportunities policy had stated that it was being introduced into the employees' contracts of employment. There was no such evidence of contractual intent in *Grant*. Note that this *Grant* litigation was separate from and parallel to the main litigation which involved an ultimately unsuccessful argument before the ECJ that EC law on sex discrimination should also cover sexual orientation; see below.

policy) Curtis J held that the policy was not part of the contract at all; it was merely a statement of aims and aspirations. Given the prevalence of various forms of policies, circulars, codes of practice or (God forbid) mission statements, this distinction is likely to be troublesome for some time to come.

In dismissal law, however, the practical effect of these matters may be diminished by the fact that the modern law on unfair dismissal is not concerned with technical questions of breach of contract but rather with the overall merits of the dismissal, and in this context it is clear that, whilst breach of the rules (whether contractual or not) may well be important in any given case, it will only be *evidence*, not a determinative factor, and the existence of works rules will in no way preclude a tribunal from looking into the overall fairness of the employer's actions. Thus, for example, in *Laws Stores Ltd v Oliphant*[274] the disciplinary section of the works rules said that cases of gross misconduct (including the disregard of till procedures which was in question) would normally result in immediate dismissal, but the EAT held that such a provision (or even one more mandatory) could not limit a tribunal's jurisdiction and held the dismissal, on the facts of the particular case, to be unfair. This case is perhaps an example of the decline in the purely contractual approach to employment.

(iii) Duties of the employer

(a) To pay wages

This obligation is so fundamental that the law relating to it is considered separately in chapter 4 below.

(b) To provide work

The general common law position has been that there is no obligation to provide work for the employee to do; there is only the obligation to pay the wages which may be due under the particular contract of employment concerned. The classic, if now rather nostalgic, statement of this rule was given by Asquith J in *Collier v Sunday Referee Publishing Co Ltd*[275]:

> 'Provided I pay my cook her wages regularly, she cannot complain if I choose to take any or all of my meals out.'

This means that in such a case the employer will not be in breach of contract by failing to provide work and so may, for example, normally give salary in lieu of notice[276].

---

274 [1978] IRLR 251. An equally good example is the imposition of a disciplinary penalty by the employer – he may technically have had the contractual power to impose the penalty in question, but it is still open to the employee to argue that on the facts of the case it was excessive (thus, for example, justifying the employee in walking out and claiming constructive dismissal): *BBC v Beckett* [1983] IRLR 43; *Cawley v South Wales Electricity Board* [1985] IRLR 89.

275 [1940] 2 KB 647 at 650, [1940] 4 All ER 234 at 236.

276 *Konski v Peet* [1915] 1 Ch 530. It is possible that in some cases, where the contract does not envisage dismissal with wages in lieu (either expressly or impliedly), such a dismissal will be a breach of contract *but* as damages have been paid in anticipation (by paying the wages due in the notice period) this will be a technical breach only and of little legal significance (except possibly where a restraint of trade clause is in issue): *Rex Stewart Jeffries Parker Ginsberg v Parker* [1988] IRLR 483, CA. See p 461 below.

However, the law recognised that in certain contracts the opportunity to work is of the essence, and so certain exceptions to the general rule evolved. In particular, it was held that there may be an obligation to provide work for an actor or singer where the publicity involved may be as important as the remuneration[277], for an employee paid on a piecework[278] or commission[279] basis where actual work is necessary for him to earn his living, and possibly for an employee engaged to fill a specific office (particularly of a professional nature)[280]. Outside such exceptional cases, however, the general rule applied, as can be seen in *Turner v Sawdon & Co*[281] where a salesman on a fixed-term contract at a fixed salary was given no work to do but still paid his salary and it was held, distinguishing *Turner v Goldsmith*[282], that this was merely a contract to retain the employee so that the employer was not in breach of contract, in spite of the employee's assertions that denial of work would make him deteriorate as a salesman. However, some doubt was cast on this principle in *Langston v Amalgamated Union of Engineering Workers*[283] where an employee involved in an industrial dispute was suspended on full pay by his employer. To succeed in his claim against the union involved under now repealed legislation[284] he had to show that the dispute had induced a breach of contract, and this would only have been so if he had a contractual right to be provided with work since the employers were continuing to pay his salary. The Court of Appeal thought that the duty to provide work might exist, and in a strong judgment Lord Denning MR said that the previous authorities such as *Collier v Sunday Referee Publishing Co Ltd* were out of date, that the courts now recognise a 'right to work' and that this was one application of it. However, it must be remembered that this decision was only at an interlocutory stage, so that the Court of Appeal had to decide only if there was an arguable case on this point – they then did not have to *decide* the point, and the judgments of the other two members of the court, Cairns and Stephenson LJJ, are much less emphatic on the point than that of the Master of the Rolls. The case was remitted to the NIRC which held in the employee's favour[285] but on much more restricted grounds than those explored by Lord Denning, for Sir John Donaldson P held that this case came within one of the existing exceptions to the old rule, since under the contract the employee was to be paid premium payments for night shifts and overtime, so that he came within the pieceworker exception in that denial of actual work meant denial of opportunity to earn the premium payments. Thus, in its result, the case is in fact compatible with the old common law rule and its established exceptions.

277 *Fechter v Montgomery* (1863) 33 Beav 22; *Bunning v Lyric Theatre* (1894) 71 LT 396; *Marbé v George Edwardes (Daly's Theatre) Ltd* [1928] 1 KB 269, CA; the obligation may be to provide not just work, but work of a particular kind or standard, eg a leading part in a play as in *Herbert Clayton and Jack Waller Ltd v Oliver* [1930] AC 209, HL.
278 *R v Welsh* (1853) 2 E & B 357; *Devonald v Rosser & Sons* [1906] 2 KB 728, CA.
279 *Turner v Goldsmith* [1891] 1 QB 544, CA; *Bauman v Hulton Press Ltd* [1952] 2 All ER 1121.
280 *Collier v Sunday Referee Publishing Co Ltd* [1940] 2 KB 647, [1940] 4 All ER 234.
281 [1901] 2 KB 653, CA. *Quaere* whether the position would be different if it was more urgent that the employee should keep in practice, as for example in the case of a surgeon.
282 [1891] 1 QB 544, CA.
283 [1974] 1 All ER 980, [1974] ICR 180, CA; see also *Breach v Epsylon Industries Ltd* [1976] ICR 316, [1976] IRLR 180; *Bosworth v Angus Jowett & Co Ltd* [1977] IRLR 374.
284 Industrial Relations Act 1971, s 96.
285 [1974] ICR 510, [1974] IRLR 182. It is made clear in the President's judgment that the employee had to work such shifts and hours as the employer stipulated, which made it easier to construe overtime as a contractual requirement; it is submitted, however, that purely voluntary overtime is not an essential part of a contract, and so failure to provide it should *not* be a breach of contract, and so not subject to the reasoning in *Langston's* case.

This question of whether and when there is a right to work (or more accurately, whether a contract requires the provision of work in addition to the payment of wages) has been dormant for many years, but was revived in an unusual context in *William Hill Organisation Ltd v Tucker*[286] . The case concerned an attempt by an employer to construct an implied 'garden leave clause'[287] from the terms of the employee's contract, quite simply because they had omitted to put an express clause in. The contract contained a long (six months') notice provision; when the employee left with only one month's notice, the employers applied for an injunction restraining him from taking work elsewhere during the six-month period, on the basis that they were prepared to pay his wages *and* had a common law right to require him during that period to do no work for them or anyone else. The Court of Appeal held that that depended on whether his contract only required payment of wages (as the employers argued) *or* required the employers to provide him with work as well (in which case the employers would be in breach of contract and the employee could leave to take up other work); they thus revived the old controversy, and for good measure seemed to take an expansive view as to who can claim to have a sufficient interest in actually performing their work in order to claim that the contract is to be interpreted as requiring work to be provided, not just payment. Far from restricting it to theatrical or piecework/ commission workers, they held that this employee, a senior 'spread betting' dealer with a betting organisation, *did* have a right to be provided with work; there was thus no inherent right for the employer to put him on garden leave[288] , and so the employer's application for an injunction was refused. Factors leading to that conclusion were that the appointment was a specific and unique one, that the skills involved were those requiring constant practice and experience and that the contract contained certain provisions (as to obligations on the employee in carrying out his duties, training and an express power of suspension) which the court thought consistent with an obligation to provide work, provided that it was available. While the first point (a specific appointment) could point to a narrow future application of this case and some of the points on construction of the contract terms are, with respect, highly arguable, it is likely that most contention in any future cases will be over the second point – who will be considered to be in a job whose skills need constant honing and exercise, so as to come within a widened class of employees with some form of 'right to work'?

Two further points might be mentioned. The first is that this uncertain area of law will only be relevant where there is no express term covering the provision of work, and where such provision is important to either of the parties, they are advised to incorporate a clause in the contract putting the matter beyond doubt. The second is that this topic may be allied to the question of the continuation of wages during stoppages of work and for present purposes it might be noted that at common law suspension without pay will only be lawful if there is an express or

---

286 [1999] ICR 291, [1998] IRLR 313, CA.

287 A 'garden leave clause' is an alternative to a restraint of trade clause, whereby an employer puts an employee on to long notice with a provision that during that notice he can be sent home by the employer (to avoid damage to the employer's business) *but* cannot take any other work while still technically employed by that employer; see p 464 below.

288 As Morritt LJ stated at the end of his judgment, the answer of course is for the employer to use an *express* garden leave clause wherever there might arguably be a right to work (more often now, in the light of this case?). Moreover, this case could also limit the hitherto widely assumed implied right of an employer to dismiss with wages in lieu; again, the preferred solution increasingly is an express wages in lieu clause in the contract; see p 462 below.

implied term in the particular contract to that effect; that failure to provide work may constitute a lay-off, thus activating certain statutory provisions (principally concerned with redundancy – Employment Rights Act 1996, sections 147–154); and that in the absence of continuing contractual payments the employee may be eligible for a statutory guarantee payment under the 1996 Act, sections 28–35.

(c) To exercise care – generally and in relation to employment references

On a general level, this matter will normally relate to care for the employee's health and safety, and so is dealt with fully in chapter 12 below, for the employer's common law duty of care is one of the bases of the law relating to the compensation of an injured employee. However, four particular applications of it are important here. The first is that one of the commonly accepted aspects of this overall duty is that the employer must provide competent and safe fellow employees[289], for example to protect the employee from practical jokers; one effect of this is that there may be a positive common law obligation upon the employer to be rid of a potentially dangerous employee and this should be a good defence to an allegation of unfair dismissal by that employee, provided the necessary procedures are used in effecting the dismissal. The second is that the general duty of care may be construed as including an obligation upon the employer to pay attention to complaints from an employee that a particular appliance, method, etc is unsafe and to act reasonably in dealing with matters of safety; if the employer does not do so, not only may the employee be justified in walking out and claiming, for the purposes of unfair dismissal, to have been constructively dismissed[290] but also that dismissal may well be automatically unfair[291]. The third is that the employer may be under an obligation to indemnify the employee against expenses necessarily incurred in the course of his employment, which may include the cost of defending legal proceedings, though not where the fault was purely that of the employee and only collateral to the performance of his duties[292]; there is, however, no implied obligation to insure the employee's activities to any greater extent than is required by law[293]. The fourth is that the specialised duty of care will in general not extend to a duty to take care of the employee's belongings[294]; any possible liability for loss of the employee's goods would have to arise on ordinary principles of tort if there was evidence of particular proximity between the particular employer and employee, not just on the employment relationship per se, or possibly under the Workplace (Health, Safety and Welfare) Regulations 1992, regulation 23 which provides for 'suitable and sufficient accommodation' for clothing not worn during working hours[295].

289 *Wilsons & Clyde Coal Co Ltd v English* [1938] AC 57, HL; *Hudson v Ridge Manufacturing Co Ltd* [1957] 2 QB 348, [1957] 2 All ER 229.
290 *British Aircraft Corpn v Austin* [1978] IRLR 332; cf *Lindsay v Dunlop Ltd* [1980] IRLR 93.
291 Employment Rights Act 1996, s 100, see p 595 below.
292 *Burrows v Rhodes* [1899] 1 QB 816; *Re Famatina Development Corpn* [1914] 2 Ch 271, CA; *Gregory v Ford* [1951] 1 All ER 121.
293 *Lister v Romford Ice and Cold Storage Co Ltd* [1957] AC 555, [1957] 1 All ER 125, HL. In a case where insurance cover is likely to be important, the employee is advised to make the position clear with the employer, especially since the decision in *Merrett v Babb* [2001] EWCA Civ 214, [2001] QB 1174, that when the employer went out of business the individual employee could be liable in damages for bad advice given during employment.
294 *Deyong v Shenburn* [1946] KB 227, [1946] 1 All ER 226, CA; *Edwards v West Herts Group Hospital Management Committee* [1957] 1 All ER 541, [1957] 1 WLR 415, CA.
295 *McCarthy v Daily Mirror Newspapers Ltd* [1949] 1 All ER 801, CA (on the equivalent provision under the old Factories Acts).

One area of considerable current interest concerns the application of a duty of care to the giving of references by an employer or ex-employer. There could, of course, be liability for a negligently written reference to the new employer[296], but the question arose whether the employee as the *subject* of the reference could sue in negligence, for breach of a duty of care. The House of Lords in *Spring v Guardian Assurance plc*[297] (reversing a more cautious decision by the Court of Appeal) held that there could be such a duty on the employer giving a reference; it lies both in tort (according to Lord Goff on a *Hedley Byrne*-style assumption of responsibility, and according to Lords Lowry, Slynn and Woolf on the basis that this extension of liability is fair, just and reasonable, and concerning a sufficiently proximate relationship) and also in contract, based upon a breach of this implied term. This decision does not prevent the giving of a bad reference, only a negligently bad reference, and their Lordships were not persuaded by the argument that to impose liability would deter people from writing references. Subsequent case law has explored this new form of liability to the subject of the reference. One key question is how comprehensive a reference needs to be in order to discharge the duty of care. This point was addressed in the most important explanatory case to date, *Bartholomew v London Borough of Hackney*[298] where the Court of Appeal adopted from defamation law the rule that the reference must be true, accurate and fair, but need not necessarily be full and comprehensive. The latter part of this means that the subject has no right to insist on particular information being in it; content remains a decision for the referee provided that the end result is not misleading (either positively or through the effect of an omission). This has been particularly important when addressing a well-known problem here – what is the referee to say when the employee left while still subject to unfinished disciplinary investigations? In *Bartholomew* a reference was requested by a potential employer on an individual who had left the referee's employment in a negotiated termination while under investigation for financial irregularities. The reference stated this as a fact and the individual was refused the post. When he sued under *Spring* the Court of Appeal held for the defendant referee; the reference was factually accurate, it did not give a misleading impression and the individual had no right to demand that it should have contained further explanatory or exculpatory material. However, in *Cox v Sun Alliance Life Ltd*[299] an ex-employer giving a reference

---

296 Under the ordinary principles of *Hedley Byrne & Co Ltd v Heller & Partners Ltd* [1964] AC 465, [1963] 2 All ER 575, HL.

297 [1994] ICR 596, [1994] IRLR 460, HL. The decision was by 4–1, with Lord Keith dissenting. The majority held that a duty of care did exist on the facts, but this does not mean that an action will always succeed in such circumstances – the question of causation must also be established (did the employee fail to get new employment because of the negligent reference?); where the plaintiff was one of many applicants, that may be difficult to prove.

298 [1999] IRLR 246, CA, applied in *Kidd v Axa Equity and Law Life Assurance Society plc* [2000] IRLR 301. In *Legal and General Assurance Ltd v Kirk* [2001] EWCA Civ 1803, [2002] IRLR 125 it was held that, the action lying in tort, an actual reference must have been given in order for a cause of action to arise: the employee cannot sue on the basis that the ex-employer is *proposing* to give a reference in terms to which he or she objects. However, in a different context, it was held in *TSB Bank Ltd v Harris* [2000] IRLR 157 that an employee (still in employment) discovering that misleading references were being given about her could leave and claim constructive dismissal on the basis of breach of the implied term of trust and respect.

299 [2001] EWCA Civ 649, [2001] IRLR 448. Part of the ex-employee's complaint was that a form of reference had been agreed as part of a termination settlement but the employer had ignored this. There could be a problem with an agreed reference as part of a settlement (a common practice) – if it was misleadingly incomplete, to hide misdeeds by the departing employee, there could be *Hedley Byrne* liability to the *recipient* (the new employer); presumably the fact of agreement between referee and subject would be no defence to such liability, provided that damage and causation could be proved.

overstepped an important line here by going beyond a factual statement that allegations had been made (at a very late stage) against the individual and gave the impression that there was substance to them (so that he may well have been dismissed if he had not resigned), even though these allegations had *not* been investigated, or even put to the individual for his reactions. The Court of Appeal upheld his claim in negligence; the basis for this was that if value judgments are to be made as to guilt and included in the reference they must (to satisfy the duty of care) be made on the basis of reasonable investigation. Mummery LJ made an interesting analogy here with the law of unfair dismissal where a dismissal for suspected misconduct will only be fair after a reasonable investigation has led to a positive belief in guilt[300]; if a dismissal requires this, so does a later reference. Short of such an investigation, the referee ex-employer should stick to factual statements and to value judgments only on any parts of the investigation that had been completed.

The law's application to employment references has thus developed out of all recognition in the last decade, though entirely in relation to the reference's subject, not it recipient. This is likely to continue because of another development in a different field. Traditionally references on employees were wholly confidential and so, even if the subject suspected that poor opinions were being expressed by the referee (for example if turned down for several jobs, having named the same referee), it was quite likely that he or she would never actually know that or be able to prove it. Now, however, there has been a major change almost by a side-wind. By virtue of the Data Protection Act 1998 an employment reference, though unavailable to the subject in the hands of the referee, *can* be demanded by the subject in the hands of the recipient (the only exception being if it refers to third parties who have their own confidentiality interest, though this is unlikely in an employment reference)[301]. Whatever the logic of this strange position may be, it is capable of revolutionising the practice of reference writing, though whether overall for the better may be arguable. The discoverability of references may well lead to yet more litigation in this area by their subjects.

Finally, one continuing problem is whether there is any implied obligation on an (ex-) employer to *give* a reference; it has normally been thought that there is no such obligation, but in the speech of Lord Woolf in *Spring* there is a passage suggesting that in certain circumstances (where references are known to be an essential element of recruitment) it may be necessary to imply just such an obligation[302]. As with the whole of the case, this could be seen against the factual background of the plaintiff seeking new employment under the LAUTRO rules (with their mandatory references), but equally both these remarks and the case itself are expressed in general terms potentially applicable either to employment generally or at least to types of employment where references play an important part in recruitment. On the other hand, Lord Slynn pointed out that it is open to the reference-giver to state specifically the parameters within which the reference is given (and any limitations on his knowledge of the employee) or, ultimately, to

300 *British Home Stores Ltd v Burchell* [1980] ICR 303n, [1978] IRLR 379; see p 583 below.
301 Data Protection Act 1998 s 7 and Sch 7 para 1. For the Information Commissioner's advice as to handling requests for references, see p 106 above.
302 [1994] ICR 596 at 647, [1994] IRLR 460 at 481. In addition, the ECJ have held that if an employer *refuses* to give a reference to retaliation for a sex discrimination complaint made by the employee, that itself can constitute unlawful sex discrimination: *Coote v Granada Hospitality Ltd* C-185/97 [1999] ICR 100, [1998] IRLR 656, ECJ, applied in *Coote (No 2)* [1999] ICR 942, [1999] IRLR 452, EAT.

rely on the *Hedley Byrne* aspect of the case to make his agreement to the employee to give the reference subject to an express disclaimer of liability. Further judicial guidance on these important points in the general context (ie not just in the financial services sector) is needed.

(d) To treat the employee with respect

In modern employment law there has been a restatement of implied duties of mutual respect between employer and employee. In certain employments, particularly of a domestic nature, this may require positive courtesy[303] while in others it may mean treating each other with such a degree of consideration and tolerance as would allow the contract to be executed. This is, of course, a vague concept which will vary with the circumstances, and if there is a more concrete area of dispute in any given case questions of want of 'respect' will be of secondary importance[304]. However, an obligation upon the employer to treat the employee with respect and not to act in a manner likely to destroy or seriously damage the relationship of trust and confidence without good cause may be seen as a corollary of the employee's general duty of faithful service, as confirmed in *British Telecommunications plc v Ticehurst*[305]. Given that the line is still strongly held that employment is *not* a fiduciary relationship and so generalised mutual duties of good faith are not to be incorporated that way[306], the development of this implied term has meant that more particular duties can be imposed when necessary in order to govern the employment relationship, in particular to restrain inequitable exercises of contractual power by the employer; at times, such duties come very close to fiduciary or 'good faith' ones but by using a more acceptable contractual analysis[307]. Moreover, it is argued above[308] that there are developments suggesting not only that this is a well-established and much-used implied term, but that it is assuming an overriding nature, capable of qualifying the ability of an employer to rely on a literal application of his rights under a contract of employment.

The development of such a term is perhaps not so surprising, for the advent of the law on unfair dismissal has restricted the employer's prerogative to dismiss so that good personnel management has become an essential, not an optional extra[309]. The overall requirement of fair dismissal procedures, for example, has meant that more notice has to be taken of the employee's viewpoint, and the employer is expected not just to assess conduct and issue warnings, but also to take more

---

303 *Wilson v Racher* [1974] ICR 428, [1974] IRLR 114, CA.
304 As in *Donovan v Invicta Airways Ltd* [1970] 1 Lloyd's Rep 486, CA.
305 [1992] ICR 383, [1992] IRLR 219, CA; see p 187 below.
306 *Nottingham University v Fishel* [2000] ICR 1462, [2000] IRLR 471.
307 For the evolution of the term generally, see Mr Justice Lindsay: 'The implied term of trust and confidence' (2001) 30 ILJ 1. Terminology may be significant; the term tends to be expressed in the negative (*not* to act in such a way as to *destroy* trust and confidence/ respect) because a positive formulation (that the employer *must* act in a particular way) could suggest a wider, reasonableness test at which courts have baulked (see p 141 above). If necessary, however, the term *can* place positive obligations on the employer: *Transco plc v O'Brien* [2002] EWCA Civ 379, [2002] ICR 721, [2002] IRLR 444, CA. One balance for the employer is the qualification that the employer must not behave in the way in question 'without reasonable and proper cause': *Hilton v Shiner Ltd* [2001] IRLR 727.
308 See p 140 above.
309 In *Cantor Fitzgerald International v Bird* [2002] IRLR 867 breach of the term came from the manner of the employer's dealings with the employeees when changing their contracts; in *Stanley Cole (Wainfleet) Ltd v Sheridan* [2003] ICR 297, [2003] IRLR 52 it came from the imposition of an unjustified disciplinary penalty.

positive action to assist or train the employee to meet any required standards of competence or conduct. Moreover, in one important area of unfair dismissal law, the concept of an implied duty of respect has taken on definite significance; this is in the area of 'constructive dismissal'. This is discussed in detail in chapter 8 below, but the essence of it is that the employee can claim to be dismissed, even though he walks out, if he can show that the employer's conduct was such that he was 'entitled' to do so[310]. In *Western Excavating (ECC) Ltd v Sharp*[311], a case which served to emphasise the underlying contractual nature of the employment relationship, the Court of Appeal held that this meant *contractually* entitled, ie where the employer's conduct went as far as to repudiate the whole contract; on the face of it, this narrowed the concept of constructive dismissal, for mere unreasonableness by the employer would not be enough per se, but the effect of this case has been considerably reduced by praying in aid the implied term of respect, for if there is such a term and the employer behaves unreasonably (ie with unacceptable disregard for the employee), the employer can be held to have broken the implied term, to have repudiated the contract, and therefore to have constructively dismissed the employee even within the narrower view taken in *Western Excavating (EEC) Ltd v Sharp*[312]. Reliance on the implied term in this context is common and can arise on a wide variety of facts, to such an extent that it can constitute something of a 'wild card' in employment law, often requiring the employer to think in terms not just of whether contemplated or proposed conduct (for example changes to working practices or terms and conditions) is strictly lawful under the wording of the individual contracts, but whether objection could legitimately be made by affected employees to the *manner* in which the management propose to pursue their goals. This potentially restraining effect may be a significant factor in good personnel/HR practice. Moreover, the trend in recent years has been for the implied term to be used more widely than just in its original home of constructive dismissal. Action which breaches it also constitutes repudiatory conduct generally which may give rise to other arguments or causes of action. Thus, for example, the implied term has been the basis for extending compensation for wrongful dismissal,[313] for freeing a employee from a restraint of trade clause after leaving because of the employer's conduct,[314] and even for receiving personal injury damages in cases of occupational stress caused by such conduct[315].

---

310 Employment Rights Act 1996, s 95; a similar definition applies to redundancy claims – s136. For an application of similar ideas of a duty of trust and confidence in a common law claim, see *Bliss v South East Thames Regional Health Authority* [1987] ICR 700, [1985] IRLR 308, CA.
311 [1978] 1 All ER 713, [1978] ICR 221, CA.
312 There is an excellent explanation of this role for the implied term of respect in the judgment of Browne-Wilkinson J in the EAT in *Woods v WM Car Services (Peterborough) Ltd* [1981] ICR 666, [1981] IRLR 347 (approved by the Court of Appeal [1982] ICR 693, [1982] IRLR 413). If employer conduct is bad enough to breach this term, that will invariably be repudiatory conduct for these purposes: *Morrow v Safeway Stores plc* [2002] IRLR 9. See also the modern case law set out at pp 140–143 above, and in particular the extension of this term to the area of employees' pension rights in *Imperial Group Pension Trust Ltd v Imperial Tobacco Ltd* [1991] ICR 524, [1991] IRLR 66.
313 *Clark v BET plc* [1997] IRLR 348; see p 486 below.
314 *Cantor Fitzgerald International v Bird* [2002] IRLR 867.
315 *Gogay v Hertfordshire County Council* [2000] IRLR 703, CA; *McCabe v Cornwall County Council* [2002] EWCA Civ 1887, [2003] ICR 501, [2003] IRLR 87.

The implied term of trust and respect finally received the approval of the House of Lords in *Malik v BCCI SA*[316] where it formed the basis for an unusual claim at common law for 'stigma damages', the employees' argument being that they had had their future job prospects materially damaged (as ex-managers in the collapsed BCCI bank) by reason of the fraudulent conduct of the bank's operations while they had been employed by it, which had breached the term of trust and respect. Lord Steyn referred to the term as a 'sound development' which had met with widespread approval, and which had to be applied to a wide range of situations in order to strike a balance between the employer's interest in managing the business and the employee's interest in not being unfairly and improperly exploited[317]. Shortly afterwards, however, in a fashion not uncommon in cases of major developments in the common law, serious uncertainty was introduced into this area as a side-effect of the subsequent House of Lords decision in *Johnson v Unisys Ltd*[318]. The principal aim in this decision was to strangle at birth a new head of recovery of wide, general damages for 'stigma' loss *on dismissal*. This had been enthusiastically taken up by claimants' lawyers after *Malik* and was viewed by their Lordships as a highly undesirable development which was to be stopped. They did so by restricting stigma damages to breaches of contract *during* employment (ie confining *Malik* to its own facts). This was achieved in two ways – (1) by holding that a common law wrongful dismissal action is not to be used to outflank the statutory action for unfair dismissal, which is what Parliament intended should be the principal remedy for unfairness in termination (including stigma), with its deliberate imposition of short time limits and a cap on the amount that can be recovered; and (2) by holding that the term of trust as respect is aimed at ensuring that the contract can *continue* in a reasonable and proper manner and so is not applicable at the dismissal stage where, by definition, questions of continuance no longer arise. It was this second ground that caused problems. If confined to the moment and mechanics of dismissal (as used in the case itself to rule out stigma damages from the manner of dismissal) it was unobjectionable. However, if ever applied more widely to the whole process leading up to dismissal, it could be disastrous for the proper treatment of employees under discipline and indeed for constructive dismissal (where the employee will normally want to rely on immediately pre-termination employer misconduct as justifying leaving). This danger was recognised by the Outer House of the Court of Session in *King v St Andrews University*[319] where an employee

316   [1997] ICR 606, [1997] IRLR 462, HL; see Brodie 'The heart of the matter: mutual trust and confidence' (1996) 25 ILJ 121 (cited with approval in the case) 'Beyond exchange: the new contract of employment' (1998) 27 ILJ 79; and 'Mutual trust and the values of the employment contract' (2001) 30 ILJ 84.

317   The Northern Ireland Court of Appeal in *Brown v Merchant Ferries Ltd* [1998] IRLR 682 and the English Court of Appeal in *Transco plc v O'Brien* [2002] EWCA Civ 379, [2002] ICR 721, [2002] IRLR 444 adopted Lord Steyn's formulation of the implied term which stressed that the test was an objective one, ie whether the employee could properly conclude that the employer was repudiating the contract, not whether the employer had intended so to act. It was also established in *Malik* (n 316 above) that the repudiatory conduct does not in law have to be aimed directly at the employee.

318   [2001] UKHL 13, [2001] ICR 480, [2001] IRLR 279. This decision is also causing problems in the law of unfair dismissal because of Lord Hoffmann's view that stigma/ manner of dismissal damages can be recovered in an unfair dismissal action, contrary to all previous authority; see p 615 below.

319   [2002] IRLR 252, Ct of Sess (OH). *R (Arthurworrey) v Haringey London Borough Council* [2002] ICR 279 can be seen as consistent with this view (injunction granted to restrain disciplinary procedures while a public inquiry was considering the whole case, because to continue such procedures would be contrary to the implied term).

was allowed to challenge allegedly improper disciplinary procedures by reliance on breach of trust and respect, even though these procedures had led to his dismissal. However, the danger then seemed to eventuate in the Court of Appeal in *Eastwood v Magnox Electric plc*[320] where employees (who had successfully brought unfair dismissal claims) sought to bring common law damages claims for stress injuries caused by the employer's treatment of them prior to dismissal, in breach of the term of trust and respect, but the employer successfully defended on the basis of *Johnson v Unisys*. The Court of Appeal held that this disapplication of the term applied not just to the moment of termination, but to any pattern of events stretching back over a period and leading up to the termination. This was, however, reconsidered shortly afterwards by a different Court of Appeal in *McCabe v Cornwall County Council*[321]. Although the facts were very similar (an employee, suspended because of complaints and later dismissed on those grounds, succeeding in unfair dismissal proceedings and then suing the employer at common law for stress injuries due to the original suspension) the court here permitted the claim to proceed, holding that it was not precluded by *Johnson v Unisys*. The ratio was that *Johnson* does not rule out a claim simply because the events finally led to dismissal, that here the complaint related to the initial suspension which was sufficiently independent of the dismissal to be a valid cause of action, and that *Eastwood* was distinguishable. Arguably, however, that distinction is thin and what these cases actually show is very different approaches to *Johnson*; the court in *McCabe* intimated that further, authoritative consideration of this conundrum is now necessary. With or without that, there will continue to be a troublesome distinction between cases where the breach of trust and respect is so closely tied in to the process of dismissal as to fall foul of *Johnson* and permit no supplementing common law action and cases where the breach relates to what Sedley LJ in *McCabe* called 'a separate and antecedent wrong', thus allowing a common law action (even where the employee has already utilised the law of unfair dismissal). The apparently simple principle from *Johnson* that the implied term of trust and respect is not applicable on termination thus contains a serious difficulty in defining 'on termination'; at the time of writing, it is the most pressing difficulty in this area.

(e) To deal promptly and properly with grievances

In *W A Goold (Pearmak) Ltd v McConnell*[322] two salesmen whose commission-based pay had been hit by a change in sales methods, tried to raise this as a grievance; in the absence of a proper procedure[323] they tried to do so on several occasions in an ad hoc manner with their manager and then with the new managing director, but with no results. When eventually they sought an interview with the company chairman and were refused they walked out. Upholding the tribunal decision

---

320 [2002] EWCA Civ 463, [2002] IRLR 447. This could lead to the odd result that the employer was better off (ie not facing stigma damages) by dismissing the employee than by merely disciplining them, eg by suspension, as pointed out by Hale LJ in *Gogay v Hertfordshire County Council* [2000] IRLR 703, CA (a case difficult to rationalise with the view in *Eastwood*, but *not* disapproved in *Johnson v Unisys*).
321 [2002] EWCA Civ 1887, [2003] ICR 501, [2003] IRLR 87.
322 [1995] IRLR 516.
323 As employees, they should have had a written note of the appropriate grievance procedure in their written ('section 1') statement of terms and conditions; see p 113 above. This point was used by the EAT to demonstrate Parliament's intention that there should be proper such procedures, properly administered.

that this was a constructive dismissal and unfair, the EAT held that it is an implied term in a contract of employment that employers will reasonably and promptly afford a reasonable opportunity to their employees to obtain redress of any grievances they may have. Moreover, this is a fundamental term, breach of which will be sufficiently serious to justify the employee in terminating the employment.

This declaration of a new (possibly overriding?) implied term was of particular significance for three reasons. First, it was a very good example of the use of implied terms set out above, as a way of the courts governing certain basic contents of the employment relationship and imposing certain standards of behaviour in employee relations. Secondly, although this point is not mentioned in the judgment of Morison J, the case could be seen as following on from at least two previous decisions in which failures to take up specific forms of complaints arising in the high-profile areas of health and safety[324] and sexual harassment[325] had been held to constitute fundamental breaches of contract for the purpose of establishing constructive dismissal when the complainant left. *Goold* in effect consolidates such disparate cases into one general principle and in doing so places new emphasis on the efficient administration of grievance procedures. Thirdly, it fits in well with two subsequent developments elsewhere, namely the extension of the ACAS Code of Practice No 1 in 2000 to cover grievance procedures as well as disciplinary procedures and the provisions in the Employment Act 2002, Schedule 2, Part 2, which make use of the new statutory 'standard grievance procedure' effectively mandatory. Failure by an employer to process a grievance properly under the latter will have its own statutory penalties[326], but *Goold* will still be important as providing the contractual breach necessary for constructive dismissal where the employer's failure makes the employee's position untenable. There is, however, a sting in the statutory tail for the employee, in that under the Employment Act 2002, section 32, if he or she fails to use a grievance procedure (in circumstances yet to be set out in Regulations at the time of writing) there are limitations on the right to complain to a tribunal at all. For all of these reasons, grievance procedures have been given an ever-higher profile in recent years and proper exhaustion of them by both parties will now usually be very advisable.

(f) To provide a reasonably suitable working environment

In *Waltons & Morse v Dorrington*[327] a non-smoking secretary in a solicitors' firm was moved into a room close to heavy smokers which she found a problem. Her complaints had only partial effects and eventually she was told to put up with the solution or leave. She left and claimed constructive dismissal, which was upheld by the EAT who held that it is now an implied term of all contracts of employment that the employer will provide and monitor for employees, so far as is reasonably practicable, a working *environment* which is reasonably suitable for the performance by them of their contractual duties. This term goes beyond the long-standing term of health and safety (above) (on the facts, for example it would probably have been too soon to show distinct health risks to her), and in formulating it (much more along 'welfare' lines) the EAT adopted much of the phraseology of

---

324 *British Aircraft Corpn v Austin* [1978] IRLR 332.
325 *Bracebridge Engineering Ltd v Darby* [1990] IRLR 3.
326 See p 543 below.
327 [1997] IRLR 488.

the Health and Safety at Work etc Act 1974, s 2(2)(e) which provides that the employer must take reasonable care for 'the provision and maintenance of a working environment for his employees that is, so far as reasonably practicable, safe, without risks to health and adequate as regards facilities and arrangements for their welfare at work'. Moreover, although not mentioned in the judgment, this implied term is also consistent with (1) modern health and safety Regulations, especially the Management of Health and Safety at Work Regulations 1999 with their emphasis on pro-active measures such as risk assessments in workplaces, and (2) the clear coverage of the 'working environment' (not just traditional health and safety) in Article 118a of the Treaty of Rome (now Art 137), under which the Working Time Directive was validly passed, even though it does not concern health or safety directly[328]. This new implied term is potentially very wide and is likely to need much interpretation in the future case law on it.

(g) Further developments: advice, confidentiality and PHI schemes

As seen above, it is, of course, always open to the courts to extend the scope of these imposed duties on employers. In that context, three developments merit mention. The first is that in *Scally v Southern Health and Social Services Board*[329] the House of Lords upheld the finding of an implied term that the employer would *inform* the employee of valuable (but obscure) rights under his pension scheme; when the employer failed to do so and the employee lost those rights due to a time limitation, the employee could therefore sue the employer for breach of contract. Clearly, the facts of this case were unusual, but Lord Bridge drew a principle that there could be such an implied term where (a) the terms of the contract had not been negotiated individually, but resulted from negotiation with a representative body or were otherwise incorporated by reference, (b) the employee could only avail himself of a valuable right under the contract by taking certain action, and (c) the employee could not, in all the circumstances, reasonably be expected to be aware of the term unless it was brought to his attention. Obligations to inform or warn are common in modern health and safety law[330], and it was interesting to see this development in mainstream employment law (albeit in the specialised context of pensions), because the traditional approach was much more in the nature of caveat employee[331]. However, subsequent case law has not shown a desire to extend *Scally*, which may eventually turn out to have been the highwater mark here, or indeed to be restricted to its

---

328 See p 242 below.
329 [1991] ICR 771, [1991] IRLR 522, HL.
330 A good example is the decision of Waite J in *Pape v Cumbria County Council* [1992] 3 All ER 211 that there was a common law duty on the employer to warn cleaning staff of the danger of dermatitis from certain cleaning chemicals (*General Cleaning Contractors Ltd v Christmas* [1953] AC 180, [1952] 2 All ER 1110, HL applied).
331 In *Lister v Romford Ice and Cold Storage Co Ltd* [1957] AC 555, [1957] 1 All ER 125, HL there was no obligation on the employer to organise all matters of insurance (see p 171 below) and in *Reid v Rush & Tompkins Group plc* [1990] ICR 61, [1989] IRLR 265, CA it was held that the employer was under no duty to warn the employee of the risk of economic loss (through not insuring himself adequately when working abroad). The question of insurance cover for the employee should preferably be covered expressly in the contract whenever it is likely to be an isue, especially since the decision in *Merrett v Babb* [2001] EWCA Civ 214, [2001] QB 1174 that when a firm of surveyors went bankrupt one of their employees could be personally liable to a client to whom he had given bad advice; unfortunately he was not insured as he was no longer covered by the firm's previous policy.

own facts. In *University of Nottingham v Eyett*[332] it was held that there was no duty on an employer to advise an employee about to retire that his pension would be higher if he delayed slightly (when all that that employee had enquired about was his entitlement on his preferred date of retirement) and in *Hagen v ICI Chemicals and Polymers Ltd*[333] there was again held to be no obligation to give positive advice on pension entitlements through a TUPE transfer; for good measure, the Court of Appeal held in *Outram v Academy Plastics*[334] (alleged breach of duty by employer as pension trustee in not advising the employee to rejoin the scheme when he renewed employment after a break) that if there is no duty under the contract of employment (given this restrictive treatment of *Scally*) the employee will not be allowed to argue for a wider duty in tort. Thus, unless a case arises which is much closer to the facts of *Scally* (which is now seen as heavily dependent on the inability of the employees to discover the true facts without information from the employer) it is unlikely that any duty to advise will be held to have arisen. One interesting side point here is that in *Hagen* the claimant employees in fact succeeded on the separate ground that certain information that they had actually been given was misleading and so, they having relied on that to their provable detriment,[335] the employer was liable in tort for negligent misstatement. Thus, if an employer chooses to give information which the employee will reasonably and foreseeably rely on care must be taken as to its accuracy *but* the post-*Scally* case law suggests that there is unlikely to be any general duty to give such information in the first place.

The second development is the possible extension of ideas of confidentiality in employment. There is a well-developed implied duty of confidence *on* an employee, but there may evolve an equal and opposite duty *towards* an employee. In *Dalgleish v Lothian and Borders Police Board*[336] an interdict was granted, preventing the employers from divulging employees' names and addresses to the Council who were chasing community charge defaulters, partly on the ground that this information was confidential, not in the public domain, and was held by the employers only for the purpose of the employer–employee relationship. Another sign of such ideas was the decision of the European Court of Human Rights in *Halford v United Kingdom*[337] that interception of telephone calls at work constituted a violation of the Convention rights to respect for private life and family life, home and correspondence. Clearly, such arguments are now likely to be buttressed by the coming into force of the Human Rights Act 1998 in October 2000, so that such matters may now be justiciable before the national courts and tribunals. In practice, however changes in the direction of greater recognition of ideas of employee privacy or confidentiality in personnel/HR practice are likely to come from a further, independent source not reliant on contractual or human rights ideas, namely data protection law as revamped by the Data Protection Act

---

332 [1999] ICR 721, [1999] IRLR 87. See also *Marlow v East Thames Housing Group Ltd* [2002] IRLR 798.
333 [2002] IRLR 31.
334 [2001] ICR 367, [2000] IRLR 499, CA.
335 This element in *Hagen* was unusual – the employees could show causation on the basis that, if their true position had been known to them, they would have objected to the TUPE transfer *and* then the employers would *not* have gone through with it. Normally, employees will have no such de facto power of veto, the transfer would happen anyway and so what they may or may not have been told in advance would have no causative effect on their later loss, which would have happened anyway.
336 [1991] IRLR 422, Ct of Sess.
337 [1997] IRLR 471, ECtHR.

1998. Although in itself lying primarily outside employment law, much effort during 2002 and 2003 was put into the production by the Information Commissioner of an Employment Code of Practice giving best practice advice on the impact of the legislation in the employment context. A significant amount of this advice is clearly of relevance to the establishment of a level of confidentiality for employees while at work that has hitherto only been argued for in theory. It is perhaps not fanciful to say that the overall approach is based on a simple yet important principle that the employer employs the employee, it does not own him or her.

The Code is split into four parts. We have already seen Part I: Recruitment and Selection at the beginning of this chapter[338]. Even at this initial stage there are provisions clearly premised on an element of employee confidentiality, in particular the advice to (a) only ask for information that is directly relevant to recruitment, (b) destroy information afterwards unless it is definitely necessary to keep as part of a personnel file and (c) only ask for sensitive personal data (especially on health record) once a prima facie decision has been made to appoint that person. Part II: Employment Records continues this approach into the question of what information to keep (and how to keep it) on employees once appointed. Key points here are to (a) only keep such records as are necessary (and inform employees what is kept), (b) ensure security of records, limiting access only to those managers who need to have it, (c) use absence records, not detailed schemes records, where possible, (d) have systems to cope with access requests by employees and third parties, (e) provide references to third parties only where the employee wishes this, (f) ensure that disciplinary records are accurate and only used when necessary and for proper purposes (for example in later investigations) and (g) have a disposal policy for old or spent information. Medical records are to be dealt with separately in the fourth part of the Code (not produced at the time of writing). However, it is the third part 'Monitoring at work' which is likely to be most controversial in the context of confidentiality. In draft at the time of writing, it is to cover not just obviously intrusive forms of monitoring such as the use of telephone tapping or CCTV cameras, but the much wider and more sensitive areas of monitoring for email and/or Internet abuse. Here, the simple approach that the machinery belongs to the employer, who can therefore do as he wants, is not sufficient because we are seeing the evolution of at least formative ideas that an employee at work has certain rights or expectations of privacy, especially where personal use is not wholly banned. Key suggestions in the Code are to (a) have clear business reasons for any monitoring, (b) have a policy on the use and abuse of electronic communications and publicise it to staff, (c) keep access to information obtained restricted, (d) use an 'impact assessment' (similar to a health and safety risk assessment) to determine what monitoring is justified by the benefits, (e) ensure that workers and others know the extent of monitoring, (f) where possible monitor traffic, not content[339], (g) try to use software solutions to present abuse at source (especially downloading of offensive material) and (h) in dealing with any allegations of Internet abuse, remember that inappropriate websites can be accessed by mistake. Technically, of course, a Code such as this is only relevant to

338 See p 103 above.
339 Although sensible generally, this might not be possible in a case of alleged harassment by electronic means where the content would be vital.

data protection issues, and breach of it for no good reason would only be of direct concern in an enforcement action under the Data Protection Act 1998. However, the cross-over into employment indirectly could be considerable for three reasons – (1) in fact the Codes are likely to have a major impact on personnel/HR practice, just as much as if they had been produced under employment law; (2) the Code on Monitoring could well have a major impact in any case concerning discipline or dismissal for email or Internet abuse (for example where the employee has breached a well-known and consistently applied employer policy, drafted in line with the Code[340]); (3) an interesting point would arise if ever an employee sought to use breach of his or her rights or expectations under the Code(s) (especially that on monitoring) to privacy at work as a reason for walking out and claiming constructive dismissal – would the courts evolve an implied term either to protect privacy generally or (less controversially) to abide by the Codes? If so, the cross-over would become formal, not just informal.

The third development concerns a modern trend in the employment of more senior employees of offering permanent health insurance ('PHI') as part of the remuneration package; paid for by the employer, this can offer major benefits to an employee who becomes permanently incapable of work through illness, but its relationship with ordinary sickness procedures and notice provisions has proved troublesome (as has the potentially difficult relationship between employer, employee and the insurance company providing the scheme[341]) especially where the PHI has been in the nature of an 'add-on' without thought as to its possible legal effects. In *Aspden v Webbs Poultry and Meat Group (Holdings) Ltd*[342] the plaintiff was a senior manager who was subject to the firm's PHI scheme for senior staff – if incapable of work for more than 26 weeks, he would be entitled to three-quarter salary until death, retirement or ceasing to be an employee. However, on engagement he had been given a standard contract which did *not* take the separate PHI scheme into account and in the case of long-term illness provided for six months' sick pay and then for dismissal. When he became ill (after altercations with the firm over reorganisations) the employers, who suspected he might have been exaggerating his illness, exercised their contractual power of dismissal before he could qualify for the PHI benefits. The employee brought an action for wrongful dismissal; normally this would have been doomed to failure because of the terms of the contract, but Sedley J upheld the employee's claim that on the facts of the case there was an implied term that, save for summary dismissal for cause[343], the employer would not terminate the contract while he was incapacitated, so as to deprive him of the PHI benefits. The

340 Particularly in the light of the hard line already taken by the EAT to such misconduct in *Thomas v Hillingdon London Borough Council* (2002) Times, 4 October.
341 In *Marlow v East Thames Housing Group Ltd* [2002] IRLR 798 the insurance company stopped paying the PHI benefits when it thought the employee was no longer incapable of work; the employee could not challenge this directly(the PHI scheme contract was between the employer and the insurance company) but established that the employer was contractually bound to take all reasonable steps to pursue her claim, on the basis of the implied term of trust and respect.
342 [1996] IRLR 521.
343 This was expressed in *Aspden* to be the important protection that the employer needs in such a case; for an example of its application, see *Briscoe v Lubrizol Ltd* [2002] EWCA Civ 508, [2002] IRLR 607. However, it now needs to be expanded to cover summary dismissal for cause *and* dismissal for bona fide redundancy, neither of which mean that the employer is trying to frustrate the PHI scheme, and so neither of which would be contrary to the implied term: *Hill v General Accident Fire and Life Assurance Corpn plc* [1998] IRLR 641, OH.

judge acknowledged that this was on the edge of permissibility for the use of implied terms, but was necessary because otherwise an unrestricted power to terminate would completely negate the working of the PHI scheme which clearly applied to the plaintiff but had been completely overlooked when his contract had been given to him. Although an adventurous decision, it has been followed by the Outer House of the Court of Session[344] and approved obiter in the Court of Appeal[345]; it marks yet a further move away from strict contract doctrine in the employment field.

One point of considerable importance for future developments here is whether the *Aspden* principle will be applied outside the PHI context. It operates by, in effect, placing a restriction on the employer's normal power to dismiss by giving notice where to do so would negate valuable PHI rights; might it evolve into a wider principle, applying to deliberate attempts by the employer to use the doctrine of notice to deprive the employee unfairly of *any* valuable rights or expectations? This would be a major inroad into the traditional law on dismissal by notice,[346] but there are signs of such an extension (certainly where there is a close analogy to PHI rights) in *Jenvey v Australian Broadcasting Corpn*[347] where an employee, alleging that his employment had been deliberately terminated in a way and at a time so as to ensure that he could not claim valuable redundancy rights, successfully bought a common law breach of contract action for the value of those rights. Elias J held that there had been a breach of a specific implied term that, where an employer has resolved to dismiss an employee by reason of redundancy, the employer will not (other than for good cause) dismiss that employee for some other reason. Thus, any advance of the law here is suitably cautious and incremental, not based on any wide generalised principle; on the other hand, the case does extend the PHI cases by analogy into an area not previously covered. As in any area of controversy, however, developments are not all in one direction, and the subsequent decision of the Privy Council in *Reda v Flag Ltd*[348] was far less adventurous. It concerned complex contractual provisions for the termination and payment of two senior executives of a Bermudan company; there were three stipulated forms of termination, each with a different compensation package spelled out. When the company dismissed them expressly under one of these (with a substantial payment) but with the effect that they could not benefit from a new share option scheme being introduced, they argued on analogy with *Aspden* that this was unlawful and that they were entitled to the benefit of the scheme. The Privy Council turned down their claims. At first sight this appears to go against the flow of the previous cases but it is suggested that the case is best viewed as reliant on its facts – the termination agreement was highly specific and was not to be assailed by reliance on implied terms (whereas such an assault may be more feasible in more normal cases where the employer is just (ab)using the ordinary doctrine of notice, with no large pay-offs); *Aspden* was distinguished, not disapproved

---

344 *Adin v Sedco Forex International Resources Ltd* [1997] IRLR 280, Ct of Sess.

345 *Brompton v AOC Int Ltd* [1997] IRLR 639, CA. In *Villella v MFI Furniture Centres Ltd* [1999] IRLR 468 a similar argument succeeded again, this time where dismissal was used to try to avoid continuing with PHI payments already being made, as in *Briscoe v Lubrizol Ltd* (n 343 above) where the Court of Appeal accepted the *Aspden* principle as established law.

346 See p 459 below and Suite and Randall *Contract Actions in Modern Employment: Developments and Issues* (2000) pp 93–95.

347 [2002] EWHC 927 (QB), [2003] ICR 79, [2002] IRLR 520.

348 [2002] UKPC 38, [2002] IRLR 747.

(and none of the other above case law was mentioned); and in any event on the facts the court clearly thought little of the merits of the employees' cases, and said that the employers had had sound commercial reasons ('reasonable cause'?) for acting as they had done. Thus, unless and until we are told to the contrary in further case law, it is suggested that *Reda* should not be seen as stopping further development in this area in suitable cases, though it does show that radical arguments such as these are not to be relied on too readily or too widely. Suitability here may well be heavily reliant on the substantive merits of the case. In *Jenvey* the employer had in fact dismissed the employee in a way that was automatically unfair (partly as revenge for tribunal proceedings brought by him over a dispute), but then pleaded that as the reason why he could not claim to have been redundant and so qualified for the enhanced redundancy rights. Faced with this deeply unattractive argument that the employer could rely on its own automatically unfair dismissal to negate the employee's rights (or at least expectations) Elias J ended his judgment with the following instructive passage:

'It follows that I find for the claimant. I confess that I am pleased to be able to do so. The defendant's position lacked merit. It would in my view have been a gross injustice if ABC were to be better off as a result of dismissing the employee for an unlawful reason than it would have been had it dismissed him lawfully by reason of the redundancy that had arisen. The need to preserve the integrity of the legal process recognised in the old adage "hard cases make bad law" may sometimes compel a court to accept a particular injustice because it cannot properly be remedied in line with legal principle. Fortunately, I am satisfied that I can here do justice without any improper distortion of the legal rules.'

(iv) Duties of the employee

(a) Obedience

In the days before employment was explained in terms of a contract, the servant's duty of obedience was taken to be a natural element of employment and indeed if one delves far enough back it was accompanied by the master's right to discipline and perhaps chastise the erring servant. It is now explained as an aspect of the contract of employment that the employer may give and the employee should obey a lawful order, and indeed it has been argued that this should be taken a step further and viewed not as a duty of obedience, but rather as an example of co-operation. The term 'lawful' order is often used but in this context it means primarily an order which is reasonably within the ambit of the employment in question so that, once again, in any given dispute much or all will depend on the terms of the individual contract of employment, whether express or implied; the task of deciding what is the scope of the employment may be facilitated by the requirements in section 1 of the Employment Rights Act 1996 of written particulars of terms of employment, particularly of the title of the job which the employee is employed to do (section 1(4)(f)). Thus, the employer cannot give orders outside the proper scope of the employment, for example orders of a 'personal' nature such as regulating the length of the employee's hair or his out-of-work activities (unless he can show some special considerations bringing such matters within the scope of employment, such as danger in having long hair when working machines or some form of special interest, employment-related, in outside activities). Also, this principle means that the employer cannot order the employee to change his contract, so that if it is clear that he is not contractually bound to be mobile or work overtime, it will not be 'lawful' to order him to work elsewhere[349] or put in hours above the basic[350].

Questions of obedience are naturally bound up with the law on dismissal, and at common law principally with the employer's right to dismiss summarily. In general, refusal to obey a proper order would usually justify summary dismissal and although such matters tend to change over time with different social attitudes this is still the basic position with regard to the common law action for wrongful dismissal. However, the statutory action for unfair dismissal is now far more important and the question of fairness depends upon all the factors in the case, not just whether the employee was technically in breach of contract[351]. In the light of this, although the employer may still dismiss summarily in cases of grave misconduct, a single act of disobedience may not necessarily render the dismissal fair, for although it would qualify as a reason concerning 'conduct' within section 98(2) of the Employment Rights Act 1996, the tribunal must go further and consider, under section 98(4), whether the employer acted reasonably in treating it as a sufficient reason for dismissal in all the circumstances of the particular case.

The duty of obedience at common law is subject to two particular qualifications. The first is that the employer may not order the employee to do something illegal[352]; if he does so the employee is entitled to refuse to obey the order, and any purported summary dismissal will be wrongful, and of more importance, very likely to be held to be unfair, as in *Morrish v Henlys (Folkestone) Ltd*[353] where the employee was dismissed because he refused to falsify accounts. The second qualification is that the employer may not order the employee into danger; in *Ottoman Bank v Chakarian*[354] an employee was held to have been justified in disobeying an order to stay in Constantinople where he had previously been sentenced to death and was in danger of being apprehended a second time. However, it appears that for this exception to apply there must be immediate and personal danger so that in *Bouzourou v Ottoman Bank*[355], expectation merely of general hostility from the Turkish authorities was not enough to justify refusal of an order to work in Mersina; likewise with an unspecific fear of IRA activity if sent to work in Eire in *Walmsley v UDEC Refrigeration Ltd*[356].

---

349 *O'Brien v Associated Fire Alarms Ltd* [1969] 1 All ER 93, [1968] 1 WLR 1916, CA; *Courtaulds Northern Spinning Ltd v Sibson* [1988] ICR 451, [1988] IRLR 305, CA; cf *Stevenson v Teesside Bridge and Engineering Ltd* [1971] 1 All ER 296 and *United Kingdom Atomic Energy Authority v Claydon* [1974] ICR 128, [1979] IRLR 6.
350 *Pengilly v North Devon Farmers Ltd* [1973] IRLR 41.
351 *Farrant v Woodroffe School* [1998] ICR 184, [1998] IRLR 176.
352 *Gregory v Ford* [1951] 1 All ER 121. Semble there must be a clear order if the employer is to be in breach of this principle: *Buckoke v Greater London Council* [1970] 2 All ER 193, per Plowman J; affd by the Court of Appeal: [1971] 1 Ch 655, [1971] 2 All ER 254, CA.
353 [1973] 2 All ER 137, [1973] ICR 482.
354 [1930] AC 277, PC.
355 [1930] AC 271, PC.
356 [1972] IRLR 80, IT.

(b) Adaptation to new methods and techniques

As was pointed out earlier in this chapter when considering changes in the terms of employment, problems may arise from the fact that jobs change but contracts tend to be static. What is to happen if the employer introduces new working methods or techniques which the employee is unwilling to accept? In such a case, the employee may argue that the changes are sufficiently fundamental to fall outside the scope of his existing contract; if this is so, the employer must be able to show a consensual variation of the relevant terms before he can insist on the employee accepting the changes[357]. There is extensive case law on this point in the law on redundancy[358], where the courts have consistently given considerable latitude to employers to alter work practices without being held to have altered the job itself. A second possibility is that the employer may have envisaged the possibility of future changes and in the light of that either framed the contractual terms (particularly the job title/description) flexibly, or given himself express contractual authority to make the changes in question. However, the question remains what is to happen where neither of these solutions applies, ie where the changes are not fundamental enough to alter the job itself, but changes in methods or techniques are not expressly covered by the contract? Can the employee refuse to adapt?

It appears that in most cases he will not be able to refuse, for he will not be deemed to have a right to continue as he always had indefinitely. There is little case law directly on this point, but it is possible that if necessary the courts would develop an implied term of adaptation. Signs of this can be seen in the judgment of Walton J in *Cresswell v Board of Inland Revenue*[359]. In that case, Inland Revenue officers and clerks refused to operate a new computerised system of PAYE administration when their employers could not guarantee that there would be no compulsory redundancies. They sought a declaration that their employers were in breach of contract in requiring them to operate the computers. It was held, however, that the change to computers was not sufficient to fall outside their contractual duties of tax gathering and that on the facts they were expected to adapt to the new methods:

'... there can really be no doubt as to the fact that an employee is expected to adapt himself to new methods and techniques introduced in the course of his employment'[360].

However, if such an implied term is to be developed, it should be noted that Walton J added a requirement of reasonableness, continuing the same passage as follows:

'Of course, in a proper case the employer must provide any necessary training or retraining. ... [I]t will, in all cases, be a question of pure fact as to whether the retraining involves the acquisition of such esoteric skills that it would not be reasonable to expect the employee to acquire them.'

---

357 On variation, see p 118, above. If no such variation is forthcoming, the employer may have to dismiss the objector employee and defend an unfair dismissal action on the ground that the dismissal was fair because of the business need to change; see p 599 below.

358 See p 631 below.

359 [1984] ICR 508, [1984] IRLR 190. Napier, 'Computerisation and employment rights' (1992) 21 ILJ 1.

Cresswell was a common law action, but this reasonableness approach would be particularly important in an unfair dismissal action where the employer, having introduced changes which were not sufficiently major to alter the contract of employment, insisted on the employee adopting the new methods but then dismissed him for incapability when he was unable so to adapt.

(c) The duty of care

An employee owes to his employer an implied duty of care in carrying out his job. The basic authority for this is usually said to be *Harmer v Cornelius*[361] even though that case actually concerned a representation that the employee possessed the necessary *skill* for the job, for in subsequent cases skill and care have been treated as roughly equivalent. This duty of care applies generally[362] and could cover, for example, care in using the employer's equipment. However, its principal legal significance arises where an employee in the course of his employment injures a third party or his goods. In these circumstances the employer may be sued for damages by the third party as being vicariously liable for the tort of the employee (see chapter 12 below). Once sued, however, the employer has a legal action against the employee for an *indemnity*, and this has caused some difficulty.

The employer's cause of action arises in two ways:

(a) He may sue the employee for breach of contract, for in incurring him in liability to pay damages the employee is in breach of his implied duty of care. The leading case on this is *Lister v Romford Ice and Cold Storage Co Ltd*[363] where it was clearly held that this implied duty exists, and the employer's insurers were awarded an indemnity against the employee who had negligently run down a third party (his own father as it happened) who had sued the employer for damages. In the House of Lords, the employee attempted to mitigate this harsh application of the duty of care by saying that in modern employment law there is a further implied term that the employer will ensure that the employee is insured against liability such as this, but this was rejected by a majority of three to two.

(b) He may sue the employee in tort, for where the employer has been held vicariously liable he and the negligent employee are in law joint tortfeasors, so that he may sue the employee for contribution or a full indemnity under the Civil Liability (Contribution) Act 1978; under this statute, the court may award such contribution as it thinks 'just and equitable having regard to the extent of [the employee's] responsibility for the damage'.

The decision in *Lister's* case caused some consternation and has been heavily criticised on the grounds that the principal rationalisation for vicarious liability is the practical one that it is the employer or his insurer who can afford to pay the damages and that a finding by a court that the employee was negligent may be just a means of fixing liability on to the employer or his insurers; on both of these grounds, a right of indemnity would be inconsistent[364]. Two ways round the

---

360 At pp 518 and 195, respectively.
361 (1858) 5 CBNS 236.
362 Theoretically breach of this duty could found an action for damages by the employer against the employee: this is most unlikely to happen, though there has been one modern example of it, on rather special facts: *Janata Bank v Ahmed* [1981] ICR 791, [1981] IRLR 457, CA.
363 [1957] AC 555, [1957] 1 All ER 125, HL.
364 Glanville Williams 'Vicarious liability and the Master's indemnity' (1957) 20 MLR 220 and 437.

decision in *Lister's* case have been suggested. The first was in *Harvey v R G O'Dell Ltd*[365] where McNair J held that the right of indemnity did not apply to an employee driving a vehicle in the course of his employment when such action was not work he was employed to do but was merely a special occasion on which the employee had assisted his employer by undertaking an unusual task; this, however, is to take a very refined view of what an employee is engaged to do. The second arises from the fact that at common law (before the new cause of action was added by statute in 1935) the rule was that there could be *no* contribution between joint tortfeasors[366]; there was, however, one longstanding exception to this where the party seeking contribution was wholly innocent[367] and only liable by some operation of law such as vicarious liability – *Lister's* case was an example of this exception, hence the common law indemnity. Thus, if some fault can be attributed to the employer who is seeking contribution, the case does not fall within the exception, but comes instead within the rule and so contribution cannot be claimed; such fault could arise, for example, if the employer had given the employee some task beyond his competence or had failed to give him proper instruction, as in *Jones v Manchester Corpn*[368] where an inexperienced doctor had caused physical injury to a patient who had sued the employing hospital board for damages, but when the board sought an indemnity from the doctor the Court of Appeal, by a majority, refused to allow it since the hospital had also been at fault in failing to provide adequate supervision for the doctor. The practical problem is that, even if one can circumvent the contractual action in this way, the court still has the discretion to apportion under the 1978 Act, and so an indemnity may still in the end be awarded against the employee, unless the court could be persuaded that it would not be 'just and equitable' to do so; 100% indemnities under the Act were awarded against employees in *Ryan v Fildes*[369], *Semtex Ltd v Gladstone*[370], *Harvey v R G O'Dell Ltd* (above) and in *Lister's* case itself.

In the light of these problems, the effects of *Lister's* case were investigated by a committee of the then Ministry of Labour[371] which concluded that while legislation could alter the position, there was no urgency since in general employers would not seek indemnities because of the effect on industrial relations, and insurers (who were most likely to be interested, since when they pay the damages awarded against the employers they are 'subrogated' into their insured's shoes and can exercise their insured's rights in their own favour – it was an insurance company which brought the action in *Lister's* case, not the employers) have a 'gentleman's agreement' not to exercise these subrogated rights to indemnity against employees (in personal injury cases, where there is no willful misconduct or collusion). This remains the position and there has been no amending legislation. However, the rights against employees still exist in law (even if not generally exercised by employers or their insurers in practice) as can be seen from *Morris v Ford Motor Co Ltd*[372] where a third party who was neither the employer nor an insurance company, claimed to have acquired the important right of subrogation through a peculiar indemnity clause in a cleaning

365 [1958] 2 QB 78, [1958] 1 All ER 657.
366 The rule in *Merryweather v Nixan* (1799) 8 Term Rep 186.
367 *Adamson v Jarvis* (1827) 4 Bing 66; *Pearson v Skelton* (1836) 1 M & W 504.
368 [1952] 2 QB 852, [1952] 2 All ER 125, CA.
369 [1938] 3 All ER 517.
370 [1954] 2 All ER 206, [1954] 1 WLR 945.
371 See Gardiner (1959) 22 MLR 652.
372 [1973] QB 792, [1973] 2 All ER 1084, CA.

contract. The third party then sought to sue the negligent employee who had (indirectly) caused him to pay damages, but the Court of Appeal by a majority refused to allow it. There was no *express* subrogation clause in the cleaning contract, so Lord Denning MR disallowed an implied one on the grounds (a) that subrogation was an equitable concept and it would not be equitable to allow it in this case and (b) that no clause would be implied in the light of industrial realities, and James LJ also disallowed it on ground (b). However, this case does *not* remove the legal right to indemnity in the industrial sphere, for two reasons – first, it contains no assault on *Lister's* case, only upon the concept of subrogation which does not directly affect the actual right to indemnity; second, the majority could only decide the case this way because there was no express subrogation provision – if there had been it could not have been negated by an implied term to the contrary, so James LJ at least would presumably have had to decide the other way and that would have produced a majority in favour of the indemnity. The possibility of an indemnity being claimed from a negligent employee therefore continues to exist even if it is rarely enforced in practice. This raises two further points of interest – first, no concerted action has been taken by trade unions to secure insurance cover for employees (the term claimed in *Lister's* case), and second, it appears to be no-one's business or interest to clear up an area where the formal legal position is in no way in accordance with general assumptions or practice.

(d) Good faith

An act which is inconsistent with the terms of the contract, express or implied, and which is injurious to the employer and his interest will amount to a breach of the duty of faithful service. Thus, a manager whose acts were injurious to the interests of the theatre he was employed to manage was held to have been rightly dismissed at common law[373], and conversely a court saved from attachment an employee who refused to produce material documents in his possession which he held merely in his role of employee, for the court would not infer that he could produce the documents without violating the duty he owed to his employer[374]. In particular, an employee must not place himself in a position in which his own interests conflict with his duty to his employer[375]. The clash of interest and duty can be seen most clearly in the leading case, *Boston Deep Sea Fishing and Ice Co v Ansell* [376]. The defendant had been employed as managing director of the plaintiff company and he had contracted with a firm of shipbuilders for the supply of certain vessels and had taken from them a commission in respect of the transaction, of which his employers knew nothing. He also possessed shares in an ice-making and fish-carrying company which paid bonuses to those of its shareholders who, being owners of fishing vessels, used the company's ice or its services as a carrier. He was held to the strictest accountability but, apart from

373 *Lacy v Osbaldiston* (1837) 8 C & P 80.
374 *Eccles & Co v Louisville and Nashville Railroad Co* [1912] 1 KB 135, CA.
375 *Pearce v Foster* (1886) 17 QBD 536, CA provides a good example; see generally Stephens 'An agent's duty to account' (1975) 28 CLP 39.
376 (1888) 39 Ch D 339, CA. Note that one of the main propositions established in this case, that at common law the employer may rely on misconduct unknown to him at the date of dismissal and only discovered subsequently in order to justify dismissal, does *not* apply to proceedings for unfair dismissal: *W Devis & Sons Ltd v Atkins* [1977] 3 All ER 40, [1977] ICR 662, HL.

that, there was clearly a breach of his duty faithfully to serve, since the temptation to use the company's ice or its services as a carrier conflicted or might conflict with his duty to consider his employer's interests in preference to his own. It was held that he was properly dismissed, and he had to account to his employer for his profits. It is true that this case concerned a managing director and directors may be under a special fiduciary duty anyway[377], but the general principle may apply to any employee who misuses his employer's property in a way which shows breach of fidelity (for example by borrowing from the till when not allowed to do so: *Sinclair v Neighbour*[378]), or improperly exploits his position of employment in order to make a secret profit or gain. In *Reading v A-G*[379] , Sergeant Reading who was stationed in Egypt agreed on a number of occasions to accompany lorries to certain destinations, his uniform guaranteeing that such lorries would avoid inspection by the police. These lorries contained illicit spirits and as a result of his services Reading secured almost £20,000. When the military authorities arrested him, they impounded the money and when he was released from prison he brought a petition of right claiming return of the money by the Crown. The House of Lords not surprisingly held against him, for he had misused his position in the service of the Crown and had to account for his profit.

Although secret profits and interests may have to be disclosed, and in certain circumstances an employee may have to inform his employer about matters in his knowledge which affect confidential interests of the employer[380], the duty of fidelity must not be taken too far. Except for the case of directors who are under a fiduciary duty[381], a contract of employment is not a contract uberrimae fidei requiring total and voluntary disclosure. Thus, an employee is not under a general duty to declare facts which may prove inimical to the employer, including his own misconduct or unsavoury aspects of his own background. This rule, dating back to the well-known authority of *Bell v Lever Bros Ltd*[382], was strongly reaffirmed in *Nottingham University v Fishel*[383] where the employers were seeking to recover damages from their employee, a leading scientist, who had been undertaking private work abroad without telling them, also using other university employees. Their victory was distinctly Pyrrhic because the primary breach of contract (working abroad in university time) had in fact benefited university research so that there was no damage; there was a secondary breach by using the other employees which gave rise to damages but not to any great amount. On the crucial allegation (for present purposes) that he was in breach by not telling them the truth, the

---

377   *Cook v Deeks* [1916] 1 AC 554, PC; *Cranleigh Precision Engineering Ltd v Bryant* [1964] 3 All ER 289, [1965] 1 WLR 1293; *Industrial Development Consultants v Cooley* [1972] 2 All ER 162, [1972] 1 WLR 443; *Thomas Marshall (Exports) Ltd v Guinle* [1978] ICR 905, [1978] IRLR 174. The Companies Act 1985, s 317 requires a director with an interest in a contract with the company to disclose that interest to the board of directors; for a newsworthy example, see *Guinness plc v Saunders* [1988] 2 All ER 940, [1988] 1 WLR 863, CA (non-disclosure leading to a constructive trust to repay £5.2m).

378   [1967] 2 QB 279, [1966] 3 All ER 988, CA.

379   [1951] AC 507, [1951] 1 All ER 617, HL.

380   *Cranleigh Precision Engineering Ltd v Bryant* [1964] 3 All ER 289, [1965] 1 WLR 1293.

381   *Regal (Hastings) Ltd v Gulliver* (1942) [1967] 2 AC 134n, [1942] 1 All ER 378, HL; *Horcal Ltd v Gatland* [1984] IRLR 288, CA.

382   [1932] AC 161, HL. Most of these cases involve attempts by an employer to recover golden handshakes given to employees who, after leaving, are discovered to have been defrauding the employer. Note that a 'spent' conviction does not have to be disclosed anyway, under the Rehabilitation of Offenders Act 1974, s 4 (for the application of this Act to unfair dismissal cases, see p 582 below).

383   [2000] ICR 1462, [2000] IRLR 471.

court held that it was important *not* to erect any contractual duties on employees to fiduciary levels and that special duties of disclosure should only exist if expressly provided for in the contract, which was not the case here. Thus, the university's claim under this head failed, very much along the lines of *Bell v Lever Bros Ltd*. However, this rule has always been subject to the qualification that the employee must not positively *mislead* the employer as to such matters[384], and in the important case of *Sybron Corpn v Rochem Ltd*[385] it was further (a) suggested that there may be a duty to disclose the employee's own misconduct which has been fraudulently concealed, and (b) held that there may be on the facts of the case a positive duty to disclose the misconduct of *other* employees (particularly in the case of an employee high in the company's hierarchy, with responsibility for those other employees) even if that involves of necessity disclosing his own misconduct[386].

From this general discussion of fidelity, we must now turn to four specific ways in which an employer might be in breach of his duty – by competition, misuse of confidential information, making his own inventions and failing to serve the employee in good faith.

(1) Competition

The courts will be most reluctant to impose restraints on a person's spare time and generally an employee's skills are his own (even if learned in the employer's time) so that normally there is no legal objection to an employee taking other employment in his spare time. The courts will, however, interfere in the untypical case where the use of the employee's skill and knowledge can be clearly shown to be harming the employer. This was the situation in the leading case of *Hivac Ltd v Park Royal Scientific Instruments Ltd*[387]. Certain employees of the plaintiff company worked in their spare time on a similar kind of highly specialised work for the defendant company, the two firms being in direct competition. There was no evidence that any of the employees (who were not parties to the action) had divulged any confidential information. It was found that the employees had agreed to do and had done work which they knew must harm their employers, that this was a breach of their duty of fidelity and that the defendant company would be restrained from employing them. The court made something of the fact that because of the abnormality of the times and the operation of an essential work order, the employees could not easily be dismissed, but it is doubtful how far this is relevant, as the principle remains that where the employee harms his employer the law may interfere:

'It would be most unfortunate if anything we said should place an undue restraint on the right of the workman, particularly a manual workman, to

---

384 Hence the importance, on recruitment, of the employer asking the right questions (eg at an interview) so that the employee cannot simply refrain from volunteering information and obtain the employment sub silentio. Deliberate fraud in gaining employment will usually be a fair ground for dismissal: *City of Birmingham District Council v Beyer* [1978] 1 All ER 910, [1977] IRLR 211. Moreover, in the light of *Fishel* (n 383 above) an employer may be advised to include in the appointed employee's contract a clause specifically requiring disclosure (eg of any other employment or activities to be undertaken) if it is likely to be a significant issue.
385 [1983] 2 All ER 707, [1983] IRLR 253, CA.
386 Applying *Swain v West (Butchers) Ltd* [1936] 3 All ER 261, CA.
387 [1946] Ch 169, [1946] 1 All ER 350, CA.

make use of his leisure for his profit. On the other hand, it would be deplorable if it were laid down that a workman could, consistently with his duty to his employer, knowingly, deliberately and secretly set himself to do in his spare time something which would inflict great harm on his master's business'[388].

There may, therefore, be cases where the courts will restrain competition, but even then it will only be during the course of employment, and will not apply to competition by an ex-employee[389]. If the employer wishes to fetter competition after the employee leaves him it will have to be by an express restraint clause (see above under head 4 – Legality and restraint of trade) and, as we have seen, even then the clause will only be valid if there is some definite element of trade secrets, customer connections or staff preservation to protect, for the courts will not allow a clause which is aimed simply at stifling competition[390].

If an employee engages in improper competition that may be a valid reason for dismissal, though as always in the realm of unfair dismissal the fact that it is a breach of contract is not conclusive (as it might have been at common law for wrongful dismissal) and the dismissal must still be fair in all the circumstances, including the procedure adopted[391]. If the employer finds that the employee is soliciting customers with a view to setting up in business when he leaves, that too may be a valid ground for pre-emptive dismissal, but once again the evidence of this will have to be clear, and may require reasonable investigation by the employer before this step is taken[392]; if the further elements of trade secrets or other confidential information being at risk are not present, however, merely planning to leave employment to work for a competitor or to set up in competition will probably not be a fair ground for dismissal[393].

(2) Misuse or disclosure of confidential information

During the course of his employment the employee is under an implied duty not to misuse confidential information belonging to his employer[394] and this is a duty which may continue to operate after the termination of his employment; however, it was pointed out by the Court of Appeal in what has for some time now been

---

388 [1946] Ch 169 at 178, [1946] 1 All ER 350 at 356, per Lord Greene MR. This dictum was applied by the EAT to an unfair dismissal claim in *Nova Plastics Ltd v Frogatt* [1982] IRLR 146, reinforcing the requirement of definite harm to the employer before an ordinary employee can be said to be in breach of this duty.

389 *JA Mont (UK) Ltd v Mills* [1993] IRLR 172, CA. The combination of the duty on an *existing* employee not to compete and a long notice provision produces a 'garden leave clause': see p 464 below.

390 *Herbert Morris Ltd v Saxelby* [1916] 1 AC 688, HL; *Faccenda Chicken Ltd v Fowler* [1986] ICR 297, [1986] IRLR 69, CA.

391 *Gibson v National Union of Dyers, Bleachers and Textile Workers* (1972) 7 ITR 324; *Golden Cross Hire Co Ltd v Lovell* [1979] IRLR 267.

392 *Hawkins v Prickett* [1976] IRLR 52, IT.

393 *Harris and Russell Ltd v Slingsby* [1973] 3 All ER 31, [1973] ICR 454; *Laughton and Hawley v Bapp Industrial Supplies Ltd* [1986] ICR 634, [1986] IRLR 245; cf, however, *Marshall v Industrial Systems and Control Ltd* [1992] IRLR 294 where a managing director, proposing to leave, had suborned two other employees and approached customers (*Laughton* distinguished), and *Adamson v B & L Cleaning Services Ltd* [1995] IRLR 193 where the foreman of a contract cleaning firm tendered for a contract in competition with his employer prior to leaving to set up his own firm, and was fairly dismissed.

394 *Bents Brewery Co Ltd v Hogan* [1945] 2 All ER 570; see generally Bryan 'The employee and trade secrets law' (1977) 30 CLP 191.

viewed as the leading modern case on the subject, *Faccenda Chicken Ltd v Fowler*[395], that there is a difference in the content and extent of the duty – in the case of an existing employee the obligation of confidentiality is wider (covering matters such as the employee's own particular skills and knowledge acquired generally during the employment) than in the case of an ex-employee whose obligations to his ex-employer are restricted to the kind of trade secrets or confidential customer connections that could be the subject of a valid restraint of trade clause[396]. To cover this latter case (of an ex-employee), in any employment where questions of confidentiality are at all likely to be material the employer is well advised to extract from the employee such an express restraint clause (or a garden leave clause) which is not only more certain, but which may in practice be more effective for, provided that it is valid, it will stop the ex-employee actually entering employment where he may be tempted to divulge confidential information, whereas the implied duty of fidelity could only be used to seek to prevent him from divulging such information once he is in the employment in question. An express clause is thus preferable, but if the employer omits to negotiate one or if there is an express clause which stops short of imposing any actual restraints on the employee, the courts will usually find an implied term as in *Robb v Green*[397] where a manager secretly copied out lists of his employer's customers, left the employment and set up in competition using the lists: the Court of Appeal upheld the injunction which had been granted restraining the ex-employee and Lord Esher MR said:

'I think that in a contract of service the Court must imply such a stipulation as I have mentioned (ie, that the servant will act with good faith towards his master), because it is a thing which must necessarily have been in view of both parties when they entered into the contract. It is impossible to suppose that a master would have put a servant into a confidential position of this kind, unless he thought that the servant would be bound to use good faith towards him; or that the servant would not know, when he entered into this position, that the master would rely on his observance of good faith in the confidential relation between them.'

Thus, in *Sanders v Parry*[398] an assistant solicitor who set up independently, taking away from his employer one of the practice's main clients whose affairs he had looked after, was held to have broken his implied duty of good faith.

In general, the same rules will apply to this implied duty as apply to express restraint of trade clauses, and these are considered under head 4 of this chapter – Legality and restraint of trade; in particular, the duty will apply essentially to trade secrets and customer connections (those being recognised by the law as protectable interests, with increasingly the addition of staff preservation), there

---

395 [1986] ICR 297, [1986] IRLR 69, CA, noted Hepple [1986] 15 ILJ 183; applied in *Roger Bullivant Ltd v Ellis* [1987] ICR 464, [1987] IRLR 491, CA and *Johnson & Bloy (Holdings) Ltd v Wolstenholme Rink plc* [1987] IRLR 499, CA.

396 Thus, in *Wallace Bogan & Co v Cove* [1997] IRLR 453, CA solicitors leaving their employer to set up their own firm played it 'by the book', doing nothing to infringe the higher duties before leaving; but *then* writing to clients of the old employer announcing the existence of the new firm. *Held* – no general restriction on this form of competition after employment, in the absence of a restraint of trade clause.

397 [1895] 2 QB 315, CA; the passage cited is at 317.

398 [1967] 2 All ER 803, [1967] 1 WLR 753. Contract on the facts *Wallace Bogan & Co v Cove* [1997] IRLR 453, CA.

must be a genuine element of secrecy attached to the information in question, the duty will not apply to ordinary skills or knowledge gained during employment, and it will not be allowed in order simply to stifle bona fide competition[399]. However, even though essentially the same principles apply, the express clause remains preferable, for it will normally restrain the ex-employee from entering certain forms of employment during a particular period, and so breach of it will readily be shown, whereas the implied duty allows other employment, only restraining the ex-employee from improper disclosure and this may be far more difficult to *prove*, particularly where there is no tangible evidence such as the deliberate copying out of plans or lists (as in *Robb v Green*)[400]. This problem arises because of the difficult borderline between the ordinary use of information and expertise, albeit gained in the previous employment, which is permissible[401], and the improper misuse of confidential information which may be restrainable; this may be further complicated if the ex-employee is using some information from each category, and the principle has been stated by Lord Denning in *Seager v Copydex Ltd*[402] thus:

> 'When the information is mixed, being partly public and partly private then the recipient must take special care to use only the material which is in the public domain. He should go to the public source to get it; or, at any rate, not be in a better position than if he had gone to the public source. He should not get a start over others by using the information which he received in confidence.'

The difficulties of applying such a principle to any particular set of facts, for example where a technical director has left his employer and gone to work for a competitor on similar work, are great, and in the light of this it may be the case in practice that although there is no legal requirement that the ex-employee should have carried the information away in some tangible (particularly written) form before the duty can be used to restrain him (and so in some cases evidence of deliberate solicitation of customers prior to leaving has been sufficient[403]), the presence of evidence of such conduct could be extremely persuasive and indeed in the lack of it the employer could have grave problems of proof. Considering

---

399 The assumption has also been hitherto that, like a restraint clause, the implied duty will lapse if the employee is wrongfully dismissed, under the rule in *General Billposting Co Ltd v Atkinson* [1909] AC 118, HL (see p 133, n 176 above). However, *Campbell v Frisbee* [2002] EWCA Civ 1374, [2003] ICR 141 raised at least the possibility of a coterminous equitable obligation of confidence on an ex-employee (in particular not to divulge *personal* information about the ex-employer) which might survive an employer repudiation. The case itself was not determinative because all that the Court of Appeal were doing was to disapprove an order for summary judgment in favour of the claimant (the model Naomi Campbell); the matter was not dealt with on its merits: see Clarke (2003) 32 ILJ 43.

400 If, however, it *is* the case that the employee leaves with written material containing confidential information, he may expect short shrift from a court, even if he argues that at least some of the information could have been carried away in his head: *Johnson & Bloy (Holdings) Ltd v Wolstenholme Rink plc* [1987] IRLR 499, CA, applying *Roger Bullivant Ltd v Ellis* [1987] ICR 464, [1987] IRLR 491, CA where Nourse LJ stated that it was still of great importance that the principle in *Robb v Green* should be steadfastly maintained.

401 *Spafax Ltd v Harrison* [1980] IRLR 442, CA; *Faccenda Chicken Ltd v Fowler*, n 395 above.

402 [1967] 2 All ER 415 at 417, [1967] RPC 349 at 368, CA. This dictum refers particularly to the position of a third party, which is considered below, but the principle is applicable to the ex-employee himself.

403 *Wessex Dairies Ltd v Smith* [1935] 2 KB 80, CA; *Thomas Marshall (Exports) Ltd v Guinle* [1978] ICR 905, [1978] IRLR 174; cf *Hawkins v Prickett* [1976] IRLR 52, IT.

this problem in *Printers and Finishers Ltd v Holloway*[404] Cross J said, in the context of the ex-employee's knowledge of the general workings of the employer's business:

> 'Recalling matters of this sort is, to my mind, quite unlike memorising a formula or list of customers or what was said (obviously in confidence) at a particular meeting. The employee might well not realise that the feature or expedient in question was in fact peculiar to his late employer's process and factory; but even if he did such knowledge is not readily separable from his general knowledge of the flock printing process and his acquired skill in manipulating a flock printing plant, and I do not think that there was anything improper in his putting his memory or particular features of his late employer's plant at the disposal of his new employer. The law will defeat its own object if it seeks to enforce in this field standards which would be rejected by the ordinary man.'

The employer failed on this particular part of the case, essentially because his case was too vague (as in *Baker v Gibbons*[405]), and this is likely to be the case wherever the employer lacks compelling evidence such as deliberate subterfuge and compilation of information[406].

If an employee or ex-employee is misusing confidential information, what remedies are available to the employer? If the employee is still in employment, it might well be a good reason for dismissal which is likely to be held to be fair[407]. If he has already left employment, the employer may seek an injunction to restrain him from passing on information or damages for breach of the implied duty as in *Sanders v Parry*[408]. A complication might arise if the ex-employee passes on confidential information to a third party, for example a competitor with whom he has taken employment or a company which he has set up in order to take advantage of his illicit knowledge. This, however, has not proved a problem, for the original employer may sue that third party, seeking an injunction restraining him from taking advantage of the information either on the narrower ground of inducement to breach of contract[409] (particularly if the employee in question is still in employment with the original employer) or on the wider ground of breach of confidence. The exact basis and extent of this latter equitable concept are still

---

404 [1964] 3 All ER 731 at 736, [1965] 1 WLR 1 at 6.
405 [1972] 2 All ER 759, [1972] 1 WLR 693.
406 This is as a matter of evidence; there is, however, no legal principle that an employee is free to use *anything* carried away only in his head: *Johnson & Bloy (Holdings) Ltd v Wolstenholme Rink plc* [1987] IRLR 499, CA, disapproving dicta in favour of such a principle by Scott J in *Balston Ltd v Headline Filters Ltd* [1987] FSR 330.
407 *Smith v Du Pont (UK) Ltd* [1976] IRLR 107, IT.
408 [1967] 2 All ER 803, [1967] 1 WLR 753. See Goulding 'Springboard injunctions in employment law' (1995) 24 ILJ 152. In *Johnson & Bloy (Holdings) Ltd v Wolstenholme Rink plc* [1987] IRLR 499, CA it was held that a plaintiff employer in such a case should normally be entitled to an injunction – it is not enough for the defendant to offer an undertaking not to use the information to compete with the plaintiff (with the prospect only of damages if there is in fact unlawful competition).
409 *Bents Brewery Ltd v Hogan* [1945] 2 All ER 570; *Hivac v Park Royal Scientific Instruments Ltd* [1946] Ch 169, [1946] 1 All ER 350, CA. The injunction may even order the new employer not to proceed with contracts already entered into: *PSM International plc v Whitehouse* [1992] IRLR 279, CA.

arguable and some fundamental questions await a definite answer[410] (for example whether there is a breach if the recipient of the information is ignorant of its source or confidential nature, and if so, what the remedy should be). Whatever be the details and developments, however, it is capable of being a useful weapon against a third party in cases such as these, as a further ground for an injunction or damages[411], or, perhaps of more value, as a ground for ordering an account of profits[412] and delivery up or destruction of the material in question[413]. Thus, to take a useful example from an Australian jurisdiction, in *Ansell Rubber Co v Allied Rubber Industries*[414] the plaintiff company made rubber gloves from machines whose parts and principles were known, but the actual construction of which was secret. One of their employees, A, left their employment and set up the defendant company using identical machines, and a fellow employee, G, remained in employment while helping A to do so. In the subsequent action, the court held (i) that the construction of a machine is capable of being a matter of confidence, albeit made from known components; (ii) that A was in breach of his contractual duty of fidelity through misuse of confidential information, G was likewise in breach for that reason and through improper competition while still employed, and the defendant company had received and misused confidential information and so was in breach of confidence; (iii) that the plaintiff company should be awarded damages against A and G, an account of profits against the defendant company and injunctions restraining any further use of the information and the machines.

One exception to the duty not to misuse or divulge confidential information arises where disclosure by the employee or ex-employee is in the public interest. This might arise where the employer is committing a criminal offence, but it might also go wider than this. The exception evolved at common law, but is now covered by statute.

(i) *Common law* In *Initial Services Ltd v Putterill*[415] the ex-employee gave to a newspaper details of an unlawful price-protection ring involving the employers (contrary to the Restrictive Trade Practices Act 1956) and of price rises attributed to Selective Employment Tax in order to disguise higher profits. The Court of Appeal held that this was capable of constituting proper disclosure in the public interest, and Lord Denning MR clearly envisaged that this exception went beyond crime and fraud and applied wherever disclosure was justified in the public interest. This principle was applied in *Fraser v Evans*[416] and *Hubbard v Vosper*[417] but

410 On breach of confidence generally see *Saltman Engineering Co Ltd v Campbell Engineering Co Ltd* [1963] 3 All ER 413n, (1965) 65 RPC 203, CA; *Seager v Copydex Ltd* [1967] 2 All ER 415, [1967] RPC 349, CA; *Sun Printers Ltd v Westminster Press Ltd* [1982] IRLR 292, CA: Report on Breach of Confidence (Law Com No 110).
411 *Seager v Copydex Ltd (No 2)* [1969] 2 All ER 718, [1969] 1 WLR 809, CA. Causation must be proved: *Universal Thermosensors Ltd v Hibben* [1992] 3 All ER 257, [1992] 1 WLR 840.
412 *Peter Pan Manufacturing Corpn v Corsets Silhouette Ltd* [1963] 3 All ER 402, [1963] RPC 45. In a rather more sensational context, the possibility of an action for an account of profits through misuse of confidential information was mentioned as a further remedy for the government against Mr Peter Wright, author of *Spycatcher*, in the light of its failure to have it suppressed in other jurisdictions; no such proceedings were brought in the event.
413 *Industrial Furnaces Ltd v Reaves* [1970] RPC 605.
414 [1967] VR 37; the judgment of Gowans J contains an extensive review of the relevant British and US authorities on confidential information. For a more recent example, see *PSM International plc v Whitehouse* [1992] IRLR 279, CA.
415 [1968] 1 QB 396, [1967] 3 All ER 145, CA.
416 [1969] 1 QB 349, [1969] 1 All ER 8, CA.
417 [1972] 2 QB 84, [1972] 1 All ER 1023, CA.

was subject to restriction in *Beloff v Pressdram Ltd*[418] by Ungoed-Thomas J who thought that it only applied to the disclosure of 'misdeeds of a serious nature' by the employer. However, this restrictive view was later disapproved by the Court of Appeal in *Lion Laboratories Ltd v Evans*[419] where it was held that public interest disclosure could apply to a wide range of matters, of which 'iniquity' on the part of the employer was only one example. Moreover, disclosure in the public interest may be particularly justified where that disclosure is to a regulatory body with power of investigation and control of the employer's business[420]. This whole area became topical with increasing concern being expressed over attempts by certain employers to prevent any form of disclosure by employees by the incorporation of 'gagging clauses' into their contracts, for example banning them from talking to the press about anything concerning their employment, and making it a disciplinary offence to do so[421]. Particular concern arose over the use of such clauses by the newly independent trusts and other bodies in the NHS[422]. While at one level the incorporation of an express clause could be likened to the (lawful) use of a restraint of trade clause (rather than relying on the general implied term of confidentiality), the suspicion was quick to arise that these clauses were really intended to go further and prevent *any* disclosure or, as it has come to be known, whistle-blowing.

(ii) *Statute* Although the above common law will continue to apply by way of a defence to a civil action, concerns such as those above allied with certain moves (eg the Nolan Committee) towards more openness about standards in public life led to calls for more direct protection for the *individual* employee making disclosures in the public interest. This came about through a Private Member's Bill, backed by the government as a commitment in the White Paper 'Fairness at Work', which became the Public Interest Disclosure Act 1998[423]. This operates by way of additions to the Employment Rights Act 1996 to establish special protection from dismissal[424]

418 [1973] 1 All ER 241 at 260. The earlier authorities would have restricted it to criminal acts or danger to the state: *Weld-Blundell v Stephens* [1920] AC 956, HL. Note that an employee may in certain circumstances be under a statutory duty to disclose certain material, eg under the Health and Safety at Work etc Act 1974, ss 27 and 28.

419 [1985] QB 526, [1984] 2 All ER 417, CA. This is an interesting case on the application of the public interest defence, containing inter alia a statement by Stephenson LJ that not all that is interesting to the public may be disclosed in the public interest, and a reminder that the press may have a private interest of their own in making disclosures, which may be a factor to be taken into account.

420 *Re a Company's Application* [1989] ICR 449, [1989] IRLR 477.

421 Lewis 'Whistleblowers and job security' (1995) 58 MLR 208.

422 Vickers 'Whistleblowers and the NHS' (1995) NLJ 57. One such clause even prevented employees from contacting their MP without going through (protracted?) internal procedures. One irony is that, at the same time as concern was mounting about this practice, doctors were themselves being placed under a contractual *obligation* to blow the whistle on allegedly negligent colleagues (though not of course on the activities of the increasing legions of hospital administrators, a breed who have rapidly overtaken undertakers, farmers, estate agents and solicitors to top the list of public hate figures).

423 Lewis 'The Public Interest Disclosure Act 1998' (1998) 27 ILJ 325 and 'Whistleblowing at work: on what principles should legislation be based?' (2001) 30 ILJ 169.

424 Employment Rights Act 1996, s 103A; such a dismissal is automatically unfair, as is any later selection for redundancy for this reason; there is no qualifying period or upper age limit; the cap on the compensatory award for unfair dismissal has been removed completely in these cases and interim relief is available. According to Public Concern at Work (the charity that was the architect of the Act) in the first three years of this new law, there was a success rate of 46% before tribunals; the highest award was £805,000, the lowest £1,000 and (perhaps most significantly) the average was £107,117, a remarkably high figure.

or action short of dismissal[425] imposed because the worker[426] has made a 'protected disclosure'. This is the disclosure of information which, in the reasonable belief of the worker making the disclosure, tends to show a criminal offence, a failure to comply with a legal obligation, a miscarriage of justice, a health and safety danger, environmental damage, or deliberate concealment of any of these[427]. As with the wider view of the common law, this goes well beyond criminal offences and to that extent the protection is wide. Moreover, in the first major case on the subject the EAT gave the legislation an extremely wide interpretation, applying 'failure to comply with a legal obligation' to what was essentially a complaint that the employee's own contractual rights had been infringed (albeit in the sensitive area of his having allegedly been dismissed for making health and safety complaints)[428]. If such an approach is taken any further, these provisions will arguably go beyond what Parliament intended (in an Act meant to apply to *public* disclosure of misdeeds, not just to add another avenue for airing *private* grievances). On the other hand, the drafting makes it clear that the Act is also meant to strike a balance and not simply to allow the whistle-blower to go straight to the press on all occasions, especially where the press in question are waving chequebooks[429]. To that extent, it has advantages to an employer too in emphasising that disclosure is primarily and initially meant to be internal[430]. This is achieved by establishing the forms of disclosure that have the protected status, with four categories of disclosure to named persons, backed up by two categories of wider disclosure which are subject to much more stringent conditions. The four 'normal' categories are disclosure:

(1) in good faith, to the employer or where the worker reasonably believes that the relevant failure relates solely or mainly to the conduct of another person or to any other matter for which another person has legal responsibility, to that person[431];

(2) to a legal adviser, in the course of obtaining legal advice[432];

---

425 S 47B.
426 The 1998 Act adopts the wider definition of 'worker' in the Employment Rights Act 1996, s 230(3), ie a person under a contract of employment *or* under any other contract to do or perform personally any work or services for another (other than a client or customer of any profession or business undertaking carried out by the person); see p 32 above. For good measure, the new s 43K specifically includes agency workers, homeworkers, work trainees and certain specified NHS staff who might not otherwise have qualified. Although the terminology of unfair dismissal is of course being used, the Act can go wider than the employment relationship because there is no requirement that the divulged information must show evil-doing by the worker's employer (though of course in many cases that will be so).
427 S 43B(1). These matters may occur in the UK or abroad: s 43B(2). The reference to the reasonable belief of the worker means that there can still be a protected disclosure if some or all of the allegations are later not substantiated: *Darnton v University of Surrey* [2003] ICR 615, [2003] IRLR 133.
428 *Parkins v Sodexho Ltd* [2002] IRLR 109. Part of the problem seems to have been that the case was brought by a litigant in person who, lacking the year's service for an ordinary unfair dismissal, cast around for areas of higher protection and ended up suing under basically an inappropriate part of the legislation.
429 '[The Act] will encourage resolution of concerns through proper workplace procedures, but it will protect those who, in the last resort, have to go public': Fairness at Work (Cm 3968, 1998), para 3.3.
430 Although there is no obligation in the Act for an employer to have a formal whistle-blowing policy, this may well be advisable so that complaints/disclosures can be dealt with effectively in-house, thus avoiding the possibility of a protected disclosure to the press.
431 S 43C.
432 S 44D.

(3) in good faith, to a Minister of the Crown (where the worker's employer is appointed by a Minister)[433];

(4) to a person prescribed by order by the Secretary of State, where the worker reasonably believes that the relevant failure falls within the order and that the information disclosed (and any allegation contained in it) are substantially true[434].

Obviously, cases may well arise where one of these is not appropriate (particularly where the person to whom disclosure is primarily meant to be made is actually the culprit – in this context of course, the employer) and so the Act then establishes two longstops, where the worker is in effect allowed to 'go public':

(1) 'disclosure in other cases'[435] – this applies where (a) the worker makes the disclosure in good faith, (b) he reasonably believes that the information disclosed (and any allegations contained in it) are substantially true, (c) he does not make the disclosure for personal gain, (d) any one of a series of conditions is met[436], and (e) in all the circumstances of the case, it is reasonable for him to make the disclosure[437];

(2) 'disclosure of exceptionally serious failure'[438] – this applies where (a) the worker makes the disclosure in good faith, (b) he reasonably believes that the information disclosed (and any allegations contained in it) are substantially true, (c) he does not make the disclosure for purposes of personal gain, (d) the relevant failure is of an exceptionally serious nature (undefined) and (e) in all the circumstances of the case, it is reasonable for him to make the disclosure[439].

The question of gagging clauses is then dealt with directly and briefly by a provision which states that any provision in any agreement between a worker and his employer[440] (*including* a settlement of legal proceedings) is void in so far as it purports to preclude the worker from making a protected disclosure[441].

---

433 S 43E.

434 S 43F. See the Public Interest Disclosure (Prescribed Persons) Order 1999, SI 1999/1549, *Harvey* R[1183].

435 S 43G.

436 The conditions are that (a) the worker reasonably believes that he will be subjected to a detriment by his employer if he makes the disclosure to him or to a prescribed person; or (b) that, where there is no prescribed person, the worker reasonably believes that it is likely that evidence relating to the relevant failure will be concealed or destroyed if he makes disclosure to his employer; or (c) that the worker has previously made a disclosure of substantially the same information to his employer or a prescribed person: s 43F(2).

437 In deciding on reasonableness, regard is to be had to (a) the identity of the person (or tabloid?) to whom disclosure is made; (b) the seriousness of the relevant failure; (c) whether the failure is continuing or likely to occur in the future; (d) whether the disclosure is made in breach of a duty of confidentiality owed by the employer to any other person; (e) in a case of previous disclosure (under s 43G(2)(c)) any action which the employer or prescribed person has taken or might reasonably be expected to have taken as a result; and (f) in a case of previous disclosure to the employer, whether the worker complied with any disclosure procedure whose use by him was authorised by the employer: s 43G(3). The final head shows the possible importance of a whistle-blowing policy in ensuring that disclosure follows the correct internal channels, rather than spilling out too easily into the public arena.

438 S 43H.

439 In deciding on reasonableness, regard is to be had in particular to the identity of the person to whom the disclosure is made: s 43H(2).

440 Whether or not a 'worker's contract' (under the extended definition in the Employment Rights Act 1996, s 230(3)).

441 S 43J. A disclosure not protected under the Act would not come under this provision and so a gagging clause covering it would be valid *unless* a court were persuaded to strike it down at common law.

Finally, one possible further statutory development should be noted which would operate in the opposite direction, ie to *increase* the liability of an individual (possibly an employee) in relation to the use of information. The Law Commission have suggested that it should become a *criminal* offence (triable on indictment) knowingly to use or disclose a trade secret belonging to another without that other's consent[442]. Clearly this would need a carefully drafted public interest defence; the consultation paper came before the Public Interest Disclosure Act 1998 and so contained its own proposed draft of such a defence (including 'any use or disclosure of information which under the law of confidence would be justified on grounds of public interest'), but any developments in this area would now need to be consistent with the 1998 Act; of equal interest will be how it is eventually proposed to define 'trade secret', still a notorious area of difficulty in the civil context after a century of case law.

(3) The employee's inventions

In the absence of an express term in the contract of employment, the common law position was that the employer was entitled to the benefit of inventions made by his employee if they were referable to the employment. Thus, in *British Syphon Co Ltd v Homewood*[443] the defendant discovered a new type of soda syphon and applied to patent it; he was employed by the plaintiffs as a chief technician to advise them generally on their business, but he had not been asked to make any new designs and there was no express agreement between them on the matter of inventions. Roxburgh J held that the plaintiffs were entitled to the benefit of the invention which had arisen out of the employment. This was a strong implied term at common law, usually explained on the basis of fidelity, and it would apply if the parties were silent or if an express term was void through being too wide; moreover, it would continue to apply even if the employee went ahead and patented the invention, for then it was held that he held the patent on trust for the employer[444]. It was even held that the employee might be under a continuing duty to do anything necessary to assist the employer to realise the patent[445]. Not every invention belonged to the employer, however, and much might depend on the nature of the invention and the position of the employee, but the employee was only really safe if the nature of the invention was clearly outside the employer's business interest[446]; however, if it was safely outside those interests, the fact that it was made during working hours or with the employer's materials would not deprive the employee of it[447] and indeed even an express term giving the benefit of *any* invention to the employer might be void as in restraint of trade[448]. Section 56(2) of the Patents Act 1949 appeared to mitigate this possibly harsh implied term by allowing the comptroller to apportion the benefits of an invention between employer and employee unless satisfied that one party was absolutely entitled, but this was construed restrictively by the House of Lords in *Sterling Engineering Co*

---

442 Misuse of Trade Secrets (Law Com No 150, 1997). One other possibility raised in the paper is an offence of dishonest acquisition of trade secrets. See generally Colling 'Should the use and disclosure of trade secrets be criminalised?' (1998) 27 ILJ 147.

443 [1956] 2 All ER 897, [1956] 1 WLR 1190. See also *British Reinforced Concrete Engineering Co v Lind* (1917) 86 LJ Ch 486.

444 *Triplex Safety Glass Co Ltd v Scorah* [1938] Ch 211, [1937] 4 All ER 693.

445 *British Celanese Ltd v Moncrieff* [1948] Ch 564, [1948] 2 All ER 44, CA.

446 *Re Selz Ltd* (1953) 71 RPC 158.

447 *Mellor v Beardmore* (1927) 44 RPC 175.

448 *Electrolux Ltd v Hudson* [1977] FSR 312.

Ltd v Patchett[449] so that it did not apply to the majority of employment cases where, by the operation of the implied term, the employer was already absolutely entitled to the invention. The whole area of patent law was overhauled, however, by the Patents Act 1977, and so the common law will now only apply (i) to inventions made before the commencement of the relevant parts of the Act[450]; (ii) where the Act does not apply, in particular where the employee was not 'mainly employed in the United Kingdom', but, under the conflict of laws rules, the matter remains generally governed by English law[451].

For present purposes, the modern legislation made two innovations – it sets out in section 39 when an invention will belong to the employer, and provides in sections 40 and 41 a scheme for compensating an employee inventor which is quite independent of contractual obligations. Now, therefore, most disputes as to employee inventions will be solved by a process of statutory interpretation, not by recourse to the common law rules. Section 39 provides that an invention belongs to the employee except in two specified instances when, for the purposes of the Act and all other purposes, it belongs to the employer; these are:

(a) if it was made *in the course of the normal duties of the employee* or in the course of duties falling *outside his normal duties, but specifically assigned to him,* and the circumstances in either case were such that an invention might reasonably be expected to result from the carrying out of his duties; or

(b) if the invention was made in the course of the duties of the employee and at the time of making the invention, because of the nature of his duties, he had a *special obligation to further the interests of the employer's undertaking*[452].

Unlike the common law position, this owes nothing to concepts of fidelity, and contentious points now are likely to be whether the invention was reasonably to be expected, and in what circumstances an employee is under the special obligation mentioned in paragraph (b) (a director under a fiduciary duty would presumably be covered, but the question is how far coverage will extend outside that special case)[453]. By section 42, any agreement purporting to diminish the employee's rights in an invention under section 39 is unenforceable to the extent that it does so diminish those rights.

Sections 40 and 41 provide in addition a statutory scheme for compensation for an inventor employee. Under this scheme, the employee may make a claim to the Patents Court or the Patents Office within a year of the expiry of the patent for compensation in one of two circumstances:

(a) where the invention belonged to the employer under section 39 and proved to be of 'outstanding benefit'[454] to that employer; or

(b) where the invention belonged to the employee under section 39 and he assigned or exclusively leased it to the employer but received benefits from that contract which were 'inadequate in relation to the benefit derived by the employer from the patent'.

---

449 [1955] AC 534, [1955] 1 All ER 369, HL.
450 Patents Act 1977, s 43(1); the 'appointed day' was 1 June 1978 – Patents Act 1977 (Commencement No 2) Order 1978, SI 1978/586.
451 S 43(2).
452 Emphasis added.
453 For detailed discussion of these provisions, see the Commentary section in the *Encyclopedia of United Kingdom and European Patent Law* and Phillips 'Employee inventors and the new Patents Act' (1978) 7 ILJ 30; *Reiss Engineering Co Ltd v Harris* [1985] IRLR 232.
454 'Outstanding' is not capable of definition and remains a question of fact in each case: *Memco-Med Ltd's Patent* [1992] RPC 403. It is a superlative term, not merely a comparative one, and so the burden of proof is a high one: *British Steel plc's Patent* [1992] RPC 117.

The court or comptroller is then empowered to award such compensation to the employee as will secure for him a 'fair share' of the actual or anticipated benefits derived from the patent. 'Fair share' is not defined, but section 41 lays down criteria to be considered. In the case of (a) above, these are:

(i) the nature of the employee's duties, his remuneration and any other advantages from his employment or the invention;
(ii) the employee's effort and skill in making the invention;
(iii) the effort and skill of any third party involved;
(iv) the significance of any contributions of the employer towards the invention (for example advice, facilities).

In the case of (b) above, they are:

(i) any conditions in any licences granted under the Act in respect of the invention or the patent;
(ii) any extent to which the invention was a joint project with a third party;
(iii) any contributions by the employer (as in (iv) above).

An order for compensation may be for a lump sum or for periodic payments or both[455]. Any agreement purporting to exclude the employee's right to statutory compensation is ineffective, but these provisions do not apply where the matter is already governed by a collective agreement[456].

The position with regard to copyright in material produced by an employee is governed by the Copyright, Designs and Patents Act 1988, section 11, which provides that, although the first owner of copyright is the author, 'where a literary, dramatic, musical or artistic work or a film is made by an employee in the course of his employment, his employer is the first owner of any copyright in the work subject to any agreement to the contrary'. This straightforward provision does not attempt any more ambitious schemes of recompensing employed authors, such as that seen above in the patents legislation, being content instead to leave the matter as essentially one for agreement between the parties. It substantially re-enacts the pre-existing law which was contained in the repealed Copyright Act 1956, section 4, whose effect can be seen from the case of *Stevenson, Jordan and Harrison Ltd v MacDonald and Evans*[457] where an accountant employed by the plaintiff company wrote a book on business management; part was based on public lectures given during his employment, part was composed while engaged on a particular assignment for the employer, and the rest was written after leaving the employment. The Court of Appeal held that the lectures were not given pursuant to his contract of employment, but that the second part (composed whilst on the assignment) was produced in the course of his employment, and so the copyright in that part lay with the employer who could restrain publication of it.

(4) Failure to serve the employer faithfully

It has been seen above that the employee must obey proper orders of the employer and that there is a general duty of fidelity upon the employee. This does not give the employer an unrestricted prerogative and in general he will be bound by the terms of the contract of employment which he cannot change unilaterally. Thus, he cannot make the employee work overtime if it is purely voluntary or change the terms of employment (for example by making a day worker work nights where there is no such provision in the contract); to this extent the employee may stand

---

455 The first reported cases of applications by employees under s 40 are set out and discussed in Wotherspoon 'Employee Inventions Revisited' (1993) 22 ILJ 119.
456 Patents Act 1977, s 40(3).
457 (1952) 1 TLR 101, CA; see also *Beloff v Pressdram Ltd* [1973] 1 All ER 241.

upon the terms of the contract, and, if necessary, withdraw his goodwill, even if this has a disadvantageous effect on the employer's business. However, there may be cases where a lack of co-operation by the employee may be construed not as a lawful insistence upon observation of the contract, but instead as in fact collective industrial action aimed at prejudicing the employer's business. Although the employee may argue that this form of action (known, for example, as 'going slow', 'working to rule' or 'working to contract') is merely the insistence on the contractual minimum, it is clear that in some cases it can, in fact, be a *breach* of contract, in particular the implied duty to serve faithfully. The line between the two arguments can be a thin one, but it exists.

Strict adherence to contractual terms (on a collective level, as part of industrial action) was held capable of being a breach of contract by the Court of Appeal in *Secretary of State for Employment v ASLEF (No 2)*[458], though the reasoning of the three judges varied. However, the leading case is now *British Telecommunications plc v Ticehurst*[459] where a college manager took part in industrial action, first by way of a go-slow and work to contract, and then escalating to a rolling campaign of strikes. The question arose[460] whether this action was lawful under the contract and the Court of Appeal held that it was a breach of the implied term 'to serve the employer faithfully within the requirements of the contract'. Adopting that formulation from the judgment of Buckley LJ in the *ASLEF* case, Ralph Gibson LJ said:

'It is, in my judgment, necessary to imply such a term in the case of a manager who is given charge of the work of other employees and who therefore must necessarily be trusted to exercise her judgment and discretion in giving instructions to others and in supervising their work. Such a discretion, if the contract is to work properly, must be exercised faithfully in the interests of the employers.'

And later:

'The term is breached, in my judgment, when the employee does an act, or omits to do an act, which it would be within her contract and the discretion allowed to her not to do, or to do, as the case may be, and the employee so acts or omits to do the act, not in the honest exercise of choice or discretion for the faithful performance of her work but in order to disrupt the employer's business or to cause the most inconvenience that can be caused.[461]'

458 [1972] 2 QB 455, [1972] 2 All ER 949, CA. The case concerned long-repealed provisions of the Industrial Relations Act 1971.
459 [1992] ICR 383, [1992] IRLR 219, CA.
460 Whether or not such action is a breach of contract is not particularly relevant in the context of unfair dismissal, since the special provisions on dismissal during industrial action (p 751 below) apply to strikes 'or other industrial action', with the latter *not* depending on proof of breach of contract. However, this case concerned the equally vital question as to whether the employer can *refuse to pay* employees taking industrial action, where the question of breach is central; that aspect of the case is considered at p 218 below.
461 [1992] ICR 383 at 398, [1992] IRLR 219 at 225, CA. In *Burgess v Stevedoring Services Ltd* [2002] UKPC 39, [2002] IRLR 810 the Privy Council also adopted the narrower views of Buckley LJ in ASLEF, rather than the wider views adopted by Lord Denning. While this case is interestig (given the scarcity of recent authority on this abstruse point), it was under Bermudian legislation which has no UK counterpart and *Ticehurst*, n 459 above (the leading UK case) was not discussed.

Although the case concerns a manager, it is suggested that the key to this is not managerial status but, much more generally, employee *discretion* in how to perform the work. It may be that, if a job was exhaustively defined in the contract, there could still be a work to contract that would not be in breach[462], *but* in modern conditions most jobs are not like that; in such circumstances, the decision in *Ticehurst* shows that such action is very likely to be a breach of the implied duty of faithful service in the contract.

Finally, it may be noted that in at least one area the employee may be under a positive obligation to co-operate with his employer, for under the Health and Safety at Work etc Act 1974, section 7(a), there is a statutory duty upon every employee 'as regards any duty or requirement imposed on his employer or any other person by or under any of the relevant statutory provisions, to co-operate with him so far as is necessary to enable that duty or requirement to be performed or complied with'.

6 CONTINUITY OF EMPLOYMENT

(i) The concept of continuity and the treatment of part-time employees

The concept of 'continuous employment' is an important one in that many accruing rights, privately negotiated or statutory, depend upon it either for qualification for a particular right, or for computation of benefits to be received under it. Thus, various periods are laid down by statute for the purposes of qualification for written particulars of employment and minimum rights during notice, qualification for redundancy pay, computation of redundancy pay, qualification for protection from unfair dismissal, and qualification for various employment protection rights (particularly those relating to maternity). These matters are considered in detail elsewhere, but are mentioned to show the direct effect of the provisions that govern the question of continuity (now contained in sections 210–219 of the Employment Rights Act 1996). The scheme for computing continuous employment was altered by the Employment Act 1982 with the effects that (a) most qualifying periods are now expressed in months and years rather than weeks, which diminishes the former technical importance of the 'week' as the unit of account, and (b) the emphasis now is upon determining when the employment started[463] and ended, and then computing the period on a more straightforward calendar basis. The main aims of the change were to simplify record keeping and to avoid some of the stranger results of the previous week-base (under which, for example, part weeks counted as full weeks so that the 52 weeks' qualifying period that used to be required in order to bring an unfair dismissal action could in some cases be satisfied where the employee had worked for 50 weeks plus a couple of odd days falling fortuitously in different weeks). Some of the case law on the old system is therefore no longer authoritative.

Four preliminary points should be noticed. The first is that continuity of employment means generally with one employer[464], and this has been construed

---

462 It could, of course, still constitute 'industrial action' for statutory purposes, see n 460 above.

463 A person 'starts work' within s 211 when his contract of employment begins, even if he does not actually take up his duties under the contract until some time later: *General of the Salvation Army v Dewsbury* [1984] ICR 498, [1984] IRLR 222.

464 *Lee v Barry High Ltd* [1970] 3 All ER 1040, [1970] 1 WLR 1549, CA; *Harold Fielding Ltd v Mansi* [1974] 1 All ER 1035, [1974] ICR 347. It also means in relation to one contract of employment: *Lewis v Surrey County Council* [1988] AC 323, [1987] ICR 982, HL.

widely to include continuity where the employee has changed department, job, seniority or even the terms of his contract of employment during the period, provided that he has remained with the same employer[465]. The second is that the Act governs which weeks count in computing a period of employment, and generally if a week does not count it will break continuity, so that the employee then loses his accrued period and must start again from scratch[466]; however, there is the qualification that certain weeks (particularly those spent on strike or, for the purpose of redundancy, abroad[467]) do not count, but at the same time are deemed not to break continuity, and thereby the position is effectively rendered neutral (the employee is not unduly penalised by losing all accrued continuity, but at the same time does not benefit because he cannot actually use the relevant period for any purpose of computation). The third is that there is a statutory presumption of continuity, unless the contrary is shown; thus, in cases of doubt (for example where there is a possibility that some relevant weeks may not count and so break continuity) the burden of proof is on the employer to show that the employee did *not* have the necessary continuity of employment[468].

The fourth, and much the most significant, point is that this area underwent major change in February 1995 due to a conflict with EC law. In domestic law the concept of continuity had always been used to achieve the secondary, less obvious aim of excluding part-timers from employment protection rights such as redundancy and unfair dismissal. This was done by providing that a week did not count unless during it the employee actually worked (or normally worked) for sixteen hours or more (or between eight and sixteen hours after five years' service). Thus, no matter how long the part-time employee worked, they never accumulated the necessary continuous period of employment for the major rights (for example two years, as it then was, in order to claim unfair dismissal) if they did not work the necessary hours. This was long-standing, deliberate policy and indeed at one time the previous government were proposing to increase the threshold to twenty hours per week, in order to carry further the deregulation of the part-time labour market[469]. However, the tide of EU law was running strongly in the opposite direction (towards extending rights to atypical employees). Although the Maastricht opt-out which was in operation at the time could be

---

465 *Wood v York City Council* [1978] ICR 840, [1978] IRLR 228, CA; *Jennings v Salford Community Service Agency* [1981] ICR 399, [1981] IRLR 76; continuity is a purely statutory concept, exhaustively covered by the statutory provisions which are not to be qualified by courts or tribunals: *Carrington v Harwich Dock Co Ltd* [1998] ICR 1112, [1998] IRLR 567 (applying Lord Denning MR's judgment in *Wood v York City Council*, above, and doubting the decision in *Roach v CSB (Moulds) Ltd* [1991] ICR 349, [1991] IRLR 200); *Sweeney v J & S Henderson Ltd* [1999] IRLR 306, EAT (going further and disapproving *Roach*).
466 S 210(4). This significance of the 'week' survived the changes in the 1982 Act.
467 Ss 216 and 215 respectively.
468 S 210(5). The effect of the presumption was considered in *Nicoll v Nocorrode Ltd* [1981] ICR 348, [1981] IRLR 163 where the EAT held that where it is unclear whether an employee had worked the necessary number of qualifying weeks, the employee need only show that *some* weeks during the qualifying period count and the burden of proof then passes to the employer to prove that there were weeks that do not count and so break continuity. However, there is an exception – in *Secretary of State for Employment v Cohen* [1987] ICR 570, [1987] IRLR 169, the EAT held that the presumption does *not* apply to a 'transfer of business' case under s 218 (see below), though Scott J emphasised that although the burden of proving continuity through such a transfer lies on the employee, a tribunal should not apply an unrealistically high *standard* of proof.
469 'Building businesses ... not barriers' (Cmnd 9794, 1986); it would appear that such a change would have removed employment protection rights at a stroke from a further 366,000 people: [1986] Employment Gazette 281.

used to prevent any direct EC pressure for more such rights by employment law Directives, the government could not rule out the possibility of a challenge under already-applicable EC law, in particular that relating to equality of pay and treatment. This happened in *R v Secretary of State for Employment, ex p Equal Opportunities Commission*[470], in which the House of Lords held that (1) the Equal Opportunities Commission (EOC) had locus standi to challenge the legality of the hours limits, (2) those limits were contrary to Article 119 and the Equal Pay Directive 75/117 (in relation to redundancy payments) and the Equal Treatment Directive 76/207 (in relation to unfair dismissal) and (3) in neither case was the discriminatory effect on women justified on the government's assertions that such limitations were necessary socially and economically in order to promote the extension of part-time employment, in the absence of substantive *evidence* that deregulation had had that effect. This bombshell decision had certain loose ends[471] but the government soon realised that they could not sensibly hold any tenable line simply by amending the hours limits, and so by the Employment Protection (Part Time Employees) Regulations 1995[472] removed these limits altogether, as from 6 February 1995. Thus, the major statutory rights can now be claimed by part-timers; as will be seen below, this in turn has had serious long-term effects on the law relating to continuity of employment, though in the short term the primary battlefield was over the entertaining (or not) of back-dated claims by employees without the necessary weekly hours dismissed prior to February 1995 wishing to bring actions for redundancy rights or unfair dismissal, not having done so initially because they assumed they would be ruled out. As the *EOC* case was a court decision determining the meaning of the EC provisions, it prima facie had full retrospective effect, but the courts conducted a desperate rearguard action to prevent a flood of old cases, not by denying that retrospective effect, but by adopting a stringent approach to the domestic limitation periods[473].

(ii) Weeks which count

(a) 'Any week during the whole or part of which the employee's relations with the employer are governed by a contract of employment'

(Employment Rights Act 1996, section 212(1).) As stated immediately above, this used to be a far more complex provision, linking continuity to the performance

---

470 [1995] 1 AC 1, [1994] ICR 317, HL; see Villiers and White (1995) 58 MLR 560.
471 As the redundancy restriction was contrary to Art. 119 itself, the decision applied directly in both public and private sectors; however, the House of Lords only held the unfair dismissal restriction to be contrary to the Equal Treatment Directive, which meant that apparently the decision could only be relied on directly in the public sector (under the principle of vertical effect of directives). Subsequently, however, the EAT held that the unfair dismissal restriction also fell under Art 119 (*Mediguard Services Ltd v Thame* [1994] ICR 751, [1994] IRLR 504). Although this point is no longer relevant in cases arising since the 1995 Regulations came into force, it could still be material if retrospective claims were to be allowed.
472 SI 1995/31.
473 *Biggs v Somerset County Council* [1996] ICR 364, [1996] IRLR 203, CA; *Setiya v East Yorkshire Health Authority* [1995] ICR 799, [1995] IRLR 348. This was possible because of the 'not reasonably practicable' test for extending the unfair dismissal time limit; it was subsequently held that such an approach preventing backdating may not work in a sex discrimination claim where the test for extending the limit is whether it is 'just and equitable' to do so: *DPP v Marshall* [1998] ICR 518.

or normal performance of sixteen hours work or more per week (or eight hours for more than five years). In that form, it required a very technical approach with much complex case law, often attempting to 'forgive' lapses in that normal hours requirement, and to count marginal hours, such as those spent on preparation work or breaks during employment. Moreover, there were several specific statutory provisions aimed at covering temporary breaks in work normally meeting the hours requirements. With the removal of these requirements in 1995, the result is a far simpler statutory provision, with the repeal of most of the special subsidiary rules. The emphasis now is on looking only at the continuing existence of the contractual relationship, and whether it covers the week(s) in question. Thus, in *Clifford v Devon County Council*[474] a dismissed employee was able to claim unfair dismissal even though for part of the two years prior to the claim she had only worked seven and a half hours per week and, most startlingly of all, in *Colley v Corkindale*[475] an employee working one five and a half-hour bar shift every *alternate* Friday was also allowed to bring an unfair dismissal action. Under the previous law the latter claim would have been doubly inadmissible, due to (i) the number of hours and (ii) the existence of the alternate weeks when no work was done or expected, which would have broken continuity anyway[476]. The test now is thus a far more general, less technical and (above all) contractual one than before. It is suggested therefore that the proper approach is to construe the new provision afresh, and to forget the substantial body of case law on the old provisions. That is not to say that the same result may not be reached in any given case. Thus, for example, there is still a requirement that the contract in question must be continuous, and so continuity might still be broken in a case of regular *but separate* contracts, as in *Hellyer Bros Ltd v McLeod*[477] where trawlermen were held not entitled to redundancy payments on the collapse of their part of the fishing industry, for although they had sailed for one particular owner for many years the court held that the proper construction was that they had been engaged on a series of separate crew agreements, each covering one voyage. Arguably this case would still be decided the same way now and so, although the continuity rules are now simpler, they still cannot be taken for granted. This was further emphasised in *Booth v United States of America*[478] where maintenance workers were put on to a series of fixed-term contracts totalling more than two years, but with very deliberate two-week gaps between each; their eventual claims for redundancy payments and unfair dismissal were disallowed for lack of continuity – the gaps broke normal continuity, which (for technical reasons, see below) could not be covered by one of the 'deemed continuity' provisions, and the bottom line was expressed by Morison P as follows:

474 [1994] IRLR 628.
475 [1995] ICR 965.
476 Thus, in *Lloyds Bank Ltd v Secretary of State for Employment* [1979] 2 All ER 573, [1979] ICR 258, an employee working one week on and one week off was *not* covered by the normal continuity rules, and only succeeded in the claim under the special 'saving' rule in s 212(3)(b) by a strained interpretation which is now probably untenable (see below). This is a good example of the sort of technicality which hopefully should now arise less frequently.
477 [1987] 1 WLR 728, [1987] ICR 526, CA.
478 [1999] IRLR 16. This is a particularly harsh decision because, although the employees were formally 'terminated' and had to complete new application forms for the next contract (after a break which the employers insisted has to be for a minimum of two weeks – strangely), in fact when they returned they were given the same employee number and used the same tools and equipment, and even the same lockers. What a coincidence.

'If, by so arranging their affairs, an employer is lawfully able to employ people in such a manner that the employees cannot complain of unfair dismissal or seek a redundancy payment, that is a matter for him. The courts simply try and apply the law as it stands. It is for the legislators to close any loopholes that may be perceived to exist.[479]'

(b) A week during which there is no subsisting contract of employment, but which is covered by special statutory provisions

In order to avoid unfortunate gaps or 'hiccoughs' in continuity, certain exceptions have always been specifically created by the legislation, and these are now contained in the Employment Rights Act 1996, section 212(3). When they were contained in the previous legislation[480], there was a problem of statutory construction because the headnote referred to 'Periods in which there is no contract of employment', but that phrase did not appear in the body of the provision. Earlier case law tended where necessary to ignore the question of whether or not the contract subsisted, and to apply the special provision (to preserve continuity) in cases where there *was* a continuing contract but it had some unfortunate hiatus or gap in it. However, in *Ford v Warwickshire County Council*[481] the House of Lords placed considerable emphasis on the requirement that there be no subsisting contract and so the decisions in those earlier cases have been dubious since then. Fortunately, the position is now simpler under the 1995 Regulations and the 1996 consolidation – that marginal note now does not appear, but (a) the simplified format (with the removal of the hours requirements) means that section 212(1) applies where there *is* a subsisting contract and subsection (3) therefore clearly applies only where there is *no* such contract (thus reinforcing the point in *Ford*) and (b) in any event there will be far less need now to try to squeeze cases within subsection (3) in order to preserve continuity, since most of the hours-based complications of sub section (1) have been removed. Subject to that caveat, the three specific cases covered by subsection (3) are now considered.

(a) Where the employee is incapable of work through sickness or illness (subsection (3)(a)). Incapable has been held to refer to the job in question and a temporary lighter job need not break continuity[482]. Absence from work does not normally, in default of express provision in the contract, terminate the contract[483]. If the contract has not been determined then the weeks of absence count under subsection (1) anyway. This head is an extension stretching into the period after the contract has been determined[484]. It is limited to 26 weeks after a week counting under subsection (1) and must be followed by a week so counting. Theoretically an employee could have a solitary week of employment followed by 26 weeks of illness and a further week of employment which would both maintain the continuity and permit a further 26 weeks of absence through illness to count.

---

479 [1999] IRLR 16 at 18. There is nothing in the White Paper 'Fairness at Work' covering this matter. If it is allowed to continue, the moral of the story seems to be that the more cynical the manipulation of these rules, the more likely the employer is to win.

480 In the Employment Protection (Consolidation) Act 1978, Sch 13, para 9(1)(a)–(d).

481 [1983] ICR 273, [1983] IRLR 126, HL.

482 *Collins v Nats (Southend) Ltd* (1967) 2 ITR 423; *Donnelly v Kelvin International Services* [1992] IRLR 496.

483 For the law as to the payment of sick pay, see pp 220–226 below.

484 There must be a causal link between the absence from work and the incapacity through sickness or injury: *Pearson v Kent County Council* [1993] IRLR 165, CA.

(b) Where the employee is absent from work on account of a 'temporary cessation of work' (subsection (3)(b)); this has been in practice the most important special case, but it is a phrase not without difficulty. No time-limit is laid down. The phrase was considered by the House of Lords in *Fitzgerald v Hall, Russell & Co Ltd*[485] where it was held that it refers to cessation of the *employee's* work for some reason, so there is no requirement that the employer's business in which the employee is engaged should have ceased. It was also held that each case under this head must be looked at in the round and, if necessary, with hindsight, to establish whether it was 'temporary' (the statute giving no guidance on this). Thus, if both parties obviously envisaged that it would be only temporary that would be cogent evidence, but the lack of it would not mean that the arrangement would necessarily be construed to be permanent:

> 'The effect of that case is that the tribunal is enjoined to look at the matter as the historian of a completed chapter of events, and not as a journalist describing events as they occur from day to day. The importance of that is this, that things are seen, as they unfold, quite differently from the way in which they are seen when one looks back and considers the whole of the chapter in context. What at the time seems to be permanent may turn out to be temporary, and what at the time seems to be temporary may turn out to be permanent.'[486]

The essence of most successful cases is that the employee has been 'stood off' in the sense that he was to be recalled later. The fact that a job is taken in the period of cessation does not destroy the position[487], but it is plainly not meant to cover the situation where an employee moves to a new employer, fails to settle, and quickly moves back to his old job. It may cover situations such as extra holiday periods taken as periods of absence with the employer's agreement at the employee's expense, and, more particularly, periods when the work-place is closed or no work is available[488] (which may arise through many causes such as a natural calamity like a fire[489], or the disruption of supplies of materials). In *Ford v Warwickshire County Council*[490] it was held to cover the case of a schoolteacher who had been employed on eight consecutive fixed-term contracts for the academic year (September to July); thus, the

---

485 [1970] AC 984, [1969] 3 All ER 1140, HL, approving *Hunter v Smith's Dock Ltd* [1968] 2 All ER 81, 3 ITR 198. 'Work' here means paid work; if that is missing, the paragraph may apply and it is not the tribunal's function to enquire into *why* the paid work is missing: *University of Aston in Birmingham v Malik* [1984] ICR 492. However, at the end of the day it must be the case that there is a 'cessation of work' available for the employee to do: if the work remains but for some reason he is not eligible to do it, the paragraph does not apply: *Bryne v Birmingham City District Council* [1987] ICR 519, [1987] IRLR 191, CA. It is that cessation that must then be 'temporary', not the employee's absence: *Flack v Kodak Ltd* [1986] ICR 775, [1986] IRLR 255, CA. This can have the unfortunate effect that if the work remains available but the employer *refuses* at certain times to offer it to a particular employee (in order deliberately to break continuity, eg by insisting on gaps between fixed term contracts), then sub-s. (3)(b) cannot apply and the employee may be unable to claim statutory rights: *Booth v United States of America* [1999] IRLR 16.

486 *Bentley Engineering Co Ltd v Crown* [1976] ICR 225 at 228, [1976] IRLR 146 at 148; in this case, periods of two years and 21 months were held still to be temporary.

487 *Thompson v Bristol Channel Ship Repairers and Engineers Ltd* (1969) 4 ITR 262; affd (1971) 5 ITR 85, CA; *Bentley Engineering Co Ltd v Crown* [1976] ICR 225, [1976] IRLR 146.

488 *Hunter v Smith's Dock Ltd* [1968] 2 All ER 81, 3 ITR 198.

489 *Newsham v Dunlop Textiles Ltd (No 2)* (1969) 4 ITR 268.

490 [1983] ICR 273, [1983] IRLR 126, HL, overruling *Rashid v ILEA* [1977] ICR 157.

periods of the summer vacations were held not to break continuity so that she could claim unfair dismissal and a redundancy payment when she did not receive a ninth contract. In interpreting the subsection, the House of Lords took a basically similar approach to that in their earlier decision in *Fitzgerald v Hall Russell Ltd* (above), holding that 'temporary' means 'transient' and adding that the application of subsection (3)(b) was not defeated either by the fact that the absences were easily foreseeable in advance or by the fact that the case concerned a series of fixed-term contracts (rather than a series of contracts terminable by notice). The 'transience' requirement makes it clear that the principle in the case cannot be applied so widely as to give previously unheard of rights to genuinely casual/seasonal workers (who, for example, only work for three or four months of each year – there, the gaps would be anything but transient); however, the case may give food for thought to any employer seeking to avoid the application of employment laws by putting an employee on a series of short-term contracts, if it transpires that in fact the gaps are relatively short by comparison with the periods of work (provided that it remains the case that it is the *work* that is temporarily unavailable, not just the fact that it is not being done by that employee[491]). The application of hindsight and an overall view of events, permissible under this subsection, could easily work to the employer's disadvantage in such a case, though it must be remarked that the categorisation of transience as a matter of fact for the tribunal would make it difficult to give definite advice in advance in a marginal case on whether the sub-paragraph will apply[492] , the lawyer being faced with the unanswerable question 'How long is short?'

In seeking to answer that question, two quite different approaches are possible. As stated above, *Fitzgerald v Hall Russell Ltd* sets out a 'broad brush' approach, looking at all the circumstances throughout the period of employment in order to see if any particular gap can be categorised as temporary. However, in *Ford v Warwickshire County Council*, Lord Diplock suggested a narrower 'mathematical' test of looking at whatever period is relevant to the claim in question[493] and, in the case of any gap during that time, comparing its length mathematically with the periods of work on either side of it to see if it was temporary. This latter approach could produce anomalies[494] and the matter was reconsidered by the Court of Appeal in *Flack v Kodak Ltd*[495] a case on very different facts from those in *Ford*. This case concerned a series of highly irregular work patterns over periods varying from

491 See *Booth v United States of America*, n 485, above.
492 See, eg, the facts in *Berwick Salmon Fisheries Co Ltd v Rutherford* [1991] IRLR 203 where salmon netters had been employed for 30 weeks on, 22 weeks off, until their final two seasons when they only worked for 23 weeks on, 29 weeks off. This point now has a particular resonance under the Fixed-term Employees (Prevention of Less Favourable Treatment) Regulations 2002, SI 2002/2034, under which these continuity-rules are applied in order to calculate whether an employee has been kept on 'successive' fixed-term contracts for four years, thus becoming a permanent employee unless the employer can objectively justify continued use of fixed-term contracts (see p 26 above).
493 For example, if the question arose as to entitlement to a redundancy payment, that period would be the last two years before the date of dismissal.
494 If in the relevant period, for example, the employee had a gap of eight weeks with periods in work of only two weeks on each side, that would not be 'temporary' on a straight mathematical comparison. If, however, that was because of short time in times of difficulties prior to his redundancy, and came as a series of late hiccoughs after years of unbroken service, the end result (no redundancy pay because not continuously employed for two years counting back from the date of dismissal) would be ludicrous.
495 [1986] ICR 775, [1986] IRLR 255, CA.

three to eleven years (the employees having been laid off and taken back on again intermittently, depending on season and demand). The tribunal applied the mathematical approach (even to the extent of expressing the gaps as percentages of their surrounding periods in work) and found that in the case of each employee continuity was broken in the vital qualifying period for redundancy payments. However, the EAT and the Court of Appeal held that this was the wrong test to apply, that the 'broad brush' approach should be taken and that the matter should be remitted to another tribunal for reconsideration. The question is where this leaves the law. Although Lord Diplock's statement in *Ford* as to the mathematical test was said to be obiter, it is clear from later cases that that test has not been disapproved. In *Sillars v Charrington Fuels Ltd* the EAT[496] suggested that the mathematical test should apply to cases like *Ford* of regular gaps, and the broad-brush approach to cases like *Flack* of irregular gaps. Unfortunately, the matter was not fully resolved when the case went to the Court of Appeal[497] for it was there held that (the case being one of seasonal employment with long, regular gaps) the mathematical test was one which it was *open* to the tribunal to have used. Although the distinction drawn by the EAT appears to have been thought too simplistic by the Court of Appeal, if one is looking for a rough rule of thumb it may not be a bad one, pending further authoritative guidance on the matter.

A lock-out is covered, and so are non-strikers laid off because a strike has disrupted production so that work is not available[498]. However, section 216(1) expressly provides that absence through strikes does not count (although, of course, by section 216(2) continuity is not broken by a strike), and so cannot be made to count by calling it a 'temporary cessation of work.' This, however was qualified in *Clarke Chapman-John v Walters*[499] where a period on strike was followed, in the employee's case, by a short period laid off pending a phased return to work; it was held by the NIRC that during that short period he was not on strike, so the predecessor of section 216(1) did not apply, and it could be construed as a 'temporary cessation of work', albeit the direct result of the actual strike.

(c) Where the employee is absent from work in circumstances such that, by arrangement or custom, he is regarded as continuing in the employment of his employer for any purpose (subsection (3)(c)). Under this head any unique local practices are covered, and some potentially unfortunate breaks in continuity avoided. It appears that the agreement or custom must exist when the absence begins, not as an ex post facto afterthought[500]; once this is

---

496 [1988] ICR 505, [1988] IRLR 180.
497 [1989] ICR 475, [1989] IRLR 152, CA. The mathematical approach was also applied to the facts of *Berwick Salmon Fisheries Co Ltd v Rutherford* [1991] IRLR 203, see n 492 above.
498 *Macartney v Sir Robert MacAlpine & Sons Ltd* (1967) 2 ITR 399.
499 [1972] 1 All ER 614, [1972] ICR 83.
500 *Murray v Kelvin Electronics Ltd* (1967) 2 ITR 622; *Todd v Sun Ventilating Co Ltd* [1975] IRLR 4; cf *Cann v Co-operative Retail Services Ltd* (1967) 2 ITR 649. 'Arrangement' requires some form of advanced discussion or agreement to the effect that the parties regard the employment as continuing; mere acquiescence or expectation that the employer would periodically lay the employees off is not enough: *Booth v United States of America* [1999] IRLR 16. An exception was created to the rule (that the arrangement or custom must already exist at the time of the absence) in *Ingram v Foxon* [1984] ICR 685, [1985] IRLR 5 where it was held that the subsection covered an agreement to reinstate on the understanding that continuity would be deemed to be unbroken, but this was disapproved in *Morris v Walsh Western UK Ltd* [1997] IRLR 562.

satisfied the cause of the absence appears to be immaterial – it could be something ad hoc, such as leave of absence for personal reasons[501] or a long-term agreement that the employer might keep the employee on a 'reserve-list' to be called upon when necessary[502]. One area of current interest where reliance has been sought on subsection (3)(c) is contractual career break schemes. These are not covered by statute; where they have been introduced voluntarily (for example as part of a family-friendly package of terms and conditions) they have caused novel problems legally[503]. One question has been whether the employee taking the break could claim that his (or, more likely her) continuity of employment was preserved under this subsection, on the basis that the scheme constituted an 'arrangement' to regard the employment as continuing. This finally came before the courts in *Curr v Marks & Spencer plc*[504], where the employee had taken a four-year break (for family purposes) under the employer's scheme. She had commenced her employment with them in 1973 and took the leave from 1990 to 1994. When she was made redundant in 1999 the employers calculated her entitltement to a reduncacy payment only back to 1994; she claimed back to 1973 (capped to the maximum twenty years) on the basis that she had continuity through the break. The scheme itself provided that an employee taking the break had to resign and forfeit continuing staff benefits (for example staff discount, loans and share options), but that the employers undertook to take the employee back into an equivalent position and that in each year of the break the employee would do two weeks' paid work (to keep up skills). A tribunal found against this employee, a sympathetic EAT allowed her appeal, but the Court of Appeal (while expressing some sympathy for her position and some criticism of the employers for not making the continuity point clear) restored the tribunal's decision. Reaffirming the point that an 'arrangement' must be mutual[505], they held that here there was no meeting of minds to the effect that the employment was to be considered as continuing, primarily in the light of the requirement on the employee to resign, and the freezing of all employee benefits. Given that this probably represented a fairly typical career break scheme, this case shows that severe problems of continuity are to be expected with such schemes, *unless* an employer (wishing to use one as a positive recruiting tool) very deliberately drafted it so as to preserve continuity by contract[506]. This apart, *semble* a scheme would only come purely within the wording of the subsection if employment was accepted as continuing 'for any purpose' (for example for pension purposes, as instanced by the Court of Appeal) which was not the case here.

501 *Moore v James Clarkson & Co Ltd* (1970) 5 ITR 298; *Taylor v Triumph Motors* [1975] IRLR 369, IT.
502 *Puttick v John Wright & Sons (Blackwall) Ltd* [1972] ICR 457; *Normanton v Southalls (Birmingham) Ltd* [1975] IRLR 74, IT.
503 An interesting parallel can be seen with PHI schemes (p 166 above), which at one point were being enthusiastically introduced as an aid to headhunting, without working out their complex legal implications.
504 [2002] EWCA Civ 1852, [2003] ICR 443, [2003] IRLR 74.
505 See n 500 above, particularly *Booth v United States of America* [1999] IRLR 16.
506 Even here there is a problem – continuity for statutory purposes cannot be established by contract where the statutory definition is not satisfied (see p 189, n 465 above and p 465 below), so the employer would need to draft a scheme operating purely in contract even when giving (wholly or partly) the statutory entitlement.

(iii) Industrial disputes

The Act defines strikes and lock-outs in similar language[507]. A lock-out involves the closing of a place of employment, the suspension of work or the refusal by an employer to continue to employ any number of his employees. A strike involves cessation of work by a body of employees acting in combination, a concerted refusal to continue work. In the case of both strikes and lock-outs these actions must be in consequence of a dispute and in each case the aim of the action must be to coerce the employees or employers, as the case may be, to accept or not to accept terms or conditions of or affecting employment. Both definitions also expressly include similar action taken to aid other employers or employees in dispute.

If an employee is on strike during a week or any part thereof, that week does not count as a period of employment by virtue of section 216(1); however, a compromise is achieved by section 216(2) which provides that the employee's *continuity* of employment is not broken by a strike. The original legislation (Contracts of Employment Act 1963) made a distinction between lawful and unlawful strikes, in an attempt to curb the latter (principally 'unofficial' strikes) but these provisions were repealed in 1965. In the case of a lock-out section 216(3) provides that continuity is not broken by the fact that an employee is absent from work because of a lock-out, but the paragraph says nothing about whether such a period can *count*, so that that question must rely on whether the contract of employment subsists during the lock-out[508]. If it does not, presumably the period will not count, though of course continuity will not be broken.

During the currency of a strike, the employer may in fact dismiss the employees, but this in itself will not affect continuity of employment for the following reasons – (i) section 216 makes no distinction between strikes where there are dismissals and those where there are not; (ii) the definition of 'employee' for the purposes of section 216, in section 230, includes an ex-employee; (iii) it was held in *Bloomfield v Springfield Hosiery Finishing Co Ltd*[509] that section 216 applies to persons who were employed at the *outset* of the strike, and that for present purposes the strike is to be considered as continuing as long as there is the possibility that normal employment will be resumed at the end of the dispute; this may mean in practice until the employer replaces the striking employees with others, closes down the department in question, or until the employees concerned find permanent employment elsewhere. Thus, if the striking employees are in fact re-engaged, their continuity will be safeguarded even if they were dismissed during the strike. Similar principles should apply to a lock-out.

As noticed above, a further extension of this is that if a striker is temporarily laid off at the end of a strike until the business picks up and there is work for him to do, that employee is not on strike during that period, but he may be considered to be absent on account of a temporary cessation of work under section 212[510], and so not only is his continuity safeguarded, but he may also count the period of lay-off.

---

507 Employment Rights Act 1996, s 235. Note that these definitions are only for stated purposes; they do not apply to the unfair dismissal provisions relating to industrial action, see p 751 below.

508 *E and J Davis Transport Ltd v Chattaway* [1972] ICR 267, 7 ITR 361.

509 [1972] 1 All ER 609, [1972] ICR 91.

510 *Clarke Chapman-John v Walters* [1972] 1 All ER 614, [1972] ICR 83; *quaere* whether this would apply if he was taken back into employment but then validly laid off under a contractual lay-off clause, in the light of the requirement that there be *no* subsisting contract if s212(3) is to apply (*Ford v Warwickshire County Council*, considered above).

(iv) Change of employment under the 1996 Act and the Transfer of Undertakings Regulations

(a) Continuity under the 1996 Act

Normally when an employee terminates his job with an employer and goes to work for another employer, his continuity ends and he must start to build up continuous service with the new employer from scratch[511]. However, there may be ways in which the continuity can be carried over, so that he is regarded as being employed by the new employer as from the date when he commenced employment with the old employer. The Employment Rights Act 1996, section 218 lays down six classes of case in which employment may be deemed to be continuous even though there is a change in employment. The six cases are as follows:

(i) Where the trade of business or undertaking is itself transferred. Subsection (2) provides that continuity is unbroken; this is of general application, but particularly important in cases of redundancy. However, to be relied upon at all, the criteria for its application must be satisfied; one is that the employee in question must have been in the relevant employment 'at the time of the transfer' (which raises the problem of a gap in employment over the period of the transfer[512]), but the primary one is – was it a transfer of business, or merely the disposal of certain assets? If the latter, the provision does not apply, even if the employee goes with the asset, so that, for example, the sale of an operating factory may not come within subsection (2) if it is seen merely as the disposal of a surplus asset, particularly if the original employer carries on his business in other establishments[513]. In *Lloyds v Brassey*[514] Lord Denning MR said:

> 'The meaning of [this provision] was considered by the Divisional Court in *Kenmir Ltd v Frizzell,* where Widgery J said "In deciding whether a transaction amounted to the transfer of business, regard must be had to its substance rather than its form ... the vital consideration is whether the effect of the transaction was to put the transferee in possession of a going concern, the activities of which he could carry on without

---

511 *Lee v Barry High Ltd* [1970] 3 All ER 1040, [1970] 1 WLR 1549, CA.

512 This was for a long time complicated by the decision of the Court of Appeal in *Teesside Times Ltd v Drury* [1980] ICR 338, [1980] IRLR 72 which permitted a gap to count, but for three different reasons; in *Clark & Tokeley Ltd v Oakes* [1998] 4 All ER 353, [1998] IRLR 577, the Court of Appeal subsequently held that it is Stephenson LJ's judgment in *Teesside Times* that is to be applied, ie that there is no hard-and-fast rule, that a 'transfer' may well take place over an extended period of time, and that continuity will be preserved, provided that the employee was still in employment at the start of that process (a question of fact for the tribunal).

513 *Kenmir Ltd v Frizzell* (1968) 3 ITR 159; *Woodhouse v Peter Brotherhood Ltd* [1972] 2 QB 520, [1972] 3 All ER 91, CA; *Crompton v Truly Fair (International) Ltd* [1975] ICR 359, [1975] IRLR 250. There must be a legal transfer of sorts, it is not enough merely that de facto control has been given to someone else: *S I (Systems and Instrumentation) Ltd v Grist* [1983] ICR 788, [1983] IRLR 391. Continuity is preserved even if there is a gap between the two employments, provided that gap is related to the machinery of the transfer: *Macer v Abafast Ltd* [1990] ICR 234, [1990] IRLR 137. Note that the presumption of continuity in s 210(5) does *not* apply to a 'transfer of business' case under s 218: *Secretary of State for Employment v Cohen* [1987] ICR 570, [1987] IRLR 169.

514 [1969] 2 QB 98 at 103, [1969] 1 All ER 382 at 384.

interruption." I think that it is the right test. If the new owner takes over the business as a going concern – so that the business remains the same business but in different hands – and the employee keeps the same job with the new owner ... his period of employment is deemed to continue without a break in the same job.'

This basic distinction between a transfer of business and a transfer of assets was approved and applied by the House of Lords in *Melon v Hector Powe Ltd*[515] to a case of the sale by the original employer of one of their two factories to another employer in the same trade; in the circumstances it was held that the tribunal had correctly decided that this was merely a transfer of assets, not a transfer of business. However, certain forms of business may be sui generis, and in *Lloyd v Brassey* the Court of Appeal held that in the case of farming the essence of the business is the land itself, so that sale of the land constitutes transfer of the business, not just the disposal of an asset; this idea was applied by analogy to the transfer of the tenancy of a hotel in *Young v Daniel Thwaites & Co*[516], but attempts to apply it more widely to other businesses have failed[517]. The question whether there has been an actual transfer is to be considered from the point of view of the dealings between the employers; if their dealings do not disclose such a transfer subsection (2) does not apply even if the employees carry on doing the same work and from *their* point of view it appears to be a transfer. In *Woodhouse v Peter Brotherhood Ltd*[518] a factory was sold and the new owner carried on using the same plant and equipment and indeed completed the order for one of the old employer's contracts, but it was held by the Court of Appeal that from the employer's point of view this was no transfer, and it was irrelevant that from the employee's point of view their 'working environment' had continued unchanged. One major factor pointing towards a transfer might be the sale of goodwill[519] which was one of the missing factors in the *Woodhouse* case. The term 'business' is defined in section 235 as including a trade or profession and any activity carried on by a body of persons, whether corporate or unincorporate[520]. It has been held to cover the transfer of *part* of a business (for example where an employer carries on business in place A and place B and sells off his whole business in place A, as in *G D Ault (Isle of Wight) Ltd v Gregory*[521]), but only if that part is genuinely severable (in its nature or location)[522] – if not, the transaction might well be viewed as again merely the disposal of an asset.

515 [1981] ICR 43, [1980] IRLR 477, HL. Notice that in this case it was the *employees* who were arguing that there was no transfer of business, in order to be able to claim their redundancy rights from the original employer; this claim was upheld by the House of Lords. See to like effect *Ward v Haines Watts* [1983] ICR 231, [1983] IRLR 285 (concerning sale of the goodwill of a professional practice).

516 [1977] ICR 877.

517 *Port Talbot Engineering Co Ltd v Passmore* [1975] ICR 234, [1975] IRLR 156 (maintenance contracts); *Bumstead v John L Cars Ltd* (1967) 2 ITR 137 (petrol station).

518 [1972] 2 QB 520, [1972] 3 All ER 91, CA.

519 *HA Rencoule (Joiners and Shopfitters) Ltd v Hunt* (1967) 2 ITR 475; *Kenmir Ltd v Frizzell* [1968] 1 All ER 414, [1968] ITR 159.

520 Explained by Diplock LJ in *Dallow Industrial Properties Ltd v Else* [1967] 2 QB 449 at 458, [1967] 2 All ER 30 at 33.

521 (1967) 2 ITR 301.

522 *McCleod v John Rostron & Sons* (1972) 7 ITR 144; *Newlin Oil Co Ltd v Trafford* [1974] IRLR 205, 9 ITR 324; *Gibson v Motortune Ltd* [1990] ICR 740.

(ii) Where an Act of Parliament causes one corporate body to replace another as employer: subsection (3).

(iii) Where the employer, not being corporate, dies and the personal representatives carry on the business: subsection (4)

(iv) Where the 'employer' is a partnership, personal representatives or trustees, and the composition of the body involved changes: subsection (5). This provision safeguards continuity when, for example, a partner retires and another is appointed. A more difficult case, however, arises where the partnership is dissolved but *one* of the partners carries on the business. On a narrow construction of subsection (5) it was held in *Harold Fielding Ltd v Mansi*[523] that this was not covered and so continuity was not preserved. The opposite conclusion was reached in the later cases of *Allen & Son v Coventry*[524] and *Jeetle v Elster*[525] but primarily on the alternative ground that, irrespective of subsection (5), such a change could constitute a 'transfer of business' under subsection (2); in each case the EAT criticised the reasoning on subsection (5) in *Mansi* but without actually overruling it.

(v) Where the employee is taken into the employment of an associated employer[526]: subsection (6).

(vi) Where an employee of the governors of a school maintained by a local education authority or that authority itself is taken into the employment of the governors of another such school or the authority: subsection (7).

(b) Automatic transfer under the Transfer of Undertakings Regulations 1981

In addition to these provisions of the 1996 Act, there are extra rules which may apply to a change of employer by virtue of the Transfer of Undertakings (Protection of Employment) Regulations 1981[527]. These Regulations (which are due to be updated at the time of writing, see below) were passed pursuant to an EC Directive[528] and contain provisions relating to rights to information and consultation[529], the continuance of union recognition through a transfer[530] and the dismissal of employees as a consequence of a transfer[531]; they also have provisions relating to the continuance of contracts of employment through such a transfer of the employer's undertaking. Thus, regulation 5(1) states that a relevant transfer does not terminate contracts of employment, which are deemed to have been originally made between the employees and the transferee employer. In terms purely of protecting continuity of employment of employees who do in

523 [1974] 1 All ER 1035, [1974] ICR 347; *Wynne v Hair Control* [1978] ICR 870.
524 [1980] ICR 9, [1979] IRLR 399.
525 [1985] ICR 389, [1985] IRLR 227.
526 For the definition of associated employers, see pp 30–32 above.
527 SI 1981/1794. See Davies and Freedland *Transfer of Employment* (1982); Hepple (1982) 11 ILJ 29; and, particularly, McMullen *Business Transfers and Employee Rights*, 'Atypical transfer; atypical workers and atypical employment structures – a case for greater transparency in transfer of employment issues' (1996) 25 ILJ 286; and 'Takeovers, transfers and business re-organisations' (1992) 21 ILJ 15. The Regulations are set out in *Harvey* R [181].
528 Council Directive 77/187/EEC, known as the Acquired Rights Directive; now Directive 2001/23/EC. The House of Lords held in *Litster v Forth Dry Dock and Engineering Co Ltd* [1989] ICR 341, [1989] IRLR 161 not only that the Directive could be used as an aid to interpretation, but also that it justified the adoption of a broad and purposive construction of the Regulations in order to effect the protective intent of the Directive.
529 See pp 91–94 above.
530 See p 79 above.
531 See pp 593 below.

fact end up working for the transferee, this actually adds little because the above provisions of the 1996 Act probably apply anyway. However, the Regulations also contain the potentially radical concept of automatic transfer (whether or not the employees and/or the transferee want it). This has caused serious problems in recent years, due to a spate of ECJ decisions on the Directive, in the light of which the Regulations must be construed; major uncertainties have arisen as to when the Regulations apply, how far their effects go, who is covered by them and, most controversial politically, how they apply to the modern phenomenon of the contracting out of services to the private sector (a key policy of the previous government, not exactly reversed by the present government but given the more acceptable title of 'Best Value' in the public sector). For the purposes of relatively straightforward exposition, these are now considered separately, though of course any given case may concern several of them (*and* the provisions in the Regulations on unfair dismissal, which are considered separately at p 593 below).

(1) Application of the Regulations

The Regulations only apply to a 'relevant transfer', which is defined as a transfer 'from one person to another of an undertaking situated immediately before the transfer in the United Kingdom, or a part of one which is so situated'[532]. The transfer may be affected by sale, some other disposition or by operation of law[533], which means that one major limitation is that the Regulations do not apply to a take-over of a business by the purchase of its shares[534]. An 'undertaking' is defined as including 'any trade or business' and was originally construed in a similar fashion to the 'transfer of business' provisions in the 1996 Act, namely as referring to a going concern, not just a sale of assets[535]. This was in line with older decisions on the Acquired Rights Directive, in particular that in *Spijkers v Gebroeders Benedik Abbattoir BV: 24/85*[536] which stressed the importance of the continuing viability of that which was transferred; that case arose in the context of the transfer of part of an undertaking where the emphasis on the transfer of significant parts of the going concern is of particular importance and so, although a relevant transfer is defined as including the transfer of *part* of a business it may still be necessary to apply a similar test of viability as a concern as under the old law, and so there may be little change there. Where, however, there has been potential for change and development is in the interpretation to be given to an 'undertaking', for in subsequent cases on the Directive the ECJ have taken a broader approach to this, looking at whether there had been a transfer of some form of *economic unit* or a change of persons *operating* the undertaking, rather than more narrowly at the

---

532 Reg 3(1).
533 Reg 3(2); *Robert Seligman Corpn v Baker* [1983] ICR 770. It may be effected by two or more transactions (see *Longden v Ferrari Ltd* [1994] ICR 443, [1994] IRLR 157) and it is declared that it may take place whether or not any property is transferred: reg 3(4), as amended by the TURERA 1993. In an untypical case, a transfer may occur over a (possibly length) period of time, rather than on one occasion: *Celtec Ltd v Astley* [2002] EWCA Civ 1035, [2002] ICR 1289, [2002] IRLR 629.
534 This limitation is found in the Directive and continues to apply, even if being used deliberately by an employer in order to avoid the application of the Regulations: *Brookes v Borough Care Services* [1998] ICR 1198 [1998] IRLR 636. It is not of great significance for continuity of employment because in a take-over of this sort the employing company remains the same, albeit under new control. It is, of course, significant in relation to union consultation (see above).
535 *Premier Motors (Medway) Ltd v Total Oil Great Britain Ltd* [1984] ICR 58, [1983] IRLR 471; *Banking Insurance and Finance Union v Barclays Bank plc* [1987] ICR 495.
536 [1986] ECR 1119, [1986] 2 CMLR 296, ECJ.

details of what tangible or intangible assets were transferred, or at legal concepts of *ownership*[537]. *Spikjers* (above) is still widely cited, in the sense of determining whether some form of 'economic entity' has been transferred. While this is still not to look at the matter wholly through the eyes of the employees affected by it, it does suggest a wider application for the Regulations; this has been particularly important in relation to tendering, and is further considered below. There used to be an important restriction written into the Regulations, stating that they were not to apply to an undertaking not in the nature of a commercial venture. However, in the light of ECJ case law which showed that this restriction was inconsistent with the Directive[538], it was removed by the Trade Union Reform and Employment Rights Act 1993.

(2) Effect on contracts – automatic transfer

As we have seen, regulation 5(1) states that a relevant transfer does not terminate a contract of employment with the transferor, and has the effect that that contract operates after the transfer as if originally made between the employee and the transferee. Regulation 5(2) goes on to state that all the transferor's rights, powers, duties and liabilities under or in connection with the contract are transferred to the transferee[539]; the Directive gives member states the option of imposing joint

---

537 This arose particularly in relation to the transfer of some form of business lease, with the employees going into the employment of the new lessee and being covered by the Directive: *Foreningen af Asbejdslederei i Danmark v Daddy's Dance Hall A/S*: 324/86 [1988] IRLR 315, ECJ; *Landsoganisationen i Danmark v Ny Molle Kro*: 287/86 [1989] ICR 330, [1989] IRLR 37, ECJ; *Berg v Besselsenn*: 144/87 [1990] ICR 396, [1989] IRLR 447, ECJ. A much-reported case showing such an approach in a more mainstream context is the *Christel Schmidt* case: C-392/92 [1994] ECR I-1311, [1995] 2 CMLR 331, ECJ; see p 210, below. There can even be a relevant transfer between two companies in the same group: *Allen v Amalgamated Construction Ltd*: C-234/98 [2000] ICR 436, [2000] IRLR 119, ECJ.

538 In particular, *Dr Sophie Redmond Stichting v Bartol*: C-29/91 [1992] IRLR 366, ECJ where the Directive applied to the transfer of a franchise between two charities. In one way, however, the Regulations go beyond the Directive; this is in reg 4 which gives protection to employees of an insolvent company that is subject to a rescue operation by way of 'hiving down' (see Davies and Fredland 'The effects of receivership upon employees of companies' (1980) 9 ILJ 95; McMullen, n 527 above; Collins 'Transfer of undertakings and insolvency' (1989) 18 ILJ 144; Pollard 'Insolvent companies and TUPE' (1996) 25 ILJ 191); the Directive does not extend to formal judicial liquidation proceedings: *Abels v Bedrijfsvereniging voor de Metaalindustrie en de Electrotechnische Industrie*: 135/83 [1985] ECR 469, [1987] 2 CMLR 406, ECJ.

539 Existing criminal liabilities of the transferor are not affected: reg 5(4). The regime of transfer has been applied more widely than just to ordinary terms and conditions; it has been held to apply to a protective award for failure to consult on collective redundancies and liability for failure to consult under TUPE itself (*Kerry Foods Ltd v Creber* [2000] ICR 556, [2000] IRLR 10; *Alamo Group (Europe) Ltd v Tucker* [2003] ICR 829, [2003] IRLR 266), the benefit of a restraint of trade clause which could be claimed by the transferee (*Morris Angel & Son Ltd v Hollande* [1993] ICR 71, [1993] IRLR 169, CA), liability for alleged sex discrimination (*DJM International Ltd v Nicholas* [1996] ICR 214, [1996] IRLR 76) and even liability for an industrial injury suffered by the employee while in the transferor's employment (*Bernadone v Pall Mall Services Group* [2001] ICR 197, [2000] IRLR 487, CA). Reg 7 excludes occupational pensions; attempts were made to evade this by arguing that, although a transferee does not have to continue to operate an existing pension scheme, he is under an obligation (under Art 3(3) of the Directive) to provide something equivalent, but this was strongly disapproved by the EAT in *Walden Engineering Co Ltd v Warrener* [1993] 3 CMLR 179, [1993] ICR 967; this exclusion is not contrary to the Directive: *Adams v Lancashire County Council* [1997] IRLR 436, CA. On the other hand, it was held in *Beckman v Dynamco Whicheloe Macfarlane Ltd* C-164/00 [2003] ICR 50, [2002] IRLR 578, ECJ that it is only the age-related refinement element of a pension scheme that does not transfer; other elements (eg allowing early and/or health retirement) mght transfer.

liability on the transferee and the transferor, but the British government did not adopt that approach and it is not to be implied into the Regulations[540]. These transfer provisions are further underpinned by regulation 8 which makes any transfer-related dismissal unfair, unless for an 'economic, technical or organisational reason' (see p 593 below). This form of automatic transfer (or statutory novation of the contract) goes beyond a mere matter of continuity of employment, which was probably safeguarded anyway, in two ways. The first is that, where the employees go with the business, not only is continuity preserved, but also their existing terms and conditions (and accrued rights, especially to redundancy payments[541]) are protected and the new employer takes them on subject to that, with a longstanding problem of when and how the transferee employer can lawfully change them (see below)[542]. The second is even more fundamental – the basic principle is that automatic transfer occurs on a relevant transfer *irrespective of the desires of the parties*. At common law, an employee could not be required to work for a particular employer without his consent[543]. That principle disappeared once the Regulations applied[544]. Moreover, a purchaser of a business who, in earlier times, would have bought it without the staff (who would have been made redundant by the old employer), can now find that he is *deemed* to be their new employer, on their existing terms and responsible for any redundancy payments, based on their years of service with their old employer. Regulation 5(5) does give the employee a right to leave (and claim constructive dismissal) but it is restricted – it only applies if 'a substantial change is made in his working conditions to his detriment'[545], and it is declared that the change in the identity of the employer is not per se such a substantial change (unless the employee can show real detriment because of it). Apart from that, the employees were as bound by automatic transfer as the transferee employer. Initially, this appeared to be very much in line with the intent of the Directive[546], but doubt was cast on that by the ECJ's decision in *Katsikas v Konstantinidis*[547] upholding the German equivalent of these Regulations which allows an employee a right of objection to the transfer, avoiding automatic transfer of his contract; the view of the ECJ was that under the Directive it is for the member state to decide whether or not to legislate for automatic transfer. In the light of that case, a hurried

---

540 *Allan v Stirling District Council* [1995] ICR 1082, [1995] IRLR 301, Ct of Sess, approving *Ibex Trading Co Ltd v Walton* [1994] ICR 907, [1994] IRLR 564.
541 See p 637 below, for the fundamental changes made to redundancy payments liability by the Regulations.
542 This is especially so in the light of (a) the decision of the Court of Appeal in *Berriman v Delabole Slate Ltd* [1985] ICR 546, [1985] IRLR 305 that seeking to 'standardise' the newcomers' terms and conditions to those of the transferee's existing workforce is *not* within the 'economic, technical or organisational' defence and (b) the leading case of *Wilson v St Helens Borough Council* [1998] ICR 1141, [1998] IRLR 706 in the House of Lords on transfer-related variations.
543 *Nokes v Doncaster Amalgamated Collieries Ltd* [1940] AC 1014, [1940] 3 All ER 549, HL.
544 *Newns v British Airways plc* [1992] IRLR 575, CA. Paradoxically, in several of the leading cases it is the *employees* arguing that the Regulations should *not* apply, because they want a break in their employment, so that they can cash in their accrued redundancy rights against the old employer and start afresh with the transferee; see, eg, *Whitewater Leisure Managment Ltd v Barnes* [2000] ICR 1049, [2000] IRLR 456.
545 On ordinary principles of constructive dismissal law, those changes must constitute a breach of contract by the employer, so that making changes which the employer is contractually permitted to make will not activate reg 5(5): *Rossiter v Pendragon plc* [2002] ICR 1063, [2002] IRLR 483, CA.
546 *Berg v Besselsen*, n 537 above.
547 C-132, 138, 139/91: [1992] ECR I-6577, [1993] 1 CMLR 845, ECJ.

amendment to the Regulations was put into the Trade Union Reform and Employment Rights Act 1993 as it was going through Parliament. The inserted regulation 5(4A) states that there is not to be automatic transfer 'if the employee informs the transferor or the transferee that he objects to becoming employed by the transferee'[548]. However, regulation 5(4B) then goes on to state that where such objection is made 'the transfer of the undertaking ... shall operate so as to terminate his contract of employment with the transferor *but he shall not be treated, for any purpose, as having been dismissed by the transferor*'. The result of this bizarre amendment is that the employee has a theoretical right of objection but if he exercises it he may be left in a state of legal limbo, with no rights against the transferee (because there is no automatic transfer of his contract), but also no recourse against the transferor for any cause of action that requires him to have been 'dismissed' (because regulation 5(4B) deems there to have been no dismissal). The potential harshness of this situation led the Court of Appeal to add a major qualification, in a particularly purposive decision[549] holding that if an employee leaves by exercising his right to do so under regulation 5(5) (substantial detrimental changes being proposed/threatened by the transferee employer), then regulation 5(4B) does *not* apply and the employee retains any remedies he may have against the transferor (which remain personal to that employer and do not pass to the transferee, because of regulation 5(4A)). This is a good example of both the complexity of these Regulations and the need occasionally for creative interpretation to avoid some of their more notable absurdities.

Following on from that point, recent domestic case law has shown two major difficulties for employers on a 'TUPE transfer' (to lapse into the jargon). The first is that if a transferee takes on employees whose existing terms of employment were made by reference to some extraneous factor affecting the transferor, the transferee will be bound by them, possibly with strange results. In *Whent v T Cartledge Ltd*[550] the transferee (the successful tenderer in a contracting-out case) took on employees whose terms on remuneration referred to collective bargains between the old employer and a recognised union, with the result that when wages were raised by the next such bargain the transferred employees successfully claimed the increase, even though by then in the employment of the transferee who was not concerned at all in the bargaining. In *Unicorn Consultancy Services Ltd v Westbrook*[551] transferred employees could claim from the transferee profit-related pay (PRP) due under their contracts, based on the *transferor's* profits and performance. This could be a serious problem – the case only involved an 'easy' version of this because the employees were claiming PRP that had already been earned by the time of the transfer. As the EAT noted, the real difficulty was the operation of such a PRP term in the *future*, after the transfer. This point arose in *MITIE Managed Services Ltd v French*[552], where (on the basis that something had to transfer, but an obligation based still on the transferor's undertaking would be unworkable) the EAT held that in such a case the obligation on the transferee would be to provide a PRP scheme of 'substantial equivalence'.

---

548 No particular form is laid down for objection, which may therefore be inferred from words or conduct: *Hay v George Hanson (Building Contractors) Ltd* [1996] IRLR 427, though notice the more cautious approach in *Senior Heat Treatment Ltd v Bell* [1997] IRLR 614.
549 *University of Oxford v Humphreys* [2000] IRLR 183, CA.
550 [1997] IRLR 153.
551 [2000] IRLR 80.
552 [2002] ICR 1395,[2002] IRLR 512.

The second point of difficulty only compounds the first. In the straightforward world of domestic contract law, it would be possible for the transferee to take on the transferred employees on their existing terms and conditions and then to negotiate changes in the normal way. However, it has been held that the protection of the Directive (and hence the Regulations) is intended to be stronger than that, with the result that a transferee may *not* lawfully change the existing terms and conditions *if* the change is 'transfer-related', and that any attempt to do so will be void, even if for good consideration and with the ostensible agreement of the employees. This particular bombshell was dropped by the EAT in *Wilson v St Helens Borough Council*[553] (with the laconic comment that this may be 'surprising ... to English legal tradition'), with the result that employees who had agreed changes to their terms on a transfer for a buy-out payment could demand restoration of the original terms over a year later[554]. By the time that this case reached the House of Lords the basic principle seemed to be accepted, and the argument at that stage was over the circumstances in which the principle might be avoided (and a contractual change lawful)[555]. Two such circumstances were accepted – (i) where either transferor or transferee dismisses the employees and re-engages them on the new terms (this being effective because domestic law does not acknowledge the possibility of a dismissal being void, even under the Directive); (ii) where the transferee can break the claim of causation by showing that the changes were *not* 'transfer-related', ie that they were made for some other, independent reason such as a reorganisation of the whole workplace involving all employees (longstanding and transferred), in which case the ordinary rules of contract law apply. Category (i) is not as attractive as it seems, because it lays the employer open to unfair dismissal actions by the employees[556], compensation possibly reflecting the net loss incurred under the new terms and conditions. Category (ii) can be fraught with problems of proof and timing (there being *no* rule of thumb that a change will not be transfer-related after a certain period from the transfer), and assumptions made by employers about their ability to impose or even negotiate changes after the transfer can sometimes be proved to have been entirely wrong[557].

---

553 [1996] ICR 711, [1996] IRLR 320; this was based on long-overlooked dicta by the ECJ in *Foreningen of Arbejdsledere i Danmark v Daddy's Dance Hall A/S*: 324/86 [1988] IRLR 315, ECJ.

554 The mechanism used was a claim for unlawful deductions from wages under Pt II of the Employment Rights Act 1996 (see p 259 below), where the limitation period (in a case of continuing deductions) only flows from the last pay day, under the new terms, before the date of the proceedings. One unresolved point is a case like this is whether the employer can reclaim from the employees the amount paid to buy out the original terms, on the basis of failure of consideration.

555 [1998] ICR 1141, [1998] IRLR 706, HL; see McMullen (1998) 28 ILJ 76. The reasons for this subtle but significant change in emphasis were that (a) the case was consolidated with the appeal in *Meade and Baxendale v British Fuels Ltd* [1996] IRLR 541 where there had been a dismissal and re-engagement on new terms, not just a contractual variation, and (b) it became apparent that the dismissal tactic had in fact also been used in *Wilson* itself, a factor which had not been thought particularly significant at EAT level.

556 The employees can claim unfair dismissal from their old *contract*, even though still in the employment of the employer under the new contract, under the rule in *Hogg v Dover College* [1990] ICR 39: see p 545 below.

557 In two cases, restraint of trade clauses negotiated into contracts by the transferee shortly after the transfer were held to be unenforceable because they were transfer-related and therefore void changes: *Crédit Suisse First Boston (Europe) Ltd v Padiachy* [1999] ICR 569, [1998] IRLR 504; *Crédit Suisse First Boston (Europe) Ltd v Lister* [1999] ICR 794, [1998] IRLR 700, CA. In the latter case, this was despite the employee having been paid £625,000 for the change in terms.

(3) Which employees are covered?

In many cases it will be obvious which employees are covered by the Regulations and the accompanying statutory protection, especially where a whole undertaking is transferred, with the whole existing workforce being kept on. However, problems have arisen in two areas. The first is where *part* of an undertaking is transferred, especially where it is a part of a complex organisation or group of companies; given that the remainder may be facing financial disaster, can an employee who worked for several or all parts of the organisation or group claim to be attached to the part transferred, and so 'jump ship' to the employment of the financially viable transferee/purchaser (at least for the purposes of bringing any redundancy or unfair dismissal claims against the latter if not kept on)? In *Sunley Turriff Holdings Ltd v Thomson*[558] two companies (LC Ltd and LC Scotland Ltd) went into receivership and the latter was sold to Co X. The employee had been company secretary and chief accountant for both companies. Although his contract had been with LC Ltd, he had done substantial work for LC (Scotland) Ltd and so, when made redundant by the receivers the EAT held that he was able to claim that he was covered by the Regulations and so technically taken on by Co X, against whom he could claim unfair dismissal. On the other hand, in *Michael Peters Ltd v Farnfield*[559] when receivers were called in to a group of a holding company and twenty-five subsidiaries, the EAT held that the chief executive of the group could not invoke the Regulations and claim to go with the transfer when (only) four viable subsidiaries were sold to Co Y. In both cases, the court applied the test laid down by the ECJ in *Botzen v Rotterdamsche Droogdok Maatschappij BV*[560], ie to look as a question of fact at 'to which part of the undertaking or business the employee was assigned' or allocated. It is clear from the first of the two EAT cases that this will not be resolved simply by looking at the technicalities of where the contract of employment lay. Other than that (which presumably must at least be a factor) this is a wide question of fact and degree with (so far) no attempt to lay down rules of thumb, such as at least x% of work being done for the part transferred, which could make advising on this point in advance of a transfer very difficult[561], especially as the EAT subsequently added that tribunals should be astute to ensure that protection of the individual (and the intent of the Directive and Regulations) should not be prejudiced by too formalistic an emphasis being placed on the intricacies of the corporate structure of the transferor organisation[562].

The second problem arose early in the convoluted history of the Regulations and involves a question of *when* the employee in question must have been in the transferor's employ. In order for these automatic transfer provisions to apply the employee must have been employed 'immediately before' the transfer of undertaking (regulation 5(3)); the question arose whether there can be a gap between the end of employment with the transferor and the transfer itself (for example over a weekend). Originally

---

558 [1995] IRLR 184.
559 [1995] IRLR 190. See also *CPL Distribution Ltd v Todd* [2002] EWCA Civ 1481, [2003] IRLR 28, where a manager's PA was held not to transfer, on similar grounds.
560 Case 186/83: [1985] ECR 519, [1986] 2 CMLR 50, ECJ. In *Michael Peters* it was held that the solution to this problem lies in applying this test, *not* in attempting to lift the veil of incorporation.
561 It may also reinforce the need, appreciated early on under these Regulations, to put indemnity clauses into business sales agreements to cover the possibility of unforeseen liabilities being placed on the transferee, contrary to the expectations of both parties.
562 *Duncan Web Offset (Maidstone) Ltd v Cooper* [1995] IRLR 633.

it was held that there could be[563], which could lead to a less technical application of the Regulations, though at the expense of considerable uncertainty (how long a gap was permissible?). However, in *Secretary of State for Employment v Spence*[564], the Court of Appeal overruled this approach and held that regulation 5 only applies to employees employed by the transferor at the precise moment of the transfer, so that a gap even of hours was fatal. This at least has the merit of certainty, important in itself in advising the parties to the transfer, but it did appear to give more scope to the purchaser/transferee who wishes to insist that the vendor/transferor dispense with the workforce before the transfer, if only marginally before (leaving the dispensed workers with rights only against the transferor who may in some cases be in a far weaker economic position than the transferee). However, this potentially major gap in the protection intended by the Regulations for employees in this position has now been rectified in two cases, not by overruling *Spence*, but rather by holding that in many cases the reasoning in that case does not go far enough. In *P Bork International A/S (in liquidation) v Foreningen af Arbejdsledere i Danmark*[565] the ECJ, construing the Acquired Rights Directive, held that if an employee is dismissed before the transfer and because of it, then Article 4(1) renders that dismissal ineffective; the result of this is that the employee is *deemed* still to be employed 'immediately before' the transfer, so that liabilities in respect of him *are* transferred to the transferee. The provisions of Article 4(1) appear in domestic law as regulation 8[566] which makes a dismissal because of the transfer automatically unfair unless it was for an 'economic, technical or organisational reason entailing changes in the workforce'. As the ECJ's decision in *Bork* produced a result contrary to that in *Spence*, the whole question had to be reconsidered as a matter of domestic law. This occurred in *Litster v Forth Dry Dock and Engineering Co Ltd*[567], where employees of the transferor company were dismissed only an hour before the transfer, but the transferee company denied that they were liable for any unfair dismissals because the employees were not employed 'immediately before the transfer' (thus leaving them to pursue any remedies only against the transferor company, which was in receivership). The House of Lords, applying *Bork*, held that regulation 5 did apply, so that the transferees were liable; *Spence* was upheld, in as much as it establishes that 'immediately before' means 'at the time of', *but* regulation 5(3) which contains that phrase must be read as if there were inserted the phrase 'or would have been so employed

---

563 *Apex Leisure Hire v Barratt* [1984] ICR 452, [1984] IRLR 224; *Secretary of State for Employment v Anchor Hotel (Kippford) Ltd* [1985] ICR 724, [1985] IRLR 452.
564 [1986] ICR 651, [1986] IRLR 248, CA, applying *Wendeboe v LJ Music ApS*: 19/83 [1985] ECR 457, [1986] 1 CMLR 476, ECJ (a case on the Acquired Rights Directive). *Spence* was one of the cases where it was the employees who did *not* want reg 5 to apply – they wanted to cash in their redundancy rights (in fact against the Secretary of State since their old employer was insolvent) and could do so only if their employment was not transferred to the new employer. However, by winning their case they appeared to worsen the position of employees in other cases who *do* wish to rely on the Regulations.
565 101/87: [1989] IRLR 41, ECJ.
566 See p 593 below.
567 [1989] ICR 341, [1989] IRLR 161, HL; see Collins (1989) 18 ILJ 144. The wide and purposive interpretation of the Regulations adopted in this case was justified (particularly by Lord Keith) on the grounds that the Regulations were passed to implement the Directive and that the previous decision of the House of Lords in *Pickstone v Freemans plc* [1988] ICR 697, [1988] IRLR 357 permitted heavy reliance on the Directive (as construed in *Bork*) as an aid to interpretation. One possible problem was that Art. 4(1) renders a dismissal because of transfer *ineffective* whereas reg 8 only renders it potentially *unfair*; however, this point is outflanked by the approach of the House of Lords in using a wide interpretation to imply wording into reg 5(3), as set out below.

[immediately before the transfer] if he had not been unfairly dismissed in the circumstances described in regulation 8(1)'. The outcome of this decision is as follows – (i) the transferee cannot escape liability under regulation 5 merely by inducing the transferor to dismiss the employee shortly before the actual time of transfer, because that Regulation is to be read subject to the unfair dismissal provisions of regulation 8; (ii) *Spence* is correct as an authority on the meaning of the phrase 'immediately before' *and* was correctly decided on its facts because in that case there *was* an 'economic ... reason' for the dismissal, so that regulation 8 did not apply; in most cases, however, that will not be so, regulation 8 will apply (in spite of any applicable gap between the dismissal and the time of transfer) and so for example – (iii) the cases of *Apex Leisure Hire* and *Anchor Hotel (Kippford) Ltd*[568] were correctly decided on their facts, but for the wrong reasons. As was pointed out in the House of Lords, this wide and purposive interpretation achieves the presumed intent of Parliament which was to give effect to the protective intent of the Directive, rather than to negative it (as the decision in *Spence*, standing alone, had been capable of doing).

(4) Application to tendering and contracting out[569]

It has been the policy of successive governments for several years now to encourage or even require bodies in the public sector to put out to tender certain services (such as catering or cleaning), on the basis that such services can be more efficiently and cheaply provided by the private sector. Similarly, large private concerns may decide to do so voluntarily, for similar reasons. When this happens, staff who previously performed these services in-house will often be taken on by the successful contractors, but it was always assumed that this was after a clean break with the old employer, so that (a) the contractor did not assume any responsibility for any accrued rights (in particular, accrued redundancy rights) and (b) he was free to take on only some of the old workforce and/or then to 'adjust' (ie diminish) their old terms and conditions, to reduce labour costs. Clearly, if the Regulations applied, neither of those assumptions would survive and the whole economic basis of contracting out would be called into question.

It initially seemed clear that under domestic law the Regulations could not apply, for two independent reasons. The first was the restriction that they did not apply to non-commercial undertakings. Thus, in *Expro Services Ltd v Smith*[570], where catering services were contracted out to a private company by the Ministry of Defence, it was held that the Regulations did not apply (and so there was no continuity of employment for an employee who transferred to the private company and was later dismissed within the magic two years then required for an unfair dismissal claim), because the catering venture had not been a commercial venture when carried out by the Ministry. The second was that, in any event, the domestic courts took the view that merely giving out a contract or tender[571] could not

---

568 See n 563, above.
569 See McMullen (1994) 23 ILJ 230; Radford and Kerr 'Acquiring rights – losing power: a case study in ministerial resistance to the impact of EC law' (1997) 60 MLR 23.
570 [1991] ICR 577, [1991] IRLR 156.
571 This could happen in two ways – (1) the old employer A could change from performing the service in-house, and contract it out to private firm B (a 'first generation contracting-out') *or* (2) the old employer A could already have contracted it out to private firm B, but on the expiry of that contract retendered and awarded the new contract to private firm C (a 'second generation contracting-out'). Problems of continuity arise if a particular employee carries on doing the same job in the same place, but moves in the first case from A to B, and in the second case from B to C.

constitute the 'transfer of an undertaking' because it fell short of a going business (even if the employees and certain premises or equipment went with it). Thus, in *Curling v Securicor Ltd*[572] the Home Office had contracted out services at a detention centre to Securicor, but when that contract came up for renewal it was awarded to another company; the employee stayed doing the same job and transferred to the employment of the other company, but it was held that regulation 5 did not apply because this mere change of contract did not constitute a transfer of undertaking.

This situation began to change when it became clear that the restriction to commercial undertakings was contrary to the Directive and so had to be removed by the Trade Union Reform and Employment Rights Act 1993[573]. At first, the then government maintained that the Regulations still would not apply to contracting out because of the second reason above (no 'undertaking' transferred). However, the axe soon fell on that with the decision of the ECJ in *Rask v ISS Kantineservice A/S*[574] that the Directive did apply where a large private company had contracted out the running of a staff canteen to a service company and an existing employee entered the latter's employment; the result was that when the service company changed one of her terms of employment she could claim the protection of the Danish legislation enacting the Directive[575]. Following on from this, it was held by the High Court in *Kenny v South Manchester College*[576] that effect must now be given to this wide approach in domestic law; thus, where prison education had been contracted out to a local authority but, as a result of re-tendering, was then contracted out to a college, the staff previously employed by the local authority on that work had to be taken on by the college, on the same terms and conditions. A similar conclusion was reached in *Wren v Eastbourne Borough Council*[577] where a mainstream example of a local authority being obliged to contract out its street cleaning and refuse collection functions led to the finding of a 'transfer of undertaking' when those functions were taken over by a private company. This approach was then taken further in three ways. First, in *Dines v Initial Health Care Services*[578] the Court of Appeal held that the inescapable logic

---

572 [1992] IRLR 549. This was another case where it was in fact the employees arguing that the Regulations did *not* apply, because they were seeking (successfully) redundancy payments from Securicor.

573 See p 202 above.

574 C-209/91: [1993] IRLR 133, ECJ.

575 At least in *Rask* it concerned an employee who wanted to be there and whom the transferee wanted to employ; automatic transfer means that a firm contracting for a service would notionally have to take on *all* the employees currently doing the job (even those he had not planned on keeping), with all their accrued rights.

576 [1993] ICR 934, [1993] IRLR 265.

577 [1993] 3 CMLR 166, [1993] ICR 955. There was a transfer even though the council retained overall responsibility for the functions being performed; this point was emphasised in *Birch v Nuneaton and Bedworth Borough Council* [1995] IRLR 518 where there was a relevant transfer when the management of a leisure centre was contracted out, even though the council built into the contract remarkably detailed controls over its running.

578 [1995] ICR 11, [1994] IRLR 336, CA. In such a case, the potential problems are unlikely to be sorted out by the parties A and B amicably (eg through price adjustments and indemnity clauses) because they are commercial competitors and indeed, in an extreme case, may not even know who the other is. In fact, the application of the Regulations could give an opportunity for disappointed tenderer A to cause problems for the successful tenderer B – there are apocryphal stories of A's last act being to double their employees' wages, so that B has to take them on at those wage rates! Another possibility is that A could assign to that contract for the last phase of the contract all the employees he most wishes to lose.

(resisted, as a matter of policy, by the EAT in that case) was that the Regulations could apply to a subsequent re-tendering exercise; thus, where the original contract for the services (in that case, for hospital cleaning) by Co A ran out and the principal body retendered and Co B won the next contract, there was a transfer of undertaking from A to B (albeit in two stages – the handing back from A to the principal body and then the granting of the new contract to B); the effect was that employees of A were either notionally taken into the employment of B for the purposes of an unfair dismissal claim, or were actually taken on by B but with their existing terms and conditions protected. The counter argument, that all that had been 'transferred' was a contract, not an undertaking, was disapproved. Second, in *Isles of Scilly Council v Brintel Helicopters Ltd*[579] it was held that there was a transfer of undertaking where the firm to which airport support services had been contracted out went into administration and the council took these services back in-house, ie a contracting *back in*. Third, this broad approach to the contracting of services (and, more generally, to the defining of a transfer of undertaking by looking generally for the continuance of an economic entity or activity with some sort of retained identity, rather than for more concrete matters such as the transfer of assets or equipment or good will) seemed to be taken to its logical conclusion by the decision of the ECJ in the *Christel Schmidt* case[580] that the Acquired Rights Directive applied where an employee who was the sole cleaner of a bank's premises was dismissed when that service function was contracted out to the firm that already provided it with other cleaning services; this was so in spite of the facts that (a) all that was concerned was a purely ancillary function (not part of the bank's principal business), (b) only one employee was involved and (c) there was no transfer whatever of any tangible assets. Intervening in the argument of the case, the British government had again tried to draw a distinction between the transfer of a business (or part thereof) and the mere entering of a contractual arrangement, but again this had fallen on deaf ears.

Those involved in contracting-out operations thus had to become accustomed to conducting them against the background of the Regulations, which were therefore giving considerable protection to the employees involved. Unfortunately, however, it could not be assumed that the Regulations would always apply, and the uncertainty caused by two subsequent ECJ cases (appearing to resile from the high point reached in *Christel Schmidt*) meant that this continued to be a troublesome area. *Rygard v Stø Mølle Akustik A/S*[581] caused some ripples by appearing to revive ideas that it may be only a contractual function that was being transferred, but it was on unusual facts and was later restrictively distinguished by the EAT and ECJ[582] and has had little effect. The case that did, however, cause most heartache even to TUPE-hardened employment lawyers was *Ayse Süzen*[583] , in

579 [1995] ICR 249, [1995] IRLR 6.
580 *Schmidt v Spar und Leihkasse der früheren Ämter Bordesholm, Kiel und Cronshagen*: C 392/92 [1994] ECR I-1311, [1995] 2 CMLR 331, ECJ. For a recent appplication of TUPE to a single employee, see *Dudley Bower Building Services Ltd v Lowe* [2003] ICR 843, [2003] IRLR 260.
581 C-48/94 [1996] ICR 333, [1996] IRLR 51, ECJ.
582 *BSG Property Services v Tuck* [1996] IRLR 134; *Allen v Amalgamated Construction Co Ltd*: C-234/98 [2000] IRLR 119, [2000] All ER (EC) 97, ECJ.
583 *Süzen v Zehnacker Gebäudereinigung GmbH Krankenhausservice*: C-13/95 [1997] ICR 662, [1997] IRLR 255, ECJ. A similar approach was taken subsequently by the ECJ in *Francisco Hernández Vidal SA v Gomez Perez*: C-127/96 [1999] IRLR 132, ECJ and *Sánchez Hidalgo v Asociación de Servicios Aser and Sociedad Cooperativa Minerva*: C-173/96 [2002] ICR 73, [1999] IRLR 136, ECJ, though (it has been argued) with more emphasis on the importance of the workforce itself as the 'economic entity' in a labour-intensive industry.

which the ECJ stated (helpfully) that a contracting-out may *or may not* be a relevant transfer, depending in many cases on whether assets and/or a significant part of the workforce were actually transferred by the commercial arrangement. Immediately after this decision the Court of Appeal held in *Betts v Brintel Helicopters Ltd*[584] that there was no relevant transfer (on a second generation contracting-out) where the new contractors for the supply of gas rigs had its own helicopters and facilities and deliberately declined to offer employment to any of the employees engaged on the service by the old contractor. A case such as this exposed the flaw in *Ayse Süzen* from the point of view of employee protection, namely that a cynical transferee could use it to make non-application of the Regulations a self-fulfilling prophecy by refusing to take on either assets or staff. This possibility has, however, been considerably lessened by the important case of *ECM (Vehicle Delivery Service) Ltd v Cox* where just such a tactic was used, again on a second generation contracting-out. The EAT[585] held that the Regulations did apply on two grounds that, they said, had not been before the ECJ in *Ayse Süzen* – (i) in a labour-intensive industry it may be relevant (as it was in *Christel Schmidt*) that the employee in question was 'dedicated' to the work that was being transferred (rather than merely being a member of staff of a large service company who, on the loss of one contract, will simply be moved on to the next one), which should point to there being a relevant transfer; (ii) in any event, as a matter of policy and purposive interpretation, a tribunal may wish to prevent an employer from deliberately using *Ayse Süzen* to avoid the Regulations. On appeal[586], point (i) was not in issue, and it may be that the EAT's view on it is of importance because arguably it goes to the heart of the economic realities of a transfer and whether the employee's continuing need of *that* job merits protection. On point (ii) the Court of Appeal dismissed the employer's appeal and held in a short judgment that *all* the circumstances of the transfer must be considered, *including* any intent to evade the Regulations, a point subsequently approved and applied in Scotland by the Inner House of the Court of Session[587]. This '*ECM* point' has continued to cause problems, splitting the Court of Appeal (2-1 in result, but unhelpfully being in effect a three-way split because of different reasoning between the majority judges) in *ADI (UK) Ltd v Willer*[588] and being subject to a less than enthusiastic analysis by another Court of Appeal in *RCO Support Services v UNISON*[589], where the refusal to accept existing staff by the transferee was agreed to be a factor in the overall assessment, but only in an objective sense (not in the original, subjective sense of being in effect a punishment for a deliberate attempt

---

584 [1997] ICR 792, [1997] IRLR 361, CA.
585 [1998] ICR 631, [1998] IRLR 416.
586 [1999] ICR 1162, [1999] IRLR 559, CA.
587 *Lightways (Contractors) Ltd v Associated Holdings Ltd* [2000] IRLR 247, Ct of Sess (contractor submitting a bid on the basis that TUPE applied was not allowed to insist later to the employees that it did not). One problem arising from *ECM* is that *Betts* (n 584 above) is not criticised, but appears to produce the opposite result on *very* similar facts (including an allegation that the refusal to take on the staff was a deliberate ploy). While each case is of course decided on its facts, it may be that *Betts* would probably be decided the other way today, and that the employees in *Betts* were extremely unlucky in the timing of their case.
588 [2001] IRLR 542, CA. Dyson LJ adopted *ECM* positively; May LJ felt bound to apply it, but reluctantly (on the basis that the recent case law had warped the original meaning of the directive); Simon Brown LJ, in a remarkably strong dissent, said that *ECM* was contrary to EC law, going beyond permissible purposive interpretation.
589 [2002] EWCA Civ 464, [2002] ICR 751, [2002] IRLR 401, CA.

to evade TUPE). The ECJ returned to the fray in *Oy Liikenne*[590] , where it was held that there was no TUPE transfer when the public bus service in the Finnish capital was re-contracted to a different tenderer, with some of the staff being taken back on but no buses being transferred. One interpretation of this case was that (under *Ayse Suzen*) there will not be a TUPE transfer in an assets-reliant industry if there is not transfer of 'significant tangible assets'. However, it was not long before this was subject to reinterpretation with the EAT opining that that was not what the case really meant, that asset transfer was only one factor and that ultimately the matter remains 'multifactorial' (a nice word, but not very helpful for those trying to advise in advance of a transfer). On that basis, currency is given to the other interpretation of *Oy Liikenne*, namely that, rather than a leading case on contracting out, it is merely the leading EC law case on the Helsinki bus industry. None of this has been getting us far in the last few years and although new case law arises regularly[591] , one despairing view would be that in effect the courts have got about as far as they can in this dreadful area. The focus now needs to shift to the long-overdue legislative reform.

(5) The new Acquired Rights Directive and proposals for reform

Directive 77/187, on which the Regulations were based was materially amended by Directive 98/50[592] . In some ways, the new Directive was a disappointment, in particular because the 'new' definition of a relevant transfer merely seeks to codify the existing decisions of the ECJ without giving clearer guidance in contracting-out cases[593] , and because the UK government's suggested way out of the *Wilson v St Helens* conundrum (ie that it should be lawful for the workforce *collectively* to agree post-transfer changes in terms) was only incorporated into the Directive in the restricted case where the employer is insolvent and it is necessary ensure the survival of the undertaking. Nevertheless, the new Directive is to mean new TUPE Regulations, but these have been subject to serious delays and still had not been produced at the time of writing. Consultation documents were issued in 2001[594] , but then nothing further happened, largely due to the near-intractable problem of how to achieve the transfer of pensions (a major change to which the government had committed itself) in any workable and/or intelligible form. At the time of writing, the government had announced that (to break this logjam) they had taken the pension issue out of TUPE reform and put it into a general review to be taken in relation to pensions generally. Hopefully, therefore, TUPE reform should be back on the agenda early in the currency of this edition. Possible changes to watch out for will be:
(1) a new regime of joint liability on both transferor and transferee;
(2) a new definition of a relevant transfer to apply specifically to contracting-out cases[595] ;

---

590 C-172/99 [2001] IRLR 171, ECJ.
591 At the time of writing, further appeal to the House of Lords was anticipated in *RCO v UNISON*.
592 See Davies 'Amendments to the ARD' (1998) 27 ILJ 365. The government enacted a power to make TUPE Regulations (under the European Communities Act 1972, s 2(2)) going beyond the requirements of the Directive: Employment Relations Act 1999, s 38.
593 See now the consolidated Directive 2001/23/EC, *Harvey* P[773].
594 See the Detailed Background Paper (URN 01/1158,DTI) and Sargeant 'New Transfer Regulations' (2002) 31 ILJ 35.
595 The idea here is to try to ensure that TUPE will always apply where it is necessary to protect the individual (whose livelihood would vanish on the transfer if he or she is not transferred) but does not apply if to do so would be ridiculous (eg where the transferor, the long-term employer, merely puts that individual on to new work when the company happens to lose that pari.tuclar contract, one of many).

(3) almost-automatic application of TUPE to public sector transfers;
(4) new obligations on existing holders of contracts to give information to other parties on the re-tendering of the contract, so that tenderers will know what staff they would have to take on;
(5) *some* relaxation of the ban on TUPE-related changes to terms and conditions of employment post-transfer, though this may not go far because it is not specifically permitted by the Directive.

One change has already been made in the public sector, but not by legislation. In response to union opposition to public-private finance initiatives and their strong concerns about such initiatives creating a 'two-tier workforce', the government issued to local authorities a Code of Practice governing contracting-out cases under its 'Best Value' programme[596]. Under this an authority is to require a potential contractor to agree not only to preserve existing terms and conditions for any staff going from authority to contractor with the work, but also to extend those protected terms and conditions to any new employees taken on to perform the work under that contract, ie a form of TUPE-plus.

596 The Code is available on www.odpm.gov.uk/news/0302/0024.htm.

Chapter 4

Wages and hours

I INTRODUCTION

It will be seen in this chapter that the law has long had a role with regard to wages in providing certain forms of protection of the right to receive wages and in establishing rights to certain forms of income replacement, especially when ill. However, the prevailing political view of the last two decades has been that the law (ie the state) should *not* be involved in setting wage levels. Not only were moves within the EC to enter this area (eg by minimum wage rates or maximum hours) vigorously opposed by the previous government, but also they progressively dismantled those legal provisions that in the past did have an effect on wage setting. Mechanisms for imposing 'fair wages' requirements in state contracts were abolished, as were legal means of trying to enforce the 'going rate for the job'. Indeed, free market economics would doubt whether there was any such thing – the only rate is the rate that the market will bear, especially in times of declining collective bargaining and increasing individual contracting. The only legally binding form of wage fixing in recent years was the wages councils, which operated in certain, very specific industries with little or no collective machinery. They remained, however, an anachronism under the new dispensation; initially the previous government curtailed their powers in 1986, and eventually abolished them in 1993, leaving only the Agricultural Wages Board which is set up under its own legislation.

The incoming New Labour government has been keen to stress its free market credentials and not to be seen to be going back to dated ideas of wages policies or wage restraint that caused so many problems for the Labour governments of the 1960s and 1970s. However, they were committed to two forms of statutory intervention strongly opposed by the previous government; those were a national minimum wage and compliance with the EC Working Time Directive, and both were enacted within the first two years of the government's first term. While these provisions enact important minima and limitations, neither of them seek to determine the actual *levels* of wages or the hours of work required (or their organisation). For most purposes, therefore, wages and hours remain primarily a question for agreement and contract, not legal intervention. As such, they have in the past been primarily a matter for the ordinary courts, not the employment tribunals, in the case of disputes as to payability, amounts owed, etc; this led in the past to an extremely unfortunate split in jurisdiction (eg a dismissed employee having to go to a tribunal for unfair dismissal, but to the county court for unpaid notice or holiday pay). We shall see, however, that there have been major inroads into this principle in recent years, by (1) the adoption of interpretations of Part II of the Employment Rights Act 1996 (originally the Wages Act 1986) which deserve a nomination for the Booker Prize for Fiction, in relation to what can constitute a 'deduction' from wages, and (2) at long last the granting to tribunals of jurisdiction to hear certain common law contractual claims (though unfortunately restricted to amounts owing on termination of employment).

2 THE RIGHT TO WAGES AT COMMON LAW

The obligation upon the employer to pay the wages which are due is a basic term of the contract of employment; details of the scale, rate or method of calculation of the remuneration should be given to the employee in writing[1], and he has a statutory right to receive an itemised pay statement upon payment of wages or salary[2]. However, it must be stressed that the details of the obligation upon the employer depend entirely upon the terms of the contract of employment, and there cannot be said to be any overall legal obligation to pay wages as such, since wages are not necessarily the consideration to be supplied by the employer for the work done or service rendered by the employee. Thus, at common law there can be a valid contract of employment, even though no set wages are payable, where the employee is to be rewarded by a commission[3], by fees, by the receipt of tips from customers[4] or by being given the *chance* to earn a salary[5]. Likewise, there will be no set wage or salary where the employee is paid on a piecework or hourly basis (with or without an agreed guaranteed minimum wage), though in such a case there may be an implied term that the employer shall provide a reasonable amount of work for the employee to do[6]. Moreover, in an extreme case it might be that the correct construction of the contract is that, in the circumstances, nothing is payable to the employee as in *Re Richmond Gate Property Co Ltd*[7] where the managing director of a company in liquidation had never had the question of his remuneration determined by the directors as required by the company's articles, and so Plowman J held that, in the circumstances, he was not entitled to receive anything for services rendered prior to the liquidation. Also, in certain older cases[8] it was held that an agreement which gives the employer the right to fix remuneration, gives him the right to give *no* remuneration. However, this is unlikely to be the case now, for where there is some reference to

---

1   Employment Rights Act 1996, s 1(4); on the significance of different forms of remuneration, see Freedland 'The obligation to work and to pay for work' (1977) 30 CLP 175.
2   S 8.
3   *Phillips v Curling* (1847) 10 LTOS 245; *Clayton Newbury Ltd v Findlay* [1953] 2 All ER 826n, [1953] 1 WLR 1194n; *Bronester Ltd v Priddle* [1961] 3 All ER 471, [1961] 1 WLR 1294, CA.
4   *Pauley v Kenaldo Ltd* [1953] 1 All ER 226, [1953] 1 WLR 187.
5   *Gaumont-British Picture Corpn v Alexander* [1936] 2 All ER 1686.
6   See p 153 above.
7   [1964] 3 All ER 936, [1965] 1 WLR 335.
8   *Taylor v Brewer* (1813) 1 M & S 290; *Roberts v Smith* (1859) 4 H & N 315. See, however, the explanation of these cases by Vaughan Williams LJ in *Loftus v Roberts* (1902) 18 TLR 532, CA.

remuneration, or some discernible understanding that there would be remuneration, or where the contract is just vague on the subject, the employee may be able to recover a reasonable sum on a quantum meruit basis, as in *Way v Latilla*[9] where the plaintiff, who had obtained gold mining concessions for the defendant (yielding a million-pound profit) on the vague understanding that the defendant would 'look after his interests', was held by the House of Lords to be entitled to £5,000 commission on a quantum meruit basis when the defendant refused to pay him anything. Likewise, in *Powell v Braun*[10] a secretary who had been offered an unspecified annual bonus (having regard to the firm's performance) in place of the usual increase in wages was held by the Court of Appeal to be entitled to a reasonable amount on a quantum meruit basis for the two years during which her employer had failed to pay any bonus at all, thus establishing that a quantum meruit action may be used to recover additional remuneration as well as ordinary wages or salary. Some of these stranger forms of remuneration (or, indeed, possible non-remuneration) may of course now have to be read subject to the national minimum wage legislation (below), but that only specifies a minimum *amount* that must eventually be payable and does *not* mean that these forms in themselves are illegal.

One theoretical problem concerning the common law right to wages has arisen where the employee does not complete the relevant obligation in the contract of employment. In strict theory it may be that *no* remuneration is payable (even on a quantum meruit action), as in the old case of *Cutter v Powell*[11] where a sailor who contracted for 30 guineas to act as second mate for a certain voyage died in the course of that voyage and his widow failed to recover any of the amount agreed upon, since the court held that partial performance of an entire obligation did not give rise to a right to any of the remuneration. This principle is most unlikely to apply to a case today, for most contracts are divisible, not entire, certainly to the extent of definite periods for payment of remuneration[12]. Even if this were not so, an employee could attempt to circumvent *Cutter v Powell* in several ways – first, by claiming that the employer had received substantial performance of the contract and so was not relieved from payment[13]; second, if complete performance was prevented by the employer, by bringing a quantum meruit action[14]; third, where the contract was frustrated[15], by claiming a just amount under the Law Reform (Frustrated Contracts) Act 1943, section 1(3); fourth, by claiming that his wages or salary are to be deemed to accrue from day to day (even though not so payable under the contract) under the Apportionment Act 1870, section 2 which thus apportions 'all rents, annuities, dividends and other periodic payments

9   [1937] 3 All ER 759, HL. See also *Craven-Ellis v Canons Ltd* [1936] 2 KB 403, [1936] 2 All ER 1066, CA.
10 [1954] 1 All ER 484, [1954] 1 WLR 401, CA.
11 (1795) 6 Term Rep 320, followed in *Sinclair v Bowles* (1829) 9 B & C 92 and *Vigers v Cook* [1919] 2 KB 475, CA.
12 Details of the periods for payment must be given to the employee in writing: Employment Rights Act 1996, s 1(4).
13 *Hoenig v Isaacs* [1952] 2 All ER 176, CA; *H Dakin & Co Ltd v Lee* [1916] 1 KB 566, CA; *Bolton v Mahadeva* [1972] 2 All ER 1322, [1972] 1 WLR 1009, CA.
14 *Planché v Colburn* (1831) 5 C & P 58.
15 See p 449 below.

in the nature of income' – section 5 states that 'annuities' include 'salaries and pensions', and it appears that 'salaries' should be taken to include wages[16].

In addition to this theoretical problem, three points might be mentioned particularly about the employee's right at common law to be paid his wages. The first is that an action for wages due, brought in the ordinary courts or a tribunal, might be used not just as an individual's remedy but also as a way of testing the legal position in what is in essence a collective dispute between employer and workforce (possibly by the device of bringing an action by one named individual, which is viewed in reality as a test case affecting an entire class of employees). In *Burdett-Coutts v Hertfordshire County Council*[17] the county council purported to vary the terms of employment of school dinner assistants without their consent (indeed, in the face of their positive dissent); they continued to work under protest, accepting the lower wages under the new terms, but brought an action in the High Court claiming, inter alia, the payment of the arrears of wages that were due under the pre-existing terms of employment; the judge held that on the facts they had *not* impliedly accepted the employer's variation by continuing to work, and gave judgment for the arrears. The validity of such an action was accepted by the Court of Appeal in *Miller v Hamworthy Engineering Ltd*[18] (enforced short-time working, not covered by the terms of the contract and not agreed to by the employee or his union) and, more importantly, in the short but emphatic decision of the House of Lords in *Rigby v Ferodo Ltd*[19] (unilateral reduction in wages by the employer, not agreed to by the employee or his union). The point about such an action (or the threat of it) is that it may oblige the employer (who wishes still to force through the new terms) to dismiss the employees formally, and then have to defend an action for unfair dismissal[20].

However, this will only work if the employee is held to have been contractually in the right. This is because the second point is that in *Cresswell v Board of Inland Revenue*[21] Walton J held that where an employee refuses to perform duties that he is contractually obliged to perform, the simple principle 'no work, no pay' applies, so that an action for wages will then fail. Of course, such a principle begs the monumental question – what duties *is* the employee contractually obliged to perform? In fact, the case hinged on this question, and whether a requirement that the staff start to operate a newly computerised system had or had not altered the nature of the job[22]. The principle has acquired particular significance in a series of cases concerning deductions from wages due to industrial action – if

---

16   *Moriarty v Regent's Garage Co Ltd* [1921] 1 KB 423 (reversed on other grounds: [1921] 2 KB 766, CA). See Matthews 'Salaries in the Apportionment Act 1870' (1982) 2 LS 302. 'Day to day' was held to mean working days, not calendar days, in the year, at least when claiming holiday pay under the Working Time Regulations: *Leisure Leagues UK Ltd v Maconnachie* [2002] IRLR 600 (disapproving *Thames Water Utilities v Reynolds* [1996] IRLR 186 on the basis that it was decided before those Regulations were introduced).

17   [1984] IRLR 91. See also *Gibbons v Associated British Ports* [1985] IRLR 376.

18   [1986] ICR 846, [1986] IRLR 461, CA.

19   [1988] ICR 29, [1987] IRLR 516, HL.

20   As in *Gilham v Kent County Council (No 2)* [1985] ICR 233, [1985] IRLR 18, CA; see p 599 below on the application of unfair dismissal laws to this class of case.

21   [1984] ICR 508, [1984] IRLR 190.

22   This aspect of the case is considered at p 170 above and p 600 below. One significance of applying such a general principle is that the employer has a freestanding right not to pay wages – it does not constitute a 'suspension' and so the employer does not have to comply with any contractual procedures that may exist before he can impose a suspension (so that *Gorse v Durham County Council* [1971] 2 All ER 666, [1971] 1 WLR 775 was distinguished in *Cresswell*).

the employee fails wholly or partly to carry out his duties, what can the employer do? An employee in breach of contract may be sued by the employer, but this is unlikely in practice; instead, the employer will wish to avoid paying some or all of the wages in the first place. If the employee fails to perform any of his duties (either through being on strike, or through only being willing to perform certain of his duties, which the employer refuses to allow, sending him home instead), then as in *Cresswell* the employer need not pay any wages. However, the position becomes more complex when the employee is permitted by the employer to perform *part* of his duties.

Here, there are two possibilities. If the part not performed is discrete and quantifiable, it seems clear that the employer may refuse to pay the amount of wages representing that part. Thus, in *Royle v Trafford Borough Council*[23] where a teacher participating in industrial action refused to accept a further five pupils into his class but continued to teach his existing 31 pupils, the education authority were allowed to deduct five thirty-sixths of his salary. Similar results were reached in *Sim v Rotherham Metropolitan Borough Council*[24] (amounts deducted from teachers' salaries representing their refusal to cover for absent colleagues as part of industrial action) and *Miles v Wakefield Metropolitan District Council*[25] (registrar normally working 37 hours per week refusing to perform marriage ceremonies in the three hours on a Saturday morning as part of industrial action; employer held correct to deduct three thirty-sevenths of his salary). However, there has been a significant divergence of view on the reasoning behind these deductions[26]; in *Sim* Scott J held that in such a case the employee could sue for his wages in full, but subject to the employer's right of equitable set-off of the amount representing the duties not performed (for which the employer could have sued the employee in separate proceedings). However, in *Miles* the House of Lords took the more fundamental approach that with regard to the three hours in question the employee had *no* right to the pay in the first place since he had failed to provide the consideration for his part of the contract, namely being ready and willing to work. In the case of a quantifiable failure to perform duties, these two approaches produce the same result, but the position becomes more difficult in the case of a more generalised and nebulous failure (for example as part of a general go-slow or withdrawal of goodwill). This could be particularly important if (a) the industrial action is 'guerilla' in nature[27], being aimed at inconveniencing the employer while at the same time allowing the employees still to earn most of their wages, (b) it involves employees who have some discretion in how they perform their work, and (c) they work in open premises from which the employer cannot simply lock them out. Under the above cases, the employer could counter the action by deducting a 'reasonable sum' (as in *Sim*) representing duties not carried out. However, two later Court of Appeal decisions (*Wiluszynski v London Borough of Tower Hamlets*[28] and *British Telecommunications plc v Ticehurst*[29]) have

23 [1984] IRLR 184.
24 [1986] ICR 897, [1986] IRLR 391.
25 [1987] ICR 368, [1987] IRLR 193, HL.
26 See the notes on *Sim* and *Miles* by McMullen (1988) 51 MLR 234 and Morris (1987) 16 ILJ 185.
27 This may now be more difficult to arrange lawfully because of the requirement of strike notice, introduced by the Trade Union Reform and Employment Rights Act 1993; see p 624 below.
28 [1989] ICR 493, [1989] IRLR 259, CA; see also *MacPherson v London Borough of Lambeth* [1988] IRLR 470.
29 [1992] ICR 383, [1992] IRLR 219, CA.

established that if the employer makes it *clear* that he will not accept the defective performance by the employees, he may lawfully refuse to pay anything *at all* (even if the employees have attended work and performed most of their duties). In *Wiluszynski* this was explained as following on from the reasoning in *Miles* (above), and the important decision in *Ticehurst* takes this further in two ways – (1) it links it in with an implied term that employees with a discretion how to perform their work will exercise that discretion so as to advance the employer's business, not so as to frustrate it[30]; (2) it shows the efficacy of one particular employer tactic when faced with guerilla action, namely to give an ultimatum that the employees must work normally as from a certain date, otherwise the employer will refuse to pay at all as from that date. One final point on this area should be noted; if the employer permits imperfect performance by his employees in such a way as to suggest acquiescence in it, he may be held to have waived the employees' breach and so lost his right to deduct (whether partially or totally)[31].

The third point raises legal complications out of proportion to its commonplace nature. What is to happen if the employee is mistakenly overpaid? Can the employer recover the overpayment?[32] What if the employee has already spent the money? Can the employee simply keep quiet about it? Such problems could arise where payment is in cash, but may be more likely to arise now, with payment by direct debit more common. The starting point is that, in the ordinary law of restitution, payments made under a mistake of law are not generally recoverable, but those made under a mistake of fact are. Thus, the first point is to categorise the mistake. Simple inadvertent overpayment (whether by quill pen or computer) is likely to constitute a mistake of fact, thus giving the employer a prima facie right to recover. This was the case in *Avon County Council v Howlett*[33] where an employee off sick was inadvertently overpaid. The principal defence to the employer's action for repayment was estoppel by representation, in relation to the whole of the overpayment in spite of the admission by the employee that he had only spent *part* of the overpaid amount[34]. This defence succeeded. However, in the subsequent House of Lords decision in *Lipkin Gorman v Karpnale Ltd*[35] (not

30 This aspect of the case is considered at p 187 above; as pointed out there, most jobs today are likely to have some discretion in them, rather than being wholly governed by the contract; and so this case doubts the legality in most cases of any form of 'work-to-contract', 'work-to-rule' or 'withdrawal of goodwill'.

31 *Bond v CAV Ltd* [1983] IRLR 360 (employer's action in not insisting on the employee working on disputed machinery and allowing him to continue working on other machinery held to constitute waiver of the employee's breach).

32 On a technical level, a deduction to recover an overpayment is not an illegal deduction under the Employment Rights Act1996, Pt II (p 262 below) since it is covered by an exception in ibid., s 14(1); however, that subsection does *not* give a positive right to recover and so the overall legality of recovery by the employer remains a common law matter, subject to the following rules.

33 [1983] 1 All ER 1073, [1983] IRLR 171, CA.

34 A peculiarity of the case, commented on adversely by Cumming-Bruce LJ, was that the evidence showed that the defendant had in fact spent *all* the overpayment before realising that he was not entitled to it. However, at the trial, counsel for the defence was instructed to proceed on the basis of only *part* expenditure, since the defendant's backers were using this as a test case, seeking to establish (for the purpose of others who had been overpaid) that even partial expenditure could defeat the employer's right to repayment.

35 [1991] 2 AC 548, [1992] 4 All ER 512, HL. Lord Goff is of course no stranger to the law of restitution. In *National Westminster Bank plc v Somer International Bank (UK) Ltd* [2001] EWCA Civ 970, [2002] QB 1286, [2002] 1 All ER 198 (a commercial case) it was held that even where estoppel is still used a court can (in its equitable jurisdiction) rule that only the part actually spent has become irrecoverable; if this is correct, *Avon CC* and *Lipkin Gorman* would now produce the same result.

itself an overpayment of wages case), Lord Goff said that in future cases such as *Howlett* should be dealt with, not on grounds of estoppel, but on grounds of a general defence of 'change of position' in the law of restitution. He said that such a defence should now be evolved in case law and so is likely to be uncertain for some time. However, one relatively certain point is that such a defence would allow only that part of the overpayment actually spent innocently to become irrecoverable, rather than the defence of estoppel which would operate, potentially unfairly, on an all-or-nothing basis.

All of this operates on the assumption that the employee has spent the money innocently. The one thing that he must not do is simply keep quiet about it if he does realise that he has been overpaid, because that can render him guilty of theft, by virtue of the Theft Act 1968, section 5(4) which provides that:

> 'Where a person gets property by another's mistake, and is under an obligation to make restoration (in whole or in part) of the property or its proceeds or of the value thereof, then to the extent of that obligation the property or proceeds shall be regarded (as against him) as belonging to the person entitled to restoration, and an intention not to make restoration shall be regarded accordingly as an intention to deprive that person of the property or proceeds.'

The Court of Appeal held in *A-G's Reference (No 1 of 1983)*[36] that this section (which does not actually create an offence, but rather supplies what might otherwise be the missing elements for a charge of theft under section 1) can apply to payment by direct debit of sorts as well as to payment in cash, and so provided the prosecution can prove dishonesty[37] the employee may be found guilty of theft through deliberately keeping the overpayment, though the Court of Appeal expressed some disquiet at the involvement of the criminal law in such cases which have the flavour predominantly of civil debt. However, there should only be criminal liability where the defendant deliberately kept it, or spent it *after* realising that he had been overpaid. If he had already spent it before so realising, then in civil law the employer would have lost his right to restitution according to the above cases and so section 5(4) ('… is under an obligation to make restoration …') would not apply.

3 WAGES DURING SICKNESS AND STATUTORY SICK PAY

In most cases, questions of pay during sickness will be governed expressly by the contract of employment, some form of 'topping up' of state sickness benefits being now very common and usually clearly set out (for example as to how many

---

36 [1985] QB 182, [1984] 3 All ER 369, CA. The Theft Act 1968, s 5(4) made a definite change here, for under the pre-1968 law an employee keeping an overpayment was not guilty of theft: *Moynes v Coopper* [1956] 1 QB 439, [1956] 1 All ER 450.

37 Dishonesty is covered by *R v Ghosh* [1982] QB 1053, [1982] 2 All ER 689, CA, and is a question whether (a) the conduct in question is dishonest by the standards of ordinary people and (b) the defendant realised that it would be thought wrong by those standards. While this may often be obvious in one of these cases, there could be latitude for a defence of no dishonesty if, for example, the employee kept the overpayment because he was already owed money by the employer who was refusing to pay him it. A jury might be sympathetic.

weeks per year are payable, whether there is any waiting period before it is payable, whether there is a qualifying period for new employees, and at what rate it is payable, bearing in mind receipts from the state)[38]. However, there have been cases where the question of whether sick pay is payable has arisen where there has been no express agreement on the matter. The question then arises whether a term is to be implied covering sick pay and, as a matter of law, this has caused problems. Theoretically, the basis of the law here is the general common law tenet that the employee's consideration for wages is 'service' (ie being ready and willing to serve), not the actual performance of work[39], and this could lead to the inference that, in the absence of anything to the contrary, wages should continue to be paid during sickness even though the employee is unable actually to perform his work. This view that there is a presumption that sick pay is payable was accepted by Pilcher J in *Orman v Saville Sportswear Ltd*[40] and was consistent with the judgment of the Court of Appeal in *Marrison v Bell*[41], as explained in later cases[42]. Such a presumption could be rebutted by factors such as payment on a piecework basis[43], a clear custom that nothing was offered or expected[44] or some form of notice by the employer that he would accept no, or restricted, liability to make any payments[45]. However, it was still arguable that it was putting matters too highly to say that there was a presumption, and fortunately the matter was clarified by the Court of Appeal in *Mears v Safecar Security Ltd*[46], an important case not only on sick pay but also on the jurisdiction of tribunals on complaints of failure to give any or proper particulars of the terms of employment[47] and on the whole question of the implication of terms into contracts of employment[48]. In this case it was clearly held that there is in law no presumption that sick pay is payable; if there is no express provision, a tribunal or court must look at all the facts of the case to determine the correct inference. Applying that approach, the Court of Appeal upheld the EAT's decision that nothing was payable on the facts of the case given that it was the employer's well-known practice not to pay, the applicant had been

38 See the statistics in the White Paper 'Income during initial sickness' (Cmnd 7864, 1980) which introduced the idea of statutory sick pay.

39 *Warburton v Co-operative Wholesale Society Ltd* [1917] 1 KB 663, CA; *Henthorn v CEGB* [1980] IRLR 361, CA; *Miles v Wakefield Metropolitan District Council* [1987] ICR 368, [1987] IRLR 193, HL; Elias 'The structure of the employment contract' [1982] CLP 95; cf, however, the different views expressed by Napier 'Aspects of the wage work bargain' [1984] CLJ 337.

40 [1960] 3 All ER 105, [1960] 1 WLR 1055.

41 [1939] 2 KB 187, [1939] 1 All ER 745, CA.

42 *Petrie v MacFisheries Ltd* [1940] 1 KB 258, [1939] 4 All ER 281, CA; *O'Grady v M Saper Ltd* [1940] 2 KB 469, [1940] 3 All ER 527, CA. The problem was that Scott LJ expressed his views on sick pay so strongly in *Marrison v Bell* that it was reported (in the law reports and the newspapers) as laying down a definite right to wages during sickness as a matter of law, leading to claims for it by people who could show little or no contractual backing for entitlement to it; this was rectified in the above two cases.

43 *Browning v Crumlin Valley Collieries Ltd* [1926] 1 KB 522; *Hancock v BSA Tools Ltd* [1939] 4 All ER 538.

44 *O'Grady v M Saper Ltd*, n 42 above.

45 *Petrie v MacFisheries Ltd*, n 42 above.

46 [1982] 2 All ER 865, [1982] IRLR 183, CA, applied by the EAT in *Howman & Son v Blyth* [1983] IRLR 139, where the implication of a term raised questions as to amount and duration of payment.

47 Employment Rights Act1996, Pt I; see pp 114–118 above. The case was brought before a tribunal under s11 to determine the correct contractual term; it was not a common law claim for actual payment.

48 See p 139 above.

ill during the course of employment and had never asked for payment, and he had only brought his claim seven months after leaving employment, not really expecting to get anything. Stephenson LJ, giving the judgment of the court, did say that there might be a residual presumption that sick pay was payable in a case where there were no factors either way to guide the court on the correct term to be implied, but that this was inherently extremely unlikely to happen, since usually there will be some evidence at least of past custom and practice.

A clear contractual term covering sick pay entitlement is a good example of the benefits to be gained from a well-drafted contract of employment[49], or proper compliance with the obligation to give written notice of terms of employment. As stated above, such terms are common and, indeed, were for many years an important area for the improvement of terms and conditions by negotiation (for example by increasing payment rates and the entitlement per year, and decreasing or eliminating any qualifying periods), particularly in times of wage restraint (though with some evidence in the 1990s of retrenchment by employers and the worsening of sick pay terms in times of recession). Thus, except in the odd case unfortunately leaving sick pay as a matter to be implied (or not), it could have been said that there was little *law* on sick pay, merely a question of construction of individual contracts. However, that has not been the case since 1983 when there came into force the present scheme of statutory sick pay (SSP) under the Social Security and Housing Benefits Act 1982 (now Part XI of the Social Security Contributions and Benefits Act 1992)[50].

This scheme came into being pursuant to a White Paper[51] which showed that contractual sick pay terms are common and quantitatively more important than state National Insurance benefits in the maintenance of income during short-term sickness[52], that such contractual schemes operated usually by taking into account amounts received from the state[53] and that most illness was in fact short-term[54]. From these findings, the government formed the view that the existing system was administratively inefficient – '... given that the great majority of claimants have available a second source of income from their employer, there is duplication of administrative machinery between employers and DSS in that evidence of incapacity has to be provided for both schemes and two sets of arrangements for the calculation and payment of income have to be maintained'[55].

---

49   One complication in some recent cases has been the provision by the employer of permanent health insurance (PHI) on top of the normal sickness provisions in the contract, without really thinking through how the two are to fit together; see p 166 above.

50   As amplified by the Statutory Sick Pay (General) Regulations 1982, SI 1982/894, *Harvey* R[198].

51   Income during initial sickness (Cmnd 7864, 1980).

52   Contractual sick pay terms were relatively uncommon in 1948 at the inception of the National Insurance System, but by 1974 (the year used in the White Paper for statistical purposes) 80% of full-time male workers and 78% of full-time female workers were covered by them; in the large majority of cases, employees qualified to claim sick pay either immediately upon becoming employed or at the most within six months.

53   In 1974, in the case of male workers, for example, full pay without deduction was payable in only 11.5% of cases; full pay *less state benefits* was payable in 55% of cases; some other scheme operated in the remaining 33.5% of cases (eg topping state benefits up to 85% of full pay).

54   '... only a very small proportion of people who qualify for (state) benefit need to draw it for any length of time. No payment is made for the first three "waiting" days of incapacity; 60% of those who qualify for sickness benefit are back at work by the end of a fortnight, 80% within a month and 90% within six weeks. Yet the effort put in by DHSS in dealing with these short-term claims is considerable': White Paper, n 51 above, para 3.

55   White Paper, n 51 above, para 3.

The new scheme was therefore designed to prevent duplication in the large majority of claims – where an employee is sick, the employer must now by law pay an amount equivalent to what that employee would have received from the state. As originally enacted, SSP was payable for a maximum of *eight* weeks (either in one period of illness or cumulatively over several illnesses) in one tax year. However, the scheme was viewed as such a success by the government that the Social Security Act 1985 contained a major extension, so that the maximum entitlement is now twenty eight weeks (put on to a rolling basis, ie not tied now to the tax year); the overall effect of this is that now the employer is liable for the payment of all short-term sickness benefit due to one of his employees (with the principal function for the DSS now being the payment of long-term benefits such as incapacity benefit once the extended SSP entitlement has been exhausted in the case of a major illness or disability). Under the original scheme, the employer recouped the full amount of the money paid out as SSP, by deducting it from his NI contributions. However, this position was gradually altered by the Statutory Sick Pay Acts 1991 and 1994, so that the current position is now that in most cases there is *no* recoupment, so that the employer actually *pays* the SSP; the only exception is that if in any income tax month the employer pays out SSP exceeding 13% of his liability to pay NI contributions in that month, he can recoup that excess[56]. This is a far cry from the original scheme under which the employer merely administered the payment of SSP.

Before looking at the details of the scheme, two important points must be noticed. First, the scheme does not in any way directly affect contractual sick pay terms which remain matters between the employer and the employee or his union. Thus, contractual sick pay is still to be paid on top of SSP if there is a contractual term to that effect; likewise, if an employer is not contractually obliged to pay sick pay, there is nothing in the statutory scheme to alter that – he will merely be obliged to discharge what was previously the function of the DSS to pay SSP. Secondly, the abolition of the separate claim for industrial injury benefit (for those injured at work or contracting a prescribed industrial disease)[57] should be seen in the light of this scheme for the administration of sick pay – employees are now eligible simply for sickness benefit when incapable of work whether or not they are injured in a work-related accident (or incapacitated by an industrial disease), and the SSP scheme will apply to any claim for such benefit by a person in employment.

Turning to the elements of the scheme, there is a legal obligation on all employers to pay SSP, with no contracting out by agreement with his employees[58]. There are three qualifying conditions for payment – (i) the day in respect of which payment is sought must form part of a 'period of incapacity for work', ie a period of four or more consecutive days (thus preserving the former rule that the claimant had to wait for three days before state sickness benefit was payable); any

---

56 Statutory Sick Pay Percentage Threshold Order 1995, SI 1995/512. This may be a contributory reason for employers increasingly looking to make savings in their occupational sick pay schemes, which were established on the basis of the state also paying its share. There has also been said to be a danger that the removal of the recoupment may make employers more wary of taking on disabled employees, or those with a poor health record, though cf now the Disability Discrimination Act 1995.

57 See p 830 below.

58 Social Security Contributions and Benefits Act 1992, s 151. SSP may not be paid in kind, or by provision of board, lodging, services or other facilities: Statutory Sick Pay (General) Regulations 1982, SI 1982/894, reg 8.

two periods of incapacity for work which are separated by not more than eight weeks are treated as one single period[59]; (ii) the day must fall within a 'period of entitlement', ie a period starting with the illness and ending with (a) the end of the illness, (b) the expiry of the maximum entitlement (formerly eight weeks, now twenty-eight weeks), (c) the termination of the contract of employment, or (d) the eleventh week before the expected date of confinement in the case of a pregnant employee[60]; (iii) the day must be a 'qualifying day', ie a day when the employee would normally be required to work[61]. There are three main disqualifications[62] – (i) where the employee has not yet started work, (ii) where the twenth-eight-week maximum entitlement is exhausted, and (iii) where at the time when the employee falls sick there is a trade dispute at his place of work; this last disqualification is the same as the well-known trade dispute disqualification from jobseeker's allowance, for it is provided that the employee can avoid it if he can prove that at no time on or before the date his sickness began did he participate in, or have a direct interest in, that trade dispute[63]. The amount of statutory sick pay which is payable after the first three days is fixed by the Act, subject to a power for the Secretary of State to increase the amount by statutory instrument[64].

The method by which a sick employee must notify that sickness to his employer is basically a matter for agreement, with residual provisions laid down by regulation[65]. In fact, it was in this sphere of the procedure for making a claim that developments had already obliged employers to consider making changes even before the introduction of the SSP scheme in 1983; this was because of the emphasis being placed on 'self certification'[66], ie allowing the employee to certify

59 S 152. All days of the week are counted for this purpose.
60 S 153. An employer may not evade paying statutory sick pay by dismissing the employee in order to end the period of entitlement prematurely: S.I. 1982 No 894, reg4.
61 S 154; see R (SSP) 1/85, para. 10 for a summary of the method of establishing qualifying days. This requirement is here to prevent a sick employee claiming payment in respect of a day on which he would not normally have worked anyway. Under s 3(2), the definition of an employee's 'qualifying days' is primarily a matter for agreement between employer and employee, with detailed statutory rules in reg 5 in default of such agreement.
62 Sch 11, para 2. Also excluded are employees who are over retirement age, or pregnant (and past the eleventh week before the expected date of confinement).
63 Sch 11, para 7; R (SSP) 1/86. The extensive case law in the jobseeker's allowance context (particularly on the concept of 'direct interest') will thus apply here too: see p 652 below.
64 S 157. There used to be three rates of SSP (depending on normal earnings) but this was reduced to two in 1987 and then to one in 1994. At the time of writing it stands at £64.35 pw. To be eligible at all, the employee must earn over the lower limit for the payment of NI contributions; *quaere* whether this could be challenged under EC law as unlawful sex discrimination, contrary to the Equal Treatment Directive, as affecting more female employees than male. There used to be a requirement for the Secretary of State to review the SSP rates each year (though it stopped short of actual index-linking), but this was repealed by the Social Security Act 1986 and the upper (now the only) rate was pegged for several years.
65 SI 1982/894, reg 7.
66 The old system was that in order to claim state sickness benefits (after the three waiting days) the employee needed a medical certificate, which could then be used in a claim for contractual sick pay from his employer. In 1982 the DHSS went over to self-certification for the first week of illness for the purposes of claiming sickness benefit (SI 1982/699). Theoretically this did not affect employers and contractual sick pay schemes (and it tended to be presented by the DHSS as merely a change in internal administrative procedure), but such was the inter-relationship between state and private schemes (as pointed out by the White Paper, n 51 above) that this immediately put pressure on employers to follow suit (especially as doctors are no longer obliged to give medical certificates until the second week of illness). Thus, self-certification was a separate development from the introduction of SSP in 1983, but naturally in practice the two went hand-in-hand and constituted (along with the fusion of injury and sickness benefits) a major alteration to previous procedures.

himself as incapable of work through illness without the need for a medical certificate, at least until the beginning of the second week of a period of sickness (thus avoiding the need for a doctor to certify short-term illness which is often of such a nature, for example the classic cold or 'flu, that such certification was of little practical value). One possible problem with self-certification is how to prevent abuse; it may well be that in most cases this will not be a significant problem[67], but in a case of persistent illnesses by one employee for periods of less than a week it may be necessary for the employer to investigate and ultimately even to treat it as a disciplinary matter[68], with deliberate fraud presumably a potentially fair ground for dismissal.

The last point to note about the SSP system is that, as stated above, it was viewed by the previous government (if not by employers who have to administer it) as a considerable success; this meant not only its major expansion by the Social Security Act 1985 but also the further possibility that it could be used as a model for other forms of income maintenance. The Social Security Bill 1986 as originally drafted was not only going to convert Family Income Supplement into Family Credit, but also make Family Credit payable through the employer in the same way as SSP. This second proposal was dropped because of employer opposition, *but* the Social Security Act 1986 as eventually passed did of course introduce the system of payment of maternity pay through the employer – statutory maternity pay (SMP)[69]. The present government have now taken the matter further in the legislation on tax credits (replacing family credit and extending similar ideas to areas of low pay generally) which are payable through the employer, as are statutory paternity pay and statutory adoption pay, introduced by the Employment Act 2002.

The whole question of income maintenance during sickness or injury has thus been the subject of important developments, which should hopefully be properly reflected in well drafted contracts of employment, though in the nature of things there will still be cases which arise partly or wholly because contractual terms do not adequately reflect current law or actual working practices. Finally, the general point should be noted that receipt of any form of sick pay normally pre-supposes that the person claiming it is still in employment and there is of course the possibility of the sick employee being dismissed. The statutory scheme provides that an employer cannot evade paying statutory sick pay by dismissing the claimant employee[70], but does not go further and declare such a dismissal to

---

67   In fact, the experience of many employers has been that self certification actually *decreased* short-term illness absences, due to the employee having to declare in writing that he had been incapable of work on each of the days on which he was away (rather than just being signed off for the week by his doctor). One possible administrative remedy for persistent absence is that if an employee has self-certified himself four times within a year, an employer may refuse to pay SSP on the fifth occasion and refer him to the DSS for formal investigation and medical checks: Employers' Guide to Statutory Sick Pay (NI 227, DSS) paras 92–95.

68   This would be aided by the approach of the EAT to persistent absence through illness in *International Sports Co Ltd v Thomson* [1980] IRLR 340.

69   See p 423 below.

70   SI 1982/894, reg 4 states that where the contract of employment is brought to an end by the employer solely or mainly for the purpose of avoiding liability for SSP, the employer remains liable to pay it for as long as it would have been payable but for the dismissal. It would appear, however, that reg 4 would not apply if the employer could claim successfully that the contract had been *frustrated* by virtue of the illness, because then it would have been brought to an end by law automatically, not by any action of the employer; in the light of the recent case law, there is still a distinct possibility that a contract could be frustrated by a serious illness, see p 449 below.

be in law unfair. However, there is no reason why such a dismissal should not be unfair on general principles, as considered in chapter 8.

4 WAGES DURING LAY-OFF OR SHORT TIME

(i) Generally

Turning to the question of wages during a lay-off or short time, this too is likely to be covered in some way by a relevant contract or collective agreement, which might define or limit the employer's right to lay off, or provide a guaranteed minimum wage or minimum number of hours per week[71]. In the absence of some express provisions or definite custom, however, the common law position is unclear. The starting point is that, unless it consisted of a dismissal by the employer followed by re-engagement later[72], a lay-off would be a suspension without pay, and there is no general common law power to do this[73]. This approach would favour the continuance of wages, and indeed in *Devonald v Rosser & Sons*[74] the Court of Appeal held that the employer had no right to close down his work and fail to provide remunerative work for his pieceworkers simply because of a lack of profitable orders. However, in *Browning v Crumlin Valley Collieries*[75] Greer J held that there was an implied term that the employer could lay off without pay where the reason for the suspension (in that case closure of the colliery for necessary repairs) was outside his control. Moreover, although the employer's argument in *Devonald v Rosser & Sons* that there was a custom allowing lay-offs in the circumstances in question failed, there may well be cases where such a custom could be shown, particularly in an industry where lay-offs are common and accepted (whatever be the usual common law position) and in such a case the court might well find suspension without pay impliedly allowed[76], thus at least bringing the law into line with the practical position. In *Puttick v John Wright & Sons (Blackwall) Ltd*[77] the NIRC held that where the employee had been available to do specific jobs for the same employer over a long period of time, being paid for the work done and then laid off until the next work was ready, the correct legal construction was that there existed an ordinary contract of employment for the whole of that period, including an implied term allowing the employer to lay him off without pay in the periods between available work. It is therefore difficult to state any particular

---

71 See, eg, *Powell Duffryn Wagon Co Ltd v House* [1974] ICR 123.
72 In which case continuity of employment is preserved if it is a 'temporary cessation of work': Employment Rights Act 1996, s 212(3).
73 *Hanley v Pease & Partners Ltd* [1915] 1 KB 698; *Gorse v Durham County Council* [1971] 2 All ER 666, [1971] 1 WLR 775; *Neads v CAV Ltd* [1983] IRLR 360.
74 [1906] 2 KB 728, CA.
75 [1926] 1 KB 522.
76 *Bird v British Celanese Ltd* [1945] KB 336, CA; *Marshall v English Electric Co Ltd* [1945] 1 All ER 653, CA.
77 [1972] ICR 457. The question whether on the facts there is a series of individual contracts or one global contract in such a case may cause difficulties; this has arisen in the context of trawlermen and the question whether they have continuity of employment between voyages; in *Hellyer Bros Ltd v McLeod* [1987] ICR 526, [1987] IRLR 232, CA it was held that there was not sufficient mutuality of obligations to establish a global contract (and so there was no continuity for redundancy payment purposes). However, in the present context it will not help the employee if the court finds a global contract but then proceeds to imply into it a lay-off clause.

common law rule, but this is of little significance, since most aspects of lay-offs will normally be covered (in a unionised industry) by a collective agreement (which may, for example, give a guaranteed minimum week, subject to safeguards for the employer who may be relieved from this obligation in the case of industrial action or events totally beyond his control, thus approximating to what may be the common law position anyway) or by a statutory provision in the modern legislation. Such provisions affect lay-offs in four main ways – (i) by preserving continuity of employment[78]; (ii) by allowing an employee subject to lay-offs or short time (in certain circumstances) to treat himself as dismissed and apply for a redundancy payment[79]; (iii) by allowing an employee on short time or lay-off to claim jobseeker's allowance, even though technically the contract of employment subsists[80]; and (iv) by providing certain minimal statutory rights to lay-off pay, either generally or in relation to certain particular forms of lay-off[81]. It is this last category that must now be considered here, ie the general right to a guarantee payment and the specific right to pay if laid off for certain health and safety reasons.

(ii) Guarantee payments

Where an employer is obliged to lay off employees, or is unable to provide them with work at a particular time, the salaried and weekly paid employees may not be affected in the short term, but those paid by the hour or by output (and those whose contracts provide for suspension without pay) may lose wages. To meet this situation, an obligation to make guarantee payments was introduced in 1975, and is now to be found in the Employment Rights Act 1996, sections 28–35. These provisions are a good example of the 'floor of rights' argument for providing statutory minima, for the amounts which may be received are meagre, but the principle is established, presumably in part to encourage the establishment and extension of more generous private schemes (for example to give a guaranteed minimum number of hours per week to hourly paid workers). This approach can be seen in two particular aspects of the statutory scheme. The first is that any contractual payments referable to the workless day are set off against the statutory right (often to the point of extinguishing it), *not* additional to it[82]. The second is that the minister may make exemption orders, exempting from these provisions employers who are parties to a collective agreement or wages order which covers the question of guaranteed remuneration to his satisfaction[83].

To qualify for a guarantee payment, the employee must have been continuously employed under a contract of employment for the month ending with the last complete week before the workless day in question[84]. This may disqualify casual workers, as in *Mailway (Southern) Ltd v Willsher*[85] where the EAT held that a woman

---

78 See n 72 above.
79 Employment Rights Act 1996, ss 148; see p 647 below.
80 See p 649 below.
81 On the various statutory and contractual possibilities in this difficult area, see Szyszczak *Partial Unemployment: The Regulation of Short-time Working in Britain* (1990).
82 Employment Rights Act 1996, s 32.
83 S 35; as at 2002, there were 26 such orders (see *Harvey* Q [659]).
84 S 29(1).
85 [1978] ICR 511, [1978] IRLR 322; aliter where the employer may *oblige* the employee to attend work when he requires him, rather than just offering him work: *Miller v Harry Thornton (Lollies) Ltd* [1978] IRLR 430, IT. In relation to the decision in *Mailway*, note that the employee now does not have to work a minimum of 16 hours per week in order to have continuity of employment.

who was registered as a part-time packer with the employers who offered her work as and when they needed her, and who on average worked more than sixteen hours per week (though she had not in fact done so in the four weeks in question), was not eligible for a guarantee payment as this relationship was only a contract to pay for services rendered, not a contract of employment. If an employee is in fact qualified he is entitled to a guarantee payment under section 28 when he is not provided with work by his employer on a day on which he would normally be required to work; the failure to provide work must be due to either (a) a diminution in the requirements of the employer's business for work of that kind, or (b) any other occurrence affecting the normal working of the employer's business in relation to that work (for example a power failure or natural disaster affecting the factory; it will not extend to extraneous matters such as factory holidays[86]). The requirement that the workless day be one on which he would normally be required to work means that this right cannot be used as a back-door method to gain remuneration for days not in fact envisaged in the contract; for example where a contract is only to work four days a week (possibly varied from an original five-day contract as an alternative to redundancy) an employee cannot claim a guarantee payment for the fifth day[87], nor can he claim one for days during an agreed annual shutdown of a factory[88].

The employee will lose his right to payment in three cases. The first is where the failure to provide work is in consequence of a strike, lock-out or other industrial action involving his employer or an associated employer[89]. The second is where the employee refuses the offer of suitable alternative work for that day, which may be work outside his contract, provided it is suited to his skill, aptitude, etc[90]. The third is where the employee fails to comply with a reasonable attendance requirement, so that the employer can in certain circumstances hold his work-force together, at least for part of the day, for example if he is still hoping that vital supplies will be delivered in time[91].

As stated above, the amount of the statutory guarantee payment is small, for although the principle is that the employee is to receive the number of working hours on that day multiplied by the 'guaranteed hourly rate' (as defined), this is all subject to a maximum of £17.30 per day at the time of writing, and any individual may only claim for a total of five workless days in any period of three months[92]. Where an employer fails to pay all or part of a guarantee payment, an employee may complain to a tribunal within three months of the last workless day (longer if the tribunal finds that it was not reasonably practicable to complain within that period), and if the tribunal upholds the claim it may order the employer to make the necessary payment[93].

86   *North v Pavleigh Ltd* [1977] IRLR 461, IT.
87   *Clemens v Richards Ltd* [1977] IRLR 332, IT; *Daley v Strathclyde Regional Council* [1977] IRLR 414, IT.
88   *York v Colledge Hosiery Co Ltd* [1978] IRLR 53, IT.
89   Employment Rights Act 1996, s 29(3).
90   S 29(4); *Purdy v Willowbrook International Ltd* [1977] IRLR 388, IT.
91   S 29(5); *Meadows v Faithful Overalls Ltd* [1977] IRLR 330, IT.
92   S 30. This includes any such workless days in respect of which contractual remuneration has already been paid – the employee cannot claim five *further* days of guarantee pay if five or more days have already been paid for under the contract within the three-month period: *Cartwright v G Clancey Ltd* [1983] ICR 552, [1983] IRLR 355.
93   S 34.

(iii) Suspension from work on medical grounds

Where an employee is suspended from work because of the operation of one of several specified health and safety provisions (for examplewhere the employer has to close down his factory or that part of it where the employee works), he is entitled to be paid a 'week's pay' (as defined in the Employment Rights Act 1996, Part XIV, Chapter II) for each week of suspension, up to a maximum of twenty-six weeks[94]. It is thus more generous than the more general provisions on guarantee payments, because of the specialised nature of the reason for the suspension; the relevant health and safety provisions have been considerably shortened and simplified, so that they now only cover parts of the Control of Lead at Work Regulations 2002, the Ionising Radiations Regulations 1999 and the Control of Substances Hazardous to Health Regulations 2002. Two general points should be noted. The first is that these sections do not give the employer a positive right to suspend when one of these provisions applies; to suspend lawfully the employer must have contractual authority to do so, and only in such a case do these sections apply to give the employee a limited right to further payments. If there is no contractual right to suspend, the employee may have an ordinary contract action for his wages in full anyway, and indeed it is specially provided that any contractual payments received during the relevant period go towards discharging the employer's obligations under the statute, and vice versa[95]. The second point is that these provisions apply to suspension through the effect of the relevant health and safety legislation on the employer's undertaking, not on the health of the employee himself. Thus, if the employee is in fact incapable of work through disease or injury during the relevant time he cannot claim payment under section 64 for that period of incapacity[96]. It seems that this exclusion would even apply where the employee was ill because of the same health risk that caused the shut down (for example if he was suffering from lead poisoning after the factory had been closed because of contraventions of the relevant lead regulations), which may seem inequitable and could cause problems if ever there was added to the list of specified provisions a health and safety requirement which operated by reference to the individual employee and not to the nature of the undertaking (eg a regulation that no one with a particular skin disease should bake bread), for then the employee would have to be suspended but, on the strict wording of the Act, would be ineligible for section 64 payments because of his incapacity for work.

As well as the illness exclusion, an employee will also be disqualified from payment if he refuses suitable alternative work or fails to comply with a reasonable attendance requirement, as in the case of guarantee payments. Complaint lies to a tribunal within three months of the last day of suspension (longer if the tribunal finds that it was not reasonably practicable to complain within that period) and the tribunal may order the employer to make the relevant payment[97].

A further form of statutory protection requiring the continuation of wages through suspension, this time where it occurs on maternity grounds, was added by the Trade Union Reform and Employment Rights Act 1993. As this is an

---

94 Employment Rights Act 1996, ss 64–65; the specified provisions may be in either statutes, regulations, or Codes of Practice issued under the Health and Safety at Work etc. Act 1974, s 16.
95 S 69(3).
96 S 65(3).
97 S 70.

integral part of the new rules on maternity enacted by that statute, it is dealt with along with those rules in chapter 6 below.

5 CALCULATION OF NORMAL WORKING HOURS AND A WEEK'S PAY

The concepts of 'normal working hours' and 'a week's pay' are important in several contexts throughout modern industrial legislation. The principal significance of 'normal working hours' used to be in deciding whether an employee worked more than the magic sixteen hours per week and so could claim statutory rights, but that hours limit has now been abandoned[98]. However, it is still necessary to know whether an employment has 'normal working hours' for the purpose of ascertaining what the 'week's pay' is and, in turn, it is necessary to know what the 'week's pay' is for the purpose of computing, inter alia, the amount of a redundancy payment, guarantee payment or basic award for unfair dismissal. Rather than being defined individually for the purpose of each statutory right where they are relevant, these two concepts are each covered for all statutory purposes in one place, namely sections 220–229 and 234 of the Employment Rights Act 1996. However, it must be added that these have always been difficult provisions and have required a considerable amount of statutory interpretation.

(i) Normal working hours[99]

In many cases it will be obvious what an employee's normal working hours are, in the sense of the number of hours which the employee is *obliged* to work by his contract; there is no overall statutory definition of this, and it is essentially a matter of interpreting the contract. Thus, where the contract expressly states the number of hours this will usually be conclusive of the matter[100], and the employee should ensure that the contractual term correctly reflects the practical position, for he will be held to that term (for example for the purpose of calculation of a redundancy payment) even if in practice he works longer hours and regards himself as bound to work those longer hours, *unless* the facts in his case are such as to support an argument that the term of the contract relating to hours has actually been varied by the parties to include the longer hours[101]. This possibility apart, however, it will normally be to no avail that the employee in fact works longer hours than those stipulated in the contract. In *ITT Components (Europe) Group v Kolah*[102] a clerk was employed under a contract specifying twenty hours per week (at a time when the necessary minimum for qualification for an unfair dismissal claim was twenty-one hours per week), but she regularly worked a further three hours each week; the EAT, reversing the tribunal decision in her favour, held that this was not in itself a contract for twenty-one hours or more per week because of the express term for twenty hours, but remitted the case to the tribunal to discover what the correct interpretation of the contract should be, since the

---

98 See p 190 above.

99 See *Harvey* CI2A.

100 *Gascol Conversions Ltd v Mercer* [1974] ICR 420, [1974] IRLR 155, CA; *Fewell v B & B Plastics Ltd* [1974] IRLR 154; *Lake v Essex County Council* [1979] ICR 577, [1979] IRLR 241, CA.

101 For a case in which it was held that there had been such a variation, see *Armstrong Whitworth Rolls Ltd v Mustard* [1971] 1 All ER 598, 9 KIR 279.

102 [1977] ICR 740, [1977] IRLR 53.

clerk had in fact been promoted to a supervisor ten months before she was dismissed, and there was at least the possibility that the relevant contractual term might have been varied on the promotion (that being a question of fact for the tribunal to consider).

If there is no express term covering the normal working hours (in spite of the statutory obligation to give written particulars of this, under the Employment Rights Act 1996, section 1(4)), the tribunal must consider the facts and what happens in practice to decide what is the correct term to infer. This may be a difficult exercise where the employee has in fact been working fluctuating hours. In *Dean v Eastbourne Fishermen's and Boatmen's Protection Society Ltd*[103] a barman worked certain set sessions and at other times when requested to do so by his employer; this produced fluctuating hours, and as the set sessions amounted to less than the twenty-one hours per week at that time required for qualification for redundancy rights the tribunal rejected his claim for a redundancy payment when he was dismissed. However, the EAT allowed his appeal, holding that as the contract was silent on the matter, the tribunal had to infer the relevant term and in a case such as this, where that term was essentially to work the hours required of him, that meant looking at what happened in practice during a period before the dismissal. The appropriate period appears to be the period required to qualify for the particular right being claimed (for example two years for redundancy, one year for unfair dismissal or six months for additional maternity leave)[104]; in *Dean's* case the EAT held that as in the qualifying period of the last 104 weeks the employee had worked for more than twenty-one hours in eighty-six of those weeks the proper interpretation was that his normal working hours exceeded twenty-one per week and so he was eligible for a redundancy payment.

Whether 'normal working hours' are expressed in the contract or left to be inferred when the need arises, one overall consideration is that in general they will *not* include overtime. This proposition may help to simplify the question, for even if a contract of employment is not specific on the normal working hours (or, to put it another way, the minimum number of obligatory hours), it might well state that overtime is payable after a certain number of hours per week have been worked and where this is the case the Employment Rights Act 1996, section 234, provides that normal working hours shall be that number of hours to be worked before overtime becomes payable. Thus, in *Fox v C Wright (Farmers) Ltd*[105] an agricultural worker was employed under a contract which did not specify a minimum number of hours to be worked, and he often worked fifty or sixty hours per week as the job demanded; the contract did, however, provide that overtime was payable for hours worked in excess of forty per week, and when he claimed a redundancy payment the EAT held that he was caught by this provision, and his normal working hours were therefore forty (for the purposes of calculating the redundancy payment). Section 234 does, however, create an exception to this in a case where the contract sets a fixed number of obligatory hours which includes a number of hours in fact payable at overtime rates (for example an obligatory week of forty hours, but with overtime rates payable from thirty-five hours). In such a case, the normal working hours will remain the obligatory figure even though that includes some overtime. The predecessor of this provision was

103 [1977] ICR 556, [1977] IRLR 143. See, to like effect, *Green v Roberts* [1992] IRLR 499.
104 *Larkin v Cambos Enterprises (Stretford) Ltd* [1978] ICR 1247.
105 [1978] ICR 98.

considered by the Court of Appeal in *Tarmac Roadstone Holdings Ltd v Peacock*[106] where Lord Denning MR said that for overtime to be included under this exception it must be fully obligatory under the contract, in the sense that the employee must work it *and* the employer must provide it; it is not sufficient if the overtime is voluntary on both sides or if the employer is obliged to work it when requested but the employer is not obliged to provide it in any particular week. Thus, this exception is restrictively construed (in line, it is submitted, with the clear wording of the provision), and so overtime will only be included in the normal working hours if it is clearly obligatory on both sides under the contract.

(ii) A week's pay[107]

The rules governing the calculation of a weeks' pay for statutory purposes are laid down in Part XIV, Chapter II of the Employment Rights Act 1996 (sections 220–229). There are four different methods of calculation, depending upon the category into which the employee concerned falls; the first three cover cases where there are normal working hours (as defined above) but differing or specialised forms of payment for the work done during those hours, and the fourth covers the case where there are no discernible normal working hours. These are now considered in turn.

(i) Where there are normal working hours and the remuneration does not vary with the amount of actual work done. This is the simplest case where, essentially, the employee is paid on a time basis, ie for the hours during which he is at work, and here the 'week's pay' is the amount payable under the contract of employment when the employee works throughout the normal hours of the week, the relevant contractual provision being that in force on the calculation date[108]. This may be simply the basic rate for a time worker, but not necessarily since it could include any further payments if they are paid on a regular basis, for example a night shift rate or a regular bonus[109].

(ii) Where there are normal working hours, but the remuneration varies with the amount of actual work done. This obviously covers pieceworkers, but also extends to persons basically on a time rate but eligible for variable bonuses or commission[110]. Here the 'week's pay' is the remuneration for the normal working hours payable at the *average hourly rate*, which is calculated by working out the total numbers of hours actually worked in a period of twelve calendar weeks preceding the calculation date, then the total amount of remuneration

---

106 [1973] 2 All ER 485, [1973] ICR 273, CA, followed in *Lotus Cars Ltd v Sutcliffe* [1982] IRLR 381, CA.

107 See *Harvey* CI2B.

108 Employment Rights Act 1996, s 221(2); calculation dates vary with the particular statutory rights involved, and are laid down individually in ss 225 and 226. This could cause injustice if, for example, the contractual term had been varied downwards by the calculation date (eg because of the firm's economic difficulties).

109 *A & B Marcusfield Ltd v Melhuish* [1977] IRLR 484. See the inclusion of a site bonus in *Donelan v Kerrby Constructions Ltd* [1983] ICR 237, [1983] IRLR 191.

110 S 221(4); *Jones v Shellabear Price Ltd* (1967) 2 ITR 36. Where, however, commission is based on the success of work (rather than on a greater amount of work being done) then, if it can still be said that remuneration does not vary with the amount of work done, the employee remains under head (i) above, which may be financially disadvantageous: *Evans v Malley Organisation Ltd* [2002] EWCA Civ 1834, [2003] ICR 432, [2003] IRLR 156, CA.

actually paid for those hours over that period (excluding any overtime premia paid), and then working out the average payment per hour[111].

(iii) Where there are normal working hours but they are to be worked at varying times and in varying amounts in different weeks. This category primarily covers employees working rotating shifts, where the pattern of work is set, but alternates from week to week, so that here it is necessary to average *both* the rate of remuneration *and* the number of hours worked in a week, once again over a period of twelve calendar weeks preceding the calculation date. The 'week's pay' here is therefore the average weekly number of normal working hours payable at the average hourly rate[112].

(iv) Where there are no normal working hours. In this residual category, which would cover, for example, the case of a university lecturer, the tribunal must determine the 'week's pay' simply by calculating the amount of the average weekly remuneration received by the employee over the period of twelve calendar weeks preceding the calculation date[113]. This form of calculation could well be the most favourable for the employee since it looks at overall remuneration, and is not tied to concepts such as basic hours, so that, for example, in *Fox v C Wright (Farmers) Ltd*[114] the agricultural worker who regularly worked fifty to sixty hours per week was trying to argue that he had no normal hours in order to put the question of averaging at large, but the EAT held that as his contract provided for overtime rates to be paid after forty hours' work per week, he was caught by section 234 (considered above) and so he was deemed to have normal working hours of forty per week.

Those being the four categories of employee covered by the provisions, four general qualifications should be noticed:

(a) The twelve-week period referred to must consist of weeks during which the employee actually worked in order to earn some pay, and it is that earned pay which is used for the purpose of calculation even if in any given week he worked (and therefore earned) considerably less than usual for some reason; this leads to a possible gap in the legal coverage in the case where work is consistently run down in the twelve weeks (or more) immediately prior to dismissal – as long as the employee actually earned *something*, those weeks will be used for calculation purposes even if they are in fact untypical and decrease what would otherwise have been his statutory entitlement. This requirement of looking at the pay actually earned in any given calculation week excludes matters such as payment during rest days[115] and the payment of fall-back or guaranteed pay for periods when not actually working[116]. If, however, the period of twelve calendar weeks includes a week when *no* work is done to earn remuneration, the tribunal must ignore that week and take an earlier week instead to bring the number up to twelve again[117]. If the employee has not been employed long enough for calculation over twelve weeks, the tribunal must apply the above provisions as nearly as it can, looking at certain other factors, such as the remuneration of other persons in

111 S 221(3).
112 S 222.
113 S 224.
114 Discussed above; see n 105 above.
115 *Mole Mining Ltd v Jenkins* [1972] ICR 282.
116 *Adams v John Wright & Sons (Blackwall) Ltd* [1972] ICR 463.
117 Employment Rights Act 1996, s 223(2). *Secretary of State for Employment v Crane* [1988] IRLR 238.

comparable employment, though if the employee has just joined the employer in question from another employer and his employment with both is deemed to be continuous, a period of employment with the previous employer can be taken into consideration if necessary[118].

(b) The emphasis remains against the inclusion of overtime rates. As seen above, overtime other than fully obligatory and guaranteed overtime is not counted towards 'normal working hours' in the first place. However, for the purpose of calculating the 'average hourly rate' under categories (2) and (3) above the tribunal must look at the hours *actually worked* during the twelve-week period, and this may include some hours worked at overtime rates; where this is so, however, section 223(3) provides that the amount of overtime premia earned is to be ignored when calculating the total remuneration for that period for the purpose of calculating the average; the employee therefore cannot take advantage of the overtime premia to increase the average, but this only applies to actual overtime, and does not disallow the inclusion of amounts under incentive or bonus schemes which may be built into the wage structure, for these are not to be treated as analogous to overtime[119].

(c) The word used throughout the scheme is 'remuneration', but its definition has been left to the case law. It obviously includes wages and salaries, and has been held to include commission[120]; moreover, the tribunal must look at the realities of an employee's pay, which may be significant in the case of certain more complicated payment systems:

'It is not possible for an employer, as a matter of law, to represent that a worker who is paid £1 as remuneration for doing an hour's work is really paid 50p for an hour's work because the parties choose to specify that the rate shall be 50p an hour but one hour's work shall count as two hours' work in calculating pay.[121]'

Contractually binding bonuses will be included, in whatever guise they are presented[122], and it is specifically provided that if such a bonus is only payable at a time outside the calculation period (for example once per year), it may be apportioned for calculation purposes in such manner as may be just, and taken into account accordingly[123]. In addition to such matters, an employee may in fact receive further indirect benefits which may cause more difficulty. He may, for example, receive an amount labelled 'expenses' which may be simply genuine reimbursement for money of his own actually expended, or may instead be a none-too-subtle form of giving increased remuneration. If the former, it is not to be included, but if the latter it may be brought into account according to the leading case of *S & U Stores Ltd v Wilkes*[124]; such an arrangement may sometimes raise a suspicion of tax evasion, but the general approach has been to ignore this, as being basically a matter for the Inland

---

118 Ss 228 and 229; on continuity of employment, see pp 188–213 above.
119 *Ogden v Ardphalt Asphalt Ltd* [1977] ICR 604; the possible intricacies of bonus and overtime schemes in this context are well illustrated by *British Coal Corpn v Cheesbrough* [1990] ICR 317, [1990] IRLR 148, HL.
120 *Weevsmay Ltd v Kings* [1977] ICR 244.
121 *Mole Mining Ltd v Jenkins* [1972] ICR 282 at 284, per Sir John Brightman.
122 *Amalgamated Asphalte Companies Ltd v Dockrill* (1972) 7 ITR 198.
123 Employment Rights Act 1996, s 229(2); *J & S Bickley Ltd v Washer* [1977] ICR 425.
124 [1974] 3 All ER 401, [1974] ICR 645.

Revenue, not the employment tribunals[125]. The case of *S & U Stores Ltd v Wilkes* also establishes that two other indirect benefits are *not* to be taken into account when quantifying remuneration; these are payments in kind, such as free accommodation or a firm's car, and payments from a person other than the employer. The latter means that a waiter cannot include cash tips in his remuneration for the purpose of calculating his 'week's pay', since these are discretionary payments by a third party[126]; this has, however, been held not to apply to a fixed service charge shared out between the employees (through a tronc system or otherwise), since that is obligatory payment in fact payable by the employer[127]. Likewise, gratuities on credit cards or cheques paid out to waiters (under Inland Revenue pressure) directly through the employer as 'additional pay' may count as part of the week's pay[128].

(d) If the week's pay calculated as above turns out to be below the applicable rate of the national minimum wage, then as a matter of policy it is the national minimum wage (NMW) rate that is to be used when working out any statutory entitlement (particularly a redundancy payment or compensation for unfair dismissal)[129].

6 STATUTORY REGULATION OF WAGES AND HOURS

(i) General

For many years the state, in pursuance of its economic policies, has sought to play a role in wage regulation though normally this has been done indirectly through extra-legal devices such as White Papers, social compacts/contracts or exhortation. Statutory regulation (outside wartime) has been rare. There have, however, been incidents of legislative intervention to try to protect employees receiving inadequately low pay, though these have been on a specific basis applying to particular industries, persons or activities, as opposed to the new legislation on the national minimum wage which puts in place a general 'floor' right.

An early device relating to low pay was the establishment in 1909 of trades boards[130], later to become known as wages councils. These covered specific industries or trades where unionism was low, as were wages, and consisted of a statutory board (equal numbers of employers and workers, with independent members and chairman) charged with setting minimum wages and (later) other

---

125 *S & U Stores Ltd v Lee* [1969] 2 All ER 417, [1969] 1 WLR 626; cf *Jennings v Westwood Engineering Ltd* [1975] IRLR 245, IT.

126 *Hall v Honeybay Caterers Ltd* (1967) 2 ITR 538; *Palmanor Ltd v Cedron* [1978] ICR 1008, [1978] IRLR 303. Note that tips not paid through the payroll also do not count as remuneration for the purposes of the national minimum wage.

127 *Tsoukka v Potomac Restaurants Ltd* (1968) 3 ITR 259; *Keywest Club Ltd v Choudhury* [1988] IRLR 51.

128 *Nerva v RL & G Ltd* [1997] ICR 11, [1996] IRLR 461, CA (a case on the repealed Wages Councils legislation, but applying the same principle); the waiters' ultimate action before the ECtHR failed: *Nerva v United Kingdom* [2002] IRLR 815.

129 *Pagetti v Cobb* [2002] IRLR 861; this obviously applies to the basic award for unfair dismissal which is mathematically based on the week's pay, but less obviously it also applies to the compensatory award which is to be based on a calculation of what the employee's net wage would have been if paid at the NMW level.

130 Trade Boards Act 1909; the first four boards covered the so-called 'sweated traders' of tailoring, box-making, lace-making and chain-making.

basic terms and conditions which were enforceable in the civil courts (and backed by criminal sanctions) through the administrative means of a wages inspectorate. Although the councils were supposed to be a temporary expedient (pending the growth of normal collective bargaining) they proved to be longlasting and their coverage spread[131], though of course they always remained the exception rather than the rule in industrial relations. With the election of a Conservative government in 1979 espousing laissez-faire free market economics, the wages council system fell into official disapproval, as being a statutory limitation on a free market in labour. Their powers were first curbed in the Wages Act 1986 (taking youth workers out of their jurisdiction and limiting them to setting basic rates) and they were finally abolished by the Trade Union Reform and Employment Rights Act 1993. The only survivor (and now the only example of a statutory minimum wage in a particular industry) was the Agricultural Wages Board which was set up under separate legislation[132]; although technically not a 'wages council' it operates in the same way and continues to set minimum wages, terms and conditions for those employed in agriculture, horticulture and growing[133]. Revival of the wages council system generally has not figured in the plans of the present government.

A second form of low pay provision was the Fair Wages Resolution, a resolution of the House of Commons in 1891 (repeated in 1946) that employers receiving government contracts should be required to pay fair wages, ie the going rate for the job, in order to prevent undercutting by driving down wages[134]. Workers or their trade union could complain of breach of the Resolution to (initially) the Industrial Court (since 1976 the Central Arbitration Committee) which resolved the matter by arbitration, the result of which was legally binding on the employer. This was supplemented by other forms of unilateral arbitration on wages for either the resolution of disputes or for the maintenance of the going rate of pay. The former was particularly the case in wartime; that applying in the Second World War lasted until 1959, but on its abolition then the legislation[135] retained one form of it whereby a claim could be made to the Industrial Court that an employer was not observing the terms and conditions established in that industry. This eventually became embodied in Schedule 11 of the Employment Protection Act 1975, enforced by the Central Arbitration Committee. This 'Schedule 11 claim' procedure was widely used in the 1970s[136]; its primary aim was to attack pockets of low pay within an industry, though towards the end of that decade it was criticised as being used for other, less noble purposes because a Schedule 11 award was not subject to the then government's pay restraint policy. With the change of government in 1979 and the radical change in economic policy, these forms of statutory and quasi-statutory intervention quickly became viewed as

---

131 The largest industries covered were retail, hotels and restaurants. In addition, there were certain rather more rarified examples, such as the ostrich feather and fancy hat council and the pin, hook and zip fasteners council. Shortly before their abolition, there were 24 councils covering 2.5 million workers.

132 Agricultural Wages Act 1948.

133 The previous government consulted on abolishing it, but to their surprise the farmer employers strongly favoured its retention. It is due for a further review during the currency of this edition, the result of which is uncertain because of the existence now of a national minimum wage.

134 Bercusson *Fair Wages Resolution* (1978).

135 Terms and Conditions of Employment Act 1959.

136 ACAS Annual Reports show conciliation in 3,092 cases between 1976 and 1980, with 1,970 arbitration by the CAC.

anachronistic, for two reasons: (1) they pre-supposed the clear establishment by collective bargaining of comprehensive national terms and conditions across an industry, whereas that model was rapidly breaking down; and (2) in any event the Conservative economic orthodoxy of the time denied outright that there was any such thing as a 'fair' or 'going' rate for a job – the only rate for the job was increasingly to be that set by a deregulated market. Thus, Schedule 11 was repealed immediately, in the Employment Act 1980, and the Fair Wages Resolution was rescinded two years later[137]. Once again, restitution of specific provisions such as these has not been suggested by the present government, and indeed would be difficult if not impossible in the current flexible, devolved and localised labour market.

With regard to hours of work, these too have not been subject to wide-ranging statutory control in mainstream employment law. Of course, the movement to restrict maximum hours, especially in factories, was a major factor in nineteenth-century social history and was eventually successful in a consistent series of factories statutes, aimed at improving what we would now call the health and safety of the workforce[138]. These provisions were, however, specific to certain places and/or industries and, although eventually extended to men, the initial thrust of them was to give extra protection to women and young persons. It was this that fed through into the modern factories legislation, and came increasingly under attack. In relation to women, the restrictions (for example on night working or overtime) were seen as unacceptably paternalistic and discriminatory (affecting questions of equal pay if women could not earn certain premium payments)[139] and they were repealed in the Sex Discrimination Act 1986. With regard to young persons, the restrictions were repealed as a deregulatory measure in the Employment Act 1989.

One unusual case where there are highly specific limitations on working hours is that of Sunday shop opening and betting. This was a highly contentious matter and, as part of the eventual political trade off, the legislation[140] creates a category of 'protected' workers who cannot be obliged to work on Sundays. Initially, this protection was only meant to be transitional, so that those already in employment when the change came in could not be forced to work on Sundays. However, due to pressure in Parliament, it was extended and so in fact enacts a legal regime covering Sunday working into the future too. It gives the right to opt out of Sunday working by giving three months' notice, and not to be prejudiced thereby; there is also provision for a protected shop or betting workers to opt back into Sunday working. Any provision in a contract which contravenes these rules is declared to be unenforceable.

Thus, in spite of a somewhat varied history, by 1997 and the change of government statutory intervention in questions of wages and hours had been

---

137 The delay was due to the need for the government to denounce an International Labour Organisation Convention which underpinned the Resolution.

138 For an excellent description of this legislation, see Cornish and Clark 'Law and Society in England 1750–1950' (1989) ch 4.

139 EOC 'Health and safety legislation: should we distinguish between men and women' (1979).

140 The main controversy was over the Sunday Trading Act 1994, which gave rise to the provisions governing 'protected shop workers'. When Sunday betting was legalised by the Deregulation and Contracting Out Act 1994, similar provisions were inserted into the Betting, Gaming and Lotteries Act 1963. All of these protective provisions are now in the Employment Rights Act 1996, Pt IV; the anti-victimisation and dismissal provisions are in ss 45 and 101, see p 598 below.

restricted to the setting of wages and conditions in agriculture and the specific rules on Sunday working in the retail and betting industries. That position has now been significantly altered by the National Minimum Wage Act 1998 (a New Labour election commitment) and the Working Time Regulations 1998 (an EC law requirement).

(ii) The National Minimum Wage Act 1998

The advantages and disadvantages of a national minimum wage have been a controversial matter in this jurisdiction for some time; it is a device that is widely used in Europe and some states in the US, and an early ILO Convention[141] encouraged such action by states. Its introduction was an election issue in 1997, and immediately on coming into office the present government established a Low Pay Commission, at first on an informal basis and then put on to a statutory footing by the legislation, to investigate and make recommendations. The government proceeded to pass the National Minimum Wage Act 1998 which operates in significant areas by giving regulation-making powers; when the Low Pay Commission made its first report[142], its recommendations were incorporated into the National Minimum Wage Regulations 1999[143], which contain much of the detailed law – while obviously the most politically contentious question is the rate at which the minimum wage is set, the most difficult questions legally tend to be those of definition (what is pay? what can be disregarded? how to average? who is covered?) which are particularly acute in a piece of legislation intended to apply to employment across the board, in all its varieties.

The Act sets out a basic entitlement for any worker (working, or ordinarily working, in the UK under his contract) to be remunerated by his employer in any pay reference period at a rate not less than the national minimum wage fixed by regulations by the Secretary of State[144]. The ambit of this duty is deliberately broad through the use of the wide term 'workers' which covers employees and any other person under a contract (whether express or implied, written or not) whereby the individual undertakes to do or perform personally any work or services for another party to the contract whose status is not that of a client or customer of any profession or business undertaking carried on by the individual[145]. Any attempt to contract out of the protection of the legislation is void[146].

141 Convention No 26 (1928) 'Minimum wage-fixing machinery'.
142 Cm 3976, 1998. For the Commission's observations on other countries' legislation, see Cash 'Lessons from the international experience of statutory minimum wages' [1998] Labour Market Trends 463. Any further investigations are to be instigated by the Secretary of State; there is no obligation on the Commission to carry out periodic investigations, or to initiate them on its own initiative: National Minimum Wage Act 1998, s 6. For the initial experience see the 2nd Report of the Law Pay Commission (Cm 4571, February 2000).
143 SI 1999/584. For detailed guidance, see the DTI 'Guide to the National Minimum Wage' (1999). Simpson 'Implementing the national minimum wage' (1999) 28 ILJ 171.
144 National Minimum Wage Act 1998, s 1. The pay reference period is a month or, in the case of a worker who is paid by reference to a period shorter than a month, that period: reg 10. This could cause problems with 'annualised hours' contracts.
145 S 54 (se p 32 above): there are subsidiary provisions in ss 34 and 35 to ensure (if necessary) that agency workers and home workers are covered. For the wide definition of 'worker' generally, see p 24, above. Voluntary workers (eg for a charity or similar organisation) are specifically excluded: s 44. At a late stage, under media pressure, au pairs and family workers were exempted: reg 2(2)–(4).

Although the introduction of the national minimum wage in 1999 was the honoring of an important commitment by New Labour, the rate at which it was set (the principal rate was £3.60 per hour) was substantially below what the unions had argued for. By October 2003, the rates had risen to:

(1) £4.50 per hour generally[147];

(2) £3.80 per hour for a worker of 22 or over who is in the first six months of employment with that employer[148];

(3) £3.80 per hour for a worker aged 18 but under 22[149].

A worker under 18 does not qualify for the national minimum wage at all; nor does a worker under 26 employed under a contract of apprenticeship and in the first twelve months of his employment or who has not attained the age of 19[150]. A survey in Spring 1998 had estimated that between 1.9m and 2.4m employees (ie between 8.4% and 10.4% of the workforce) earned below the projected level of £3.60 (£3.00 for those aged 18–22), and that by commencement in April 1999 between 1.7m and 2.1m were likely to be affected[151]. This fitted the Low Pay Commission's own estimate that about 2m employees should benefit, with a total recurring cost to industry of £2.4bn (0.6% of the national average wage bill); however, the government have been keen to argue that there should be significant offsetting savings to business in lower absenteeism and staff turnover costs, both of which tend to be higher in sectors of low pay[152].

In order to determine whether the legal minimum is being paid, it is of course necessary to work out the current hourly rate for the particular individual, which may be easier said than done where the contracting and/or pay arrangements are complex or flexible. The established formula is to take the total of remuneration for the reference period minus the total of reductions to be made, and divide it by the total hours worked in that period[153]. However, the question of 'total hours' is a potential stumbling block, and to try to cover this, the legislation divides work into four possible catgegories:

---

146 S 49. The Secretary of State has power to exclude or modify the right in relation to particular persons but, in response to concerns expressed about the width of this when the Bill war going through Parliament, it is specifically stated that this cannot be on the basis of specifying different areas, sectors of employment, sites of undertakings or occupations: ss 3, 4. In the event, this power has been used in relation to workers of certain ages.

147 Reg 11.

148 Reg 13(2). The worker must not have been previously employed by that employer or an associated employer, and must be required to take part in accredited training on at least 26 days in the six-month period.

149 Reg 13(1).

150 Reg 12(1), (2). Being under a contract of apprenticeship includes being engaged in a Modern Apprenticeship. Workers participating in certain designated training or employment schemes also do not qualify: reg 12(5).

151 Wilkinson 'Who are the low paid?' [1998] Labour Market Trends 617. Over half of those affected are women working part time; the percentage is highest in hotels and restaurants, with the highest actual numbers in wholesale and retail.

152 'The Low Pay Commission have confirmed the view taken by Government that sustainable economic growth and job creation cannot hinge on low pay alone. The rates introduced by these Regulations should encourage fairer competition by preventing undercutting based on unduly low wages and will reinforce companies which compete through quality, service and timeliness of delivery rather than just price and wage costs': Consultation Document URN: 98/885 (September 1998) Annex 5, para. 13. This argument primarily relates to competition with other *national* firms who are also subject to the minimum wage; international competition is another matter.

153 Reg 14.

(1) 'time work', ie work that is paid for by reference to the time worked (even if depending on the worker's output per hour)[154];

(2) 'salaried hours work', ie where there are ascertainable basic hours in return for an annual salary, not varying with hours actually worked (except for any performance bonus)[155];

3) 'output work', ie work that is paid for wholly by reference to the number of pieces made or processed by the worker, or to some other measure of output (for example number or value of sales or transactions)[156];

4) 'unmeasured work', ie work not within the previous categories, in particular where there are no specified hours and the worker is required to work when needed or when work is available[157].

Calculating the hours worked is simplest in the case of time work, where it is simply the number of hours actually worked in the relevant pay reference period. Likewise, there is a simple averaging process over the salary year in the case of salaried hours work *if* only the basic hours are worked. If, however, the salaried worker actually works more than this, a more complicated calculation is set out to take the extra hours into account[158]. More generalised problems are bound to arise with output work and unmeasured work because of the variability of the hours put in by the worker in discharging the duties. Prima facie, the measure here has to be the total number of hours *actually* worked in the reference period, but this could be administratively difficult where there are significant fluctuations, and so the Regulations permit the worker and employer to agree in writing what the worker's *normal* hours are likely to be, so determining what the 'ascertained hours' are to be for the pay reference period[159]. In the case of output work, this must be a 'fair estimate', bearing some relationship to the speed at which an average piece worker would work, and backed by records of actual hours kept by the worker. In the case of unmeasured work, it must be a 'realistic average' of the hours likely to be spent on the contractual duties. As will be seen below, this approach is similar to that in the Working Time Regulations, laying down default rules but placing major emphasis on fitting the requirements to individual jobs by agreement (though with the difference that in relation to working time the emphasis is largely on collective forms of agreement, whereas here it is on individual agreement). An employer may have much to gain in entering such

---

154 Reg 3. In relation to time work, time spent while available for work and required to be available (eg on a stand-by arrangement at or near the employer's premises) is to count (reg 15(1)). Time when a worker may sleep has caused problems: reg 15(1A) appears to exclude it but the courts have construed this narrowly to apply only where the worker may sleep while waiting to work, not applying where the worker's job is to be available on shift in case of need, cf a nightwatchman or person available to answer request for help: *British Nursing Association v Inland Revenue* [2002] IRLR 480; *Scottbridge Construction Ltd v Wright* [2003] IRLR 21, Ct of Sess (IH). On the other hand, a 24-hour carer living in the client's home in case of problems was held to be on 'unmeasured work' and so able to enter a 'realistic average' agreement for only certain hours to count for NMW purposes: *Walton v Independent Living* [2003] EWCA Civ 199, [2003] ICR 688, [2003] IRLR 469. The potential conflict between these cases could cause problems. Time when the worker is absent from work does not count, and this is expressed to include rest breaks and industrial action: reg 15(5)–(7). Time spent on training counts: reg 19.

155 Reg 4. This heading was added to the original draft Regulations, and gives rise to some of the most complex provisions in the Regulations.

156 Reg 5.

157 Reg 6.

158 Reg 22; see the DTI Guide, paras. 155–172.

159 Regs 24–29.

agreements, especially where fluctuating or ungovernable work patterns may mean at times being technically in breach of the legislation, in the absence of agreed averages. One final point in ascertaining hours, possibly a problem with any of the four categories, is travelling time; this is dealt with specifically, the general rule being that work-related travelling (and necessary waiting times) are counted, but travelling from home to work is not[160].

The other variable which has to be calculated in order to determine whether the worker is being paid the legal minimum is of course the pay in the relevant reference period. The 'total of remuneration' is defined as all moneys paid by the employer to the worker in (or in respect of) that reference period, plus any permitted charge for living accommodation[161]. From this gross amount, there are then a series of reductions to be made[162], essentially in order to comply with the Low Pay Commission recommendation that (however the pay is calculated) it is components that comprise pay for standard working that are to count towards the national minimum wage, not premia or other additions for non-standard work.

The worker has a statutory right of access to the records which the employer must keep[163], In a case of non-compliance with the minimum, the individual worker is given a statutory entitlement under his contract to 'additional remuneration' representing the shortfall[164]. The legislation does not give any special procedure for recovery, and so this amount would have to be claimed in an ordinary breach of contract action (in the county court or, on termination, in a tribunal) or as an unlawful deduction for wages under Part II of the Employment Rights Act 1996; in any such proceedings there is a reversal of the burden of proof[165]. There is, however, in an interesting parallel with the old wages council system, an alternative form of enforcement which may be to an individual worker's advantage. The Secretary of State is given power to appoint minimum wage inspectors with wide powers to inspect records, require information and enter premises for these purposes[166]. If such an officer finds non-compliance with the minimum, he may serve an enforcement notice on the employer, requiring future

---

160 See the DTI Guide, para. 127.
161 Reg 30. Benefits in kind are excluded (including exchangeable vouchers such as luncheon vouchers), as are (1) loans or advances of wages, (2) any pension or compensation for loss of office, (3) any tribunal award or settlement amount (other than for an amount contractually due), (4) any redundancy payment and (5) any amount under a suggestions scheme: Regs. 8 and 9.
162 These cover – (1) payment for work done in a previous reference period, (2) payment for time absent from work, (3) (crucially) overtime or shift premium, (4) special allowances (eg for dangerous work, antisocial hours or being on standby; however, performance or incentive payments *do* count), (5) tips or gratuities paid directly by customers and not through the payroll, (6) reimbursement of business expenses, (7) certain deductions which have been made by the employer (eg for purchase of tools, equipment or clothing), (8) certain payments by the worker to the employer (similar to the deductions in (7)) and (9) deductions for living accommodation in excess of a set figure per day (£3.50 as at October 2003): Regs 31–37.
163 S 10; the worker may complain of failure to provide access to an employment tribunal (subject to the usual three month time limit) and if the complaint is upheld the tribunal must make a declaration to that effect and award compensation of 80 times the hourly amount of the minimum wage: s 11. Details of the records to be kept are set out in Reg 38, and because of employer pressure at draft stage they are much less onerous than as originally proposed.
164 S 17.
165 S 28. Refusal or wilful neglect to pay the national minimum wage is a criminal offence, punishable on summary conviction by a fine not exceeding level 5 on the standard scale: s 31.
166 Ss 13, 14.

compliance and the payment of arrears to the individual(s) concerned[167]. If the notice is not complied with, the inspector may bring proceedings for the arrears on behalf of the worker in a tribunal (under Part II of the 1996 Act) or by way of other civil proceedings[168] *and* may serve a penalty notice for a financial penalty equal to twice the hourly minimum rate (in respect of each underpaid worker) for each day of failure to comply[169]. Finally, the individual worker is given a right not to be subjected to any detriment by his employer because of any action taken by him or on his behalf under this legislation, because the employer has been prosecuted, or because he qualifies for the legal minimum[170]; in line with other areas of specialised protection in other contexts, a dismissal on these grounds is declared to be automatically unfair[171].

(iii) The Working Time Regulations 1998

The Working Time Regulations 1998[172], which came into force on 1 October 1998, enact the Working Time Directive (93/104/EC) and certain provisions of the Young Workers Directive (94/33/EC)[173], applying statutory limits or entitlements in four main areas – the forty-eight hours maximum working week, night working, rest breaks and paid annual holiday. The Working Time Directive had a complicated history, which has had important effects politically and in relation to the drafting of the eventual Regulations[174]. The previous government took part in some of the negotiations on the Directive which eventually took on a much watered-down form, with major 'derogations' which a member state can adopt in order to lessen the effect of the main requirements. However, even in this form it turned out to be politically unacceptable to the previous government who refused to agree it, on the assumption that that meant that it could not be passed. However, the remaining member states proceeded to adopt it under Article 118 a (now Art 137) of the Treaty of Rome, which permits the adoption of 'health and safety' directives by qualified majority voting. This meant that the UK government could neither block it nor use the then-existing opt-out; they instead brought proceedings in the ECJ to have the Directive annulled, arguing that working time was not a health and safety issue. This challenge was, however,

---

167 S. 19. The employer may appeal against the notice to an employment tribunal, but only on certain enumerated grounds: ibid.

168 S. 20.

169 S. 21. Again, there is a right of appeal to a tribunal on enumerated grounds: s 22.

170 S. 23. Complaint lies to an employment tribunal, subject to the same procedure as other classes of detriment (Employment Rights Act 1996, ss 48 and 49): s 24.

171 S. 25, adding the Employment Rights Act 1996, s 104A. Adopting the usual 'package' approach, a subsequent redundancy on these grounds is also unfair, no qualifying period is required and the upper age limit does not apply. There is, however, no entitlement to higher levels of compensation.

172 SI 1998/1833.

173 They do so in relation to young persons (ie between 15 and 18, and over school leaving age); these provisions were tightened by the Working Time (Amendment) Regulations 2002, SI 2002/3128, primarily to restrict a young worker's working time to 8 hours in any day or 40 hours in any week, and to ban night working except in restricted circumstances. In relation to children under that age, the Directive was transposed by the Children (Protection at Work) Regulations 1998, SI 1998/276. On this basis it was held by the EAT that a child cannot claim under the Working Time Regulations (eg for paid holidays): *Addison v Ashby* [2003] 3 ICR 667, [2003] IRLR 211.

174 See Bercusson *European Labour Law* (1996) ch 21.

eventually rejected by the ECJ[175] who took a broader approach to health and safety generally, pointing in particular to the phrasing of Article 118a itself which refers to 'improvements, especially in the *working environment*, as regards the health and safety of workers'; on this broader, 'welfare' approach, all elements of the Directive were upheld (except for one minor provision relating to Sunday normally being a rest day). The incoming New Labour government immediately made clear its intention to transpose the Directive willingly and, after a consultation exercise[176], produced the 1998 Regulations[177]. Although that willingness was in contrast to the attitude of their predecessors, the Regulations as drafted are in fact more notable for continuity of approach because they adopt in full all of the derogations negotiated by the previous government. The Regulations are in fact relatively short, largely adopting the 'copy out' technique of implementation, so that (1) much of the wording comes from the Directive itself and (2) the Regulations are quite difficult to use because of the precision of drafting and the (logical but non-user-friendly) sequence of first setting out the obligations and only later the derogations that are adopted. To counteract this, and to give some practical guidance as to the *possible* interpretations and effects in the substantial number of grey areas, the government has issued DTI Regulatory Guidance[178] which aims to be easier to understand in its format; its use is recommended. It remains the case, however, that (as with the minimum wage provisions) this one set of Regulations is meant to apply to the whole diverse workforce, and so the areas of doubt and possible debate are widespread, and likely to remain so for some time. As in other areas of employment law, it may be necessary to adopt the approach that, on any given question of application, it may only be possible to advise or adopt a *possible* or *arguably tenable* interpretation or application, not *the* indisputably correct one. Moreover, as these provisions had no direct predecessors in UK law (unlike in other countries in the EU, apart from Ireland, which have a long history of working time laws) there will be ways in which they are hard to reconcile with other employment laws (a good example being how the holiday entitlement is to operate where the worker is on long-term sickness leave or maternity leave). Ultimately, these Regulations have to be applied as they stand, even if they produce odd results – a lawyer might put it that (as in tax law) there is no equity to the legislation; a lay person might put it that common sense may have little part to play in applying it.

---

175 *United Kingdom v EU Council*: C-84/94 [1997] ICR 443, [1997] IRLR 30, ECJ; see Fitzpatrick 'Straining the definition of health and safety?' (1997) 26 ILJ 115. The ECJ gave its decision on 12 November 1996 and the Directive came into force 11 days later; there was therefore a considerable period during which the UK was in breach. Not surprisingly, given our litigeous nature and literal approach, the first case law on the subject concerned the legal position during this period of non-implementation. In *R v A-G for Northern Ireland, ex p Burns* [1999] IRLR 315 it was held that a private sector worker could bring a *Francovich* action against the government based on the non-implementation. In the public sector, the EAT at first held that a worker could rely directly on the Directive, but this was reversed by the Court of Appeal: *Gibson v East Riding of Yorkshire Council* [2000] IRLR 598.

176 DTI consultation document URN 98/645, April 1998.

177 The Regulations are set out at *Harvey* R[1072]. A useful source of discussion in the IDS Employment Law Supplement 'Working Time Regulations 1998' (October 1998); see also Barnard 'The Working Time Regulations 1998', (1999) 28 ILJ 61.

178 Available on www.dti.gov.uk/er. It was updated in 2000, but unfortunately in less detailed form.

(a) Application

As with the minimum wage provisions, the Regulations use the wide definition of 'worker', as being an individual under a contract of employment *or* any other contract, whether express or implied, oral or written, whereby they undertake to do or perform personally any work or services for another party to the contract whose status is not that of a client or customer of any profession or business undertaking carried out by the individual[179]. The breadth of this approach is then immediately qualified by the first major exclusion (contained in the Directive) namely that three sectors of activity are excluded from the Regulations altogether – (a) air, rail, road, sea, inland waterway and lake transport[180], sea fishing and other work at sea, (b) the activities of doctors in training[181] and (c) activities of services such as the armed forces, police and civil protection services 'which inevitably conflict with the provisions of these Regulations'[182].

(b) Agreements to vary or exclude

The various powers to vary or exclude the principal obligations (known in the Regulatory Guidance as 'flexibilities') are so important to these Regulations that it is necessary at the outset to set out the three forms of agreement specifically allowed by the drafting; in ascending order of potential protection for individual workers, these are.

- *individual agreement*: in itself, this only applies in relation to opting out of the maximum 48 hours per week;
- *a 'relevant agreement'*: this is defined as a workforce agreement, any provision of a collective agreement which forms part of a contract between the worker and his employer, or any other agreement in writing which is legally enforceable as between the worker and his employer[183]. As this may include an individual agreement (provided in writing and legally binding, eg as part of a contract of employment), this format tends to be used for definitional issues (eg what may constitute working time), rather than outright exclusions;
- *a 'collective agreement or workforce agreement'*: this format, importing an obvious collective element of protection, is adopted for some of the major exclusions.

Clearly, the most important development here is the introduction of the concept of the 'workforce agreement' which is meant to apply to workers who do not have

---

179 Reg 2(1); see p 32 above. Thus, the paid holiday right could be claimed by Schedule D paying, self-employed sub-contractors working for only one employer on a long-term basis: *Byrne Bros (Farmwork) Ltd v Baird* [2002] ICR 667, [2002] IRLR 96. There are subsidiary provisions in regs 36 and 42 to ensure that agency workers and non-employed trainees are covered.

180 This is a major exception, especially as the Regulatory Guidance suggests that it applies not just to transport firms, but also to other firms which run their 'own account' transport operations (eg supermarkets). Moreover, the exception applies to all working in the transport industry, even non-mobile workers such as secretaries: *Bowden v Tuffnells Parcels Express Ltd* C-133/00 [2001] IRLR 838, ECJ. These exceptions are narrowed by amending legislation as from August 2003.

181 The previous government were particularly concerned to have this exclusion written into the Directive; for the issues involved in lengthy trainee doctors' hours, see *Johnstone v Bloomsbury Health Authority* [1991] ICR 269, [1991] IRLR 118, CA, p 142 above.

182 Reg 18. There is a further exclusion in Reg 19 of domestic service in a private household, which relates to maximum working hours, night work and pattern of work; this does not appear in the Directive but is justified as being part of the general exclusion of such activities from domestic health and safety law.

183 Reg 2(1).

any terms and conditions set by a collective bargain[184]. Such an agreement must be in writing, have a specified length of not more than five years, apply to either all the relevant members of the workforce or to all those in a particular group[185], and be signed by either the representatives of the workforce or group, or (if the employer employs twenty or fewer workers) either by such representatives or by the majority of the workers[186]. Where use is made of representatives, they must have been 'duly elected' and the Regulations provide the basic electoral rules that must be complied with[187]. There could be overlaps here with representatives elected for other consultative purposes, and this development could be seen as a further 'carrot' towards de facto works councils of sorts. There is, however, one possible trap because, although the point is not made expressly in the Regulations, the Regulatory Guidance takes the view that, while dual (or more) use of the same representatives is possible, 'it would have to be made clear to those voting that the representatives were being elected for both purposes'. Thus, technically the use of *existing* consultative machinery for this further purpose might not be lawful (another similarity with the health and safety consultation requirements and difference from those applying to collective redundancies and TUPE). The answer in the longer term is to ensure that next time a consultative body is elected it is made express for what specific purposes the body is being constituted.

(c) Two principal exceptions

In addition to the excluded sectors, the Regulations adopt from the Directive's permissible derogations two broad exceptions which, while not applying across the board, do apply to the majority of the rights and limitations. By virtue of regulation 20 ('Unmeasured working time') the provisions on the forty-eight-hour maximum week, the length of night working and daily/weekly rest and rest periods do not apply 'in relation to a worker where, on account of the specific characteristics of the activity in which he is engaged, the duration of his working time is not measured or predetermined or can be determined by the worker himself'. The interpretation of this extremely vague exception could prove to be crucial to the effectiveness or otherwise of the Regulations, since so many modern forms of flexible working have at least *some* element of unmeasured time, and discretion in working hours. How great that element needs to be proved to be

---

184 To this extent, it follows the precedent of the Health and Safety (Consultation with Employees) Regulations 1996, which only allow consultation with directly elected worker representatives where there is *no* existing representation by a recognised union. This is achieved in these Regulations by defining the 'relevant members of the workforce' as 'all workers employed by a particular employer, *excluding* any worker whose terms and conditions of employment are provided for, *wholly or in part*, in a collective agreement': Sch 1, para. 2 (emphasis added).

185 This is defined as a group undertaking a particular function, working at a particular workplace or belonging to a particular department or unit: ibid.

186 Sch. 1, para. 1(a)–(d); note that a worker disagreeing but in a minority is bound by the agreement. Before making an agreement available for signature, the employer must have provided all the affected workers with copies of the text and such guidance as they may reasonably require in order to understand it fully: para. 1(e).

187 The number of representatives is to be determined by the employer; candidates must be relevant members of the workforce or group; no eligible candidate must be unreasonably excluded from standing; all relevant members of the workforce or group must be entitled to vote, and able to vote for as many candidates as there are to be representatives; there must be secret voting (as far as is reasonably practicable) and the votes must be fairly and accurately counted: Sch 1, para. 3.

highly controversial. A teacher, for example, will have set teaching hours, but may put in many hours over and above those in preparation and marking. On behalf of a broad construction, the original Regulatory Guidance[188] stressed that it is impossible to lay down comprehensively who is and is not covered. On the other hand, the examples given in the Regulation ('managing executives or other persons with autonomous decision-making powers', family workers and religious celebrants) are very narrow, and the Guidance suggested that only those with *complete* control over their hours would come within the exclusion[189]. This uncertainty caused problems, partly due to assumptions being made in certain sectors that this regulation would apply (for example in law firms) which may or may not have been correct. In addition, employers nationally expressed their concerns over the uncertainty, with a result that (to the annoyance of the unions) the government amended the 1998 Regulations only a year later[190], to add a paragraph to regulation 20 stating that where *part* of a worker's working time is measured or predetermined or cannot be determined by the worker himself, but the specific characteristics of the activity are such that, *without being required to do so* by the employer, he may also do work which is *not* measured or predetermined (or can be determined by the worker himself), then the provisions on the forty-eight-hour week and night working only apply to the first part, ie the 'voluntary' part will not be subject to those provisions. What is to be the effect of this? One possibility is that it will simply legalise practices which were already assumed to be outside the Regulations (see the teacher and lawyer examples above). On the other hand, some employers may see it as extending the exception well down the management ladder from the managing executive. In an attempt to counter criticism of appearing to be saying different things to the TUC and the CBI about this amendment, the government said that the answers would be found in new guidance from the DTI, but when this appeared it was fairly anodyne and not of much help in the most marginal cases. Perhaps the key to the new paragraph is the meaning to be given to 'without being required to do so by the employer'. What if the pressure comes from the *amount* of work to be done, rather than any instructions? What if the unwritten *ethos* of the workplace is for long hours to be put in? What if promotion in practice depends on it, though without it being a formal requirement? One irony here is that if the Directive and Regulations were supposed to help to counter our long-hours culture, this amendment may actually exempt just the sort of workers most in need of coverage. The guidance will only take us so far; the first court decisions are awaited with great interest.

The second principal exception is contained in regulation 21 ('Other special cases') which again raises as many questions as it answers in relation to its likely breadth of interpretation. It states that the provisions on length of night working and daily/weekly rest and rest periods do not apply in relation to a worker:

'(a) where the worker's activities are such that his place of work and place of residence are distant from one another or his different places of work are distant from one another;

(b) where the worker is engaged in security and surveillance activities requiring a permanent presence in order to protect property and

---

188 Para 2.2.2.
189 One interesting question is whether this is to be construed much more narrowly than the provisions in the minimum wage legislation on 'output workers' and 'non-hours workers'; homeworkers, for example might come under these 'pay' categories, but are a long way from managing executives.
190 Working Time Regulations 1999, SI 1999/3372.

persons, as may be the case for security guards and caretakers or security firms;

(c) where the worker's activities involve the need for continuity of service or production, as may be the case in relation to—

    (i) services relating to the reception, treatment or care provided by hospitals or similar establishments, residential institutions and prisons;

    (ii) work at docks or airports;

    (iii) press, radio, television, cinematographic production, postal and tele-communications services and civil protection services;

    (iv) gas, water and electricity production, transmission and distribution, household refuse collection and incineration;

    (v) industries in which work cannot be interrupted on technical grounds;

    (vi) research and development activities;

    (vii) agriculture;

(d) where there is a foreseeable surge of activity, as may be the case in relation to—

    (i) agriculture;

    (ii) tourism; and

    (iii) postal services;

(e) where the worker's activities are affected by—

    (i) an occurrence due to unusual and unforeseeable circumstances, beyond the control of the worker's employer;

    (ii) exceptional events, the consequences of which could not have been avoided despite the exercise of all due care by the employer; or

    (iii) an accident or the imminent risk of an accident.'

Once again, the original Regulatory Guidance was at pains to point out that it is the actual nature of the work that is to be considered and that the examples given are *only* examples. The bottom line was the statement (helpful?) that it is for the employer to take a view as to 'whether the conditions are satisfied for each individual worker's situation'[191]. The equal vagueness and potential significance of these categories mean that they are likely to be widely claimed and disputed.

(d) Maximum weekly working time

A worker's working time, including overtime, is not to exceed an average of forty-eight hours for each seven days in any particular reference period[192]. The fact

---

191 Para 2.2.3. The Guidance stated that head (e) relates essentially to emergency situations, and is not to be used on a routine basis.

192 Reg 4(1). Time on call only counts when the employee is at the place of employment, not when elsewhere (especially at home) but available to be called in: *Sindicato de Médicos de Asistencia Pública (SIMAP) v Conselleria de Sanidad y Consumo de la Generalidad Valenciana* C-303/98 [2000] IRLR 845, ECJ. Reg 4(6), (7) set out the formula for calculating the average, and days of annual, sickness and maternity leave that are not to count. Note that where a worker works for more than one employer, the average applies to the aggregated hours; the Regulations are silent on what the employer(s) is or are to do in these circumstances, but the original Guidance para. 2.1.3 intimated that it is up to the employer to find out if a worker is working elsewhere and if necessary to adjust working arrangements accordingly; it did not say on *which* employer any primary responsibility to do so may rest. With regard to overall impact, in Summer 1998 29.8% of male full time employees and 11.6% of female full time employees worked more than 48 hours per week: [1998] Labour Market Trends 599.

that this is an averaging process is fundamental, because it does not necessarily mean a maximum of forty-eight hours per week, and up to a point fluctuations can be accommodated. The question becomes over how long a period the averaging can be done, hence the importance of the 'reference period'. In the first instance this is stated to be seventeen weeks[193], but where one of the 'Other special cases' in regulation 21 (above) applies, this is increased to twenty-six weeks. Further, it can be raised by a collective or workforce agreement to a maximum of fifty-two weeks 'for objective or technical reasons or reasons concerning the organisation of work' (!), which could be highly advantageous to employers wanting variations in hours over certain prolonged seasons in the year[194]; protection for the worker lies in the collective nature of the necessary agreement

The forty-eight-hour average maximum is then further subject to the most striking exception in the Regulations, namely that it does not apply *at all* to a worker who has agreed in writing with his employer that it should not apply in his case[195]; this individual agreement may be either for a specified period or indefinite, but a worker may terminate it by giving written notice (of a maximum of three months in the agreement or, in default of coverage in the agreement, of seven days). The *quid pro quo* for an exclusion agreement was originally an obligation on the employer to keep specified records of actual hours which were to be open to inspection by a Health and Safety Inspector; however, in another rapid volte-face, the Amendment Regulations in 1999 watered this down very considerably, so that now the only requirement is to keep a record of *who* has signed the opt-out[196]. One possible point of controversy not covered by the Regulations is what is to happen to the worker's wages if he or she does *not* opt out and their hours have to be reduced to meet the new forty-eight-hour average? This will be primarily a matter of contract so that if, for example, the worker is paid at a fixed amount per hour the wage will have to go down pro rata to the new number of hours, whereas a worker paid a salary for work done (over however many hours it takes) would have a good argument for breach of contract if the employer reduced that salary (simply because of a new maximum on hours) without his or her consent. One possible complication could arise if most workers agreed to keep existing hours (and pay) but a particular individual refused to agree and insisted on the forty-eight-hour maximum, suffering a pay cut in consequence – could he or she claim that this constituted a 'detriment' (for not entering an agreement) which is outlawed by the Regulations[197]? The original Guidance suggested that a purely pro rata wage reduction because of reduced working time should not be considered a 'detriment' but that any 'excessive' wage reduction might be[198].

---

193 Reg 4(3); a relevant agreement can lay down *which* 17-week periods are to be used; failing that, the average must be met over '*any* period of 17 weeks in the course of his employment', which could be less advantageous for an employer with predictable variations in hours required.

194 Reg 23(b).

195 Reg 5(1).

196 Reg 4(2), as amended.

197 Reg 31, adding the Employment Rights Act 1996 s 45A. This could raise complicated issues such as those arising in the context of detriment on union membership grounds in *Associated Newspapers Ltd v Wilson; Associated British Ports v Palmer* [1995] ICR 406, [1995] IRLR 258, HL; see p 571 below. Would it be viewed as a 'detriment' by way of a pay cut, or just a natural inability to continue paying the higher wages of those agreeing to the longer hours?

198 Para 1.4.

(e) Limits on night working

A night worker's normal hours of work in any reference period are not to exceed an average of eight hours in each twenty-four hours[199]. A 'night worker' is defined as a worker who normally works at least three hours of his daily working time during night time, or such proportion of his annual working time as may be specified in a collective agreement or workforce agreement[200]. As with maximum weekly hours, the averaging process is vital, and the reference period is seventeen weeks; a relevant agreement can set out *which* succeeding 17-week periods are to be used, but in default it means *any* seventeen weeks (ie a rolling period)[201]. There is, however, an exception to the averaging process where the night work involves 'special hazards or heavy physical or mental strain', in which case the limit is eight hours in *any* twenty-four-hour period in which night work is done[202]. On the question of night work, much is left to be determined by agreement, and this goes beyond matters of definition because ultimately it is possible for the rules themselves to be modified or excluded completely by a collective agreement or workforce agreement[203], a particularly striking example of collective protection being thought sufficient.

Arguably, the night working provisions are most closely related to the health and safety provenance of the Regulations, and the Directive itself makes clear in its preamble the assumption on which this is based, one of the recitals being:

'Whereas research has shown that the human body is more sensitive at night to environmental disturbances and also to certain burdensome forms of work organisation and that long periods of night work can be detrimental to the health of workers and can endanger safety at the workplace.'

In the light of this, two further obligations are laid on employers of night workers, going beyond the regulation of hours. The first is that no adult worker is to be assigned to night work without at least an opportunity for a free health assessment (unless there is an existing such assessment still in operation), and each night worker must then have the opportunity of further assessments at regular intervals

---

199 Reg 6(1).
200 Reg 2(1). The original Guidance, para. 3.1.3 suggested that employers and workers may wish to clarify what constitutes 'normal' working in a collective or workforce agreement too. 'Night time' means a period set out in a relevant agreement, lasting at least seven hours and including the period between midnight and 5am; in default of agreement, it means 11pm to 6am: reg 2(1). An employer could use this to push back the definition so that workers working late (eg up to 2am in a bar or night club) do *not* work the three hours in the period necessary to be a night worker.
201 Reg 6(3). The formula for the average is set out in reg 6(5).
202 Reg 6(7); the actual circumstances in which this applies are left to be determined by a collective agreement or workforce agreement, or in a risk assessment required by the Management of Health and Safety at Work Regulations 1992, SI 1992/2051. If neither of these avenues is used, there could be a health and safety breach by the employer, though the Regulations do not say so specifically.
203 Reg 23(a). This is subject to the requirement of compensatory rest under reg 24 (below), though on its wording (applying where 'a worker is ... required ... to work during a period which would otherwise be a rest period or rest break') it is more difficult to apply to night working than to the rules on rest breaks.

appropriate to his case[204]. A young worker must have the opportunity of such assessments (as to health *and capacity*) whenever assigned to work during the period from 10pm to 6am[205]. Secondly, the employer must transfer a night worker on to non-night work if a registered medical practitioner advises that he is suffering health problems related to night working and it is possible to transfer the worker to suitable work not at night[206]. Significantly, there are no permissible derogations to these duties.

(f) Rest periods

An adult worker is entitled to the following rest periods:
(i)   a daily rest period of not less than eleven hours in each twenty-four hours work period[207];
(ii) a weekly rest period of not less than twenty-four hours in each seven day work period[208];
(iii) a rest break of at least twenty minutes (subject to any longer time agreed in a collective agreement or workforce agreement) where daily working time is more than six hours[209].

In the case of young workers, these entitlements are increased to twelve hours daily rest, forty-eight hours weekly rest and a rest break of at least thirty minutes after four and a half hours work[210].

As well as the normal derogations (including the ability to modify or exclude entirely all the adult entitlements by collective agreement or workforce agreement[211]), there are special provisions relating to daily and weekly rest periods in the case of shift workers being potentially in breach when changing shifts and, more generally, in the case of 'workers engaged in activities involving periods of work split up over the day, as may be the case for cleaning staff.'[212]

---

204 Reg 7(1). This rather stark paragraph was considerably fleshed out by paras 4.1.2 and 4.1.3 of the original Guidance which suggest that (i) while very few people will be unfit to work at night at all, there could be problems with diabetes, heart/circulatory disorders, stomach/intestinal disorders, sleep conditions, chest disorders and others requiring regular medication; (ii) the health assessment (undefined) could start with a screening questionnaire carried out by the employer, with professional opinion being involved in the interpreting of the questionnaire and any necessary follow-up action; (iii) while the Regulations are silent on how regularly to re-assess, a rule of thumb might be to administer the questionnaire annually.

205 Reg 7(2); this does not apply where the work is 'of an exceptional nature' (undefined): reg 7(4). As stated above, the emphasis (since the amendment in 2002) is on the young worker normally not working nights at all.

206 Reg 7(6). If the health problems constituted a 'disability' within the Disability Discrimination Act 1995, this might be required in any event as a reasonable adjustment.

207 Reg 10(1).

208 Reg 11(1). The employer may vary this to two 24-hour rests or one 48-hour rest in a 14-day period: reg 11(2). The relevant seven-day period is to be laid down in a relevant agreement, or, in default of that, is to be a week beginning with Monday: reg 11(6). The weekly rest period is not to include any daily rest period, 'except where this is justified by objective or technical reasons or reasons concerning the organisation of work': reg 11(7).

209 Reg 12(1)–(3). Whether such rest breaks are to be with pay is a matter of contract, as the Regulations are silent on the matter.

210 Regs 10(2), 11(3), 12(4); the derogations applying to adult workers' rest periods do not apply to young workers, but there is a *force majeur* exception applying to them in reg 27 (unforeseen or exceptional circumstances) in relation to daily rest and rest breaks.

211 Reg 23(a).

212 Reg 22.

(g) Compensatory rest

Although the derogations are of great importance to the overall scheme of the Regulations, there is one complication to some of them that could cause considerable difficulty in practice. This is that it is stated that where the application of any provision is excluded by regulation 21 ('other special cases') or 22 ('shift workers'), or is modified or excluded by a collective agreement or workforce agreement under regulation 23(a) and a worker is accordingly required by his employer to work during a period which would otherwise be a rest period or rest break, the employer must wherever possible allow him to take an *equivalent period of compensatory rest*[213]. The original Guidance stated that an equivalent period of rest should be considered to be a period as long as that the worker was entitled to but not able to take, and that it should be provided within a reasonable time from when the entitlement to rest was modified (in the case of daily rest, this being within a couple of weeks; in the case of weekly rest, within a couple of months)[214]. This may help where there are regular fluctuations of work on a short cycle (so that rest breaks can be disapplied at the busy peaks and compensatory rest given during the slack periods) but this may not be possible where rest breaks are disapplied because of a sustained *season* of heavy work possibly lasting for several months (as may be envisaged, for example, in several of the 'special cases' set out in regulation 21, for example a 'foreseeable surge of activity' in agriculture or tourism). In such cases there will be important questions of interpretation as to the meaning of 'wherever possible' and whether compensatory rest is legally acceptable if it only comes at the end of an extended season of consistent work.

(h) Annual leave

Along with the forty-eight-hour maximum working week, the aspect of the Regulations to which most publicity was given on their introduction was the entitlement to a statutory minimum period of paid leave in each leave year, set initially at three weeks (utilising a derogation in the Directive), but rising to four weeks as from November 1999[215]. The leave year is primarily left to be determined by a relevant agreement; in default of that, the general rule is that it runs from the date of commencement of employment[216], but of course that could be inconvenient for an employer who will normally wish to stipulate a standardised holiday year for all employees.

---

213 Reg 24(a). In exceptional cases where this is not possible for objective reasons, the employer must 'afford such protection as may be appropriate in order to safeguard the worker's health and safety': reg 24(b); the original Guidance para. 6.2.4 stated that such cases will be rare and that this flexibility is not to be used on a routine basis. This raises a question of interpretation – are reg 24(a) and (b) exhaustive, ie can (a) only be disapplied if (b) applies? *Or* can there be middle ground where it is not possible to give compensatory rest but for reasons which do not activate the requirements of (b)?

214 Para 5.25.

215 Reg 13. The worker is entitled to be paid a 'week's pay' for each week of leave, which is to be worked out by applying the Employment Rights Act 1996, ss 221–224 (see p 232 above): reg 16. Contractual remuneration is offset against the statutory amount, and vice versa. Reg 15 covers the case of a worker leaving part of the way through the holiday year.

216 Reg 13. Where an employee joins part of the way through a leave year, he or she is entitled to a holiday period on a pro rata basis: reg 13(5).

Given the existing contractual entitlements of most full-time employees[217], it may seem that this new entitlement was hardly revolutionary, even after November 1999, but the provisions may bite in two particular ways:

(i) This entitlement applies simply to 'workers', which may include certain casual or temporary workers previously without holiday rights by contract. At first the government tried to minimise this effect by providing, in effect, a thirteen-week qualifying period for a new employee before having the statutory holiday right but there was no authority for this in the Directive; it was successfully challenged in the ECJ by a union representing many workers in broadcasting who were adversely affected because kept on separate short-term contracts (often not individually going beyond the thirteen weeks)[218] and the government had to amend the Regulations in 2001 to remove the qualifying period and provide instead that entitltement accures on a monthly basis in the first year of employment[219].

(ii) It is specifically provided that the statutory holiday period must be actually *taken*, in the sense that it may not (in whole or, particularly, in part) be either carried forward into the next holiday year or bought out by a payment in lieu (except on termination of employment)[220]. This is of course in line with the health and safety provenance of the Regulations (ie that people should actually have the holiday period to rest, in spite of some evidence that holidays with the family can in some cases rate on the stress scale as highly as moving house, public speaking or Christmas!). It could, however, have an effect (especially with the full four-week minimum entitlement) in industries such as agriculture with a tradition of buying out holiday entitlements.

In cases where neither of these points arise, the initial temptation for employers was to think that, if they complied with the prescribed length of annual holidays by contract (four weeks or more), they could simply carry on as before. However, the case law to date has shown this to be a dangerous assumption. Ordinary contractual rules continue to apply to any entitlement above the statutory (for example the fifth week where the contract provides for five weeks a year) *but* in relation to the first four weeks the statutory rules must always be complied with; if necessary they will override any inconsistent contractual rules and, given that they are novel and not linked into existing laws, applying them literally can produce strange (if legally logical) results. One of the earliest cases, *Witley and District Men's Club v Mackay*[221], concerned the interaction of holiday pay and

217 In summer 1998, 85% of permanent full-time staff already had 20 or more working days holiday per annum: Hours and Holidays 1998 (IDS Study No 657).

218 *R v Secretary of State for Trade and Industry, ex p BECTU* C-173/99 [2001] ICR 1152, [2001] IRLR 559, ECJ.

219 Working Time (Amendment) Regulations 2001, SI 2001/3256, amending reg 13 and adding a new reg 15A containing the accrual system. Of course, those on genuinely short-term contracts will not normally want to take holidays, so the key change is that they will be due for accrued holiday *pay* at the end of the hiring.

220 Reg 13(9). Subject to a relevant agreement, the general rules on the timing of holidays are that a worker may give notice of intention to take a certain period, of a length twice as long as the time to be taken off; equally, an employer may require a worker to take a particular period by similar notice, or may notify the worker of time that is not to be taken as holiday by notice of a length equal to that to be taken off: reg 15. This gives the employer considerable ability to time holidays, either to bunch them (eg for annual shutdowns) or to spread them among employees to ensure continuity of production. Moreover, there is no magic to public or bank holidays, which are treated as any other day and so, where given, can count towards the statutory minimum.

221 [2001] IRLR 595.

summary dismissal. When the employee was dismissed summarily for fraud the employers refused payment of accrued holiday pay, as was specifically allowed under the collective agreement incorporated into his contract. Regulation 14 governs the payment of accrued pay when a worker leaves part of the way through the holiday year (normally giving them a right to pro rata payment in lieu of holiday) and allows a relevant agreement to fix 'such sum' as is to be payable. That seemed to cover this case but did not. The EAT held (regretfully) that on a plain wording interpretation 'such sum' could not cover 'no sum'. Thus, the collective agreement term expressly covering this eventuality was unlawful under the Regulations and the employee was entitled to the pro-rata entitlement in the regulation, even though dismissed for gross misconduct[222], These termination provisions also arose in *Hill v Chapell*[223] but in reverse – what is to happen when the worker has taken *more* than his pro rata entitlement when leaving in the course of the holiday year? Previously, the general law would allow the employer to recoup holiday pay in respect of those unearned days, for example from moneys outstanding to the worker. That was done in this case but the worker successfully sued for it back – regulation 14(4) states that a relevant agreement 'may' provide for recovery by the employer and this was held by the EAT to be exhaustive, ie the employer can *only* recover overpaid holiday pay if there is a relevant agreement (usually meaning an express term in a written contract) to that effect.

Turning to the form of payment, one device historically used by employers, particularly in cases of sporadic employment where there may be administrative difficulties in working out exact holiday entitlements, was to 'roll up' holiday pay into an enhanced basic pay rate. In *Gridquest Ltd v Blackburn*[224] the employers did this but without telling the workers who, when asking for their holiday pay, were told that they had already had it through their weekly wages. Economically, this was true but the Court of Appeal held that the practice was ineffective if not contained in a contractual power to do it – regulation 16(5) allows set off of contractual holiday pay, so non-contractual amounts were not within the Regulations. The workers could have the amount twice[225]. What if the workers do know their entitlement but do not take it? As already seen, a rather nebulous duty seems to be cast on the to the employer to ensure that the statutory four weeks are actually taken, and one side effect of this was seen in *List Design Group Ltd v Douglas*[226] where the worker had not asked for his full entitlement; not surprisingly, the employer only paid for the holidays taken but the worker was held entitled to receive payment for the full statutory period (thus introducing the novel concept of a year for payment purposes being anything up to fifty-

---

222 Perhaps the oddest part of this is that if the agreement had provided for the dismissed worker to receive £1, 1p or a peppercorn that would have been 'such sum' and so lawful.
223 [2003] IRLR 19.
224 [2002] EWCA Civ 1037, [2002] ICR 1206, [2002] IRLR 604.
225 Technically, the court did not decide if rolling up *would* be lawful if there *were* a contractual provision to that effect. In *MPB Structures Ltd v Munro* [2002] IRLR 601 the Scottish EAT had gone further and held that rolling up is always unlawful, on the policy ground that holidays are meant to be taken and that lower paid workers are less likely to do so if they have no lump-sum holiday pay at the time. In *Gridquest* the court declined to decide this point, though they did point out that reg 16(5) had not been considered in *MPB*, and it is suggested that the overall logic of their decision strongly suggests that a contractual provision allowing it would be effective. However, on further appeal in *MPB Structures* the Inner House of the Court of Session upheld the EAT's decision on policy grounds that rolling up is always unlawful ([2003] IRLR 350). There is thus a disagreement on a point of law between the English and Scottish courts on this point.
226 [2002] ICR 686, [2003] IRLR 14.

sixweeks!). However, the prize for the strangest decision to date must go to *Kigass Aero Components Ltd v Brown*[227] where it was held that workers off work with long-term sickness still qualify for paid holidays even though physically unable to take them and not having any work to take a holiday *from*. As always, the logic was impeccable (the term 'worker' only requires the person to be under a contract which qualifies, it does *not* require the person actually to perform any work) but the result is strange, particularly as the health and safety aim behind this part of the Regulations is to have holidays taken to avoid the worker becoming ill! The reasoning in the case would apply even if the worker was absent for the whole holiday year (this possibly having the boomerang effect of giving an incentive to the employer to dismiss the long-term sick worker earlier than he would normally have done) and by analogy could apply to an employee on maternity leave, especially as it went up to a whole year in 2003 (though here the common sense answer of dismissing the employee instead would only be adopted by an employer with a death wish). The point is clearly seen from these cases that these holiday provisions operate on their own terms and independently of existing contractual provisions (or even other areas of statutory employment law such as maternity) in relation to the first four weeks of holiday entitlement per year.

(i) Pattern of work – the loose end

The Working Time Directive, Article 13 contains the rather Delphic provision that member states are to take the measures necessary to:

> 'ensure that an employer who intends to organise work according to a certain pattern takes account of the general principle of adapting work to the worker, with a view, in particular, to alleviating monotonous work and work at a predetermined work-rate, depending on the type of activity, and of safety and health requirements, especially as regards breaks during working time.'

This is potentially a wide provision, arguably in line with the modern emphasis on the working *environment* generally. When, however, the government consulted on implementing the Directive they said that they thought the intention of Article 13 was 'unclear'[228] and that it appeared to replicate Article 6(2)(d) of the Health and Safety Framework Directive[229]. In the result, the only attempt at transposition in the Working Time Regulations is in regulation 8, which picks up only on the specific point of rest breaks:

---

227 [2002] ICR 697, [2002] IRLR 312. The decision in this case could be particularly useful for the long-term sick employee who has exhausted SSP and contractual sick pay, as it gives an entitlement to a further four weeks pay while ill; *quaere* whether any provision inserted into the contract to prevent this situation would be void under reg 35 (no contracting out of the protection of the Regulations). Note that in *Kigass* in one of the three consolidated appeals the employer had paid the sick worker five days' holiday pay as specifically provided for in such circumstances by the governing collective agreement; as in *Witley and District Men's Club v Mackay* (n 221 above) this provision was overruled by the Regulations.

228 URN 98/645, para 117.

229 Directive 89/391/EEC, see p 889 below. Note, however, that originally Art 6(2) was not specifically transposed in the enacting Management of Health and Safety at Work Regulations 1992, being left instead to be covered by the much more general (existing) provisions of the Health and Safety at Work etc Act 1974. Interestingly, it *was* specifically transposed when the Management Regulations were reissued in 1999 (SI 1999/3242, reg 4, Sch 1).

'Where the pattern according to which an employer organizes work is such as to put the health and safety of a worker employed by him at risk, in particular because the work is monotonous or the work rate is predetermined, the employer shall ensure that the worker is given adequate rest breaks.[230]'

This falls well short of any general obligation to fit the work to the worker; unless it can be argued that Article 13 is transposed in some other way (expressly or impliedly), it could be argued that there has been a failure to transpose, which might be relevant in independent proceedings (eg a civil action for damages for occupational stress), though there may be less scope for this now that it has been held that the Directive (or at least parts of it) does not have direct effect[231].

(j) Enforcement

The way in which the Regulations effectively straddle employment law and health and safety law is particularly noticeable in the area of enforcement. The so-called 'limitations' relating to the forty-eight-hour maximum working week, night working and patterns of work are enforceable under the health and safety system, with primary responsibility on the Health and Safety Executive[232]. Thus, the principal obligations in these areas are that the employer must 'take all *reasonable* steps' to ensure that the weekly maximum and the night working limit are observed. There is an obligation on employers to maintain records adequate to show compliance, and to keep them for two years[233].

On the other hand, the 'entitlements' to rest breaks and paid annual leave are enforceable by complaint by an individual worker to an employment tribunal which may make a declaration, award compensation (not subject to a maximum amount) and, where the complaint is of failure to pay holiday pay, order the employer to pay the amount due[234]. In spite of this specific provision, the EAT held in *List Design Group Ltd v Douglas*[234a] that the worker retains the option to recover unpaid holiday pay under Part II of the Employment Rights Act 1966 (unlawful deduction from wages) which may be important if there is some tactical advantage in doing so (in particular if, as in this case, the time limitation under Part II is more generous). The individual worker is not given a statutory right to complain of breach of the maximum working week or night work (or pattern of work) provisions, but it is possible that breach of these obligations could be used *indirectly* by an individual in three ways – first, it could be used as evidence of unreasonable conduct by the employer in another form of claim, such as for

230 The original Guidance, para 6.1.3 merely stated that this may mean *regular* rest breaks.
231 *Gibson v East Riding of Yorkshire Council* [2000] IRLR 598, CA.
232 Reg 28. It is an offence to fail to comply, carrying a fine on either summary conviction or conviction on indictment: reg 29. The HSE (or local authority where that is the enforcing authority) must make adequate arrangements for enforcement (reg 28(2)), but when the Regulations came into force the HSE made clear that they lacked the resources for proactive enforcement by inspector; it may be that enforcement turns out to be reactive, ie following on accidents or other notified events.
233 Reg 9.
234 Reg 30. The time limit is the usual three-month period, subject to the 'not reasonably practicable' power to extend: reg 30(2). Complaint must be that the employer has 'refused' to permit the worker to exercise the right in question, not just that he has 'failed' to do so. This could be an important distinction, eg where the employer has *offered* to comply with the Regulations but the workforce have not wanted this because of the possible effect on pay – where is the employer 'refusal'?
234a [2002] ICR 686, [2003] IRLR 14.

constructive dismissal or in a personal injury action (for example for stress-related illness); secondly, it is possible that the Regulations could be held to support civil liability, so that in a case of non-compliance causing definable harm to the worker he or she could sue the employer for breach of statutory duty[235]; thirdly, in a highly purposive judgment in *Barber v RJB Mining (UK) Ltd*[236] Gage J held that it is an implied term of the contract of employment that the employer will comply with the maximum working week requirement, so that if an employee is made to work past the forty-eight-hour average (without agreeing to do so) by an employer who assumes that this can 'only' be challenged by health and safety procedures, that employee may have a breach of contract action, or may even (according to the judge) calculate when he has done sufficient hours in that reference period to average forty-eight per week and then *stop* until the beginning of the next reference period. Thus, there are several possibilities here that do not appear on the face of the Regulations.

Any provision in an agreement (whether or not a contract of employment) is void if it purports to exclude or limit the application of the Regulations or to preclude a person from bringing proceedings before an employment tribunal (subject to the usual exceptions for ACAS-conciliated (COT 3) settlements and compromise agreements)[237].

In line with most other recent protective legislation, it is provided that any dismissal because of refusal to comply with a breach of the Regulations, to forego a right or to sign a workforce agreement, or because of being or seeking to be a worker representative, is automatically unfair[238]; likewise, a worker has a right not to suffer a detriment (short of dismissal) for similar reasons[239].

(k) Effects and future

The general impression to date has been that the Working Time Regulations have had little effect in practice. The only notable litigation has been over the holiday entitlement and even there it has been primarily about holiday pay. As far as the pursuit of the wider social goals of limiting working hours and patterns are concerned, little change can be discovered and indeed surveys quoted in the media have tended to suggest that, if anything, working hours on average have tended to go *up* since the Regulations came into force. Health and safety enforcement has not happened. Some of this will no doubt be due to the Regulations simply being ignored. However, it is also the case that the exceptionally wide derogations and exceptions make the Regulations easy to avoid lawfully; the opting out of the maximum working week by simple written

---

235 This possibility was expressly envisaged in the government's consultation document URN 98/645 para 184. Such liability would not be automatic under the Health and Safety at Work etc. Act 1974, s 47(2) because the Regulations were passed under the European Communities Act 1972, not under the 1974 Act; it would therefore be necessary to prove Parliamentary intent that they should support civil liability in the usual way. Given this possibility, an employer might be advised to keep records for at least *three* years (the limitation period in personal injury actions) not just the statutory two years.

236 [1999] ICR 679, [1999] IRLR 308.

237 Reg 35.

238 Reg 32, adding the Employment Rights Act 1996, s 101A. Asserting a right under the Regulations is protected by s 104 of the Act.

239 Reg 31, adding the Employment Rights Act 1996, s 45A.

agreement is the most obvious example. Is this likely to change? It must be remembered that the negotiation of the directive by the previous UK government caused some annoyance among our EU partners, in particular in relation to the inclusions of the wide derogations which have made the UK Regulations so weak. There have already been moves to restrict the major exceptions, with agreement reached to bring seafaring and the transport industry at least partly within the Directive and to start progressive coverage of trainee doctors (down initially to fifty-eight hours a week and only to forty-eight hours by 2012). However, the most interesting aspect politically here is that the Directive states that the major derogations are to be reviewed by November 2003. Will our partners press for adoption of the pure form of the original Directive, without most or even all of the derogations? What would be the reaction of the UK government, given the serious effects for the UK economy of a Directive that actually meant what it said? Putting it colloquially, is it to be pay-back time for perfidious Albion?

7 PROTECTION OF WAGES

(i) The repeal of the Truck Acts and the effect on cashless pay

One of the longest standing pieces of social legislation in English law was the Truck Acts 1831–1940, designed and basically put into place early in the nineteenth century to protect the employee in his free enjoyment of his earnings[240]. They served two distinct purposes:

(a) the original Act of 1831 gave a legal right to payment in 'current coin of the realm', designed to prevent abuse of the then prevalent 'tommy shop' system whereby an employer might pay at least part of the employee's wages in tokens to be spent at the employer's own shop[241];

(b) the later legislation (particularly the Truck Act 1896) then placed restrictions on the making of deductions from wages, principally in respect of the provisions of goods and services by the employer, fines or bad workmanship; these were of great complexity, but in essence they usually provided that the deduction had to be authorised in writing and be fair and reasonable in the circumstances.

The principal limitation of the legislation was that it only applied to *manual* workers[242] (with certain limited extensions to shop assistants). Persons not covered were therefore left to their contractual rights on both payment methods and deductions[243]. It was recognised for years that the legislation was in need of, at the least, revision, and indeed the last major case on it showed just how

---

240 For the details of this legislation, see the third edition of this book, at pp. 389–394. The archaic meaning of 'truck' was to exchange or barter; one of the few current usages is the phrase 'to have no truck' with something, in the sense of not wishing to have any dealings with it. The word 'truck' was not actually used in the wording of the legislation.

241 Such a system was not necessarily vicious, since the employer might have the benefit of discount buying, but obviously it was open to abuse.

242 This distinction caused great difficulties and a considerable amount of old case law; for a modern example of the problem, see *Brooker v Charrington Fuel Oils Ltd* [1981] IRLR 147, Co Ct.

243 On deduction, however, there was at least the statutory right to have deductions notified, as part of the statutory itemised pay statement under the Employment Rights Act 1996, s 8.

unpredictable and unreliable its coverage was[244]. However, the previous government became interested in the area not because of anything concerning deductions, but rather because of the first of the above two effects, that of the right to payment in cash. Britain had long lagged behind other western countries in the move towards cashless pay (ie pay by cheque or credit transfer)[245]. It is true that the strict requirement in the 1831 Act of current coin of the realm had been qualified by the Payment of Wages Act 1960 which permitted cashless pay with the employee's written agreement, but the problem was that that agreement could always be revoked by written notice and so a manual worker could re-invoke his rights under the Truck Act. Banks have of course been interested in extending cashless pay, and sometimes they and employers have offered cash incentives to go over to it; the problem with the 1960 Act was that any such agreement was *not* irrevocable. The government therefore decided to deregulate this area by the repeal of the Truck Acts and the Payment of Wages Act 1960. However, to do so simpliciter would also remove all protection with regard to deductions and eventually this was thought to be too sweeping, particularly in the light of media coverage of certain cases of highly inequitable deduction clauses in employment contracts, particularly in certain areas of retailing[246]. The compromise was contained in Part I of the Wages Act 1986 which repealed the Truck legislation (and other related statutes)[247] but also enacted entirely new provisions giving at least partial protection in relation to deductions; the principal feature in favour of this scheme is that it applies to *all* employees, not just to manual workers; one criticism of it, however, is that (with the exception of certain extra protection for retail workers, considered below) the new provisions largely relate to the *mechanics* of making deductions (the principal requirement normally being the employee's written consent), rather than any concept of the substantive *fairness* or otherwise of the deductions – in this sense, they are not as interventionist as the old Truck Act provisions, and the question of the reason for the deduction in question is left largely as a matter of contract.

As seen above, however, the matter of deductions was (if not an afterthought) at least a subsidiary matter in the eyes of the government. The principal point was the removal of blockages to cashless pay, and this has been achieved. The repeal of the Truck Acts means that there is now no freestanding legal right to payment

---

244 In *Bristow v City Petroleum Ltd* [1988] ICR 165, [1987] IRLR 340 the House of Lords finally held that a deduction from a shop worker's wages in respect of a stock or till deficiency could be a 'fine' within the Truck Act 1896, s 1, thereby resolving a conflict of opinion between different Divisional Courts on the issue. This final decision came too late to affect the decision to repeal the legislation.

245 In the early 1980s it was estimated that 50% of all workers in Britain and 78% of manual workers were still paid in cash. This compared with 20% of all workers in Holland and Sweden, 10% in France, 5% in West Germany and Canada and 1% in the USA. Approximately 400,000 workers in Britain were changing to cashless pay each year, but this was considered slow progress.

246 One area much in the news at the time was petrol stations, where contracts of employment often included a term requiring the attendant to refund out of his wages any stock or till deficiencies arising during his shift *whether through his default or not*, thus covering the motorist who deliberately drove off without payment. In *Bristow v City Petroleum Ltd*, n 244 above, the deductions had averaged 17% of net pay over a period of five weeks but there was anecdotal evidence of far greater deductions in some cases, even to the extent of leaving little pay left after the deductions. See Goriely 'Arbitrary deductions from pay and the proposed repeal of the Truck Acts' (1983) 12 ILJ 236.

247 The Payment of Wages Act 1960; the Shop Clubs Act 1902; the Payment of Wages in Public-houses Prohibition Act 1883; the Checkweighing in Various Industries Act 1919; and various older statutes concerning coal-mines.

in cash and so an employer taking on a new employee (manual or otherwise) may lawfully make it a term of the contract that payment will be by cheque or credit transfer. However, it is important to note that the Wages Act did *not* give an employer a right to insist unilaterally on existing employees who were paid in cash changing to cashless pay. If there is a contractual term (express or implied from past conduct) for payment in cash, that may still only be varied by agreement[248]. The important point for the employer in such a case, however, is that if the employee does so agree that will be final since there is now no right to revert to cash.

The Wages Act 1986 was repealed by the Employment Rights Act 1996, and the provisions relating to deductions are now contained in Part II (sections 13–27) of that Act; in employment lawyers' jargon, however, there remains a tendency to refer to an action before a tribunal to recover an unlawful deduction from wages as 'a Wages Act claim'.

(ii) Deductions from wages

Section 13 provides that an employer shall not make deductions from the wages of a worker employed by him unless the deduction is (i) required or authorised by statute (for example PAYE, NI contributions or an attachment of earnings order), (ii) required or authorised by a provision in the contract of employment which has either been given to him or notified to him previously in writing, or (iii) agreed to by the employee in writing prior to the making of the deduction[249].

(a) Application

From such humble beginnings, these provisions became subject to quite remarkable development, for one procedural reason which had little to do with their origins. Until 1994, we were afflicted with a split jurisdiction, so that in the past employment tribunals could not deal with common law matters such as non-payment of wages, which had to go to the ordinary courts (doubly annoying if, for example, the ex-employee was already bringing a tribunal action for unfair dismissal). However, a way round this was discovered – if an employee was complaining about a refusal to pay wages, holiday entitlements etc, could that be *called* a 'deduction'? If so, the employee could (on the assumption that there was no prior written consent) complain to a tribunal under the Wages Act for its 'recovery'. This reasoning has been largely successful, as can be seen from the

---

248 One difficult point would arise if an employer managed to negotiate a change to cashless pay with all but one or two of a large staff; would it be fair to dismiss them on the grounds of business need after taking all reasonable steps to persuade them to change? On dismissals and business need, see p 599 below.

249 S 15 has equivalent provisions concerning the making of payments by workers to employers, instead of operating by way of deduction. 'Worker' is defined widely in s 230(3), as covering not only a person under a contract of service or apprenticeship, but also under a contract to do or perform personally work or services for another party (other than in a professional–client relationship). The requirement of *prior* written agreement means prior to the event causing the deduction, not just to the deduction itself: *Discount Tobacco and Confectionery Ltd v Williamson* [1993] ICR 371, [1993] IRLR 327; *York City and District Travel Ltd v Smith* [1990] ICR 344, [1990] IRLR 213. To be relied on, a contractual provision must be notified to the employee individually, not just by a factory notice: *Kerr v Sweater Shop (Scotland) Ltd* [1996] IRLR 424.

very high number of 'Wages Act cases' brought in recent years[250]; it operated as a de facto transfer of certain common law, contractual claims to tribunals. It had been hoped that when an order was finally made by the government giving common law jurisdiction to tribunals, this would be in general terms, and would end the need to extend what is now Part II of the 1996 Act to perform a function it was probably not intended for. However, this simple hope has not come about, for two reasons – (1) the order[251] in fact only gives common law jurisdiction to tribunals in cases arising on or out of *termination* of employment, and so challenges to non-payment or under-payment of wages or other benefits *during* employment can still only be brought before a tribunal by squeezing them under Part II; (2) even on termination, it may still be tactically advantageous to the ex-employee to claim amounts not paid under Part II rather than directly under the order, since the latter is subject not only to a monetary limit (set relatively highly at £25,000) but also, and far more importantly, to an express power of counterclaim by the employer which can be avoided by claiming under Part II (leaving the employer to pursue any claim he may think he has through the ordinary courts, which in practice is highly unlikely to happen). Thus, claims under Part II are likely to continue at their present high level, and the reported cases show that such an action can be used as a relatively quick and certainly effective way of challenging an attempt by an employer to force through a unilateral variation of contractual terms[252].

As a matter of law, this development raised two questions of interpretation of the Act – what is a 'deduction' and what are 'wages'? On the first question, section 13(3) gives a broad definition[253] and certain cases have shown an equally broad approach, so that for example there can still be a deduction even if it is so large that it actually extinguishes the wage payment altogether[254], and the phasing out of a special bonus from a payment system was held to qualify as a deduction[255]. However, the crucial question was whether simple non-payment would qualify – on a straightforward application of section 13 it would, but it could also be argued as a matter of English that non-payment was different in kind from a deduction from wages paid. On the second question, section 27 gives a lengthy inclusive

250 In 2001/02 ACAS received 37,591 cases under Part II for individual concilation, of which 25,808 were settled or withdrawn. Taken together with the 28,804 cases under the Extension of Jurisdiction Orders (n 251 below), these cases comprised 38% of all tribunal applications referred to ACAS concilation: ACAS Annual Report 2001/02. Using the tribunals' system of counting applicants, not applications, the figure was 29%: ETS Annual Report 2001/02.
251 The Industrial Tribunals Extension of Jurisdiction (England and Wales) Order 1994, SI 1994/1623; the Scottish order is SI 1994/1624; see p 528 below. A further point of difference is that Part II applies to the wider category of 'worker' (including some self-employed) but the Extension Order only applies to 'employees' properly so called: *Robertson v Blackstone Franks Investment Management Ltd* [1998] IRLR 376, CA.
252 *Bruce v Wiggins Teape (Stationery) Ltd* [1994] IRLR 536 (withdrawal of shift bonus); *Morgan v West Glamorgan County Council* [1995] IRLR 68 (disciplinary salary cut in breach of contract); *Saavedra v Aceground Ltd* [1995] IRLR 198 (employer allocating part of waiters' tronc for tips to himself). In each case the employers' actions were held to be unlawful 'deductions'. See Miller (1995) 24 ILJ 162.
253 'Where the total amount of any wages that are paid on any occasion by an employer to any worker employed by him is less than the total amount of the wages that are properly payable by him to the worker on that occasion …'
254 *Alsop v Star Vehicle Contracts Ltd* [1990] ICR 378, [1990] IRLR 83.
255 *McCree v Tower Hamlets London Borough Council* [1992] ICR 99, [1992] IRLR 56.

and exclusive definition[256], although not specifically covering one of the most contentious areas, wages in lieu of notice on a dismissal; could such amounts, if kept by the employer, be recovered under the Act?

Both of these questions caused major disagreements between different divisions of the EAT, but the matter was largely settled by the decisions of the Court of Appeal and House of Lords in the leading case of *Delaney v Staples*[257]. The facts were refreshingly simple. The employee was dismissed, being owed £55.50 commission and holiday pay and £82 in lieu of notice. She claimed both of these amounts, not in the county court, but before a tribunal under the Wages Act. This neatly raised both of the above questions. The Court of Appeal held that the £55.50 could be recovered, because a simple non-payment such as this *does* qualify as a 'deduction', on a literal interpretation of section 13(3), and there was here no prior agreement. That point was not subject to further appeal and so remains governed by the Court of Appeal's decision. However, the matter of the £82 in lieu went on further appeal to the House of Lords and raised the second question – are payments in lieu of notice 'wages'? Here, the matter was resolved not primarily by the wording of the Act, but by a broader consideration of the nature of payments in lieu. Lord Browne-Wilkinson said that the essential characteristic of wages (at common law and under the Act) was as 'payments in respect of the rendering of services during the employment'. He then analysed 'wages in lieu' as covering four different possibilities[258]; in only one (where the employer formally gives the correct notice, pays during that period, but does not actually require the employee to work during it, for example in a 'garden leave' case) does the payment still constitute wages during employment, to which the Act could apply. In the case itself, the in lieu payment came into the much more common category of anticipatory *damages* for the employer's breach of contract in dismissing the employee instantly, without proper notice. It was therefore not 'wages' and so the non-payment could not be challenged before a tribunal. Thus, the end result is that non-payment of wages accrued during the employment can be subject to a statutory action under Part II before a tribunal, but in most cases non-payment of wages in lieu cannot be (though of course, as such a case by definition arises on termination, such amounts outstanding *can* now be claimed before a tribunal quite separately under the Transfer of Jurisdiction Order). One further class of case deserves mention. If it is the *employee* who is in breach of contract by leaving without giving his contractual notice, the employer may be very tempted to hang on to any final wages, holiday pay etc, still owing to that employee, as 'damages'. In the light of *Delaney's* reasoning and two earlier cases[259]

---

256 'Wages' means 'any sums payable to the worker by his employer in connection with his employment'; there are then six categories specifically included and five specifically excluded. The first included is 'any fee, bonus, commission, holiday pay or other emolument referable to his employment, whether payable under his contract or otherwise'. The last two words meant that the Act's procedure could be used to challenge non-payment of a *discretionary* or *ex gratia* payment, provided the making of such a payment was clearly anticipated: *Kent Management Services Ltd v Butterfield* [1992] ICR 272, [1992] IRLR 394. See also the recovery of commission by a self employed person in *Robertson v Blackstone Franks Investment Management Ltd* [1998] IRLR 376, CA. However, there must be a legal obligation of sorts to pay the amount in question: *New Century Cleaning Co Ltd v Church* [2000] IRLR 27, CA.

257 [1991] ICR 331, [1991] IRLR 112, CA; affd [1992] ICR 483, [1992] IRLR 191, HL. The previous EAT decisions now do not need to be considered.

258 These are set out at p 461 below, in the discussion of dismissal by notice.

259 *Pename Ltd v Paterson* [1989] ICR 12, [1989] IRLR 195; *Chiltern House Ltd v Chambers* [1990] IRLR 88.

this is likely to be unlawful in the absence of prior written consent. The moral is simple; if the employer wants a power to retain accrued wages in the event of the employee leaving in breach of his notice obligation (especially where the employer wants to be able to rely on that obligation, for example so as to have time to find a replacement) the employer should ensure that there is a clear written term to that effect in the employee's contract.

(b) Exceptions

Section 14 contains a series of exceptions[260] : thus the provisions of section 13 do not apply to deductions in respect of –
(a) overpayment of wages, or expenses;
(b) disciplinary proceedings held by virtue of any statutory provision;
(c) a statutory requirement to deduct from wages and pay over to a public authority;
(d) payments agreed to by the worker which are to be made over by the employer to a third party;
(e) a strike or other industrial action in which the worker took part; or
(f) the satisfaction of a court or tribunal order requiring the worker to pay something to the employer.

The primary point to notice about these exceptions is that they do *not* establish an independent, unilateral right for the employer to make such deductions; they only state that deductions made on these grounds do not infringe the procedural requirements of section 13. In any given case, the question of the overall legality of a deduction may well depend on the contractual or other common law propriety of making it at all. If there is no contractual authority to make the deduction, the employee can sue for it in the county court in the normal way. However, the question again arose whether an action could be brought instead in a tribunal. At first that seemed possible, for in *Home Office v Ayres*[261] it was held that the exclusions in section 14 only apply to deductions *lawfully* made on the above grounds; it was therefore open to the employee to argue that the deduction (a) was unlawful at common law[262], (b) was therefore not covered by the relevant exclusion in section 14, and (c) was therefore recoverable under the Act, in the absence of prior written consent. However, this reasoning was later repudiated by the EAT in *Sunderland Polytechnic v Evans*[263] where it was held, by exercising the courts' new power to consider *Hansard*[264] that Parliament's intention was that section 14 and its exceptions were to be applied literally, leaving any question of the contractual lawfulness of the deduction in question to be fought over in the ordinary courts[265].

---

260 There is also an exception in s 13(4) relating to errors of computation of wages, but this is to be construed narrowly: *Yemm v British Steel plc* [1994] IRLR 117; *Morgan v West Glamorgan County Council* [1995] IRLR 68.
261 [1992] ICR 175, [1992] IRLR 59.
262 The case itself concerned a deduction to recover an overpayment; the employers relied on s 14 but the employee argued that there was no common law right to recover the amount because he had spent it innocently. The employee succeeded in a tribunal action.
263 [1993] ICR 392, [1993] IRLR 196, applied in *SIP Industrial Products Ltd v Swinn* [1994] ICR 473, [1994] IRLR 323.
264 *Pepper v Hart* [1993] AC 593, [1993] 1 All ER 42, HL.
265 The case itself concerned a deduction for taking part in industrial action (s. 14(5)), where this policy consideration is perhaps particularly strong; however, the reasoning should apply to all the heads of s 14.

(c) Retail employment

Due to the discussions prior to the introduction of the 1986 Act and concerns expressed as to certain inequitable deductions made in certain service industries, sections 17–22 of the 1996 Act impose a further limitation on deductions from the wages of workers in retail employment[266]. Where such a deduction is made in respect of cash shortages or stock deficiencies, the maximum that may be deducted is 10% of the gross amount of wages for that particular pay day. While such an extra provision is to be welcomed, two further points should be noticed – (i) this limitation only applies to the *amount* deductible, not to the grounds for deduction, since there is still no requirement that those grounds be fair and reasonable[267]; (ii) there is nothing to stop the full amount of a contractually recoverable deficiency being carried forward over successive pay days until fully recovered, provided that only 10% is taken on each occasion and indeed section 22 states that the 10% rule does not apply to the final pay day if the employee's employment is terminated, when the whole of any outstanding deficiency could be set against the wages payable.

(d) Remedies

A complaint that deductions have been made (or payments demanded) in contravention of section 13 may be presented to an employment tribunal within three months of the date of the last deduction or payment, or if that is not reasonably practicable within such further period as the tribunal thinks reasonable[268]. If the tribunal finds the complaint well-founded, it is to make a declaration to that effect and order the repayment of amounts improperly deducted[269]. Four final points should be noted on these provisions. The first is that section 205(2) states that '[t]he remedy of a worker in respect of any contravention of [sections 13ff] shall be by way of a complaint under section 23 *and not otherwise*'. At first sight, that may appear to rule out a common law action for wages (the traditional remedy to recover improper deductions). However, that is not so since, as pointed out above, all that the Act does is to apply to deductions from wages certain (albeit important) procedural requirements, particularly as to prior written agreement to the making of such deductions. There may well still be cases where the employee is objecting not just to the procedure adopted (which may have complied with section 13), but rather to the legality of making a deduction at all in those circumstances. In such a case the employee retains the option of a common law action in the county court[270]. The second point is that there is a measure of overlap between these provisions and the right in section 11 of the 1996 Act to bring tribunal proceedings against an

---

266 'Retail employment' is defined in s 17(2), referring principally to the direct supply to the public or other individuals in a personal capacity of goods or services (including financial services).

267 It is therefore still lawful to incorporate a contractual term requiring the refunding of, for example, till deficiencies at a petrol station, even where those deficiencies are not the attendant's fault (as, for example, where caused by fraud by a customer).

268 S 23. For the case law on the 'reasonably practicable' escape clause in the context of an unfair dismissal action, see p 512 below.

269 Moreover, those amounts are *not* then to be treated as properly recoverable by further deductions (by whatever means) or by action in the ordinary courts, ie the employer loses the right to them altogether: s 25; *Potter v Hunt Contracts Ltd* [1992] ICR 337, [1992] IRLR 108.

270 *Rickard v PB Glass Supplies Ltd* [1990] ICR 150, CA.

employer for failing to give proper notification of deductions from wages in the statutory-required itemised pay statement[271]; section 26 provides that both actions can be brought, but that if that happens there is not to be double recovery of the deduction. The third point is that, in potentially an important extension of the tribunal's powers under the Act, the EAT have held that even if the employer does have prior written consent to make a deduction on a particular ground, the employee can argue that the *amount* deducted was excessive and not justified by the written consent; this permits the tribunal to consider whether that particular deduction was sustainable in fact[272]. The fourth point is that special protection is given to an employee making a complaint under Part II. One problem always was that, although such a complaint is not subject to any qualifying period and so may be brought by a new employee, if such an employee did not have the necessary qualifying period for unfair dismissal he could be dismissed because of the complaint without protection. Now, however, the Employment Rights Act 1996 provides that if an employee is dismissed for asserting certain statutory rights (which include those under Part II), not only is that dismissal automatically unfair, but (crucially) the normal qualifying period does not apply[273].

8 RIGHTS ON THE EMPLOYER'S INSOLVENCY

Where an employer becomes bankrupt or insolvent, the general rule is that wages or salary due to an employee in respect of the four months before the bankruptcy or insolvency are a preferential debt, subject to a maximum of £800[274]. Beyond that, they constitute an unsecured debt. The Employment Protection Act 1975 introduced new measures to improve the position of the employee of a bankrupt employer in two ways; they are now in the Insolvency Act 1986 and Part XII of the Employment Rights Act 1996. First the Insolvency Act 1986, Schedule 6 provides that certain other amounts are to be treated as wages and so preferential debts. These are amounts owed by the employer in respect of a guarantee payment, remuneration during suspension on medical grounds, payment for time off for union duties, to attend ante-natal care and to look for other work and remuneration under a protective award[275]. Secondly, the Employment Rights Act 1996, section 182 gives the employee rights to claim certain amounts due to him from his employer from the Secretary of State instead, who is to pay them out of the National Insurance Fund[276]. The amounts in question are those relating to arrears of pay (up to a maximum of eight weeks), wages during the statutory

---

271 S 8.
272 *Fairfield Ltd v Skinner* [1992] ICR 836, [1993] IRLR 4.
273 See p 597 below. These provisions were introduced by the Trade Union Reform and Employment Rights Act 1993.
274 Insolvency Act 1986, s 386, Sch 6, para 9; para 10 covers holiday pay. Where the employer goes into administration or receivership and the employee is kept on, there may be a continuing liability on the administrator or receiver for 'qualifying liabilities' (wages, holiday pay, sick pay and pension contributions) if his contract is adopted by the administrator or receiver, and only from the *date* of adoption: Insolvency Act 1994. This Act (amending the 1986 Act) was rushed through Parliament to negative the effects of the decisions of the Court of Appeal and then the House of Lords in *Powdrill v Watson* [1995] 2 AC 394, [1995] 2 All ER 65, HL.
275 Insolvency Act 1986, Sch 6, para 13.
276 The Secretary of State may also make redundancy payments directly out of the Fund where he is satisfied that the employer is insolvent; Employment Rights Act 1996, s 167.

minimum notice period[277], holiday pay (up to a maximum of six weeks), a basic award for unfair dismissal and a reasonable sum to reimburse all or part of any fee paid by an apprentice or articled clerk; further, 'pay' is deemed to include any outstanding amounts by way of guarantee payment, remuneration during suspension on medical grounds, payment for statutory time off work or remuneration under a protective award. Where any of these sums is to be computed by reference to weekly pay (for example arrears of wages) the maximum amount that can be used for computation purposes at the time of writing is £260[278]. The employee may also request the Secretary of State to make up any contributions to his occupational pension scheme left unpaid due to his employer's insolvency. Any further sums outstanding can still be claimed by the employee as unsecured debts.

Where the Secretary of State makes one of the above payments to the employee, the rights and remedies which the employee had in the employer's bankruptcy in respect of that amount become vested in the Secretary of State[279]. However, the employee may still be the ultimate beneficiary from this statutory scheme (apart from gaining from its administrative convenience for him) for the amount which he can claim from the Secretary of State may be greater than that which the Secretary of State can then claim as a preferential debt in the bankruptcy, for two reasons. First, the amount claimable from the Secretary of State may be greater than the £800 maximum preferred debt for wages and salaries; second, certain items in respect of which the employee can claim from the Secretary of State are still not deemed to be preferred debts (for example the amount of a basic award for unfair dismissal). In the case of any such amounts, the Secretary of State must

---

277 Laid down in the Employment Rights Act, s 86. If for any reason wages during the notice period would not have been payable by the employer, they are not payable by the Secretary of State under s 182; *Secretary of State for Employment v Wilson* [1978] ICR 200, [1977] IRLR 483; this imports the common law notion of mitigation of damage, so that if the ex-employee in fact earns money during what should have been his notice period, those earnings are deducted from the amount payable by the Secretary of State: *Secretary of State for Employment v Jobling* [1980] ICR 380. The major practical problem that arose was whether unemployment benefit received during what should have been the notice period should be deducted – application of the doctrine of mitigation would suggest that it should, but this would lead (in the case of an ex-employee becoming long-term unemployed) to the ex-employee's (then) one-year entitlement to unemployment benefit running out sooner than it would have done if he had received proper notice, without any recompense. After protracted litigation, the House of Lords finally held in *Westwood v Secretary of State for Employment* [1985] ICR 209, [1984] IRLR 209, HL, that the amount recoverable from the Secretary of State, though by a statutory right, represented damages for wrongful dismissal, so that the duty to mitigate applied, and this included deducting unemployment benefit (though they suggested a method of doing so that in fact recompensed the ex-employee). After this decision the position was altered to allow the employee to get the (net) s 182 payment, but then receive what would otherwise have been his full entitlement to unemployment benefit (now jobseekers allowance).

278 This figure was substituted as from February 2003 and is subject to annual review under the Employment Relations Act 1999, s 34. Applying the principle in *Westwood* (n 277 above), the amount to be paid by the Secretary of State is the amount of the employee's *net* loss, so that from gross wages owed there is to be deducted the amounts normally payable as tax and NI contributions, and any mitigating amounts such as benefit received and/or any amounts earned elsewhere during the period in question: *Secretary of State for Employment v Cooper* [1987] ICR 766. However, for the purpose of applying the statutory maximum for a week's pay, the Secretary of State is correct to apply that maximum to the *gross* loss, and only then deduct the above amounts: *Morris v Secretary of State for Employment* [1985] ICR 522, [1985] IRLR 297; heads, the Secretary of State wins, tails ...?

279 Employment Rights Act 1996, s 189.

pay them to the employee, claim as much as possible as a preferred debt and then claim the balance simply as an unsecured debt; it is thus the NI which bears the risk in such a case, not the individual employee.

Chapter 5

Discrimination in employment

1 INTRODUCTION[1]

The common law placed no restrictions on an employer's freedom to decide whether to hire a particular individual, an approach deeply rooted in *laissez-faire* philosophy and encapsulated in the following dictum of Lord Davey in *Allen v Flood*[2] :

> 'an employer may refuse to employ [an individual] for the most mistaken, capricious, malicious or morally reprehensible motives that can be conceived, but [that individual] has no right of action against him.'

Thus, a refusal to employ on grounds of sex, race, marital status, disability or on any other ground was not unlawful[3], still less did the courts reveal any concern to enforce equality in the terms of employment. Indeed, in *Roberts v Hopwood*[4], Lord Atkinson in the House of Lords castigated the Poplar Council's policy of providing equal pay to men and women performing the same work as motivated by 'misguided principles of socialistic philanthropy'. The merest hint of a willingness to intervene in cases of sex discrimination on grounds of public policy can perhaps be discerned in the decision of the Court of Appeal in *Nagle v Feilden*[5], where it was held that the Jockey Club's 'arbitrary and capricious' refusal to grant a licence to a woman trainer infringed her 'right to work'. However, the 'right to work' principle is at best of dubious authority, and it is highly unlikely that the

---

1 See generally McColgan *Discrimination Law: Text, Cases and Materials* (2000); Townshend-Smith *Discrimination Law: Text, Cases and Materials* (1998); Fredman *Discrimination Law* (2002); Fredman *Women and the Law* (1998); Donohue *Foundations of Employment Discrimination Law* (1997); McColgan *Just Wages for Women* (1997); Bourne and Whitmore *Anti-Discrimination Law in Britain* (1996); Dine and Watt (eds) *Discrimination Law: Concepts, Limitations and Justifications* (1996); McCrudden, Smith and Brown *Racial Justice at Work* (1991); O'Donovan and Szyszczak *Equality and Sex Discrimination Law* (1988).
2 [1898] AC 1 at 172.
3 See eg *Weinberger v Inglis (No 2)* [1919] AC 606, HL; *Bebb v Law Society* [1914] 1 Ch 286, CA; *Short v Poole Corpn* [1926] Ch 66, CA.
4 [1925] AC 578, HL.
5 [1966] 2 QB 633, [1966] 1 All ER 689, CA; see p 603 below.

courts would have been able (or indeed willing) to develop it into a broad principle capable of combating discrimination in employment generally.

Given the disinterest of the common law in tackling discrimination at work, it is to legislation that the victim of discrimination must look. The first legislative intervention, the Sex Disqualification (Removal) Act 1919, had a narrow scope, removing the restrictions on the employment of women in certain occupations and vocations (for example as civil servants or solicitors); crucially, it did not outlaw discrimination on grounds of sex in the appointment to those occupations or in the terms of employment. The Race Relations Act 1965 tackled discrimination in certain public places, and established the Race Relations Board, but it was a further three years before the Race Relations Act 1968 prohibited discrimination in employment on grounds of colour, race, ethnic or national origins. However, that Act relied for its enforcement on a combination of voluntary procedures and the institution of proceedings by the Race Relations Board, and was widely considered to have been a failure. The Equal Pay Act 1970[6] introduced a new right to equal terms and conditions for men and women in certain circumstances, but did not prohibit other forms of discrimination between the sexes, in particular discrimination at the point of hiring and in the provision of training. The turning point came with the enactment of the Sex Discrimination Act 1975, which introduced broad protection against direct and indirect discrimination in employment (and also in certain other specified areas such as education and the provision of goods and services) on the grounds of sex and marital status, with a right of complaint to a tribunal in employment cases; that Act also established the Equal Opportunities Commission (EOC) to oversee the operation of the legislation and to enforce it by bringing court proceedings or through the issue of non-discrimination notices. The Race Relations Act 1976 closely followed the provisions of the Sex Discrimination Act 1975, and established the Commission for Racial Equality (CRE) with powers similar to those of the EOC.

In the two decades that followed the enactment of the Sex Discrimination Act 1975, the developments in this area mostly occurred as a result of the influence of European law. As will be seen below, European law has had a profound impact on UK sex discrimination law[7], stretching it into areas which were not originally considered to fall within the scope of the domestic legislation, such as equal pay for work of equal value, benefits on death or retirement, and discrimination on grounds of gender reassignment. The principal measure is Article 141[8] of the EC Treaty, which provides that 'Each Member State shall ensure that the principle of equal pay for male and female workers for equal work or work of equal value is applied'[9]. In a series of landmark decisions[10], the ECJ has established that Article 141

6 Commencement of the Act was delayed for five years to enable employers to remove discrimination in terms and conditions; the Act was heavily amended by the Sex Discrimination Act 1975, and both Acts came into force on the same date.

7 See generally Bercusson *European Labour Law* (2nd edn, 2001); Barnard *European Employment Law* (2nd edn, 2000); Hervey and O'Keeffe *Sex Equality Law in the European Union* (1996); Ellis *European Community Sex Equality Law* (1992); McCrudden (ed) *Women, Employment and European Equality Law* (1987).

8 Art 141 was formerly Art 119, but was renumbered in the Amsterdam Treaty. In the interests of readability, this chapter generally refers to Art 141 throughout, irrespective of whether the decisions predate the Amsterdam Treaty.

9 Before the Amsterdam Treaty modifications, Art 119 (as it then was) only mentioned equal pay for *equal work*, not equal pay for *work of equal value*, but it was nevertheless held to cover work of equal value even before the amendment to the wording by the Amsterdam Treaty.

10 Beginning with *Macarthys Ltd v Smith* Case 129/79 [1980] ICR 672, [1980] IRLR 210, ECJ.

and its associated Directives (which extend the principle to pay and conditions and to work of equal value[11]) differ from the domestic law in several important respects, not least of which is that the definition of 'pay' under Community law is significantly wider than under domestic law. This is significant for several reasons: first, the supremacy of EC law over the national law of member states means that our domestic equality laws can be measured by the yardstick of Article 141, which prevails over any conflicting provisions of domestic law, in effect overriding them[12] ; if domestic law fails properly to implement Community law, the European Commission can bring enforcement proceedings in the European Court in order to enforce compliance[13], and a person with sufficient standing can bring judicial review proceedings in the Divisional Court for the purpose of securing a declaration that UK primary legislation is incompatible with EC law[14]; secondly, Article 141 has direct effect[15], in the sense that a complainant may rely upon it before a domestic court or employment tribunal[16], which must set aside any incompatible provision of domestic law to give effect to the supremacy of EC law; thirdly, the two associated Directives have 'vertical' direct effect[17], ie a complainant may rely upon them before a domestic court or tribunal, but only against the state or an 'organ of the state'[18] (the reasoning being that as it is the state that should

---

11   Directives 76/207/EEC (the Equal Treatment Directive) and 75/117/EEC (the Equal Pay Directive).

12   European Communities Act 1972, s 2(1). See *Amministrazione delle Finanze dello Stato v Simmenthal SpA* [1978] ECR 629, ECJ.

13   As in Case 61/81 *EC Commission v United Kingdom* [1982] ICR 578, [1982] IRLR 333, where the ECJ held that the existing Equal Pay Act 1970 did not comply with the requirements of the Equal Pay Directive 75/117/EEC by allowing a woman to demand equal pay for work of equal value where there was no job evaluation scheme in force; this led to the introduction into domestic law in 1983 of the concept of equal pay for work of equal value (see p 333 below). See also Case 165/82 *EC Commission v United Kingdom* [1984] ICR 192, [1984] IRLR 29, ECJ, concerning small firm and private household exceptions, discriminatory collective agreements and midwives.

14   As in *R v Secretary of State for Employment, ex p EOC* [1995] 1 AC 1, [1994] ICR 317, HL, where the House of Lords declared that the statutory provisions subjecting part-time employees to different qualifying conditions for unfair dismissal from those applicable to full-time employees were incompatible with EC law as they indirectly discriminated against women; this led to the repeal of the offending provisions and the harmonisation of qualifying periods for full-time and part-time workers (see p 558 below).

15   *Defrenne v SABENA (No 2)* [1976] ECR 455, [1976] ICR 547, ECJ.

16   *Secretary of State for Scotland v Wright and Hannah* [1991] IRLR 187, EAT; *Livingstone v Hepworth Refractories plc* [1992] ICR 287, [1992] IRLR 63, EAT.

17   See *Marshall v Southampton and South-West Hampshire Area Health Authority (Teaching)* [1986] ICR 335, [1986] IRLR 140, ECJ, where the ECJ held that the compulsory retiring of a woman at an earlier age than a man in the same occupation (then lawful under English law) infringed the Equal Treatment Directive. The decision led to a major revision of the domestic law relating to compulsory retirement ages by the Sex Discrimination Act 1986, but while an employee in the public sector could rely on the Equal Treatment Directive to demand equal compulsory retirement ages even before that Act, an employee in the private sector could not.

18   Ie 'a body, whatever its legal form, which had been made responsible pursuant to a measure adopted by a public authority, for providing a public service under the control of that authority and had for that purpose special powers beyond those which resulted from the normal rules applicable in relations between individuals'; *Foster v British Gas plc* [1991] 1 QB 405, [1991] ICR 84, ECJ; the House of Lords subsequently held ([1991] 2 AC 306, [1991] ICR 463, HL) that the nationalised British Gas Corporation was an organ of the state against which the directive could be directly relied upon by its employees to establish discrimination in compulsory retirement ages. Contrast *Doughty v Rolls Royce plc* [1992] ICR 538, [1992] IRLR 126, CA (Rolls Royce not an organ of the state despite the fact that the state was the sole shareholder prior to its privatisation, as it had not been made responsible for providing a public service, nor was there any evidence that it had special powers).

have put the Directive properly into effect, which, ex hypothesi, has not been done, the state should not be allowed to rely on its own failure to implement the Directive)[19]; fourthly, the domestic courts and tribunals are obliged to interpret national law as far as possible in such a way as to achieve the result sought by the Directive[20], if that can be done without unduly distorting the meaning of the domestic legislation[21]; this is so whether or not the national law in question pre-dates the relevant Directive[22]; and finally, the ECJ held in the landmark case of *Francovich v Italy*[23] that an individual who has suffered loss as a result of the failure of a member state to implement Community law fully may in certain circumstances sue the state for damages. This is potentially a highly significant prospect in view of the continuing uncertainty over the requirements of Community law in this area, particularly for private sector employees, who (as seen above) have no remedy against their employer where the state has failed to implement a Directive, although there are a number of demanding hurdles that must be overcome before such a claim can succeed[24].

While European law has been a fertile source of developments in sex discrimination law, until recently it had no role to play in the development of laws prohibiting discrimination on other grounds. Domestically, the next big leap forward came with the enactment of the Disability Discrimination Act 1995, the first piece of UK legislation to tackle discrimination against disabled people, which, inter alia, prohibited discrimination against disabled people in relation

19 A directive does not have 'horizontal' direct effect against individuals or non-state bodies (such as a private-sector employer). The ECJ has stated that Directive 75/117 (the equal pay directive) does not extend Art 141 but is simply designed 'to facilitate the practical application' of the principle outlined in the article, and 'in no way alters the content or scope of that principle as defined in the Treaty'. This suggests that Directive 75/117 has both vertical and horizontal direct effect: *Jenkins v Kingsgate (Clothing Productions) Ltd* [1981] ICR 592, [1981] IRLR 228, ECJ.

20 By this means a domestic court may be able to give indirect effect to a directive even if is not directly effective (eg because the complainant is not employed by an organ of the state); see eg *Pickstone v Freemans plc* [1988] ICR 697, [1988] IRLR 357, HL, where the House of Lords construed s 1(2)(c) of the Equal Pay Act 1970 purposively in order to bring it into line with Art 141; cf Lord Oliver: 'so to construe a provision which, on its face, is unambiguous involves a departure from a number of well-established rules of construction.' See also *Webb v EMO Air Cargo (UK) Ltd* [1992] 4 All ER 929, [1993] ICR 175, HL.

21 See eg *Duke v GEC Reliance Ltd* [1988] ICR 339, [1988] IRLR 118, HL, where the House of Lords held that it was not possible to construe s 6(4) of the Sex Discrimination Act 1975 (exclusion in respect of provisions in relation to death or retirement) so as to prohibit differential compulsory retirement ages, because s 6(4) was in fact intended to preserve discriminatory retirement ages, and was therefore unambiguously at variance with EC law.

22 *Marleasing SA v La Comercial Internacional de Alimentación SA* [1990] ECR I-4135, [1992] 1 CMLR 305, ECJ, approved by the House of Lords in *Webb v EMO Air Cargo (UK) Ltd.* [1992] 4 All ER 929, [1993] ICR 175, HL.

23 [1995] ICR 722, [1992] IRLR 84, ECJ. See Curtin (1992) 21 ILJ 74; Parker (1992) 108 LQR 180.

24 In *Brasserie du Pêcheur SA v Germany; R v Secretary of State for Transport, ex p Factortame (No 3)* [1996] All ER (EC) 301, [1996] IRLR 267, ECJ, the ECJ set out three conditions: (i) the rule of Community law infringed must be intended to confer rights upon individuals; (ii) the breach must be 'sufficiently serious' (ie did the member state 'manifestly and gravely' disregard the limits on its discretion in implementing the requirements of Community law?); and (iii) there must be a direct causal link between the breach of the obligation resting on the state and the damage sustained by individuals. Cf *R v HM Treasury, ex p British Telecommunications plc* [1996] IRLR 300, ECJ, where the test was given a narrow interpretation.

to employment, the provision of goods, facilities and services, and the sale and letting of property. The Act was the result of a well-co-ordinated and vociferous campaign for the introduction of legislation protecting the civil rights of disabled people which saw no fewer than fourteen abortive Private Members' Bills before the government was driven to act. The tragic death of Steven Lawrence and the subsequent Public Inquiry conducted by Sir William Macpherson[25] led to the introduction of the Race Relations (Amendment) Act 2000, which implemented the recommendations of the inquiry report and also placed a positive duty on a wide range of public authorities to promote race equality. The latter development is highly significant, in that it marks a movement away from the traditional, reactive approach to tackling discrimination, which puts the responsibility onto individuals to seek remedies via the courts and tribunals, towards a more proactive approach which 'mainstreams' equality by requiring public authorities to take equality issues into account in the development of their policies and programmes[26]. The duty to promote equality is already well-established in Northern Ireland, where section 75 of the Northern Ireland Act 1998 places a statutory duty on public authorities, in carrying out their functions relating to Northern Ireland, to have 'due regard to the need to promote equality of opportunity' on grounds of religious belief, political opinion, racial group, age, marital status, sexual orientation, gender, disability, and persons with and without dependants. The government has indicated that it intends to extend the duty to promote equality more widely to include the other strands of anti-discrimination law when legislative time allows, but other than provisions concerning specific public authorities[27], there had been no further legislative developments in this direction at the time of writing. The extension of a duty to promote equality to public authorities across the rest of the UK is surely inevitable. Whether that duty will in time be extended to the private sector remains to be seen.

At the time of writing, the main impetus for the further extension and development of the domestic law on discrimination in employment was once again coming from Europe, as a result of the inclusion into the EC Treaty (by the Treaty of Amsterdam) of Article 13, which provides a new legal basis for community-wide action to combat discrimination on grounds of sex, racial or ethnic origin, religion or belief, disability, age or sexual orientation[28]. In 1999 the European Commission brought forward two Directives under Article 13, a Race Directive combating discrimination on grounds of racial or ethnic origin in a wide range of areas, including employment, education, social security, cultural activities and access to goods and services, and a framework Employment Directive dealing with discrimination in employment and occupation on grounds of religion or belief, disability, age or sexual orientation. The Race Directive[29] was

25 *The Stephen Lawrence Inquiry: Report of an Inquiry by Sir William Macpherson* (Cm 4262–I, 1999).
26 See Fredman 'Equality: A New Generation?' (2001) 30 ILJ 145; Hepple, Coussey and Choudhury *Equality: A New Framework* (2000).
27 See eg the Greater London Authority Act 1999, s 404, which imposes a duty on the Greater London Authority, Metropolitan Police Authority and London Fire and Emergency Planning Authority to 'have regard to the need (a) to promote equality of opportunity for all persons irrespective of their race, sex, disability, age, sexual orientation or religion; (b) to eliminate unlawful discrimination; and (c) to promote good relations between persons of different racial groups, religious beliefs and sexual orientation'.
28 See Waddington (1999) 28 ILJ 133; (2000) 29 ILJ 176.
29 Directive 2000/43/EC.

adopted in June 2000, and implemented in Great Britain by Regulations amending the Race Relations Act 1976[30]. The Employment Directive[31] was adopted in November 2000, and will be implemented by a series of Regulations amending the Disability Discrimination Act 1995[32], and introducing new measures prohibiting discrimination in employment on grounds of religion or belief[33], sexual orientation[34], and age[35]. The implementing Regulations were preceded by a lengthy consultation process[36] which in the case of age discrimination was still ongoing at the time of writing[37]. The amendments to the existing law on race and disability discrimination, and the new measures on sexual orientation and religion or belief discrimination, are discussed below. For the most part, the government has attempted to achieve coherence and consistency across the different strands by using common concepts and terminology, in line with its Equality Statement of November 1999 which stated that 'we will where practicable harmonise the provisions of the Race Relations Act, Sex Discrimination Act and Disability Discrimination Act'.[38] Unfortunately, however, this laudable objective has been undermined by the decision to implement the new Directives by Regulations[39] rather than by primary legislation, which has made it impossible to rationalise the old and new provisions (the obstacle being that as parts of the existing anti-discrimination legislation lie outside the scope of EC law, they are not amenable to modification via secondary legislation). The result is a proverbial dog's breakfast, with significant differences *between* the strands (for example between the domestic provisions on sex discrimination and those which apply to the other strands[40]), and even differences *within* the strands, depending on whether the provisions relate to areas falling within the scope of one of the new Directives.

The current chaotic state of British anti-discrimination legislation brings the law into disrepute, and primary legislation harmonising the provisions across the various strands is urgently needed. One way of achieving this would be through a single Equality Act covering all the new and existing strands[41], an approach which has already been adopted in several other jurisdictions, including Australia, New

30 Race Relations Act 1976 (Amendment) Regulations 2003, SI 2003/1626; in force from 19 July 2003; see p 365.
31 Directive 2000/78/EC.
32 Disability Discrimination Act 1995 (Amendment) Regulations 2003, SI 2003/1673; in force from 1 October 2004; see p 383.
33 Employment Equality (Religion or Belief) Regulations 2003, SI 2003/1660; in force from 2 December 2003; see p 377.
34 Employment Equality (Sexual Orientation) Regulations 2003, SI 2003/1661; in force from 1 Decemner 2003; see p 363.
35 The age strand of the Employment Directive does not have to be implemented until October 2006.
36 *Towards Equality and Diversity: Implementing the Employment and Race Directives* (DTI, 2001); *Equality and Diversity: The Way Ahead* (DTI, 2002); *Equality and Diversity: Making it Happen* (DTI, 2002).
37 *Equality and Diversity: Age Matters* (DTI, 2003)
38 Cabinet Office, Equality Statement, 30 November 1999.
39 Under the European Communities Act 1972, s 2.
40 The Commission has brought forward an Equal Treatment Amendment Directive (Directive 2002/73/EC) which amends Directive 76/207/EEC to reflect ECJ case law and to bring the provisions on sex discrimination into line with the Race and Employment Directives, but the Amendment Directive does not require implementation until 5 October 2005.
41 The arguments for and against a single Equality Act are considered in Hepple, Coussey and Choudhury *Equality: A New Framework* (2000) ch 2; the authors recommend that there should be such an Act in Britain.

Zealand, Ireland, the US and Canada, but the present government has shown no enthusiasm for such a development[42]. A more likely prospect is the establishment of a single Equality Commission[43] to take over the existing functions of the EOC, CRE and Disability Rights Commission and to perform a similar role in relation to the new strands not presently covered by a commission (ie sexual orientation, religion or belief and age). Such a body would be able to offer integrated advice, guidance and support on equality matters across all the strands and would help to ensure a coherent approach to equality issues; arguably it would also be more effective in dealing with cases of multiple discrimination (particularly where a person believes he or she has been unfairly treated but does not know the reason). There is, however, a danger that a single commission might be too unwieldy, that there might be a loss of focus, and possibly of expertise, on some of the strands, and that some strands might lose out to others in the inevitable internal battle for resources. At the time of writing, the government had issued a consultation document[44] on the future of the equality institutions which explored several options for reform, including: (i) a fully integrated single equality body covering all the strands, with an internal structure organised either on a functional basis or with units based on individual strands; (ii) a 'single gateway' approach, with a single point of contact providing basic information and advice, and acting as a gateway to the existing commissions (and possibly to new bodies covering the new strands); and (iii) an 'overarching' commission, with representatives from each strand, overseeing the existing commissions and new strand bodies, with a strategic role in relation to overall priorities and strategy. Major changes to the existing institutional machinery were not expected to be in place before 2006, although special (and presumably temporary) arrangements are to be made to support the implementation of the strands on sexual orientation and religion or belief[45].

The other potential source of further developments in this area is the Human Rights Act 1998, 'bringing home' the European Convention on Human Rights into domestic law[46]. At first glance the Convention appears to have major significance for the law on discrimination in employment, as Article 14 provides that 'the enjoyment of the rights and freedoms set forth in this Convention shall be secured without discrimination on an any ground such as sex, race, colour, language, religion, political or other opinion, national or social origin, association with a national minority, property, birth or other status'. However, Article 14 does not confer a free-standing right not to be discriminated against; it merely confers a right not to be discriminated against in the enjoyment of the other rights and

---

42   Better Regulation Task Force *Review of Anti-Discrimination Legislation in Great Britain* (May 1999).

43   As in Northern Ireland, where the Equality Commission for Northern Ireland, established by the Northern Ireland Act 1998, replaced the Fair Employment Commission, Equal Opportunities Commission for Northern Ireland, Commission for Racial Equality for Northern Ireland and Northern Ireland Disability Council.

44   DTI *Equality and Diversity: Making it Happen* (2002). See also O'Cinneide 'A Single Equality Body: Lessons from Abroad' (2002).

45   DTI *Equality and Diversity: Making it Happen*, Part 10. Regrettably, the government does not intend to replicate the investigatory and legal advice/representation functions of the existing commissions for the new strands 'in the short term': see para 10.4.

46   See generally Ewing (ed) *Human Rights at Work* (2000); O'Dempsey et al *Employment Law and the Human Rights Act 1998* (2001); Hepple 'The Impact on Labour Law' in Markesinis (ed) *The Impact of the Human Rights Bill on English Law* (1998); Ewing 'The Human Rights Act and Labour Law' (1998) 27 ILJ 275; Palmer 'Human Rights: Implications for Labour Law' (2000) 59 CLJ 168; and see p 42.

freedoms guaranteed by the Convention, and employment is not a Convention right. The position would change radically if the UK government were to ratify Protocol 12 to the Convention, which requires that 'the enjoyment *of any right set forth by law* shall be secured without discrimination . . . etc[47]', thus providing a general prohibition on discrimination, but there was no sign of this happening at the time of writing. There is no doubt that certain types of employment discrimination can fall within the scope of the Convention, as was seen in *Smith and Grady v United Kingdom*[48], where the European Court of Human Rights held that the investigations into the sexuality of members of the British armed forces, and their subsequent discharge from the armed forces on the sole ground of their sexual orientation (pursuant to the Ministry of Defence's policy on homosexuals) constituted a violation of their right to respect for their private lives under Article 8 of the Convention[49]. The protection of freedom of religion under Article 9 is also of potential significance for the law on discrimination in employment, although previous attempts to challenge religious discrimination in employment as a violation of Article 9 have been unsuccessful[50]. In practice, it seems likely that the main impact of the incorporation of the Convention on the law on employment discrimination will stem from the duty placed on the domestic courts and tribunals, so far as possible, to interpret domestic legislation so as to accord with the Convention.

2 SEX DISCRIMINATION IN EMPLOYMENT

(i) Relationship between the Sex Discrimination Act 1975 and the Equal Pay Act 1970

The Sex Discrimination Act 1975 came into force in December 1975, at the same time as the Equal Pay Act 1970. While the statutes are clearly complementary and wherever possible are to be construed 'so as to form a harmonious code'[51], it remains the case that they are mutually exclusive in their operation, so that an action must be brought under the correct statute[52]. The borderline is that the Equal Pay Act 1970 applies to contractual terms of employment, amenable to inclusion in the statutory 'equality clause', whereas the Sex Discrimination Act 1975 applies to discrimination on grounds of sex in matters outside the contract (such as recruitment, promotion and dismissal) and is thus much wider. The Race Relations Act 1976 was modelled on the Sex Discrimination Act 1975 (although it makes no distinction between pay and other aspects of employment), and cases decided under one Act will normally also be precedents for the other[53].

---

47 Italics supplied.
48 [1999] IRLR 734, ECtHR. See p 361 below. Cf also *Pearce v Governing Body of Mayfield Secondary School* [2003] IRLR 512, HL.
49 Art 8 could also conceivably be used to challenge employers' dress and appearance rules; see p 304 below.
50 See eg *Ahmad v Inner London Education Authority* [1978] 1 All ER 574, CA; see p 377.
51 *Steel v UPOW* [1978] ICR 181 at 186, [1977] IRLR 288 at 290, per Phillips J; *Jenkins v Kingsgate (Clothing Productions) Ltd (No 2)* [1981] ICR 715, [1981] IRLR 388, EAT.
52 *Oliver v J P Malnick & Co (No 2)* [1984] ICR 458, IT is a good example. For an illustration of the difficulties raised by the distinction, see *Barclays Bank plc v James* [1990] ICR 333, [1990] IRLR 90; the case was subsequently settled on the understanding that the EAT's decision was wrong: [1990] IRLR 499.
53 Although this may not be the case where the substantive provisions have diverged, eg as a result of the recent amendments to the Race Relations Act 1976 to implement the Race Directive.

The existence of two principal Acts concerning sex discrimination has given rise to complexity and confusion in this area, a situation exacerbated by the impact of EC law, and in particular Article 141 of the EC Treaty. As seen above, although ostensibly concerned with 'pay', Article 141 (as explained and expanded by its supporting Directives) is much wider in scope than the Equal Pay Act 1970, and many of the cases decided by the ECJ have concerned matters which, in English domestic law, would fall within the ambit of the Sex Discrimination Act 1975. With hindsight, the law would have been much more straightforward and transparent if the drafters of the 1975 Act had simply torn up the Equal Pay Act 1970 and started again with a clean sheet of paper. The EOC has long recommended the replacement of the two Acts by a single Sex Equality Act, incorporating EC law and based on the principle of a fundamental right to equal treatment between men and women[54], but as was seen in the introduction to this chapter, the present government has indicated[55] that it does not believe that major legislative change of that type is appropriate at this stage.

(ii) Application of the Sex Discrimination Act 1975

The aim of the Sex Discrimination Act 1975 is to prevent discrimination on the grounds of sex in several areas, including employment; although drafted in terms of women being the object of the discrimination, the Act is equally applicable to men[56] and also covers discrimination against a person on the ground of his or her marital status[57]. The parts which are relevant here apply to discrimination in 'employment' which is defined as employment under a contract of service or apprenticeship, or under a contract personally to execute any work or labour[58]; a person outside this definition may not claim the benefit of the relevant provision[59], except in the case of 'contract workers' (ie people working for A who have in fact been engaged by B and hired to A under a contract of supply of labour), who are included[60]. The Act prohibits discrimination at all stages of employment, whether in relation to the arrangements which the employer makes for selecting employees, the terms on which he offers employment, access to promotion, transfer, training or other benefits, or dismissal. It can also apply to post-termination discrimination, provided there is a sufficient connection with the employment relationship[61]. However, as seen above, once the employment has

---

54 EOC *Equality in the 21st Century: A New Sex Equality Law for Britain* (1998). The EOC also recommended, inter alia, the introduction of compulsory gender monitoring of the workforce, and of a legal duty on public authorities to work towards eliminating unlawful discrimination and to promote equality of opportunity.

55 The government's response was heavily influenced by the Better Regulation Task Force's *Review of Anti-Discrimination Legislation in Great Britain* (May 1999).

56 Sex Discrimination Act 1975, s 2.

57 Sex Discrimination Act 1975, s 3. *Hurley v Mustoe* [1981] ICR 490, [1981] IRLR 208. For a rare recent example, see *Chief Constable of the Bedfordshire Constabulary v Graham* [2002] IRLR 239, EAT. It is not unlawful to discriminate against a single person on the ground of his or her marital status.

58 Sex Discrimination Act 1975, s 82(1). This is a deliberately extended definition, capable of taking in certain categories of the self-employed as well as employees: *Quinnen v Hovells* [1984] ICR 525, [1984] IRLR 227; *Gunning v Mirror Group Newspapers Ltd* [1986] 1 All ER 385, [1986] ICR 145, CA. The tribunal's jurisdiction is not dependent on the existence of an enforceable contract: *Leighton v Michael* [1995] ICR 1091, [1996] IRLR 67, EAT.

59 *Knight v A-G* [1979] ICR 194, EAT.

60 Sex Discrimination Act 1975, s 9. *Rice v Fon-a-Car* [1980] ICR 133, EAT.

61 *Rhys-Harper v Relaxion Group plc* [2003] IRLR 484, HL (see p 312 below).

commenced any complaint relating to inequality in the terms and conditions of employment must be brought under the Equal Pay Act 1970[62]. The 1975 Act also gives a trade union member a right not to be discriminated against by the union on the ground of sex in matters of admission, expulsion and provision of union benefits, facilities, etc[63] .

The Act specifies certain exclusions, some of which are particularly relevant to discrimination in employment. Thus, the application of the Act is modified in the case of the police, prison officers and ministers of religion[64], and cases where the alleged discrimination relates to the provision of services by the employer to the woman qua member of the public, rather than qua employee, are excluded[65]. On its introduction the Act contained a blanket immunity for the armed forces, but it was applied to them in 1995, albeit with an exemption for acts 'done for the purpose of ensuring the combat effectiveness of the armed forces'[66] (a dispensation which has been widely and controversially used in order to exclude women from certain sections of the armed forces). This more limited exemption was itself the subject of legal challenge in *Sirdar v Army Board* [67], where the ECJ held that the Royal Marines were not in breach of the Equal Treatment Directive by not engaging a woman as a cook, despite the seemingly tenuous connection between catering and combat effectiveness, on the grounds that their policy of 'inter-operability' meant that all members of the Marines had to be capable of serving as front-line commandos. The ECJ held that there is no general exception to the principle of equal treatment under Community law permitting the blanket exclusion of women from the armed forces, but that their exclusion from service in special combat units such as the Marines 'may' be justified under Article 2(2), provided the principle of proportionality is observed (ie that the exclusion is within the limits of what is appropriate and necessary in order to achieve the aim of protecting public security)[68].

There was previously an important (and extremely troublesome) exclusion for provisions in relation to death or retirement[69], which was considered necessary because discrimination in retirement provision (state and private) has historically been firmly entrenched, based on differential state pensionable ages. However, that exclusion became increasingly untenable in the light of the ECJ's rulings on the scope of Article 141and the associated Directives, culminating in *Barber v Guardian Royal Exchange Assurance Group*[70], where the ECJ held that a pension paid under a contracted-out, private occupational pension scheme falls within the scope of Article 141. The government was therefore forced to reconsider the whole question of equality of treatment in pensions provision, and the Pensions Act 1995 introduced important new provisions requiring equal treatment in both

---

62 *Oliver v J P Malnick & Co (No 2)* [1984] ICR 458, IT.
63 Sex Discrimination Act 1975, s 12. See Homans (1984) 13 ILJ 262.
64 Sex Discrimination Act 1975, ss 17–19.
65 Sex Discrimination Act 1975, s 6(7).
66 Sex Discrimination Act 1975, 85(4), as substituted by SI 1994/3276, with effect from 1 February 1995.
67 [2000] ICR 130, [2000] IRLR 47, ECJ.
68 Art 2(2) of the Equal Treatment Directive permits a derogation from the principle of equal treatment in the case of occupational activities where the sex of the worker 'constitutes a determining factor'. See *Kreil v Bundesrepublik Deutschland* Case C-285/98 [2000] ECR I-69, where the ECJ interpreted the derogation very narrowly.
69 Sex Discrimination Act 1975, s 6(4), as substituted by the Pensions Act 1995, s 66(3). The equivalent exclusion in the Equal Pay Act 1970, s 6(1A) and (2), was substituted by s 66(1) of the 1995 Act.
70 [1991] 1 QB 344, [1990] ICR 616, ECJ.

membership of and rights under occupational pension schemes[71], repealing the existing exclusion in the sex discrimination and equal pay legislation for provisions in relation to death or retirement[72]. The issue is explored further below[73].

Two further exclusions may be relevant. The first is where questions of national security arise[74] and the second is where the discriminatory act is done under statutory authority[75]. The latter exclusion was significantly restricted by the Employment Act 1989. As originally enacted, section 51 of the Sex Discrimination Act 1975 gave a blanket exemption from liability for discriminatory acts which were necessary to comply with a statute or regulation in force before the passage of that Act. That provision was designed to avoid any conflict between the 1975 Act and the many, long-standing provisions in the Factories Act 1961 and other industrial safety legislation which gave special protection to women (for example by restricting night working or the number of hours that they could work in a factory). Many of the restrictions on women's employment had increasingly been seen as archaic and unnecessary, and most of the restrictions on the hours of work and working conditions of women were removed by the Sex Discrimination Act 1986[76]. However, a number of restrictions remained in force, and in October 1986 the European Commission issued a reasoned opinion alleging that section 51 was inconsistent with the requirements of the Equal Treatment Directive 76/207/EEC. In consequence the Employment Act 1989 narrowed the scope of the section 51 exemption[77], restricting it to discriminatory actions which are necessary to comply with a statutory provision concerning 'the protection of women' as regards pregnancy, maternity or other circumstances giving rise to risks specifically affecting women[78], and removed all remaining discriminatory provisions, such as the prohibition on the employment of women underground[79], other than those which could be justified on the basis of reproductive hazards[80]. Under the amended section 51 a discriminatory action will be lawful if it was 'necessary' in

71 Pensions Act 1995, ss 62–66; see further, p 359 below.
72 Sex Discrimination Act 1975, s 66(1), (3). Note, however, that s 6(4) (as substituted by the 1995 Act) does not outlaw discrimination in relation to membership of, or rights under, an occupational scheme where such discrimination is not prohibited by the 1995 Act.
73 See p 352 below.
74 Sex Discrimination Act 1975, s 52. The system whereby a minister could issue a conclusive certificate that national security was involved had to be discontinued (in the employment context) because of the decision of the ECJ in *Johnston v Chief Constable of the Royal Ulster Constabulary* Case 222/84 [1987] ICR 83, [1986] IRLR 263 that such a certificate was not conclusive in an action brought under the Equal Treatment Directive.
75 Sex Discrimination Act 1975, s 51, as substituted by the Employment Act 1989, s 3(3). On the equivalent provision in the Race Relations Act 1976, see *Hampson v Department of Education and Science* [1990] ICR 511, [1990] IRLR 302, HL.
76 For further details, see the fourth edition of this book, ch 11.
77 Employment Act 1989, s 3(3). The 1989 Act went no further than was considered necessary to comply with European obligations, so that in areas other than employment and vocational training (the only areas covered by the Directive) the exemption for discriminatory requirements which pre-date the 1975 Act still applies.
78 The list of restrictions which are still valid includes those on the employment of women in factories within four weeks of childbirth, the employment of women in work involving lead products, or exposure to ionising radiations, and the employment of women at sea or on aircraft during pregnancy: Employment Act 1989, s 4.
79 The lifting of all restrictions on women working underground required the government to denounce ILO Convention 45 and Art 8(4)(b) of the European Social Charter.
80 Exceptionally, s 5 permits discrimination in connection with certain educational appointments, eg in Oxbridge women's colleges and religious schools.

order to comply with a statutory requirement for the protection of women. In interpreting the word 'necessary' under the original section 51, the EAT in *Page v Freight Hire (Tank Haulage) Ltd*[81] was prepared to accept a broad measure of managerial prerogative, holding that an employer could defend his refusal to allow a woman to drive lorries containing dimethylformide (which could be harmful to women of child-bearing age) on the basis that this discriminatory action was 'reasonably necessary' to enable him to comply with his general duty under the Health and Safety at Work etc. Act 1974, section 2[82].

Finally, one of the most controversial issues in discrimination law in recent years has been whether the prohibition of discrimination 'on the grounds of sex' extends to discrimination on grounds that are more generally *related* to sex, including gender reassignment and sexual orientation. As will be seen below[83], the courts have consistently refused to find that sex discrimination includes discrimination on grounds of sexual orientation, and it has been necessary to introduce separate measures prohibiting sexual orientation discrimination. The position as regards gender reassignment discrimination is, however, different, as in *P v S and Cornwall County Council*[84] the ECJ held that the dismissal of a transsexual who was proposing to undergo male to female gender reassignment did in fact infringe the Equal Treatment Directive. It was argued on behalf of the employers in that case that as long as they would also have dismissed someone previously a woman who had undergone an operation to become a man, there was no discrimination on grounds of sex, but in a bold (and so it seemed at the time, potentially far-reaching) decision, the ECJ held that the principle of Community law that there should be 'no discrimination whatsoever on grounds of sex' was simply the expression of the fundamental Community law principle of equality, and that the scope of the Directive could not be confined to discrimination based on the fact that a person is of one or other sex, but also applied to discrimination arising from gender reassignment, the point being that 'such discrimination is based, essentially if not exclusively, on the sex of the person concerned'. In *Chessington World of Adventures Ltd v Reed*[85], the EAT in turn reinterpreted the Sex Discrimination Act 1975 as applying to a case where the complainant had been discriminated against after declaring an intention to undergo gender reassignment, holding that where the reason for unfavourable treatment is sex-based, there is no requirement for the usual male/female comparison to be made. To formalise the position, the government subsequently introduced Regulations amending the Sex Discrimination Act to make it unlawful to treat a person less favourably than others would be treated because that person 'intends to undergo, is undergoing or has undergone gender reassignment'[86]. Problems remain, however, not least because gender reassignment can give rise to some difficult and highly sensitive issues in the workplace. Some of these are

---

81   [1981] ICR 299, [1981] IRLR 13.
82   See p 871 below.
83   See p 359 below.
84   [1996] All ER (EC) 397, [1996] IRLR 347, ECJ. See Wintemute (1997) 60 MLR 334; Skidmore (1987) 26 ILJ 51.
85   [1997] IRLR 556, EAT.
86   Sex Discrimination Act 1975, s 2A(1), added by the Sex Discrimination (Gender Reassignment) Regulations 1999, SI 1999/1102. The new protection only applies to direct discrimination in employment and vocational training. Interestingly, in this context any discrimination in relation to pay falls to be dealt with under the Sex Discrimination Act, not the Equal Pay Act: s 6(8).

specifically addressed in the legislation; so, for example, a person who is absent from work as a result of undergoing gender reassignment has a right to be treated no less favourably than would be the case if the absence was due to sickness or injury, or to some other cause such that, having regard to the circumstances, it is reasonable for him to be treated no less favourably[87] ; and there are specific 'genuine occupational qualifications' (GOQs) which apply to transsexuals, for example where objection might reasonably be taken to the employment of a person who is undergoing or has undergone gender reassignment on grounds of privacy or decency, or where the job involves the job holder being liable to be called upon to perform intimate physical searches pursuant to statutory powers[88]. Historically much of the difficulty in this area has resulted from the fact that UK law has traditionally refused to recognise gender reassignment as having any effect on a person's legal gender, which remained as it was at birth[89]. However, in the landmark case of *Goodwin v United Kingdom*[90] the European Court of Human Rights held that by failing to give legal recognition to the gender reassignment of a post-operative male-to-female transsexual, the UK had failed to comply with its obligation to respect her private life under Article 8 of the European Convention. The implications of *Goodwin* for the treatment of post-operative transsexuals in the workplace and for the GOQ exception was considered in *A v Chief Constable of the West Yorkshire Police*[91]. The applicant, a post-operative male-to-female transsexual, applied to join West Yorkshire Police as a police constable, but was rejected on the grounds that she would not be capable of performing the full duties of the post, as these included conducting intimate searches which by law had to be carried out by an officer 'of the same sex as the person searched'. The EAT had held that the applicant had to be regarded as male in law, and that the GOQ exceptions should be considered on that basis, but the Court of Appeal held that in the light of the decision in *Goodwin* (which was delivered after the EAT's decision) in the context of employment law it was no longer possible to regard a post-operative male-to-female transsexual as being other than female, except where there were significant factors of public interest to weigh against the interests of the individual applicant in obtaining legal recognition of her gender reassignment. It followed that if the Chief Constable was bound to treat the applicant as female, it was not open to him to discriminate against her on the basis that she was a transsexual, and that no possibility of invoking the GOQ exception could arise.

While the decision in *A v Chief Constable of the West Yorkshire Police* helps to clarify the position of post-operative transsexuals, the position of those who are undergoing the process is still problematic. As the Advocate General observed in *P v S and Cornwall County Council*[92], transsexuals do not constitute a third sex, and the question therefore arises, at what point in time does a person undergoing gender reassignment have a right to be treated as a member of the sex to which they aspire? Here it is important to appreciate that the Sex Discrimination Act gives a person the right not to be treated less favourably than 'other persons' on grounds of gender reassignment. It does not in terms give a transsexual the right

---

87 Sex Discrimination Act 1975, s 2A(3).
88 Sex Discrimination Act 1975, s 7A, 7B. The GOQs for sex discrimination are discussed at p 302.
89 *Corbett v Corbett* [1970] 2 WLR 1306.
90 [2002] IRLR 664, ECtHR.
91 [2002] EWCA Civ 1584, [2003] IRLR 32.
92 [1996] All ER (EC) 397, [1996] IRLR 347, ECJ.

to insist on being treated no less favourably than a person of the sex to which that person aspires, as was graphically illustrated in *Croft v Royal Mail Group plc*[93]. In that case, the applicant, a pre-operative transsexual, had already been employed at a sorting office in Leicester for more than ten years when she embarked on her 'real life test' of living exclusively as a woman, prior to making a decision on whether to undergo gender reassignment surgery. Discussions took place with management about how to deal with the changed circumstances, including the need to remind colleagues of the organisation's harassment code, and initially the applicant agreed to use the unisex disabled toilet. However, this arrangement soon proved unsatisfactory to her, and she indicated that she wished to use the female toilet. Her request was refused by the employer on the grounds that other female employees objected to sharing their facility (which was also used as a changing room) with a person whom they had known as a man for many years, and that the applicant would only be allowed to use the female facilities once a suitable period of communication and consultation with the workforce had been undertaken. The applicant resigned, claiming that the employer's refusal constituted unlawful gender reassignment discrimination. The Court of Appeal upheld the decision of the employment tribunal and the EAT that her claim should fail, pointing out that while the protection against gender reassignment discrimination includes those at all stages of gender reassignment[94]: 'it does not follow that all such persons are entitled immediately to be treated as members of the sex to which they aspire. Nor does it follow that, until the final stage is reached, they can necessarily be required, in relation to lavatories, to behave as if they were not undergoing gender reassignment.' Given the unacceptability of both of these approaches, the court took a pragmatic approach, acknowledging that although a moment would come when a person in the applicant's position was entitled to use female toilets, the timing would depend on all the circumstances, not on the choice of the applicant[95], and that in the meantime the employer was entitled to make separate arrangements for those undergoing the change.

(iii) The meaning of 'discrimination'

(a) Direct discrimination

The Sex Discrimination Act 1975 defines three types of discrimination, direct and indirect discrimination, and discrimination by way of victimisation. Direct discrimination is defined in section 1(1)(a) as where the employer, on the ground of a woman's sex, treats her less favourably than he treats or would treat a man. The scope of section 1(1)(a) is wide, particularly as the House of Lords has made clear in the leading case of *James v Eastleigh Borough Council*[96] that in determining whether there as been direct discrimination the motive or purpose or intention

---

93 [2003] EWCA Civ 1045, [2003] IRLR 592.
94 Cf Sex Discrimination Act 1975, s 82: '"gender reassignment" means a process which is undertaken under medical supervision for the purpose of reassigning a person's sex by changing physiological or other characteristics of sex, *and includes any part of such a process.*' (italics supplied)
95 'Acquiring the status of a transsexual does not carry with it the right to choose which toilets to use', although 'with respect to other facilities, the employee's self-definition may be a very important factor in determining the sex in which the employee is entitled to be treated', per Pill LJ at 599.
96 [1990] ICR 554, [1990] IRLR 288, HL; revsg [1989] ICR 423, [1989] IRLR 318, CA.

of the alleged discriminator is irrelevant. In that case the applicant, a man of 61, complained that he had been discriminated against by the local authority because he had been charged 75p to swim in the municipal swimming baths, while his wife of the same age had been admitted free under the authority's policy of allowing free entry to those who had reached the state pensionable age of 65 for men and 60 for women. The Court of Appeal had held (distinguishing an earlier House of Lords decision to the effect that a subjective motive or intention to discriminate is not a condition of liability[97]) that there had not been less favourable treatment on the ground of sex because the reason for the concession was to benefit pensioners and not to discriminate against men. In the words of the Vice-Chancellor, Browne-Wilkinson VC: 'In my judgment there is a clear distinction between the ground or reason for which a person acts and his intention in so acting.' However, on further appeal the House of Lords overturned this decision, rejecting the subjective approach and instead affirming that the correct approach is an objective one: 'Would the complainant have received the same treatment but for his sex?' On the facts it was clear that the less favourable treatment would not have occurred but for the complainant's sex, and so there was direct discrimination. The fact that the council did not intend to discriminate against the applicant, and that its reason for adopting the policy of concessions to pensioners was an honourable one[98], was considered to be irrelevant.

It follows that a good motive on the part of the employer (for example a belief that the discriminatory action is in the applicant's own best interests) is no excuse for what is, on the wording, an act of discrimination[99], nor is the fact that the employer has been pressurised to discriminate by a third party, for example a trade union, or the applicant's fellow employees[100]. Given that one of the aims of the legislation is to discourage the treatment of women or men *en masse* as capable of certain things and incapable of others, general stereotypical assumptions (for example that women cannot do heavy work or that men are not suited to secretarial work or to working in the caring professions) are likely to be held to be discriminatory, and an employer who acts on such assumptions may well contravene the statute[101].

For there to be a finding of direct discrimination the applicant must show that the employer has treated her 'less favourably than he treats or would treat a man' on the grounds of her sex. Unlike the Equal Pay Act, which works on the basis of a comparison between the treatment of the applicant and that of a named comparator (or comparators), the Sex Discrimination Act is based on a comparison

---

97   *Birmingham City Council v Equal Opportunities Commission* [1989] AC 1155, [1989] IRLR 173, HL.

98   The case is a good illustration of the fact that, other than the GOQ's (see p 302 below), there is no 'justification' defence in a complaint of direct discrimination. Cf Bowers and Moran 'Justification in Direct Sex Discrimination Law: Breaking the Taboo' (2002) 31 ILJ 307.

99   *Peake v Automotive Products Ltd* [1977] ICR 480, [1977] IRLR 105 (reversed on other grounds, [1977] ICR 968, [1977] IRLR 365, CA); *Grieg v Community Industry* [1979] ICR 356, [1979] IRLR 158; *Din v Carrington Viyella Ltd* [1982] ICR 256, [1982] IRLR 281. While motive is not relevant when determining whether discrimination has occurred, it may be relevant when deciding the level of compensation to be awarded: *Chief Constable of the Greater Manchester Police v Hope* [1999] ICR 338, EAT.

100 *R v Commission for Racial Equality, ex p Westminster City Council* [1985] ICR 827, [1985] IRLR 426, CA (a race relations case).

101 *Skyrail Oceanic Ltd v Coleman* [1981] ICR 864, [1981] IRLR 398, CA; *Horsey v Dyfed County Council* [1982] ICR 755, [1982] IRLR 395.

with a hypothetical comparator ('treats or would treat'), and the comparison 'must be such that the relevant circumstances in the one case are the same, or not materially different, in the other'[102]. The identification of the appropriate comparator, and the determination of which circumstances are to be considered as relevant, are key elements in any discrimination claim, often requiring difficult judgments as to which of the differences between any two individuals are relevant and which are irrelevant, and the choice of characteristics 'may itself be determinative of the outcome'[103]. It may, of course, be possible to find an actual comparator whose circumstances are the same or not materially different to those of the applicant, in which case that person can perform the role of the statutory comparator, but in most cases this will not be possible, and in such circumstances the tribunal must[104] make a hypothetical comparison, by considering how the employer would have treated a male employee in comparable circumstances. One way of doing this is see how the employer acted 'in cases which, while not identical, were also not wholly dissimilar'[105], as that evidence may provide a sound basis for inferring how the employer would have treated a male employee in the same circumstances as the applicant.

Direct discrimination is based around the concept of 'less favourable' treatment. Differential treatment does not in itself amount to discrimination: 'If discrimination is to be established, it is necessary to show not merely that the sexes are treated differently, but that the treatment accorded to one is less favourable than the treatment accorded to the other'[106]. The need to show treatment which is 'less favourable', and not merely different, is problematic, not least because it can give rise to the kind of tendentious 'separate but equal' arguments once used to justify racial segregation in the US[107]. On the whole the courts have been robust in resisting such arguments, and have generally accepted that differential treatment is detrimental, although not without the occasional unfortunate lapse. Indeed, in the first case under the 1975 Act to come before the Court of Appeal, *Peake v Automotive Products Ltd*[108], the court was prepared to disregard differential treatment on the grounds that it was too minor. In that case, the employer allowed women to leave the factory five minutes before the men, in the interests of safety and to avoid women being caught in the rush to the gates. One of the men complained to a tribunal that this was unlawful discrimination against men. The EAT upheld his claim, but the Court of Appeal unanimously rejected it, on the grounds that the different treatment was in the interests of safety and good administration (in the words of Lord Denning MR: 'it is not discriminatory for mankind to treat womankind with the courtesy and chivalry which we have been

102 Sex Discrimination Act 1975, s 5(3). This requirement has been especially problematic in cases involving pregnancy discrimination, where for obvious reasons it is not possible to make the necessary comparison. The point is discussed further below, at p 439.

103 *Shamoon v Chief Constable of the Royal Ulster Constabulary* [2003] UKHL 11, [2003] IRLR 285 at 292, per Lord Hope,

104 A tribunal commits an error of law if it does not construct a hypothetical comparator, where one is required, against which to test the alleged discriminatory treatment: *Balamoody v United Kingdom Central Council for Nursing, Midwifery and Health Visiting* [2001] EWCA Civ 2097, [2002] IRLR 288, CA. See also *Chief Constable of West Yorkshire v Vento* [2001] IRLR 124, EAT.

105 *Balamoody v United Kingdom Central Council for Nursing, Midwifery and Health Visiting* [2001] EWCA Civ 2097, [2002] IRLR 288 at 306, per Lord Rodger.

106 *Smith v Safeway plc* [1996] IRLR 456 at 458, CA, per Phillips J.

107 Such arguments are excluded in the case of the Race Relations Act 1976, which specifically provides in s 1(2) that racial segregation is less favourable treatment; see p 368 below.

108 [1977] ICR 968, [1977] IRLR 365, CA, restrictively interpreted by the EAT in *Grieg v Community Industry* [1979] ICR 356, [1979] IRLR 158.

taught to believe is right conduct in our society'), and that in any event the employer's action was harmless and could be disregarded under the de minimis principle. In the later case of *Ministry of Defence v Jeremiah*[109] the Court of Appeal reconsidered the approach taken in *Peake*. In that case it was held that requiring a man employed in an ordnance factory to perform dirty and unpleasant work making 'colour-bursting' shells when women working in the factory were excused from such work was less favourable treatment within the meaning of the Act, and therefore unlawful. Lord Denning MR stated that the approach to the definition of direct discrimination taken in *Peake* (ie exempting 'sensible administrative arrangements' in the interests of health or chivalry) was wrong and that the decision was only supportable on the alternative ground given (ie that on the facts the discrimination was too minor to be effective, under the de minimis principle). On the facts in *Jeremiah* it was held that requiring only the men to do the work in question was unlawful, and the fact that they were paid extra to do it was irrelevant.

While the approach of the Court of Appeal in *Jeremiah* showed a stronger adherence to the actual wording of the Act, it still seemed to allow some scope for the de minimis defence. In subsequent cases the courts have tended to take a more robust approach, particularly where the alleged less favourable treatment involves the denial of an opportunity afforded to persons of the opposite sex. In *Jeremiah*, Brightman LJ suggested that as differentiation is not necessarily discriminatory, a mere deprivation of choice might not of itself be unlawful[110]. However, in *Birmingham City Council v Equal Opportunities Commission*[111] (a case involving access to grammar schools), the House of Lords held that in order to establish less favourable treatment on the grounds of sex, it is enough that members of one sex are deprived of a choice which is valued by them and which (even though others may take a different view) is a choice obviously valued on reasonable grounds by many others. A similarly broad approach to the concept of less favourable treatment was taken in *Gill v El Vino Co Ltd*[112], where the Court of Appeal held that it was unlawful for a wine bar to refuse to serve women at the bar. In that case Eveleigh LJ stated:

> 'I find it very difficult to invoke the maxim de minimis non curat lex in a situation where that which has been denied to the plaintiff is the very thing that Parliament seeks to provide, namely facilities and services on an equal basis[113].'

There is, however, an important caveat that needs to be entered, as the question of whether there is less favourable treatment is an objective one for the tribunal to decide; the fact that a complainant subjectively considers that she has been less favourably treated does not of itself establish that there is 'less favourable treatment' within the meaning of section 1(1)(a)[114]. The House of Lords has recently confirmed that in order for treatment to constitute a detriment, the

109 [1979] 3 All ER 833, [1979] IRLR 436, CA.
110 [1979] 3 All ER 833 at 840, [1979] IRLR 436 at 440.
111 [1989] IRLR 173, HL.
112 [1983] IRLR 206, CA.
113 [1983] IRLR 206 at 208.
114 *Burrett v West Birmingham Health Authority* [1994] IRLR 7 at 8, EAT, per Knox J. See p 305 below.

tribunal must find that 'a reasonable worker would or might take the view that the treatment was in all the circumstances to his [sic] detriment'[115], although the test is not wholly objective, in that it must be applied by considering the issue from the point of view of the victim[116]. A similar approach was taken in *Stewart v Cleveland Guest (Engineering) Ltd*[117], where the EAT refused to overturn the tribunal's finding that the employers had not discriminated against the complainant on grounds of sex by allowing male employees to display nude pin-ups in the workplace, even though they knew that the pictures were offensive to her. According to the EAT, there is room for disagreement as to what is or is not less favourable treatment, and the employment tribunal is best placed to make a decision on the facts of a particular case.

A further difficulty with the need to show 'less favourable' treatment is that it enables an employer to argue that, because he treats his male and female employees equally badly, his treatment of one sex is no less favourable than his treatment of the other[118]. The tribunals have in the past been able to circumvent this line of argument, particularly in harassment cases, by holding that conduct which is 'gender-specific' is sexually discriminatory per se, without the need for any comparison[119]. However, in *Pearce v Governing Body of Mayfield Secondary School*[120], the House of Lords rejected this approach: 'The fact that harassment is gender specific in form cannot be regarded as of itself establishing conclusively that the reason for the harassment is gender-based: "on the ground of her sex".[121]' It therefore seems that the only remaining circumstance in which the courts are prepared to find that conduct is sexually discriminatory per se, without the need for any comparison, is in the context of pregnancy discrimination, where the comparative approach breaks down because of the absence of an appropriate (actual or hypothetical) male comparator[122].

Finally, it must be remembered that the complainant has to be able to show the necessary causal connection between the less favourable treatment and the sex or marital status of the complainant; if there is some other genuine reason for the less favourable treatment which is untainted by discrimination (for example the employer genuinely needs someone strong or experienced and the woman in question is weak or inexperienced), then that is not 'on the ground of her sex' and discrimination is not established. So for example, in *Bullock v Alice Ottley School*[123], the employers maintained a retirement age of 60 for teaching and domestic staff (who were primarily female) and 65 for gardeners and maintenance staff (who were all male). The applicant, a domestic worker who was retired at 60,

---

115 *Shamoon v Chief Constable of the Royal Ulster Constabulary* [2003] UKHL 11, [2003] IRLR 285 at 301, per Lord Scott; *Chief Constable of West Yorkshire Police v Khan* [2003] UKHL 11, [2001] IRLR 830 at 835, per Lord Hoffmann.
116 'If the victim's opinion that the treatment was to his or her detriment is a reasonable one to hold, that ought, in my opinion, to suffice': [2003] IRLR 285 at 301, per Lord Scott.
117 [1996] ICR 535, [1994] IRLR 440, EAT. See p 308 below.
118 An argument customarily referred to by the authors as the 'bastard' defence (as in 'But I'm a bastard to everyone').
119 See eg *British Telecommunications plc v Williams* [1997] IRLR 668, EAT. See p 307 below.
120 [2003] IRLR 512, HL.
121 [2003] IRLR 512 at 516, per Lord Nicholls. Note the different approach taken to sexual harassment under EC law, where it is deemed to be discrimination on the grounds of sex: see p 310 below.
122 See p 439 below.
123 [1993] ICR 138, [1992] IRLR 564, CA. The decision confirms that there is nothing unlawful about having different retirement ages for different jobs, provided there is no direct or indirect discrimination based on a prohibited ground.

complained that she had been treated less favourably because of her sex, but the Court of Appeal held that there was no direct discrimination on grounds of sex because there was no evidence that a man in the same job would have been treated any differently. Greater difficulties arise where the employer acts from mixed motives, not all of which constitute unlawful discrimination. It is clearly established that the unlawful motive need not be the sole reason for the employer's action. In *Owen and Briggs v James*[124], a race discrimination case, the Court of Appeal held that where there is more than one operating cause, it is enough if the unlawful motive is an 'important factor' in the employer's decision; in other words, the unlawful motive must be of sufficient weight in the decision-making process to be treated as a cause, but not necessarily the sole cause, of the act thus motivated[125].

(b) Indirect discrimination

Discrimination can, of course, take more subtle forms than the overt form envisaged above. In particular, it could take the form of a rule, policy, criterion or practice which, while not expressly mentioning sex or marital status, in practice puts those of one sex or marital status at a disadvantage because it has a disproportionate impact on the members of that group; for example a requirement that applicants for a particular post be between 17 and 28, while gender-neutral on its face, may be held to discriminate indirectly against women because in practice many women would be unavailable for work between those ages because of family commitments[126]. Similarly, a rule that a candidate for a job should not have young children could be said to discriminate indirectly against married women in that it would tend to rule out large numbers of such persons[127]. On the other hand, it could be the case that the factor causing the discriminatory effect is in fact necessary for the efficient performance of the job, and so a balance has to be struck so that legitimate business needs are not jeopardised, while at the same time recognising that the fact that the discrimination is indirect will often make it, if anything, more insidious. The statutory compromise is the concept of indirect discrimination, which enables an applicant to raise an inference of discrimination by showing that a rule, etc, of the employer has an adverse impact on women, but then permits the employer to rebut that inference by showing that there is some objective justification for the application of that rule, etc, despite its adverse impact. Until 2001, there was one definition of indirect discrimination which applied for the purposes of both the sex and race discrimination legislation. That definition, contained in section 1(1)(b) of both Acts, provides that a person discriminates against a woman when the following four conditions are satisfied:

(i) the employer applies to her a requirement or condition which he also applies or would apply equally to a man;

---

124 [1982] ICR 618, [1982] IRLR 502, CA. Compare *Seide v Gillette Industries Ltd* [1980] IRLR 427, where the EAT suggested that the applicant must be able to show that the discrimination was the activating or the substantial cause. Both cases must now, of course, be considered in the light of the objective test laid down in *James v Eastleigh Borough Council* above.

125 *Nagarajan v Agnew* [1995] ICR 520, [1994] IRLR 61, EAT.

126 *Price v Civil Service Commission* [1978] ICR 27, [1977] IRLR 291.

127 *Thorndyke v Bell Fruit (North Central) Ltd* [1979] IRLR 1, IT; *Hurley v Mustoe* [1981] ICR 490, [1981] IRLR 208, EAT.

(ii) the requirement or condition is such that the proportion of women who can comply with it is considerably smaller than the proportion of men who can comply with it;

(iii) the employer cannot show the requirement or condition to be justifiable irrespective of the sex of the person to whom it is applied; and

(iv) the requirement or condition is to the complainant's detriment because she cannot comply with it.

In 2001 a new, less technical definition of indirect discrimination was introduced by the Sex Discrimination (Indirect Discrimination and Burden of Proof) Regulations 2001[128], implementing the Burden of Proof Directive[129]. Under the new definition, which only applies to claims of indirect sex discrimination in the employment field, there is indirect discrimination when the following four conditions are satisfied:

(i)   the employer applies a provision, criterion or practice which he applies or would apply equally to a man;

(ii) the provision, criterion or practice is such that it would be to the detriment of a considerably larger proportion of women than of men;

(iii) the employer cannot show the provision, criterion or practice to be justifiable irrespective of the sex of the person to whom it is applied; and

(iv) the provision, criterion or practice is to the complainant's detriment.

To complicate matters still further, the Regulations implementing the Race and Employment Directives[130] contain yet another definition of indirect discrimination[131] which applies for the purposes of race discrimination[132] (or, more accurately, those parts of the Race Relations Act which are within the scope of the Race Directive), sexual orientation discrimination[133] and discrimination on grounds of religion or belief[134]. Under this third definition, there is indirect race discrimination if:

(i)   the employer applies a provision, criterion or practice which he applies or would apply equally to a person not of the same race or national or ethnic origins as the applicant;

(ii) that provision, criterion or practice puts or would put persons of the same race or national or ethnic origins as that person at a particular disadvantage when compared with other persons;

(iii) the employer cannot show the provision, criterion or practice to be a proportionate means of achieving a legitimate aim; and

---

128 SI 2001/2660.
129 Directive 97/80/EC. Art 2(2) of the Burden of Proof Directive defines indirect discrimination as 'an apparently neutral provision, criterion or practice [which] disadvantages a substantially higher proportion of the members of one sex unless that provision, criterion or practice is appropriate and necessary and can be justified by objective factors unrelated to sex'.
130 Directive 2000/43/EC (Race Directive) and Directive 2000/78/EC (Employment Directive).
131 Art 2(2) of the Race Directive provides that indirect discrimination is taken to occur 'where an apparently neutral provision, criterion or practice would put persons of a racial or ethnic origin at a particular disadvantage compared with other persons, unless that provision, criterion or practice is objectively justified by a legitimate aim and the means of achieving that aim are appropriate and necessary.' The same definition applies, mutatis mutandis, to discrimination within the scope of the Employment Directive.
132 Race Relations Act 1976 (Amendment) Regulations 2003, SI 2003/1626, reg 3 (inserting new s 1(1A) into the Race Relations Act 1976).
133 Employment Equality (Sexual Orientation) Regulations 2003, SI 2003/1661, reg 3(1)(b).
134 Employment Equality (Religion or Belief) Regulations 2003, SI 2003/1660, reg 3(1)(b).

(iv) the provision, criterion or practice puts the complainant at a disadvantage. The unfortunate consequence is that, at the time of writing, there were no fewer than three definitions of indirect discrimination in force in the UK. This unsatisfactory state of affairs could have been avoided if the government had chosen to implement the Directives via primary legislation, as it would then have been possible to enact one common definition of indirect discrimination across the whole of UK discrimination law, including those aspects currently outside the scope of EC law and therefore not amenable to modification via secondary legislation. The failure to do so is particularly regrettable in view of the extensive consultation that took place in the three years between the adoption of the Race and Employment Directives and the introduction of the implementing Regulations. Harmonisation will no doubt come in time, but meanwhile the approach taken in this section is to examine the different elements of the original Sex Discrimination Act definition, and to consider at each stage the extent to which the new definitions are likely to lead to different outcomes.

The need for the complainant to show a specific 'requirement or condition' has been a major obstacle to a successful claim of indirect discrimination. In several of the earlier sex discrimination cases the EAT gave the phrase 'requirement or condition' a broad construction, holding that it was capable of including any kind of employment practice[135], but in *Perera v Civil Service Commission. (No 2)*[136] the equivalent provision in the Race Relations Act 1976 was interpreted far more narrowly by the Court of Appeal as meaning an absolute barrier or a 'must'. However, in *Falkirk Council v Whyte*[137], the Scottish EAT declined to apply this stricter test to a case under the Sex Discrimination Act involving selection criteria for a job which were stated to be 'desirable' rather than an absolute bar. The EAT held that the tribunal was entitled to give a liberal interpretation to the meaning of 'requirement or condition' under the Sex Discrimination Act, and to find on the facts that a criterion was a 'requirement or condition', even though it was only stated to be a desirable factor, where it was clear that it had been a decisive factor in the selection process. Significantly, the EAT further held that the race discrimination cases, and in particular *Perera*, would not be followed in the sex discrimination context if the case turned on whether a factor had to be an absolute bar for the post in question. This broader, purposive approach is more in tune with EC law, as under Article 141, indirect sex discrimination can be established without the need to show the application of a 'requirement or condition'[138]. In *Enderby v Frenchay Health Authority*[139], the ECJ considered an equal pay claim by a group of predominantly female speech therapists who were receiving less pay than a group of predominantly male clinical psychologists and pharmacists. It was not possible to identify any requirement or condition applied by the employer which had an adverse impact on the former group, but the ECJ nevertheless held that a prima facie case of sex discrimination under Article 141 had been made out. Statistics revealed an appreciable difference in pay between two jobs of equal

---

135 *Clarke v Eley (IMI) Kynoch Ltd* [1983] ICR 165, [1982] IRLR 482; *Watches of Switzerland Ltd v Savell* [1983] IRLR 141; *Home Office v Holmes* [1984] ICR 678, [1984] IRLR 299.
136 *Perera v Civil Service Commission (No 2)* [1983] ICR 428, [1983] IRLR 166, CA; affd in *Meer v Tower Hamlets London Borough* [1988] IRLR 399, CA.
137 [1997] IRLR 560, EAT.
138 There was no statutory definition of indirect discrimination in EC law until the Burden of Proof Directive, that concept having been developed in the jurisprudence of the ECJ interpreting the principle of equal treatment: see eg *Jenkins v Kingsgate Clothing Productions* [1981] ICR 592, [1981] IRLR 228, ECJ.
139 [1994] 1 All ER 495, [1994] ICR 112, ECJ.

value, one of which was carried out almost exclusively by women and the other predominantly by men, and that was sufficient to shift the burden of proof onto the employer to show an objective justification for the difference in pay. It was widely anticipated that the ECJ decision in *Enderby* would signal the end of the narrow approach in *Perera*, at least in sex discrimination cases. However, in *Bhudi v IMI Refiners Ltd* [140], the EAT surprisingly held that, notwithstanding *Enderby*, it was still essential under section 1(1)(b) of the Sex Discrimination Act for the complainant to show that the employer had applied a requirement or condition. *Enderby* was said to be concerned with the EC provisions relating to equal pay, not equal treatment, where different considerations apply; and furthermore, even if under EC law indirect discrimination could be proved without having to show the application of a requirement or condition, it was not possible to construe section 1(1)(b) so as to accord with the EC position, since the wording did not allow such an interpretation [141]. The decision in *Bhudi* seemed unnecessarily narrow. The very fact that the UK courts before *Perera* were prepared to give the words 'requirement or condition' a broader, more purposive interpretation undermined the claim that it was not possible to construe section 1(1)(b) so as to accord with *Enderby*. In any event, for those areas within the scope of the three new Directives this is no longer a live issue, as the applicant need only show that the employer has applied a 'provision, criterion or practice', which is a much looser test.

Under the original definition, the next stage involves the applicant in showing that the proportion of women who can comply with the requirement or condition is considerably smaller than the proportion of men who can comply with it. This stage involves two questions: what is the appropriate comparison, and what is meant by 'considerably smaller'? The selection of the appropriate pool of comparison is often the crucial issue in an indirect discrimination claim. The law requires a comparison to be made between the proportion of women who can comply, as compared with the proportion of men, but this begs the question: should the comparison cover the entire workforce, or only those who are qualified for the job in question, or only those at the employer's workplace, or perhaps some other category? The selection of the pool of comparison is generally regarded as a question of fact for the tribunal [142], sometimes with unfortunate results. In *Kidd v DRG (UK) Ltd* [143], the complainant argued that a 'part-timers first' redundancy selection procedure was indirectly discriminatory on grounds of sex (because a greater proportion of women work part-time) and marital status (because part-

---

140 [1994] ICR 307, [1994] IRLR 204, EAT. See also *Meade-Hill v British Council* [1995] IRLR 478, CA, where it was held that the inclusion of a contractual term (in that case, a mobility clause) imposing an obligation on a party to the contract constitutes the application of a requirement or condition, even if not invoked.

141 Cf *Webb v EMO Air Cargo (UK) Ltd* [1992] 4 All ER 929, [1993] ICR 175, where the House of Lords held that the UK courts should construe domestic legislation in any field covered by a Directive so as to accord with the interpretation of the Directive, as laid down by the ECJ, if that can be done without distorting the meaning of the domestic legislation.

142 *Price v Civil Service Commission* [1978] ICR 27, [1977] IRLR 291; *Perera v Civil Service Commission (No 2)* [1982] ICR 350, [1982] IRLR 147, EAT.

143 [1985] ICR 405, [1985] IRLR 190. The case demonstrates that the law on indirect discrimination can only work properly if the tribunal looks at what happens in practice (eg that most children are in fact still cared for by women, not by men); it founders if a tribunal looks instead at what might be considered desirable in the way of sex equality (eg men undertaking a greater degree of responsibility for looking after children).

time workers are more likely to be married women with children), but the tribunal took as the pool for comparison those households where there are small children, and were not prepared to accept as a generalisation that in such households more women than men look after children, so that the claim of indirect discrimination failed. In *Jones v University of Manchester*[144], the university advertised a post of careers adviser as being for 'a graduate, preferably aged 27–35 years with a record of successful experience in an industrial, commercial or public service setting.' The complainant, although well qualified for the post, was not shortlisted, apparently due to the fact that she was aged 46 at the time, having obtained her degree as a mature student. The tribunal upheld her complaint that the age requirement indirectly discriminated on grounds of sex against women who were mature students, as statistics showed that the proportion of women graduates obtaining their degrees as mature students who could comply with the age requirement was considerably smaller than the proportion of male graduates. The EAT reversed the tribunal on this point, holding that the wrong pool for comparison had been used, and this view was upheld on further appeal. The Court of Appeal held that the appropriate pool for comparison was all men and women with the required qualifications for the job, not including the requirement complained of (ie all graduates with the required experience, not just those who had graduated as mature students), and warned of the dangers of allowing the pool for comparison to be sub-divided or altered in a way that might allow the outcome to be manipulated. As Ralph Gibson LJ put it, the legislation demands comparison of like with like, '… but that [does] not authorise an applicant to subdivide her sex. There would be many who could demonstrate disadvantage if they could elect their own parameters'[145]. Undoubtedly the most controversial application of the definition in recent years (and one which could be said to show that the reverse of the above statement is equally true[146]) occurred in *Coker and Osamor v Lord Chancellor*[147], where the applicants challenged the appointment by the Lord Chancellor of a special adviser, Garry Hart, without open advertisement, claiming that the selection of the successful candidate from within a small, mostly male, mostly white group of people who were already known to the Lord Chancellor indirectly discriminated against them on grounds of sex and race. The employment tribunal held that the requirement to be personally known to the Lord Chancellor was indirectly discriminatory on grounds of sex, because the group of otherwise qualified people who satisfied that criterion included more men than women[148]. The decision was reversed by the EAT[149], and a further appeal by the applicants was dismissed by the Court of Appeal, which held that the appointment could not constitute indirect sex or race discrimination because 'those members of the elite pool who were personally known to the Lord Chancellor were, on the unchallenged evidence, reduced to a single man'. The requirement could have no disproportionate effect on the different groupings

144 [1993] ICR 474, [1993] IRLR 218, CA.
145 [1993] IRLR 218 at 224. See also *R v Secretary of State for Education, ex p Schaffter* [1987] IRLR 53, DC, where Schiemann J (at 56) cautioned against reducing the size of the pool to a very small size, because there is 'very real risk that you have incorporated an act of discrimination into your definition'.
146 Ie that there would be many respondents who could demonstrate an *absence* of disadvantage if they could elect their own parameters.
147 [2001] EWCA Civ 1756, [2002] IRLR 80, CA.
148 Martha Osamor's claim failed on the facts, on the grounds that she did not meet the requirements of the position.
149 [2001] IRLR 116, EAT.

within the pool, because '[h]owever many other persons there may have been who were potential candidates, whatever the proportions of men and women or racial groups in the pool, the requirement excluded the lot of them, except Mr Hart.' The logical implication of this startling piece of reasoning is that the rules on indirect sex and race discrimination do not apply when making an appointment from within a closed group of family, friends and acquaintances, and that it is possible to circumvent the prohibition on discrimination in selection arrangements 'by the simple expedient of not having any selection arrangements'[150]: 'The test of indirect discrimination focuses on the effect that the requirement objected to has on the pool of potential candidates. It can only have a discriminatory effect . . . if a significant proportion of the pool are able to satisfy the requirement. Only in that situation will it be possible for the requirement to have a disproportionate effect on the men and women, or the racial groups, which form the pool.' It would be a very brave (and probably certifiable) lawyer who advised a client to rely on a tribunal taking a similarly lenient approach in a less high profile case.

Having established the appropriate pool for comparison, the next stage for the tribunal under the original definition is to determine whether the proportion of women who 'can comply with' the requirement or condition is 'considerably smaller' than the proportion of men who can comply with it. The EAT has held that 'can comply with' means 'can comply in practice with', so that it is not enough for an employer to argue that it was theoretically physically possible for a woman to comply with the requirement, if in practice it would be harder for her to do so than it would be for a man. Thus, a requirement for a particular post that the applicant had to be between 17 and 28, which applied to both sexes, was held to be capable of being indirectly discriminatory because, although it was, of course, physically possible for a woman to comply, the tribunal accepted that a considerable number of women would be unable to apply when between those ages because of child-rearing commitments[151].

The crux of the original definition is the need to show that a 'considerably smaller' proportion of women than men can comply with the requirement or condition. In *R v Secretary of State for Education, ex p Schaffter*[152], Schiemann J explained the proper application of the test in the following terms:

'. . . The subsection would seem to indicate that what you should do is to establish: first, the proportion of all women who can comply with the requirement – I shall call this X per cent; secondly, the proportion of all

---

150 Rubenstein, [2001] IRLR 116 at 115.
151 *Price v Civil Service Commission* [1978] ICR 27, [1977] IRLR 291; affd by the House of Lords in the important race relations case of *Mandla v Dowell Lee* [1983] ICR 385, [1983] IRLR 209.
152 [1987] IRLR 53, DC. This test was approved by the Court of Appeal in *Jones v University of Manchester* [1993] ICR 474, [1993] IRLR 218. See also *McCausland v Dungannon District Council* [1993] IRLR 583, a case under the Fair Employment (Northern Ireland) Act 1989, in which the Northern Ireland Court of Appeal held that a considerably smaller proportion of Catholics could comply with a condition of being an existing employee, where 1.5% of all Catholics and 2.1% of all Protestants were able to meet the condition. At first sight the difference between the two figures might appear to be insignificantly small, but when one is expressed as a percentage of the other, the proportion of Catholics who could comply was only 71% of the other, which was held to be a considerably smaller proportion.

men who can comply with the requirement – I shall call this Y per cent; thirdly, compare X and Y and determine whether one is considerably smaller than the other.'

Under the original definition, the applicant was usually expected to produce statistical evidence in support of her claim that a considerably smaller proportion of women could comply with a particular requirement or condition[153], but there were no clear guidelines as to what constituted a 'considerably smaller' proportion, and the higher courts ducked the issue by ruling it to be a question of fact for the tribunal, the words 'considerably smaller' being 'ordinary words in common usage'[154]. In particular, there is no rule of thumb in the UK similar to the 'four-fifths rule' which is used in the US, whereby if the proportion of women who can comply with a requirement or condition is less than four-fifths of the proportion of men who can comply, that disparity is sufficient to establish a prima facie case of indirect discrimination. In principle, it is difficult to see why the *extent* of the disparity should be relevant in the first place: all that the applicant should have to do in order to pass the burden of proof on to the employer to show justification is to establish that a particular practice does in fact have *some* disparate impact on women. The extent of the disparity is only relevant in so far as it confirms the reliability of the statistical evidence – in other words, a test of statistical significance. On this view, the only purpose of the requirement to show that a *considerably* smaller proportion of women can comply is to ensure that any difference in compliance rates is in fact due to sex discrimination, rather than to chance, and where the quality of the statistical evidence is good, a tribunal should be prepared to find that a 'considerably smaller' proportion of women than men can comply where the difference in the compliance rates is statistically significant. Surprisingly, the UK courts have been reluctant to accept that a disparity of impact will be 'considerable' if it is statistically significant, although they came very close to it in *R v Secretary of State for Employment, ex p Seymour-Smith (No 2)*[155], when the House of Lords acknowledged that the quality of the statistical information is relevant in determining what degree of disparate impact need be shown in order to establish indirect sex discrimination. In that case the applicants, who were dismissed from their employment in 1991, sought judicial review of the then two-year qualifying period for bringing an unfair dismissal complaint on the grounds that it indirectly discriminated against women, contrary to the Equal Treatment Directive. The House of Lords held, following a reference to the ECJ, that the statistical evidence for the period from 1985 to 1991 demonstrated that in 1991 the two-year qualifying period had a considerably greater adverse impact on women than on men, so as to amount to indirect discrimination contrary to Article 141[156]. Significantly, their Lordships held that a considerable disparity can be more readily established if

---

153 Cf *Perera v Civil Service Commission (No 2)* [1982] ICR 350, [1982] IRLR 147; affd [1983] ICR 428 [1983] IRLR 166, CA, where the Court of Appeal cautioned that as the question is the *proportion* who can comply, not necessarily the *number*, over-elaborate statistical evidence may not be relevant.

154 *Staffordshire County Council v Black* [1995] IRLR 234, EAT.

155 [2000] IRLR 263, HL *(No 2)*; see also [1999] IRLR 253, ECJ; [1997] IRLR 315, HL; [1995] ICR 889, [1995] IRLR 464, CA; [1994] IRLR 448, DC.

156 Lord Nicholls, Lord Goff and Lord Jauncey, Lord Slynn and Lord Steyn disagreeing on this point. The ECJ had indicated that in its view the statistics for 1985 did not appear to show that a considerably smaller percentage of women than men was able to fulfil the two-year requirement; [1999] IRLR 253 at para 64. On the facts, their Lordships held, by a 3:2 majority, that any adverse effect was in fact justified: see at p 294 below.

the statistical evidence covers a long period and the figures show a persistent and relatively constant disparity[157] : 'In such a case a lesser statistical disparity may suffice to show that the disparity is considerable than if the statistics cover only a short period or if they present an uneven picture'[158]. This looks remarkably like a test of statistical significance.

As seen above, the new definitions of indirect discrimination take a rather different approach to the comparison. The Burden of Proof Directive states that indirect discrimination exists where a provision etc 'disadvantages a substantially higher proportion' of the members of one sex, and this is translated in the amended Sex Discrimination Act as requiring the applicant to show that the provision would be to the detriment of 'a considerably larger proportion' of women than of men. The requirement to show a 'substantially higher' or 'considerably larger' proportion suggests that this aspect of the new definition may not differ very much in practice from the original SDA/RRA definition. However, the Race and Employment Directives take a different approach, as they merely require proof that a provision would put persons of (for example) a racial or ethnic origin 'at a particular disadvantage' compared with other persons, and a similar form of words is used in the implementing Regulations[159]. The amended wording is significant, in that it appears to downplay the importance of statistical evidence in establishing indirect discrimination, and may in practice make it easier for an applicant to bring a claim. It also facilitates hypothetical comparisons, as instead of having to show that the proportion of the disadvantaged group 'who *can* comply' with the requirement is considerably smaller than the proportion of the comparator group, the applicant only need show that the requirement 'puts *or would put*' persons of his or her group at a particular disadvantage.

While the new definition should make it easier to use non-statistical evidence to establish a case, it would be wrong to assume that under the original SDA/RRA definition the tribunals always insisted on a mountain of statistical evidence in order to establish indirect discrimination. This is because a tribunal was entitled to take account of its own knowledge and experience[160], particularly in a traditionally male occupation where the number of women employed was so small as to make a purely statistical comparison unreliable. In *London Underground v Edwards (No 2)*[161], the applicant, a female train operator, complained that a change in the employer's rostering arrangements indirectly discriminated against her, because the proportion of female train operators who could comply with the new arrangements was considerably smaller than the proportion of male operators. The relevant statistics were that 100% of the 2,023 of the male train operators

157 On this point their Lordships echoed the view of the ECJ that statistical evidence revealing 'a lesser but persistent and relatively constant disparity over a long period' could also be evidence of indirect sex discrimination: [1999] IRLR 253, para 61.

158 Per Lord Nicholls at 270.

159 Race Relations Act 1976 (Amendment) Regulations 2003. SI 2003/1626, reg 3 (inserting new s 1(1A) into the 1976 Act); Employment Equality (Religion or Belief) Regulations 2003, SI 2003/1660, reg 3(1)(b); Employment Equality (Sexual Orientation) Regulations 2003, SI 2003/1661, reg 3(1)(b).

160 *Briggs v North Eastern Education and Library Board* [1990] IRLR 181, NICA. Cf *Kidd v DRG (UK) Ltd* above, where the EAT held that a tribunal may decline to act 'on generalised assumptions which it regards as too unsafe for acceptance' (eg in that case, that women's domestic responsibilities make it more difficult for them to work full-time).

161 [1999] ICR 494, [1998] IRLR 364, CA.

could comply with the new arrangements, compared with 95.2% (or 20 out of 21) of the 21 female train operators (the applicant being the only existing female train operator who could not comply)[162]. The Court of Appeal held that the tribunal was entitled to find that the change was indirectly discriminatory, even though statistically the percentage difference did not appear to be very great, because the tribunal was entitled to have regard to the comparatively small numbers of women involved, and to its common knowledge of the proportionately larger number of women than men with primary responsibility for the care of children[163]. Such arguments are likely to become more commonplace under the new, less technical definition of indirect discrimination.

Some of the greatest difficulty with the original definition of indirect discrimination was experienced with the defence of justification, which often lies at the heart of an indirect discrimination case. Initially, a stringent view of the defence was taken. Phillips J held in *Steel v Union of Post Office Workers* [164] that generally there is a heavy onus on an employer asserting justification, and that in particular he must be able to show that the discriminatory requirement or condition in question was necessary for his business, not merely convenient. However, the strictness of this test was progressively watered down in a series of cases under the equivalent provision in the Race Relations Act 1976, in particular by the Court of Appeal in *Ojutiku v Manpower Services Commission*[165] where the necessity test was rejected in favour of an approach based on the existence of reasons which would be 'acceptable to right-thinking people as sound and tolerable reasons'[166]. It seemed for a time as though the tests of justification in sex and race discrimination cases had diverged as a result of the decision of the House of Lords in the equal pay case of *Rainey v Greater Glasgow Health Board*[167], where the stricter test of objective justification laid down by the ECJ in *Bilka-Kaufhaus GmbH v Weber von Hartz*[168] was applied to the test of genuine material difference under section 1(3) of the Equal Pay Act 1970. In *Rainey*, Lord Keith stated that there was no material distinction in principle between the need to show 'objectively justified grounds' of difference in order to establish a defence under section 1(3) of the Equal Pay Act, and the need to justify a requirement or condition in a case of indirect discrimination under the Sex Discrimination Act, a comment which seemed to lend support to the argument that *Ojutiku* had been

---

162 As the new arrangements only involved a change to existing terms and conditions, the Court of Appeal agreed that relevant pool for comparison was all the *existing* drivers.

163 Potter LJ noted that if only one other female operator had been unable to comply, that would immediately have put the percentage of women who could not comply up to 10%. The case is a good illustration of the fact that where small numbers are involved, statistical comparisons can become unreliable.

164 [1978] ICR 181, [1977] IRLR 288, followed in *Hurley v Mustoe* [1981] ICR 490, [1981] IRLR 208, EAT.

165 [1982] ICR 661, [1982] IRLR 418, CA. See *Singh v Rowntree MacKintosh Ltd* [1979] ICR 554, [1979] IRLR 199, EAT and *Panesar v Nestlé Co Ltd* [1980] ICR 144n, [1980] IRLR 64, CA.

166 Per Eveleigh LJ at 421 (see also Kerr LJ to similar effect). Stephenson LJ preferred an approach based on the objective balancing of the discriminatory effect against the discriminator's need for it.

167 [1987] ICR 129, [1987] IRLR 26, HL: see p 342 below.

168 Case 170/84 [1987] ICR 110, [1986] IRLR 317, ECJ. The *Bilka* test requires the employer to show that the measures chosen correspond to a real need on the part of the undertaking, are appropriate to achieve that objective and are necessary to that end (see p 343 below).

impliedly overruled by *Rainey*. However, in *Hampson v Department of Education and Science*[169], the Court of Appeal said that there was no significant difference between the test adopted by Stephenson LJ in *Ojutiku*[170] and that adopted by the House of Lords in *Rainey*, and ruled that whether a requirement or condition is justifiable requires an objective balance to be struck between the discriminatory effect of the requirement or condition and the reasonable needs of the person who applies it[171]. The test in *Hampson* was subsequently approved by the House of Lords in *Webb v EMO Air Cargo (UK) Ltd* [172]. This is clearly the preferable view, for it would be unsatisfactory to expect courts or tribunals to apply a different standard of justification in sex and race discrimination cases when the two statutes are in fact in pari materia on this point.

In *Cobb v Secretary of State for Employment* [173], Wood J explained the correct approach to the question of justification in the following terms:

> 'It was for the respondent to satisfy the Tribunal that the decisions which he took were objectively justified for economic, administrative or other reasons. It was for the Tribunal to decide what facts it found proved, and to carry out the balancing exercise involved, taking into account all the surrounding circumstances and giving due emphasis to the degree of discrimination caused against the object or aim to be achieved – the principle of proportionality.[174]'

Cobb involved a challenge to the eligibility criteria for admission to the Community Programme, a government scheme which provided temporary employment for the long-term unemployed. In *R v Secretary of State for Employment, ex p Seymour-Smith (No 2)*[175], which involved a challenge under Article 141 to the legality of the two-year qualifying period for claiming unfair dismissal, the House of Lords held that where the complaint relates to legislative measures implementing social policy aims, the onus is on the member state to show (1) that the allegedly discriminatory rule reflects a legitimate aim of its social policy, (2) that this aim is unrelated to any discrimination based on sex, and (3) that the member state could reasonably consider that the means chosen were suitable for attaining that aim[176]. It was also held that the test of justification applied in the lower courts was too stringent, and that member states should be afforded a broad measure of discretion

169 [1989] IRLR 69; overruled on other grounds [1991] 1 AC 171, [1990] ICR 511, HL.
170 [1982] ICR 661, [1982] IRLR 418, CA. Balcombe LJ considered that neither Eveleigh LJ nor Kerr LJ in *Ojutiku* had indicated what they considered the test to be.
171 This test was approved by the Northern Ireland Court of Appeal in *Briggs v North Eastern Education and Library Board* [1990] IRLR 181, and by the EAT in *Greater Manchester Police Authority v Lea* [1990] IRLR 372.
172 [1992] 4 All ER 929, [1993] ICR 175, HL. Lord Keith stated expressly that the *Hampson* test must now be regarded as the appropriate one and as superseding that expressed by Eveleigh LJ in *Ojutiku*.
173 [1989] ICR 506, [1989] IRLR 464, EAT.
174 At 468. Note also Wood J's observation that the employer 'is under no obligation to prove that there was no other way of achieving his object, however expensive and administratively complicated.'
175 [2000] IRLR 263, HL.
176 On the facts, the House of Lords held that the Secretary of State had discharged the burden of showing that the increase in the qualifying period in 1985, and its retention in 1991, were objectively justified.

('margin of appreciation') in pursuing their social policy aims (although generalised assumptions, lacking any actual foundation, would not be good enough)[177]. Significantly, however, the House of Lords held that if a government introduces a measure which proves to have a disparately adverse impact, it has a duty to take reasonable steps to monitor the working of that measure by reviewing the position periodically, because if the benefits hoped for do not materialise, the retention of such a measure may no longer be objectively justifiable[178]. There is no reason in principle why this duty to keep indirectly discriminatory policies and practices under periodic review should not also be applied to employers in both the public and private sector.

The question of justification is an issue of fact for the tribunal[179], with the result that a tribunal's decision on the matter will be difficult if not impossible to challenge provided it applies the correct tests[180]. This approach has been criticised for leading to an undesirable level of uncertainty and inconsistent decisions in this sensitive area[181], but it is very much in line with the 'anti-legalism' drive by the courts discussed in Chapter 8. A good illustration of the potential for inconsistency may be seen by comparing two decisions of the EAT concerning refusal to allow a female employee to return to work part-time after maternity leave. In the first, *Home Office v Holmes*[182], the EAT upheld a tribunal decision that a refusal to allow a woman with children to transfer to part-time working constituted indirect sex discrimination (the 'requirement or condition' in question being the obligation to work full time) which, on the facts, was not justifiable. The potential effect of such a decision is considerable, particularly when allied to the woman's statutory right to return to work after maternity (the eventual outcome possibly being to leave full-time work and return to part-time work, at least where the employer cannot show good reason to refuse this)[183]. However, the case also demonstrates how difficult it can be to predict the outcome of indirect discrimination claims, for while the decision was hailed in the press as a major step forward in women's rights, in fact it was no such thing. At the end of his judgment, Waite P went out of his way to state that the decision was taken entirely on the particular facts of the case ('It is easy to imagine other instances, not strikingly different from hers, where the result would not be the same'), and the

177 See to like effect *Kutz-Bauer v Freie und Hansestadt Hamburg* [2003] IRLR 368, ECJ. Significantly, the ECJ rejected arguments that budgetary considerations (ie the desire to reduce costs) could constitute an aim pursued by a member state's social policy and thereby justify sex discrimination. Cf also *Jorgenen v Foreningen af Speciallaeger* [2000] IRLR 726, ECJ.

178 Per Lord Nicholls, [2000] IRLR 263 at 271. His Lordship also observed: 'The greater the disparity of impact, the greater the diligence which can reasonably be expected of the government'.

179 A point stressed by the House of Lords in the important race discrimination case of *Mandla v Dowell Lee* [1983] ICR 385, [1983] IRLR 209, HL.

180 In *University of Manchester v Jones* [1992] ICR 52 the EAT suggested that the exercise of a judicial discretion 'may be re-examined where irrelevant factors have been taken into consideration or where relevant considerations have been omitted in its exercise'. (The decision of the EAT was affirmed by the Court of Appeal: [1993] ICR 474, [1993] IRLR 218.)

181 See in particular the remarks of Browne-Wilkinson J in *Clarke v Eley (IMI) Kynoch Ltd* [1983] ICR 165, [1982] IRLR 482.

182 [1984] ICR 678, [1984] IRLR 299. See also *London Underground Ltd v Edwards (No 2)* [1999] ICR 494, [1998] IRLR 364, CA, where the employer was unable to show that indirectly discriminatory rostering arrangements were justified.

183 The Part-Time Workers Directive protects part-time workers from less favourable treatment by reason of their part-time status, but it does not give any right to insist on a transfer to part-time work. See p 24 above.

point was subsequently reinforced by the decision of the Scottish EAT in *Greater Glasgow Health Board v Carey*[184], where on facts very similar to those in *Holmes* it was held that a refusal to allow a return to work part-time after maternity leave was justified by considerations of administrative efficiency[185].

The new definitions of indirect discrimination in the Regulations implementing the Burden of Proof, Race and Employment Directives take a different approach to the justification defence, but it is unlikely that the change in terminology will lead to any significant change in outcome. All three Directives use similar language: under the Burden of Proof Directive, the test is whether the provision, criterion or practice 'is appropriate and necessary and can be justified by objective factors unrelated to sex', whereas under the Race and Employment Directives the test is whether the provision etc 'is objectively justified by a legitimate aim and the means of achieving that aim are appropriate and necessary.' The Regulations implementing the Burden of Proof Directive simply reiterate the existing SDA/RRA test (ie is the provision etc 'justifiable irrespective of the sex of the person to whom it is applied') but those implementing the Race and Employment Directives take a leap into the unknown by dispensing with the familiar SDA/RRA test and asking instead whether the provision etc is 'a proportionate means of achieving a legitimate aim.' The government's explanation for this new approach (as set out in the explanatory memoranda to the new Regulations), is that the addition of the words 'objectively justified' would not add anything to the requirement for the discriminator to demonstrate the existence of a legitimate aim, and that the term 'proportionate' was used, first, because both the Directives and the ECJ use that term interchangeably with 'appropriate and necessary' anyway; and secondly, because there was a risk that the UK courts might interpret the term 'necessary' as a very strict requirement (in accordance with the usual English law approach to the concept of necessity) whereas the term 'appropriate and necessary' in the European context 'does not set out an absolute test but, rather, one of proportionality involving balancing between the discriminatory effects of a measure and the importance of the aim pursued.[186]' It remains to be seen whether the new wording is interpreted in that spirit by the courts.

(c) Victimisation

The Sex Discrimination Act 1976 creates a third form of discrimination, victimisation, which applies where a person is subjected to less favourable treatment because he or she has brought proceedings or given evidence in proceedings against the discriminator under the Act or the Equal Pay Act 1970, or made allegations in good faith of breaches of one of these Acts[187]. However, to benefit from the statutory protection the applicant must show that the reason for the less favourable treatment is because he or she has done one of the protected acts. At one time it

---

184 [1987] IRLR 484.

185 For a further example of conflicting decisions on similar facts (this time in the context of part-timers-first redundancy selection procedures), compare *Clarke v Eley (IMI) Kynoch Ltd* [1983] ICR 165, [1982] IRLR 482 with *Kidd v DRG (UK) Ltd* [1985] ICR 405, [1985] IRLR 190. The decision in *Kidd* has been heavily criticised: see p 246.

186 Explanatory memorandum to the Employment Equality (Religion or Belief) Regulations 2003, reg 14. The explanatory memorandum to the Employment Equality (Sexual Orientation) Regulations contains an explanation in identical terms.

187 Sex Discrimination Act 1975, s 4. For the comparable provision in the context of race discrimination, see the Race Relations Act 1976, s 2.

was thought that in order to establish victimisation there had to be some conscious motivation in the mind of the alleged discriminator which caused him to treat the complainant less favourably than other persons[188], but in *Nagarajan v London Regional Transport*[189], the House of Lords held that in complaints of victimisation under the Race Relations Act (and by analogy, under the Sex Discrimination Act) the motive of the alleged discriminator is irrelevant, and the question to be asked is the simple causative one, ie whether the complainant would have been treated in that way but for his race[190]. While the motive of the alleged discriminator is irrelevant, a claim of victimisation will still fail if the employer did not treat the complainant any less favourably than he would have treated a person who had not done one of the protected acts, and this once again raises the vexed question of who the appropriate comparator is. Put simply, should the treatment afforded to the complainant be compared with the treatment of other employees who have not made discrimination complaints against the employer? Or should the comparison be with other employees who have not made any type of complaint against the employer? This point was considered in *Chief Constable of West Yorkshire v Khan*[192], in which the House of Lords revisited some of the issues previously considered in *Nagarajan*. The facts were that the complainant had made a number of unsuccessful applications for promotion, which had led him to bring a race discrimination complaint against West Yorkshire Police. While that claim was still outstanding he applied to another force for a more senior post, but West Yorkshire Police refused to provide him with a reference, on the grounds that it might prejudice the case before the tribunal. The complainant then added a complaint of victimisation in respect of the refusal of the reference, claiming that he had been treated less favourably than others by reason of having brought his original discrimination complaint, in that references were normally provided on request for those applying for new employment. The victimisation complaint succeeded up to the Court of Appeal, which applied a straightforward 'but for' test (would a reference have been provided but for the fact that he had a discrimination complaint pending?), but the House of Lords allowed the appeal, holding that the Court of Appeal had applied the wrong test. On the issue of the comparator, the House of Lords held that the appropriate comparison was with another employee who had not made a tribunal complaint, and so the complainant had in fact been treated less favourably than the employer would have treated other persons; however, their Lordships considered that the complainant's case failed the second part of the test (was the less favourable treatment 'by reason that' the complainant had brought proceedings under the Act?), as this was considered to involve a higher threshold than the 'but for' test. Their Lordships considered that the reference was not withheld 'by reason that' the complainant had brought discrimination proceedings, but rather because the employers wished to preserve their position in the pending discrimination proceedings. Unfortunately, the speeches are not entirely consistent, and some of their Lordships appeared to want to reintroduce motive as relevant consideration[193],

188 See eg *Aziz v Trinity Street Taxis Ltd* [1988] ICR 534, [1988] IRLR 204, CA.
189 [1999] ICR 877, [1999] IRLR 572, HL, reversing the Court of Appeal.
190 This is the *James v Eastleigh Borough Council* test which applies in complaints of direct discrimination under s 1: see p 280. Dicta to the contrary in *Aziz v Trinity Street Taxis Ltd* [1988] ICR 534, [1988] IRLR 204 were said to be incorrect. Cf the strong dissenting judgment of Lord Browne-Wilkinson, who said that he did not understand how one could victimise someone subconsciously.
192 [2001] IRLR 830, HL.
193 See eg Lord Nicholls at 833 and Lord Scott at 837.

but Lord Hoffmann's clearsighted analysis, explaining the issue as a question of causation[194], is highly persuasive and more easily reconciled with *Nagarajan.*

Finally, the protection against victimisation for having made an allegation of discrimination only applies where the allegation is that the discriminator has committed an act 'which . . . would amount to a contravention' of the anti-discrimination legislation[195]. The implications of this were graphically demonstrated in *Waters v Metropolitan Police Comr*[196], where the employee alleged that she had been victimised by the employer for alleging sexual harassment by a work colleague. The Court of Appeal held that for the protection against victimisation to apply in such a case, the alleged act must be one for which the employer would be vicariously liable, and as the alleged harassment was not committed in the 'course of employment', the employer could not be held vicariously liable for it, and could not therefore be held to have victimised the complainant for making the allegations[197]. At one time, the protection against victimisation was believed[198] not to apply to events occurring after the end of the employment relationship (for example the provision of an adverse reference in retaliation for making a discrimination complaint), but in *Coote v Granada Hospitality Ltd*[199], the ECJ held that the Equal Treatment Directive requires member states to introduce measures protecting workers from discrimination after the employment relationship has ended, and the EAT subsequently reinterpreted the 1975 Act as covering victimisation by an ex-employer[200]. The House of Lords has recently confirmed (in the joined appeal in *Rhys-Harper v Relaxion Group plc*[201]) that the Sex Discrimination Act, Race Relations Act and Disability Discrimination Act should all be interpreted as covering discriminatory conduct (including victimisation) after the end of employment, provided there is a substantive connection between the conduct complained of and the employment relationship, and this has been further reinforced by an amendment to the SDA to put the matter beyond doubt[202].

(d) Positive discrimination[203]

The Sex Discrimination Act is based on a neutral or symmetrical model of equality. It gives each individual, male or female, the right not to be treated less favourably on grounds of his or her sex or marital status. As *James v Eastleigh Borough Council*[204] demonstrated, the fact that the defendant acted from a good or worthy

---

194 See [2001] IRLR 830 at 835.
195 Sex Discrimination Act 1975, s 4(1)(d).
196 [1997] ICR 1073, [1997] IRLR 589, CA. See p 317 below.
197 The practical importance of the decision has arguably been reduced by the broad approach to vicarious liability taken in some recent cases: see p 317.
198 Based on the ruling in *Nagarajan v Agnew* [1995] ICR 520, [1994] IRLR 61, EAT (a case under the RRA).
199 [1999] ICR 100, [1998] IRLR 656, ECJ.
200 *(No 2)* [1999] IRLR 452, EAT.
201 [2003] IRLR 484, HL.
202 Sex Discrimination Act 1975 (Amendment) Regulations 2003, SI 2003/1657; see p 312 below. A similar amendment has been made to the RRA (see p 369 below) and the DDA is to be amended to like effect from October 2004.
203 See Fredman 'Reversing Discrimination' (1997) 113 LQR 575; Pitt 'Can Reverse Discrimination Be Justified?' in Hepple and Szyszczak (eds) *Discrimination: the Limits of Law* (1992), ch 16; McCrudden 'Rethinking positive action' (1986) 15 ILJ 219.
204 [1990] IRLR 288, HL. See also *Jepson and Dyas-Elliott v Labour Party* [1996] IRLR 116, IT (women-only shortlists unlawful), although note now the Sex Discrimination (Election Candidates) Act 2002.

motive is no defence to a complaint of unlawful discrimination. It follows that any preferential treatment aimed at redressing the historic disadvantage experienced by women and enabling them to compete equally will normally be illegal if it involves the less favourable treatment of a man. Such measures – generally referred to as 'positive discrimination' – must be distinguished from measures which do not involve preferential treatment of one group but which are designed to promote a greater degree of equality of opportunity within the workplace (so-called 'positive action'). While positive discrimination will normally be unlawful, 'positive action' is not prohibited. The Code of Practice issued by the EOC suggests a number of such measures, including the introduction of a monitoring policy and the taking of positive steps to identify and remove potential barriers to the recruitment and advancement of women[205]. Other measures aimed at promoting equal opportunities which fall short of positive discrimination might include the development of policies and practices designed to assist disadvantaged groups (for example 'family-friendly' policies), encouraging applications from under-represented groups, and the setting of targets to reduce under-representation.

One exception to the prohibition on positive discrimination is section 47, which allows discrimination in favour of one sex in vocational training where it appears that in the previous twelve months there were no persons of that sex employed in the work in question in Great Britain, or an area within Great Britain, or the number was comparatively small[206]. Where such under-representation is established, it is not unlawful to provide women-only or men-only training facilities to help fit the under-represented sex for that work. There is also a special exemption targeted at those in special need of training because they have been out of full-time employment discharging domestic or family responsibilities[207]. This provision enables employers to run training courses targeted at women returning to work after maternity leave, irrespective of whether there is a general under-representation of women in that kind of work.

This is an area in which UK law has generally been in step with EC law, although the position is not entirely clear. In general terms, EC law has tended to adopt the same symmetrical approach to equality as English law. Article 2(4) of the Equal Treatment Directive provides that the Directive 'shall be without prejudice to measures to promote equal opportunity for men and women, in particular by removing existing inequalities which affect women's opportunities', which appears to permit preferential treatment for women to enable them to compete more equally, but the ECJ has interpreted this provision narrowly, and has been reluctant to accept it as legitimising positive discrimination other than within very narrow limits. In *Kalanke v Freie Hansestadt Bremen*[208], the ECJ considered the legality of a so-called 'tie-break' provision in the relevant domestic provisions, whereby women who had the same qualifications as men for the same post were

---

205 EOC Code of Practice, paras 37–40.
206 See Sacks 'Tackling Discrimination Positively' in Hepple and Szyszczak (eds) *Discrimination: the Limits of Law* (1992). Employers are also permitted to target training on under-represented groups within their organisation: Sex Discrimination Act 1975, s 48. There are parallel provisions in the Race Relations Act 1976, ss 37 and 38.
207 Sex Discrimination Act 1975, s 47(3).
208 [1996] ICR 314, [1995] IRLR 660, ECJ.

to be given priority in sectors where they were underrepresented. The ECJ held that national rules which guarantee women absolute and unconditional priority for appointment or promotion go beyond promoting equal opportunities and overstep the limits of the exception to the principle of equal treatment in Article 2(4)[209]; the exception was interpreted strictly, as permitting national measures relating to access to employment 'which give a specific advantage to women with a view to improving their ability to compete in the labour market and to pursue a career in an equal footing with men'. The decision in *Kalanke* was greeted with dismay (not least by the European Commission), and when the ECJ next had an opportunity to consider the issue, in *Marschall v Land Nordrhein-Westfalen*[210], there was a noticeable softening of the tone. That case also involved a tie-break provision giving women priority for promotion in the event of equal suitability, competence and professional performance, but with the crucial addition of a 'saving clause' whereby women were not to be given priority if reasons specific to an individual male candidate tilted the balance in his favour. The ECJ noted that even where male and female candidates are equally qualified, male candidates tend to be promoted because of prejudices and stereotypes concerning the role and capacities of women in working life, and the fear that women will interrupt their working lives more frequently, be less flexible in their working hours because of household and family duties, and be absent from work more frequently because of pregnancy or childbirth. The ECJ acknowledged that because of these factors, the mere fact that male and female candidates are equally qualified 'does not mean that they have the same chances', and held that although a national rule which guaranteed absolute and unconditional priority for women would not be lawful, a rule which counteracted the prejudicial effects of the attitudes and behaviour described above by giving preferential treatment to equally qualified women candidates could be lawful if it contained a saving clause which guaranteed 'that the candidatures will be the subject of an objective assessment which will take account of all criteria specific to the individual candidates and will override the priority accorded to the female candidates where one or more of the criteria tilts the balance in favour of the male candidate' (all of which begs the question of what 'equally qualified' means in this context). A similar approach was taken in the case of *Badeck*[211], where the ECJ upheld a programme aimed at eliminating the under representation of women in the public sector which, inter alia, gave priority to equally qualified women applicants in sectors where they were underrepresented and allocated at least half the available training places to women in occupations in which they were underrepresented, the decisive point being that, as in *Marschall*, the programme did not automatically and unconditionally give priority to women when women and men were equally qualified. One of the more interesting (and, it must be said, ingenious) aspects of the programme in *Badeck* was the approach taken to the evaluation of the candidates' qualifications, in that the scheme in effect sought to redefine 'merit' for the purposes of the comparison by providing that in assessing their qualifications, certain factors were to be taken into account (for example capabilities and experience acquired by looking after children or persons requiring care, in so far as they were of importance for the suitability of applicants),

209 The ECJ held that the provisions in question fell outside this exception by substituting for equal opportunity 'the result which is only to be arrived at by providing such equality of opportunity'.
210 [1998] IRLR 39, ECJ.
211 *Badeck's Application* [2000] IRLR 432, ECJ.

while other factors (for example family status, income of the partner, part-time work, leave or delays in completing training as a result of looking after children or dependants) were to be left out of the equation. Another novel aspect of the scheme in *Badeck* was that instead of leaving the all-important assessment of the individual situations of the candidates at large, the saving clause identified five situations which justified overriding the tie-break rule for the advancement of women, including promoting disabled persons, ending a period of long-term unemployment or giving preferential treatment to those who, for family reasons, worked part-time and wished to resume full-time employment. The scheme in *Badeck* probably represents the high-water mark of positive discrimination programmes accepted as valid to date by the ECJ[212]. In contrast, the scheme in *Abrahammsson v Fogelqvist*[213], which required the appointment of a suitably qualified candidate of the underrepresented sex even if they were less highly qualified than a candidate of the opposite sex, was considered to overstep the boundaries of positive discrimination permitted by Article 2(4).

Finally, as a result of an amendment made by the Amsterdam Treaty, the EC Treaty now contains an express provision permitting positive measures aimed at promoting equality. Article 141(4) states: 'With a view to ensuring full equality in practice between men and women in working life, the principle of equal treatment shall not prevent any Member State from maintaining or adopting measures providing for specific advantages in order to make it easier for the under-represented sex to pursue a vocational activity or to prevent or compensate for disadvantages in professional careers.' On the face of it this would seem to permit a wider range of positive discrimination measures than Article 2(4), but in *Abrahammsson* the ECJ considered that the selection method in that case was not justified by Article 141(4), as it was 'disproportionate to the aim pursued'. It must therefore be doubted whether Article 141(4) permits anything more than the limited type of tie-break scheme sanctioned in *Marschall* and *Badeck*. As far as the UK is concerned, the present government has shown no inclination to date to exploit, or indeed to permit employers to exploit, the limited scope for positive discrimination under EC law.

(iv) Discrimination before employment

The first and perhaps most difficult stage at which a woman may encounter discrimination in employment is when she applies for a job. It is unlawful under section 6(1) for an employer to discriminate against a woman in the arrangements[214] he makes for the selection procedure, in the terms on which he offers her employment[215], or by refusing or deliberately omitting to offer her the

---

212 Although cf *Lommers v Minister van Landbouw, Natuurbeheer en Visserij* [2002] IRLR 430, ECJ, where a scheme giving female employees priority for subsidised nursery places was upheld so long as nursery places were available on the same terms to male single parents.
213 [2000] IRLR 732, ECJ.
214 On the meaning of 'arrangements', see *Brennan v J H Dewhurst Ltd* [1984] ICR 52, [1983] IRLR 357 (biased interview).
215 Where the terms in question are amenable to inclusion in an 'equality clause', the claim should be under the Equal Pay Act 1970, not the Sex Discrimination Act 1975, s 8. On equal pay, see pp 325–359 below.

employment[216]. Once again, a certain amount of realism is necessary in construing these provisions, so that for example it is not necessarily unlawful for an employer to ask a woman a question at an interview which would not be asked of a man (particularly questions about the suitability of a woman for a job where the employment of a man has been normal in the past); the issue is whether, by asking the question, the woman was treated less favourably on grounds of her sex than a man would be treated[217]. The law against discriminatory selection arrangements is indirectly strengthened by section 38, which makes it unlawful to publish or cause to be published a job advertisement which indicates or might reasonably be understood as indicating an intention to discriminate[218]. Only the Equal Opportunities Commission may bring proceedings against a publisher or advertiser under section 38[219]. At one time it was thought that a discriminatory advertisement qualified as an 'arrangement' for selection and therefore constituted unlawful discrimination under section 6(1), but the EAT has held that this is not so[220], and that only the statutory enforcement agencies can bring proceedings in respect of an advertisement which indicates an intention to discriminate. According to the EAT, it is necessary to distinguish between an intention to do an act of discrimination, and an act of discrimination; placing a discriminatory advertisement indicates an intention to do an act of discrimination, but it is not an act of discrimination in itself[221]. In practice the most difficult obstacle facing a woman who believes that she may have been discriminated against at the appointment stage is to prove her case. The vexed question of proving discrimination is considered below[222].

Section 7 creates a statutory exemption from liability for unlawful discrimination in selection for employment where being a man or a woman is a genuine occupational qualification (GOQ) for the job. The GOQ defence is an important exception to the normal rule that motive is irrelevant in cases of direct discrimination. It is designed to avoid some of the more obvious absurdities of complete equality, but it is important that the boundaries of the exception are not stretched too far, lest the protection against discrimination be undermined, and the EAT has held that section 7 lays down exhaustively the categories of job which come within the GOQ defence[223]. Thus, an employer can advertise for and appoint a man where the job calls for a man for physiological reasons (though this does not mean strength and stamina simpliciter), where for reasons of

216 The Court of Appeal held in *Post Office v Adekeye* [1997] ICR 110, [1997] IRLR 105 that the parallel provision in the Race Relations Act does not cover a dismissed employee seeking reinstatement on appeal, but the Sex Discrimination Act has now been amended to cover post-termination discrimination: see p 312 below.

217 *Saunders v Richmond-upon-Thames London Borough Council* [1978] ICR 75, [1977] IRLR 362. The EOC's Code of Practice, para 23, advises against asking questions about the candidate's marriage or family intentions.

218 It seems that this will include an advertisement which is indirectly discriminatory: *Commission for Racial Equality v Dutton* [1989] QB 783, [1989] IRLR 8, CA.

219 Sex Discrimination Act 1975, s 72.

220 *Cardiff Women's Aid v Hartup* [1994] IRLR 390, EAT (a case under the equivalent provisions in the Race Relations Act 1976, s 4(1)(a)).

221 Quaere whether the outcome would have been different if the complainant had actually applied for and been refused the job in question?

222 At p 312.

223 *Grieg v Community Industry* [1979] ICR 356, [1979] IRLR 158, EAT.

authenticity a male actor is needed for a stage part, where the job needs to be held by a man to preserve decency or privacy (for example a lavatory attendant or possibly a tailor)[224], where the job entails living in a private home in close contact with the employer (for example an old lady's companion)[225], where the job involves living on the premises, and the location is such that personal facilities can only reasonably be expected for men (the case of the proverbial lighthouse keeper), and where the work is in a men's hospital or prison and should not reasonably be done by a woman. Also included in the list are welfare or educational services which can 'most effectively be provided' by a man[226], jobs involving duties abroad in a country where those duties, by law or custom, are performed by men, and the employment of a man as half of a husband and wife team (for example chauffeur and housekeeper). The exemption will not apply if there are other employees who are capable of performing the duties in question and whom it would be reasonable for the employer to employ on those duties, provided they already[227] exist in sufficient numbers to meet the employer's likely requirements without undue inconvenience[228]. In other areas of discrimination law, the GOQ defence is being replaced by a new and almost certainly narrower exception based on the EC law concept of a 'genuine occupational requirement'[229], and the same modification will no doubt be made to the Sex Discrimination Act in due course.

(v) Discrimination during employment

Under section 6(2) it is unlawful for an employer to discriminate against a woman during her employment in the way he affords or refuses to afford her access to opportunities for promotion, transfer or training[230], or to any other benefits, facilities[231] or services. It is also unlawful if he discriminates against her by subjecting her to any 'detriment'. In *Ministry of Defence v Jeremiah*[232] the Court of Appeal held that subjecting to any detriment is to be given its ordinary, common-sense meaning of 'putting under a disadvantage'.[233] Doubt had arisen over whether this was the correct test as a result of the EAT decision in *Coker v Lord*

---

224 See eg *Sisley v Britannia Security Systems* [1983] ICR 628, [1983] IRLR 404, EAT.
225 There used to be a formal exemption in the case of domestic servants but this (along with the small firm exemption) was repealed by the Sex Discrimination Act 1986 in the wake of the decision of the ECJ in *EC Commission v United Kingdom* Case 165/82 [1984] ICR 192, [1984] IRLR 29; the exemption for private homes is all that remains.
226 This phrase also appears in the equivalent provision of the Race Relations Act, s 5(2)(d); for its interpretation in that context, see *Tottenham Green Under Fives' Centre v Marshall* [1989] ICR 214, [1989] IRLR 147, EAT; *Tottenham Green Under Fives' Centre v Marshall (No 2)* [1991] ICR 320, [1991] IRLR 162, EAT; *Lambeth London Borough v Commission for Racial Equality* [1990] ICR 768, [1990] IRLR 231, CA.
227 See *Lasertop Ltd v Webster* [1997] ICR 828, [1997] IRLR 498, EAT.
228 S 7(4); see *Etam plc v Rowan* [1989] IRLR 150 (employer could have employed male assistant in women's clothing shop because there were sufficient female assistants to preserve decency). See also *Wylie v Dee & Co (Menswear) Ltd* [1978] IRLR 103 (inside leg measurements).
229 See eg p 370.
230 This could occur in a redundancy situation where a new job is created but the employer refuses to transfer a person of a particular sex to it (subject to the genuine occupational qualification defence): *Timex Corpn v Hodgson* [1982] ICR 63, [1981] IRLR 530, EAT.
231 This refers to facilities which already exist: *Clymo v London Borough of Wandsworth* [1989] ICR 250, [1989] IRLR 241, EAT.
232 [1979] 3 All ER 833, [1979] IRLR 436, CA, disapproving the reasoning on this point in *Peake v Automotive Products Ltd* [1977] ICR 968, [1977] IRLR 365, CA – see p 283 above.
233 [1979] IRLR 436 at 438, per Lord Brandon.

Chancellor[234], in which the view was expressed that the applicant needed to demonstrate 'some physical or economic consequence' in order to establish 'detriment', but in *Shamoon v Chief Constable of the Royal Ulster Constabulary*[235], the House of Lords confirmed the orthodox position. Their Lordships also confirmed that the test of detriment contains both subjective and objective elements, approving Brightman LJ's formulation in *Jeremiah* that 'a detriment exists if a reasonable worker would or might take the view that the [treatment] was in all the circumstances to his detriment[236]'; according to Lord Scott, the test must be applied 'by considering the issue from the point of view of the victim. If the victim's opinion that the treatment was to his or her detriment is a reasonable one to hold, that ought . . . to suffice.[237]' The emphasis on the reasonableness of the victim's view of the treatment means that 'an unjustified sense of grievance cannot amount to 'detriment'.[238]' The need to establish detriment means that differentiation between sexes is not in itself unlawful discrimination, for there must be some element of disadvantage, although the courts have generally been prepared to find that differential treatment is detrimental[239]; it may also be possible for a tribunal or court to consider a claimed disadvantage to be so minor as to be disregarded on the de minimis principle, although as seen earlier the scope of the de minimis defence is probably very narrow[240]. Once there is a detriment, however, it will not be a defence for an employer to show that he takes the detriment into account by compensating those who experience it (for example where only men are obliged to do certain disagreeable work, but receive an extra payment in respect of it); there may still be unlawful discrimination even though special rates of pay are given for that work[241]. Two issues which have given rise to particular difficulty, and therefore warrant special attention, are dress and appearance rules, and sexual harassment.

(a) Dress and appearance rules

It is not uncommon for employers to impose rules on employees concerning their dress and appearance while at work. This may be done for operational reasons (for example in the interests of safety and hygiene), or simply because the employer is seeking to promote a particular corporate image which involves the employees wearing a uniform or observing restrictions on, for example, their hair-style or the wearing of jewellery. Such rules often impose different requirements on men and women, reflecting current perceptions of conventional appearance, yet it could be argued that under the test of direct discrimination approved by the House of Lords in *James v Eastleigh Borough Council*[242], any such differentiation necessarily constitutes discrimination on the grounds of sex, because 'but for' a person's sex, the gender-specific appearance requirement would not have been

---

234 [2001] IRLR 116, EAT. See also *Jiad v Byford* [2003] EWCA Civ 135, [2003] IRLR 232.
235 [2003] UKHL 11, [2003] ICR 337, [2003] IRLR 285.
236 [1979] IRLR 436 at 440.
237 [2003] UKHL 11, [2003] IRLR 285 at 301. Note also that to amount to a 'detriment', the disadvantage must arise 'in the field of employment': per Lord Hope at 291.
238 [2003] UKHL 11, [2003] IRLR 285 at 291, per Lord Hope. See also *Barclays Bank plc v Kapur (No 2)* [1995] IRLR 87.
239 See p 283 above.
240 See p 283 above.
241 See *Ministry of Defence v Jeremiah* [1978] ICR 984, [1978] IRLR 402; affd by CA: [1979] 3 All ER 833, [1979] IRLR 436.
242 [1990] IRLR 288, HL; see p 280.

applied[243]. Furthermore, the underlying rationale of the Sex Discrimination Act was to tackle discrimination which results from gender-stereotyping, yet arguably what is regarded as 'conventional' in terms of appearance is itself permeated by gender stereotyping, and therefore inherently sexually discriminatory.

The approach of the courts and tribunals to this issue has been to skirt around the problem by holding that there is no infringement of the Act where the employer imposes an appearance code which has different rules for men and women, as long as the code enforces a common principle of smartness or conventionality, and taken as a whole neither gender is treated less favourably. So, for example, in *Schmidt v Austicks Bookshops Ltd* [244], the employer imposed a rule that women could not wear trousers at work and had to wear overalls, while men were not allowed to wear tee-shirts. A female employee complained that the rule against trousers was unlawful under the Act, but the EAT held against her on the ground that the employer applied rules on clothing to all employees, although in the nature of things the rules were not the same given the difference between the sexes[245]. According to the EAT, an employer is entitled to a large measure of discretion in controlling the image of his establishment, including the appearance of the staff, especially where they come into contact with the public. The *Schmidt* approach was approved by the Court of Appeal in *Smith v Safeway plc*[246]. In that case, the employers' appearance code placed restrictions on hair length which applied to men only; women were allowed to have long hair provided it was tied back. The complainant was dismissed because he refused to cut off his pony-tail. The tribunal, following *Schmidt*, held that the treatment of the complainant was not less favourable than that which would have been accorded to a woman because the code, although different for men and women, enforced a common standard of smartness and conventionality, and taken as a whole it could not be said that either gender was treated less favourably. The EAT upheld the employee's appeal[247], holding that since the employers' rules restricted only the hair length of men, the treatment of the complainant was self-evidently less favourable, and that the employer's requirements with respect to hairstyle were capable of being applied to both men and women in such a way as to take account of convention (for example by allowing men to have a pony-tail), without placing a restriction on hair length for men only. The EAT also placed emphasis on the fact that, unlike other appearance requirements concerning uniform, hairstyle and jewellery, a restriction on hair length extends beyond working hours, and thereby affects individual choice detrimentally at all times (the implication being that such a restriction requires a stronger justification). However, the Court of Appeal overturned the EAT in favour of a more conventional interpretation of *Schmidt*. According to Phillips LJ, the starting point of the reasoning in *Schmidt*, which he considered to be 'plainly correct', was that it was necessary to show not merely that the sexes were treated differently, but that the treatment accorded to one was less favourable than the treatment accorded to the other; in his view, the

243 See Cunningham (1995) 24 ILJ 177; Wintemute (1997) 60 MLR 334.
244 [1978] ICR 85, [1977] IRLR 360, EAT.
245 See also *Burrett v West Birmingham Health Authority* [1994] IRLR 7, EAT, where it was held that a female nurse who was required to wear a cap as part of her uniform was not less favourably treated on grounds of sex than male nurses who were not required to wear a cap, since the requirement to wear a uniform applied equally to male and female nurses. Her honestly held belief that the requirement to wear a cap was demeaning was held not to be determinative of whether or not there was less favourable treatment (see p 283 above).
246 [1996] ICR 868, [1996] IRLR 456, CA.
247 [1995] ICR 472, [1995] IRLR 132, EAT, Pill J dissenting.

most important element of the *Schmidt* approach was that, looking at the code as a whole, neither sex was to be treated less favourably as a result of its enforcement, and the tribunal's decision to that effect should therefore be upheld[248].

There are, however, three reasons why the existing case law on dress and appearance codes should be approached with caution. First, the imposition of restrictions on how a person chooses to present himself or herself could be seen as an infringement of that person's right to respect for private and family life under Article 8 of the European Convention on Human Rights[249]; secondly, where a person adopts a particular form of dress in accordance with the customs or requirements of their religion, the imposition of a dress code that conflicts with the requirements of that religion could constitute unlawful discrimination on grounds of religion or belief[250]; and thirdly, what is regarded as 'conventional' in relation to dress and appearance may change with time, and employers may be expected to modify their dress and appearance rules to reflect those changes. In *McConomy v Croft Inns Ltd*[251], a case on discrimination in the provision of goods and services under Part III of the Act, it was held to be unlawfully discriminatory for a public house to refuse to serve a man for wearing earrings where there was no similar objection to women wearing earrings. The court stressed that while account must be taken of certain basic rules of human conduct, such as the ordinary rules of decency accepted in the community, which might permit or require different dress regulations as between men and women, in today's conditions it is not possible to say that the circumstances are different as between men and women as regards the wearing of personal jewellery or other items of personal adornment. The recent employment tribunal decisions in which dress codes prohibiting women from wearing trousers at work have been held to be discriminatory[252] confirm the inherently transient nature of conventions of dress and appearance and indicate that standards of what is 'conventional' in relation to appearance have shifted somewhat in the years since *Schmidt*, but the decision in *Smith v Safeway plc* suggests that the courts are not yet ready to accept as conventional a man who turns up for work wearing a pony-tail, let alone lipstick and high heels[253].

(b) Sexual harassment[254]

At the present time[255] the Sex Discrimination Act does not expressly prohibit sexual harassment, but it is well-established that sexual harassment is capable of constituting a 'detriment' for the purposes of section 6(2) of the 1975 Act. One of the main drawbacks in attempting to tackle sexual harassment through anti-discrimination law is that, as seen above, the law on direct discrimination is based

---

248 According to Phillips LJ, the fact that a restriction applied to permanent characteristics such as hair length or colour, and therefore extended beyond the workplace, was a factor to be taken into account in considering whether a code treats one sex less favourably than the other, but does not affect the test itself.
249 See p 42.
250 See p 376.
251 [1992] IRLR 561, NIHC.
252 See eg *Owen v Professional Golfers' Association* (January 2000, unreported), ET.
253 Cf Cunningham, n 243 above, at p 181.
254 See Dine and Watt 'Sexual Harassment: Moving Away From Discrimination' (1995) 58 MLR 343; European Commission Report 'The Protection of the Dignity of Men and Women at Work', OJ 97B (1992).
255 A new definition of sexual harassment will be in force from October 2005: see p 310 below.

around the concept of less favourable treatment, so that strictly speaking a woman complaining of sexual harassment would need to show that she had been less favourably treated than a man on the grounds of her sex in order to obtain a remedy. This could be hard to prove where the employer argues that there has been no disparate treatment because both male and female employees would have been treated alike[256], as where the conduct in question is equally offensive to both sexes. One widely used way of circumventing such arguments in harassment cases has been to place the emphasis on the sexual nature of the harassment, the argument being that if the acts complained of are gender-specific, then it may readily be assumed that they are discriminatory – in other words, that if the *form* of the harassment is dictated by the gender of the victim, that of itself indicates the *reason* for the harassment. So, for example, in one of the early sexual harassment cases, *Porcelli v Strathclyde Regional Council*[257], the Court of Session held that a woman who had been subjected to persistent[258] personal insults, obscene language, suggestive remarks and unwanted physical contact by two male colleagues with the intention of forcing her to apply for a transfer had been less favourably treated on the ground of her sex than a man would have been treated. The court held that if any material part of the unfavourable treatment to which a woman is subjected includes a significant sexual element to which a man would not be vulnerable, the treatment is on the grounds of her sex within the meaning of section 1(1)(a) of the 1975 Act[259]. The court managed to overcome the problem of establishing less favourable treatment on the ground of sex by finding that while an equally disliked male colleague would have been subjected to equally unpleasant treatment, that treatment would not have been of a sexual nature[260], and it could therefore be said that the treatment of the complainant was different in a material respect from that which would have been inflicted on a male colleague.

This approach was taken an important stage further (and, it now appears, a stage too far) in *British Telecommunications plc v Williams*[261], where the EAT held that in sexual harassment cases there is no need to look for a comparator, and that it is no defence to a complaint of sexual harassment that a person of the opposite sex would have been similarly treated, because the conduct which constitutes sexual harassment is itself gender-specific (ie sexual harassment is discriminatory per se). However, the House of Lords has now held in *Pearce v Governing Body of Mayfield Secondary School* that this is the wrong approach, and that: 'the fact that the harassment is gender-specific in form cannot be regarded as of itself establishing conclusively that the reason for the harassment is gender-based: "on the ground of her sex".[262]' Lord Nicholls observed that the expression 'sexual harassment' is ambiguous, because the adjective 'sexual' may describe the *form* of the harassment (for example verbal abuse in explicitly sexual terms) or the

---

256 The so-called 'bastard' defence. See p 284 above.

257 [1986] ICR 564, [1986] IRLR 134, Ct Sess (an unfortunately named case, since the acts complained of arose from the behaviour of male chauvinist *porcelli*).

258 This is not a necessary requirement, as a single act is capable of amounting to harassment: see below.

259 The Court of Session adopted the broad definition of 'detriment' from *Ministry of Defence v Jeremiah* [1979] 3 All ER 833, [1979] IRLR 436 as meaning any conduct which places the applicant at a disadvantage.

260 Lord Grieve described the harassment of the complainant as a 'sexual sword' which 'had been unsheathed and used because the victim was a woman'.

261 [1997] IRLR 668, EAT.

262 [2003] IRLR 512 at 516, HL, per Lord Nicholls.

reason for the harassment (for example if a male employee makes office life difficult for a female employee because he does not wish to share his office with a woman): 'It is only in the latter sense that, although not as such prohibited by the Sex Discrimination Act, sexual harassment may nevertheless be within the scope of the Act as less favourable treatment accorded on the ground of sex. A claim under the Act cannot get off the ground unless the claimant can show she was harassed because she was a woman.[263]' In many cases this may not be a major hurdle to overcome, because where the harassment is gender-specific in form a tribunal may readily draw the inference that the reason for the harassment was gender-based[264], but the *Pearce* test is more problematic where the conduct is sexual in nature but the motivation of the harasser is not sexual, and it seems certain to give rise to some very difficult questions over the identification of the appropriate comparator[265], questions which the 'discrimination per se' approach had neatly avoided. Consider for example *Stewart v Cleveland Guest (Engineering) Ltd*[266], in which the EAT refused to overturn the tribunal's finding that the employers had not discriminated against the complainant on the grounds of her sex by allowing male employees to display pin-ups of nude women in the workplace, even though they knew that the pictures were offensive to her. The tribunal had held that the display of pin-ups was 'neutral', in that a man might have found that sort of display just as offensive as the complainant did, and that as a result she had not succeeded in establishing that she had been treated less favourably than a man would have been treated. The problem with this line of reasoning is that it fails to recognise that pin-ups of nude women are not gender-neutral, because women are more vulnerable to them than are men[267]. The case is a good illustration of how the choice of comparator in harassment cases (as in other areas of discrimination law) can often predetermine the outcome. A new definition of harassment must be introduced by October 2005, implementing the Equal Treatment Amendment Directive[268], and this will in effect restore the position in *British Telecommunications plc v Williams* because it deems harassment to be discrimination without the need for a comparator. Until that time, it seems that the *Pearce* test will apply[269].

Another major difficulty in this area is in defining what sexual harassment actually is. There is no statutory definition (although this is to change from October 2005, as will be seen below), but the European Commission has issued a Recommendation and Code of Practice[270] which defines sexual harassment as 'unwanted conduct of a sexual nature, or other conduct based on sex affecting the dignity of women and men at work'. The Code of Practice states that such conduct is unacceptable if: (a) it is unwanted, unreasonable and offensive to the

---

263 [2003] IRLR 512 at 515.
264 Lord Rodger referred to the 'classic cases of sexual harassment, where the motivation of the conduct is sexual', as where a male manager pursues a female member of staff and, despite her objections, fondles her, tries to kiss her and makes suggestive remarks; [2003] IRLR 512 at 535.
265 McColgan (1995) 24 ILJ 181.
266 [1996] ICR 535, [1994] IRLR 440, EAT; see p 284 above. See also *Balgobin v London Borough of Tower Hamlets* [1987] ICR 829, [1987] IRLR 401, EAT.
267 Cf *Insitu Cleaning Co Ltd v Heads* [1995] IRLR 4, where the EAT refused to equate a remark by a man about a woman's breasts ('Hiya, big tits') with a remark by a woman about a bald head or a beard: 'One is sexual, the other is not' (per Morison J, at 5).
268 Directive 2002/73/EC.
269 Although note that the new definition applies to race discrimination in the employment field with effect from 13 July 2003: see below, at p 369.
270 Commission Recommendation 92/131/EEC on the protection of the dignity of men and women at work.

recipient; (b) a person's rejection of or submission to such conduct on the part of employers or workers (including superiors or colleagues) is used explicitly or implicitly as a basis for a decision affecting that person's access to training or employment, or their continued employment, promotion, salary or other employment decisions; and/or (c) such conduct creates an intimidating, hostile or humiliating work environment for the recipient. Although not legally binding on the UK courts and tribunals, this definition has been increasingly heavily relied upon in recent years[271].

One of the most difficult issues in this area is whether a tribunal considering an allegation of sexual harassment should apply a wholly subjective test, or whether the test should contain an objective element. The problem with a subjective test is that it enables an over-sensitive complainant who takes offence unreasonably at an innocent comment to bring a claim for sex discrimination. On the other hand, the use of an objective test could be considered objectionable because it allows scope for value-judgments about the extent to which certain words and conduct are painful or offensive to the members of a particular sex (or, in the case of race discrimination, a particular racial group). The definition of sexual harassment in the EC Code of Practice contains both subjective ('unwanted') and objective ('unreasonable') elements, and the case law is not wholly clear on the correct balance between these two approaches. In *Reed and Bull Information Systems Ltd v Stedman*[272], the EAT considered that the test of whether conduct amounts to sexual harassment is a subjective one : 'The essential characteristic of sexual harassment is that it is words or conduct which are unwelcome to the recipient and it is for the recipient to decide for themselves what is acceptable to them and what they regard as offensive'[273]. In contrast, in *De Souza v Automobile Association*[274] (a case under the equivalent provisions of the Race Relations Act), the Court of Appeal suggested that the conduct must be such that 'a reasonable worker would or might take the view that he had been thereby disadvantaged in the circumstances in which he had thereafter to work', and in *Driskel v Peninsula Business Services*[275] the EAT observed that if the facts simply disclosed hypersensitivity on the part of the complainant to conduct which was reasonably not perceived by the alleged discriminator as being to her detriment, no finding of discrimination could follow. In that case, the complainant was told the evening before an interview for promotion that she had better turn up the following day 'in a short skirt and see-through blouse, showing plenty of cleavage'. The employment tribunal found in the employer's favour, heavily influenced by the fact that she did not make an immediate complaint, but the EAT questioned the significance of this, pointing out that 'any instinct to complain must perforce be inhibited by the fact that she wanted the promotion that would come from the approval of [the alleged harasser].[276]' The EAT also stressed that where a number

---

271 See eg *Wadman v Carpenter Farrer Partnership* [1993] IRLR 374, EAT; *British Telecommunications plc v Williams* [1997] IRLR 668, EAT.
272 [1999] IRLR 299, EAT.
273 Per Morison J. See also *Wileman v Minilec Engineering Ltd* [1988] ICR 318, [1988] IRLR 144. Lack of intent is not a defence (although cf the comment of Holland J in *Driskel v Peninsula Business Services Ltd* [2000] IRLR 151, EAT, that 'the understanding, motive and intention' of the alleged discriminator is one of the factors to be considered by the tribunal).
274 [1986] ICR 514, [1986] IRLR 103, CA.
275 [2000] IRLR 151, EAT.
276 [2000] IRLR 151, per Holland J. Cf also *Wileman v Minilec Engineering Ltd*, above, n 273 (a tribunal should be slow to infer that the conduct was not unwelcome from the mere fact that the complainant does not complain or delays in making her complaint).

of specific incidents are alleged to constitute harassment, the tribunal should not carve up the case into a series of incidents and try to measure the harm in relation to each of them, but should instead consider the cumulative effect of such behaviour, lest it fall into the trap of 'ignoring the impact of the totality of successive incidents, individually trivial'[277]. On the other hand, a single act may be so clearly unwelcome as to be 'unwanted'[278], thus avoiding the argument that conduct cannot be said to be unwanted until it has been tried and rejected: 'A woman does not, for example, have to make it clear in advance that she does not want to be touched in a sexual manner'[279]; at the other end of the scale, where a woman appears to be unduly sensitive to what might otherwise be regarded as unexceptional behaviour, the question becomes whether by words or conduct she has made it clear that she finds such conduct unwelcome: 'Provided that any reasonable person would understand her to be rejecting the conduct of which she was complaining, continuation of the conduct would, generally, be regarded as harassment'[280].

The effect of the action complained of on the complainant will be highly relevant when assessing compensation, because the amount of compensation will depend on the extent of the detriment that the complainant has suffered as a result of sexual harassment. Here, the fact that the complainant's attitude to matters of sexual behaviour is such that she was unlikely to be very upset by conduct of an overtly sexual nature will have a direct bearing on the compensation awarded. So, for example, in *Snowball v Gardner Merchant Ltd*[281] the tribunal admitted evidence of the complainant's sexual exploits and that fact that she was in the habit of referring to her bed as a 'playpen', and in *Wileman v Minilec Engineering Ltd*[282] the tribunal took notice of the fact that the complainant sometimes wore what was described as provocative clothing to work. Significantly, however, the EAT held in that case that the complainant's willingness to pose for a national newspaper in a flimsy costume was not inconsistent with a finding that she had been sexually harassed by her employer: 'A person may be happy to accept the remarks of A or B in a sexual context, and wholly upset by similar remarks made by C'[283].

Finally, as has already been mentioned, a new definition of harassment (based on the definitions in the Race, Employment and Equal Treatment Amendment Directives[284]) is in the process of being rolled out across UK anti-discrimination law[285].

277 [2000] IRLR 151 at 154. ('That which in isolation may not amount to discriminatory detriment may become such if persisted in notwithstanding objection, vocal or apparent', per Holland J at 154).
278 See eg *Insitu Cleaning Co Ltd v Heads* [1995] IRLR 4; *Bracebridge Engineering Ltd v Darby* [1990] IRLR 3, EAT.
279 [2000] IRLR 151, per Morison J.
280 [2000] IRLR 151, per Morison J.
281 [1987] ICR 719, [1987] IRLR 397
282 [1988] ICR 318, [1988] IRLR 144.
283 [1988] ICR 318, [1988] IRLR 144, per Popplewell J.
284 The Equal Treatment Amendment Directive differs from the other two Directives in that it contains *two* definitions, one of 'harassment' (ie 'where an unwanted conduct related to the sex of a person occurs with the purpose or effect of violating the dignity of a person, and of creating an intimidating . . . etc environment'), and the other of 'sexual harassment' (ie 'where any form of unwanted verbal, non-verbal or physical conduct of a sexual nature occurs, with the purpose or effect of violating the dignity of a person, in particular when creating an intimidating . . . etc environment').
285 The new definition will apply in race discrimination cases (or, more accurately, those within the scope of the Race Directive) from July 2003, in sexual orientation discrimination and religion or belief discrimination cases from December 2003, and in disability discrimination cases from October 2004; the deadline for the implementation of the new definition in sex discrimination cases is October 2005.

The new definition provides that harassment takes place where, on one of the prohibited grounds, a person engages in 'unwanted' conduct which has the purpose or effect of either violating another person's dignity, or 'creating an intimidating, hostile, degrading, humiliating or offensive environment' for that person[286]. This definition differs from that which appears in the Directives in that the two limbs (violation of dignity and offensive (etc) environment) are expressed as alternative rather than cumulative requirements, this apparently because the definition in the Directives was seen as potentially containing an additional hurdle not present under the existing UK law. Crucially, under the new definition harassment is not constructed as a form of discrimination, but is defined as an unlawful act distinct from direct and indirect discrimination. This has the advantage of enabling the concept to shed a great deal of troublesome baggage, including the need to show that the harassment constitutes less favourable treatment on one of the prohibited grounds. The other highly significant aspect of the new definition is that it expressly incorporates an objective element. Conduct is only to be considered as having the effect of violating a person's dignity or creating an offensive (etc) environment for that person if, taking into account all the circumstances, 'it should reasonably be considered as having that effect'[287]; the subjective perceptions of the victim are also relevant, however, as there is a requirement to have regard in particular to the victim's perception of the conduct.

(vi) Discrimination on, and after, termination of employment

Under section 6(2) it is unlawful to discriminate against a woman by dismissing[288] her, and this could give rise to a complaint to a tribunal of discrimination in the ordinary way, with the tribunal empowered to give compensation and make a recommendation, which could include reinstatement of the woman. However, it is likely that in such a case the woman would also have a good claim for unfair dismissal[289], which has three advantages over the straight discrimination claim – the preliminary burden of proof in the unfair dismissal case is on the employer, there can be an order of reinstatement or re-engagement and, if the remedy is to be compensation, it will include a basic award. On the other hand, the discrimination claim has the distinct advantage that the one-year qualifying period for unfair dismissal does not apply, the tribunal is expressly empowered to award a sum for injury to feelings[290], and there is no upper limit on the compensation which can be awarded for discrimination[291]. It may therefore be wise for the dismissed woman to bring her complaint to the tribunal under both heads; if she does so, she cannot be doubly compensated, as the compensation for discrimination cannot take into account any head of loss already included in the compensation for unfair dismissal, and vice versa.

---

286 See eg the Race Relations Act 1976, s 2A(1), as inserted by the Race Relations Act 1976 (Amendment) Regulations 2003, SI 2003/1626.
287 Race Relations Act 1976, s 2A(2).
288 Dismissal here includes a constructive dismissal: Sex Discrimination Act 1975, s 82(1A).
289 A dismissal through an act of unlawful indirect discrimination is not automatically unfair in law, though in practice it is likely to be found unfair: *Clarke v Eley (IMI) Kynoch Ltd* [1983] ICR 165, [1982] IRLR 482, EAT.
290 Sex Discrimination Act 1975, s 66(4) (as applied by s 65(1)(b)); see p 321 below.
291 See p 323 below.

While it is clear that the Sex Discrimination Act applies to a discriminatory dismissal, the position as regards post-termination discrimination has until recently been more uncertain. As originally enacted, the 1975 Act did not expressly refer to discriminatory acts done by an employer after the end of employment, and case law under the Race Relations Act (which was drafted in the same terms as the SDA) appeared to establish that discrimination against a former employee was not unlawful[292]. However, in *Coote v Granada Hospitality Ltd*[293], the ECJ held that Article 6 of the Equal Treatment Directive requires member states to introduce measures protecting workers from discrimination after the employment relationship has ended, and in the resumed hearing[294], the EAT reinterpreted the 1975 Act as covering victimisation by an ex-employer. That decision was narrowly interpreted by the EAT in *Rhys-Harper v Relaxion Group plc*[295] as only covering post-termination victimisation, not other acts of discrimination occurring after the end of employment (in that case, the employer's alleged failure to investigate an allegation of sexual harassment made during an internal appeal against dismissal), and the EAT's decision was upheld by the Court of Appeal. On a further consolidated appeal addressing the same point under the sex, race and disability discrimination legislation, the House of Lords held[296] that it is unlawful for a person to discriminate against former employees 'if there is a substantive connection between the discriminatory conduct and the employment relationship'[297], whenever the discriminatory conduct arises. In the wake of the decision, the government introduced the Sex Discrimination Act 1975 (Amendment) Regulations 2003[298], which expressly prohibit unlawful discrimination after the end of the employment relationship which 'arises out of and is closely connected to the [employment] relationship'[299]. The wording of the amended SDA is wide enough to cover a broad range of claims by ex-employees, including the conduct of internal appeals against dismissal, and the provision of references[300].

(vii) Proving discrimination

Establishing the liability of an employer in a discrimination case can be highly problematic. Proof can be extremely difficult in these cases, as there will usually be little or no direct evidence of discrimination. Traditionally, the burden of

---

292 *Nagarajan v Agnew* [1995] ICR 520, [1994] IRLR 61, EAT (provision of an adverse reference to a former employee); *Adekeye v Post Office* [1997] ICR 110, [1997] IRLR 105, CA (discrimination in the conduct of an internal appeal against dismissal).
293 [1998] IRLR 656, ECJ (refusal to provide a reference to a former employee).
294 *(No 2)* [1999] ICR 942, [1999] IRLR 452, EAT.
295 [2000] IRLR 810, EAT.
296 *Rhys-Harper v Relaxion Group plc; D'Souza v London Borough of Lambeth; Jones v 3M Healthcare Ltd* [2003] IRLR 484, HL.
297 Per Lord Rodger at 510. Cf Lord Hobhouse at 501 ('a substantive and proximate connection between the conduct complained of and . . . employment by the alleged discriminator'); Lord Nicholls at 489 ('the obligation not to discriminate applies to all the incidents of the employment relationship, whenever precisely they arise').
298 SI 2003/1657, inserting new ss 20A and 35C into the Sex Discrimination Act 1975.
299 SI 2003/1657, reg 3, inserting new s 20A. The same wording appears in the new regulations implementing the Race and Employment Directives.
300 The House of Lords emphasised that the refusal of an employer to provide a reference to an ex-employee would only be discriminatory if the employer treated the applicant less favourably than other ex-employees on one of the prohibited grounds.

proof has been on the applicant to show, on the balance of probabilities, that he or she has been discriminated against[301], but in practice the courts developed an approach whereby, if the applicant was able to show less favourable treatment in circumstances consistent with discrimination, the tribunal would look to the employer for an explanation, and if no explanation was put forward, or if the tribunal considered the explanation to be inadequate or unsatisfactory, the tribunal could[302] legitimately infer unlawful discrimination[303]. There was no formal reversal of the burden of proof, which remained on the applicant[304], but in practice the ability of the tribunals to infer discrimination in the absence of reasonable explanation by the employer meant that there was probably little difference (other than one of terminology) between the de facto position and a formal reversal of the burden of proof.

In recognition of the difficulties faced by complainants attempting to prove discrimination, and after an extremely long gestation period[305], all member states other than the UK adopted a Burden of Proof Directive[306] in 1997 which requires the burden of proof to be shifted onto the respondent in sex discrimination cases when the complainant establishes facts from which it may be presumed that there has been direct or indirect discrimination[307]. The UK government acceded to the Directive in July 1998[308], and it was duly implemented by the Sex Discrimination (Indirect Discrimination and Burden of Proof) Regulations 2001[309], which introduced a new section 63A into the 1975 Act. This provides that where the complainant proves facts from which the tribunal could conclude, in the absence of an adequate explanation, that the respondent has committed an unlawful act of discrimination against the complainant, the tribunal must uphold the complaint unless the respondent proves that he did not commit that act. The government's view[310], shared by most commentators, is that the implementation of the Directive is unlikely to make much difference in practice, given the existing approach of the UK courts and tribunals described above[311], although clearly it is important symbolically. In the first case to come before the EAT on the new provisions, *Barton v Investec Henderson Crosthwaite Securities Ltd*[312],

301 *Oxford v Department of Health and Social Security* [1977] ICR 884, [1977] IRLR 225.
302 Such an inference was not mandatory: see *Glasgow City Council v Zafar* [1998] IRLR 36, HL.
303 *King v Great Britain – China Centre* [1992] ICR 516, [1991] IRLR 513, CA, approved in *Zafar v Glasgow City Council* [1998] IRLR 36. See also: *North West Thames Regional Health Authority v Noone* [1988] ICR 813, [1988] IRLR 195, CA; *West Midlands Passenger Transport Executive v Singh* [1988] ICR 614, [1988] IRLR 186, CA; *Baker v Cornwall County Council* [1990] ICR 452, [1990] IRLR 194, CA.
304 A point stressed by the EAT in *Barking and Dagenham London Borough Council v Camara* [1988] ICR 865, [1988] IRLR 373, and in *Carrington v Helix Lighting Ltd* [1990] ICR 125, [1990] IRLR 6.
305 A Directive on the burden of proof in sex discrimination cases was first proposed by the European Commission in 1988.
306 Directive 97/80/EC.
307 The Race and Employment Directives make similar provision in relation to discrimination on grounds of race, religion or belief and sexual orientation: see below.
308 Directive 98/52/EC.
309 SI 2001/2660.
310 Cf the Cabinet Office Guidance on the Regulations, which stated: 'we do not think it will make any significant difference to the outcome of cases.'
311 Cf *Nelson v Carillion Services Ltd* [2003] IRLR 428, EAT: 'the effect of s 63A was to codify rather than alter the pre-existing position established by case law', per Simon Brown LJ at 432.
312 [2003] IRLR 332, EAT.

the EAT gave useful guidance[313] on how the burden of proof is now to be approached[314]:

(1) It is for the applicant who complains of sex discrimination to prove on the balance of probabilities facts from which the tribunal could conclude, in the absence of an adequate explanation, that the respondents have committed an act of discrimination against the applicant which is unlawful.

(2) If the applicant does not prove such facts he or she will fail.

(3) It is important to bear in mind in deciding whether the applicant has proved such facts that it is unusual to find direct evidence of sex discrimination. Few employers would be prepared to admit such discrimination, even to themselves. In some cases the discrimination will not be an intention but merely based on the assumption that 'he or she would not have fitted in'.

(4) In deciding whether the applicant has proved such facts, it is important to remember that the outcome at this stage of the analysis by the tribunal will therefore usually depend on what inferences it is proper to draw from the primary facts found by the tribunal.

(5) It is important to note the word is 'could'. At this stage the tribunal does not have to reach a definitive determination that such facts *would* lead it to the conclusion that there was an act of unlawful discrimination. At this stage a tribunal is looking at the primary facts proved by the applicant to see what inferences of secondary fact *could* be drawn from them[315].

(6) These inferences can include, in appropriate cases, any inferences that it is just and equitable to draw from an evasive or equivocal reply to a questionnaire[316] or any other questions that fall within section 74(2) of the 1975 Act[317].

(7) Likewise, the tribunal must decide whether any provision of any relevant code of practice is relevant and if so, take it into account in determining such facts pursuant to section 56A(10) of the 1975 Act. This means that inferences may also be drawn from any failure to comply with any relevant code of practice.

(8) Where the applicant has proved facts from which inferences could be drawn that the respondents have treated the applicant less favourably on the grounds of sex, then the burden of proof moves to the respondent.

(9) It is then for the respondent to prove that he or she did not commit (or, as the case may be, is not to be treated as having committed) that act.

(10) To discharge that burden it is necessary for the respondent to prove, on the balance of probabilities, that the treatment was in no sense whatsoever on the grounds of sex, since 'no discrimination whatsoever' is compatible with the Burden of Proof Directive.

(11) That requires a tribunal to assess not merely whether the respondent has proved an explanation for the facts from which such inferences can be

---

313 Based heavily on the old law as set out by Neill LJ in *King v Great Britain – China Centre* [1992] ICR 516, [1991] IRLR 513.

314 In *Shamoon v Chief Constable of the Royal Ulster Constabulary* [2003] UKHL 11, [2003] ICR 337, [2003] IRLR 285, HL, the facts of which arose prior to the implementation of s 63A, the House of Lords suggested that in cases of direct discrimination it may be convenient for the tribunal to begin by deciding the reason for the treatment rather than whether the applicant was less favourably treated. Unfortunately, the potential impact of s 63A was not considered in any of the speeches.

315 Italics supplied.

316 Ie in accordance with the Sex Discrimination Act 1975, s 74(2)(b). The statutory questionnaire is considered below at p 320.

317 See p 320 below.

drawn, but further that it is adequate to discharge the burden of proof on the balance of probabilities that sex was not any part of the reasons for the treatment in question.

(12) Since the facts necessary to prove an explanation would normally be in the possession of the respondent, a tribunal would normally expect cogent evidence to discharge that burden of proof. In particular, the tribunal will need to examine carefully explanations for failure to deal with the questionnaire procedure and/or code of practice.

In practice the main hurdle for the applicant will often be the need to provide factual evidence of discrimination sufficient to shift the burden of proof onto the employer. Unreasonable treatment by the employer will not of itself suffice, as the House of Lords has held that the fact that an employer has acted unreasonably towards an employee and that no satisfactory explanation has been given does not oblige the tribunal to infer that there has been less favourable treatment on grounds of sex or race, as the employer could have treated other employees in the same unreasonable manner[318]; having said that, unreasonable behaviour by the employer is likely to require an explanation, and whether the tribunal is satisfied with the explanation 'will depend not on a theoretical possibility that the employer behaves equally badly to employees of all races (sic) but on evidence that he does.[319]' One particularly difficult issue is the extent to which the tribunal may draw inferences of discrimination from statistical evidence, for example, that the employer's workforce is composed almost entirely of men[320]. On the one hand, the fact that in practice within a workplace there is occupational segregation along gender lines, with men doing one kind of work and women another, will not per se contravene the statute, provided that the employer does not give preferential treatment to men in the former occupation or women in the latter. Thus, for example, in *Noble v David Gold & Son Ltd*[321], the Court of Appeal found nothing discriminatory about the fact that in a packaging plant men in fact did the heavier tasks and women the lighter, even when the employer, faced with a fall-out of work, decided to run down the lighter side, which in practice meant making some of the women redundant. However, in the context of race discrimination the Court of Appeal has accepted that statistical evidence drawn from ethnic monitoring which reveals a discernible pattern in the treatment of a particular group to which the complainant belongs (for example a regular failure of members of the group to obtain promotion to particular jobs, or under-representation in such jobs) may justify the inference that 'the real reason for the treatment is a conscious or unconscious racial attitude which involves stereotyped assumptions about members of that group[322]'. In other words, statistical evidence,

---

318 *Zafar v Glasgow City Council* [1998] IRLR 36.
319 *Anya v University of Oxford* [2001] EWCA Civ 405, [2001] ICR 847, [2001] IRLR 377 (a race discrimination case)
320 The complainant may use the statutory 'Questions and Replies' procedure (Sex Discrimination Act 1975, s 74; Race Relations Act 1976, s 65) to obtain information from the employer; adverse inferences may be drawn from a failure to reply (s 74(2)(b); s 65(2)(b)). This procedure is in addition to the normal power of the tribunal to order discovery, on which see *Science Research Council v Nassé* [1979] ICR 921, [1979] IRLR 465, HL (discovery of confidential documents may be ordered, with suitable safeguards, where necessary to dispose fairly of the proceedings).
321 [1980] ICR 543, [1980] IRLR 252, CA.
322 *West Midlands Passenger Transport Executive v Singh* [1988] ICR 614, [1988] IRLR 186, CA, per Balcombe LJ. In that case the Court of Appeal ordered discovery of statistics showing the ethnic origins of those who had applied for the post of inspector in the preceding two years, and those whose applications had been successful.

although not in itself conclusive, may be sufficient to raise an inference of discrimination which, in the absence of a satisfactory explanation by the employer, will be sufficient for the complainant to succeed on the balance of probabilities. This, of course, assumes that there is statistical evidence available[323], and here the problem for potential complainants is that there is no legal duty on employers to conduct gender monitoring of the workforce[324]. The EOC has recommended that employers should be required to conduct gender monitoring on at least an annual basis, and to make the information obtained via monitoring available to employees, their representatives and the EOC[325], but that proposal has not been accepted by the government.

In at least one respect the complainant in a discrimination case receives some help from the statute, for section 41(1)[326] makes the employer vicariously liable for discrimination by the complainant's fellow employees in the course of their employment, whether or not done with the employer's knowledge or approval[327]. This could be particularly important in a sexual harassment case where the harassment is coming from fellow employees rather than from a superior[328], especially since an employee cannot be held directly liable under the employment-related provisions of the Act, which apply only to employers. However, the position is qualified by section 41(3), which provides a defence if the employer can prove that he took such steps as were reasonably practicable to prevent the fellow employees' conduct, and it has been held[329] that this defence is made out where it is shown that an employer (with no knowledge of the conduct) has maintained adequate supervision of the employees and publicised his policy of equal opportunities. In *Jones v Tower Boot Co Ltd*[330] (a case under the equivalent provisions of the Race Relations Act), the Court of Appeal explained the purpose of the 'reasonable steps' defence as exonerating a conscientious employer who has used his best endeavours to prevent harassment, and encouraging all employers to take the steps necessary to make the defence available in their own workplace. It follows that an employer who has not taken reasonably practicable steps will not be exculpated simply because the employee's conduct was such that, even if those steps had been taken, they would not have prevented the discriminatory acts in question from occurring[331]. The correct approach is to identify what steps, if any, have been taken, and to consider whether there were any further reasonably practicable steps that could have been taken, irrespective of whether taking those steps would have been successful in preventing the discriminatory acts.

---

323 Disclosure of statistics may not be ordered if the material is not readily to hand and it would be unreasonable to order it to be produced: *West Midlands Passenger Transport Executive v Singh* [1988] ICR 614, [1988] IRLR 186. See also *Carrington v Helix Lighting Ltd* above, n 304 (disclosure limited to the production of documents in being).

324 The position as regards ethnic monitoring is now different, as a result of the Race Relations (Amendment) Act 2000: see p 373 below.

325 EOC *Equality in the 21st Century: A New Sex Equality Law for Britain* (1998).

326 There are parallel provisions in the other anti-discrimination provisions.

327 Cf Sex Discrimination Act 1975 (Amendment) Regulations 2003, SI 2003/1657, which amend the 1975 Act to make Chief Constables vicariously liable for acts of sex discrimination by police officers.

328 See eg *Porcelli v Strathclyde Regional Council* [1986] ICR 564, [1986] IRLR 134, Ct Sess.

329 *Balgobin v London Borough of Tower Hamlets* [1987] ICR 829, [1987] IRLR 401, EAT.

330 [1997] ICR 254, [1997] IRLR 168, CA.

331 *Canniffe v East Riding of Yorkshire Council* [2000] IRLR 555, EAT (sexual assaults on a disabled female colleague).

The principal limitation on the vicarious liability of an employer in this context is the requirement that the person causing the disadvantage to the complainant was acting 'in the course of his employment'. In the earlier cases on this provision it was held that the statutory test of vicarious liability was the same as the common law test (ie whether the employee's act was merely an unauthorised or prohibited mode of doing an authorised act, as distinct from an act which was outside the sphere of what he was employed to do[332]). The problem with this approach, particularly in cases involving sexual or racial harassment, was that the worse an employee's acts, the less likely it was that he would be held to be acting in the course of his employment; indeed, taken to its logical conclusion it might even mean that no employer could ever be held responsible for such acts, as no employee is employed to harass other employees. It is therefore to be welcomed that the application of the common law test in this context was comprehensively rejected by the Court of Appeal in *Jones v Tower Boot Co Ltd*[333]. In that case, the complainant had been subjected to a number of extreme incidents of racial harassment by fellow employees, including being branded with a hot screwdriver, whipped across the legs and verbally abused. The EAT had overturned the tribunal's finding that the perpetrators were acting in the course of their employment, holding that the acts complained of could not 'by any stretch of the imagination' be described as an improper mode of performing authorised tasks. The Court of Appeal reversed the EAT's decision and held the employer liable; giving the principal judgment, Waite LJ held that a purposive approach should be taken to the statutory test, and that the words 'in the course of his employment' should be interpreted in the sense in which they are employed in everyday speech, unclouded by any parallels drawn from the common law of vicarious liability. This wide interpretation places heightened emphasis on the importance for the employer of being able to rely on the 'reasonable steps' defence, discussed above. In subsequent cases, the test has been interpreted as extending even to social activities occurring outside working hours, where those activities are work-related[334]; there are, however, limits, as was shown in *Waters v Metropolitan Police Comr*[335], where the Court of Appeal held that no tribunal applying the statutory test (as interpreted in *Tower Boot*) could find that an alleged sexual assault by a male police officer on a female officer was committed 'in the course of his employment', where both parties were off duty at the time, and the man was a visitor to her room[336].

Where the employer is held vicariously liable under section 41(1), the employee responsible for the discriminatory act may himself be held personally

---

332 See eg *Irving and Irving v Post Office* [1987] ICR 949, [1987] IRLR 289, CA (on the equivalent provision in the Race Relations Act 1976, s 32).

333 Above, n 330.

334 *Chief Constable of Lincolnshire Police v Stubbs* [1999] ICR 547, [1999] IRLR 81, EAT (police authority held liable for harassment of a female police officer while off-duty at a pub with her work colleagues, and while at a work-related leaving party).

335 [1997] ICR 1073, [1997] IRLR 589, CA. See p 298 above. On appeal ([2000] ICR 1064, [2000] IRLR 720), the House of Lords found for the applicant on the grounds that the Commissioner had acted negligently in failing to protect her from victimisation and harassment which might cause her physical or mental harm, in breach of the duty of care both under contract of employment and under the common law principles of negligence.

336 See also *Sidhu v Aerospace Composite Technology Ltd* [2001] ICR 167, [2000] IRLR 602, CA (violence at a social function organised by the employers outside working hours where most of those present were not employees of the employer held to be outside the course of employment).

liable under section 42(1) for knowingly aiding the employer's breach[337], which means that in effect the employee can be held liable for aiding and abetting his own acts! By this convoluted process it is possible to hold an employee responsible in law for discriminatory acts even though the statutory duty not to discriminate applies only to employers. The House of Lords has held that in this context the word 'aids' is to be given its ordinary, everyday meaning[338], but that something more than a general attitude of helpfulness and co-operation is needed[339]. The employee remains liable even if the employer is able to make out the section 41(3) defence by showing that he took reasonably practicable steps to prevent the employee from doing the act in question[340], thus producing the intriguing result that the employee who committed the act can only be held liable for aiding and abetting the employer, who in turn is only liable through being vicariously liable for the employee's act, and who may himself be able to make out a defence under section 41(3). The law is a curious beast at times.

The vicarious liability principle in section 41 only makes employers liable for discriminatory acts committed by their servants or agents, not for the acts of third parties (for example harassment of employees by a customer). However, in *Burton v De Vere Hotels*[341], the EAT held that an employer could be held *directly* liable for the acts of a third party in certain circumstances. In that case the complainants, who were both black, were employed as casual waitresses at a Round Table dinner at which Bernard Manning was the guest speaker. During his speech Mr Manning made a number of jokes about the sexual organs and sexual activities of black men, and used racially offensive language. Some of his remarks were directed at the complainants, and a number of the diners joined in the racial abuse. Both women brought complaints against the employer under the Race Relations Act. The tribunal dismissed their complaints on the grounds that, while they had undoubtedly suffered a detriment within the meaning of the Act, it was not the employer who had subjected them to it. The EAT allowed the appeal, holding that an employer 'subjects' an employee to the detriment of harassment if he causes or permits the harassment to occur in circumstances in which he can control whether it happens or not, in the sense that he could have prevented or reduced the harassment by the application of 'good employment practice'. This principle, which had obvious implications for employers whose employees are at risk of racial or sexual harassment by customers or the general public, was reconsidered by the House of Lords in *Pearce v Governing Body of Mayfield Secondary School*[342], in which their Lordships held that *Burton* was wrongly decided because it treated an employer's inadvertent failure to take reasonable steps to protect employees from harassment by third parties as discrimination 'even though the failure had nothing

---

337 *Read v Tiverton District Council* [1977] IRLR 202; *Enterprise Glass Co Ltd v Miles* [1990] ICR 787, EAT; *AM v WC and SPV* [1999] ICR 1218, [1999] IRLR 410, EAT.

338 *Anyanwu v South Bank Students' Union* [2001] UKHL 14, [2001] IRLR 305 (under the parallel provisions in the RRA): 'While there is no exact synonym, the words help, assist, co-operate, or collaborate, convey more or less the right nuance.' (per Lord Steyn at 310); the help does not have to be substantial or productive, provided it is 'not so insignificant as to be negligible' (per Lord Bingham at 306).

339 *Hallam v Avery* [2001] IRLR 312, HL (also under the RRA).

340 Sex Discrimination Act 1975, s 42(2); see *Yeboah v Crofton* [2002] EWCA Civ 794, [2002] IRLR 634 (on the parallel provisions in the RRA).

341 [1997] ICR 1, [1996] IRLR 596, EAT.

342 [2003] IRLR 512, HL. See also p 307 below.

to do with the sex or race of the employees'.[343] It seems therefore that in order for an employer to be liable for the discriminatory acts of third parties, it is necessary to show that the employer treated the employee less favourably than he would have treated a person of the opposite sex, or a person from some other racial group. Lord Nicholls acknowledged that 'there is, surely, everything to be said in favour of a conclusion which requires employers to take reasonable steps to protect employees from racial or sexual abuse by third parties', but was unrepentant: 'It is not for the courts to extend the ambit of the discrimination legislation, however desirable this may seem, under the guise of interpretation of provisions which are unambiguously clear. As the legislation stands, the employer cannot be in a worse position regarding sexual or racial harassment of an employee by a third party for whose behaviour he is not vicariously liable than he is regarding sexual or racial harassment committed by himself. [344]'

(viii) Remedies

An employee or ex-employee may bring to a tribunal a complaint of any of the above forms of discrimination in employment[345]; the time limit for the presentation of complaints is three months[346] beginning when the act complained of was done[347], or, in the case of a deliberate omission, when the person in question decided upon it[348], although the tribunal has a wide discretion to consider a complaint out of time if it considers that it is 'just and equitable' to do so[349]. The courts have on the whole been reluctant to extend the time-limit in discrimination complaints where the delay was caused by the applicant awaiting the resolution of internal grievance or appeal procedures before embarking on litigation[350],

---

343 [2003] IRLR 512 at 517, per Lord Nicholls. The evidence in *Burton* was apparently that the manager's failure to take steps to protect the black waitresses was not connected with their ethnic origin, and that the employer would have treated white waitresses in the same way.

344 [2003] IRLR 512.

345 Sex Discrimination Act 1975, s 63. For a critique of the handling of sex discrimination cases by tribunals, see Alice Leonard *Judging Inequality* (1987, Cobden Trust, London).

346 Or six months for those serving in the armed forces, because of the need to follow the service redress procedures before making a complaint to a tribunal: Sex Discrimination Act 1975, s 76(1)(b).

347 Sex Discrimination Act 1975, s 76(1). Where the act complained of is dismissal, the date of the dismissal for these purposes is not necessarily the same as the 'effective date of termination' for unfair dismissal purposes: *Lupetti v Wrens Old House Ltd* [1984] ICR 348 (under the Race Relations Act 1976); *Gloucester Working Men's Club and Institute v James* [1986] ICR 603 cf.

348 Sex Discrimination Act 1975, s 76(6)(c). See *Swithland Motors plc v Clarke* [1994] ICR 231, [1994] IRLR 275, EAT ('decided' means 'decided at a time and in circumstances when he is in a position to implement that decision').

349 Sex Discrimination Act 1975, s 76(5). This is a much wider formulation than the usual 'reasonably practicable' escape clause: see *Hutchinson v Westward Television Ltd* [1977] ICR 279, [1977] IRLR 69, EAT; *Clarke v Hampshire Electro-Plating Co Ltd* [1992] ICR 312, [1991] IRLR 490, EAT; *Hawkins v Ball* [1996] IRLR 258, EAT; *British Coal Corpn v Keeble* [1997] IRLR 336, EAT; *DPP v Marshall* [1998] ICR 518, EAT. Cf *London Borough of Southwark v Afolabi* [2003] IRLR 220, CA (a case under the parallel provisions in the RRA, in which a complaint was allowed nearly nine years after the expiry of the three-month limit).

350 *Apelogun-Gabriels v London Borough of Lambeth* [2001] EWCA Civ 1853, [2002] ICR 713, [2002] IRLR 116, CA, approving *Robinson v Post Office* [2000] IRLR 804, EAT, and disapproving *Aniagwu v London Borough of Hackney* [1999] IRLR 303, EAT.

although the general position as regards the extension of time limits for beginning tribunal proceedings has now changed as a result of the measures contained in the Employment Act 2002 making statutory dismissal, disciplinary and grievance procedures an implied term in every contract of employment[351]. Discrimination often takes the form of a continuing act extending over a period of time, in which case the time limit runs from the end of that period[352]. However, a continuing act of discrimination must be distinguished from a single act or event of discrimination which has continuing consequences, where the time limit runs from the act itself[353]. So, for example, in *Calder v James Findlay Corpn Ltd*[354], the employer's refusal to allow the complainant access to a mortgage subsidy scheme was held to be a continuing act of discrimination, entitling her to bring her complaint more than three months after the refusal. In contrast, in *Sougrin v Haringey Health Authority*[355], a case under the Race Relations Act, a grading decision was held by the Court of Appeal to be a single act with continuing consequences, not a continuing act of discrimination. The distinction can be extremely difficult to draw, especially where a single act of discrimination is repeated or reaffirmed on subsequent occasions[356]. A succession of specific instances of discrimination (for example a failure to re-grade over a number of years, or the reaffirmation of a refusal to allow an employee to job-share) may, however, indicate the existence of a discriminatory policy or regime (formal or informal), which can constitute a continuing act extending over a period[357]. In *Hendricks v Metropolitan Police Comr*[358] the Court of Appeal reviewed the authorities and took a broad view of the concept of a continuing act, holding that the focus should be on whether there is an 'ongoing situation or a continuing state of affairs' in which the alleged incidents of discrimination were linked to one another, rather than on whether it was possible to identify some 'policy, rule, scheme, regime or practice' in accordance with which decisions affecting the treatment of workers were taken. This is a less demanding approach than that taken in some of the earlier authorities, and should make it easier in practice for applicants to establish that a succession of discriminatory acts are not unconnected or isolated, but constitute an act extending over a period.

If the tribunal finds the complaint well founded, it may make three orders – a declaration that the employee's rights have been infringed, an order for compensation and a recommendation that the employer take action suggested by the tribunal within a specified period in order to remove the discrimination[359]. The latter recommendation is just that; it is not a positive order and should not

---

351 See further at p 540.
352 Sex Discrimination Act 1975, s 76(6)(b).
353 See eg *Amies v Inner London Education Authority* [1977] 2 All ER 100, [1977] ICR 308, EAT (failure to appoint to a particular post held not to be a continuing act of discrimination). See also *Tyagi v BBC World Service* [2001] EWCA Civ 549, [2001] IRLR 465 (alleged discriminatory recruitment policy not a continuing act).
354 [1989] ICR 157n, [1989] IRLR 55, EAT, approved by the House of Lords in *Barclays Bank plc v Kapur* [1991] ICR 208, [1991] IRLR 136 (under the Race Relations Act). See also *Littlewoods Organisation plc v Traynor* [1993] IRLR 154, EAT (failure to take promised remedial action in relation to a complaint of discrimination was a continuing act of discrimination by the employer).
355 [1992] ICR 650, [1992] IRLR 416, CA.
356 See eg *Rovenska v General Medical Council* [1998] ICR 85, [1997] IRLR 367, CA.
357 *Owusu v London Fire and Civil Defence Authority* [1995] IRLR 574, EAT (re-grading); *Cast v Croydon College* [1998] ICR 500, [1998] IRLR 318, CA (job-share).
358 [2003] IRLR 96, CA.
359 Sex Discrimination Act 1975, s 65(1)(a), (b) and (c).

be framed as such[360], although the EOC has recommended that the tribunals should be given the power to order reinstatement, re-engagement, appointment or promotion, as appropriate[361]. If the employer fails to comply with a recommendation without reasonable justification, the complainant may go back to the tribunal which may award increased compensation if it considers it just and equitable to do so[362]. In such proceedings the tribunal must take a realistic approach and one of the main factors in deciding whether the employer had reasonable justification may be whether he has had sufficient time to put matters right, for the provisions relating to the recommendation clearly envisage the possibility of longer-term measures[363].

On the question of compensation, the tribunal is empowered to award it on the same basis as if the complainant had brought an action for damages in tort before an ordinary court, so that, as best as money can do it, the applicants must be put into the position they would have been in but for the unlawful conduct of the employer[364]. There is an express power to award damages for injury to feelings[365], difficult though this may be to quantify. An award for injury to feelings has been said to be 'almost inevitable' in a sex discrimination case[366], but this does not mean that it is automatic, as the applicant must still prove that some injury has been sustained[367]. The Court of Appeal has indicated that while damages for injury to feelings in discrimination cases should not be minimal[368] (since this would tend to trivialise the issue and diminish respect for the law), the awards should be restrained, as to award sums which are generally felt to be excessive would do almost as much harm to the policy of the legislation as to make nominal awards[369]. In the earlier cases, awards for injury to feelings tended to be fairly small; however, in *Armitage, Marsden and HM Prison Service v Johnson*[370], a race discrimination case, the EAT upheld an award for injury to feelings of £21,000,

360 *Ministry of Defence v Jeremiah* [1978] ICR 984, [1978] IRLR 402; affd [1979] 3 All ER 833, [1979] IRLR 436. The recommendation may not include an increase of salary (*Prestcold Ltd v Irvine* [1981] ICR 777, [1981] IRLR 281, CA) or an instruction to appoint or promote the applicant to the next available vacancy, where he or she has not been appointed or promoted because of discrimination (*North West Thames Regional Health Authority v Noone* [1988] ICR 813, [1988] IRLR 530, CA; *British Gas plc v Sharma* [1991] ICR 19, [1991] IRLR 101, EAT).
361 EOC *Equality in the 21st Century: A New Sex Equality Law for Britain* (1998).
362 Sex Discrimination Act 1975, s 65(3).
363 *Nelson v Tyne and Wear Passenger Transport Executive* [1978] ICR 1183.
364 Sex Discrimination Act 1975, s 65(1)(b). See *Alexander v Home Office* [1988] ICR 685, [1988] IRLR 190, CA (under the Race Relations Act 1976) and *Ministry of Defence v Cannock* [1994] ICR 918, [1994] IRLR 509, EAT, which contain detailed guidance on the assessment of damages in discrimination cases.
365 Sex Discrimination Act 1975, s 66(4). The injury to feelings must arise directly from the sex discrimination, not from other, more remote, consequences: *Skyrail Oceanic Ltd v Coleman* [1981] ICR 864, [1981] IRLR 398, CA.
366 *Murray v Powertech (Scotland) Ltd* [1992] IRLR 257, EAT.
367 *Ministry of Defence v Cannock* [1994] ICR 918, [1994] IRLR 509, EAT. In *Cannock*, the EAT suggested that it will often be easy to prove injury, as no tribunal will take much persuading that the anger and distress caused by the discriminatory act has injured the applicant's feelings. In sexual harassment cases, the EAT has held that compensation must relate to the degree of detriment suffered; this has led to an uncomfortably close examination of the applicant's character and antecedents in some cases: see eg *Snowball v Gardner Merchant Ltd* [1987] ICR 719, [1987] IRLR 397; *Wileman v Minilec Engineering Ltd* [1988] ICR 318, [1988] IRLR 144, EAT.
368 £500 is 'at or near the minimum': *Sharifi v Strathclyde Regional Council* [1992] IRLR 259.
369 *Alexander v Home Office* [1988] ICR 685, [1988] IRLR 190, CA.
370 [1997] IRLR 162, EAT. The EAT also upheld awards of £500 each against two prison officers personally.

holding that the award was not grossly or obviously out of line with the general range of awards in personal injury cases. In one race discrimination case, an employment tribunal awarded £100,000 for injury to feelings plus aggravated damages of £25,000, although this award was highly exceptional and reflected the appalling nature of the conduct complained of and the devastating impact on the complainant[371]. In *Vento v Chief Constable of West Yorkshire Police (No 2)*[372], the Court of Appeal expressed concern at awards of that magnitude, and attempted to limit the size of awards for injury to feelings by identifying three broad bands into which such awards should fall: the top band, for the most serious cases (such as where there has been a lengthy campaign of sexual or racial harassment) should normally be between £15,000 and £25,000; only in 'the most exceptional case' should an award for injury to feelings exceed £25,000; the middle band of between £5,000 and £15,000 should be used for serious cases not meriting an award in the highest band; and awards of between £500 and £5,000 are appropriate for less serious cases, such as isolated or one-off acts of discrimination; awards of less than £500 should be avoided altogether 'as they risk being regarded as so low as not to be a proper recognition of injury to feelings[373]' The tribunal can also award damages for personal injury (including an award for psychological harm caused by the discrimination)[374], and the EAT has held that, unlike a common law claim for negligence, a personal injury claim in a discrimination complaint is not limited to harm that is reasonably foreseeable, and that all the applicant need show is a direct causal link between the act of discrimination and their loss[375]. Aggravated damages are available where, for example, the defendant has behaved in a high-handed, malicious, insulting or oppressive manner in committing the discriminatory act[376], or where the defendant has defended the discrimination claim in a manner which was designed to be intimidatory and to cause the maximum unease and distress to the applicant[377], but it has been held that a tribunal cannot award exemplary damages in sex and race discrimination cases[378]. Until 1993, compensation under the Sex Discrimination Act was subject to two major limitations: first, it was subject to the same upper limit as the compensatory award for unfair dismissal[379] ; and secondly, in a complaint of indirect discrimination under section 1(1)(b), compensation could only be awarded if the employer applied the requirement or condition with the *intention* of discriminating on the ground of sex (although the tribunal could still make a declaration and recommendation). However, as in so many other areas of UK sex

---

371 *Virdi v Metropolitan Police Comr* (8 December 2000, unreported).
372 [2002] EWCA Civ 1871, [2003] ICR 318, [2003] IRLR 102. The tribunal's award of £50,000 for injury to feelings plus £15,000 aggravated damages was held to be excessive, and the Court of Appeal substituted awards of £18,000 and £5,000 respectively; damages for psychiatric injury were left at £9,000.
373 [2003] IRLR 102 at 110, per Mummery LJ.
374 *Sheriff v Klyne Tugs (Lowestoft) Ltd* [1999] ICR 1170, [1999] IRLR 481, CA (under the parallel provisions in the RRA).
375 *Essa v Laing Ltd* [2003] IRLR 346, EAT (also under the RRA).
376 *Alexander v Home Office* above, n 364; *Armitage, Marsden and HM Prison Service v Johnson* above, n 370; *Ministry of Defence v Meredith* [1995] IRLR 539, EAT.
377 *Zaiwalla & Co v Walia* [2002] IRLR 697, EAT (£7,500 aggravated damages awarded for the way in which the defendant firm of solicitors conducted their defence).
378 *Deane v Ealing London Borough Council* [1993] ICR 329 [1993] IRLR 209, EAT, following the decision of the Court of Appeal in *Gibbons v South West Water Services Ltd* [1993] QB 507, [1993] 1 All ER 609. See also *Ministry of Defence v Meredith* [1995] IRLR 539.
379 See p 609.

discrimination law, EC law has made its mark in this area, and both these limitations have been removed. In *Marshall v Southampton and South-West Hampshire Area Health Authority (No 2)*[380], the ECJ held that the upper limit on compensation infringed Article 6 of the Equal Treatment Directive, which requires the provision of adequate remedies which compensate the complainant in full for the loss and damage sustained as a result of the discrimination. This decision led to the removal of the upper limit in sex discrimination cases[381]; the limit in race discrimination cases was also subsequently abolished[382], bringing the two Acts into line once again. The effect of this change was demonstrated in dramatic fashion by the complaints brought against the Ministry of Defence by servicewomen dismissed on the grounds of pregnancy, where awards of compensation in excess of £300,000 were made in some cases[383]. The removal of the upper limit means that it may be preferable to challenge a discriminatory dismissal under the discrimination legislation rather than in a claim for unfair dismissal, although the normal rules concerning mitigation and discounting for future uncertainties will still apply[384].

The ruling in *Marshall* also brought into doubt the bar on the award of damages for unintentional indirect discrimination, long seen as a significant weakness in the domestic provisions. In *London Underground v Edwards*[385], the EAT managed to circumvent this bar by holding that an intention to discriminate could be inferred where the employer applied a requirement or condition with the knowledge of its unfavourable consequences for a woman, but in *MacMillan v Edinburgh Voluntary Organisations Council*[386], the EAT held that the provisions excluding compensation for unintentional indirect discrimination were unambiguous, and could not be construed to accord with the provisions of the Directive[387]. The uncertainty was subsequently resolved by the introduction of further Regulations allowing the tribunal to award compensation for unintentional indirect discrimination where it is satisfied that the power to make a declaration and recommendation is not sufficient, and it is just and equitable to award compensation[388], thus bringing domestic law into line with the Directive.

In addition to the remedies available to the aggrieved employee, the EOC, set up under the Act[389], is empowered to take certain direct steps to secure compliance with the statute. In particular it may conduct a formal investigation into any alleged

380 [1994] QB 126, [1993] ICR 893, ECJ.
381 Sex Discrimination and Equal Pay (Remedies) Regulations 1993, SI 1993/2798. The Regulations also empowered tribunals to award interest on compensation, in line with the ECJ's ruling in *Marshall*; see now the Employment Tribunals (Interest on Awards in Discrimination Cases) Regulations 1996, SI 1996/2803.
382 Race Relations (Remedies) Act 1994.
383 See *Ministry of Defence v Cannock* [1994] ICR 918, [1994] IRLR 509, EAT; *Ministry of Defence v Hunt* [1996] ICR 554, [1996] IRLR 139, EAT.
384 See *Ministry of Defence v Cannock* [1994] ICR 918, [1994] IRLR 509, EAT; *Ministry of Defence v Hunt* [1996] ICR 554, [1996] IRLR 139, EAT. See also *Ministry of Defence v Wheeler* [1998] ICR 242, [1998] IRLR 23, CA.
385 [1995] ICR 574, [1995] IRLR 355, EAT; see also *J H Walker Ltd v Hussain* [1996] ICR 291, [1996] IRLR 11, EAT, a case under the Race Relations Act, where it was held that a person will be taken to have intended the unfavourable consequences to follow from his acts 'if he knew when he did them that those consequences would follow and if he wanted those consequences to follow', per Mummery J at 15.
386 [1995] IRLR 536, EAT.
387 The decision in *London Underground v Edwards* was not mentioned in the judgment. As a private-sector employee, the complainant was unable to rely on the direct effect of the Directive.
388 Sex Discrimination Act 1975, s 65(1B), inserted by SI 1996/438.
389 Sacks 'The Equal Opportunities Commission – ten years on' (1986) 49 MLR 560.

contraventions, which may result in the issue of a non-discrimination notice if it discovers breaches of the Act; such a notice requires the discontinuance of the act of discrimination or discriminatory practice in question, and it may contain requirements to be met by the employer, who has six weeks in which to appeal against it to a tribunal. If there is no appeal, or an appeal is dismissed, the notice becomes final, and any further contraventions of it may be restrained by injunction at the suit of the Commission[390]. There are also further, more specific powers given to the Commission to take action against discriminatory advertisements[391], to seek an injunction to restrain 'persistent discrimination' (ie where an employer appears likely to commit further unlawful acts within five years of receiving a non-discrimination notice, or being found liable for an act of unlawful discrimination[392]), and to give practical help to individuals to bring discrimination claims against their employers[393]. In recent years the EOC, in addition to supporting individual claimants before the courts and tribunals, has sought to make use of the machinery of judicial review in pursuance of its statutory duty to work towards the elimination of discrimination, with stunning results. In *Birmingham City Council v Equal Opportunities Commission*[394] the Commission successfully applied for judicial review to establish that the authority was in breach of its obligations under the 1975 Act in failing to provide as many grammar school places for girls as for boys. Initially the EOC's attempts to use judicial review to challenge the legality of domestic legislation under Community Law met with more limited success. In *R v Secretary of State for Social Security, ex p Equal Opportunities Commission*[395] the Commission unsuccessfully sought a declaration that the UK state pension scheme infringed EC Directive 79/7 (which establishes the principle of equal treatment in social security schemes) by requiring men to pay contributions for longer than women in order to qualify for the same state pension, the ECJ ruling that the unequal treatment was covered by the exception in Article 7(1) which allows member states to fix the state pensionable age[396]; however, in *R v Secretary of State for Employment, ex p Equal Opportunities Commission*[397], the House of Lords held that the EOC had locus standi to challenge by judicial review the legality under Community law of the legislative provisions which subjected part-time workers to different qualifying conditions for redundancy pay and compensation for unfair dismissal from those which applied to full-time employees[398] and, furthermore, that those qualifying thresholds were

---

390 Sex Discrimination Act 1975, ss 67–70. On the nature of an appeal against a non-discrimination notice, see *Commission for Racial Equality v Amari Plastics Ltd* [1982] ICR 304, [1982] IRLR 252, CA; if the formal investigation is not carried out in accordance with the stipulated procedure, any resulting non-discrimination notice is void: *Re Prestige Group plc, Commission for Racial Equality v Prestige Group plc* [1984] ICR 473, [1984] IRLR 166, HL. The EOC has recommended an extension of its powers to issue non-discrimination notices, and the introduction of a power to accept legally binding commitments as an alternative: *Equality in the 21st Century: A New Sex Equality Law for Britain* (EOC, 1998).
391 Sex Discrimination Act 1975, s 72.
392 Sex Discrimination Act 1975, s 71.
393 Sex Discrimination Act 1975, s 75.
394 [1989] AC 1155, [1989] IRLR 173, HL. This case is an important authority on the significance of a discriminatory motive or intent: see p 281 above.
395 Case C-9/91 [1992] ICR 782, [1992] IRLR 376, ECJ.
396 The vexed question of discrimination in relation to pension schemes is considered more fully at p 352.
397 [1995] 1 AC 1, [1994] ICR 317, HL.
398 The Court of Appeal had held (by a majority, Dillon LJ dissenting) that the EOC lacked a sufficient interest to bring judicial review proceedings against the government or a minister for failure to fulfil obligations under Community law.

incompatible with Community law as they were indirectly discriminatory (the vast majority of part-time workers being women), and had not been shown to be objectively justified by reference to the extra costs to employers and the impact on the availability of part-time work[399]. This momentous ruling led to the repeal of the offending provisions, and the harmonisation of qualifying periods for full-time and part-time workers.

3 EQUAL PAY[400]

The Equal Pay Act 1970, as amended by the Sex Discrimination Act 1975, is aimed at preventing discrimination between men and women as regards terms and conditions of employment. As such, it only applies to cases where a contractual relationship already exists between the complainant and his or her employer[401]; if a case arises concerning alleged discrimination in an area other than terms and conditions of employment (for example advertising vacancies, recruitment, refusal of employment or promotion), that will come under the Sex Discrimination Act 1975[402]. The 1970 Act, once passed, was held in abeyance for five years in order to give employers time to make necessary arrangements for compliance and it finally came into force on 29 December 1975. In its early years the Act led to a significant shift in relative pay levels as between men and women[403], but after it had been in operation for several years it became clear that it was subject to certain limitations which meant that it could go so far and no further. However, since the early 1980s the whole area has been revitalised by the impact of EC law, and in particular Article 141 of the EC Treaty, which provided (before the Amsterdam Treaty modifications[404]) that each member state shall 'ensure and subsequently maintain the principle that men and women shall receive equal pay for equal work'. As explained earlier in this chapter[405], this is important for a number of reasons, not least that Article 141 prevails over conflicting provisions of domestic law, and if domestic law is found wanting when measured against the yardstick of EC law, enforcement proceedings can be brought in the ECJ in order to enforce compliance. In Case 61/81 *EC Commission v United Kingdom*[406], the ECJ held that the Equal Pay Act 1970 did not comply with the treaty requirements by allowing a woman to demand equal pay for work of equal value. This led to the major amendments in 1983 instituting (by Regulations) the 'equal value claim' which is considered below. More recently, the ECJ's broad interpretation of Article 141, and in particular its landmark decision in *Barber v Guardian Royal Exchange Assurance Group*[407] that benefits under a contracted-out, private occupational

---

399 See p 293 above.
400 See McColgan *Just Wages for Women* (1997).
401 The definition of 'employment' is wide enough to cover an independent contractor who executes work personally, as well as an employee: Equal Pay Act 1970, s 1(8); for the cases on the similar provision in the Sex Discrimination Act 1975, see p 275 above.
402 See p 276.
403 By 1977, women's pay as a proportion of men's had risen to 75.5%, compared with 63% in 1970.
404 As modified in the Amsterdam Treaty, Art 141 now expressly confers a right to equal pay for work of equal value: 'Each Member State shall ensure that the principle of equal pay for male and female workers for equal work *or work of equal value* is applied' (italics supplied).
405 See p 269.
406 [1982] ICR 578, [1982] IRLR 333, ECJ.
407 [1991] 1 QB 344, [1990] ICR 616, ECJ. See p 354 below.

pension scheme fall within the scope of the word 'pay', led to the repeal of the exclusion in the 1970 Act for provisions made in connection with death or retirement, the enactment in the Pensions Act 1995 of a new right to equal treatment in occupational pension schemes, and the equalisation of state pensionable ages at 65[408]. Unusually, the ECJ held in *Barber* that its decision was not to operate retrospectively, so that Article 141 could not be relied upon in order to claim entitlement to equal pension benefits for periods of service before the ruling in that case; however, the temporal limitation in *Barber* was held not to apply to the right to *join* a pension scheme[409], and the impact of Community law was graphically illustrated by the ECJ's decision in *Preston v Wolverhampton Healthcare NHS Trust*[410] (a test-case for some 60,000 part-time workers excluded from occupational pension schemes) that workers unlawfully excluded from such schemes were in principle entitled to backdate their membership to 8 April 1976 (ie the date on which the ECJ first held that Article 141 had direct effect).

While EC law has undeniably revitalised the domestic law on equal pay, the current position is far from satisfactory. The relevant principles and procedures are extremely complex and time-consuming (one well-known case involving a group of NHS speech therapists took 14 years to resolve[411]), yet the statistics indicate that the pay gap between men and women is stubbornly resistant to further reduction. Despite over thirty years of equal pay legislation, the average hourly pay of female full-time workers is still only 82% of that of male full-time workers, and the gender pay gap for part-time workers is 39%[412]. The reasons for the continuing disparity in pay levels are complex, but they include matters such as the disproportionate number of women in lower grades, the fact that women are still heavily concentrated in employment sectors which have a high degree of gender-segregation and where pay levels are generally low, and the effect of family responsibilities on women's working patterns and career development[413]. Over the years there have been regular calls for reform of the equal pay laws to address the continuing gender pay gap, but these have met with limited success. In 1998 the EOC called for a radical overhaul of equal pay and sex discrimination law, including the enactment of a single Sex Equality Act and the introduction of a duty on employers to review their pay systems and take action to close the gender pay gap[414]. It also recommended that employment tribunals be empowered to hear group actions and to make general findings of discrimination (rather than simply ruling on the individual case in hand), and that equal pay procedures be streamlined to make justice more speedy and straightforward.

In October 1999, the EOC set up an independent Equal Pay Task Force[415] to investigate pay discrimination in the workplace. In its report, *Just Pay*, the Task Force analysed the reasons for the continued gender pay gap between women's

---

408 See p 359 below.
409 *Vroege v NCIV Institut voor Volkshuisvesting BV* [1995] ICR 635, [1994] IRLR 651, ECJ.
410 Case C-78/98, [2000] ICR 961, [2000] IRLR 506. See p 350 below.
411 *Guardian*, 8 May 2000, reporting a £12m settlement for 351 NHS staff, negotiated between the Department of Health and MSF union; the legal action in the case is discussed at p 343 below.
412 EOC *Equality in the 21st Century: A New Sex Equality Law for Britain* (1998).
413 See Cabinet Office *Women's Incomes over a Lifetime* (2000).
414 See n 412.
415 The 12-member Task Force included senior figures from the private and public sectors, from employers and trade unions, as well as experts in pay equality and gender issues. The Chair was Bob Mason from BT.

and men's pay[416], and found that three main factors contribute to it: occupational segregation (ie the concentration of women in low-paid jobs such as shop assistants, secretaries, nurses and teachers), the unequal impact of women's family responsibilities, and pay discrimination. The Task Force considered that 25%-50% of the pay gap was attributable to discrimination, and advised that with concerted action by all the key players, that part of the gender pay gap attributable discrimination in the workplace could be reduced to 50% within five years, and eliminated entirely within eight years. Five main barriers to closing the gender pay gap were identified in the report: lack of awareness and understanding of the issue; ineffective, time-consuming and cumbersome equal pay legislation; lack of expertise in addressing the problem; lack of transparency and accountability for implementing equal pay; and social and economic measures that have failed to keep pace with women's changing place in the labour market. The Task Force proposed a 'multi-levered' approach to addressing the problem, focused on: raising levels of awareness and developing a common understanding of what the pay gap leans; reforming and modernising the equal pay legislation; capacity-building to ensure that employers and trade unions know how to implement equal pay; enhancing transparency and developing accountability for delivering pay equality; and amending social, economic and labour market policies to complement equal pay measures. The report also contained a series of recommendations for the reform of equal pay legislation, the principal one being a call for the enactment of a legal duty on employers to carry out regular equal pay reviews: 'Our evidence suggests[417] that the vast majority of employers do not believe they have a gender pay gap and therefore do not believe an equal pay review is necessary. We are firmly of the view that there will be little or no progress in closing the pay gap unless employers take the essential first step of examining whether they have gender inequalities in their pay systems. However, the overwhelming evidence to date is that most will not do so voluntarily.' In addition, the Task Force recommended, inter alia, reforms to streamline the tribunal process in equal pay cases, the use of hypothetical comparators, and the extension of the statutory questionnaire procedure for discrimination claims to equal pay cases.

In the wake of the Task Force report, the government commissioned its own review of women's employment and pay, which reported in December 2001. The Kingsmill Review[418] contained a far more modest set of recommendations, focusing mainly on voluntary measures to improve 'human capital management' by helping employers to appreciate 'the overwhelming business case for the effective use of the talents and abilities of women' which was seen as offering 'the greatest potential for reducing the pay gap'. The one specific recommendation for reform of the law on equal pay was the introduction of a right for individual employees to obtain information about the pay of named colleagues, and predictably on this occasion the government heeded the call for reform by legislating to extend the statutory questionnaire procedure to equal pay claims[419]. Under the new procedure, people who believe they may not have received equal pay are entitled to write to their employer asking for information that will help to

416 The UK has the widest pay gap in Europe: Grimshaw and Rubery *The Gender Pay Gap: a research review* (EOC, 2001) ch 3 (international comparisons).
417 See Morrell et al *Gender Equality in Pay Practices* (EOC, 2001). The report indicated that employers have misplaced confidence that their payment systems lack bias.
418 *Kingsmill Review of Women's Employment and Pay* (2001).
419 Equal Pay Act 1970, s 7B, inserted by the Employment Act 2002.

establish whether in fact they are receiving less favourable pay and contractual terms and conditions than a colleague or colleagues of the opposite sex, and if not, what the reasons are. The employer does not have to reply, but if the employer deliberately fails to reply within eight weeks, without reasonable excuse, or replies in an evasive or ambiguous way, the tribunal can take this into account, and can draw inferences from it, for example by concluding that the employer did not provide a proper explanation for a difference in pay because there was no genuine reason for the difference. No such inference can be drawn if the employer has a reasonable excuse for failing to respond, which might include the fact that the comparator does not want confidential information relating to his or her pay package or appraisal review disclosed[420].

The remainder of the Task Force recommendations (for example for mandatory pay reviews in both the public and private sectors) had not been acted upon at the time of writing, although the government had undertaken that all its departments and agencies would carry out equal pay reviews and prepare action plans to close any pay gaps by April 2003, and had responded to criticism over its failure to implement other aspects of the Task Force report by pointing to other initiatives (such as the improvements to maternity leave, new rights for part-time workers, National Minimum Wage, National Childcare Strategy and spreading best practice through 'fair pay champions' and the Castle awards[421]) which it believes will have a positive impact on the gender pay gap. In turn, the EOC has established an Equal Pay Forum, developed an Equal Pay Review Kit based on an Equal Pay Review Model, and produced a series of useful guidance notes on matters such as avoiding discrimination in job evaluation schemes, starting pay, working time payments (for example overtime and shift pay), bonus payments, progression, grading and performance-related pay; a revised version of the EOC's Code of Practice on Equal Pay[422] was in preparation at the time of writing.

(i) The equality clause

Under section 1(1) of the Act, every woman's contract is deemed to include an 'equality clause' to the effect that (i) if any term in her contract is less favourable than a similar term in a man's contract, that term is to be treated as modified so that it is not less favourable than the man's term, and (ii) if her contract does not include a beneficial term which appears in a man's contract, her contract shall be treated as including that term[423]. For the equality clause to operate one of three

---

420 The Guidance Notes to the questionnaire suggest that employers may be able to preserve the anonymity and confidence of their workers by answering detailed questions in a general way, or by anonymising the information. The Guidance Notes also state that the questionnaire does not override the common law duty of confidence or the Data Protection Act 1998.

421 Named after Barbara Castle, these are intended to recognise employer excellence in addressing equal pay and related issues.

422 *Code of Practice on Equal Pay* (1997). The Code aims to provide practical guidance and to recommend good practice to those with responsibility for, or an interest in, pay arrangements. It is admissible in evidence in proceedings under the Sex Discrimination Act or Equal Pay Act, and must be taken into account by the tribunal where relevant.

423 Equal Pay Act 1970, s 1(2); although framed in terms of women being at a disadvantage, these provisions apply equally if a man is at a disadvantage: s 1(3). The effect of an equality clause was considered by the House of Lords in *Hayward v Cammell Laird Shipbuilders Ltd* [1988] ICR 464, [1988] IRLR 257, considered below.

tests must be satisfied: the woman must be employed either on 'like work' with a man 'in the same employment', or on 'work rated as equivalent' with a man in the same employment, or on 'work of equal value' to that of such a man. As there is no statutory reversal of the burden of proof[424], it will be for the applicant to show that her case falls within one of the three heads[425]. Where the applicant succeeds, a presumption will be raised that the difference in terms is due to sex discrimination, and her contract will be modified by the equality clause, unless the employer is able to rebut the presumption by showing that the difference in terms is genuinely due to some material factor other than the difference of sex between the applicant and her comparator, ie that the reason for the difference is not tainted by sex discrimination. The modification via the equality clause operates on a term-by-term basis. The tribunal is not empowered to act as a general wage-fixing body, deciding for example that the woman's work is worth 80% of the value of the man's work and ordering any necessary wage adjustments accordingly. Neither is it possible to offset any disadvantageous terms in the applicant's contract by pointing to other terms in her contract which are more favourable that those enjoyed by her comparator, a point established in *Hayward v Cammell Laird Shipbuilders Ltd*[426], one of the first cases on the equal value provisions to come before the higher courts. Miss Hayward (supported by her union and the EOC) won on her substantive claim, but then the question arose as to what she was entitled to. She claimed the same basic rate of pay as her male comparator as a term of her contract under the equality clause, but the employers objected to this, pointing out that although her basic rate had been less, she had enjoyed other terms of employment (particularly as to sickness benefits, holidays and meal breaks) which were better than her comparator's, which offset the disadvantage on pay. Thus, if one took a 'term-by-term' approach she could succeed in her claim for the same basic pay, but if one took a broader, 'package' approach to her terms and conditions as a whole she would fail. The Court of Appeal opted for the package approach, but her appeal was allowed by the House of Lords which held, as a matter of construction of section 1(2), that the correct approach is to examine the two contracts term by term; she was therefore entitled to keep the benefit of those terms which were better than those of her comparator, while still being entitled to the equality of basic pay that she had sought all along[427], Lord Mackay LC adding for good measure that this approach is consistent with EC law[428]. The term-by-term approach may seem counter-intuitive, but one possible rationale for it is the difficulty that a court might face in making an overall assessment and comparison of all the non-wage elements of the two contracts.

424 Compare the position under the Sex Discrimination Act 1975: see p 313.

425 Note, however, that in *Handels-og Kontorfunktionaerernes Forbund i Danmark v Dansk Arbejdsgiverforening (acting for Danfoss)* Case 109/88 [1991] ICR 74, [1989] IRLR 532, the ECJ stated that by virtue of EC Directive 75/117, where a pay system is marked by a 'total lack of transparency' the burden of proof will be on the employer to show that the pay system was not discriminatory.

426 [1988] ICR 464, [1988] IRLR 257, HL (noted Napier (1988) NLJ 341); revsg [1987] ICR 682, [1987] IRLR 186, CA.

427 An obvious danger in this approach is the potential disruption of differentials in pay and conditions, particularly where the employer's payment system involves employees in choosing from a menu of non-wage benefits. The scope to be given to the defence of 'genuine material factor' (below) could be crucial in such cases (see *Hayward*, per Lord Goff).

428 This was confirmed by the ECJ in *Barber v Guardian Royal Exchange Assurance Group* [1991] 1 QB 344, [1990] ICR 616, ECJ. See also *Jorgensen v Foreningen af Speciallaeger* [2000] IRLR 726 ECJ; *Brunnhofer v Bank der Osterreichischen Postsparkasse AG* [2001] IRLR 571 ECJ.

(a) Like work

This is defined in section 1(4) as work 'of the same or a broadly similar nature', such that any differences between the things the woman does and the things done by the male comparator 'are not of practical importance in relation to terms and conditions of employment'. Three points might be made on this definition. The first is that in deciding whether work is the same or broadly similar, the tribunal should take a wide view. Thus, in *Capper Pass Ltd v Lawton*[429] a female cook who prepared 10 to 20 lunches for directors was held to be employed on like work with two male assistant chefs who helped to provide many more meals at more times of the day in the works canteen, particularly as it was a generally similar type of work involved, with similar skill and knowledge required to do it. In deciding upon similarity or otherwise, the tribunal is not confined to the detailed physical processes performed by the employees in question, but may consider more general matters such as differences in responsibility (as in the case of two buyers, where the higher paid male buyer is in fact employed to buy more expensive goods, thereby incurring greater responsibility if he buys poor goods[430]), or the status of the complainant as a 'trainee'[431]. If matters such as these are taken into account in a bona fide grading scheme, under which the man and the women are genuinely on different grades, then the man and the woman will not be held to be on 'like work' and the woman will not be able to claim equality[432]. The second point is that in looking to see whether any differences are of practical importance the tribunal should take an equally broad approach, for the very concept of 'broadly similar' work necessarily implies differences in detail. However, these should not defeat a claim for equality unless they are such as the tribunal would expect in practice to be reflected in different terms and conditions of employment[433]. Also, section 1(4) itself states that in comparing work 'regard shall be had to the frequency or otherwise with which any such differences occur in practice as well as to the nature and extent of the differences'. Thus, the tribunal must look at the duties actually performed, not those theoretically possible. In *Shields v Coomes (Holdings) Ltd*[434] a male counterhand at a betting shop was paid at a higher hourly rate than a female counterhand, the claimed difference being that the man was there partly as a deterrent to potential troublemakers; the Court of Appeal held that the woman was entitled to equal pay, since there was no evidence of the man in question being particularly skilled or specially trained for this extra function or of there in fact ever having been any particular trouble for him to deal with, so that any difference was in practice only one of sex and the tribunal, in finding for the employer, had paid too much attention to bare contractual obligations and too little to the practicalities. The third point is that the tribunal, in making its comparison, must look at the duties performed by the woman and the man, not at the time at which they are performed. In *Dugdale v Kraft Foods Ltd*[435] female quality control workers performed prima facie similar work to that done by male quality

---

429 [1977] ICR 83, [1976] IRLR 366.
430 *Eaton Ltd v Nuttall* [1977] ICR 272, [1977] IRLR 71.
431 *De Brito v Standard Chartered Bank Ltd* [1978] ICR 650, EAT.
432 *Capper Pass Ltd v Allan* [1980] ICR 194, [1980] IRLR 236, EAT.
433 *Capper Pass Ltd v Lawton* [1977] ICR 83 at 87H, [1976] IRLR 366 at 367.
434 [1978] ICR 1159, [1978] IRLR 263, CA; see also *Redland Roof Tiles v Harper* [1977] ICR 349, EAT.
435 [1977] ICR 48, [1976] IRLR 368. See also *Electrolux Ltd v Hutchinson* [1977] ICR 252, [1976] IRLR 410.

control workers, but the men were paid at a higher basic rate because they worked night shifts and certain Sundays. The tribunal thought that this was a material difference, but the EAT reversed this decision and remitted the case to another tribunal, which eventually awarded equal pay to a majority of the applicants in the case[436].

However, it must be remembered that the Act is aimed at securing treatment that is not less favourable than that given to a man in the circumstances, not at securing mathematical equality of pay packets at the end of the day, so that if the male comparator does in fact perform similar work but at anti-social hours, or in unfavourable conditions, this may amount to a material difference justifying the payment of extra remuneration (special premia for overtime, night working, Sunday shifts, etc) provided that such premia genuinely reflect the extra inconvenience and are not so large that they are seen as simply a way of indirectly reintroducing a sex-based distinction:

'... this does not mean that men, or women, cannot be paid extra for working at night or at weekends, or at other inconvenient times; if the additional remuneration is justified by the inconvenience of the time at which it is done the claim [for equality] will not succeed. For, while every contract of employment is deemed to include an equality clause, it only has to take effect so that the terms of the woman's contract shall be treated as so modified as not to be less favourable than the man's. Thus the industrial tribunal – without falling into the error of setting itself up as a wage-fixing body – may adjust the woman's remuneration upon a claim by her so that it is at the same rate as the man's, discounting for the fact that he works at inconvenient hours, and she does not.[437]'

What has been said on this third point so far, however, assumes that there is a sex-based difference in the working patterns. Where, however, both men and women work at inconvenient times, there is no requirement that all those who work, for example at night, shall be paid the same basic rate as all those who work normal day shifts. Thus, a woman who works days cannot use the principle (of disregarding the time of performing similar work) in order to claim equality with a man on a higher basic rate for working nights if in fact there are women working nights on that rate too, and the applicant herself would be entitled to that rate if she changed shifts[438].

Finally, it is implicit in what has already been said that a claim under this head should not be defeated simply on the grounds that the applicant and her comparator have different qualifications (although that may be give rise to a 'genuine material factor' defence: see below). However, in *Angestelltenbetriebsrat der Wiener Gebietskrankenkasse v Wiener Gebietskrankenkasse*[439], the ECJ surprisingly held that for the purposes of Article 141 and the Equal Pay Directive, graduate psychologists employed as psychotherapists were not to be regarded as doing the 'same work' as trained doctors employed to do the same job, 'where the same

436 *Dugdale v Kraft Foods Ltd* [1977] IRLR 160, IT.
437 *National Coal Board v Sherwin* [1978] ICR 700 at 740D, [1978] IRLR 122 at 124 per Phillips J (cf, on the facts, *Thomas v National Coal Board* [1987] ICR 757, [1987] IRLR 451, EAT).
438 *Kerr v Lister & Co Ltd* [1977] IRLR 259, EAT.
439 Case C-309/97 [2000] ICR 1134, [1999] IRLR 804, ECJ. See also *Glasgow City Council v Marshall* [2000] ICR 196, [2000] IRLR 272, HL.

activities are performed over a considerable length of time by persons the basis of whose qualification to exercise their profession is different'. The decision can perhaps be defended on its facts, on the grounds that the difference in the qualifications of the two groups probably meant that their level of performance was qualitatively different, but as a general proposition it is respectfully doubted.

(b) Work rated as equivalent

A woman is to be regarded as being on work rated as equivalent to that of a man if it has been given an equal value with that of his (in terms of the demands made on her under various headings such as effort, skill and decision) by a job evaluation scheme covering that employment[440]. The Act does not lay down detailed requirements for such a scheme[441], but it is in mandatory terms, so that where there has been such a study a tribunal should act upon its recommendations, even if the parties who drafted it are no longer happy with it[442] ; once the scheme has been worked out, it will be binding for the purposes of the Act and may be relied on by the claimant, even if the employer has not in fact put it into effect[443]. However, to be binding the job evaluation scheme must be a valid scheme, in the sense that it must be non-discriminatory, objective and capable of impartial application:

'... subsection (5) can only apply to what may be called a valid evaluation study. By that, we mean a study satisfying the test of being thorough in analysis and capable of impartial application. It should be possible by applying the study to arrive at the position of a particular employee at a particular point in a particular salary grade without taking other matters into account except those unconnected with the nature of the work ... One which does not satisfy that test, and requires the management to make a subjective judgment concerning the nature of the work before the employee can be fitted into the appropriate place in the appropriate salary grade, would seem to us not to be a valid study for the purposes of subsection (5).[444]'

It may therefore be possible to challenge the validity of a scheme (indeed subsection (5) allows a tribunal to 'correct' a scheme which is based on different

---

440 Equal Pay Act 1970, s 1(5). In *Springboard Sunderland Trust v Robson* [1992] ICR 554, [1992] IRLR 261, the EAT held that where a job evaluation scheme operates by awarding points for different criteria, what matters is whether the woman and her comparator have been placed in the same grade under the scheme, and not the precise number of points awarded.

441 For some guidance on standard forms of schemes, see *Eaton Ltd v Nuttall* [1977] ICR 272 at 278, [1977] IRLR 71 at 74; also *ACAS Guide No 1*.

442 *Greene v Broxtowe District Council* [1977] ICR 241, [1977] IRLR 34, EAT.

443 *O'Brien v Sim-Chem Ltd* [1980] ICR 573, [1980] IRLR 373, HL. For this principle to apply, however, the scheme must have been worked out and accepted as valid by the parties who had agreed to carry it out: *Arnold v Beecham Group Ltd* [1982] ICR 744, [1982] IRLR 307.

444 *Eaton Ltd v Nuttall* [1977] ICR 272 at 277H, [1977] IRLR 71 at 74. In *Bromley v H & J Quick Ltd* [1988] ICR 623, [1988] IRLR 249 the Court of Appeal held that, to be valid under s 1(5) an employer-commissioned job evaluation must be 'analytical' in nature, ie based on the demands made on employees under various discrete headings, rather than on any job 'ranking' or 'felt fair' basis which would be too vague. Art 1 of the Equal Pay Directive (Directive 75/117/EEC) also has a requirement that an evaluation study must be fair, in the sense of being based on the same criteria for men and women, and so drawn up as to exclude any discrimination on the grounds of sex: see *Rummler v Dato-Druck GmbH* Case 237/85 [1987] ICR 774, [1987] IRLR 32, ECJ.

values for men and women, by looking to see if the work would have been rated equally but for that particular false premise). However, it should be noted that such a challenge might not in practice be of much assistance to the applicant for, having disposed of the scheme as it stood, she may not then rely on what she thinks the scheme should have provided, for no such different scheme ever existed and the tribunal may not undertake its own evaluation exercise under this head[445] .

(c) Work of equal value

The European Court of Justice ruled in Case 61/81 *EC Commission v United Kingdom*[446] that the existing equal pay laws did not comply with the requirement of the Equal Pay Directive[447] that a woman should be able to claim equal pay for work of equal value; this was only permitted under the existing laws if the employer had voluntarily undertaken some form of job evaluation (head (b) above), so did not avail the majority of women in employments not subject to such a study. In order to comply with this judgment, the government introduced by Regulations[448] a right to equal pay for work of equal value[449], but subjected it to an exceptionally complicated, not to say tortuous procedure.

The change was achieved by an amendment to section 1 of the Equal Pay Act 1970, adding a third category of entitlement to equal pay, where a woman is employed on work which (though not being like work or work rated as equivalent)[450] 'is, in terms of the demands made on her (for instance under such headings as effort, skill and decision), of equal value to that of a man in the same employment'[451]. The immediate problem is that this takes the tribunals away from matters of relatively observable fact (Is the work the same or similar? Has the employer got a job evaluation study that applies to this woman?) and into the realm of assessment of value and the almost religious mysteries of job evaluation, for which arguably a tribunal as a judicial body is not particularly well suited. The compromise has been to keep the procedure judicial, but to make it heavily dependent in practice on the opinion of an independent expert, ie a person appointed by ACAS from a panel kept by them of persons knowledgeable in the techniques of job evaluation.

---

445 *England v Bromley London Borough Council* [1978] ICR 1, EAT.
446 [1982] ICR 578, [1982] IRLR 333, ECJ.
447 Council Directive 75/117/EEC. Before the Amsterdam amendments, Art 141 did not expressly confer a right to equal pay for work of equal value: the only explicit reference to that head was in the Equal Pay Directive.
448 The Equal Pay (Amendment) Regulations 1983, SI 1983/1794, amending the Equal Pay Act 1970, s 1 and inserting new s 2A, dealing with the main substantive changes.
449 Rubenstein *Equal Pay for Work of Equal Value* (1984); Hepple *Equal Pay and the Industrial Tribunals* (1984); Lester and Wainright *Equal Pay for Work of Equal Value: Law and Practice* (1984); McCrudden 'Equal pay for work of equal value' (1983) 12 ILJ 197 and (1984) 13 ILJ 50; Szyszczak 'Pay inequalities and equal value claims' (1985) 48 MLR 139; McCrudden (ed) *Women, Employment and European Equality Law* (1987) ch 7.
450 See on this requirement *Pickstone v Freemans plc* [1988] ICR 697, [1988] IRLR 357, HL, discussed under (d) below.
451 In *Murphy v Bord Telecom Eireann* Case 157/86 [1988] ICR 445, [1988] IRLR 267, ECJ the employer raised the astonishing defence in an equal value case that the women who were paid less than the male comparator could not claim equality because they were in fact engaged on work of *higher* value than his; this was held by the ECJ to be contrary to Art 141 and so, under EC law at least, a woman can claim equal pay for work that is at least of equal value to that of the male comparator.

The equal value procedure has been highly controversial, not least because of the excessive delays which have bedevilled it since its introduction. In the early years, the average time taken to resolve equal value cases was over two and a half years, and some claims took far longer, particularly where the employer decided to fight the claim at each stage. It was widely thought that the decline in the number of equal pay complaints during the 1980s was (at least in part) a result of the length and complexity of the tribunal processes concerned[452], and some even went so far as to suggest that the system was designed to deter claims. By the early 1990s the case for a radical overhaul of the equal value procedures had become overwhelming. The President of the EAT described the procedures as in need of 'urgent review', and as giving rise 'to delays which are properly described as scandalous and amount to a denial of justice to women seeking remedy through the judicial process'.[453] In 1990, the EOC published a series of proposals for the reform of the equal pay laws[454], designed in part to tackle the inordinate delays in processing equal value cases. Most of the recommendations were not proceeded with, although some limited (and, it could be said, half-hearted) reforms were introduced in 1994, requiring independent experts to set a timetable for the production of reports, and preventing employers from raising the genuine material factor defence twice. After a further period of consultation[455], another series of reforms were introduced in 1996[456], reducing the role of the independent expert and restricting the circumstances in which employers can raise the 'genuine material factor' defence. However, despite these changes, the procedure in equal value claims is still extremely complex and prone to excessive delay, with even the less complicated cases taking an average of twenty months to decide.

Turning to the detail of the equal value procedures[457], the initial emphasis in an equal value claim is, as usual, upon ACAS conciliation, but if that is not successful the first major stage is, in effect, a preliminary hearing in order to decide whether the case should be remitted to an expert for the compilation of a formal report. At this stage, a tribunal may dismiss the claim without considering it on its merits if it is satisfied that there are 'no reasonable grounds for determining that the work is of equal value', ie if it considers that the claim is so weak that it has no reasonable prospect of success[458]. One particular case is spelled out as having no reasonable prospect of success; this is where the employer has already undertaken a job evaluation study which shows that the man and woman in question are not performing work of equal value. Such a study will thus be a good defence to the

---

452 ACAS Annual Report, 1992, p 23; EOC Annual Report, 1991, p 6.
453 *Aldridge v British Telecommunications plc* [1989] ICR 790, [1990] IRLR 10, per Wood J.
454 *Equal Pay for Men and Women: Strengthening the Acts* (EOC, 1990). The proposals included the automatic application of successful decisions to similarly placed employees, the removal of the initial requirement to show that the case has a reasonable chance of success, the appointment of full-time independent experts, and the removal of the bar on equal value claims where there is an existing job evaluation scheme.
455 *Resolving Employment Rights Disputes: Options for Reform* (1994).
456 SI 1996/438.
457 See the Employment Tribunals (Constitution and Rules of Procedure) Regulations 2001, SI 2001/1171, Sch 3 (The Employment Tribunals (Equal Value) Complementary Rules of Procedure 2001), hereinafter referred to as 'CRP'.
458 Equal Pay Act 1970, s 2A. The tribunal should not dismiss the claim without giving the parties an opportunity to adduce their own evidence at a further hearing: *Wood v William Ball Ltd* [1999] IRLR 773, EAT. The EOC has recommended that the 'no reasonable grounds' defence should be abolished on the grounds that it 'allows traditional stereotypes and attitudes to go unchallenged': *Equality in the 21st Century: A New Sex Equality Law for Britain* (EOC, 1998).

employer, even if commissioned after the commencement of the proceedings[459], unless it was itself 'made on a system which discriminates on grounds of sex'[460]. The burden of proof will be on the employer to show that the existing job evaluation study is untainted by sex discrimination[461]. Finally, the defence of 'genuine material factor' (considered below) may be raised at this preliminary stage[462], for it would be a waste of time and money to commission the report if the tribunal was then to rule out the claim on the basis of this particular defence. Originally, the employer was allowed two bites of this particular cherry, as the raising of the genuine material factor defence at the preliminary stage was expressly stated to be 'without prejudice' to further consideration of that defence after the expert had reported. However, the rules were changed in 1994 to avoid the possibility of the defence being raised twice[463], so that where the genuine material factor defence has been raised by the employer and considered by the tribunal at the preliminary hearing, the position now is that the employer will not be able to raise it a second time after the expert has reported.

If the claim is not rejected under the 'no reasonable grounds' defence, the tribunal must then decide whether to commission a report by an independent expert. Originally, the tribunal had no discretion whether or not to commission a report, even where the applicant's case was so strong (or so weak) that there seemed little point in doing so, but the procedure was amended in 1996 to give the tribunal such a discretion[464]. Where a report is commissioned, the tribunal must adjourn the proceedings pending receipt of it. The procedure for the expert to follow is set out[465] and in particular it requires him to listen to and consider representations from the parties; this could be an important stage for the parties, since their grounds of challenge once the report is written are restricted. He may also require the disclosure of evidence or documents, through application to the tribunal[466]. Job evaluation is an inexact science, with several different (though equally acceptable) approaches, but the Act does not require any particular method to be used[467], and in practice it is likely to be difficult to

---

459 *Dibro Ltd v Hore* [1990] ICR 370, [1990] IRLR 129, EAT. The tribunal may be unwilling to stay proceedings in order to allow such a study to come into operation: *Avon County Council v Foxall* [1989] ICR 407, [1989] IRLR 435, EAT.

460 This is defined in s 2A(3) as a system under which 'a difference, or coincidence, between values set by that system on different demands under the same or different headings is not justifiable irrespective of the sex of the person on whom those demands are made'. This might be the case if more brownie points are given under the system for traditionally male attributes (eg strength) than for traditionally female attributes (eg dexterity), even though each attribute may be equally important in the job concerned. The study itself (to be valid under s 1(5) and therefore under s 2A) must be conducted on an analytical basis: *Bromley v H & J Quick Ltd* [[1988] ICR 623, [1988] IRLR 249, CA..

461 *Bromley v H & J Quick Ltd*, n 460 above

462 SI 1993/2687, r 9 (2E); if the defence is made out at this stage, the tribunal must dismiss the claim without commissioning a report: *Reed Packaging Ltd v Boozer* [1988] ICR 391, [1988] IRLR 333.

463 CRP, SI 2001/1171, r 11(2E).

464 SI 1996/438. See *Wood v William Ball Ltd* [1999] IRLR 773, EAT.

465 CRP, SI 2001/1171, r 10A.

466 CRP, SI 2001/1171, r 4(5A).

467 In *Leverton v Clwyd County Council* [1989] ICR 33, [1989] IRLR 28, HL, it was suggested that the independent expert has to carry out what is in effect an ad hoc job evaluation study, and assess the demands of the job on a qualitative rather than a quantitative basis. The EOC has recommended that the expert be required to draw up job descriptions of both the applicant's and comparator's jobs: EOC *Equality in the 21st Century: A New Sex Equality Law for Britain* (1998).

challenge the method in fact adopted. The original rules envisaged the report being submitted to the tribunal within six weeks, but in practice this timetable proved to be impossibly optimistic, with reports frequently taking over a year to be completed. In an effort to speed up the process, new rules were introduced in 1993 requiring the expert to notify the Secretary of State, within fourteen days of his appointment or as soon as practicable thereafter, of the date by which he expects to send his report to the tribunal. If he is unable to fix the date he must explain the reasons why, and if there is any subsequent delay in the production of his report he must again notify the Secretary of State, giving his reasons, and must indicate the date by which he expects his report to be available. The tribunal may require him to submit a progress report, acting of its own volition or on the request of a party, and in cases of unjustifiable delay it may revoke the appointment and appoint another expert in his place[468].

Once the report has been prepared and submitted, the tribunal convenes a resumed hearing. Its first function is to decide whether to accept the report; it may reject it if (a) the expert has not followed the correct procedure, (b) the conclusions are perverse (in the accepted sense) or (c) the report is unsatisfactory for some other material reason. The importance of this stage must not be underestimated, for it is provided[469] that this is the only stage at which the parties may give evidence or question any witness on any matter of fact on which the expert's report is based. If the report is admitted, the tribunal proceeds to determine the case on the basis of the whole of the available evidence, of which the expert's report will be an important part[470]. The expert may be required to attend to be cross-examined; each party (though in practice this will mean the party against whom the expert has found) 'may, on giving reasonable notice of his intention to do so to the tribunal and to any other party to the claim, call one witness to give expert advice on the question on which the tribunal has required the expert to prepare a report' and this evidence is subject to cross-examination. This is to prevent a situation where a party may claim to win on the basis of five experts to four.

Finally, while the criticisms of the equal value provisions are undoubtedly well-founded, it could be argued that the success or otherwise of those provisions cannot be measured entirely in terms of the number of successful tribunal applicants, for they act as a background to collective negotiations on the subject of pay and job comparisons, and the prospect of a tribunal application if negotiations fail may well influence the outcome of those negotiations. Just how significant that prospect is as a factor in pay negotiations is of course a matter of debate.

468 CRP, SI 2001/1171, r 10A.
469 CRP, SI 2001/1171, r 11(2C). In *Hayward v Cammell Laird Shipbuilders Ltd*, p 329 above, the employers had not challenged the report at this stage and were ruled out when they tried to do so later; the tribunal emphasised that the employer must maintain a challenge at this stage, and may do so by commissioning his own study as evidence. There are two exceptional cases where matters of fact may be raised at a later stage: (i) where the employer raises the defence of genuine material factor; (ii) where the expert's investigations have been frustrated by the failure of a party to comply with an order of disclosure under Rule 4 (so that the tribunal itself may proceed to consider questions of fact, possibly to the detriment of the party in breach of the disclosure order).
470 S 2A(1). Recent cases have tended to play down the significance of the expert's report, emphasising that while it must be admitted in evidence, it is not conclusive of the question of equal value: *Tennants Textile Colours Ltd v Todd* [1989] IRLR 3, NICA; *Aldridge v British Telecommunications plc* [1989] ICR 790, [1990] IRLR 10, EAT.

(d) The area of comparison

Unlike the Sex Discrimination Act, which works on the basis of a comparison between the treatment of the applicant and that of a hypothetical comparator, the Equal Pay Act is based on a comparison with a named comparator (or comparators). The requirement to identify an actual comparator can be a major hurdle for an applicant, particularly if she works for an organisation where jobs are de facto segregated along gender lines, as it may be impossible for her to find an appropriate comparator. The general rule on the area of comparison in the Act is that the comparator must be 'in the same employment' as the applicant, in the sense that he is employed by her employer (or by an 'associated employer', as defined[472]) at the same establishment, or at another establishment at which common terms and conditions of employment are observed, either generally or for employees of relevant classes[473]. In *Leverton v Clwyd County Council*[474], the House of Lords held that the requirement of common terms and conditions refers to the terms and conditions at the establishment at which the woman is employed and the establishment at which her comparator is employed, rather than to common terms and conditions as between the applicant and her comparator; in that case, the requirement was satisfied since both establishments were covered by the same collective agreement covering male and female employees of the employer, regardless of the establishment at which they worked[475]. 'Common terms and conditions' in this context means 'broadly similar' rather than 'the same'. In *British Coal Corpn v Smith*[476], some 1,286 women employed as canteen workers or cleaners at forty-seven different establishments claimed equal pay for work of equal value with 150 male comparators employed as clerical workers or surface mineworkers at fourteen different establishments. The House of Lords held that the applicants were in the same employment as their comparators because the terms and conditions of the comparators were governed by national agreements which also applied (or would apply) to men of the same class employed at the applicant's establishment, even though local variations relating to incentive bonuses and entitlement to concessionary coal meant that the terms and conditions at different establishments for the same classes of worker were not the same. Lord Slynn interpreted the phrase 'common terms and conditions' purposively:

'The real question is what the legislation was seeking to achieve. Was it seeking to exclude a woman's claim unless, subject to de minimis exceptions, there was complete identity of terms and conditions for the comparator at his establishment and those which applied or would apply to a similar male worker at her establishment? Or was the legislation seeking to establish that the terms and conditions of the relevant class were sufficiently similar for a fair comparison to be made, subject always to the employer's right to

---

472 See p 30.
473 Equal Pay Act 1970, s 1(6). There is no statutory definition of 'establishment'; for its construction in the context of redundancy consultation (where it is similarly not defined), see p 87 above.
474 [1989] ICR 33, [1989] IRLR 28, HL. The case is a good illustration of the fact that, where there are common terms and conditions, there need be no male employees at the woman's establishment, and no women need be employed at the establishment where the male comparator works.
475 A situation described by Lord Bridge as the paradigm case.
476 [1996] IRLR 404, HL (reversing the Court of Appeal on this point).

establish a "material difference" defence .... If it was the former then the woman would fail at the first hurdle if there was any difference (other than a de minimis one) between the terms and conditions of the men at the various establishments, since she could not then show that the men were in the same employment as she was. The issue as to whether the differences were material so as to justify different treatment would then never arise. I do not consider that this can have been intended.'[477]

Provided she is able to overcome this hurdle, the complainant may choose the man with whom she wishes to be compared[478] ; there is no express requirement that the chosen comparator be 'fairly representative' of a group of workers[479], although the Court of Appeal has indicated that where the chosen comparator is from a separate establishment, it is implicit 'that the male comparator must be representative of the group or class to which he belongs'[480]. It is firmly established that an equal pay claim will not be undermined by the existence of a token male on the same terms and conditions as the complainant, as long as there is a man within the permitted area of comparison who is more favourably treated. At one time it seemed as if this basic principle was in danger of abrogation in an equal value claim; this was because the relevant provision, section 1(2)(c), states that it applies to work 'not being work in relation to which paragraph (a) [like work] or (b) [work rated as equivalent] above applies'. In *Pickstone v Freemans plc*[481] the question arose whether this prevented a woman doing job A from claiming equality of pay through work of equal value with a man doing job B if the employer simply pointed out that there were in fact other men doing job A, and so on 'like work'. This literal interpretation (which raised the possibility of an employer being able to avoid an equal value claim by employing a token male in an otherwise all-female workforce on job A) was upheld by the Court of Appeal[482] but disapproved on further appeal by the House of Lords, who held that an equal value claim can be brought in such circumstances – all that the wording in section 1(2)(c) means is that the chosen comparator must not be doing like work or work rated as equivalent; the existence of another male doing such work will be irrelevant.

The wording of the Equal Pay Act envisages a comparison between a man and a woman working together for the same employer (or an associated employer) at the same time. However, under European sex discrimination law the permitted comparison is wider. In *Defrenne v SABENA*[483], the ECJ referred to employment 'in

477 [1996] IRLR 404 at 408.
478 *Ainsworth v Glass Tubes and Components Ltd* [1977] ICR 347, [1977] IRLR 74, EAT. There is no time-limit on the period in respect of which comparisons can be made: *Kells v Pilkington plc* [2002] IRLR 693, EAT.
479 *Thomas v National Coal Board* [1987] ICR 757, [1987] IRLR 451. In *McPherson v Rathgael Centre for Children and Young People and Northern Ireland Office (Training Schools Branch)* [1991] IRLR 206, the chosen comparator had been placed on a higher rate by mistake; the Northern Ireland Court of Appeal left open the question whether an anomalous comparator could be disregarded as inappropriate.
480 *British Coal Corpn v Smith; North Yorkshire County Council v Ratcliffe* [1994] ICR 810, [1994] IRLR 342 at 358, CA, per Balcombe LJ (reversed on other grounds; see, n 476 above).
481 [1988] ICR 697, [1988] IRLR 357, HL.
482 [1987] ICR 867, [1987] IRLR 218, CA. The Court of Appeal proceeded to consider the claim under Art 141 of the EC Treaty and upheld it independently on that ground (see at 232). Thus, while the House of Lords disapproved of the Court of Appeal's narrow interpretation of English law, they in fact upheld the eventual decision, and found it unnecessary to pronounce upon the correctness or otherwise of the Court of Appeal's views on EC law.
483 [1976] ECR 455, [1976] ICR 547.

the same establishment or service, whether public or private', and this has led to a significant broadening of the scope of the permitted comparison under the Equal Pay Act. So, for example, in *Macarthys Ltd v Smith*[484] the ECJ held, on a reference from the Court of Appeal, that a woman has the right under Article 141 to compare her pay with that of her male predecessor in the same job, a decision which was subsequently applied by the Court of Appeal at the resumed hearing[485] ; and in *Diocese of Hallam Trustee v Connaughton*[486] the EAT allowed a comparison to be made with a male successor. These two decisions represent a fairly modest stretching of the boundaries of domestic law, but more recent cases have raised the fundamental question of whether an applicant may rely on Article 141 in order to choose a comparator who is not employed by her employer (or by an associated employer), on the grounds that they meet the *Defrenne* criteria of employment 'in the same establishment or service'. The issue first arose in the UK in *Scullard v Knowles*[487], where the EAT held that the applicant, who was employed by a regional education advisory council, could compare herself with a man employed by a different regional advisory council, even though the two public authorities were not 'associated employers' within the meaning of the Act. A similar approach was taken in *South Ayrshire Council v Morton*[488], where the EAT held that a female primary school head could compare her pay with that of a male secondary school head employed by a different education authority because the education system in Scotland constituted one 'service', in a loose and non-technical sense. The decision was upheld on appeal[489], but on the different (and potentially much wider) ground that a cross-employer comparison was permissible on the facts because the discrimination arose from a national collective agreement that set the salaries for both primary and secondary school heads. According to the Court of Session, the *Defrenne* criteria of employment 'in the same establishment or service' were merely examples of cases falling within Article 141, which was said to cover forms of discrimination 'which have their origin in legislative provisions or in collective labour agreements', a line of reasoning which appeared to open the way for widespread cross-employer equal pay claims[490]. The ECJ had an opportunity to clarify the matter in *Lawrence v Regent Office Care Ltd*[491], but unfortunately the decision in that case has only increased the uncertainty. The applicant was a school catering assistant whose job had been contracted-out

---

484 [1979] 3 All ER 325, [1979] ICR 785, CA.
485 Case 129/79 [1980] ICR 672, [1980] IRLR 210, ECJ; apld [1980] ICR 672, [1980] IRLR 210, CA. Note, however, that in such a case there may not be an order for equality (even under Art 141) if there are genuine economic or other circumstances accounting for the difference in pay between the woman and her predecessor; ie there is under the Article a justification defence analogous to the 'genuine material difference' defence to a claim under the Act: *Albion Shipping Agency v Arnold* [1982] ICR 22, [1981] IRLR 525.
486 [1996] IRLR 505, EAT.
487 [1996] ICR 399, [1996] IRLR 344, EAT. The advisory councils were not 'associated employers' within the meaning of s 1(6) because that definition only applies to companies, yet as Mummery J observed (at 346), under Art 141 no distinction is drawn between work carried out in the same establishment or service of limited companies and of other employers, whether incorporated or not.
488 [2001] IRLR 28, EAT.
489 [2002] ICR 956, [2002] IRLR 256, Ct Sess.
490 In *Milligan v South Ayrshire Council* [2003] IRLR 153, the Court of Session allowed a contingent claim by a *male* primary school teacher comparing himself to a female primary school teacher, which was stayed pending the outcome of her claim in relation to a male secondary school headteacher (thus preserving his entitlement to back-pay from the time when his claim was lodged).
491 [2003] ICR 1092, [2002] IRLR 822, ECJ.

by North Yorkshire County Council to the respondents, a private catering firm, with a consequent drop in pay. She claimed equal pay with former male colleagues still employed by the local authority, whose work had been rated of equal value to hers under a local government job evaluation scheme[492]. The claim was dismissed by the EAT, on the grounds that 'there is nothing about this case which would distinguish it from any other case where an applicant claimed equal pay with a comparator employed by another company, not necessarily even engaged in the same industry.[493]' The Court of Appeal referred the matter to the ECJ, which acknowledged that there is nothing in the wording of Article 141 to suggest that it is limited to situations in which men and women work for the same employer. However, where (as here) the differences identified in the pay conditions of workers performing equal work or work of equal value 'cannot be attributed to a single source', such a situation does not come within the scope of Article 141 because 'there is no body which is responsible for the inequality and which could restore equal treatment.' It seems therefore that cross-employer comparisons may now be possible in circumstances where the difference in pay can be traced to a common source, for example where the applicant and her comparator work for the same legal person or group of persons, or for public authorities operating under joint control, or where their pay is covered by the same collective agreement or legislative provision. The ECJ's ruling is likely to be particularly significant within the public sector, where claims (such as that in *South Ayrshire Council v Morton*) involving comparators from different public authorities operating under the control of the same government department are likely to become commonplace. It remains to be seen to what extent it will permit comparisons across the public/ private sector divide, or indeed wholly within the private sector, particularly where the basis of the claim is that two private sector employers are covered by the same industry-wide collective agreement[494]. This development comes close to turning the equal pay laws into a mechanism for the fixing of fair wages, and it is respectfully doubted whether this was ever intended by those who drafted the Equal Pay Act, or indeed Article 141.

Finally, while the ability of an applicant in a equal pay case to choose her comparator may often work to her advantage (at least in raising an initial presumption of discrimination), there is a catch, because having chosen her comparator, she will not subsequently be able to argue that there are other factors (for example greater length of service) entitling her to terms which are *more* favourable than those of her comparator. In *Evesham v North Hertfordshire Health Authority*[495] the applicant, a speech therapist, succeeded in establishing that she was employed on work of equal value with her named male comparator, a clinical

492 The female catering assistants had previously successfully challenged a reduction in their pay by the local authority to enable it to compete in the tendering process (see *Ratcliffe v North Yorkshire County Council* [1995] IRLR 439, HL; p 344 below). As a result of that ruling, their pay was equalised with that of the men, but the authority lost the tender for the provision of catering and cleaning services, and some of the staff were re-employed by the contractors.
493 [1999] ICR 654, [1999] IRLR 148, EAT.
494 Problems are likely to arise where an industry-wide agreement lays down *minimum* standards that are improved upon locally, as the applicant's employer will not be in a position to explain any difference, or why it is objectively justified. Significantly, Advocate General Geelhoed's opinion in *Lawrence* referred to cases in which 'a *binding* collective agreement . . . applies' (para 54, emphasis supplied), which may provide a basis for limiting the impact of the ECJ's ruling, that being a concept generally unknown in the UK.
495 [2000] ICR 612, [2000] IRLR 257, CA.

psychologist, and was entitled to be placed on the pay scale for clinical psychologists. However, she had longer service than her comparator, and claimed that instead of being placed on the same point as him on his pay scale, she should be placed on that scale at a higher point, reflecting her additional years of service. The Court of Appeal rejected her claim, holding that the Equal Pay Act only requires equality of treatment by the employer of the applicant and the comparator whom she has chosen: 'were Mrs Evesham to enter, at the relevant date, the pay scale enjoyed by her comparator but at an incremental level higher than her comparator, the effect would be that from that date she received pay at a level in excess of that received by her comparator with whom she had established equal value, and commensurate with the pay scale of somebody with whom she had not established equal value.'

(ii) Genuine material differences and factors

Even if there is a prima facie case of inequality, the applicant may still fail if the employer can show, on a balance of probabilities[496], that the difference in terms is genuinely due to a material factor which is not the difference of sex[497]. The most obvious examples of genuine material factors justifying differential treatment are personal differences between the applicant and her comparator, for example factors such as long service, superior qualifications, higher output or different geographical location[498], or where the man is on a higher grade under a bona fide, impartial grading scheme, so that, although in fact performing the same sort of work, he is rated more highly at doing it (for example he works more efficiently, or more reliably and so subject to less supervision)[499]. Unfortunately, the precise formulation of the genuine material factor defence differs according to the category in which the applicant's claim falls. In cases of like work or work rated as equivalent, the employer must show that the genuine material factor is a *material difference* between the woman's case and the man's, whereas in equal value claims that requirement does not apply, and the employer need only show that the variation is genuinely due to a *material factor*. It appears that the aim of this exercise in inspired gobbledegook was to admit more matters by way of defence in equal value cases than were thought to be admissible under the existing material difference defence, and in particular to give full rein to arguments based on market forces and economic realities[500], but ironically the material difference defence

496 *National Vulcan Engineering Insurance Group Ltd v Wade* [1978] ICR 800, [1978] IRLR 225. This is consistent with EC law, which places the burden of proof on the employer where a pay system is marked by a 'total lack of transparency': *Handels-og Kontorfunktionaerernes Forbund i Danmark v Dansk Arbejdsgiverforening (acting for Danfoss)* Case 109/88 [1991] ICR 74, [1989] IRLR 532.

497 Equal Pay Act 1970, s 1(3), as substituted by the Equal Pay (Amendment) Regulations 1983, SI 1983/1794. The employer must prove (i) that the variation is genuinely due to a material factor, and (ii) that this is not due to the difference of sex: *Financial Times Ltd v Byrne (No 2)* [1992] IRLR 163; see also *Barber v NCR (Manufacturing) Ltd* [1993] IRLR 95, EAT.

498 *Navy, Army and Air Force Institutes v Varley* [1977] ICR 11, [1976] IRLR 408, EAT.

499 *National Vulcan Engineering Insurance Group Ltd v Wade* [1978] ICR 800, [1978] IRLR 225, CA.

500 The distinction between material factors and material differences was introduced by the Equal Pay (Amendment) Regulations 1983, SI 1983/1794 apparently to circumvent the decision in *Clay Cross (Quarry Services) Ltd v Fletcher* [1979] ICR 1, [1978] IRLR 361, CA, discussed below. See McCrudden (1983) 12 ILJ at 211.

was given such a wide interpretation by the House of Lords in *Rainey v Greater Glasgow Health Board*[501] that the gap between a 'material difference' and a 'material factor' has been substantially narrowed, if not entirely removed.

The issue in *Rainey* was whether a material difference under section 1(3) could relate to matters outside the personal equation, such as the operation of 'market forces'. The case concerned the expansion of a national health prosthetics department by the recruitment of prosthetists (all male, as it happened) from the private sector on their existing level of remuneration, which was higher than that paid to the existing National Health Service prosthetists (who were principally female and included the applicant). The applicant sought equal pay with one of the male entrants, who it was accepted was employed on like work with her. The employer's genuine material difference defence had seemed doomed to fail, as the Court of Appeal had previously held in *Clay Cross (Quarry Services) Ltd v Fletcher*[502] that the payment of higher wages to a male clerk than to a longer-serving female clerk on the basis that when his job was advertised he was the only suitable candidate and could only be induced to take the job by the offer of a higher salary than that already being paid to her, went outside the bounds of permissible personal differentials envisaged in section 1(3), and that any other conclusion could render the statute a dead letter by allowing employers simply to say that they paid the man more because he asked for more, or that they paid the woman less because she was willing to work for less. However, in *Rainey*[503], the House of Lords held that the genuine material difference defence under section 1(3) is not limited to personal differences, but is capable of extending to other objectively justified[504] grounds for the woman being paid less:

'In my opinion these statements [in *Fletcher*] are unduly restrictive of the proper interpretation of section 1(3). The difference must be "material", which I would construe as meaning "significant and relevant", and it must be between "her case and his". Consideration of a person's case must necessarily involve consideration of all the circumstances of that case. These may well go beyond what is not very happily described as "the personal equation", i.e. the personal qualities by way of skill, experience or training which the individual brings to the job. Some circumstances may on examination prove to be not significant or not relevant, but others may do so, though not relating to the personal qualities of the employee. In particular, where there is no question of intentional sex discrimination whether direct or indirect (and there is none here) a difference which is connected with economic factors affecting the efficient carrying on of the employer's business or other activity may well be relevant.[505]'

---

501 [1987] ICR 129, [1987] IRLR 26, HL.

502 [1979] ICR 1, [1978] IRLR 361, CA; this case is also authority for the proposition that it is no defence for an act of unlawful discrimination to say that it was unintentional.

503 Above; the Scottish EAT and the Court of Session had distinguished *Fletcher* (though the grounds of distinction were difficult to see), but the House of Lords reconsidered the whole matter. The case is noted by McLean (1987) 46 CLJ 224; Schofield (1987) 50 MLR 379 and Townshend-Smith (1987) 16 ILJ 114.

504 Lord Keith, giving judgment, states that the test here is the same as that under the Sex Discrimination Act 1975, s 1(1)(b)(ii) for the justification of a requirement or condition which indirectly discriminates against women.

505 [1987] ICR 129 at 140, [1987] IRLR 26 at 29, per Lord Keith.

On the facts of the case, the House of Lords held that the applicant's case failed because there was objective justification for putting the male entrant on to a higher scale (given the need to expand the prosthetic service within a reasonable time), and for not raising the wages of the applicant and other existing prosthetists to that higher rate (since there were 'sound objectively justified administrative reasons' for maintaining their existing position within the overall Whitley Council scale). In so holding, the House of Lords adopted the 'objective justification' test for indirect discrimination under Article 141 set out by the ECJ in *Bilka-Kaufhaus GmbH v Weber von Hartz*[506], where it was held that in determining whether there were any objectively justified grounds for the variation in pay, the court should consider whether the measures adopted by the employer:

'correspond to a real need on the part of the undertaking, are appropriate with a view to achieving the objectives pursued and are necessary to that end[507].'

While the decision on the facts in *Rainey* can perhaps be defended on the basis of the employer's need to recruit prosthetists against a specific labour market shortage, by breaching the 'personal equation' rule in such a comprehensive manner it was feared that the House of Lords might have opened something of a Pandora's Box, particularly if the courts and tribunals were to accept too readily the sort of argument put forward in *Clay Cross*, ie that an employer was justified in paying a woman less because she was willing to work for less. The danger of such an approach is that it simply reinforces historic labour market inequalities in pay between men and women, and could render the equal pay laws a dead letter. In subsequent cases the courts have on the whole taken a cautious approach to market forces defences[508]. In *Enderby v Frenchay Health Authority*[509], the ECJ held, in a case under Article 141, that 'the state of the employment market, which may lead an employer to increase the pay of a particular job in order to attract candidates, may constitute an objectively justified economic ground' for a difference in pay, but crucially also held that 'it is for the national court to determine, if necessary by applying the principle of proportionality, whether and to what extent the shortage of candidates for a job and the need to attract them by higher pay constitutes an objectively justified economic ground for the difference in pay between the jobs in question'. In other words, an employer will not be able to justify the whole of the difference in pay on the basis of market forces (or indeed any other objectively justifiable reason) where only part of the difference in pay is attributable to that reason[510]. In a further blow to the market forces defence, in *Ratcliffe v North Yorkshire County Council*[511], the House of Lords refused to accept that the imposition of a

---

506 Case 170/84 [1987] ICR 110, [1986] IRLR 317, ECJ. The case is discussed further below.
507 In *Rainey*, Lord Keith added ([1987] ICR 129 at 143, [1987] IRLR 26 at 30) that he considered that the ECJ's ruling 'would not exclude objectively justified grounds which are other than economic, such as administrative efficiency in a concern not engaged in commerce or business'.
508 For an unfortunate lapse, see *Calder v Rowntree Mackintosh Confectionery Ltd* [1993] ICR 811, [1993] IRLR 212, CA.
509 [1994] ICR 112, [1993] IRLR 591, ECJ.
510 The ECJ's ruling on this point casts doubt on the correctness of the Court of Appeal decision in *Calder v Rowntree Mackintosh Confectionery Ltd* [1993] ICR 811, [1993] IRLR 212, CA, where the employers were only able to explain part of the shift premium paid to male shift-workers as representing compensation for working unsocial hours.
511 [1995] 3 All ER 597, [1995] ICR 883, HL.

pay cut for a group of predominantly female school catering assistants to enable the employer to tender for work at a commercially competitive rate was due to a material factor which was not the difference of sex. In that case, the council had established a direct service organisation (DSO) for the provision of school meals following the introduction of compulsory competitive tendering, but its catering staff were forced to take a pay cut after it became apparent that the DSO was unable to compete for the school dinner contracts with commercial organisations, who employed only women, while continuing to pay the staff on their existing local government rates. The Court of Appeal held that the material factor which led to the lower rates of pay, the need to compete effectively with rival bidders, was genuinely due to the operation of market forces, and that those market forces were gender-neutral in the sense that they were unconnected with the difference of sex. However, the House of Lords upheld the appeal and restored the tribunal's decision that the material factor was in fact due to the difference of sex, in that the labour market for catering staff was almost exclusively female, whereas the council employees employed on work of equivalent value (road sweepers, gardeners, refuse collectors and leisure attendants) were mostly men:

> 'Though conscious of the difficult problem facing the employers in seeking to compete with a rival tenderer, I am satisfied that to reduce the women's wages below that of their male comparators was the very kind of discrimination in relation to pay which the Act sought to remove[512].'

It could perhaps be concluded that where an employer pays one group of workers more, for example to combat a specific labour shortage, as in *Rainey*, the difference in pay will be justifiable under section 1(3) provided the employer can demonstrate that the difference is genuinely gender-neutral; but where the difference in pay between two groups of employees is simply a reflection of historic inequalities in the labour market, for example where the work in question is sex-segregated, as in *Ratcliffe*, the employer will find it difficult to show that paying lower rates of pay to a predominantly female group of employees is genuinely gender-neutral.

As seen above, in *Rainey* the House of Lords held that in order to discharge the burden of proof under section 1(3), it is necessary for the employer to show that the difference in pay is objectively justified, applying the test laid down by the ECJ in the *Bilka-Kaufhaus* case[513]. The test was usefully restated by the EAT in *Barton v Investec Henderson Crosthwaite Securities Ltd*[514], in which the applicant, a female financial analyst in the City, successfully challenged the disparity in salary and bonus payments between herself and her male colleagues. The EAT stated that the burden was on the respondents to prove: (1) that there were objective reasons for the difference; (2) unrelated to sex; (3) corresponding to a real need on the part of the undertaking; (4) appropriate to achieving the objective pursued; (5) it was necessary to that end; (6) that the difference conformed to the principle of

---

512 [1995] 3 All ER 597 at 604, per Lord Slynn. The fact that two men were employed on the same work at the same rate of pay as the applicants did not detract from this conclusion: 'It means no more than that the two men were underpaid compared with other men doing jobs rated as equivalent' ([1995] 3 All ER 597 at 603).

513 The correctness of the test was confirmed by the ECJ in *Brunnhofer v Bank der Österreichischen Postsparkasse AG* [2001] IRLR 571 ECJ.

514 [2003] IRLR 332, EAT.

proportionality; and (7) that was the case throughout the period during which the differential existed. On the facts, the employer's claim that secrecy is a 'vital component' of the City bonus culture was unequivocally rejected by the EAT, which declared that: 'no tribunal should be seen to condone a City bonus culture involving secrecy and/or lack of transparency because of the potentially large amounts involved, as a reason for avoiding equal pay obligations.'

Until recently, it was believed that to make out a section 1(3) defence, an employer had to show an objective justification for a difference in pay in all cases. However, in *Strathclyde Regional Council v Wallace*[515] the House of Lords held that the requirement to show some objective justification for a variation in terms only arises where the factor which the employer is relying upon to explain the variation is itself directly or indirectly sexually discriminatory. Where there is no element of sex discrimination, 'the employer establishes [the section 1(3) defence] by identifying the factors which he alleges have caused the disparity, proving that those factors are genuine and proving further that they were causally relevant to the disparity in pay complained of'[516]. According to Lord Nicholls in *Glasgow City Council v Marshall*[517], the requirement that the factor be 'material' simply means that it must be significant and relevant in a causal sense, rather than in a justificatory sense. If this is correct[518], it follows that where a difference in pay is genuinely caused by a factor which is not itself tainted by direct or indirect sex discrimination (for example where there is an historic explanation for the variation[519], or where it resulted from a careless mistake[520]) the employer is under no obligation to prove a 'good' reason for the pay disparity, even if it could not possibly be objectively justified. Moreover, although Lord Nicholls stated in *Marshall* that once the applicant had shown that she was doing like work, work rated as equivalent or work of equal value to that of a man, a rebuttable presumption of sex discrimination arises and the burden of proof passes to the employer to show that the explanation for the variation is not tainted with sex[521], in *Nelson v Carillion Services Ltd*[522], the Court of Appeal held that the burden of proof remains on the applicant to show, on the balance of probabilities, that the matter complained of has had a disproportionate adverse impact upon her sex, just as in an ordinary indirect sex discrimination claim under the 1975 Act[523]. The unfortunate implication of this decision is that in an equal pay claim, the applicant now has *two* hurdles to overcome in order to raise an inference of discrimination sufficient to pass the burden onto the employer to show some objective justification

---

515 [1998] ICR 205, [1998] IRLR 146, HL.
516 [1998] ICR 205, [1998] IRLR 146, per Lord Browne-Wilkinson. Cases such as *Rainey*, *Enderby* and *Ratcliffe* can all be explained as cases where the factor relied upon was one which affected a considerably higher proportion of women than men, and which therefore required objective justification.
517 [2000] ICR 196, [2000] IRLR 272, HL.
518 Cf *Brunnhofer v Bank der Osterreichischen Postsparkasse AG* [2001] IRLR 571, where the ECJ required objective justification for the difference in pay even though the facts did not appear to reveal any indirect discrimination.
519 As in *Marshall*, where the difference in pay between two groups of very similar gender composition (instructors and teachers) was due to different collective bargaining structures; significantly, the applicants had accepted that there was no sex discrimination.
520 See eg *Tyldesley v TML Plastics Ltd* [1996] ICR 356, [1996] IRLR 395, EAT.
521 [2000] IRLR 272 at 202.
522 [2003] IRLR 428, CA.
523 Significantly, the Court of Appeal stated that the burden of proof in indirect discrimination cases should be approached in the same way, irrespective of whether they are brought under Art 141, the 1975 Act or the 1970 Act.

for the difference in pay; first, she must satisfy the section 1(2) hurdle of showing that she is doing like work etc with a man in the same employment; and secondly, she must show that the matter complained of has had a disproportionate adverse impact upon her sex. The problem with this is that under the Equal Pay Act scheme, as traditionally understood, the first hurdle is supposed to *replace* the need to prove disparate adverse impact, not to be a mere preliminary to it. It seems inevitable that the approach adopted in *Nelson* will make it even more difficult for applicants to succeed in equal pay claims.

The section 1(3) defence has given rise to particular difficulties in three areas. The first concerns the application of the section 1(3) defence to part-timers[524], an area of particular significance in the development of the law on equal pay because it was in cases involving part-timers that the legislation was reinterpreted to cover practices which indirectly discriminate against women. In the early cases it appeared to be established that the fact that a woman worked part-time was a genuine material difference, so that she could not claim equality of hourly pay rates with a man working full time, even if he was doing exactly the same work[525]. However, in *Jenkins v Kingsgate (Clothing Productions) Ltd (No 2)*[526], the EAT (following a reference to the ECJ) reinterpreted section 1(3), and held that the fact of being part-time can be a genuine material difference only if the employer can show that the lower rate for part-timers is reasonably necessary to achieve some objective (probably economic) unrelated to sex. The overall effect of this was to introduce into equal pay law a concept of indirect discrimination akin to that in sex discrimination law, in that if the effect of the particular factor claimed to be the genuine material factor operates particularly harshly against women, it will only be permitted as a defence under section 1(3) if the employer can justify it objectively, on grounds other than sex.

Subsequent cases have graphically demonstrated the unwillingness of the courts to accept part-time working as a justification for indirect sex discrimination, unless some objective justification unrelated to any discrimination on grounds of sex can be shown[527]. In *Bilka-Kaufhaus GmbH v Weber von Hartz*[528], the ECJ held that the exclusion of part-time workers from an occupational pension scheme is contrary to Article 141 if the exclusion affects significantly more women than men, unless the employer can show that the exclusion is objectively justified on economic grounds relating to the management of the organisation[529]. In that

---

524 Part-time workers now have a right to equal treatment under the Part-Time Workers Directive and the implementing Regulations (see p 24) and are therefore less likely to need to argue indirect sex discrimination in the future.

525 *Handley v H Mona Ltd* [1979] ICR 147, [1978] IRLR 534.

526 [1981] ICR 715, [1981] IRLR 388, EAT

527 Although there have been cases which have bucked the trend: see eg *Stadt Lengerich v Helmig* [1996] ICR 35, [1995] IRLR 216, where the ECJ held that it was not discriminatory for an employer to pay an overtime supplement only to those working more than normal full-time working hours, so that part-time female employees were not entitled to the enhanced rate unless they worked more than 39 hours a week. The ECJ held that since on the facts the overall pay for full-time and part-time employees was the same for the same number of hours worked, there was no unequal treatment and therefore no discrimination, so that the question of objective justification did not arise.

528 [1981] ICR 110, [1981] IRLR 317, ECJ. In *Kowalska v Freie und Hansestadt Hamburg* [1992] ICR 29, [1990] IRLR 447, ECJ, the *Bilka-Kaufhaus* test was applied to a collective agreement which excluded part-timers from severance payments; see also *Nimz v Freie und Hansestadt Hamburg* [1991] ECR I-297, [1991] IRLR 222, ECJ (seniority rules).

529 This test was subsequently adopted by the House of Lords in *Rainey* when reconstruing the s 1(3) defence: see p 343 above.

case, the ECJ held that the exclusion of part-time workers from the pension scheme could in fact be justified by reference to the needs of the business, as it was the aim of the employer to employ as few part-time workers as possible. In *Rinner-Kühn v FWW Spezial-Gebäudereinigung GmbH & Co KG*[530], the ECJ adopted the same approach in holding that a provision in national legislation excluding part-timers from state sickness benefits was in breach of Article 141, unless the member state could establish that the means selected corresponded to an objective necessary for its social policy and were appropriate and necessary to the attainment of that objective. The decision in *Rinner-Kuhn* was in turn applied by the House of Lords in the landmark case of *R v Secretary of State for Employment, ex p Equal Opportunities Commission*[531] to strike down the hours per week qualifying thresholds for redundancy pay and unfair dismissal compensation on the grounds that they indirectly discriminated against women and were therefore incompatible with European law. In that case, the Secretary of State had claimed that the discriminatory qualifying thresholds were objectively justified, as they were designed to reduce the costs to employers of employing part-time workers and therefore to bring about an increase in the availability of part-time work. However, while the House of Lords was prepared to accept that increasing the availability of part-time work was a necessary aim of social policy, it held that the Secretary of State had failed to establish an objective justification for the threshold provisions because it had not been shown that they were suitable and requisite for achieving that aim. Perhaps the most startling aspect of the decision was the unwillingness of the House of Lords to accept at face value the Secretary of State's assertion that the threshold provisions had actually resulted in greater availability of part-time work than would have been the case without them, and were therefore requisite to achieve the stated aim. Lord Keith described the evidence for the Secretary of State on this point as not containing 'anything capable of being regarded as factual evidence demonstrating the correctness of these views[532] .'

The second area of difficulty concerns collective bargaining, and the extent to which an employer can argue that the separate bargaining processes for two groups of workers constitutes a genuine material factor which justifies a variation in terms between the two groups. On one view, as long as each bargaining process is in itself non-discriminatory, the different bargaining arrangements could be said to represent an objectively justified reason for the difference in outcome[533]; against that, however, it could be argued that the key issue is whether the difference in outcome between the two pay structures can *itself* be justified, so that the mere fact that pay is regulated by separate collective agreements will not of itself justify a difference[534]. The issue arose in stark form in *Enderby v Frenchay*

---

530 Case 171/88 [1989] ECR 2743, [1989] IRLR 493, ECJ. See also *Arbeiterwohlfahrt der Stadt Berlin eV v Bötel* [1992] 3 CMLR 446, [1992] IRLR 423, ECJ (legislative provisions limiting compensation available to part-timers for time off to undergo training).

531 [1995] 1 AC 1, [1994] ICR 317, HL.

532 [1995] 1 AC 1 at 30. Note, however, the approach of the ECJ in *Nolte v Landesversicherungsanstalt Hannover* [1996] All ER (EC) 212, [1996] IRLR 225, and *Megner v Innungskrankenkasse Vorderpfalz* [1996] All ER (EC) 212, [1996] IRLR 236, where member states were said to have a 'broad margin of discretion' in exercising their competence to choose the measures capable of achieving their social and employment policy objectives.

533 As was held in *Reed Packaging Ltd v Boozer* [1988] ICR 391, [1988] IRLR 333, EAT, where the genuine material factor defence was held to apply as the applicant and her comparator were employed under separate pay structures which were not in themselves discriminatory.

534 See *Barber v NCR (Manufacturing) Ltd* [1993] IRLR 95, where the EAT held that the fact that the difference in pay had arisen from collective bargaining did not constitute an objective factor which justified the result which had been produced.

Health Authority[535], where the applicant, one of a group of predominantly female speech therapists employed by the health authority, claimed that her work was of equal value with the predominantly male pharmacists and clinical psychologists, who were paid substantially more. The employer argued that the variation in pay was due to historical differences in the collective bargaining arrangements for the two groups, and that since those arrangements were not in themselves discriminatory, they constituted a genuine material factor which justified the difference. The EAT found for the employer[536], holding that if the factor causing the disparate impact has no taint of gender, there is nothing which requires justification. The Court of Appeal referred the matter to the ECJ[537], which held that the fact that the respective rates of pay of two jobs of equal value, one carried out almost exclusively by women and the other predominantly by men, were arrived at by collective bargaining processes which, although carried out by the same parties, were distinct and which, considered separately, were not in themselves discriminatory, is not sufficient objective justification for the difference in pay between those two jobs. The ECJ considered that if an employer could rely on the absence of discrimination within each of the collective bargaining processes taken separately as sufficient justification for the difference in pay, he could easily circumvent the principle of equal pay by using separate bargaining processes[538]. Under this approach, it is the *result* of the collective bargaining process which has to be justified by objective factors; the fact that the difference in pay arises from separate collective bargaining processes, while relevant[539], does not of itself constitute an objective justification for that difference. Having said that, the House of Lords has since held[540] that the need for the results of separate bargaining processes to be objectively justified only arises where the difference in terms results from sex discrimination (for example, where there is evidence that the difference in bargaining processes has a disparate adverse impact on women and is therefore prima facie indirectly discriminatory[541]). If the separate bargaining structures do not impact disproportionately on one sex, there is no obligation on the employer to justify the disparity in the terms which result from that process[542].

The third area of difficulty under section 1(3) concerns the 'red circling' cases[543]. These arise where male employees are paid more than female employees on like or equally rated work because the pay of the men is protected, or 'red circled', because of some event in the past; examples of this would be where the man was injured and put permanently on to lighter work but at his previous higher wage, or where the man's job was down-graded but rather than being made

---

535 [1994] ICR 112, [1993] IRLR 591, ECJ. The case is also an important authority on the need to establish a requirement or condition in cases of indirect discrimination (see p 287), and on whether the whole or only part of a difference in pay need be objectively justified (see p 343 above).
536 [1991] ICR 382, [1991] IRLR 44, EAT.
537 [1994] ICR 112, [1992] IRLR 15, CA.
538 [1994] ICR 112, [1993] IRLR 591 at 595.
539 See *Specialarbejderforbundet i Danmark v Dansk Industri, acting for Royal Copenhagen* [1996] ICR 51, [1995] IRLR 648, ECJ.
540 See *Glasgow City Council v Marshall* [2000] ICR 196, [2000] IRLR 272, HL.
541 An inference of discrimination can arise where 'significant' numbers of the disadvantaged group are female: see *British Road Services Ltd v Loughran* [1997] IRLR 92, NICA.
542 As in *Glasgow City Council v Marshall* above. Note, however, the ECJ decision in *Brunnhofer v Bank der Osterreichischen Postsparkasse AG* [2001] IRLR 571 ECJ.
543 Some care is needed, for 'red circle' must not be considered to be a term of art: *National Coal Board v Sherwin* [1978] ICR 700 at 706F, [1978] IRLR 122 at 125; *Methven v Cow Industrial Polymers Ltd* [1980] ICR 463, [1980] IRLR 289, CA, per Dunn LJ.

redundant he was kept on at the lesser job but again at his previous higher wage. In both of these cases there may be women also doing the lighter or lesser work, but at the ordinary rate for that work, so that they are paid less. A genuine red circle case may well come within section 1(3) so that a woman cannot claim to be put on to the man's protected rate, as can be seen from the judgment of the EAT in *Charles Early and Marriott (Witney) Ltd v Smith and Ball*[544], but in the consolidated appeal in *Snoxell v Vauxhall Motors Ltd*[545] the EAT in fact held that the red circle argument failed, since it appeared that the existence of the men's protection was partly due to past discrimination on sexual grounds. Thus, the important principle is that the tribunal should inquire into the original reason for the protection of the man's wages and should only accept the red circle as a genuine material factor if it had its origins in genuine factors other than any form of direct or indirect sexual discrimination. In *Methven v Cow Industrial Polymers Ltd*[546] the Court of Appeal emphasised that in 'red circling' cases the tribunals should not lose sight of the wording of the Act and accepted that three questions arise: (i) was there a variation between the woman's contract and the man's? (ii) was there a material difference (other than the difference of sex) between her case and his? (iii) have the employers proved on the balance of probabilities that the variation in wages was due to the material difference (a matter of causation)? While it is clear that in an appropriate case red circling can provide a defence indefinitely[547], the EAT has stressed that even where a red circling agreement is genuine and reasonable at the time of its inception, its continuation indefinitely would be likely to cause bad feelings among those not thus protected, so that in the light of good industrial relations practice it might be expected that the employer would phase it out after a reasonable period, with the implication that if this is not done the employer might find after the expiry of such a period that he cannot use it as a defence to a claim for equal pay[548]. In *Benveniste v University of Southampton*[549], the Court of Appeal confirmed that this reasoning also applies in the reverse situation, ie where a person has been appointed on less favourable terms than normal because of temporary financial considerations. In that case the applicant had been appointed at a lower rate than would normally have been the case because of financial constraints then operating on the employer, but it was held that the employer could not use this as a defence under section 1(3) once those financial constraints had eased.

(iii) Remedies

A claim for equal pay may be brought before an employment tribunal[550]. On such a claim[551], the tribunal may declare the existence of the equality clause, to ensure treatment no less favourable. However, this is dependent upon a finding that

---

544 [1977] ICR 700, [1977] IRLR 123.
545 [1977] ICR 700, [1977] IRLR 123.
546 [1980] ICR 463, [1980] IRLR 289; *Ministry of Defence v Farthing* [1980] ICR 705, [1980] IRLR 402, CA; *Avon and Somerset Police Authority v Emery* [1981] ICR 229, EAT.
547 *Charles Early and Marriott (Witney) Ltd v Smith and Ball* [1977] ICR 700, [1977] IRLR 123.
548 *Outlook Supplies Ltd v Parry* [1978] ICR 388, [1978] IRLR 12, EAT.
549 [1989] ICR 617, [1989] IRLR 122, CA.
550 Equal Pay Act 1970, s 2.
551 In which the applicant may be assisted by the EOC if a question of principle is raised, or a complicated point is involved: Sex Discrimination Act 1975, s 75.

there is like work/work rated as equivalent, or work of equal value; if that is not so, the tribunal has no jurisdiction to make any order, even if the women concerned are being poorly treated, and the gap in the remuneration between men and women is in no way commensurate to the difference in the work that they do: the Act does not enable a tribunal to act as a general wage-fixing body[552]. However, once there is a valid claim for equality, the applicant may be awarded arrears of pay or damages for contravention of the equality clause.

As originally enacted, the Equal Pay Act contained two limitation periods which were both successfully challenged as incompatible with EC law. Section 2(4) stated that a claim had to be brought within six months of the end of employment; and section 2(5) placed a limit of two years from the date of commencement of proceedings on any award of arrears of remuneration (ie back pay) or damages. It is a fundamental principle of EC law that in the absence of Community rules on the matter, it is for domestic legal systems to lay down procedural rules governing the enforcement of Community rights, provided they are not less favourable than those governing similar domestic actions (the principle of equivalence), and do not render the exercise of rights conferred by Community law virtually impossible or excessively difficult (the principle of effectiveness). Both time limits were held by the ECJ to infringe these principles, and the limits were duly amended by the Equal Pay Act 1970 (Amendment) Regulations 2003[553]. The original six-month limit in section 2(4) was held by the ECJ to infringe the principle of effectiveness in *Preston v Wolverhampton Healthcare NHS Trust*[554], because the limit applied at the end of *each* contract of employment, even in cases where there had been a succession of separate short-term contracts in respect of the same employment, and thus made the enforcement of the right conferred by EC law excessively difficult[555] (the problem being that, as originally enacted, the Equal Pay Act contained no provisions analogous to those in the employment rights legislation preserving continuity of employment through a succession of fixed-term contracts[556]). Under the amended section 2(4), proceedings before an employment tribunal must now be instituted on or before the 'qualifying date'[557]; as before, this is normally six months after the last day on which the woman was 'employed in the employment[558]' in question, but the limit is now modified in three circumstances; first, where the employer and employee had a 'stable employment relationship', the qualifying date is six months after the end of that relationship, irrespective of the fact that there may have been more than one contract of employment during that period[559]; secondly, where the employee was

---

552 *Maidment v Cooper & Co (Birmingham) Ltd* [1978] ICR 1094, [1978] IRLR 462.
553 SI 2003,/1656, with effect from 19 July 2003.
554 Case C-78/98, [2000] ICR 961, [2000] IRLR 506, ECJ. The case was part of the litigation concerning the exclusion of part-time workers from occupational pension schemes; see p 358 below.
555 Surprisingly, the House of Lords subsequently held ([2001] UKHL 5, [2001] ICR 217, [2001] IRLR 237) that the six-month limit did not breach the principle of equivalence, because taken overall it was not less favourable than the six-year limitation period for bringing a claim for breach of contract.
556 See p 188 above.
557 Equal Pay Act 1970, s 2ZA, as inserted by SI 2003/1656.
558 Cf *National Power plc v Young* [2001] IRLR 32, EAT, where this phrase in the pre-2003 provisions was held to refer to her employment with the employer, rather than the actual job for that employer in respect of which her claim was made.
559 Equal Pay Act 1970, s 2ZB(4). Sub-s (2) expressly provides that the period of a stable employment relationship can include a time when no contract of employment is in force, and thus has as similar role to the provisions that preserve continuity of employment through a temporary cessation of work: see p 193 below.

under a disability[560], the qualifying date is six months after she ceased to be under a disability[561]; and thirdly, where the employer deliberately concealed relevant facts[562] from the employee, the qualifying day is six months after she discovered (or could with reasonable diligence have discovered) the information in question[563]. The provisions on concealment were introduced to meet the point which arose in *Levez v T H Jennings (Harlow Pools) Ltd*[564], where the ECJ held that the six-month limit infringed the principle of effectiveness because it did not make allowance for an applicant who delayed bringing proceedings as a result of a deliberate misrepresentation by the employer. In *Levez*, the ECJ also considered the two-year limit on arrears of remuneration. The ECJ held that the two-year limit did not in itself infringe the principle of effectiveness[565], and that it was for the national courts to determine whether the rule in question infringed the principle of equivalence through being less favourable than the rules applying to similar domestic actions. The EAT subsequently ruled[566] that the two-year limit did in fact contravene the principle of equivalence, in that it was less favourable than the six-year limitation period governing similar claims under domestic law (for example for breach of contract or discrimination on grounds of race or disability), and the EAT disapplied the two-year limit as being incompatible with EC law, holding that the normal six-year time limit applied instead. In *Preston v Wolverhampton Healthcare NHS Trust*[567], the ECJ clarified the position by holding that in relation to those excluded from occupational pension schemes, the two-year limit on the back-dating of membership infringed the principle of effectiveness, and the House of Lords subsequently held[568] that an employer could not rely on the two-year limit to prevent an employee from retroactively gaining access to a pension scheme, and that in principle pension rights could be back-dated as far back as 8 April 1976[569] (subject to the proviso that in a contributory scheme the employee would have to pay any contributions owing in respect of the period for which retrospective membership was being claimed). The amended section 2(5) now provides that if proceedings under the Equal Pay Act are successful, the tribunal may award back-pay or damages back to the 'arrears date'[570], which is normally six years before the institution of proceedings[571]. This is still less generous than the position under the Sex Discrimination Act, where there is no ceiling on the compensation that may be awarded.

560 Ie a minor or of unsound mind: Equal Pay Act 1970, s 11(2A), as amended.
561 Equal Pay Act 1970, s 2ZA(6). The exception applies if she was under a disability at any time during what would otherwise have been the six-month limitation period.
562 Ie facts which are relevant to the proceedings, without knowledge of which the woman could not reasonably have been expected to institute the proceedings: Equal Pay Act 1970, s 2ZA(2).
563 Equal Pay Act 1970, s 2ZA(5). The exception applies if she did not discover (or could not reasonably have discovered) the information until after the last day of employment, or after the end of a stable employment relationship, as the case may be.
564 [1999] ICR 521, [1999] IRLR 36, ECJ.
565 Although on the facts that principle was found to be infringed because of the lack of any provision on deliberate concealment: see above.
566 *Levez v T H Jennings (Harlow Pools) Ltd (No 2)* [1999] IRLR 764, EAT.
567 Case C-78/98 [2000] ICR 961, [2000] IRLR 506, ECJ.
568 *Preston v Wolverhampton Healthcare NHS Trust (No 2)* [2001] UKHL 5, [2001] ICR 217, [2001] IRLR 237, HL.
569 Ie the date of the *Defrenne* judgment, in which the ECJ first held that Art 141 had direct effect.
570 Equal Pay Act 1970, s 2ZB, as inserted by SI 2003/1656.
571 Equal Pay Act 1970, s 2ZB(3). Special provision is again made for cases involving disability and/or deliberate concealment, where the arrears date is the date of the contravention to which the proceedings relate: s 2ZB(2), (4). There are separate rules for claims by service personnel in the armed forces: s 7A.

(iv) Death or retirement

As originally enacted, the Equal Pay Act contained a blanket exclusion for any provision made in connection with death or retirement[572], considered to be necessary because of the differential state pensionable age upon which many such provisions have traditionally been based. However, during the 1980s it became increasingly clear that the breadth of the exclusion in the domestic legislation was incompatible with EC law, in that while the differential state pensionable age itself was outside the scope of Article 141[573], retirement benefits (and indeed retirement ages) which are based on the state pensionable age are not. As a result, the government was forced to introduce legislation outlawing discrimination in provisions made in connection with retirement, initially in relation to promotion, transfer, training, demotion or dismissal[574], and later in the area of occupational pensions also[575]. The picture is a complex and difficult one, but the impact of EC law in this area has tended to crystallise around four main issues, of ascending practical importance.

The first concerns what might be considered the incidents, or 'perks', of retirement; in *Garland v British Rail Engineering Ltd*[576], the ECJ gave an early indication that the definition of 'pay' in Article 141 was to be interpreted widely[577], and that the exclusion for death or retirement in the domestic legislation would have to be construed narrowly in order to comply with it. In *Garland*, the employer discriminated in the provision of travel concessions to retired employees by providing concessions for the families of male former employees but not for those of female former employees. The Court of Appeal applied the exclusion widely and held that it ruled out the complaint in English law; on further appeal, the House of Lords remitted the matter to the ECJ, which held that travel facilities accorded to employees after retirement are 'pay' within the meaning of Article 141, and that the discrimination was therefore contrary to EC law. In the light of this, the House of Lords gave the exclusion a narrow construction in order to comply with EC law[578], and held that the travel concessions infringed English law since they were not directly the result of 'provisions in relation to death or retirement'[579].

---

572 Equal Pay Act 1970, s 6. There was an equivalent exclusion in the Sex Discrimination Act 1975, s 6(4).

573 Art 7 of EEC Directive 79/7 on Social Security allows member states to exclude 'the determination of pensionable age for the purposes of granting old-age and retirement pensions' from the principle of equal treatment, but does not in terms extend to provisions which are tied to the state pensionable age. See *R v Secretary of State for Social Security, ex p Equal Opportunities Commission* [1992] ICR 782, [1992] IRLR 376, ECJ.

574 Sex Discrimination Act 1986, s 2 (see p 353 below)

575 Pensions Act 1995, ss 62–66 (see p 359 below).

576 [1983] 2 AC 751, [1982] ICR 420, ECJ.

577 Art 141 provides that 'pay' means 'the ordinary basic or minimum wage or salary and any other consideration, whether in cash or in kind, which the worker receives, directly or indirectly, in respect of his employment from his employer'. *Garland* gave an early indication of the wide interpretation which the ECJ was prepared to give to the word 'pay'.

578 The extent to which the national courts and tribunals are required to interpret domestic legislation in the light of EC law is considered above at p 270.

579 [1982] ICR 420, [1982] IRLR 257, HL. As there was no contractual entitlement to the benefits in question, the case came under the Sex Discrimination Act 1975.

The second issue which then arose was whether it was lawful for an employer to insist on discriminatory retirement ages (for example retiring a man at 65, but a woman at 60); it was clear that this widespread practice could be detrimental to a woman, both financially[580] and through premature loss of job satisfaction, but as it was directly linked to provisions in relation to retirement, it seemed fairly clear that it was lawful under English law[581]. However, the breakthrough here came in *Marshall v Southampton and South West Hampshire Area Health Authority (Teaching)*[582], where discriminatory compulsory retirement ages were held by the ECJ to be contrary to the Equal Treatment Directive. Significantly the ECJ rejected the argument that as differential retirement ages simply reflected the differential state pensionable age, they were covered by the exemption in the Social Security Directive[583], and held that the exclusion of social security matters from the scope of the Equal Treatment Directive must be interpreted strictly. The Equal Treatment Directive itself was held to be directly effective (ie giving rights directly enforceable in the national courts by a person such as Mrs Marshall), but the ECJ approved the prevailing theory that a Directive (as opposed to an Article of the Treaty) can only have 'vertical' direct effect, ie only as against the state or one of its organs; this meant that the newly won EC right to equal retirement ages only itself applied to public sector employment[584]. This was clearly an untenable situation, and so *Marshall*'s case led to an important legislative amendment in the Sex Discrimination Act 1986, section 2, which amended both the Equal Pay Act 1970 and the Sex Discrimination Act 1975 so that it became unlawful (in either public or private sector employment) to discriminate against a woman in provisions relating to retirement, in the area of promotion, transfer, training, demotion or dismissal; it is the last that is particularly important in a case like *Marshall*, as it renders illegal the compulsory retiring of a woman at an earlier age than a man in the same position[585].

The third issue is, however, that these developments did not appear to affect differential *pension* ages (the principal reason for the exclusion for death or retirement in the first place). In particular, it was thought that occupational pension schemes, which traditionally have tended to adopt the state differential pension ages of 65 for a man and 60 for a woman, were not amenable to challenge under EC law because the Social Security Directive expressly permits member states to continue to fix their own pension ages[586]. To that extent, *Marshall* and the 1986 Act appeared to have created an anomaly, by requiring equal retirement

---

580 In view of the likely difference between her earnings and her pension, and the fact that her pension entitlement might well depend on her final salary, so that by retiring five years earlier than a man, that salary could be substantially lower than it would have been five years later, with corresponding effect on her level of pension.

581 *Burton v British Railways Board (No 2)* [1982] ICR 329, [1982] IRLR 116, ECJ.

582 Case 152/84 [1986] ICR 335, [1986] IRLR 140, ECJ.

583 Directive 79/7/EEC. See, n 573 above.

584 The direct effect of Directives is discussed above at p 269.

585 It was also necessary to amend the Employment Protection (Consolidation) Act 1978 (see now the Employment Rights Act 1996, s 109) to equalise the relevant ages in the 'normal retiring age' exclusion in complaints of unfair dismissal, see p 559 below.

586 But cf *Worringham v Lloyds Bank Ltd* Case 69/80 [1981] ICR 558, [1981] IRLR 178, ECJ and [1982] ICR 299, [1982] IRLR 74, CA, where the ECJ held that Art 141 applied to a pension scheme under which the employer made extra pensions contributions for male employees under 25, on the basis that those additional sums were included in the calculation of gross salary and determined the calculation of other salary-related benefits, such as redundancy payments. Contrast *Newstead v Department of Transport*: 192/85 [1988] ICR 332, [1988] IRLR 66, ECJ.

ages between men and women while still allowing pensions to be payable at different ages. However, this whole area was thrown into confusion by the ruling of the ECJ in the landmark case of *Barber v Guardian Royal Exchange Assurance Group*[587]. In that case Mr Barber had been made redundant at the age of 52, and complained that while a woman in those circumstances would have been entitled under the pension scheme in question to an immediate pension at 50, he would not be so entitled until he reached the age of 55 (a difference obviously based on the difference in the state pensionable ages). The ECJ ruled that benefits paid under a contracted-out, private occupational pension scheme fell within the definition of 'pay' in Article 141, so that a differential entitlement as between men and women under such a scheme infringed Article141, irrespective of the fact that the difference simply mirrored the state pension age[588]. Put simply, the effect of *Barber* was to require equalisation of benefits under contracted-out, private occupational pension schemes. However, the ECJ's decision raised as many questions as it answered, and it took a series of further references to the ECJ before the full implications of the decision were finally clarified. The uncertainty centred on two main areas, firstly, the scope of the *Barber* ruling (did other types of benefits and pension schemes also fall within the definition of 'pay' in Article 141?); and secondly, its practical implementation (did it require all benefits paid after the date of the judgment to be paid on an equal basis, or only those payable in respect of periods of service after that date? Did it require the levelling up of benefits, or was it permissible for employers to equalise benefits by reducing the advantage of those previously favoured?). On the first point, it is now clear that the definition of 'pay' in Article 141 covers all pension benefits paid to a worker by reason of the employment relationship[589], including those paid under a non-contracted-out occupational scheme[590], and also covers a survivor's pension provided by an occupational pension scheme[591]; it has also been established that Article 141 may be relied upon by employees and their dependants against the trustees of a pension scheme[592]. However, Article 141 does not apply to benefits which derive from additional voluntary contributions by employees[593], or to transfer benefits and capital-sum benefits[594] (the significant point here being that the ECJ has ruled that it is not a breach of Article 141 for actuarial factors which vary according to sex[595] to be used in determining the employers' contribution rates and in

---

587 Case C-262/88: [1991] 1 QB 344, [1990] ICR 616, ECJ

588 One of the ironies of *Barber* is that it overrode Social Security Directives 79/7 and 86/378, which required equal treatment in occupational pension schemes but permitted member states to defer the implementation until 1 January 1993; see p 358 below.

589 *Bestuur van het Algemeen Burgerlijk Pensioenfonds v Beune* [1994] ECR I-4471, [1995] IRLR 103, ECJ. In that case the ECJ also held that legislation which applies different rules for calculating the occupational pensions of married men and married women infringes Art 141.

590 *Coloroll Pension Trustees Ltd v Russell* [1995] ICR 179, [1994] IRLR 586, ECJ; see also *Moroni v Firma Collo GmbH* [1995] ICR 137, [1994] IRLR 130, ECJ.

591 *Ten Oever v Stichting Bedrijfspensioenfonds voor het Glazenwassers-en Schoonmaakbedrijf* [1995] ICR 74, [1993] IRLR 601, ECJ.

592 *Coloroll Pension Trustees Ltd v Russell* [1995] ICR 179, [1994] IRLR 586. As the requirement of equal treatment takes precedence over the rules of the pension scheme, employers and trustees must do everything within their powers to ensure that the scheme complies with the principle of equal treatment, including where necessary having recourse to the national courts to amend the scheme.

593 *Coloroll Pension Trustees Ltd v Russell* [1995] ICR 179, [1994] IRLR 586.

594 *Coloroll Pension Trustees Ltd v Russell* [1995] ICR 179, [1994] IRLR 586.

595 Eg the actuarial assumption that women live longer than men and that their pensions are therefore more expensive to maintain.

calculating transfer values and capital lump sums[596]). A state pension is not 'pay' for the purposes of Article 141, and a particularly difficult problem therefore arises where the payments made to an employee under an occupational pension scheme are reduced to take account of the amount of state pension which the employee is entitled to receive. In such a case, a choice has to be made between requiring formal equality under the scheme itself, irrespective of any entitlement to a state pension, and seeking to achieve overall substantive equality by taking entitlement to a state pension into account. This was the issue in *Roberts v Birds Eye Walls Ltd* [597], where the applicant, who had retired early on grounds of ill-health at the age of 57, complained that she had been discriminated against on the grounds of sex because the bridging pension which she received from her occupational pension scheme was reduced by £749 when she reached 60 (that being the amount of the state pension which it was assumed she would be receiving from that age), whereas a man taking early retirement at the same age as her would not have suffered any such reduction in entitlement until he reached the state pension age for men, ie 65. The EAT had held that the reduction in her bridging pension from the age of 60 was discriminatory, even though this gave rise to the seemingly absurd result that the achievement of 'equality' in her case meant that she would in fact be £749 per annum better off than her male comparator! However, the ECJ held that it is not contrary to Article 141 for an employer to reduce the amount of a bridging pension to take account of the amount of the state pension which the employee will receive, even though, in the case of men and women aged between 60 and 65, the result is that a female employee will receive a smaller bridging pension than that paid to her male counterpart[598]. As the court observed, 'to maintain the amount for women at the same level as that which obtained before they received the state pension would give rise to unequal treatment to the detriment of men who do not receive the state pension until the age of 65.' The mechanism for ensuring overall equality of treatment (ie the deduction of the state pension from the bridging pension) was considered to be 'neutral', and therefore not discriminatory[599]. Taken at face value, the ECJ's decision could be seen as supporting the position that direct discrimination can be objectively justified under Community law (a view considered as little short of heresy by discrimination lawyers), but the court made no express ruling to that effect, and it is unlikely that it was intending to lay down any such general principle. Rather, the ECJ's decision is probably best seen as a pragmatic response to an untypical situation where the alleged discriminatory treatment is an attempt to achieve substantive equality by counteracting an existing inequality.

On the second point, in an attempt to restrict the impact of its ruling, the ECJ held in *Barber* that the decision was not to operate retrospectively, and that Article 141 could not be relied upon in order to claim entitlement to a pension with

---

596 *Neath v Hugh Steeper Ltd* [1995] ICR 158, [1994] IRLR 91, ECJ.
597 [1994] ICR 338, [1994] IRLR 29, ECJ.
598 For good measure, the ECJ held that the employer was entitled to take account of the full state pension, even if the pension which the woman was in fact receiving was a widow's pension, or if she had exercised the married woman's option of paying reduced NI contributions in return for a reduced state pension.
599 Significantly, the ECJ stated that 'the principle of equal treatment laid down by Art 141 . . . presupposes that the men and women to whom it applies are in identical situations . . .', a requirement which, taken to its logical conclusion, would seem to undermine the application of Art 141 in cases of pregnancy discrimination: see p 439 below.

effect from a date before the ruling in that case (ie 17 May 1990)[600], except in the case of those who had already initiated legal proceedings or raised an equivalent claim[601] under the applicable national law before that date. After much initial uncertainty over the scope of this temporal limitation, the ECJ has confirmed[602] that Article 141 may only be relied upon in relation to benefits payable in respect of periods of service after the date of the *Barber* judgment; where a benefit is not linked to the length of actual service (as in the case of a lump-sum payment in the event of the employee's death-in-service), the principle of equal treatment applies where the operative event occurred after the date of that judgment[603]. On the vexed question of levelling-up versus levelling-down, the position is unfortunately very confusing: the ECJ has held that Article 141 does not preclude the adoption of measures which implement the principle of equal treatment by reducing the advantages of the favoured class (ie by levelling-down), but that in relation to periods of employment between the date of the *Barber* judgment and the date on which the scheme adopted measures to achieve equal treatment, the equalisation of benefits must be at the more favourable level (ie levelling-up)[604]; in relation to periods of employment before the *Barber* judgment, the ECJ has held that Community law imposes no obligation which would justify retroactive reduction of the advantages which women enjoyed[605]. So, to take the example of a scheme which, pre-*Barber*, assumed a pension age of 65 for men and 60 for women, this would mean that periods of service before the *Barber* judgment are unaffected, but that for the period between the date of the judgment and the date on which the scheme adopted measures to achieve equality, the pension rights of men would have to be calculated on the basis of a retirement age of 60. It seems that most occupational pension schemes have in fact equalised pension ages upwards, by raising the retirement age for women, and the ECJ has held that where the retirement age is raised, Article 141 does not permit transitional measures designed to soften the blow for women adversely affected thereby as regards future periods of service[606].

Last but certainly not least is the important question of access to occupational pension schemes, and in particular the position of part-time workers denied access to such schemes. Section 6 of the Equal Pay Act, which excluded provisions made in connection with death or retirement from the scope of that Act, did not apply to access to occupational pension schemes[607], where a right of equal access was first introduced in 1975[608]. However, that right only prohibited direct

---

600 This temporal limitation on the *Barber* ruling was subsequently endorsed in a Protocol to the Treaty on European Union (the Maastricht Treaty).

601 In *Howard v Ministry of Defence* [1995] ICR 1074, [1995] IRLR 570, EAT, this was taken to mean that the dispute must have been raised before an independent third party with power to determine the matter (eg an arbitrator), and that merely asserting a claim would not be sufficient.

602 *Ten Oever v Stichting Bedrijfspensioenfonds voor het Glazenwassers-en Schoonmaakbedrijf*; see also *Coloroll Pension Trustees Ltd v Russell* [1995] ICR 74, [1993] IRLR 601.

603 *Coloroll Pension Trustees Ltd v Russell* [1995] ICR 179, [1994] IRLR 586.

604 *Smith v Avdel Systems Ltd* [1995] ICR 596, [1994] IRLR 602, ECJ. That case also establishes that Art 141 precludes a scheme from retrospectively raising the retirement age for women in relation to the period between 17 May 1990 and the date of entry into force of the measures designed to achieve equal treatment, even if there are objectively justifiable considerations relating to the needs of the undertaking or of the scheme itself.

605 *Smith v Avdel Systems Ltd* [1995] ICR 596, [1994] IRLR 602.

606 *Smith v Avdel Systems Ltd* [1995] ICR 596, [1994] IRLR 602. See also *Van Den Akker v Stichting Shell Pensioenfonds* [1995] ICR 596, [1994] IRLR 616, ECJ.

607 Equal Pay Act 1970, s 6(1A)(a), as amended by the Pensions Act 1995, s 66(1).

608 Social Security Pensions Act 1975, s 53(2) (see now the Pension Schemes Act 1993, s 118).

discrimination between the sexes[609], and was therefore of no assistance to part-time workers who were indirectly discriminated against by being denied access to pension schemes. The turning-point came in *Bilka-Kaufhaus GmbH v Weber von Hartz*[610], where the ECJ held that the conditions for admission to an occupational pension scheme fall within the scope of Article 141 (provided the benefits paid to employees under the scheme are paid in respect of employment), and that excluding part-timers from a pension scheme constitutes unlawful indirect discrimination if the exclusion affects a much greater proportion of women than men, unless the employer can show that the exclusion is objectively justified. This decision was reaffirmed in *Vroege v NCIV Institut voor Volkshuisvesting BV*[611], where the ECJ crucially held that the temporal limitation in the *Barber* judgment and the Protocol only applies to benefits under an occupational pension scheme, and does not apply to the right to join a pension scheme in the first place[612].

This ruling raised the fascinating prospect of part-time workers who had previously been excluded from an occupational pension scheme claiming the right to join a scheme retroactively, potentially as far back as 8 April 1976 (that being the date when the ECJ first ruled that Article 141 had direct effect[613]). However, in *Fisscher v Voorhuis Hengelo BV*[614], the ECJ held that there are two crucially important limitations on this right: first, a worker who claims the right to join a pension scheme retroactively cannot avoid paying the employee contributions for the period of membership in question, which is likely to be a major disincentive to bringing such a claim for many potential applicants; and secondly, the national (ie domestic) rules relating to time-limits for bringing actions under national law apply to workers asserting their right under Community law to join a pension scheme, provided that they are not less favourable than those which apply to similar actions under domestic law (the principle of equivalence), and that they do not render the exercise of rights conferred by Community law impossible in practice (the principle of effectiveness). In the wake of the *Vroege* and *Fisscher* judgments, some 60,000 part-time workers in both the public and private sectors in the UK commenced proceedings before tribunals claiming that they had been unlawfully excluded from membership of various occupational pension schemes. In a belated attempt at damage-limitation, the government introduced Regulations[615] prohibiting (as from 31 May 1995) all direct or indirect discrimination on grounds of sex regarding membership of any occupational pension scheme, requiring such claims to be brought within six months of the end of the employment in question, and limiting any backdated award to a maximum period of two years

609 Cf Pension Schemes Act 1993, s 118(1), which states: '. . . the equal access requirements in relation to an occupational pension scheme are that membership of the scheme is open to both men and women on terms which are the same as to age and length of service needed for becoming a member.'
610 [1987] ICR 110, [1986] IRLR 317, ECJ.
611 [1995] ICR 635, [1994] IRLR 651, ECJ.
612 For a recent illustration of the difficulty in distinguishing complaints over access to benefits under a pension scheme from complaints over level of benefits under such a scheme, see *Quirk v Burton Hospitals NHS Trust* [2002] EWCA Civ 149, [2000] ICR 602, [2002] IRLR 353.
613 *Defrenne v SABENA (No 2)* [1976] ECR 455, [1976] ICR 547, ECJ. Significantly, in *Dietz v Stichting Thuiszorg Rotterdam* [1996] IRLR 692, the ECJ ruled that a part-timer unlawfully excluded from a pension scheme can backdate beyond the *Barber* date in relation to both membership and benefits.
614 [1995] ICR 635, [1994] IRLR 662, ECJ.
615 The Occupational Pension Schemes (Equal Access to Membership) Amendment Regulations 1995, SI 1995/1215. The regulations came into force on 31 May 1995, and apply to claims lodged on or after that date.

from the institution of proceedings (in effect applying the time-limits which applied to claims under the Equal Pay Act), but as those Regulations did not have retrospective effect, they could not affect the many thousands of claims which had already been lodged before they came into force. As seen earlier, in *Preston v Wolverhampton Healthcare NHS Trust* [616], the ECJ ruled that the two-year limit on the back-dating of membership of occupational pension schemes under the Equal Pay Act[617] infringed the principle of effectiveness, and the House of Lords subsequently confirmed[618] that workers unlawfully excluded from such schemes are in principle entitled to claim a right to back-date their membership to 8 April 1976, although any employee contributions due in respect of the period for which retrospective membership was being claimed would have to be paid. It should also be remembered that the decision in *Preston* does not give a part-time employee an *automatic* right to retrospective membership of her employer's pension scheme: she would still need to show that the exclusion of part-timers had a disproportionate impact on women and was therefore indirectly sex discriminatory, and even she if overcame that hurdle, the employer would have an opportunity to argue that there was some objective justification unrelated to sex (for example administrative complications) for the exclusion of part-time workers from the scheme.

The issue of equal treatment in occupational pension schemes had been high on the agenda within the EC for several years before the *Barber* judgment. In July 1986, the EC Council issued Directive 86/378 on the implementation of the principle of equal treatment for men and women in occupational social security schemes, with a deferred implementation date of 1 January 1993, and the Social Security Act 1989 contained a series of provisions designed to implement the requirements of the Directive[619]. Article 9 of the Directive appeared to allow member states to defer application of the principle of equal treatment in relation to differential pensionable ages in occupational pension schemes until equality in pensionable ages is achieved in statutory schemes, or is required by a further Directive[620], and Schedule 5 to the 1989 Act contained an exemption to that effect[621]. However, before those provisions were brought into force they were overtaken by the decision of the ECJ in *Barber*[622], which went significantly further than the Directive by holding that differential pensionable ages in occupational schemes are contrary to Article 141, even if based on statutory schemes. In the light of *Barber* (and the subsequent ECJ decisions explaining and clarifying it), it

---

616 Case C-78/98 [2000] ICR 961, [2000] IRLR 506. The ECJ's ruling on the validity of the six-month time-limit on the presentation of claims is discussed at p 350 above.

617 As modified by the Occupational Pension Schemes (Equal Access to Membership) Regulations 1976, SI 1976/142, which, inter alia, provide that the only remedy under the 1970 Act for a failure to comply with the equal access requirements is a declaration that the employee is entitled to be admitted to the scheme, subject to a limitation period of two years before the date on which the proceedings were instituted (regs 11 and 12).

618 *Preston v Wolverhampton Healthcare NHS Trust (No 2)* [2001] UKHL 5, [2001] ICR 217, [2001] IRLR 237, HL; see p 351 above.

619 Social Security Act 1989, s 23 and. Sch 5.

620 It was because Directive 86/378 appeared to allow an exception for the consequences of differences in state pensionable ages that the ECJ in *Barber* placed a limitation on the retrospective effect of its judgment, the point being that before that case it was reasonable for people to rely on the Directive and to assume that Art 141 did not apply to differential pensionable ages in occupational pension schemes.

621 Social Security Act 1989, para 2(4).

622 See p 354 above.

was clear that further legislation was necessary, and this was introduced in the Pensions Act 1995 which, in addition to laying down a new regulatory regime for occupational pension schemes, equalising the state pension ages of men and women at 65 (from 2020), and abolishing Guaranteed Minimum Pensions[623], introduced new provisions requiring equal treatment in relation to membership of and rights under occupational pension schemes[624]. The Pensions Act provisions echo those in the Equal Pay Act (and are to be construed as one with that Act[625]) by enacting that a statutory equal treatment rule (equivalent to an equality clause under the 1970 Act) is to be included in all occupational pension schemes, the effect of which is to require any term of a scheme which concerns access to or benefits[626] under the scheme, and which is less favourable to a woman than to a man, to be modified so as to be not less favourable, where the woman is employed on like work, work rated as equivalent or work of equal value with the man[627]. As with the Equal Pay Act, there is a defence if the trustees or managers of the scheme can prove that the difference in treatment is genuinely due to a material factor which is not the difference of sex[628]. The provisions are however subject to two limitations: first, the requirement for equality in relation to the treatment of members of an occupational pension scheme applies only to pensionable service on or after 17 May 1990 (in line with the temporal limitation on the *Barber* judgment, discussed above)[629] ; and secondly, the Act permits a variation in treatment as between a man and a woman where that variation consists of the application of actuarial factors[630] to the calculation of employers' contributions or the determination of benefits (an exception permitted by Directive 86/378 until July 1999)[631].

4 SEXUAL ORIENTATION DISCRIMINATION IN EMPLOYMENT[632]

One of the most controversial issues in discrimination law in recent years has been whether the prohibition of discrimination 'on the grounds of sex' in the Sex Discrimination Act 1975 extends to discrimination on related grounds, such as

623 On these aspects of the Act, see Nobles (1996) 59 MLR 241.
624 Pensions Act 1995, ss 62–66. The equal treatment provisions of the Act are supplemented by the Occupational Pension Schemes (Equal Treatment) Regulations 1995, SI 1995/3183 paras 5 and 6 of Sch 5 to the 1989 Act (on unfair maternity and family leave provisions) are adopted by s 63(3) of the 1995 Act; the remainder of Sch 5 would appear to be a dead letter.
625 Pensions Act 1995, s 63(4).
626 Including benefits for dependants: Pensions Act 1995, s 63(1).
627 Pensions Act 1995, s 62(1)–(3). The requirement of equal treatment also applies to any terms which confer a discretion on the trustees or managers of the scheme, or on any other person, and to the effect of the exercise of such a discretion: Pensions Act 1995, s 62(5).
628 Pensions Act 1995, s 62(4).
629 Pensions Act 1995, s 63(6); as before, the temporal limitation does not apply to access to membership of a pension scheme: see p 357 above.
630 Within limits prescribed by regulations: see SI 1995/3183.
631 Pensions Act 1995, s 64(3); this exception may be repealed by regulations: Pensions Act 1995, s 64(4).
632 Stonewall found that 15% of lesbians and gay men had suffered at least one experience of discrimination in their working lives ('Less equal than others: A Survey of Lesbians and Gays at Work' (1993), while the National Survey of Sexual Attitudes and Lifestyles (1990) found that over 20% of lesbian and gay workers had been harassed due to their sexuality: DTI 'Regulatory Impact Assessment for the Employment Equality (Sexual Orientation) Regulations 2003'.

sexual orientation and gender reassignment. Initial attempts to argue that the 1975 Act should be interpreted as covering discrimination against gays and lesbians were rebuffed by the courts. In *R v Ministry of Defence, ex p Smith*[633] the policy of the Ministry of Defence barring homosexuals from serving in the armed forces was challenged as being in breach of the EC Equal Treatment Directive. The Court of Appeal declined to accept that the Directive had any application in such a case on the grounds that it is aimed at sex discrimination, not sexual orientation discrimination, and held that where an employer refuses to accept homosexuals of either sex, that is discrimination on grounds of sexual orientation, not on grounds of gender. On this narrow interpretation, the only situation in which discrimination on grounds of sexual orientation could be brought within sex discrimination law would be if a gay man was treated less favourably than a lesbian, or vice versa[634]. However, when the ECJ ruled in *P v S and Cornwall County Council*[635] that the dismissal of a person proposing to undergo gender reassignment infringed the Equal Treatment Directive because 'such discrimination is based, essentially if not exclusively, on the sex of the person concerned[636]', there was widespread optimism that in due course the ECJ would hold that the Equal Treatment Directive also covered discrimination on grounds of sexual orientation. The first opportunity the ECJ had to consider the matter was in *Grant v South-West Trains*[637], where a female employee of a railway company complained that she had been discriminated against because her female partner had been denied travel concessions under a company policy, a condition of which restricted such concessions to workers living in a stable relationship with a person of the opposite sex. Despite the opinion of the Advocate-General that the case was indistinguishable from *P v S and Cornwall County Council*, the ECJ dismissed her claim, holding that since the condition applied in the same way to male and female workers, it could not be regarded as constituting discrimination directly based on sex, since a male homosexual would also have been refused a travel concession for his male partner[638].

In the wake of the decision in *Grant*, another reference to the ECJ which was pending at the time, in *R v Secretary of State for Defence, ex p Perkins*[639], was withdrawn, on the basis that the ECJ had already settled the issue. In some respects *Perkins* was a far stronger case than *Grant* as it involved another challenge to the MoD's policy on gays and lesbians in the armed forces, not just the loss of fringe benefits for a partner, and with hindsight it was unfortunate that it was *Grant* in which the ECJ first got the opportunity to rule on the issue. That was not the end of the matter, however, for four dismissed service personnel then challenged the MoD's policy before the European Court of Human Rights, which held (in *Smith and*

---

633 [1996] 1 All ER 257, [1996] IRLR 100, CA.
634 *Smith v Gardner Merchant Ltd* [1999] ICR 134, [1998] IRLR 510, CA.
635 [1996] All ER (EC) 397, [1996] IRLR 347, ECJ. See Wintemute (1997) 60 MLR 334; Skidmore (1987) 26 ILJ 51.
636 See p 278.
637 [1998] ICR 449, [1998] IRLR 206, ECJ.
638 Cf Wintemute above, n 635, at p 347, who argues persuasively that sexual orientation discrimination is simultaneously discrimination based on sex, since if one applies the 'but for' test of direct discrimination laid down in *James v Eastleigh Borough Council* (see p 280), it is clear that the applicant would not have been treated in the same way 'but for' her sex, as the appropriate comparison would be the treatment accorded to a male employee with a female partner.
639 [1997] IRLR 297, QBD (referring the matter to the ECJ); *(No 2)* [1998] IRLR 508, QBD (withdrawing the reference).

Grady v United Kingdom[640]), that the way in which their sexuality had been investigated, and their subsequent discharge from the armed forces on the grounds of their sexual orientation, violated the right to respect for private life under Article 8 of the European Convention on Human Rights[641]. The UK government had claimed that the interference was justified under Article 8(2) as being 'necessary in a democratic society in the interests of national security . . . for the prevention of disorder', because the presence of homosexuals within the armed forces would have a substantial and negative effect on morale and consequently on the fighting power and operational effectiveness of the armed forces, but the court rejected the argument, observing that when the restrictions concern 'a most intimate aspect of an individual's private life', there must be 'particularly serious reasons' before such interference can be justified. According to the ECHR, the problems identified by the MoD as a threat to fighting power and operational effectiveness represented 'a predisposed bias' on the part of a heterosexual majority against a homosexual minority, and such negative attitudes could not amount to sufficient justification for the interference with the applicants' rights 'any more than similar negative attitudes towards those of a different race, origin or colour[642] '.

This landmark decision raised the intriguing prospect that the UK courts and tribunals might be persuaded to reinterpret the Sex Discrimination Act as covering sexual orientation discrimination, in order to comply with their duty under the Human Rights Act 1998[643], and in *MacDonald v Ministry of Defence*[644], which involved yet another challenge to the MoD's policy, the Scottish EAT did just that. The revolution was however short-lived, because on appeal a majority of the Court of Session held[645] that on a proper construction of the SDA, discrimination 'on the ground of . . . sex' is restricted to discrimination on the basis of gender and does not include sexual orientation discrimination. The appropriate comparator for a male member of the RAF dismissed because he was homosexual was a woman employed in the armed forces who was also attracted to her own sex, and as the MoD's policy was even-handedly intolerant towards gays and lesbians, the applicant had not been treated less favourably than a woman would have been in comparable circumstances. Lord Prosser dissented on this point, arguing that as the SDA requires the 'relevant circumstances' of the applicant and the comparator to be 'the same, or not materially different'[646], the appropriate comparator for a man having or wanting a male partner was a woman having or wanting a male partner, and it was clear that a heterosexual woman would not have been dismissed. The gist of this argument, persuasively advanced by Wintemute in a highly influential article[647], is that sexual orientation

---

640 [1999] IRLR 734, ECtHR. Cf the contemporaneous decision in *Lustig-Prean and Beckett v United Kingdom* (1999) 29 EHRR 548 to the same effect.
641 There was also held to be a violation of Art 13, in that they had no effective remedy before a national authority in relation to the violation of their right under Art 8.
642 [1999] IRLR 734, para 90. In the wake of the ECHR decision, the Armed Forces Minister announced that the ban on homosexuals was to be replaced by a redrafted Code of Discipline covering inappropriate conduct generally, whether by heterosexuals or homosexuals.
643 As public authorities, courts and tribunals have a duty under the Human Rights Act 1998 to act in accordance with the Convention: see p 44.
644 [2000] ICR 1, [2000] IRLR 748, EAT.
645 *Secretary of State for Defence v MacDonald* [2001] IRLR 431, Ct Sess.
646 Sex Discrimination Act 1975, s 5(3); see p 282.
647 Wintemute (1997) 60 MLR 334.

discrimination is simultaneously discrimination based on gender, since the application of the 'but for' test[648] permits only the sex of the applicant to be changed when making the comparison, and to compare the treatment of the applicant, a male employee with a male partner, with that of a female employee with a female partner involves changing not only the sex of the applicant, but also the sex of the applicant's partner. The competing argument is that the applicant's sexuality *is* a 'relevant circumstance' for the purposes of the SDA, which means that in making the statutory comparison it is necessary to compare the treatment of a gay man with that of a lesbian.

The issue came before the courts again in *Pearce v Governing Body of Mayfield Secondary School*[649], albeit in a very different context. The applicant was a lesbian teacher who had been driven out of her job by an appalling catalogue of homophobic abuse by pupils. The EAT and Court of Appeal found that this did not amount to sex discrimination because a male teacher subjected to homophobic abuse would not have been treated more favourably; the fact that the abuse was gender-specific, in that the terms directed at her ('dyke', 'lezzie', 'lemon' etc) were not terms which would have been directed at a male homosexual, was considered to be beside the point: 'she was not abused because she was a woman, but rather, because she was or was believed to be a lesbian: her harassment resulted from her sexual orientation, or the perception of it . . . there is nothing to suggest that apart from the actual words of abuse a male homosexual teacher . . . would have been treated any differently by the pupils.[650]' It was argued that the Sex Discrimination Act should be construed so as to provide a remedy against sexual orientation harassment, in order to ensure compatibility with the Convention right to respect for private life under Article 8, but in the Court of Appeal only Hale LJ was prepared to acknowledge the force of that argument[651]. Both *MacDonald* and *Pearce* were subsequently considered by the House of Lords in a joined appeal[652], and the narrow approach taken by the Court of Session and the Court of Appeal was upheld. Their Lordships were agreed that for the purposes of the Sex Discrimination Act, 'sex' means 'gender', not 'sexual orientation', and there was no justification for interpreting 'on the ground of her sex' so as to include cases of discrimination on the grounds of sexual orientation. As to the argument that to compare gays with lesbians was an inappropriate comparison, the House of Lords were unanimously of the view that sexual orientation cannot be treated as irrelevant for the purposes of the statutory comparison. Section 5(3) requires the 'relevant circumstances' (ie those taken into account by the alleged discriminator when deciding how to treat the applicant) to be 'the same or not materially different', and so all the characteristics of the applicant which had a bearing on the way in which he or she was treated must also be found in the comparator; in both these cases, the sexual orientation of the applicant was considered to be a relevant circumstance, and so the appropriate comparison was with a homosexual person of the opposite gender, 'otherwise one would not be comparing like with like.[653]'

648 Ie the test of direct discrimination laid down in *James v Eastleigh Borough Council* [1990] ICR 554, [1990] IRLR 288, HL; see p 280.
649 [2003] IRLR 512, HL; [2002] ICR 198, [2001] IRLR 669, CA; [2000] ICR 920, [2000] IRLR 548, EAT.
650 [2001] IRLR 669, per Judge LJ.
651 The facts arose before the Human Rights Act 1998 came into force.
652 [2003] IRLR 512, HL.
653 [2003] IRLR 512 at 515, per Lord Nicholls.

It is clear that the decisions in *MacDonald* and *Pearce* were reached in the knowledge that protection against sexual orientation discrimination was already in the legislative pipeline as a result of Article 13 of the EC Treaty[654] and the EC Employment Directive[655] (indeed, the very fact that such legislation was on the way seems to have influenced the approach taken to the interpretation of the SDA, despite the obvious circularity in reasoning). The Employment Equality (Sexual Orientation) Regulations 2003[656] implement the UK's obligations under the Directive[657] by prohibiting discrimination on grounds of sexual orientation in employment[658] and vocational training. 'Sexual orientation' is defined as being a sexual orientation towards persons of (i) the same sex (covering gay men and lesbians); (ii) the opposite sex (covering straight men and women); or (iii) both sexes (covering bisexual men and women)[659]. The Regulations are broadly similar in structure and form to the SDA and the RRA, but are narrower in scope, reflecting the more limited scope of the Directive[660]. In so far as the SDA and RRA have diverged as a result of the recent amendments to the RRA implementing the Race Directive (for example in relation to the amended definition of indirect discrimination and the new definition of harassment), the Sexual Orientation Regulations follow the RRA approach. Direct discrimination is defined in similar terms to the SDA and RRA: it occurs where, on grounds of sexual orientation, A treats B less favourably than he treats or would treat other persons[661]. The use of the expression 'on grounds of sexual orientation' mirrors the wording of the RRA[662], and is wide enough to include discrimination based on A's perception of B's sexual orientation, whether right or wrong, and cases where a person is discriminated against by reason of someone else's sexual orientation, for example where a person is discriminated against for associating with gay friends, or for refusing to carry out an instruction to discriminate against gays or lesbians. Indirect discrimination is defined in similar terms to the RRA[663]: it occurs where A applies to B a provision, criterion or practice which A applies equally to other persons, but which puts persons of B's sexual orientation at a particular disadvantage, and puts B at that disadvantage, unless A can show that it is proportionate means of achieving a legitimate aim[664]. Discrimination by way of victimisation is also prohibited[665], just as under the SDA and RRA, and there is

654 Art 13 provides a legal basis for Community legislation to combat discrimination on grounds (inter alia) of sexual orientation; see p 271 above.
655 Directive 2000/78/EC; see p 272.
656 SI 2003/1661. The regulations come into force on 1 December 2003.
657 Other than in respect of occupational pensions, which are to be the subject of separate regulations.
658 This is defined in similar terms to the SDA, RRA and DDA: see p 275. The regulations also apply, inter alia, to contract workers, office-holders, police, barristers, partnerships, the providers of vocational training and employment agencies There is an exception for national security.
659 SI 2003/1661, reg 2.
660 Hence the importance of the decision in *Pearce* [2003] IRLR 512, which closes off any possibility of using sex discrimination law to tackle sexual orientation discrimination in areas outside the scope of the Regulations.
661 Employment Equality (Sexual Orientation) Regulations 2003, SI 2003/1661, reg 3(1)(a).
662 See p 367.
663 Employment Equality (Sexual Orientation) Regulations 2003, SI 2003/1661, reg 3(1)(b).
664 The new definition is discussed at p 285.
665 Employment Equality (Sexual Orientation) Regulations 2003, SI 2003/1661, reg 4. Victimisation is discussed at p 296.

an express prohibition of harassment[666]. The scope of the protection is also defined in similar terms to the SDA and RRA, covering discrimination against job applicants and employees before, during and on termination of employment[667], and after the employment relationship has ended[668].

There are a number of exceptions, some of which have already generated controversy. The widest is a general exception for 'genuine occupational requirements' which allows an employer to treat job applicants and, in certain circumstances, employees[669] differently on grounds of sexual orientation where, having regard to the nature of the job or the context in which it is carried out, being of a particular sexual orientation is a 'genuine and determining occupational requirement', and it is proportionate to apply it[670]. This GOR defence also applies in other areas of discrimination law[671], but in this context there is another, more controversial exception which applies where employment is for the purposes of an organised religion, and which allows employers to discriminate against gays and lesbians in order to comply with the doctrines of the religion, or 'to avoid conflicting with the strongly held religious convictions of a significant number of the religion's followers'.[672] This exception has been strongly criticised by the Lesbian and Gay Christian Movement as institutionalising homophobia by permitting religious employers to sack gay and lesbian staff, although an organised religion exception is not unprecedented[673]. The government has claimed that the organised religion exception is consistent with Article 4 of the Directive because 'a requirement which meets the criteria defined in regulation 7(3) is necessarily a genuine and determining occupational requirement which is applied proportionately[674]', although if this were so the requirement would presumably be covered by the standard GOR exception anyway, making the organised religion exception redundant. Another important exception applies to benefits that are dependent on marital status, for example survivor benefits in an employer's occupational pension scheme that are available only to the widow or widower of the deceased employee[675]. These are excluded for the technical reason that treatment by reference to marital status is outside the scope of the Directive, distinctions between the rights of married and unmarried people being outside the scope of Community competence. Pension schemes which allow survivor benefits to unmarried opposite sex partners but not to same sex partners will be caught by the Regulations. Finally, there is an exception which permits positive action in relation to access to facilities for

666 Employment Equality (Sexual Orientation) Regulations 2003, SI 2003/1661, reg 5. The same definition is used for the purposes of discrimination on grounds of race, religion or belief and disability (from 1 October 2003). Harassment is discussed at p 306.
667 SI 2003/1661, reg 6.
668 SI 2003/1661, reg 21. This provision mirrors the new provisions in the SDA and RRA on post-termination discrimination: see p 311.
669 The employer may rely on a GOR when promoting, transferring or training persons for a post, or when dismissing persons from a post:. SI 2003/1661, reg 7(1).
670 SI 2003/1661, reg 7(2).
671 Other than sex discrimination, as the new exception has not yet been applied in that context: see p 303.
672 SI 2003/1661, reg 7(3).
673 There is a similar exception in the Sex Discrimination Act 1975, s 19, permitting discrimination on grounds of sex or gender reassignment in the case of employment for purposes of an organised religion 'so as to comply with the doctrines of the religion or avoid offending the religious susceptibilities of a significant number of its followers.'
674 Explanatory Memorandum to the Draft Regulations, para 24.
675 Employment Equality (Sexual Orientation) Regulations 2003, SI 2003/1661, reg 25.

training, or encouraging persons of a particular sexual orientation to take advantage of work opportunities[676]. Unlike the similar provisions in the SDA and RRA, however, it is not necessary to show evidence that persons of a particular sexual orientation are under-represented in particular jobs, for the obvious reason that statistical evidence is unlikely to be available. Instead, the positive action should 'prevent or compensate for disadvantages linked to sexual orientation' suffered by those at whom the provisions are aimed.

As far as enforcement is concerned, the Regulations follow very closely the SDA and RRA model, with complaints brought in an employment tribunal within the usual three-month time-limit, which may make a declaration or recommendation, or order (potentially unlimited) compensation to be paid[677]. As is now usual, the burden of proof is on the respondent once the applicant has made out a prima facie case[678], and provision is made for the vicarious liability for employers and for secondary liability for employees for aiding unlawful acts[679]. The government's Regulatory Impact Assessment assumes a maximum of 1,000 tribunal cases a year under the new Regulations, with annual recurring compliance costs to business of around £2 million, although that figure is apparently based on an assumption that employers have complied with the legislation and will win all those cases!

5 RACIAL DISCRIMINATION IN EMPLOYMENT

As seen in the introduction to this chapter, while race relations legislation in England and Wales dates back to 1965, the present provisions in the Race Relations Act 1976 are closely modelled on the Sex Discrimination Act 1975, and much of the discussion under head 2 above applies, mutatis mutandis, to racial discrimination as well. The approach taken in this section will therefore be to highlight those areas where the law differs from that which applies to sex discrimination. There are some highly significant differences: first, unlike the law on sex discrimination, race discrimination law is not bedevilled by separate legislation on equal pay: all complaints lie under the 1976 Act[680]; secondly, as a result of the reforms introduced by the Race Relations (Amendment) Act 2000, the Race Relations Act now places a positive duty on a wide range of public authorities to promote race equality, and in the case of certain authorities this includes a specific duty to conduct ethnic monitoring of the workforce; and thirdly, the Race Relations Act has recently been amended[681] to comply with the EC Race Directive[682], which establishes for the first time a minimum standard of legal

---

676 SI 2003/1661, reg 26.
677 SI 2003/1661, regs 28 (jurisdiction), 30 (remedies) and 34 (time-limit).
678 SI 2003/1661, reg 29. The applicant may use the questionnaire procedure to obtain information relating to their complaint: reg 33.
679 SI 2003/1661, regs 22, 23 respectively.
680 See eg *Wakeman v Quick Corpn* [1999] IRLR 424, CA (complaint that Japanese managers working for a Japanese firm in the UK were being paid more than locally recruited managers; the complaint failed on the facts because the necessary causal link could not be established).
681 Race Relations Act 1976 (Amendment) Regulations 2003, SI 2003/1626.
682 Directive 2000/43/EC, agreed by the Council of Ministers in June 2000. Directive 2002/73/EC, which amends the Equal Treatment Directive, will in due course require similar amendments to be made to sex discrimination law, but not until 5 October 2005.

protection against racial discrimination across the EU[683]. Most of the employment-related areas covered by the Directive were already covered under UK law (this being one area where the UK has been ahead of some other member states), but there were a number of areas where the Race Relations Act required amendment in order to implement the Directive fully; so, for example, there is a new definition of indirect discrimination[684], because Article 2 of the Directive defines indirect discrimination in broader, less technical terms than the original RRA definition; a definition of harassment has been included[685], reflecting the definition in Article 3 of the Directive; a new exception for 'genuine occupational requirements'[686] replaces the existing genuine occupational qualification defence; the burden of proof is shifted from the complainant to the respondent once the complainant has established facts from which it may be presumed that there has been direct or indirect racial discrimination[687]; and some of the exceptions originally permitted under the Race Relations Act (for example the exceptions for private households, charities and small partnerships) have been removed because they are not permitted under the Directive. Unfortunately, however, the decision was taken to implement the Race Directive by Regulations[688] rather than by primary legislation, which means that the Race Relations Act could only be amended to the extent necessary to comply with the Directive, the important point being that in certain crucial respects the Directive has a narrower scope than the Act. In particular, the Directive only applies to discrimination on grounds of racial or ethnic origin and national origin[689]; it does not apply to discrimination on grounds of colour or nationality. The result is that the recent amendments only apply to those areas of the Act that fall within the scope of the Directive; the old provisions continue to apply to discrimination falling outside the scope of the Directive. The CRE's gloomy assessment of the implications of this complex picture are well worth repeating:

'There will be two definitions of indirect discrimination; two definitions of harassment; two definitions of "genuine occupational qualification"; two burdens of proof; and effectively, two classes of equality. Courts and tribunals may have to use different standards for different aspects of a case, if one part is covered by the Directive and another is not. Individuals and organisations will be left unsure of their rights and responsibilities under the Race Relations Act 1976, as amended by these regulations. Litigation is likely to increase, leading to more delay and expense. Hearings will become more complex, and therefore longer and more expensive.[690]'

683 The Directive applies to discrimination on grounds of racial or ethnic origin in employment and training, and also in matters such as education, social protection and social security, 'social advantages' of an economic or cultural nature (eg concessionary travel, reduced prices at cultural events and subsidised school meals) and access to and the supply of goods and services.

684 Race Relations Act 1976, s 1(1A), inserted by the Race Relations Act 1976 (Amendment) Regulations 2003, SI 2003/1626. The new definition is discussed above, at p 286.

685 SI 2003/1626, reg 2A. See p 310 above.

686 SI 2003/1626, reg 4A. See p 370 below.

687 SI 2003/1626, reg 54A. This mirrors the position as regards the burden of proof in sex discrimination cases following the implementation of the Burden of Proof Directive; see p 313 above.

688 Under the European Communities Act 1972, s 2.

689 Art 2 of the Directive only refers to racial and ethnic origin, but it has been interpreted by the government as also extending to discrimination on grounds of national origin: DTI, *Equality and Diversity: The Way Ahead* (2002), para 71.

690 Commission for Racial Equality *Which Way Equality* (2002).

Turning to the details, the 1976 Act prohibits discrimination on 'racial grounds', defined in section 3(1) as relating to colour, race, nationality, or ethnic or national origins. In *Mandla v Dowell Lee*[691], the complainant, a Sikh boy, was refused entrance to a private school unless he gave up wearing his turban and had his hair cut, a requirement which conflicted with his religion; the House of Lords held that Sikhs constitute an ethnic group within the meaning of the Act, Lord Fraser commenting that for a group to constitute an ethnic group it must regard itself, and be regarded by others, as a distinct community with a long shared history and a cultural tradition of its own. It is clearly established that Jews[692] and gypsies[693] constitute identifiable ethnic groups, but Rastafarians have been held not to, on the grounds that although they have certain identifiable characteristics, they have not established a separate identity by reference to their ethnic origins[694]. The fact that some faith groups have been able to obtain protection against religious discrimination indirectly via the Race Relations Act while others have not has been a source of considerable grievance, hence the importance of the new provisions prohibiting religious discrimination[695]. 'Nationality' in this context points to citizenship, and to the existence of a recognised state at the material time, but 'national origin' is a wider concept, turning on the existence of a nation at some point in time, established by reference to history and geography. Thus, in *Northern Joint Police Board v Power*[696], the issue was whether the applicant, who claimed that he had been rejected for a post of Chief Constable in Scotland because he was English, had been discriminated against on racial grounds. The tribunal held that there was no discrimination on grounds of nationality, as 'within the context of England, Scotland, Northern Ireland and Wales the proper approach to nationality is to categorise all of them as falling under the umbrella of British'; however, discrimination against an English person, or a Scot, was held to constitute discrimination on grounds of national origin, since it could not be in doubt that both England and Scotland were once separate nations[697]. In *BBC Scotland v Souster*[698], which involved the non-renewal of the contract of an English journalist to a post as a television sports presenter in Scotland, the Court of Session took a broad, subjective view of the concept of 'national origins', holding that it is not limited to 'nationality' in the legal sense, nor to the citizenship acquired by an individual at birth, and that a person can become a member of a racial group defined by reference to 'origins' through adherence (for example by marriage) or adoption, or through being perceived to have become a member of that racial group. The burden of proof is, however, on the applicant to prove he is English, whether by virtue of national origins, or because he has acquired English nationality, or because he is perceived to be English.

The use of the expression 'on racial grounds' means that unlike the Sex Discrimination Act, which applies where discrimination is 'on the grounds of

---

691 [1983] ICR 385, [1983] IRLR 209, HL. The decision shows how the 1976 Act can sometimes be used to outlaw discrimination on religious grounds, even though religious discrimination is not directly prohibited under the Act.
692 *Seide v Gillette Industries Ltd* [1980] IRLR 427, EAT.
693 *Commission for Racial Equality v Dutton* [1989] QB 783, [1989] 1 All ER 306, CA.
694 *Dawkins v Department of the Environment* [1993] IRLR 284, CA.
695 See p 376 below.
696 [1997] IRLR 610, EAT.
697 The same reasoning naturally applies to Wales and Ireland, although in *Gwynedd County Council v Jones* [1986] ICR 833, the EAT held that the 1976 Act does not apply to discrimination on the grounds of not being able to *speak* Welsh.
698 [2001] IRLR 150, Ct Sess.

her sex', the 1976 Act can apply where a person suffers a detriment on the basis of *another* person's race, for example where a white person is dismissed for refusing to apply a colour bar. In *Weathersfield Ltd v Sargent*[699], the complainant resigned from her job with a vehicle hire firm after being told not to hire vehicles to black or Asian prospective customers. The Court of Appeal held that she had been discriminated against on racial grounds, even though it was the race of the prospective customers that was at issue, and not her own race.

As seen above, the 1976 Act was originally modelled on the Sex Discrimination Act 1975 in its scheme and its remedies, and despite the recent changes they still have much in common. Thus, section 1(1) of the 1976 Act defines direct discrimination in substantially the same terms as those in section 1(1) of the 1975 Act, save that the comparator is a person not of that racial group. As with sex discrimination[700], conduct which is 'race-specific' (for example racial harassment) has in the past been held to constitute less favourable treatment on racial grounds, without the need for a comparison[701], but that approach must now be considered unsound as a result of the House of Lords' decision in *Pearce v Governing Body of Mayfield Secondary School*[702], which confirms that a comparison is required in every case. Segregation on racial grounds is declared in section 1(2) to qualify automatically as 'less favourable treatment' for the purpose of direct discrimination (thus forestalling any 'separate but equal' arguments). As seen above, in cases of indirect discrimination the test to be applied will depend upon whether the case involves discrimination on grounds of race or ethnic or national origins. If so, the new definition will apply, and the applicant will have to show that the employer has applied a 'provision, criterion or practice' which put persons of the same race or national or ethnic origins as the applicant 'at a particular disadvantage.[703]' Under the old definition, which still applies where the discrimination is on grounds of colour or nationality, the EAT has taken a narrower approach to the meaning of 'requirement or condition' under the 1976 Act than under the Sex Discrimination Act[704], but the approach to justification now seems to be the same[705], requiring an objective balance between the discriminatory effect of the requirement or condition and the reasonable needs of the employer[706]. Thus, in *Singh v Rowntree MacKintosh Ltd*[707] the employers operated a rule prohibiting the wearing of beards by employees in contact with the factory's products; this prima facie indirectly discriminated against Sikhs, but the EAT held that it was 'justifiable' within section 1(1)(b)(ii) in the interests of commercial hygiene.

---

699 [1999] ICR 425, [1999] IRLR 94, CA. The case also establishes the important point that a constructive dismissal is a detriment for the purposes of the anti-discrimination legislation. See also *Showboat Entertainment Centre Ltd v Owens* [1984] ICR 65, [1984] IRLR 7, EAT.
700 See p 284.
701 *Sidhu v Aerospace Composite Technology* [1999] IRLR 683, EAT.
702 [2003] IRLR 512, HL.
703 Race Relations Act 1976, s 1(1A), inserted by the Race Relations Act 1976 (Amendment) Regulations 2003, SI 2003/1626. The new definition is discussed in detail at p 286.
704 *Perera v Civil Service Commission (No 2)* [1983] ICR 428, [1983] IRLR 166, CA; affirmed in *Meer v Tower Hamlets London Borough* [1988] IRLR 399, CA. See p 287 above.
705 *Hampson v Department of Education and Science* [1989] ICR 179, [1989] IRLR 69, CA, approved in *Webb v EMO Air Cargo (UK) Ltd* [1992] 4 All ER 929, [1993] ICR 175, HL. See p 294 above.
706 For a case illustrating the difficulties which can sometimes arise in identifying the relevant pool for comparison under the RRA, see *Orphanos v Queen Mary College* [1985] IRLR 349, HL.
707 [1979] ICR 554, [1979] IRLR 199. The 'no turban' rule in a school in *Mandla v Dowell Lee* (above) was held not justifiable on the facts.

Discriminatory employment practices are defined in the same way as in the Sex Discrimination Act[708] (ie applying to selection, benefits, etc., during employment or dismissal[709] or other detriment). Previously harassment was not expressly mentioned in the 1976 Act, although it was clear that racial harassment could constitute a 'detriment'[710]. However, a definition has now been introduced (albeit only in respect of claims of harassment on the grounds of race or ethnic or national origin), which provides that harassment occurs when there is unwanted conduct which has the purpose or effect of violating a person's dignity or creating an intimidating, hostile, degrading, humiliating or offensive environment[711]. At one time it seemed that, the scope of the protection under the 1976 Act was narrower than under the 1975 Act, as it was held not to extend to racial discrimination after the end of employment, for example[712]. That gap has now been comprehensively filled, first, by an amendment to the 1976 Act which expressly provides that a claim can be brought in respect of an act of discrimination or harassment on the grounds of race or ethnic or national origins occurring after the end of employment, where the discrimination or harassment 'arises out of, and is closely connected to' the employment relationship'[713]; and secondly, because the House of Lords has recently confirmed (in the joined appeal in *Rhys-Harper v Relaxion Group plc*[714]) that the Race Relations Act, along with the Sex Discrimination Act and the Disability Discrimination Act, should be interpreted as covering discriminatory conduct after the end of employment, provided there is a substantive connection between the conduct complained of and the employment relationship. Section 5 lays down certain exempted categories of employment where being a member of a particular racial group is a 'genuine occupational qualification' (GOQ) for a job, for example where the holder of the job provides persons of that racial group with 'personal services promoting their welfare', and those services 'can most effectively be provided by persons of that racial group'[715], or where the job involves participation in a dramatic performance, working as an artist's or photographic model, or working in a bar or restaurant, where a person of a particular racial group is required 'for reasons of authenticity'[716]. In order to comply with the Race Directive, the GOQ exception

---

708 Race Relations Act 1976, s 4.
709 'Dismissal' in this context includes constructive dismissal: *Derby Specialist Fabrication Ltd v Burton* [2001] IRLR 69, EAT.
710 Cf *De Souza v Automobile Association* [1986] ICR 514, [1986] IRLR 103, CA (racial insult by a fellow employee not enough, by itself, to constitute a 'detriment'); see also *Thomas v Robinson* [2003] IRLR 7, EAT.
711 Race Relations Act 1976, s 2A, inserted by the Race Relations Act 1976 (Amendment) Regulations 2003, SI 2003/1626. The new definition is discussed at p 310.
712 *Post Office v Adekeye* [1997] ICR 110, [1997] IRLR 105, CA. Compare *Coote v Granada Hospitality Ltd (No 2)* [1999] ICR 942, [1999] IRLR 452, where the EAT reinterpreted the Sex Discrimination Act as covering discrimination by an ex-employer in order to comply with a ruling of the ECJ: see p 312 above.
713 Race Relations Act 1976, s 15A, inserted by the Race Relations Act 1976 (Amendment) Regulations 2003, SI 2003/1626.
714 [2003] IRLR 484, HL.
715 See *Tottenham Green Under Fives' Centre v Marshall* [1989] ICR 214, [1989] IRLR 147, EAT; *(No 2)* [1991] ICR 320, [1991] IRLR 162, EAT; *Lambeth London Borough v Commission for Racial Equality* [1990] ICR 768, [1990] IRLR 231, CA.
716 See Pitt 'Madam Butterfly and Miss Saigon: Reflections on Genuine Occupational Qualifications', in Dine and Watt (eds) *Discrimination Law: Concepts, Limitations and Justifications* (1996).

has been part-repealed[717], and in its place a new exception based on the concept of a 'genuine occupational requirement' has been introduced[718]. This exception allows employers to recruit employees on the basis of their race or ethnic or national origins if it can be shown that, having regard to the nature of the employment or the context in which it is carried out, being of a particular race or of particular ethnic or national origins is a 'genuine and determining occupational requirement', and it is proportionate for that requirement to be applied in the particular case[719]. The new exception is almost certainly narrower than the GOQ exception, and will probably only apply where the employer can show that the employee's race or ethnic or national origin is an essential, defining feature of the job. There is a related exemption in section 4(3) which allows employers to discriminate on racial grounds when they are employing someone to work in a private household, but this too has been part-repealed in order to being the Race Relations Act in line with the Race Directive, and now only applies to discrimination on the grounds of colour and nationality[720]. The exemptions for partnerships of fewer than six partners, and for charities, which were permitted to employ staff for certain support roles on the basis of race, nationality or ethnic or national origins, have also been part-repealed[721].

Discrimination by way of victimisation on racial grounds is covered by section 2. The case law on victimisation under the 1976 Act has clarified several important points in recent years, although some grey areas still remain[722]; thus in *Nagarajan v London Regional Transport*[723], the House of Lords held that in complaints of victimisation the motive of the alleged discriminator is irrelevant, the relevant question simply being whether the complainant would have been treated in that way but for his race; and in *Chief Constable of West Yorkshire v Khan*[724], the House of Lords held, in a victimisation complaint arising from the Chief Constable's refusal to provide a reference for an officer who had a claim of race discrimination outstanding, that the proper comparator was an officer who did not have a complaint outstanding, rather than an officer who had a complaint outstanding but not under the Race Relations Act. Had the decision been otherwise, it would have been a defence for the Chief Constable to claim that he would similarly have refused to provide a reference to another officer who was suing the police authority on some other ground, which would have undermined the protection. On the facts, however, their Lordships allowed the Chief Constable's appeal on the grounds that the reference was not withheld 'by reason that' the complainant had brought discrimination proceedings, but rather because the employers

---

717 The repeal only applies to discrimination on the grounds of race or ethnic or national origin; the existing GOQ exception will continue to apply in cases involving colour or nationality.
718 Race Relations Act 1976, s 4A, inserted by the Race Relations Act 1976 (Amendment) Regulations 2003, SI 2003/1626.
719 Race Relations Act 1976, s 4A(2).
720 Race Relations Act 1976, s 4(3), as amended by the Race Relations Act 1976 (Amendment) Regulations 2003, SI 2003/1626.
721 Race Relations Act 1976, s 10(1A) (partnerships) and s 34(1)(a) (charities), as amended by the Race Relations Act 1976 (Amendment) Regulations 2003, SI 2003/1626. Small partnerships may continue to discriminate on grounds of colour and nationality, and charities may still discriminate on grounds of nationality (discrimination on grounds of colour by charities was never permitted).
722 The case law on victimisation under the Race Relations Act is considered more fully at p 296 in the context of sex discrimination.
723 [1999] ICR 877, [1999] IRLR 572, HL. See p 297 above.
724 [2001] ICR 1065, [2001] IRLR 830, HL. See p 297 above.

wished to preserve their position in the pending discrimination proceedings. The decision in *Khan* is not easy to reconcile with the earlier decision in *Nagarajan*[725].

Procedures and remedies in race discrimination cases are similar to those under the Sex Discrimination Act, but with the important difference that no compensation may be awarded for indirect discrimination under the Race Relations Act if the respondent proves that the discrimination was unintentional[726]. The practical impact of this restriction has to some extent been alleviated by the decision in *J H Walker Ltd v Hussain*[727], where the EAT held that a person will be taken to have intended the unfavourable consequences to follow from his acts 'if he knew when he did them that those consequences would follow and if he wanted those consequences to follow'[728]. Complainants in race discrimination cases may encounter the same difficulties in relation to proving discrimination[729] and obtaining disclosure of documents[730], but the position of those claiming discrimination on grounds of race or ethnic or national origin has been strengthened by the shifting of the burden of proof onto the respondent once the complainant has established a prima facie of discrimination[731]. The Commission for Racial Equality (CRE), set up under the 1976 Act, has similar powers to those of the EOC, in particular powers to conduct formal investigations[732], to issue and enforce non-discrimination notices[733], to take action against discriminatory advertisements[734] and persistent discrimination[735], and to help individuals to bring discrimination claims against their employers[736]. It also has a range of powers and responsibilities as regards the duty to promote equality, discussed below. The CRE has produced a Code of Practice on racial equality in employment which came into force in 1984[737], setting out the relevant law and suggesting good employment practices on matters such as equal opportunity policies, recruitment (including the possible discriminatory effects of

---

725 See p 297 above.
726 The restriction was removed in sex discrimination cases by SI 1996/438: see p 323 above. The CRE has recommended that compensation for unintentional indirect discrimination be made available under the 1976 Act: *Reform of the Race Relations Act 1976* (CRE, 1998).
727 [1996] ICR 291, [1996] IRLR 11, EAT.
728 [1996] IRLR 11 at 15, per Mummery J.
729 See p 312 above. The fact that an alleged discriminator is related by marriage to people from one ethnic group does not justify an inference that he did not racially abuse a person from a different ethnic group: *Robson v IRC* [1998] IRLR 186, EAT.
730 See *Science Research Council v Nassé* [1979] ICR 921, [1979] IRLR 465, HL. In *West Midlands Passenger Transport Executive v Singh* [1988] ICR 614, [1988] IRLR 186, the Court of Appeal held that statistical material showing the numbers of white and non-white applicants for similar posts was logically probative of whether the employers had discriminated against the applicant on racial grounds, and was thus potentially subject to disclosure. On disclosure generally, see p 315 above.
731 Race Relations Act 1976, s 54A, inserted by the Race Relations Act 1976 (Amendment) Regulations 2003, SI 2003/1626. See p 313.
732 Such an investigation must stem from an existing belief that discrimination is taking place by a named person, who must be allowed to make representations: *Hillingdon London Borough Council v Commission for Racial Equality* [1982] AC 779, [1982] IRLR 424, HL; *Re Prestige Group plc* [1984] ICR 473, [1984] IRLR 166, HL.
733 Race Relations Act 1976, s 58. The person against whom a notice is issued may appeal against it under s 59; the complexity and time-consuming nature of the statutory appeal structure can be seen from *Commission for Racial Equality v Amari Plastics Ltd* [1982] ICR 304, [1982] IRLR 252, CA.
734 Race Relations Act 1976, ss 29 and 63.
735 Race Relations Act 1976, s 62.
736 Race Relations Act 1976, s 66.
737 SI 1983/1081. The text of the Code is set out in *Harvey* S[311].

recruitment by word of mouth or through trade unions), cultural or religious needs, language training, the analysis and monitoring of the racial mix of the workforce[738] and positive action in training (the only area where this is legally permissible); the Code also considers the responsibilities of fellow employees, trade unions and employment agencies.

The CRE has a duty under section 43 of the Race Relations Act to keep the working of the Act under review and, if it thinks necessary, to make recommendations for amending it. To date, the CRE has carried out three reviews of the Act. The first, in 1985, elicited no response from government, while the second, in 1992, received a detailed response which rejected most of the proposals. In the third review, in 1998, the CRE recommended some 50 changes to the existing law[739], some of which built on the earlier proposals for reform of the law enforcement aspects of the 1976 Act, while others were aimed at establishing good equal opportunities practice within organisations. In particular, the CRE proposed the enactment of a broad right not to be discriminated against by public bodies (thereby extending the original RRA provisions, which only applied to discrimination in employment and training and the provision of goods, facilities and services, to areas such as policing and the treatment of prisoners), and a positive duty on all public bodies to work for the elimination of racial discrimination and to promote equality of opportunity and good race relations. Other reforms proposed by the CRE included the adoption of a wider, less technical definition of indirect discrimination, extending the scope of the 1976 Act to cover office-holders and volunteers, empowering the CRE to enter into legally binding undertakings and to conduct formal investigations on its own initiative, clarifying the law on positive action, making ethnic monitoring compulsory for all employers with more than 250 employees, extending the power of employment tribunals to make recommendations on future conduct, and giving tribunals the power to consider group or class actions.

The case for reform of the Race Relations Act was given significant added impetus in February 1999 by the publication of the Stephen Lawrence Inquiry Report[740], which found clear evidence of institutional racism[741] within the Metropolitan Police, and accepted the CRE's submission that institutional racism is widespread in other institutions. One of the key recommendations of the Inquiry Report was that the full force of the race relations legislation should apply to all police officers, and that chief officers of police should be made vicariously liable for the acts and omissions of their officers relevant to that legislation[742]. In the wake of the Inquiry Report, the government introduced the Race Relations (Amendment) Act 2000, which extends the scope of the Race Relations Act to

---

738 The Code was taken into consideration in *West Midlands Passenger Transport Executive v Singh* (n 730 above) as a factor in altering the previous judicial approach to ethnic monitoring (and the discovery of material relating thereto). In *Carrington v Helix Lighting Ltd* [1990] ICR 125, [1990] IRLR 6, the EAT indicated that failure to monitor as recommended by the Code may lead to an adverse inference being drawn by the tribunal.

739 CRE *Reform of the Race Relations Act 1976* (1998).

740 *The Stephen Lawrence Inquiry: Report of an Inquiry by Sir William Macpherson* (Cm 4262-I, 1999).

741 Defined in the Inquiry Report as: 'The collective failure of an organisation to provide an appropriate and professional service to people because of their colour, culture or ethnic origin. It can be seen or detected in processes, attitudes and behaviour which amount to discrimination through unwitting prejudice, ignorance, thoughtlessness and racist stereotyping which disadvantage minority ethnic people.'

742 Cm 4262-I, 1999, recommendation 11.

cover all of the functions of all public bodies (not just the police)[743], thus making it unlawful for a public authority to discriminate directly or indirectly on racial grounds when performing any of its functions. In a new departure for British anti-discrimination law[744], the Act also imposes a statutory duty on a wide range of public authorities to promote race equality. Section 71(1) of the amended Race Relations Act requires listed[745] public authorities to have 'due regard' in carrying out their functions[746] to the need (a) to eliminate unlawful racial discrimination; (b) to promote equality of opportunity; and (c) to promote good relations between persons of different racial groups. The general duty to promote equality extends to sixty categories of public bodies, covering around 40,000 organisations. In addition to the general duty, the Secretary of State is also empowered to impose specific duties on some or all of the public authorities covered by the general duty, for the purpose of ensuring the better performance of their general duty[747]. These specific duties include the duty to publish a Race Equality Scheme setting out how the authority intends to fulfil its general duty, and the duty to carry out ethnic monitoring of the workforce (referred to as the 'employment duty'). The introduction of these positive duties to promote race equality represent a highly significant shift in thinking as regards the use of the law to tackle discrimination. Unlike the existing anti-discrimination laws, which are essentially reactive, they reflect a more proactive and strategic approach to tackling discrimination. The imposition of a duty to conduct ethnic monitoring is particularly significant, as it has long been argued that monitoring is an essential tool in the identification of inequality and discrimination, and in the assessment of progress (or lack of it) in removing barriers to equality of opportunity.

The Commission for Racial Equality has issued a statutory Code of Practice on the Duty to Promote Race Equality[748] containing practical guidance for authorities on how to perform their general and specific duties, and has also issued non-statutory guidance for public authorities on using the Code, including a guide to conducting ethnic monitoring. The Code sets out four 'guiding principles' governing the efforts of public authorities in meeting their general duty to promote race equality: (1) the duty is 'obligatory' for all listed public authorities, meaning that all such authorities 'must make race equality a central part of their functions'; (2) public authorities must meet the duty to promote race equality 'in all relevant functions'; (3) the weight given to race equality should be

---

743 There are a few exceptions, including the core functions of the intelligence and security services (other than employment, which remains covered), judicial acts by courts and tribunals, and of course immigration and nationality decisions, which by definition involve discrimination on grounds of nationality and ethnic or national origin: Race Relations Act 1976, s 71A.

744 Although not for Northern Ireland, where the Fair Employment legislation has imposed a duty to promote equality for some time. See p 380.

745 Sch 1A to the 1976 Act lists, inter alia, Ministers of the Crown and government departments, the National Health Service, local government, education and housing bodies and the police. A further range of public bodies were brought within the scope of the general duty by the Race Relations Act 1976 (General Statutory Duty) Order 2001, SI 2001/3457.

746 Only the public functions of a listed public authority are covered by the duty.

747 Race Relations Act 1976, s 71(2), as substituted by the Race Relations (Amendment) Act 2000. The specific duties are contained in the Race Relations Act 1976 (Statutory Duties) Order 2001, SI 2001/3458, issued under s 71(2) (hereinafter the RRA (Statutory Duties) Order 2001).

748 The Code is issued under s 71C of the 1976 Act. As a statutory Code, it is admissible in evidence in legal proceedings before a court or tribunal, and must be taken into account where relevant: Race Relations Act 1976, s 71C(11).

'proportionate' to its relevance[749]; and (4) the three elements of the duty are 'complementary'; they all support each other, and may in practice overlap, but they are all necessary to meet the whole duty[750]. In meeting its general duty, each public authority should identify which of its functions (including employment) are relevant to the duty, prioritise those most relevant to race equality, and then assess whether the way those functions are being carried out meets the duty. The Code stresses that the general duty is a continuing duty, and that what a public authority may have to do to meet it may change over time as its functions or policies change[751].

The specific duties apply to a narrower range of public bodies. They are designed to help public authorities to meet the general duty, and are therefore best seen as a means to an end rather than as an end in themselves[752]. The duty to publish a Race Equality Scheme is restricted to, inter alia, government departments, armed forces, National Health Service, local government, police, regulatory bodies, complaints authorities and commissions[753]. In its Race Equality Scheme, a public authority is required to identify those of its functions and policies which it has assessed as relevant to the performance of its general duty[754], and to set out its arrangements for: assessing and consulting on the likely impact of its proposed policies on the promotion of race equality; monitoring its policies for any adverse impact on the promotion of race equality; publishing the results of such assessments, consultations and monitoring; ensuring public access to information and services which it provides; and training staff in connection with its duty to promote race equality[755]. The Code suggests that public authorities may find it useful to include in their schemes the arrangements they make to meet the employment duty. Many public authorities already had more general equality and diversity strategies and action programmes in place before the new duty to promote race equality was enacted, and the Code confirms that a Race Equality Scheme can be part of such a plan 'as long as it can be easily identified as meeting all the statutory requirements.[756]'

A wider range of public bodies (including for example non-departmental public bodies, libraries and museums, public corporations, nationalised industries and research councils, but not all of the bodies subject to the general duty), are subject to the employment duty[757]. This consists of a duty to monitor the numbers of staff in post, and of applicants for employment, training and promotion, by reference to the racial group to which they belong[758]. In addition, public

---

749 So, for example, greater consideration and resources might need to be given to functions or policies that have most effect on the public, or on the authority's employees
750 Code of Practice, para 3.2.
751 Code of Practice, para 3.7.
752 Code of Practice, para 4.1.
753 The bodies covered by this duty are listed in appendix 2 of the Code of Practice. The listed authorities were required to publish a race equality scheme by 31 May 2002.
754 The assessment must be reviewed at least every three years: RRA (Statutory Duties) Order 2003, art 2(3).
755 Code of Practice, para 2(2).
756 Code of Practice, para 4.8.
757 The bodies covered by the employment duty are listed in appendix 3 of the Code or Practice. Schools and further and higher education establishments are bound by separate employment responsibilities: RRA (Statutory Duties) Order 2003, art 3.
758 The Code encourages public authorities to use the same ethnic classification system as was used in the 2001 census.

authorities with 150 or more full-time staff are required to monitor the numbers of staff from each racial group who receive training, benefit or suffer detriment as a result of its performance assessment procedures, are involved in grievance procedures, are the subject of disciplinary procedures, or cease employment[759]. The aim of the employment duty is to provide a framework for measuring progress in equality of opportunity in public sector employment, and to provide information to guide initiatives that could lead to a more representative workforce (for example setting recruitment targets or targeting job training for under-represented racial groups)[760]. The results of this ethnic monitoring must be published annually. Having collected the ethnic monitoring data, the Code indicates that the public authority should analyse it to find any patterns of inequality, and take whatever steps are needed to remove barriers and promote equality of opportunity[761]. If the monitoring shows that current employment policies, procedures and practice are leading to unlawful racial discrimination, the authority should take steps to end the discrimination; if the monitoring reveals adverse impact on equal opportunities or good race relations falling short of unlawful discrimination, the authority should consider changing its policies or procedures so that they do not harm equality of opportunity or race relations[762]. The CRE's guide to ethnic monitoring gives detailed guidance on the conduct of ethnic monitoring; for example, it encourages public authorities to carry out an audit of all employees by grade, type of contract, pay and benefits, length of service, sex, disability and racial group; to compare the information collected with information on the wider population from which recruitment is normally made; to check for differences in success rates depending on racial group; if differences are identified, to ask whether recruitment and selection procedures improve or reduce chances according to racial group; to remove any barriers to equal opportunities, and revise any policy or practice that puts employees or job applicants from some racial groups at a disadvantage; to consider using positive action to tackle under-representation; to carry out regular reviews of personnel policies and procedures, especially on training, appraisal, grievance and discipline; and to make sure that all staff know about and understand any changes made to employment policies and procedures, and that they have the necessary skills and knowledge to put them into practice.

Enforcement of the specific duties to promote race equality is the responsibility of the CRE[763], which may issue a compliance notice on an authority if it is satisfied that the authority has 'failed to comply with, or is failing to comply with' any of its specific duties. The notice will instruct the authority to meet its duty, and to inform the CRE, within twenty-eight days, of what steps it has taken (or is taking) to comply[764]. If after three months the CRE considers that the authority has not complied with the notice, the CRE can apply to the county court for an order requiring compliance, and failure to obey such an order may result in the authority being found in contempt of court. There is no similar statutory procedure for enforcement of the general duty, which may be enforced by an

---

759 Code of Practice, para 5.
760 Code of Practice, para 5.4.
761 Code of Practice, para 5.9.
762 Code of Practice, paras 5.10 and 5.11.
763 Race Relations Act 1976, s 71D.
764 In the compliance notice the CRE can ask for written evidence that the authority has complied.

application to the High Court for judicial review by a person or group of people with a sufficient interest in the matter, or by the CRE.

6 RELIGION OR BELIEF DISCRIMINATION IN EMPLOYMENT[765]

There has been legislation tackling race discrimination on the UK statute book since 1965, but apart from Northern Ireland, where discrimination in employment on grounds of religious belief or political opinion has been unlawful since 1976[766], there has been nothing directly addressing discrimination on grounds of religion. As was seen in Part 5, some religious groups have enjoyed de facto protection against religious discrimination for many years under the Race Relations Act 1976. The RRA does not expressly refer to religious discrimination, but some religious groups (for example Sikhs[767] and Jews[768]) have been held to constitute a 'racial group' within the meaning of the RRA because their members have a common ethnic origin[769]. However, the fact that some religious groups have been able to claim the protection of the law in this way has merely served to heighten the sense of injustice felt by other faith groups (for example Muslims, Hindus, Buddhists and Christians) whose members may experience religious discrimination and harassment in the workplace but are unable to obtain any remedy via the RRA[770]. In theory, human rights law should offer some protection against religious discrimination[771], as Article 9 of the European Convention on Human Rights declares that 'Everyone has the right to freedom of thought, conscience and religion', including the freedom 'either alone or in community with others . . . to manifest his religion or belief, in worship, teaching, practice, and observance'. Article 9 does not itself provide for equal treatment on grounds of religion, but Article 14 of the Convention provides that 'The enjoyment of the rights and freedoms set forth in this Convention shall be secured without discrimination on any ground such as . . . religion.[772]' However, even though these two Articles, in conjunction, appear to provide a basis for tackling religious discrimination (albeit only directly against public authorities), the fact is that the freedom to manifest one's religion in Article 9 is not an absolute right, but may be subject to restrictions which are 'prescribed by law and . . . necessary in a democratic society . . . for the protection of the rights and freedoms of others[773]', and case law under

---

765 On the incidence of religion discrimination, see Weller, Feldman and Purdam 'Religious discrimination in England and Wales' Home Office Research Study 220 (2001). The 1999 British Social Attitudes Survey estimated that there are about 4.65 million men and women in employment who actively participate in religious activities, and the DTI's Regulatory Impact Assessment assumes that about 2% (roughly 94,000) of those may have experienced some form of employment discrimination.

766 See now the Fair Employment and Treatment (Northern Ireland) Order 1998, SI 1998/3162. See p 380.

767 *Mandla v Dowell Lee* [1983] 2 AC 548, [1983] 1 All ER 1062, HL.

768 *Seide v Gillette Industries Ltd* [1980] IRLR 427.

769 See p 367.

770 One possible source of protection for religious groups is via indirect race discrimination, but for this to work the action causing a detriment to eg Muslims must amount to indirect discrimination against a racial group that is predominantly Muslim: see eg *JH Walker v Hussain* [1996] ICR 291, [1996] IRLR 11, EAT.

771 See p 42.

772 This is not a free-standing right, but can only be claimed in conjunction with one of the specified Convention rights; see p 273. The UK government has not yet signed Protocol 12 to the Convention, which would provide a general prohibition on discrimination.

773 European Convention on Human Rights, Art 9(2).

the Convention has revealed that the requirements of religious observance are likely to take second place to commercial and business considerations, and the primacy of contractual obligations[774]. Those looking for laws that offer reliable and robust protect against religious discrimination must look elsewhere.

As in the case of sexual orientation discrimination, the turning point came with the Treaty of Amsterdam, which introduced Article 13 into the EC treaty. This provides a legal basis for community-wide action to combat discrimination on a range of grounds, including 'religion or belief', and in November 2000 the Council adopted the Employment Directive[775], which requires member states to introduce measures prohibiting discrimination inter alia on grounds of religion or belief by 2 December 2003. The Employment Equality (Religion or Belief) Regulations 2003[776] implement the UK's obligations under the Directive[777] by prohibiting discrimination on grounds of religion or belief in employment[778] and vocational training. The key issue here, and one which presents an extremely difficult challenge to any legislator intruding into this highly sensitive area, is the definition of the protected group. Which faith groups and their members are to benefit from the protection against discrimination[779]? Should an attempt be made to define 'religion', or to draw up a list of officially recognised religions, or, recognising that any such attempt is likely to be highly invidious, should the protection be extended to all religious beliefs, including the often obscure religious cults that spring up from time to time? And what of those who experience discrimination on account of their atheism or agnosticism, or their adherence to ethical, secular belief systems? Predictably, the approach taken in Article 13 and the Employment Directive is to side-step these difficult issues by prohibiting discrimination on grounds of 'religion *or* belief', thereby avoiding the need to define religion. That approach is mirrored in the Religion or Belief Regulations, which simply provide that 'religion or belief' means 'any religion, religious belief or similar philosophical belief.[780]' The regulatory guidance states that 'this does not include any philosophical or political belief unless that belief is similar to a religious belief', which rather begs the question[781]. Ultimately it will be for the humble employment tribunals to attempt to make sense of all this, as the government clearly intends: 'Given the wide variety of different faiths and beliefs in this country, we have reached the view that we should not attempt to define "religion or belief", and that it would be better to leave it to the courts to resolve

---

774 See eg *Ahmad v Inner London Education Authority* [1978] 1 All ER 574; *Ahmad v United Kingdom* (1981) 4 EHRR 126; *Stedman v United Kingdom* (1997) 23 EHRR CD 168.
775 Directive 2000/78/EC.
776 SI 2003/1660. The regulations come into force on 2 December 2003. See Vickers (2003) 32 ILJ 23.
777 Other than in respect of occupational pensions, which are to be the subject of separate regulations.
778 This is defined in similar terms to the SDA, RRA and DDA: see p 275. The regulations also apply, inter alia, to contract workers, office-holders, police, barristers, partnerships, the providers of vocational training and employment agencies There is an exception for national security.
779 See Hepple and Choudhury 'Tackling religious discrimination: practical implications for policy-makers and legislators' Home Office Research Study No 221 (2000), part 3.
780 Employment Equality (Religion or Belief) Regulations 2003, SI 2003/1660, reg 2.
781 Notes on Regulations, Para 5. The notes also suggest that the courts and tribunals may consider a number of factors when deciding what is a 'religion or belief', 'eg collective worship, clear belief system, profound belief affecting way of life or view of the world'.

definitional issues as they arise[782].' As an exercise in legislative buck-passing, this takes some beating.

Turning to remainder of the Religion or Belief Regulations, they are broadly similar in structure and form to the SDA and RRA, albeit narrower in scope as they only apply to employment and vocational training. Not surprisingly, the closest similarity is with the contemporaneous Sexual Orientation Regulations. Direct discrimination is defined as occurring where, on grounds of religion or belief, A treats B less favourably than he treats or would treat other persons[783]. The use of the expression 'on grounds of religion or belief' again mirrors the wording of the RRA, and includes discrimination based on A's perception of B's religion or belief, and discrimination by reason of the religion or belief of someone else, for example where a person is discriminated against for refusing to carry out an instruction to discriminate against Muslims. One potentially very difficult issue is the appropriate comparison to be made in cases of alleged direct religious discrimination. Most workplaces in the UK are still based around a Christian calendar, with employees enjoying Sunday as a rest day, and holidays at the main Christian festivals of Easter and Christmas. It is likely, therefore, that many employees who adhere to the Christian faith are able to follow the observance requirements of their religion without having to request any special treatment from their employer[784]. The question therefore arises, if for example a Muslim employee approaches his employer requesting time off work to celebrate a Muslim holy day, is the appropriate comparator: (i) an employee who has requested time off to celebrate a different religious festival; (ii) an employee who has requested time off for some other non-religious purpose, for example to attend a football match; or (iii) an employee who does not need to request time off to celebrate his religious festivals because he is a Christian and the employer's workplace already operates according to a Christian calendar? It is submitted that the appropriate comparator must be an employee who has also requested time off from the employer (although whether (i) or (ii) is uncertain), because to choose (iii) would in effect be to impose a duty on the employer to make adjustments to working arrangements in order to accommodate other religious faiths[785] (there being no justification defence in the case of direct discrimination). This means that the employer does not automatically have to grant all requests for leave for religious observance, but he must not refuse a request for leave simply on grounds of the employee's religion or belief, where another employee would have been treated more favourably in comparable circumstances.

Indirect discrimination is also defined in similar terms to the RRA[786]: it occurs where A applies to B a provision, criterion or practice which A applies equally to other persons, but which puts persons of B's religion or belief at a particular disadvantage, and puts B at that disadvantage, unless A can show that it is proportionate means of achieving a legitimate aim[787]. So, for example, an employer that applies rules on leave, or on dress and appearance at work, which particularly

---

782 DTI *Towards Equality and Diversity: Implementing the Employment and Race Directives* (2001), para 13.4.
783 Employment Equality (Religion or Belief) Regulations 2003, SI 2003/1660, reg 3(1)(a).
784 Cf the right of shop workers and betting workers to object to Sunday working: Employment Rights Act 1996, Pt IV.
785 Cf Moon and Allen [2000] EHRLR 580, explaining the case against a duty to make adjustments in this context.
786 SI 2003/1660, reg 3(1)(b).
787 The new definition is discussed at p 286.

disadvantage certain religious or belief groups in comparison with others may be found to have discriminated indirectly, unless the those rules can be objectively justified as being a proportionate means of achieving a legitimate aim. The potential impact of these provisions on working conditions can be seen from the government's own impact assessment:

'Under the new legislation, and in line with best practice, employers may need to accommodate a wide variety of religious and cultural needs of workers such as different dietary requirements and prayer room facilities. Employers may also need to be flexible in order to accommodate cultural or religious holidays and restrictions on hours of work. People should not be discriminated against in recruitment decisions if they cannot work on particular days of the week; particular times of the day; or in particular areas of a business (for example, the meat and alcohol section of a supermarket) unless this can be objectively justified.[788]'

Discrimination by way of victimisation is prohibited[789], and again there is an express prohibition of harassment[790]. The scope of the protection is also defined in similar terms to the SDA and RRA, covering discrimination against job applicants and employees before, during and on termination of employment[791], and after the employment relationship has ended[792].

As usual there are a range exceptions, including the general 'genuine occupational requirements' (GOR) exception which allows an employer to treat job applicants and, in certain circumstances, employees[793] differently on grounds of religion or belief where, having regard to the nature of the job or the context in which it is carried out, being of a particular religion or belief is a 'genuine and determining occupational requirement', and it is proportionate to apply it[794]. This would cover a requirement for example 'that the post of Church of England chaplain in the armed forces should be held by an Anglican Minister'[795]. There is also a highly controversial exception for organisations with 'an ethos based on religion or belief'; this is similar to the general GOR, but *without* the requirement to show that religion or belief is a determining (ie decisive, or defining) occupational requirement[796]. It is unclear what an organisation will need to show in order to qualify as having an ethos based on religion or belief (can an organisation acquire such an ethos merely by proclamation, or must it be of a certain type, and have a suitable track record, in order to qualify?), and even if it

---

788 DTI *Regulatory Impact Assessment on the Religion or Belief Regulations* para 6.
789 Employment Equality (Religion or Belief) Regulations 2003, SI 2003/1660, reg 4. Victimisation is discussed at p 296.
790 SI 2003/1660, reg 5. The same definition is used for the purposes of discrimination on grounds of race, sexual orientation and disability (from 1 October 2003). Harassment is discussed at p 306.
791 SI 2003/1660, reg 6.
792 SI 2003/1660, reg 21. See p 311.
793 The employer may rely on a GOR when promoting, transferring or training persons for a post, or when dismissing persons from a post: SI 2003/1660, reg 7(1).
794 SI 2003/1660, reg 7(2).
795 DTI *Towards Equality and Diversity: Implementing the Employment and Race Directives* (2001) para 13.11.
796 SI 2003/1660, reg 7(3). The 'religious ethos' GOR is permitted under Art 4(2) of the Directive, which refers to a situation where a person's religion or belief 'constitute a genuine, legitimate and justified occupational requirement, having regard to the organisation's ethos'.

overcomes that hurdle, the employer will still need to show that that religion or belief is a genuine occupational requirement for the job in question, and that it is proportionate to apply it. It remains to be seen how much latitude employers will be granted under this GOR, but it is submitted that it should be interpreted narrowly, as an exception to the principle of equal treatment[797]. There is also an exception which protects Sikhs from discrimination for not wearing safety helmets on construction sites; this provides that where an employer requires a Sikh to wear a safety helmet on a construction site, this is to be treated as indirect discrimination which cannot be justified[798]. Finally, there is the usual exception permitting positive action in relation to access to facilities for training, or encouraging persons of a particular religion or belief to take advantage of work opportunities[799]. As with the Sexual Orientation Regulations, and unlike the SDA and RRA, it is not necessary to show evidence that persons of a particular religion or belief are under-represented in particular jobs, because of the difficulties in collecting statistics. Instead, the positive action should 'prevent or compensate for disadvantages linked to religion or belief' among those to whom the positive action relates. The provisions on enforcement again follow the SDA and RRA model as regards bringing complaints, the burden of proof and remedies etc[800]. The government's Regulatory Impact Assessment assumes around 1,000 tribunal cases a year under the new Regulations, with annual recurring compliance costs to business of around £2 million, although as with the identical figures for sexual orientation, that figure is based on an assumption of full compliance, and so does not include cases won by the applicant.

Finally, as mentioned above, there has been 'fair employment' legislation prohibiting religious and political discrimination in Northern Ireland since 1976[801], and those measures provide a fascinating contrast with anti-discrimination laws in the rest of the UK, not least in the use of the concept of 'fair participation'[802], and the imposition of requirements (backed by a range of civil, criminal and economic sanctions) in relation to registration, annual monitoring, three-yearly review, and mandatory affirmative action (linked to goals and timetables) to remedy under-representation. The fair employment provisions were consolidated and extended by the Northern Ireland Act 1998 and the Fair Employment and Treatment (Northern Ireland) Order[803]. Two of the reforms

---

797 Significantly, Art 4(2) of the Directive states that the religious ethos GOR 'should not justify discrimination on another ground'.

798 SI 2003/1660, reg 26. This is consistent with the existing exemption of Sikhs from the requirement to wear safety helmets in the Employment Act 1989, s 11, which is not to be treated as giving rise to discrimination against any other person: reg 26(2).

799 SI 2003/1660, reg 25.

800 See SI 2003/1660, regs 27–34. The provisions are virtually identical to those in the Sexual Orientation Regulations, discussed at p 365.

801 The Fair Employment (Northern Ireland) Acts 1976 and 1989. The 1976 Act prohibited direct discrimination on grounds of religion or politics in public and private-sector employment; the 1989 Act extended the coverage to indirect discrimination, and established the Fair Employment Commission, with powers which are considerably wider than those of the EOC or the CRE. For a comprehensive analysis of the 1989 Act, see Magill and Rose (eds) *Fair Employment Law in Northern Ireland: Debates and Issues*; McLaughlin and Quirk (eds) *Policy Aspects of Employment Equality in Northern Ireland*; McVey and Hutson (eds) *Public Views and Experiences of Fair Employment and Equality Issues in Northern Ireland* (SACHR, 1997).

802 See McCrudden (1992) 21 ILJ 170.

803 SI 1998/3162. On the background to the new provisions, see *Employment Equality: Building for the Future* (Cm 3684, 1997), and the White Paper, *Partnership for Equality* (Cm 3890, 1998). See also Fitzpatrick (1999) 28 ILJ 336.

introduced in that process are worthy of special mention, not least because of their 'read across' implications for the rest of the UK[804]. First, the 1998 Act established the Equality Commission for Northern Ireland, replacing the Fair Employment Commission, the Equal Opportunities Commission for Northern Ireland, the Commission for Racial Equality for Northern Ireland and the Northern Ireland Disability Council[805]. Secondly, section 75 of the 1998 Act places a statutory duty on a public authority, in carrying out its functions relating to Northern Ireland, to have 'due regard to the need to promote equality of opportunity' in relation to religious belief, political opinion, racial group, gender, marital status, disability, and (most significantly) age, sexual orientation and persons with and without dependants. The duty thus extends well beyond the current scope of discrimination law in the UK. Public authorities were required to submit an 'equality scheme' to the Equality Commission for Northern Ireland within six months of the commencement of the provisions (on 1 January 2000) showing how they proposed to fulfil the duty to promote equality[806]. As seen in the introduction to this chapter, a similar duty has since been applied to public authorities in the rest of the UK in relation to race equality[807], and the extension of the duty to promote equality more generally across the other strands of anti-discrimination law is surely inevitable.

7 DISABILITY DISCRIMINATION IN EMPLOYMENT[808]

Statistics indicate that disabled people account for nearly a fifth of the working-age population in Great Britain, but for only about one-eighth (or 12%) of all people in employment. There are over 6.5 million people with a work-limiting, long-term disability or health problem in Great Britain, but disabled people are only half as likely as non-disabled people to be in employment[809]. Disabled employees earn on average two-thirds of the wages of non-disabled employees[810], and are more likely to be employed in manual and unskilled occupations than are non-disabled employees[811]. To some extent this can be explained by the effect which a physical or mental impairment might have on a disabled person's capacity to perform the work in question, but there is also strong evidence to suggest that disabled people suffer systematic discrimination in relation to employment, often as a result of ill-informed, stereotypical assumptions on the part of employers about the impact of particular disabilities on the work-capacity of such employees and the difficulty of adapting working arrangements and premises to accommodate them[812]. Until 1995 there was no legislation tackling the problem of

---

804 Hepple (1990) 10 OJLS 408.
805 Northern Ireland Act 1998, s 73. The new Commission came into being on 1 October 1999.
806 Northern Ireland Act 1998, Sch 9, para 2.
807 See p 271.
808 See generally, Thomas *The New Law on Disability Discrimination* (1996), Doyle *Disability Discrimination: Law and Practice* (Jordans, 4th edn, 2003). See also 'Monitoring the Disability Discrimination Act (DDA) 1995', (DfEE Research Series RR119, 1999).
809 Labour Force Survey (Summer 1999).
810 Martin, White and Meltzer *Disabled Adults: Services, Transport and Employment* (OPCS, 1989).
811 Prescott-Clarke *Employment and Handicap* (SCPR, 1990).
812 Honey, Meager and Williams *Employers' Attitudes towards People with Disabilities* (IMS, 1993).

discrimination against disabled people in the workplace, successive governments having maintained (in what has become a familiar refrain) that the issue was most appropriately tackled by education and persuasion rather than by anti-discrimination legislation. However, following an intensive and well-organised campaign for the introduction of comprehensive civil rights legislation for disabled people, and no fewer than 14 abortive attempts to introduce Private Members' Bills on the subject, the Conservative government introduced the Disability Discrimination Act 1995[813] (DDA), the first legislative attempt to tackle discrimination against disabled people. The DDA prohibited discrimination against disabled people in relation to employment, the provision of goods and services, and the sale and letting of property; it also required schools, colleges, universities and LEAs to provide fuller information about their arrangements and facilities for disabled pupils and students[814], and imposed some modest requirements as regards accessible public transport for disabled people. In the area of employment, the DDA tries to strike a balance between the interests of disabled people (in terms of access to employment and equal treatment in the workplace etc) and the interests of employers, by making it unlawful for an employer to discriminate against a disabled employee or job applicant by treating that person less favourably than he treats or would treat others for a reason relating to his or her disability, and by placing a duty on an employer to make reasonable adjustments to working arrangements and premises (by providing special equipment, altering working hours, arranging training, adapting premises, etc), in order to accommodate a disabled person who would otherwise be at a substantial disadvantage in comparison with non-disabled persons, while at the same time allowing an employer to claim that discrimination against a disabled person is justified in certain circumstances. The right not to be discriminated against is enforceable in an employment tribunal, as in the case of sex and race discrimination. The DDA repealed much of the Disabled Persons (Employment) Act 1944, including the system of voluntary registration of disabled persons, the requirement for those employing more than 20 employees to employ a quota of at least 3% registered disabled employees (with preferential treatment for disabled candidates until the quota is met), and the designated employment scheme whereby certain occupations were reserved for disabled employees. The 1944 Act had been widely criticised for its ineffectiveness; the only sanction was criminal proceedings brought by the Secretary of State, and prosecutions were very rare, despite widespread evidence of non-compliance[815] ; indeed, the number of people registered as disabled under the Act had fallen to such an extent (due at least in part to a fear of being discriminated against for carrying that label) that in practice it would not have been be possible for all employers to meet the 3% quota anyway.

The DDA was given only a qualified welcome by disabled rights campaigners, on account of the perceived deficiencies in its provisions. In particular, concern

---

813 The Act was heralded by a consultation document on *Government Measures to Tackle Discrimination Against Disabled People* (produced following the furore surrounding the 'talking-out' of the Civil Rights (Disabled Persons) Bill in 1994), and by a White Paper, *Ending discrimination against disabled people* (Cm 2729) which was published on the same day as the Bill. The employment provisions of the DDA came into force on 2 December 1996.

814 The DDA did not apply to the provision of educational services, but this omission has since been remedied by the Special Educational Needs and Disability Act 2001.

815 There were only ever ten prosecutions, the last one in 1975.

was expressed at the narrowness of the definition of disability[816], the extent to which employers were able to claim that discrimination against disabled persons was justified, and (at the outset) the absence of a commission similar to the EOC and the CRE with powers to investigate complaints, assist individuals in enforcing their legal rights or take enforcement action on its own account. By far the greatest criticism was levelled at the exemption of small businesses from the employment provisions of the Act[817], which was estimated to exclude 96% of employers from the duty not to discriminate against disabled persons. The incoming Labour government addressed some of the main criticisms by establishing a Disability Rights Commission, with powers similar to those of the EOC and CRE[818], and reducing the small employer threshold from 20 to 15. The government also set up a Disability Rights Task Force to examine the whole question of disability rights legislation, and the Task Force's Report in late 1999 made over 150 recommendations, including key reforms to the DDA's employment provisions such as the lowering of the small employer threshold to two, extending the scope of the provisions to cover, for example partnerships, police and prison officers, fire-fighters and the armed forces, restricting disability-related enquiries before the offer of a job is made, removing the justification defence in the case of the duty to make reasonable adjustments, and giving tribunals power to order reinstatement or re-engagement where a disabled person is unlawfully dismissed, and to make recommendations regarding future conduct[819]. The case for reform of the DDA was given a major boost by the reaching of agreement in October 2000 on the Employment Directive[820], brought forward under Article 13 of the EC Treaty, which requires member states to introduce laws tackling, inter alia, disability discrimination in employment. Implementation of the Directive requires some changes to be made to the DDA, many of which were anticipated in the Task Force's report, for example the ending of the exemption for small firms and the extension of the DDA to cover many of those sectors of employment currently excluded from its protection, including police officers, prison officers and fire-fighters. The Directive also necessitates some changes to the DDA's definition of discrimination, and the availability of the justification defence. The Disability Discrimination Act 1995 (Amendment) Regulations 2003[821] implement the provisions of the Directive so far as it relates to disability discrimination. At the time of writing the government had not yet brought forward legislation in response to the other recommendations of the Task Force, although it had indicated its intention to implement some of them[822], including allowing employment tribunals to order re-instatement or re-engagement, and the introduction of an obligation on public authorities to promote equality of opportunities for disabled people. In May 2003, the Disability Rights Commission produced its first review

---

816 Although the definition was broadened during the Act's passage through Parliament, it still does not cover some categories who might fall within a broader definition of disability, eg those with a reputation for disability.

817 Disability Discrimination Act 1995, s 7. The exclusion mirrored the 1944 Act, under which the duty to employ a 3% quota of registered disabled employees only applied to firms employing 20 or more.

818 Disability Rights Commission Act 1999.

819 Disability Rights Task Force *From exclusion to inclusion* (1999).

820 Directive 2000/78/EC. See p 272.

821 SI 2003,/1673, in force as from 1 October 2004. In the text that follows, footnote references to the DDA also include the renumbered sections, as from October 2004.

822 DfEE *Towards Inclusion: Civil Rights for Disabled People* (2001).

of the DDA[823], in which it proposed wide-ranging reforms to the provisions relevant to employment, including (i) the extension of the definition of disability to include, inter alia, all progressive conditions from the point of diagnosis, genetic predispositions, and those in receipt of specified disability benefits; and (ii) placing a duty on employers to anticipate the requirements of potential disabled employees and applicants, restricting disability-related enquiries before a job is offered, empowering tribunals to order re-employment and to recommend changes in employment practices, and extending the DDA to the armed forces. The government had not yet responded to the review at the time of writing.

A notable feature of the DDA is the extent to which it leaves many fundamental issues and concepts to be clarified and expanded upon by Regulations, ministerial guidance and codes of practice. There are two principal sets of employment-related Regulations[824], and the Secretary of State has issued guidance on 'matters to be taken into account in determining questions relating to the definition of disability', and a Code of Practice 'for the elimination of discrimination in the field of employment against disabled persons or persons who have had a disability'. The Guidance and the Code of Practice are both admissible in evidence in proceedings before a tribunal, and must be taken into account where relevant. Some of the concepts and terminology used in the Act were borrowed from the sex and race discrimination legislation (for example 'less favourable treatment', 'any other detriment'), but the Court of Appeal has warned that a textual comparison between the disability discrimination legislation and the legislation relating to sex and race discrimination is not helpful, and may even be misleading:

> 'Contrary to what might be reasonably assumed, the exercise of interpretation is not facilitated by familiarity with the pre-existing legislation prohibiting discrimination in the field of employment (and elsewhere) on the grounds of sex (Sex Discrimination Act 1975) and race (Race Relations Act 1976). Indeed, it may be positively misleading to approach the 1995 Act with assumptions and concepts familiar from experience of the workings of the 1975 Act and the 1976 Act.[825]'

(i) The meaning of 'disability'

The key to the Act's provisions is the definition of disability in section 1(1), which states that a person has a disability 'if he has a physical or mental impairment which has a substantial and long-term adverse effect on his ability to carry out normal day-to-day activities'. This definition has been described as a 'common-sense' definition which fits 'a generally acceptable perception of what disability means to employers, service providers, disabled people and the nation at large'[826];

---

823 DRC *Disability Equality: Making it Happen* (2003).
824 The Disability Discrimination (Meaning of Disability) Regulations 1996, SI 1996/1455, and the Disability Discrimination (Employment) Regulations 1996, SI 1996/1456.
825 *Clark v Novacold Ltd* [1999] ICR 951, [1999] IRLR 318 at para 30, CA, per Mummery LJ. Cf the government's 'Equality Statement' from November 1999, which stated that 'we will where practicable harmonise the provisions of the Race Relations Act, Sex Discrimination Act and Disability Discrimination Act'.
826 Minister of State, *Hansard* HC Standing Committee E, col 73.

however, it has also been criticised for being too narrow, and for adopting a medical as opposed to a social model of disability[827], by defining disability in terms of impairments rather than focusing on the ways in which disabled people are disadvantaged by the organisation, structure and attitudes of the society in which they live and work. In *Goodwin v Patent Office*[828], the EAT held that the tribunal should adopt a purposive approach to the interpretation of the definition, and should construe the language of the Act in a way which gives effect to the stated or presumed intention of Parliament, but with due regard to the ordinary and natural meaning of the words.

The definition, which is fleshed out by Regulations and guidance[829], has the following key elements : (i) there must be a 'physical or mental impairment'; these terms are not defined, but are intended to cover all forms of impairment, including sensory impairments. Mental illness only counts as a mental impairment if it is 'a clinically well-recognised illness'[830] (a requirement apparently designed to avoid 'the possibility of claims based on obscure conditions unrecognised by reputable clinicians'[831]), and the EAT has stressed that the existence or not of a mental impairment 'is very much a matter for qualified and informed medical opinion', and that 'some loose description such as 'anxiety', 'stress' or 'depression' of itself will [not] suffice', unless there is credible and informed evidence of a clinically well-recognised illness[832]. Problems have arisen over the dividing line between physical and mental impairment, particularly where an impairment affects a person physically (for example pain) but it is not clear whether the cause of that impairment is physical or mental[833]. The Court of Appeal set out the correct approach to that issue in *McNicol v Balfour Beatty Rail Maintenance Ltd*[834], holding that the term 'impairment' bears its ordinary and natural meaning, that it 'may result from an illness or it may consist of an illness'[835], and, crucially, that 'it is not necessary to consider how an impairment was caused'.[836] It follows that in applying the statutory definition, the focus should be on whether a physical or mental function or activity is affected, rather than on whether the cause of the impairment is physical or mental (a particularly helpful approach, given how difficult it can be to distinguish between physical and mental conditions, especially where the impairment is multi-factorial in origin). A number of conditions are deemed

---

827 See eg Doyle (1996) ILJ 1.
828 [1999] ICR 302, [1999] IRLR 4, EAT.
829 See p 384. Note also the Disability Discrimination (Blind and Partially Sighted Persons) Regulations 2003, SI 2003/712, which deem a person certified as blind or partially sighted to be disabled. Cf *Vicary v British Telecommunications plc* [1999] IRLR 680, where the EAT stated that the Guidance will only be of assistance in marginal cases.
830 Disability Discrimination Act 1995, Sch 1, para 1(1). The EAT has identified four possible routes to establishing the existence of a mental impairment: (i) proof of a mental illness specifically mentioned as such in the World Health Organisation's International Classification of Diseases; (ii) proof of a mental illness specifically mentioned as such in a similar publication; (iii) proof by other means of a medical illness recognised by a respected body of medical opinion; (iv) proof by substantial and specific medical evidence of a mental impairment which neither results from nor consists of a mental illness: *Morgan v Staffordshire University* [2002] ICR 475, [2002] IRLR 190.
831 Minister of State, *Hansard*, HC Standing Committee E, col 104.
832 *Morgan v Staffordshire University* [2002] ICR 475, [2002] ICR 475, [2002] IRLR 190, EAT.
833 As in the condition known as psychological or functional 'overlay', where a person experiences pain which has no apparent physical cause.
834 [2002] EWCA Civ 1074, [2002] ICR 1498, [2002] IRLR 711.
835 [2002] IRLR 711 at 713, per Mummery LJ. See to like effect Lindsay J in *College of Ripon & York St John v Hobbs* [2002] IRLR 185 at para 32.
836 [2002] EWCA Civ 1074, [2002] ICR 1498, [2002] IRLR 711, citing with approval Part 1 of the Guidance (see n 829 above).

not to be impairments for the purposes of the Act (for example dependency on alcohol, nicotine or other non-prescribed substance, pyromania, kleptomania, a tendency to physical or sexual abuse of others[837], exhibitionism, voyeurism and hayfever[838]), although it is necessary to distinguish between such excluded conditions and impairments which may result from them[839]; (ii) the impairment must have a 'substantial' effect[840]; this is not defined, although the intention is only to include impairments having an effect which is 'more than minor or trivial'[841]. In *Goodwin v The Patent Office*[842], the EAT emphasised that the Act is concerned with the effect of an impairment on a person's *ability* to carry out activities: 'The focus of attention required by the Act is on the things that the applicant either *cannot* do or can only do with difficulty, rather than on things that the person *can* do'. This approach avoids the danger of a tribunal concluding that as there are many things that an applicant can do, the adverse effect of the impairment cannot be substantial[843]. The Guidance suggests that in determining whether the effect of an impairment is substantial, account should be taken of factors such as the time taken to carry out the activity (para A2) and the way in which it is carried out (para A3), in comparison with what might be expected if the person did not have the impairment[844]; (iii) the impairment must have a 'long-term' effect; conditions which are only temporary, such as short-term illness, are not disabilities within the meaning of the Act. An impairment will be treated as having a long-term effect if it has lasted, or is likely to last, for at least 12 months[845], or if it is likely to last for the rest of a person's life (as in the case of a terminal illness)[846]. Where the impairment is intermittent or sporadic (for example epilepsy or multiple sclerosis), it will be treated as continuing to have a long-term adverse effect, even through periods of remission, if it is likely to recur[847]; (iv) the impairment must have an adverse effect on a person's ability 'to carry out normal day-to-day activities'. Schedule 1 contains an exhaustive list[848] of activities which are to be treated as

---

837 See eg *Murray v Newham Citizens Advice Bureau* [2003] IRLR 340, where the EAT surprisingly held that such conditions are only excluded if they are' freestanding', and not the direct consequence of a physical or mental impairment falling within s 1(1) (eg a tendency to violence resulting from paranoid schizophrenia).

838 Disability Discrimination (Meaning of Disability) Regulations, SI 1996/1455, regs 3 and 4.

839 *Power v Panasonic UK Ltd* [2003] IRLR 151, EAT (depression resulting from alcohol addiction still capable of being an impairment within the meaning of the Act).

840 Sch 1, para 3 provides that a severe disfigurement will be treated as an impairment having a substantial adverse effect; deliberately acquired disfigurements such as tattoos or decorative body piercing are excluded: Disability Discrimination (Meaning of Disability) Regulations, SI 1996/1455, reg 5.

841 *Goodwin v Patent Office* [1999] ICR 302, [1999] IRLR 4; *Vicary v British Telecommunications plc* [1999] IRLR 680, EAT.

842 *Goodwin v Patent Office* [1999] ICR 302, [1999] IRLR 4, per Morison J (emphasis supplied).

843 *Leonard v Southern Derbyshire Chamber of Commerce* [2001] IRLR 19, EAT.

844 The Guidance also advises that it may be appropriate to consider the cumulative effects of the impairment on a range of normal day-to-day activities (para A4), and the cumulative effects of more than one impairment (para A6).

845 The material time at which the disability must be assessed is the time of the alleged discriminatory act, not the date of the hearing (*Cruickshank v VAW Motorcast Ltd* [2002] ICR 729, [2002] IRLR 24, EAT), although the Guidance states (at para E8) that in assessing the likelihood of an effect lasting for any period, account should be taken of the total period for which the effect exists, including time before and after the point when the discriminatory act occurred. Cf also *Greenwood v British Airways plc* [1999] ICR 969, [1999] IRLR 600, EAT.

846 Disability Discrimination Act 1995, Sch 1, para 2(1).

847 Disability Discrimination Act 1975, Sch 1, para 2(2).

848 Regulations may deem an impairment to affect a person's ability to carry out normal day-to-day activities, and vice versa: Disability Discrimination Act 1975, Sch 1, para 4(2).

normal day-to-day activities for these purposes, namely: mobility; manual dexterity; physical co-ordination; continence; ability to lift, carry or otherwise move everyday objects; speech, hearing or eyesight; memory or ability to concentrate, learn or understand; or the perception of the risk of physical danger. 'Normal day-to-day activities' are the activities of an ordinary average person, not a person with specialised skills or abilities. In deciding whether an activity is a normal day-to-day activity, the Guidance states that account should be taken 'of how far it is normal for most people and carried out by most people on a daily or frequent or fairly regular basis' (para C2). In *Vicary v British Telecommunications plc*[849], normal day-to-day activities were held to include making beds, doing housework, sewing and cutting with scissors, minor DIY tasks, filing nails, curling hair and ironing, since they are all 'activities which most people do on a frequent or fairly regular basis'[850]. In *Ekpe v Metropolitan Police Comr*[851], the tribunal at first instance had held that the ability of a woman to put rollers in her hair and to use her right hand to apply makeup were not normal day-to-day activities because they were 'activities carried out almost exclusively by women', but the EAT, allowing the appeal, stated that what is 'normal' for these purposes may be best understood 'as anything which is not abnormal or unusual', and that the exclusion of any activity done by women rather than men (or vice versa) was 'plainly wrong'[852]. The Guidance states that 'normal day-to-day activities' do not include work of any particular form, 'because no particular form of work is "normal" for most people'[853]. This is not to say, however, that the effect of a person's impairment whilst at work is irrelevant, for the following reasons; first, the work they perform may include some normal day-to-day activities, and evidence of how they are able to perform those activities while at work will be relevant to the tribunal's assessment of their case[854]; and secondly, the effects of an impairment may be exacerbated by conditions at work (for example exposure to fumes), and 'it would risk turning the Act on its head' if the employer were able to avoid any obligations under the Act (for example to make reasonable adjustments) by arguing that the employee was not disabled because the impairment only had a substantial adverse effect on normal day-to-day activities while the employee was at work[855].

One difficult practical issue for the tribunal is the weight to be placed on medical evidence. It is for the tribunal to decide whether the applicant has an impairment which has a substantial adverse effect on normal day-to-day activities, and the EAT has held that a tribunal makes an error of law if it relies too heavily on medical opinion on those issues[856]. The medical report should be confined to the doctor's diagnosis of the impairment, the doctor's observation of the applicant carrying out normal day-to-day activities and the ease with which he was

849 [1999] IRLR 680, EAT.
850 [1999] IRLR 680 at 682, per Morison P. See also *Abadeh v British Telecommunications plc* [2001] IRLR 23, [2001] ICR 156, EAT (travelling by Underground and flying held to be normal day-to-day activities because they were normal means of transport used by most people on a daily or frequent or fairly regular basis).
851 [2001] IRLR 605, EAT.
852 [2001] IRLR 605 at 609.
853 Guidance, para C3. See eg *Quinlan v B & Q plc* (EAT 1386/97) (assistant at garden centre not disabled within the meaning of the Act because, although unable to lift heavy objects following heart surgery, he was capable of lifting everyday objects).
854 *Law Hospital NHS Trust v Rush* [2001] IRLR 611, Ct Sess.
855 *Cruickshank v VAW Motorcast Ltd* [2002] ICR 729, [2002] IRLR 24, EAT (occupational asthma exacerbated by exposure to fumes at work).
856 *Vicary v British Telecommunications* [1999] IRLR 680, EAT.

able to perform those functions, together with any relevant opinion as to prognoses and the effect of medication[857]. On the other hand, while a tribunal is not obliged to accept uncontested medical evidence[858], it may not disregard such evidence in favour of its own impression of the applicant formed in the course of the hearing[859].

A number of further points can be made in relation to the definition. First, the statutory protection extends to those who have had a disability in the past, even if they have made a full recovery and are no longer disabled[860]. This is in recognition of the fact that a person with a history of disability (for example a person with a history of mental illness) may continue to experience discrimination even when no longer disabled; it is an example of the Act adopting a more 'social' model of disability. Secondly, the effect of an impairment on normal day-to-day activities must be considered without taking into account any measures (for example medical treatment[861], or the use of a prosthesis or other aid) which are being taken to treat or correct the impairment[862], the rationale again being that such a person may experience discrimination even if the potentially disabling condition is controlled; so for example, in the case of a person with diabetes which is controlled by medication, whether or not the effect of the condition is substantial must be decided by reference to what the effects of the condition would be if that person were not taking his or her medication[863]. Difficulties can arise here where it is not clear whether an impairment would in fact have a substantial adverse effect if the medical treatment were to be discontinued, and on this the Court of Appeal has taken a strict line, requiring the applicant to prove his or her alleged disability 'with some particularity': 'Those seeking to invoke [this] particularly benign doctrine . . . should not readily expect to be indulged by the tribunal of fact. Ordinarily . . . one would expect clear medical evidence to be necessary'.[864] The other limitation on the doctrine is that where the medical treatment creates a *permanent* improvement, the effects of that treatment *should* be taken into account in assessing the disability, as measures are no longer needed to treat or correct it once the permanent improvement has been established[865]. Thirdly, a person suffering from a progressive condition, such as cancer, multiple

---

857 *Abadeh v British Telecommunications plc* [2001] ICR 156, [2001] IRLR 23, per Nelson J.

858 Eg where the evidence on the basis of which a doctor has formed an opinion is rejected by the tribunal, or where it is clear that the medical witness has misunderstood the evidence which he was invited to consider in expressing his opinion.

859 *Kapadia v London Borough of Lambeth* [2000] IRLR 699, CA. Cf Pill LJ at 703: by consenting to a medical examination on behalf of the employer, the applicant was consenting to the disclosure to the employer of a report resulting from that examination, so that no further consent for disclosure was required. See also *London Borough of Hammersmith & Fulham v Farnsworth* [2000] IRLR 691, EAT (an occupational health physician was not bound by any duty of confidence owed to the applicant not to disclose details of the applicant's medical history to the employer, because the applicant had consented to medical information about her being provided to the employer).

860 Disability Discrimination Act 1995, s 2.

861 This can include attendance at therapy or counselling sessions: *Kapadia v London Borough of Lambeth* [2000] IRLR 699.

862 Disability Discrimination Act 1995, Sch 1, para 6. This does not apply to those with impaired sight which is correctable by spectacles or contact lenses or some other prescribed method.

863 Ie the tribunal must consider the 'deduced effects' of the impairment: *Goodwin v Patent Office* [1999] ICR 302, [1999] IRLR 4.

864 *Woodrup v London Borough of Southwark* [2002] EWCA Civ 1716, [2003] IRLR 111.

865 *Abadeh v British Telecommunications plc* [2001] ICR 156, [2001] IRLR 23, EAT (although note that a person whose disabling impairment has been successfully treated remains protected by virtue of the provisions on past disability).

sclerosis, muscular dystrophy or infection by HIV, will be deemed to fall within the definition of a disabled person from the point in time when, as a result[866] of that condition, that person has an impairment which has some adverse effect (which need not be substantial) on that person's ability to carry out normal day-to-day activities, if the condition is likely to result in an impairment which has a substantial adverse effect[867]. The burden of proof is on the applicant to show, on the balance of probabilities, that the condition is likely to have a substantial adverse effect at some stage in the future[868], and this may prove difficult where the applicant has a condition which is variable in nature, such as multiple sclerosis, where the prognosis may be uncertain[869]. The provision for progressive conditions is in recognition of the fact that a person who is diagnosed as suffering from such a condition may suffer discrimination as a result of that diagnosis well before the condition can be said to have a substantial adverse effect on that person's ability to carry out normal day-to-day activities. However, the protection only arises from the point when the condition begins to have some effect; it does not apply while the condition, although diagnosed, remains latent, and it could therefore be said to provide a positive incentive to discriminate before a person begins to manifest any symptoms. In view of these concerns, the government has indicated that it intends to change the law to ensure that HIV infection counts as a disability from the time at which it is diagnosed, and that people with cancer count as disabled from the time at which the cancer is diagnosed as being a condition that is likely to require substantial treatment[870]. Those diagnosed with other progressive conditions will however remain unprotected until the condition becomes symptomatic, as will a person diagnosed as having a genetic predisposition to a potentially disabling condition[871]. Finally, the burden of proof in establishing an impairment is on the applicant[872]. The tribunal does not have a duty 'to conduct a free-standing inquiry of its own[873]', nor is it required to obtain evidence or to ensure that adequate medical evidence is obtained by the parties[874].

---

866 An impairment which is a result of standard treatment to relieve a progressive condition (eg urinary incontinence resulting from surgery for prostate cancer) rather than a direct result of the condition itself, still falls within this exception: *Kirton v Tetrosyl* [2003] IRLR 353, CA.

867 DDA, Sch 1, para 8. 'Likely' here means 'more probable than not': Guidance, para 87.

868 Eg by medical evidence of the likely prognosis, or by statistical evidence.

869 See eg *Mowat-Brown v University of Surrey* [2002] IRLR 235, EAT. Cf Rubenstein at [2002] IRLR 227: 'This decision . . . highlights a problem with the drafting of the DDA. Applicants with progressive conditions do not want them to get worse and it seems invidious, both for them and their doctors, to require them to prove that this is more likely than not to happen.'

870 DfEE *Towards Inclusion: Civil Rights for Disabled People* (2001) para 3.11.

871 On the potential for genetic discrimination in employment, see the report of the Human Genetics Advisory Council 'The Implications of Genetic Testing for Employment' (1999). The DRC has called for the Act's protection to be extended to those with a genetic predisposition: see *Disability Equality: Making it Happen* (2003).

872 Note that as from October 2004, implementing the Employment Directive, the burden of proof will shift to the respondent where the complainant proves facts from which the tribunal could conclude that the respondent has acted unlawfully: DDA, s 17A(1C).

873 *Rugamer v Sony Musical Entertainment UK Ltd* [2001] IRLR 644 at 652, clarifying the comment of Morison J in *Goodwin v Patent Office* [1999] IRLR 4 that the role of the tribunal 'contains an inquisitorial element'. See also *Morgan v Staffordshire University* [2002] IRLR 190 at 194, EAT.

874 *NcNicol v Balfour Beatty Rail Maintenance Ltd* [2002] IRLR 711 at 714, per Mummery LJ. In this respect, the duty of an employment tribunal differs from that of a medical or other tribunal dealing with a disablement issue as part of a benefits claim.

It may however exercise its discretion to grant an adjournment to enable the applicant to obtain further evidence, particularly where the applicant is not only in person but also suffers some mental weakness[875].

(ii) The scope of the protection

Section 4 echoes the other anti-discrimination legislation by prohibiting discrimination against a disabled person in all aspects of employment[876]. It makes it unlawful for an employer to discriminate against a disabled applicant for employment in the arrangements which he makes for recruitment, in the terms on which employment is offered, or by refusing or deliberately omitting to offer employment[877]; it also makes it unlawful for an employer to discriminate against a disabled person 'whom he employs'[878] in relation to the terms of employment, the way he affords or refuses to afford him opportunities for promotion, transfer, training or other benefit, or by dismissing him[879] or 'subjecting him to any other detriment'[880] (a phrase which has been interpreted in other contexts as covering any type of disadvantage)[881]. As originally enacted, the DDA contained a range of excluded categories, some of which were very controversial. In particular there was an exemption for small businesses (originally, those employing fewer than twenty employees[882]) from the employment provisions of the Act[883], which was estimated to exclude 96% of employers from the duty not to discriminate against disabled persons. The small employer threshold was reduced from twenty to fifteen in 1998[884], thereby extending the protection to a further 45,000 employers and 60,000 disabled employees[885]. However, the Employment Directive allows no exceptions based on the size of the undertaking, and so the exception for small employers is to be removed with effect from October 2004. Also excluded from the protection are police and prison officers, fire-fighters, the armed forces and people in partnerships, and these exclusions are also to be removed in 2004

---

875 *Morgan v Staffordshire University* [2002] IRLR 190 at 195, per Lindsay P (the President's guidance was approved by the Court of Appeal in *McNicol* [2002] IRLR 711).

876 The protection extends to employees and applicants for employment, including contract workers (s 12; new s 4B from October 2004), office-holders (new ss 4C–4F, from October 2004); apprentices and self-employed workers who contract personally to do any work (s 68(1)). Certain occupations (eg armed forces, police, prison officers and fire-fighters), are currently excluded, but all these categories (except the armed forces) will be included from October 2004: s 64, as will people in partnerships (new ss 6A–6C), and barristers and advocates (new ss 7A–7D)

877 DDA, s 4(1).

878 The SDA and RRA use a slightly different form of words ('employed by him') but the House of Lords held in *Rhys-Harper v Relaxion Group plc* [2003] IRLR 484 that nothing turns on the difference.

879 A dismissal which is unlawful under the DDA is not automatically unfair under the Employment Rights Act 1996: *H J Heinz Co Ltd v Kenrick* [2000] ICR 491, [2000] IRLR 144, EAT.

880 DDA, s 4(2).

881 See p 303 above.

882 Those employed by associated employers are not to be included in the calculation: *Hardie v CD Northern Ltd* [2000] ICR 207, [2000] IRLR 87, EAT.

883 Disability Discrimination Act 1995, s 7. The exclusion mirrored the 1944 Act, under which the duty to employ a 3% quota of registered disabled employees only applied to firms employing 20 or more.

884 SI 1998/2618. There was a statutory requirement to review the exclusion within four years of the provisions coming into force: s 7(5).

885 DTI Regulatory Impact Assessment.

(with the exception of the armed forces, as the Employment Directive allows member states to exempt them from the provisions on disability and age discrimination).

The DDA does not expressly refer to harassment, although as in other areas of discrimination law, disability-related harassment is clearly capable of constituting a 'detriment'. From October 2004, the DDA will contain a new provision (implementing the Employment Directive) making it unlawful in relation to employment to subject a disabled person to harassment[886], and defining harassment as unwanted conduct, for a reason related to the disabled person's disability, which has the purpose or effect of violating that person's dignity, or creating an intimidating, hostile, degrading, humiliating or offensive environment for him.[887]' As originally enacted, the DDA did not state whether 'by dismissing him' includes constructive dismissal, and there is conflicting case law on the point[888], but the post-2004 provisions make it explicit that constructive dismissal situations are covered by the DDA[889]. Another point of controversy (as in several other areas of anti-discrimination law) has been whether a claim can be brought under the DDA in respect of post-termination discrimination[890]. It had been thought that the wording of the Act did not allow for such a claim, and the post-2004 provisions therefore contain a new provision expressly prohibiting post-employment discrimination where it 'arises out of and is closely connected to the [employment] relationship'[891]; ironically, however, while the amending Regulations were before Parliament, the House of Lords held[892] (on a consolidated appeal addressing the same point under sex, race and disability discrimination law) that it is unlawful for a person to discriminate against former employees 'if there is a substantive connection between the discriminatory conduct and the employment relationship'[893], whenever the discriminatory conduct arises (a test which is more or less the same as that contained in the new Regulations). Significantly, their Lordships left open the question whether the duty to make reasonable adjustments continues after the end of the contract of employment. Section 11 of the 1995 Act makes special provision for discriminatory job advertisements, by raising a presumption of discrimination in favour of a disabled person who applies for and is not offered a particular job, if the advertisement[894] for that job indicates (or might reasonably be taken to

---

886 Disability Discrimination Act 1995 (Amendment) Regulations 2003, SI 2003/1673, reg 5, inserting new s 4(3).

887 DDA, s 3B(1). The new EC definition of harassment is discussed at p 310.

888 *Metropolitan Police Comr v Harley* [2001] ICR 927, [2001] IRLR 263, EAT (DDA does not apply to constructive dismissal); compare *Catherall v Michelin Tyres plc* [2003] ICR 28, [2003] IRLR 61, EAT (DDA does apply to constructive dismissal).

889 Disability Discrimination Act 1995 (Amendment) Regulations 2003, SI 2003/1673, reg 5, inserting new s 4(5)(b).

890 Eg arising out of a post-termination appeal against dismissal, the provision of a reference from a former employer, a failure to reinstate after dismissal, or some other post-termination benefit arising from the employment relationship.

891 SI 2003/1673, reg 15, inserting new s 16A.

892 *Rhys-Harper v Relaxion Group plc; D'Souza v London Borough of Lambeth; Jones v 3M Healthcare Ltd* [2003] IRLR 484, HL.

893 [2003] IRLR 484 at 510, per Lord Rodger. Cf Lord Hobhouse at 501 ('a substantive and proximate connection between the conduct complained of and . . . employment by the alleged discriminator'; Lord Nicholls at 489 ('the obligation not to discriminate applies to all the incidents of the employment relationship, whenever precisely they arise').

894 This includes every form of advertisement or notice, whether to the public or not: DDA, s 11(3).

indicate) that the employer might discriminate against a disabled applicant[895]; the employer can rebut the presumption by showing that the failure to offer the job to that person was not related to his disability[896]. In contrast, the SDA and RRA make it unlawful to publish a discriminatory job advertisement, and place enforcement in the hands of the Commissions[897]. The post-2004 provisions introduce a similar regime into the DDA, with the Disability Rights Commission empowered to take action in relation to the publication of a discriminatory advertisement[898]. The Act contains no specific provisions dealing with pre-employment health screening, despite evidence that it is a common source of discrimination against disabled applicants[899], but it might be held to be unlawful for an employer to insist on a medical check for a disabled applicant if the same requirement is not applied to other, non-disabled applicants. The protection against dismissal operates alongside the existing law of unfair dismissal, but the two are not co-extensive because under the 1995 Act the employer is under a duty to make reasonable adjustments to arrangements and premises in order to overcome a disabled employee's disadvantage (see below), which may involve the employer in, for example, reallocating work or transferring the disabled employee to another vacancy. This duty is stricter than any obligation on an employer under the unfair dismissal legislation in the case of a dismissal for incapability or ill-health[900].

(iii) The meaning of 'discrimination'

The definition of discrimination in section 5 of the DDA differs in several respects from that used in the other anti-discrimination legislation. In particular, the DDA does not require a like-for-like comparison, it permits less favourable treatment to be justified in certain circumstances, it uses a concept of reasonable adjustment in place of indirect discrimination, and it allows positive discrimination in favour of disabled people. In the main, the definition of discrimination in the DDA is consistent with the approach taken in the Employment Directive, but some changes will be necessary in order to bring domestic law into line with EC law.

(a) Less favourable treatment and 'direct discrimination'[901]

The DDA provides[902] that an employer discriminates against a disabled person 'if, for a reason which relates to the disabled person's disability, he treats him less

895 DDA, s 11(1).
896   DDA, s 11(2).
897 See p 302 below.
898 Disability Discrimination Act 1995 (Amendment) Regulations 2003, reg 15, inserting new s 16B, with effect from October 2004. S 11 is repealed by reg 12.
899 The Disability Rights Task Force recommended restrictions on disability or disability-related pre-employment enquiries (*From Exclusion to Inclusion*, recommendations 5.32 and 5.33) but the government has not accepted the need for change.
900 See ch 8 below.
901 In other areas of discrimination law, less favourable treatment on one of the prohibited grounds is usually referred to as 'direct discrimination', but in this context the two terms are not synonymous: see below.
902 Disability Discrimination Act 1995, s 5(1)(a). A revised definition of discrimination covering the whole of Part II applies as from 1 October 2004. The new definition, in s 3A of the Act, is very similar to the existing definition: Disability Discrimination Act 1995 (Amendment) Regulations 2003, reg 4.

favourably than he treats or would treat others to whom that reason does not or would not apply'. At first sight this looks very similar to the definition of discrimination which is used in the SDA and RRA[903]; however, the DDA does not require the like-for-like comparison that is applied in the other anti-discrimination legislation[904], and the employer may have a defence if he can show that the treatment in question is justified (see below).

The scope of the protection offered by this section turns on two fundamentally important issues: first, who is the appropriate comparator when determining whether there has been 'less favourable treatment'[905]?; and secondly, what degree of knowledge of the complainant's disability is required on the part of the employer? The first issue arose for consideration in *Clark v Novacold Ltd* [906], where the applicant was dismissed for long-term sickness absence following an accident at work. The EAT identified two possible approaches to the comparison required by section 5(1)(a); the first involves a like-for-like comparison between the treatment of the disabled person and the treatment of a person who was also unable to fulfil all the requirements of the job, but for a reason unrelated to disability (ie someone who had been absent from work for the same amount of time as the applicant, but for a reason other than disability); the second involves a comparison between the treatment of the disabled person and the treatment of a person who was able to fulfil all the requirements of the job (ie someone who had not been absent from work at all, or who had the same absence record as the applicant when any disability-related absences were discounted). In practice, the second approach is far more likely to lead to a finding of less favourable treatment, thus putting the onus on the employer to show justification for that treatment; the first approach is unlikely to lead to a finding of less favourable treatment (unless the employer has discriminated against the applicant simply because he has a disability) which means that the need to show justification is less likely to arise. The EAT preferred the first approach, and held that the applicant had not been less favourably treated for a reason which related to his disability, because he was treated no differently than a person in similar circumstances who was not disabled would have been treated. In sharp contrast, in *British Sugar v Kirker*[907], the EAT held that the DDA does not require a like-for-like comparison, but 'simply requires the applicant to show that he was less favourably treated than other employees where the reason for the treatment, that is a reason related to his disability, does not apply to those other employees' (ie the straightforward causative test of the second approach); it was unnecessary to identify other employees with whom to compare the treatment of the disabled applicant, other than for the purpose of determining the causation question. On appeal, the Court of Appeal in *Clark v Novacold Ltd*[908] reversed the EAT's decision,

---

903 And, as from December 2003, the Sexual Orientation Regulations and Religion or Belief Regulations.
904 In particular, unlike eg the SDA, s 5(3), the DDA does not require that in making the comparison 'the relevant circumstances in the one case are the same, or not materially different, in the other'.
905 Ie in the words of DDA, s 5(1)(a), who are the 'others to whom that reason does not or would not apply'?
906 [1998] ICR 1044, [1998] IRLR 420, EAT.
907 [1998] IRLR 624, EAT. The earlier EAT decision in *Clark v Novacold Ltd* was not mentioned in the judgment.
908 [1999] ICR 951, [1999] IRLR 318, CA.

and applied the second, causative approach: 'The test of less favourable treatment is based on the reason for the treatment of the disabled person and not on the fact of his disability. It does not turn on a like-for-like comparison of the treatment of the disabled person and of others in similar circumstances.' One objectionable aspect of the DDA as originally enacted was that an employer could try to justify direct discrimination even where the less favourable treatment of a disabled person was simply because that person had a disability, rather than on the basis of that person's ability to do the job (ie where the treatment was essentially for reasons of prejudice). This is not permitted by the Employment Directive, and so the DDA has been modified to say that less favourable treatment cannot be justified if it amounts to 'direct discrimination' ie if, on the ground of the disabled person's disability, the employer treats the disabled person less favourably than he would treat a person not having that particular disability 'whose relevant circumstances, including his abilities, are the same as, or not materially different from, those of the disabled person.[909]'

Turning to the second issue, the degree of knowledge required on the part of the employer, in *O'Neill v Symm & Co Ltd*[910], the first EAT decision on the DDA provisions, the EAT held that the use of the words 'for a reason which relates to the disabled person's disability' means that that the employer must have knowledge of the employee's disability, or at least the material features of it, and not merely knowledge of one or other equivocal symptom. In that case, the employee was dismissed as a result of absences from work due to chronic fatigue syndrome. The EAT held that she had not been discriminated against for a reason which related to her disability, because her employers had no knowledge of her condition, and had dismissed her solely on the grounds of uncertified absence. However, in *H J Heinz Co Ltd v Kenrick*[911] the EAT disagreed with *O'Neill*, and held that it was not necessary for the employer to have knowledge of the disability in order to be said to have acted for a reason 'which relates' to the disability; according to the EAT, the reason may include a 'reason deriving from how the disability manifests itself even where there is no knowledge of the disability as such'. The EAT used the example of a postman who successfully conceals from the employer the fact that he has an artificial leg, and who is dismissed for making his rounds too slowly. If he can show that his slowness is attributable to his artificial leg, then according to the EAT he would have been treated less favourably than others 'to whom that reason does not apply' (ie others who do their rounds at an acceptable pace) for a reason which related to his disability, whether or not the employer knew before the dismissal that the reason for the slowness was that he was disabled.

The decision in *Heinz* is consistent with the approach of the Court of Appeal in *Clark v Novacold Ltd*[912], in that it applies an objective test of whether or not there is a causal connection between the less favourable treatment complained of and the applicant's disability, rather than a subjective test through the eyes of the employer: 'Unless the test is objective, there will be difficulties with credible and honest yet ignorant or obtuse employers who fail to recognise or acknowledge the obvious'[913]. The effect in practice is to place much greater emphasis on the question of justification, where absence of knowledge of the disability on the part

---

909 DDA, s 3A(5), in force from 1 October 2004.
910 [1998] ICR 481, [1998] IRLR 233, EAT.
911 [2000] IRLR 144, EAT.
912 [1998] IRLR 420.
913 [2000] IRLR 144 at 147, per Lindsay P.

of the employer may be highly material[914]. The importance of establishing a causal connection between the conduct complained of and the applicant's disability has been illustrated in several EAT decisions. For example in *British Gas Services Ltd v McCaull*[915], the EAT overturned the tribunal's finding that that the applicant had been treated less favourably by the employer's failure to supply him with information about an alternative job because there was no evidence as to the reason for that failure, which could have been the result of managerial oversight or incompetence or some other reason which had nothing to do with the applicant's disability. Similarly, in *London Clubs Management Ltd v Hood* [916], the EAT held that the employer's refusal to pay sick pay to the applicant was because of a policy not to pay sick pay generally, and was not for a reason which related to the applicant's disability.

The employer has a defence to a complaint of less favourable treatment if he can show that the less favourable treatment is justified[917]. The availability of a justification defence in such circumstances is a recognition of the fact that a person's disability may have a bearing on their ability to do a job, but there is clearly a danger that if the defence is applied too widely, it could undermine the statutory protection[918]. The Act states that treatment is justified if the reason for it 'is both material to the circumstances of the particular case[919] and substantial'[920] ; this is amplified by the Code of Practice[921], which states that the reason must relate to the individual circumstances in question, and must not be trivial or minor, a test which has been judicially described as a 'very low threshold'[922]. In *Baynton v Saurus General Engineers Ltd*[923], the EAT held that in applying the test of justification the tribunal must carry out a balancing exercise between the interests of the disabled employee and the interests of the employer, but as the EAT subsequently observed in *Heinz*, in undertaking such an exercise the comparatively limited requirements of the justification test must be borne in mind. The leniency of the test was confirmed in *Jones v Post Office*[924], where the Court of Appeal held that in

914 Note that the employer's duty to make reasonable adjustments does not arise if the employer does not know and could not reasonably be expected to know that the person has a disability: DDA, s 6(6).
915 [2001] IRLR 60, EAT.
916 [2001] IRLR 719, EAT.
917 DDA, s 5(1)(b) (s 3A(1)(b) from October 2004). As from October 2004, it will no longer be possible to argue justification if the treatment amounts to 'direct discrimination': s 3A(3); see p 394.
918 Concern has been expressed in particular at the danger of employers using health and safety requirements as a 'false excuse' for not employing or continuing to employ disabled people, rather than taking positive steps to overcome health and safety barriers to the recruitment or retention of disabled people: *Health, Safety and Disability: Are there conflicts at work?* (IRS, 2003).
919 The relevant circumstances include the circumstances of both the employer and the employee: *Baynton v Saurus General Engineers Ltd* [2000] ICR 375, [1999] IRLR 604, EAT.
920 DDA, s 5(3) (s 3A(3) from October 2004). Where an employer is under a duty to make a reasonable adjustment, but has failed without justification to comply with that duty, the employer cannot justify less favourable treatment of that person unless that treatment would have been justified even if the employer had made the adjustment: s 5(5) (s 3A(6) from October 2004).
921 Code of Practice 'For the elimination of discrimination in the field of employment against disabled persons or persons who have had a disability' para 4.6.
922 *H J Heinz Co Ltd v Kenrick* [2000] IRLR 144 at 146, per Lindsay P.
923 Above, n 919.
924 [2001] EWCA Civ 558, [2001] ICR 805, [2001] IRLR 384. Cf *Murray v Newham Citizens Advice Bureau Ltd* [2003] IRLR 340, EAT (standard of investigation required to satisfy the DDA test of justification is higher for existing employees than for job applicants); also *Surrey Police v Marshall* [2002] IRLR 843, EAT (admissibility of expert evidence in applying the test of justification).

determining whether there is material and substantial reason for the discrimination, the function of the tribunal 'is not very different from the task which they have to perform in cases of unfair dismissal' – in other words, a 'range of reasonable responses' test. Under the Employment Directive, the test of objective justification that applies in disability cases is the same as that which applies in other areas of discrimination law, and as interpreted by the ECJ this requires the employer to show that the measures in question 'correspond to a real need on the part of the undertaking, are appropriate with a view to achieving the objectives pursued and are necessary to that end.[925]' It is unlikely that the test approved in *Jones v Post Office* accords with that standard.

(b) Failure to make a reasonable adjustment

Unlike the other anti-discrimination legislation, the DDA does not expressly prohibit indirect discrimination against a disabled person on the grounds of disability; instead, the Act[926] places a duty on the employer to make reasonable adjustments to his arrangements[927] (for example interview and selection procedures, job offers, contractual arrangements, working conditions and arrangements for redeployment[928]) or to any physical feature[929] of his premises[930] (for example doors which are too narrow for wheelchairs, lighting which is too dim for someone with restricted vision), where they place a disabled employee or a disabled applicant for employment at a 'substantial disadvantage' (not defined) in comparison with persons who are not disabled[931]. Failure to comply with the duty to make reasonable adjustments will constitute unlawful discrimination[932]. As originally enacted, the DDA allowed employers to argue that a failure to make a reasonable adjustment was justified, where the reason for the failure was 'both material to the circumstances of the particular case and substantial[933]'. However, the justification defence for failure to make a reasonable

---

925 *Bilka-Kaufhaus GmbH v Weber von Hartz* [1987] ICR 110, [1986] IRLR 317, ECJ. See p 293.

926 DDA, s 6 (s 4A from October 2004).

927 As defined in s 6(2), this applies to arrangements for determining to whom employment should be offered, and to any term, condition or arrangements on which employment, promotion, a transfer, training or any other benefit is offered or afforded. As from October 2004, 'arrangements' will be replaced by 'provision, criterion or practice', consistent with the wording of the Employment Directive. Although not expressly stated in the Act, the duty has been held to apply to the dismissal of a disabled employee: *Morse v Wiltshire County Council* [1998] ICR 1023, [1998] IRLR 352, EAT.

928 *Kent County Council v Mingo* [2000] IRLR 90, EAT.

929 As defined in the Disability Discrimination (Employment) Regulations 1996, reg 9.

930 The duty applies only to premises occupied by the employer; if the employer's premises are leased, the terms of the lease may be overriden if the landlord unreasonably withholds consent to the alterations, to enable the occupier to comply with the duty to make adjustments: DDA, s 16.

931 The EAT provided useful guidance for a tribunal dealing with an alleged failure to make reasonable adjustments in *Morse v Wiltshire County Council* [1998] ICR 1023, [1998] IRLR 352, but it is not an error of law for a tribunal not to apply that guidance, provided they properly applied themselves to considering whether the statutory requirements were satisfied: *Beart v H M Prison Service* [2003] IRLR 238, CA.

932 A complaint of a failure to make a reasonable adjustment does not depend upon showing that there has been less favourable treatment: *Clark v Novacold Ltd* [1998] ICR 1044, [1998] IRLR 420, EAT.

933 DDA, s 5(2), (4). This is the same test of justification as in cases of less favourable treatment. The fact that the employer has no knowledge of the disability does not preclude the employer from arguing that he was justified in not making an adjustment: *Quinn c Schwarzkopf Ltd* [2002] IRLR 602, Ct Sess; *Callagan v Glasgow City Council* [2001] IRLR 724, EAT.

adjustment is to be removed from October 2004 on the grounds that it is entirely covered by the need for adjustments only to be reasonable, and is therefore redundant.

The Act contains a number of examples of steps which an employer might have to take to comply with this duty; they include: making adjustments to premises; reallocating duties to other employees; transferring a disabled employee to an existing vacancy; altering his working hours; assigning him to a different place of work; giving him time off during working hours for rehabilitation, assessment or treatment; arranging training; acquiring or modifying equipment; modifying instructions or reference manuals; modifying procedures for testing or assessment; and providing a reader or interpreter[934]. In *Kenny v Hampshire Constabulary*[935], the EAT held that the duty to make reasonable adjustments to the employer's 'arrangements' only applies to job-related arrangements, and does not extend to a duty to provide a personal carer to assist with the personal needs of a disabled employee. The Act also lists five factors[936], embracing issues of cost, practicability and effectiveness, which must be taken into account in determining whether it is reasonable for an employer to have to take a particular step; they are (i) the extent to which taking the step would prevent the effect in question; (ii) the extent to which it is practicable for the employer to take the step; (iii) the financial and other costs which would be incurred by the employer in taking the step and the extent to which taking it would disrupt any of his activities; (iv) the extent of the employer's financial and other resources; v) the availability to the employer of financial or other assistance. In October 2004, two additional factors will join this list, reflecting the fact that the Act will thereafter apply to small employers; they are: (vi) the nature of the employer's activities and the size of his undertaking; and (vii) where the step would be taken in relation to a private household, the extent to which taking it would disrupt that household, or disturb any person residing there. The Act contains a power to put a financial ceiling on the cost of making adjustments[937], but this has not been exercised to date, with the result that the question of what is a reasonable cost for an employer to have to bear is left to the judgment of the employment tribunals[938] (with obvious implications for consistency of treatment).

It is for the employer to satisfy the tribunal that the duty to make reasonable adjustments has been satisfied. It will not be good enough for the employer to show that the applicant was unable to think of any satisfactory adjustments if the employer has given no thought to the matter[939]. On the other hand, if there were no particular steps which the employer ought reasonably to have taken in all the circumstances, the employer will have a defence, even if he gave no consideration to the matter. As the EAT stated in *British Gas Services Ltd v McCaull*[940], the test under section 6 is an objective one: 'The test of whether it was reasonable for an employer to have to take a particular step . . . does not relate to what the employer

---

934 DDA, s 6(3) (s 18B from October 2004, at which time 'giving, or arranging for, training or mentoring (whether for the disabled person or any other person)' will be added to the list of examples).
935 [1999] ICR 27, [1999] IRLR 76, EAT.
936 DDA, s 6(4) (s 18B(1) as from October 2004).
937 DDA, s 6(9).
938 The Compliance Cost Assessment for the Act estimated an average cost of £200 per disabled employee for the 10% of cases where a disabled employee is likely to require an adjustment.
939 *Cosgrove v Caesar and Howie* [2001] IRLR 653, EAT.
940 [2001] IRLR 60, EAT.

considered but to what he did and did not do'; an employer does not fail to comply with the duty merely because he has not consciously considered what steps might reasonably be taken; it followed that '[an] employer might take all reasonable steps as contemplated by section 6 while remaining ignorant of the statutory provision itself.' The duty to make adjustments does not arise if the employer does not know, and could not reasonably be expected to know, that the person has a disability which is likely to place him at a substantial disadvantage in comparison with non-disabled persons[941]. This raises the difficult question of just when an employer can be expected to draw an inference that an employee is disabled, and/or at a substantial disadvantage. In *Ridout v TC Group*[942], the applicant stated in her job application that she had photosensitive epilepsy controlled by medication, and was disabled. She was interviewed in a room which had bright fluorescent lighting. She entered the interview room wearing sunglasses around her neck (at 5 pm on a February afternoon) and remarked that she might be disadvantaged by the lighting. The interview proceeded, and she was not offered the job. She subsequently complained that the employers had failed to make a reasonable adjustment in respect of the physical arrangements for the interview. The EAT upheld the tribunal's decision that the applicant had not been unlawfully discriminated against on grounds of her disability. The EAT stated that tribunals should be careful not to impose on disabled people seeking employment a duty to give a long explanation as to the effects of their disability merely to cause the employer to make adjustments which probably should have been made in the first place, but neither should an employer be required to ask a number of questions as to whether a disabled person feels disadvantaged, questions which would not have been asked of somebody who was able-bodied. On the facts, the EAT held that the tribunal was entitled to conclude that no reasonable employer would be expected to know, without being told in terms by the applicant, that the arrangements which the employer made for the interview might disadvantage the applicant, given that the applicant's form of epilepsy was rare. Whether the prospective employers should have taken any other steps as a result of what was said at the interview was said to be a matter of fact and evidence for the tribunal.

(iv) Remedies

The remedies available for unlawful disability discrimination are similar to those which apply in other discrimination complaints[943], as are the procedures. Complaints must be presented to an employment tribunal within three months of the act complained of[944], and if the tribunal finds the complaint well-founded, it may make a declaration that the employee's rights have been infringed, order the employer to pay compensation, and/or recommend that the employer take action specified by the tribunal to remove the adverse effect of the

---

941 DDA, s 6(6) (s 4A(3) as from October 2004). In the case of a disabled applicant, the duty only applies in relation to a person who is, or has notified the employer that he may be, an applicant for the employment: s 6(5) (s 4A(2) as from October 2004).

942 [1998] IRLR 628, EAT. *Quaere* whether the decision in this case is affected by *H J Heinz & Co Ltd v Kenrick* [2000] ICR 491, [2000] IRLR 144, EAT (see p 394 above).

943 See p 319 above.

944 DDA, s 8(1), Sch, para (s 17A(1) as from October 2004).

discrimination[945]. If the employer fails without reasonable justification to comply with such a recommendation, the tribunal may make an increased award of compensation if it thinks it just and equitable to do so[946]. Compensation will be calculated on the same basis as an action for damages in tort, and may include compensation for injury to feelings[947]. A medical expert may be required if the parties are unable to agree the evidence. There is no upper limit on the amount of compensation which may be awarded under the Act. The highest award to date was in *British Sugar v Kirker*[948], where the applicant was awarded £103,146.

The remaining provisions concerning remedies (for example on contracting-out, protection against victimisation, questionnaires and vicarious liability) are very similar to those in the other anti-discrimination legislation[949]. Until recently, the most significant difference was unquestionably the absence of a Commission equivalent to the EOC or the CRE[950], but that controversial omission was remedied by the Disability Rights Commission Act 1999[951], which established a Commission of that name with powers to investigate complaints of discrimination, assist individuals in bringing complaints before the courts and tribunals, and take strategic enforcement action on its own account. In an interesting innovation, the Commission is empowered to enter into a legally binding written agreement with a person it has reason to believe may have committed, or may be committing, an unlawful act[952], thus providing a less severe procedure than the usual alternatives of prosecution or formal investigation. The Commission has already had a major impact on the scene, spreading awareness of disabled people's rights, campaigning hard (and effectively) for further legal reform[953], and assisting individuals in bringing tribunal claims.

8 AGE DISCRIMINATION IN EMPLOYMENT

To date there has been no legislation prohibiting age discrimination in the UK, despite widespread evidence that discrimination on grounds of age is endemic at the recruitment stage (for both younger and older workers) and in selection for redundancy, and not to mention the fact that the whole concept of a retirement age is itself an example of deeply ingrained ageism. As seen above, age

---

945 DDA, s 8(2) (s 17A(2) as from October 2004). Tribunals are not able to order reinstatement or re-engagement under these provisions.
946 DDA, s 8(5) (s 17A(5) as from October 2004).
947 DDA, s 8(3) and (4) (s 17A(3) and (5) as from October 2004). On assessment of compensation under the Sex Discrimination Act 1975, see p 321 above. The normal tribunal procedures for fixing compensation are not well suited to DDA cases, which may hinge on disputed medical opinion, and the tribunal will usually need to have a directions hearing involving, amongst other things, an exchange of statements of case and any witness statements: *Buxton v Equinox Design Ltd* [1999] ICR 269, [1999] IRLR 158, EAT.
948 [1998] IRLR 624, EAT.
949 See p 312ff above.
950 The National Disability Council, established under s 50 of the DDA, was only empowered to advise the government on general issues relating to discrimination against disabled people.
951 The provisions of the Act establishing the DRC came into force on 6 August 1999: SI 1999/2210.
952 Disability Rights Commission Act 1999, s 5.
953 The Commission's first review of the DDA, *Disability Equality: Making it Happen* (2003), is considered in the introduction to this Part.

discrimination is one of the strands covered by the Employment Directive[954], and legislation implementing the Directive's requirements will need to be introduced in due course. However, progress towards implementation has been slower than the other strands as the Directive allows member states until October 2006 to implement the provisions, reflecting the complexity of the issues involved.

Even without legislation expressly prohibiting age discrimination, certain forms of age discrimination are capable of being tackled via other strands of discrimination law. For example age discrimination can constitute indirect sex discrimination (for example where an employer operates an age requirement which has an adverse impact on women)[955], and in *Nash v Mash/Roe Group*[956], an employment tribunal boldly disapplied the provisions in the Employment Rights Act 1996 which prevent employees over normal retirement age from claiming unfair dismissal or statutory redundancy payments[957], on the grounds that they indirectly discriminate against men (because more men than women work beyond 65) and are therefore contrary to Article 141 of the EC Treaty. A similar conclusion was reached in *Rutherford v Towncirle Ltd and Secretary of State for Trade and Industry (No 2)*[958], where the tribunal surprisingly held that the Secretary of State was unable to show that the statutory upper age limits were objectively justifiable because they were tainted by sex discrimination, being originally linked to the different state pensionable ages for men and women. An appeal to the EAT was pending at the time of writing. It has also been argued that an employee whose contract of employment includes an equal opportunities clause in which, inter alia, the employer undertakes not to discriminate on grounds of age may be able to claim a contractual right not to be discriminated against on grounds of age, but as a matter of construction such a clause is unlikely to be held to override an express contractual retirement policy[959], which of its very nature discriminates against people on grounds of age.

Before the 1997 General Election, the Labour Party indicated that, if elected, it intended to legislate against age discrimination, but no such legislation was forthcoming. Instead, the government issued a Code of Practice on Age Diversity in Employment[960], which sets out a series of action points ('principles') for employers in six aspects of the employment cycle: recruitment, selection, promotion, training and development, redundancy and retirement. The action points include, for example, avoiding the use of age limits or age ranges in job advertisements, or using phrases which imply age restrictions, such as 'young graduates' or 'mature person'; using where possible a mixed age interviewing panel, and selecting on merit; ensuring that promotion opportunities are advertised through open competition; ensuring that age is not a barrier to training, and that all employees are aware of the training and development opportunities that are available and are encouraged to use them; using objective, job-related criteria when considering candidates for redundancy, and making sure age is not a criterion (potentially very significant in an unfair dismissal claim based on

---

954 Directive 2000/78/EC; see p 272.
955 See eg *Price v Civil Service Commission* [1978] ICR 27, [1977] IRLR 291, EAT.
956 [1998] IRLR 168, EAT. Sadly the appeal was never heard by the EAT because the applicant died before the appeal hearing could take place.
957 Employment Rights Act 1996, ss 109 and 156. See p 559 below.
958 [2002] IRLR 768, EAT.
959 *Taylor v Secretary of State for Scotland* [2000] 3 All ER 90.
960 DfEE 1999; see Desmond [1999] 28 ILJ 186. The Code was preceded by a report: *Action on Age; Report of the Consultation on Age Discrimination in Employment* (DfEE, August 1998).

unfair redundancy selection); and not seeing age as the sole criterion when operating early retirement schemes, and using flexible retirement schemes and phased retirement where possible. Laudable though these principles are, the main weakness in the Code is that it lacks any method of enforcement; it is entirely voluntary, issued on a non-statutory basis, and unlike other Codes of Practice in the employment field, there is no legal requirement on tribunals to take it into account where relevant. The signs are that the Code has made little impact on age discrimination in the workplace[961].

Draft Regulations implementing the age strand of the Employment Directive had not yet been published at the time of writing, but the government had issued a separate consultation document on age discrimination[962], following up the earlier, more general consultations on the new Directives[963]. It seems very likely that the Regulations on age will mirror the other new strands as regards their terminology and scope, but the key (and, at the time of writing, unresolved) issue is the extent to which employers will be permitted to justify treating people differently on the grounds of age. The Employment Directive gives little guidance on the matter (consistent with its status as a framework Directive), meaning that member states have a broad margin of discretion in terms of how to implement the age provisions. Article 6 of the Directive states that 'Member States may provide that differences of treatment on grounds of age shall not constitute discrimination, if, within the context of national law, they are objectively and reasonably justified by a legitimate aim, including legitimate employment policy, labour market and vocational training objectives, and if the means of achieving that aim are appropriate and necessary'. It goes on to state that such differences of treatment '*may include, among others*': (i) the setting of special conditions on access to employment and vocational training, including remuneration conditions, for young people, older workers and persons with caring responsibilities, in order to 'promote their vocational integration or ensure their protection'; (ii) the fixing of *minimum* conditions of age, professional experience or seniority in service for access to employment or advantages linked to employment; and (iii) the fixing of a *maximum* age for recruitment based on the training requirements of the post in question or the need for a reasonable period of employment before retirement[964]. The government is considering setting out a list of specific aims which could in principle justify age discrimination, with the onus on the employer to show, by reference to those aims, that treating a person differently on grounds of age is 'appropriate and necessary in the particular circumstances'. The specific aims referred to in the consultation document are: health welfare and safety; facilitation of employment planning; training requirements of the post in question; encouraging and rewarding loyalty; and the need for a reasonable period of employment before retirement. On the vexed question of retirement age, the consultation document states that retirement ages set by employers will be unlawful under the Directive unless objectively justified, and that the government is still 'seeking views' on whether the legislation should provide for employers,

---

961 In September 1999, research conducted for the Employers Forum on Age found that one in three employers were completely unaware of the Code, and fewer than one in ten intended to make any changes in the way they recruit and train.

962 *Equality and Diversity: Age Matters* (DTI, 2003).

963 *Towards Equality and Diversity: Implementing the Employment and Race Directives* (DTI, 2001); *Equality and Diversity: The Way Ahead* (DTI, 2002); *Equality and Diversity: Making it Happen* (DTI, 2002).

964 Employment Directive 2000/78/EC (italics supplied).

exceptionally, to be able to justify mandatory retirement ages, and whether there should be a 'default age' of 70 at or after which employers could require employees to retire without having to justify their decision.

Chapter 6

Maternity and parental rights

I INTRODUCTION[1]

The new Labour government came into office in May 1997 committed to a review of the existing law on maternity rights, and the introduction of new 'family-friendly' measures to help workers strike a balance between work and home[2]. Since that time, the law in this area has been transformed almost beyond recognition, first by the Employment Relations Act 1999, which introduced a new framework of maternity rights, replacing the existing substantive provisions in the Employment Rights Act 1996 with a series of enabling powers which were subsequently fleshed out by supporting regulations[3]; and secondly by the Employment Act 2002, which brought further major restructuring and extension of maternity rights, new rights to paternity leave and adoption leave, and a right for parents of young children to request flexible working.

That the existing law on maternity rights was long overdue for reform was not in doubt. The existing provisions had developed piecemeal since the Employment Protection Act 1975 first introduced three statutory rights relating to maternity – the right not to be unfairly dismissed because of pregnancy, the right to return to work after pregnancy or childbirth and the right to maternity pay. A fourth right, to time off work for ante-natal care, was introduced in the Employment Act 1980. The right to maternity pay was superseded in April 1987 by the statutory maternity pay (SMP) provisions, introduced in the Social Security Act 1986 and subsequently consolidated in the Social Security Contributions and Benefits Act 1992. The maternity provisions were notorious for their complexity, and were widely criticised, not least because it was possible for a minor, technical slip-up to cost the employee her rights. In one case, the provisions were memorably described as being 'of inordinate complexity exceeding the worst

1   See McRae *Maternity Rights in Britain* (1991); Fredman *Women in Labour: Parenting Rights at Work* (1995); McColgan (2000) 29 ILJ 125; Conaghan (1993) 20 JLS 71.
2   *Fairness at Work* (Cm 3968, 1998) ch 5.
3   Maternity and Parental Leave etc (MPL etc) Regulations 1999, SI 1999/3312.

excesses of a taxing statute'[4]. The position was exacerbated by the fact that the qualifications for the different rights differed in several important respects (for example there were different qualifying dates and notice requirements for the right to return and for SMP).

The whole area was the subject of major change in 1993 by the Trade Union Reform and Employment Rights Act 1993, implementing the Pregnant Workers Directive[5]. The 1993 Act introduced a new right to fourteen weeks' maternity leave, and gave improved protection against dismissal on grounds of pregnancy or childbirth, in both cases regardless of length of service[6]. It also introduced a right to be suspended from work on maternity grounds where continued employment would be unlawful or contrary to a Code of Practice. The 1993 Act provided an excellent opportunity for a thorough overhaul of the law in this area and the removal of unnecessary complexity, but unfortunately that opportunity was missed. The new provisions were simply overlaid onto the existing law, and it took a greater than usual degree of fortitude to attempt to unravel them. Some improvement flowed from the consolidation of employment rights in the Employment Rights Act 1996, but as a consolidating statute, that Act was bound to have only limited success in attempting to fashion the proverbial silk purse out of the raw materials. Nearly two decades after Browne-Wilkinson J uttered the remarks quoted above, Ward LJ was moved to state in the Court of Appeal[7], in a case on the interpretation of the provisions on maternity leave and the right to return to work (which by that stage had been in force since 1975), that 'it is surely not too much to ask of the legislature that those who have to grapple with this topic should not have to have a wet towel around their heads as the single most important aid to the understanding of their rights'[8].

As redrawn in the 1999 Act and the associated regulations, the maternity leave provisions were undoubtedly an improvement on what had gone before. The notification requirements, notoriously complicated under the pre-1999 law, were rationalised and simplified, and some notorious grey areas were clarified, in particular the status of the contract of employment during maternity leave. However, there was a groundswell of opinion that the reforms had not gone far enough: 'Employers and employees alike are bewildered by, or unaware of, the existing legislation on maternity pay and leave. As it stands the system is a minefield of qualification periods and dates, variable leave lengths, different calculation periods and short notification requirements.[9]' The reforms that were intended to achieve the other stated objective, that of making employment law more 'family-friendly', also received a lukewarm response. The 1999 Act extended the right to 'ordinary' maternity leave from fourteen to eighteen weeks, and reduced the qualifying period for 'additional' maternity leave from two years to

---

4   As was illustrated in *Lavery v Plessey Telecommunications Ltd* [1982] ICR 373, [1983] IRLR 180 at 182, EAT, per Browne-Wilkinson J. In *Lavery* the giving of five days' notice of intention to return to work after maternity leave instead of the seven then required robbed the employee of her right to return.

5   Directive 92/85/EC. The directive, which was agreed in October 1992, was brought forward as a health and safety measure under Article 118A of the Treaty of Rome, and as such required only qualified majority approval; the UK government abstained in the vote on its adoption.

6   A right to pay during the 14-week maternity leave period was introduced via reforms to the SMP provisions.

7   *Halfpenny v IGC Medical Systems Ltd* [1999] ICR 834, [1999] IRLR 177, CA.

8   To which prescription both authors would probably wish to add a couple of aspirins or a large whisky, or quite possibly both.

9   DTI *Work and Parents: Competitiveness and Choice, a framework for simplification* (May 2001).

one, but these were only modest improvements on the previous position. More significant was the introduction of a right to parental leave for mothers and fathers, and a right to emergency leave ('time off for dependants'), implementing the Parental Leave Directive[10], but here again the new provisions were open to criticism for example in relation to the restriction of the entitlement to parental leave to the parents of children under five, and the fact that there was no provision for any part of the leave to be paid.

No doubt stung by these criticisms, in 2000 the government embarked on yet another major review of maternity and parental rights, this time with a much wider remit. The Green Paper, *Work and Parents: Competitiveness and Choice*[11], put forward a wide range of options for further reform, designed 'to balance improving choice for parents and enhancing competitiveness for business'. The responses indicated that the greatest levels of support were for further simplification of the arrangements for maternity leave and pay, the introduction of new rights to paid paternity leave[12] and paid adoption leave, and a new right to flexible working for parents. In June 2001 the government set up the Work and Parents Taskforce, headed by Professor Sir George Bain, to consider how best to implement a right to flexible working for the parents of young children, and the Taskforce reported later that year[13]. The Taskforce recommended the introduction of a new right to *apply* for flexible working, falling well short of a right to insist on working flexibly. Legislation underpinning that right was introduced in the Employment Act 2002, along with measures implementing the other reforms mentioned above. The new framework for maternity leave and pay deserves a special mention, as it represents a considerable (and long overdue) simplification, rationalisation and enhancement of the existing provisions, and should be good news for both employees and employers[14]. The extension of the maternity leave period may, however, be an irrelevance to the many employees who simply cannot afford to stay at home for a year[15].

The government has claimed with some justification that, in addition to the above reforms, measures introduced in other areas will assist parents in balancing work and family life[16], in particular the introduction of Child Tax Credit and Working Tax Credit to provide support for families with children and those in work on low incomes, the implementation of the Working Time Directive, which (in principle, if not in practice) attacks the long-hours culture that can be so destructive of family life and gives all workers the right to four weeks' paid holiday, and the Part-Time Workers Directive, which indirectly benefits working mothers (many of whom work part-time) by prohibiting discrimination against part-time workers. The government has also instituted a Work-Life Balance campaign to

10   Directive 96/34/EC.
11   Cm 5005, December 2000.
12   On work-life balance for fathers, see Hatton, Vinter and Williams 'Dads on Dads: Needs and expectations at home and at work' (EOC, 2002).
13   Work and Parents Taskforce *About Time: Flexible Working* (November 2001).
14   The more generous the maternity provision, the higher the proportion of women returning to work after childbirth: Callender, Millward, Lissenburgh and Forth *Maternity Rights and Benefits in Britain* DSS Research Report No 67 (1997); see also Forth, Lissenburgh, Callender and Millward *Family-Friendly Working Arrangements in Britain* DfEE Research Report No 16 (1997).
15   Only a quarter of eligible employees took all or nearly all of the maximum entitlement even before the recent increases: DTI *Work and Parents: Competitiveness and Choice, a framework for simplification* (May 2001).
16   HM Treasury/DTI *Balancing work and family life: enhancing choice and support for parents* (January 2003).

raise awareness among employers and employees of the positive advantages of introducing flexible working options for all staff[17] . In practice, one of the most important factors for mothers and fathers seeking to find a satisfactory balance between work and family life is the availability of high quality, convenient and affordable childcare. It remains to be seen whether the government's much-vaunted Childcare Strategy, which aims to encourage the provision of good quality childcare through a range of initiatives, will be more successful than the previous government-sponsored initiatives in this area[18] .

Finally, while the focus of this chapter is on work and parents, and the extent to which the law assists working parents in achieving a satisfactory work-life balance, it is important to remember that a good work-life balance is an objective desired not just by working parents but by employees of all types, irrespective of their family commitments. One of the least satisfactory aspects of the current laws promoting work-life balance is that they tend to focus on the needs of parents (and often the parents of very young children) while doing little to meet the expectations of employees with other types of commitment, for example employees with aged parents, or disabled partners, or simply harbouring a desire to spend more time gardening or following the Barmy Army around the cricketing venues of the Southern Hemisphere. The danger of a law that only promotes the work-life balance of parents is that it can breed resentment among those who do not fall within the protected class, particularly if they feel that their own quality time outside the workplace is being sacrificed in the interests of their working parent colleagues. On that point, it should be remembered that, as in other areas of employment law, the statutory provisions outlined below represent a minimum entitlement which may in practice be replaced by more generous contractual arrangements, and while the law may give preferential treatment to working parents, it is clear that many employers with flexibility policies extend the benefit of those schemes to all employees, not just to working parents. One leading example is Asda, which has had its efforts in promoting flexible working and equal pay recognised by the government through a Castle Award, and by its own employees voting it top of the *Sunday Times 100 Best Companies to Work For*. Asda provides a wide range of flexible working practices and family-friendly policies, including shift-swapping, job-sharing, childcare leave, term-time working and (he noted enviously) 'Benidorm' leave, in the form of a three-month unpaid winter holiday. At the time of writing, Asda had just announced another ground-breaking policy whereby women undergoing IVF treatment will be entitled to a certain number of days of paid leave. Such policies are likely to become more widespread as employers wake up to the economic and business case for flexibility, and as firms increasingly see cutting-edge flexibility policies as a cost-effective means of recruiting, retaining and motivating the best staff.

17 See DfEE *Changing Patterns in a Changing World: A discussion document* (March 2000); DfEE *Creating a Work-Life Balance: A good practical guide for employers* (September 2000); DfEE *Work-Life Balance 2000: Baseline study of work-life balance practices in Great Britain* (November 2000).
18 The inter-departmental Childcare Review *Delivering for Children and Families* (2002) led to a doubling of resources for childcare in the 2002 Spending Review, although that includes spending on early years; and from April 2002, the childcare element of Working Tax Credit extends to those using approved childcare in their own homes.

2 DISMISSAL AND DETRIMENT FOR FAMILY REASONS

All employees have the right not to be dismissed or subjected to any detriment by their employer for reasons connected with pregnancy or childbirth or for other specified family reasons, regardless of their age or length of service. Until 1993, the protection against dismissal on grounds of pregnancy or childbirth was seriously deficient, in that it only applied where the employee satisfied the normal qualifying period of continuous employment for unfair dismissal (which was still two years at that time). The effect of this was to exclude some 40% of working women from the protection[19]. All was not lost, however, for a woman dismissed for pregnancy within two years of employment could complain that her dismissal was unlawful sex discrimination (such complaints not being subject to any qualifying period of continuous employment). In 1993, the protection against pregnancy dismissal was extended to all employees by the Trade Union Reform and Employment Rights Act 1993, implementing the Pregnant Workers Directive[20], with the result that a woman dismissed on grounds of pregnancy or childbirth within the first year of employment does not have to claim sex discrimination in order to obtain a remedy. There may, however, still be advantages in doing so, not least being the fact that compensation for sex discrimination is not subject to any upper limit. The significance of sex discrimination law in this area is considered below[21].

The provisions on pregnancy dismissal were further amended by the Employment Relations Act 1999, which simplified the existing provisions, and extended the unfair dismissal protection to dismissal for other family reasons (including the fact that the employee took parental leave, or time off for dependants), as required by the Parental Leave Directive; similar provisions prohibiting dismissal for taking paternity or adoption leave were introduced in 2002. The opportunity was also taken in 1999 to introduce for the first time a parallel right not to suffer detriment short of dismissal for family reasons. Section 99 of the 1996 Act, which used to contain the substantive provisions on dismissal for pregnancy and childbirth, is now a framework provision conferring a power to make regulations concerning dismissal for family reasons, and the detailed provisions on dismissal and other detriment are to be found in the Maternity and Parental Leave (MPL) Regulations[22] and the Paternity and Adoption Leave (PAL) Regulations[23].

---

19 1989 Labour Force Survey, *Employment Gazette*, December 1990, p 633. The problem was particularly acute for part-time workers (ie those working less than 16 hours per week) who at that time needed to work for five years in order to qualify.

20 Directive 92/85/EC.

21 See p 439.

22 MPL etc. Regulations 1999, reg 20.

23 PAL Regulations, reg 29.

(i) Dismissal for family reasons

The Maternity and Parental Leave (MPL) Regulations provide that a dismissal will be automatically unfair if the reason or principal reason for the dismissal[24] is connected with: (i) the pregnancy of the employee[25]; (ii) the fact that she has given birth to a child[26]; (iii) her suspension from work on maternity grounds[27]; (iv) the fact that she took, or sought to take, ordinary maternity leave, additional maternity leave, parental leave or time off for dependants; (v) the fact that she availed herself of the benefits of ordinary maternity leave[28]; (vi) the fact that she failed to return to work after ordinary or additional maternity leave where the employer had failed to notify her of the date of return[29]; (vii) the fact that she refused to sign a workforce agreement in relation to parental leave[30]; or (viii) the fact that she performed (or proposed to perform) any functions or activities of a workforce representative (including standing as a candidate) for the purposes of the provisions on parental leave. Similar provision is made for paternity and adoption leave by the Paternity and Adoption Leave (PAL) Regulations, which provide that a dismissal will be automatically unfair if the reason or principal reason for the dismissal is connected with the fact that: (i) the employee took, or sought to take paternity or adoption leave; (ii) the employer believed that the employee was likely to take adoption leave; or (iii) the fact that the employee failed to return to work after additional adoption leave where the employer had failed to notify the employee of the date of return[31]. Special rules apply in the case of redundancy. First, a dismissal will be unfair if the employee is made redundant and it is shown that he or she was selected for redundancy in preference to other comparable employees for one of the family reasons set out above[32]. Secondly, where a redundancy situation arises during the employee's ordinary or additional maternity or adoption leave which makes it impracticable for the employer to continue to employ her under her original contract of employment, the employee is entitled to be offered alternative employment with her employer (or with a successor, or an associated employer) where there is a suitable available vacancy, ie where the work to be done is of a kind which is suitable in relation to the employee, appropriate for her to do in the circumstances, and on terms and conditions (including the capacity and place in which she is to be

---

24 As in other unfair dismissal cases, it will be for the employer to show the reason for the dismissal. An employee dismissed while pregnant or during ordinary or additional maternity leave is entitled to a written statement of the reasons for dismissal, without requesting it, and regardless of her length of service: s 92(4), as amended.

25 Before the 1993 Act, this was the only ground upon which a pregnancy dismissal could be held automatically unfair. As under the old provisions, the dismissal must be causally connected with the pregnancy: it is not sufficient that the employee was dismissed while pregnant: see, on the old law, *Del Monte Foods Ltd v Mundon* [1980] ICR 694, [1980] IRLR 224, EAT.

26 The protection under this head only applies during the employee's ordinary or additional maternity leave: MPL etc. Regulations 1999, reg 20(4).

27 Ie under a relevant statutory requirement or relevant recommendation in a Code of Practice, as defined by s 66(2) of the 1996 Act; see p 426 below.

28 Ie that during her ordinary maternity leave period, she availed herself of the benefit of any of the terms and conditions of her employment preserved under s 71: MPL etc. Regulations 1999, reg 20(5), applying reg 19(3).

29 This head was added by the Maternity and Parental Leave (Amendment) Regulations 2002, SI 2002/2789.

30 See p 434 below.

31 PAL Regulations, reg 29.

32 MPL etc. Regulations 1999, reg 20(2); PAL Regulations, reg 29(2).

employed) not substantially less favourable to her than if she had continued to be employed under her previous contract[33]. If the employer has a suitable alternative vacancy available, but makes the employee redundant during ordinary or additional maternity or adoption leave without first offering it to her, the redundancy dismissal will be unfair[34]. If, however, there is no suitable alternative work available which could be offered to her, she will not be regarded as unfairly dismissed.

There are two further significant limitations on the protection against dismissal, both of which were originally introduced by the Employment Act 1980 in an attempt to redress what was seen by the government of the day as an imbalance in the maternity leave provisions in favour of employees. First, if the employer is a small employer employing only five or fewer people (including any employees employed by an associated employer) at the time when the employee's additional maternity or additional adoption leave ends, and the employer can prove that it is not reasonably practicable to permit the employee to return to her old job or to a similar job which is both suitable for the employee and appropriate for her to do in the circumstances, the employee will not be regarded as automatically unfairly dismissed when the employer does not allow the employee to return to work at the end of the maternity leave or adoption leave period[35]. Secondly, if the employer can prove that it is not reasonably practicable (for a reason other than redundancy) to permit the employee to return to her old job or to a similar job which is both suitable for the employee and appropriate for her to do in the circumstances, and an associated employer has offered suitable alternative employment which the employee has accepted or unreasonably refused, then once again the employee will not be regarded as automatically unfairly dismissed when not allowed to return to work at the end of maternity leave or adoption period[36]. Both these exceptions are a major limitation on the right to return to work after maternity or adoption leave; the only comfort given to an employee in this situation is that the burden of proof is placed squarely upon the employer to show (a) that it is not reasonably practicable to permit the employee to return in the normal way, and (b) that he or an associated employer has offered the employee alternative employment 'which is both suitable for her and appropriate for her to do in the circumstances'[37]. The concept of an offer of suitable alternative employment is well known in the law on redundancy[38] and there may be a tendency to apply redundancy precedents to this maternity leave provision (though the wording of the two provisions is not the same), but it is submitted that in construing the maternity provision a tribunal should consider

33   MPL etc. Regulations 1999, reg 10; PAL Regulations, reg 23. The offer of alternative employment must be made before the end of her existing contract, and the new contract must take effect immediately on the ending of the previous contract.
34   MPL etc. Regulations 1999, reg 20(1)(b); PAL Regulations, reg 29(1)(b). If the employer offers her a suitable alternative vacancy and she unreasonably refuses it, she may lose her right to a redundancy payment. It was held under the old provisions that whether a vacancy is 'available' is a question of objective fact, not of reasonableness: *Community Task Force v Rimmer* [1986] ICR 491, [1986] IRLR 203, EAT.
35   MPL etc. Regulations 1999, reg 20(6); PAL Regulations, reg 29(4).
36   MPL etc. Regulations 1999, reg 20(7); PAL Regulations, reg 29(5).
37   MPL etc. Regulations 1999, reg 20(8); see also PAL Regulations, reg 29(6). The requirement in redundancy cases that the terms and conditions of the alternative employment be not substantially less favourable to her than if she had continued to be employed under her previous contract does not apply here.
38   See p 641.

it as very much the exception to the normal rule, for to allow it to apply too readily would be to jeopardise an important employment right.

Before the 1993 amendments, a pregnancy dismissal was not unfair where the employer could prove that the employee was incapable of doing her job properly because of her pregnancy (for example where her job involved lifting)[39], or that she could not carry on working without contravening some statutory provision (for example the regulations prohibiting the exposure of pregnant women to ionising radiations or lead)[40]. Those exceptions no longer apply, but where the employee's continued employment would be unlawful or contrary to the recommendations of a Code of Practice, the employee may now be suspended from work on maternity grounds (see below), and a dismissal connected with such suspension will be unfair.

In the case law on the pre-1993 provisions, the words 'reason connected with pregnancy' were broadly construed. In *Brown v Stockton-on-Tees Borough Council* [41], the applicant, a care supervisor on a youth training scheme, was selected for redundancy on the basis that she was pregnant. The employers argued that they were justified in selecting the applicant for redundancy because otherwise they would have had to arrange a replacement for her during maternity leave. The EAT and the Court of Appeal held that this was not a case of dismissal 'for a reason connected with pregnancy', but was instead purely a redundancy situation[42]. However, in a judgment of some importance the House of Lords held that the dismissal fell within the section and was therefore unfair; the section was to be construed in its own terms, as 'part of social legislation passed for the specific protection of women and to put them on an equal footing with men', and it could not have been the intention of Parliament 'that an employer should be entitled to take advantage of a redundancy situation to weed out his pregnant employees' (per Lord Griffiths). As seen above, the redrafted provisions now expressly provide that selection for redundancy for family reasons will be automatically unfair, but the decision is arguably still important, for it shows that the courts will be prepared to interpret the provisions purposively where necessary in order to achieve the social policy objectives of the legislation.

(ii) Protection from detriment for family reasons

The statutory protection from detriment for family reasons was introduced in the Employment Relations Act 1999. Before that Act there was no explicit right not to suffer detriment for family reasons, although in practice detrimental treatment on grounds of pregnancy or childbirth will almost invariably constitute unlawful sex discrimination[43]. The new provisions bring the protection from detriment in line with the unfair dismissal protection, although there are some differences between the two.

---

39 See eg *Brear v Wright Hudson Ltd* [1977] IRLR 287.
40 The only exception was where the employer had failed to offer her a suitable available vacancy, in which case the dismissal was unfair.
41 [1988] ICR 410, [1988] IRLR 263, HL. See also *Clayton v Vigers* [1989] ICR 713, [1990] IRLR 177, EAT.
42 The argument on behalf of the employer being that cases of unfair redundancy selection were not subject to s 99.
43 See p 439 below.

Section 47C of the Employment Rights Act 1996 (as fleshed out by the Maternity and Parental Leave etc. Regulations[44] and the Paternity and Adoption Leave Regulations[45]) gives an employee the right not to be subjected to any detriment[46] (other than dismissal) by the employer for the reason that the employee: (i) is pregnant; (ii) has given birth to a child; (iii) has been suspended from work on maternity grounds; (iv) has taken, or sought to take, ordinary maternity leave, additional maternity leave, parental leave or time off for dependants, paternity leave or adoption leave; (v) has availed herself of the benefits of ordinary maternity leave; (vi) has failed to return to work after ordinary or additional maternity leave, or additional adoption leave, where the employer had failed to notify the employee of the date of return; (vii) has refused to sign a workforce agreement in relation to parental leave; or (viii) has performed (or proposed to perform) any functions or activities of a workforce representative (including standing as a candidate) for the purposes of the provisions on parental leave[47].

The remedy for an infringement of the right not to be subjected to a detriment for family reasons operates through the usual procedures in Part V of the Employment Rights Act for protection from suffering detriment in employment. Complaint lies to an employment tribunal, within three months of the act, or deliberate failure to act complained of (or within a further reasonable period where not reasonably practicable)[48], and if the tribunal upholds the complaint it must make a declaration to that effect, and may award the employee such compensation as it considers just and equitable in all the circumstances[49].

3 ORDINARY MATERNITY LEAVE

All pregnant employees are entitled to at least twenty-six weeks' ordinary maternity leave, irrespective of length of service or hours of work, during which the contract of employment continues (unless either party expressly ends it, or it expires), and the employee is entitled 'to the benefit of the terms and conditions of employment which would have applied if she had not been absent'[50] (apart from remuneration, which is specifically excluded[51]). The right to ordinary maternity leave was first introduced by the Trade Union Reform and Employment Rights Act 1993, implementing the Pregnant Workers Directive. At the outset the entitlement was restricted to fourteen weeks, but the ordinary maternity leave period was extended first to eighteen weeks by the Employment Relations Act

---

44 MPL etc. Regulations 1999, reg 19, as amended by the MPL (Amendment) Regulations 2002, reg 13.
45 PAL Regulations, reg 28.
46 This includes detriment by any act or by deliberate failure to act: MPL etc. Regulations, reg 19(1); PAL Regulations, reg 28(1).
47 For the detailed interpretation of these grounds, see the discussion of the parallel provisions concerning dismissal. As with dismissal, the protection for childbirth only applies where the detriment takes place during the employee's ordinary or additional maternity leave: reg 19(5).
48 Employment Rights Act 1996, s 48, as amended.
49 Employment Rights Act 1996, s 49, as amended.
50 Employment Rights Act 1996, s 71(4), as amended by the Employment Relations Act 1999, Sch 4.
51 Employment Rights Act 1996, s 71(5). Remuneration is defined for these purposes as 'sums payable to an employee by way of wages or salary': MPL etc. Regulations 1999, reg 9. On entitlement to pay during maternity leave, see p 423 below.

1999, and then to twenty-six weeks from April 2003[52]. Employees with at least twenty-six weeks' continuous service[53] have a right to a further twenty-six weeks of leave (termed 'additional maternity leave' to distinguish it from the shorter period of 'ordinary maternity leave') but for those who do not qualify for that right, and have no independent contractual right to maternity leave, the right to twenty-six weeks' ordinary maternity leave may be invaluable, particularly where the start of the ordinary maternity leave period can be delayed until just before childbirth, thereby allowing several months of leave after childbirth before having to return to work. The distinction between ordinary and additional maternity leave is important, because during ordinary maternity leave an employee has a statutory right to continue to benefit from all her normal terms and conditions of employment, except those providing for wages or salary[54] (unless, of course, she has a contractual right to receive wages or salary during maternity leave). This means that she is entitled to continue to benefit from any terms and conditions concerning, for example, the use of a company car or mobile phone, membership of clubs and societies, reimbursement of professional subscriptions and participation in employee share-ownership schemes. She is also entitled to any other benefits which would have accrued if she had been at work (for example holiday entitlement) as if she had been at work and not on maternity leave. The period of ordinary maternity leave counts towards her period of continuous employment for the purposes of qualifying for statutory employment rights, and because the contract continues throughout, the period also counts when assessing matters such as her seniority, pension rights and other similar rights which depend on length of service (for example contractual pay increments). In contrast, during additional maternity leave a woman is entitled to the benefit of a much narrower range of terms and conditions of employment, unless her contract provides otherwise. A woman who also enjoys a contractual right to ordinary maternity leave may not exercise the two rights separately, but may take advantage of whichever right is, in any particular respect, the more favourable[55]. An employee returning to work from an isolated period of ordinary maternity leave is entitled to return to the job in which she was employed before her absence[56], with her seniority, pension rights and similar rights as they would have been if she had not been absent, and on terms and conditions not less favourable than those which would have applied if she had not been absent[57]; if, however, her ordinary maternity leave was taken after another period of statutory leave (for example a period of additional maternity leave or additional adoption leave), and it is not reasonably practicable for the employer to permit her to return to her old job, she only has a right to return to another job which is both suitable for

52 MPL etc Regulations 1999, reg 7, as amended by MPL (Amendment) Regulations 2002, reg 8. The extended period applies to employees whose expected week of childbirth began on or after 6 April 2003.
53 The qualifying period for additional maternity leave was reduced from two years to one by the Employment Relations Act 1999, and then to 26 weeks by the MPL (Amendment) Regulations 2002.
54 MPL etc. Regulations 1999, reg 9, as substituted by the MPL (Amendment) Regulations 2002.
55 MPL etc. Regulations 1999, reg 21. This is commonly referred to as a 'composite' right. For the interpretation of this provision in relation to additional maternity leave, see p 416 below.
56 MPL etc. Regulations 1999, reg 18(1), as substituted by the MPL (Amendment) Regulations 2002; this is also the position if she returns to work after two or more consecutive periods of statutory leave which do not include any additional maternity or additional adoption leave, or parental leave of more than four weeks.
57 MPL etc Regulations 1999, reg 18A, as inserted by the MPL (Amendment) Regulations 2002.

her and appropriate for her to do in the circumstances[58]. This is to avoid a scenario where an employee who has taken, say, additional maternity leave followed by *another* period of ordinary maternity leave might be in a better position than an employee returning to work after additional maternity leave.

(i) Commencement and duration

Within certain limits, an employee is free to choose the date on which her ordinary maternity leave starts[59]. However, she cannot choose a start date earlier than the beginning of the eleventh week before the expected week of childbirth (EWC)[60], and her maternity leave period will be *automatically* triggered by any day on which she is absent from work wholly or partly because of pregnancy after the beginning of the fourth week before the EWC[61]. The thinking behind the latter provision is apparently to prevent a woman from delaying the start of her ordinary maternity leave until the last possible moment (thus ensuring the maximum amount of leave after childbirth) by taking sick leave instead of maternity leave, but it could have the unfortunate consequence of encouraging a woman to continue working during the latter stages of pregnancy, even though medically unfit to do so, in order to prevent her maternity leave period from being automatically triggered. While the impact of the automatic triggering provision has been ameliorated by the reduction of the relevant period from six weeks before the EWC to four, this still seems a strange way of giving effect to a Directive which is intended to protect the health and safety of pregnant women[62]. If childbirth occurs prematurely, the maternity leave period begins with the day following the day of childbirth[63], and the employer must be notified of the date of birth as soon as is reasonably practicable.

Ordinary maternity leave normally lasts for a maximum of 26 weeks, but provision is also made for two weeks' 'compulsory maternity leave'[64], beginning with the day of childbirth, and if the compulsory maternity leave period extends beyond the date on which ordinary maternity leave would have ended, the ordinary maternity leave period will be deemed to continue until the end of compulsory maternity leave[65]. The ordinary maternity leave period is also deemed to continue

---

58 MPL etc Regulations 1999, reg 18(2), as substituted by the MPL (Amendment) Regulations 2002.
59 Employment Rights Act 1996, s 71(3). MPL etc. Regulations 1999, reg 6, as amended by the MPL (Amendment) Regulations 2002.
60 MPL etc. Regulations 1999, reg 4(2)(b).
61 MPL etc. Regulations 1999, reg 6(1)(b), as amended by the MPL (Amendment) Regulations 2002, reducing the period within which the automatic triggering provisions operate from the sixth week before the EWC. Absence from work due to time off for ante-natal care does not count. 'Childbirth' is defined as 'the birth of a living child or the birth of a child whether living or dead after 24 weeks of pregnancy': reg 2; the same definition appears in the Employment Rights Act 1996, s 235(1).
62 The employer can of course choose to disregard days of pregnancy-related illness if the employee wishes to defer the start of her maternity leave period.
63 MPL etc. Regulations 1999, reg 6(2), as amended by the MPL (Amendment) Regulations 2002.
64 It is an offence under the Public Health Act 1936 to permit a woman to work in a factory within four weeks after the date of childbirth.
65 Employment Rights Act 1996, s 72 (as amended) and MPL etc. Regulations 1999, reg 8. The requirement is compulsory on *both* sides, and an employer who infringes the prohibition is liable on summary conviction to a fine not exceeding level 2 on the standard scale; there is no provision for any sanction on the employee in such a case.

beyond the normal twenty-six weeks where the employee is prohibited by law from working, by reason of having recently given birth[66]. The Act specifically provides for a right to return to work at the end of the ordinary maternity leave period, but such a provision is arguably unnecessary given that the contract of employment continues to exist throughout that period. An employee who wishes to return to work *before* the end of her ordinary maternity leave period may do so, on giving twenty-eight days' notice to the employer[67], although she must still observe the compulsory maternity leave period. Dismissal during the ordinary maternity leave period brings that period to an end[68]. Such a dismissal will normally be automatically unfair[69], as will a dismissal at the end of ordinary maternity leave (for example where the employee is not given her job back) although special provision is made for redundancy during ordinary maternity leave[70], in that where a redundancy situation arises during the employee's ordinary maternity leave which makes it impracticable for the employer to continue to employ her under her original contract of employment, she is entitled to be offered alternative employment with her employer (or with a successor, or an associated employer) where there is a suitable available vacancy. Failure to offer such a vacancy will make the redundancy dismissal automatically unfair[71].

(ii) Notice requirements

To take advantage of her right to ordinary maternity leave, the employee must satisfy certain notice requirements. These requirements, long criticised for their complexity, were simplified by the Employment Relations Act 1999 and the regulations issued thereunder, and further modified by the Maternity and Parental Leave (Amendment) Regulations 2002[72]. The employee is now required to notify her employer, at least fifteen weeks[73] before her expected week of childbirth (EWC)[74]: (i) that she is pregnant; (ii) when the expected week of childbirth will be; and (iii) the date on which she intends her ordinary maternity leave to start. If she gives birth before she has notified a date, or before the date she has notified, her maternity leave will start automatically on the day following the day of childbirth, and she must notify her employer as soon as is reasonably practicable (in writing, if so requested) that she has given birth, and of the date on which childbirth occurred[75]. Before the 2002 reforms, notification did not

---

66 MPL etc. Regulations 1999, reg 7(2).
67 MPL etc. Regulations 1999, reg 11, as amended by the MPL (Amendment) Regulations 2002. See p 415 below.
68 MPL etc. Regulations 1999, reg 7(5).
69 MPL etc. Regulations 1999, reg 20. See p 408 above.
70 MPL etc. Regulations 1999, reg 10. See p 408 above. Similar provisions apply to redundancy during additional maternity leave: see p 420 below.
71 MPL etc. Regulations 1999, reg 20(1)(b).
72 MPL etc. Regulations, reg 4, as amended by the MPL (Amendment) Regulations 2002.
73 To be precise, notification must be 'no later than the *end* of the 15th week before the EWC': para 4(1)(a), as amended.
74 Or, where this is not reasonably practicable, as soon as is reasonably practicable. Cf *Nu-Swift International Ltd v Mallinson* [1979] ICR 157, [1978] IRLR 537, decided under the old provisions, where it was suggested that a woman may only be allowed to use this exception if she did not know of the time limit and was not put on inquiry about it.
75 MPL etc. Regulations 1999, reg 4(4), as amended by the MPL (Amendment) Regulations 2002.

have to be given until twenty-one days before the date on which the employee intended her maternity leave to start, which in practice often gave employers very little opportunity to make alternative arrangements, such as recruiting a temporary replacement. Under the new rules, the employer will usually have more warning, particularly if the employee decides to delay the start of her maternity leave until closer to the expected date of childbirth. She is, however, allowed to vary the intended start-date, provided she does so at least twenty-eight days before the date varied, or twenty-eight days before the new date, whichever is the earlier (or, if this is not reasonably practicable, as soon as reasonably practicable thereafter)[76]. Notification does not have to be in writing, but the employer is entitled to ask for written notification of the intended start date of maternity leave, or of any subsequent variation of that date[77], and may demand to see a medical certificate verifying the expected week of childbirth[78]. One important new requirement is that an employer who has received notification of the intended start-date of maternity leave must respond by notifying the employee of the date on which her maternity leave (ordinary or additional, depending on her entitlement) will end[79]. Failure to do so will mean that the employee will be protected against detriment or dismissal if she fails to return to work on the due date[80]. There is no need for the employee to give notice to the employer of her intention to return to work – it is assumed that she will return on the date notified to her by the employer as the end of her ordinary maternity leave period – but if she wishes to return to work *earlier* than that date she may do so, on giving the employer twenty-eight days' notice of the date on which she intends to return[81]. If she attempts to return without giving the correct period of notice, the employer is entitled to postpone her return until twenty-eight days have elapsed (although not to a date after the end of the ordinary maternity leave period)[82], although the employer will be unable to prevent her from returning early if he has failed to notify her of the date on which her maternity leave period will end[83].

4 ADDITIONAL MATERNITY LEAVE

An employee who has at least twenty-six weeks' continuous employment with her employer at the beginning of the fourteenth week before the expected week of

---

76 MPL etc. Regulations 1999, reg 4(1)(a), as inserted by the MPL (Amendment) Regulations 2002.
77 MPL etc. Regulations 1999, reg 4(2), as amended by the MPL (Amendment) Regulations 2002.
78 MPL etc. Regulations 1999, reg 4(1)(b). There is no longer a requirement for an employee wishing to take additional maternity leave to inform the employer at this stage that she intends to exercise that right.
79 MPL etc. Regulations 1999, reg 7(6), as inserted by the MPL (Amendment) Regulations 2002. The notification must normally be given within 28 days of receiving the employee's notification: reg 7(7).
80 See pp 408 and 411 above.
81 MPL etc. Regulations 1999, reg 11(1), as amended by the MPL (Amendment) Regulations 2002. Under the pre-1999 provisions, only seven days' notice of the intended date of early return was required.
82 MPL etc. Regulations 1999, reg 11(2), (3), as amended by the MPL (Amendment) Regulations 2002. If the employer has postponed the employee's return, the employer is under no obligation to pay her if she still insists on returning before that date: reg 11(4).
83 MPL etc. Regulations 1999, reg 11(5), as inserted by the MPL (Amendment) Regulations 2002.

childbirth[84] is entitled to a period of additional maternity leave of up to twenty-six weeks from the end of ordinary maternity leave[85], after which she is entitled to return to the same job, on terms and conditions no less favourable than if she had not been absent from work[86]. This represents a major change over the pre-2003 position, when the additional leave period was twenty-nine weeks, but measured from the week of childbirth, which meant that each week of ordinary maternity leave taken after the week of childbirth was in effect subtracted from the entitlement to additional leave. Under the new entitlements, the combined ordinary and additional leave period will now be fifty-two weeks, irrespective of when the employee started her maternity leave; under the old regime, the combined leave was usually no more than 40 weeks, and often less if the employee delayed starting her ordinary leave beyond the eleventh week before the expected week of childbirth.

As with ordinary maternity leave, the statutory right to additional maternity leave may be supplemented by more generous contractual arrangements. Where this is the case, the employee may not exercise the two rights separately, but may take advantage of whichever right is in any particular respect the more favourable[87]. However, this is not necessarily as generous as it may seem, as under the pre-1999 provisions the EAT held in *Bovey v Board of Governors of the Hospital for Sick Children*[88] that it does not allow the employee licence to carve out bits of each scheme in order to put together the most advantageous amalgam possible. In that case the employee, employed as a full-time grade 1 physiotherapist before taking maternity leave, told the employers that she wanted to return on a part-time basis only; the employers agreed, provided she returned on a lower grade. She did so, but later claimed that she should be employed as a part-timer at the grade 1 level, on the basis that she could use the contractual agreement to return part-time, but then rely on the statutory provisions that her terms of employment should be no less favourable in order to remain at the grade 1 level. The EAT dismissed this claim, on the grounds (inter alia) that the employee could not subdivide an essentially indivisible contractual arrangement and simply take out that part which was most favourable to her. In exercising a composite right, the employee must still comply with the statutory requirements, modified to give effect to any more favourable terms in her contract[89].

(i) Qualification and notice requirements

In order to qualify for additional maternity leave, the employee must be entitled to ordinary maternity leave (see above), and she must have been continuously

---

84 Ie at least 40 weeks' continuous employment before the EWC: MPL etc. Regulations 1999, reg 5, as amended by the MPL (Amendment) Regulations 2002.
85 MPL etc. Regulations 1999, reg 7(4), as amended by the MPL (Amendment) Regulations 2002.
86 MPL etc. Regulations 1999, reg 18, as amended by the MPL (Amendment) Regulations 2002. Special rules apply where it is not reasonably practicable for her to return to her old job: see p 420 below.
87 MPL etc. Regulations 1999, reg 21(2). Some private contractual schemes are modelled for certain purposes on the state scheme, but here some care is needed, for if the state scheme is altered, that will not per se alter the private scheme, which must be changed independently by agreement and redrafting: CAC Award 82/7.
88 [1978] ICR 934, [1978] IRLR 241, EAT.
89 Note however the cases under the pre-1999 law where an employee was able to circumvent the statutory requirements altogether by claiming that her contract continued during her maternity absence: see eg *Lucas v Norton of London Ltd* [1984] 86, EAT.

employed[90] for at least twenty-six weeks at the beginning of the fourteenth week before the expected week of childbirth[91]. Under the pre-1999 provisions, if the employee did not continue to be employed up to the eleventh week before (for example if she resigned earlier in the pregnancy, or was dismissed), she lost her entitlement[92], although she did not have to be actually performing work up to that date as long as her contract still subsisted[93]. Premature resignation was therefore a major trap, being a sure way of losing the statutory right to return. The position appears to be the same under the redrafted provisions.

One of the most important changes in this area in recent years has been the relaxation of the notice requirements for additional maternity leave. It used to be the case that the employee had to inform her employer before her maternity leave commenced that she intended to return to work at the end of her maternity leave. Furthermore, the employer could write to her during her maternity leave seeking confirmation of her intention to return to work. Failure to comply with either requirement could seriously jeopardise the employee's position. Those requirements no longer apply, so that the employee will be entitled to additional maternity leave as long as she has satisfied the notice requirements for ordinary maternity leave (assuming, of course, that she has the necessary period of continuous employment). In fact, the only notification requirement under the present provisions is on the employer, who must notify the employee of the date on which her maternity leave will end[94]. The removal of the need to give notice of intention to return to work after maternity leave has helped to reduce the risk of employees losing their rights through failure to comply with technical notice requirements. That this was a very real danger under the old provisions was graphically demonstrated in *Nu-Swift International Ltd v Mallinson*[95] where the employee failed to give notice of her intention to return to work at the correct time because she could not make up her mind whether she wished to return to work or not. The EAT held that it had been reasonably practicable for her to give notice in time and therefore she had lost her right to return. Perhaps Mrs Mallinson was being too conscientious, for under the old provisions the employer had no recourse against an employee who gave notice saying that she intended to return to work but then changed her mind, or who gave notice while still undecided because she wanted to keep her options open. Indeed, pregnant employees were invariably advised to give notice that they intended to return to work, just as a matter of precaution. The removal of the need to give notice reflects the fact that, in practice, the giving and receiving of notice was an empty gesture which served only to trap the unwary or (as in Mrs Mallinson's case) the indecisive.

Another notification requirement that has been removed is the requirement to give the employer at least twenty-one days' written notice before returning to

90 See ch 3 above.
91 MPL etc. Regulations 1999, reg 5, as amended by the MPL (Amendment) Regulations 2002. Before the 1999 reforms, the qualifying period was two years; it was reduced to one year in 1999, and to 26 weeks in 2003.
92 *Mitchell v Royal British Legion Club* [1981] ICR 18, [1980] IRLR 425; *Williams & Co Ltd v Secretary of State for Employment* [1978] IRLR 235, IT. The tribunals were reluctant to interpret a statement by an employee that she did not intend to return to work as a resignation: *Hughes v Gwynedd Area Health Authority* [1978] ICR 161, [1977] IRLR 436.
93 *Satchwell Sunvic Ltd v Secretary of State for Employment* [1979] IRLR 455; *Secretary of State for Employment v Doulton Sanitaryware Ltd* [1981] ICR 477, [1981] IRLR 365, EAT.
94 MPL etc. Regulations 1999, reg 7(6), as inserted by the MPL (Amendment) Regulations 2002. The notification must normally be given within 28 days of receiving the employee's notification: reg 7(7).
95 [1979] ICR 157, [1978] IRLR 537.

work, which was repealed in 1999. This final technical hurdle was a major obstacle at which many women fell[96]. To make matters worse, the requirement to give notice was held to be an absolute one, which meant that a failure to give the required notice disentitled the employee from returning to work at all[97]. There is no such requirement under the present provisions. The assumption is that an employee who takes additional maternity leave will be returning to work on the date notified to her by the employer; she does not have to give notice of her intended date of return. As with ordinary maternity leave, she only need give notice to the employer to return to work if she wishes to return *before* the end of her additional maternity leave, in which case she must give at least twenty-eight days' notice of the date on which she intends to return[98]. If she attempts to return early without giving the correct period of notice, then, as with ordinary maternity leave, the employer may postpone her return until twenty-eight days' notice has been given, although not to a date later than the end of her additional maternity leave[99], and as before, the employer will be unable to prevent her from returning early if he has failed to notify her of the date on which her maternity leave period will end[100].

Under the pre-1999 provisions, the employer and the employee could postpone the return to work in certain circumstances: the employer could postpone the employee's return for up to four weeks, provided a reason was given for doing so and a new date for her return was specified; and the employee could postpone her return for up to four weeks where she was unable to return on the notified date due to illness, or where she was prevented from returning on that date because of an interruption of work due to industrial action or some other reason. There is no provision in the current regulations for either party to postpone the return to work. If an employee is unable to attend work at the end of additional maternity leave due to sickness, the normal sickness absence procedures under her contract of employment will apply. If the employer decides to dismiss her because of her inability to return to work, the employee will be able to claim that the dismissal was unfair on general principles, and if the employer responds more harshly to her sickness absence than he would to other employees in comparable circumstances, that could amount to sex discrimination.

(ii) Rights during and after additional maternity leave

The basic position is that an employee who is entitled to ordinary maternity leave and who has completed twenty-six weeks' continuous service by the beginning of the fourteenth week before the expected week of childbirth is entitled to a period of additional maternity leave which starts on the day after the last day of her ordinary maternity leave, and finishes at any time up to twenty-six weeks from the

---

96 The Court of Appeal held in *Crees v Royal London Mutual Insurance Society Ltd; Kwik Save Stores Ltd v Greaves* [1998] IRLR 245, that once the employee had give notice of her intended date of return, her right to return crystallised, even if she was then unable through illness to return on the notified date, but in *Halfpenny v IGE Medical Systems Ltd* [2001] IRLR 96, the House of Lords held that she also had to demonstrate that she was acting in accordance with her contract.

97 See eg *Lavery v Plessey Telecommunications Ltd* [1983] ICR 534, [1983] IRLR 202, CA.

98 MPL etc. Regulations 1999, reg 11(1), as amended by the MPL (Amendment) Regulations 2002.

99 MPL etc. Regulations 1999, reg 11(2), (3), as amended by the MPL (Amendment) Regulations 2002.

100 MPL etc. Regulations 1999, reg 11(5), as inserted by the MPL (Amendment) Regulations 2002.

day on which it started[101] (so that when taken together with ordinary maternity leave, the total period of absence will now be fifty-two weeks, irrespective of when the ordinary maternity leave period started). The employee's contract of employment continues during her additional leave period (unless either party expressly ends it, or it expires), but during that period she is entitled to the benefit of a much narrower range of terms and conditions of employment than she enjoyed during her ordinary maternity leave, unless her contract provides otherwise. In the absence of an agreement to the contrary, she is entitled during the additional maternity leave period to the benefit of her employer's implied obligation to her of trust and confidence, and any terms and conditions of her employment relating to notice of termination by the employer, redundancy compensation, or disciplinary or grievance procedures; concomitantly, she is bound during that period by her implied obligation to her employer of good faith, and any terms and conditions of her employment relating to notice of termination by her, disclosure of confidential information, the acceptance of gifts or other benefits, or her participation in any other business[102].

An employee who takes additional maternity leave is generally entitled to return to the job in which she was employed before her absence, on terms and conditions not less favourable than those which would have applied if she had not been absent from work, and with her seniority, pension rights and other similar length-of-service rights as they would have been if the period of employment before the start of her additional maternity leave and after her return to work were continuous[103]. The effect of the latter provision is that while her continuity of employment for statutory purposes continues to accrue during additional maternity leave[104], the period of additional leave does not count in the computation of non-statutory rights (in the absence of any contractual provision to the contrary), which could be significant, for example in the operation of a 'last in first out' redundancy procedure[105]. This contrasts with ordinary maternity leave, which does count for the purpose of assessing such rights.

The right to return to the same job does not necessarily mean that a woman is entitled to go back into exactly the same job as before. The definition of 'job' for these purposes as 'the nature of the work which she is employed to do in accordance with her contract and the capacity and place in which she is so employed[106] ' clearly implies that the employee does not have a right to return to exactly the same post doing exactly the same work in the same department or under the same person; it may be sufficient if the employer takes her on again in the same general kind of work, particularly if the work in question is subject to a

---

101 MPL etc. Regulations 1999, regs 5, 6(3) and 7(4), as amended by the MPL (Amendment) Regulations 2002. Where the employee is dismissed during additional maternity leave, the period ends at the time of the dismissal. Such a dismissal will normally be automatically unfair: see p 408.

102 MPL etc. Regulations 1999, reg 17.

103 MPL etc. Regulations 1999, reg 18A(1), as inserted by the MPL (Amendment) Regulations 2002.

104 Under the old provisions there was an express provision to this effect in s 212(2), but it was repealed by the 1999 Act because the contract of employment now continues through additional maternity leave in every case.

105 Note, however, the Social Security Act 1989, Sch 5, para 5, implementing Directive 86/378/EC on equal treatment in occupational social security schemes, which requires credit to be given for the period of paid maternity absence for the purposes of employment-related benefit schemes. These provisions were adopted by the Pensions Act 1995, s 63(3): see p 359 above.

106 MPL etc. Regulations 1999, reg 2.

comprehensive grading scheme with the employee being taken back at the same grade, and in such a case there may be certain necessary administrative changes in the organisation of the woman's work which she must accept and which are too minor to be capable of altering the nature of the job[107]. On the other hand, the tribunal will look at her overall position after maternity leave, and if for example there are any new and less favourable terms in her employment (for example affecting the security of her job) this may mean that the employer has not complied with his duty to allow her to return to the same job[108], even if in other respects her terms and conditions and the grade on which she is employed remain the same.

An employee who is not permitted to return to her old job at the end of additional maternity leave will normally be regarded as unfairly dismissed. However, the right to return is not absolute, for there are four situations in which the employee will not be entitled to return to her old job. The first is where there is some reason (other than redundancy) which makes it not reasonably practicable for the employer to permit her to return to her original job. In such a case, her entitlement is to return to another job which is both suitable for her and appropriate for her to do in the circumstances[109], and on terms and conditions no less favourable to her than if she had continued to be employed in her old job. Secondly, as with ordinary maternity leave, special provision is made for redundancy during additional maternity leave, in that where a redundancy situation arises during the employee's additional maternity leave which makes it impracticable for the employer to continue to employ her under her original contract of employment, the employee is entitled to be offered alternative employment with her employer (or with a successor, or an associated employer) where there is a suitable available vacancy[110]. Failure to offer such a vacancy will make the redundancy dismissal automatically unfair[111]. Thirdly, if it is not reasonably practicable for the employee to return to her old job, or to be offered a suitable alternative job, and the employer is a small employer employing no more than five people, the employee will not be regarded as unfairly dismissed if she is not permitted to return to work at the end of her additional maternity leave[112]. Finally, it is not unlawful for an employer to dismiss an employee during or after the end of maternity leave for a reason other than the fact that she has taken or availed herself of the benefits of maternity leave (or any of the other family reasons for which a dismissal will be automatically unfair[113]), unless of course the dismissal is unfair for some other reason. In all the above cases, however, the employer will need to take great care to ensure that there is no discrimination on grounds of sex or marital status (see below).

One of the most significant changes to the provisions on additional maternity leave in the Employment Relations Act 1999 was that it was made clear that the contract of employment continues throughout additional maternity leave. Under the old provisions, the right to return to work after maternity leave operated independently of the contract of employment. In most cases, it did not matter whether the employee's contract continued to exist during maternity absence: the statute gave her a right to return to work, irrespective of the status of her

107 *Edgell v Lloyd's Register of Shipping* [1977] IRLR 463, IT.
108 *McFadden v Greater Glasgow Passenger Transport Executive* [1977] IRLR 327, IT.
109 MPL etc. Regulations 1999, reg 18(2).
110 MPL etc. Regulations 1999, reg 10. See p 408 above.
111 MPL etc. Regulations 1999, reg 20(1)(b).
112 MPL etc. Regulations 1999, reg 20(6). See p 409 above.
113 See p 408 above.

contract during maternity absence, provided she complied with the complex statutory notice requirements. If she was denied her right to return to work, whether by a total refusal to take her back or by being taken back on disadvantageous terms, she was *deemed* to have been dismissed on the 'notified date of return' (ie the date on which she intended to return to work). The provisions worked tolerably well where the employee complied to the letter with all the notice requirements, and was physically able to return to work on the notified date, but serious difficulties arose for the employee if she was not able to satisfy those requirements, in that she lost her statutory right to return (a problem exacerbated by the lack of any saving provision whereby minor or technical defaults could be overlooked). The problems were graphically illustrated by *Lavery v Plessey Telecommunications Ltd*[114] where the giving of five days' notice of intention to return (instead of the seven days then required) robbed the employee of her right to return, even though if she had understood the requirement she could in fact have given the required seven days' notice easily. The case contains strong criticism of the statutory provisions at that time, which were described as being 'of inordinate complexity exceeding the worst excesses of a taxing statute'[115]. Happily, that type of problem should no longer arise, as the employee's contract continues throughout maternity leave.

Three further general points should be noted. The first point is that an employer (particularly in a small business) may need to take on a replacement to take the place of an employee on maternity leave. Such an employer is given qualified protection by section 106 which provides that if the employer informs the replacement in writing at the time of engagement that his or her employment will cease when the original employee returns to work, and then dismisses him or her in order to take that original employee back, that will constitute half a defence to an allegation of unfair dismissal in that it is deemed to be a substantial reason capable of justifying dismissal (within section 98), but the tribunal must still proceed to consider whether he acted reasonably in all the circumstances in actually dismissing the replacement, which may be difficult if there was a vacancy available elsewhere that the replacement might readily have filled. This provision was less important while the qualifying period for unfair dismissal was two years, as it was unlikely that a replacement would work for long enough to qualify to bring an unfair dismissal claim, but now that the qualifying period has been reduced to one year, and the combined ordinary and additional maternity leave period has been increased to one year, it assumes a much greater practical significance.

The second general point is that one major perceived deficiency of the statutory right to return is that it does not give a woman the right to return to work on *different* terms and conditions (for example on a part-time basis or with flexible working hours), yet for many women this may be the only way of reconciling the competing demands of work and family responsibilities, especially in view of the limited availability of affordable child care in certain areas. However, the Employment Act 2002 has given a woman returning to work after maternity leave the right to request flexible working[116], and it is possible that the return-to-work provisions could be outflanked by the argument that a refusal to allow a woman previously in

---

114 [1983] ICR 534, [1983] IRLR 202, CA.
115 Per Browne-Wilkinson J, [1982] IRLR 180 at 182, EAT. His remarks were endorsed by the Court of Appeal, [1983] ICR 534, [1983] IRLR 202, CA.
116 See p 437.

full-time employment to return to work part-time is indirect sex discrimination. This is what happened in *Home Office v Holmes*[117] where the woman used the return-to-work provisions to return full-time, but also claimed that the requirement to continue working full-time constituted unjustifiable indirect sex discrimination (in that compliance with it was particularly difficult for women with children). This argument succeeded in the case, which was widely reported in the press and said by the EOC to be a significant development. However, it does not stretch the imagination to suppose that there could be many circumstances in which a requirement to work full-time might be held to be justifiable[118] in economic terms, and the EAT's decision was based very much upon the facts of the particular case[119], as can be seen from the subsequent case of *Greater Glasgow Health Board v Carey*[120], where on similar facts it was held that the employer's refusal to allow a full-time health visitor to return on a part-time basis was indirectly discriminatory but was justified by the need for continuity of care by the same visitor.

The third general point is that in certain sectors (particularly local government, banks, computer companies, the retail sector and oil companies) there have been significant moves towards allowing women employees to take far more substantial 'career breaks' in order to have a family – breaks of anything up to seven years are mentioned, and with the possibility of attending several days' training per year during the break in order to maintain contact with colleagues and keep up with changes. For present purposes the main point to notice is that any such scheme can come about only by agreement and as a matter of contract; such breaks are not provided for in the statutory maternity leave scheme. Employers' schemes which improve upon the statutory entitlement can have a sting in the tail, however, particularly where they involve a lengthy career break, because the effect of the career break may be to break her continuity of employment, with potential disastrous consequences for her employment rights. This issue arose for consideration in *Curr v Marks & Spencer plc*[121] where the employee was accepted onto a four-year child break scheme, a condition of which was that she resigned from the company. At the end of the break she returned to work, but was subsequently made redundant. She claimed a redundancy payment covering all her years of service, both before and after the career break, but the employers argued that she was only entitled to count the period since her return from the child break. The Court of Appeal held that the terms of the career break did not constitute a contract of employment, so that her continuity was not preserved on the basis that her contract continued throughout, but neither could she claim that continuity was preserved under section 212(3)(c) of the Employment Rights Act 1996[122] because the employer did not regard her as continuing in

---

117 [1984] ICR 678, [1984] IRLR 299.
118 See p 293 above.
119 It is important these days not to be too sanguine about cases as precedents; at its most basic, all that the EAT were doing was to say that in this case the tribunal were not manifestly wrong in holding that the requirement to work full time was (a) discriminatory and (b) unjustifiable on the facts before them.
120 [1987] IRLR 484. In coming to this conclusion, the EAT applied the obiter remarks in *Rainey v Greater Glasgow Health Board Eastern District* [1987] ICR 129, [1987] IRLR 26, HL that administrative efficiency, if sufficiently demonstrated, may be an important factor in the justification defence under the Sex Discrimination Act 1975, s 1(1)(b)(ii); see above.
121 [2002] EWCA Civ 1852, [2003] ICR 443.
122 Ie that there was an 'arrangement' by which she was absent from work in circumstances such that she was regarded as continuing in employment: see p 196.

employment during the child break (an odd conclusion, it must be said, given that the employee maintained contact with the employer during the break, including returning to work for two weeks each year, but reached on the basis that the terms of the career break agreement were quite unlike a contract of employment). The upshot was that Mrs Curr paid a heavy financial penalty for her career break, and the lesson for an employee is to be very cautious about the effect of a career break on her contract of employment, and on her continuity of employment.

5 STATUTORY MATERNITY PAY

A pregnant employee who meets certain qualifying conditions based on her length of service and average earnings is entitled to receive statutory maternity pay (SMP) from her employer for up to twenty-six weeks, the first six weeks at nine-tenths of the employee's normal pay, and the remaining twenty weeks at a flat rate. The employer, in turn, is entitled to recover most of the amount paid out as SMP from the state, by deducting it from PAYE and National Insurance contributions. In effect, therefore, SMP can be seen as a state maternity benefit which is administered via employers. To understand how this convoluted state of affairs has come about, it is necessary to delve a little into the history of the current provisions.

Until April 1987 a pregnant employee leaving work to have a baby would normally qualify for the state maternity allowance, but on top of that she could qualify (if she had at least two years' service) for maternity pay from her employer; this latter was payable for the first six weeks of absence, at nine-tenths of her week's pay (less the amount of the maternity allowance and any remuneration paid by the employer under a contractual maternity scheme), and was payable whether or not the employee wished to return to work after her maternity absence, ie it was not dependent upon continuation in some form of the employment relationship. From the point of view of drafting this position was neat since the principal conditions for entitlement were the same as for maternity leave, so that the two major rights went hand in hand. However, the system was viewed as wasteful by the government since it involved duplication of administrative effort by the State and the employer, and as the whole amount paid out as maternity pay could be recouped from the State-run Maternity Pay Fund, the employer was in reality simply performing a social security role.

The whole system was reformed in 1987 in order to require the employer to make all the payments, by the introduction of statutory maternity pay (SMP), payable at two levels depending on length of service, but with the employer able to recover the amount paid out by deducting it from National Insurance contributions; the obvious model was statutory sick pay[123], introduced by the government four years earlier for the same reasons of rationalisation and administrative ease (for the government, that is, not for employers). The structure of the SMP scheme was very different from what had gone before, but the end result as far as most employees were concerned was very similar to the pre-1987 position, in that SMP was payable for up to eighteen weeks at a lower rate (in effect replacing the state maternity allowance), but an employee with two years' continuous service

123 See p 220 above.

was entitled to SMP at a higher rate of nine-tenths of her normal weekly earnings for the first six weeks (corresponding to the old maternity pay scheme).

The SMP scheme was subject to major reforms in 1994 to bring it into line with the requirements of EC Directive 92/85 (the Pregnant Workers Directive), which provides for a minimum entitlement of fourteen weeks' paid maternity leave for all pregnant employees[124], during which a woman is entitled to be paid an amount equivalent to the amount of state benefit she would receive if she were absent from work due to sickness. The Directive was implemented in the UK by equalising lower rate SMP with statutory sick pay, and granting all those entitled to SMP the right to receive it at the higher rate for the first six weeks. To meet the additional cost to the state of this enhanced entitlement, the amount of SMP which employers were able to recover was reduced to 92%[125], albeit with special help for small employers[126], who are still able to recover the full amount[127]. When the ordinary maternity leave period was increased from eighteen to twenty-six weeks in 2003, the length of the SMP entitlement was similarly increased to bring it into line, and the notice requirements and qualifying periods for maternity leave and SMP were harmonised. The SMP provisions are currently to be found in Part XII of the Social Security Contributions and Benefits Act 1992, and the flesh is added to the bones by several sets of regulations[128].

(i) Qualification[129]

To qualify at all, the employee must satisfy a number of complex conditions: (i) her earnings must have been at or above the lower earnings limit for the payment of National Insurance contributions (set at £77 per week for the tax year 2003/04)[130]; (ii) she must have been employed by that employer[131] for a continuous period of at least twenty-six weeks ending with the week immediately preceding the fourteenth week before the expected week of childbirth[132]; (iii) she must give the employer medical evidence of the expected week of childbirth[133], and at least

---

124 The Directive permits entitlement to pay during the maternity leave period to be made conditional on periods of previous employment of up to 12 months before the expected date of childbirth.
125 Statutory Maternity Pay (Compensation of Employers) and Miscellaneous Amendment Regulations 1994, SI 1994/1882, amended by SI 2003/672.
126 Ie those whose National Insurance liability does not exceed £40,000 for the qualifying tax year. Some small employers may now be able to claim funding in advance.
127 Small employers are also entitled to recover an additional 4.5% of the SMP paid, to compensate for other costs: SI 2002/225 (amending SI 1994/1882).
128 Principally the Statutory Maternity Pay (General) Regulations 1986, SI 1986/1960, as amended. Practical guidance is given in some detail (with worked examples) in the Employer's Guide to Statutory Maternity Pay (NI 257, DSS).
129 Social Security Contributions and Benefits Act 1992, s 164, as amended by the Employment Act 2002, s 20.
130 The EAT has held that the application of the lower earnings limit as a qualifying condition for SMP is not contrary to Art 141 (ex 119) of the EC Treaty or the Pregnant Workers Directive: *Banks v Tesco Stores Ltd* [1999] ICR 1141, EAT.
131 A woman may not count her previous employment with another employer for these purposes; in this respect the system differs from that applying to statutory sick pay.
132 Compare the position with the right to additional maternity leave, where she must have 26 weeks' continuous employment at the beginning of the fourteenth week before the expected week of childbirth. The two dates are in fact the same, but expressed differently.
133 This should be given not more than 20 weeks before the expected week of childbirth. The employer cannot start paying SMP until the certificate has been received.

twenty-eight days' notice of the date on which she expects his liability to pay SMP to begin (ie the date on which she expects to start her ordinary maternity leave); (iv) she must have reached the eleventh week before the expected week of childbirth, or have recently given birth (although she does not need to remain in employment beyond the qualifying week); and (v) she must have stopped work.

(ii) The right to payment

If she can satisfy these conditions, the employee qualifies for SMP at the higher, earnings-related rate for six weeks, and thereafter at the lower rate for the remainder of the maternity pay period, subject to an overall maximum of twenty-six weeks. Once entitlement to SMP is established in the qualifying week, the employee is entitled to receive her full entitlement to twenty-six weeks' SMP, even if she leaves the employer's employment before her SMP was due to start. Alternatively, she may continue working right up to the date of childbirth, and still retain her full entitlement to twenty-six weeks' SMP. The lower rate of SMP is fixed by regulations (at the time of writing, it stands at £100pw[134]). The higher rate of SMP is set at nine-tenths of her week's pay (averaged, if necessary, over the eight weeks prior to the fourteenth week before the expected week of childbirth[135]). Payments of SMP must be offset against any contractual payments for the weeks in question (for example under a contractual maternity scheme) and vice versa. Under the pre-1994 provisions, an employee lost a week of her SMP entitlement for each week that she continued to work beyond the sixth week before the expected week of childbirth, but this rule no longer applies, and the maternity pay period will normally begin when the ordinary maternity leave period starts, and run contemporaneously with it for twenty-six weeks. However, to ensure consistency with the maternity leave provisions, the maternity pay period is automatically triggered where a woman is absent from work wholly or partly because of pregnancy or childbirth after the fourth week before. The SMP period usually lasts for the full twenty-six weeks, but it is not payable for any week in which the employee does any work for her employer, and if she starts work for a new employer after childbirth, the entitlement to SMP stops completely.

An employee who does not qualify for SMP but who earns at least £30 per week on average[136] may be entitled to claim the state Maternity Allowance from the Benefits Agency.

---

134 Statutory Maternity Pay (General) Regulations 1986, SI 1986/1960, reg 6 (as amended with effect from April 2003). If her earnings related rate is *less* than the prescribed weekly rate, she will receive the lower of the two rates for the remaining 20 weeks.

135 Social Security Contributions and Benefits Act 1992, s 166, as substituted by the Employment Act 2002, s 19. If the employer subsequently grants a back-dated pay rise which affects that eight-week period, her earnings must be recalculated taking into account the arrears: SI 1996/1335 (implementing *Gillespie*; see p 443 below). Quaere whether pay rises taking effect *after* the eight-week referencing period must also be taken into account in calculating earnings-related SMP: see *Alabaster v Woolwich plc* [2002] IRLR 420, where the Court of Appeal referred that question to the ECJ.

136 This applies to a woman whose expected date of childbirth falls on or after 20 August 2000. Before that date, entitlement to maternity allowance was conditional on earnings reaching the lower earnings level for NI contributions.

6 RISK ASSESSMENT AND SUSPENSION FROM WORK ON MATERNITY GROUNDS

All employers have a duty under the Management of Health and Safety at Work (MHSW) Regulations 1999 to assess the risks to health and safety to which their employees are exposed whilst they are at work[137]. In addition, as a result of an amendment to the MHSW Regulations in 1994 (implementing the Pregnant Workers Directive[138]) employers of women of child-bearing age have a specific duty to carry out a further risk assessment where the work is of a kind which could involve a risk to the health and safety of a new or expectant mother[139], or to that of her baby, from any processes or working conditions, or from physical, biological or chemical agents[140]. Where that risk assessment identifies a risk to the health and safety of a new or expectant mother or her baby, the employer is under a duty in the first instance to take action to prevent her from being exposed to the risk by following the requirements of any relevant health and safety regulations (for example by removing the hazard or by providing protective clothing). If the risk cannot be avoided by such means, and it is not reasonable for the employer to alter the employee's working conditions or hours of work, or such an alteration would not avoid the risk, the employer must remove the employee from the risk by suspending her from work for as long as is necessary to avoid the risk[141]. An employer must also suspend an employee from work on maternity grounds where the employee is a new or expectant mother who works at night, and she has a certificate from a registered medical practitioner or registered midwife which shows that it is necessary for her health and safety that she should not be at work for any period of night work identified in the certificate[142].

Under the MHSW Regulations, the duty to take action by altering working conditions or hours of work, or by suspending an employee from work, does not arise until the employee has notified the employer in writing that she is pregnant, has given birth within the preceding six months or is breast-feeding[143], although even in the absence of written notification of pregnancy, an employer who fails to take reasonable action to protect an employee who is known to be pregnant or breast-feeding might well be in breach of the general duty to protect the health and safety of his employees. The duty to conduct a pregnancy risk assessment in the first place is triggered whenever the employer employs a woman of child-bearing age, and does not depend upon there being an employee who is pregnant[144].

137 SI 1999/3242, reg 3. The MHSW Regulations are discussed at p 889 below.
138 Directive 92/85/EC.
139 Defined as employees who are pregnant, have given birth within the preceding six months or are breastfeeding.
140 MHSW Regulations, reg 16(1). These are said to include the list of agents set out in Annexes I and II of the Pregnant Workers Directive.
141 MHSW Regulations, reg 16(2), (3).
142 MHSW Regulations, reg 17.
143 MHSW Regulations, reg 18. If the employee has given the employer a medical certificate which arguably indicates that she is pregnant, but without expressly stating that fact, the burden may pass to the employer to show that there was no notification: *Day v T Pickles Farms Ltd* [1999] IRLR 217, EAT.
144 *Day v T Pickles Farms Ltd* above. That case also established that an employer's failure to carry out such a risk assessment may amount to sex discrimination if a new or expectant mother can show that she has suffered a detriment. See also *Hardman v Mallon t/a Orchard Lodge Nursing Home* [2002] IRLR 516, EAT; see p 250 below.

The employer's duty under the MHSW Regulations is mirrored by a series of rights enjoyed by employees suspended from work on maternity grounds[145]. These rights were introduced by the Trade Union Reform and Employment Rights Act 1993, implementing the Pregnant Workers Directive[146]. First, before being suspended from work on maternity grounds, an employee has the right to be offered suitable alternative employment by her employer where there is an available vacancy[147], with a right to complain to a tribunal if the employer fails to make such an offer[148]. The work must be suitable in relation to the employee, appropriate for her to do in the circumstances, and on terms and conditions which are not substantially less favourable than those under which she normally works[149]. Secondly, an employee who is suspended from work on maternity grounds has the right to be paid her normal remuneration by her employer during the period of suspension, unless she has unreasonably refused an offer of suitable alternative work for the period in question, in which case no remuneration is payable for the period during which the offer applies[150]; once again, there is a right of complaint to a tribunal that the employer has failed to pay the amount due[151], and where the tribunal finds the complaint well-founded it will order the employer to pay the unpaid remuneration to the employee.

7 TIME OFF FOR ANTE-NATAL CARE

A pregnant employee has a right not to be unreasonably refused time off during working hours to attend ante-natal care on the advice of a registered medical practitioner, registered midwife or registered health visitor[152], irrespective of her length of service. After the first visit, the employer may require the employee to produce a certificate from the doctor, midwife or health visitor confirming that she is pregnant, and an appointment card or other document showing that an appointment has been made[153], but for obvious reasons this is not necessary for the first visit. Ante-natal care is not defined in the Act, but it can include relaxation and parentcraft classes, as well as medical examinations, provided of course that the attendance is on the advice of a doctor, midwife or health visitor. The right to

---

145 See now the Employment Rights Act 1996, ss 66–68. Suspension must be in consequence of a 'relevant requirement' or a recommendation in a Code of Practice issued or approved by the Health and Safety Commission under s 16 of the Health and Safety at Work etc. Act 1974: s 66(1). The Suspension from Work (on Maternity Grounds) Order, SI 1994/2930, specifies reg 17 of the MHSW Regulations as a relevant requirement for these purposes. Cf also the Suspension from Work on Maternity Grounds (Merchant Shipping and Fishing Vessels) Order, SI 1998/587.

146 Directive 92/85/EC. See p 404 above.

147 Employment Rights Act 1996, s 67(1).

148 Employment Rights Act 1996, s 70(4). The right of complaint is subject to the usual three-month time limit, calculated from the first day of suspension: s 70(5); where the tribunal upholds the complaint it may make an award of compensation: s 70(6).

149 See *British Airways (European Operations at Gatwick) Ltd v Moore and Botterill* [2000] ICR 678, [2000] IRLR 296, EAT, where an offer of ground work to two pregnant cabin crew workers failed the test because it did not include the flying allowances which they received while working as cabin crew.

150 Employment Rights Act 1996, s 68.

151 The time limit here is three months (or a further reasonable period where not reasonably practicable) from the day in respect of which the remuneration was not paid: s 70(2).

152 Employment Rights Act 1996, s 55.

153 Employment Rights Act 1996, s 55(2).

time off is not absolute: the Act states that an employee has the right not to be *unreasonably* refused time off, which implies that there may be circumstances where it would be reasonable for the employer to refuse time off; for example it might be reasonable for an employer to refuse time off to a part-time worker who could reasonably be expected to arrange her ante-natal care outside her working hours.

The employee is entitled to be paid at her normal rate of pay during the period of time off[154]. Complaint of unreasonable refusal to give time off, or of failure to pay wages during time off may be made to a tribunal within three months of the day of the appointment concerned (or within a further reasonable period if the tribunal accepts that it was not reasonably practicable for the complaint to be presented within the three-month period)[155].

8 PATERNITY LEAVE AND PAY

While entitlement to maternity leave is now well established, until recently there was no entitlement for fathers to take paternity leave in order to care for the child or support the child's mother in the weeks after childbirth. In the absence of any contractual entitlement to paternity leave, the only option for fathers who wanted some time at home following the birth of a child was to use whatever holiday entitlement they had, or to take parental leave, which is unpaid. The introduction of a right to paid paternity leave was one of a range of possible reforms floated in the government's review of working arrangements for parents[156], and it received a very positive response; the new right was duly introduced by the Employment Act 2002. The entitlements are modest – only two weeks' paid leave, to be taken within eight weeks of childbirth, at a flat rate of only £100 per week – but the provisions are nevertheless significant, as they are the first legal recognition of the fact that fathers have responsibilities around the time of childbirth that are capable of overriding the needs of employers. Paternity leave is also available to employees following the adoption of a child, although here the adoptive parents may be able to choose which parent takes paternity leave and which takes adoption leave.

(i) Qualification and notice requirements

In order to qualify for paternity leave in relation to the birth of a child, an employee must: (i) have been continuously employed for at least twenty-six weeks at the 15th week before the expected week of childbirth[157]; (ii) be either the child's biological father or the mother's husband or partner; and (iii) have, or expect to have, responsibility for the child's upbringing[158]. The notice requirements are similar to those applying to maternity leave: the employee must inform his

154 Employment Rights Act 1996, s 56. See *Gregory v Tudsbury Ltd* [1982] IRLR 267, IT. The amount of pay will usually be calculated by dividing her week's pay by the number of normal working hours in a week.

155 Employment Rights Act 1996, s 57. Dismissal or redundancy selection for taking time off for ante-natal care is likely to be automatically unfair under s 99: see p 408 above.

156 *Work and Parents: Competitiveness and Choice* (DTI, December 2000).

157 Special provision is made for cases where the child is born prematurely before the 14th week before the expected week of childbirth: PAL Regulations, reg 4(3).

158 PAL Regulations, reg 4(2). An employee who is the mother's husband or partner but not the child's father must have 'the main responsibility (apart from any responsibility of the mother) for the upbringing of the child'.

employer (in writing, if the employer so requests) of his intention to take paternity leave by the fifteenth week before the expected week of childbirth, unless this is not reasonably practicable, and must tell the employer (i) the expected week of the child's birth; (ii) the amount of leave which the employee wishes to take (see below); and (iii) the date on which he wants his leave to start[159]. After the child is born, he must notify the employer, as soon as reasonably practicable, of the date of childbirth[160]. An employer who wants some evidence of the employee's entitlement to paternity leave is entitled to ask for a signed declaration from the employee (in effect, a self certificate) that the leave is for the purpose of caring for a child or supporting its mother, and that he meets the eligibility criteria[161], but the employer is not entitled to ask for any further evidence of entitlement.

There are parallel provisions for paternity leave in relation to adoption, in which case the employee must: (i) have been continuously employed for at least twenty-six weeks ending with the week in which notice is given of having been matched with a child[162]; (ii) be either married to or the partner of the child's adopter; and (iii) have, or expect to have, the main responsibility (apart from the responsibility of the adopter) for the child's upbringing[163]. As with paternity leave at the time of childbirth, the employee must inform the employer that he intends to take paternity leave, in this case no later than seven days after notification of being matched with a child, unless this is not reasonably practicable, and the notice must specify (i) the date of notification of being matched with a child; (ii) the date on which the child is expected to be placed with the adopter; (iii) the length of the leave period which the employee wishes to take; and (iv) the date on which he wants his leave to start[164]. The employer can also require the employee to self-certify that the leave is for the purpose of caring for a child or supporting its adopter, and that he meets the eligibility criteria[165].

(ii) Extent of the entitlement

An employee who satisfies the eligibility criteria and notice requirements set out above can choose to take either one week or two consecutive weeks of paternity leave. There is no option to take odd days, or even two separate weeks, and unlike parental leave (where there is an entitlement for each child) only one period of paternity leave can be claimed in the event of a multiple pregnancy. The employee can choose to start his leave on the date of the child's birth (whenever that occurs), or on a date which is a chosen number of days or weeks after the child's birth, or on a predetermined date[166], but the leave must be taken within fifty-six days of the

---

159 PAL Regulations, reg 6. The employee can vary the chosen start-date by giving the employer notice at least 28 days in advance, unless this is not reasonably practicable: reg 6(4).
160 PAL Regulations, reg 6(7).
161 PAL Regulations, reg 6(3).
162 This requires notification to the adopter of a match with a child by an approved adoption agency: PAl Regulations, reg 2(4).
163 PAL Regulations, reg 8(2).
164 PAL Regulations, reg 10.
165 PAL Regulations, reg 10(3).
166 If the employee chooses a predetermined date and the child has not yet been born at that date, he must choose another date and notify the employer as soon as reasonably practicable: PAL Regulations, reg 6(6).

date of childbirth[167]. Similar rules apply where paternity leave is claimed in connection with adoption, except that the timings run from the date on which the child is placed for adoption[168]. During statutory paternity leave, most employees will be entitled to receive Statutory Paternity Pay (SPP) from their employer, for either one or two weeks, depending on the length of paternity leave chosen[169]. This is fixed at the same rate as standard-rate SMP, ie £100 per week, or 90% of average weekly earnings if this is less than £100. Any paternity pay received under the employee's contract during paternity leave will be offset against the statutory entitlement, and vice versa[170]. Employees whose average weekly earnings are below the Lower Earnings Limit for National Insurance purposes[171] will not qualify for SPP, but may be able to claim Income Support while on paternity leave. As seen above, in the case of adoption the adoptive parents can elect whether to take paternity leave or adoption leave, but for obvious reasons a parent who has elected to receive statutory adoption pay cannot receive SPP.

During paternity leave a man is in a similar position as regards contractual entitlements as a woman on ordinary maternity leave, in that (unless his contract provides otherwise) he will be entitled to the benefit of all his normal terms and conditions of employment, except for terms relating to wages or salary[172]. The similarity with ordinary maternity leave continues after the end of paternity leave, in that an employee returning to work after a period of paternity leave is entitled to return to the job in which he was employed before his absence[173], with his seniority, pension rights etc as they would have been if he had not been absent, and on terms and conditions no less favourable than those which would have applied if he had not been absent[174]. An employee taking paternity leave is also protected against dismissal or detriment for taking or seeking to take paternity leave.[175]

9 ADOPTION LEAVE AND PAY

The introduction of adoption leave was another of the reforms introduced by the Employment Act 2002 after the idea received strong support in the review of maternity rights[176]. The entitlements mirror those of a woman to ordinary and additional maternity leave, ie twenty-six weeks' paid ordinary adoption leave and a further twenty-six weeks' unpaid additional adoption leave for an adoptive

---

167 PAL Regulations, reg 5. If the child is born prematurely, leave can be taken within 56 days of the beginning of the expected week of childbirth. Where the employee has chosen the date on which leave is to begin, the notice to the employer must specify that date: PAL Regulations, reg 6(1)(c).
168 PAL Regulations reg 9.
169 Social Security Contributions and Benefits Act 1992, s 171ZA, as inserted by the Employment Act 2002. Employers can recover SPP in the same way as they can recover SMP, ie 92% of the amount paid out, or more if eligible for small employer's relief.
170 Social Security Contributions and Benefits Act 1992, s 171ZG.
171 Ie £77 per week from April 2003.
172 PAL Regulations, reg 12.
173 PAL Regulations, reg 13. As with ordinary maternity leave, the position may be different if the paternity leave is not an isolated period of leave, but follows another period of statutory leave: see p 412.
174 PAL Regulations, reg 14.
175 PAL Regulations, reg 28, 29; see p 408.
176 DTI *Work and Parents: Competitiveness and Choice* (December 2000).

parent when a child is newly placed for adoption[177]; there are however some significant differences, particularly in relation to qualification and entitlement to pay during adoption leave. The leave can be taken by an individual person who adopts, or by one member of a couple who adopt jointly. In the latter case the couple may elect which partner takes adoption leave[178]; the other partner may be eligible for paternity leave. To be eligible for adoption leave, an employee must be the child's adopter (ie he or she must have been matched with a child for adoption by an approved adoption agency), and must have been continuously employed by the employer for at least twenty-six weeks ending with the week in which the employee receives notification of having been matched with a child[179]. Unlike maternity leave, the twenty-six week qualifying period applies both to ordinary and additional adoption leave. The adopter can choose to start ordinary adoption leave from the date of the child's placement, or from a predetermined date up to fourteen days in advance of the expected date of placement[180]. As in the case of maternity leave, the adopter must notify the employer that he or she intends to take adoption leave, and the requirement is a tight one – notice must be given within seven days of being notified by the adoption agency that they have been matched with a child, although this limit can be extended if it was not reasonably practicable for the employee to comply. The notice must specify the date when the child is expected to be placed with the adopter, and when the adopter wishes the adoption leave to start[181]. The employer can also ask for evidence of the employee's entitlement to adoption leave, in the form of a 'matching certificate' issued by the adoption agency[182], but the employee will need to provide this in any event in order to claim Statutory Adoption Pay. Once the employer has received notification of the intended start-date, the employer must respond within twenty-eight days by writing to the employee setting out the date on which the adoption leave will end (assuming that the employee takes advantage of the full entitlement)[183]. If the employer fails to do so, the employee will be protected against detriment or dismissal if he or she fails to return to work on the due date.

During ordinary adoption leave, employees are entitled to the benefit of all their normal terms and conditions of employment, with the exception of terms relating to wages or salary, just as in the case of ordinary maternity leave[184]. The adopter will also be entitled to receive Statutory Adoption Pay (SAP) from the employer for twenty-six weeks at the same rate as standard SMP – ie £100 per week, or 90% of average weekly earnings if less than that amount – unless the adopter's average weekly earnings are below the Lower Earnings Limit for National

---

177 PAL Regulations, reg 18(1), 20(2). If the placement ends prematurely during the adoption leave period, the entitlement to leave normally continues for another eight weeks after the end of the placement: reg 22.
178 PAL Regulations, reg 2(1), (4).
179 PAL Regulations, reg 15. The employee must also have notified the adoption agency that he agrees to the placement of the child, and the timing of the placement.
180 PAL Regulations, reg 16.
181 PAL Regulations, reg 17(1), (2). This date can be varied on giving 28 days' notice, unless not reasonably practicable to do so.
182 PAL Regulations, reg 17(3). The certificate must contain certain specified information about the agency, the child, the date of notification of being matched with a child, and the expected date of placement.
183 PAL Regulations, reg 17(7).
184 PAL Regulations, reg 19.
185 Ie £77 per week from April 2003.

Insurance purposes[185]. Unlike SMP, however, in this context there is no higher, earnings-related rate for the first six weeks. Employers are entitled to recover the amount of SAP paid out in the same way and to the same extent as they can recover SMP (ie 92%, or in the case of small employers, 100% plus an additional amount to cover extra National Insurance contributions). The usual rules requiring contractual payments during leave to be offset against entitlement to SAP apply. During additional adoption leave the employee's position is the same as during additional maternity leave: the contract of employment continues in existence, but only for a limited range of purposes[186]. The employee does not have to notify the employer before returning to work, unless he or she wishes to return early, in which case twenty-eight days' notice of their intended date of return must be given[187]. Returnees from adoption leave are in a similar position to those returning to work after maternity leave. After ordinary adoption leave, adoptive parents are entitled to return to the job in which they were employed before their absence, with their seniority, pension rights etc as they would have been if they had not been absent, and on terms and conditions no less favourable than those which would have applied if they had not been absent; the basic position is the same for those returning after additional adoption leave, except that if there is a reason which makes it not reasonably practicable for the employer to permit the employee to return to her original job, the entitlement is to return to another job which is both suitable for her and appropriate for her to do in the circumstances, and on terms and conditions no less favourable to her than if she had continued to be employed in her old job[188]. Finally, as with other types of family-related leave, employees taking adoption leave are protected against dismissal or detriment for taking or seeking to take adoption leave[189].

10 PARENTAL LEAVE

As seen in the introduction to this chapter, the Employment Relations Act 1999 introduced a new right to parental leave for male and female employees, implementing the Parental Leave Directive[190]. The detailed provisions on parental leave are contained in the Maternity and Parental Leave etc. (MPL) Regulations 1999[191], which set out who has a right to parental leave, and certain key elements which apply to everyone. Employers and employees are free to agree a detailed parental leave scheme, via a collective or workforce agreement, which will be valid provided it does not contradict any of the key elements in the regulations. The regulations also contain a set of 'default' provisions on parental leave, in the form of a 'model' scheme which will automatically come into operation unless the parties agree on their own scheme.

---

186 PAL Regulations, reg 21.
187 PAL Regulations, reg 25.
188 PAL Regulations, reg 26, 27. As with maternity leave, if a redundancy situation arises during ordinary or additional adoption leave, the employee is entitled to be offered any suitable available vacancy: PAL Regulations, reg 23; see p 408.
189 PAL Regulations, reg 28, 29; see p 408.
190 Directive 96/34/EC. The Directive was extended to the UK by Directive 97/75/EC.
191 MPL etc. Regulations 1999, SI 1999/3312, as amended by the MPL (Amendment) Regulations 2001 and 2002.

(i) Entitlement to parental leave

The right to parental leave is available to an employee who has been continuously employed for at least one year, and who has, or expects to have, 'parental responsibility' for a child within the meaning of the Children Act 1989[192]. Such an employee is entitled to at least thirteen weeks' parental leave in respect of each child, for the purpose of caring for that child[193]. If the employee works part time, the entitlement to leave is proportionate to the time for which the employee normally works[194], and if the leave is taken in shorter periods than the employee's normal working week, the individual periods of leave are aggregated together[195]. Employees have a right not to be dismissed or subjected to any detriment by their employer for taking or seeking to take parental leave[196].

Controversy arose over the way in which the Parental Leave Directive was originally implemented in the UK, because of the requirement that parental leave had to be taken before the child's fifth birthday[197] (under the Directive the government could have allowed leave to be taken up to the age of eight) and could not be claimed in respect of a child born before 15 December 1999[198]. The latter restriction was challenged by the TUC in judicial review proceedings as being in breach of the requirements of the Directive[199], and the entitlement to parental leave was duly extended to those with children born before 15 December 1999 by the Maternity and Parental Leave (Amendment) Regulations 2001[200]. The other major bone of contention is that parental leave is unpaid, unless the employer agrees otherwise. In practice, this means that many employees who might wish to take some parental leave may simply be unable to do so because of the financial consequences.

During the period of parental leave, the employee remains in employment but, in the absence of an agreement to the contrary, is in the same position as an employee on additional maternity leave, ie the employee is only entitled to the benefit of the employer's implied obligation of trust and confidence, and any terms and conditions of employment relating to notice of termination by the employer, redundancy compensation, or disciplinary or grievance procedures. During that period the employee is bound by the implied obligation to the employer of good faith, and any terms and conditions of employment relating to notice of termination by the employee, disclosure of confidential information, the acceptance of gifts or other benefits, or the employee's participation in any other business[201]. As in the case of ordinary maternity or adoption leave or paternity leave, an employee who takes parental leave of four weeks or less is entitled to

---

192 MPL etc. Regulations 1999, reg 13.
193 MPL etc. Regulations 1999, reg 14(1). In the case of multiple births, an employee is entitled to thirteen weeks' leave for each child. Parents of disabled children are entitled to up to 18 weeks' leave: reg 14(1A).
194 MPL etc. Regulations 1999, reg 14(2).
195 MPL etc. Regulations 1999, reg 14(4).
196 MPL etc. Regulations 1999, reg 19, 20.
197 In the case of an adopted child, the leave may be taken up to the fifth anniversary of the date on which the child was placed for adoption, or the child's eighteenth birthday, whichever is the sooner; the parent of a child who is entitled to disability living allowance is allowed to take parental leave up to the date of the child's eighteenth birthday: reg 15.
198 An exception was made in the case of a child adopted by the employee, or placed with the employee for adoption, on or after that date.
199 *R v Secretary of State for Trade and Industry, ex parte Trades Union Congress* [2000] IRLR 565.
200 SI 2001/4010.
201 MPL etc. Regulations 1999, reg 17.

return to work after parental leave to the job in which he or she was employed before taking leave[202], with seniority, pension rights etc as they would have been if the employee had not been absent, and on terms and conditions not less favourable than those which would have been applicable to the employee had he or she not been absent[203]. If the period of parental leave is more than four weeks, or the leave is taken immediately after additional maternity leave or additional adoption leave, the employee is entitled to return to the old job or, if that is not reasonably practicable, to another job which is both suitable and appropriate for the employee in the circumstances.[204]

(ii) Collective or workforce agreements

In line with the current political emphasis on 'partnership' in the workplace, the MPL etc. Regulations allow employers and employees to agree a detailed parental leave scheme via a collective or workforce agreement which is incorporated into the contracts of employment of individual employees[205]. Such a scheme may improve upon the entitlements set out in the regulations (for example by allowing parental leave after a child's fifth birthday), but it may not contradict any of the key elements in the regulations (for example by imposing lower age limits, or a later birth or adoption date). The regulations contain a 'model' scheme which automatically comes into operation if the parties do not agree on their own scheme (see below). A 'workforce agreement' is defined for these purposes in similar terms to those used in the Working Time Regulations[206]. To be valid, a workforce agreement must (a) be in writing; (b) have effect for a specified period not exceeding five years; (c) apply to all the members of the workforce, or all the members of a particular group of workers who share a function, workplace or organisational unit (excluding those whose terms and conditions are provided for, wholly or in part, by a collective agreement); and (d) be signed by all the elected workforce representatives (although if the employer employs 20 or fewer employees on the date when the agreement is first made available for signature, it is sufficient if the agreement is signed by a majority of the workforce). In addition, before the agreement is made available for signature, the employer must have provided all the employees to whom it was intended to apply with copies of the agreement, together with such guidance as they might reasonably require to help them understand it[207]. The MPL etc. Regulations set out the requirements for the election of workforce representatives[208], including matters such as candidature, entitlement to vote and the conduct of the ballot[209].

202 MPL etc. Regulations reg 18(1), as substituted by the MPL (Amendment) Regulations 2002.
203 MPL etc. Regulations 1999, reg 18A, as inserted by the MPL (Amendment) Regulations 2002.
204 MPL etc. Regulations 1999, reg 18(2), as substituted by the MPL (Amendment) Regulations 2002.
205 MPL etc. Regulations 1999, reg 16. A 'collective agreement' is defined for these purposes as an agreement or arrangement made between one or more independent trade unions and one or more employers or employers' associations: MPL etc. Regulations 1999, reg 2.
206 See p 244 below.
207 MPL etc. Regulations 1999, Sch 1.
208 Workforce representatives have a right not to be dismissed or subjected to any detriment by the employer for performing (or proposing to perform) any functions or activities as a workforce representative or a candidate for election as a workforce representative: see p 408.
209 These requirements are similar to those which apply to the election of workforce representatives under the Working Time Regulations: see p 245 above.

(iii) The model scheme

As seen above, the MPL etc. Regulations contain a model scheme[210] on parental leave which automatically comes into operation if the parties do not make their own collective or workforce agreement. The key elements of the model scheme are as follows: (i) parental leave may not be taken in periods other than a week or multiple of a week (except in the case of a child entitled to disability living allowance); (ii) an employee may not take more than four weeks' leave in respect of any individual child during a particular year; (iii) the employee must give the employer at least twenty-one days' notice of the taking of parental leave, and its duration; (iv) fathers wishing to take parental leave immediately after the baby is born must give the employer notice at least twenty-one days before the beginning of the expected week of childbirth; (v) employees wishing to take parental leave immediately after the date of placement of an adopted child must give the employer notice at least twenty-one days before the beginning of the week in which placement is expected to occur, or as soon as reasonably practicable thereafter; (vi) the employer may ask for reasonable evidence of the employee's entitlement to parental leave (for example evidence of the child's date of birth, or date of placement for adoption); (vii) the employer may postpone a period of parental leave (other than leave on birth or adoption) where the employer considers that the operation of his business would be unduly disrupted if the employee took leave during the period identified in the notice; (viii) leave may not be postponed for more than six months, and the employer must notify the employee of the postponement in writing within seven days of receiving the employee's notice, giving the reason for the postponement and specifying the dates on which the period of leave will begin and end.

11 TIME OFF FOR DEPENDANTS

In addition to the right to parental leave, the Employment Relations Act 1999 also introduced a right for employees to take a reasonable amount of unpaid time off to deal with incidents involving a 'dependant'[211]. Like the provisions on parental leave, the provisions on time off for dependants were designed to implement the Parental Leave Directive, which gives a right to time off in family emergencies. The hope and expectation is that the new provisions will lead to a reduction in the number of employees taking odd days off sick in order to care for sick children or to cope when domestic arrangements (for example child-minding arrangements) go awry at short notice.

Although colourfully (and sometimes mischievously) portrayed in certain sections of the media as giving employees carte blanche to take time off whenever they wish to attend to the needs of leaking washing machines or sick poodles, the right to time off for dependants is in fact more limited than this. An employee has the right to be permitted to take a 'reasonable amount' of time off (not further defined or explained) during working hours to take action which is necessary: (a) to provide assistance when a dependant falls ill, gives birth, or is injured or assaulted; (b) to make arrangements for the provision of care for a dependant who is ill or injured; (c) when a dependant dies; (d) because of the unexpected

---

210 MPL etc. Regulations 1999, Sch 2.
211 Employment Rights Act 1996, ss 57A and 57B, added by the Employment Relations Act 1999.

disruption or termination of arrangements for the care of a dependant; or (e) to deal with an incident which involves a child of the employee and which occurs unexpectedly during school hours or other time when the child's school is responsible for the child[212]. A 'dependant' of an employee is defined for these purposes as a spouse, child, parent, or a person who lives in the same household as the employee, otherwise than as an employee, tenant, lodger or boarder[213]. For the purposes of heads (a) and (b) above, 'dependant' also includes a person who reasonably relies on the employee (i) for assistance on an occasion when the person falls ill or is injured or assaulted, or (ii) to make arrangements for the provision of care in the event of illness or injury; and for the purposes of head (d), it includes any person who reasonably relies on the employee to make arrangements for the provision of care. Where time off is taken under these provisions, the employee must tell the employer the reason for the absence as soon as reasonably practicable, and how long the employee expects to be absent from work[214].

A complaint that an employer has unreasonably refused time off under these provisions lies to an employment tribunal, within three months of the refusal, or within a further reasonable period where the tribunal is satisfied that it was not reasonably practicable for the complaint to be brought within that period[215]. Where the tribunal upholds the complaint, it must make a declaration to that effect, and may order the employer to pay compensation to the employee of such amount as the tribunal considers just and equitable in all the circumstances, having regard to the employer's default, and any loss suffered by the employee which is attributable to the matters complained of. An employee also has the right not to be dismissed or subjected to any detriment by his or her employer for taking or seeking to take time off for dependants[216]. The extent of the entitlement to time off under this head was considered for the first time by the EAT in *Qua v John Ford Morrison Solicitors*[217]. In that case, the applicant was dismissed for absenteeism having been absent from work for seventeen days over a ten-month period as a result of medical problems suffered by her young son. The employment tribunal dismissed her complaint that she was unfairly dismissed for taking time off for dependants[218], on the grounds that she had failed to comply with her obligation to tell the employer as soon as reasonably practicable the reason for her absence and how long she expected to be absent, and that her absences went beyond what was reasonable. The EAT, allowing the appeal, gave useful guidance on the interpretation of the statutory provisions, pointing out that the right is to take a reasonable amount of time off in order to deal with unexpected or sudden events affecting dependants, and to make any necessary longer-term arrangements for their care. The right to time off to provide assistance under head (a) 'does not in our view enable employees to take time off in order themselves to provide care for a sick child, beyond the reasonable amount necessary to enable them to deal with the immediate crisis.' The EAT rejected the argument that each individual request for time off should be considered in isolation, confirming that where an

212 Employment Rights Act 1996, s 57A(1). No qualifying period of continuous employment is required.
213 Employment Rights Act 1996, s 57A(3).
214 Employment Rights Act 1996, s 57A(2).
215 Employment Rights Act 1996, s 57B.
216 MPL etc. Regulations 1996, regs 19, 20.
217 [2003] ICR 482, [2003] IRLR 184, EAT.
218 She argued her case on this ground because she lacked the necessary continuous employment to being an ordinary unfair dismissal complaint.

employee has exercised the right on more than one previous occasion, the employer can take into account the number and length of previous absences in order to determine whether the time sought to be taken off is reasonable and necessary. However, in determining what is a reasonable amount of time off, the EAT considered that 'the disruption or inconvenience caused to an employer's business by the employee's absence are irrelevant factors, which should not be taken into account', on the grounds that the 'operational needs of the employer cannot be relevant to a consideration of the amount of time an employee reasonably needs' to deal with emergency situations. On the particular issue raised by the case, that of a parent with a child suffering from a chronic illness, the EAT gave the provisions a narrow interpretation: 'The legislation contemplates a reasonable period of time off to enable an employee to deal with a child who has fallen ill unexpectedly and thus the section is dealing with something unforeseen. Once it is known that the particular child is suffering from an underlying medical condition, which is likely to cause him to suffer regular relapses, such a situation no longer falls within the scope of . . . section 57A at all.' On the issue of whether the applicant had complied with the duty under section 57A(2) to inform the employer, the EAT held that there is no duty on an employee to report to the employers 'on a daily basis' whilst taking time off work; she must tell the employer the reason for her absence, and how long she expects to be absent, but 'there is no continuing duty on an employee to update the employer as to her situation, though of course many employees would no doubt do this as a matter of course.'

12 FLEXIBLE WORKING

One of the greatest obstacles faced by working parents trying to reconcile the competing demands of work and family life is that they usually have very little control over the pattern of their working lives. This is a particular problem for women returning to work after maternity leave, as the statutory provisions on maternity leave give a woman the right to return to the job in which she was employed before maternity leave; they do not confer any right to change the job specification to make it easier for her to return to work.

As seen in the introduction to this chapter, the introduction of a right to work flexibly received a high level of support in the government's review of maternity and parental rights, and provisions on flexible working were duly brought forward in the Employment Act 2002[219]. However, those measures fell well below expectations, because they do not give employees an automatic right to work flexibly: they merely give a right to *apply* to work flexibly, and even that right is very restricted in its scope. The gist of the provisions is that employees who have (or expect to have) responsibility for the upbringing of a child under 6[220] may request a change in their terms and conditions relating to the hours they work, the times when they are required to work, or where they are required to work (ie as between home or on the employer's premises), to enable them to care for the child[221]. To

---

219 Employment Rights Act 1996, Pt 8A, as inserted by the Employment Act 2002, s 47. Pt 8A is supplemented by the Flexible Working (Procedural Requirements) Regulations 2002, SI 2002/3207, and the Flexible Working (Eligibility, Complaints and Remedies) Regulations 2002, SI 2002/3236.
220 Or a disabled child under 18. The application must be made at least 14 days before the child's 6th (or, if disabled, 18th) birthday.
221 Employment Rights Act 1996, s 80F, as inserted by the Employment Act 2002, s 47.

be eligible, the employee must be either the mother, father, adopter, guardian or foster parent of the child, or the spouse or partner of any of these, and must have twenty-six weeks' continuous service with the employer at the date of the application[222]. The procedure for making and responding to requests for flexible working is set out in detail in the Act and the accompanying regulations. The employee must apply in writing[223], and the application must explain what effect, if any, the employee thinks making the change applied for would have on the employer and how in the employee's opinion any such effect might be dealt with[224]. The employer's duty is merely to consider the request; there is no automatic right to work flexibly. The Act specifies the grounds on which an employer may refuse a request, viz, (i) the burden of additional costs; (ii) detrimental effect on ability to meet customer demand; (iii) inability to re-organise work among existing staff; (iv) inability to recruit additional staff; (v) detrimental impact on quality; (vi) detrimental impact on performance; (vii) insufficiency of work during the periods the employee proposes to work; (viii) planned structural changes; and (ix) any other grounds specified in regulations[225]. It can be seen that this list provides an employer who is minded to resist an application to work flexibly with plenty of ammunition for doing so, particularly when one appreciates that the employer's refusal is not subject to any test of reasonableness or proportionality. The employer must respond to the employee's application within twenty-eight days of receipt, either by agreeing to it (with notification to the employee in writing) or by arranging a meeting with the employee to discuss the application[226]. The employee is entitled to be accompanied at that meeting by a fellow employee[227]. Within fourteen days of the meeting the employer must notify the employee in writing of his decision. If the application is rejected, the notice must specify the particular ground or grounds for the refusal from the above list, and explain why those grounds apply in the circumstances[228]; it must also set out the appeal procedure, which gives the employee a right of appeal within fourteen days[229]. The appeal process is essentially a re-run of the original meeting, with the employer again required to provide reasons if the application is still refused[230]. If the employer fails to follow the procedure correctly, the employee has a right to complain to an employment tribunal, which may issue a declaration, order the employer to reconsider the request and award compensation of up to eight weeks' pay[231]. The tribunal cannot order the employer to permit an employee to work flexibly. Employees to have a right not to be dismissed or subjected to any detriment for requesting flexible working, or seeking to exercise or enforce any rights thereto[232].

---

222 Flexible Working (Eligibility, Complaints and Remedies) Regulations 2002, reg 3.
223 Flexible Working (Eligibility, Complaints and Remedies) Regulations 2002, reg 4. The application must state whether the employee has made a previous application, and if so, when.
224 Employment Rights Act 1996, s 80F(2).
225 Employment Rights Act 1996, s 80G, as inserted by the Employment Act 2002.
226 Flexible Working (Procedural Requirements) Regulations 2002, reg 3.
227 Flexible Working (Procedural Requirements) Regulations 2002, reg 14. The companion may address the meeting, and may confer with the employee during the meeting, but may not answer questions on behalf of the employee. In the event of a failure to comply, the employee may complain to an employment tribunal, which may award compensation of up to two weeks' pay,: reg 15.
228 Flexible Working (Procedural Requirements) Regulations 2002, reg 5.
229 Flexible Working (Procedural Requirements) Regulations 2002, regs 6, 7.
230 Flexible Working (Procedural Requirements) Regulations 2002, regs 8–10.
231 Employment Rights Act 1996, ss 80H, 80I.
232 See p 408.

Modest though they may be, there are some potential pitfalls for employees in these new procedures: first, any contract variation that results from an application under these procedures will be permanent, unless otherwise agreed at the outset; there is no automatic right to revert to the old terms; and secondly, an employee may only make one variation application per year[233], up to the child's sixth birthday, and each application will be considered by the employer in the light of the employer's circumstances at that time. The combination of these two factors means that an employee who succeeds in achieving flexibility in working arrangements in the short term may be unable to revert to his or her original terms and conditions if circumstances change. There are also potential pitfalls for employers, not least the fact that there are potential sex discrimination implications if applications for flexible working from male and female employees are not treated equally.

13 PREGNANCY, MATERNITY AND SEX DISCRIMINATION[234]

In the last ten years or so, the law on maternity rights in the UK has been completely transformed by a series of landmark ECJ decisions in which it has been held that adverse treatment of a woman on grounds of pregnancy or maternity can constitute unlawful direct[235] discrimination on grounds of sex. The possibility of challenging adverse treatment on grounds of pregnancy as sex discrimination was particularly attractive in the UK because of the gaps in the protection for pregnancy and maternity under the employment rights legislation: until 1993, the statutory protection against dismissal on grounds of pregnancy was significantly weakened by the requirement to satisfy the normal two-year qualifying period of continuous employment, and parallel protection against detriment short of dismissal for reasons of pregnancy was not introduced until December 1999. Since the 1993 reforms, the need to challenge a dismissal under sex discrimination law has been greatly reduced, although there may still be advantages in doing so, as sex discrimination claims are not subject to any upper limit on compensation.

Initially, there was some doubt as to whether adverse treatment on grounds of pregnancy fell within the scope of sex discrimination law *at all.* This might seem strange to those uninitiated in the mysteries of the Sex Discrimination Act 1975 – after all, one might be forgiven for thinking that adverse treatment on grounds of pregnancy must necessarily be sexually discriminatory, given the inescapable biological fact that men cannot become pregnant. The doubts arose because in determining whether a woman has been treated less favourably than a man on the ground of sex, the 1975 Act requires the comparison between the treatment of the applicant and that of a man to be such that the relevant circumstances in the one case 'are the same, or not materially different, in the other'[236], and so it seemed that in cases involving pregnancy the necessary comparison could not be made[237]. However, in *Hayes v Malleable Working Men's Club and Institute*[238], the EAT managed to avoid this conclusion by holding that the correct approach under

233 Employment Rights Act 1996, s 80F(4).
234 See Fredman (1994) 110 LQR 106; Szyszczak (1996) 59 MLR 589; Wintemute (1998) 27 ILJ 23; Honeyball (2000) 29 ILJ 43.
235 Protection against indirect sex discrimination (eg in relation to a transfer to part-time work after maternity leave) is considered at p 295 above.
236 Sex Discrimination Act 1975, s 5(3).
237 *Turley v Allders Department Stores Ltd* [1980] ICR 66, [1980] IRLR 4, EAT.
238 [1985] ICR 703, [1985] IRLR 367.

the 1975 Act was to compare the treatment of a pregnant woman with that of a man in comparable circumstances (for example a man suffering from some temporary disability). While this 'sick man' approach was open to the objection that it treated pregnancy as analogous to illness, it did at least succeed in bringing pregnant women within the protection of the Sex Discrimination Act, which was crucially important at the time for those dismissed within the first two years of employment.

It soon became apparent that there was a further highly significant dimension to this issue, in the form of EC Directive 76/207 (the Equal Treatment Directive). In a series of cases, beginning with *Dekker v Stichting Vormingscentrum voor Jong Volwassenen (VJV – Centrum) Plus*[239], the ECJ held that less favourable treatment of a woman on account of her pregnancy constituted unlawful direct discrimination on the grounds of sex, contrary to the Equal Treatment Directive, irrespective of how a hypothetical male would have been treated in comparable circumstances. In *Dekker*, the employer refused to appoint the complainant on learning that she was pregnant (the reason being that under Dutch law the employer would have been required to pay Mrs Dekker her full salary while on maternity leave, but could not have recovered that amount from its insurers because her pregnancy was known at the time her appointment would have commenced). The ECJ ruled that as pregnancy is a condition unique to women, to refuse a woman employment on the ground of pregnancy constituted direct discrimination on grounds of sex, contrary to the Directive; this was held to be the case even though the refusal of employment was on account of the adverse financial consequences to the employer of her absence due to pregnancy, as the refusal was still based on the fact of pregnancy itself. In *Handels-og Kontorfunktionaerernes Forbund i Danmark (for Hertz) v Dansk Arbejdsgiverforening (for Aldi Marked A/S)* [240], decided on the same day as *Dekker*, the ECJ held that the same principle applied to a dismissal on account of pregnancy, although on the facts the court held that a dismissal some eighteen months after the end of maternity leave due to absence for prolonged post-natal illness would not be sexually discriminatory if a man absent from work due to illness for a similar period would have been treated in the same way.

The apparent conflict between domestic and Community law on this issue was first considered by the UK courts in *Webb v EMO Air Cargo (UK) Ltd*[241]. In that case the applicant, recruited to provide temporary cover for another employee who was about to take maternity leave, was dismissed when she discovered shortly after starting work that she too was pregnant. The industrial tribunal dismissed her claim that her dismissal constituted unlawful discrimination on grounds of sex under the 1975 Act, holding that the reason for her dismissal was her anticipated inability to carry out the primary task for which she had been recruited (ie to cover for an absent colleague) and that if a man recruited for the same purpose had told the employer that he needed to be absent for a similar period of time, he too would have been dismissed. The EAT and the Court of Appeal upheld the tribunal's decision, rejecting the argument that the fact that pregnancy is specific to women means that a dismissal for pregnancy must automatically be discriminatory, and applying the comparative approach by comparing the

---

239 Case 177/88 [1992] ICR 325, [1991] IRLR 27, ECJ.
240 Case C-179/88 [1992] ICR 325, [1992] ICR 332, [1991] IRLR 31, ECJ.
241 [1990] ICR 442, [1990] IRLR 124, EAT; affd [1992] ICR 445, [1992] IRLR 116, CA; [1993] ICR 175, [1993] IRLR 27, HL; refd [1994] ICR 770, [1994] IRLR 482, ECJ; revsd *(No 2)* [1995] ICR 1021, [1995] IRLR 645, HL. The applicant was unable to complain under s 99 because she lacked the necessary period of continuous employment.

treatment of the pregnant applicant and the treatment which would have been accorded to a man in comparable circumstances (for example a man with a medical condition requiring him to be absent from work for a similar period of time). On appeal to the House of Lords, Lord Keith (giving the leading judgment) conceded that as child-bearing and the capacity for child-bearing are characteristics of the female sex, '. . . in general to dismiss a woman because she is pregnant or to refuse to employ a woman of child-bearing age because she may become pregnant is unlawful direct discrimination,' as it involves the application of a gender-based criterion[242]. However, he considered that on the facts the reason for the dismissal was not gender-based, since the applicant was dismissed not because she was pregnant but because of her unavailability for work at the critical period, and it was therefore appropriate to compare her treatment with that of a hypothetical man who would also be unavailable (for whatever reason) at the critical time[243]. As it was unclear whether under Community law the unavailability for work rather than the pregnancy would be regarded as being the real reason for dismissal, the House of Lords referred the case to the ECJ, which rejected the comparative approach, holding that under the Equal Treatment Directive the dismissal of an employee for pregnancy constitutes direct discrimination and is therefore unlawful per se. Significantly, however, the ECJ's ruling indicated two possible limitations on the scope of the protection: first, the ECJ accepted that in the case of a dismissal for an illness attributable to pregnancy which manifests itself after maternity leave, it would be appropriate to adopt a comparative approach with the treatment of a sick man in analogous circumstances[244] ; and secondly, the ECJ emphasised that Ms Webb had been engaged under a contract of employment of indefinite duration, the implication being that had she been engaged simply as a temporary replacement on a fixed-term contract, the outcome might have been different. When the case returned to the House of Lords, Lord Keith reinterpreted the 'more precise' test of unlawful discrimination under the 1975 Act so as to accord with the ECJ's ruling: 'It seems to me that the only way of doing so is to hold that, in a case where a woman is engaged for an indefinite period, the fact that the reason why she will be temporarily unavailable for work at a time when to her knowledge her services will be particularly required is pregnancy is a circumstance relevant to her case, being a circumstance which could not be present in the case of a hypothetical man[245].' As the applicant had been recruited for an unlimited term, her dismissal was unlawful under the 1975 Act. However, Lord Keith indicated that the outcome might have been different if the employment had been for a fixed period during the *whole* of which the employee would have been unavailable for work because of her pregnancy, commenting that if such a situation were not to be distinguished, 'the result would be likely to be perceived as unfair to employers and as tending to bring the law on sex discrimination into disrepute.[246]' The legal basis for a distinction between

242 Applying the 'but for' test approved by the House of Lords in *James v Eastleigh Borough Council* [1990] ICR 554, [1990] IRLR 288, HL, discussed at p 280 above.

243 One obvious objection to this line of reasoning is that it could allow a gender-based dismissal to be disguised as gender-neutral, the point being that if the underlying reason for the woman's unavailability for work is her pregnancy, it is strongly arguable that the dismissal is in fact gender-based, as *but for her sex* she would not have been pregnant, and *but for her pregnancy* she would not have been unavailable for work.

244 As in *Hertz* above n 240.

245 [1995] IRLR 645 at 647, HL.

246 Cf *Caruana v Manchester Airport plc* [1996] IRLR 378, where the EAT held that any special rule for fixed-term contacts must be restricted to cases where the employee would be unavailable for the *whole* of the term of the contract.

indefinite and fixed-term contracts in such cases clearly owed more to pragmatism than to principle, and it came as no surprise that the ECJ, when given the opportunity to approve a fixed-term contract exception in *Tele Danmark A/S v Handels-og Kontorfunktionaerernes Forbund i Danmark (for Brandt-Nielsen)*[247], held the line and refused to do so. In that case the applicant had applied for a temporary job on a six-month contract knowing that she was pregnant, and that she would be unable to perform a substantial part of her contract. She was dismissed for failing to inform the employers of her pregnancy when she was recruited, and the ECJ was asked to rule on whether the dismissal contravened the Equal Treatment Directive. The ECJ's ruling was unequivocal: 'Since the dismissal of a worker on account of pregnancy constitutes direct discrimination on grounds of sex, whatever the nature and extent of the economic loss incurred by the employer as a result of her absence because of pregnancy, whether the contract of employment was concluded for a fixed or an indefinite period has no bearing on the discriminatory character of the dismissal. In either case, the employee's inability to perform her contract of employment is due to pregnancy.[248]'

In the cases since *Webb (No 2)*, the extent of the special protection from pregnancy discrimination has been clarified, and a robust approach has been taken. It is now well established that any adverse treatment on grounds of pregnancy will be unlawful per se[250], provided the necessary causal connection can be established. The EAT gave useful guidance on this latter point in *O'Neill v Governors of St Thomas More RCVA School*[251]. In that case, the complainant, a religious education teacher at a Roman Catholic school, was dismissed after becoming pregnant as a result of a relationship with a local Roman Catholic priest. The tribunal had held that the dismissal, although unfair, was not discriminatory, as pregnancy was not the predominant cause of the dismissal, but the EAT allowed the complainant's appeal. According to Mummery J: 'The basic question is: what, out of the whole complex of facts before the tribunal, is the "effective and predominant" cause or the "real and efficient" cause of the act complained of?' He considered that the other factors surrounding the pregnancy which had led to her dismissal ('the paternity of the child, the publicity of that fact and the consequent untenability of the applicant's position as a religious education teacher') were all causally related to the fact that she was pregnant, and so it could be said, on an objective consideration of all the surrounding circumstances, that her pregnancy 'precipitated and permeated the decision to dismiss her'.

---

247 [2001] IRLR 853, ECJ.

248 See also *Jimenez Melgar v Ayuntamiento de Los Barrios* [2001] IRLR 848, ECJ (non-renewal of a pregnant worker's fixed-term contract constitutes direct sex discrimination contrary to the Equal Treatment Directive where the reason for the non-renewal is related to the worker's pregnancy).

250 See eg *Mahlburg v Land Mecklenburg-Vorpommern* [2001] ICR 1032, [2000] IRLR 276, ECJ (unlawful to refuse a pregnant woman appointment to a post of unlimited duration on the grounds that a statutory prohibition on her employment because of her pregnancy prevented her from being employed in that post from the outset and for the duration of her pregnancy); see also *Hardman v Mallon t/a Orchard Lodge Nursing Home* [2002] IRLR 516 (failure to conduct a risk assessment in respect of a pregnant woman was unlawful sex discrimination, without the need for a male comparator).

251 [1997] ICR 33, [1996] IRLR 372, EAT; see also *Shomer v B & R Residential Lettings Ltd* [1992] IRLR 317, CA; *P & O European Ferries (Dover) Ltd v Iverson* [1999] ICR 1088, EAT.

The 'special protection' is, however, subject to certain temporal limits, as the decision in *Hertz* showed. In *Handels-og Kontorfunktionaerernes Forbund i Danmark (for Larsson) v Dansk Handel & Service (for Fotex Supermarked A/S)*[252], the ECJ held that it was lawful for an employer to take into account periods of absence due to pregnancy-related illness outside the maternity leave period in calculating whether there are grounds for dismissal, provided a man with a similar record of sickness absence would also have been dismissed. To the extent that the decision in *Larsson* seemed to imply that an employer could take account of pregnancy-related absence before the beginning of maternity leave, it appeared to conflict with the basic principle established in *Dekker* and *Webb (No 2)*, and it was no surprise that when the ECJ next had an opportunity to reconsider the matter, in *Brown v Rentokil Ltd*[253], it confirmed that when considering a dismissal for sickness absence, it is unlawful to take account of absences due to pregnancy-related illness that have occurred between the start of pregnancy and the start of maternity leave[254]. Indeed, in that case the ECJ took the rare step of expressly disapproving the distinction drawn in *Larsson* between absence for pregnancy-related illness during pregnancy and during maternity leave. After *Brown v Rentokil Ltd*, it is now possible to state with some assurance that the special protection against dismissal on grounds of pregnancy applies from the start of pregnancy to the end of maternity leave. Within that period, a dismissal (or other adverse treatment) for absence caused by pregnancy-related illness will be unlawful. After the end of maternity leave, the comparative approach applies, so that such treatment will only be unlawful if a man would have been treated more favourably in comparable circumstances (ie the sick man comparison applies)[255]. In making that comparison, however, it will be unlawful to take into account any period of pregnancy-related sickness absence occurring between the start of pregnancy and the end of maternity leave.

While the decisions in *Dekker* and *Webb (No 2)* clarified the law in one area, they in turn gave rise to a further, related issue: if adverse treatment on grounds of pregnancy or maternity leave is unlawful, does this mean that a woman on maternity leave is entitled to claim the benefit of the terms and conditions of employment which she would have enjoyed if still at work? This issue first arose for consideration by the ECJ in *Gillespie v Northern Health and Social Services Board*[256], where it was argued that a woman should be entitled to receive full pay during maternity leave, on the grounds that if the only reason she does not receive full pay is that she is on maternity leave, that must be direct discrimination on the grounds of sex contrary to Community law, since that reason can only affect women. In a decision which owed more to pragmatism than to logic, but which no doubt

---

252 [1997] IRLR 643, ECJ.

253 [1998] ICR 790, [1998] IRLR 445, ECJ.

254 The fact that her contract contained a term allowing the employer to dismiss after a stipulated number of weeks of absence was held to make no difference.

255 See eg *British Telecommunications plc v Roberts* [1996] ICR 625, [1996] IRLR 601, EAT (request to jobshare after maternity leave not covered by the special protection, but subject instead to the comparative approach).

256 [1996] All ER (EC) 284, [1996] IRLR 214, ECJ. The ECJ also held that where the amount of maternity pay is calculated on the basis of pay received before the maternity leave begins, a woman on maternity leave is entitled to the benefit of a pay-rise awarded during that period (including a retrospective award) when calculating her maternity pay: see p 425 above.

caused a huge collective sigh of relief amongst employers, the ECJ ruled that women taking maternity leave 'are in a special position which requires them to be afforded special protection, but which is not comparable either with that of a man or with that of a woman actually at work'; consequently it was not unlawful under Community law to pay women on maternity leave at a level which is less than their full pay for the period of the leave. The Court considered that it was for the national legislature to set the amount of maternity pay, provided this was not so low as to undermine the purpose of maternity leave. In subsequent cases on this issue, the ECJ has maintained a clear distinction between a woman's rights (i) while she is pregnant and still working; (ii) during maternity leave; and (iii) following her return to work. While pregnant and still working, the *Dekker* principle applies, so that any adverse treatment on grounds of pregnancy will be unlawful per se[257]. During maternity leave, her rights are those set out in the Pregnant Workers Directive (unless enhanced under national law or by her contract of employment); she cannot compare herself with the position of a man or woman actually at work, nor is she entitled to compare herself with a man or woman absent from work on sick leave[258], or on holiday[259]. Following her return to work, however, the comparative approach applies.

While the basic principles are now tolerably clear (albeit thoroughly muddled conceptually), they can be difficult to apply in practice, particularly where the tricky issue of the pro-rata-ing of benefits in proportion to periods of absence arises. While the ECJ in *Gillespie* stepped back from the brink of accepting a right to full pay during maternity leave, this left open the question of whether an employee continues to build up entitlement to other contractual benefits (for example the accrual of holiday or pension entitlement or annual bonuses) during maternity leave, particularly where those benefits are not dependent on actual performance of work. Subsequent cases have established that it is permissible under Article 141 and the Equal Treatment Directive for entitlement to (or accrual of) such benefits to be limited to the minimum fourteen-week maternity leave period guaranteed under the Pregnant Workers Directive . In *Boyle v Equal Opportunities Commissions*[260], the applicant challenged several aspects of the EOC's maternity scheme, including a clause whereby annual holiday leave ceased to accrue during periods of supplementary contractual maternity leave after the end of the minimum fourteen-week leave period. The ECJ held that such a clause was not precluded by European law, since the period of contractual maternity leave was a special advantage available only to women, so the fact that annual leave ceased to accrue during that period could not amount to less favourable treatment of women[261]. The ECJ also held that a clause requiring the repayment of any

---

257 See eg *Handels-og Kontorfunktionaerernes Forbund i Danmark (for Pedersen) v Faellesforeningen for Danmarks Brugsforeninger (for Kwickly Skive)* [1999] IRLR 55, ECJ (held to be unlawful to pay a woman absent from work with a pregnancy-related illness *before* the start of maternity leave a lower level of sick pay than was paid to other employees).

258 *Boyle v Equal Opportunities Commission* [1998] IRLR 717, ECJ; see also *Todd v Eastern Health and Social Services Board; Gillespie v Northern Health and Social Services Board (No 2)* [1997] IRLR 410, NICA.

259 *Edwards v Derby City Council* [1999] ICR 114, EAT.

260 Above, n 258.

261 This, of course, begs the question of whether the benefit in question is one which is awarded retrospectively as a reward for past service (in which case it may be reduced pro-rata for periods of maternity leave after the 14-week minimum) or merely depends on the employee being in current employment when the benefit is awarded: see *Lewen v Denda* [2000] ICR 648, [2000] IRLR 67, ECJ (a case on the Parental Leave Directive).

contractual maternity pay over and above the level of SMP if a woman did not return to work after maternity leave was not unlawful (rejecting the comparison with a man or woman absent on sick leave, who would not have been required to repay sick pay on not returning to work), nor was a clause providing for the triggering of maternity leave where a woman absent on sick leave gave birth during such absence. A clause prohibiting an employee from taking sick leave during the minimum fourteen-week period unless she elected to return to work and terminate her maternity leave was held to be unlawful (although not so in relation to a period of supplementary maternity leave), as was a clause limiting the accrual of occupational pension rights during the minimum fourteen-week period to the period during which the woman received contractual or statutory maternity pay. In *Caisse Nationale d'Assurance Vieillesse des Travailleurs Salaries v Thibault* [262], the applicant was denied an annual performance assessment (and with it the possibility of qualifying for promotion) because the relevant collective agreement restricted such assessments to employees who had been present at work for at least six months in the relevant year, and she was unable to qualify because she had been away from work on maternity leave. She argued that to deny her the assessment was discriminatory, since if she had not taken maternity leave, she would have qualified for an assessment. In a brief (and unfortunately rather delphic) judgment which is difficult to reconcile with *Boyle*, the ECJ upheld her complaint, on the grounds that a woman who continues to be bound to her employer by an employment contract during maternity leave should not be deprived of the benefit of working conditions which apply to both men and women and which are a result of that relationship. A similar approach was taken in *GUS Home Shopping Ltd v Green* [263] where the applicants were denied payment under a loyalty bonus scheme because they were absent from work during the relevant period. The EAT held that this was unlawful sex discrimination because their absence from work was due to pregnancy-related illness or maternity leave, and the case therefore fell within the mainstream principle established by *Webb* and *Thibault*.

Finally, while most of the cases in this area have been brought by women, the question arises whether a man is able to complain that he has been discriminated against on grounds of sex through being denied benefits enjoyed by women in connection with pregnancy. The short answer to this is that such a claim is likely to fail. Section 2(2) of the Sex Discrimination Act provides that it is not unlawful for an employer to discriminate by affording 'special treatment' to women in connection with pregnancy or childbirth, and this is reinforced by Article 2(3) of the Equal Treatment Directive, which provides an exception to the principle of equal treatment for 'provisions concerning the protection of women, particularly as regards pregnancy and maternity'. In *Abdoulaye v Régie Nationale des Usines Renault SA* [264], a group of male employees claimed equal pay with women, who were entitled to receive a lump-sum maternity allowance while on maternity leave, in addition to their *full* pay. The applicants claimed that the refusal of the employers to pay an equivalent allowance to fathers was a breach of the principle of equal pay in Article 141 of the EC Treaty. The ECJ reaffirmed the principle that the position of women on maternity leave is not comparable with that of men, and held that the principle of equal pay in Article 141 does not preclude the payment of a lump-sum exclusively to female workers who take maternity leave, where that payment is designed to offset the occupational disadvantages which arise for them as a result of their being away from work.

262 [1998] IRLR 399, ECJ.
263 [2001] IRLR 75, EAT.
264 [1999] IRLR 811, ECJ.

Chapter 7

Contracts of employment (2): discharge at common law

I MODES OF TERMINATION OTHER THAN DISMISSAL

Certain common law and statutory rights depend upon an employee being dismissed, but there are certain ways in which employment may be terminated other than simply by dismissal. These are now considered, and one of the themes that runs through them is that they are founded on old common law principles established at a time when an employee had few rights and so the concept of continuity of employment was of little significance, but they are now heavily qualified (though not actually abrogated) by specialised statutory provisions aimed at mitigating their potentially harsh application to modern employment rights. One such provision is the Employment Rights Act 1996, section 136 which (along with section 139) provides that, for the purposes of claiming redundancy payments, where an act of the employer or an event affecting the employer (including his death) has the effect of terminating the contract of employment by operation of law, that is deemed to be a termination by the employer (ie a dismissal) and is further deemed to be by reason of redundancy if that is the real reason behind the failure to continue employing the employee. This will go far towards safeguarding the employee's redundancy rights in most cases of death, dissolution or frustration. However, there remain areas not yet covered by ameliorating statutory provisions where the industrial lawyer (particularly when representing the employee) has to beware of the sudden emergence of arguments based on common law notions of discharge of employment which, if accepted, can do great harm to statutory rights; a good example is the effect of the doctrine of frustration on certain unfair dismissal actions.

(i) Death or dissolution of the enterprise

At common law, death would bring the contract of employment to an end, whether it be the death of the employee[1] or the employer, as in *Farrow v Wilson*[2] where the

---

1   *Stubbs v Holywell Rly Co* (1867) LR 2 Exch 311; *Graves v Cohen* (1929) 46 TLR 121.
2   (1869) LR 4 CP 744.

personal representatives were held not to be liable to continue the engagement of the employee. The employee is discharged from further performance on the death of the employer, not through any breach of contract, but as the result of an implied condition that the continued existence of the parties is an essential of the contract. This position is now qualified by statute in three ways. First, if the business does not carry on after the employer's death, the termination of employment is deemed to be a dismissal for redundancy under the Employment Rights Act 1996, sections 136, 139, above, so the employee may claim a redundancy payment from the employer's personal representatives[3]. Secondly, if the deceased employer's business is carried on by his personal representatives and the employee continues to work for them there is deemed to be no termination for redundancy purposes[4], and his continuity of employment for general purposes is not broken[5]. Thirdly, where it is the employee who dies, any pending proceedings of his before an employment tribunal may be instituted or continued by his personal representatives (or by other persons appointed by the tribunal if there are no personal representatives) and if he dies whilst under notice of dismissal he will be treated for the purposes of unfair dismissal and redundancy as if he had actually been dismissed[6].

In practice of course most employees will be employed by partnerships or companies which do not die, but they may be dissolved or wound up in certain ways, and the operation of these processes of law upon the contracts of employment concerned must now be considered.

In the case of a partnership, where a partners dies and there is a consequent dissolution of the partnership, the contract of employment will be discharged wherever it is one related to the personal conduct of the deceased person. In *Harvey v Tivoli (Manchester) Ltd*[7] the death of a member of a troupe of three music-hall artists was held to discharge the contract though he had been replaced, and the troupe was ready to appear. In *Phillips v Alhambra Palace Co*[8] one of the defendant partners had died after a contract had been entered into with the plaintiffs, who were also music-hall artists. In this case it was held that the obligation continued despite the death of the partner, for the obligation was not of a personal character and the partners, when they booked the artists to appear, were not individually known. In the first case the contract was with three specific persons – in the second case it was with a firm and the personal element was not paramount. A dissolution of a partnership on account of the retirement of a partner will operate as a wrongful dismissal at common law[9], but a continuance of employment under a firm containing some of the old partners will amount to a waiver of common law rights of action[10]. Under statute, even if the dissolution did not constitute a dismissal per se (which it almost certainly does) it would be deemed to be such for redundancy purposes under section 136 of the 1996 Act, above, and where

3   Employment Rights Act 1996, s 206(3).
4   S 174. It must be shown on the acts that the personal representatives did renew the contract or re-engage the employee, but in practice the longer he continues to work for them the easier this will be to infer (in the absence of express agreement): *Ranger v Brown* [1978] ICR 603, EAT.
5   S 218(4).
6   S 206; Employment Tribunals Awards (Enforcement in case of Death) Regulations 1976, SI 1976/663.
7   (1907) 23 TLR 592; *Tunstall v Condon* [1980] ICR 786.
8   [1901] 1 KB 59.
9   *Brace v Calder* [1895] 2 QB 253, CA; *Briggs v Oates* [1990] ICR 473, [1990] IRLR 472.
10 *Hobson v Cowley* (1858) 27 LJ Ex 205.

the employee continues in the reconstituted firm's employment his continuity of employment is safeguarded by section 218(5) of that Act.

In the case of a company, the legal position is complex[11]. The position seems to be as follows. An order of the court for a compulsory winding up of the company operates as notice of dismissal to its employees[12]. The effect of a voluntary winding up depends upon whether the business is to be carried on in some form (as for example where it has been taken over by another company); if it is to carry on *Midland Counties District Bank Ltd v Attwood*[13] decided that it does not operate as notice of dismissal, but if there is no intention of carrying on, then it may so operate, as in the case of a compulsory order[14]. The appointment of a receiver is a less drastic step than an immediate winding up, but once again the rules are complicated. The appointment of a receiver by the court terminates contracts of employment[15], but the appointment of a receiver out of court by the debenture holders, as agent for the company, does not have that effect[16], except perhaps in four cases:

(a) where the receiver is appointed to act as agent for the creditors only, not for the company[17];
(b) where the receiver sells the business, so that there is no continuation;
(c) where the receiver enters a new contract of employment with the employee in question which is inconsistent with the existence of the old one;
(d) where the continuation of the contract of employment is inconsistent with the appointment of the receiver because of the nature of the employment; this may be the case with a managing director, but is not necessarily so and will depend upon all the facts of the case[18].

The case law on these points is at times confusing, for though most of the cases envisage the effect of one of these events, if any, to be the giving of notice, some are capable of pointing to instant dismissal (as by operation of law) which, as has been pointed out[19], could jeopardise common law rights of the employee – though it might be noted that some of the cases concern managers on fixed-term contracts, in whose case any termination (whether with or without notice) may constitute wrongful dismissal and so, for example, free the manager from any restraint of trade clause he may have signed which would otherwise have bound him[20].

---

11 See Freedland *The Contract of Employment* (1976) pp 332–339; Graham 'The effect of liquidation on contracts of service' (1952) 15 MLR 48; Davies and Freedland 'The effects of receivership upon employees of companies' (1980) 9 ILJ 95; Pollard *Corporate Insolvency: Employment and Pension Rights* (2nd edn, 2000). Questions of continuity of employment may be covered separately by the Transfer of Undertakings (Protection of Employment) Regulations 1981, SI 1981/1794; see p 200 above.
12 *Re General Rolling Stock Co (Chapman's Case)* (1866) LR 1 Eq 346; *Re Oriental Bank Corpn Ltd (MacDowall's Case)* (1886) 32 Ch D 366.
13 [1905] 1 Ch 357.
14 *Fowler v Commercial Timber Co Ltd* [1930] 2 KB 1, CA: *Reigate v Union Manufacturing Co Ltd* [1918] 1 KB 592, CA; *Fox Bros (Clothes) Ltd v Bryant* [1979] ICR 64, [1978] IRLR 485, EAT.
15 *Reid v Explosives Co* (1887) 19 QBD 264, CA; *Re Foster Clark Ltd's Indenture Trusts* [1966] 1 All ER 43, [1966] 1 WLR 125; cf *Pambakian v Brentford Nylons Ltd* [1978] ICR 665, EAT.
16 *Re Foster Clark Ltd's Indenture Trusts* [1966] 1 All ER 43, [1966] 1 WLR 125; *Re Mack Trucks (Britain) Ltd* [1967] 1 All ER 977, [1967] 1 WLR 780; *Nicoll v Cutts* [1985] BCLC 322, CA.
17 *Hopley Dodd v Highfield Motors (Derby) Ltd* (1969) 4 ITR 289.
18 On exceptions (b)–(d), see *Griffiths v Secretary of State for Social Services* [1974] QB 468, [1973] 3 All ER 1184.
19 *Re Patent Floor Cloth Co* (1872) 41 LJ Ch 476 at 477, per Bacon V-C.
20 *Measures Bros Ltd v Measures* [1910] 2 Ch 248, CA.

(ii) Frustration of the contract

It is a general principle of the law of contract that a contract will be terminated automatically if it is frustrated[21], that is if a change of law or circumstances is such as to mean that the contract becomes impossible of performance or that performance of the contractual obligation would produce a result radically different from that which was originally undertaken in the contract. This doctrine of frustration applies to contracts of employment. Thus in *Morgan v Manser*[22] it was held that the calling-up for military service of a music-hall artist frustrated the contract which he had with his manager, and Streatfeild J formulated the test as follows:

> 'If there is an event or change of circumstances which is so fundamental as to be regarded by the law as striking at the root of the contract as a whole, and as going beyond what was contemplated by the parties and such that to hold the parties to the contract would be to bind them to terms which they would not have made had they contemplated that event or those circumstances, then the contract is frustrated by that event immediately and irrespective of the volition or the intention of the parties, or their knowledge as to that particular event, and this even though they have continued for a time to treat the contract as still subsisting.'

The effects of this doctrine on the contract of employment are threefold:

(i) If the contract is frustrated it is terminated automatically, and immediately upon the happening of a frustrating event; there is no need, for example, for the employer to take any steps to terminate the contract or even to indicate that he regards it as terminated[23].

(ii) As a consequence of (a), there is no right to any back pay from the date of frustration until any other date (for example a date, if any, on which the employer indicated that he thought the contract had ended)[24]. However, any wages due up to the date of frustration may be claimed under the Law Reform (Frustrated Contracts) Act 1943, either under section 2(4) if the contract can be regarded as divisible and the employee has fully performed those severable parts before the date of frustration, or under section 1(3) if the wages concerned were not actually due at that date but it would be just in all the circumstances for the court to award a sum representing the work done up to that date.

(iii) If the contract of employment is frustrated, its termination is due to the operation of law, and not to dismissal (either at common law or under the Employment Rights Act 1996, sections 95 or 136) which could have a serious effect on certain common law and statutory rights, particularly unfair dismissal, which may only be claimed if the employee is dismissed. However, where the

---

21 *Davis Contractors Ltd v Fareham UDC* [1956] AC 696, [1956] 2 All ER 145, HL. See Mogridge 'Frustration, employment contracts and statutory rights' [1982] NLJ 795.

22 [1948] 1 KB 184, [1947] 2 All ER 666; the passage cited is at 191 and 670 respectively.

23 *Marshall v Harland & Wolff Ltd* [1972] 2 All ER 715, [1972] ICR 101, disapproving suggestions to the contrary in *Thomas v John Drake & Co Ltd* (1971) 6 ITR 146; it is not necessary to be able to date the frustrating event precisely, which is particularly significant in the case of frustration through illness. See also *Egg Stores (Stamford Hill) Ltd v Leibovici* [1977] ICR 260, [1976] IRLR 376, EAT.

24 *Unger v Preston Corpn* [1942] 1 All ER 200.

frustrating event is one relating to the employer (for example his death or the destruction of his business), section 136(5) of the 1996 Act safeguards the employee's rights to a redundancy payment by deeming that termination to be a dismissal, and this will apply even if the event applies to both employer and employee (for example the passing of new legislation making the whole employment in question illegal), for it is enough that some of the effect is upon the employer[25].

For an event or circumstance to frustrate the contract of employment it must be exceptionally grave. Certain wartime factors have been held to have the effect of frustration, such as being called up or interned[26]. However, in practice the most important event is illness on the part of the employee, for if it is sufficiently grave to frustrate the contract the employee will lose any potential rights which he may have to claim unfair dismissal or redundancy (the latter because this is not an event befalling the employer, so not covered by the Employment Rights Act 1996, section 136(5)). In *Poussard v Spiers*[27] an opera singer was ill during rehearsals for the opera for which she was engaged, and could not take part in the first four performances; this was held to frustrate the contract so that her employer was entitled to treat the contract as ended. This was also the case in *Condor v Barron Knights Ltd*[28] where the employee was physically unable to play with the pop group in question for seven nights per week through illness and this was held to be a frustration, particularly as the group could not operate on anything less than full-time and could not reasonably operate with a part-time substitute. However, some care may be needed with certain theatrical cases, for a court or tribunal may be more ready to find frustration in the case of a short-term contract entered with a particular performance or set of performances in mind. It may be more difficult to establish in the case of a long-standing employment of a permanent nature[29], particularly in view of the old common law principle that in general the consideration for wages is readiness and willingness to serve on the employee's part, not necessarily the performance of actual work[30]. As the question of frustration through illness is so important in the context of the statutory rights, it was reviewed by the NIRC in *Marshall v Harland and Wolff Ltd*[31] where Sir John Donaldson P laid down the following matters as factors which should be weighed by a tribunal in deciding whether a contract was frustrated:

(a) the terms of the contract, including any provisions as to sick pay;
(b) how long the employment was likely to last in the absence of sickness, for a temporary or specific hiring is more likely to be frustrated;
(c) the nature of the employment, in particular whether the employee was in a 'key post' which had to be filled permanently if his absence was prolonged[32];

25 *Fenerty v British Airports Authority* (1976) 11 ITR 1.
26 *Horlock v Beal* [1916] 1 AC 486, HL; *Marshall v Glanvill* [1917] 2 KB 87; *Morgan v Manser* [1948] 1 KB 184, [1947] 2 All ER 666; *Unger v Preston Corpn* [1942] 1 All ER 200. However, even something as potentially drastic as internment must have a substantial effect and not be merely transitory: *Nordman v Rayner and Sturges* (1916) 33 TLR 87.
27 (1876) 1 QBD 410; cf *Bettini v Gye* (1876) 1 QBD 183, where a singer's illness incapacitated her for the rehearsals but not for any of the performances, and this was held *not* to be a frustration.
28 [1966] 1 WLR 87.
29 See eg *Storey v Fulham Steel Works Co* (1907) 24 TLR 89, CA.
30 *Warburton v Co-operative Wholesale Society Ltd* [1917] 1 KB 663, CA; *Henthorn v Central Electricity Generating Board* [1980] IRLR 361, CA.
31 [1972] 2 All ER 715, [1972] ICR 101.
32 *Hebden v Forsey & Son* [1973] ICR 607, [1973] IRLR 344.

or whether it was such that it could be held open for a considerable period[33];

(d) the nature of the illness, how long it has continued and the prospects of recovery; this may interact with (c) in that if there is no urgency for a replacement, a more distant prospect of recovery may keep the contract alive;

(e) the period of past employment, for 'a relationship which is of long standing is not so easily destroyed as one which has but a short history'.

Tribunals have regularly followed these guidelines, but in *Egg Stores (Stamford Hill) Ltd v Leibovici*[34] the EAT pointed out that they raise a particular difficulty in the case of short-term periodic contracts of employment, which may be determined at short notice, for although the doctrine of frustration is necessary in longer-term contracts if it has become impossible for the employee to perform his part, in the case of the short-term contract the employer has the more ready remedy of dismissal on relatively short notice, which may be more appropriate in the circumstances than reliance upon frustration. In the light of this, although frustration has succeeded in such cases (and the EAT reaffirmed that where this is the case it operates automatically without the necessity of any steps being taken by the employer), in these cases more emphasis may be placed upon whether the employer has thought it right to dismiss the absent employee, for if he has not done so, the tribunal *might* infer that the reason was that he did not think that enough time had elapsed to make it a proper course to take, and that would be a strong inference against frustration. The EAT then said that a short-term periodic contract could be subject to an event (for example a crippling accident) so drastic that it was obvious that it was frustrated, but that in the more normal case of a lingering illness there are further matters to be taken into account along with those in *Marshall*'s case; these are:

(f) the risk to the employer of incurring obligations (in respect of redundancy payments and unfair dismissal) to an employee meant to be a replacement;

(g) whether wages have continued to be paid;

(h) the acts and statements of the employer in relation to the employment, in particular whether there has been a dismissal of sorts and if not, why not[35];

(i) whether in all the circumstances a reasonable employer could be expected to wait any longer.

All of these factors must be weighed by the tribunal which will probably be loath to find frustration; if the contract is not frustrated and the employer is found to have dismissed the employee, a claim for unfair dismissal may proceed which must be decided in the normal way[36], and it has been stated that the tests laid down in *Marshall*'s case are those for frustration, *not* those for deciding whether a dismissal for ill health is reasonable[37], though if the further factors in the *Egg Stores* case are applied, in particular factor (i) above, the two tests do begin to look somewhat similar[38].

33 *Maxwell v Walter Howard Designs Ltd* [1975] IRLR 77, IT.
34 [1977] ICR 260, [1976] IRLR 376, further discussed in *Hart v AR Marshall & Sons (Bulwell) Ltd* [1977] ICR 539, [1977] IRLR 51 and *Williams v Watsons Luxury Coaches Ltd* [1990] ICR 536, [1990] IRLR 164.
35 Emphasised in *Hart v A R Marshall & Sons (Bulwell) Ltd* [1977] ICR 539, [1977] IRLR 51.
36 See p 576 below.
37 *Tan v Berry Bros and Rudd Ltd* [1974] ICR 586, [1974] IRLR 244.
38 *Egg Stores (Stamford Hill) Ltd v Leibovici* [1977] ICR 260 at 264G, [1976] IRLR 376 at 378, per Phillips J.

At one point, the whole question of the application of the doctrine of frustration to contracts of employment was thrown into confusion by the decision of the EAT in *Harman v Flexible Lamps Ltd*[39] where it was held not only that the applicant's illness did not frustrate her contract on the facts, but further that the doctrine as a matter of law should only apply to long-term contracts not terminable by notice. However desirable such an approach may be as a matter of policy, the decision was fatally flawed as a precedent since it did not even cite either *Marshall v Harland and Wolff Ltd* or *Egg Stores (Stamford Hill) Ltd v Leibovici* (above), with both of which it was inconsistent. Not surprisingly, therefore, when the issue went to the Court of Appeal in *Notcutt v Universal Equipment Co (London) Ltd*[40] orthodoxy was re-established – it was accepted that Bristow J was correct to state in *Harman* that a court should be *cautious* about applying frustration to contracts easily terminable by notice (particularly if it is being used as a means of avoiding statutory rights), but to go further and suggest that the doctrine itself is not applicable was incorrect. In the case itself illness absence of eight months due to a coronary was held to have frustrated the contract of employment of an employee of twenty-seven years' service, who was entitled by law to twelve weeks' notice. The employee's claim was in fact a common law claim in the county court for sick pay (which in the event was not payable due to the frustration of the contract) but it is clear that the decision is also applicable to a statutory action, particularly an action for unfair dismissal. While the court did state that defences of frustration should be treated carefully[41], it must be accepted that the decision does leave considerable scope for frustration in sickness cases – twelve weeks was not an unduly long notice period, and the dominant factor in the case appears to be that the illness led immediately to total and lasting incapacity for work, which is not going to be a rare occurrence in cases of major illness or accident. In such an event, however, the position may now be complicated by a modern tendency in some employments to offer (as part of enhanced terms and conditions) 'permanent health insurance' covering generously employees who are permanently unable to work – in such a case, could this factor be used to defeat an argument for frustration, on the basis that the illness was fully covered by the contract and so not an *unforeseen* frustrating event?[42] If so, could the argument eventually be taken even further and applied to an employment covered by an *ordinary* sick pay term, at least where it is relatively generous and envisages a long period off work while still receiving pay?

Varying views as to the proper approach to be taken to frustration can also be seen in the other major area for its potential application to employment contracts, the effect of imprisonment of the employee. Here the complicating factor is not whether the contract is terminable on short notice, but rather whether imprisonment constitutes 'self induced frustration', for it is usually

---

39   [1980] IRLR 418.
40   [1986] ICR 414, [1986] IRLR 218, CA, followed in *F C Shepherd & Co Ltd v Jerrom* [1986] ICR 802, [1986] IRLR 358, CA.
41   Further, it was accepted by Mustill LJ in *F C Shepherd & Co Ltd v Jerrom* (n 40 above) that the existence of a disciplinary procedure covering the event in question (in that case, imprisonment) might be a factor against finding frustration.
42   This argument was accepted in *Villella v MFI Furniture Centres Ltd* [1999] IRLR 468. For the effect of such permanent health insurance schemes on the giving of notice to persons subject to them, see p 166 above.

said that the frustrating event must not be self-induced[43]. In *Hare v Murphy Bros Ltd*[44] the Court of Appeal held that a contract of employment was automatically terminated when the employee was sentenced to twelve months' imprisonment for an assault unconnected with his employment. Lord Denning clearly said that the contract was frustrated and that it was not a case of self induction for the frustrating event was the imposition of the sentence (even though that was of course originally caused by the criminal behaviour). The problem was, however, that the other two judgments were not unequivocally in agreement with this approach, and a major disagreement arose between different EATs as to whether the doctrine of frustration should apply to imprisonment cases. In one sense the end result might be much the same since even if frustration does not apply and an unfair dismissal action proceeds, it is likely that the dismissal of an employee who has received an immediate and substantial term of imprisonment will be fair, provided it is sensibly handled by the employer[45]. However, it remains of considerable interest legally whether the employer can go further and stop an unfair dismissal action dead in its tracks in such a case by pleading frustration. A finding of frustration through imprisonment was upheld in *Harrington v Kent County Council*[46] (even though the employee's sentence was under appeal, which was ultimately successful), and was assumed to be possible (though not proved on the facts) in *Chakki v United Yeast Co Ltd*[47]; to the contrary, however, it was held in *Norris v Southampton City Council*[48] that a contract of employment is *not* frustrated by imprisonment, as a matter of law. The point was eventually resolved by the Court of Appeal in *F C Shepherd & Co Ltd v Jerrom*[49] which concerned an unfair dismissal action by an apprentice who lost his employment when sentenced to borstal training for offences of violence half-way through his apprenticeship. The EAT[50] held that imprisonment can frustrate a contract of employment, that *Hare v Murphy Bros Ltd* (above) does support that proposition and that *Norris* is wrong. However, they upheld the tribunal's decision that there was no frustration here on rather novel grounds – seeking to restrict the operation of the doctrine, Waite P added the gloss that where, as here, the contract contained a prescribed termination procedure covering the event in question (in this case, incorporated from a national joint agreement governing apprenticeship) that event cannot be an *unforeseen* eventuality and so cannot be a frustrating event. However, this interesting and positive gloss was disapproved by the Court of Appeal who allowed the employer's appeal and held the doctrine to be applicable to cases of imprisonment simpliciter. That left one remaining problem – was not this

---

43   *Bank Line Ltd v Arthur Capel & Co* [1919] AC 435 at 452, HL, per Lord Sumner; *Denmark Productions Ltd v Boscobel Productions Ltd* [1969] 1 QB 699, [1968] 3 All ER 513, at 736, CA and 533 respectively, per Harman LJ. It is for the party relying on frustration to prove it, but for the other party to prove that it was self-induced (if that be their allegation): *Joseph Constantine Steamship Line Ltd v Imperial Smelting Corpn Ltd* [1942] AC 154, [1941] 2 All ER 165, HL.
44   [1974] 3 All ER 940, [1974] ICR 603, CA.
45   *Kingston v British Railways Board* [1984] ICR 781, [1984] IRLR 146, CA.
46   [1980] IRLR 353, EAT.
47   [1982] 2 All ER 446, [1982] ICR 140, EAT.
48   [1982] ICR 177 [1982] IRLR 141. The decision in this case involved a strained reading of *Hare v Murphy Bros Ltd*, n 44 above and, arguably, entirely misplaced reliance on *London Transport Executive v Clarke* [1981] ICR 355, [1981] IRLR 166, CA, p 553 below, which concerned a case of clear repudiation of contract, not frustration.
49   [1986] ICR 802, [1986] IRLR 358, CA.
50   [1985] ICR 552, [1985] IRLR 275. The case was newsworthy when decided by the EAT; the idea of a boy sent to borstal for offences of violence receiving compensation of £7,000 for being refused his job back was not treated sympathetically in the tabloid press.

frustration self-induced? Further, was it not the case that frustration must not be the fault of *either* party?[51] This was resolved in two ways – Balcombe LJ accepted Lord Denning MR's view in *Hare v Murphy Bros Ltd* that the frustrating event was actually the imposition of the sentence, not the misconduct by the employee, but Lawton and Mustill LJJ took a more fundamental approach – that, properly understood, the rule against self-induction only meant that neither party could rely on his *own* misconduct to establish a defence of frustration. As the employer was relying on the *employee's* fault here, that requirement was satisfied and frustration could succeed; to hold otherwise would allow a party at fault to benefit from his own misdeeds, which would not be tolerated. As with *Notcutt's* case in the context of sickness, this decision of the Court of Appeal resolved an unfortunate division of opinion on frustration, and did so by applying a fairly straightforward and orthodox approach again. It leaves one (possibly unanswerable) question – how long does the sentence of imprisonment have to be in order to justify a finding of frustration? This presumably remains a question of fact for the tribunal or court.

(iii) Expiry of fixed term contracts

There used to be a presumption that a general hiring (ie one with no fixed duration) was a hiring for a year, the significance of this being that it guaranteed agricultural labourers employment through all four seasons. This, however, no longer has any place in employment law, and a general hiring now is regarded as a hiring for an indefinite period, determinable by reasonable notice[52]. However, the employer and employee may agree that a contract shall be for a fixed period only (possibly for a probationary period) and at common law that contract terminates automatically at the expiry of the period[53]. Clearly this point had to be taken into account by the framers of the modern statutory employment law, though for many years this was done in a rather ambiguous way. On the one hand, the expiry of a fixed term contract has always been deemed to be a 'dismissal' for the purposes of unfair dismissal and redundancy law;[54] to have failed to do so would have left a huge gap in the legal protection by allowing the employer to avoid it simply by making the employee's contract fixed term. On the other hand, for many years the employer was allowed to restrict his liability in defined circumstances, in that an employee could sign away his unfair dismissal rights in a fixed term contract of one year or more and his redundancy rights in a fixed term contract of two years or more.[55] The present government have repealed both of these provisions, the first by the Employment Relations Act 1999 and the

---

51 See, in a commercial context, *Paal Wilson & Co A/S v Partenreederei Hannah Blumenthal* [1983] 1 AC 854, [1983] 1 All ER 34, HL.
52 *De Stempel v Dunkels* [1938] 1 All ER 238, CA; *Richardson v Koefod* [1969] 3 All ER 1264, [1969] 1 WLR 1812, CA.
53 *R v Secretary of State for Social Services, ex p Khan* [1973] 2 All ER 104, [1973] 1 WLR 187, CA. See also *Brown v Knowsley Borough Council* [1986] IRLR 102 (contract expressed to be subject to continued external funding held to terminate automatically when that funding ceased).
54 Employment Rights Act 1996 ss 95(1)(b), 136(1)(b); see p 546 below.
55 S 197, now wholly repealed.

second by the Fixed-term Worker (Prevention of Less Favourable Treatment) Regulations 2002[56].

Given this involvement of statute, questions of interpretation not surprisingly arose, and two in particular go to the root of the meaning of fixed term. The first, and most immediately pressing in the early case law, was the possible conflict between a statement that a contract is for a fixed term and the inclusion in it of a provision for termination by notice. In *BBC v Ioannou*[57] the contract in question was for a fixed period, but with a provision for termination by three months' notice, and this was held not to be a 'fixed-term contract', so that the purported written surrender of redundancy and unfair dismissal rights was ineffective. Termination by notice was held to be inconsistent with a fixed-term contract, which had to be for that term and not terminable during it. In this case the Court of Appeal were attempting to safeguard the position of those on fixed term contracts by ensuring that only those *genuinely* on such contracts could sign away their rights (as the law then allowed). When, however, this reasoning was applied to the statutory definition of dismissal it had potentially dire results for the employee[58], for it meant that if the employer put him on a contract which was ostensibly for a fixed term but used the ploy of inserting a notice provision of sorts, the employer could then have argued that, under *BBC v Ioannou*, that was *not* a fixed-term contract, and so when it expired that was *not* the expiry of a fixed term contract under the Employment Rights Act 1996, sections 95(1)(b) and 136(1)(b) and so, as it would not qualify as an ordinary dismissal under sections 95(1)(a) and 136(1)(a), there would have been no 'dismissal' and so no possible claims for unfair dismissal or redundancy. This was argued by an employer in *Dixon v BBC*[59], but in that case the Court of Appeal recognised the absurdity that would arise from this application of *BBC v Ioannou* and so, not wishing to establish two different definitions for 'fixed term' depending on whether the case concerned (a) or (b) above, they reversed as per incuriam that part of *BBC v Ioannou* which dealt with the definition of 'fixed term', and held that a contract for a set period remains a fixed-term contract for statutory purposes even if it also contains a provision for termination by notice during its currency. Thus *Dixon v BBC* is now the ruling case, and so the employer cannot use this simple device to rule out the employee's action, but must instead accept that when a fixed-term contract expires (whether or not there is a notice provision in it), that is a 'dismissal' under sections 95 and 136 and, in an unfair dismissal case, be prepared to justify his reasons for not renewing the contract[60].

The second question has become even more fundamental and has led to a significant recent change – what form of expiry is necessary before a contract comes within this category at all? The case law on the legislation as it stood until 2002 made the clear distinction that that a fixed-term contract is one which is to

---

56 The redundancy provision was repealed as from 1 October 2002; any existing clause excluding redundancy rights continued to be effective at the end of the contract but after that date no new or renewed contract could lawfully contain such a clause. The main purposes of the 2002 Regulations are to enact a regime of less favourable for fixed-term employees and to place limitations on the length of time that an employer can keep an employee on successive fixed-term contracts; see p 26 above.
57 [1975] 2 All ER 999, [1975] ICR 267, CA.
58 See Hepple and Napier 'Temporary workers and the law' (1978) 7 ILJ 84.
59 [1979] ICR 281, [1979] IRLR 114, CA.
60 *Terry v East Sussex County Council* [1977] 1 All ER 567, [1976] ICR 536, approved by the Court of Appeal in *Fay v North Yorkshire County Council* [1986] ICR 133, [1985] IRLR 247, CA.

expire on a definable *date*, not on the happening of a particular event or the completion of a particular task at some time in the future[61]. There was therefore the possibility of such a 'task' or 'purpose' contract (for example employment until a particular building is demolished) terminating automatically without there being a dismissal in law, which could, of course, materially prejudice statutory rights[62]. If, however, the event or completion in question (for example the end of a particular course in a short-term teaching contract) could in fact be dated with reasonable precision, then it was held that that should be treated as sufficient for the existence of a fixed-term contract; if it were otherwise, it might be easy for an employer to avoid the statutory definition of dismissal by putting the contract in the *form* of an engagement pending a particular event, even if the date of that event could be discerned. This was, however, subject to major change in October 2002 under the Fixed-term Employees (Prevention of Less Favourable Treatment) Regulations 2002 in order to comply with the wider definition in the Fixed-term Worker Directive 1999/70/EC, which covers task or purpose contracts. Moreover, this change applies not only under the Regulations themselves, but also to the basic definitions in the above sections in the Employment Rights Act 1996. Both the unfair dismissal and redundancy payments provisions now state that there is deemed to be a dismissal where the employee 'is employed under a limited-term contract[63] and that contract terminates by virtue of the limiting event without being renewed under the same contract'. Inserted definitions define 'limited-term contract' as being where '(a) the employment under the contract is not intended to be permanent and (b) provision is accordingly made in the contract for it to terminate by virtue of a limiting event'; 'limiting event' is defined as the expiry of a fixed term, the performance of a specific task in contemplation of which the contract is made or the occurrence or non-occurrence of an event where the contract provides for termination on such occurrence or non-occurrence.[64] Thus, task or purpose contracts are now included in the statutory definitions and, as there has not in the past been any divergence between statute and common law concepts of fixed-term contracts (given that they have been so closely intertwined), it is to be assumed that this new approach would, if ever necessary, be applied at common law too.

(iv) Mutual consent

As with other contracts, a contract of employment may in general be terminated by the mutual agreement of the employer and employee so to do (just as they may agree to vary the agreed terms of the contract during its operation, provided that the variation is voluntary and without undue pressure on the employee[65]). Thus in *S W Strange Ltd v Mann*[66] the defendant was employed as the plaintiff company's manager under a contract which included a restraint clause, restricting his post-

61 *Wiltshire County Council v NATFHE* [1980] ICR 455, [1980] IRLR 198, CA.
62 *Brown v Knowsley Borough Council*, n 53 above, is an extreme example of this.
63 This change of terminology here is curious because the Regulations themselves (which of course use substantially the same definition) retain the term 'fixed-term contract'.
64 Employment Rights Act 1996, s 235(2A), (2B).
65 *Marriott v Oxford and District Co-operative Society Ltd (No 2)* [1970] 1 QB 186, [1969] 3 All ER 1126, CA.
66 [1965] 1 All ER 1069, [1965] 1 WLR 629; cf *Cowey v Liberian Operations Ltd* [1966] 2 Lloyd's Rep 45.

employment activities. After certain disagreements the parties agreed that the defendant should cease to be manager and instead take over the running of only one department. When he was eventually dismissed, the plaintiff tried to enforce the restraint clause, but the court held for the defendant on the ground, inter alia, that the original contract had been terminated by mutual consent, and the new contract which was entered did not contain the relevant clause. As with other common law concepts, however, 'mutual consent' gained renewed significance with the advent of the new statutory rights, often dependent upon continuity of the employment, and the fact of dismissal. While the concept of mutual consent in fact worked in the employee's favour in *Strange Ltd v Mann*, it would be more likely to jeopardise an employee's statutory rights if found too readily, for it could break continuity and provide the employer with an argument that there had in fact been no dismissal, only a voluntary parting of the ways. In *McAlwane v Boughton Estates*[67] an employee was given notice to terminate his employment on 19 April, but during the notice period he asked if he could leave on 12 April. The employer agreed, and, when the employee claimed a redundancy payment and unfair dismissal, argued that there was no dismissal because the contract had been terminated by mutual consent on 12 April. The NIRC rejected this argument, holding that this merely constituted an agreed variation of the notice period, so that the employee was still dismissed by the employer. Sir John Donaldson P said:

'We would further suggest that it would be a very rare case indeed in which it could properly be found that the employer and the employee had got together and, notwithstanding that there was a current notice of termination of the employment, agreed mutually to terminate the contract, particularly when one realises the financial consequences to the employee involved in such an agreement. We do not say that such arrangement cannot arise; we merely say that, viewed in a real life situation, it would seem to be a possibility which might appeal to a lawyer more than to a personnel manager[68].'

This decision, and this dictum in particular, was applied by the Court of Appeal (by a majority) in *Lees v Arthur Greaves Ltd*[69] where, on similar facts, it was once again held that there was no termination by mutual consent.

Mutual consent will therefore be difficult to establish, particularly in a statutory context; this is particularly so in an unfair dismissal action, for the Employment Rights Act 1996, section 95(2) provides that where an employee under notice gives his employer notice that he wishes to leave before the expiry of the employer's notice, the employee is deemed still to have been dismissed by the employer for unfair dismissal purposes. The applicants in *McAlwane* and *Lees* could not rely upon the equivalent provisions in the legislation at the time[70] since they then required *written* notice by the employee, and this had not been given. The requirement of writing was deleted for unfair dismissal purposes by the Employment Protection Act 1975, but not for redundancy purposes where it

---

67 [1973] 2 All ER 299, [1973] ICR 470.
68 [1973] 2 All ER 299 at 302, [1973] ICR 470 at 473.
69 [1974] 2 All ER 393, [1974] ICR 501, CA. See also *Glacier Metal Co Ltd v Dyer* [1974] 3 All ER 21, [1974] IRLR 189.
70 Industrial Relations Act 1971, s 23(3) (later the Trade Union and Labour Relations Act 1974, Sch 1, para 5(3)) and the Redundancy Payments Act 1965, s 4(2).

is still required[71]. However, termination by mutual consent does remain a possibility as can be seen from *Lipton Ltd v Marlborough*[72] where an employee, faced with the loss of his job on a reorganisation, began to look for other employment, but was hindered by his contract which required him to give six months' notice and contained a restraint of trade clause. During negotiations he requested that he be released from his contract immediately and the employer agreed. When he later claimed unfair dismissal the tribunal found that he had been constructively dismissed (on the basis that the employer intended to phase out his job), but the EAT allowed the employer's appeal and held that this was a termination by mutual agreement, not a dismissal, Bristow J stating:

> 'The whole difference between termination by mutual agreement in this context and constructive dismissal is that in the first case the employee says "Please may I go?" and the employer says "Yes". In the second case the employee says "You have treated me in such a way that I'm going without a by-your-leave".'

Such a case will, however, remain a rarity (either in the specific context of a cross-notice to end employment or more generally) and the fact that the employee did not object to his own dismissal (for example on an agreed redundancy) will not normally prevent it from still being a dismissal[73]; the usual narrow approach was reaffirmed by the EAT in *Tracey v Zest Equipment Co Ltd*[74] where termination of employment following a failure to return on time from holiday (when the employee, who had been late back before, had agreed beforehand that his employment would be terminated in the event of lateness) was held not to have been terminated by mutual consent, but rather to have been repudiatory conduct leading to dismissal, thus allowing the tribunal to consider the substantive question of fairness.

As against that, termination by mutual consent was subsequently found by the Court of Appeal in *Birch v University of Liverpool*[75] in the case of two academics taking early retirement under a scheme adopted by universities and their relevant unions. The facts were exceptional in that the scheme required a high degree of mutual agreement and clearly envisaged that statutory redundancy payments (which the two applicants were now claiming) would *not* be payable on top; the case does, however, show an important potential application of the idea of mutual consent in modern circumstances particularly where, as Ackner LJ pointed out, the employer calls for resignations well in advance of decreases in the workforce, there is no compulsion and the employer offers financial inducements well in excess of what would be payable under the ordinary redundancy payments scheme.

---

71 Employment Rights Act 1996, s 136(3).
72 [1979] IRLR 179.
73 *Burton, Allton and Johnson Ltd v Peck* [1975] ICR 193, [1975] IRLR 87. In *Lassman v De Vere University Arms Hotel* [2003] ICR 44 a hotel manager whose job was being downgraded was given the choice (only) of going part-time or taking redundancy; when she reluctantly chose the latter, it was held that she had still been dismissed and so could claim unfair dismissal.
74 [1982] ICR 481, [1982] IRLR 268. The case is in line with the restrictive approach taken at the same time to the analogous area of 'constructive resignation' or 'self dismissal', as seen in *London Transport Executive v Clarke* [1981] ICR 355, [1981] IRLR 166, CA (see below) which is cited in the judgment of the EAT.
75 [1985] ICR 470, [1985] IRLR 165, CA, distinguishing *Burton, Allton & Johnson Ltd v Peck*, n 73 above; noted Freedland (1985) 14 ILJ 243.

The decision in *Birch* was taken one step further by the EAT in *Scott v Coalite Fuels & Chemicals Ltd*[76] where it was held that there was mutual termination where employees took voluntary early retirement while already under notice of dismissal for redundancy. While such a decision may make good industrial sense in a case where early retirement (with a lump-sum payment, but a reduced weekly pension) is negotiated as an *alternative* to redundancy, it does call into question the dictum of Sir John Donaldson cited at the beginning of this section that mutual termination during a current notice period would only be found in 'a very rare case indeed'. Perhaps cases involving genuine early retirement schemes should be treated as sui generis.

2 DISMISSAL BY NOTICE

Most contracts of employment may be terminated by either party giving the necessary notice of termination. The period of notice may be agreed expressly by the parties[77] and, more unusually, the parties may agree to restrict the reasons behind the giving of notice[78]. More usually, however, the right to give notice will not be so restricted and only the mechanics of the period to be given will be laid down. If there is no such express provision, and no term can be ascertained from custom or trade usage[79], the law will read into a contract of employment that it is terminable upon 'reasonable notice'. It may then be a litigious matter to quantify what is reasonable; as this is a matter of construction of the contract it has in the past been within the jurisdiction of the civil courts, but it could now be raised in proceedings before tribunals, under their common law jurisdiction on termination of employment[80]. There are many reported cases on this question of quantification and all that can be said is that each case must depend upon its own facts such as the position of the employee within the firm, his or her professional standing and, in some cases, the intervals for payment[81]. To be effective (since it has such a drastic effect) the notice must be definite and explicit. Thus in *Morris v Bailey*[82] it was held that a notice of termination given to the plaintiff's union but not to him personally was not effective to dismiss him, even though most of his contract of employment (including the notice provisions) consisted of terms incorporated from the union's collective agreement. Moreover, the details of the

---

76 [1988] ICR 355, [1988] IRLR 131 (see also *Logan Salton v Durham County Council* [1989] IRLR 99, where an employee under threat of disciplinary proceedings negotiated severance terms and was held to them). It remains the case, however, that there will still be a dismissal (even if in form there appears to be mutual agreement) if either (a) all that the employee has done is to volunteer to be dismissed for redundancy, or (b) there has been pressure put on the employee to agree to go (see p 545 below).

77 Written particulars of the notice period should be given to the employee within two months of commencement: Employment Rights Act, s 1(4)(e).

78 *McClelland v Northern Ireland General Health Services Board* [1957] 2 All ER 129, [1957] 1 WLR 594, HL. It has been held that there is an *implied* restriction on giving notice to a long-term sick employee where there is a permanent health insurance scheme in operation under the contract; see p 166 above.

79 *George v Davies* [1911] 2 KB 445.

80 See p 528 below.

81 Thus in *Grundy v Sun Printing and Publishing Association* (1916) 33 TLR 77, CA, an editor was entitled to 12 months' notice, but in *Fox-Bourne v Vernon & Co Ltd* (1894) 10 TLR 647 another editor was only entitled to six months'. For a more modern example of this process of quantification, see *Hill v CA Parsons & Co Ltd* [1972] Ch 305, [1971] 3 All ER 1345, CA.

82 [1969] 2 Lloyd's Rep 215, CA.

notice that is to be given must be made known to the employee, so that a mere warning of impending dismissal (for example for redundancy) will not constitute notice[83]. However, once an effective notice has been given by one of the parties, he may not withdraw it unilaterally, and so withdrawal of the notice may only be by mutual consent[84].

Under the common law of employment, the availability to the employer of dismissal by notice could in practice negate what rights an employee might have; for example an employee might be justified in refusing to obey an order which was illegal or outside the scope of his employment and the employer could not summarily dismiss him for that refusal, but there was nothing to stop the employer from giving him notice because of the incident, since a dismissal on proper notice was lawful regardless of the motive behind it. If the notice period was only a matter of days or even hours, that could be a powerful threat to the employee. This position is now heavily overlaid by the statutory provisions as to redundancy and unfair dismissal (particularly as the latter entails scrutiny of the merits of the dismissal, not just its technical correctness), but the question of notice was first affected by statute in the Contracts of Employment Act 1963[85] which attempted to alter the common law in two ways – first, by gearing the period of notice to the length of continuous service, not simply to the status of the employee; secondly, by safeguarding certain employee rights during the period of notice. The present provisions relating to these two points will now be considered.

The common law rules proved to be inadequate in that they made no distinction for the long-serving employee. Thus an employee on a weekly contract would only be entitled to a week's notice whether he worked for his employer for one week or forty years. Large scale redundancies emphasised this defect, and certain minimum notice periods are now laid down by statute. Under the Employment Rights Act 1996, section 86, the minimum notice period for an employee with under two years' continuous employment is one week; where there is over two years' continuous employment, the employee is entitled to one week's notice for each year up to a maximum of 12 weeks. As for the employee, the statutory minimum which he must give to terminate his employment is one week if he has been employed for four weeks or more. The section states that it does not affect the right of either party to terminate the contract through the other party's conduct, and does not prevent either party from waiving his right to notice on any particular occasion[86]. Subsection (3) also states that the section does not prevent a party from accepting a payment in lieu of notice[87]. 'Wages in lieu' is a common phenomenon, whereby the employer gives the employee the wages which he would have earned during the notice period, and instructs him not to work out

---

83   *Morton Sundour Fabrics Ltd v Shaw* (1966) 2 ITR 84; *Pritchard-Rhodes Ltd v Boon and Milton* [1979] IRLR 19; *International Computers Ltd v Kennedy* [1981] IRLR 28; *Doble v Firestone Tyre and Rubber Co Ltd* [1981] IRLR 300; *Haseltine Lake & Co v Dowler* [1981] ICR 222, [1981] IRLR 25. This is particularly important in the context of the giving of counter-notice by an employee, for the purposes of redundancy law; see p 625 below.

84   *Riordan v War Office* [1959] 3 All ER 552, [1959] 1 WLR 1059 (affd [1960] 3 All ER 774n, [1961] 1 WLR 210, CA); *Harris and Russell Ltd v Slingsby* [1973] 3 All ER 31, [1973] ICR 454.

85   Later the Contracts of Employment Act 1972, and now to be found in the Employment Rights Act 1996, ss 86–91.

86   Waiver of notice includes waiver of any right to payment for the notice period (especially in a voluntary severance case): *Trotter v Forth Ports Authority* [1991] IRLR 419, Ct of Sess; *Baldwin v British Coal Corpn* [1995] IRLR 139.

87   *Staffordshire County Council v Secretary of State for Employment* [1987] ICR 956, [1988] IRLR 3 (reversed on other grounds, [1989] ICR 664, [1989] IRLR 117, CA).

the notice period, so that the employer is rid of him immediately. This is perfectly lawful if both parties agree to it, and this is as far as the subsection goes. One contentious point, however, is whether the employer has a *right* to give wages in lieu if the employee wishes to work out the notice period. The old tenet of employment law that the employer's only obligation is to provide wages, not work, suggested that dismissal with wages in lieu would be lawful[88], except in one of the exceptional cases where work also had to be provided[89]. However, the more modern approach has been to look more closely at *how* the dismissal is effected. The renewed interest in this point is not because of its direct effect on wrongful dismissal (since, even if the dismissal is wrongful, the prima facie measure of damages, the wages themselves, have already been paid[90]), but rather because of four incidental matters which may be affected – (1) whether the protection against unlawful deductions in Part II of the Employment Rights Act 1996 applies to any non-payment of the wages[91]; (2) what is the effective date of termination of the dismissal[92]; (3) whether any restraint of trade clause in the contract survives the termination[93]; (4) whether an employee deprived of the qualifying period for unfair dismissal by a instant dismissal just before reaching it can claim loss of compensation for unfair dismissal in a wrongful dismissal action[94]. In *Delaney v Staples*[95], the leading case on deductions from wages, Lord Browne-Wilkinson analysed the law on dismissal with wages in lieu; adopting his classification, the position in relation to the above matters appears to be as follows.

(i)　The employer gives the employee proper notice, but then tells him that he need not work it out; in such a case (including a 'garden leave' case) the dismissal is lawful, with advance payment of 'wages', the effective date of termination is the end of the notice period, and any restraint clause may continue to apply.

(ii)　The contract itself provides for termination by notice *or* by wages in lieu; here, the dismissal is lawful, the payment is not 'wages' for the purposes of Part II of the 1996 Act (because not paid under a subsisting contract of employment), the effective date of termination is the date the wages in lieu are given (*not* the end of the period of notice) and any restraint clause may continue to apply[96].

88　*Konski v Peet* [1915] 1 Ch 530.
89　See p 152 above. This point was particularly taken up (in the context of garden leave) in *William Hill Organisation Ltd v Tucker* [1999] ICR 291, [1998] IRLR 313, CA which showed a broader approach to who can claim an interest in having the work itself provided.
90　Though it can still affect whether the nature of the employee's right is damages or *debt* (in which case there is no obligation to mitigate loss, and so earnings in new employment need not be taken into account): *Gregory v Wallace* [1998] IRLR 387, CA.
91　If it does, the ex-employee may challenge any non-payment (total or partial) of the wages in lieu before an employment tribunal, instead of before the ordinary courts; see p 259 above.
92　See p 553 below. This is relevant because (a) by that date the employee must have the necessary qualifying service and (b) the three-month time limit for claiming unfair dismissal flows from that date. It is thus in the employer's interest to have the EDT early, ie when the employment actually ends, not the (later) date on which notice would notionally have expired.
93　If the dismissal is wrongful, the restraint clause falls: see p 132 above.
94　See p 486 below; if there is an express wages in lieu clause, the instant termination is not wrongful and so no damages can be claimed, even though the employee has still lost the unfair dismissal rights: *Morran v Glasgow Council of Tenants' Associations* [1998] IRLR 67, Ct of Sess.
95　[1992] ICR 483, [1992] IRLR 191, HL.
96　*Rex Stewart Jeffries Parker Ginsberg Ltd v Parker* [1988] IRLR 483, CA, explaining the earlier decision in *Dixon v Stenor Ltd* [1973] ICR 157, [1973] IRLR 28.

(iii)   At the end of the employment, the employer and employee agree ad hoc that it will end forthwith, on the payment of the sum in lieu; the results here are as in (ii), it being a lawful variation of the normal notice term.

(iv)   The employer summarily dismisses the employee, without his agreement, but tenders a payment in lieu of notice; here, the employer is in breach of contract and so the dismissal is wrongful, which means that the payment is *damages*, not 'wages' (but they extinguish any *claim* for damages), the effective date of termination remains the date of the summary dismissal and payment in lieu, *but* any restraint of trade clause now becomes invalid because of the wrongful dismissal.

From this analysis, it can be seen that the employer now has much to gain from putting into the contract of employment a term expressly permitting dismissal with wages in lieu, since it provides the optimum position of a lawful dismissal, no challenge to the payment in tribunal proceedings, an early effective date of termination and the preservation of any restraint of trade clause. From the employee's point of view, the existence of an express payment in lieu clause is both advantageous and disadvantageous. On the positive side, as the dismissal is lawful, the employee may claim any unpaid wages in lieu as a debt due under the contract, not as damages for breach of it; this means that the employee is not under a duty to mitigate his loss, which may be of particular importance for a highly paid employee on long notice, who has obtained new employment during what would have been the notice period but who does *not* have to bring those new (equally high?) earnings into account, and so may receive and retain both sums of money in full[97]. On the negative side, however, the fact that the payment in lieu is contractual means that the amount paid is taxable in the employee's hands, since it cannot be construed as 'damages' and hence not subject to income tax (as remains the case with a non-contractual payment, under head (iv) above)[98].

In addition to laying down minimum periods of notice, the legislation also safeguards certain employee rights during the period of notice[99], though it should be noted that these provisions do not apply where the notice to be given by the employer under the contract is more than a week longer than the statutory minimum as laid down in section 86[100]. These provisions differ slightly, depending upon whether or not the employee who is under notice works 'normal working hours'. The construction of that phrase is therefore important, and essentially

---

97   *Abrahams v Performing Right Society* [1995] ICR 1028, [1995] IRLR 486, CA. This case also contains some extremely dubious dicta, to the effect that even if the dismissal had been unlawful (ie under category (iv)) there would still have been no duty to mitigate; this is contrary to established principle (on mitigation, see p 489 below), contrary to the speech of Lord Browne-Wilkinson in *Delaney v Staples* (n 95 above, at 493, 194), contrary to dicta in the earlier House of Lords case of *Westwood v Secretary of State for Employment* [1985] ICR 209, [1984] IRLR 209 where mitigation was in issue (see particularly per Lord Bridge at 219, 211), and best tactfully forgotten. It was discreetly ignored subsequently in *Gregory v Wallace* [1998] IRLR 387, CA. According to *Cerberus Software Ltd v Rowley* [2001] EWCA Civ 78, [2001] ICR 376, [2001] IRLR 160, where there is an in lieu clause but the employer refuses to pay under it, the employee is restricted to an action in damages and so must mitigate (even though this in effect allows the employer to benefit from his own misdeed in dismissing wrongfully, rather than lawfully under the in lieu clause).

98   *EMI Group Electronics Ltd v Coldicott* [1999] IRLR 630, [1999] STC 803, CA; applied to a negotiated settlement in *Richardson (IT) v Delaney* [2001] IRLR 663. It is, however, now clear that a non-contractual payment in lieu of notice (PILON) will not always be free from tax, because the Inland Revenue have issued new guidance restricting non-taxability to payments which are genuinely damages: Tax Bulletin, February 2003, p 999.

99   Employment Rights Act 1996, ss 87-91.

100 S 87(4). *Scotts Co (UK) Ltd v Budd* [2003] IRLR 145, EAT.

the test is whether the contract of employment lays down a certain or minimum number of hours which the employee must work; if so, he works 'normal working hours'. Prima facie this might be expected to be exclusive of overtime, but under section 234(3) of the 1996 Act some overtime may count if it is included in the number of hours which the employee must work (for example if he is contractually bound to work forty hours per week, and overtime rates begin to be payable after thirty-seven hours, then that is still normal working hours of forty per week); to qualify under this extension, however, the overtime must be compulsory in the sense of being obligatory for the employee and guaranteed by the employer[101]. Where the employee works normal working hours and actually works during the notice period he will be contractually entitled to the correct payment without assistance from the legislation but section 88(1) ensures that he continues to be paid at the relevant rate for any periods when (a) he is ready and willing to work but the employer has no work for him, (b) he is incapable of work through sickness or injury, or (c) he is away on proper holiday; it is provided[102] that where the employee draws sickness or industrial injury benefit that is to be taken into account in computing the employer's liability to him, since otherwise he might be doubly entitled, through drawing the benefit and receiving full pay from the employer. Where the employee does not work normal working hours, the employer must pay him a week's pay (calculated in accordance with Part XIV of the 1996 Act[103]) for each week of the period of notice, provided that he is ready and willing to do work of a reasonable nature and amount to earn it; once again, the employee is specifically entitled to payment during absence through sickness or injury, or whilst on proper holiday. The legislation contains three main qualifications upon these rights to payment:

(a) the employee is not entitled to be paid during time off which he has requested (including time off governed by statute[104]);

(b) if the employee breaks the contract during the period of notice and is justifiably summarily dismissed, he is not entitled to further payment as from that dismissal;

(c) if it is the employee who has given notice and he goes on strike during the notice period, he is not entitled to payment under these provisions at all; where it is the employer who has given notice this qualification does not apply, so that the employee will be contractually entitled to payment for that part of the notice period when he was not on strike[105].

If an employer fails to give the statutory notice, the rights laid down in these provisions are to be taken into account in assessing damages, and it is further provided that if the employer breaks the contract of employment during the

---

101 See, in the context of the *computation* of the number of normal working hours, *Tarmac Roadstone Holdings Ltd v Peacock* [1973] 2 All ER 485, [1973] ICR 273, CA, applied to the present context of the *definition* of normal working hours in *Fox v C Wright (Farmers) Ltd* [1978] ICR 98. The questions of 'normal working hours' and what constitutes 'a week's pay' are discussed at p 230 above.

102 Employment Rights Act 1996, s 90. The rationale behind this was queried by Dillon LJ in *Notcutt v Universal Equipment Co (London) Ltd* [1986] ICR 414, [1986] IRLR 218, CA, since it may mean paying sick pay during notice to an employee not normally entitled to it; however, as the court held that the contract was frustrated by the sickness the matter did not arise.

103 This calculation is considered at p 232 above.

104 Employment Rights Act 1996, Part VI; Trade Union and Labour Relations (Consolidation) Act 1992, ss 168, 170.

105 For the effect on redundancy entitlements of a strike during the notice period, see the 1996 Act, ss 140 and 143.

period of notice (for example by wrongfully terminating it summarily) the benefits that the employee will receive anyway under these provisions are to go towards mitigating any damages payable to the employee[106].

One final point to notice on the common law doctrine of notice is that it has increasingly been used by employers to safeguard trade secrets or (in businesses which are highly reliant on skilled employees) to prevent head-hunting by other firms, by the incorporation into sensitive contracts of employment of 'garden leave' clauses. These provide for long periods of notice on either side, during which the employee will be remunerated in full but not necessarily required to work. Thus, an employee wishing to leave may be required to give, say, six months' or a year's notice during which time (provided the employer pays him his full entitlement to wages and benefits) he continues to be subject to the implied term not to compete or breach confidence[107], or preferably to an express term to like effect. Compared with the traditional restraint of trade clause[108], this is expensive *but* it is probably more reliable since restraint clauses are notoriously difficult to draft and enforce. In an appropriate case, a garden leave clause may be enforced by injunction[109], but it must be remembered that ultimately an injunction is a discretionary remedy and may be refused by a court if it appears that the clause is unconscionable as, for example, if there is little or no chance of the employer suffering actual damage if the employee does take up a particular new job (albeit in breach of the clause)[110]. Moreover, the efficacy of garden leave clauses generally may now be subject to some limitation because of the decision of the Court of Appeal in *William Hill Organisation Ltd v Tucker*[111]; the ratio of the case is that a court will not *imply* a garden leave clause in any case where it is arguable that the employee has an interest in doing the work not just receiving payment[112], and to this extent it is unexceptionable (merely stressing the advantage of an express term) but at the end of the judgment Morritt LJ said obiter that it should not be too readily assumed that a garden leave clause will succeed where a restraint clause might fail; he said that:

> 'if injunctive relief was sought then it had to be justified on similar grounds to those necessary to the validity of the employee's covenant in restraint of trade. The court should be careful not to grant interlocutory relief to enforce a garden leave clause to any greater extent than would be covered by a justifiable covenant in restraint of trade previously entered into by an employee.'

---

106 Employment Rights Act 1996, s 91(5).
107 See p 175 above.
108 See p 124 above. It is possible to have both a garden leave clause and (then) a restraint of trade clause in a contract, though a court would need to consider the reasonableness of them taken together: *Crédit Suisse Asset Management Ltd v Armstrong* [1996] ICR 882, [1996] IRLR 450, CA.
109 *Evening Standard Co Ltd v Henderson* [1987] ICR 588, [1987] IRLR 64, CA (clause requiring a year's notice enforced to prevent a newspaper production manager from taking up employment during that time with a new newspaper venture, the employers undertaking to pay in full during the year); *Euro Brokers Ltd v Rabey* [1995] IRLR 206 (six-month garden leave clause enforced against a money broker wishing to move to a competitor firm); see Freedland (1989) 18 ILJ 112; and Gouldring 'Injunctions and contracts of employment: the *Evening Standard* doctrine' (1990) 19 ILJ 98.
110 *Provident Financial Group plc v Hayward* [1989] ICR 160, [1989] IRLR 84, CA (injunction to restrain financial director from taking up new employment towards the end of a long notice period refused because there was little evidence of any actual detriment to the employers).
111 [1998] IRLR 313, CA; applied in *Symbian Ltd v Christiensen* [2001] IRLR 77, CA.
112 For this aspect of the case, see p 154 above.

This may mean that in future there may be more emphasis on the *extent* of the garden leave, what interests it is protecting, and a tougher line on severing or reducing an unreasonably wide clause[113]. Further developments in this area will be important.

3 DISMISSAL FOR CAUSE

At common law an employer may dismiss an employee summarily (ie without notice) if he has sufficient cause to do so. In old cases, from the nineteenth century and before, this was viewed as a natural and necessary aspect of the relationship between master and man, and the servant's duty of obedience. The judgment of Parke B in *Callo v Brouncker*[114] was treated for many years as laying down set rules on summary dismissal which, he said, could be for moral misconduct (pecuniary or otherwise), wilful disobedience or habitual neglect. However, with the move in the nineteenth century towards viewing employment in a contractual light, the emphasis changed so that the right to dismiss summarily became explicable on the ground that the conduct of the employee was such that it showed a repudiation by him of the contract of employment which the employer then accepted and treated as terminating the contract immediately[115]. In *Laws v London Chronicle (Indicator Newspapers) Ltd*[116], Lord Evershed MR said:

> '... the proper conclusion ... is that, since a contract of service is but an example of contracts in general, so that the general law of contract will be applicable, it follows that the question must be – if summary dismissal is claimed to be justifiable – whether the conduct complained of is such as to show the servant to have disregarded the essential conditions of the contract of service.'

This will apply as a general principle, not just to the particular categories listed by Parke B, but to any context in which the employee's conduct is sufficiently grave as to be repudiatory, so that, for example, an employee may be summarily dismissed for going on strike[117]. The principal effect of this contractual approach is that every case must be viewed on its own facts to determine whether the conduct in question was grave enough, and the question is not to be solved by searching for absolute rules covering each particular context (with the result that decided cases may be of little or no assistance). Thus:

---

113 For example, in *GFI Group Inc v Eaglestone* [1994] IRLR 119 an over-long garden leave clause was saved by being reduced in length by the court (and then enforced for that shorter period), but this is just what a court will *not* normally do with a restraint clause which usually has to stand or fall as originally drafted.

114 (1831) 4 C & P 518. Several of the points raised below are considered at greater length in Smith and Randall *Contract Actions in Modern Employment Law: Developments and Issues* (2000) ch 8.

115 *Boston Deep Sea Fishing and Ice Co v Ansell* (1888) 39 Ch D 339, CA, particularly per Bowen LJ at 364–365; *Laws v London Chronicle (Indicator Newspapers) Ltd* [1959] 2 All ER 285, [1959] 1 WLR 698, CA; *Pepper v Webb* [1969] 2 All ER 216, [1969] 1 WLR 514, CA.

116 [1959] 2 All ER 285 at 287, [1959] 1 WLR 698 at 700.

117 *Simmons v Hoover Ltd* [1977] 1 All ER 775, [1977] ICR 61, not following the distinction between those strikes with and those without strike notice drawn in *Morgan v Fry* [1968] 2 QB 710, [1968] 3 All ER 452, CA; the common law position on strikes is now considerably affected by statute.

'... the true question is whether the acts and conduct of the party evince an intention no longer to be bound by the contract.[118]'

'... in every case the question of repudiation must depend on the character of the contract, the number and weight of the wrongful acts or assertions, the intentions indicated by such acts and words, the deliberation or otherwise with which they are committed or uttered and on the general circumstances of the case.[119]'

Much will therefore depend upon the context and the nature of the reason, so that for example, a relatively minor instance of dishonesty may warrant summary dismissal, particularly if the employee's job involves dealing with money[120], whereas mere negligence may in most cases be amenable only to dismissal by notice and a summary dismissal may be wrongful[121], unless there are other particular factors, such as endangering life by neglect[122]. Also, while an employer may not be justified in dismissing summarily for a single 'offence', a previous history of similar transgressions, even if not as serious as the one leading to dismissal, may be important evidence in the employer's favour[123]. Any particular case should also be viewed with a certain amount of realism, so that in *Jupiter General Insurance Co Ltd v Shroff*[124] the Privy Council said:

'Their Lordships would be very loath to assent to the view that a single outbreak of bad temper, accompanied, it may be, by regrettable language, is sufficient ground for dismissal. Sir John Beaumont CJ [in the court below] was stating a proposition of mere good sense when he observed that in such cases we must apply the standard of men and not angels and remember that men are apt to show temper when reprimanded.'

The court went on to make two observations which might be borne in mind. The first was that summary dismissal is a strong measure justified only in exceptional circumstances; the second was that the test to be applied in determining whether a dismissal was justified must vary with the nature of the business and the position held by the employee and that decisions in other cases are of little value. This variable approach can also be seen more recently in *Neary v Dean of Westminster*[125] where ideas taken from the modern law on the implied term of trust and respect were also introduced, looking at whether the employee's conduct was such as to undermine completely that element of the employment relationship. In the light of all these factors (and particularly the number of old or very old cases on

---

118 *Freeth v Burr* (1874) LR 9 CP 208 at 213, per Lord Coleridge CJ, applied by the House of Lords in *General Billposting Co Ltd v Atkinson* [1909] AC 118, HL.
119 *Re Rubel Bronze and Metal Co and Vos* [1918] 1 KB 315 at 322, per McCardie J.
120 *Sinclair v Neighbour* [1967] 2 QB 279, [1966] 3 All ER 988, CA.
121 See eg *Gould v Webb* (1855) 4 E & B 933.
122 It has been held, however, that the court should look primarily at the negligent act, and not at the consequences which flowed from it, as the latter could be too harsh and involve too much hindsight: *Savage v British India Steam Navigation Co Ltd* (1930) 46 TLR 294.
123 See eg *Clouston & Co Ltd v Corry* [1906] AC 122, PC (intoxication); *Pepper v Webb* [1969] 2 All ER 216, [1969] 1 WLR 514, CA (unsatisfactory work), discussed in *Wilson v Racher* [1974] ICR 428 [1974] IRLR 114, CA.
124 [1937] 3 All ER 67, PC.
125 [1999] IRLR 288 (Lord Jauncey, sitting as a Special Commissioner for the Visitor to Westminster Abbey).

the subject), another important factor may be changing attitudes, modes of organisation or *mores* in general. Thus in *Wilson v Racher*[126], Edmund Davies LJ said:

'Reported decisions provide useful, but only general guides, each case turning upon its own facts. Many of the decisions which are customarily cited in these cases date from the last century and may be wholly out of accord with the current social conditions. What would today be regarded as almost an attitude of Czar-serf, which is to be found in some of the older cases where a dismissed employee failed to recover damages would, I venture to think, be decided differently today.'

Good examples of responsiveness to new needs are the decision in *Denco Ltd v Joinson*[127] that almost any form of deliberate computer misuse during employment will justify summary dismissal and the decision in *Thomas v Hillingdon London Borough Council*[128] that this is also likely to be the case in most instances of Internet and/or email abuse at work, particularly when it concerns downloading pornography. The advent of the modern statutory rights for employees has of course had an effect on summary dismissal, but usually indirectly, since the presence or absence of notice is a procedural matter and as such only of paramount importance in a common law action for wrongful dismissal; the statutory action for unfair dismissal requires an examination of the substantive fairness of the dismissal, and so any question of the presence or absence of notice will be of secondary importance. Under the legislation, the employer is not deprived of his right to dismiss summarily, and the continuance of this common law concept is clearly envisaged in the Employment Rights Act 1996, section 86(6) (rights to minimum periods of notice not to affect cases where summary termination is justified) and the ACAS Code of Practice, 'Disciplinary and grievance procedures'[129]. However, the existence of the unfair dismissal legislation is likely to make employers more wary of dismissing summarily and may perhaps make them more likely to punish misconduct by action short of dismissal (for example suspension) or by dismissal by notice after exhausting a set procedure of warnings and a hearing; this might particularly be the case where the ground for dismissal is incompetence or negligence. The absence of notice would not per se make the dismissal unfair[130], but might sway the tribunal against the employer on the question whether he acted reasonably. Also, the employer might be mindful of paragraph 9(xi) of the Code of Practice which states that a disciplinary procedure should 'ensure that, except for gross misconduct, no employees are dismissed for a first breach of conduct' – this applies to *any* dismissal, whether with or without notice, and shows that the modern emphasis is generally against hasty action on dismissal, even if summary dismissal may still be justified in certain extreme cases. Moreover, the advent of the unfair dismissal action has placed new emphasis on *procedures*

126 [1974] ICR 428, [1974] IRLR 114, CA.
127 [1991] ICR 172, [1991] IRLR 63; see Napier 'Computerisation and Employment Rights' (1992) 21 ILJ 1.
128 (2002) Times, 4 October.
129 Particularly para 7.
130 *Treganowan v Robert Knee & Co Ltd* [1975] ICR 405, [1975] IRLR 247; *BSC Sports and Social Club v Morgan* [1987] IRLR 391. See the discussion of the different bases for wrongful and unfair dismissal in the judgment of Judge Clark in *Farrant v Woodroffe School* [1998] ICR 184, [1998] IRLR 176.

and so an employer might be advised to exercise his rights to dismiss summarily in the light of modern personnel management techniques, in particular the desirability of such matters as laying down in the company's rules what conduct may warrant summary dismissal, ensuring that the decision to dismiss is taken at a reasonably high level (certainly higher than immediate superiors), and providing for an appeal structure[131].

The common law on dismissal for cause is thus heavily qualified by statute and the modern statutory provisions owe little to the existing common law rules. For example at common law a dismissal would be lawful if the employer acted on reason A which was quite inadequate, but later found out about reason B which could in fact justify dismissal[132], but under the unfair dismissal legislation the relevant reason is the one upon which the employer acted at the time of dismissal, and not anything that he only discovered later[133]. Moreover, at common law there was no obligation upon the employer to give his reasons, but under the Employment Rights Act 1996, section 92, an employee with one year's continuous service has a statutory right to be provided with a written statement giving particulars of the reasons for his dismissal[134].

4 WRONGFUL DISMISSAL

(i) Meaning

As can be seen from the discussion above, the common law on dismissal looks basically at form, not at substance so that, except in the case of a purported dismissal for cause, the concept of wrongful dismissal is essentially procedural and largely dependent upon the actual terms of the contract in question. Thus, if a contract is for a fixed term, or expressly stated to be terminable only in certain ways[135], and it is terminated before the term expires or in an improper way, that may be a wrongful dismissal. More typical, however, is the case where the employer dismissed the employee with no or inadequate notice, or purported to dismiss him for cause where the facts did not justify such action. This common law action for wrongful dismissal must therefore be kept separate from the statutory action for unfair dismissal which entails an examination of the substantive merits of the dismissal. For many years, there was also a formal split of forum, with a unfair

---

131 Code of Practice, paras 7, 9(vii) and 9(xiv) respectively. This is now particularly the case, with the mandatory procedures in Sch 2 to the Employment Act 2002. Even where conduct warranting such dismissal is expressed, it must be clear that it is summary dismissal that is envisaged, given the gravity of the action to be taken: *Skilton v T & K Home Improvements Ltd* [2000] ICR 1162, [2000] IRLR 595, CA (reference to 'instant dismissal' is not enough to mean summary dismissal in a case of missing quarterly sales targets; employee still entitled to wages in lieu of notice).

132 *Boston Deep Sea Fishing and Ice Co v Ansell* (1888) 39 Ch D 339, CA; *Cyril Leonard & Co v Simo Securities Trust Ltd* [1971] 3 All ER 1313, [1972] 1 WLR 80, CA.

133 *W Devis & Sons Ltd v Atkins* [1977] AC 931, [1977] 3 All ER 40, HL.

134 See p 527 below.

135 This is rare in practice: *McClelland v Northern Ireland General Health Services Board* [1957] 2 All ER 129, [1957] 1 WLR 594, HL is an unusual example. In modern circumstances, it might arise if an employer agreed to a contractually binding 'no compulsory redundancy' deal; any redundancy dismissal during its currency would then be wrongful and arguably the damages should not be restricted (as is usual) to wages for the notice period, but should be for the rest of the period of the agreement, subject to mitigation and a discount for the possibility of lawful dismissal (ie on non-redundancy grounds) during that period.

dismissal claim going to an employment tribunal, but a wrongful dismissal claim having to go to the ordinary civil courts; since 1994, however, tribunals have been given jurisdiction over contractual claims on termination of employment[136], and so can hear a claim for wrongful dismissal (up to the statutory limit of £25,000).

(ii) Remedies

(a) The rule against enforcement

While the idea of wrongful dismissal is explicable on a contractual basis (ie that the employer has repudiated the contract by his actions), it is when one comes to the nature of the remedies open to the dismissed employee that the inadequacies of contract theory and, as a consequence, the practical ineffectiveness of the common law become obvious[137]. The starting point is the general principle that the courts will not enforce a contract of employment, either directly by specific performance or indirectly by injunction or any other means[138], the principal explanation being that the contract is of a personal nature, not amenable to enforcement. Thus, in *De Francesco v Barnum*[139] Fry LJ said:

'I should be very unwilling to extend decisions the effect of which is to compel persons who are not desirous of maintaining continuous personal relations with one another to continue those personal relations. I think the courts are bound to be jealous lest they should turn contracts of service into contracts of slavery; and ... I should lean against the extension of the doctrine of specific performance and injunction in such a manner.'

Moreover, this is now enshrined in statute as far as such an order against an employee is concerned, for the Trade Union and Labour Relations (Consolidation) Act 1992, section 236 provides that no court shall issue an order compelling an employee to do any work or attend at any place for the doing of any work. This sentiment has been applied by the courts equally to cases where the order is sought against the employer, who may not be made to continue employing a particular individual, and so at common law there has never been any general remedy of reinstatement. If an employee is wrongfully dismissed the general rule is that his remedy lies in damages[140].

Such a rule (of automatic termination) may, or may not, make practical sense but it is difficult to explain in contractual terms, for in contract law a repudiation is usually of no effect unless accepted by the innocent party – '... an unaccepted repudiation is a thing writ in water and of no value to anybody'[141] – and so in

---

136 Employment Tribunals (Extension of Jurisdiction) Orders 1994, SI 1994/1623 and SI 1994/1624 (one order applying to England and Wales, another to Scotland); see p 528 below.
137 For an analysis of the difficult case law on remedies and possible developments, see Ewing 'Remedies for breach of the contract of employment' [1993] CLJ 405.
138 *Whitwood Chemical Co v Hardman* [1891] 2 Ch 416, CA. For a peculiar application of this on the facts (employee not seeking to continue his contract per se, but rather to continue to exercise his contractual rights as a shop steward in spite of being suspended), see *City and Hackney Health Authority v NUPE* [1985] IRLR 252, CA.
139 (1890) 45 Ch D 430 at 438.
140 Or, in an appropriate case, a quantum meruit action: *Planché v Colburn* (1831) 8 Bing 14.
141 *Howard v Pickford Tool Co Ltd* [1951] 1 KB 417 at 421, CA, per Asquith LJ. See *White and Carter (Councils) Ltd v McGregor* [1962] AC 413, [1961] 3 All ER 1178, HL.

theory an employee faced with wrongful dismissal should be entitled to refuse to accept this repudiation and insist on carrying on in the employment. This, however, used not to be the prevailing view and it was said that contracts of employment form an exceptional category in which the employee has no choice but to accept the repudiation and sue for damages, so that the employer's repudiation automatically terminates the contract[142]. Thus, for example in *Sanders v Ernest A Neale Ltd* [143] Sir John Donaldson P said:

'The obvious, and indeed the only, explanation is that the repudiation of a contract of employment is an exception to the general rule. It terminates the contract without the necessity for acceptance by the injured party.'

In *Vine v National Dock Labour Board*[144] a dismissal was held to be invalid on the peculiar facts of the case (considered below), but Viscount Kilmuir LC was at pains to point out that:

'This is an entirely different situation from the ordinary master and servant case; there, if a master wrongfully dismisses the servant, either summarily or by insufficient notice, the employment is effectively terminated, albeit in breach of contract.'

and he approved the decision of Jenkins LJ in the Court of Appeal[145] that:

'... in the ordinary case of master and servant the repudiation or the wrongful dismissal puts an end to the contract, and the contract having been wrongfully put an end to a claim for damages arises. It is necessarily a claim for damages and nothing more. The nature of the bargain is such that it can be nothing more.'

On the other hand, this doctrine of automatic (or 'unilateral') termination was doubted in cases such as *Decro-Wall International SA v Practitioners in Marketing Ltd*[146]; *Hill v CA Parsons & Co Ltd*[147] and *CH Giles & Co Ltd v Morris*[148]. This counter-argument is that the rule against enforcement is not a rule of law, but only a question of fact (albeit frequently recurring fact) in that in nearly all cases the basis of mutual confidence has been destroyed and it would be futile to keep the employment relationship in being. Subsequently, this alternative doctrine of elective (or 'acceptance') termination gained ground, with the result that in some cases it can be argued that the employee did not accept the employer's repudiation of the contract (although in most cases in practice such acceptance will be easy to infer). This can be seen in the judgment of Megarry V-C in *Thomas*

---

142 *Denmark Productions Ltd v Boscobel Productions Ltd* [1969] 1 QB 699, [1968] 3 All ER 513, CA.
143 [1974] 3 All ER 327 at 333, [1974] ICR 565 at 571.
144 [1957] AC 488 at 500, [1956] 3 All ER 939 at 944, HL.
145 [1956] 1 QB 658 at 674, [1956] 1 All ER 1 at 8, CA.
146 [1971] 2 All ER 216, [1971] 1 WLR 361, CA, per Salmon and Sachs LJJ; aliter per Buckley LJ. The majority judgments are cogently criticised by Sir John Donaldson P in *Sanders v Ernest A Neale Ltd* [1974] 3 All ER 327, [1974] ICR 565.
147 [1972] Ch 305, [1971] 3 All ER 1345, CA, per Lord Denning MR and Sachs LJ. The more traditional view that there is a rule of law against enforcement is well set out in Stamp LJ's dissenting judgment at 322 and 1357 respectively.
148 [1972] 1 All ER 960 at 970, [1972] 1 WLR 307 at 318, per Megarry J.

Marshall (Exports) Ltd v Guinle[149], in the majority decision of the Court of Appeal in *Gunton v Richmond-upon-Thames London Borough Council*[150] and in the judgment of Hodgson J in *Dietman v Brent London Borough Council*[151]. In practice the difference in common law claims between the automatic and elective theories may not be great, for in *Gunton's* case the majority, having clearly decided in favour of the latter, went on to stress (a) that in most cases the employee will have no option in reality but to accept the employer's repudiation and seek a remedy in damages[152], and (b) that the rule of practice against specific enforcement of contracts of employment remains strong and may operate independently of the elective theory so that while, for some purposes[153], an employee may wish to argue that he did not accept the employer's repudiation, he will not normally be allowed to do so in order to claim specific performance (directly or indirectly). These severe limitations on the elective theory can be seen in *Gunton's* case where the theory was invoked to attack the validity of a dismissal which had omitted proper observance of a contractually binding disciplinary procedure, the plaintiff claiming that he never accepted this repudiation by the employer; to that extent it succeeded, but given that the employer could have dismissed lawfully by going through the procedure properly the court held that the normal rule on damages for wrongful dismissal applied and all that the plaintiff was entitled to was his wages until the date on which a proper dismissal could have been achieved after exhaustion of the procedure. The plaintiff thus succeeded in invalidating the original dismissal, but only obtained a short stay of execution and a few weeks' extra pay (representing the time it would have taken to exhaust the procedure). He certainly did not get his job back, though the elective theory would in theory help to allow room for an atypical case where a court might be persuaded to enforce a contract of employment (where the usual factors against enforcement do not apply) as in *Hill v CA Parsons & Co Ltd*, which is considered below. Moreover, swings continue to swing and roundabouts to turn; in *R v East Berkshire Health*

---

149 [1978] 3 All ER 193, [1978] ICR 905.
150 [1980] ICR 755, [1980] IRLR 321, CA, per Buckley and Brightman LJJ. Shaw LJ dissented on the reasoning, adopting the automatic approach, but concurred in the result on the facts. The later decision of the Court of Appeal in *London Transport Executive v Clarke* [1981] ICR 355, [1981] IRLR 166, CA, though of fundamental importance on the statutory definition of dismissal, was ambiguous on this point of theory.
151 [1987] ICR 737, [1987] IRLR 259; upheld on appeal [1988] ICR 842, [1988] IRLR 299, CA.
152 See eg *Dietman v Brent London Borough Council* (n 151 above) where the acceptance theory was applied, but the court found acceptance established on the facts fairly readily. In *Delaney v Staples* [1992] ICR 483 at 489, [1992] IRLR 191 at 93, HL, Lord Browne-Wilkinson spoke of an unequivocal instant (wrongful) dismissal being 'effective to put an end to the employment *relationship*, whether or not it unilaterally discharges the contract of employment'. Moreover, in *Marsh v National Autistic Society* [1993] ICR 453 it was held that, even if the elective theory is applied, the demise of the employment relationship will mean that the employee may not sue in debt for continuing wages, but will be confined to the (restricted) action for damages.
153 See eg the continued existence of the contractual term restricting the employee's activities during employment in *Thomas Marshall (Exports) Ltd v Guinle* (n 149 above) in spite of the employee's wrongful resignation, the desire in *CH Giles & Co Ltd v Morris* (n 148 above) to put the plaintiff into employment in the first place, if only so that his remedies would be better when then dismissed, and the (unsuccessful) attempt to enforce a shop steward's contractual right to enter the employer's premises in spite of being under suspension in *City and Hackney Health Authority v National Union of Public Employees* [1985] IRLR 252, CA. More recently, there have been attempts to seek specific enforcement of contracts of employment in order to insist on disciplinary procedures being properly applied – see p 482 below.

Authority, ex p Walsh[154] in the Court of Appeal May LJ stated unequivocally that he preferred the dissenting judgment of Shaw LJ in *Gunton* and the automatic view, and Sir John Donaldson MR was clearly not ecstatic about the overruling by the majority in *Gunton* of his own previous decision in *Sanders v Ernest A Neale Ltd*[155], and in *Boyo v Lambeth London Borough Council*[156] the Court of Appeal applied the ratio of *Gunton* (to allow wages for a short extra period that it would have taken the employer to go through the contractual disciplinary procedure properly), but stated their unease at doing so, making it clear that they had grave doubts about the reasoning of the majority in that case.

The question of which theory (elective or automatic) is to be preferred remains at best undecided; in the context of common law claims it has the same intellectual fascination as the question as to how many angels may dance on the head of a pin and (except perhaps in a case where some collateral or incidental matter relies upon the technical continued existence of the contract) about as much practical relevance, though there is an outside possibility that the provisions of the Employment Act 2002 enacting a legally required minimum disciplinary procedure spark renewed interest in this area, along the lines of *Gunton* (above).

However, when one turns to the possible impact of these theories on statutory rights on dismissal, the picture becomes much more complicated, and in fact it is in the statutory context (usually of unfair dismissal) that most of the active dispute has arisen. One problem is that if the automatic theory is applied to the statutory definition of dismissal[157] it can support the idea of 'self dismissal', ie that if an employee misbehaves sufficiently badly he can be said to have repudiated his contract of employment, thus automatically terminating it; if this is so, there is no 'dismissal' by the employer and so the tribunal is denied jurisdiction to hear a claim of unfair dismissal. The elective theory in fact fits the statutory definition of dismissal much better, for if acceptance of a repudiation is required the termination of the misbehaving employee's contract is brought about by the employer's acceptance of the repudiation and *is* thus 'dismissal' by the employer[158]; on the other hand if the *employer* repudiates the contract, termination is brought about by the employee's acceptance, but this is specifically covered by statute which deems it to be a 'constructive dismissal'[159]. The *elective* theory is thus important for the actual definition of dismissal. However, the second problem is that equal difficulties arise if one applies it to the *date* of dismissal. It is important to know precisely the date for the purpose of applying the stringent time limits in the statute (particularly the limitation period for starting an unfair dismissal action of three months from the 'effective date of termination'[160]), but if an employee could claim that he had in fact refused to accept the employer's repudiation he could argue that the time limit either never started to run or, at least, started to run at some time significantly later than the wording of the statutory

154 [1984] ICR 743, [1984] IRLR 278, CA.
155 N 143 above.
156 [1994] ICR 727, [1995] IRLR 50, CA. Appearing in person, the employee (who was on a month's notice) had initially argued that, as he had not accepted the employer's repudiation, he was entitled to his wages up to the year 2000(!).
157 Contained in the Employment Rights Act 1996, s 95 (in relation to unfair dismissal) and s 136 (in relation to redundancy).
158 Within ss 95(1)(a) and 136(1)(a).
159 Within ss 95(1)(c) and 136(1)(c); see p 546 below.
160 See p 553 below.

definition of 'effective date of termination' would suggest. In the interests of certainty, therefore, it is important that the *automatic* theory be applied to questions of limitation.

One commentator has made a strong case for adopting this differential approach in the statutory context[161], and this now seems to be the position in practice – in *London Transport Executive v Clarke*[162] the Court of Appeal by a majority disapproved of the idea of 'self dismissal', applying the elective theory, whereas in *Brown v Southall and Knight*[163] and *Robert Cort & Son Ltd v Charman*[164] the EAT rejected arguments based upon that theory when determining the effective date of termination, preferring instead an automatic termination approach based on (a) the wording of the statutory definition of effective date of termination and (b) the need for certainty on this vital concept. As long as this practical compromise is maintained, the position now seems to be satisfactory, but if there were in the future any real danger of the reintroduction of the sort of uncertainty that existed prior to this case law (and which may still exist in the case of a common law claim), the time would surely be ripe for legislative clarification.

Returning to the common law position, and accepting that there is at least a rule of practice (if not an absolute rule of law) against enforcing contracts of employment in most cases, we must now consider certain establishment exceptions.

(b) Exceptions to the rule against enforcement

A. A negative restraint clause

Where the employee has agreed in the contract not to do certain things (for example not to perform for any other theatre owner during the currency of the contract, or not to work for a competitor within a certain period after leaving the employment[165]), the court will hold him to his promise and enforce that negative stipulation (even if it would not enforce the positive obligations in the contract)[166]. It is immaterial that this may indirectly persuade the employee to remain in the employment (ie that it may have indirectly a positive effect), but on the other hand it is well established that the clause must be bona fide, in particular that it must not be in reality a positive obligation merely expressed in a negative way[167]. Moreover, an injunction will not be granted if the practical effect would be to compel the employee to perform his side of the contract or starve (for example where the stipulation is that he will not take *any* employment for a period after leaving the employment)[168].

---

161 J McMullen in his very useful article 'A synthesis of the mode of termination of contracts of employment' [1982] CLJ 110.
162 [1981] ICR 355, [1981] IRLR 166, CA.
163 [1980] ICR 617, [1980] IRLR 130.
164 [1981] ICR 816, [1981] IRLR 437, approved by the Court of Appeal in *Stapp v Shaftesbury Society* [1982] IRLR 326, CA.
165 See pp 124–134, 'Legality and Restraint of Trade', above.
166 *Lumley v Wagner* (1852) 1 De GM & G 604.
167 *Davis v Foreman* [1894] 3 Ch 654; *Warner Bros Pictures Inc v Nelson* [1937] 1 KB 209, [1936] 3 All ER 160.
168 *Rely-a-Bell Burglar and Fire Alarm Co Ltd v Eisler* [1926] Ch 609; *Warner Bros Pictures Inc v Nelson* [1937] 1 KB 209, [1936] 3 All ER 160; *Page One Records Ltd v Britton* [1967] 3 All ER 822, [1968] 1 WLR 157; *Warren v Mendy* [1989] ICR 525, [1989] IRLR 210, CA.

B. Where the dismissal is a nullity

In certain restricted cases, a dismissed employee may be able to invoke certain administrative law remedies to argue that his dismissal was invalid; if this is accepted, the legal result is that there was no effective dismissal, and so the contract of employment will be indirectly enforced. The two principal bases for challenge are that the dismissal was contrary to the rules of natural justice or was in some way ultra vires[169]. There has been considerable case law on this question, though in the modern case law the emphasis has switched to consideration of how this confusing area of law fits in with the procedure for claiming judicial review under RSC Order 53. In turn, this has coincided with increased interest in this area of employment law since it is well appreciated now that in unfair dismissal cases tribunals hardly ever order reinstatement or re-engagement; thus any remedy that may in fact *keep the employee in employment* such as this may well be worth pursuing, certainly in cases arising in the public sector. The following attempt[170] at explanation proceeds by examining first the older case law and then the more recent case law on Order 53. It is tempting to think of the former as establishing the principles and the latter as determining the remedy but, as will be seen, that would be an oversimplification.

The older case law In *Ridge v Baldwin*[171] a chief constable who was dismissed without a proper opportunity to be heard in his own defence was granted a declaration that the decision to dismiss him was a nullity as it was in breach of natural justice[172]. Remedies such as this are familiar in the context of expulsion from a trade union and indeed if a dismissal involved jeopardising trade union rights (as in *Taylor v National Union of Seamen*[173] where dismissal as branch secretary disqualified the individual from later standing for office in the union) the safer course is to rely upon the denial of those rights, not the dismissal. However, in the ordinary case

---

169 Ganz 'Public law principles applicable to dismissal from employment' (1967) 30 MLR 288; Freedland *The Contract of Employment* (1976) pp. 278–292; Davidson 'Judicial review of decisions to dismiss' (1984) 35 NILQ 121 (written before the decision in *ex p Walsh*, below); Fredman and Lee 'Natural justice for employees' (1986) 15 ILJ 15; Ewing and Grubb 'The emergence of a new labour injunction?' (1987) 16 ILJ 145; Fredman and Morris 'Public or private? State employees and judicial review' (1991) 107 LQR 298; Sedley 'Public law and contractual entitlement' (1994) 23 ILJ 201; Laws 'Public law and employment law: abuse of power' [1997] PL 455; Freedland (1990) 19 ILJ 199, (1991) 20 ILJ 72; Carty (1991) 54 MLR 129; Smith and Randall *Contract Actions in Mondern Employment Law: Developments and Issues* (2002) ch 10. Presumably other public law grounds of challenge such as perversity would be applicable, though less likely to succeed: see *R v Hertfordshire County Council, ex p NUPE* [1985] IRLR 258, CA.

170 Humility is, it is said, a virtue. Any over-confident lawyer wishing to learn it should consider the case law that follows in some depth. He or she is likely to come away from it feeling at best chastened and at worst an *ursus mentis parvae*.

171 [1964] AC 40, [1963] 2 All ER 66, HL; applied in *Chief Constable of the North Wales Police v Evans* [1982] 3 All ER 141, [1982] 1 WLR 1155, HL.

172 One possible limitation on the effectiveness of natural justice (even if locus standi can be shown) may be the decision in *R v Chief Constable of the Thames Valley Police, ex p Cotton* [1990] IRLR 344, CA, that in order to succeed the applicant employee must show not just a breach of the procedural requirements of natural justice, but also actual prejudice caused to him; if this allows a defence that in fact it made no difference to the outcome it is inconsistent with developments in unfair dismissal law where just that defence (to procedural failure) was disapproved by the House of Lords in *Polkey v A E Dayton (Services) Ltd* [1988] ICR 142, [1987] IRLR 503: see p 569 below.

173 [1967] 1 All ER 767, [1967] 1 WLR 532; *Stevenson v United Road Transport Union* [1977] 2 All ER 941, [1977] ICR 893, CA.

of dismissal the application of these remedies has been confused and illogical. In *Malloch v Aberdeen Corpn*[174] Lord Wilberforce said:

> 'A comparative list in which persons have been held entitled or not entitled to a hearing, or to observation of rules of natural justice, according to the master and servant test, looks illogical and even bizarre. A specialist surgeon is denied protection which is given to a hospital doctor; a University professor, as a servant, has been denied the right to be heard, a dock labourer and an undergraduate have been granted it.[175]'

This confusion arises because if one thing is certain in this area it is that these remedies are not available in 'ordinary master and servant cases'. Thus, in *Ridge v Baldwin* Lord Reid said[176]:

> 'The law regarding master and servant is not in doubt. There cannot be specific performance of a contract of service and the master can terminate his contract with the servant at any time and for any reason or for none[177]. But if he does so in a manner not warranted by the contract he must pay damages for breach of contract. So the question in a pure case of master and servant does not at all depend on whether the master has heard the servant in his own defence; it depends on whether the facts emerging at the trial prove breach of contract.'

The problem therefore becomes to determine how to distinguish between ordinary master and servant cases and those rare cases in which the remedies may be invoked. In *Ridge v Baldwin*[178] Lord Reid envisaged the doctrine of natural justice as applicable to an 'office-holder' who could only be dismissed for some measure of cause, and in *Malloch v Aberdeen Corpn*, where a Scottish teacher whose employment was heavily qualified by statute was held by a majority of the House of Lords to have been entitled to a hearing before dismissal, Lord Wilberforce said[179]:

> 'One may accept that if there are relationships in which all requirements of the observance of rules of natural justice are excluded ... , these must be confined to what have been called "pure master and servant cases", which I take to mean cases in which there is no element of *public employment or service*, no support by *statute*, nothing in the nature of an *office or a status* which is

---

174 [1971] 2 All ER 1278 at 1294, [1971] 1 WLR 1578 at 1595, HL; *Jones v Lee and Guilding* [1980] ICR 310, [1980] IRLR 67, CA.

175 See *Barber v Manchester Regional Hospital Board* [1958] 1 All ER 322, [1958] 1 WLR 181; *Palmer v Inverness Hospitals Board* 1963 SC 311; *Vidyodaya University of Ceylon v Silva* [1964] 3 All ER 865, [1965] 1 WLR 77, PC; *Vine v National Dock Labour Board* [1957] AC 488, [1956] 3 All ER 939, HL; *Glynn v Keele University* [1971] 2 All ER 89, [1971] 1 WLR 487.

176 [1964] AC 40 at 65, [1963] 2 All ER 66 at 71, HL.

177 The case was decided before the introduction of the unfair dismissal provisions in the Industrial Relations Act 1971.

178 [1964] AC 40, [1963] 2 All ER 66, HL.

179 [1971] 2 All ER 1278 at 1294, [1971] 1 WLR 1578 at 1595, emphasis added. Lord Morris (dissenting) took a narrower view of the application of the remedies to employment cases, as he had done in his decision in *Vidyodaya University of Ceylon v Silva* [1964] 3 All ER 865, [1965] 1 WLR 77, PC, but in his speech in *Malloch's* case Lord Wilberforce doubted the correctness of that case on this point (see at 1295 and 1596 respectively).

capable of protection. If any of these elements exist, then, in my opinion, whatever the terminology used, and even though in some inter partes aspects the relationship may be called that of master and servant, there may be essential procedural requirements to be observed, and failure to observe them may result in a dismissal being declared to be void.'

It is submitted that this is one of the clearest statements of the position in the older cases, but even here the difficulties are numerous, for although his Lordship talks of 'any' of these elements existing, it is clear that they are not necessarily enough by themselves; for example many employees are in 'public employment' but at too lowly a level to claim protection[180]. This means that there will be some need for additional 'status', as in the third element mentioned, but it is this very 'status' that is the elusive factor. Moreover, the question arises whether an office holder in purely private, commercial employment (for example a company secretary) would be able to challenge his dismissal in this way – in theory there is no reason why not, but so far the cases have all been in the context of public employment of sorts, except in *Stevenson v United Road Transport Union*[181] where the dismissed employee was employed by a trade union as an officer of that union.

The position is little clearer when one turns from questions of natural justice to a challenge on the basis of the dismissal being ultra vires. In *McClelland v Northern Ireland General Health Services Board*[182] the House of Lords appear to have held by a majority that a dismissal for a reason other than one expressly permitted in the particular contract of employment in question was ultra vires in the sense of not being allowed under the contract. Normally, however, such a dismissal would only give rise to an action for damages for wrongful dismissal, and if that case is correct the reasoning can only apply where the contract is particularly explicit on the permissible reasons for dismissal. More normally, a challenge on the basis of ultra vires will be based upon a statutory scheme or requirement governing the employment, as in *Vine v National Dock Labour Board*[183] where a registered dock worker employed by the Board (under the now-repealed statutory scheme designed to dispense with casual labour on the docks) was dismissed for refusing a valid order, but his dismissal was effected by a committee which, on the true construction of the statutory scheme, did not have power to do so. The House of Lords held the dismissal to be ultra vires, and gave a declaration that it was a nullity. Viscount Kilmuir LC stressed that the existence of the special statutory scheme took the employee out of the 'ordinary master–servant' category[184]:

---

180 See eg *Forbes v Johnston* [1971] NZLR 117. The point is taken up in the case law on Order 53, below. In *R v BBC, ex p Lavelle* [1983] ICR 99, [1982] IRLR 404, Woolf J suggested that *any* employment protected by procedural rules before dismissal might have the necessary office-holding status; this would have had enormous repercussions since most permanent employments these days would come into that category, with disciplinary rules written into their terms of employment. This idea has not been taken any further in the subsequent case law (see eg the narrow approach to 'office' in *R v Hertfordshire County Council, ex p NUPE* [1985] IRLR 258, CA).

181 [1977] 2 All ER 941, [1977] ICR 893, CA; cf *Taylor v National Union of Seamen* [1967] 1 All ER 767, [1967] 1 WLR 532.

182 [1957] 2 All ER 129, [1957] 1 WLR 594, HL.

183 [1957] AC 488, [1956] 3 All ER 939, HL; *Taylor v Furness, Withy & Co Ltd* [1969] 1 Lloyd's Rep 324, 6 KIR 488.

184 [1957] AC 488 at 500, [1956] 3 All ER 939 at 944.

'Here, the removal of the plaintiff's name from the register being in law a nullity, he continued to have the right to be treated as a registered dockworker with all the benefits which, by statute, that status conferred on him. It is therefore right that, with the background of this scheme, the court should declare his rights.'

Challenge on the basis of ultra vires has, however, been restrictively construed, and will not apply simply because the employment in question is in some way governed by statute; even if it has a 'strong statutory flavour' it may still be deemed to be an ordinary master-servant case[185], and in *Francis v Municipal Councillors of Kuala Lumpur*[186] Lord Morris said that relief could only be given in such cases if there were 'special circumstances'; in *Vine's* case, those circumstances were the all-embracing nature of the statutory scheme and the fact that the employee could not work as a docker *at all* if dismissed from the Board's employment.

Thus, the cases where a dismissal has been successfully challenged as a nullity have been uncommon in the past, and the principles upon which they have succeeded are uncertain, though usually revolving round some sort of elusive office-holding status. Theoretically that has been no great hardship for we now have the laws relating to unfair dismissal, where matters of natural justice[187] and compliance with internal disciplinary procedures may be important, if only indirectly. However, the practical position may be slightly different with, as stated above, renewed interest generally in common law and/or administrative law remedies for dismissed employees, given the low instance of reinstatement by tribunals and, in some cases, the desire to use the vehicle of an individual challenge in order to prevent or deter abuse of disciplinary procedures by the employer[188]. We can now turn to the later case law but here we find procedural complications.

The problem of Order 53 Order 53 was introduced into the Rules of the Supreme Court in 1977 in order to simplify procedure, so that now there can be one application for 'judicial review' which can lead, if successful, to the granting of any one of the appropriate remedies (certiorari, mandamus, prohibition, declaration, injunction or, possibly, damages). It contains an anti-technicality rule in Order 53, rule 9(5) whereby an application under the Order can, if it transpires that that is the wrong procedure, be deemed to have been commenced instead by writ, and proceed accordingly. Essentially it was a liberalising reform though it does import certain restrictions (especially a time limit) and, more important here, has led to a position in which the division between 'public law' and 'private law' is thrown into higher relief than previously[189]. This has happened

---

185 *Barber v Manchester Regional Hospital Board* [1958] 1 All ER 322, [1958] 1 WLR 181.
186 [1962] 3 All ER 633, [1962] 1 WLR 1411, PC.
187 Ideas derived from natural justice permeate the Code of Practice no 1 'Disciplinary practice and procedure in employment', particularly paras 10(e), (f), (g), and 11. Also, there have been cases where rules of natural justice have been applied directly when considering procedural unfairness; see eg *Ayanlowo v IRC* [1975] IRLR 253; CA; *Khanum v Mid-Glamorgan Area Health Authority* [1979] ICR 40, [1978] IRLR 215; cf *Slater v Leicestershire Health Authority* [1989] IRLR 16, CA.
188 See p 482 below.
189 This distinction may now have yet more significance with the enactment of the Human Rights Act 1998; see Morris 'The Human Rights Act and the public/private divide' (1998) 27 ILJ 293.

through a series of House of Lords cases[190] in which their Lordships have been concerned to establish the proper relationship between the new public law remedy in Order 53 and ordinary private law claims, so that hopefully the Order will be neither abused nor so construed as to restrict unduly (or even prejudice) genuine private law claims. The position basically is that application is to be made under Order 53 if, but only if, the subject matter of the complaint relates to public law (as that is in the process of being defined). Thus, tests have been evolving as to when the *Order 53 remedy* is available but the problem in the employment law field is that those tests may not be exactly the same as the principles that evolved under the previous case law as to when *some sort of remedy* should be given by the courts to a dismissed employee (usually in the past by way of a declaration or injunction); in other words, the older principles and the new remedy may not be co-terminous.

The leading case is *R v East Berkshire Health Authority, ex p Walsh*[191] in which a senior nursing officer (employed under a contract which pursuant to regulations and with the approval of the Secretary of State incorporated terms and conditions jointly agreed for the health service) sought to challenge his dismissal on the grounds of breach of natural justice (through not being given a proper hearing) and ultra vires (having been dismissed, he argued, by an official who did not have the power to do so under the relevant contractual term). He applied for judicial review under Order 53, seeking an order of certiorari to quash the dismissal; he was successful at first instance but the Court of Appeal unanimously rejected the application. They held that the dismissal did not raise the sort of issues of public law necessary under Order 53 to attract the remedy of certiorari. What is the basis for such a decision? The one thing that is clear is that the fact that the applicant was employed by a public body of sorts is *not* enough without more to attract public law remedies; if it were otherwise a substantial proportion of the workforce would be able to seek remedies on dismissal from the Divisional Court, thus potentially outflanking the employment tribunal system which, according to the Court of Appeal, is a far more appropriate forum for the sort of issues that arise on dismissal. The relevant distinction must therefore lie elsewhere. As seen above, in the older case law the courts tended to look at *the status of the applicant*. In *ex p Walsh* however the court clearly looked instead at *the nature of his complaint* – did it raise matters categorisable as public law? It is true that Mr Walsh's contract was made by reference to regulatory provisions and subject (ultimately) to sanctioning by the Secretary of State. However, he was not complaining that his contract had not been made in accordance with the correct statutory procedures; his complaint was in essence quite simply that, having been properly made, his contract had then been *broken* by the Health Authority by the manner of his

---

190 *O'Reilly v Mackman* [1983] 2 AC 237, [1982] 3 All ER 1124, HL; *Cocks v Thanet District Council* [1983] 2 AC 286, [1982] 3 All ER 1135, HL; *Davy v Spelthorne Borough Council* [1984] AC 262, [1983] 3 All ER 278, HL; *Wandsworth London Borough Council v Winder* [1985] AC 461, [1984] 3 All ER 976; *Roy v Kensington, Chelsea and Westminster Family Practitioner Committee* [1992] 1 All ER 705, [1992] IRLR 233, HL. For an interesting application in the employment context, see *Doyle v Northumbria Probation Committee* [1991] 4 All ER 294, [1992] ICR 121. A different, less technical, approach applies in Scotland: *West v Secretary of State for Scotland* [1992] IRLR 399, Ct of Sess.

191 [1984] ICR 743, [1984] IRLR 278, CA, noted Cripps [1984] CLJ 214, Collins (1984) 13 ILJ 174; *R v Derbyshire County Council, ex p Noble* [1990] ICR 808, [1990] IRLR 332, CA. Where the applicant is a civil servant, an application for judicial review can raise fundamental questions as to the contractual position for Crown servants: see p 107 above and in particular *R v Lord Chancellor's Department, ex p Nangle* [1991] ICR 743, [1991] IRLR 343.

dismissal. Breach of contract, said the Court of Appeal, remains a matter of private law (even when the employment is in the public sector with some measure of public control):

> 'The ordinary employer is free to act in breach of his contracts of employment and if he does so his employee will acquire certain private law rights and remedies in damages for wrongful dismissal, an order for reinstatement or re-engagement and so on. Parliament can underpin the position of public authority employees by directly restricting the freedom of the public authority to dismiss, thus giving the employee "public law" rights and at least making him a potential candidate for administrative law remedies. Alternatively, it can require the authority to contract with its employees on specified terms with a view to the employee acquiring "private law" rights under the terms of the contract of employment. If the authority fails or refuses thus to create "private law" rights for the employee, the employee will have "public law" rights to compel compliance, the remedy being mandamus requiring the authority so to contract or a declaration that the employee had those rights. If, however, the authority gives the employee the required protection, a breach of that contract is not a matter of "public law" and gives rise to no administrative law remedies[192].'

> 'The only remedies sought by Mr. Walsh arise solely out of his contract of employment with them as opposed to any public duty imposed upon the Health Authority[193].'

Thus the requirements for Order 53 were not satisfied. In the subsequent case of *McClaren v Home Office*[194] the doyen of modern administrative law, Woolf LJ, developed this approach into four principles which constitute valuable guidance in this maze.

(i) In relation to a personal claim against the employer, an employee of a public body is normally in exactly the same situation as other employees and can bring proceedings in the ordinary way for damages, a declaration or an injunction (except in relation to the Crown)[195].

(ii) An employee of a public body can seek judicial review and obtain a remedy which would not be available to an employee in the private sector where there exists some disciplinary or other body established under the prerogative or by statute to which the employer or employee is entitled or required to refer disputes affecting their relationship.

(iii) In addition, if an employee of a public body is adversely affected by a decision of general application by his employer, he can be entitled to challenge that decision by way of judicial review on grounds that it is flawed.

(iv) Judicial review will *not* be available where disciplinary procedures are of a purely domestic nature, albeit that their decisions might affect the public.

192 Per Sir John Donaldson MR at 752 and 281, respectively.
193 Per Purchas LJ at 769 and 288, respectively.
194 [1990] ICR 824, [1990] IRLR 338, CA. The case is primarily of importance as a statement of the contractual status of civil servants: see p 107 above. The following passage is merely a precis; Woolf LJ's erudite judgment deserves reading as a whole.
195 In the case itself a prison officer was seeking to sue the Home Office for *breach of contract*; it was therefore the Home Office who were arguing that his remedies properly lay in judicial review (for which his application would have been out of time). The restrictive approach to Ord 53 thus worked in the employee's favour on the facts.

At first sight, it may appear that what the Court of Appeal were doing in these cases was to lay down new principles to replace those in the older case law as to when any form of remedy is to be given, and to do so restrictively in an attempt to minimise the use of administrative law remedies and have dismissal cases dealt with before the proper forum of employment tribunals (a strong and patent policy factor). However, the position is not so simple because there is a further stage. As explained above, under Order 53, rule 9(5) an action wrongly commenced under the Order can be transformed at the court's discretion into an action begun by writ. In *ex p Walsh*, the employee applied for this to be done but that application was refused by the Court of Appeal on procedural grounds. Thus although *ex p Walsh* is the leading case on Order 53 and dismissal cases, it does not answer the further question – if rule 9(5) is applied (or indeed if an action is commenced by writ in the first place seeking a declaration or injunction on the grounds of breach of natural justice or ultra vires), what principles are *then* to apply to determine whether relief should be given? Here it seems that the principles in the older cases still apply, and we are back to the status of the employee. As Purchas LJ put it:

> 'It is important to remember that the three categories of employment described by Lord Reid in *Ridge v Baldwin* and referred to in *Malloch v Aberdeen Corpn* were directed to the question of the right to be heard and not to the procedural question [ie under Order 53] which is central to the instant appeal. ... It is important, in my judgment, to distinguish the two concepts involved. The first is the well-debated problem as to whether or not an obligation to obey the rules of natural justice in master and servant cases encapsulated in the expression "audi alteram partem" is imported into a contract of employment. The second is whether that invokes of necessity the supervisory powers of the court.[196]'

To sum up, an application under Order 53 to challenge a dismissal will only be successful if the nature of the applicant's complaint is such as to raise issues of public law and *ex p Walsh*, the leading case, establishes that a complaint that is essentially one of breach of contract by the employer is *not* categorisable as a matter of public law. Even if Order 53 is inapplicable, a court may in its discretion treat the application as if begun by writ for a declaration or injunction (or indeed the applicant may have proceeded in that manner in the first place). In such a case the court may still have jurisdiction to intervene (even though this leads to the logically unsatisfactory position of applying public law concepts such as breach of natural justice or ultra vires in cases to which ex hypothesi the principal public law procedure of Order 53 is not applicable). Moreover, the grounds for interfering appear to be wider, for the test to be applied is *not* that contained in *ex p Walsh* of the nature of the complaint (ie the criterion for coming under Order 53), but rather the old test based upon the status of the employee. The older case law on this (considered above) tended to look for something in the nature of, or analogous to, 'officeholding' and, while it stands independently of the recent case law on Order 53, the tenor of the latter suggests that here too a restrictive approach is likely to be taken, for fear of opening the way for a multitude of cases (especially from the public sector) being brought before the ordinary

---

196 At 768 at 287, respectively.

courts which, in the opinion of the Court of Appeal in *ex p Walsh*, should be dealt with instead by employment tribunals[197].

C. The decision in *Hill v CA Parsons & Co Ltd*[198]

In this case, the plaintiff refused to join a union which had negotiated a closed shop with his employers, who therefore gave him one month's notice of dismissal. He had been employed by them for 35 years as a chartered engineer, and had two years to go to retirement, so that the dismissal would affect his pension rights; moreover, the unfair dismissal legislation was due to come into force within six months of the dismissal. The plaintiff sued the employers for wrongful dismissal and claimed an interim injunction restraining them for treating the notice as terminating his employment. This could be construed as enforcing the contract of employment, but the Court of Appeal by a majority (Lord Denning MR and Sachs LJ, Stamp LJ dissenting) granted the interim injunction. The imminence of the new legislation was obviously a strong background factor (and hence the finding that proper notice would have been at least six months for a man in his position), but to find in the plaintiff's favour the majority had to go against the normal rule against enforcement (the application of which was the basis of Stamp LJ's dissent). To do so they held that that rule is not a fixed rule of law, but a question of fact which therefore permits exceptions in cases where the usual reasons against enforcement do not apply, in particular where there is continued confidence between the parties (as in this case, where both the parties wanted to continue the employment and the pressure to terminate it came from the trade union[199]). Further, Lord Denning said that in this case damages were not an adequate remedy, so it was right that an injunction should be granted, on the principle 'ubi jus ibi remedium'[200] which would allow the court to 'step over the trip-wires of previous cases and to bring the law into accord with the needs of today'. It may certainly be argued that justice was done to the plaintiff in this case, but it left many questions open which would have had to have been solved had this area of law not been effectively superseded by the new unfair dismissal action, particularly as the case cast doubt on the general principle discussed above that when an employer repudiates a contract of employment, that automatically terminates the contract and the employee must accept the repudiation and sue for damages; this raised the problem of what circumstances would put a case into the category in which the employer's repudiation might not have this automatic effect, and opened the way for rather refined arguments based on the concept of repudiation which at times, it is submitted, could stray a long way from the realities of employment[201]. In the event, the case did not lead to a radical reappraisal of enforcement of contracts of employment at common law, and was restrictively

197 The Scottish courts have shown a consistently strict view on the matter, not allowing judicial review of what are essentially contractual matters: *West v Secretary of State for Scotland* [1992] IRLR 399, Ct of Sess. In *Blair v Lochaber District Council* [1995] IRLR 135 the Court of Session refused review to a chief executive allegedly suspended contrary to the authority's own rules, which was held to remain essentially a contractual matter. Distinguishing *Malloch*, above (itself a Scottish decision, but now apparently out of favour) it was held that even if the older case law had to be considered, the chief executive here did *not* have the necessary 'status' as an office holder. If he did not, who does?
198 [1972] Ch 305, [1971] 3 All ER 1345, CA; noted [1972A] CLJ 49, (1972) 35 MLR 310.
199 This view of the facts was disputed by Stamp LJ.
200 'Where there is a right, there is a remedy', but in this context perhaps best translated as 'where there is a will, there is a way'.
201 See, eg, *Shields Furniture Ltd v Goff* [1973] 2 All ER 653, [1973] ICR 187, NIRC.

construed in subsequent cases as a rare case on its facts, relying upon the continued existence of mutual confidence between the parties, which is unlikely to be so in many cases[202]. However, the case is a decision of the Court of Appeal and at least shows that there may be *some* scope for enforcement of the contract as a remedy at common law.

At times subsequently, interest has been rekindled to some extent in the possibility of such a common law remedy – in *Irani v Southampton and South West Hampshire Health Authority*[203] Warner J applied *Hill v C A Parsons & Co Ltd* to grant an injunction restraining a dismissal in breach of quasi-statutory disciplinary procedures; a similar result was reached by Mervyn Davies J in *Wadcock v London Borough of Brent* [204] and by Morland J in *Robb v London Borough of Hammersmith and Fulham*[205] in the case of contractually binding disciplinary procedures; in *Powell v London Borough of Brent*[206] the Court of Appeal granted an interlocutory injunction restraining the employers from depriving the employee of a promotion for which she had successfully applied; in *Hughes v London Borough of Southwark* [207] Taylor J granted an interlocutory injunction restraining the employers from insisting on the employees taking on work which the latter argued was not within their contractual obligations; in *Anderson v Pringle of Scotland Ltd*[208] Lord Prosser granted an interim interdict to restrain a redundancy dismissal in breach of a LIFO redundancy agreement which was assumed to be part of the employee's individual contract and in *Peace v City of Edinburgh Council* [209] Lord Penrose restrained the disciplining (*short* of dismissal) of the employee under a new procedure which he argued he had not consented to as part of his contract. In these cases, the basis of the court's power to intervene is clearly seen as the (argued) continued

---

202   *GKN (Cwmbran) Ltd v Lloyd* [1972] ICR 214; *Sanders v Ernest A Neale Ltd* [1974] 3 All ER 327, [1974] ICR 565; *Chappell v Times Newspapers Ltd* [1975] 2 All ER 233, [1975] ICR 145, CA; *City and Hackney Health Authority v NUPE* [1985] IRLR 252, CA. In *GKN (Cwmbran) Ltd v Lloyd* Sir John Donaldson P suggested (at 221) that a further material factor in *Hill v CA Parsons & Co Ltd* was that the actual dismissal had not taken place, so that the court was restraining a proposed dismissal, not putting an employee back into employment after he had been effectively dismissed. This point was also stressed by Lord Prosser in the Court of Session in *Anderson v Pringle of Scotland Ltd* [1998] IRLR 64.

203   [1985] ICR 590, [1985] IRLR 203.

204   [1990] IRLR 223.

205   [1991] ICR 514, [1991] IRLR 72.

206   [1988] ICR 176, [1987] IRLR 466, CA; after the plaintiff's successful application for the senior post, one of the unsuccessful applicants claimed that the council's equal opportunity policy had been infringed and so the council purported to negate the promotion and readvertise the post.

207   [1988] IRLR 55. In *Ali v London Borough of Southwark* [1988] ICR 567, [1988] IRLR 100 a challenge to threatened disciplinary proceedings that the plaintiff said would be irregular failed on two grounds: (a) no continued mutual confidence; (b) the court will not normally step in in advance to restrain *pending* disciplinary proceedings (applying the similar rule in trade union cases, in *Longley v National Union of Journalists* [1987] IRLR 109, CA).

208   [1998] IRLR 64, OH. Lord Prosser stated that 'such exceptional cases as there have been give no very clear picture of the criteria for intervention', but justified his order on the grounds that (a) there was no evidence of loss of trust in the employee (this being a redundancy case) and (b) court intervention was possible *before* the dismissal was due to take place.

209   [1999] IRLR 417, OH. Here it was important that it was a breach of contract *during* employment that was being restrained, and that both parties were assuming that the contract was to continue.

existence of mutual confidence between the parties[210]. However, the point remains that these are *not* ordinary, everyday dismissal cases (indeed, *Powell, Hughes* and *Peace* are not dismissal cases at all) and while they may point to interesting and useful developments in the use (or threatened use) of the common law to restrain employer misuses of contractually binding disciplinary procedures[211], it would be premature to consider them as showing a resurgence of common law actions aimed at preserving employment in wrongful dismissal cases generally, particularly as it is equally possible to point to recent decisions refusing similar relief for traditional reasons[212]. There is, however, one procedural innovation which might have some influence here. What is now Part 24 of the Civil Procedure Rules (originally Order 14A of the Rules of the Supreme Court) was introduced to allow a court to determine any question of law or construction of any document at any stage in the proceedings where it appears to the court that (a) such question is suitable for determination without a full trial of the action and (b) such determination will finally determine the entire cause or matter or any claim or issue therein. This de facto power to issue a declaration of the meaning of, for example, a contract of employment, was used by Chadwick J in *Jones v Gwent County Council*[213] to declare that a letter of dismissal was not validly issued within the contract and, on that basis, to grant injunctions restraining the employers from acting on it. Technically, this power does not 'enforce' the contract of employment, but if its use became more widespread the question would have to be faced as to whether it constituted unacceptable back-door enforcement.

(c) Damages for wrongful dismissal

The remedies for wrongful dismissal are limited not only by the rule against enforcement, but also by the restricted measure of damages recoverable in many cases. The restriction arises once again from the doctrine of notice, for if an employer wrongfully dismisses an employee who should have had, say, two weeks' notice, what has the employee in fact lost? He cannot be said to have lost his long-term livelihood, for at common law he could have been dismissed at any time merely by being given two weeks' notice. Thus, all that he has lost is his two weeks' notice, and so his measure of damage is restricted to his pay during that

---

210 This means either no loss of confidence on the facts or, possibly, that any such loss by the employer is on irrational grounds, and so rectifiable. In *Hughes*, Taylor J said that mutual confidence should not be considered to have gone merely because the employer and employee are in genuine dispute as to the construction or application of certain contractual terms or duties. Note, however, that in *Robb* Morland J took a slightly different approach saying that, while continued trust and confidence is important where the employee is trying to get his job back, if (as in that case) the employee was only interested in securing use of the disciplinary procedure in order to air his grievances the test should be whether a court order would actually be workable.

211 Similar proceedings can be seen in *Deitman v Brent London Borough Council* [1988] IRLR 299, CA.

212 *Alexander v Standard Telephones and Cables plc* [1990] ICR 291, [1990] IRLR 55; *Jakeman v South West Thames Regional Health Authority and London Ambulance Service* [1990] IRLR 62; *Wishart v NACAB Ltd* [1990] ICR 794, [1990] IRLR 383, CA.

213 [1992] IRLR 521.

period[214]. This is backed by the general principle that, in a damages action, the employers must be assumed to have discharged their contractual duties towards the employee in the way least onerous to them, which will usually mean assuming that they would have ended the contract in any event, as quickly as they could lawfully have done so (usually by giving notice)[215]. Basically, therefore, a wrongfully dismissed employee is entitled to damages equal to his wages or salary during his notice period[216]. Moreover, the common law was always wary of giving further damages under other heads. Thus, in *Addis v Gramophone Co Ltd*[217] an employee who was paid at a fixed salary plus commission was wrongfully dismissed and claimed damages under the following heads – (i) salary for the six-month notice period, (ii) reasonable commission for a six-month period, (iii) damages for the humiliating manner of dismissal, (iv) damages for loss of reputation leading to future difficulty in obtaining employment. The House of Lords held by a majority that only heads (i) and (ii) were recoverable. Also, the law only looked at the definite contractual liabilities of the employer in assessing damages, not at what the employee might in fact have received (eg a discretionary bonus which he might have received during the notice period). In *Lavarack v Woods of Colchester Ltd*[218] an employee who was wrongfully dismissed had been on a five-year contract with a fixed salary subject to periodic discretionary bonuses. After he had been dismissed (but during the period for which the contract should have continued) the employers discontinued the bonus scheme and increased the wages of their staff. The Court of Appeal held by a majority that the increase in wages should not be taken into account when assessing the damages, since the only fully contractual obligation upon the employers was to pay the fixed salary and anything on top of that was discretionary (whether a bonus or an increase in wages). Lord Denning MR, dissenting, took the wider view that the dismissed employee was

214 A gloss here is that if a contractually binding disciplinary procedure has been breached, a court may look at when the contract could *lawfully* have been terminated, awarding damages for a short period representing the time necessary to have operated the procedure properly and *then* the notice period: *Gunton v Richmond-upon-Thames London Borough Council* [1980] ICR 755, [1980] IRLR 321, CA; *Boyo v Lambeth London Borough Council* [1994] ICR 727, [1995] IRLR 50, CA. However, a court or tribunal cannot go farther and speculate on the *chances* of the employee having been kept on if the proper procedure had gone in his favour: *Focsa Services (UK) Ltd v Birkett* [1996] IRLR 325; *Janciuk v Winerite Ltd* [1998] IRLR 63, EAT.
215 This principle, taken from the majority decision in *Laverack v Woods of Colchester Ltd* [1967] 1 QB 278, [1966] 3 All ER 683, CA (below), was applied strongly in *Janciuk v Winerite Ltd* (above) and *Morran v Glasgow Council of Tenants' Associations* [1998] IRLR 67, Ct of Sess.
216 One slight extension here is that the employee may also claim any benefit that he would have *qualified* for, had he been given and served out the proper length of notice: *Silvey v Pendragon plc* [2001] EWCA Civ 789, [2001] IRLR 685 (proper notice would have taken the employee past the age of 55, which was significant for pension purposes; damages awarded to reflect this). Australian case law departing from the harsh common law rule and allowing general damages in such cases is considered in Ewing 'Remedies for breach of the contract of employment' [1993] CLJ 405 at 428.
217 [1909] AC 488, HL, reaffirmed in *Bliss v South East Thames Regional Health Authority* [1987] ICR 700, [1985] IRLR 308, CA. See *Alexander v Standard Telephones and Cables Ltd (No 2)* [1991] IRLR 286. The employee's remedy lies in damages; he may not sue instead in debt for continuing wages into the future: *Marsh v National Autistic Society* [1993] ICR 453.
218 [1967] 1 QB 278, [1966] 3 All ER 683, CA; *Bold v Brough, Nicholson and Hall Ltd* [1963] 3 All ER 849, [1964] 1 WLR 201. Damages for loss of rights under a share option scheme were refused because of a literal interpretation of the scheme's rules in *Micklefield v SAC Technology Ltd* [1991] 1 All ER 275, [1990] IRLR 218.

entitled to recover all that he would *in fact* have earned but for the employers' breach of contract.

To this harsh general rule on damages, there are exceptions. The *first* is that where the contract of employment is for a fixed term, not terminable by notice, the damages recoverable are the amount which the employee would have earned under the contract during the remainder of the term, after the wrongful dismissal (subject to mitigation, which is considered below). The *second* is that certain untypical contracts of employment may be construed as envisaging a greater reward for the employee than the bare wage or salary, so that damages in respect of this further loss can be recovered in addition. Thus in *Marbé v George Edwardes (Daly's Theatres) Ltd*[219] an American actress wishing to establish her reputation in London contracted to play a particular part for the defendant, who undertook to give her full publicity. When she was wrongfully denied the chance to play the part, the Court of Appeal held that she could recover the salary due to her for the period of the contract *plus* an amount representing loss of reputation. The extent of this exception outside the theatre is uncertain (*quaere*, for example, whether it would apply to any case where the courts found that there was a contractual obligation to provide the employee with actual work, not simply to pay wages[220]), but one case which is at least analogous is *Dunk v George Waller & Son Ltd*[221] where the plaintiff, an apprentice, was wrongfully dismissed during the four-year term in question and was held entitled to his net loss of wages for the rest of the term plus an amount representing loss of tuition and training and diminution of future prospects. One possible variant of this may be where the extra 'benefit' that the employee expects under the contract is so important that the court will imply a term that the employer will not use the normal power to dismiss by notice so as to deprive the employee of that benefit. This has arisen in the 'PHI cases', where a long-term sick employee is deprived of major financial benefits under a permanent health insurance (PHI) scheme, provided by the employer, though the employer dismissing him by notice before he can qualify under the scheme[222]. In such cases, courts have impliedly restricted the power to give notice in sickness absences where the result would be deprivation of PHI rights. Thus, a dismissal (otherwise lawful under the contractual notice provision) may become wrongful, with the prospect opening up of *general* damages for loss of those rights. An open question then becomes whether the PHI cases could be extended to other analogous contexts. This was done in *Jenvey v Australian Broadcasting Corpn*[223], where damages were awarded for the loss of valuable redundancy rights under the contract due to an unlawful early dismissal held to be wrongful because of its effect. Another interesting possibility might be where an employee is taken on specifically in order to bring with him particular trade, contacts or contracts to the new employer; could it be argued that it is an implied term that he will not be dismissed (other than for gross misconduct) as long as the employer retains that

219 [1928] 1 KB 269, CA. See also *Herbert Clayton and Jack Waller Ltd v Oliver* [1930] AC 209, HL; *Withers v General Theatre Corpn Ltd* [1933] 2 KB 536, CA.

220 See pp 166–168 above.

221 [1970] 2 QB 163, [1970] 2 All ER 630. *Quaere* whether the reasoning in this case applies only to apprenticeship, or might be applicable to any contract of employment envisaging vocational training or retraining.

222 *Aspden v Webbs Poultry and Meat Group (Holdings) Ltd* [1996] IRLR 521; *Adin v Sedco Forex International Resources Ltd* [1997] IRLR 280, Ct of Sess.

223 [2002] EWHC 927 (QB), [2003] ICR 79, [2002] IRLR 520; see p 167 above.

trade, etc, so that general damages for wrongful dismissal could be awarded for any such dismissal?[224]

A third exceptional case has been suggested for some time. This may arise where the employer breaks the contract of employment by dismissing the employee with no or short notice, thereby depriving him of his statutory rights (especially the right to claim unfair dismissal) by advancing the effective date of dismissal to *within* the qualifying period[225]. In such a case, the employee would be debarred from claiming unfair dismissal (if that were the right in question) but may be able to bring an action in the ordinary courts for *wrongful* dismissal claiming extra damages representing the loss to him of his potential statutory rights[226]. This would seem to be a practical answer to the possible problem of an employer being able to rely on the relatively rigid rules on dates of termination and qualifying periods through deliberate breach of contract on his own part, and an award of damages on this basis was finally permitted by the EAT in *Raspin v United News Shops Ltd*[227] where a summary dismissal three weeks short of the unfair dismissal qualifying period was held to have been wrongful *and* in breach of a contractually binding disciplinary procedure, proper exhaustion of which would have taken long enough to have allowed the employee to reach the qualifying period.

The fourth exception arises from potentially significant applications of the modern term of trust and respect[228] and even wider ideas borrowed from administrative law to the area of damages. In *Clark v BET plc*[229], a wrongful dismissal claim by a highly paid chief executive on a three-year fixed-term contract, liability was conceded but a major question arose as to quantification of damages because the executive had been heavily reliant for much of his pay package on salary increases and bonuses which, while regularly paid in the past, remained discretionary. On a strict approach (typified by the *Laverack* case considered above and the principle that the employer should normally be assumed to have discharged the contract in the way least onerous to himself) the executive would not have been awarded anything for these heads, because technically the employer could have decided to give *nothing* for the remainder of the contract. However, Walker J avoided that harsh result by looking at what the employers were likely to have paid out (given the firm's known performance over the relevant period) if they had continued to exercise their discretion *in good faith*. Although only at

---

224 General damages could cause particular problems of quantification in a context such as this; a court or tribunal would have to fix some sort of 'multiplier' to assess the likely period of loss, but without the highly developed 'tariff' system available to perform a similar task in personal injury cases.

225 This is consistent with the better view of the meaning of 'effective date of termination', that it occurs when the dismissal in practice takes effect (see p 454, below); this remains so even where the dismissal is in breach of contract (and even if that breach is deliberate): *Stapp v Shaftesbury Society* [1982] IRLR 326, CA.

226 *Robert Cort & Son Ltd v Charman* [1981] ICR 816, [1981] IRLR 437, per Browne-Wilkinson J, approved by the Court of Appeal in *Stapp v Shaftesbury Society*, n 225 above. This analysis does not work if there is a *express* payment in lieu of notice clause in the contract, because then the instant dismissal is not wrongful: *Morran v Glasgow Council of Tenants' Associations* [1998] IRLR 67, Ct of Sess.

227 [1999] IRLR 9. It is possible that this argument may be strengthened by the Employment Act 2002, s 30, which deems the new statutory (minimum) disciplinary and grievance procedures in Schedule to be incorporated into all contracts of employment. However, there are now doubts whether this will be brought into force.

228 See p 158 above.

229 [1997] IRLR 348.

first instance, this is clearly an important decision in any case where significant elements of remuneration are discretionary, and it does show a significant departure from the straight *Laverack* approach. A similar result can be seen in *Clark v Nomura International plc*[230] where an employee who had been a highly successful trader, receiving large annual bonuses clearly linked to his trading profits for the company, was dismissed and awarded a nil bonus for his final year, even though his trading had continued to be profitable. Burton J (now President of the EAT, which may become significant in this area) felt able to quantify what the employee should normally have received on past experience and awarded that as damages. However, he did not do so under the term of trust and respect (which he thought could cause problems of application here, especially if cast in terms of 'capriciousness'), but on the other hand to apply an ordinary test of reasonableness to cases like this would be too low a threshold for controversial legal intervention. His solution was to import the concept of *perversity*, the basis of adjudication being whether the exercise of the employer's discretion was such that no reasonable employer would have behaved in that way (the employer on the facts failing that test here). Of course, any importation of public/administrative law principles into private law will be both significant and controversial[231]. It was therefore important that this line was then adopted by the Court of Appeal in *Mallone v BPB Industries plc*[232] where an executive, dismissed due to genuine concerns by the company about his performance, subsequently had his (vested) rights to valuable share options cancelled by the company. This was technically within its powers under the terms of the share option rules (ie within the employer's 'absolute discretion') but damages for loss of the options were granted on the basis that the company had acted *irrationally* in coming to this decision (especially as there was no documentation showing *how* it had been reached). Arguably, what we are seeing here is the law on damages being used increasingly to control employer discretion, even where that discretion is clearly and deliberately provided for in the contract. Moreover, the end result is coming close to Lord Denning's dissenting view in *Lavavack v Woods*[233] that the employee should be compensated for what, in some sense, he or she *should* have received in practice. Several implications of this are immediately obvious. The first is that employers may increasingly not just have to justify their actions on the strict wording of the contract, but in the light of how and why they exercised the rights or discretions given by that wording (especially on or after dismissal, if there is any suggestion of motives of revenge). The second is that reliance on ideas of perversity or irrationality can provide a wide form of challenge, possibly going beyond pure breach of contract (note that in both *Clark v Nomura* and *Mallone* the dismissals were lawful, and the damages were awarded for the deprivation of the benefits as such, not as part of a wrongful dismissal action). This could provide a wider range of remedies on termination than under traditional analysis. A third implication could arise from ideas expressed in *Mallone* that the vested share option rights were akin to property rights. Deprivation of such rights can be seen as validating the importation of administrative law ideas; in which case,

---

230 [2000] IRLR 766.
231 See the discussion of possible public law remedies of enforcement of the contract of employment at pp 474–481 above.
232 [2002] ICR 1045, [2002] IRLR 452, CA; see the discussion in Smith and Randall *Contract Actions in Modern Employment Law: Developments and Issues* (2002) at pp 101–103.
233 See n 218 above.

need they stop at perversity? If emphasis is to be placed on the rationality of the employer's decision (see the concerns of the Court of Appeal about inadequate records), could the employee argue that he or she has a right to *participate* in the decision making process (ie a right to be heard)? Might ideas of unlawful *bias* surface here (for example if two of the three directors on the committee deciding on annual bonuses or the exercise of share options had been responsible for the employee's dismissal in the first place)? This whole area will need much more judicial exploration, but for the moment it seems that at least the foundations have been laid.

A fifth exception, again possibly opening up wider damages (this time *general* damages for injury to feelings and/or manner of dismissal), recently seemed to arise at the highest level, but was immediately heavily restricted, being seen as the movement too far in this volatile area. In *Malik v BCCI SA (in liquidation)*[234] ex-employees of the failed BCCI bank claimed damages in respect of injury to their reputation and future employment prospects caused by the bank conducting a dishonest or corrupt business. The House of Lords upheld this claim on the grounds that the conduct of the employer was a serious breach of the implied term of trust and respect (to the evolution of which they gave their clear support[235]). *Addis* was subject to considerable scrutiny by Lords Nicholls and Steyn, giving the principal judgments, and was side-stepped partly on the basis that it principally concerned a claim for injury to feelings caused by the wrongful dismissal whereas the claim in *Malik* was clearly for future financial loss caused by the employer's conduct, and partly on the basis that *Addis v Gramophone* (above) was decided well before the development of the term of trust and respect which now occupies a central position in employment law. This new genus of 'stigma damages' caused much interest and was enthusiastically pursued by claimants' lawyers because it seemed to open up a vista into general damages for wrongful dismissal, even though (a) the case was *not* in fact one of wrongful dismissal but one of breach of contract during employment, and (b) both Law Lords ended their speeches with warnings that the facts in *Malik* were extreme and that in many, more ordinary cases there could be severe problems of causation, remoteness and mitigation[236]. Thus, the case posed the question – a claimant's Pandora's Box or an interesting decision on unusual facts? The argument that *Malik* was *not* meant to allow damages for injury to feelings was accepted by the Court of Appeal in *French v Barclays Bank plc*[237], a common law damages claim involving breach of trust and respect where a head of claim relating to stress and anxiety caused by the breach was disallowed. This was consistent, however, with the view that stigma damages for financial loss would now be claimable, including in a wrongful *dismissal* case, but that view has now been stopped by the further (and very different) decision of the House of Lords in *Johnson v Unisys Ltd*[238]. This was a difficult case on rather unusual facts, since the employee (who had suffered from work-induced stress prior to being summarily dismissed) had already succeeded in an unfair dismissal action, and then brought a substantial claim for damages for wrongful dismissal to the tune of £400,000, alleging that as a result

---

234 [1997] ICR 606, [1997] IRLR 462, HL; see McMullen (1997) 26 ILJ 245.
235 They added that the trust-destroying conduct did not have to be aimed at the individual, and that it was not necessary that that individual became aware of the conduct while still an employee.
236 The claim did indeed finally fail on its facts: *BCCI SA (in liq) v Ali (No 3)* [2002] IRLR 460, CA.
237 [1998] IRLR 646, CA.
238 [2001] ICR 480, [2001] IRLR 279, HL.

of it he had suffered a nervous breakdown and was unable to work (thus arguably covering both injured feelings *and* future financial loss, through admittedly not in the usual 'stigma' manner). Ruling this claim out, the House of Lords confined stigma damages to the (highly unusual) case of an employee suing the employer for breach of contract *during* employment. Such damages, they said, are *not* available on termination (ie in a wrongful dismissal action) for two reasons. The first was that, on an analytical level, the implied term of trust and respect (the basis for *Malik*) was aimed at keeping the contract alive and so, ex hypothesi, was not applicable on termination[239]. The second was the interesting and novel constitutional point that the common law was not to be developed in such a way as to evade or negative statutory employment law. Parliament has provided the law of unfair dismissal to deal with employer abuses of power on termination, but has laid down limitations such as the short time limit and (crucially) the statutory cap on the amount of compensation that can be claimed and awarded. A new law on stigma damages in a common law wrongful dismissal action could be used to side-step unfair dismissal which, said Lord Hoffmann, was the proper action in which to claim damages for manner of dismissal, injury to feelings, etc[240].

Once the prima facie amount of damages has been ascertained, it is subject to reduction in three ways:

A. Mitigation

The employee is under a duty to mitigate his loss, and in the context of the contract of employment this will mean essentially finding another job. This will be particularly important in the case of the wrongful termination of a fixed-term contract which had several years to run, but will apply generally to all wrongful dismissals[241]. What constitutes reasonable steps to mitigate will be a question of fact in each case, but two general points might be made. The first is that the courts apply a realistic standard, so that the dismissed employee is not expected to take any job immediately, irrespective of his former position; thus, he may be allowed a certain time to look around for a position of equal status before resorting to lesser employment, and it may not be reasonable to expect him to take another post inside the firm that dismissed him, if that is offered, particularly if it involves a reduction in status[242]. The second is that matters other than another job could

---

239 This has caused problems with the correct meaning to give to 'or termination' – does this mean only the actual process of dismissal or does it stretch back further (with possibly harsh results for the employee)? See p 160 above.

240 This constitutional approach meant that the old authority of Addis was not central to the argument of the majority who accepted that the common law could evolve away from that case but held that it was undesirable to do so. Lord Steyn (dissenting on the reasoning but agreeing with the result of the facts) would have effected such an evolution. Lord Hoffmann's remark that manner of dismissal damages are available in an unfair dismissal action went against previous authority and caused problems in that context; see p 615 below.

241 If the dismissal is not wrongful, the employee may sue for unpaid wages for the notice period in an action for debt, to which the obligation to mitigate does not apply: *Abrahams v Performing Right Society Ltd* [1995] ICR 1028, [1995] IRLR 486, CA; dicta in this case suggesting that the obligation does not apply even where dismissal is wrongful must be considered to be wrong; see p 462 n 97 above.

242 *Yetton v Eastwoods Froy Ltd* [1966] 3 All ER 353, [1967] 1 WLR 104; *Shindler v Northern Raincoat Co Ltd* [1960] 2 All ER 239, [1960] 1 WLR 1038. The general principles of mitigation in the employment context were summed up by Potter LJ in *Wilding v BT plc* [2002] ICR 1079, [2002] IRLR 524, CA.

constitute mitigation, but before allowing them as such (with the resultant decrease in the amount of damages to be paid by the defendant employer) the court should be satisfied that they are not too remote to be taken into consideration. In *Lavarack v Woods of Colchester Ltd*, the facts of which are given above, the employee was debarred by the contract of employment from engaging in, or holding shares in, any other business during his employment. After his dismissal, he became employed by M Ltd (purchasing half of its stock) and invested in V Ltd. The defendant employers claimed that the profits on these investments should be taken into account to mitigate his damages; the Court of Appeal held that the profits from his shares in M Ltd were to be taken into account, since his dismissal had left him free to *partake* in M Ltd and thereby increase the value of those shares, but the profits from his shares in V Ltd were not to be taken into account, since these were too remote, and the mere fact that he could not have invested while in the defendant's employment was not enough to alter that.

B. Taxation

The general rule on the taxation of damages, laid down by the House of Lords in *British Transport Commission v Gourley*[243], is that where a head of damage is based on an estimate of lost wages, the court should make allowance for the tax that would have been paid, and so deduct that figure and award the damages net of tax. This applies to damages for wrongful dismissal. However, the basis for the rule is that the amount awarded as damages is not taxable in the claimant's hands, and at the time of *Gourley* this was generally the case. Now, however, under the Income Tax (Earnings and Pensions) Act 2003, section 403 (previously, and for many years, the Income and Corporation Taxes Act 1988, section 148) such 'post-cessation receipts' are taxed to the extent that they exceed £30,000. The end result is that the rule in *Gourley*'s case applies to the first £30,000 of damages for wrongful dismissal, which must be awarded net of tax, but not to any amount over and above that, which must be awarded gross (and will then be taxed by the Inland Revenue)[244].

C. Deduction of other benefits received

Where a person is unable to work and claims damages because of that, it is likely that he will receive benefits from various sources during the period out of employment; the question then arises whether the amount of those benefits should be deducted from the damages which the defendant must pay. This is obviously of great importance in personal injury claims, where it is well established

---

243 [1956] AC 185, [1955] 3 All ER 796, HL.
244 *Parsons v BNM Laboratories Ltd* [1964] 1 QB 95, [1963] 2 All ER 658, CA. The tax position must be considered realistically, taking into account any tax rebates due to the employee being unemployed after the dismissal: *Hartley v Sandholme Iron Co Ltd* [1975] QB 600, [1974] 3 All ER 475 (a personal injury case). See also *Bold v Brough, Nicholson and Hall Ltd* [1963] 3 All ER 849, [1964] 1 WLR 201; *Basnett v J & A Jackson Ltd* [1976] ICR 63, [1976] IRLR 154; and *Shove v Downs Surgical plc* [1984] ICR 532, [1984] IRLR 17; Harvey A5A(1); Powell 'The taxation of payments received on termination of employment' (1981) 10 ILJ 239; Bishop and Kay 'Taxation and damages: the rule of Gourley's case' (1987) 104 LQR 211. This is, of course, all on the assumption that the amount recovered by the claimant is *damages*; if it is simply a debt under the contract (eg a payment in lieu under an *express* 'in lieu' clause in the contract), it is taxable in the hands of the claimant anyway: *EMI Group Electronics Ltd v Coldicott* [1999] IRLR 630, [1999] STC 803, CA; *Richardson v Delaney* [2001] IRLR 663.

that insurance payments provided by the claimant's own foresight and payment of the premia are not deductible[245], whereas most social security benefits are now (since the Social Security Act 1989) recoverable in full by the state through the system of civil recoupment[246]. Outside those areas, however, the position is less clear, particularly since the decision of the House of Lords in *Parry v Cleaver*[247] which showed a modern tendency not to deduct benefits[248] and concentrated on public policy and overall fairness rather than the older, more technical test for deductibility, such as remoteness, whether the benefit was received as of right and whether the plaintiff had contributed to the scheme providing the benefit. The problem is that the case itself only concerned a contributory police disablement fund and indeed their Lordships declined to consider the deductibility of other benefits (such as those more relevant to the dismissed employee)[249], so that any effect that this case may have on other benefits must be by implication. While in some respects courts subsequently have taken a more straightforward view of quantifying the claimant's actual loss[250], the approach in *Parry v Cleaver* was strongly reaffirmed by the House of Lords in *Smoker v London Fire and Civil Defence Authority*[251] where it was held in a personal injury case that private pension benefits were not to be deducted from the plaintiff's damages for loss of earnings and this was applied directly to an action for wrongful dismissal in *Hopkins v Norcros plc*[252]. As the law stands at present, with regard to other benefits particularly applicable to wrongful dismissal cases, it appears that contractual payments by the employer such as sick pay are deductible (even if provided under an insurance policy maintained by the employer)[253], that jobseekers allowance (previously unemployment benefit) received by the dismissed employee during the period by which the damages are calculated is deductible[254],

245 *Bradburn v Great Western Rly Co* (1874) LR 10 Exch 1.
246 Social Security (Recovery of Benefit) Act 1997; see p 844 below. This special recoupment system does *not* apply to damages for wrongful dismissal.
247 [1970] AC 1, [1969] 1 All ER 555, HL. See generally on this question Lewis 'Deducting collateral benefits from damages: principle and policy' (1998) 18 LS 15, and 'The overlap between damages for personal injury and work related benefits' (1998) 27 ILJ 1.
248 See also *Daish v Wauton* [1972] 2 QB 262, [1972] 1 All ER 25, CA.
249 See [1970] AC 1 at 19 and 39, [1969] 1 All ER 555 at 562 and 579, per Lord Reid and Lord Wilberforce.
250 *Dews v National Coal Board* [1987] ICR 602, [1987] IRLR 330, HL; *Hodgson v Trapp* [1989] AC 807, [1988] 3 All ER 870, HL.
251 [1991] ICR 449, [1991] IRLR 271, HL; see also *Longden v British Coal Corpn* [1998] 1 All ER 289, [1998] ICR 26, HL.
252 [1994] ICR 11, [1994] IRLR 18, CA; this meant on the facts of the case that the wrongfully dismissed company chairman received £99,604 twice, once from the pension fund and once as damages for lost income. The judge at first instance had pointed out that provision could be made expressly either in an employment contract or in the rules of a pension scheme to prevent such double recovery.
253 *Hussain v New Taplow Paper Mills Ltd* [1988] ICR 259, [1988] IRLR 167, HL. In an industrial injury case, one way to prevent the employer (by paying sick pay) effectively subsidising the tortfeasor is to provide in the sick pay clause that, in the event of the injured employee later recovering damages from a third party, amounts paid to the employee as sick pay are refundable to the employer; this should enable damages to be awarded to the employee in full, without deduction of sick pay. Such clauses have been used, for example, in agricultural, railway and police contracts.
254 *Parsons v BNM Laboratories Ltd* [1964] 1 QB 95, [1963] 2 All ER 658, CA; *Foxley v Olton* [1965] 2 QB 306, [1964] 3 All ER 248n; *Cheeseman v Bowater UK Paper Mills Ltd* [1971] 3 All ER 513, [1971] 1 WLR 1773, CA. In *Nabi v British Leyland (UK) Ltd* [1980] 1 All ER 667, CA, the Court of Appeal applied the *Parsons* case, but thought that the rule was due for reconsideration. However, the House of Lords applied *Parsons* without demur in *Westwood v Secretary of State for Employment* [1985] ICR 209, [1984] IRLR 209, HL.

and after considerable doubt over a long period the Court of Appeal held that the same rule of deductibility applies to supplementary benefit (now income support)[255]. The other major benefit which might be relevant is a redundancy payment and while there was some authority in earlier cases[256] against deductibility (on the basis that the payment is due on dismissal anyway, whether or not the dismissal is wrongful) the Court of Appeal have held that such a payment *is* deductible, except possibly in a rare case where it can be shown that the employee would have been made redundant anyway[257].

(iii) Wrongful dismissal and unfair dismissal

The obvious contrast between the two is that the statutory action for unfair dismissal involves an enquiry into the overall merits of the dismissal whereas the common law action for wrongful dismissal looks basically to the *form* of the dismissal (except in cases where the employer purported to dismiss summarily for cause and the employee alleges that he gave no such cause). Thus, at common law an employer could dismiss for any reason provided he gave the correct length of notice (or wages in lieu thereof), but for the purposes of unfair dismissal this previously all-important question of notice is of evidential value only, if that, and the fact that proper notice was given will certainly not mean that the dismissal is necessarily fair. Thus, although a dismissal could be both wrongful and unfair, it could also easily be one but not the other. Fundamental concepts, such as the meaning of 'dismissal', can vary from one to the other and so for example a finding that an employee was unfairly dismissed will not necessarily put him at an advantage if he wishes later, in some other context, to claim that the dismissal was also wrongful[258]. Also, the separate principles of compensation operate independently[259] and indeed in theory the primary remedy for unfair dismissal is reinstatement of re-engagement, a remedy which, as seen above, the common law would only countenance in highly unusual cases.

There used to be a further difference in the appropriate forum. In *Treganowen v Robert Knee & Co Ltd*[260] an employee was dismissed without notice because of a personality clash between her and her colleagues for which she was to blame; the tribunal held that this reason rendered the dismissal fair, but considered that

---

255 *Lincoln v Hayman* [1982] 2 All ER 819, [1982] 1 WLR 488, CA (a personal injury case).
256 *Yorkshire Engineering and Welding Co Ltd v Burnham* [1973] 3 All ER 1176, [1974] ICR 77; *Millington v TH Goodwin & Sons Ltd* [1975] ICR 104, [1974] IRLR 379; *Basnett v J and A Jackson Ltd* [1976] ICR 63, [1976] IRLR 154. In each of these cases the decision of Arnold J in *Stocks v Magna Merchants Ltd* [1973] 2 All ER 329, [1973] ICR 530 that a redundancy payment should be deducted was not followed.
257 *Colledge v Bass Mitchells & Butlers Ltd* [1988] ICR 125, [1988] IRLR 163, CA (another personal injury case, where the judge at first instance had made a finding of fact that it was unlikely that the plaintiff would have been made redundant but for the accident).
258 *Turner v London Transport Executive* [1977] ICR 952, [1977] IRLR 441, CA. There is certainly no question of issue estoppel as such as between the unfair and wrongful dismissal actions, but on the other hand there are cases where a finding of fact by a tribunal has been treated as res judicata in later civil proceedings: *Green v Hampshire County Council* [1979] ICR 861; *Automatic Switching Ltd v Brunet* [1986] ICR 542, EAT.
259 *Norton Tool Co Ltd v Tewson* [1973] 1 All ER 183, [1972] ICR 501; *Everwear Candlewick Ltd v Isaac* [1974] 3 All ER 24, [1974] ICR 525; there is, however, a duty to mitigate loss as at common law, imposed specifically by the provisions relating to the compensatory award: Employment Rights Act 1996, s 123(4).
260 [1975] ICR 405, [1975] IRLR 247, applied in *BSC Sports and Social Club v Morgan* [1987] IRLR 391.

she should not have been dismissed summarily, but should instead have received six weeks' pay in lieu of notice, though they did not have jurisdiction to award this sum. The employee appealed claiming that they did have jurisdiction since the lack of notice was capable of making the dismissal unfair. The EAT dismissed the appeal, clearly holding that, while lack of notice could possibly be of evidential value in deciding some of the points necessary for an unfair dismissal action, it could not per se make a dismissal unfair that was otherwise fair, since it only gave rise to an action for *wrongful* dismissal which had to be brought in the ordinary courts, not before a tribunal at that time. While this case remains an instructive one on the distinction between the two actions, the forum point has been altered by the Employment Tribunals (Extension of Jurisdiction) (England and Wales) Orders 1994[261] which give tribunals the power to hear claims for breach of contract on termination of employment (up to a maximum of £25,000) and at long last have rid us of the previous, very unfortunate, split jurisdiction.

(iv) The residual importance of wrongful dismissal

The common law doctrine of notice meant that wrongful dismissal was only a theoretical remedy for a large number of employees, since they were on relatively short notice, so that even if such an employee went to the trouble and expense of bringing a common law action, his damages would be small, since they were so rigidly tied to the amount of wages during the notice period. The statutory action for unfair dismissal, whilst not abolishing wrongful dismissal, is now far more important in practice, with its easier procedure, the possibility (at least in theory) of reinstatement or re-engagement and the more liberal and realistic approach to compensation. On the other hand, there may still be some atypical cases where wrongful dismissal is still important. One class of case would be where the employee does not qualify for the statutory action, in particular where he is in an excluded category or where he lacks the necessary period of continuous service; indeed, in the latter case it has been held that if he falls short of that qualifying period because of the action of the employer in wrongfully dismissing him, he may claim loss of statutory rights as a head of damage in a common law wrongful dismissal action[262]. The most important case, however, would be that of a highly paid employee either on a fixed-term contract or entitled to a substantial period of notice, for the compensation for unfair dismissal is subject to statutory maxima[263] which, though perhaps adequate for many employees (certainly when compared with the small amounts recoverable by them for wrongful dismissal), may be a real restriction in the case of the high earner who, if dismissed unfairly *and* wrongfully, may have more to gain by an action for wrongful dismissal which is not subject to the statutory maxima. Such an action continues to be governed by the law as set out above, but for most practical purposes a modern dismissal case is likely to proceed on the statutory basis and be subject to the separate body of law on unfair dismissal, to which we must now turn.

---

261 SI 1994/1623 in England and Wales; SI 1994/1624 in Scotland; see below.
262 See p 486 above.
263 At the time of writing, the maximum basic award is £7,800; the maximum compensatory was for many years kept at a low level, *not* keeping up with inflation, so that as late as 1999 it was only £12,000. It was raised to £50,000 by the Employment Relations Act 1999 and at the time of writing stands at £53,500, but that could still be a low ceiling in the case of a very high earner.

Chapter 8

The law and procedure of unfair dismissal

'If we are not careful, we shall find the [employment] tribunals bent down under the weight of the law books or, what is worse, asleep under them. Let principles be reported, but not particular instances.'[1]

'We must not strive to create a body of judge-made law supplementing the law as laid down in the Employment Protection (Consolidation) Act 1978. The Act itself provides quite enough law in all conscience ...'[2]

'This is a Tribunal which, rightly in our view, preferred to drink at the pure waters of the section rather than allow itself to be diverted into the channels created by judicial decisions ... in other cases in different circumstances.'[3]

'Deciding these cases is the job of [employment] tribunals and when they have not erred in law neither the appeal tribunal nor [the Court of Appeal] should disturb this decision unless one can say in effect: "My goodness, that must be wrong"[4].'

'... [T]he only truth lies in learning to free ourselves from insane passion for the truth[5].'

---

1 *Walls Meat Co Ltd v Khan* [1979] ICR 52 at 57, [1978] IRLR 499 at 501, CA, per Lord Denning MR.
2 *Kearney & Trecker Marwin Ltd v Varndell* [1983] IRLR 335 at 340, CA, per Eveleigh LJ.
3 *Siggs & Chapman (Contractors) Ltd v Knight* [1984] IRLR 83 at 85, per Waite P.
4 *Neale v Hereford and Worcester County Council* [1986] ICR 471 at 483, [1986] IRLR 168 at 173, per May LJ.
5 Umberto Eco *The Name of the Rose* (1984) p 491.

I EMPLOYMENT TRIBUNALS AND THE EMPLOYMENT APPEAL TRIBUNAL

The large majority of all employment and industrial relations litigation is handled by employment tribunals, which from inauspicious beginnings under the Industrial Training Act 1964 have expanded to assume wide new jurisdictions under the modern employment legislation and in 1994 were at last given common law jurisdiction over breach of contract claims, at least on termination of employment[6]. They started life as 'industrial tribunals' but were renamed 'employment tribunals' in 1998[7], for no apparently compelling reason. As 'industrial juries' they are designed to provide a means of speedy resolution of industrial cases which will often turn very heavily upon their particular facts, and the Donovan Report in 1968[8] referred to their potential advantages as being ease of access, informality, speed and inexpensiveness. Rules of procedure (including pre-trial procedures, such as the simplified pleadings) are drafted with this aim in mind, and the tribunals have wide powers to decide most cases in a common sense way, having regard to 'good industrial practice'. The paradox here, however, is that while the tribunals' procedure may be simplified, the law which they have to apply is often of great complexity and hence the major controversy over how 'legalistic' the proceedings and decisions of tribunals should be. Simple, common sense access to quick justice may be a worthy aim, but there is still a lot of hard law which must be complied with in most of the statutory actions.

This controversy over legalism will be one of the major themes throughout this chapter; it is viewed in many quarters as little less than a disease infecting the tribunal system[9] and, while views in the courts have varied over time (at times involving a clear difference of opinion between the Employment Appeal Tribunal (EAT) and the Court of Appeal), the modern approach has come down strongly in favour of the anti-legalism camp, with the Employment Rights (Dispute Resolution) Act 1998 and the Employment Act 2002 making at least piecemeal attempts at reform. The aim of this part of the chapter is to look briefly at the constitution of tribunals and the EAT (and at certain proposals for reform) and then to consider the assault on legalism, suggesting that the problem is not quite as one-dimensional as some would suggest.

(i) Employment tribunals

Tribunals sit in most local centres of population, under the auspices in England and Wales of twenty-one local offices, all under the control of the Central Office of Employment Tribunals (COET) in London, and in Scotland three local offices

---

6   See p 528 below.
7   Employment Rights (Dispute Resolution) Act 1998, s 1. The Industrial Tribunals Act 1996 was renamed the Employment Tribunals Act 1996. All references to these bodies pre-1998 (in cases and legislation) will of course be to 'industrial tribunals'.
8   Royal Commission on Trade Unions and Employers Associations (Cmnd 3623, 1968).
9   See eg ACAS Annual Report 1983, paras 5.8–5.10 and Annual Report 1984, pp 63–66. The most obvious manifestation of legalism is the involvement of lawyers at tribunals (and indeed before, eg at conciliation), but the application of the phrase goes much deeper, calling into question the very role of the law, the appellate courts and any concept of precedent in the resolution of industrial law cases. For a refutation of the current anti-legalism arguments, see Leslie 'Legalism in industrial tribunals?' [1985] Employment Gazette 357, and in particular the strong defence of the tribunal system in MacMillan 'Employment tribunals: philosophies and practicalities' (1999) 28 ILJ 33.

under the control of the COET in Glasgow. Since 1997 the general administration of the whole system is undertaken by an executive agency, the Employment Tribunals Service. A tribunal consists of three people, a legally qualified chairman and two lay members, one from a panel kept by the Secretary of State representing employers' interests and one from a panel kept representing employees' interests. The theory is that, although expressly appointed from each side of industry, the lay members are to act as independent members of the bench, not in a partisan manner, and so they are full members of the tribunal which decides its cases if necessary by a majority (even in the unusual case of the chairman being in the minority). One of the principal functions of the side members is to use their industrial experience to help the tribunal to come to a sensible and practicable decision; however, this approach must not be taken too far, and the Court of Appeal has warned that knowledge of the industrial background and industrial common sense (though of great importance in many cases) may *not* be used to take a decision directly against the plain meaning of a statutory provision, even if the side members consider the end result of applying that plain meaning to be unfair or ridiculous[10].

The Trade Union Reform and Employment Rights Act 1993 amended these provisions as to the composition of a tribunal by establishing a class of case to be heard by a chairman alone; this was partly to deal with withdrawn or non-contested cases, but it also covered Wages Act cases, applications for interim relief and the common law proceedings that may now be heard by a tribunal, *unless* they raise matters of fact or law such that they should be heard by a full tribunal. This process was taken further by the Employment Rights (Dispute Resolution) Act 1998 which extended the categories of chairman-alone hearings (covering, for example, guarantee payments and redundancy payments and cases involving union subscriptions) against the background of a significant increase in tribunal applications[11]. This trend towards chairman-only hearings may be taken further under new tribunal Regulations to be made under the Employment Act 2002, awaited at the time of writing. The 1998 Act also provided for the appointment of 'legal officers' to assist the tribunal, in particular by dealing with certain preliminary or interlocutory matters.

The tribunal is administered by a clerk who is a full-time official. The applicant may conduct his case before the tribunal in person or be represented by any other person (sometimes a lawyer, sometimes a trade union official, and the respondent employer may often be represented by a member of the firm's personnel or legal staff[12]); there is no legal aid for representation, and little sign

---

10   *British Coal Corpn v Cheesbrough* [1988] ICR 769, [1988] IRLR 351, CA.
11   Applications rose sharply from 34,697 in 1990/91 to 71,821 in 1992/93; they peaked at 130,408 in 2000/01 and fell back only slightly to 112,227 in 2001/02..
12   Dickens et al *Dismissed: a Study of Unfair Dismissal and the Industrial Tribunal System* (1985) found that 23% of applicants had legal representation, 22% had trade union representation and 9% had some other form of representation; 41% of employers had legal representation, 52% had internal company representation and 5% were represented by an employers' association. The Genn Report (The Effectiveness of Representation at Tribunals; Report to the Lord Chancellor, 1989) found broadly the same, with 28% of applicants having legal representation, 16% trade union representation and 18% some other form of representation; 42% of employers had legal representation, 49% internal company representation and 8% employers' association representation. The report has a wealth of information on the effects of representation; see Mullen (1990) 53 MLR 230 and Genn 'Tribunals and Informal Justice' (1993) 56 MLR 393. See also Banerji, Smart and Stevens 'Unfair dismissal cases in 1985–6 – impact on parties' [1990] Employment Gazette 547; Tremlett and Banerji *1992 Survey of Industrial Tribunal Applications* (1994).

of it coming, though a dismissed employee may be eligible to obtain free preliminary advice from a solicitor, and may also be able to turn to his trade union or to the CAB.

Costs are not usually awarded; this has generally been thought to be a fundamental and desirable element of the tribunal system. However, there is always some pressure politically to curb what are seen as unworthy or time-wasting applications (at the very least adding a significant 'nuisance value' to applications, leading – so the argument goes – to too many undeserving cases being bought off by employers, regardless of their merits). In recent years, this has coincided with the desire of successive governments to curb the major increase in the number of tribunal applications. There has always been a residual power to award costs. Originally this only covered frivolous or vexatious conduct by a party; in 1980 this was widened to cover cases brought 'otherwise unreasonably' and in 2001 the current rule was introduced under which costs may be awarded where the party or their representative acted 'vexatiously, abusively, disruptively or otherwise unreasonably, or the bringing or conducting of the proceedings by a party has been misconceived'.[13] The significance of the 'misconceived' heading was that for the first time a costs application could be made based on the weak *merits* of the case, not just the way it was handled. Even this change was not thought enough by the present government when drafting the Employment Act 2002. At original Bill stage, this contained the remarkably radical proposal to introduce an ordinary costs rule (loser pays) into the tribunals, as a major assault on increasing applications. This, however, proved to be too controversial and was withdrawn (at least for the present). However, the Act does contain powers to make two other significant changes. The first is to allow an employer to claim costs based not just on its legal expenditure, but on its own in-house costs in dealing with the case. The second is to allow the making of what elsewhere are called wasted costs orders against paid representatives whose conduct has needlessly wasted tribunal time. Costs are thus a live issue, with new tribunal Regulations awaited at the time of writing. On the other hand, tribunal chairmen remain generally wary of introducing wider costs rules into their jurisdiction and, in spite of previous changes, actual orders for costs remain relatively rare.

Apart from specific rules, such as that on costs, the tribunals have wide powers to determine their own procedure by virtue of the Rules of Procedure laid down in regulations[14], which are considered below.

(ii) The Employment Appeal Tribunal

Appeal from a tribunal decision lies to the EAT, a body set up under the Employment Protection Act 1975[15] in much the same form as the National Industrial Relations Court which existed under the Industrial Relations Act

---

13 R 14. The power to strike out the entire claim under rule 15(2) was also extended to 'misconceived' applications. In 2001/02 there were 636 costs orders (169 to applicants, 467 to respondents); the average award was £983: ETS Annual Report 2001/02.

14 Employment Tribunals (Constitution and Rules of Procedure) Regulations 2001, SI 2001/ 1171, *Harvey* R[1317] (in Scotland SI 2001/1170). Rulle 11 in particular gives a wide discretion: *Dean v Islamic Foundation* [1983] ICR 36, [1982] IRLR 290, CA.

15 Now the Employment Tribunals Act 1996, Pt II.

1971. The EAT, a superior court of record, consists of a High Court judge and either two or, more unusually, four lay members, once again giving equal representation to both sides of industry, though once again the members should not act in a partisan manner and the decision of the EAT is by simple majority, if necessary[16]. Where a tribunal has consisted of a chairman sitting alone (as now permitted since the Trade Union Reform and Employment Rights Act 1993), an appeal may be heard by the judge alone. The constitution of the EAT is laid down in the Employment Tribunals Act 1996, which expressly gives it the powers of the High Court *and* those of the employment tribunals[17]. Its procedure is contained in the EAT Rules laid down in Regulations[18]. As in the case of tribunal proceedings, the parties may be represented by anyone and costs are not normally awarded, unless the EAT considers that the appeal was 'unnecessary, improper or vexatious' or there was 'unreasonable delay or other unreasonable conduct in bringing or conducting the proceedings'[19].

The most important point about the appeal to the EAT is that it is an appeal on a point of law *only* (except on an appeal from a decision of the Certification Officer on the registration or certification as independent of a union, where appeal may be on law or fact)[20]; this is a deliberate policy to minimise appeals. The practical significance of this is that the parties must ensure that they argue the facts properly and fully before the tribunal, for if they do not and they lose on the facts (for example, by not calling all the relevant evidence or by not presenting it sufficiently persuasively) they may not take the matter to the EAT for a second chance. To appeal to the EAT, the party must be able to show that the tribunal were wrong in law. It has been authoritatively stated in *British Telecommunications plc v Sheridan*[21] by the Court of Appeal that this means one of two things – either (a) an ex facie error of law or (b) that the tribunal's decision was perverse. There had been said to be a third category, ie where the tribunal misunderstood or misapplied the facts[22], but that was specifically disapproved in *Sheridan*, since it would have permitted the EAT to allow an appeal simply by taking a different view of the facts[23]. The judicial approach to perversity has undergone considerable changes in the last ten years and these are considered below, for it is suggested that the present restricted approach is an integral part of the attack on legalism. In addition to such policy considerations, perversity appeals also face another problem; it is now well established that a tribunal must not simply substitute its

---

16   This has caused some debate, particularly after the case of *Nethermere (St Neots) Ltd v Gardiner* [1983] ICR 319, [1983] IRLR 103 (extending rights to homeworkers), the argument being that if appeal to the EAT is so stringently confined to a point of law, then should there be two non-lawyers with the power to outvote a High Court judge? The point made about side members in employment tribunals above (p 496 above) also applies to side members in the EAT.

17   Ss 28, 33.

18   SI 1993/2854, *Harvey* R[714]. These rules are supplemented by the EAT *Practice Direction* reissued in December 2002 and set out at [2003] IRLR 65.

19   Rule 34. *Ravelin v Bournemouth Borough Council* (1986) Times, 19 July, CA.

20   TULR(C)A 1992, s 9. The EAT will not hear appeals where the dispute has in fact been resolved, even if one or both of the parties wish to have a particular point resolved as a matter of principle: *IMI Yorkshire Imperial Ltd v Olender* [1982] ICR 69. Likewise, if there is no real dispute between the parties, who want a ruling for some extraneous purpose: *Baker v Superite Tools Ltd* [1986] ICR 189.

21   [1990] IRLR 27, CA.

22   *Watling v William Bird & Son Contractors Ltd* (1976) 11 ITR 70, per Philips J.

23   Note, however, that if there can be said to be *no* evidence to support a particular finding of fact, that is an error of law under head (a).

own view of what would have been reasonable in the circumstances for that of the employer, but must consider (in an unfair dismissal case) whether dismissal was an option which *a* reasonable employer might have chosen, even if others might not (the 'range of reasonable responses' test, see p 568 below). Thus, if a tribunal's decision on reasonableness is to be challenged as perverse the appellant has, in effect, a double hurdle – he must show that *no* reasonable tribunal could possibly have come to the conclusion that *a* reasonable employer could have decided to dismiss (where the appellant is the employee) or that *no* reasonable employer could have decided to dismiss (where the appellant is the employer).

Appeal on a point of law is thus tightly circumscribed and the point has been made repeatedly that the EAT must exercise considerable self-restraint in cases where it disagrees profoundly with the decision of the tribunal on the facts but where there is no definable error of law; in such a case it must not interfere[24]. Likewise, there have been repeated warnings by the Court of Appeal to appellants and, more particularly, their legal advisers, that points of fact are not to be dressed up in the garb of points of law in order to bring an appeal[25].

Three further points about the EAT are worth noting. The first is that it will be most reluctant to admit fresh evidence unless, exceptionally, the existence of the fresh evidence could not have been reasonably known of or foreseen (akin to the 'reasonable diligence' test applied generally by the Court of Appeal)[26]; this rule is not to be circumvented by remitting the case to the tribunal for a re-hearing including the otherwise inadmissible evidence[27]. This reinforces the point made above that it is essential that all relevant evidence is placed before the tribunal at the hearing. The second point is that, although the EAT is empowered on appeal to substitute its own decision for that of the tribunal if it allows the appeal[28], if the decision on appeal entails the finding of further facts or the reconsideration of certain existing facts the proper course will normally be to remit the case to the tribunal for further consideration in the light of the EAT's decision[29]. The third point is that as a matter of precedent the EAT is not bound by a previous decision of its own[30]. Thus, there have been many instances, in cases raising bona fide matters of law, of a later EAT decision altering the direction of an area of law away from previous authorities. However, there have

---

24 *Retarded Children's Aid Society Ltd v Day* [1978] ICR 437, [1978] IRLR 128, CA; *Martin v Glynwed Distribution Ltd* [1983] ICR 511, [1983] IRLR 198, CA; *O'Kelly v Trusthouse Forte plc* [1983] ICR 728, [1983] IRLR 369, CA; *Spook Erection v Thackray* [1984] IRLR 116, Ct of Sess. The decision of the EAT in *Woods v WM Car Services (Peterborough) Ltd* [1981] ICR 666, [1981] IRLR 347 (upheld on appeal: [1982] ICR 693, [1982] IRLR 413, CA) is a good example of the necessary self denial; see also the judgment of Mummery P in *Stewart v Cleveland Guest (Engineering) Ltd* [1996] ICR 535, [1994] IRLR 440. This will be particularly so in matters of procedure which fall primarily within the discretion of the tribunal chairman: *Dietmann v London Borough of Brent* [1987] IRLR 146, CA.

25 See eg *Hollister v NFU* [1979] ICR 542, [1979] IRLR 238, CA; *Thomas and Betts Manufacturing Ltd v Harding* [1980] IRLR 255, CA.

26 *Borden (UK) Ltd v Potter* [1986] ICR 647 (overruling the previous 'reasonable explanation' test in *Bagga v Heavy Electricals (India) Ltd* [1972] ICR 118); for an example of the application of this test (and the further requirement that the new evidence would have an important influence on the outcome of the case) see *Wileman v Minilec Engineering Ltd* [1988] ICR 318, [1988] IRLR 144. Similarly, the EAT will not normally allow a party to argue a point of law not taken at the tribunal, unless it is a point that the tribunal should have considered on its own motion: *Langston v Cranfield University* [1998] IRLR 172.

27 *Kingston v British Railways Board* [1984] ICR 781, [1984] IRLR 146, CA.

28 Employment Tribunals Act 1996, s 33.

29 *O'Kelly v Trusthouse Forte plc* [1983] ICR 728, [1983] IRLR 369, CA.

30 *Secretary of State for Trade and Industry v Cook* [1997] ICR 288, [1997] IRLR 150.

also been in the past instances of a division of the EAT simply producing a decision inconsistent with previous authority. In a court as busy as the EAT this has sometimes merely been a case of the left hand not knowing what the right is doing, but equally there have been cases where previous authority has been suddenly departed from simply because that particular division of the EAT disagreed with the previous case law[31]. This has caused problems of uncertainty in the past (a point commented on particularly in previous editions of this book), for while flexibility on points of fact may be desirable, it must not be forgotten that employment law has to be applied initially by industrial relations practitioners (in unions and in management) who do look for certainty, at least on points of law that concern them. It is suggested therefore that, in this area, ready departure from established case law may be a luxury that should not be afforded. Fortunately, however, most of the outstanding examples of blatant differences of opinion on major points of law have been resolved over the past few years and the problem now seems to be much less.

(iii) The attack on legalism

As stated above, the attack on the perceived problem of over-legalism in the employment tribunals has been a major feature of modern employment law. It explains certain procedural changes, for example the consistent statements from the Court of Appeal that tribunals do *not* now have to give their reasons as exhaustively (as to fact and law) as a normal court would; presumably the policy behind this is to discourage the losing side's lawyers from poring over the written reasons looking for any technical slip or omission in order to mount an appeal[32]. Further, the Rules of Procedure were altered in 1985 to allow a tribunal to give its reasons in summary form only, in the first instance[33]; where this is done, either party may still require full reasons for the purpose of mounting an appeal, but the onus is upon them to do so. Another procedural example was the institution in 1985 of a special procedure in cases involving appeals on the grounds of perversity (the most suspect ground from the modern point of view, since it can come closest to trying to get the EAT simply to *review* the tribunal's decision on

---

31   A prime example was the decision of Kilner Brown J in *Norris v Southampton City Council* [1982] ICR 177, [1982] IRLR 141 that, contrary to previous authority, a contract of employment *cannot* be rendered void for frustration if the employee is imprisoned. The judgment contains this passage: 'None of this makes the task of Chairmen of Industrial Tribunals any easier. All that we can say by way of comfort is that where there are conflicting decisions of the EAT an Industrial Tribunal may prefer the two decisions previously promulgated and no one would criticise them if they did.' Fortunately, the position has now been set straight, and orthodoxy re-established by the Court of Appeal in *F C Shepherd & Co Ltd v Jerrom* [1986] ICR 802, [1986] IRLR 358, CA: see p 453 above. For a further example, see *Barking and Dagenham London Borough v Camara* [1988] ICR 865, [1988] IRLR 373, where the EAT under Wood P disapproved and declined to apply the approach to the burden of proof in discrimination cases established by previous EATs in two cases in 1981.

32   See p 524 below. Not only does this mean that tribunal decisions are not to be upset on narrow grounds, but also there is the potentially even more significant point that, given that the reasons do not have to be exhaustive, the EAT and Court of Appeal will *not* draw the inference that because the tribunal omitted to mention a particular fact or argument, therefore they must have overlooked it; this could make an appeal on perversity difficult to maintain.

33   Employment Tribunals (Constitution and Rules of Procedure) Regulations 2001, SI 2001/1171, reg 12, *Harvey* R [1343].

the facts); this was extended in 1997 and 2002, so that now all cases are subject to active case management, which will often involve a short preliminary hearing in order to weed out cases which do not appear to the EAT to raise any genuine point of law[34].

These procedural changes are important in themselves but the principal attacks have come on three substantive fronts – the classification of as many issues as possible as 'ultimately questions of fact for the [employment] tribunal to decide'[35], the disapproval of the previous practice of appellate courts laying down guidelines for tribunals to follow in frequently recurring instances, and finally (as, arguably, an integral part of the first two) a consistently narrow approach to what can constitute a 'perverse' decision on the facts by a tribunal. The first two of these will now be considered separately (though of course they do tend to run into one another). Looking first at the classification as fact aspect, examples of this abound and will be found throughout this chapter. The following examples of matters classified as pure questions of fact will suffice for present purposes (and illustrate the breadth of the modern approach which is not confined to major areas of unfair dismissal law): whether a contract is a contract of employment or a contract for services[36]; whether an employer's conduct is bad enough to constitute a constructive dismissal[37]; whether an employee resigned or was forced to do so[38]; contributory fault[39]; whether it was reasonably practicable to present an unfair dismissal claim in time[40]; when discovery is to be ordered[41]; what is 'reasonable' time off work[42]; whether a requirement that indirectly discriminates against women is justifiable[43]. A stir was caused here by the decision of the House of Lords in *Davies v Presbyterian Church of Wales*[44] where Lord Templeman stated that the matter before the court (whether a Methodist minister was an employee) was a question of law, so that the tribunal's decision was reviewable on appeal. However, this dictum in the event has not led to any major change of direction, and was restrictively construed by Slade LJ in *Hellyer Bros Ltd v McLeod*[45], as being confined to cases where the decision on employment status depends wholly on the interpretation of documents. It would therefore take a considerably more unambiguous decision of the House of Lords than *Davies* to reverse the current trend.

---

34 EAT Practice Direction (December 2002) para 9.
35 If it moves classify it.
36 *O'Kelly v Trusthouse Forte plc* [1983] ICR 728, [1983] IRLR 369, CA; *Nethermere (St Neots) Ltd v Gardiner* [1984] ICR 612, [1984] IRLR 240, CA. Presumably the *tests* to be applied remain a question of law, but that may mean little here since arguably there are *no* clear tests as to the existence of a contract of employment, see p 10 above.
37 *Pedersen v Camden London Borough Council* [1981] ICR 674n, [1981] IRLR 173, CA; *Woods v WM Car Services (Peterborough) Ltd* [1982] ICR 693, [1982] IRLR 413, CA; see p 646 below.
38 *Martin v Glynwed Distribution Ltd* [1983] ICR 511, [1983] IRLR 198, CA.
39 *Hollier v Plysu Ltd* [1983] IRLR 260, CA; see p 618 below.
40 *Palmer v Southend-on-Sea Borough Council* [1984] ICR 372, [1984] IRLR 119, CA; see p 512 below.
41 *Medallion Holidays Ltd v Birch* [1985] ICR 578 [1985] IRLR 406, disapproving *British Library v Palyza* [1984] ICR 504, [1984] IRLR 306, which had held that a tribunal's decision on procedure was fully reviewable on appeal. See also *Dietmann v London Borough of Brent* [1987] IRLR 146, CA on appeals on procedural matters generally.
42 *Thomas Scott & Sons (Bakers) Ltd v Allen* [1983] IRLR 329, CA.
43 *Home Office v Holmes* [1984] ICR 678, [1984] IRLR 299; *Greater Glasgow Health Board v Carey* [1987] IRLR 484, EAT.
44 [1986] ICR 280, [1986] IRLR 194, HL.
45 [1987] ICR 526, [1987] IRLR 232, CA. This explanation was later approved in *Lee Ting Sang v Chung Chi-Keung* [1990] ICR 409, [1990] IRLR 236, PC and *Clifford v Union of Democratic Mineworkers* [1991] IRLR 518, CA.

Where a matter is clearly classified as one of fact, the losing party cannot appeal on the ground that the tribunal misdirected itself in law, and so will probably be thrown back on the ground that the tribunal's decision was perverse. It is here that the narrow approach to perversity comes in (with the corresponding warnings to the EAT not to reverse a tribunal decision merely because they think it wrong on the facts). In *RSPB v Croucher*[46] Waite P went as far as to call cases of perversity 'exceptional' and said:

> 'We have to remind ourselves of our duty and our functions as an appellate tribunal. We have to remember that it is our duty loyally to follow findings of fact by an industrial tribunal which has enjoyed the advantages, which can never be ours, of having seen witnesses, sensed the atmosphere prevailing in a particular work-place, gauged the qualities of the different personalities, weighed the impact of their effect each upon the other; and that cases must be very rare indeed where we take upon ourselves to reach the conclusion that a tribunal has arrived at a result not tenable by any reasonable tribunal properly directed in law.'

This narrow approach to perversity was approved by the Court of Appeal in *Neale v Hereford and Worcester County Council*[47] where May LJ said that an appellate court should only reverse a tribunal's decision if it could be said 'My goodness, that must be wrong'[48]. Indeed, even this well-known explanation was thought possibly too liberal in *Piggott Bros & Co Ltd v Jackson*[49] by Lord Donaldson MR who thought that it might tempt an interventionist EAT into the forbidden land of fact. However, his preferred solution (that perversity could normally only be shown by an error of law or a total lack of evidence) was arguably capable of removing perversity as a separate heading. Subsequently, Wood P in the EAT in *East Berkshire Health Authority v Matadeen*[50] complained that *Piggott* was causing difficulties in appeals, and sought to lean back towards the *Neale* approach, stating that the EAT could interfere if the members[51] were satisfied that the tribunal decision was not a permissible option, or was one which offended reason, or was one which no reasonable tribunal could have reached, or was so clearly wrong that it could not stand. This formulation would leave perversity as a freestanding ground, which seems now to have been accepted at Court of Appeal level, though with the clear warnings that any perversity challenge must be fully particularised, and should only be upheld by the appellate body if an 'overwhelming case' has been made out[52].

46 [1984] ICR 604, [1984] IRLR 425; the passage cited is at 609 and 428, respectively. Note, however, that on its facts this case was later restrictively construed in *John Lewis plc v Coyne* [2001] IRLR 139.

47 [1986] ICR 471, [1986] IRLR 168, CA; moreover it was held in *Campion v Hamworthy Engineering Ltd* [1987] ICR 966, CA that if a case goes to the Court of Appeal on perversity, that court's function is to apply the *Neale* test to the tribunal's decision, *not* to consider whether the EAT's decision on the point was correct.

48 This is known in some quarters as the 'Biggles test' (see (1987) 16 ILJ 213) due to a flippant remark in the *Harvey* bulletin that although this statement is entirely consistent with the modern approach, its phraseology may appear over-reliant on the writings of Captain W E Johns ('Gosh' said Biggles as a shell ripped off his right leg).

49 [1992] ICR 85, [1991] IRLR 309, CA.

50 [1992] ICR 723, [1992] IRLR 336.

51 One strong argument by Wood P is that the lay members are there to contribute their industrial expertise, and are capable of applying such tests of perversity 'when viewed against appropriate industrial experience and practice'.

It is not being argued here that the whole movement towards classification as fact is ill-founded, and the policy reasons behind the desire to 'return decision making to the tribunals' can easily be appreciated. What is suggested, however, is that this process has in the past been taken too far and has in certain cases been extended into areas more properly categorisable as matters of law, particularly areas of statutory interpretation, which could lead to major uncertainties as to the ground rules that are to be applied by the tribunals. The clearest example of this occured under the Trade Union and Labour Relations (Consolidation) Act 1992, section 238 which (after an initial eight-week period) removes the jurisdiction of a tribunal where an employee is dismissed for taking part in 'a strike or other industrial action' unless, inter alia, others taking part were not dismissed (ie there has been victimisation). The phrase 'other industrial action' is not defined in the Act and one might have expected it to be a matter of statutory interpretation as to how the phrase is to be applied to the various forms that industrial action can take, ie a question of law on which the EAT should pronounce. However, the Court of Appeal held that what constitutes 'other industrial action' is a question of *fact* for the tribunal[53]. Thus, a tribunal in Manchester might decide one day that, in a strike-dismissal case, taking part in a ban on voluntary overtime *was* industrial action, while the next day a tribunal in Leeds in a similar case might decide that such a ban was *not* industrial action, with the result that the bar on jurisdiction in section 238 would apply in one case but not in the other; however, the point would then be that, as it is a question of fact, *both* tribunals would be right and (except in the 'exceptional' case of a finding of perversity on appeal) both decisions would be upheld[54]. What is the lawyer to say if asked, for example, by an employee client whether he will be able to claim unfair dismissal if he takes part in a voluntary overtime ban and is dismissed (naively expecting there to be an answer to his question)? This particular problem under section 238 occurred in *Naylor v Orton and Smith Ltd*[55] and was subject to strong criticism by Browne-Wilkinson P:

'... [A] decision to impose an immediate overtime ban could reasonably be considered as not constituting taking industrial action, as the Industrial Tribunal held: it could also reasonably be considered to constitute industrial action. Since both views are reasonable, we cannot interfere with the Industrial Tribunal decision. ... Whether such employees have a claim for unfair dismissal will depend on whether or not the Industrial Tribunal they chance to come before takes the view that they were taking part in industrial action. ... In our view it is not in the best interests of orderly industrial relations that such severe consequences to both employers and employees should depend on which of two, equally correct but diametrically opposite, views is subsequently adopted by the Industrial Tribunal before which the case may come.'

---

52   *Yeboah v Crofton* [2002] IRLR 634, [2002] EWCA Civ 794.

53   *Coates v Modern Methods and Materials Ltd* [1982] ICR 763, [1982] IRLR 318, CA; see p 757 below.

54   To paraphrase a character from NF Simpson's play *A Resounding Tinkle* – isn't the world wonderful, and if it had all been totally different, that would have been pretty wonderful too.

55   [1983] IRLR 233; the passage cited is at 237. Remarks about the length of tribunal members' feet might also have been appropriate.

However, in the light of the later case law, the voice of this particularly learned President of the EAT has been as one crying in the wilderness, for subsequently the possibility of this sort of major inconsistency has been said to be an inherent, if unfortunate, aspect of the flexibility of the tribunal system[56], a price which has to be paid. Part of that price is that it might be difficult, if not impossible, to bring a case before a tribunal or, indeed, an appeal to the EAT in order to set a clear precedent, in the nature of a 'test case' (for example, where there are likely to be several or indeed many other employees in a similar position); likewise, cases which are reported and seem to mark a significant development in the law should be treated with caution for the same reason – to take one example, the case of *Home Office v Holmes*[57] which was widely reported in the press (and greeted enthusiastically by the EOC) as a major breakthrough allowing women to claim (well in advance of the new Regulations on part-time working) to work part-time through the use of the concept of indirect sex discrimination is, when looked at in the light of this modern approach, nothing of the sort, as in fact Waite P was at pains to point out at the end of his judgment, and indeed subsequently in *Greater Glasgow Health Board v Carey*[58] the EAT held in a similar case that although there might be indirect discrimination, it was justified on the facts and so the claim failed; a sobering example is set by another 'breakthrough', that in *Clarke v Eley (IMI) Kynoch Ltd*[59] that operating a 'part-timers first' rule on redundancy may constitute indirect sex discrimination, for in the subsequent case of *Kidd v DRG (UK) Ltd*[60] the EAT upheld a tribunal decision entirely to the contrary.

Turning now to the other major limb of the attack on legalism, the discouragement of judicial guidelines, a similar picture emerges but here, if anything, the law has seen more definable swings. During the 1970s, under the NIRC and in the early days of the EAT (especially under the presidency of Phillips J), a need was perceived to put some flesh on to the bare bones of the new statutory provisions on unfair dismissal – after all, a statute that simply says that a tribunal is to look at how reasonably an employer behaved in the light of equity and the substantial merits of the case, or that an employee who is a union officer has a right to reasonable time off, is not immediately self-explanatory. Moreover, in the law on unfair dismissal, it soon became obvious that the overall test of fairness was having to be applied by tribunals in many cases to frequently recurring fact situations (for example, suspected theft, long-term illness, business reorganisation), so that some consistency of approach was needed in order to avoid a completely 'palm tree justice' approach. The answer was for the appellate court to lay down

---

56 See eg *Kidd v DRG (UK) Ltd* [1985] ICR 405 at 417, [1985] IRLR 190 at 196, per Waite P, and *Gilham v Kent County Council (No 2)* [1985] ICR 233 at 240, [1985] IRLR 8 at 22, CA, per Griffiths LJ ('endemic in a system where there is no appeal on fact') and at 244 and 23, per Dillon LJ ('inherent in the system which Parliament has set up'). In the latter case it was clearly held that the fact (put forward by the appellant) that two other tribunals had previously reached the opposite conclusion in very similar cases (concerning councils effecting cuts by altering dinner ladies' contracts) was *no* basis for an argument that the tribunal's decision was perverse. For a further example, contrast the end results of two cases of dismissals arising during the miners' strike – *McLaren v National Coal Board* [1988] ICR 370, [1988] IRLR 215, CA and *Dillett v National Coal Board* [1988] ICR 218, CA.

57 [1984] ICR 678, [1984] IRLR 299; see p 295 above.

58 [1987] IRLR 484.

59 [1983] ICR 165, [1982] IRLR 482; such a rule would now be specifically illegal under the Part-time Worker Regulations 2000, unless objectively justified.

60 [1985] ICR 405, [1985] IRLR 190. Once again, what is the lawyer to say if an employer seeks his advice, asking 'Is it lawful to make redundancies on a part-timers-first basis?'

judicial guidelines for the tribunals on major aspects of unfair dismissal law. These were not rules of law, so that it was never the case that failure to apply a relevant guideline was automatically an appealable error of law[61]. However, if a tribunal did apply such a guideline its decision would probably not be upset on appeal. Moreover, this approach fitted in well with the then prevailing views on when a tribunal decision should be held to be perverse. A much wider approach was taken in this time of judicial activism, and in particular a decision that was thought to be 'contrary to good industrial practice' by all three members of the EAT (the two wingmen taking that decision in the light of their industrial experience) was likely to be held to be perverse[62]; 'good industrial practice' in many instances was to be found in the existing and often-applied guidelines. This gave the appellate court a considerable supervisory jurisdiction and had the merit of a desirable amount of certainty; however the other, less desirable effect was the growth of a formidable body of precedent on unfair dismissal law, a proliferation of appeals, what was seen to be an unnecessarily high level of legalism, and the danger of turning employment law into a heavy case-law subject (especially with the large scale reporting of the cases in the specialist law reports). These negative factors, along with the general feeling that the tribunals' discretion was being unduly restricted and real decision-making being taken away from them contrary to Parliament's intention, led to a major attack on judicial guidelines by the Court of Appeal, principally in *Bailey v BP Oil (Kent Refinery) Ltd*[63] in which Lawton LJ said:

> 'Each case must depend on its own facts. In our judgment it is unwise for this Court or the Employment Appeal Tribunal to set out guidelines, and wrong to make rules and establish presumptions for Industrial Tribunals to follow or to take into account when applying [the statutory test of fairness].'

The implication of this (ie that there is *no* value in guidelines) was contested by the EAT under the presidency of Browne-Wilkinson J who, while accepting the argument that judicial intervention had gone too far[64], considered the position taken by the Court of Appeal to be an over-reaction and tried to take a middle course. This consisted of continuing to develop guidelines but with more circumspection and with more stress on their evidential value only; *Williams v Compair Maxam Ltd*[65] is the best example of this, with its comprehensive re-examination of the circumstances in which a redundancy dismissal (normally

---

61   See *Jowett v Earl of Bradford (No 2)* [1978] ICR 431 at 436, per Bristow J.
62   This approach was summarised by Phillips P writing extra-judicially in 'Some notes on the Employment Appeal Tribunal' (1978) 7 ILJ 137, 140. For a rare subsequent application of this approach, see the judgment of Nolan J in *Payne v Spook Erection Ltd* [1984] IRLR 219.
63   [1980] ICR 642, [1980] IRLR 287, CA; the passage cited is at 648 and 289 respectively. See also *Thomas and Betts Manufacturing Ltd v Harding* [1980] IRLR 255, CA and *UCATT v Brain* [1981] ICR 542, [1981] IRLR 224, CA. One problem is that, as Browne-Wilkinson P pointed out in *Grundy (Teddington) Ltd v Plummer* [1983] ICR 367, [1983] IRLR 98, the Court of Appeal at the time on at least two occasions specifically approved existing guidelines laid down by the EAT: *W Weddel & Co Ltd v Tepper* [1980] ICR 286, [1980] IRLR 96, CA and *W & J Wass Ltd v Binns* [1982] ICR 486, [1982] IRLR 283, CA (though the latter case was later overruled by the House of Lords, see p 569 below).
64   See the Hon Mr Justice Browne-Wilkinson 'The role of the EAT in the 1980s' (1982) 11 ILJ 69.
65   [1982] ICR 156, [1982] IRLR 83. See also *Grundy (Teddington) Ltd v Plummer*, in n 63 above.

fair) can become unfair on general principles. However, the approach of the Court of Appeal continued unaltered[66] and with the change of presidency in 1983 it soon became clear that under Waite P the EAT itself would apply the law as laid down by the Court of Appeal, and enthusiastically rather than reluctantly[67], an approach also adopted by his successor, Popplewell P[68]. Indeed, whereas it was possible to argue that what the Court of Appeal was saying initially on the question of guidelines was 'so far and no further', the approach particularly of Waite P was to call into question even well-established guidelines and cases which for years have been considered central to the developing law on unfair dismissal[69].

As in the case of classification as fact, the narrow approach to what can constitute perversity aided this approach materially, for under this approach not only would it not be a ground for perversity that the tribunal failed to apply an established guideline, but ironically the only certain ground for perversity would be that a tribunal felt itself *bound* to follow a guideline rather than applying a more general test based upon the wider wording of the statute[70]. It is of course true that a tribunal might choose to apply existing and well-applied guideline authority, and hopefully in many instances would continue to do so. The uncertainty inherent in this modern approach arose from the fact that a *failure* to follow the commonly accepted pattern in frequently recurring cases would *not* be an appealable error of law. Perhaps fortunately, the pendulum received a healthy pull back towards the centre under the presidency of Wood P who, from the beginning of his term, showed himself more sympathetic to the constructive use of guideline authority[71], and (as will be seen throughout the parts of this book dealing with individual employment law) handed down a series of lucid and highly useful judgments on approaches or procedures to be adopted when dealing with frequently occurring employment problems, in what may be considered a particularly fruitful period in the EAT's short history. His successors, Mummery P, Morison P and Lindsay P, have continued this more active approach, which has been emphasised by the sudden increase during this time of cases in which the EAT has had to consider complex questions of EC law and its effect on domestic employment legislation (which certainly cannot be shunted off into limbo by being called a matter of fact, and on which detailed guidance to tribunals has been essential). Moreover, the novel approach of appointing a specialist employment lawyer fully to the EAT (first in the person of Judge Clark and most recently with the appointment as President of Burton J, in his time a leading employment law silk) has had an effect in producing judgments reassessing and re-evaluating certain longstanding rules or guidelines in the light of modern employment conditions. However, it remains the case that in general the use of

---

66   *Varndell v Kearney & Trecker Marwin Ltd* [1983] ICR 683, [1983] IRLR 335, CA; see the dictum cited at the beginning of this chapter on the primacy of the wording of the statute.

67   Sir John Waite 'Lawyers and laymen as judges in industry' (1986) 15 ILJ 32.

68   Sir Oliver Popplewell 'Random thoughts from the President's chair' (1987) 16 ILJ 209; at 213 he states, 'So far as the present EAT is concerned, we have striven continuously to discourage the constant or indeed any citing of authorities wherever that is possible'.

69   See particularly *Anandarajah v Lord Chancellor's Department* [1984] IRLR 131, EAT.

70   *Rolls-Royce Motors Ltd v Dewhurst* [1985] ICR 869, [1985] IRLR 184, EAT.

71   Sir John Wood 'The EAT as it enters the 1990s' (1990) 19 ILJ 133; note particularly his approving references to (now) Lord Browne-Wilkinson's presidency and his remarks on perversity and the role of the EAT's industrial members.

guidelines today has to be not only constructive, but also circumspect, and we have not necessarily heard the last word[72].

To reiterate the point made above about the first line of attack on legalism, the argument here is *not* that a drive to decrease legalism and formalism in employment tribunals is misconceived, especially given the widespread criticism of over-legalism from *both* sides of industry. The point that is being made is that it is possible to take the attack too far and produce a situation of equal but opposite imbalance, in which the disadvantages of rampant uncertainty and difficulty (if not impossibility) of advising in advance of problems outweigh the advantages of what is perceived to be desirable non-legalism[73]. The clarion call to return decision making to the tribunals and keep the lawyers out[74] may be superficially of great attraction to practitioners of industrial relations, but one may wonder whether the attraction would be as great if the corresponding disadvantages were properly explained, particularly the disadvantage of not being able to get a relatively simple answer to a simple question from a lawyer consulted on the legality or otherwise of a projected course of action; if taken to its logical conclusion, the only answer to most questions, given an extreme anti-legalism approach, would be that it would depend on the reaction of the particular tribunal on the day in question. A danger of this would be that if employers were convinced that tribunals operated in an unpredictable, or even random, manner[75], unfair dismissal law could lose much of its normative value as an instrument for the promotion of fair employment practices, in that employers might take the view that there was little point in trying to act in a way that could predictably be judged as good industrial relations practice, and that they might as well simply proceed in any way that seemed most expedient in the circumstances and hope, if challenged, to strike lucky with a sympathetic tribunal.

Given that there is a serious problem over the balance to be struck between flexibility and informality on the one hand and certainty and normative effect on the other, one possible way out of the log-jam was perceived at one stage to be the updating and, more importantly, the expansion of the original ACAS Code of Practice No 1 on disciplinary practice and procedures[76]. The idea was that such a Code would be a more far-reaching document giving guidance on the handling, not just of dismissals generally, but of dismissals and disciplinary proceedings

---

72 A very different Court of Appeal approach can be seen in *Foley v Post Office* [2000] ICR 1283, [2000] IRLR 827, CA, where the court not only resolved a major problem in unfair dismissal law as to the correctness of the range of reasonable responses test (see p 574 below), but did so without any qualms as to instructing the tribunals on the right approach, and even expedited the hearing of the appeal in order to lay down this 'guidance'.

73 One argument might be that if non-legalism is the dominant aim, the best way to achieve it would be to do away with the whole tribunal system and replace it with a system of compulsory arbitration in dismissal cases: see heading (iv) below. For a strong refutation of this view, see MacMillan 'Employment tribunals: philosophies and practicalities' (1999) 28 ILJ 33, and see to the contrary Clark 'Adversarial and investigative approaches to the arbitral resolution of dismissal disputes' (1999) 28 ILJ 319.

74 'The first thing we do, let's kill all the lawyers' (*Henry VI, Part 2*, IV ii) is merely an exaggerated form of such a sentiment.

75 In such matters, objective fact may be less important than received opinion; an example of this is the resilience of the myth that employers are guilty until proved innocent in tribunal proceedings, in which they stand little chance of success, whereas in practice for years the employee applicant has had a less than evens chance of success before a tribunal.

76 See p 530 below. See, eg, the support given to this idea by Sir John Waite, above, n 67.

concerning some of the more common problems encountered in practice. After much work, ACAS produced a draft Code which, while giving guidance largely gleaned from the decided cases, could have been relied on as a *distillation* of that case law, without reference to a battery of law reports (and, arguably, without the need for it to be supplemented by further case law). The middle ground could have been reoccupied without falling into the trap of over-legalism. However, when the draft Code was submitted to the then Secretary of State for Employment, Lord Young, he refused to approve it[77]. The basis for this deeply regrettable decision was largely that the Code was thought to be too long and detailed ('aimed primarily at lawyers and personnel managers in larger firms') and would be difficult for a small firm to apply[78]; the irony here is that it is precisely these small firms, without professional personnel staff, who could be said to be most in need of straightforward guidelines (indeed, check-lists) on the various problems likely to be encountered in practice which could lead to a dismissal, and although the draft Code as a whole was quite long, the individual chapters were not and any complications were largely the result of the legal complications inevitably arising in such a diverse area. The Secretary of State invited ACAS to redraft the Code and resubmit it. Instead of doing so, they used much of the material to produce an advisory handbook 'Discipline at Work' which covers rules and procedures, counselling, disciplinary interviews, disciplinary action and appeals; in addition, it gives guidance on the substantive areas of criminal charges, absence, substandard work, ill health and failure to return from leave, and contains check-lists, precedents and the text of the Code of Practice[79]. As this is not formally a Code of Practice, it does not have to be considered by a tribunal, but on the other hand there is no reason why it could not be put to a tribunal by either party as evidence of good practice or otherwise. It should certainly be read and borne in mind by students and practitioners of this subject, particularly as it gives a good flavour and overview of many of the detailed legal rules that follow in this chapter.

(iv) Suggested reforms

Partly due to concerns about over-legalism, real or perceived, suggestions for reform of the employment tribunal system have been put forward with some frequency. Three in particular are worth mentioning here for their historical context, before considering the current position. The first is that there has been a longstanding argument that unfair dismissal cases should be dealt with by arbitration rather than through tribunals. As the legislation is drafted, it seems to be assumed that arbitration should be at least a viable alternative, since by virtue of section 110 of the Employment Rights Act 1996 the parties to a dismissal

---

77 See p 64 above. The text of the Secretary of State's letter to the Chairman of ACAS setting out his reasons is in [1987] Employment Gazette 150.

78 Other reasons related to the danger of the Code itself giving rise to case law on its interpretation (leading to frequent need for revision) and the criticism that the Code mixed up substantive law with general advice so that it was difficult to tell what was actually obligatory. It is interesting to note that the latter criticism was made of the Codes of Practice on the closed shop and on picketing, which were produced by the previous government.

79 The Code itself was reissued in 2000 in slightly expanded form (in particular covering grievance procedures). Some of the provisions on dispute resolution in the Employment Act 2002 (laying down the mandatory basic disciplinary and grievance procedures) can also be seen as trying to minimise litigation by setting out statutory 'guidelines'.

procedure agreement (for example, as part of a collective agreement) may apply to the Secretary of State to 'contract out' of unfair dismissal law (ie that any dismissals will be dealt with *solely* under the procedure, with no right to apply to a tribunal). In the event, however, only the electrical contracting industry ever took advantage of this procedure, which has fallen into disuse[80]. It has always been arguable that more use could be made of contracting out, particularly in large industries with sophisticated disciplinary procedures, often culminating in ACAS-organised arbitration[81], and the case has been made for a large-scale transfer of functions[82].

The second significant set of suggestions were contained in the Justice Report 'Industrial Tribunals' (1987) which is highly recommended reading on this subject. The committee which produced the report saw considerable scope for reforms to the present tribunal system; these included the following: (1) wider selection of side members to be more representative; (2) increased training for both chairmen and side members; (3) specialised training for those who are to sit on sex discrimination and race relations cases[83]; (4) the appointment of 'tribunal officers' whose task it would be to investigate cases at a preliminary stage and isolate the issues to be tried if and when a case came before the tribunal itself[84]; (5) the transfer of most common law claims on the contract of employment from the ordinary courts to the tribunals[85]; (6) the transfer of the tribunals' current jurisdiction over cases between a member and his trade union to the ordinary courts or the Certification Officer; (7) the encouragement of collective contracting out (above); (8) the laying down of guidelines by ACAS in regularly reviewed Codes of Practice[86] and (9) a power to award interest on tribunal awards, which should be made easier to enforce.

80 Two reasons are put forward for this: (1) an over-rigid approach by the DE (as it was), insisting that any exempt procedure should mirror unfair dismissal law closely, and (2) simple ignorance today of the possibility of contracting out.

81 If there is no contracting out order, a dismissed employee can go through the whole internal procedure and, if he loses, then go to a tribunal (provided he submitted his claim within the three-month limitation period). In practice, however, when this happens, the tribunal usually comes to the same conclusion as the arbitrator.

82 Rideout 'Unfair dismissal – tribunal or arbitration' (1986) 15 ILJ 84.

83 This would have to be handled carefully – the report argues that these cases are special in that frequently there will be no *direct* evidence of discrimination and so the issue will be as to the inferences that should properly be drawn; on the other hand, if badly handled, a recommendation such as this might appear to be a sophisticated form of jury knobbling.

84 This would be in addition to ACAS conciliation, and would *not* be done by ACAS; the officer would produce a written dossier for the tribunal, and would increase the inquisitional function of the system generally. In a successful case, the officer could investigate the possibility of re-employment. This suggestion goes much further than the 'legal officers' appointable under the Employment Rights (Dispute Resolution) Act 1998.

85 Such a transfer occurred in 1994, but unfortunately only in relation to claims arising on termination of employment. The case for going further and having full 'labour courts' is made by Wedderburn 'The social charter in Britain – labour law and labour courts' (1991) 54 MLR 1, esp at 25ff.

86 This proposal is of interest in the light of the discussion under heading (iii) above. Discussing the modern anti-legalistic approach, the report states (p 53), 'The result of this reduction of the appellate function and the abandonment of guidelines has been to devalue the EAT. It has in effect condoned a great degree of inconsistency between tribunals hearing similar cases in different parts of the country. Little practical guidance can now be obtained from EAT decisions by industrial relations practitioners who wish to avoid facing an industrial tribunal'.

The report then goes on to consider a more radical set of reforms, involving a complete restructuring[87]. Their suggested system would be two-tier: (i) a lower tier of tribunals hearing the bulk of cases with increased reliance on preliminary investigation to sift the facts (by the tribunal officer suggested above) and an improved inquisitorial procedure aimed at lessening the need for legal representation[88]; (ii) a reconstituted EAT sitting as an Industrial Court with appellate jurisdiction from the lower tier on points of law, but also original jurisdiction to hear cases assigned to it because they involve either points of law, complex facts or importance as test cases. In contrast to the improved inquisitorial function of the lower tier, the Industrial Court would have improved representation before it (with legal aid), relying on a more traditional adversarial approach, though staffed by a more specialised judiciary and more highly trained side members.

The third set of suggestions came in 1994 with the publication of the long-promised Green Paper on the future of the tribunals[89]. Given some urgency by the doubling of the number of cases registered before tribunals in four years[90] with little sign of any slow down, the paper was generally less wide-ranging than the Justice Report and more concerned with procedural reforms aimed at cost-reducing efficiencies, such as easier disposal of weak or unpursued cases, extending the scope of compromise agreements, more chairman-only hearings and improved liaison with ACAS. However, two ideas were floated that are of greater interest in principle. The first was the possibility of placing more emphasis on the exhaustion by an employee of internal procedures within the firm or organisation before going to a tribunal; the second was the re-emergence of the voluntary arbitration option, as a binding (and cheaper) alternative to tribunal proceedings, with the clear understanding that the arbitrator would not primarily be applying unfair dismissal law as applied by the tribunals, but would instead be applying the parties' own rules and expectations, as reflected in the terms of reference[91]. The previous government stated their intent to proceed with most of the Green Paper proposals; on the change of government in 1997, this was one of the first areas to show the likely continuity of approach by the new government which, after a further consultation exercise, produced and passed the Employment Rights (Dispute Resolution) Act 1998 (their first legislation in the area) which (i) renamed the tribunals 'employment tribunals', (ii) increased the incidence of determinations without full hearings or by chairman alone, (iii) introduced the possibility of appointing legal officers to deal with preliminary issues, (iv) broadened the rules on compromise agreements, (v) placed penalties on employees seeking unfair dismissal awards without first going through internal procedures, and (vi) gave the statutory basis for the ACAS arbitration alternative in

87   Appendix 1 to the report contains comparative material on the approach to labour courts taken in certain foreign jurisdictions.
88   This suggestion is of course the very reverse of the well-known statement of the EAT on the desirability of normally following usual court procedures and rules of evidence in tribunal cases: *Aberdeen Steak Houses Group plc v Ibrahim* [1988] ICR 550, [1988] IRLR 420, see p 523 below.
89   Resolving employment rights disputes – options for reform (Cm 2707, 1994); see Cockburn (1995) 24 ILJ 285 – he refers to the Green Paper as a 'pot pourri of ideas that the authors have assembled and put under various subject headings', ie with little internal coherence.
90   See p 496 n 11 above
91   In this context, the Green Paper drew heavily on Lewis & Clark *Employment rights, industrial tribunals and arbitration: the case for alternative dispute resolution* (Institute of Employment Rights, 1993).

unfair dismissal cases[92]. Conceptually it was this last development which was the most fundamental, though at the time of writing the take-up rate is extremely low.

The position of the tribunals and their procedures have become topical again recently, with the present government's stated aim being not just to arrest the increase in tribunal applications but actually to reverse it. The idea mentioned above of requiring exhaustion of internal procedures before recourse to a tribunal features heavily in the dispute resolution provisions in the Employment Act 2002 which sets out standard disciplinary and grievance procedures which are to become in effect mandatory, with serious penalties for parties not going through them.[93] Moreover, the Act gives powers to produce new procedure Regulations requiring more and earlier disclosure of the parties' cases in tribunal applications, wider costs rules, wider powers to strike-out weak cases and greater use of chairman-only and/or paper hearings. Even when these changes are in force (the timing of this being uncertain at the time of writing) that will not be an end of the matter because the government have established the Employment Tribunal Task Force to monitor tribunal proceedings. Their first report[94] recommended yet more emphasis on dispute resolution measures and earlier disclosure of information by parties, improved infrastructure, better IT links and better preparation of cases before the hearing. Major changes on a continuing basis can thus be anticipated through the currency of this edition, particularly as in March 2003 the Lord Chancellor announced that the employment tribunals and EAT are to be amalgamated with the proposed new (unified) Tribunal Service, covering most of the present separate forms of administrative tribunals, as advocated in the Leggatt report on tribunals[95].

2 PROCEDURE

The rules of procedure have been deliberately simplified in tribunal and EAT cases[96], particularly as regards pre-trial matters such as pleadings, which are on simplified standard forms and administered through the tribunal offices. One innovation in the 2001 reissue of the rules was the inclusion of an 'overriding objective' to deal with cases justly. This is stated to include (a) ensuring that the parties are on an equal footing, (b) saving expense, (c) dealing with the case in ways which are proportionate to the complexity of the issues and (d) ensuring that it is dealt with expeditiously and fairly. While in one sense these are fairly obvious and hardly controversial per se, the intention presumably was to human-rights-proof the rules, or at least to allow human rights issues to be dealt with internally, rather than externally under the Human Rights Act 1998 itself[97].

---

92 See p 529 below.
93 See p 540 below.
94 See www.employmenttribunalsystemtaskforce.gov.uk and Jones and Coley 'The 21st century employment tribunal' [2002] NLJ 1843.
95 Tribunals for Users; One System, One Service (March 2001, HMSO).
96 Tribunal procedure is governed by the Employment Tribunals (Constitution and Rules of Procedure) Regulations 2001, SI 2001/1171 (in Scotland SI 2001/1170); see *Harvey* R [1317] and [1421].
97 In *Goldman Sachs Services Ltd v Montali* [2002] ICR 1251 the EAT used the overriding objective to hold that tribunals should apply to interlocutory orders the principles set out in the Civil Procedure Rules. In *Somjee v UK* [2002] IRLR 886, ECHR extreme delays in a tribunal action were held to contravene art 6 (right to a fair hearing); *quaere* whether such a case would now be better dealt with under head (d) above.

The detailed rules of procedure are considered in full elsewhere[98], but certain of the more important aspects are considered now in outline.

(i) Time limits

As in the case of actions to enforce other employment protection rights such as guarantee payments, payment during suspension on medical grounds and time off work[99], an action for unfair dismissal is subject to a fairly stringent three-month time limit, ie the action must be commenced within three months of the effective date of termination[100]. The aim is obviously to promote speedy trial of the matter, but an absolute rule could cause hardship, so in each statutory provision which is modelled on the unfair dismissal one there is a qualification in this form: '… or within such further period as the tribunal considers reasonable in a case where it is satisfied that it was not reasonably practicable for the complaint to be presented before the end of the period of three months.' There are three leading cases on the construction of the 'not reasonably practicable' exception; the first is the decision of the Court of Appeal in *Dedman v British Building and Engineering Appliances Ltd* [101] that the test is whether the applicant had just cause or excuse for not complying with the limit. Ignorance of his rights (or knowledge of his rights but ignorance of the time limit) will not normally be sufficient (particularly as unfair dismissal has now been with us for some time, and a dismissed employee has various sources of information and advice, for example posters and leaflets at employment offices); the applicant will have to show some further factor:

'… does total ignorance of his rights inevitably mean that it was impracticable for him to present his complaint in time? In my opinion, no. It would be necessary to pay regard to his circumstances and the course of events. What were his opportunities for finding out that he had rights? Did he take them? If not, why not? Was he misled or deceived? Should there prove to be an acceptable explanation of his continuing ignorance of the existence of his rights, it would not be appropriate to disregard it, relying on the maxim "ignorance of the law is no excuse". The word "practicable" is there to

---

98   *Harvey* Div. T.
99   An action for a redundancy payment is subject to a six-month limit which operates in a different way – Employment Rights Act 1996, s 164(1).
100 S 111(2); see *Harvey* T [186]. Sub-s (3) allows a complaint to be presented before the effective date of termination provided that the complainant is under notice at the time; this includes notice given by the employee himself where he resigns but claims constructive dismissal: *Presley v Llanelli Borough Council* [1979] ICR 419, [1979] IRLR 381. In this context, 'presented' means actually received; *House v Emerson Electric Industrial Controls* [1980] ICR 795; *Post Office v Moore* [1981] ICR 623. On the posting of an application, see *St Basil's Centre v McCrossan* [1992] ICR 140, [1991] IRLR 455; *Birmingham Midshires Building Society v Horton* [1991] ICR 648, EAT and *Consignia plc v Sealy* [2002] EWCA Civ 878, [2002] ICR 1193, [2002] IRLR 624.
101 [1974] 1 All ER 520, [1974] ICR 53, CA. When *Dedman* was decided, the relevant wording was 'not practicable'; however, that was construed in such a way that the addition of 'reasonably' in 1974 was held not to alter the test: *Times Newspapers Ltd v O'Regan* [1977] IRLR 101. The phrase 'reasonably practicable' was criticised by Waite P as too imprecise (*Croydon Health Authority v Jaufurally* [1986] ICR 4); he thought that Parliament should either spell out the exceptions or leave the whole matter in the discretion of the tribunal, to extend time simply if it was 'fair' to do so. Similar sentiments were expressed by the Master of the Rolls in *London International College Ltd v Sen* [1993] IRLR 333, CA.

moderate the severity of the maxim and to require an examination of the circumstances of his ignorance. But what if, as here, a complainant knows he has rights but does not know that there is a time limit? Ordinarily, I would not expect him to be able to rely on such ignorance as making it impracticable to present his claim in time. Unless he can show a specific and acceptable explanation for not acting within [three months] he will be out of court[102].'

Secondly, in *Walls Meat Co Ltd v Khan*[103] the applicant knew of his rights and of the three months limit, but mistakenly thought that his unfair dismissal claim would be covered by the same procedure and heard by the same tribunal as his concurrent claim for unemployment benefit; he did not discover his mistake until the three month period had elapsed, but the Court of Appeal allowed him to bring his claim, on the basis that his genuine mistake constituted just cause or excuse. However, Lord Denning MR (in addition to stressing that the application of the test lies very much within the discretion of the tribunal) said that tribunals should be 'fairly strict' in enforcing the time limit, and so wherever possible the dismissed employee should ensure that an application goes in within the period – it may not be enough to say that he thought it better to wait the outcome of some other event before applying (for example, the decision of a court in a pending criminal action against him, on the ground of which he was dismissed[104]). The applicant will not be in any better position if he seeks the help of a 'skilled adviser' (such as a lawyer, trade union official or the Citizens' Advice Bureau[105]), for if that adviser makes a mistake as to the time limit, or omits to advise him about it (even where the adviser was primarily being consulted on another matter[106] such as defending a pending criminal action, as in the above example), the applicant may not use that mistake or omission as a ground for seeking an extension of time:

'But what is the position if he goes to skilled advisers and they make a mistake? The English court has taken the view that the man must abide by their mistake. There was a case where a man was dismissed and went to his trade association for advice. They acted on his behalf. They calculated the three months wrongly and posted the complaint two or three days late. It was held that it was "practicable" for it to have been posted in time. He was not entitled to the benefit of the escape clause: see *Hammond v Haigh Castle & Co Ltd*[107]. I think that was right. If a man engages skilled advisers to act

---

102 [1974] 1 All ER 520 at 528; [1974] ICR 53 at 64, per Scarman LJ.
103 [1979] ICR 52, [1978] IRLR 499, CA.
104 *Norgett v Luton Industrial Co-operative Society Ltd* [1976] ICR 442, [1976] IRLR 306; *Porter v Bandridge Ltd* [1978] ICR 943, [1978] IRLR 271, CA; *Walls Meat Co Ltd v Khan*, n 103, above, at 56 and 501 respectively, per Lord Denning MR.
105 *Riley v Tesco Stores Ltd* [1980] ICR 323, [1980] IRLR 103, CA. However, reliance on bad advice from a tribunal official *may* be acceptable: *Rybak v Jean Sorelle Ltd* [1991] ICR 127, [1991] IRLR 153; even if a solicitor has also been consulted: *London International College v Sen* [1993] IRLR 333, CA.
106 *Norgett v Luton Industrial Co-operative Society Ltd*, n 104 above; cf *Union Cartage Co Ltd v Blunden* [1977] ICR 420, [1977] IRLR 139, though the approach in this case was doubted by Lord Denning MR in *Walls Meat Co Ltd v Khan*, n 103 above and the approach in *Norgett's* case preferred by the Court of Appeal in *Riley v Tesco Stores Ltd*, n 105 above. Confusion between the employee and the adviser as to who was to make the application will not be enough: *Dowty Aerospace Gloucester Ltd v Ballinger* (1993) Times, 5 March, EAT.
107 [1973] ICR 148, [1973] IRLR 91, NIRC.

for him – and they mistake the time limit and present it too late – he is out. His remedy is against them[108] .'

The third leading case is *Palmer v Southend-on-Sea Borough Council* [109] which sets the previous case law into the context of the modern approach to unfair dismissal law by stressing that the application of the exemption is essentially a question of fact. The Court of Appeal did consider the test to be applied and May LJ suggested that the question is whether it was 'reasonably feasible' to have presented the claim in time[110] . Having said that, however, it was stated clearly that it is for the employment tribunal to decide as a matter of fact (with little chance of a successful appeal) and so, in line with the modern approach, the most that can be said of the previous case law is that it suggests 'factors' which a tribunal may decide to take into account when applying the test:

'Dependent upon the circumstances of the particular case, an industrial tribunal may wish to consider the manner in which and reason for which the employee was dismissed, including the extent to which, if at all, the employer's conciliatory appeals machinery has been used. It will no doubt investigate what was the substantial cause of the employee's failure to comply with the statutory time limit; whether he had been physically prevented from complying with the limitation period for instance by illness or a postal strike, or something similar. It may be relevant for the industrial tribunal to investigate whether at the time when he was dismissed and if not then when thereafter, he knew that he had the right to complain that he had been unfairly dismissed; in some cases the tribunal may have to consider whether there has been any misrepresentation about any relevant matter by the employer to the employee. It will frequently be necessary for it to know whether the employee was being advised at any material time and, if so, by whom; of the extent of the adviser's knowledge of the facts of the employee's case; and of the nature of any advice which they may have given to him. In any event it will probably be relevant in most cases for the industrial tribunal to ask itself whether there had been any substantial fault on the part of the employee or his adviser which has led to the failure to comply with the statutory time limit. Any list of *possible relevant considerations,* however, cannot be exhaustive and, as we have stressed, at the end of the day *the matter is one*

---

108 *Dedman's* case, n 101 above, at 526 and 61 respectively, per Lord Denning, MR; *Croydon Health Authority v Jaufurally* [1986] ICR 4. The logic of this was doubted obiter by Sir Thomas Bingham MR in *London International College v Sen* [1993] IRLR 333, CA, but it was accepted as an established approach.
109 [1984] ICR 372, [1984] IRLR 119, CA. The judgment of the court, given by May LJ, contains a particularly full and useful review of the previous authorities. The factual nature of the apparent 'rules' on this point was again stressed by the Court of Appeal in *London International College v Sen,* n 105 above. A generally more liberal approach was taken in a case of illness towards the end of the three-month period in *Schultz v Esso Petroleum Co Ltd* [1999] 3 All ER 338, [1999] IRLR 488, CA.
110 The desire for an alternative formulation was prompted by a feeling that to construe the phrase 'reasonably practicable' in the sense simply of 'reasonable' was too wide, but that to construe it as meaning 'reasonably capable of being done' (as in the factory legislation) would be too restrictive. 'Feasibility' was thought to express a middle way; note, however, that in other contexts the Court of Appeal have held that courts or tribunals should *not* place glosses on to the plain wording of the statute.

of fact for the industrial tribunal taking all the circumstances of the given case into account.'[111]

In addition to these general principles, three particular problems deserve mention. The first arises where the dismissed employee does not put in his complaint within three months because he spends that time trying to regain his job through the firm's internal appeal structure, not wishing to jeopardise that procedure by also making a tribunal application. This problem was potentially more acute when the time limit was twenty-eight days[112], but could still arise with the present three-month limit, for if the ex-employee uses the internal appeal and *fails* it is well established that the effective date of termination (from which the three months run) is the date of the initial dismissal, *not* the date of the rejection of the appeal[113]. In such circumstances, the dismissed employee is best advised to put in his application to safeguard his position, if only to make an immediate request to the tribunal to postpone any proceedings pending the outcome of the internal appeal. What is to happen, however, if he does not do so? In *Crown Agents for Overseas Governments and Administration v Lawal*[114] the EAT expressed the opinion that the exhaustion of internal remedies should in most cases be a good reason for a tribunal to allow an extension of time. However, confusion was caused by the subsequent EAT decision in *Bodha v Hampshire Area Health Authority*[115] saying precisely the opposite, ie that there should be *no* extension. The facts of *Palmer v Southend-on-Sea Borough Council* (considered above) raised this very point and the Court of Appeal stated unequivocally that *Bodha* was to be preferred, thus settling the matter[116]. This may be seen as a very unfortunate decision on two grounds, first that it makes it more difficult to integrate internal and external forms of challenging a dismissal, and second that the law should encourage such internal appeals, just as it encourages other forms of voluntary settlement without recourse to a tribunal (such as ACAS conciliation and compromise agreements); this decision provides no such encouragement[117]. On that basis, the Employment Act 2002, section 33 contains

---

111 At 385 and 125 respectively, per May LJ (emphasis added).

112 Under the Industrial Relations Act 1971.

113 *J Sainsbury Ltd v Savage* [1981] ICR 1, [1980] IRLR 109, CA, approved in *West Midlands Co-operative Society v Tipton* [1986] ICR 192, [1986] IRLR 112, HL. In *Batchelor v British Railways Board* [1987] IRLR 136, CA it was held that it is irrelevant that the dismissal was in breach of a contractually binding procedure – that cannot be relied on to advance the date of termination (to within the three-month period).

114 [1979] ICR 103, [1978] IRLR 542.

115 [1982] ICR 200. This was a good example of the confusion that can be caused when one EAT simply declines to follow the decision of a previous EAT (see p 499 above). In his judgment Browne-Wilkinson P said that there ought to be amending legislation specially providing that time should not run until after the exhaustion of an internal appeal, but there has been no sign of this happening, even under the Employment Rights (Dispute Resolution) Act 1998 which in other ways tried to emphasise the importance of going through internal procedures.

116 This was even applied where an internal procedure resulted in an offer of re-engagement which was then dishonoured: *London Underground Ltd v Noel* [2000] ICR 109, [1999] IRLR 621, CA.

117 It is of course arguable that the law should not encourage (by extending time limits) attempts to regain employment by the organisation of industrial action to put direct pressure on the employee; after all, one of the aims of the unfair dismissal legislation was to lessen the incidence of strikes over dismissals. However, that rationale does *not* apply to the use of internal grievance procedures.

a power for the Secretary of State to make regulations governing time limits in any matter to which one of the new statutory procedures (on discipline, dismissal and grievances, see p 540 below) applies. If and when eventually exercised (during the currency of this edition) this could have a significant effect on the harshness of the existing case law on pursuing internal procedures; the extent of any new power or obligation to extend the statutory time limit is such cases will depend on the eventual formulation of the new rules.

The second particular problem arises where the employee does not learn of a material fact until more than three months after the date of the dismissal. In *Churchill v A Yeates & Sons Ltd*[118] the employee was dismissed ostensibly for redundancy, but more than three months later discovered that someone had been taken on to do his job, thus raising the inference that the redundancy was in fact a sham and his dismissal may have been unfair. The EAT held that the tribunal was acting properly in extending the time limit. This decision was later approved by the Court of Appeal in *Machine Tool Industry Research Association v Simpson*[119], where a similar decision was taken. Again, the case concerned a 'sham redundancy' and it is possible that that is the only area in which this principle is likely to apply in practice (though its importance in that area should not be underestimated[120]).

The third particular problem has been of particular concern in recent years, and arises where there has been a change in the law through a court decision, in particular where a long-standing assumption or rule of domestic law has been successfully challenged under EC law and 'disapplied'. Can employees who thought that they had no cause of action when dismissed prior to that court decision now seek to bring an unfair dismissal case? This happened in particular with the ruling in *R v Secretary of State for Employment, ex p Equal Opportunities Commission*[121] by the House of Lords that the old sixteen hours per week qualification was contrary to EC sex equality requirements. This raised the potential for a flood of cases by employees under that limit who had been dismissed before that decision. However, the courts (faced with that prospect) have taken a stringent view, (a) applying the domestic limit even where the claim is at least partly under EC law, (b) holding that there was technically nothing to have stopped the employee challenging the old qualification prior to the *EOC* case, and (c) refusing to exercise the power to extend the period because what was involved in these cases was an error of *law* by the employee, not the sort of error of fact that could lead to a finding that it had not been reasonably practicable to present the claim at the time of the actual dismissal[122].

118 [1983] ICR 380, [1983] IRLR 187.

119 [1988] ICR 558, [1988] IRLR 212, CA. The Court of Appeal added the gloss that in such a case the tribunal does not have to decide on the truth of the alleged further facts – it is sufficient (for the purposes of extending the time limit, to establish jurisdiction) to show their effect on the applicant's state of belief.

120 Many employers, particularly in small business, seem to assume that redundancy means getting rid of X and not replacing him *for about six months*; there is no legal validity for the latter, even if in practice there may be something to it as a rule of thumb. This case may have some effect in attacking at least *blatant* attempts to misapply the rules on redundancy.

121 [1994] ICR 317, [1994] IRLR 176, HL; see p 190 above.

122 *Biggs v Somerset County Council* [1996] ICR 364, [1996] IRLR 203, CA (in which the applicant, who had worked 14 hours per week had tried to claim unfair dismissal based on the termination of her employment in 1976). On the other hand, it has been held that the *Biggs* decision does *not* apply to the backdating of a sex discrimination claim where the power to extend the time limit is differently worded ('just and equitable'): *British Coal Corpn v Keeble* [1997] IRLR 336, EAT.

(ii) Originating procedure[123]

An applicant to a tribunal claiming, for example, unfair dismissal commences his action, not by writ, but by submitting an 'originating application' to the appropriate local tribunal office in England, or to the COET in Scotland. This application, usually made in standard form on document IT1[124], requires the applicant to state certain particulars about himself, the relief he is claiming, and, in an unfair dismissal case, the reasons for which he says he was dismissed and what remedy he is seeking. The application is then sent to the respondent employer who should enter an appearance within twenty-one days of receiving the application; the employer does so by completing standard form IT3 which asks, inter alia, whether the employer intends to resist the claim, whether he accepts that the applicant was dismissed and on what grounds he intends to defend the case. Failure to enter an appearance means that the employer will not be allowed to take part in the hearing, though he can apply for the twenty-one days to be extended[125]. It is at this stage, if not before, that the employer should consult his lawyers if the case is going to be contentious for, although he is not absolutely bound by what he puts on form IT3, he may weaken his case if the grounds put down in it are not fully consistent with the way in which he wishes to defend the case before the tribunal. Likewise, the applicant should make sure that he raises all the allegations and various causes of action that he wants considering because, on ordinary principles of issue estoppel[126], the eventual tribunal decision will finally decide the points raised *and* all *others* that could with reasonable diligence have been raised at the same time[127].

In preparation for a tribunal hearing, either side may request of the other further and better particulars of the matters raised in the pleadings and discovery of documents. If a party refuses a request, the other party may refer the question to the tribunal which may order further particulars or discovery as part of its general powers of case management[128]. The question of discovery of documents

---

123 See *Harvey* T [291]ff.
124 Use of the form IT1 is not mandatory; a letter may be sufficient to constitute an originating application provided that it is clear that that is the intention: *Smith v Automobile Proprietary Ltd* [1973] ICR 306, 8 ITR 247; *Alex Munro (Butchers) Ltd v Nicol* [1988] IRLR 49. Whether it is the standard form or a letter, the application should contain the basic information required by r 1(1), though an incomplete application may be accepted and then cured by the power to amend: *Dodd v British Telecom plc* [1988] ICR 116, [1988] IRLR 16.
125 EAT Rules, rr 3(3) and 17.
126 *Henderson v Henderson* (1843) 3 Hare 100 at 114: 'The plea of res judicata applies ... not only to points on which the court was actually required by the parties to form an opinion and pronounce a judgment, but to every point which properly belonged to the subject of litigation and which the parties, exercising reasonable diligence, might have brought forward at the time', per Sir James Wigram V-C.
127 *Divine-Bortey v Brent London Borough Council* [1998] ICR 886, [1998] IRLR 525, CA; *Hancock v Doncaster Metropolitan Borough Council* [1998] ICR 900; *Sheriff v Klyne Tugs (Lowestoft) Ltd* [1999] IRLR 481, CA. These were relatively stringent applications of the rule in *Henderson*, given that tribunals in other contexts are supposed to be inquisitorial in nature. In a non-employment case the House of Lords took a more liberal view that *Henderson* should not be allowed to stifle legitimate complaints (*Johnson v Gore Wood* [2001] 1 All ER 481, HL) and such an approach was adopted by the Court of Appeal in an employment context (though on particularly strong facts) in *Friend v Civil Aviation Authority* [2001] EWCA Civ 1204, [2001] IRLR 819. There is thus currently some uncertainty as to how strongly the estoppel rules should be applied here.
128 R 4; *West Midlands Passenger Transport Executive v Singh* [1988] ICR 614, [1988] IRLR 186, CA. Important guidance on discovery was given by Wood P in *Byrne v Financial Times Ltd* [1991] IRLR 417.

may be sensitive where the documents in question are of a confidential nature and, although there are provisions for safeguarding confidentiality and holding hearings in private[129] , the courts have held in the context of discrimination cases that discovery of confidential documents such as references and personal files should only be granted subject to restrictive conditions[130] , and the EAT have held that this should also apply in unfair dismissal cases[131] .

(iii) Conciliation and settlement[132]

As often seen elsewhere in industrial law, emphasis is placed upon reaching agreed settlements. To this end, copies of all application documentation are sent to the ACAS conciliation officers[133] who are under a statutory duty to attempt to conciliate at the request of either party or, in the absence of such a request, where the officer considers that he could act with a reasonable prospect of success[134] ; in doing so, the officer should have regard to the desirability of the parties using established grievance procedures. In unfair dismissal cases, the legislation states that the conciliation officer should seek to promote reinstatement or re-engagement on terms which seem to him to be equitable, and only seek to promote agreement on compensation where the applicant does not wish to have his job back, or where it would not be practicable; in practice, however, this hardly even happens and compensation is the only realistic remedy pursued. Any information or statement communicated to a conciliation officer during the course of conciliation is not admissible in evidence at a subsequent tribunal hearing without the consent of the person who communicated it[135] .

It is important that the parties, particularly the applicant, should understand the significance of statutory conciliation. If they reach an agreed settlement they may submit it to the tribunal for promulgation as a formal decision which will bring an end to the case.[136] However, the agreement may still be binding without this formal step if it is reached after the involvement of the conciliation officer, for in such a case (usually resulting in the officer recording the agreement on form COT 3) the legislation provides that the agreement is an exception to the rule that the parties cannot by contract or agreement exclude the right to bring a case before a tribunal and so the applicant cannot then go back on the agreement and renew his tribunal application[137] . This drastic effect can place ACAS officers

---

129 R 8(3); matters conveyed to the conciliation officer are confidential: Employment Tribunals Act 1996, s 18(7).

130 *Science Research Council v Nassé* [1979] 3 All ER 673, [1979] IRLR 465, HL; *West Midlands Passenger Transport Executive v Singh* (n 20, above).

131 *Crown Agents v Lawal* [1979] ICR 103, [1978] IRLR 542.

132 See *Harvey* T [676] and [726].

133 In 2001/02, 75% of applications notified to conciliation officers in this way were settled or withdrawn without proceeding to a hearing: ACAS Annual Report 2001/02.

134 Employment Tribunals Act 1996, s 18(2); see ACAS *Individual Employment Rights – ACAS Conciliation between Individuals and Employers*.

135 S 18(7).

136 Rules of Procedure, r 15(2)(b).

137 Employment Rights Act 1996, s 203(2)(e); *Moore v Duport Furniture Products Ltd* [1982] ICR 84, [1982] IRLR 31, HL. An agreement is also binding if signed by the employee's adviser (eg a CAB adviser): *Freeman v Sovereign Chicken Ltd* [1991] ICR 853, [1991] IRLR 408. There is no legal requirement that an agreement be recorded in writing – an oral agreement is binding if it is reached through ACAS: *Gilbert v Kembridge Fibres Ltd* [1984] ICR 188, [1984] IRLR 52. An attempt to have an agreement declared invalid through economic duress failed in *Hennessy v Craigmyle & Co Ltd* [1986] ICR 461, [1986] IRLR 300, CA.

in a difficult position – the emphasis is upon reaching settlements, but where are justice and fairness to fit in? Here there is a major divergence between the law and the practice. Case law (largely brought by applicants with second thoughts wishing to evade their agreements to settle) has given ACAS a very wide discretion here; in particular, the House of Lords has held that a conciliation officer does not have to investigate the 'fairness' of an agreement that is simply presented to him after being worked out between the parties[138] and, more generally, the EAT has held that there is no legal obligation on a conciliation officer to explain his legal rights to an applicant before he agrees to settle[139]. However, it is clear from the following passages (among many) that that is not how ACAS see their functions in practice:

> 'During 1984 the Service pointed out to a number of commentators and interested organisations that, for the purposes of providing a valid conciliation settlement, a conciliation officer cannot simply rubber stamp or verify an existing agreement which either or both parties regard as binding. Officers endeavour to ensure that the parties, particularly the individual employees concerned, are making decisions on a properly informed basis concerning their rights, the options open to them and the implications of their decision. This necessitates private discussions with employees or their representatives which can result in changes being made to previous agreements.'[140]

> '… [A]n important part of the conciliation officer's work in trying to promote a settlement is to ensure that both sides are adequately informed, and fully understand the range of options open to them and the consequences of the different decisions they may take.[141]

ACAS found particular difficulty with this balancing act when faced with a steep rise in the late 1980s of cases being referred to them for rubber-stamping of an existing agreement where there had not even been a complaint presented to a tribunal ('non-IT1 cases'). As a result of this, they decided on a policy of only exceptionally dealing with such cases, which by 1992 had produced a radical decrease in their number[142].

The point remains, however, that while ACAS officers may (commendably) take this more positive view of their role generally, if for any reason (except possibly mala fides) a conciliation officer does not take this approach (particularly by omitting to offer relevant advice to an applicant) that will *not* be a good ground for challenging the validity of the agreement to settle, once the fact of agreement and the involvement of ACAS have been shown.

ACAS conciliation is expected to be made subject to a major (and controversial) change during the currency of this edition. Under the Employment Act 2002,

---

138 *Moore v Duport Furniture Products Ltd*, n 137 above. The Justice report *Industrial Tribunals* (1987) para 2.28 points out that one view is that ACAS may be *too* impartial, in that any existing imbalance between employer and employee is perpetuated, not ameliorated, by a neutral stance in conciliation.

139 *Slack v Greenham (Plant Hire) Ltd* [1983] ICR 617, [1983] IRLR 271, EAT.

140 ACAS Annual Report 1984, p 63.

141 *Individual Employment Rights – ACAS Conciliation between Individuals and Employers*, n 134 above.

142 See p 60 above for the figures and a statement of the current policy.

section 24 it is proposed that there should be a fixed period of conciliation during which a party would not be allowed to proceed to a tribunal. At the time of writing, it is suggested that this should be thirteen weeks (with a 'fast track' of seven weeks in cases concerning deductions from wages, breach of contract on termination and redundancy payments). Conciliation would thus in effect become compulsory, in another attempt to decrease the number of tribunal cases by promoting more settlements. After the compulsory period, ACAS would be under no further duty to conciliate in the case (and would only do so in prescribed circumstances). Views have varied as to whether this will work, or just postpone the common door-of-the-tribunal settlements by thirteen/seven weeks. Much will depend on whether the attitudes and practices of employment law practitioners can be changed, not just the law.

If a settlement is reached without the involvement of ACAS, the position was originally that it was not binding on the parties because of the rule that the employee may not contract out of the protection of the legislation; it was therefore always possible for the employee to pocket the money on offer and still proceed to bring an action, although in such a case a tribunal finding in his favour might decide it was not just and equitable to award any compensation[143]. However, the law here was materially altered by the Trade Union Reform and Employment Rights Act 1993 which introduced the concept of a legally binding 'compromise agreement' *without* the involvement of ACAS (presumably to take the place of what used to be the 'non-IT1 cases', above). Such an agreement became legally binding if (a) it is in writing, (b) it relates to the particular proceedings, (c) the employee received independent advice as to the terms and effect of the proposed agreement and in particular its effect on his ability to pursue his rights before a tribunal, (d) the adviser was professionally insured, (e) the agreement identifies the adviser and (f) it states that these statutory conditions regulating compromise agreements are satisfied. Originally, the independent advice (the crux of the employee's protection) had to be from a qualified lawyer, but this was widened in an attempt to increase the use of compromise agreements yet further by the Employment Rights (Dispute Resolution) Act 1998, and so now the advice can come from a qualified lawyer, an authorised trade union official, an authorised advice centre worker, or any other person specified by order of the Secretary of State (though to date no such order has been made). This regime applies not only to the settlement of unfair dismissal actions, but also to other statutory actions in modern employment law. Common law claims arising on termination, which may now be brought before a tribunal, are subject to a general ability to settle (as in the county court) without the above safeguards. Compromise agreements, after a relatively slow start, have now become part of the landscape, but they received a warning as to possible over-use from the EAT in *Lunt v Merseyside TEC Ltd*[144] where it was pointed out that the reference in the legislation to 'particular proceedings' being compromised means that one of these agreements cannot be used for an 'all claims settlement'; it can be used to settle multiple claims, but these must be specified in the agreement. COT 3 settlements can be used on an 'all claims' basis, provided that all the claims in question are ones in respect of

---

143   *Courage Take Home Trade Ltd v Keys* [1986] ICR 874, [1986] IRLR 427. For the deductibility of ex gratia payments from compensation, see p 612 below.
144   [1999] ICR 17. As originally drafted, the Employment Bill 2002 contained a provision reversing *Lunt*, but this was dropped during the Bill's Parliamentary passage.

which ACAS have conciliatory jurisdiction and that the terms of the settlement are construed as having that effect[145].

(iv) Pre-hearing reviews

In a further attempt to keep to a minimum the number of cases actually going before a tribunal, there was introduced in 1980 a further stage (if conciliation fails). This was the pre-hearing assessment, whereby a tribunal could (at the request of one of the parties, or of its own motion) hold a preliminary review of a case on the basis of the pleadings and written and oral submissions by the parties (but without witnesses). The aim was not actually to strike out cases which are unlikely to succeed, but it was provided that if the tribunal indicated that in its opinion an application was unlikely to succeed, or that any particular contention of either of the parties has no reasonable prospect of success, that the party in question (if he continued with the case) could be at risk under the rule on costs (considered above). The figures suggest that this procedure could be effective; for example, in 1990–91 73% of those applicants who had been given a 'costs warning' at a pre-hearing assessment settled or withdrew their applications, and of the twenty-one applicants who proceeded to a tribunal hearing in spite of a costs warning, eighteen failed (with seven actual orders for costs).

However, in other ways the picture was much less encouraging. First, the take-up rate declined substantially, from a peak of 3,555 assessments in 1983 to only 196 in 1992–93. Secondly, concern was expressed by ACAS that even when the number was high the assessment procedure could also have a 'backlash' effect in making ordinary conciliation more difficult (and making an employee *less* likely to settle if an employer in fact failed to secure a costs warning in an assessment)[146]. Thirdly, the Justice Report[147] considered that on the whole the assessment procedure had not been a success and should be repealed.

However, far from going for repeal, the previous government decided to try to strengthen the procedure. The result is the present replacement for assessments, the pre-hearing review (PHR). The statutory basis for this was laid by the Trade Union Reform and Employment Rights Act 1993 and the procedure is contained in rule 7 of the Employment Tribunal Rules of Procedure. As with the previous procedure, either party may apply for a review or the tribunal may hold one of its own motion, and if (on consideration of the originating application and notice of appearance, and any written or oral representation) the tribunal considers that a party's contentions have 'no reasonable chance of success' it may make a costs warning[148]. However, the novelty of this procedure is that in addition the tribunal may make an order requiring that that party pay a deposit of up to £500 as a condition of continuing with the application or response. If the party continues, loses and has an award of costs made against him, the deposit goes

---

145 *BCCI SA (in liquidation) v Ali* [2001] UKHL 8, [2001] ICR 337, [2001] IRLR 292. A court may be particularly unwilling to hold that a settlement bars certain future claims, of which the employee was not and could not be aware (see Harvey T [668.01]); see eg *Royal National Orthopaedic Hospital Trust v Howard* [2002] IRLR 849.
146 ACAS Annual Report 1984, p 67.
147 *Industrial Tribunals* (1987), para 2.34.
148 Members who sit on a PHR may not then sit on any eventual hearing: r 7(9). Although theoretically there is a right of appeal from a PHR ruling, such an appeal is very unlikely to succeed: *Mackie v John Holt Vintners Ltd* [1982] ICR 146, [1982] IRLR 236, EAT.

towards those costs; further, the fact of the deposit having been ordered is itself a factor in deciding whether to make a costs order[149].

(v) Procedure at the tribunal hearing

Exceptionally, the tribunal may wish to consider certain points relating to jurisdiction (territorial or otherwise) as a preliminary issue[150]. Normally, however, the case will be set down for one hearing, though the standard practice is to hear the parties first on the question of liability, only going on to arguments over remedies once there is a finding in favour of the applicant[151]. The tribunal has power to postpone the hearing if other proceedings relating to the dismissal are pending elsewhere (for example, in the High Court or Crown Court); the decision whether to postpone is in the discretion of the tribunal chairman and his decision will not usually be altered on appeal (in the absence of a clear error of law)[152], though a decision to postpone may be particularly appropriate where identical issues are likely to arise in parallel court proceedings (for example, for wrongful dismissal), especially as there is a danger of a tribunal decision raising an issue estoppel in any subsequent court proceedings[153]. Each side has the right to call witnesses, give evidence, cross-examine witnesses called by the other side and address the tribunal at the conclusion[154]. In unfair dismissal cases, the respondent employer will usually present his case first, as he bears the burden of proving that the dismissal was not unfair; if, however, the employer disputes that there was ever a dismissal (for example, in a constructive dismissal case) it will be for the employee to begin and argue that he was in fact dismissed[155].

Although it is for the parties to conduct their own case, as in an ordinary court, the tribunal chairman may take steps to ensure that a party's case is considered fully if he is not represented, which may mean that the chairman adopts a more 'inquisitorial' role. The extent to which such a role should be adopted by the tribunal generally has been the subject of mixed messages in recent cases. On the one hand, there are EAT decisions saying that a tribunal should if necessary

---

149 R 14(7).
150 There is a specific power to do so in r 6, but its desirability has been the subject of debate within the EAT; one leading authority was in favour generally of discouraging the practice, which is viewed as often a false economy giving rise to problems on appeal, and being particularly hostile to any practice of having preliminary points considered by a chairman alone: *Sutcliffe v Big C's Marina Ltd* [1998] ICR 913, [1998] IRLR 428.
151 Such a 'split hearing' may encourage a settlement on remedies if there is a finding of unfairness. However, if such a procedure is to be adopted, the tribunal must make this clear at the beginning and state how the evidence is to be called: *Iggesund Converters v Lewis* [1984] ICR 544, [1984] IRLR 431. Tribunals should not normally entertain a submission of no case to answer half-way through the case: *Ellis v Ministry of Defence* [1985] ICR 257, EAT.
152 *Carter v Credit Change Ltd* [1979] ICR 908, [1979] IRLR 361, CA.
153 *First Castle Electronics Ltd v West* [1989] ICR 72; *Warnock v Scarborough Football Club* [1989] ICR 489; *Bowater plc v Charlwood* [1991] ICR 798, [1991] IRLR 340. On issue estoppel, see *Green v Hampshire County Council* [1979] ICR 861; *O'Laoire v Jackel International Ltd (No 2)* [1991] ICR 718, [1991] IRLR 170, CA.
154 R 11(2).
155 The burden of proof may assume substantive importance at the end of the case – if the tribunal is genuinely stuck on a point of fact it may resort to the burden of proof to resolve it, though with the caveat that this approach should *not* be resorted to over-hastily, where the tribunal is merely having difficulty in making up its mind: *Morris v London Iron and Steel Co Ltd* [1987] ICR 855, [1987] IRLR 182, CA.

consult the ACAS Code of Practice on its own initiative[156], and that there are certain rules of unfair dismissal laws (for example, on redundancy selection) that are so well accepted that they should automatically be considered by a tribunal even if not specifically raised by a party, especially if unrepresented[157]. On the other hand, in more procedural contexts, the emphasis has been placed more strongly on the responsibility on the parties themselves to raise and argue all relevant points; if they do not, then (a) it will not be a ground of appeal that the tribunal did not decide on an issue not specifically relied on[158], and (b) any later attempt to raise such a point in separate proceedings could be struck out on the grounds of issue estoppel and res judicata[159].

The proceedings are usually marked by a greater degree of informality than in an ordinary court[160] and the Rules specifically state that a tribunal is not bound by 'any enactment or rule of law relating to the admissibility of evidence in proceedings before the courts of law'[161]; thus, for example, in a case concerning dismissal for suspected crime a tribunal may hear evidence that would be inadmissible in a criminal trial, such as hearsay, complaints, previous convictions and even improperly obtained confession evidence[162]. However, this emphasis on informality is subject to at least two caveats. First, with regard to the wider discretion on evidence, this only works one way – a tribunal may receive evidence otherwise inadmissible but may *not* exclude evidence which would normally be admissible (as being relevant and probative)[163]. Secondly, this whole question has been considered by Wood P in *Aberdeen Steak Houses Group plc v Ibrahim*[164], in terms which suggest that in practice there should normally be less informality than rule 11 would at first sight allow. The principal point made is that too much informality may be counter-productive and too loose a procedure may lead to perceived unfairness. Normal laws of procedure and evidence do not have to be followed slavishly, but on the other hand Wood P points out that those laws (unlike the laws and usages of Gormenghast) do not exist just for the sake of it, or merely because things have always been done that way[165] – they are there so that both sides know the rules of the game and are less likely to be ambushed. Thus, the

156 *Lock v Cardiff Rly Co Ltd* [1998] IRLR 358.
157 *Langston v Cranfield University* [1998] IRLR 172.
158 *Mensah v East Hertfordshire NHS Trust* [1998] IRLR 531, CA; for the position where it is the employer who has not raised all necessary points before the tribunal, see *Church v West Lancashire NHS Trust (No 2)* [1999] ICR 586, [1998] IRLR 492.
159 *Divine-Bortey v Brent London Borough Council* [1998] ICR 886, [1998] IRLR 525, CA; *Hancock v Doncaster Metropolitan Borough Council* [1998] ICR 900; *Sheriff v Klyne Tugs (Lowestoft) Ltd* [1999] IRLR 481, CA; see p 517 above. A generally more libaral approach has been taken towards allowing the re-litigation of an issue that a party had withdrawn, for whatever reason (*Sajid v Sussex Muslim Society* [2001] EWCA Civ 1684, [2002] IRLR 113; *Ako v Rothschild Asset Management Ltd* [2002] EWCA Civ 236, [2002] IRLR 348) but this has yet to feed through into this more direct form of estoppel, though cf *Friend v Civil Aviation Authority* [2001] EWCA Civ 1204, [2001] IRLR 819.
160 R 11(1) states that 'the tribunal shall so far as appears to it appropriate seek to avoid formality in its proceedings ...'.
161 R 11(1), making express (as from 1980) what had already been established in the case law: *Coral Squash Clubs Ltd v Matthews* [1979] ICR 607, [1979] IRLR 390, EAT.
162 *Morley's of Brixton Ltd v Minott* [1982] ICR 444, [1982] IRLR 270; *Dhaliwal v British Airways Board* [1985] ICR 513, EAT.
163 *Rosedale Mouldings Ltd v Sibley* [1980] ICR 816, [1980] IRLR 387; this was doubted in *Snowball v Gardner Merchant Ltd* [1987] ICR 719, [1987] IRLR 397, but that case was in turn doubted subsequently in *Aberdeen Steak Houses Group plc v Ibrahim*, n 164 below, and so *Rosedale* appears to be still good law.
164 [1988] ICR 550, [1988] IRLR 420.
165 Even in Norfolk.

present guidance of the EAT is that normally it should be for the parties to run their own cases, call witnesses and ensure that all relevant evidence is adduced[166]; the party opening the case should call all his evidence and then close his case, leaving the field to the other side and the normal rules of cross-examination should apply; although normally inadmissible evidence may be admitted, it should be remembered that there is usually good reason for not admitting it, which may mean here treating it with caution. The case may be seen as a useful statement of desirable practice but, on the other hand, (a) it sits oddly alongside the usual criticism that tribunals are already *too* legalistic, and (b) it raises the question as to whether these are 'guidelines' to be followed by tribunals and, if so, whether it will be an appealable error of law for a tribunal to depart from them without good reason.

At the conclusion of the case the tribunal gives its decision (either immediately or in reserved form). However, although there is a mandatory requirement to give reasons[167], this area has seen two important developments (one legislative, one judicial) as part of the current campaign to curb 'legalism' in tribunal procedure. The first is that in 1985 what is now rule 12 was amended to allow a tribunal to give its reasons *in summary form only*; however, full reasons must be given in four cases – (a) in cases concerning equal pay, sex discrimination or race discrimination; (b) where a party requests full reasons orally at the hearing; (c) where a party submits a written request for full reasons within twenty-one days of the document recording the summary reasons being sent to the parties or (d) where the tribunal considers that summary form would not sufficiently explain the grounds for its decision. Thus, by virtue of (b) and (c) a party still has a right to full reasons, which is of course important for a party wishing to appeal to the EAT. The second development was a reconsideration by the Court of Appeal of what is meant by 'reasons' in the first place; in particular, how detailed they need to be. As noted above, reasons have to be given and they will form the basis for any appeal[168]. However, in a series of cases[169] the Court of Appeal stressed that there is no obligation on the tribunal to set out the facts in full with the arguments put for both sides and a closely reasoned conclusion; the fact that many tribunal decisions are in this form does not mean that it is obligatory and, indeed, merely to point out that a particular fact or argument is not expressly referred to in the reasons will not be sufficient to show that the tribunal's decision was perverse. As a way of discouraging appeals, this approach is possibly something of a blunt instrument and the EAT subsequently qualified it, at least to the extent of (a) holding that where there is a conflict of fact on a particular issue the tribunal should make that clear in its decision and state which version of the facts is believed[170] and (b) stating that a case may be remitted to the tribunal if the EAT

---

166 This includes the normal rule that if a party specifically states that he will not be calling particular evidence, he should normally be bound by that statement.

167 R 12(3); *Guest v Alpine Soft Drinks Ltd* [1982] ICR 110, EAT.

168 *Owen and Briggs v James* [1982] ICR 618, [1982] IRLR 502, CA. In the light of the more restrictive approach adopted by the Court of Appeal (n 169 below), however, the tribunal chairman's note of evidence may assume more significance, especially in an appeal on the grounds of perversity: *Martin v Glynwed Distribution Ltd* [1983] ICR 511, [1983] IRLR 198, CA.

169 *UCATT v Brain* [1981] ICR 542, [1981] IRLR 224, CA; *Martin v Glynwed Distribution Ltd*, n 168 above; *Varndell v Kearney & Trecker Marwin Ltd* [1983] ICR 683, [1983] IRLR 335, CA; *Morris v London Iron and Steel Co Ltd*, n 155 above.

170 *Levy v Marrable & Co Ltd* [1984] ICR 583.

is unable to see from the reasons *why* the tribunal reached its decision[171]. The latter point can also be seen in a subsequent Court of Appeal decision[172] in which (i) the court (though purporting to apply the previous case law) upheld the EAT's decision to allow an appeal on the basis of inadequate reasons, and (ii) Bingham LJ stated that tribunals should outline their factual conclusions and reasoning at least sufficiently for the parties and an appellate court to see why the decision went that way and whether any point of law is involved. However, it may take more than one decision to swing the pendulum back in this area.

The reasons, in either summary or full form, are put into writing, signed by the chairman, transmitted to the central office for entering in the Register and sent to the parties. Until a decision is entered in the Register, the tribunal has the same inherent power as a court to alter any mistakes in it, though this power is to be used sparingly and after giving the parties the opportunity to be heard further[173]. An order by a tribunal for monetary compensation is enforceable by county court order[174].

(vi) Review and appeal[175]

Under rule 13 of the Rules of Procedure, a party to a tribunal hearing may apply to have the decision reviewed on certain grounds. This procedure is appropriate, rather than an appeal, where an error of law *or fact* is discovered soon after the decision. The party must make his application within fourteen days of the decision being sent to the parties (unless he actually makes it at the end of the hearing), and it must be in writing stating grounds for requesting a review *and* the reasons why that party says that the tribunal decision was wrong[176]. The application is considered by the chairman of the tribunal that heard the case, who may refuse it on the ground that he considers it has no reasonable chance of success. If it is not refused, it is heard by that tribunal (or another if it is not practicable to remit it to the same one) which may vary or revoke its decision, or order a re-hearing before a different tribunal. The grounds for review set out in rule 13 are (a) that the decision was wrong through an error made by the tribunal staff, (b) that a party did not receive notice of the proceedings leading to the decision, (c) that the decision was made in the absence of a party entitled to be heard, (d) that new

---

171 *Yusuf v Aberplace Ltd* [1984] ICR 850.
172 *Meek v City of Birmingham District Council* [1987] IRLR 250, CA. Bingham LJ (at 251) also suggested that it was highly desirable that the tribunal 'should give guidance to employers and trade unions as to practices which should or should not be adopted', which appears to be doubly heretical in the light of the prevailing views on guidelines.
173 *Hanks v Ace High Productions Ltd* [1978] ICR 1155, [1979] IRLR 32, doubting the reasoning (though not the decision) in *Jowett v Earl of Bradford* [1977] 2 All ER 33, [1977] ICR 342. A tribunal should not use this power to go back on primary findings of fact and change the whole basis of its decision: *Lamont v Fry's Metals Ltd* [1985] ICR 566, [1985] IRLR 470, CA. Unfortunately, however, in the latter case the Court of Appeal only assumed (without deciding) that there is a power to amend an oral decision; some doubt was expressed about that power in *Spring Grove Service Group plc v Hickinbottom* [1990] ICR 111 by the EAT, and the matter remains in need of an authoritative ruling.
174 Employment Tribunals Act 1996, s 15.
175 See *Harvey* T [1111] and [1401].
176 *Drakard & Sons Ltd v Wilton* [1977] ICR 642. The decision of the EAT in *Ladup Ltd v Barnes* [1982] ICR 107, [1982] IRLR 7 to use the power of review to alter a decision in the light of subsequent events is open to criticism as (a) an extension of the true purpose of a review and (b) possibly introducing a large measure of uncertainty.

evidence has become available which could not reasonably have been known of or foreseen at the time of the hearing, or (e) that the interests of justice require such a review. If a party wishes to rely on (c) he will have to show good cause for his failure to attend[177], and likewise under (d) he will have to show that the new evidence could have an important bearing on the decision and is genuinely 'new', not just something which could have been adduced at the hearing by the use of due diligence[178]. Moreover, ground (e) has not been construed so as to short-circuit the other grounds (particularly (d)), since it is also in the 'interests of justice' that tribunal decisions should be as final as possible once handed down[179].

A tribunal decision is subject to appeal on a point of law to the EAT. The appeal must be instituted by serving on the EAT a notice of appeal together with a copy of the decision or order within forty-two days of the date on which the decision was sent to the appellant[180]; the EAT has power to extend this period, though the appellant must show cause why this should be done[181]. The notice of appeal is served on the respondent who must make his reply if he intends to contend the issue and may at this stage cross-appeal. Consistently with the EAT's overriding objective of fairness in handling cases and the modern emphasis on case management, appeals are sifted by either a judge or the registrar to determine the best way to proceed. While some cases may be assigned for a full hearing immediately (possibly on a fast-track basis if urgent), most can expect to be subject to a preliminary hearing, held in order to establish that there is a genuine point of law involved in the appeal[182]. At the hearing, fresh evidence will only rarely be heard and the EAT will rely primarily upon the written decision of the tribunal and, if necessary, upon the chairman's notes made at the tribunal hearing. The decision of the EAT is by simple majority, if necessary, and it is expressly given all the powers of an employment tribunal to make relevant orders to dispose of the case, or it may decide to remit the whole matter to the same or another tribunal for a rehearing[183]; the EAT may be particularly disposed to remit the case if there are, in the light of its decision, further factual matters to consider before coming to a final conclusion[184]. The EAT has power to review its own decisions once given[185], and on points of law appeal then lies to the Court of Appeal and then to the House of Lords.

177 *Morris v Griffiths* [1977] ICR 153, EAT.

178 *Flint v Eastern Electricity Board* [1975] ICR 395, [1975] IRLR 277.

179 [1995] ICR 395 at 404, [1975] IRLR 277 at 281, per Phillips J; *General Council of British Shipping v Deria* [1985] ICR 198; *Ironside Ray & Vials v Lindsay* [1994] ICR 384, [1994] IRLR 318.

180 EAT Rules 1993, r 3. Note that if separate decisions are given on liability and remedy, the 42-day period flows from *each*, not just from the date of the later decision.

181 Appeals out of time are governed by the EAT *Practice Direction* (dated December 2002, see [2003] IRLR 65) and the guidelines laid down in *United Arab Emirates v Abdelghafar* [1995] ICR 65, approved in *Aziz v Bethnal Green City Challenge Co Ltd* [2000] IRLR 111, CA.

182 EAT Practice Direction, para 9.

183 Employment Tribunals Act 1996, s 35. *Dobie v Burns International Security Services (UK) Ltd* [1984] ICR 812, [1984] IRLR 329, CA.

184 *Askew v Victoria Sporting Club Ltd* [1976] ICR 302. However, a case should not be remitted in order to hear evidence that was in fact available but not given at the original hearing: *Kingston v British Railways Board* [1984] ICR 781, [1984] IRLR 146, CA.

185 EAT Rules 1993, r 33; this power should not normally be used to challenge rulings of law in the decision, where the proper recourse is to an appeal, not to a review: *Blockleys plc v Miller* [1992] ICR 749.

(vii) Statements of reasons for dismissal

One further point of procedure to be noticed in the context of an unfair dismissal action is that under the Employment Rights Act 1996, section 92 an employee with one year's qualifying service who is under notice or who has been dismissed has a right to be provided by the employer (within fourteen days of making the request) with a written statement of reasons for his dismissal; there was no such common law right. If the employer unreasonably fails to give such a statement, the ex-employee may complain to the tribunal on that ground (or on the ground that a statement given under this section is inadequate or untrue[186]) and the tribunal has powers (a) to make a declaration as to what it finds were the employee's real reasons for the dismissal, and (b) to award the employee two weeks' pay. A small but important change was made to the wording by the Trade Union Reform and Employment Rights Act 1993. Previously, an employer was liable if he *refused* to give a statement, and this led to case law on the subtle difference between refusal and mere failure. However, the wording was altered in 1993 to extend to *failure* to provide the statement, and so that previous case law is no longer applicable[187]. However, it remains the case that, once 'failure' has been shown the tribunal must still go on to consider whether that failure was 'unreasonable'; the most important type of case raising this point is where the employer refuses to give a statement because he denies that there was a dismissal *at all* (for example. where the employee walked out and now wants to claim constructive dismissal, which is contested by the employer) – where the employer can show that he reasonably believed that there was no dismissal, a tribunal will probably hold his failure to have been reasonable and so not contrary to the section[188].

The section does not say how detailed the statement has to be, but at the least it must be such that anyone reading it can tell on its face why the employee was dismissed; thus, in *Horsley, Smith and Sherry Ltd v Dutton*[189] it was held by the EAT that it is not enough to refer *solely* to reasons given in earlier conversations or separate documents; however, in the subsequent case of *Gilham v Kent County Council*[190] the Court of Appeal narrowed the scope of that decision by holding

---

186 *Harvard Securities plc v Younghusband* [1990] IRLR 17, EAT.
187 One further change in the 1993 Act is that where an employee is dismissed while she is pregnant (or after childbirth but in circumstances in which her maternity leave period is ended by dismissal), she is entitled to a s 92 statement (a) without having to request it and (b) whether or not she has the one-year qualifying period: s 92(4). This now also applies to an employee dismissed while on adoption leave: s 92(4A).
188 *Broomsgrove v Eagle Alexander Ltd* [1981] IRLR 127, stressing the objective nature of the test; in the slightly earlier case of *Brown v Stuart Scott & Co* [1981] ICR 166 the EAT had put it in terms of whether the employer had a 'conscientious' and bona fide belief that there was no dismissal (though stressing that the tribunal must first decide whether there had in fact been a dismissal). The objective view in *Broomsgrove* is more consistent with the requirement of 'unreasonable' failure.
189 [1977] ICR 594, [1977] IRLR 172. Where, however, the document or letter to which reference is made was explicit as to the reasons, there may be a 'refusal' but it may in the circumstances be a *reasonable* refusal: *Marchant v Earley Town Council* [1979] ICR 891, [1979] IRLR 311. It is not enough for the employer to rely on the fact that he has entered an appearance to the ex-employee's unfair dismissal application stating the grounds for dismissal; s 92 assumes some form of independent documentation directly to the ex-employee: *Rowan v Machinery Installations (South Wales) Ltd* [1981] ICR 386, [1981] IRLR 122.
190 [1985] ICR 227, [1985] IRLR 16, CA.

that there was compliance with the section where the employer replied to the ex-employee's request by referring to reasons set out in two previous letters, copies of which were attached to the reply.

The procedural significance of section 92 is that, by subsection (5), a written statement provided under the section is expressly made admissible in subsequent proceedings; a section 92 request may therefore be a useful 'first shot' for an ex-employee claiming unfair dismissal and the respondent employer might be advised to seek legal advice upon receipt of it in any case likely to be difficult to defend for, although he will not be absolutely bound by what he says in the written statement (in the sense of only being able to rely on points of law raised in it), any basic inconsistency between the terms of the statement and his defence as actually put forward before the tribunal could seriously weaken his case.

(viii) Contract claims

One of the long-standing criticisms of the tribunal system for many years after its inception was that tribunals could not deal with common law claims for breach of contract, which had to go to the county court. In practice, such cases could be heard if they could be squeezed under the 'deductions' rules in the Wages Act 1986 (now Part II of the Employment Rights Act 1996), but that was less than satisfactory and so eventually the government exercised its long-standing power[191] to extend common law jurisdiction to tribunals. This was done in the two Employment Tribunals (Extension of Jurisdiction) Orders of 1994[192], with effect from July 1994. The first point to notice is that such contract claims can only be brought before a tribunal if they arise or are outstanding on the *termination* of the employee's employment. While it is to be welcomed that a tribunal can now, for example, deal with a claim for notice pay or holiday pay outstanding at the same time as hearing an unfair dismissal action, it is unfortunate that, due to this limitation, they cannot hear a claim for amounts alleged to be outstanding *during* the employment, at least directly under the Orders. Certain common law claims are excluded[193], and the claim must be brought within three months of termination (subject to the usual 'not reasonably practicable' power to extend). The procedure for bringing such a claim is the same as that (above) for statutory claims, but two peculiarities must be noted – (i) the Orders specifically give the employer a right of counter-claim (within six weeks of receiving the originating application for the employee's claim, subject again to the power of extension); (ii) the employee's claim is subject to a statutory maximum of £25,000 in respect of any one contract (regardless of the number of claims brought on it). As this maximum is relatively high (a little under half the limit for the compensatory award for unfair dismissal, and indeed twice that award when it previously stood at only £12,000) it has given scope (when both breach of contract and unfair dismissal are being claimed) for the employee's representatives to seek to bring as much of the immediate loss as possible under the heading of the contract

---

191   Previously contained in the Employment Protection (Consolidation) Act 1978, s 131 (hence references to these as 'section 131 orders'), but now contained in the Employment Tribunals Act 1996, s 3.

192   The England and Wales Order is SI 1994/1623; the Scotland Order is SI 1994/1624. See *Harvey* R [778], [788].

193   Art 5 excludes claims relating to the employee's living accommodation, intellectual property, confidence and restraint of trade. The Employment Tribunals Act 1996, s 3 excludes claims for damages for personal injuries.

claim, thus freeing the compensatory award to reflect future loss more fully, at least in the case of a higher earner, for example on a longer notice period.

Although these orders are an important development and the figures show a consistently high take-up rate[194], there may still be many cases where employees and their representatives continue to use the 'deduction' provisions of Part II of the 1996 Act instead for two reasons: (i) because in any case arising during employment that remains the only way to challenge breaches of contract before a tribunal rather than a court; (ii) even where a case arises on termination, the action under Part II may be used to avoid the possibility of a counterclaim under the Orders.

(ix) ACAS arbitration in unfair dismissal and flexible working cases

Voluntary arbitration organised through ACAS has always been available, though (in common with arbitration generally) its incidence has been declining. Moreover, it is not a true *alternative* solution, since an employee failing at this arbitration stage still has the right to bring a claim before a tribunal. For some time now, ideas have been mooted of producing a special statutory scheme that would indeed act as a true alternative to the tribunal system[195]. Faced with the steep rise in tribunal applications, the previous government looked with favour on this idea[196] and the present government proceeded with it by giving the necessary powers in the Employment Rights (Dispute Resolution) Act 1998[197], permitting ACAS to produce a scheme for the approval of the Secretary of State. The scheme was introduced in relation to unfair dismissal claims, after considerable delay, in May 2001[198], and then extended to the new statutory right to request flexible working in April 2003[199].

Views vary considerably as to its desirability[200], partly depending on one's views of whether tribunals are too legalistic, because it can be argued that it is meant to produce a form of alternative dispute resolution which was the original aim of the tribunals themselves. The scheme as finally established works as follows. The parties have to agree to use the arbitration alternative, and sign a COT 3 or compromise to that effect, thus giving up *totally* their rights to go to a tribunal. ACAS then organise for the case to be heard by a single arbitrator (from a panel already appointed for that purpose). The parties submit written statements of

---

194 The ACAS Report 2001/02 shows a total of 28,804 breach of contract claims received by them for conciliation (out of an overall total of 165,093 cases in all jurisdictions). The total for claims under Pt II of the 1996 Act ('Protection of Wages') was 37,591. Added together, these two jurisdictions amounted to 40% of all applications.

195 Particularly influential was Lewis and Clark *Employment Rights Industrial Tribunals and Arbitration: the Case for Alternative Dispute Resolution* (1993).

196 Green Paper 'Resolving employment rights disputes: options for reform' (Cm 2707, 1994).

197 Adding new ss 212A and 212B to the Trade Union and Labour Relations (Consolidation) Act 1992.

198 ACAS Arbitration Scheme (England and Wales) Order 2001, SI 2001/1185, *Harvey* R [1443].

199 ACAS (Flexible Working) Artibration Scheme (England and Wales) Order 2003, SI 2003/694, *Harvey* R [1719]. For the statutory right to request flexible working, see p 437 above.

200 Contrast to hostile view of a Regional Chairman of Tribunals in MacMillan 'Employment tribunals – philosophies and practicalities' (1999) 28 ILJ 33 with the view of one of the scheme's original proponents in Clark 'Adversarial and investigative approaches to the arbitral resolution of dismissal disputes' (1999) 28 ILJ 319.

case and the hearing takes place locally. Legal representation is discouraged, and the hearing is to be relatively informal, with no prolonged cross-examination and a relatively inquisitorial role for the arbitrator. The result is an award by the arbitrator, issued through ACAS, with the arbitrator having all the remedies powers of a tribunal. In line (controversially) with ordinary arbitrations, there is *no* appeal (only certain, restricted grounds of challenge for procedural irregularity under the Arbitration Act 1996). The advantages of the scheme are speed (the aim being to have the hearing within two months of the reference to ACAS), less expense, more informality, relative confidentiality and a greater possibility of re-employment. The disadvantages are its finality (for the party losing), a more 'basic' approach to disputed facts, reliance on a single-member forum and the fact that *only* an unfair dismissal or flexible working claim can be heard (with any other allegations, for example of discrimination, having to go to a tribunal). The lack of an appeal may certainly cause employers to be nervous of it, particularly with the raising of the maximum compensatory award from £12,000 to the present £53,500, which is in the arbitrator's 'gift'.

In addition, there is one other uncertainty, of a more principled nature. What *standard* should an arbitrator apply when judging the fairness of a dismissal? The aim is to have a less legalistic forum, not dependent on the citation and use of legal authority, from which it would follow that the arbitrator (often not legally trained) would tend to apply what is sometimes described as an 'industrial relations' or 'felt-fair' standard, possibly reflecting the standards and assumptions of the parties themselves in that particular industry. Some lawyers would therefore fear double standards, with the tribunals continuing to apply a more legally refined standard based on case precedents. On the other hand, (a) this issue may in practice be lessened by the heavy reliance of arbitrators on ACAS publications (in particular, the Code of Practice on Discipline and Grievances and the handbook 'Discipline at Work') which to an extent distil the wisdom of the case law, and (b) arguably double standards are nothing new and were inherent in the system as it was first set up thirty years ago, when the assumption was that *most* cases would be dealt with by internal procedures (often including voluntary arbitration), with tribunals operating only as long-stops. In large part due to these concerns and a background of widespread hostility among employment lawyers, the unfair dismissal scheme has had a very slow start indeed, with only thirteen references to arbitration in 2001/02. Future development will be watched with interest, because it is not certain that the scheme will ever prosper here. Equally, however, it will be interesting to see if the take-up is eventually higher in the context of flexible working where it might be considered more appropriate, especially as by definition both parties are still in the employment relationship, which may point more towards this form of quasi-internal dispute resolution system.

3 CODES OF PRACTICE AND DISCIPLINARY AND GRIEVANCE PROCEDURES

Fair procedures have always been a major concern of modern employment law. The ACAS Code of Practice No 1 on discipline and dismissal has been the most important single document in individual employment law since the inception of unfair dismissal in 1971. The redrafted (2000) Code was extended to give advice on grievance procedures (whose significance has been increasing over the years) and now, at the time of writing, the Employment Act 2002 is to put in place standard procedures for both discipline/dismissal and grievances which are to be in effect compulsory, as a way of furthering government policy to require exhaustion of internal remedies first, and to halt the hitherto inexorable rise in tribunal applications. It is necessary to look first at the Code of Practice idea itself, then the longstanding law on disciplinary measures (including warnings and hearings), and then the proposals under the 2002 Act (with the caveat that at the time of writing their finalised form remained a matter of speculation).

(i) The Code of Practice as a legal device

Increasing use has been made of Codes of Practice in modern industrial law in an attempt to apply necessarily vague general principles to the wide variety of industrial practices. In the area of discipline and dismissal this is particularly so for three reasons. First, it has long been established in unfair dismissal law that there is a distinct head of 'procedural unfairness', so that a dismissal for a substantive reason which is prima facie fair may still be unfair if the wrong procedure was adopted[201]; this therefore puts emphasis upon determining what is the *right* procedure. Second, tribunals are consistently encouraged to reach their decisions in the light of 'good industrial relations practice' which up to a point is amenable to distillation into Codes of Practice. Third, the advent of the modern legislation has led to increased formalisation and legalisation of many aspects of employment, including questions of discipline and the procedures leading up to dismissal[202], in which previously there was little law involved; now however there is a considerable body of law involved, and Codes of Practice have figured largely in this intervention. What then is the legal status of a Code of Practice? It is not law in itself, though it has to be issued by ACAS in accordance with a set procedure[203]. Thus contravention of one of its provisions by someone does not render that person directly liable to any form of proceedings (by way of enforcement or otherwise); however, it is expressly provided[204] that it is admissible in evidence before a tribunal (or the CAC) and, further, that if any of its provisions are relevant to the proceedings in question 'it shall be taken into account in determining that question'. As with the Highway Code, a person ignores it at his peril, particularly if that person is an employer wishing to dismiss an employee without risking a finding of unfair dismissal. Compliance with Code provisions on matters of discipline and dismissal will therefore be most material to an employer's claim that he acted reasonably and fairly although, as the Code does not have the force of law, failure to comply with it will not make the action in question automatically unfair[205], for there may be good reasons for not complying

---

201 *Earl v Slater and Wheeler (Airlyne) Ltd* [1973] 1 All ER 145, [1972] ICR 508, NIRC, approved by the House of Lords in *W Devis & Sons Ltd v Atkins* [1977] ICR 662, [1977] IRLR 314, HL.

202 Questions of discipline are intertwined with the law on dismissal, for dismissal may be seen as the ultimate form of disciplining, and the procedures for each may to a large extent be the same; therefore much of what follows is applicable to both.

203 Trade Union and Labour Relations (Consolidation) Act 1992, s 200; under s 203 the Secretary of State may also issue Codes of Practice, after consultation with ACAS; this power has been exercised in the politically controversial areas of picketing and balloting.

204 S 207; a COP produced by the Secretary of State is also admissible in court proceedings.

205 *Lewis Shops Group v Wiggins* [1973] ICR 335, [1973] IRLR 205.

on the facts of a particular case[206]. The EAT have reaffirmed the continuing importance of the Code, stating that it may be part of the tribunal's inquisitorial function to consult it wherever relevant, even if it is not specifically referred to by the parties[207].

The provisions relevant to discipline and dismissal were introduced in the highly influential ACAS Code of Practice No. 1 *Disciplinary Practice and Procedures in Employment* and many employers now have definite rules and procedures (often in works rules or handbooks) drafted in the light of the Code's recommendations. The Code itself (reissued in expanded form in 2000) places great emphasis on involvement of employees and their representatives in the drafting of procedures covering grievances, discipline and appeal structures. Union agreement is not essential in order to have an effective disciplinary procedure, for such matters lie in the first place within the management's responsibilities and in any event only a minority of employees are now union members or covered by any form of collective bargaining. However, the fact that the procedure is an agreed one will greatly add to its authority, and to the authority which may be exercised by the management when they take action clearly in accordance with the agreed rules; tribunals will naturally tend to pay great attention to an agreed procedure as a question of fact and evidence[208]. Where there are set rules on discipline, grievances and appeals (whether agreed or not) the employer must give the employee written notice of them within two months of the commencement of his employment[209]. For the guidance of employers when drawing up rules and procedures, the Code makes the following general points:

> 'Disciplinary procedures should not be viewed primarily as a means of imposing sanctions. Rather they should be seen as a way of helping and encouraging improvement amongst employees whose conduct or standard of work is unsatisfactory.'

> 'When drawing up disciplinary rules, the aim should be to specify clearly and concisely those that are necessary for the efficient and safe performance of work and for the maintenance of satisfactory relations within the workforce and between workers and management . . . whatever set of rules are eventually drawn up they should not be so general as to be meaningless.'

(ii) Disciplinary measures

Although certain forms of disciplinary action may still lie entirely within the managerial prerogative (for example, transferring a general labourer to a different job or refusing to give a discretionary bonus), many other forms will impinge upon the rights and expectations of the disciplined employee (for example, fines, suspension, demotion) and so the crucial point about lawful disciplinary measures is that the employer must have the power to impose them, and normally this will involve having the contractual authority (express or implied) to do so. If the employer goes outside this authority the employee may in theory maintain a

---

206 *Retarded Children's Aid Society Ltd v Day* [1978] ICR 437, [1978] IRLR, 128, CA.
207 *Lock v Cardiff Rly Co Ltd* [1998] IRLR 358.
208 *Securicor Ltd v Smith* [1989] IRLR 356, CA.
209 Employment Rights Act 1996, s 3, see p 113 above.

common law action (for example, to recover the amount of a fine unlawfully deducted)[210]; of much greater significance in modern employment law is the possibility that the wrongly disciplined employee may walk out and claim to have been constructively dismissed, for the purpose of bringing an unfair dismissal action. Thus, although some managers remain suspicious of setting down their disciplinary powers in writing on the basis that it restricts managerial prerogative, the modern tendency is to put down in written form the company's policy on discipline (which will of course vary from industry to industry) and the procedures to be adopted, which may then form part of the employment contract either expressly or by implication. A leading survey referred to a 'massive spread of formal disciplinary and dismissal procedures across British industry and commerce' in the 1970s as a 'remarkable development in British industrial relations'. Their findings in 1990 showed that 97% of establishments recognising a union operated a disciplinary and dismissal procedure and (perhaps even more significantly) so did 83% of those not recognising a union; 93% of procedures were written, 74% provided for union representation of employees and 65% were jointly agreed[211]. On the other hand, *compliance* with procedures may sometimes be a different matter and a DTI survey in 1998 found that when one looked at cases actually brought to tribunals (itself arguably a sign of failure of the system) they were characterised by a relatively high incidence of lack of procedures or failure to operate them[212]; one reason for this was that the small firm sector produces a disproportionate number of tribunal cases, and that sector was particularly covered by the survey (which also found evidence of continued widespread reliance on informality and flexibility, especially in smaller firms, ie still viewing formal disciplinary procedures only as a last resort).

Turning to the detailed provisions of the ACAS Code, the primary suggestion is that where a disciplinary procedure is established it should be clear and unambiguous so that the individual employee may know what is expected of him; in particular, he should be made aware of the likely consequences of breaking the rules and the type of conduct which may warrant summary dismissal[213]. Although it is therefore desirable to lay down the major forms of unacceptable conduct in the circumstances of the particular industry involved, and the likely

---

210 *Gorse v Durham County Council* [1971] 2 All ER 666, [1971] 1 WLR 775. In the example given, there may also be a statutory action under the Employment Rights Act 1996, s 13.
211 Millward et al 'Workplace industrial relations in transition' (the ED/ESRC/PSI/ACAS Survey) (1992) ch 6. A similar pattern was found in the preliminary results of the 1998 exercise: Cully et al 'The 1998 Workplace Employee Relations Survey: the First Findings' (ESRC/ACAS/PSI, 1998; URN 98/934).
212 Earnshaw, Goodman, Harrison and Marchington 'Industrial Tribunals, Workplace Disciplinary Procedures and Employment Practice' (DTI Employment Relations Research Paper, 1998); see Edwards (1998) 27 ILJ 362.
213 COP, para 7; a statement that an employee is 'liable to' dismissal for particular misconduct is probably strong enough: *Procter v British Gypsum Ltd* [1992] IRLR 7. If the rules are ambiguous as to the seriousness of a particular matter but then the employer dismisses for the *first* breach (ie without warning), a tribunal may well consider that unfair: *Trusthouse Forte (Catering) Ltd v Adonis* [1984] IRLR 382. On the other hand, however, the fact that particular conduct is absolutely banned by the rules and stated to warrant mandatory dismissal does not mean that such a dismissal will automatically be fair, for the rules cannot oust the jurisdiction of the tribunal to look into the overall merits: *Laws Stores Ltd v Oliphant* [1978] IRLR 251; *Ladbroke Racing Ltd v Arnott* [1983] IRLR 154, Ct of Sess; *Taylor v Parsons, Peebles NEI Bruce Peebles Ltd* [1981] IRLR 119. This may cause problems in striking a reasonable balance between certainty and flexibility: see p 581 below.

consequences of each form, the list should not necessarily be exhaustive otherwise novel forms of transgression could be construed as permissible (in the sense of not attracting a valid penalty).

A system of warnings (considered below) may be an integral part of a disciplinary system (as well as leading up to a dismissal), but if warnings are ignored and the misconduct repeated the employer, in a case not warranting dismissal, may wish to impose a lesser sanction. Fines or deductions must be permissible under the contract of employment if they are to be valid, and must also comply with the requirements of Part II of the Employment Rights Act 1996[214]. Suspension with pay will usually be lawful[215], and may be the proper step to take for a brief period while a serious allegation against the employee is under investigation[216]; for any longer period, however, it is tantamount to a holiday and the more obviously punitive sanction is suspension *without* pay. It is here, however, that the question whether the employer has contractual authority to act becomes particularly vital for, in the absence of express or implied incorporation into the contract, there is *no* common law power to suspend without pay, for this would contravene the employer's basic obligation to pay wages[217]. Thus, as in the case of lay-offs, the employer is clearly allowed to suspend without pay only where he incorporates a clause to that effect in the contract, either directly or via the works rules or a collective agreement. Other discipline may take forms such as reprimands, temporary withdrawal of privileges or demotion or transfer; once again these are in theory only lawful if allowed by the contract though the practical position, particularly in the case of demotion or transfer, may be that even if the legality is dubious the employer may go ahead and then, if the employee walks out and claims constructive dismissal, accept that there was a dismissal but argue that it was fair because of the urgent need to remove the employee from his previous position. These are, however, all matters which are amenable to inclusion in a contract of employment in the first place (possibly via a set disciplinary Code for the firm) and so an employer who finds himself unable to take certain disciplinary action (or the subject of an unfair dismissal action for doing so) may have only himself to blame for the lack of foresight.

The Code of Practice, paragraph 9, should be considered when drafting a disciplinary procedure, for it states that such procedures should:
(i)   be in writing;
(ii)   specify to whom they apply;
(iii) be non-discriminatory;
(iv)   provide for matters to be dealt with without undue delay;
(v)   provide for proceedings, witness statements and records to be kept confidential;
(vi)   indicate the disciplinary actions which may be taken;
(vii) specify the levels of management which have the authority to take the various forms of disciplinary action;

214 See p 259 above.
215 Except perhaps in cases where the employee claims a right actually to work, not just to be paid wages: *Langston v AUEW* [1974] 1 All ER 980, [1974] ICR 180, CA. This category of case might expand in the light of *William Hill Organisation Ltd v Tucker* [1998] IRLR 313, CA, which emphasis the advantage to an employer of having an express power to suspend with pay.
216 COP, para 13.
217 *Hanley v Pease & Partners Ltd* [1915] 1 KB 698; *Bird v British Celanese Ltd* [1945] KB 336, [1945] 1 All ER 488, CA.

(viii)   provide for workers to be informed of the complaints against them and where possible all relevant evidence before any hearing;
(ix) provide workers with an opportunity to state their case before decisions are reached;
(x) provide workers with the right to be accompanied;
(xi) ensure that, except for gross misconduct, no worker is dismissed for a first breach of discipline;
(xii)   ensure that disciplinary action is not taken until the case has been carefully investigated;
(xiii) ensure that workers are given an explanation for any penalty imposed;
(xiv)   provide a right of appeal – normally to a more senior manager – and specify the procedure to be followed.

(iii) Warnings and hearings

A system of warnings has become an integral part of modern employment procedures, particularly where there is a possibility of dismissal. Warnings may seem particularly appropriate to cases of misconduct by the employee, but the general requirement for them has also been applied to cases of lack of capacity (such as inefficiency, bad workmanship and incompetence)[218] and, in line with the principle that discipline should be constructive as well as punitive, a warning to the employee should not just point out the unsatisfactory conduct but may also be expected to specify any required improvements. Many employers will have a definite warning procedure built into their disciplinary Code (which may be in the firm's rules or jointly agreed with a trade union), and may operate on a 'rule of thumb' basis such as 'one oral and two written'; there is no magic in a particular combination, but paragraph 15 of the Code does lay down this general advice:

'Where the facts of a case appear to call for formal disciplinary action a formal procedure should be followed. The type of procedure will vary according to the circumstances of the organisation. Depending on the outcome of the procedure some form of disciplinary action may be taken as follows:

First Warning:

Oral. In the case of minor infringements the worker should be given a formal oral warning. Workers should be advised of the reason for the warning, that it constitutes the first step of the disciplinary procedure and of their right to appeal. A note of the oral warning should be kept but should be disregarded for disciplinary purposes after a specified period (eg, six months). Or

Written. If the infringement is regarded as more serious the worker should be given a formal written warning giving details of the complaint, the improvement or change in behaviour required, the timescale allowed for this and the right of appeal. The warning should also inform the worker

---

218 *Winterhalter Gastronom Ltd v Webb* [1973] ICR 245, [1973] IRLR 120, NIRC.

that a final written warning may be considered if there is no sustained satisfactory improvement or change. A copy of the written warning should be kept on file but should be disregarded for disciplinary purposes after a specified period (for example, twelve months).

Final written warning – Where there is a failure to improve or change behaviour during the currency of a prior warning, or where the infringement is sufficiently serious, the worker should normally be given a final written warning. This should give details of the complaint, warn the worker that failure to improve or modify behaviour may lead to dismissal or to some other action short of dismissal and refer to the right of appeal. The final written warning should normally be disregarded for disciplinary purposes after a specified period (eg, 12 months).

Dismissal or other sanction – If the worker's conduct or performance still fails to improve the final step might be disciplinary transfer, disciplinary suspension without pay, demotion, loss of seniority, loss of increment (provided these penalties are allowed for in the contract) or dismissal. The decision to dismiss should be taken only by the appropriate designated manager and the worker should be informed as soon as reasonably practicable of the reasons for the dismissal, the date on which the contract between the parties will terminate, the appropriate period of notice (or pay in lieu of notice) and information on the right of appeal including how to make the appeal and to whom. The decision to dismiss should be confirmed in writing. Employees with one year's continuous service or more have the right, on request, to have a "written statement of particulars of reasons for dismissal".'

Further to this general statement, three particular points should be noticed. First, the existence of a warning system places emphasis upon writing and the keeping of detailed personnel records by the employer[219] who must be able, if necessary, to provide documentary proof of previous warnings; this leads, for example, to the practices of giving written confirmation even of an 'oral' warning, and of requiring the employee's signature of acknowledged receipt of a warning. This may lead to an increased personnel function within a firm, but is inevitable with the modern movement towards increased legalisation. Second, the employer's system should include some time limit on warnings, so that after a set period they lapse[220]. Third, a warning should be reasonably specific, identifying the precise ground of complaint by the employer. One consequence of this is that a warning on ground A (for example, swearing) should not be used as a step in the procedure to dismiss on ground B (for example, bad workmanship), so that one employee may be subject to more than one series of warnings concurrently if he is deficient in different respects; this must be viewed realistically, however, and there may come a point when a multitude of warnings on different matters add

---

219 COP, para 32. The warning should usually be given to the employee personally; giving it to his trade union may not be enough: *W Brooks & Son v Skinner* [1984] IRLR 379, EAT.
220 A firm's disciplinary procedure may permit an appeal against a warning; a warning which is under appeal may be considered by an employer when dismissing, but the fact that the appeal has not yet been heard should also be taken into account: *Tower Hamlets Health Authority v Anthony* [1989] ICR 656, [1989] IRLR 394, CA.

up overall to reasonable grounds to dismiss, particularly if some of the grounds are not dissimilar, and the employer may genuinely issue one final warning on generally unsatisfactory conduct[221].

The presence or absence of warnings may be a most important factor in determining the fairness or otherwise of a dismissal, though as always on matters of procedure it is not necessarily conclusive. Thus, there may be circumstances in which lack of a warning is reasonable; summary dismissal for gross misconduct is still permissible[222], and a warning might also be dispensed with where the employee has made it clear that he does not intend to 'improve' (for example, where he is at odds with the company's policy)[223], where his incapability is so bad as to be irredeemable or where (as in the case of senior management) the employee already knows exactly what is required of him, so that a warning would be irrelevant[224].

In addition to warnings, the employee who is in danger of dismissal should normally be allowed a hearing of sorts, which may be built into the firm's disciplinary procedures, or be arranged ad hoc. This may perform two functions, first to ascertain the true facts of the incident in question and second to allow the employee to make representations on the question whether he ought on those facts to be dismissed (when he may wish to refute the charges against him, or accept them but put forward matters such as length of service or previous good conduct in mitigation); where these two functions are separated (for example, where the second is considered by a higher level of management), the employee should normally be given a proper opportunity to be heard at each stage[225].

It will usually be of the essence of a fair hearing that the employee must be made aware of the charges against him[226] (unless they are obvious[227]), but the precise form of the required hearing will vary with the circumstances and the emphasis is on the overall failures of the procedure adopted, rather than any rigidly prescribed format[228]. Although the basic requirement of a hearing is akin to the rules of natural justice (which are sometimes prayed in aid in such cases), it must be remembered that these are *not* court proceedings, and so there is no inalienable right to appear in person[229], to receive witness statements[230], or to be

---

221 *Auguste Noel Ltd v Curtis* [1990] ICR 604, [1990] IRLR 326 is a particularly strong case on this point. One innovation in the draft ACAS Code on discipline and dismissal (which the Secretary of State refused to accept – p 64 above) was the concept of a 'first and final' warning, to apply to cases of serious misconduct just falling short of warranting dismissal; this would have provided more flexibility, with a half-way house between instant dismissal and exhaustion of the full warning system. The idea was finally taken up in the 2000 revision of the Code and is implicit in the warnings system (see above).

222 See p 465 above.

223 *Retarded Children's Aid Society Ltd v Day* [1978] ICR 437, [1978] IRLR 128, CA.

224 *James v Waltham Holy Cross UDC* [1973] ICR 398, [1973] IRLR 202.

225 *Budgen & Co v Thomas* [1976] ICR 344, [1976] IRLR 174; *Tesco (Holdings) Ltd v Hill* [1977] IRLR 63. It is normally for the employer to take the initiative in operating the procedure; it is not enough to say that the employee could have used the *grievance* procedure: *Clarke v Trimoco Motor Group Ltd* [1993] ICR 237, [1993] IRLR 148, EAT.

226 *Louies v Coventry Hood and Seating Co Ltd* [1990] ICR 54, [1990] IRLR 324; *Spink v Express Foods Group Ltd* [1990] IRLR 320, EAT.

227 *Fuller v Lloyds Bank plc* [1991] IRLR 336, EAT.

228 There is, however, a very useful summary of the key points normally expected of a fair hearing in the judgment of Wood P in *Clark v Civil Aviation Authority* [1991] IRLR 412 at 415.

229 *Ayanlowo v IRC* [1975] IRLR 253, CA. Moreover, it has been emphasised that the rules of natural justice do not constitute an independent head of challenge to the fairness of a dismissal in this context: *Slater v Leicestershire Health Authority* [1989] IRLR 16, CA.

230 *Hussain v Elonex plc* [1999] IRLR 420, CA; on the facts, the tribunal had taken the view that the employee had been made sufficiently aware of the allegations in other ways.

allowed to cross-examine 'witnesses'[231]. On the other hand, a fair hearing procedure (in whatever form) should normally give the employee a reasonable opportunity to hear the allegations against him and to attempt to refute them[232]. However, the analogy with the rules of natural justice must not be exaggerated, especially in the difficult area of potential bias, for it may not always be practicable to expect a complete separation of powers between the person dismissing and the person holding the disciplinary hearing (or appeal), since they may both be ordinary line managers; as long as there is substantive fairness in the internal procedure (and such procedures are, of course, to be encouraged), it is not to be attached with rules of natural justice on bias which evolved in different contexts[233]. Where the employee is to attend a formal hearing, he should normally be allowed to be represented if he so wishes (by a trade union representative or a fellow employee); this has always been good practice, but in addition the Employment Relations Act 1999, sections 10–13 now give a statutory right to be accompanied at a disciplinary hearing[234] by a trade union official or another of the employer's workers; that person is to be permitted to address the hearing (but not answer questions on behalf of the worker[235]) and to confer with him or her during the hearing, and is to be given paid time off work for the purpose[236]. If the chosen companion is not available at the time proposed for the hearing, the employer must postpone it to an alternative time proposed by the worker (provided it is reasonable and falls within the next five working days). Complaint of breach of this right lies to an employment tribunal (subject to the usual three-month time limitation provisions), which may order compensation of up to two weeks' pay.

In addition to a hearing, most disciplinary procedures in other than small firms will include some form of appeal from an adverse decision; this is suggested by the Code of Practice, paragraph 9(xiv) (set out above) and may take many

---

231 *Khanum v Mid-Glamorgan Area Health Authority* [1979] ICR 40, [1978] IRLR 215; *Santamera v Express Cargo Forwarding* [2003] IRLR 273. There may, in particular, be cases where an informant wishes to remain anonymous for fear of reprisals; Wood P laid down guidance on how to deal with the situation in *Linfood Cash and Carry Ltd v Thomson* [1989] ICR 518, [1989] IRLR 235, EAT.

232 *Bentley Engineering Co Ltd v Mistry* [1979] ICR 47, [1978] IRLR 437. For subsequent examples of findings of unfair dismissal based on breach of natural justice (in these cases, the rule on potential bias) see *Moyes v Hylton Castle Working Men's Social Club and Institute Ltd* [1986] IRLR 482 and *Campion v Hamworthy Engineering Ltd* [1987] ICR 966, CA; cf, however, *Slater v Leicestershire Health Authority*, n 229 above.

233 *Rowe v Radio Rentals Ltd* [1982] IRLR 177, where the (unsuccessful) ground of challenge was that the person hearing the appeal had been told of the facts beforehand by the person who dismissed the employee, and the latter person had been present at the appeal hearing: *R v Chief Constable of South Wales, ex p Thornhill* [1987] IRLR 313, CA. However, wherever possible (especially in a large organisation), it is highly desirable to have separate levels of management dealing with the different stages: *Sartor v P&O European Ferries (Felixstowe) Ltd* [1992] IRLR 271, CA; *Byrne v BOC Ltd* [1992] IRLR 505, EAT.

234 This means a hearing that could result in a formal warning, the taking of some other action or the confirmation of either: Employment Relations Act 1999, s 13(4); what the employer calls it is not particularly relevant, as it is the statutory definition that must be applied: *London Underground Ltd v Ferenc-Batchelor* [2003] IRLR 252. Note that this right also applies to grievance hearings 'which concern the performance of a duty by an employer in relation to the worker': s 13(5). Guidance on this right is found in s 3 of the ACAS Code of Practice.

235 The wide definition of 'worker' is used in relation to this right, which is itself extended to cover agency workers and home workers: Employment Relations Act 1999, s 13(1)–(3).

236 S 10(6), (7). Section 12 extends the usual package of employment protection measures (concerning detriment and dismissal) to both the worker relying on this right and the chosen companion (when in that employer's employment).

forms, from a simple further hearing by a more senior manager up to a formal appeal hearing by a joint management-union committee or even ACAS-organised arbitration. The importance of such an appeal as an integral part of the internal procedure (lack or denial of which may per se make the dismissal unfair) has been recognised by the House of Lords[237]; this has been emphasised even further subsequently by the evolution of the rule that a bad initial dismissal may be 'cured' by a fair appeal, *provided* that the appeal takes the form of a full re-hearing of the facts (rather than just a review of the initial decision)[238].

As in the case of a warning, a hearing and appeal may well be expected in most cases, but lack of them will not necessarily make a dismissal unfair. There may be definite classes of case where it is highly arguable that a hearing would have been inappropriate, such as where the employee clearly refuses to accept the employer's legitimate requirements, where the employee's conduct 'is of such a nature that, whatever the explanation, his continued employment is not in the interests of the business'[239] (particularly where the employment in question is of a delicate or sensitive nature[240]) or where the employee is already being investigated by the police with a view to criminal charges being brought[241]. More generally, however, this is clearly an area where views may differ, and indeed we have seen definite changes of judicial approach to the whole question of fair procedure over the years. In the 1970s (in the infancy of the unfair dismissal law) great emphasis was placed on proper procedures, but this was then perceived to have gone too far and a reaction set in, from two directions – first, through a generally more relaxed approach to procedural requirements beginning with the decision of the Court of Appeal in *Hollister v NFU*[242], taking the view that a lapse in procedure (such as failure to give a hearing) is merely one factor to take into account and, secondly and more specifically, through the evolution and widespread application of the rule in *British Labour Pump Co Ltd v Byrne*[243] that an element of procedural unfairness (such as the lack of a hearing) may be 'forgiven' if the employer could show that even if the proper procedure had been carried out it would have made no difference. The potential inroad of the *Byrne* principle into any general requirement of a hearing hardly needed to be spelled out. That is why its overruling in the leading House of Lords decision in *Polkey v A E Dayton Services Ltd*[244] was of such great importance, and led to a general swing back of the pendulum, with more emphasis again being placed on procedure in general, and hearings in particular. The court emphasised that the task of a tribunal is to

237 *West Midlands Co-operative Society Ltd v Tipton* [1986] ICR 192, [1986] IRLR 112, HL.
238 *Whitbread & Co plc v Mills* [1988] ICR 776, [1988] IRLR 501; *Clark v Civil Aviation Authority* [1991] IRLR 412; approved by the Court of Appeal in *Sartor v P&O European Ferries (Felixstowe) Ltd*, n 233 above. In *Post Office v Marney* [1990] IRLR 170 an EAT held a fair initial decision cures a bad appeal, sed quaere whether this goes against *Tipton*, n 237 above.
239 *James v Waltham Holy Cross UDC* [1973] ICR 398, [1973] IRLR 202.
240 *Alidair Ltd v Taylor* [1978] ICR 445, [1978] IRLR 82, CA.
241 *Carr v Alexander Russell Ltd* [1979] ICR 469n, [1976] IRLR 220, applied in *Parker v Clifford Dunn Ltd* [1979] ICR 463, [1979] IRLR 56, EAT.
242 [1979] ICR 542, [1979] IRLR 238, CA.
243 [1979] ICR 347, [1979] IRLR 94, EAT.
244 [1988] ICR 142, [1987] IRLR 503, HL; see p 569 below and Collins (1990) 19 ILJ 39. Arguably, however, the later interpretation of *Polkey* in *Duffy v Yeomans Ltd* [1995] ICR 1, [1994] IRLR 642, CA has within it certain unfortunate echoes of *Byrne*: see p 569 below. Moreoever, a modified form of the *Byrne* principle is to be re-introduced by the Employment Act 2002, s 34 (introducing a new s 98A ('Procedural fairness') into the Employment Rights Act 1996), see p 542 below.

assess the reasonableness of what the employer actually did at the time, not what he might have done, and that the question whether at the end of the day the employee actually suffered injustice goes only to compensation, *not* to liability. The case of *McLaren v National Coal Board*[245] is a good example of the result of once again taking procedures seriously. The employee was accused of assaulting a working miner during the strike; normally the matter would have been investigated by the local manager but in the circumstances this was thought to be impracticable and so it was left to the police and the court – once the employee was convicted, he was automatically dismissed without a hearing. The tribunal held that this was fair given the surrounding circumstances of industrial warfare, but the Court of Appeal held that it was unfair, Sir John Donaldson MR stating:

> '[N]o amount of heat in industrial warfare can justify failing to give an employee an opportunity of giving an explanation. ... You have the position that acceptable reasons for dismissing may change in a varying industrial situation, but *the standards of fairness never change. They are immutable but are applied in a different situation.*' (Emphasis added.)

The pendulum may therefore be on its way at least partially back; there will still be cases where lack of a hearing is explained sufficiently to the tribunal's satisfaction to produce a finding of fair dismissal, and it remains ultimately a matter of fact for the tribunal[246]. However, in entertaining an employer's case that it was reasonable to dispense with a hearing a tribunal might do well to bear in mind the words of Megarry V-C in *John v Rees*[247]:

> '[T]he path of the law is strewn with examples of open and shut cases which, somehow, were not; of unanswerable charges which, in the event, were completely answered; of inexplicable conduct which was fully explained; of fixed and unalterable determinations that, by discussion, suffered a change. Nor are those with any knowledge of human nature who pause to think for a moment likely to underestimate the feelings of resentment of those who find that a decision against them has been made without their being afforded any opportunity to influence the course of events.'

(iv) The new 'standard procedure' for dismissal and discipline

A fundamental part of the government's programme in the Employment Act 2002 to reduce the number of tribunal applications by encouraging alternative dispute resolution is the enactment of a new 'standard procedure' to be used in disciplinary and dismissal cases. This was backed by research commissioned by the Department of Trade and Industry (DTI) which showed a worrying level of

---

245 [1988] ICR 370, [1988] IRLR 215, CA; the passage cited is at 377 and 218 respectively.
246 This can be seen from the decision of a differently constituted Court of Appeal in *Dillett v National Coal Board* [1988] ICR 218, where on facts similar to those in *McLaren* they confirmed a decision that a dismissal without a hearing in the middle of the miners strike was *fair*, but largely on the ground that that had been the view of the tribunal on the particular facts of the case and it was not open to an appellate court to reverse them (see p 504 above).
247 [1970] Ch 345 at 402, [1969] 2 All ER 274 at 309.

tribunal cases in which either no or virtually no use had been made of any form of internal procedures in order to resolve the issue without recourse to a tribunal.[248] The Act itself lays down the outlines of what is to be the new system, but a great amount is left to be fleshed out by regulations. At the time of writing, these had not been produced and so some of what follows remains speculative; the commencement date was also uncertain, but these provisions are almost certain to come in during the currency of this edition.

The standard procedure is laid down in Schedule 2, Part 1 to the 2002 Act. It states that the employer must set out in writing the employee's alleged conduct or characteristics, or other circumstances, which lead him to contemplate dismissing or taking disciplinary action against the employee, send this to the employee, inviting them to attend a meeting. This must take place before action is taken (except for suspension) and after the employee has been informed of the basis of the employer's grounds and has had a reasonable opportunity to consider his response[249]. The employee must take all reasonable steps to attend the meeting[250]. After it, the employer must inform the employee of his decision and notify him of the right to appeal. If the employee notifies the employer of his wish to appeal, the employer must invite him to a further meeting, which again the employee must take all reasonable steps to attend. After the appeal meeting the employer must inform the employee of the final decision[251]. Four general requirements are set out for any of the statutory procedures – (1) each step and action must be taken without unreasonable delay; (2) the timing and location of meetings must be reasonable; (3) meetings must be conducted in a manner that enables both employer and employee to explain their cases[252]; (4) at an appeal meeting, the employer should, so far as reasonably practicable, be represented by a more senior manger than at the first meeting[253]. The normal statutory right to be accompanied by a follow employee or union official is stated to apply[254].

Enforcement of these new requirements is to be by novel provisions, using both contract law and unfair dismissal law. The statutory procedure may be deemed to be incorporated into all contracts of employment[255]. Moreover, if in a statutory

---

248 'Findings of the 1998 Survey of Employment Tribunal Applications (Surveys of Applicants and Employers)' (Employment Relations Research Services, No 13, DTI, 2002). A survey of 2,700 ET cases found that only 58% of employers and 32% of applicants said that existing procedures had been fully followed; 65% of employers and 60% of applicants said that there had been no meeting between them to try to resolve the dispute; 39% of employers and 35% of applicants said that there had been no internal attempts at all to try to resolve the dispute.

249 Employment Act 2002, Sch 2, paras 1, 2(1), (2). There is a 'modified procedure' in paras 4 and 5 which consists of setting out the employer's grounds and allowing an appeal (ie with no preliminary meeting stage); it is thought that this may be applied to summary dismissal cases.

250 Sch 2, para 2(3). Failure to do so would put the employee in breach of the procedure which could have serious consequences, as set out below. This provision might be particularly difficult to apply in an occupational stress case where the employee claims to be too stressed to attend a meeting, even though this might lead to an impasse. At what stage will the employer be justified in proceeding in the employee's absence?

251 Sch 2, paras 2(4), 3.

252 This is in line with existing unfair dismissal law which requires *overall* fairness but stops short of any inalienable rights, eg to conduct cross-examination (see p 537 above).

253 Sch 2, paras 11–13.

254 Sch 2, para 4. See p 538 above.

255 Employment Act 2002, s 30. This may have the side-effect that any dismissal in breach of the procedure will constitute a *wrongful* dismissal at common law, in addition to the consequences specifically set out in the Act. As well as (at least technically) opening up an action for damages, this could affect a case where the employer wants to rely on a post-termination restraint clause or garden leave clause, which might be invalidated.

action before a tribunal leading to an award of compensation, it appears to the tribunal that the procedure had not been completed, there is to be an increase in compensation (where the employer was to blame) or a decrease in compensation (where the employee was to blame) by between 10 and 50%, unless there are 'exceptional circumstances' making it unjust or inequitable to do so[256]. From the employer's point of view, however, it will be even more fundamental because the new Employment Rights Act 1996, section 98A ('Procedural fairness') will state that a dismissal without completion of the standard procedure (wholly or mainly attributable to the failure of the employer) *will be unfair* space with (in addition to the above provisions on compensation) on extra award of four weeks pay.

What will be the effects of these new statutory rules? Four points are ventured. The first is that it is vital to remember that they do *not* replace or invalidate the ACAS Code of Practice which provides for more subtle procedures (for example, the new standard procedure does not mention warnings, which will continue to come within the ACAS Code) and will still be essential evidence for a tribunal determining the fairness of a dismissal. It is likely that, for an employer seeking to establish a fair dismissal, compliance with the new statutory procedure will be a necessary condition, but *not* a sufficient one[257]. The second is that many good employers have far more sophisticated procedures of their own. How will these interact with the new statutory procedure? The latter will have to be complied with anyway, but some managers might be tempted towards 'dumbing down' to apply only the statutory version. This, it is submitted, would be most unwise. Tribunals will still look at the ACAS Code (at the very least) and an employer will still gain significant brownie points by being seen to go through a more sophisticated system than that. Moreover, the new section 98A will contain a major advantage for such an employer. It will state that, in relation to any part of a procedure that is more advanced than the standard procedure, if an employer fails to follow any of that part the dismissal will still *not* be unfair if the employer 'shows that he would have decided to dismiss the employee if he had followed the procedure'[258]. This is a strong argument against dumbing down. The third point is that many detailed points remain (at the time of writing) to be resolved by the eventual regulations – at what point in a disciplinary procedure will the new standard procedure apply (presumably not to a first oral warning)? How will 'failure to comply' be defined? What permissible excuses will there be for a party not to go through the procedure? Although it is clear that the new procedure applies to misconduct and incapability cases, how will it apply to redundancy dismissals (where the current law is that an individual hearing is *not* always required)? The fourth point concerns application. The new procedure is clearly aimed to put pressure on to the bad employer to do at least *something* by way of a reasonable procedure before the case spills out into a tribunal. However, it will apply to *all* employers. There may be a temptation for the good employer to think

---

256 S 31.

257 One view, put forward by many employment lawyers and the TUC, was that if the government wanted to enact a basic, mandatory procedure they should simply have enacted the ACAS Code, rather than slipping a sub-ACAS procedure underneath it, potentially clouding the waters.

258 This in effect reintroduces into procedures in excess of the standard procedure the old 'it made no difference' defence in *British Labour Pump Ltd v Byrne* [1979] ICR 347, [1979] IRLR 94 which was overruled in *Polkey v AE Dayton Services Ltd* [1988] ICR 142, [1987] IRLR 503, HL: see p 539 above.

that nothing needs to be done because they already have a superior system anyway. While there may be much truth in this, it must still be remembered that the standard procedure *must* be complied with in detail, and so even the good employer must ensure that its existing procedure requires full compliance with the new statutory one, particularly as the latter is backed by the regime of automatic unfairness.

(v) Grievances and the new standard procedure

Grievance procedures have long been an important element in good industrial practice and this has been reflected in employment law. There is an implied term in a contract of employment that an employer will deal properly and timeously with a grievance[259], and when the ACAS Code of Practice was reissued in 2000 it contained for the first time detailed advice on the drafting of such a procedure. This process is to be taken further when the new dispute resolution procedures are brought into force, under the Employment Act 2002. In parallel with the new standard procedure for dismissal and discipline considered above, Schedule 2, Part 2 to the 2002 Act contains a standard grievance procedure, which again may be deemed part of all contracts of employment. Under this, the employee must set out the grievance in writing and send it to the employer who must invite the employee to attend a meeting to discuss it. The employee must inform the employer of the basis for the grievance and the employer must have a reasonable opportunity to consider his response; the employee must take all reasonable steps to attend the meeting[260]. After the meeting the employer must inform the employee of his decision and notify him of the right to appeal. If the employee informs the employer that he wishes to appeal, the employer must invite him to a further meeting, which the employee must take all reasonable steps to attend. After this, the employer must inform the employee of his final decision[261].

As before, much remains to be fleshed out by regulations. One key point will be the setting out of the circumstances in which an employee will be excused from the requirement to use the procedure, eg where to do so would endanger the employee's mental or physical well-being, especially in harassment or victimisation cases.

Enforcement measures are set out in the legislation. Not only will non-compliance be subject to the 10 to 50% increase or decrease of compensation (depending on whether the non-compliance was due to the fault of the employer or employee)[262], but from the employee's perspective there are even stronger initial incentives to use the standard procedure. Subject to any exceptions or modifications in regulations, the statute states that an employee who has not gone through the first stage of the procedure (setting out the grievance in writing

---

259 See p 161 above.
260 Employment Act 2002, Sch 2, paras 6, 7(1)–(3). The four 'general requirements' set out above in relation to the disciplinary procedure also apply here; see n 253 above. As with the disciplinary procedure there is a modified grievance procedure in paras 9 and 10, comprising only a written statement of grievance and a written response by the employer; at the time of writing, its potential use remained uncertain.
261 Sch 2, paras 7(4), 8. Again, the statutory right to be accompanied by a fellow employee or union official applies: para 14.
262 S 31; see n 256 above in the context of the disciplinary procedure.

and sending it to the employer) will be barred from presenting a claim to a tribunal in respect of that matter; where that first stage has been complied with, there will still be a twenty-eight-day delay before tribunal proceedings can be commenced, to allow the employer to respond. There will thus be considerable pressure on an employee to go through the standard procedure and not have recourse immediately to tribunal proceedings. This may have an indirect effect on constructive dismissal. Hitherto there has been *no* legal obligation on a leaving employee to tell the employer why he or she is going (let alone raise a formal grievance); thus an employee might leave without the employer realising that there had been a problem, and still claim unfair dismissal[263]. That rule will not be directly altered, *but* once the standard grievance procedure is in place that particular form of constructive dismissal (which gives the employer no chance to put matters right) may well become much less common, because of the procedural disadvantages to the employee of so acting. If this is indeed to be the effect, it will be very much in line with the government's stated policy aims in this area generally.

4 THE DEFINITION OF DISMISSAL AND THE DATE OF TERMINATION

(i) Dismissal

The existence of a dismissal is a vital jurisdictional factor in the laws relating to unfair dismissal and redundancy. In most cases it is obvious that there has been a dismissal, but in cases of doubt the onus is upon the applicant to prove that he is dismissed; if he fails to do so, he cannot proceed with his claim. In particular, a tribunal will have no jurisdiction to hear the claim if the true construction of the facts is that the termination of employment was brought about by some factor other than dismissal (for example, frustration or mutual consent)[264] or that the employee resigned (see below). Dismissal is therefore a central concept in this area of law and has not been without its problems[265].

(a) The definition of dismissal[266]

Dismissal is defined for the purposes of unfair dismissal and redundancy in sections 95 and 136 respectively of the Employment Rights Act 1996. These definitions are similar and envisage dismissal arising in one of three situations:
(a) where the contract is terminated by the employer either with or without notice;
(b) where a limited-term contract expires or otherwise terminates without being renewed;
(c) where the *employee* terminates the contract, with or without notice, in circumstances such that he is *entitled* to terminate it without notice by reason of the employer's conduct.

Category (a) covers the usual case of dismissal, where the employer clearly dispenses with the employee's services either summarily or by giving him notice (or by giving him wages in lieu thereof). As it means the termination of a particular

---

263 *Weatherfield Ltd v Sargent* [1999] IRLR 94, CA; see p 551 below.
264 For modes of termination other than dismissal, see pp 446–459 above.
265 See Elias 'Unravelling the concept of dismissal' (1978) 7 ILJ 16 and 100.
266 See *Harvey* DI [201].

contract, there can be a category (a) dismissal (and hence a claim for unfair dismissal) even though the employee is still working for the same employer under a new contract (which may be particularly useful for the employee where the employer has unilaterally insisted on radically different terms of employment, sufficient to constitute a 'new' contract, rather than just a modification of the existing one)[267]. It has also been held to cover cases where at first sight the employee appears to have resigned, but evidence then clearly establishes that the resignation was procured by the employer either by fraud[268], pressure[269] or ultimatum ('resign or be sacked')[270]; this has been done by concentrating, as a matter of fact, on the question – who *really* terminated the employment. This question may also be of importance where there is an ambiguous or hot-headed 'resignation'; while an employer may rely on a clear statement by the employee, there may be an onus on him to investigate further if there are special factors or circumstances leading up to the employee's actions, and failure to do so may mean that what eventually occurred was actually a dismissal and in all likelihood an unfair dismissal[271]. One point of historical importance to note (explaining certain older cases) is that at one time the tribunals and courts sought to extend this head of dismissal to cover matters now covered by category (c) (ie constructive dismissal), because that category (c) for redundancy purposes used to be more narrowly drafted[272], and for unfair dismissal purposes was not expressly included in the legislation until 1974[273]; thus in certain cases category (a) was stretched to cover applicants who would otherwise have fallen outside the legislation for one of these reasons, but there is now no need for this stretching and so such cases should not necessarily be viewed as good law in this context, since the type of dismissal in question should now be considered under category (c)[274].

267 This is the rule in *Hogg v Dover College* [1990] ICR 39 which, while only likely to apply on strong facts (of a major change in terms imposed by the employer on a reluctant workforce), was affirmed and applied in *Alcan Extrusions v Yates* [1996] IRLR 327. Its importance is that, unlike constructive dismissal (the usual possibility in a case of unilateral change by the employer), the employees can claim unfair dismissal while keeping their jobs.

268 *Makin v Grews Motors (Bridport) Ltd* (1986) Times, 18 April, CA.

269 *Caledonian Mining Co Ltd v Bassett* [1987] ICR 425, [1987] IRLR 165, applying *Martin v Glynwed Distribution Ltd* [1983] ICR 511, [1983] IRLR 198, CA; *Hellyer Bros Ltd v Atkinson* [1992] IRLR 540, EAT; *Lassman v De Vere University Arms Hotel* [2003] ICR 44.

270 *East Sussex County Council v Walker* (1972) 7 ITR 280; *Martin*, n 269 above. However, these cases must be carefully distinguished from – (i) cases where the employer has merely indicated a general intention to dismiss at some time in the future (eg on a planned future factory closure): *Haseltine Lake & Co Ltd v Dowler* [1981] ICR 222, [1981] IRLR 25; *International Computers Ltd v Kennedy* [1981] IRLR 28, (ii) cases where an employee under threat of dismissal reaches acceptable terms on which to leave (see p 551 n 303 below). These will be ordinary resignations.

271 *Kwik Fit (GB) Ltd v Lineham* [1992] ICR 183, [1992] IRLR 156. One problem is, of course, that in such extreme circumstances the language used tends not to be that contained in s 95; more often a tribunal will have to decide instead whether telling the employer where to insert the job, in graphic anatomical detail, constitutes an unambiguous resignation.

272 For category (c) to apply, the employee had to leave *without* notice (Redundancy Payments Act 1965, s 3(1)(c), now repealed): *Marriott v Oxford and District Co-operative Society Ltd (No 2)* [1970] 1 QB 186, [1969] 3 All ER 1126, CA.

273 See the Industrial Relations Act 1971, s 23(2), in force between 1971 and 1974; the NIRC filled this gap by construing category (a) as extending to constructive dismissals for unfair dismissal purposes in *Sutcliffe v Hawker Siddeley Aviation Ltd* [1973] ICR 560, [1973] IRLR 304, NIRC.

274 See the explanation of *Marriott*'s case by Lord Denning MR in *Western Excavating (ECC) Ltd v Sharp* [1978] ICR 221 at 227, [1978] IRLR 27 at 29, CA.

Where under category (a) an employee is given notice of dismissal, he may wish to leave his job before expiry of that notice (for example, where, being about to be made redundant, he finds another job which he wishes to start immediately). In such circumstances he would normally be in a difficult position for if he gave notice to leave he might be construed as having resigned or terminated the employment by mutual consent with his employer[275]; in either case there would be no dismissal and so he would lose his unfair dismissal and redundancy rights. To avoid this pitfall, the legislation includes the concept of 'early notice'[276], so that if, during the currency of the employer's notice, the employee gives counter-notice to terminate the employment at an earlier date he may leave and still be taken to have been dismissed by the employer. It must be noted here, however, that the provisions relating to early notice for redundancy purposes are narrower than those for unfair dismissal purposes in two ways – (i) the employee must give his counter-notice in writing, and (ii) the counter-notice must be given during the *obligatory* period of the employer's notice (ie the period which the employer must by law give, either under the individual contract, or by virtue of the minimum notice requirements[277], whichever is the longer). These requirements used to exist for unfair dismissal purposes also, but were removed by the Employment Protection Act 1975.

The original version of category (b) existed to safeguard the position of employees under fixed term contracts and used that terminology. In practice, most cases under this heading will still concern fixed-term (ie time limited) contracts, but in 2002 the wording was altered to cover all forms of limited-term contracts, to be consistent with the Fixed-term Worker Directive (in particular to cover 'task' or 'purpose' contracts). Expiry (whether by time or some other limiting event) without renewal is deemed to be a dismissal, so that in an unfair dismissal action, the employer will have to show that the reason for failure to renew was a fair one[278]. The meaning of 'limited term contract' is considered above[279].

(b) Constructive dismissal

While categories (a) and (b) have not been without difficulties, it is category (c) which has been most contentious. This sets out the statutory definition of 'constructive dismissal' which, as seen above, was always in the redundancy payments legislation and was read into the unfair dismissal provisions[280] before being expressly included in 1974. Constructive dismissal occurs where, although it is the employee who appears to terminate the employment by walking out, it can be said that the real reason for termination was in some way the prior conduct of the employer; it is necessary in order to avoid the employer being able to force

---

275 See p 456 above, under 'Mutual consent'.
276 Employment Rights Act 1996, ss 95(2) and 136(3). The counter-notice given by the employee may be of any length; it does not have to be of the length required by his contract (or even the statutory minimum of one week under s 86): *Ready Case Ltd v Jackson* [1981] IRLR 312; *quaere* what if it was only a few hours, or even minutes? The employer must have given *actual* notice for these provisions to apply; it is not enough that he has made some general statement of a possible future dismissal: see p 460 n 83 bove.
277 S 86.
278 *Terry v East Sussex County Council* [1976] ICR 536, [1976] IRLR 332, approved by the Court of Appeal in *Fay v North Yorkshire County Council* [1986] ICR 133, [1985] IRLR 247.
279 P 454 above, under 'Expiry of fixed term contracts'.
280 *Sutcliffe v Hawker Siddeley Aviation Ltd* [1973] ICR 560, [1973] IRLR 304, NIRC.

or goad the employee to leave his employment and then say that the employee in fact resigned and so was not dismissed. When it is established, it means that for statutory purposes the contract is terminated by the employer and so, for example, under these definitional provisions there has never been any continuing obligation on the employee to exhaust established grievance procedures – he could simply leave and make an immediate claim for unfair dismissal[281]. This is clearly the most contentious kind of dismissal, for there is no express act of dismissal by the employer. It must be remembered, however, that a constructive dismissal is *not* necessarily unfair and so a tribunal, even if it finds in the employee's favour on constructive dismissal, must still go on to consider fairness in the ordinary way; in many cases there will be little argument on this and the dismissal will, in the nature of things, be unfair, but this is not automatically so and there may be cases where, even though the employee had technically the right to walk out, the employer may be able to show that it was fair to act as he did[282].

The key element of the definition of constructive dismissal is that the employee must have been *entitled* to leave without notice because of the employer's conduct. What does 'entitled' mean? There were two possible interpretations of this crucial word – first that the employee could leave when the employer's behaviour towards him was so unreasonable that he could not be expected to stay, and second that the employer's conduct had to be so grave that it constituted a repudiatory breach of the contract of employment, ie that the employee was *contractually* entitled to leave. Clearly the second is a narrower approach, and it was argued that the first was more in line with the overall approach in unfair dismissal cases of looking at the reasonableness of the employer's conduct. Following an initial period of uncertainty, with conflicting decisions, the Court of Appeal held in *Western Excavating (ECC) Ltd v Sharp*[283] that the contractual approach is the correct one, Lord Denning MR defining it as follows:

'If the employer is guilty of conduct which is a significant breach going to the root of the contract of employment, or which shows that the employer no longer intends to be bound by one or more of the essential terms of the contract, then the employee is entitled to treat himself as discharged from any further performance. If he does so, then he terminates the contract by reason of the employer's conduct. He is constructively dismissed. The employee is entitled in those circumstances to leave at the instant without giving any notice at all or, alternatively, he may give notice and say that he is leaving at the end of the notice. But the conduct must in either case be sufficiently serious to entitle him to leave at once.'

---

281 *Seligman and Latz Ltd v McHugh* [1979] IRLR 130. There is an interesting overlap here with the law on jobseeker's allowance – if the employee leaves 'voluntarily without just cause' he can be disqualified for benefit for up to 26 weeks (see p 656 below); if, however, he had enough reason to leave for the purposes of establishing constructive dismissal, he should normally be able to show 'just cause', and so he can leave the employment and validly claim benefit.

282 *Savoia v Chiltern Herb Farms Ltd* [1982] IRLR 166, CA. Note, however, the unenthusiastic approach taken to this distinction by the EAT in *Cawley v South Wales Electricity Board* [1985] IRLR 89 where it was said that in a case where the two stages (constructive dismissal and then fairness under s 98) raise the same issues a constructive dismissal should almost invariably be held to be unfair; *sed quaere*.

283 [1978] ICR 221, [1978] IRLR 27, CA; the passage cited is at 226 and 29 respectively; *Courtaulds Northern Spinning Ltd v Sibson* [1988] ICR 451, [1988] IRLR 305, CA.

Thus, in a constructive dismissal case the tribunal is looking primarily for conduct by the employer[284] which is clearly a breach of one of the terms of the contract, and sufficiently important to be repudiatory on the part of the employer[285]. Certain examples may be fairly obvious, such as a refusal to pay wages[286], an unjustified demotion or suspension[287], failure to follow a contractually binding disciplinary procedure[288], unilateral alteration of job content without contractual authority[289], or insistence upon an unlawful or illegal order or the imposition of a penalty disproportionate to the offence[290]. It may, however, go wider than this, for the breach in question may be of an implied term as well as an express one, and therefore it is important to be able to say exactly which term it is claimed that the employer broke, and whether any such term ever actually existed in the contract[291]. The question of definition of contractual terms, considered in chapter 3 above, has thus been given renewed significance.

The contractual test as laid down in *Western Excavating (ECC) Ltd v Sharp* appears to be much narrower and more precise than the 'reasonableness' test, and at first seemed to be a significant restriction on constructive dismissal. However, this has

284 Conduct by an immediate superior (eg a supervisor) may be enough to justify walking out, even if the employer later argues that that superior did not actually have the power to dismiss: *Hilton Industrial Hotels (UK) Ltd v Protopapa* [1990] IRLR 316.

285 It has been held by the Court of Appeal that the question of whether a particular breach of contract is sufficient to be repudiatory (for the purpose of establishing constructive dismissal) is one of mixed fact and law, so that the EAT should rarely interfere with a tribunal's decision on this point, provided there was some evidence on which to base that decision: *Pedersen v Camden London Borough Council* [1981] ICR 674n, [1981] IRLR 173, CA. In *Dutton & Clark Ltd v Daly* [1985] ICR 780, [1985] IRLR 363 the EAT went further and held that the range of reasonable responses test (p 571 below) should be applied by the tribunal when deciding this question, but it is arguable that ultimately this is inconsistent with the contractual test in *Western Excavating*. Although the test is contractual, seriously unreasonable conduct by the employer may be powerful *evidence* of breach of contract (in particular, the implied term of trust and respect): *Brown v Merchant Ferries Ltd* [1998] IRLR 682, NICA.

286 Even this major term is not sacrosanct, however, as every case must be considered on its facts; even a failure to pay wages might not be repudiatory in exceptional circumstances: *Adams v Charles Zub Associates Ltd* [1978] IRLR 551. Further, there is no implied term of an annual wage rise, so failure to give one will not necessarily amount to repudiatory conduct by the employer: *Murco Petroleum Ltd v Forge* [1987] ICR 282, [1987] IRLR 50; likewise, there is no implied term that there will never be a pay decrease: *White v Reflecting Roadstuds Ltd* [1991] ICR 733, [1991] IRLR 331; on the other hand, the Court of Appeal held in *Cantor Fitzgerald International v Callaghan* [1999] ICR 639, [1999] IRLR 234 (a common law action, but on the same point) that failure to pay any element of remuneration, however minor, will usually be repudiatory. For detailed consideration of matters held to be repudiatory in the past, see *Harvey* DI [425].

287 *McNeill v Charles Crimm (Electrical Construction) Ltd* [1984] IRLR 179, EAT.

288 *Post Office v Strange* [1981] IRLR 515, EAT. This could take on renewed significance under the Employment Act 2002, s 30, which provides for the new statutory minimum disciplinary procedure (in Sch 2) to be part of all contracts of employment.

289 *Millbrook Furnishing Industries Ltd v McIntosh* [1981] IRLR 309; where the alteration is only temporary and for pressing business need, it *may* be arguable that it is not enough to be repudiatory, but such an argument failed in the *Millbrook* case. The practical answer for the employer is to incorporate a flexibility clause in the contract in the first place.

290 *BBC v Beckett* [1983] IRLR 43; *Cawley v South Wales Electricity Board* [1985] IRLR 89; this class of case is more interesting, for here the employer may technically have the contractual power to impose the penalty in question, but semble must still act in accordance with some sort of proportionality which is presumably implied into the contractual disciplinary rules; these cases are considered at p 142 above.

291 A good example is *Dryden v Greater Glasgow Health Board* [1992] IRLR 469 (no implied term allowing smoking); it was also held there that if a change of practice is lawful under the contract (there, the imposition of a no-smoking policy) the fact that it bears more heavily on one employee than on others is *not* a ground for constructive dismissal.

not been so, principally for two reasons. The first is that the Court of Appeal, while firmly basing the law upon ideas of contract, did not mean to impose a rigid test and envisaged some flexibility in its application; this can be seen particularly in the judgment of Lawton LJ:

'... I do not find it either necessary or advisable to express any opinion as to what principles of law operate to bring a contract of employment to an end by reason of an employer's conduct. Sensible persons have no difficulty in recognising such conduct when they hear about it. ... Lay members of the industrial tribunals ... do not spend all their time in court and when out of court they may use, and certainly will hear, short words and terse phrases which describe clearly the kind of employer of whom an employee is entitled without notice to rid himself. This is what [constructive dismissal] is all about; and what is required for the application of this provision is a large measure of common sense.[292] '

The second, and more far-reaching, reason is that in subsequent cases, the EAT has shown itself ready to read into contracts of employment a new term obliging the employer to treat the employee with trust and respect (though this has been variously expressed)[293] . To a large extent this development has outflanked the more purely contractual approach of the Court of Appeal in *Western Excavating (ECC) Ltd v Sharp*, so that harsh and unreasonable conduct by the employer might be construed by the tribunal as breach of this implied term of mutual respect, giving rise to a constructive dismissal[294]. Thus, in the outcome, the contractual approach may differ little from a simple 'reasonableness' approach[295] , and indeed a tribunal or court may now be impatient with an excessively contractual or technical argument by an employer which is aimed at frustrating the protective policy behind constructive dismissal[296]. However, there remain two main qualifications. The first is that if the 'conduct' in question consists simply of the

---

292 [1978] ICR 221 at 229, [1978] IRLR 27 at 30, CA. Generally speaking, the test is objective, in that the employer's conduct does *not* have to be intentional or in bad faith before it may be repudiatory: *Post Office v Roberts* [1980] IRLR 347. In line with this, 'seriously unreasonable' conduct can be *evidence* of contractual breach: *Brown v Merchant Ferries Ltd* [1998] IRLR 682, NICA. However, one class of case has imported a potentially subjective test – in *Frank Wright & Co (Holdings) Ltd v Punch* [1980] IRLR 217 it was held that where there is a genuine dispute as to the meaning of a contractual term and the employer insists on implementing his genuine (but possibly mistaken) version of it, that it *not* a repudiatory breach (even if he is later proved to have been wrong). This principle has backing from the normal law of commercial contracts (see *Woodar Investment Development Ltd v Wimpey Construction (UK) Ltd* [1980] 1 All ER 571, [1980] 1 WLR 277, HL) but its application to the specialised area of constructive dismissal could have an unfortunately restrictive effect (see the strong criticisms in *Harvey*, D [486]ff); it was treated with caution in *Financial Techniques (Planning Services) Ltd v Hughes* [1981] IRLR 32, CA, but mentioned with approval obiter by Sir John Donaldson MR in *Bridgen v Lancashire County Council* [1987] IRLR 58, CA, and so the point remains unresolved.
293 See p 158 above.
294 Conduct which is serious enough to breach the term of trust and respect will always be serious enough to constitute a repudiatory breach by the employer for the purpose of establishing constructive dismissal: *Morrow v Safeway Stores* [2002] IRLR 9.
295 See *British Aircraft Corpn v Austin* [1978] IRLR 332 at 334, per Phillips J.
296 In *Greenaway Harrison Ltd v Wiles* [1994] IRLR 380 an employer, trying to force through a change of terms (normally giving rise to a constructive dismissal) in fact threatened to give the employees proper notice of dismissal in doing so. He contested their claim for constructive dismissal on the basis that he had acted *lawfully* under the contract, but the EAT refused to accept that and found for the employees, largely as a matter of policy.

employer exercising one of his definite contractual rights (for example, to make the employee move from site to site, where there is a mobility clause in the contract), the employee who refuses to comply *should* not, under the contractual approach, be able to claim constructive dismissal for there has been no breach of contract; however, it is argued elsewhere[297] that this may be changing, with the development by the courts of possible *overriding* implied terms, particularly that of trust and respect, which may impose limits on the *way* in which even express terms are applied and in so doing increase the scope for constructive dismissal. The second is that a particularly contractual approach has been taken by the Court of Appeal to the question of *anticipatory* breach by the employer; this is unlikely to occur often in practice but if it does (for example, by an employer announcing that he intends to implement unilateral changes of terms and conditions at some time in the future) it has been held that the employer may retract his intended repudiation as long as he does so before the employee has unequivocally accepted it and terminated the contract in anticipation[298].

Although the theory behind constructive dismissal is that it is the employer who terminates the contract for statutory purposes, in practice it will usually be the employee who takes the final step by resigning and walking out, thus showing that he has accepted the employer's repudiation as concluding the contract. If the employee does not take such action, or does so after a delay, there is the danger (particularly in cases where the employer's conduct consists of a unilateral proposal to change the terms of employment) of this being construed as an agreement by the employee to a variation in the contract; if this is so there is no constructive dismissal, even if the employee later resigns. To avoid this danger, the employee should make up his mind quickly whether to leave[299], or, if his economic circumstances are such that he feels he has to continue working for a short period following the conduct in question, he should let it be known that he does not agree to that conduct and is working under protest. The courts and tribunals have taken a realistic view of this[300], but of course the employee cannot work under protest indefinitely and is expected to decide what his final response is to be within a reasonable period. This is because it remains the legal position that the employee must be able to show that he left *in response to* the employer's conduct (ie the causal link must be shown). However, this itself is to be viewed realistically (given the employee's difficult position), and so it has been held

---

297 See p 140 above.
298 *Norwest Holst Group Administration Ltd v Harrison* [1985] ICR 668, [1985] IRLR 240, CA.
299 *Western Excavating (ECC) Ltd v Sharp* [1978] ICR 221 at 226, [1978] IRLR 27 at 29, respectively per Lord Denning MR; *Land and Wilson v West Yorkshire Metropolitan County Council* [1981] ICR 334, [1981] IRLR 87, CA. Note, however, that even if the employee must be taken to have consented to previous repudiations by the employer, it may be possible to rely on the *fact* of those repudiations having occurred as evidence of overall breach of the general implied term of trust and respect: *Lewis v Motorworld Garages Ltd* [1986] ICR 157, [1985] IRLR 465, CA. One problem is that if the employee leaves without another job to go to, he may face a disqualification of up to 26 weeks for jobseeker's allowance (see p 656 below); if that happens he should appeal, arguing that he had 'just cause' because of his position in employment law and the need to protect his legal rights.
300 *Marriott v Oxford and District Co-operative Society Ltd (No 2)* [1970] 1 QB 186, [1969] 3 All ER 1126, CA; *Shields Furniture Ltd v Goff* [1973] 2 All ER 653, [1973] ICR 187; *Sheet Metal Components Ltd v Plumridge* [1974] ICR 373, [1974] IRLR 86; *W E Cox Toner (International) Ltd v Crook* [1981] ICR 823, [1981] IRLR 443. See too, in the context of *wrongful* dismissal, *Bliss v South East Thames Regional Health Authority* [1987] ICR 700, [1985] IRLR 308, CA.

that (1) there can still be a constructive dismissal if the employee waits to leave until he has found another job to go to[301] , and (2) as a matter of law there is no absolute requirement on the employee to tell the employer the real reason for leaving (given that the worse the employer's behaviour, the less likely the employee may be to want to dispute the position before getting out)[302] . The latter rule (highly inconvenient for HR professionals who may not have had reason to know what was going wrong until the employee left, thus giving them no chance to put it right) may be subject to qualification under the Employment Act 2002, section 32 (and supporting Regulations, still to be produced at the time of writing) which will place restrictions on the ability of an employee to complain to a tribunal unless they have raised a grievance with the employer in writing. Technically this will not reverse the case authority on the meaning of constructive dismissal, but it is clearly intended to be a considerable practical disincentive to an upset employee intending to leave without using internal grievance procedures first.

(c) Resignation by the employee

An employee may resign from his employment for any reason or none; if there is a reason and it is connected with the employer's conduct he may argue that he has been constructively dismissed, but otherwise he may not claim unfair dismissal or a redundancy payment for there is no dismissal[303] . An express resignation may be by unambiguous wording or, if the wording is ambiguous, by a combination of wording and circumstances from which a reasonable employer would understand the employee to be resigning[304] . However, the concept of resignation has caused problems when attempts have been made to apply it in circumstances other than those of express resignation by the employee, usually in order to deprive the tribunals of the jurisdiction to assess the merits in an unfair dismissal action by establishing that there was no dismissal in the first place.

Such problems have arisen in two principal ways. The first occurs where the employee simply walks out or where, as in *British Leyland (UK) Ltd v Ashraf*[305] the

---

301 *Jones v F Sirl & Son (Furnishers) Ltd* [1997] IRLR 493; *Waltons and Morse v Dorrington* [1997] IRLR 488, EAT.

302 *Weathersfield Ltd v Sargent* [1999] IRLR 94, CA, overruling on this point *Holland v Glendale Industries Ltd* [1998] ICR 493. Failure to make clear the reason for leaving when that might reasonably be expected could cast doubt on the genuineness of that reason, but only as a question of factual causation, not as a matter of law.

303 Also a resignation under threat of dismissal may constitute a dismissal (see p 545 above), unless the parties reach a mutually satisfactory agreement of terms (usually monetary) upon which the employee agrees to go; in that case it is a genuine resignation in spite of the previous threats – compare *Sheffield v Oxford Controls Co Ltd* [1979] ICR 396, [1979] IRLR 133 with *Thames Television Ltd v Wallis* [1979] IRLR 136. If the employer has already given the employee notice and the employee resigns during that period by giving counter-notice, he may still be 'dismissed' by virtue of ss 95(2) and 136(3) (see p 546 above).

304 *BG Gale Ltd v Gilbert* [1978] ICR 1149, [1978] IRLR 453; *Sothern v Franks Charlesly & Co* [1981] IRLR 278, CA. There may, however, be problems with a 'hotheaded' resignation which the employee seeks to retract almost immediately – theoretically a retraction would need the consent of the employer, but there have been cases where it has been said that a tribunal should take a broader, more common sense approach to whether the employee must be taken to have unequivocally resigned (even if, for example, the wording at the time left little to the imagination!): *Barclay v City of Glasgow District Council* [1983] IRLR 313; *Martin v Yeoman Aggregates Ltd* [1983] ICR 314, [1983] IRLR 49; *Sovereign House Security Services Ltd v Savage* [1989] IRLR 115, CA; *Kwik-Fit (GB) Ltd v Lineham* [1992] ICR 183, [1992] IRLR 156, EAT.

employee is allowed a definite period of leave from which he does not return on time. It is arguable that there needs to be a concept of 'resignation by conduct' to cover the first of these examples (ie where the employee never returns), but the problem with the second example was that it was tied in frequently with rather more spurious arguments on mutual termination or termination by agreement, for in such cases the employer may have allowed the leave on terms that 'if you do not return on time, your employment will terminate'; when the employee arrived back late, he was then told that his contract had ended automatically, without the need for a dismissal. This argument by the employer succeeded in *Ashraf*'s case, but its wider implications soon became obvious and a very different approach was taken. *Ashraf*'s case was first distinguished by the EAT[306], and finally overruled by the Court of Appeal in *Igbo v Johnson Matthey Chemicals Ltd*[307], on the ground that such an agreement for automatic termination (on failure to return from leave of absence) was void for contravening the Employment Rights Act 1996, section 203 which invalidates any agreement (whether in a contract of employment or not) which 'purports ... to exclude or limit the operation of any provision of this Act ...'[308] – this agreement limited the operation of sections 95 and 98 which give the right to claim unfair dismissal. The advantage from the employee's point of view of this reasoning is that even if he signs such an agreement in full knowledge of what he is signing (for example, because the employer will only grant leave if he does so), the agreement will still be of no legal effect under the anti-contracting-out provisions of the section.

The second way in which problems arose had a far greater potential for driving the proverbial horse-drawn transport through the unfair dismissal legislation. This was the idea (known variously as 'constructive resignation' or 'self-dismissal') that in some cases the employee may commit such a grave breach of contract that he must be considered to have resigned by his own act[309]. Once again, this meant that there was no dismissal, and so no action for unfair dismissal. Moreover, such an agreement might arise not only from unusual or drastic facts, but could also possibly be set up by an employer phrasing a final warning in terms that 'if this happens again, you will be considered as having dismissed yourself'. The employer succeeded in showing self-dismissal in *Gannon v Firth*[310] where the employees (pursuant to a dispute) walked out without informing the management and leaving the plant in a dangerous state; the EAT held that this repudiatory conduct terminated their employment, they had not been dismissed, and so they could not claim unfair dismissal. This was a short decision, citing no authority, but was followed in subsequent cases[311]. Fortunately, the position was clarified by the Court of Appeal in *London Transport Executive v Clarke*[312] which concerned the taking of unauthorised leave by an employee in the knowledge that if he did so his name would be 'removed from the books'. When he returned the employers

---

305 [1978] ICR 979, [1978] IRLR 330. For termination by mutual consent generally, see pp 456–459 above.
306 *Midland Electric Manufacturing Co Ltd v Kanji* [1980] IRLR 185; *Tracey v Zest Equipment Co Ltd* [1982] ICR 481, [1982] IRLR 268.
307 [1986] ICR 505, [1986] IRLR 215, CA.
308 See *Harvey* Q [827].
309 The theoretical basis for this in contract law can be found in the previously current idea that contracts of employment formed an exception to the normal rule that a repudiation is only effective when accepted by the innocent party; thus, on this 'automatic termination' theory (see p 470 above) the contract was in fact ended by the *employee's repudiation of it*, which did not need any further action on the part of the employer and did not constitute a 'dismissal'.
310 [1976] IRLR 415.

refused to take him back and he claimed unfair dismissal. The majority of the Court of Appeal (Templeman and Dunn LJJ) held that he had in fact been dismissed, applied the 'elective theory'[313] to repudiation of contracts of employment so that the employment was terminated by the employer's acceptance of the employee's repudiation, and overruled *Gannon v Firth* and the cases that had followed it; Lord Denning MR, dissenting, would have continued to apply the concept of self-dismissal, but the majority decision is clearly against it. Employers should not, however, throw up their hands in despair at this decision, for it was always arguable that the concept of self-dismissal was not particularly necessary anyway – if the employee's conduct was so drastic as to have been clearly repudiatory, then in most cases a tribunal is going to find his dismissal fair anyway (as was the ultimate conclusion of the Court of Appeal in *Clark*'s case, unanimously). The advantage of the majority's decision is that at least the fairness of the employer's conduct can be tested in such cases, rather than the employee's (possibly weak) claim being ruled out altogether on the jurisdictional point that technically there had been no dismissal[314].

(ii) The date of termination[315]

In the law relating to unfair dismissal and redundancy it is necessary for several reasons[316] to know when the employment ended; for unfair dismissal purposes this is known as the 'effective date of termination' and for redundancy purposes the 'relevant date'. The principal rules relating to these dates are found in the Employment Rights Act 1996, sections 97 and 145, and are as follows:

(a) Where the contract is terminated by notice (whether given by the employer or employee) – the date that the notice expires (whether or not the notice was of proper length)[317].

(b) Where the contract is terminated without notice – the date on which the termination takes effect[318].

(c) Where a fixed-term or other limited-term contract expires without renewal – the date on which the termination takes effect.

(d) Where the employee under notice gives counter-notice to terminate the employment sooner – the date of expiry of the counter-notice.

These rules are relatively straightforward, except in the case of head (b) above, which unfortunately has attracted a difference of judicial opinion on one of its most important applications. It is clear that (b) applies to summary dismissals, and in *Stapp v Shaftesbury Society*[319] the Court of Appeal affirmed that the simple

---

311 Particularly *Smith v Avana Bakeries Ltd* [1979] IRLR 423 and *Kallinos v London Electric Wire* [1980] IRLR 11.

312 [1981] ICR 355, [1981] IRLR 166, CA.

313 See p 470 above.

314 Presumably there is now also the secondary ground that if the purported self-dismissal came from an agreement that 'if you do that again, you will be deemed to have dismissed yourself', that agreement itself will be void under s 203 (applying *Igbo v Johnson Matthey Chemicals Ltd*, n 307 above).

315 See *Harvey* DI [704].

316 Eg for calculating the period of continuous employment (for calculation and possibly for qualification purposes) and for determining the date from which the three and six-month limitation periods run.

317 *TBA Industrial Products Ltd v Morland* [1982] ICR 686, [1982] IRLR 331, CA.

318 This may even mean a precise *time* on the date in question: *Octavius Atkinson & Sons Ltd v Morris* [1989] ICR 431, [1989] IRLR 158, CA.

rule that the date of termination is the date of the summary dismissal applies even if (i) that summary dismissal is affected while the employee is already under ordinary notice and (ii) the effect of the summary dismissal bringing the date of termination forward is to deprive the employee of the qualifying period for unfair dismissal which he would otherwise have attained. However, summary dismissal is only one aspect.

Far more common as a form of dismissal in practice is dismissal with wages in lieu of notice whereby the employer is rid of the employee immediately (particularly vital where the employee under notice would otherwise have access at work to the firm's computers or confidential information) but with payment of what the employee would have earned had he worked out his notice period. What is to be the date of termination – the date when the notice would have expired (ie under (a) above) or the date when the employee in fact leaves, albeit with a payment in lieu (ie under (b) above)? This could be particularly material on the question of whether a claim is brought in time, especially when the notice period is several weeks (for example, from which date does the three-month limit for bringing an unfair dismissal action run?), and could also affect whether the employee has satisfied the qualifying period for the right in question. The interests of certainty would be best served by simply opting for the date when the employee actually leaves (ie treating it as under (b) above, as if a summary dismissal), and this was for several years thought to be the case, after the decision of the Court of Appeal in *Dedman v British Building and Engineering Appliances Ltd*[320] . However, confusion was caused by the decision of the EAT in *Adams v GKN Sankey Ltd* [321] where it was suggested that the date of termination depends on the true construction to be placed on the dismissal – if it was expressed as a dismissal by notice (but with the employee not actually required to work out that notice), the date of termination should be the date of expiry of the notice; if, however, it was expressed as an instant dismissal (but with the payment of wages in lieu of notice as, in effect, compensation for wrongful dismissal), the date of termination should be the date the employee left. This distinction seems a thin one on which to base such an important concept as the date of termination and in practice may, one suspects, owe more to fortune than reality in its application. It certainly means that letters of dismissal should be drafted carefully, from the employer's point of view.

This 'construction' approach can also be seen in *Chapman v Letheby and Christopher Ltd* [322] where it was stated that the mere fact that a dismissal was stated to be with payment in lieu did not mean that it constituted an instant dismissal, and that the effect of the dismissal depended on the construction which would

---

319 [1982] IRLR 326, CA. It was suggested by the court that if the employee loses his statutory rights because of the summary dismissal, he should bring an action for *wrongful* dismissal claiming loss of statutory rights as a head of damage; see p 486 above. The fact that the summary dismissal was in breach of a contractually binding disciplinary procedure which would have taken some time to go through properly *cannot* be used to advance what is otherwise under the section the effective date of termination: *Batchelor v British Railways Board* [1987] IRLR 136, CA.

320 [1974] 1 All ER 520, [1974] ICR 53, CA, the leading case on the extension of time limits for commencing tribunal actions.

321 [1980] IRLR 416.

be placed on it by an ordinary, reasonable employee. However, in *Robert Cort & Son Ltd v Charman*[323] the EAT reverted to the straightforward *Dedman* view, stressing (i) the proper interpretation of the wording of section 97 and (ii) the need for absolute certainty on the effective date of termination, especially in the context of limitation periods (though the case itself concerned the question whether the employee had served the necessary qualifying period for an unfair dismissal action). This left the law in an uncertain state. The question was canvassed before the Court of Appeal in *Stapp v Shaftesbury Society*[324], but that case concerned a different aspect of dismissal without notice (considered above)[325]. However, Stephenson LJ, giving the principal judgment, did allude to the present problem at two stages; at one point he expressly approved of the statement of Browne-Wilkinson J in *Chapman v Letheby and Christopher Ltd* that any ambiguity in a dismissal notice should be construed against the employer (though without commenting on the construction approach generally), but later said:

> 'But the effect of summary dismissal in fixing the effective date of termination cannot be questioned. The case of *Cort* is a very recent application of what was laid down by this court some years ago in the case which it followed, *Dedman v British Building and Engineering Appliances Ltd.*'

The judgment in *Stapp*, is therefore at best ambiguous and subsequently in *Leech v Preston Borough Council*[326] the EAT pointed out that the well-worn phrase 'wages in lieu of notice' has two distinct meanings[327] and applied the 'construction' approach in *Adams* and *Chapman*. That must now be considered to be the correct approach, since it is consistent with the explanation of dismissal with wages in lieu generally by Lord Browne-Wilkinson in the leading case on deductions from wages, *Delaney v Staples*[328]; he in fact isolated *four* possible forms of such a dismissal[329], but they include the two principal forms alluded to in *Leech* and as, in his judgment, he explained that they operate on different grounds, it is reasonable to conclude that the EDT will be different, as the majority of the case law suggests.

322 [1981] IRLR 440; the facts in the case were distinctly ambiguous, showing the difficulties that this 'construction' approach can cause, though the EAT did say that ultimately any ambiguity should be construed against the employer, who should have drafted the letter of dismissal more carefully. *Quaere* – how would this apply to an oral dismissal with wages in lieu where no one can remember exactly what was said?

323 [1981] ICR 816, [1981] IRLR 437 (*Chapman v Letheby and Christopher Ltd* not referred to). The principal significance of the EAT's emphasis on the statutory interpretation of s.97 was that it enabled them to dispose of the employee's subtle arguments based on contractual ideas of repudiation and acceptance (see p 470 above); hopefully this case is authority that the 'elective' theory of repudiation does *not* apply for the purpose of fixing the date of termination for statutory purposes, so that an employee cannot push forward that date for some unspecified time simply by arguing that he never in fact accepted the employer's repudiation.

324 [1982] IRLR 326.

325 The case was principally argued on the point whether an employer could avoid statutory rights by wrongfully dismissing the employee (and after having given him proper notice at that). It was, however, a case of dismissal with wages in lieu (in effect, though not in the usual way), for he had been given notice, then when summarily dismissed during the notice period was told that he would in fact be paid for the whole of the rest of what should have been his notice period.

326 [1985] ICR 192, [1985] IRLR 337; *Cort*'s case is not cited in the judgment.

327 The 'grammatically accurate sense of compensation for summary dismissal without notice' or the 'more colloquial sense of payment to someone who is excused or prohibited from attending the workplace during the notice period'.

Four further points should be noted. The first is that where the employee is dismissed by being given less notice than the employer is obliged to give him by statute[330] , the date of termination is deemed to be the date it would have been had that statutory minimum been given, for certain purposes. Those purposes are computation of the qualifying period for claiming unfair dismissal and demanding a written statement of reasons for dismissal, calculation of the basic award for unfair dismissal, computation of the two-year qualifying period for a redundancy payment and calculation of the period of continuous employment by which such a payment is determined[331]. The second point is that if the employee has been dismissed, the fact that he is actively pursuing an appeal under the firm's grievance procedure does *not* mean that the date of termination is extended to the completion of that appeal process[332] . Moreover, this is likely to be of most significance when deciding when the three-month time limit for an unfair dismissal action begins to run and the Court of Appeal affirmed strongly that the fact of pursuing an internal appeal will *not* be a good reason to extend the three months' period in the tribunal's discretion[333] ; this inconvenient and possibly counter-productive rule (given the desirability of internal procedures being used rather than a tribunal complaint) is to be subject to relaxation by Regulations (yet to be made, at the time of writing) under the Employment Act 2002, section 33. The third point is that sections 97 and 145 do not state what the date of termination is to be in a case of constructive dismissal; it has been held that the EDT is the date of acceptance of the employer's repudiation of the contract, which will normally mean the date when the employee walks out, but it has also been held that an employee cannot use this argument to prolong the EDT past the date the employment *actually* ended[334] . The fourth, final, and perhaps most fundamental point on the EDT is that ultimately it is for the employer to get it right, so that any ambiguity is likely to be construed in the employee's favour[335] . In particular, there is in general no doctrine of *constructive* notice of dismissal, so that a dismissal by letter will only take effect when it is actually

328 [1992] ICR 483, [1992] IRLR 191, HL.
329 These are set out at p 461 above, along with the suggested EDTs, in the light of this discussion.
330 Employment Rights Act 1996, s 86. The employee can only claim an extension by the period of his *statutory* entitlement, not by the period of any more generous notice entitlement agreed in his contract: *Fox Maintenance Ltd v Jackson* [1978] ICR 110, [1977] IRLR 306. Note, however, that s 86(6) preserves the employer's right to dismiss summarily for gross misconduct, and so if an employer does so justifiably there can be *no* extension under the statute: *Lanton Leisure Ltd v White and Gibson* [1987] IRLR 119, EAT.
331 Employment Rights Act 1996, ss 97(2) and 145(5). The statutory extension is for these purposes *only*, it is not of general application: *Slater v John Swain & Son Ltd* [1981] ICR 554, [1981] IRLR 303; *Secretary of State for Employment v Cameron Iron Works* [1988] ICR 297 (revsd on other grounds [1989] ICR 664, [1989] IRLR 117, CA). In particular, note that it does *not* apply for the purposes of the three/six-month limitation periods for bringing tribunal proceedings.
332 *J Sainsbury Ltd v Savage* [1981] ICR 1, [1980] IRLR 109, CA. If however, the appeal is successful there is no break in continuity, as the appeal decision applies as from the date of the original dismissal: *Howgate v Fane Acoustics Ltd* [1981] IRLR 161, EAT.
333 *Palmer v Southend-on-Sea Borough Council* [1984] ICR 372, [1984] IRLR 119, CA; see p 514 above.
334 Contrast *G W Stephens & Son v Fish* [1989] ICR 324 with *BMK Ltd v Logue* [1993] ICR 601. Note, however, that there was introduced in 1982 an extension of time for certain purposes (akin to those in n 331 above) in the case of a constructive dismissal, the extension period being the amount of notice that should have been given under s 86 if it had been the employer who was terminating the employment: s 97(4).

received by the employee, even if that is later than expected by the employer (who will thus often be well advised to communicate the dismissal directly to the employee, or at the very least to use registered or recorded post so that the date of service can be ascertained)[336].

5 UNFAIR DISMISSAL

Just under 40% of the cases heard by tribunals each year concern claims of unfair dismissal. As is immediately obvious, such a claim is a much more realistic action to bring in most cases than the common law action for wrongful dismissal, and since its inception in 1971[337] this branch of industrial law has given rise to an enormous amount of case law. It is therefore particularly important in this context to bear in mind the dictum of Lord Denning MR cited at the beginning of this chapter and to appreciate that the only way to cope successfully with the intimidating case law is to concentrate on those cases which establish principles, points of interpretation or (at least when they are in fashion) general guidelines for the tribunals, and consider the rest as mere illustrations, interesting though they may be. One simple truth, so easy to overlook when surrounded by industrial law reports, is that unfair dismissal is *not* primarily a case law subject – primacy must remain with the relevant wording of the statute. Further, the statute in most contexts puts matters into the discretion of the tribunals (and expressly gives a restricted right of appeal to the EAT, on points of law only) and so, although for the sake of exposition the following discussion will look at the law under certain headings and will concentrate on the evolving rules relating to certain categories of dismissal of practical importance, it must be remembered that in many instances the seeming rules of law under discussion may only be guidelines to the factors to be taken into consideration by the tribunal in deciding upon what is usually the central issue in an unfair dismissal case, namely whether the employer's conduct in the dismissal was reasonable.

---

335 *Widdicombe v Longcombe Software Ltd* [1998] ICR 710 (ambiguous correspondence between employer and absent employee; EDT fixed as the date of the final, clearest letter, which came within the limitation period).

336 *McMaster v Manchester Airport plc* [1998] IRLR 112 (sick employee not receiving dismissal letter on the expected day of delivery because on a day trip to France; limitation period only flowed from the day of his return).

337 The provisions relating to unfair dismissal were first enacted in the Industrial Relations Act 1971; they were re-enacted in the first Schedule to the Trade Union and Labour Relations Act 1974, amended by the Employment Protection Act 1975, and then consolidated, first in the Employment Protection (Consolidation) Act 1978 and then in the Employment Rights Act 1996. The scheme of the provisions follows ILO Recommendation 119 (1963); revised ILO standards on dismissal worked out subsequently have not been adopted; see (1984) 13 ILJ 130. For detailed consideration of this branch of law, see *Harvey* Division DI, to which more detailed references are made below; also Dickens et al *Dismissed* (1983); Collins 'The meaning of job security' (1991) 20 ILJ 227; and, for a fundamental critique of the existing law, Collins *Justice in Dismissal* (1992) and Pitt 'Justice in dismissal – a reply to Hugh Collins' (1993) 22 ILJ 251.

(i) The right and the exclusions[338]

Subject to certain exclusions, the Employment Rights Act 1996, section 94 gives to every employee the right not to be unfairly dismissed. There are two principal qualifications for this right: first, the employee must have been 'dismissed' (a concept which is considered in head 4 above) and second, on the effective date of termination the employee must have been continuously employed by his employer for the necessary qualifying period, now one year (unless dismissed for a reason stated specifically not to require such qualifying service, such as one relating to membership or non-membership of a trade union, maternity, health and safety complaints, assertion of statutory rights or acting as an employee trustee of a pension scheme or as an elected employee representative). Initially, this period was six months, but it was raised by the previous government, first to a year in 1979 and then to two years in 1985[339]. The imposition of any such period had two aims. A long-term aim was to exclude (indirectly) part-timers from the right to claim unfair dismissal; this happened because in order to count time worked towards the required period of continuous employment at all, the employee had to work more than sixteen hours per week (or more than eight hours per week for five years). The second aim under the previous government, in line with its free market and deregulatory economic policy, was to lessen what have been perceived to be the adverse effects of employment law on business and the creation of jobs[340]; this aim was particularly important with regard to the significant lengthening of the period. This however was controversial; although it is the case that a qualifying period has the bona fide effect of allowing an employer to operate a fairly lengthy trial period for a new employee and assess suitability without having to face an unfair dismissal application, it was argued that the very long period of two years was operated more as a blanket initial immunity, and in recent years there was at least anecdotal evidence of some employers cynically using that immunity (particularly in areas of high labour turnover) by taking employees on for only eighteen months or thereabouts and then dismissing them as a matter of policy.

Both of these aims of the qualifying period have been subject to attack under EC law. The exclusion of part-timers no longer works because the sixteen-hour rule (and eight hours for five years rule) had to be removed[341] in order to comply with the ruling of the House of Lords in *R v Secretary of State for Employment, ex p Equal Opportunities Commission*[342] that those hours limitations had a disproportionate effect on female employees and so constituted indirect sex discrimination (contrary to Article 119 and the Equal Treatment Directive) which was not justified

---

338 See *Harvey* DI [24] ff.
339 Unfair Dismissal (Variation of Qualifying Period) Order 1985, SI 1985/782.
340 Lifting the Burden (Cmnd 951, 1985) ch 5.
341 Employment Protection (Part-time Employees) Regulations 1995, SI 1995/31; see p 190 above.
342 [1994] ICR 317, [1994] IRLR 176, HL. This seemed to open the floodgates to many backdated claims (under EC law, not under the prospective-only regulations) by employees who had not claimed unfair dismissal at the time because they worked too few hours. However, the courts prevented this happening by applying a very stringent approach to the three-month limitation period: *Biggs v Somerset County Council* [1996] ICR 364, [1996] IRLR 203, CA (where the applicant sought unsuccessfully to claim that she had been unfairly dismissed in 1976!); *Setiya v East Yorkshire Health Authority* [1995] ICR 799, [1995] IRLR 348 (refusal of late appeal to EAT).

by the Government's arguments on economic necessity. Thus, an employee with two years' continuous employment could claim unfair dismissal regardless of their hours of work[343]. However, the matter did not rest there, for the next stage was to attack the two-year qualifying period *itself* as sexually discriminatory (thus negativing the second aim). This was done in *R v Secretary of State for Employment, ex p Seymour-Smith*[344] in which the application for a declaration that the increase of the qualifying period in 1985 to two years was contrary to the Equal Treatment Directive was granted by the Court of Appeal; at further appeal, the House of Lords remitted the question to the ECJ which gave an exceptionally Delphic reply[345]. When the House of Lords reconsidered the case in the light of this, they finally held that the 1985 increase was *not* discriminatory (three Lords holding that any adverse effect was justified and two that there was no significant adverse effect in the first place)[346]. By this time, however, the present government had lowered the period to *one year* in any event legislatively[347], a far more satisfactory method of reform. The one-year period applies to a dismissal occurring on or after 1 June 1999 and, given that the challenge in *R v Secretary of State for Employment, ex p Seymour-Smith* failed, we have been spared any problems of backdating.

The right to bring an action is also subject to certain general exceptions, so that the following employees are excluded:
(a) *An employee who is over the retirement age on the effective date of termination* Section 109 excludes an employee who:

'… on or before the effective date of termination … has attained—
(a) in a case where—
(i) in the undertaking in which the employee was employed there was a normal retiring age for an employee holding the position held by the employee, and
(ii) the age was the same whether the employee holding that position was a man or a woman,
that normal retiring age, and
(b) in any other case, the age of sixty five.'

This formulation was substituted as from November 1987 by the Sex Discrimination Act 1986; the previous wording had allowed two forms of sex discrimination – first, there could be different contractual retiring ages for men and women, and secondly the 'fall back' in (b) was 65 for a man and 60 for a woman. Enforced retirement of a woman at an earlier age than a man could adversely affect her rights (especially pension rights when based on her *final* salary), and was held by the ECJ to be contrary to Directive 76/207/ EEC in *Marshall v Southampton and South West Hampshire Area Health Authority (Teaching)*[348], leading to the substitution of the present formulation.

The subsection thus creates two ages, the normal retiring age of the job (provided that it is sexually neutral) and the 'statutory' retiring age of 65,

---

343 In *Colley v Corkindale* [1995] ICR 965 an employee working one 51/2 hour bar shift every other Friday was able to claim unfair dismissal.
344 [1995] ICR 889, [1995] IRLR 464, CA.
345 C-167/97 [1999] ICR 447, [1999] IRLR 253, ECJ.
346 [2000] IRLR 263, HL.
347 Unfair Dismissal and Statement of Reasons for Dismissal (Variation of Qualifying Period) Order 1999, SI 1999/1436.
348 152/84: [1986] ICR 335, [1986] IRLR 140, ECJ; *Beets-Proper v F Van Lanschot Bankiers NV*: 262/84 [1986] ICR 706, ECJ.

and on the wording as it was originally cast it was generally understood that attainment of the latter excluded reliance on the former, so that if the normal retiring age for a job was 70 and the employee was dismissed when 68, he could not claim unfair dismissal because he had already reached the statutory age of 65. However, the House of Lords in *Nothman v Barnet London Borough*[349] held by a majority of 3–2, in an exercise in statutory interpretation astonishing to many people (including Lord Diplock in the minority), that that is not the correct interpretation of the section, for the majority decision was that the section does not create one test with two hurdles for the employee to clear, but instead creates two separate hurdles, one applying where there *is* a normal retiring age for the job and the other (the statutory 65) only applying if there is *no* such normal retiring age. Thus Miss Nothman, a teacher subject to a contractual retiring age of 65, was able to claim unfair dismissal when sacked at the age of 61, as she had not reached her 'normal retiring age'; the fact that she was over 60 was irrelevant, since that statutory retiring age (as it then stood) was not applicable to her. Thus, if there *is* a normal retiring age the tribunal must look at that; it is only if there is no such retiring age that it can apply the statutory 65 as the exclusory age. This is now made clearer in the present statutory wording ('... (b) *in any other case*, the age of sixty five.')

It may therefore be essential to decide whether in any given case there is a normal retiring age and, if so, what it is. This caused considerable problems over a series of cases, but is now governed by two House of Lords decisions. In *Waite v Government Communications Headquarters*[350] the House was faced with the problem of a discrepancy between what the contract said about retirement and what was argued to be the practical position of employees frequently being allowed to work past the contractual age. The decision was that the contractual age is presumed to be the normal retiring age, but that this presumption can be displaced by evidence that in practice persons in the position of the employee in question[351] have a reasonable expectation of working past the contractual age to some further age, which can then be considered as the normal retiring age. On the other hand, if the evidence only shows that employees regularly work past the contractual age to a variety of ad hoc ages, then there is *no* normal retiring age and so the statutory age of 65 applies. This was put clearly by Lord Fraser:

'The proper test ... is to ascertain what would be the reasonable expectation or understanding of the employees holding that position at the relevant time. The contractual retiring age will prima facie be the normal, but it may be displaced by evidence that it is regularly departed from in practice. The evidence may show that the contractual retiring age has been superseded by some definite higher age, and, if so, that will have become the normal retiring age. Or the evidence may

349 [1979] ICR 111, [1979] IRLR 35, HL; for the continuing story of Miss Nothman, see [1980] IRLR 65, CA.
350 [1983] ICR 653, [1983] IRLR 341, HL; previous case law in the EAT and Court of Appeal is now redundant: *Mauldon v British Telecommunications plc* [1987] ICR 450. Several of those cases had arisen in the same context as *Waite*, ie the policy of the Civil Service of a gradual reduction of the retirement age.
351 One problem with the idea of looking at the expectations of the *class* of employee is that if an employer gives a personal assurance to keep one employee on after his contractual retirement age that will not be sufficient since there is no class involved: *Age Concern Scotland v Hines* [1983] IRLR 477, EAT.

show merely that the contractual retiring age has been abandoned and that employees retire at a variety of higher ages. In that case there will be no normal retiring age and the statutory alternatives of 65 for a man and 60 for a woman will apply.[352] '

The application of these principles can be seen in *Hughes v DHSS*[353]; this was a case where the Civil Service conditions of employment stated 60 as the retirement age, but the practice was to allow employees (subject to conditions) to remain until 65. However, the applicants in question, having worked past 60, were caught by a change in departmental policy lowering the actual retirement age to 60. When they were compulsorily retired they claimed unfair dismissal but the House of Lords held that they fell within the exclusion – their 'reasonable expectation' may have been initially to work until 65, but by the date of their dismissal (which is the relevant time at which to apply the *Waite* principles) that expectation must have changed with the well-publicised change of departmental policy, which was thus effective to change the 'normal retiring age' within section 109. There have been moves to attack the age limitation under EC law. In *Nash v Mash/Roe Group Ltd*[354] an adventurous tribunal held that the age limitation is contrary to EC sex discrimination law (impacting disproportionately on men, who tend to work on past retiring age more often than women, and not being objectively justified) and so is to be disapplied. Initially, this apparently rogue decision seemed to lead nowhere, but a similar decision was then reached by another tribunal (on remission from the EAT) in *Rutherford v Town Circle (t/a Harvest)*[355]. This litigation may be appropriately timed because the whole question of age discrimination is now to be addressed under EC law in any event[356]; this may well lead to the abandonment of this age limitation on dismissal claims altogether.

(b) *Two miscellaneous categories of excluded persons* – share fishermen and the police[357].

---

352 [1983] ICR 111 at 662, [1983] IRLR 341 at 344. 'Abandoned' here merely refers to the existence of sufficient evidence to show significant departure from the contractual age: *Secretary of State for Scotland v Meikle* [1986] IRLR 208; statistical evidence may be important here: *Whittle v Manpower Services Commission* [1987] IRLR 441, EAT.

353 [1985] ICR 419, [1985] IRLR 263, HL, applied in *Highlands and Islands Development Board v MacGillivray* [1986] IRLR 210, Ct of Sess; *Whittle v Manpower Services Commission* (above), *Brooks v British Telecommunications plc* [1992] ICR 414, [1992] IRLR 66; CA and *Barber v Thames Television plc* [1992] ICR 661, [1992] IRLR 410, CA. A further point established in this case is that Lord Fraser's reference in *Waite* to the 'group' of employees holding the 'position' held by the applicant is covered by the statutory definition of 'position' in s 235, ie as pertaining to 'his status as an employee, the nature of his work and his terms and conditions of employment'. There can still be a normal retiring age where occasional, specific exceptions are made to it: *Barclays Bank plc v O'Brien* [1994] ICR 865, [1994] IRLR 580, CA; this case contains a very useful summary of the applicable principles by Peter Gibson LJ.

354 [1998] IRLR 168, ET.

355 [2002] IRLR 768, ET. For the EAT remission, see [2001] IRLR 599. A further appeal is expected at the time of writing.

356 The Equal Treatment Directive 2000/78/EC requires age discrimination to be covered by 2006, see p 399 above. The government intend to start consultation on the potentially widespread effects of this change in late 2003.

357 Employment Rights Act 1996, ss 199 and 200 respectively. On the meaning of 'share fisherman', see *Goodeve v Gilsons* [1985] ICR 401, CA. Employment protection legislation was in the main extended to the armed forces by the Trade Union Reform and Employment Rights Act 1993.

(c) *An employee governed by a dismissal procedures agreement designated by the Secretary of State's order as operating in substitution for the statutory scheme*[358] .

(d) *An employee whose dismissal was for the purpose of safeguarding national security*[359].

The Employment Relations Act 1999 made two important changes to the exceptions to the right to claim unfair dismissal. First, it repealed the provisions in the Employment Rights Act 1996, section 197 which used to permit an employer to put into a fixed-term contract of one year or more a clause excluding unfair dismissal rights on termination. There had been long-standing criticisms of this power, on the basis of abuse by employers (especially by the device of putting employees on to successive such contracts, possibly over a long period of time), and the government decided to abolish it altogether. Secondly, the 1999 Act also repealed section 196 of the 1996 Act, which used to disapply most of the rights in the latter (including unfair dismissal) where 'under the employee's contract of employment he ordinarily works outside Great Britain'. There was considerable case law on this wording[360], which tended to help a British employee sent temporarily to work abroad, but equally tended to prejudice a foreign employee temporarily working in Britain, as was seen particularly in *Carver v Saudi Arabian Airlines*[361] . When the Employment Relations Bill was before the House of Lords, a modest amendment to make this area fairer to foreign employees was proposed, but the government minister undertook (on a withdrawal of the amendment) to consider the matter. In fact, when the matter returned to the Lords the government suggested a far more radical solution, namely to repeal s 196 altogether. By now, the real impetus behind this was the need to comply with the Posted Workers Directive 96/71/EC which requires workers sent to work in another member state to have the same rights as workers in that state. Removal of the territorial bars in section 196 was perceived to be one way of doing this, and so this was done. What is to replace it? The government simply said that the matter would now be satisfactorily covered by the well-known rules of private international law(!), and a DTI press release said that the normal provisions of the Brussels and Rome Conventions should be used. However, it is possible that this was a serious mistake, because while these rules and provisions are capable of governing the proper law of, and jurisdiction in relation to, a *contract* (such as a contract of employment) it is arguable that they cannot govern the position in relation to a purely statutory right such as unfair dismissal[362] . If this is correct, what the government have done is to create a *hole* in the 1996 Act, so that we have

---

358 S 110. Only one industry (electrical contracting) opted for this form of collective contracting out and this was terminated in 2001. In some industries, ACAS arbitration on a voluntary basis could be resorted to under a firm's own procedures. As, however, they are not formally within s110 a dismissed employee could go to arbitration and *then* (if unsuccessful) claim unfair dismissal. In practice this is unlikely to happen, but it can – see, eg, *Cawley v South Wales Electricity Board* [1985] IRLR 89, EAT.

359 Employment Tribunals Act 1996, s 10. Note that this is an ad hoc security power; the long-term national security exclusion used in the GCHQ case was contained in the Employment Rights Act 1996 s 193, which was substantially narrowed by the Employment Relations Act 1999, Sch 8.

360 The leading cases were *Wilson v Maynard Shipbuilding Consultants AB* [1978] ICR 376, [1977] IRLR 491, CA; *Todd v British Midland Airways Ltd* [1978] ICR 959, [1978] IRLR 370, CA; and *Janata Bank v Ahmed* [1981] ICR 791, [1981] IRLR 457, CA.

361 [1999] 3 All ER 61, [1999] IRLR 370, CA.

362 There is no implied contractual right not to be unfairly dismissed: *Focsa Services (UK) Ltd v Birkett* [1996] IRLR 325, EAT.

a statute giving rights *without* the necessary statutory provisions on territorial jurisdiction[363]. The result would be that it would become a matter of statutory interpretation (not private international law) as to what was intended with regard to jurisdiction. Looking at the Parliamentary debate (which was short, on a very late amendment) the only clue is that the government stated that an employee should only be able to use a British tribunal if there was a 'proper connection with the UK'[364]. What this means will have to be explored judicially; in the meantime, the position in particular of employees of British companies working abroad or sent to work abroad remains uncertain.

(ii) What is an unfair dismissal?

Once the employee has proved that he was dismissed (if that is a live issue in the case) the burden of proof then passes on to the employer, under section 98 of the 1996 Act, to show two things:

1. what was the reason for the dismissal (or the principal reason if more than one);
2. that it fell within one of the enumerated categories of prima facie fair dismissals, namely that the reason was
   (a) related to the capability or qualifications of the employee for performing his work,
   (b) related to the conduct of the employee,
   (c) that the employee was redundant,
   (d) that the employee could not continue to work in that position without contravention of a legislative provision[365],
   (e) 'some other substantial reason of a kind such as to justify the dismissal'.

It is then for the tribunal to decide whether in the circumstances (having regard to equity and the substantial merits of the case) the employer acted reasonably in treating that reason as a sufficient reason for dismissing the employee (section 98(4)).

This basic structure of an unfair dismissal action should be borne in mind (except in cases where the statute expressly provides that a certain type of dismissal shall be automatically fair or unfair), and the significance of the burden of proof being upon the employer is that if he fails to satisfy the tribunal at either of the first two stages the dismissal will be held to be unfair.

---

363 Contrast this with the far more sensible amendments to the discrimination legislation in the Equal Opportunities (Employment Legislation) (International Limits) Regulations 1999, SI 1999/3163 (again seeking compliance with the Posted Workers Directive) which simply removed the wording 'or mainly' from the exclusion of employees working 'wholly or mainly outside Great Britain'. There may now be disputes over what is meant by 'wholly' outside GB (eg what level of involvement within GB could be ignored as de minimis), but at least we still have a statutory provision here to apply.

364 HL Official Report, 8 July 1999, col 1089.

365 Eg where an employee employed wholly or principally to drive a vehicle is disqualified and there is no alternative work for him: *Appleyard v FM Smith (Hull) Ltd* [1972] IRLR 19, IT; *Fearn v Tayford Motor Co* [1975] IRLR 336, IT. The tribunal must still go on to consider whether the dismissal was reasonable under s 98(4), as this is not an automatically fair reason for dismissal: *Sandhu v DES* [1978] IRLR 208. A mistaken belief by the employer that he cannot lawfully continue to employ the employee does not come under this heading, but may qualify as 'some other substantial reason': *Bouchaala v Trust House Forte Hotels Ltd* [1980] ICR 721, [1980] IRLR 382, EAT.

(a) Stage one: the reason[366]

The first stage is that the employer must show what the real reason was for the dismissal[367]; if he clearly relies upon one particular reason and the tribunal disbelieves him, the finding should be one of unfair dismissal and he should not normally be allowed to try to rely upon an entirely different reason either at the tribunal hearing (without applying for leave to amend his defence) or on appeal[368]. However, tribunal proceedings are not meant to be as formal as High Court proceedings, and it must be accepted that, in the light of the complexity of certain of these areas of law, the employer may not always initially put the correct legal interpretation on the factors determining his decision to dismiss[369]. The general approach has therefore been that the tribunal's task is to discover the reason actually motivating the employer at the time of the dismissal. In *Abernethy v Mott, Hay and Anderson*[370], Cairns LJ said:

> 'A reason for the dismissal of an employee is a set of facts known to the employer, or it may be of beliefs held by him, which cause him to dismiss the employee. If at the time of his dismissal the employer gives a reason for it, that is no doubt evidence, at any rate as against him, as to the real reason, but it does not necessarily constitute the real reason. He may knowingly give a reason different from the real reason out of kindness or because he might have difficulty in proving the facts that actually led him to dismiss; or he may describe his reasons wrongly through some mistake of language or of law.'

Thus, a wrong label given by the employer is not fatal to his case and, further, it is clear from the cases that the approach here is basically subjective particularly in cases where it is a *belief* on the part of the employer which led him to dismiss. The obvious example here is a belief that the employee is guilty of a crime (see below, under 'conduct'), for in such cases, as with other 'belief' cases, it has been consistently held that what the employer is required to prove is his genuine

---

366 See *Harvey* DI [801].
367 The burden of proof is on the employer; if he leads evidence supporting his contention that he dismissed for reason A, that may cast an evidential burden on the employee to adduce some evidence to doubt reason A and/or suggest reason B; if he does so, the legal burden of proof remains with the employer at the end of the day: *Maund v Penwith District Council* [1984] ICR 143, [1984] IRLR 24, CA. If dismissal is with notice, it may be necessary to look at the reason(s) operating both at the giving and expiry of the notice: *Parkinson v March Consulting Ltd* [1998] ICR 276, [1997] IRLR 308, CA; *West Kent College v Richardson* [1999] ICR 511, EAT.
368 *Nelson v BBC* [1977] ICR 649, [1977] IRLR 148, CA. This is certainly so on appeal as *Nelson* shows, if only because it is contrary to natural justice to decide an appeal on a ground that was not fully argued before the tribunal; a similar rule applies before the tribunal itself, but here a change of label may be permissible where the employee is in fact given a proper opportunity to refute the new ground: *Murphy v Epsom College* [1985] ICR 80, [1984] IRLR 271, CA; *Hotson v Wisbech Conservative Club* [1984] ICR 859, [1984] IRLR 422; *Burkett v Pendletons (Sweets) Ltd* [1992] ICR 407. Likewise, if the employer fails to establish the reason put forward, the tribunal should not cast around to try to find some other dismissible reason: *Adams v Derby City Council* [1986] IRLR 163, EAT.
369 'Redundancy' for example may cover a multitude of sins in layman's use, but in law it has a precise and restricted meaning.
370 [1974] ICR 323, [1974] IRLR 213, CA; the passage cited was approved by the House of Lords in *W Devis & Sons Ltd v Atkins* [1977] ICR 662, [1977] IRLR 314, HL. For an example of wrong labelling, see *Hannan v TNT–IPEC (UK) Ltd* [1986] IRLR 165, EAT.

belief, *not* that his belief was factually correct[371]. However, in the nature of things the approach cannot be totally subjective, for the employer has to *prove* that he held the belief in question and so in practice will have to go on to adduce some supporting evidence of the facts upon which he based his belief (even though it does not have to amount to clear proof of the correctness of that belief), otherwise there is the danger that the tribunal will not believe him.

At the heart of the matter of labelling lies a question of balance. It is clearly important in practice that a relatively lax approach should be taken to the label applied by the employer. On the other hand, too lax an approach could leave too much leeway for an employer to operate a 'shotgun' defence – to make multiple allegations, under different headings, against the employee and hope that one or two are accepted by the tribunal. A major step towards preventing improper use of such tactics was taken by the House of Lords in *Smith v City of Glasgow District Council*[372]. The employer put forward a mixture of reasons for dismissal, relating to incompetence and misconduct, crystallised into three substantive allegations; the tribunal found that one of them had not been made out but proceeded to find the dismissal generally fair. This reasoning was disapproved by the House of Lords, since what appeared to be an integral part of the reason for dismissal had not been proved (or, at least, proved to have been the subject of reasonable belief by the employer). This case does *not* mean that an employer cannot plead several reasons and win; it does mean, however, that if one of several reasons put forward collapses the employer must go further and show that the collapsed reason was not, or did not form a significant part of, the principal reason for the dismissal (ie that the remaining reasons were more important and justified the dismissal by themselves); according to the House of Lords, that had not been shown on the facts of this case. Clearly, the more reasons the employer loads into the shotgun (and the more he eventually fails to prove), the more difficult this will be to establish.

Two further points on this first stage of the action should also be noticed. The first is that the House of Lords held in *W Devis & Sons Ltd v Atkins*[373] that the employer can only rely on the facts as known to him at the date of dismissal; contrary to the position in a common law action for wrongful dismissal[374], therefore, the employer cannot rely upon subsequently discovered misconduct (as in a case where there is a dubious dismissal for inefficiency, following which the employer checks the books and finds clear evidence of embezzlement by the ex-employee – there must still be a finding of unfair dismissal in such a case, though the subsequently discovered misconduct may be relevant on the question of compensation, see below).

371 *Trust House Forte Leisure Ltd v Aquilar* [1976] IRLR 251.
372 [1987] ICR 796, [1987] IRLR 326, HL.
373 [1977] ICR 662, [1977] IRLR 314, HL. Date of dismissal here means the effective date of termination, so that if the facts change between the giving and the expiry of notice (eg a redundancy situation is affected by the receipt of a new order during that period), the tribunal should look at the facts as known at the expiry date: *Stacey v Babcock Power Ltd* [1986] ICR 221, [1986] IRLR 3. Thus, further evidence coming to light during the notice period can be taken into account: *Alboni v Ind Coope Retail Ltd* [1998] IRLR 131, CA (employer's reasonable conduct looking for an alternative to dismissal during the notice period taken into account); *White v South London Transport Ltd* [1998] ICR 293 (further medical evidence during notice period backed up the original ill-health dismissal).
374 *Boston Deep Sea Fishing and Ice Co v Ansell* (1888) 39 Ch D 339, CA.

There is one major qualification to this fundamental rule. Where an initial decision to dismiss is subject to an internal appeal, further evidence may come to light during the course of the appeal and it has been held that the tribunal can look at this (it being unrealistic to do otherwise) *provided* that the new evidence relates to the original ground of dismissal[375]. However, this must not be taken too far and it has been held that (a) this exception does not allow an employer to use evidence from the appeal to set up an entirely new ground for dismissal[376] and (b) it does not render admissible evidence of matters occurring after the conclusion of the appeal[377]. The series of EAT decisions that established these principles were strongly affirmed by the House of Lords in *West Midland Co-operative Society Ltd v Tipton*[378], where the approach was taken that internal appeal procedures are an integral part of the dismissal procedure and so should be taken into account; to do so does *not* offend the principle in *Devis & Sons Ltd v Atkins*. Indeed, the *Tipton* case takes matters one stage further and holds that a *refusal* by an employer to allow an internal appeal may itself be evidence of unfairness.

The second point is that section 107 of the 1996 Act provides that in determining the reason for dismissal the tribunal may *not* take into account any industrial pressure (whether by strike or lesser action) which was exercised on the employer in order to procure the dismissal, or which was such that it was foreseeably likely to lead to dismissal[379]. This might apply where action was taken by a union or group of fellow employees against an employee who had refused to join in a strike, and if the employer sacks him solely because of the pressure, section 107 leads to the artificial position before the tribunal that the only reason for dismissal has to be ignored. The employer will then be found to have dismissed the employee unfairly, no reason having been shown, and, unless there was unreasonable conduct or undue obstinacy on the employee's part during the dispute, the employer may have to pay full compensation[380]. Where, however, the pressure was exercised on the employer because of the non-membership of a union of the applicant, it is now provided that an action may be brought against the union (or other person exercising the pressure) either by the employer or by the applicant himself and the union or other person may be ordered to pay some or all of the compensation awarded to the applicant[381]. These provisions supplement section 107 without replacing it.

(b) Stage two: prima facie fair grounds

The second stage of the action is that the employer must prove that the reason for the dismissal fits into one of the enumerated categories. These are considered below, but it should be noted here that the final residual category, 'some other substantial reason justifying dismissal', is deliberately wide and not to be restricted

---

375 *National Heart and Chest Hospitals v Nambiar* [1981] ICR 441, [1981] IRLR 196; *Sillifant v Powell Duffryn Timber Ltd* [1983] IRLR 91.
376 *Monie v Coral Racing Ltd* [1981] ICR 109, [1980] IRLR 464, CA.
377 *Greenall Whitley plc v Carr* [1985] ICR 451, [1985] IRLR 289.
378 [1986] ICR 192, [1986] IRLR 112, HL.
379 *Ford Motor Co Ltd v Hudson* [1978] ICR 482, [1978] IRLR 66, EAT.
380 *Hazell Offsets Ltd v Luckett* [1977] IRLR 430; *British United Trawlers (Grimsby) Ltd v Carr* [1977] ICR 622; *Colwyn Borough Council v Dutton* [1980] IRLR 420. Although it is easiest to imagine this section applying to normal industrial disputes, it could also possibly apply to a case of pressure from a workforce, eg to dismiss an AIDS sufferer.
381 TULR(C)A 1992, s 160.

by being construed ejusdem generis with the previous categories[382]. Dismissal of a replacement for a woman temporarily absent on maternity leave (or for a person subject to compulsory medical suspension[383]) is expressly stated to be for a substantial reason (provided the replacement was told of the temporary nature of the job when engaged)[384], as is a dismissal because of a transfer of the employer's undertaking (see p 593 below), but other than that all that can be said is that the question of what can be a substantial reason is an open one in respect of which the onus is clearly upon the employer to satisfy the tribunal on the facts of the particular case; the wider it is construed by the tribunals, the wider ostensibly is the area of management prerogative[385], though of course any particular dismissal still has to be shown to be fair, even if for a substantial reason[386]. It has been held in the past to cover a range of miscellaneous reasons including an employer's mistaken belief that he had other fair grounds on which to dismiss,[387] dismissal at the behest of an important customer[388], personality clashes[389], sexual orientation[390] and the dismissal of the spouse of a person already dismissed where they were engaged as a pair[391]; as will be seen at p 599 below, it has been particularly important in cases of dismissals following necessary business reorganisations.

(c) Stage three: fairness[392]

The third stage is that the tribunal must consider under section 98(4) whether the employer acted reasonably in actually 'activating' the reason in question and

---

382 *RS Components Ltd v Irwin* [1973] ICR 535, [1973] IRLR 239. See *Harvey* DI [1854].

383 Under the Employment Rights Act 1996, s 64.

384 S 106. This could be of renewed importance with the raising of statutory maternity leave to a year (meaning that the replacement may have the qualifying period of employment for an unfair dismissal action).

385 Bowers and Clark 'Unfair dismissal and managerial prerogative: a study of "other substantial reason"' (1981) 10 ILJ 34.

386 *Gilham v Kent County Council (No 2)* [1985] ICR 233, [1985] IRLR 18, CA. A defence of some other substantial reason requires the tribunal 'to consider the reason established by the employer and decide whether it falls within the category of reason which could justify the dismissal of *an* employee – not *that* employee, but *an* employee – holding the position which that employee held': *Dobie v Burns International Security Services (UK) Ltd* [1984] IRLR 329 at 331, CA per Sir John Donaldson MR; the next stage is to consider whether the dismissal of *that* employee was fair on the facts, within s 98(4).

387 *Taylor v Co-operative Retail Services Ltd* [1981] ICR 172, [1981] IRLR 1; affd [1982] ICR 600, [1982] IRLR 354, CA (mistaken belief that employer obliged to dismiss under a closed shop agreement); *Bouchaala v Trust House Forte Hotels Ltd* [1980] ICR 721, [1980] IRLR 382 (mistaken belief that continued employment would contravene a statutory enactment).

388 *Scott Packing and Warehousing Ltd v Paterson* [1978] IRLR 166; *Grootcon (UK) Ltd v Keld* [1984] IRLR 302; *Dobie v Burns International Security Services (UK) Ltd* [1984] ICR 812, [1984] IRLR 329, CA. As with pressure from co-workers (s 107, n 380 above) this could be relevant in the dismissal of an AIDS sufferer; on such a dismissal generally, see Napier 'AIDS, discrimination and employment law' (1989) 18 ILJ 84 and Watt 'HIV, discrimination, unfair dismissal and pressure to dismiss' (1992) 21 ILJ 280.

389 *Treganowan v Robert Knee & Co Ltd* [1975] ICR 405, [1975] IRLR 247.

390 *Boychuk v HK Symons Holdings Ltd* [1977] IRLR 395 (the 'Lesbians Ignite' case); *Saunders v Scottish National Camps Association Ltd* [1980] IRLR 174; affd briefly by the Ct of Sess [1981] IRLR 277 (dismissal of homosexual from employment in children's camp). Note that new laws to outlaw discrimination on the grounds of sexual orientation are to be introduced in late 2003, see p 359 below.

391 *Kelman v Oram* [1983] IRLR 432 (dismissal of publican's wife after (unfair) dismissal of publican).

392 See *Harvey* DI [952].

dismissing the employee; this demonstrates clearly that it is not enough to show that the employer had a reason which would normally justify dismissal – it has to be shown that, in all the circumstances of the case, it actually justified the particular dismissal in question. Unlike a wrongful dismissal action, this is not a technical exercise, looking at the parties' contractual entitlements and rights, but instead entails examination of the *substance* of the dismissal and consideration of the wider circumstances such as the employer's business needs (for example, in a case of inefficiency or ineptitude by the employee) and any factors in mitigation of the employee's default, such as long service, lack of prior grounds for complaint and the possibilities of improvement. While the burden of proof on this overall question of fairness is technically neutral, the House of Lords in *Smith v City of Glasgow District Council*[393] approved the view of the Court of Session below that it remains logical to expect the employer to prove that the reason in question has been established – it cannot be reasonable to treat that reason as sufficient to justify dismissal unless the employer has shown either that it is true or that he believed it to be true. Although other factors (such as procedural considerations) may have to be considered, this emphasis on isolating the real reason(s) for dismissal may mean that in many cases the issue of overall fairness will tend to merge with the question of establishing the reason (on which the employer does still bear the burden of proof).

In applying the test of fairness, the tribunal must consider the reasonableness of the employer's conduct, *not* the injustice (or lack of it) done to the employee. This fundamental principle was reaffirmed by the House of Lords in *Polkey v AE Dayton Services Ltd*[394], probably the most important decision on unfair dismissal since *W Devis & Sons Ltd v Atkins*[395] ten years earlier. An employee dismissed without warning for redundancy and sent home immediately had his claim for unfair dismissal turned down by the tribunal because they found that proper consultation would not have made any difference, ie they looked at the eventual lack of injustice to the employee. The House of Lords clearly held this to be wrong and remitted the case to another tribunal, who were to apply the correct test of looking at the reasonableness of the employer's conduct in deciding not to consult or warn; the question of the amount of injustice done to the employee should only be relevant at the later stages of assessing compensation. This reasonableness test in section 98(4) has two overall effects. The first is that it is primarily responsible for giving the tribunals their wide discretion to reach just and equitable decisions in the light of 'good industrial practice' (the relevant wording in section 98(4) being 'in accordance with equity and the substantial merits of the case'); in the exercise of this discretion the tribunals have considerable freedom of action and in general the EAT will be reluctant to interfere with their decisions on such matters. The second effect is that it is the existence of section 98(4) which has led to the importance attached to the concept of 'procedural unfairness', ie the possibility that a dismissal may be unfair if an unfair procedure is adopted by the employer (for example, no warnings, lack of a hearing), even if there is prima facie a good substantive reason for the dismissal. This concept, not to be found expressly stated in the legislation, was developed at an early stage in the history of the action[396] and remains a

---

393 [1987] ICR 796, [1987] IRLR 326, HL; *Post Office (Counters) Ltd v Heavey* [1990] ICR 1, [1989] IRLR 513, EAT.
394 [1988] ICR 142, [1987] IRLR 503, HL.
395 See p 565 n 373.
396 *Earl v Slater and Wheeler (Airlyne) Ltd* [1973] 1 Al ER 145, [1972] ICR 508; approved by the House of Lords in *W Devis & Sons Ltd v Atkins* [1977] ICR 662, [1977] IRLR 314, HL.

significant element in it. It has been subject to definable fluctuations in the amount of emphasis to be placed on it. Four particular phases can be seen. First, procedural fairness was a dominant factor in the early years of the new unfair dismissal law, during most of the 1970s while it was bedding in; the prospect of almost any lapse in procedure being held unfair concentrated employers' minds and meant that the new law had a rapid and significant normative effect on personnel practices. Secondly, however, procedural fairness suffered a definite wane in the later years of that decade and during the first half of the 1980s for two reasons – (i) a generally less enthusiastic attitude by the Court of Appeal, seen most clearly in *Hollister v NFU* [397] with a tendency to view procedural matters as merely one of the background factors; (ii) the evolution and widespread application of the rule in *British Labour Pump Co Ltd v Byrne* [398], to the effect that even if the employer failed to use the proper procedure on dismissal, it would still be fair if he could prove on a balance of probabilities that even if he had gone through the proper procedure the employee would still have been dismissed (and that dismissal would then have been fair) – ie a lapse by the employer could be forgiven if with hindsight it made no difference. Thirdly, however, we saw a swing back of the pendulum in 1987 with the decision of the House of Lords in *Polkey v A E Dayton Services Ltd* [399] in which *Byrne*'s case was overruled [400] for two reasons – (i) it is inconsistent with *W Devis & Sons Ltd v Atkins* [401] since the tribunal should be considering what the employer actually did at the date of dismissal (and with his state of knowledge then), not what he might have done with hindsight; (ii) more significantly, the *Byrne* approach was based on consideration of the (lack of) injustice to the employee, not the reasonableness of the employer's actions and, as we have seen above, that is a fundamentally flawed approach. In addition, the case of *Polkey* also shows a generally more favourable approach to procedural unfairness [402]; Lord Mackay LC said that a lapse of procedure will not automatically make a dismissal unfair and accepted that (taking the facts of the case) a redundancy dismissal without consultation or warning might still be fair, *but* that would only be so if the employer could show that the decision not to consult or warn was a positive decision taken reasonably in the circumstances at the time, not justified merely as an ex post facto afterthought once the deed had been done [403].

397 [1979] ICR 542, [1979] IRLR 238, CA. See also *Retarded Children's Aid Society v Day* [1978] ICR 437, [1978] IRLR 128, CA and *Bailey v BP Oil (Kent Refinery) Ltd* [1980] ICR 642, [1980] IRLR 287, CA.
398 [1979] ICR 347, [1979] IRLR 94.
399 N 394 above. In his speech, Lord Mackay LC, giving the judgment of the court, relied heavily on the strong criticisms of *Byrne*'s case by Browne-Wilkinson P in *Sillifant v Powell Duffryn Timber Ltd* [1983] IRLR 91.
400 Also overruled is *W & J Wass Ltd v Binns* [1982] ICR 486, [1982] IRLR 283 in which the Court of Appeal had approved *Byrne*'s case, and 'all decisions supporting it'.
401 See n 373 above.
402 See also the post-*Polkey* decisions in *McLaren v National Coal Board* [1988] ICR 370, [1988] IRLR 215, CA; *Whitbread & Co plc v Mills* [1988] ICR 776, [1988] IRLR 501; *Spink v Express Foods Group Ltd* [1990] IRLR 320; *Stocker v Lancashire County Council* [1992] IRLR 75, CA; and Collins 'Procedural fairness after *Polkey*' (1990) 19 ILJ 39.
403 The formulation of this exception caused problems. Lord Bridge in *Polkey* said that it should only apply where the employer had *actually* (subjectively) considered the matter at the time of dismissal and concluded that consultation would be useless. However, in *Duffy v Yeomans & Partners Ltd* [1995] ICR 1, [1994] IRLR 642 the Court of Appeal applied Lord Mackay's view that it can apply where the employer *could reasonably have* so concluded. This could be seen as capable of reviving at least parts of *Byrne*'s case and the 'it made no difference' defence, if not quite as purely retrospectively as in *Byrne*. See Wynn (1995) 24 ILJ 272.

We saw, therefore, the reinstating of procedural fairness, not just as *a* factor, but as one of *the* factors that are likely to dominate an unfair dismissal action, even if this stopped short of a return in full to its heyday in the early years of the unfair dismissal jurisdiction. The fourth phase is recent, and indeed still to come into force in its finalised form at the time of writing. In addressing the perceived problem of too many cases being taken to tribunals, the present government took the view that, of those so taken in the unfair dismissal jurisdiction, too many were based on procedural unfairness only (ie where the employer had good cause to dismiss but mishandled it). The Employment Act 2002 therefore contains an attempt to limit procedural cases[404], but in a relatively subtle way. We have seen that Schedule 2 contains a statutory minimum procedure to be followed in all cases[405]. On the other hand, many employers will have their own procedures which are more extensive than this (even if only because they follow the ACAS Code of Practice), any breach of which (even if technical) has been capable of making the dismissal unfair (even if the tribunal proceeds to award little or no compensation). Section 34 of the 2002 Act takes this distinction into account when enacting a new section 98A ('Procedural fairness') into the Employment Rights Act 1996, as follows:

'(1) An employee who is dismissed shall be regarded for the purposes of this Part as unfairly dismissed if —

    (a) one of the procedures set out in Part I of Schedule 2 to the Employment Act 2002 (dismissal and disciplinary procedures) applies in relation to the dismissal,

    (b) the procedure has not been completed, and

    (c) the non-completion of the procedures is wholly or mainly attributable to failure by the employer to comply with its requirements.

(2) Subject to subsection (1), failure by an employer to follow a procedure in relation to the dismissal of an employee shall not be regarded for the purposes of section 98(4)(a) as by itself making the employer's action unreasonable if he shows that he would have decided to dismiss the employee if he had followed the procedure.'

The effect of this differential approach (achieved legislatively by the phrase 'subject to subsection 1' in subsection 2) is that any failure to comply with the basic Schedule 2 procedure *will* be unfair[406], but that in relation to any elements of the employer's own procedures going *beyond* Schedule 2's requirements there is a statutory re-introduction of the rule in *British Labour Pump Co Ltd v Byrne* (above), ie the 'it made no difference' defence the effect of which is that if the employer can prove to the tribunal that he would have dismissed even if a wholly fair procedure had been adopted, the result is not just that little compensation is likely to be awarded (the *Polkey* solution) but that the dismissal will be *fair*. This is a significant change,[407] the practical meaning of which is likely to become apparent during the currency of this edition.

404 The government's approach is that these cases, producing a basic finding of unfairness and little by way of compensation, have been a waste of tribunal time. Not all tribunal chairmen would agree.
405 See p 540 above.
406 Sub-ss (3)–(6) of the new s 98A provide for any award of compensation to be increased by four weeks' pay in such a case.
407 It may be useful in countering any arguments by managers for abandoning more sophisticated procedures (ie for dumbing down to the Sch 2 procedures only, on the basis that that is all that the law says is compulsory) because a technical glitch in the more sophisticated procedure may well now *not* produce an unfair dismissal.

(d) The correct approach: the 'range of reasonable responses' test

One aspect of section 98(4) has caused considerable disagreement in the cases; that is whether the approach of the tribunal should be subjective or objective. To any lawyer versed in criminal law or tort, the concept of 'reasonableness' is clearly objective, and in earlier cases on section 98(4) the approach was indeed objective, viewing the tribunal as an 'industrial jury' with full powers to review the employer's conduct from their standpoint and decide, in the light of standard industrial practice (hence the lay membership), whether on the facts they would have dismissed[408]. Some later cases, however, adopted the view that the approach should be subjective (at least in part) particularly in cases where the employer's belief in a set of facts at the time of dismissal is important, so that the employer's own view that he acted reasonably should have some effect[409]. Thus, in *Alidair Ltd v Taylor*[410], where an airline pilot's instant dismissal after damaging an aircraft in a faulty landing was held to be fair, Lord Denning MR said,

'... it must be remembered that [section 98] contemplated a subjective test. The tribunal have to consider the employer's reason and the employer's state of mind. If the company honestly believed on reasonable grounds that this pilot was lacking in proper capability to fly aircraft on behalf of the company, that was a good and sufficient reason for the company to determine the employment then and there. ... They clearly had no further confidence in him. He could not be trusted to fly their aircraft on their behalf. That being their honest belief on reasonable grounds, they were entitled to dismiss him. They acted reasonably in treating it as a sufficient reason for dismissing him.'

Reinforcing this, his Lordship then said:

'If a man is dismissed for stealing, as long as the employer honestly believed it on reasonable grounds, that is enough to justify dismissal. It is not necessary for the employer to prove that he was in fact stealing. Whenever a man is dismissed for incapacity or incompetence it is sufficient that the employer honestly believes on reasonable grounds that the man is incapable or incompetent. It is not necessary for the employer to prove that he is in fact incapable or incompetent.'

However, the approach cannot be totally subjective (otherwise the tribunal's discretion would be minimal when faced by an employer unshaken in his assertion that he thought he had acted reasonably), as can be seen from the above references to belief *on reasonable grounds*. Moreover, some later cases reaffirmed an objective element:

'... the industrial tribunal, while using its own collective wisdom, is to apply the standard of the reasonable employer; that is to say, the fairness or unfairness of the dismissal is to be judged ... by the objective standard of

408 *Bessenden Properties Ltd v Corness* [1977] ICR 821n, [1974] IRLR 338, CA.
409 *Ferodo Ltd v Barnes* [1976] ICR 439, [1976] IRLR 302; *Post Office v Mughal* [1977] ICR 763, [1977] IRLR 178.
410 [1978] ICR 445, [1978] IRLR 82, CA; the passages cited are at 450–451 and 84–85 respectively; *Vickers Ltd v Smith* [1977] IRLR 11. Cf *ILEA v Lloyd* [1981] IRLR 394, CA.

the way in which a reasonable employer in those circumstances, in that line of business, would have behaved[411].'

Thus, the correct position must lie in a combined approach, namely that the tribunal must have to gauge the employer's conduct by *some* objective yardstick, but at the same time take into account the honest beliefs of the employer where they are relevant. It may seem unsatisfactory not to be able to give a clear answer to what appears to be a fundamental question – subjective or objective? – but in practice it may in most cases be an empty question in the light of two aspects of section 98 which *are* clear and which may be seen as embodying elements of objectivity and subjectivity respectively:

(1) It is clear that, in all but the most blatant and obvious case of misconduct or incapability, the employer must have made a proper investigation of the grounds of his complaint against the employee and come to proper, tenable conclusions if he is to convince the tribunal that he had reasonable grounds for any belief which he is putting forward as a reason for the dismissal. Thus, in a suspected theft case the employer must show reasonable investigations, reasonably allowing him to point the finger of accusation at the employee. Moreover, the requirement of reasonable investigation means that an employer cannot rely upon his own ignorance at the time of dismissal of a particular point in the employee's favour if a reasonable investigation would have revealed it, ie the tribunal may look at the facts of which the employer knew *or ought to have known*[412]. To this extent at least, the test is objective as can be seen from the formula 'belief on reasonable grounds', and if the employer can show these reasonable grounds he may be in a strong position[413]. The test cannot be wholly objective, however, as can be seen from the second point.

(2) If the tribunal could adopt an entirely objective approach, there would be nothing to stop them looking at the facts of every case *de novo* and simply applying their own view of those facts, deciding whether they would have done what the employer did in the circumstances. However, the courts have consistently held that this is what a tribunal must *not* do[414]. Instead, they have to look at what the employer in fact did and decide whether that was a course of action which a reasonable employer could have taken in those circumstances (applying the standard of the reasonable employer as envisaged in the wording of section 98(4) itself). This becomes of particular significance in a case where in the circumstances the employer had several courses of action open to him, all of which were potentially what a reasonable employer might do, eg where the misconduct was such that he could dismiss, suspend without pay or fine and he chose to dismiss, or where in a redundancy case he could dispense with A or B or C and he chose A. In such a case, the

411 *Watling & Co Ltd v Richardson* [1978] ICR 1049 at 1056, [1978] IRLR 255 and 257, per Phillips J, explaining *Vickers Ltd v Smith* (n 410 above); see also *Mitchell v Old Hall Exchange Club Ltd* [1978] IRLR 160.

412 *St Anne's Board Mill Co Ltd v Brien* [1973] ICR 444, [1973] IRLR 309, approved by the House of Lords in *W Devis & Sons Ltd v Atkins* [1977] ICR 662, [1977] IRLR 314, HL.

413 *Post Office v Mughal* [1977] ICR 763, [1977] IRLR 178.

414 *Trust House Forte Hotels Ltd v Murphy* [1977] IRLR 186; *Meridian Ltd v Gomersall* [1977] ICR 597, [1977] IRLR 425; *Mansfield Hosiery Mills Ltd v Bromley* [1977] IRLR 301; *Watling & Co Ltd v Richardson* [1978] ICR 1049, [1978] IRLR 255.

tribunal should not consider which course they would have taken and decide whether the dismissal was fair or not in accordance with that (for example, holding dismissal unfair if they would on balance have decided upon suspension, or holding the dismissal of A unfair if on balance they would have dismissed C). Instead, they should decide whether the course of action in fact chosen was one which a reasonable employer *could* have decided upon, ie whether the employer acted *within the area of discretion covered by what would have been reasonable in the circumstances.* Thus, in *Trust House Forte Leisure Ltd v Aquilar*[415], Phillips J said,

'... when the management is confronted with a decision to dismiss an employee in particular circumstances there may well be cases where reasonable managements might take either of two decisions: to dismiss or not to dismiss. It does not necessarily mean if they decide to dismiss that they have acted unfairly because they are plenty of situations in which more than one view is possible.'

In *Watling & Co Ltd v Richardson*[416] the same judge, using the redundancy example given above as a warning to tribunals not simply to apply their own views, said:

'It has to be recognised that there are circumstances where more than one course of action may be reasonable ... In such cases ... if an industrial tribunal equates its view of what itself would have done with what a reasonable employer would have done, it may mean that an employer will be found to have dismissed an employee unfairly although in the circumstances many perfectly good and fair employers would have done as that employer did.'

Indeed the development of this 'range of reasonable responses' approach has been a major feature of unfair dismissal law and has had the effect of broadening the area of managerial discretion – it does not apply a test entirely subjective to the respondent employer, but it does enjoin the tribunals to look at the matter from an employer standpoint generally (albeit that of a reasonable employer). This approach was approved by the Court of Appeal in *British Leyland (UK) Ltd v Swift*[417], where Lord Denning MR said:

'The correct test is: was it reasonable for the employer to dismiss him? If no reasonable employer would have dismissed him, then the dismissal was unfair. But if a reasonable employer might reasonably have dismissed him, then the dismissal was fair. It must be remembered that in all these cases there is a band of reasonableness, within which one employer might reasonably take one view; another quite reasonably take a different view ... if it was quite reasonable to dismiss him, then the dismissal must be upheld as fair: even though some other employers may not have dismissed him.'

---

415 [1976] IRLR 251 at 254.
416 [1978] ICR 1049 at 1056, [1978] IRLR 255 at 258; *Grundy (Teddington) Ltd v Willis* [1976] ICR 323, [1976] IRLR 118.
417 [1981] IRLR 91, CA. The principle was well expounded by the EAT in *Rolls-Royce Ltd v Walpole* [1980] IRLR 343 and *British Gas plc v McCarrick* [1991] IRLR 305, CA is a strong decision reaffirming it.

The 'range of reasonable responses' approach has been universally accepted for years and was particularly well set out by Browne-Wilkinson P in *Iceland Frozen Foods Ltd v Jones*[418] as follows:

'... [T]he correct approach for the Industrial Tribunal to adopt in answering the question posed by [section 98(4) of the 1996 Act] is as follows: (1) the starting point should always be the words of [section 98] themselves; (2) in applying the section an Industrial Tribunal must consider the reasonableness of the employer's conduct, not simply whether they [the members of the Industrial Tribunal] consider the dismissal to be fair; (3) in judging the reasonableness of the employer's conduct an Industrial Tribunal must not substitute its decision as to what was the right course to adopt for that of the employer; (4) in many (though not all) cases there is a band of reasonable responses to the employee's conduct within which one employer might reasonably take one view, another quite reasonably take another; (5) the function of the Industrial Tribunal, as an industrial jury, is to determine whether in the particular circumstances of each case the decision to dismiss the employee fell within the band of reasonable responses which a reasonable employer might have adopted. If the dismissal falls within the band the dismissal is fair; if the dismissal falls outside the band it is unfair.'

A bombshell was dropped in late 1999 by the EAT under Morison P (in one of his final judgments in that court) in *Haddon v Van den Bergh Foods Ltd*[419], where they stated that in their opinion the range of reasonable responses test is *wrong* (being said to be an unhelpful 'mantra', along with the general point that a tribunal should not substitute its own view for that of the employer). This revisionism was based on the argument that the 'range' test made it too difficult for an employee to succeed in a misconduct case, and that it was too close to the administrative law concept of perversity (see note 418). However, the reasoning in the case was suspect and its authority weak (going against so much prior case law). The point at issue was so fundamental that the Court of Appeal expedited the hearing of the appeal in another case raising the same point and in *Foley v Post Office*[420] unambiguously disapproved *Haddon*, emphasising the correctness of the range of reasonable responses test. Subsequent case law has followed this line, confirming that the test applies not just to the actual dismissal decision but also to the adequacy of the procedures adopted[421] and, in a misconduct case, to

---

418 [1982] IRLR 439 at 442. The EAT was at pains to point out that this did not mean (as may have appeared from *Vickers Ltd v Smith* [1977] IRLR 11) that a dismissal could only be unfair if *perverse* (ie no reasonable employer could possibly have decided to dismiss); the test is not as stringent as that. In a case depending on the credibility of a witness, the question is whether the employer could reasonably believe him, *not* whether the tribunal does: *Linfood Cash and Carry Ltd v Thomson* [1989] ICR 518, [1989] IRLR 235, EAT.
419 [1999] ICR 1150, [1999] IRLR 672. The tribunal had held that the test forced them to find fair the dismissal of a employee who had been invited to a drinks party to celebrate 15 years good service, who was then summarily dismissed for not returning for the last 1½ hours of his shift because he had been drinking! Arguably, the EAT could just have reversed this on ordinary grounds of perversity.
420 [2000] ICR 1283, [2000] IRLR 827, CA.
421 *Whitbread plc v Hall* [2001] EWCA Civ 268, [2001] ICR 699, [2001] IRLR 275.

the reasonableness of the investigation carried out by the employer prior to the dismissal.[422]

(iii) Particular cases

Having considered the basis of an unfair dismissal action generally, we can now turn to eight particular cases of practical importance. The first three (capability, conduct and redundancy) are the major headings contained in section 98(2), the fourth (dismissal on a transfer of undertaking) has been added by Regulations; the fifth and sixth (dismissals for making health and safety complaints and for asserting statutory rights) were added by the Trade Union Reform and Employment Rights Act 1993; the seventh concerns special protection added by subsequent legislation; the eighth (changing business needs and reorganisation) is not specifically covered by statute but is treated separately because of its practical significance and because it involves a complicated interaction of laws relating to unfair dismissal, redundancy, construction of contracts of employment and variation of such contracts. The other heads of unfair dismissal (maternity dismissal, trade union reasons and dismissal while taking part in industrial action) are treated separately in the context in which they arise elsewhere in the book (in chapters 6, 10 and 11); they tend to be subject to more specialised rules, though some of the general principles discussed here lie behind them.

The following discussion of these headings (cross-referred to *Harvey* for further, exhaustive consideration) is, however, subject to the major caveat discussed at pp 607–615 above, that the modern approach is to treat the accumulation of case law in these areas circumspectly and to deprecate over-reliance on previous authorities (however venerable) if that either over-complicates the issue before the tribunal, or leads the tribunal to stray from the clear wording of the statute. Put shortly, precedents in this area are, to adapt Noël Coward's saying on wit, to be taken like caviar, not like marmalade.

(a) Capability or qualifications[423]

The first category of prima facie fair dismissals in section 98(2) is where the reason for dismissal is related to the capability or qualifications of the employee for performing his work. 'Capability' is defined in section 98(3) as capability assessed by reference to skill, aptitude, health or any other physical or mental quality, and 'qualifications' as any degree, diploma or other academic, technical or professional qualification relevant to the employee's position[424]. Lack of capability is of course the more important of these two categories, though the EAT have said that it should be viewed relatively narrowly as applying principally

---

422 *Sainsbury's Supermarkets Ltd v Hitt* [2002] EWCA Civ 1588, [2003] IRLR 23. In the context of misconduct, *Thomas v Hillingdon London Borough Council* (2002) TImes, 4 October is a particularly interesting (and strong) application of the test to the topical issue of Internet abuse and downloading porn.

423 See *Harvey* DI [1101] and Q [722]n. Practical advice on handling cases of absence (medical and otherwise) and poor work performance is given in the 2000 reissue of the ACAS Code of Practice on Disciplinary and Grievance Procedures, paras 19–25.

424 *Blue Star Ship Management Ltd v Williams* [1978] ICR 770, [1979] IRLR 16.

to cases where the employee is *incapable* of satisfactory work[425]; where the employee is capable of it, but refuses to exercise his ability, skills, etc, that should preferably be viewed as a case of misconduct, with the result that the employer should apply his warnings procedure more strictly and with more emphasis on the disciplinary aspect[426].

In the realm of dismissal for incapability, it is important that the employer's business should not have to suffer, to the detriment of all concerned, through the ineptitude or inefficiency of a particular employee. However, it is also important that the employee whose work is causing dissatisfaction should be treated fairly. The question for the tribunal is whether the employer has satisfied them that he genuinely believed on reasonable grounds that the employee was incapable[427]. The requirement of reasonable grounds means that the employer should make a proper and full investigation into the facts of the case, and give careful consideration to the decision to dismiss[428]; amongst other things, this consideration may include as a factor whether the employee was given proper training for the job, adequate supervision and, where appropriate, proper support from the employer. Also, it is well established that this area is amenable to the application of a warnings procedure[429], though the emphasis may be different from that in misconduct cases, for here the constructive side of a warning may be more important, not only pointing out the employer's ground for complaint but also instructing the employee how to improve and giving him reasonable time in which to do so. Of course, warnings are not essential in every case, and may perhaps be irrelevant where it is clear that the employee is completely incapable of improvement or where he already clearly knows that is expected of him[430]. That apart, however, the importance of a fair procedure in this area should not be underestimated, and lack of it (particularly if it leads to inadequate investigation by the employer) may make dismissal of an incompetent employee unfair (though it may still be open to the employer to argue that there should be little or no compensation where there was wilful default on the part of the employee, such as failure or refusal to improve[431]). One of the ways in which the ACAS Code of Practice on Disciplinary and Grievance Procedures was expanded in 2000 was by the inclusion (in paragraphs 22–25) of guidance on sub-standard work, which adopts and simplifies very much the results of this case law.

One particular aspect of incapability which has given rise to much litigation is where the employee is incapable of performing his work due to prolonged and/or frequent illness. Three preliminary points may be made on this subject. The first is that an exceptionally severe and incapacitating illness could have the effect of frustrating the contract of employment, in which case there would be no dismissal and so no action could be brought; frustration is considered elsewhere[432], and in general it should not be found readily by a tribunal because

---

425 *Sutton and Gates (Luton) Ltd v Boxall* [1979] ICR 67, [1978] IRLR 486.
426 *Littlewoods Organisation Ltd v Egenti* [1976] ICR 516, [1976] IRLR 334.
427 *Alidair Ltd v Taylor* [1978] ICR 445, [1978] IRLR 82, CA.
428 *Cook v Thomas Linnell & Sons Ltd* [1977] ICR 770, [1977] IRLR 132.
429 *Winterhalter Gastronom Ltd v Webb* [1973] ICR 245, [1973] IRLR 120, NIRC.
430 *James v Waltham Holy Cross UDC* [1973] ICR 398, [1973] IRLR 202.
431 *Sutton and Gates (Luton) Ltd v Boxall* [1979] ICR 67, [1978] IRLR 486, explaining *Kraft Foods Ltd v Fox* [1978] ICR 311, [1977] IRLR 431.
432 Pp 449–454. The applicability of the doctrine of frustration in this context was reaffirmed by the Court of Appeal in *Notcutt v Universal Equipment Co (London) Ltd* [1986] ICR 414, [1986] IRLR 218.

of its drastic effect on the employee's rights. The tests for a frustrating illness are therefore stringent, and are not the tests to be applied to the separate question whether a dismissal for illness was fair[433]. The second point is that many employees are covered by contractual sick pay schemes which will provide for payment during sickness up to a maximum period. A sick employee in most cases will expect to remain 'employed' during an illness at least until the sick pay period elapses. There is, however, no necessary link-up in law between the sick pay period and the question of dismissal for illness for (a) a contractual sick pay term only covers payment while still employed and, although it would not normally be reasonable to dismiss before the end of the sick pay period, there may be cases where the employer's business needs are so urgent that dismissal (and replacement) *during* that period could be reasonable; (b) on the other hand, it is not necessarily fair to apply a policy of dismissing automatically once the sick pay period expires[434]. Thus, the two matters are conceptually separate. The third point is that if the medical cause of the absence is likely to be long term and have a significant effect on the employee's life, the employer may now have to consider whether it could constitute a 'disability' within the Disability Discrimination Act 1995, in which case the following unfair dismissal law considerations may have to be supplemented by others under that Act, in particular any reasonable adjustments that might have to be made to help the employee to return[435].

Subject to these three points, it is well established by leading cases such as *East Lindsey District Council v Daubney*[436] that the approach of the tribunal in assessing the reasonableness of the employer's decision to dismiss should be to consider whether it was reasonable to expect the employer to wait any longer before dismissing, in the light of such factors as the nature of the illness, the actual and potential length of the absence, the circumstances of the individual employee, the urgency of the need to fill the employee's job and the size and nature of the employer's undertaking. The procedural steps to be taken by the employer will vary widely according to the facts of the case but, although a 'warning' as such is hardly appropriate, in most cases the employer will be expected to consult the employee and discuss the nature of his illness and his future prospects, bearing

---

433 *Tan v Berry Bros and Rudd Ltd* [1974] ICR 586, [1974] IRLR 244, NIRC.
434 *Hardwick v Leeds Area Health Authority* [1975] IRLR 319. For a later confirmation of this point, on rather unusual facts, see *Smiths Industries Aerospace and Defence Systems Ltd v Brookes* [1986] IRLR 434. In addition, it may be necessary also to consider the rules on statutory sick pay, discussed at pp 222–226 above, which may have an indirect effect particularly if there was evidence that one of the reasons behind the dismissal was the avoidance of payment of sick pay. It is increasingly possible that to dismiss before exhausting sick pay, even if fair on the facts, might be viewed as breach of contract in a common law action, on analogy with the 'PHI cases', see p 166 above.
435 For disability discrimination law, see p 381 above.
436 [1977] ICR 566, [1977] IRLR 181. This long-standing approach was reaffirmed (and said to be in line with the leading case on procedure generally, *Polkey v A E Dayton Services Ltd* [1988] ICR 142, [1987] IRLR 503, HL) in *A Links & Co Ltd v Rose* [1991] IRLR 353, Ct of Sess.
437 *Spencer v Paragon Wallpapers Ltd* [1977] ICR 301, [1976] IRLR 373. There may however be special factors, perhaps in the nature of the job itself, rendering consultation unnecessary: *Leonard v Fergus and Haynes Civil Engineering Ltd* [1979] IRLR 235; *Taylorplan Catering (Scotland) Ltd v McInally* [1980] IRLR 53. Note also that persistent absenteeism through a series of unrelated medical complaints (often impossible to verify medically) may in fact be more amenable to treatment as misconduct (with warnings and a final decision) than under the illness principles in *Spencer* and *Lindsey*: *International Sports Co Ltd v Thomson* [1980] IRLR 340; *Lynock v Cereal Packaging Ltd* [1988] ICR 670, [1988] IRLR 510; this may be particularly so under the current system of *self*-certification for the first week of sickness.

in mind the employer's need to have the work done[437]. The employer may also be expected to make such investigations as are necessary to establish the true facts of the case, which may mean taking further medical advice on the nature of the illness. It has been stressed by the EAT that the eventual decision whether to dismiss remains a managerial one, not a medical one[438], but in the nature of things the employer may reasonably have to rely heavily upon a medical prognosis (even if it later turns out to have been wrong). Even if the employee is likely to be away for a considerable period and his position needs to be filled, the employer may still be expected to consider the possibility of alternative (perhaps lighter) work for the employee instead of dismissal; this may particularly be the case where the employer is a large concern, though even then it probably stops short of an obligation to create an entirely new job for that employee[439]. There is, however, a very different possibility at the other end of the spectrum – if it becomes clear that the work is causing illness in that particular employee and there is *no* other work for him, might the employer argue that there is a common law obligation *to* dismiss, on health and safety grounds, which should make the dismissal fair? Older case law was less paternalistic[440], but in *Coxall v Goodyear GB Ltd*[441] (concerning occupational asthma) the only ground on which the employer was liable in tort for negligence was in not removing the employee from that work, the judge speculating that in an appropriate case the employer (faced with the desire of the employee to carry on and run the risks) might be 'under a duty in law to dismiss him for his own good so as to protect him against physical danger'

Once again, one of the changes in the ACAS Code of Practice on Disciplinary and Grievance Procedures in 2000 was the addition of a section (paragraphs 19 and 20) giving guidance on absence handling, drawing heavily on the case law.

It has been argued that these rules may have to be applied even more circumspectly and sympathetically if the incapacity was in fact the fault of the employer in the first place. At one point the EAT took the purist approach 'that the origin of the incapacity was irrelevant and that no different rules should apply', but a different EAT later resiled from this and held that an origin in the employer's own fault may well be a relevant factor for both liability and compensation.[442]

It will be clear from the above that the obtaining of reliable medical evidence on the sick employee is of great importance. Medical confidentiality could be a problem since the employer may not simply demand a report from the employee's

---

438 *East Lindsey District Council v Daubney* [1977] ICR 566, [1977] IRLR 181. The managerial role would be particularly important in the case of an employee either with, or suspected of being with, AIDS, and faced by reaction from fellow employees and/or customers; some practical (and educative) advice has been given in the joint DE/HSE booklet *AIDS and Employment*.

439 *Merseyside and North Wales Electricity Board v Taylor* [1975] ICR 185, [1975] IRLR 60.

440 In *Withers v Perry Chain Co Ltd* [1961] 3 All ER 676, [1961] 1 WLR 1314, CA, Devlin LJ put it pithily that 'The relationship between employer and employee is not that of a schoolmaster and pupil'. See *Munkman on Employer's Liability* (13th edn, 2001) at p 144 for the previous case law.

441 [2002] EWCA Civ 1010, [2002] IRLR 742, CA. Simon Brown LJ did allude to the paradox that the law here is becoming more paternalistic (in the light of health and safety concerns) at the same time that a human rights approach elsewhere is stressing the autonomy of the individual, including the individual employee.

442 *Edwards v Governors of Hanson School* [2001] IRLR 733, disapproving *London Fire and Civil Defence Authority v Betty* [1994] IRLR 384. One topical application here would be in cases of absence through work-related stress (as in *Edwards* itself).

own doctor. He may of course invite the employee to allow such a report to be compiled and released to him; if the employee agrees, that covers the matter of confidentiality. However, there is now the further complication that the Access to Medical Reports Act 1988 gives the employee a right to see such a report by his own doctor (provided he follows the prescribed procedure) in advance of its disclosure to the employer and, further, a right to object to part or all of it and, ultimately, to refuse to allow it to be disclosed (though of course in the latter, extreme, case there would be nothing to stop the employer drawing his own adverse inferences from the refusal and so in practice this may not be a realistic option). However, the Act is limited to reports compiled by the employee's *own* doctor, and so does not apply to a report compiled by an in-house company doctor, or an independent doctor nominated by the employer[443]. This factor now gives even more importance to the incorporation of a term into contracts of employment (as is now commonly done) that specifically gives the employer the right to require the employee to undertake a medical examination by a doctor nominated by the employer, with the results divulged to the employer. If there is no such term, the employer may only *request* such an examination.

The above discussion of illness has primarily envisaged physical illness as the incapacitating factor. Similar principles apply to mental illness, though in such a case it may be that the problem is more delicate and requires an even more understanding approach by the employer (particularly if he hired the employee knowing of his actual or potential condition). If, however, the employee actively concealed a mental condition when applying for the job, that may be a good reason for dismissal when the employer finds out (depending perhaps on the nature of the job) for that would not be primarily a dismissal for illness but rather for misconduct, as in other cases where an employee is taken on in some way under false pretences[444].

(b) Conduct[445]

As seen above[446], dismissal for misconduct was an important concept at common law, primarily in the context of wrongful dismissal where the main factor was whether the misconduct was so bad that it repudiated the whole contract and so justified summary dismissal. In the modern context of unfair dismissal, dismissal for misconduct is obviously important (as one of the principal heads of prima facie fair dismissals) but it operates on a much broader base than at common law, so that the misconduct may or may not be dealt with by summary dismissal. The reason for this is that the tribunals can now look into the substantive fairness of

---

443 This limitation is achieved indirectly by the drafting of the definition of 'medical report' in s 2(1), as 'a report ... prepared by a medical practitioner who is or has been responsible for the clinical care of the individual'. Section 3 states that the employer must have the consent of the employee before requesting the report in the first place; s 7 contains exceptions where the doctor may withhold parts of the report if disclosure could cause the employee serious physical or medical harm. On the Act generally, see Pitt (1988) 17 ILJ 239.

444 *O'Brien v Prudential Assurance Co Ltd* [1979] IRLR 140. Likewise, fraudulent use of a sick note might be good grounds for dismissal for misconduct: *Hutchinson v Enfield Rolling Mills Ltd* [1981] IRLR 318, EAT.

445 See *Harvey* DI [1351] and Q [722]n. Practical advice on handling disciplinary matters is given in the ACAS advisory handbook *Discipline at Work* chs 3–7; criminal offences by employees are covered in ch 8.

446 Pp 465–468 above.

any dismissal for misconduct, whereas at common law if an employer wished to be rid of an employee guilty of some lesser form of misconduct than that which would justify summary dismissal, he could just dismiss him with notice and, provided that notice was of the proper length, there could be no legal redress for the employee. Thus, the legal rules relating to the modern and the common law approaches to misconduct are different, so that many dismissals which at common law were unexceptionable can now be challenged as unfair; likewise, a dismissal could be wrongful at common law (because the conduct was not grave enough to warrant the summary dismissal which was inflicted upon the employee) but a tribunal might still hold that in the circumstances it was fair[447]. On the other hand, there will remain a practical relationship between the modern and the common law actions in that certain major heads of misconduct accepted as justifying summary dismissal at common law will remain major categories of fair dismissals, for example failure to obey proper and lawful orders[448], breach of confidence by the employee by unfairly competing with the employer or prejudicing confidentiality necessary to his business[449] and computer misuse by the employee[450]. One further influence of the common law could arise in the case of an employee who consistently plays practical jokes or is inclined to show physical aggression, for in such a case there is a common law duty upon the employer to take reasonable care for the safety of that employee's *fellow* employees[451], which may ultimately require his dismissal.

These overlaps apart, misconduct in the modern statutory context fits into the overall pattern of unfair dismissal law in being essentially a matter of assessing the reasonableness of the employer's reaction to it in all the varied circumstances of the case, including any extraneous matters such as length of service and previous good conduct which may act in mitigation of the offence; it is a particularly wide category of dismissal, ranging from gross misconduct (still justifying summary dismissal) such as theft, violence, wilful refusal to obey an order and gross negligence, down to lesser matters such as swearing and poor timekeeping which may only become serious if committed regularly. Faced with this wide diversity, there is sometimes an unfortunate tendency to attempt to over-classify, as if for example the many decided cases established a 'law on fighting at work'; while collecting together all the cases on one kind of misconduct may have some value, it must be stressed that that value is restricted to attempting to point out certain factors which *may* be important in certain of the more typical cases. Further than that, these matters remain clearly within the factual jurisdiction of the tribunals. Swearing is a good example of this, for there are ample cases on it but it remains purely a question of fact whether a particular incident merited dismissal, usually depending on factors such as the nature and place of the employment, the effect

---

447 *Treganowen v Robert Knee & Co Ltd* [1975] ICR 405, [1975] IRLR 247.
448 As at common law, the employee may refuse to obey an unlawful order: *Morrish v Henlys (Folkestone) Ltd* [1973] ICR 482, [1973] IRLR 61, NIRC.
449 *Mansard Precision Engineering Co Ltd v Taylor* [1978] ICR 44; *Golden Cross Hire Co Ltd v Lovell* [1979] IRLR 267; *Nova Plastic Ltd v Frogatt* [1982] IRLR 146.
450 *Denco Ltd v Joinson* [1991] ICR 172, [1991] IRLR 63; *Thomas v Hillingdon London Borough Council* (2002) Times, 4 October.
451 *Hudson v Ridge Manufacturing Co Ltd* [1957] 2 QB 348, [1957] 2 All ER 229; see p 847 below. Various statutory duties upon the employer to ensure compliance with safety regulations and the use of safety devices may be an important factor in the dismissal of an employee who consistently acts to the peril of himself and other employees.

upon the recipient, whether it was gratuitous or provoked and any previous incidents; thus, for example, words used to a fellow employee in the course of work on a building site could give rise to different considerations if used to a customer by an assistant at a perfume counter.

Except in cases of dismissal for a single act of gross misconduct, this area of dismissal is a prime one for the application of a warnings system (and in most cases for the granting of a hearing to allow the employee to put forward either his view of the facts, or mitigating circumstances having a bearing upon the question whether to dismiss[452]). A series of warnings may be particularly important in cases of persistent minor misconduct where it is primarily the fact of repetition which may eventually justify dismissal. Moreover, the emphasis in the warnings in this context will normally be disciplinary and so the employer should ensure that they are given in accordance with any procedure laid down in the employee's contract or in the works rules; to this end, it is usually advisable for such terms or rules to lay down any types of misconduct which are particularly relevant to the job in question and the likely consequences of transgressions[453]. Some employers may feel that by laying down such rules they are fettering their discretion, but this should not be the case for in general disciplinary rules, if properly phrased, need not be viewed as exhaustive (and so the employee cannot claim that he cannot be disciplined because what he did does not fall neatly within a particular category in the rules[454]); moreover, the employer stands to gain, for if he wishes to treat as particularly heinous (in his circumstances) something which normally would not be viewed as serious (such as smoking at work or drinking at lunch time), he is well advised to say so in his rules – if not he may have difficulty showing that a dismissal is fair when the subject matter of it would not normally be viewed as a dismissable offence in other contexts[455].

The major conceptual problem here is in trying to achieve the right balance between certainty and flexibility. On the one hand, it is said to be an important principle that people committing like offences should be treated alike (equality is equity), which argues in favour of a consistent application of disciplinary rules, regardless of who the culprit is[456]. On the other hand it is said that the key to unfair dismissal is flexibility by the employer, judging each case on its merits and

---

452 The importance of following proper procedures in misconduct cases was given a welcome reaffirmation by the Court of Appeal in *McLaren v National Coal Board* [1988] ICR 370, [1988] IRLR 215 (dismissal without any form of hearing unfair, even though it was impossible to operate the normal procedures in the middle of the miners' strike); cf however the different decision on the facts in *Dillett v National Coal Board* [1988] ICR 218, CA (a pre-*Polkey* case).

453 An important and topical example of this is the desirability of clear policies on email and Internet abuse by employees working with computers (given the potential legal difficulties for the employer, eg through the downloading and misuse of porn, especially if used for harassment of others). Such policies are strongly advised by the Data Protection Code of Practice, Pt III 'Monitoring of Employees'. If the correct procedures are carried out, dismissal for downloading porn at work is likely to be fair: *Thomas v Hillingdon London Borough Council* (2002) Times, 4 October.

454 *Distillers Co (Bottling Services) Ltd v Gardner* [1982] IRLR 47; *Macari v Celtic Football & Athletic Co Ltd* [1999] IRLR 787, Ct of Sess. An ambiguous approach by an employer (eg when setting out disciplinary rules) may however render a dismissal for a *first* breach of a particular rule unfair: *Trusthouse Forte (Catering) Ltd v Adonis* [1984] IRLR 382, EAT.

455 *Dairy Produce Packers Ltd v Beverstock* [1981] IRLR 265. One example might be particularly high standards of hygiene in food-processing establishments.

456 *Post Office v Fennell* [1981] IRLR 221, CA.

not simply adopting a 'tariff' approach to misconduct based upon rigid disciplinary rules[457]. In as much as the latter point means the matters of *mitigation* should be considered in each individual case (for example, length of service, previous work record) it is consistent with a more certain approach to the offence itself (as in the former point) and so one possible approach (particularly in a larger organisation) is that the employer should *start* by considering from the personnel records whether there have been any similar previous incidents and how they were dealt with, before going on to consider the specific facts and any mitigation in the instant case[458]. One thing that can be stated with some confidence, however, is that tribunals should be wary of simple 'disparity' arguments by applicants because, as any lawyer knows, few cases are so similar as to be directly comparable, particularly when the element of mitigation is taken into account[459].

Suspension pending fuller investigation by the employer may be appropriate in serious cases (provided the employer has contractual authority to do so); the Code of Practice[460] states that normally this should be with pay and only for a brief period and so in reality the employer may not be expected to do so for any great length of time and may reasonably have to take the decision to dismiss once he has had time to make reasonable investigations, even if other eventualities such as a criminal trial of the employee are still pending[461]; indeed, any greater delay before the employer takes decisive action could conceivably make the eventual dismissal unfair[462]. As well as the application of warnings and hearings, dismissal for misconduct is also a prime area for the application of the principle that the function of the tribunal is to decide upon the reasonableness of the action taken by the employer, not simply to substitute their views for his; in a case as heavily dependent upon its facts as a misconduct case, there may well be a considerable area of discretion in which several solutions might have been reasonable and as long as dismissal was within that area the employer is not to be penalised for choosing it in preference to any lesser measure[463].

The type of misconduct case which has caused most concern is the case where the employee has committed a criminal offence, particularly (though not necessarily) theft. Proved theft from the employer will usually be a clear ground for dismissal (regardless of the amount taken)[464] as will wilful concealment of previous convictions when applying for a job[465] unless the conviction is 'spent' within the meaning of the Rehabilitation of Offenders Act 1974, in which case the employee is not obliged to disclose it and a dismissal because of it will be unfair[466]. The problems arise in cases where there is only a *suspicion* that the

457 *Taylor v Parsons Peebles NEI Bruce Peebles Ltd* [1981] IRLR 119; *Hadjioannou v Coral Casinos Ltd* [1981] IRLR 352, EAT.
458 *Procter v British Gypsum Ltd* [1992] IRLR 7; *Harrow London Borough v Cunningham* [1996] IRLR 256.
459 *Paul v East Surrey District Health Authority* [1995] IRLR 305, CA.
460 Para 13.
461 *Conway v Matthew Wright & Nephew Ltd* [1977] IRLR 89, EAT.
462 Cf *Refund Rentals Ltd v McDermott* [1977] IRLR 59.
463 *Trust House Forte Leisure Ltd v Aquilar* [1976] IRLR 251; *Trust House Forte Hotels Ltd v Murphy* [1977] IRLR 186. See p 571 above.
464 *Murphy*'s case, n 463 above.
465 *Torr v British Railways Board* [1977] ICR 785, [1977] IRLR 184, EAT.
466 *Property Guards Ltd v Taylor* [1982] IRLR 175. Certain categories of persons, primarily professional or connected with law enforcement, are excluded: Rehabilitation of Offenders Act 1974 (Exceptions) Order 1975, SI 1975/1023. *Harvey* R [40]. These categories were significantly extended in 2001 in relation to employments involving contact with children and vulnerable adults: see p 104 below.

employee has committed an offence, for the employer may feel that he ought to dismiss the employee immediately even though it may be some time before a criminal case can be brought against the employee (which may of course result in his eventual acquittal). Where the criminal offence arose outside the employment (for example, theft from another person or the commission of a sexual or drug offence outside working hours), the employer should not normally dismiss before the employee has been found guilty[467] and even then should only do so if on the facts (looking at the nature of the offence, the type of job and the potential effects on customers and fellow employees) the commission of that offence renders the employee unsuitable for the job in question[468]. The Code of Practice, paragraph 26 puts it thus:

> '*Criminal charges or convictions outside employment.* These should not be treated as automatic reasons for dismissal. The main consideration should be whether the offence is one that makes workers unsuitable for their type of work. In all cases employers, having considered the facts, will need to consider whether the conduct is sufficiently serious to warrant instituting the disciplinary procedure. For instance, workers should not be dismissed solely because a charge against them is pending or because they are absent as a result of being remanded in custody.'

One possible complicating factor, yet to be elaborated upon, is the suggestion that, in a case of misconduct away from work, it may be reasonable to expect a *large* employer at least to consider whether there was any other employment to which the employee could be transferred, rather than being dismissed[469]. The idea of alternative work is, of course, well known in capability and redundancy cases, but could be difficult to apply here.

Where the crime arises within the employment (the obvious example being theft of the employer's property) the employer's need to dismiss may appear to him to be more urgent, but at the same time the employee under suspicion must not be treated arbitrarily. The position as it has evolved (particularly since the decision of the EAT in *British Home Stores Ltd v Burchell*[470], approved by the Court

---

467 *Securicor Guarding Ltd v R* [1994] IRLR 633. In the contrary case, where a criminal conviction comes *before* an internal disciplinary hearing, it will normally be reasonable for the employer to rely on the court's finding of guilt (including where the employee has pleaded), without going behind that finding, even where the employee still maintains his innocence: *P v Nottinghamshire County Council* [1992] ICR 706, [1992] IRLR 362, CA; *Secretary of State for Scotland v Campbell* [1992] IRLR 263, EAT.

468 See *Nottinghamshire County Council v Bowly* [1978] IRLR 252; *Norfolk County Council v Bernard* [1979] IRLR 220; *Moore v C & A Modes* [1981] IRLR 71; *Mathewson v RB Wilson Dental Laboratory Ltd* [1988] IRLR 512. 'Conduct means actions of such a nature, whether done in the course of employment or outwith it, that reflects in some way on the employer–employee relationship': *Thomson v Alloa Motor Co* [1983] IRLR 403 at 404, per Lord McDonald.

469 *P v Nottinghamshire County Council*, n 6 above. If the employer does look for other work before dismissing, however, that is *not* to be used by the employee as an argument that the misconduct could not have been too serious: *Hamilton v Argyll and Clyde Health Board* [1993] IRLR 99, EAT.

470 [1980] ICR 303n, [1978] IRLR 379; see also *Ferodo Ltd v Barnes* [1976] ICR 439, [1976] IRLR 302; *Alidair Ltd v Taylor* [1978] ICR 445 at 451, [1978] IRLR 82 at 85, CA, per Lord Denning MR. The requirement is of actual belief, not just suspicion. However, a well-founded belief in the employee's *intent* to commit the offence may suffice, if he has been found out before committing it: *British Railways Board v Jackson* [1994] IRLR 235, CA. The principles in *British Home Stores Ltd v Burchell* apply to all forms of misconduct, not just to dishonesty cases: *Distillers Co (Bottling Services) Ltd v Gardner* [1982] IRLR 47; they were reaffirmed in *ILEA v Gravett* [1988] IRLR 497 and *Whitbread & Co plc v Mills* [1988] ICR 776, [1988] IRLR 501.

of Appeal in *W Weddel & Co Ltd v Tepper*[471] and *Whitbread plc v Hall*[472] and fully in line with the current, post-*Polkey* approach) is that the employer may dismiss if he has a genuine belief in the employee's guilt, which is based upon reasonable grounds; he does not have to be able to *prove* the employee's guilt and so provided the employer has his genuine belief it is irrelevant if the employee is later acquitted of the offence (or indeed if the police decline to bring charges)[473]. Thus, it is not the function of the tribunal to try the criminal action against the employee and the employer certainly does not have to prove guilt beyond reasonable doubt – the inquiry is a much more general one than that[474], looking into the bona fides and reasonableness of the employer's claimed belief. The reasonableness of his belief will depend primarily upon whether the employer made a reasonable investigation to establish the facts and drew tenable conclusions from the results.

What constitutes a reasonable investigation will of course vary with the circumstances, so that in the case of red-handed theft with little attempt at explanation, the requirement may not be onerous. In less obvious cases, the employer should make a careful inquiry[475], allowing the employee to be heard in his own defence, but there is a major qualification on this for the EAT have suggested that where the employee's actions are being actively investigated by the police with a view to criminal proceedings it may be improper for the employer to hold a full investigation of his own and to expect the employee to explain his conduct[476]. However, on at least one occasion[477], the EAT have suggested that in such a case the employer might at least give the employee an opportunity to make representations particularly on the question whether the employer ought to go as far as to dismiss (which may involve matters in mitigation, such as long and satisfactory service); in many cases, the employer might in fact gain from doing so, for he will be seen to be acting in the spirit of a fair procedure and also any failure by the employee to put forward his point of view might be held against

471 [1980] ICR 286, [1980] IRLR 96, CA.
472 [2001] EWCA Civ 268, [2001] ICR 699, [2001] IRLR 275.
473 *Da Costa v Optolis* [1976] IRLR 178; *Harris (Ipswich) Ltd v Harrison* [1978] ICR 1256, [1978] IRLR 382. A difficult case might arise if an employee, having been (fairly) dismissed for theft, was later proved to have been innocent and brought defamation proceedings against the employer. Presumably the defence of justification would not be available and so the employer would have to rely on the protean defence of qualified privilege. For an example of findings of fair dismissal after acquittals by a criminal court, see *Dhaliwal v British Airways Board* [1985] ICR 513, EAT.
474 The strict rules of criminal evidence do not apply so that, for example, evidence of previous dishonesty is admissible, and indeed may be highly relevant: *Docherty v Reddy* [1977] ICR 365; *Coral Squash Clubs Ltd v Matthews* [1979] ICR 607, [1979] IRLR 390.
475 Even under the Employment Act 2002, s 34 (introducing the new Employment Rights Act 1996 s 98A (2) which reintroduces a qualified form of the rule in *British Labour Pump Co Ltd v Byrne* [1979] ICR 347, [1979] IRLR 94 that a dismissal may be fair in spite of a defective procedure if the employer can prove that he would have dismissed anyway, see p 570 above) it is unlikely that a definable failure to investigate would be 'forgiven', as it is central under *BHS v Burchell* and unlikely to be considered a merely technical slip.
476 *Carr v Alexander Russell Ltd* [1979] ICR 469n, [1976] IRLR 220; *Conway v Matthew Wright & Nephew Ltd* [1977] IRLR 89; *Tesco (Holdings) Ltd v Hill* [1977] IRLR 63; *Parker v Clifford Dunn Ltd* [1979] ICR 463, [1979] IRLR 56. If the employee chooses to remain silent because of impending criminal charges, it may still be reasonable for the employer to dismiss on the basis of other evidence available: *Harris v Courage (Eastern) Ltd* [1981] ICR 496, [1981] IRLR 153.
477 *Harris (Ipswich) Ltd v Harrison* [1978] ICR 1256, [1978] IRLR 382.

him. When carrying out his investigation, the involvement of the police may be important for if they give to the employer definite information about their findings that may go far towards confirming the employer's suspicions[478]; on the other hand, the mere fact of police investigation may not be sufficient in itself to constitute reasonable grounds for a belief in guilt and likewise an employer should not simply 'delegate' the matter to the police and the courts (for example, deciding not to investigate for himself, but merely to await the outcome of the court case, dismissing automatically if the employee is found guilty)[479].

The employer must therefore have a genuine belief in the employee's guilt based upon such investigations as were reasonable in the circumstances; primarily the belief must relate to the guilt of the particular individual though it has been held by the Court of Appeal that if the employer can only narrow it down to one of two employees, but he genuinely believes it must be one or other of them, it may be reasonable to dismiss *both*, which seems distinctly hard on the innocent one[480]. Once the employer has the necessary belief, he will normally be acting reasonably in dismissing in the standard case of theft (in the absence of exceptionally strong mitigating factors of which he knew or ought to have known). It should be noted, however, that there have been suggestions that, as in the other misconduct cases, it depends upon the facts of the case whether the offence is grave enough to warrant dismissal; in particular, it has been suggested that minor participation in theft, or theft from someone other than the employer (for example, from a fellow employee) *might* not warrant dismissal in some cases[481], though it remains clear that theft from the employer himself will be a good ground for dismissal in almost all cases.

(c) Redundancy[482]

The conceptual problem with redundancy in this context is that it is a dismissal which is at the same time ostensibly fair (in that the employer has no option but to dismiss) and unfair (in that the employee has done no wrong). The basic approach has therefore been to make it subject to a separate Code (now Part XI of the 1996 Act, governing the statutory rights to redundancy payments), but to acknowledge that in some redundancy cases the employer may still be said to have acted unfairly, especially procedurally. With this background in mind we must look at the detailed rules.

Redundancy is a prima facie fair ground for dismissal. The employer must establish that redundancy was the principal reason for dismissal, since the statutory presumption of redundancy for the purposes of the redundancy

---

478 As in *Carr's* case and *Parker's* case, n 15, above. However, actual police presence at an internal disciplinary hearing may well be held to render it invalid because of the pressure put on the employee: *Read v Phoenix Preservation Ltd* [1985] ICR 164, [1985] IRLR 93.

479 *McLaren v National Coal Board* [1988] ICR 370, [1988] IRLR 215, CA. It will, however, normally be reasonable for the employer to rely on the *fact* of conviction when making his decision, see n 467 above.

480 *Monie v Coral Racing Ltd* [1981] ICR 109, [1980] IRLR 464, CA. This decision was applied to a case of suspected *negligence* by one of two fitters in *McPhie v Wimpey Waste Management Ltd* [1981] IRLR 316 and to a case of incapability in *Whitbread & Co plc v Thomas* [1988] ICR 135, [1988] IRLR 43. In *Parr v Whitbread & Co plc* [1990] ICR 427, [1990] IRLR 39 it was applied to one of four; the case contains useful guidance from Wood P.

481 *Johnson Matthey Metals Ltd v Harding* [1978] IRLR 248, EAT.

482 See *Harvey* DI[1602], Q[722]n.

483 Employment Rights Act 1996, s 170(2).

484 *Midland Foot Comfort Centre Ltd v Richmond* [1973] 2 All ER 294, [1973] IRLR 141.

payments scheme[483] is not applicable in an unfair dismissal claim[484]; once he has done so, a tribunal may not look behind that reason and consider whether the employer really was obliged to make employees redundant and if so whose fault it was – that economic decision remains with the employer[485], and if he succeeds in showing it as the principal reason his primary liability will only be to make the statutory redundancy payments. In a simple redundancy case, for example upon a properly conducted liquidation[486], that will be the appropriate action to bring, but it is also possible for a dismissed employee to claim both a redundancy payment and unfair dismissal[487], since a redundancy dismissal is only prima facie fair and may become unfair either under special statutory provisions, or under the general test of reasonableness contained in section 98(4).

A redundancy dismissal is deemed to be unfair by a combination now of section 153 of the Trade Union and Labour Relations (Consolidation) Act 1992 and section 105 of the Employment Rights Act 1996 if the employee can show that the circumstances producing the redundancy applied equally to other comparable employees[488] in the same undertaking who were not dismissed, and the applicant employee was chosen for dismissal because of union membership or activities, or non-membership[489] or for an 'inadmissible reason' (covering the categories where dismissal is made automatically unfair, for example where the reason for dismissal is contrary to the special protection afforded to pregnancy or childbirth, making health and safety complaints, asserting statutory rights, being a protected shopworker, acting as an employee representative or pension fund trustee, exercising rights to the national minimum wage or under the Working Time Regulations, Part-time Worker Regulations or Fixed-term Employee Regulations or the protection given to whistleblowers). The aim of these provisions is to prevent an employer from using the more subtle technique of getting rid of perceived troublemakers or difficult cases by a later redundancy selection (an immediate dismissal on any of these grounds now being declared automatically unfair, see below).

There used to be a second ground of statutory unfair redundancy dismissal, which was where the dismissal was in breach of a collectively agreed redundancy procedure (or arrangement)[490]. The aim of this long-standing provision was to give statutory backing to such procedures. However, by 1994 the previous government took the view that it was out of line with their current thinking (being an element of the collective co-determination model of industrial relations that they had spent years dismantling); traditionally, such procedures had been heavily based on LIFO (last-in-first-out) which was seen by unions as, at least, the less unfair way of selecting employees[491]. However, in times of recession and declining union influence and recognition, many managers were seeking to move away from LIFO and towards far more rigorous procedures of selection on

---

485 *Moon v Homeworthy Furniture (Northern) Ltd* [1977] ICR 117, [1976] IRLR 298; *James W Cook & Co (Wivenhoe) Ltd v Tipper* [1990] ICR 716, [1990] IRLR 386, CA.

486 *Fox Bros (Clothes) Ltd v Bryant* [1979] ICR 64, [1978] IRLR 485.

487 Though he cannot receive double compensation: Employment Rights Act 1996, s 122(4).

488 *Powers v A Clarke & Co (Smethwick) Ltd* [1981] IRLR 483.

489 This head of unfair dismissal generally is considered at p 685 below.

490 This used to be contained in the Employment Protection (Consolidation) Act 1978, s 59(1)(b); for its interpretation in the case law, see the fifth edition of this book, at pp 371–372.

491 In 1990 length of service as the criterion was found in 70% of workplaces with a recognised union but in only 35% of workplaces without such recognition: Millward et al *Workplace Industrial Relations in Transition* (1992), p 325. The survey also found that, where redundancy procedures still existed, there was no evidence of LIFO becoming less common.

merit and ability, regardless of length of service. Redundancy procedures were thus being radically altered or scrapped altogether (at a time when large numbers of redundancies were having to be made, and when selection on merit was seen as an essential aid to business survival)[492] and so the decision was taken to repeal the statutory protection for redundancy procedures altogether[493]. The present government have shown no intention to reinstate it.

This removal of collectively based safeguards in redundancy cases has placed even more emphasis on what has been the most important development in this branch of unfair dismissal law, namely that (in addition to any special statutory provisions) an employee may claim that his dismissal for redundancy was unfair *generally*, ie that, under section 98(4), the employer's conduct was unreasonable having regard to equity and the substantial merits of the case. This significant widening of the approach to redundancy cases was originally approved by the Court of Appeal in *Bessenden Properties Ltd v Corness*[494] and remains as important head of unfair dismissal, primarily because of the greater compensation available than the amount recoverable as a simple redundancy payment. This widening allows a tribunal some discretion to review the overall fairness of the dismissal and has led in the cases to the evolution of three general requirements upon an employer who is about to make an employee redundant[495]. The first is that he must not select that employee unfairly; blatant unfairness may be challenged in this way, but in many cases it will be difficult to establish for many different factors may be involved and so questions such as efficiency and suitability of the employee may arguably be just as reasonably relied upon as a general LIFO principle. The second is that the employer should make reasonable efforts where practicable to look for alternative employment within the firm (or possibly within the group to which the firm belongs[496]), though tribunals should not expect unrealistic efforts to be made in what may be difficult circumstances[497]. The third is that, as a rule,

---

492 This was commented on particularly in the ACAS Annual Reports 1991, p 16 and 1992, p12.

493 Deregulation and Contracting Out Act 1994, s 36.

494 [1977] ICR 821n, [1974] IRLR 338, CA.

495 These three requirements are now so well established that they should automatically be considered by a tribunal in an unfair redundancy case, even if not specifically raised by an applicant (eg where he or she is a litigant in person): *Langston v Cranfield University* [1998] IRLR 172, EAT.

496 *Vokes Ltd v Bear* [1974] ICR 1, [1973] IRLR 363; *Modern Injection Moulds Ltd v Price* [1976] ICR 370, [1976] IRLR 172. However, a requirement to look within the group, not just within the firm itself, was looked on with disfavour by the Scottish EAT in *Barratt Construction Ltd v Dalrymple* [1984] IRLR 385, and by the English EAT in *MDH Ltd v Sussex* [1986] IRLR 123, EAT.

497 *British United Shoe Machinery Co Ltd v Clarke* [1978] ICR 70, [1977] IRLR 297. In *Thomas and Betts Manufacturing Ltd v Harding* [1980] IRLR 255, CA, it was said that s 98 is so wide that this may mean looking for other jobs for A to do, even if that means dismissing B instead (if B has less seniority than A), ie a 'bumping' redundancy (though cf the problems with this concept, p 630 below); once again, however, the Scottish EAT has been unwilling to apply this wider approach: *Green v A&I Fraser (Wholesale Fish Merchants) Ltd* [1985] IRLR 55. Note that statutory preference (in finding other work) is given to (a) women on maternity leave when made redundant (Maternity and Parental Leave etc Regulations 1999, SI 1999/3312, reg 10), (b) employees on adoption leave when made redundant (Paternity and Adoption Leave Regulations 2002, SI 2002/2788, reg 23) and (c) disabled employees, where the employer is making reasonable adjustments (Disability Discrimination Act 1995, s 6(3)(c); *Kent County Council v Mingo* [2000] IRLR 90).

the employer should consult the employee and give him reasonable warning of impending redundancy[498]; this requirement has been said to increase in importance the more the employer moves away from easily applied criteria for selection such as LIFO, towards more judgemental criteria based on work performance and company need[499]. On a general level, its importance was strengthened by the renewed emphasis on procedure in *Polkey* (below), itself a redundancy dismissal case, in the light of which it has been subsequently said by the EAT that 'the importance of such consultation cannot be over-emphasised'[500].

These guidelines were reaffirmed and recast by the EAT in *Williams v Compair Maxam Ltd*[501], giving additional emphasis to two further criteria. The first is that where the employer recognises a union the necessary consultations will normally of course be with that union, and where this is the case the employer should give as much warning as possible of the impending redundancies, seek to agree criteria for selection with the union, review the eventual selection with the union to consider whether it is in accordance with those criteria and consider union representations on selection. This point will now have to be expanded to include the case where there is no recognised union but, because of the added rules requiring consultation with employee representatives[502], there are collective redundancies requiring by law such consultation; lack of it may affect the fairness of any eventual individual redundancies. One major point of difficulty is whether there has to be *double* consultation, ie with both union or employee representatives and individual employee. In *Walls Meat Co Ltd v Selby*[503] the Court of Appeal declined to lay down any principle requiring such two-stage consultation; on the other hand, Balcombe LJ did say that in a particular case good industrial practice might require it. The court did uphold a tribunal decision of unfair dismissal based on failure to consult the individual as well as the union, and other cases have assumed the need to involve the individual as well[504]. This will therefore be a matter heavily dependent on the circumstances of a particular case, with much discretion given to a tribunal, and resulting uncertainly for an employer in knowing whether he has done enough to resist an individual challenge of unfair dismissal. The second is that when working out criteria for selection (whether or not with union agreement) the emphasis must be on criteria which leave as little

---

498 *Clarkson International Tools Ltd v Short* [1973] ICR 191, [1973] IRLR 90; *Kelly v Upholstery and Cabinet Works (Amesbury) Ltd* [1977] IRLR 91; *British United Shoe Machinery Co Ltd v Clarke* [1978] ICR 70, [1977] IRLR 297; cf *Atkinson v George Lindsay & Co* [1980] IRLR 196, Ct of Sess. The importance of this factor was reaffirmed by the EAT in *Freud v Bentalls Ltd* [1983] ICR 77, [1982] IRLR 443 and *Holden v Bradville Ltd* [1985] IRLR 483. The requirement is for warning *and* consultation, not just one: *Rowell v Hubbard Group Services* [1995] IRLR 195, EAT.
499 *Graham v ABF Ltd* [1986] IRLR 90; *Ferguson v Prestwick Circuits Ltd* [1992] IRLR 266. Small size of an enterprise may affect the level of consultation, but cannot excuse total lack of it: *De Grasse v Stockwell Tools Ltd* [1992] IRLR 269, EAT.
500 *Dyke v Hereford and Worcester County Council* [1989] ICR 800 at 807, per Wood J. A particularly useful summary of the consultation requirements is to be found in the judgment of Judge Clark in *Mugford v Midland Bank plc* [1997] ICR 399, [1997] IRLR 208.
501 [1982] ICR 156, [1982] IRLR 83.
502 See p 85 above.
503 [1989] ICR 601, CA.
504 In *Huddersfield Parcels Ltd v Sykes* [1981] IRLR 115 it was held that union consultation was not enough if the employee himself is left in the dark, and the general guidance on handling redundancies by Wood P in *Dyke v Hereford and Worcester County Council* [1989] ICR 800 assumes that, at least in most cases, consultation will be with both; *Rolls-Royce Motor Cars Ltd v Price* [1993] IRLR 203 is to like effect.

as possible to subjective assessments by the people making the selection, but rather are capable of being objectively applied on the basis of matters such as length of service, experience and efficiency[505].

The reaction to *Williams v Compair Maxam Ltd* has been mixed. It initially fared badly in the Scottish courts with the Scottish EAT showing itself unwilling to apply it to redundancies in smaller firms, especially when they are not unionised[506], and the Court of Session in *Buchanan v Tilcon Ltd*[507] taking a broader, less specific approach to redundancy cases, assuming that it will be relatively easy for an employer to show a redundancy dismissal to have been fair generally, once he has shown compliance with the specific statutory requirements. The English EAT, however, applied it[508], but subject to the qualification that this is an area in which it is particularly important that the tribunal should apply the 'range of reasonable responses' test[509] and not simply impose its own view as to how its members might have handled the redundancy[510]. As seen several times already, *Polkey v AE Dayton Services Ltd*[511], with its emphasis on the contiuing importance of procedures, was a landmark case generally, and in this context it is useful to remember that it was in fact an unfair redundancy case. Curiously, *Williams v Compair Maxam Ltd* was not specifically approved but, although Lord Mackay LC did not hold that a breach of normal procedure would invariably make a dismissal unfair, the overall effect of *Polkey* in reinstating procedural fairness as a central factor must be taken as backing for *Williams*. This was certainly the tenor of subsequent reported cases[512], a point of some significance given the generally high level of unfair redundancy claims in recent years, especially during times of recession.

However, possibly as a reaction to that high level of claims, two later Court of Appeal decisions have shown yet another potential change in emphasis, placing qualifications on findings of unfairness, and demonstrating again the volatility of this area of law. The first qualification concerns those cases where the normal procedures can reasonably be dispensed with. As stated above, *Polkey* does not require slavish adherence to procedures in cases where they could have no effect. The tendency was to look to Lord Bridge's speech for the exceptional case[513], which he described as being where the employer (subjectively) thought reasonably *at the time* that to go through the usual procedures would be meaningless; in such a case, the dismissal could still be fair. However, in *Duffy v Yeomans & Partners Ltd*[514] the Court of Appeal held that the proper description

---

505 Thus, in *Williams v Compair Maxam Ltd* the redundancy was held to be unfair, partly on the ground that the criteria established by the employer (that those retained would be those 'who, in the opinion of the managers concerned, would be able to keep the company viable') lacked the necessary objectivity.
506 *Meikle v McPhail (Charleston Arms)* [1983] IRLR 351; *A Simpson & Son (Motors) v Reid and Findlater* [1983] IRLR 401; *Gray v Shetland Norse Preserving Co Ltd* [1985] IRLR 53.
507 [1983] IRLR 417, Ct of Sess.
508 *Grundy (Teddington) Ltd v Plummer* [1983] ICR 367, [1983] IRLR 98.
509 See p 571 above.
510 *Grundy (Teddington) Ltd v Willis* [1976] ICR 323, [1976] IRLR 118; *Watling & Co Ltd v Richardson* [1978] ICR 1049, [1978] IRLR 255.
511 [1988] ICR 142, [1987] IRLR 503, HL.
512 *Walls Meat Co Ltd v Selby* [1989] ICR 601, CA; *Dyke v Hereford and Worcester County Council* [1989] ICR 800; *Ferguson v Prestwick Circuits Ltd* [1992] IRLR 266; *De Grasse v Stockwell Tools Ltd* [1992] IRLR 269; *Rolls-Royce Motor Cars Ltd v Price* [1993] IRLR 203, EAT.
513 See *Robertson v Magnet Ltd* [1993] IRLR 512, EAT.
514 [1995] ICR 1, [1994] IRLR 642, CA.

of the exception is that given by Lord Mackay LC, ie an objective test of whether the employer *could reasonably have concluded* at the time that to go through the usual procedures would be meaningless. This is more than semantics because the latter, objective, test could (if applied too loosely) come to bear an unfortunate resemblance to the old 'but it made no difference' test in *British Labour Pump Co Ltd v Byrne*[515], which was disapproved in *Polkey*. There is a difference in principle (under *Duffy* the tribunal must still look at the date of dismissal, whereas *Byrne* allowed the unrestrained use of hindsight), but it is a point that may need careful handling by the tribunals.

The second qualification poses an even more fundamental question – given that (a) a tribunal cannot rule upon the business need for the redundancy, (b) it is therefore confined to judging the fairness of the *handling* of the situation by the employer, and (c) the modern tendency has been to replace more simple LIFO-based criteria with more complex and judgmental assessments of skill and worth (often on a points-scoring, 'brownie points', system), how closely should a tribunal investigate the fairness of the *application* of such a system? Should it just look at the general fairness of the system set up by the employer, or should it (as the applicant will probably want) investigate in detail the scoring of *all* the employees involved, in order to decide whether the applicant had been wrongly scored or harshly treated, and so unfairly selected? One point of procedure which may act as the focus for this whole question is the power of the tribunal to order discovery; if the employee chosen has been given his score, but the employer has refused to divulge the scores of the other employees under consideration, should a tribunal accede to that employee's request for an order for discovery of that further information (without which a detailed analysis of the application of the employer's selection scheme probably cannot be made in practice)? In *Eaton Ltd v King*[516] a selected employee was not given the scores of others not selected; moreover, at the tribunal hearing the only employer witness was the plant manager who had *reviewed* all the employee assessments but had not carried them out and could not say why any particular scores had been awarded. In spite of this, the Scottish EAT held that the dismissal was not unfair, commenting that all that the employer has to prove is that the method of selection was fair, and was generally applied reasonably by the responsible manager(s); moreover effective consultation did not require the divulging of information on other employees. In itself, this case could merely have been an example of the more trenchant approach normally taken by the Scottish courts to redundancy dismissal cases[517]. However, the same approach was taken (and the case approved) subsequently by the Court of Appeal in *British Aerospace plc v Green*[518], where an order for discovery was refused and, on the substantive point at issue, Waite LJ summed up the view of the whole court as follows:

---

515 [1979] ICR 347, [1979] IRLR 94; see p 569 above.
516 [1995] IRLR 75 (revsd on other grounds by the Court of Session: sub nom *King v Eaton Ltd* [1996] IRLR 199).
517 See p 589 above. In particular, the EAT relied on the decision of the Court of Session in *Buchanan v Tilcon Ltd* [1983] IRLR 417.
518 [1995] ICR 1006, [1995] IRLR 433, CA. There may be a novel complication, given recent developments, concerning the lawfulness of disclosing information on other employees and whether to do so might contravene the data protection legislation; see particularly the Data Protection Employment Code of Practice, Part II: Employee Records.

'Employment law recognises, pragmatically, that an over-minute investigation of the selection process by the tribunal members may run the risk of defeating the purpose which the tribunals were called into being to discharge – namely, a swift, informal disposal of disputes arising from redundancy in the workplace. So in general the employer who sets up a system of selection which can reasonably be described as fair and applies it without any overt sign of conduct which mars its fairness will have done all that the law requires of him.[519]'

It must be said at the outset that there was indeed a 'pragmatic' reason for refusing discovery in this case because of its very scale – it involved the making redundant (following the cancellation of a fighter contract) of 530 employees out of a workforce of approximately 7,000. However, only one judge (Stuart-Smith LJ) made any reference to the court's approach being restricted to mass redundancy cases, and the two other judgments are in broad terms, which are capable of causing severe problems because their premise is a denial that redundancy selection operates on a comparative and competitive basis at all:

'Documents relating to retained employees are not likely to be relevant in any but the most exceptional circumstances. The question for the industrial tribunal, which must be determined separately for each applicant, is whether the applicant was unfairly dismissed, *not whether some other employee could have been fairly dismissed.*[520]'

This cannot, with respect, be correct; given that X redundancies have to be made (which cannot be challenged) and that an inherently competitive points-scoring system has been put into place to effect that, any consideration of the fairness of selecting employee A *must* involve their comparison with those not chosen, and whether the criteria have been properly applied; however distasteful it may be, a challenge to the fairness of selecting A must include within it at least an implied assertion that B or C should have been chosen instead. *British Aerospace* denies this completely. Moreover, only two months later the EAT in *FDR Ltd v Holloway*[521] effectively ignored *British Aerospace* and upheld an order for discovery of information on employees not selected[522], stating that this was essential in order to dispose of the issue of whether the selection criteria had been applied fairly, and that a

---

519 [1995] ICR 1006 at 1010, [1995] IRLR 433 at 434.
520 [1995] ICR 1006 at 1019, [1995] IRLR 433 at 438, per Millett LJ (emphasis added).
521 [1995] IRLR 400. Quantitatively the case is at the opposite end of the scale, involving the making redundant of one employee out of eight.
522 On the question of discovery, the case is distinguishable – in *British Aerospace* the employees wanted the information to see if there were any faults in the selection, and this was disallowed on the ordinary principle of discovery that the court will not allow it for a 'fishing expedition'; in *FDR* the EAT held that 'an issue' had already arisen (to which discovery could be attached) because the employee's suspicions were aroused by the retention of an employee with less service and a poorer record. In spite of this, it must be said that the EAT's treatment of *British Aerospace* is on the cavalier side of brusque – the judgment is short, citing hardly anything of the Court of Appeal judgments, and dismissing their ratio decidendi as 'certain observations' which had been 'misread' by counsel for the employers. Lord Denning himself could hardly have done better.
   Where a recognised trade union is involved, it may be able instead to seek the information required on a collective level, under TULR(C)A, s 181, since the CAC have held that redundancy selection methods may remain in the sphere of collective bargaining, for the purpose of disclosure of bargaining information: see p 81 n 100 above.

tribunal was *not* to take at face value an employer's assertion that it had all been done properly. These decisions are, quite simply, conflicting and in spite of the pure argument of precedent that the decision of the Court of Appeal should always apply it would be dangerous for an employer to assume that simple reliance could be placed on that decision in order to refuse disclosure of other scores as a matter of course. The Scottish EAT in *John Brown Engineering Ltd v Brown*[523] upheld a tribunal decision of unfair dismissal where the employers had refused to divulge scores (either to individuals or their representatives), stating that such a refusal may make individual consultation worthless, and the Court of Session in *King v Eaton Ltd (No 2)*[524] (the remedies stage of the original decision) simply stated in passing that 'the general reasons for trying to avoid that kind of inquiry [ie into individual scores] do not seem to us to be absolute'. As far as one can gather, the general approach in the tribunals has been to continue to order discovery of other employees' scores where appropriate, though it must be accepted that there is a problem of law here because of the uncompromising language in *British Aerospace*, which may eventually have to be referred to the House of Lords (for further guidance to follow on from that given in *Polkey*).

In addition to these general developments, there has been another, quite different, specific development which might add a further layer of complexity to redundancy cases. This was the decision of the EAT in *Clarke v Eley (IMI) Kynoch Ltd*[525] that a woman who is unjustifiably prejudiced on the grounds of sex by a selection procedure for redundancy may complain of indirect discrimination under the Sex Discrimination Act 1975[526]. In that case, the EAT held that a selection procedure based on part-timers going first was unlawful sexual discrimination (even though it was a procedure jointly agreed with a union and, under the unfair dismissal rules *alone*, probably fair), because of the predominance of women in part-time work. Thus, a redundancy selection may now have to be judged according to the sex discrimination legislation as well as the unfair dismissal provisions; if unlawful under the former, it will probably be unfair under the latter (even if ostensibly in line with the ordinary rules on fair and unfair redundancies). However, the volatility and indeed unpredictability of this area of law (particularly when allied to the modern approach of treating almost everything as a question of fact) is shown by the subsequent decision of the EAT in *Kidd v DRG (UK) Ltd*[527] upholding, on similar facts, a decision of an industrial tribunal that the dismissing as redundant of part-timers first was *not* unlawful discrimination (on the grounds of either sex or marital status) and that even if it was it was justified. However, even if *Clarke* is now thought generally applicable

---

523 [1997] IRLR 90; analytically, the case is less than helpful, because all it does is to rehearse the arguments for both sides and then decide it as a question of fact; arguably it is the actual *decision* that is significant.

524 [1998] IRLR 686; see particularly para 21.

525 [1983] ICR 165, [1982] IRLR 482.

526 See p 295 above.

527 [1985] ICR 405, [1985] IRLR 190. Waite J stressed the flexibility (a euphemism for unpredictability?) of the concept of indirect discrimination (see p 504 above) and added, 'It would be unwise and unsafe, therefore, for anyone with a taste of drawing generalised conclusions to set the decision in the present case beside, for example, ... the earlier decision of the appeal tribunal in *Clarke v Eley (IMI) Kynoch Ltd* for the sake of deriving supposed differences of principle from the fact that in apparently similar contexts they have arrived at opposite results. Any difference follows only from the application by the tribunals in those cases of flexible criteria to the varied circumstances confronting them' ([1985] ICR 405 at 417, [1985] IRLR 190 at 196).

the effect in practice on redundancy might not be as disruptive as at first sight, for two reasons. First, in the course of his judgment, Browne-Wilkinson J took pains to point out that, while 'part-timers first' may be of dubious legality (unless the company can clearly show justification), an ordinary application of LIFO will not be held to constitute unlawful sex discrimination; even if it may have some discriminatory effect (in that women often have been employed for shorter periods than men), that effect is too limited to be unlawful and in any event (as was pointed out by Wood P in *Brook v London Borough of Haringey*[528]) would readily be held to be justifiable in the light of the hitherto widespread acceptance of LIFO in industrial relations[529] . Secondly, a simple 'part-timers first' policy now comes within the Part time Workers (Prevention of Less Favourable Treatment) Regulations 2000 and so there would be an obligation on the employer to justify it, presumably on grounds similar to those required by sex discrimination law. A similar development has taken place in relation to any 'fixed-termers first' policy because of the Fixed-term Employees (Prevention of Less Favourable Treatment) Regulations 2002[530] .

(d) Dismissal on a transfer of undertaking[531]

A further head of unfair dismissal (arising where a business is transferred from one employer to another) was added by the Transfer of Undertakings (Protection of Employment) Regulations 1981[532] , regulation 8, which states that the dismissal of any employee of the transferor or transferee on the transfer of an undertaking (whether before or after the transfer) is automatically unfair if the reason or principal reason for the dismissal was the transfer (or some reason connected with it). This can apply either where dismissal is due to the actual transfer taking place, or to the likelihood of an imminent transfer (for example, where the undertaking is being 'slimmed down' with a view to a sale), as long as the causal link can be shown[533] . However, regulation 8(2) goes on to provide a defence to the employer if the dismissal was for an 'economic, technical or organisational reason entailing changes in the workforce of either the transferor or the

---

528 [1992] IRLR 478, EAT.
529 In the case itself, the (part) LIFO arrangement which was being challenged as discriminatory had been agreed by employer, union and ACAS. On the other hand, the case does perhaps show that if, in difficult times, employers (and unions) fall back on 'tried and tested' solutions, that may negate any advances made in other contexts towards greater equal opportunities.
530 This has, of course, been a common policy in the past (especially where fixed-term contracts were due to expire anyway) but it had not been challenged under discrimination law in the way that 'part-timers first' had been. Ironically, shortly before the 2002 Regulations came in, there arose the first major, successful challenge to a 'fixed-termers first' policy on the basis of sex discrimination: *Whiffen v Milham Ford Girls' School* [2001] EWCA Civ 385, [2001] ICR 1023, [2001] IRLR 468. For the Part-time Worker Regulations, see p 24 above; for the Fixed-term Employee Regulations, see p 26 above.
531 See *Harvey* DI [2201], R [188]; McMullen *Business Transfers and Employee Rights* ch 6; Collins 'Dismissals on transfers of a business' (1986) 15 ILJ 244; McMullen 'Takeovers, transfers and business reorganisations' (1992) 21 ILJ 15. The fundamental (and always difficult) question of when the regulations apply *at all* is considered at p 201 above.
532 SI 1981/1794, *Harvey* R [181]. It is anticipated that there will be new TUPE Regulations soon into the currency of this edition, see p 212 above.
533 *Morris v John Grose Group Ltd* [1998] ICR 655, [1998] IRLR 499, following on this point *Harrison Bowden Ltd v Bowden* [1994] ICR 186 and disapproving the narrower view in *Ibex Trading Co Ltd v Walton* [1994] ICR 907, [1994] IRLR 564, EAT.

transferee'; this is a defence in as much as the dismissal is then deemed to be for a 'substantial reason' (within section 98(1)), but the employer must then go on to show that he acted reasonably in dismissing (within section 98(4))[534]. The potential effect of this, greatly to the transferee employer's disadvantage, was disclosed by the decision of the Court of Appeal in *Berriman v Delabole Slate Ltd*[535] that 'changes in the workforce' in the defence means changes in the composition of the workforce; mere changes in the terms and conditions of the workforce are not enough. On the other hand, if there are actual changes to the jobs of those transferred (for example, as part of a reorganisation, but with a knock-on effect on terms and conditions) it was subsequently held in *Crawford v Swinton Insurance Brokers Ltd*[536] that that *can* constitute a 'change in the workforce' and so give rise to the regulation 8(2) ('ETO') defence. Clearly, there could be a thin line between these two outcomes, with allegations by the employees that the job changes were a sham, aimed at avoiding the Regulations. If, however, a transferee employer falls on the wrong side of the line, he will face the problem that if he buys the undertaking wishing to keep the existing workforce (or, indeed, simply *having* to take them because of the provisions in regulation 5 on automatic transfer of contracts), but then proceeds to alter their terms and conditions (for example to bring them into line with terms and conditions in the establishments that he already runs), the workforce could walk out, claim constructive dismissal and the defence in regulation 8(2) would *not* apply. The boomerang effect of this could have been that, far from *protecting* the employment of those in the transferred undertaking, it put the emphasis on the transferee employer making it a condition of purchase that the transferor dismisses the workforce as redundant before the sale, in an attempt to ensure that the transferee did not 'inherit' them at all[537]. However, as pointed out at p 207 above, this form of evasion has been effectively countered by the decision of the House of Lords in *Litster v Forth Dry Dock and Engineering Co Ltd*[538]. The end

534 *McGrath v Rank Leisure Ltd* [1985] ICR 527, [1985] IRLR 323. Where the reg 8(2) defence works in a redundancy context, the tribunal should go on to decide on fairness on the ordinary principles of unfair redundancy selection (above): *Warner v Adnet Ltd* [1998] IRLR 394, CA. In *Whitehouse v Chas A Blatchford & Sons Ltd* [1999] IRLR 492 the Court of Appeal held (contrary to previous understanding) that a dismissal must be *either* because of transfer (reg. 8(1)) *or* because of an ETO reason (reg 8(2)).
535 [1985] ICR 546, [1985] IRLR 305, CA, noted McMullen (1986) 49 MLR 524.
536 [1990] ICR 85, [1990] IRLR 42, EAT.
537 This appeared possible in the light of the decision in *Secretary of State for Employment v Spence* [1986] ICR 651, [1986] IRLR 248, CA that the continuity of employment provisions only apply to those in employment with the transferor at the moment of transfer.
538 [1989] ICR 341, [1989] IRLR 161, HL, applying the decision of the ECJ in *P Bork International A/S (in liquidation) v Foreningen af Arbejdsledere i Danmark*: 101/87 [1989] IRLR 41, to the effect that the continuity provisions in reg 5 must be read subject to these provisions in reg 8, so that if a dismissal is contrary to the latter the employee is to be deemed still in the transferor's employment at the time of transfer, for the purposes of reg 5. According to the Scottish EAT in *Anderson v Dalkeith Engineering Ltd* [1985] ICR 66, [1984] IRLR 429 the transferor employer may have the reg 8(2) defence ('economic, technical or organisational' reasons), if he shows that he was obliged to sack the workforce by the intending purchaser as a condition of sale; however, this was not followed by the English EAT in *Wheeler v Patel* [1987] ICR 631, [1987] IRLR 211 for two reasons: (1) it did too much violence to the employee's rights under reg 8(1); (2) 'economic' was to be read *ejusdem generis* with 'technical' and 'organisational', so that the reason must relate to the conduct of the business itself, not just its attractiveness to a buyer; this decision was subsequently followed by the Scottish EAT (rather than *Anderson*) in *Gateway Hotels Ltd v Stewart* [1988] IRLR 287. There is nothing in the decision of the House of Lords in *Litster* to contradict this later interpretation of the defence; indeed, it is entirely in line with their Lordships' views in that case as to the interpretation of the Regulations generally.

result is a considerable level of legal protection through the actual transfer for employees covered by the Regulations, and their existing terms and conditions. Indeed, that protection was taken further by the decision of the EAT in *Wilson v St Helens Borough Council*[539] that any transfer-related change of terms of employment by the transferee employer is *void*, even if (as a matter of ordinary contract law) freely agreed to by the employees and for good consideration (for example, a lump sum buy out of some of the old terms). This bombshell decision led to much inventiveness in ways to escape the conundrum that it posed for employers trying to rationalise terms and conditions after the transfer. One such way involved construction of regulation 8 indirectly – on appeal, *Wilson* became joined with another case[540] where the tactic had been adopted of firing the staff and re-hiring them on the new terms; was this effective? It was argued for the employees that it was not, but that involved arguing that regulation 8 meant (in order to apply the Acquired Rights Directive properly) that a dismissal in breach of it was *invalid*. This approach was adopted by the Court of Appeal[541] but was arguably too radical an approach for ordinary domestic employment law and, when the two cases were finally heard by the House of Lords[542], an element of orthodoxy was reasserted – in a 'fire and re-hire' case, the dismissals are effective, and the staff are taken back on by the transferee employer on the *new* terms. However, the disadvantage to the employer is that in such a case the staff, though still in his employment, could claim unfair dismissal from their previous contracts; indeed, it could be argued that compensation for unfair dismissal would amount to the 'price' of the change of terms. In the unfair dismissal action, regulation 8(1) would of course apply and, on the facts and in the light of its interpretation above, regulation 8(2) would be unlikely to afford a defence where the only employer motive was a transfer-related rationalisation of terms. As spelled out by the House of Lords, the only way out of the conundrum other than the fire and re-hire tactic (with the danger of unfair dismissal actions) is to break the causal link between the transfer and the change of terms (for example, where it can be shown that wider changes were being made anyway to all employees' jobs and terms), so that the initial *Wilson* invalidity does not apply.

(e) Health and safety protection

In order to comply with the Framework Directive on the introduction of measures to encourage improvements in the safety and health of workers at work[543], the Trade Union Reform and Employment Rights Act 1993 inserted what is now section 100 of the Employment Rights Act 1996. This makes a dismissal

---

539 [1996] ICR 711, [1996] IRLR 320; see p 205 above.
540 *Meade and Baxendale v British Fuels Ltd* [1996] IRLR 541.
541 [1998] ICR 387, [1997] IRLR 505, CA.
542 Sub nom *British Fuels Ltd v Baxendale; Wilson v St Helens Borough Council* [1998] ICR 1141, [1998] IRLR 706, HL.
543 Directive 89/391/EEC; most of the requirements of this Directive were put into domestic law by the Management of Health and Safety at Work Regulations 1992 (reissued in 1999); see p 889 below. However, the Directive also contains (in arts 7.2, 8.4, 8.5 and 11.4) directions to member states requiring protection for workers and workers' representatives from detrimental treatment and rights to take direct action to counter imminent dangers.

automatically unfair if the reason (or, if more than one, the principal reason) was that the employee:

(1) having been designated by the employer to carry out health and safety functions, carries out or proposed to carry out such activities;

(2) being a safety representative or member of a safety committee, performed or proposed to perform such functions, or acted as an elected worker representative of employee safety (or took part in an election for such position)[544];

(3) (where there was no representative or committee, or it was not reasonably practicable to raise the matter with them) brought to his employer's attention, by reasonable means, harmful or potentially harmful circumstances;

(4) left the place of work, or refused to return to it, in circumstances of danger which he reasonably believed to be serious or imminent and which he could not reasonably have been expected to avert[545]; or

(5) in such circumstances, took or proposed to take appropriate steps to protect himself or others from the danger[546].

In addition to the automatic unfairness, extra protection is achieved in the following ways:

(1) the normal qualifying period and age limit do not apply;

(2) any selection for redundancy because of the above factors is automatically unfair;[547]

(3) the normal exclusions of tribunal jurisdiction in cases of dismissal while taking part in industrial action do not apply[548];

(4) interim relief is available[549];

(5) crucially, the statutory cap on the compensatory award for unfair dismissal does not apply[550];

(6) in addition to these unfair dismissal provisions, section 44 of the 1996 Act gives an employee a right not to have action *short of* dismissal taken against

---

544 See p 885 below. To have this protection, the safety representative must have been acting within the scope of his responsibilities or jurisdiction: *Shillito v Van Leer (UK) Ltd* [1997] IRLR 495 (a case under the parallel provisions of s 44 on victimisation short of dismissal on these grounds); once that is the case, the protection is wide, covering the exercise of the functions *and* the manner of doing so: *Goodwin v Cabletel UK Ltd* [1998] ICR 112, [1997] IRLR 665, EAT.

545 The danger in question can cover threats from another employee, not just for machinery or chemicals: *Harvest Press Ltd v McCaffrey* [1999] IRLR 778, EAT.

546 Whether steps were appropriate must be judged by reference to all the circumstances, including the employee's state of knowledge, and the facilities and advice available to him: s 100(2). The special protection in (5) does not apply if the employer shows that it was so negligent for the employee to take those steps that a reasonable employer might have dismissed him for taking them: s 100(3). This derogation is specifically permitted by art 8(3) of the Directive. The reference to danger to 'others' primarily means other employees *but* it has been held that it an apply more widely, eg to customers or members of the public: *Masiak v City Restaurants (UK) Ltd* [1999] IRLR 780, EAT.

547 This protection is neutral; it does not put the representative/complainant into a *better* position in redundancy selection: *Smiths Industries Aerospace and Defence Systems v Rawlings* [1996] IRLR 656, EAT.

548 For those exclusions, see p 751 below.

549 For interim relief see p 688 below.

550 Employment Rights Act 1996, s 124(1A); this also applies to dismissal of a whistleblower under s 103A: see below.

551 This is closely modelled on the remedy for action short of dismissal taken on union or non-union grounds: see p 676 below.

him on the above grounds, and a right to complain to a tribunal of any such detrimental treatment[551].

While an employee dismissed for making health and safety complaints had some protection previously under the ordinary unfair dismissal law, it was patchy[552]. These provisions are therefore an important step forward. Unlike most of unfair dismissal law, they are the product of an EC Directive and this may mark them apart for two reasons: (1) arguments may arise that they in fact do not go far enough to meet the standards required by the Directive (in which case an applicant may try to claim rights directly under the directive, if not covered by the new domestic provisions); (2) in any event, in the light of the purposive interpretation to be given to domestic provisions enacting EC Directives[553], it may be necessary for a tribunal considering a claim under this new law to keep an eye on the wording and intent of the directive as a guide to interpretation[554]. One further point to note is that a person making health and safety complaints in a more public arena may now also have protection under the Public Interest Disclosure Act 1998, as a protected 'whistleblower'[555].

(f) Assertion of statutory rights

The Trade Union Reform and Employment Rights Act 1993 inserted a new provision (now section 104 of the Employment Rights Act 1996) making a dismissal automatically unfair if the reason (or principal reason) for it was that the employee had brought proceedings against the employer to enforce a 'relevant statutory right' or had alleged infringement by the employer of such a right[556]; this does not apply if the dismissal was because of an allegation that was false and not made in good faith. The following rights are laid down as 'relevant statutory rights':

(1) any right conferred by the 1996 Act, for which the remedy is by way of a complaint to an employment tribunal;
(2) the right to notice laid down in section 86 of the 1996 Act;
(3) the rights conferred by the Trade Union and Labour Relations (Consolidation) Act 1992 relating to deductions from pay, union activities and time off;
(4) the rights conferred by the Working Time Regulations 1998.

As with health and safety complaints (above), any redundancy selection because of such assertion of statutory rights is made automatically unfair and the normal qualifying period and age limit do not apply. The latter point may be particularly

---

552 An employee without the necessary continuous employment was unprotected, unless he could show that the dismissal was for trade union reasons; however, a health and safety complaint taken up on an individual basis was unlikely to qualify as 'union activities': *Chant v Aquaboats Ltd* [1978] 3 All ER 102, [1978] ICR 643, EAT.

553 *Litster v Forth Dry Dock and Engineering Co Ltd* [1989] ICR 341, [1989] IRLR 161, HL.

554 Smith, Goddard, Killalea and Randall *Health and Safety – the New Legal Framework* (2nd edn, 2000) ch 3.

555 See p 181 above. The decision in *Parkins v Sodexho Ltd* [2002] IRLR 109 (itself concerning a health and safety complaint) gives a very wide interprestation to this specific protection).

556 There are two gaps in the protection, due to this emphasis on the employee having complained of infringement – (1) if the employer has allowed the right in question (eg to time off for public duties), but then dismisses (before the qualifying period is served) because tired of having to allow it, that is not within the statutory protection; (2) it is not enough that on the facts the employee *could* have brought a complaint: *Mennell v Newell & Wright (Transport Contractors) Ltd* [1997] IRLR 519, CA.

significant where the alleged breach relates to the provisions on unlawful deductions (originally in the Wages Act 1986 and now in Part II of the 1996 Act), since that protection has no qualifying period, but in the past the exercise of the employee's rights under it was always dangerous if that employee lacked the qualifying period for ordinary unfair dismissal.

(g) Further specific protection

We have seen recently the addition to the long-standing general rules on unfair dismissal of several specific categories of special protection to meet particular concerns. As seen above, the Trade Union Reform and Employment Rights Act 1993 gave such protection to health and safety representatives/complainants and to those asserting their statutory rights. In addition, there is now special coverage for (1) protected shop workers and betting workers, who may not be dismissed for refusing to work on Sundays[557], (2) employees appointed as member-nominated trustees of their pension fund, under the Pensions Act 1995, who may not be dismissed for exercising their functions as such[558], (3) employees elected (or seeking election) as employee representatives for the purposes of consultation over collective redundancies or transfers of undertakings, who may not be dismissed for performing, or proposing to perform, any such functions or activities[559], and (4) employees exercising rights under the Working Time Regulations 1998, the Public Interest Disclosure Act 1998, the National Minimum Wage Act 1998, the Tax Credits Act 2002 or the Employment Act 2002, section 47 (flexible working)who may not be dismissed for any such reason[560]. In addition, the Part-time Worker Regulations 2000 and the Fixed-term Employee Regulations 2002 contain their own provisions rendering automatically unfair a dismissal due to exercising rights under the relevant Regulations[561]. In each case, there is also protection from victimisation short of dismissal.

The form of the special protection is becoming familiar (in effect now being adopted 'off the peg' by the draftsman) – a dismissal on these grounds is automatically unfair, as is any later selection for redundancy; the normal qualifying period for unfair dismissal does not apply, and neither does the normal age limit. In the case of whistleblowing, the statutory cap on compensation is removed (bringing it into line with the special protection for health and safey representative and complainants (above) with which it shares much ground). In the cases of pension trustees, employee representatives and complaints by whistleblowers or under the Working Time Regulations there are further provisions making interim relief available. The need for the extra protection for employee representatives is presumably strengthened by the fact that it is backed by EC Directives, which could give rise to arguments that any lesser provision failed to enact those Directives fully; with this background, there is a further protective provision in their case,

---

557 Employment Rights Act 1996, s 101; for the status of protected shop or betting workers, see p 237 above.
558 S 102.
559 Collective Redundancies and Transfer of Undertakings (Protection of Employment) (Amendment) Regulations 1995, SI 1995/2587, reg 14; for the election of representatives, see p 85 above.
560 Employment Rights Act 1996, ss 101A, 103A, 104A, 104B, 104C respectively.
561 SI 2000/1551, reg 7; SI 2002/2034, reg 6. There are similar protective provisions in the Transnational Information and Consultation of Employees ('European Works Council') Regulations 1999, SI 1999/3323, reg 28.

namely that (as in the case of health and safety representatives/complainants and working time complainants who are also covered by EC Directives) the normal exclusions of tribunal jurisdiction in cases of dismissal while taking part in unofficial or official industrial action do not apply, so that the employer cannot use those immunities as a cover for getting rid selectively of elected representatives.

(h) Changing business needs and reorganisation[562]

Although cases where employees are dismissed consequent upon a reorganisation are not treated separately in the legislation, they are worth special consideration since they form one particular head of 'some other substantial reason' which has evolved through the cases and which demonstrates how difficult it is to draw the line between fairness and unfairness where there is a clear conflict between the employer's legitimate business interests and the employee's contractual rights. The problem arises where the employer wishes to re-organise his operation in such a way that there will have to be changes in the employee's job, or in the way he carries it out (for example, changes relating to hours, shifts, wages, job content or location); the employee's contract, however, is static and so prima facie he can insist upon continued performance of it as it stands. To achieve a sensible balance, the employer must somehow be allowed to make changes necessary for the efficiency (and in an extreme case the survival) of the enterprise[563], but in ordinary contract law he may not make unilateral alterations to existing contracts of employment. If he attempts to do so the employee has a common law action for breach of contract[564] and, more significantly, may under the legislation walk out because of it and claim to have been constructively dismissed through the employer's breach[565]; alternatively, the employer may dismiss the employee who refuses to change by giving him proper notice, which is lawful at common law but is of course a dismissal for statutory purposes and so either way the employer lays himself open to an unfair dismissal claim. From the decided cases, it appears that there are three possibilities in such a case:

(1) It may be that the proposed changes are such that, on a proper construction, they fall within the permissible range of managerial discretion to organise the work[566] or indeed within the proper ambit of the contractual job description for that employee anyway. This will be particularly so if the changes are minor or of an administrative nature, if they can be construed merely as

---

562 See *Harvey* DI [1854].
563 This has been recognised in the context of redundancy law: *Chapman v Goonvean and Rostowrack China Clay Co Ltd* [1973] 1 All ER 218, [1973] ICR 50; *Johnson v Nottinghamshire Combined Policy Authority* [1974] ICR 170, [1974] IRLR 20, CA; *Lesney Products & Co Ltd v Nolan* [1977] ICR 235, [1977] IRLR 77, CA.
564 This can take the form of an action for wages due under the old contract, on the old terms, and can be an effective tactic: *Burdett-Coutts v Hertfordshire County Council* [1984] IRLR 91 (concerning unilateral changes to dinner ladies' terms and conditions, a fruitful source of important case law in the mid-1980s); *Rigby v Ferodo Ltd* [1988] ICR 29, [1987] IRLR 516, HL; see p 217 above. Unless the employer can show a variation of contract, assented to by the employee, he will lose the common law action, and will then have to force the issue by dismissing those who refuse to accept the changes and taking his chances in an unfair dismissal action (discussed below).
565 *Greenaway Harrison Ltd v Wiles* [1994] IRLR 380, EAT.
566 See p 151 above.

an up-dating of essentially the same job (seen in the light possibly of an implied term of the contract that the employee will adapt to new methods and techniques reasonably required of him[567]), or if the job description in fact covers jobs A and B but the employee, used to doing only A in practice, refuses to do B instead, for it is the contractual term which counts, not any particular practice which evolved, and so a skilfully drafted contractual job description (and/or a flexibility clause) could perhaps anticipate and cover subsequent re-organisations. If this is the case, the changes are not sufficiently major to constitute a breach of contract and so if the employee still refuses to accept them and is dismissed, that will be a dismissal for refusal to obey a lawful order and so probably fair; likewise, if the employee walks out because of such changes, it will not constitute constructive dismissal (unless there was something seriously objectionable about the way it was handled, capable of independently producing a breach of contract). He will therefore not receive a redundancy payment or compensation for unfair dismissal[568].

(2) If the changes are more major and would actually cause a decrease in the employee's work, that may constitute redundancy within the definition in the Employment Rights Act 1996, section 139[569]. If so, the dismissed employee may be eligible for a redundancy payment but, as redundancy is a prima facie fair ground for dismissal, he may not be able to claim unfair dismissal[570] (unless the redundancy was itself unfair – see (c) 'Redundancy', above). This solution (probably highly acceptable to the employer) is more likely to occur now, with the emphasis of the Court of Appeal in *Murphy v Epsom College*[571] on looking at the 'kind of work' that the dismissed employee was employed to do; if on the reorganisation it can be said that the kind of work changed and the employee was incapable of performing the new kind of work, then he may be dismissed as redundant even though a new employee (skilled in the new kind of work) is taken on to replace him, ie where there is *no* net loss in the number of employees required at the end of the day.

(3) If the changes are major but do not produce in law a redundancy (for example, where the work is undiminished but the hours and remuneration have to change), it is well established that the reorganisation *can* constitute 'some other substantial reason' within section 98(1), in which case there will be no

---

567   *Cresswell v Board of Inland Revenue* [1984] ICR 508, [1984] IRLR 190 (computerisation of PAYE system still within the ambit of the existing contracts of those operating the system, who were expected to adapt); see p 170 above.

568   *George Wimpey & Co Ltd v Cooper* [1977] IRLR 205; *Glitz v Watford Electric Co Ltd* [1979] IRLR 89. In the latter case the EAT pointed out that in a small firm or unit the job descriptions may necessarily be more vague, allowing the employer to expect greater flexibility and adaptability from his employees.

569   See p 628 below.

570   *Wilson v Underhill House School Ltd* [1977] IRLR 475; *Robinson v British Island Airways Ltd* [1978] ICR 304, [1977] IRLR 477, EAT.

571   [1985] ICR 80, [1984] IRLR 271, CA (dismissal of plumber held to be for redundancy where a modern heating system installed and a heating engineer appointed to replace him). The case also shows that an employer can run *both* redundancy *and*, in the alternative, some other substantial reason (through reorganisation) as defences, provided both are properly considered at the tribunal hearing.

572   *RS Components Ltd v Irwin* [1973] ICR 535, [1973] IRLR 239; *Wilson's* case and *Robinson's* case, n 507 above; *Hollister v National Farmers' Union* [1979] ICR 542, [1979] IRLR 238, CA; *Genower v Ealing, Hammersmith and Hounslow Area Health Authority* [1980] IRLR 297; *Farrant v Woodroffe School* [1998] ICR 184, [1998] IRLR 176. Cf, however, *Labour Party v Oakley* [1988] ICR 403, [1988] IRLR 34, CA where the reorganisation was shown on the facts to be a pretext for dismissing someone they had already decided to dispense with.

redundancy payment and the employee may not be able to succeed in a claim for unfair dismissal[572]. This is the type of case which causes most problems, for to reach that result the tribunal in effect has to give precedence to the employer's business needs over the employee's normal contractual and statutory rights, and allow the employer to insist upon a unilateral variation of the contract without incurring a finding of unfair dismissal[573]. It is the section 98(4) concept of reasonableness which holds the balance – given that the reorganisation is a substantial reason which *can* justify dismissal, was the dismissal of the recalcitrant employee *in fact* justified on the facts of the particular case? The tribunal is therefore looking at the reasonableness of the employer's handling of the change, and in essence looking to see whether the time had come when the employer had no further option but to dismiss the employee in order to put into effect the necessary changes. In doing so, the tribunal may have to consider three questions –

(a) Was the reorganisation necessary? Although it is not for the tribunal to decide how the employer ought to run his business and the employer's genuine belief in the necessity for changes is likely to be paramount, a tribunal may expect the employer to lead evidence showing why he thought change necessary and how he reached the particular decisions in question[574]. In one of the original cases, *Ellis v Brighton Co-operative Society Ltd*[575], the EAT seemed to assume that in order to justify eventual dismissals for non-compliance, the changes had to be so vital that if they were not put into effect the whole business would be brought to a standstill, but this was held by the Court of Appeal to be too restrictive in *Hollister v National Farmers' Union*[576] where it was said that it is sufficient if there is a good, sound business reason for the reorganisation. This approach leaves a great deal in the employer's discretion, and indeed the area of business reorganisations has produced many findings of fair dismissal. In *Evans v Elemeta Holdings Ltd*[577] the EAT appeared to move in the direction of redressing this imbalance by concentrating more upon examining the changes imposed by the employer and considering whether it was *reasonable for the employee to reject them* (the case itself concerning major changes to overtime obligations, disadvantageous to the employee). However, in the event this case did not lead to a significant development

---

573 The existence of a 'dismissal' will normally be clear, through either (a) an express dismissal by the employer of the refusenik, (b) a constructive dismissal if the employee leaves, or (c) an application of the rule that a unilateral change can be so fundamental as the constitute termination of the old contract by the employer, even where the employee in fact carries on working (under, in effect, a new contract), as in *Hogg v Dover College* [1990] ICR 39, affirmed in *Alcan Extrusions Ltd v Yates* [1996] IRLR 327, EAT.

574 *Banerjee v City and East London Area Health Authority* [1979] IRLR 147; *Ladbroke Courage Holidays Ltd v Asten* [1981] IRLR 59; in *Orr v Vaughan* [1981] IRLR 63 it was said that, while business reorganisations are basically for the employer to decide upon, the tribunal must be satisfied that, at the least, the employer came to his decision on reasonable information reasonably acquired.

575 [1976] IRLR 419.

576 [1979] ICR 542, [1979] IRLR 238; *Bowater Containers Ltd v McCormack* [1980] IRLR 50. Outside pressure for change, eg from customers or insurers, may be a relevant factor, but the employer must still establish that he handled the pressure reasonably: *Scott Packing and Warehousing Ltd v Paterson* [1978] IRLR 166; *Dobie v Burns International Security Services (UK) Ltd* [1984] ICR 812, [1984] IRLR 329, CA.

577 [1982] ICR 323, [1982] IRLR 143.

in this area, for it did not decide what was to happen in the most difficult class of case, ie where it was reasonable for the employee to reject the changes because of their effect on his livelihood, but equally it was reasonable for the employer to insist upon them because of the needs of his business; the fact that one party was acting reasonably does *not* mean that the other was therefore acting unreasonably. On those grounds, a differently constituted EAT soon afterwards refused to follow *Evans* in *Chubb Fire Security Ltd v Harper*[578]. In that case, a middle way of sorts was suggested, namely that a tribunal might consider whether the employer had acted reasonably in deciding that the advantages of the reorganisation to him outweighed the disadvantages to the employee. This is an interesting approach but it was stressed subsequently that this is only a *factor* (not a test) for a tribunal to consider when deciding whether the dismissal was fair within section 98(4) (as being within the range of reasonable responses that an employer faced with the employee's refusal to change might have adopted)[579]; this is ultimately the test and its application, here as elsewhere, is a question of fact for the tribunal, as the Court of Appeal has emphasised[580].

(b) Given the reorganisation plan, was it necessary to insist upon changing the employee's job in order to put that plan into effect? In many cases, the answer may simply be 'Yes', particularly where the employee is in a key position. It may be, however, that if only one or two employees are holding out, and their concurrence is not absolutely vital, the employer may be expected to consider any minor alterations to his plan which might accommodate those employees without frustrating the reorganisation[581].

(c) Was there sufficient consultation? Consultation with the employee and perhaps his union has been seen in the past as one of the major requirements of a fair dismissal in these cases and it is clear that if the employer does negotiate a reorganisation with the relevant union or with the majority of the employees and one employee still holds out, that agreement will considerably strengthen his hand if he then dismisses that employee. Thus, it has been said by the EAT that there must be proper consultation, not just the presentation of a fait accompli or ultimatum[582], and that the employer should consider any counter-proposals put forward by the employee, and should bear in mind the position of the individual employee, which may not be done if he treats

---

578 [1983] IRLR 311; applied in *Catamaran Cruisers Ltd v Williams* [1994] IRLR 386.
579 *Richmond Precision Engineering Ltd v Pearce* [1985] IRLR 179. One point in this case had to be rectified subsequently, for it was suggested that the test is the reasonableness of the employer's *offer*; in fact, the correct test (under s 98) is the reasonableness of the decision to *dismiss* because of the employee's *refusal* of the offer: *St John of God (Care Services) Ltd v Brooks* [1992] ICR 715, [1992] IRLR 546. Further factors to consider may include how many other employees had accepted the changes and the attitude of any trade union involved: *Caramaran Cruisers Ltd v Williams* [1994] IRLR 386. The existence of a financial inducement to 'buy out' the old terms may also be relevant.
580 *Gilham v Kent County Council (No 2)* [1985] ICR 233, [1985] IRLR 18, CA.
581 *Martin v Automobile Proprietary Ltd* [1979] IRLR 64.
582 *Ellis v Brighton Co-operative Society Ltd* [1976] IRLR 419.
583 *Martin v Automobile Proprietary Ltd* [1979] IRLR 64. Presumably this would require some form of individual consultation in the case of a non-unionist.
584 N 576 above.

all cases as one, for example by just consulting a weak union or staff association[583]. However, in *Hollister v National Farmers' Union*[584] the Court of Appeal held that too much emphasis had been placed upon consultation in past cases, to the point that the EAT was in danger of putting a gloss upon the simple reasonableness test in section 98(4) – consultation is only one of the factors to be considered when looking at the circumstances of the case, and so lack of it (as in that case, where the changes were just announced to the employee) is not necessarily fatal to the employer's case. It is possible, however, that (if and when the matter is tested again) there will be a move back towards more emphasis on consultation in this area in the light of (a) the decision of the House of Lords in *Polkey v A E Dayton Services Ltd*[585], which concerned consultation in the context of redundancy dismissals, but in the subsequent case law has taken on wider significance and (b) legislative developments in the next few years to enact the Information and Consultation Directive[586] which will require (at least in firms of fifty or more employees, by 2008, and in larger organisations sooner) mechanisms for informing and consulting the workforce on, inter alia, 'decisions likely to lead to substantial changes in work organisation as in contractual relations' – this change would operate directly only at a collective level, but it might well have an indirect effect at this individual level in helping to define reasonable handling of one of these difficult cases in the future.

Thus, to recap, the employer who wishes to reorganise parts of his business should first attempt to gain the agreement of the affected employees to variations in their contractual terms. If this is not forthcoming but the changes are still necessary, he may order unilaterally such changes as are permissible within the scope of the contracts of employment (and the amount of managerial discretion left to him under their terms); if an employee refuses to accept this category of change he may be dismissed for disobedience. Alternatively, if the changes alter the kind of work required and lead to a definite diminution in the requirements for the kind of work that the employee was engaged to perform, then the employee may be made redundant (with a redundancy payment but, provided a proper procedure was adopted, no compensation for unfair dismissal). However, if the case falls outside these two possibilities (ie where there is no redundancy, but the changes are major enough to involve definite variations of contract) the employer should usually follow some consultative procedure (depending on the facts of the case), but if an employee still refuses to change he may dismiss him, or insist upon the changes and be prepared to concede that that employee was constructively dismissed if he still refuses and walks out; in either event, he can then argue that the dismissal (actual or constructive[587]) was fair in the light of the necessity for change, the need to alter the employee's job within the scheme of the reorganisation and the consultative procedure which he adopted. However, it must be remembered in these cases that a finding of fairness jeopardises what would normally be the employee's contractual and statutory rights, and so should not be arrived at lightly.

---

585 [1988] ICR 142, [1987] IRLR 503, HL; see p 539 above.
586 See p 97 above.
587 The fact that a dismissal is constructive does not automatically mean that it is unfair: see p 547 n 282 above, and particularly *Savoia v Chiltern Herb Farms Ltd* [1982] IRLR 166, CA.

(iv) Remedies for unfair dismissal

The statutory rules governing remedies for unfair dismissal were altered by the Employment Protection Act 1975 which split compensation into a basic award and a compensatory award, and sought to strengthen the provisions relating to the direct remedies of reinstatement and re-engagement in an attempt to make them the primary remedies in practice as well as in theory; the figures have consistently shown that this aim has not been achieved[588], and so compensation remains the prime remedy in most cases. The rules governing remedies are contained in sections 111–132 of the Employment Rights Act 1996. In addition, now that dismissal for trade union reasons is covered by the Trade Union and Labour Relations (Consolidation) Act 1992, there are special provisions in sections 161–166 of that Act relating to 'interim relief' which may serve to keep a contract of employment subsisting while a complaint in such cases is considered; such interim relief was extended by the Trade Union Reform and Employment Rights Act 1993 to the new head of dismissal for health and safety reasons and then to cases involving pension trustees, employee representatives, working time complaints and whistleblowers, and so equivalent provisions now appear in the 1992 and 1996 Acts. The normal remedies are now considered in turn, along with the important concepts of contributory fault and mitigation, either of which may decrease an award of compensation. As elsewhere in unfair dismissal law, it must be remembered that, although case law may be important in filling out the legislative bones (particularly in the area of the compensatory award), it is the wording of the statute which remains of paramount importance and the majority of cases are merely illustrations of the application of that wording.

(a) Reinstatement and re-engagement[589]

If a tribunal finds that a dismissal was unfair, it then proceeds to hear the parties on the question of remedies and by virtue of section 112 it must explain to the complainant the possible orders for reinstatement and re-engagement and ask whether he wishes the tribunal to make such an order[590]. An order for reinstatement means that the employer must take him back into his job; as he is in effect treated as not having been dismissed this means that he is entitled to any benefits he might reasonably have expected to receive during his period of dismissal, principally back pay (including any *improvement* of terms and conditions which he would have received during that period had he not been dismissed, but deducting any amounts actually received from the employer by way of wages in lieu or ex gratia payments, or from any employment during that period with another employer[591]); further, any other rights and privileges such as seniority and pension rights must be restored to him, and the tribunal must specify the

---

588   In 2001/02, 9,143 unfair dismissal cases went to a tribunal hearing. 57% were dismissed and 43% upheld. There were only 11 orders for reinstatement or re-engagement (0.1% of cases heard). Remedy was left to the parties in 1,343 cases and compensation was awarded in 2,579 cases: ETS Annual Report 2001/02.

589   See *Harvey* D [2371]. Dickens, Hart, Jones and Weeks 'Re-employment of unfairly dismissed workers: the lost remedy' (1981) 10 ILJ 160; Williams and Lewis 'The aftermath of tribunal reinstatement and re-engagement' DE Research Paper No 23 (1981).

590   The mandatory nature of this wording is not what it seems; a tribunal decision will *not* be rendered void by a failure to comply with this requirement: *Cowley v Manson Timber Ltd* [1995] ICR 367, [1995] IRLR 153, CA.

591   Employment Rights Act 1996, s 114.

date upon which reinstatement is to take effect. An order for re-engagement means that the employee must be taken back on by the employer (or by a successor or an associated employer[592]) in 'employment comparable to that from which he was dismissed or other suitable employment' on terms which are, so far as reasonably practicable, as favourable as if he had been reinstated; this too carries rights to back pay and preservation of accrued interests, and here the tribunal must specify not only the effective date of the order but also the identity of the re-engaging employer, the nature of the employment and the rate of remuneration. In the case of either kind of order, the employee's continuity of employment is preserved and the time between dismissal and re-employment counts as a period of employment[593].

In a case where an employee expresses a desire for reinstatement or re-engagement, section 116 lays down a definite procedure to which the tribunal must adhere[594]. The tribunal must first decide whether to make an order for reinstatement and only if it decides not to do so should it go on to consider whether to order re-engagement and, if so, on what terms. In both exercises, it must take into account (a) the expressed wishes of the complainant, (b) whether it is *practicable* for the employer to comply with an order for reinstatement or re-engagement and (c) whether the complainant caused or contributed to his dismissal and if so whether it would be just to make an order[595]. An employer who does not wish to take the dismissed employee back may therefore at this stage make representations on grounds (b) and (c) and, although (c) is important in ruling out important remedies for a 'rogue', it is (b) and the question of practicability which is likely to be the most pressing. It is for the employer to show impracticability, and as this is such an important matter he must discharge that onus properly – it is not enough for the tribunal to take a lax approach and decide that perhaps it would not be 'expedient' to put the employee back into employment[596]. Impracticability is a question of fact in each case, but may arise from inability to perform the work, unsuitability for it, definite opposition to his return among the workforce (either collectively or individually)[597], inability to take him back without having to dismiss another employee[598], continued

---

592 Defined in the Employment Rights Act 1996, s 231; see p 30, above. A tribunal should stick to the wording of the statute and make orders for either reinstatement or re-engagement, not just make an order that the employer should *offer* to re-employ: *Lilley Construction Ltd v Dunn* [1984] IRLR 483. An order may not be made to re-employ on significantly better terms: *Rank Xerox (UK) Ltd v Stryczek* [1995] IRLR 568.

593 Employment Protection (Continuity of Employment) Regulations 1996, SI 1996/3147, *Harvey* R [1034]. These regulations apply where either there has been an application to a tribunal, or an agreed re-employment after the involvement of an ACAS conciliation officer or through a compromise agreement; thus an employee negotiating re-employment is advised to do so through ACAS or by a formal compromise agreement, otherwise there may be a break in continuity even if the employer had voluntarily taken the employee back: *Morris v Walsh Western UK Ltd* [1997] IRLR 562, EAT.

594 *Pirelli General Cable Works Ltd v Murray* [1979] IRLR 190, EAT.

595 Lewis 'Interpretation of "practicable" and "just" in relation to re-employment in unfair dismissal cases' (1982) 45 MLR 384. Contributory conduct here is the same in content as contributory fault in a compensation case (see below): *Boots Co plc v Lees-Collier* [1986] ICR 728, [1986] IRLR 485, EAT.

596 *Qualcast (Wolverhampton) Ltd v Ross* [1979] ICR 386, [1979] IRLR 98, EAT.

597 *Coleman v Magnet Joinery Ltd* [1975] ICR 46, [1974] IRLR 343, CA; *Langston v AUEW (No 2)* [1974] ICR 510, [1974] IRLR 182; *Meridian Ltd v Gomersall* [1977] ICR 597, [1977] IRLR 425.

598 *Freemans plc v Flynn* [1984] ICR 874, [1984] IRLR 486, EAT.

breakdown of trust and confidence between the parties[599] or through an intervening factor arising since the dismissal such as redundancy or potential overmanning (though in such a case the tribunal should be satisfied that it is genuine)[600]. In *Enessy Co SA v Minoprio*[601] the Scottish EAT stated obiter that practicability may depend inter alia upon the size of the employer and that reinstatement into a small concern where a close personal relationship has to exist should only be ordered in exceptional cases; this may be a factor, particularly in domestic or quasi-domestic employment as in that case itself, but it is submitted that this approach should not be applied too widely, for as a principle it could come to bear an unfortunate resemblance to the old common law rules against enforcement of contracts of employment[602].

If an order for reinstatement or re-engagement is made and the employee is taken back but the employer does not comply fully with the terms of the order, the employee may complain under section 117 to the tribunal[603] which is to order such compensation as it thinks fit having regard to the loss caused to the employee by the employer's actions. The more common form of complaint, however, will be that the employer has not complied with the order *at all* and has refused to take the employee back. In this case, section 117(3) provides that the tribunal shall make an award of compensation in the normal way instead[604] *and* an award of 'additional compensation' of between twenty-six and fifty-two weeks' pay. A 'week's pay' is subject to the same maximum as that in force at the time for the ordinary basic award[605] and, as the additional compensation is not expressly limited to compensation for loss actually suffered by the employee because of the employer's refusal to comply, it can include a punitive element[606].

Once again, it is a defence to the granting of the additional compensation if the employer can satisfy the tribunal that it was not practicable to comply with the order; this may seem a strange provision as it allows the employer a second opportunity to plead impracticability. In *Timex Corpn v Thomson*[607] Browne-Wilkinson P held that the test effectively was the same (the latter stage *not* being confined to matters arising since the date of the order), so that it was possible for

---

599   *Wood Group Heavy Industrial Turbines Ltd v Crossan* [1998] IRLR 680, EAT.
600   *Cold Drawn Tubes Ltd v Middleton* [1992] ICR 318, [1992] IRLR 160, EAT.
601   [1978] IRLR 489. As pointed out in the DE Working Paper No 23 (n 589 above) a further problem is that, in fact many firms in Britain could claim to be 'small' for this purpose, and in many of them trade union representation will be weak.
602   See p 469 above.
603   One problem is whether s 117 can be relied upon where an employer uses more subtle tactics, eg taking the employee back but subtly victimising him; also, where the employer takes the employee back on normally, but then *later* changes the terms of his employment (eg by downgrading him), that would have to be the subject of a separate unfair dismissal action. The tribunal decision in *Nensi v Vinola (Knitwear) Manufacturing Co Ltd* [1978] IRLR 297, IT that a re-employed employee fell between two stools in such a case is per incuriam since his continuity should in fact have been preserved by the 1996 Regulations (n 593 above), so that he had the necessary qualifying period and so should have been allowed his separate unfair dismissal action.
604   If the tribunal finds that the employee himself unreasonably prevented the order being complied with, that is to be considered as failure to mitigate his loss, with a view to decreasing the award of compensation: Employment Rights Act 1996, s 117(8).
605   As from February 2003, the figure is £260, giving a maximum additional award of £13,520. For the calculation of a week's pay, see p 232 above.
606   *George v Beecham Group* [1977] IRLR 43; IT; *Morganite Electrical Carbon Ltd v Donne* [1988] ICR 18, [1987] IRLR 363, EAT.
607   [1981] IRLR 522, applied in *Freemans plc v Flynn* [1984] ICR 874, [1984] IRLR 486 and *Boots Co plc v Lees-Collier* [1986] ICR 728, [1986] IRLR 485.

a tribunal merely to 'have regard' to practicability at the first stage and, if necessary, make the order on a fairly speculative basis and leave it to the employer to raise impracticability as a defence at this second stage if it did not work out in practice. This approach was generally approved by the Court of Appeal in *Port of London Authority v Payne*[608] where it was said that, although a determination of sorts has to be made at the first stage, that will be 'of necessity provisional' and without prejudice to a fuller consideration of practicability at the second stage if necessary, with the burden of proof clearly on the employer (though only to show impracticability, not absolute impossibility). Finally, it should be noted that the statute provides that the fact that the employer has hired a replacement for the dismissed employee is not to be taken into account when deciding upon impracticability (at either stage at which it may arise) unless the employer can show that it was not practicable for him to arrange for the work to be done without engaging a permanent replacement, or (at the first stage, when deciding whether to make an order) that he only engaged the replacement after a reasonable period without hearing from the dismissed employee, and then had to do so in order that the work could be done[609].

In the light of these detailed legal rules (and the elevation of reinstatement/re-engagement into an 'order' in 1975) it is surprising that it is ordered in so few cases. Research has shown a patchy picture (even in geographical terms) with many reasons being accepted by tribunals for not making an order and, indeed, considerable reluctance among ex-employees to press for one[610]. Overall, it has been suggested that, in spite of the term 'order' being used, the emphasis before tribunals is still to look for an element of *agreement* on the part of the employer to re-employ and, in the absence of that, to be very wary about going further. This may be in line with general ideas of good industrial relations practice (ie looking to see what the likely long-term effects are of an order), but it must have a severely depressing effect on prospects for re-employment[611]. If this is correct, it casts doubt on whether any alterations in the law could have much effect on what is basically a question of attitude (given the failure of the redrafting in 1975 to increase the incidence of re-employment, as it was clearly meant to do). However, certain reforms have been suggested[612], including enacting a special statutory action for victimisation after re-employment[613], the use of trial periods (at present restricted to redundancy cases), the abolition of 'practicability' as a criterion for the making of an order (leaving 'impracticability' as a defence for an employer on a complaint of failure to comply with an order) and, perhaps the most

608 [1994] ICR 555, [1994] IRLR 9, CA, reversing the decision of the EAT which had been inconsistent with *Timex*. The case itself held the record for a tribunal hearing, having lasted 189 days.
609 Reg 116(5), (6).
610 Williams and Lewis 'The aftermath of tribunal reinstatement and re-engagement' DE Research Paper No 23 (1981). There is also a suggestion that increased legal representation (and hence less of an inquisitorial approach by the tribunal) may have a depressing effect on the incidence of re-employment. For the experience of ACAS on the factors leading to low levels of re-employment, see the ACAS Annual Report 1983, para 5.11.
611 It certainly means that ideas of practicability are not tied to the physical existence of a job for the applicant to do.
612 Research Paper No 23, pp 40–41.
613 See n 603 above.

interesting, extending the application of interim relief to any case where an employee wants reinstatement[614].

(b) Compensation

The scheme of the present provisions on compensation is that the employee is eligible for a 'basic award' which is calculated mechanically in the same way as a redundancy payment and so rewards long service, and a 'compensatory award' which aims to put a realistic figure upon the employee's actual loss. The maximum for the basic award is determined by the maximum amount for a 'week's pay' for this purpose, and the compensatory award is subject to a maximum set figure in the statute[615]. This latter figure was allowed to fall behind inflation for much of the 1980s and 1990s, so that by 1999 it still stood at only £12,000, which had a depressing effect on unfair dismissal compensation[616], and caused problems when the equivalent maximum was removed from discrimination cases, so that it was in an applicant's interests to seek to bring a dismissal case as a discrimination claim whenever possible. The present government at first proposed in the White Paper Fairness at Work to remove the limit altogether, but were prevailed upon only to raise it instead; this was done in the Employment Relations Act 1999 which increased it to £50,000, and at the same time instituted a system for raising all the award limits anually in line with the Retail Prices Index[617]. One earlier, but also significant reform in this area was that tribunals were eventually given the power to award interest on their awards[618].

(1) The basic award [619]

The calculation method for this is similar to that for a redundancy payment; it is dependent upon the length of the employee's continuous employment as at the effective date of termination, and under section 119 the employee is to receive one and a half week's pay for each year of employment over the age of 41, one week's pay for each year between 22 and 41 and half a weeks' pay for each year under the age of 22; a maximum of 20 years may be counted and, as stated above, the maximum week's pay for this purpose is limited to a fixed amount, subject to review; special provisions apportion the amount claimable where dismissal takes place in the employee's retirement year. The basic award is subject to reduction (a) by the amount of any redundancy payment received (either under the Act or by virtue of a private scheme)[620], (b) where the tribunal finds that there was

---

614 There is a precedent of sorts here in the extension of interim relief by the Employment Act 1982 to employees being dismissed for non-membership of a union, pursuant to a closed-shop agreement, where the previous government clearly wanted the remedy of reinstatement to be effective.

615 As from February 2003 the maximum for a week's pay is £260 pw, giving a maximum basic award of £7,800.

616 Given that the figure stood at £6,250 in 1980, by the late 1990s inflation alone should have raised it to £30,000–40,000. The latter figure was suggested by the CBI and IPD in their responses to Fairness at Work.

617 With effect from February 2003 the maximum compensatory award stood at £53,500.

618 Employment Tribunals (Interest) Order 1990, SI 1990/479, Harvey R [459].

619 See Harvey DI [2503].

620 S 122(4); any excess over the amount of the basic award (which is thereby extinguished) is deducted from the compensatory award: s 123(7).

contributory fault on the part of the employee[621] (see below), (c) where the ex-employee has refused an offer of, in effect, reinstatement[622] and (d) where the employer has made an ex gratia payment meant to offset or extinguish all legal rights (in as much as that amount may be set off against both basic and compensatory awards, if large enough)[623].

The basic award used to be subject to a minimum of two weeks' pay, but this was abolished by the Employment Act 1980, which also extended the idea of contributory fault to cover any conduct by the employee prior to the dismissal (not just conduct known to the employer and contributing positively to the decision to dismiss). A combination of these two reforms to the basic award ensured that an employee who is unfairly dismissed on ground A (for example, unsatisfactory work) but who is later discovered to have been dismissable on ground B (for example, concealed fraud, only coming to light after he left) cannot now claim the minimum basic award of two weeks; the reforms were in response to fears expressed by the House of Lords in *W Devis & Sons Ltd v Atkins*[624] that the minimum basic award could be a 'rogue's charter' in such cases.

As will be seen below, there is now a minimum basic award (£3,500 at the time of writing) where an employee is unfairly dismissed for being or not being a union member; these provisions were extended in 1993 to the new ground of dismissal for acting as a health and safety representative, and subsequently to the unfair dismissal of pension trustees, elected employee representatives, or persons acting as workforce representatives under the working time provisions.

(2) The compensatory award[625]

Various aspects of the compensatory award can cause problems of quantification, and it is part of the tribunal's function to ensure that the relevant heads of compensation are considered[626]. However, since this award is meant to constitute realistic recompense and as such has to be approached from first principles in each case, the onus lies primarily upon the employee to adduce evidence of his losses[627]; the tribunal should not speculate unduly, but on the other hand the EAT has pointed out that only a realistic standard should be expected of the employee (who may have difficulty gaining certain evidence, even with the aid of discovery against the employer) and the tribunal should not hide behind the burden of proof where major problems of quantification arise[628].

The basis of the compensatory award is contained in section 123(1) which provides that:

---

621 S 122(2).
622 S 122(1).
623 *Chelsea Football Club and Athletic Co Ltd v Heath* [1981] ICR 323, [1981] IRLR 73, EAT.
624 [1977] ICR 662, [1977] IRLR 314, HL.
625 See *Harvey* DI [2524]; on the calculation of compensation generally, see Upex *Termination of Employment* (3rd edn, 1991); Collins 'The just and equitable compensatory award' (1991) 20 ILJ 201, Hough and Spowart-Taylor 'Liability, compensation and justice in unfair dismissal' (1996) 25 ILJ 308; and Crump, Pugsley and Ashtiany 'Butterworths Compensation Calculations' (1999).
626 *Tidman v Aveling Marshall Ltd* [1977] ICR 506, [1977] IRLR 218.
627 *Adda International Ltd v Curcio* [1976] ICR 407, [1976] IRLR 425; *Lifeguard Assurance Ltd v Zadrozny* [1977] IRLR 56; *Smith, Kline and French Laboratories Ltd v Coates* [1977] IRLR 220.
628 *Barley v Amey Roadstone Corpn Ltd (No 2)* [1978] ICR 190, [1977] IRLR 299.

'... the amount of the compensatory award shall be such amount as the tribunal considers just and equitable in all the circumstances having regard to the loss sustained by the complainant in consequence of the dismissal in so far as that loss is attributable to action taken by the employer.'

In a potentially important and expansive decision, the Inner House of the Court of Session held in *Leonard v Strathclyde Buses Ltd*[629] that this statutory language is to be applied as it stands, and is not to have grafted on to it common law tests such as whether damage claimed was foreseeable or too remote; thus, when an unfairly dismissed employee had to sell back 6,000 company shares on leaving at the current price of £1.70, only to see them rise to £5.85 some months later (on a takeover), it was held that it was 'just and equitable' to award the difference on the facts, and that this was not to be defeated by technical arguments on remoteness of damage taken from other areas of the law. Such an expansive approach (leaving much in the discretion of the tribunal) became particularly important with the raising of the statutory limit to £50,000 in 1999. On the other hand, it must also be remembered that ultimately the aim of an award is to reimburse the employee, not to punish the employer[630] , and this principle can have certain overall effects. In particular, it means that if the employee has in fact lost nothing, he is entitled to no compensatory award (only the basic award) and this may be held to be the case where it is clear that it would have made no difference even if he had not been unfairly dismissed; for example in a redundancy dismissal where it is held to have been unfair through lack of consultation but it is clear that he would have been made redundant anyway, or in an incapacity or misconduct case where the dismissal was unfair because the proper procedure was not followed but it is clear that the employee would have been dismissed in any event[631] . In such a case it has long been clear that there may be a nil compensatory award, or a very limited one (for example where in a case of lack of redundancy consultation it appears that proper consultation would have lasted for four weeks but then the employee would have been dismissed; in such a case the compensatory award may only reflect four weeks' loss of wages)[632] .

As we have already seen (p 569 above) the decision of the House of Lords in *Polkey v A E Dayton Services Ltd*[633] means that it is *not* now open to a tribunal to find a dismissal substantively fair merely because with hindsight a procedural lapse in fact made no difference, but on the other hand that decision does accept (and, indeed, emphasise) the important point being made here, namely that the injustice (or lack of it) to the employee at the end of the day *is* to be taken into

629 [1998] IRLR 693, Ct of Sess; *Balmoral Group Ltd v Rae* (2000) Times, 25 January, EAT.
630 *Clarkson International Tools Ltd v Short* [1973] ICR 191, [1973] IRLR 90; *Lifeguard Assurance Ltd v Zadrozny* [1977] IRLR 56. It was said in *Townson v Northgate Group Ltd* [1981] IRLR 382 that the tribunal could look at *how unfair* the dismissal was when assessing compensation but this was later disapproved in *Morris v Acco Ltd* [1985] ICR 306.
631 *Clarkson International Tools Ltd v Short* [1973] ICR 191, [1973] IRLR 90; *British United Shoe Machinery Co Ltd v Clarke* [1978] ICR 70, [1977] IRLR 297; *Barley v Amey Roadstone Corpn Ltd (No 2)* [1978] ICR 190, [1977] IRLR 299; *Clyde Pipeworks Ltd v Foster* [1978] IRLR 313; *Brittains Arborfield Ltd v Van Uden* [1977] ICR 211.
632 Note, however, that ultimately this remains a question of fact and what would be just and equitable, so that there is no 'tariff' of two or three weeks: *Elkouil v Coney Island Ltd* [2002] IRLR 174 (employers knew of redundancies ten weeks before telling employees; compensation given for ten weeks' loss of job searching opportunity).
633 [1988] ICR 142, [1987] IRLR 503, HL.

account in fixing compensation, and that approach has been applied strongly in the post-*Polkey* case law[634]. This may mean that the tribunals have to be more pro-active on this point, investigating the likelihood of continued employment or lack thereof, and if necessary making a percentage estimate of that likelihood (known in the jargon as the 'Polkey reduction')[635].

Moreover, an employee may be said to have lost nothing if his conduct is such that it is not just and equitable to give any compensatory award, in spite of the finding of unfairness. This would be the case for example where the employer unfairly dismissed the employee on a weak ground (for example, incapability) but then later found out about a cast-iron ground for dismissal (for example, embezzlement) which the employee had kept hidden from him. In such a case, the House of Lords held in *W Devis & Sons Ltd v Atkins*[636] that that subsequently discovered reason could not affect the fairness of the dismissal, or activate the provisions on contributory fault, for both of these matters have to be judged according to the employer's knowledge at the time of the dismissals; it could, however, justify the tribunal making a nil or nominal compensatory award on the ground of justice and equity, quite independently of any question of contributory fault[637].

Given such general considerations, tribunals have to have a system of dividing up possible heads of loss, and this is well established, principally following the early NIRC case *Norton Tool Co Ltd v Tewson*[638] which also established that the tribunal should set out in their judgment the relevant heads of compensation and the amounts awarded under each, not just one global sum[639]. The emphasis is very clearly upon pecuniary loss, and the following are the major heads:

(1) *Loss up to the date of hearing.* This head requires a relatively simple mathematical calculation of the employee's actual loss of income during the period between the dismissal and the hearing; it is aimed at realistic compensation, so, as in the case of future loss (below), the relevant figure is his previous weekly take-

---

634 See particularly *Mining Supplies (Longwall) Ltd v Baker* [1988] ICR 676, [1988] IRLR 417; *Slaughter v C Brewer & Sons Ltd* [1990] ICR 730, [1990] IRLR 426; *Red Bank Manufacturing Co Ltd v Meadows* [1992] ICR 204, [1992] IRLR 209; *Campbell v Dunoon and Cowal Housing Association Ltd* [1993] IRLR 496, Ct of Sess; *Britool Ltd v Roberts* [1993] IRLR 481; *Rao v Civil Aviation Authority* [1994] ICR 495, [1994] IRLR 240, CA.

635 *Dunlop Ltd v Farrell* [1993] ICR 885; *Wolesley Centers Ltd v Simmons* [1994] ICR 503; *Fisher v California Cake & Cookie Ltd* [1997] IRLR 212. The EAT have suggested two glosses to this rule, where the tribunal should not consider future likelihoods – (i) where the unfairness comes from a defect of substance (eg improper selection criteria) rather than of procedure: *Steel Stockholders (Birmingham) Ltd v Kirkwood* [1993] IRLR 515 (criticised by the Court of Appeal in *O'Dea v ISC Chemicals Ltd* [1996] ICR 222, [1995] IRLR 599, but reaffirmed by the Inner House of the Court of Session in *King v Eaton (No 2)* [1998] IRLR 686); (ii) where the unfairness comes from positive steps taken by the employer (eg wrong application of criteria), rather than a sin of omission: *Boulton & Paul Ltd v Arnold* [1994] IRLR 532. Arguably, both of these are unfortunate complications in an already difficult area.

636 [1977] ICR 662, [1977] IRLR 314, HL.

637 I[1977] ICR 662 at 680, [1977] IRLR 314 at 319, per Lord Dilhorne. This point was reaffirmed by the Court of Appeal in *Tele-Trading Ltd v Jenkins* [1990] IRLR 430.

638 [1973] 1 All ER 183, [1972] ICR 501. For a criticism of this whole approach, see Collins (1991) 20 ILJ 201. Lord Hoffmann in *Johnson v Unisys Ltd* [2001] UKHL 13, [2001] ICR 480, [2001] IRLR 279 stated that *Norton Tool* was too narrow in relation to the heading of 'manner of dismissal' (see below). This has caused considerable uncertainty but does not seem to apply to the rest of the case, which has been a foundation authority for 30 years.

639 See also *Adda International Ltd v Curcio* [1976] ICR 407, [1976] IRLR 425, EAT.

home pay (net of tax and National Insurance contributions) which may include matters such as overtime and tips which may *not* be counted under the stricter rules for calculating a 'week's pay' for the purpose of the basic award[640]. From this amount which the employee would have earned but for the dismissal the tribunal must deduct any sums earned in alternative employment during the period, or indeed in self employment[641]. There is, however, one qualification – where the employee earns money during what should have been his notice period, that amount will normally *not* be deducted from the compensation ordered under this head; this is in contravention of the requirement of mitigation, but is justified on the basis of good industrial relations practice[642]. A problem then arose that there were attempts to extend the qualification to cases where the employer had dismissed with wages in lieu of notice; if this amount too could be disregarded, the employer would end up paying for the notice period twice and the problem was that this would be a material disincentive to the making of voluntary payments to dismissed employees, whereas it is clearly within the policy of the statute to try to encourage settlements of disputes without going to a tribunal. Moreover, if voluntary payments of wages in lieu were disregarded, could it logically be argued that ex gratia payments *generally* should not? Once again, this could have had a serious effect on settlements. Fortunately, the position was rectified by the important decision of the Court of Appeal in *Addison v Babcock FATA Ltd*[643] – non-deductibility may apply to earnings during the notice period from elsewhere, but it does *not* apply where the ex-employer has properly discharged the contract by paying wages in lieu of notice – there, the normal principle of mitigation applies and the employer is permitted to set that payment off against the compensation otherwise payable under this head; the employer will therefore *not* lose out by having to pay twice by reason of attempting to settle the case by, inter alia, the

---

640 *Brownson v Hire Service Shops Ltd* [1978] ICR 517, [1978] IRLR 73; *Palmanor Ltd v Cedron* [1978] ICR 1008, [1978] IRLR 303. Tax matters should not be considered in too great detail by the tribunal which may, for example, ignore minor tax rebates: *MBS Ltd v Calo* [1983] ICR 459, [1983] IRLR 189. If there is a dispute as to what is the correct amount of wage payable at the date of dismissal, that must be resolved by the tribunal which is deciding upon compensation: *Kinzley v Minories Finance Ltd* [1988] ICR 113, [1987] IRLR 490, EAT.

641 *Ging v Ellward (Lancs) Ltd* (1978) [1991] ICR 222n; *Lee v IPC Business Press Ltd* [1984] ICR 306. This remains the case, even if the employee obtains new, permanent employment at *higher* pay, which eats into the compensation: *Dench v Flynn & Partners* [1998] IRLR 653, CA, disapproving on this point *Whelan v Richardson* [1998] IRLR 114.

642 *TBA Industrial Products Ltd v Locke* [1984] ICR 228, [1984] IRLR 48 (disapproving a contrary decision in *Tradewinds Airways Ltd v Fletcher* [1981] IRLR 272 and reverting to the original rule as laid down in *Norton Tool Co Ltd v Tewson* (above)), approved in *Addison v Babcock FATA Ltd*, n 643 below. The word 'normally' is used in the text because there is an exception – if in what should have been the notice period the ex-employee in fact earns a considerable sum, it may not be in the interests of good industrial relations practice to disregard that fact and award some or all of the wages for the period against the ex-employer: *Isleworth Studios Ltd v Rickard* [1988] ICR 432, [1988] IRLR 137 (ex-employee setting up in business and making £10,000 *more* than he would have earned in the remaining 29 weeks of his fixed-term contract; *held* the money made in the new business *was* to be taken into account as mitigation). The drawing of this particular line could be very difficult; it serves to show that the rule in *TBA Industrial Products* is an exception to normal principles.

643 [1987] ICR 805, [1987] IRLR 173, CA, overruling *Finnie v Top Hat Frozen Foods* [1985] ICR 433, [1985] IRLR 365, EAT.

payment of wages in lieu. Moreover, it is clear that this principle applies to ex gratia payments generally[644] – again, the employer will normally[645] be given credit for such payments and be able to set them off against any compensation awarded later[646].

As well as salary, wages and other monetary receipts, the employee can claim compensation for past (and future) loss of other benefits such as a company car, a low interest mortgage or loan, free or cheap accommodation and other fringe benefits such as medical insurance and school fees; also, section 123(2) expressly includes any expenses reasonably incurred as a result of the dismissal (for example expenses incurred in seeking other employment) though this does not include the expense of bringing the unfair dismissal action itself.

(2) *Future loss.* In contrast to the relative certainties of the first head, compensation for future loss may require the tribunal to perform a highly speculative exercise. The actual loss per week may be easy to quantify (either where the ex-employee has not obtained other employment, or has done so at a lower wage) and it may include the extra matters and perks mentioned above, but the tribunal has to fix a 'multiplier' (as in personal injury cases) of a number of weeks, months or even years during which this loss might continue[647]; the state of the local labour market and conditions in the industry concerned will be factors, but there will be other discounting factors, such as the possibilities that the employee might have resigned in the future anyway, moved from the area, had a child, etc. Also, the principle mentioned above that the employee will not be compensated if he has in fact suffered no loss must be borne in mind, so that if he would probably have lost his employment in the near future anyway (for example, through impending redundancies) he may only be compensated in respect of that short extra period of likely employment[648]. The number of factors in any particular case may thus be considerable and so, although as in other aspects of compensation the

---

644 *Horizon Holidays Ltd v Grassi* [1987] ICR 851, [1987] IRLR 371, EAT.
645 Once again the word 'normally' is used because there is an exception – if an ex gratia payment is made on dismissal which would have been made to the employee *anyway* even if no unfair dismissal had taken place (eg where a redundancy dismissal is unfair for lack of warning, but the facts show that the same ex gratia payment would have been made even if proper warning had been given), then it may be argued that that particular payment should *not* be taken into account as mitigation: *Roadchef Ltd v Hastings* [1988] IRLR 142; one complication in *Addison* was that there was (in addition to the payment in lieu) an ex gratia payment which was not taken into account, but it was for this reason.
646 Though even here the employer may lose out, for if the eventual amount of compensation is going to be over the statutory maximum, it has been held that the tribunal must deduct the ex gratia payment and *then* apply the maximum to what is left, which means that the employer may end up paying in total *more* than the statutory maximum: *McCarthy v BICC plc* [1985] IRLR 94; for the order of making deductions, see p 621 below. Thus the employer must be careful with ex gratia payments and, certainly in the case of higher earners, might be better advised to seek a binding *settlement* (either under the aegis of ACAS or under the rules on binding compromise agreements) rather than attempting a simple pay-off.
647 See, eg, *Cartiers Superfoods Ltd v Laws* [1978] IRLR 315. This must be viewed in the context of that individual claimant so that if his personal circumstances render new employment more difficult, the compensation may reflect that: *Fougère v Phoenix Motor Co Ltd* [1976] ICR 495, [1976] IRLR 259; *Gilham v Kent County Council (No 3)* [1986] ICR 52, [1986] IRLR 56, EAT.
648 *Young's of Gosport Ltd v Kendell* [1977] ICR 907, [1977] IRLR 433.

tribunal should explain in its decision how it arrived at the multiplier it used[649], this is not an exercise in precision and so that multiplier may be one general approximation of several different factors and, unless very clearly misguided, will not usually be altered by the EAT. In the past, even rough calculations could soon reach the low statutory maximum, rendering further precision unnecessary, but the raising of that maximum to £50,000 in 1999 was expected to mean much more argument on exact calculation, in order to maximise compensation within (and up to) that limit, especially in cases of higher earners and/or likely long-term unemployment; in the large majority of cases, however, this will not be so and the multiplier will be relatively modest[650].

(3) *Loss of accrued rights.* When an employee is dismissed and takes other employment, he loses any statutory (or other) rights against the dismissing employer which depend upon continuous service (for example, redundancy and the employment protection rights) and must begin to accrue new rights against his new employer. This head of loss established in *Norton Tool Co Ltd v Tewson*, was meant to reflect that disadvantage and initially caused some problems. Now, however, the major loss (of accrued redundancy rights) is in effect taken into account by the institution of the basic award and so any further compensation under this head will be less, though the EAT held in *Daley v A E Dorsett (Almar Dolls) Ltd*[651] that the right to the longer notice that accrues with service is itself valuable (particularly in times of economic recession) so that, independently of the power that a tribunal now has to award common law damages for loss of wages during the notice period, it is open to it to make an award including an amount reflecting the employee's loss of accrued statutory rights to longer notice[652].

(4) *Loss due to the manner of dismissal.* It was decided in 1972 (the year after the law on unfair dismissal was introduced) in *Norton Tool Co Ltd v Tewson* (above) that the compensatory award was clearly tied to pecuniary loss and so, as at common law[653], no amount could be awarded for loss of dignity, anguish, etc, simpliciter; an amount could only be granted under this head if the manner of dismissal could be said to affect the employee's future employment prospects, for example by blackening his name in the industry or in some way rendering him unfit for immediate re-employment[654]. This nostrum was

---

649 *Qualcast (Wolverhampton) Ltd v Ross* [1979] ICR 386, [1979] IRLR 98. There is *no* 'conventional sum' of between 6 and 12 months – the period is to be determined by the tribunal in the light of all the evidence, subject only to the statutory maximum amount that can be awarded: *Morganite Electrical Carbon Ltd v Donne* [1988] ICR 18, [1987] IRLR 363 (impossible to say that an award covering 82 weeks was excessive).

650 In 2001/02 the median award was £2,563 and the average award £5,917. 54% of awards were for under £3,000. Only 6.3% were for over £20,000: ETS Annual Report 2001/02.

651 [1982] ICR 1, [1981] IRLR 385. Compensation may also reflect the loss of any *extra* redundancy rights that the ex-employee may have had under this contract over and above his ordinary statutory entitlement: *Lee v IPC Business Press Ltd* [1984] ICR 306.

652 The EAT quantified this amount as half the wages for the statutory minimum of eight weeks' notice to which he was entitled. However, in the subsequent case of *S H Muffett Ltd v Head* [1987] ICR 1, [1986] IRLR 488 the EAT thought that in most cases it would be more appropriate merely to award a nominal sum of £100 under this head.

653 *Addis v Gramophone Co Ltd* [1909] AC 488, HL; *Bliss v South East Thames Regional Health Authority* [1987] ICR 700, [1985] IRLR 308, CA; see p 484 above.

654 *Norton Tool Co Ltd v Tewson*, n 638 above; *Vaughan v Weighpack Ltd* [1974] ICR 261, [1974] IRLR 105; *Brittains Arborfield Ltd v Van Uden* [1977] ICR 211, EAT.

followed consistently for three decades, until challenged entirely unexpectedly in a case concerning a very different point of law. *Johnson v Unisys Ltd*[655] was a common law claim for what had become known as 'stigma damages', ie manner of dismissal damages as part of a *wrongful* dismissal action[656]. In a strong decision putting an end to their development, one of the reasons given was that the common law should not be extended in such a way as to outflank or compromise statute law; in this context, that meant that manner of dismissal damages should not be given at common law *because it was the function of unfair dismissal to do so*. This bombshell was contained in Lord Hoffmann's speech, in this short passage:

> 'I know that in the early days of the NIRC it was laid down that only financial loss could be compensated: see *Norton Tool Co Ltd v Tewson* ... It was said that the word 'loss' can only mean financial loss. But I think that is too narrow a construction. The emphasis is upon the tribunal awarding such compensation as it thinks just and equitable. So I see no reason why in an appropriate case it should not include compensation for distress, humiliation, damage to reputation in the community or to family life.'[657]

Not unsurprisingly, this was rapidly taken up by claimants' lawyers and representatives as a significant extension to unfair dismissal compensation. However, it split tribunals with some granting such awards and others declining to. The problem is whether this passage is *ratio* or merely *obiter*. On the one hand, the case was based on common law, not statutory unfair dismissal. The contrary argument is that the passage and its argument is so closely tied into the decision (no damages at common law *because* already covered by the statutory action) as to be part of the *ratio*. This is a significant point, particularly with the raising of the cap for the compensatory award to its present level. One problem is that, if such an award can be made the House of Lords gave no indication as to how it is to be calculated; one solution would be to adopt by analogy the case law on awards for injury to feelings in discrimination cases (see p 321 above). It is to be hoped that this troublesome point will be determined one way or the other early in the currency of this edition.

(5) *Loss of pension rights.* Where the dismissed employee cannot find new employment, or can or may find new employment to which he cannot transfer his existing pension rights, this head of compensation may produce a considerable sum. It is, however, perhaps the most complicated head of all and the EAT have stressed that the tribunal should adopt a broad approach so that actuarial evidence, though of considerable help (bearing in mind that the claimant must adduce evidence of loss), is not conclusive. Once again the tribunal is aiming for a realistic, if approximate, estimate of actual

---

655 [2001] UKHL 13, [2001] ICR 480, [2001] IRLR 279.
656 For this aspect of the case, see p 488 above.
657 [2001] UKHL 13, [2001] ICR 480 at 500, [2001] IRLR 279 at 288.
658 Where there is an option the choice lies with the employee, who is not to be penalised by the tribunal if he opts not to take the deferred pension: *Sturdy Finance Ltd v Bardsley* [1979] ICR 249, [1979] IRLR 65. Deferment of pension has been the normal position in the pension scheme since the Social Security Pensions Act 1975, though the amended pensions regime since 1986 puts more emphasis on personal, 'portable' pensions which may go with the person and the present government's intentions in relation to 'stakeholder pensions' remain in line with this, in which case there will be less of a problem of quantification under this head.

loss so that if no loss is sustained overall, nothing is payable under this head; this might occur if the employee has to take, or opts for[658], a deferred pension from his existing entitlement and can build up a suitable further entitlement from new employment, or if he moves to employment with a better pension scheme (for example, from a contributory to a non-contributory scheme), or if he can simply transfer his pension. In *Copson v Eversure Accessories Ltd* [659] the NIRC said that there is no one correct way to quantify loss of pension rights, but isolated two types of loss – (a) loss of present pension position and (b) loss of future pension opportunity (ie the opportunity, had he not been dismissed, to improve his pension position during further service with that employer). Except in cases where the employee is close to retiring age (where the better approach may be to capitalise the cost of an annuity to produce a sum equal to the likely pension, discounting if for accelerated payment), the starting point for both (a) and (b) will be the contributions already paid to the scheme. The employee may have received back his own contributions, but can also claim (except in cases of transfer or deferment) credit for his legitimate interest in the contributions paid by the employer (plus interest thereon) which may be viewed as an adjunct to his salary[660]. As well as being the primary measure for the detriment to his present pension loss, lack of the employer's future contributions will be a guide to any future loss when compared with the position under any actual or likely pension scheme in new employment; the factors to be taken into account here may be numerous. Having arrived at a prima facie figure for loss, however, it is incorrect for the tribunal just to apply that for the number of years left to retirement age, because account must be taken of many contingencies, such as future resignation, future dismissal, early death, possible tax advantages and the fact that any capital sum is being paid sooner than normal. This discounting process is achieved by the fixing of the tribunal of a multiplier to take all of these factors into account[661]; this may considerably decrease the possible compensation under this head and inevitably imports an element of uncertainty. In an attempt to lessen the uncertainty generally, a committee of tribunal chairmen in conjunction with the Government Actuary's Department produced in 1991 a report suggesting methods of quantifying loss of pension rights; it contains examples of cases which might be likely to arise in practice, and certain basic actuarial material[662]. It is not necessarily determinative, though in the sea of actuarial uncertainty it may appear to a tribunal to be the only lifeline[663], and it may prove difficult to introduce independent actuarial evidence based on different calculation methods[664]. However, this remains an area of difficulty and development as the EAT have indicated that, ten

---

659 [1974] ICR 636, [1974] IRLR 247, NIRC.
660 *Copson's* case; *Hill v Sabco Houseware (UK) Ltd* [1977] ICR 888; *Smith, Kline and French Laboratories Ltd v Coates* [1977] IRLR 220; *Sturdy Finance Ltd v Bardsley* [1979] ICR 249, [1979] IRLR 65.
661 *Powrmatic Ltd v Bull* [1977] ICR 469, [1977] IRLR 144, EAT.
662 Sara, Crump and Puglsey *Employment Tribunals: Compensation of Loss of Pension Rights.*
663 Its predecessor (by the GAD itself) was relied on in *Manpower Ltd v Hearne* [1983] ICR 567, [1983] IRLR 281 and *Mono Pumps Ltd v Froggatt* [1987] IRLR 368. However, the EAT in *Bingham v Hobourn Engineering Ltd* [1992] IRLR 298 pointed out that a tribunal is not bound to follow it.
664 See the views of the EAT on this point in *Tradewinds Airways Ltd v Fletcher* [1981] IRLR 272. While a tribunal will properly not expect an employee to come armed with complex actuarial evidence, it is surely another matter actually to exclude it if the employee wishes to put it forward, especially where pension loss is a major factor.

years on, there is a need for a further attempt at guidance[665]. The large amounts of money involved in the loss of pension position (just on moving jobs, let alone on being dismissed) are yet another reason for amazement that the levels of compensation awards in practice are so low (see n 650 above); perhaps one reason is that in the past the low level of the statutory maximum on the compensatory award has had a depressing effect on arguing this head of loss – it may need expensive actuarial evidence, which was hardly worthwhile if any eventual claim was to be severely restricted by the maximum. With the raising of the limit to £50,000 in 1999 and the subsequent annual increases, we may expect more effort to be put into proving pension loss.

One final point may be noted about the compensatory award. What is the position if the employee has received unemployment benefit (now jobseeker's allowance) or income support prior to the date of the hearing? Before 1977, this was treated in the same way as receipt of income from another source during that period, and so was deductible. However, that meant that the employer was paying less compensation through a 'subsidy' from the state. Under the Employment Protection (Recoupment of Jobseeker's Allowance and Income Support) Regulations 1996[666], the position now is that the tribunal is not to deduct the amount representing jobseeker's allowance or income support paid up to the date of the hearing, but instead must instruct the employer not to pay immediately that amount of the compensation it has awarded which represents loss of income during the period (ie head 1 above, called in the Regulations the 'prescribed element'). The DTI will then serve upon the employer a recoupment notice (or a notice that no such notice will in fact be served) which requires him to pay back to them from the prescribed element the amount representing jobseeker's allowance or income support paid to the claimant prior to the hearing; after this has been done, the remainder of the prescribed element may be paid to the successful claimant. Thus, the DTI obliges the employer to repay to them amounts made payable by them because of the unfair dismissal and the claimant still only receives what he has in fact lost. If no jobseeker's allowance or income support was in fact claimed during the period, the Regulations do not apply. Thus, the tribunal is relieved of the task of deducting benefits from the award (in return for the administrative chore of explaining the procedure to the parties) and, moreover, need not take the possibility of further receipt of benefit into account when deciding upon future loss (head 2 above) either, for where compensation is awarded based on future loss for a set period of X weeks, months or years, the claimant is disqualified from receiving benefit during that period.

---

665 *Clancy v Cannock Chase Technical College* [2001] IRLR 331, where the EAT suggested that the existing guidelines did not cope well with a pension scheme which includes a lump sum entitlement in addition to the weekly amount (as opposed to constituting commuttation of part of that weekly amount).

666 Ie 1996/2349, *Harvey* R [1007], replacing the original 1977 Regulations. *Mason v Wimpey Waste Management Ltd* [1982] IRLR 454. The Regulations do not apply to the settlement of an unfair dismissal action, so such a settlement may well take into account the state benefits in fact received, and those benefits will not be recoverable by the state. This may be an inducement to the employer to settle, since he may end up paying less.

(3) Contributory fault[667]

If a tribunal, having found in the claimant's favour on liability, considers that the dismissal was to any extent caused or contributed to by any action of the complainant, it must reduce both the basic award and the compensatory award by such proportion as it considers just and equitable[668]. The 'action' of the claimant must constitute blameworthy conduct in some way (so that it will not apply to proper and lawful activity on his part, such as refusing to obey an improper or unlawful order[669]) and this provision is aimed at giving the tribunal discretion to reach a just solution when both parties have been to blame[670], as in the case of contributory negligence in a tort action. Contributory fault constitutes a separate stage in the inquiry, once the tribunal has put a figure on the compensation, and should be explained by the tribunal as such[671]. In *Maris v Rotherham Corpn*[672] the NIRC said that the tribunal should approach this question in a broad common sense manner, looking at all the circumstances of the case and the employee's overall conduct (even if the actual ground of unfairness is a narrow, technical one); a slight change in the wording in 1975 strengthened this view[673]. The actual figure thus lies predominantly within the tribunal's discretion and may be difficult to challenge on appeal, provided that it has been properly considered at the hearing[674].

Where the ground for dismissal was misconduct, but the dismissal is held to have been unfair (for example, because of lack of warnings or a hearing) in spite of evidence of actual misconduct, that may be a clear case for reduction of compensation. Indeed, in *W Devis & Sons Ltd v Atkins*[675] Lord Dilhorne,

---

667 See *Harvey* DI [2707].
668 Employment Rights Act 1996, ss 122(2) and 123(6) ; by a combination of the Employment Acts 1980 and 1982 the contributory fault provision in the case of the basic award was widened to cover *any* conduct before the dismissal making it just and equitable to decrease that award; the reason for this is discussed below. The procedure to be adopted (especially in a 'split' hearing) is considered by the EAT in *Iggesund Converters Ltd v Lewis* [1984] ICR 544 at 552, [1984] IRLR 431 at 435. There is no requirement that the basic and compensatory awards have to be reduced by the same percentage once contributory fault is found: *Charles Robertson (Developments) Ltd v White* [1995] ICR 349 (reviewing the previous, inconsistent case law); *Optikinetics Ltd v Whooley* [1999] ICR 984.
669 *Morrish v Henlys (Folkestone) Ltd* [1973] ICR 482, [1973] IRLR 61, approved by the Court of Appeal in *Nelson v BBC (No 2)* [1980] ICR 110, [1979] IRLR 346, CA.
670 The matter must be looked at between employer and employee, *not* involving the actions of third parties (eg other employees at fault): *Parker Foundry Ltd v Slack* [1992] ICR 302, [1992] IRLR 11, CA. Contributory fault can be applied even if the dismissal was constructive for, looking at the history of the matter, the employee may have been partly responsible for the employer taking the actual repudiatory action: *Garner v Grange Furnishing Ltd* [1977] IRLR 206; *Morrison v ATGWU* [1989] IRLR 361, NICA; *Polentarutti v Autokraft Ltd* [1991] ICR 757, [1991] IRLR 457 (not following *Holroyd v Gravure Cylinders Ltd* [1984] IRLR 259). 'Fault' on the part of the employee can include fault on the part of his agent, eg his solicitor: *Allen v Hammett* [1982] ICR 227, [1982] IRLR 89.
671 *Nudds v W and JB Eastwood Ltd* [1978] ICR 171.
672 [1974] ICR 435, [1974] IRLR 147.
673 *Brown v Rolls-Royce (1971) Ltd* (1977) 12 ITR 382 at 386, per Phillips J. There must still be a causal link between the conduct and the dismissal: *Hutchinson v Enfield Rolling Mills Ltd* [1981] IRLR 318, at least in the case of the compensatory award, though that link has been deliberately loosened in the case of the basic award.
674 *Sutcliffe and Eaton Ltd v Pinney* [1977] IRLR 349; *Hollier v Plysu Ltd* [1983] IRLR 260, CA.
675 [1977] ICR 662, [1977] IRLR 314, HL, disapproving in this context dicta in *Kemp v Shipton Automation Ltd* [1976] ICR 514, [1976] IRLR 305 and *Trend v Chiltern Hunt Ltd* [1977] ICR 612, [1977] IRLR 66. See *Marley Homecare Ltd v Dutton* [1981] IRLR 380 and *Chaplin v H J Rawlinson Ltd* [1991] ICR 553.

disapproving earlier dicta that there may be a limit on the amount of reduction (for example, 80% maximum reduction), held that there is nothing inconsistent in finding unfairness but then using contributory fault in an extreme case to reduce compensation to nil or a merely nominal amount. The position, however, is more difficult in the case of a dismissal for incapacity, for can an employee's unfortunate incapacity ever be considered to be 'fault' on his part? In *Kraft Foods Ltd v Fox*[676] the EAT held that it could not, but in the subsequent case of *Moncur v International Paint Co Ltd* [677] it was explained that that was too sweeping a proposition and that the *Kraft* case envisaged the sort of incapability that was entirely outside the employee's control; even there, the EAT in *Moncur's* case doubted whether it was an absolute rule that such incapability could *never* amount to contributory fault and a reduction in such circumstances was approved subsequently in *Finnie v Top Hat Frozen Foods*[678]. In *Slaughter v C Brewer & Sons Ltd*[679] a different tack was taken; the EAT said that a reduction of contributory fault would be rare in an incapability case *but* if it was clear that, even if the employee had been treated fairly, the employment would have had to end shortly, then compensation can be reduced accordingly under the general 'just and equitable' basis to the compensatory award, thus achieving much the same result. One matter that is well established is that where the incapability is in any way within the employee's control (for example, where he is negligent, lazy or unwilling to improve), that can clearly be contributory fault and indeed, according to the case of *Sutton and Gates (Luton) Ltd v Boxall* [680] (where a similar view was taken of the *Kraft* case), it may warrant a sizeable reduction.

A particular problem with contributory fault arose where the employer unfairly dismisses on one ground but then subsequently discovers other grounds which would certainly have justified dismissal. The House of Lords in *W Devis & Sons Ltd v Atkins*[681] held that in such a case the subsequently discovered misconduct cannot alter the finding of unfairness under section 57(3) *and* cannot be used as contributory fault for, being unknown at the time of dismissal, it could not have 'caused or contributed to' the dismissal. In such a case, however, justice could be done by giving a nil award under the general 'just and equitable' basis for compensation, *but* in that particular case the House of Lords were applying the old law on compensation which operated *before* the basic award was introduced in 1975. Once that award was introduced, the problem arose that a tribunal could not impose a nil basic award because the calculation is mathematical (not based on what is just and equitable) and it could only be reduced by contributory fault, which did not include subsequently discovered misconduct. Thus, in such a case, the employee whose dishonesty only came to light after being unfairly dismissed for laziness might still get a nil compensatory award but remain eligible for a basic award. Lord Diplock called this a 'rogue's charter' and in the Employment Act 1980 the previous government took steps to prevent it, in two ways. First, the statutory minimum basic award of two weeks' pay was abolished; secondly, the tribunals were given a wider power to decrease (and possibly

---

676 [1978] ICR 311, [1977] IRLR 431.
677 [1978] IRLR 223; *Brown's Cycles Ltd v Brindley* [1978] ICR 467.
678 [1985] ICR 433, [1985] IRLR 365 (overruled later on other grounds in *Addison v Babcock FATA Ltd* [1987] ICR 805, [1987] IRLR 173, CA).
679 [1990] ICR 730, [1990] IRLR 426.
680 [1979] ICR 67, [1978] IRLR 486.
681 N 675 above.

extinguish) a basic award where the conduct of the complainant before the dismissal was such that it would be just and equitable to reduce the award. This is wider than the previous rule on contributory fault per se (which still applies to the compensatory award) in that it does not require a definite causal link between the conduct and the dismissal[682]. Thus, the undisclosed rogue may now be awarded no compensation at all.

(4) Mitigation

Under section 123(4), the dismissed employee must take the same reasonable steps to mitigate his losses as he would have to at common law[683]; these might include answering job advertisements and going to the local job centre, though of course it might not be reasonable in the circumstances to expect him to take any job that occurs. Refusal of an offer of reinstatement by the same employer can constitute failure to mitigate[684], but failure to use the company's appeal procedure once dismissed probably will not on general principles[685]; it may be reasonable in certain circumstances to leave one industry altogether and retrain for another, even if that necessarily means a longer period without work[686]. If the employee unreasonably refuses to mitigate, that can lead to a reduction in his compensatory award[687], though (on general principles) the onus lies upon the employer to prove failure to mitigate[688].

These general principles may now be subject to two legislative developments. First, the Employment Act 2002 contains a form of statutory 'mitigation', providing that an employee who fails to comply with the statutory disciplinary or grievance procedure (in Schedule 2, see p 540 above) or fails to exercise a right of appeal under it may have any award of compensation reduced by between 10 and 50%,

---

682 Employment Rights Act 1996, s 122(2).
683 See p 489 above. See particularly Potter LJ's summary of the approach to be taken by a tribunal in *Wilding v BT plc* [2002] EWCA Civ 349, [2002] IRLR 524. In that case Sedley LJ suggested that a test akin to the range of reasonable responses test should be applied (so that the employee would only fail to mitigate if no reasonable employee would have acted in that way) but the other two lords justices did not mention or support this idea.
684 *Sweetlove v Redbridge and Waltham Forest Area Health Authority* [1979] ICR 477, [1979] IRLR 195; *Gallear v J F Watson & Son Ltd* [1979] IRLR 306; cf *Tiptools Ltd v Curtis* [1973] IRLR 276, where the offer of re-engagement included demotion. In *Wilding v BT plc*, n 683 above, Potter LJ said that a tribunal may have to take into account in such a case the attitutde of the former employer, the way the employee was treated and the employee's state of mind. The test may thus be both objective and subjective.
685 *Seligman and Latz Ltd v McHugh* [1979] IRLR 130; cf *Hoover Ltd v Forde* [1980] ICR 239. The rule was approved (and *Hoover* not followed) in *William Muir (Bond 9) Ltd v Lamb* [1985] IRLR 95. This is now subject to the Employment Act 2002; see n 689 below.
686 *Sealey v Avon Aluminium Co Ltd* [1978] IRLR 285, IT.
687 By taking it into account when fixing the multiplier: *Smith, Kline and French Laboratories Ltd v Coates* [1977] IRLR 220; *Peara v Enderlin Ltd* [1979] ICR 804. Note that the basic award is *not* subject to mitigation (except in the special case where the employee unreasonably refuses an offer of re-employment: s 122(1)), so that if the dismissed employee obtains new employment immediately he may get little or no compensatory award, but he remains eligible for the basic award (reflecting his loss of accrued employment rights).
688 *Bessenden Properties Ltd v Corness* [1977] ICR 821n, [1974] IRLR 338, CA; *Fyfe v Scientific Furnishings Ltd* [1989] ICR 648, [1989] IRLR 331 (disapproving statements to the contrary in *Scottish and Newcastle Breweries plc v Halliday* [1986] ICR 577, [1986] IRLR 291).

unless there are exceptional circumstances making such a reduction unjust and inequitable[689]. Secondly, the raising of the statutory limit on the compensatory award to its present level may lead to more arguments by respondent employers on failure to mitigate, as part of a generally greater emphasis on calculating compensation.

(5) The order of deductions

In complex cases, where there may be several deductions to be made from an award of compensation (for example, for mitigatory amounts, contributory fault, a *Polkey* reduction and, of course, the statutory limit) a long-standing problem has been the order in which such deductions are to be made. This sounds very technical, but in practice can make a difference of thousands of pounds to the eventual award. It becomes particularly acute where the mitigatory amount in question is an ex gratia payment by the employer who, of course, wants to get full benefit of it when compensation is awarded. This, however, will only happen if that amount is deducted last (ie after the award has been subjected to all the other necessary adjustments). After years worth of confusing and often inconsistent case law, the EAT reviewed the whole question in *Digital Equipment Co Ltd v Clements (No 2)*[690] and produced a definitive order of deductions, *starting* with mitigatory amounts including ex gratia payments (thus meaning that an employer may *not* get the full benefit of such a payment[691]). When the case was appealed to the Court of Appeal[692], a complication was introduced – on the facts of the case the ex gratia payment was in fact a non-statutory (ie more generous) redundancy payment and the court held that Parliament's intent[693] was that such payments were to be encouraged by being set off in full (subject only to the statutory limit), which could only be done by deducting them later. To that extent they allowed the employers' appeal; however, it is submitted that most of the reasoning of the EAT stands, subject only to this one qualification. On that basis, the order of deduction is:

(i) any mitigatory amounts (from the ex-employer or new employment) *other than* a non-statutory redundancy payment exceeding the statutory amount;

(ii) any *Polkey* reduction;

---

689 Employment Act 2002, s 31(2), (4). These provisions are to be supplemented by Regulations, not yet produced at the time of writing. They replace weaker provisions enacted by the Employment Rights (Dispute Resolution) Act 1998, which only provided for a reduction by up to two weeks' pay. Note that under s 31(3) if there is a failure to complete a statutory procedure due to the employer's fault there can be an increase in the award by similar amounts

690 [1997] ICR 237, [1997] IRLR 140. The case concerned a *Polkey* reduction of 50% and an ex gratia payment of £20,685, against a total loss of £43,136. If the *Polkey* reduction was taken off first, eventual compensation was £883. If the ex gratia payment was taken off first eventual compensation was £11,225 (reduced to the then maximum of £11,000). The EAT held for the latter approach.

691 A simple ex gratia pay-off (or attempt thereat) has thus always been inadvisable – it cannot be legally binding (Employment Rights Act 1996, s 203(1) which invalidates any attempt to contract out of the Act); finality can only be achieved by an ACAS (COT 3) settlement or a compromise agreement (s 203(2)–(4)).

692 [1998] ICR 258, [1998] IRLR 134, CA, awarding compensation of £883.

693 As evidenced by the Employment Rights Act 1996, s 123(7) which provides that any redundancy payment (statutory or otherwise) exceeding the basic award is to be set off then against the compensatory award.

(iii) any contributory fault;
(iv) any non-statutory redundancy payment;
(v) the statutory limit, if applicable.
It is to be hoped that order has now been introduced into this complex area (and also that the statutory limit will now be less of a complication in many cases, after being raised from £12,000 to £50,000 in 1999).

Chapter 9

Redundancy rights and benefits for unemployment

I INTRODUCTION

Questions of redundancy figure largely in the news in times of recession, and this was reflected, for example, in the case load of ACAS in the 1990s. Compulsory redundancy leads to significant problems in employment law, and the question of the fairness of a redundancy dismissal has already been considered in chapter 8 above. However, research has shown[1] that, even in recessionary times with the strong emphasis on 'down sizing'[2], compulsory redundancy is *not* the first option chosen and that other methods of reduction or reorganisation of the workforce are usually considered more desirable, including natural wastage, redeployment, early retirement and voluntary redundancy. Compulsory redundancy tends to be more common in the private sector, particularly where there is no recognised trade union[3]. Although therefore the majority of workforce reductions will be done in ways which, by and large, do not involve litigation (actual or potential) in employment law and will normally be dealt with by agreement (either long standing or ad hoc), it is now necessary to consider the redundancy rights of those not so dealt with. In addition, this chapter also considers the rules relating to what is now the jobseeker's allowance (replacing unemployment benefit); although this usually comes under the heading of social security law, it does have significant overlaps with employment law, and it is an area about which the employment lawyer should have some knowledge in order to give all-round advice (just as a lawyer advising on personal injuries needs to know the social security background of the various forms of sickness and injury benefits).

1 Millward et al 'Workplace industrial relations in transition' (the ED/ESRC/PSI/ACAS Survey) (1992) ch 9.
2 Large sections of British management no longer communicate in English.
3 A significant finding, relating to times of major restructuring in the economy, is that in 1990 compulsory redundancies were reported by 30% of all establishments; this consisted of 52% in private manufacturing and 35% in private services, but only 4% in the public sector. Overall, compulsory redundancies were reported in 46% of workplaces without recognised unions, compared with 17% where recognised unions were present: n 1 above, pp 321, 324.

2 REDUNDANCY PAYMENTS

(i) The redundancy payments scheme

The scheme requiring employers to make compulsory payments to redundant employees was introduced by the Redundancy Payments Act 1965; this Act was repealed and the relevant provisions are now found in Part XI of the Employment Rights Act 1996. A first basic point to make about the scheme is that it is entirely separate from the dismissed employee's right to claim benefit; in one of the early cases on the 1965 Act Lord Denning MR said:

'... As I read the Act, a worker of long standing is now recognised as having an accrued right in his job, and his right gains in value with the years. So much so that, if the job is shut down, he is entitled to compensation for loss of the job ... It is not unemployment pay. I repeat "not". Even if he gets another job straightaway, he nevertheless is entitled to full redundancy payment. It is, in a real sense, compensation for long service.[4]'

There has been some controversy over the overall purpose of the legislation; ideas of increasing mobility of labour, giving greater job security, reducing the number of strikes over redundancies and rewarding long service have been advanced, but none are complete answers and all are open to doubt[5]. Moreover, one major criticism from a legal point of view is that the legislation is arguably far too complicated for its modest aims, particularly as it is subject to a relatively low maximum payment and in practice yields on average much lower amounts than that[6]. The argument that the whole scheme is itself redundant is now supported by the existence of compulsory consultation procedures in cases of impending redundancy[7] and the redundancy aspects of the law on unfair dismissal (which of course did not exist in 1965), which is now a more important claim than one for straightforward redundancy pay. On the other hand many employers now have private redundancy schemes[8], often more generous than the legislative scheme, and it may be that it was the legislation which gave the spur to these improved schemes, while retaining some residual importance in ensuring that an employee who is not subject to such a scheme at least receives *something* if he is fairly dismissed because of economic conditions outside the control of himself or his employer.

In order to claim a redundancy payment, the ex-employee must have been 'dismissed', and that dismissal must have been 'by reason of redundancy'. The

---

4   *Lloyd v Brassey* [1969] 2 QB 98 at 102, [1969] 1 All ER 382 at 383, CA. Thus, receipt of a redundancy payment does not disentitle a person from jobseeker's allowance.

5   See Fryer 'The Myths of the Redundancy Payments Act' (1973) 2 ILJ 1.

6   As from February 2003 the maximum amount is £7,800.

7   See pp 84–91 above.

8   Also, certain specific redundancy schemes have in the past been established by statute in the public sector, eg the steelworkers' redundancy scheme, that relating to British shipbuilders and the scheme for dock workers, following the abolition of the national dock labour scheme; the scheme relating to the coal mining industry was of considerable importance in a time of contraction, but has been discontinued.

statutory definition of dismissal has already been considered[9], but three particular points may be noted. The first is that dismissal may not be necessary in certain cases if there has been instead a lay-off or short-time working; this matter is considered below. The second is that 'dismissal' cannot be stretched to include failure to employ in the first place. Thus, in *North East Coast Shiprepairers Ltd v Secretary of State for Employment*[10] it was argued that an apprentice was redundant for statutory purposes when he could not be taken on by the employer as a journeyman fitter at the end of his contract of apprenticeship, because there was no such work available. The EAT held, however, that there was no dismissal, only a refusal to employ him in a different capacity upon the proper termination of the previous contract. The third point is that the legislation attempts to safeguard the position of an employee under notice of dismissal who wishes to leave early (for example, to take up other employment). The Employment Rights Act 1996, section 136(3) provides that he is still deemed to have been dismissed if he leaves during the obligatory period of the employer's notice and gives written[11] counter-notice of his intention to do so during that period. If, however, the employer has good reason to want him to stay for the full period and gives him a further written notice to that effect, but the employee still leaves early, he will only be eligible for a payment if the tribunal thinks it just and equitable that he should receive some or all of his entitlement, after considering the strength of the employer's reasons for wanting to prolong the employment and the employee's reasons for wanting to leave early[12]. One major restriction on these provisions is that the employee's counter-notice is only effective if given during the 'obligatory' period of the employer's notice; this means the amount of time which, by statute[13] or under the individual contract of employment, the employer *has* to give to terminate the contract and so if the employer is generous and in fact gives longer notice than in law he has to, the employee must wait until he is within the obligatory period before giving the counter-notice, otherwise that counter-notice is invalid and he may be deemed to have resigned on his own initiative, not to have been dismissed[14]. This is a potential trap for the employee who, under longer notice than he is contractually entitled to, finds a new job and needs to leave immediately to take it up, thus not being able to rely on section 136(3) if still outside the obligatory period. However, the EAT has

---

9   Pp 544–553 above. See *Harvey* E [401]. As seen at pp 456–459 above, termination of contract by mutual consent will rarely be found in employment law, for it robs tribunals of jurisdiction; however, one application of it is particularly important here, namely a finding of mutual termination (not dismissal) on a voluntary early retirement/severance on satisfactory terms; in such a case, the volunteer *cannot* claim a redundancy payment as well: *Birch v University of Liverpool* [1985] ICR 470, [1985] IRLR 165, CA; *Scott v Coalite Fuels and Chemicals Ltd* [1988] ICR 355, [1988] IRLR 131, EAT.

10   [1978] ICR 755, [1978] IRLR 149.

11   In s 95(2), the equivalent provision for unfair dismissal purposes, there is no longer the requirement of writing; before the requirement was dropped it caused problems in cases where there was no notice in writing and the employer then contended that termination of the contract was in fact due to mutual agreement, not dismissal: *Lees v Arthur Greaves (Lees) Ltd* [1974] 2 All ER 393, [1974] ICR 501, CA; *McAlwane v Boughton Estates Ltd* [1973] 2 All ER 299, [1973] ICR 470. There appears to be no good reason why the requirement should remain in the redundancy provision.

12   Employment Rights Act 1996, s 142.

13   S 86.

14   *Armit v McLauchlin* (1965) 1 ITR 280; *Pritchard-Rhodes Ltd v Boon and Milton* [1979] IRLR 19; *Doble v Firestone Tyre and Rubber Co Ltd* [1981] IRLR 300, EAT.

suggested[15] a possible way round in one class of case; this is where the employee *requests* that he be allowed to leave early and the employer *agrees*. This is not a section 136(3)case (which is where the employee serves formal notice of his *intention* to leave early) and so can be construed on wider principles; in particular, it may be construed as a consensual variation of the employer's original notice, meaning that the employee leaves at the earlier date, is still 'dismissed' by the employer, and can claim his redundancy payment. However, it must be remembered (a) that the employer must still have given *actual notice* in the first place (not just made vague statements about future job losses)[16], and (b) that this alternative approach only works if there is definite agreement between employer and employee – if the employee wants to (or has to) act unilaterally he must still comply with section 136(3) and beware the 'obligatory period' trap.

A dismissed employee may present a claim for a redundancy payment to an employment tribunal within six months of the 'relevant date' of dismissal, though the tribunal may also hear the claim if presented during the six months following that period if it appears just and equitable to do so, having regard to the employee's reasons for failing to comply with the normal time limit[17]. In such proceedings, one crucial factor is that there is in section 163(2) a statutory presumption that the dismissal was for redundancy, so that the burden of proof is upon the *employer* to prove on a balance of probabilities, that the dismissal was for some other reason[18]. This leads to one problem of at least theoretical importance to which there is no definite answer, and that is – is the test to be applied subjective (what the employer *thought* was the dominant reason for dismissal) or objective (what the overall facts suggest)? The problem arises where there was on the facts prima facie a 'redundancy situation', but the employer states that he genuinely believed at the time that some other ground existed (for example, incompetence, suspected dishonesty) and that he was acting on that ground in dismissing; does that discharge his burden of proof and defeat the claim, or should the tribunal look at the facts objectively? The majority decision of the

---

15   *CPS Recruitment Ltd v Bowen* [1982] IRLR 54, approving *Tunnel Holdings Ltd v Woolf* [1976] ICR 387.

16   Thus, certain previous cases such as *Pritchard-Rhodes Ltd v Boon and Milton* (n 14 above) remain good law and are reconcilable with *Bowen*'s case on the ground that the employer had not actually given notice, and so there was no notice there to be varied by agreement. On the requirement of notice, see p 459 above.

17   S 164; 'relevant date' is defined in s 145 as (a) the date the employer's notice takes effect, (b) the date the dismissal takes effect, if no notice is given, (c) the date of termination of a limited-term contract, (d) the 'relevant date' (as already defined) of the last contract where there has been one or more trial periods, or (e) the date of expiry of the employee's notice where he has given valid early notice under s 136(3). Where, however, any notice given (including the case where no notice is given) is shorter than the legal minimum which is required by s 86, the relevant date may be deemed to be the later date of the notional expiry of that legal minimum period, for three purposes – the calculation of the two years' qualifying period, the computation of the length of service for calculation of the payment and the determination of the relevant statutory maximum on a 'week's pay' for calculation purposes (ie where that maximum has been raised by Regulations between the dismissal and the claim). The purpose of this complicated provision is to prevent an employer gaining an advantage in these three areas by wrongfully dismissing the employee with short or no notice.

18   He may then have to prove that that other reason, if accepted by the tribunal, was fair, if unfair dismissal is also being claimed. However, the presumption of redundancy will *not* apply to the latter claim: *Midland Foot Comfort Centre Ltd v Richmond* [1973] 2 All ER 294, [1973] ICR 219. For a relatively rare example of a case being decided by recourse to the statutory presumption, see *Willcox v Hastings* [1987] IRLR 298, CA.

Court of Appeal in *Hindle v Percival Boats Ltd* [19] has been said to be clear authority in favour of the subjective approach and indeed Sachs LJ said:

'... once the tribunal is satisfied that the ground put forward by the employer is genuine and is the one to which the dismissal is mainly attributable the onus is discharged – and it ceases to be in point that the ground was unwise or based on a mistaken view of facts.[20]'

However, Lord Denning MR's dissent (on the decision and on this point) is a strong one, clearly favouring an entirely objective test[21] and the third judgment, that of Widgery LJ, is less than clear on the point, for although he expresses agreement with Sachs LJ, he states that he finds the distinction between objective and subjective tests neither helpful nor conclusive, and later says:

'... the lesson of the *MacLaughlan* case in my opinion is that the tribunal must not accept the explanation put forward by the employer however honestly, without looking at the whole of the evidence to see if it positively established that the dismissal was not mainly due to a diminution in the requirement of the business for employees on work of a particular kind[22].'

However, even if a general subjective test can be constructed from this case, it is certainly not an unqualified one, and in practice the following qualifications may make the gap between it and an objective approach unimportant in many cases – first, the tribunal clearly does not have to take the employer's word at face value and may look behind it, at the very least to confirm that it is supported by facts (per Widgery LJ, above); second, the tribunal may look behind it to ensure that the employer has not 'misdirected' himself [23] or used the wrong label[24] in calling it redundancy; third, in reorganisation cases (which can prove some of the most difficult) the tribunal can clearly investigate whether it is a genuine reorganisation and not just a cover for redundancies[25]; fourth, in any case where the tribunal is left in real doubt as to the truth of the employer's assertions (especially if they are at variance with some of the facts) the statutory presumption can decide the case in the employee's favour. There may, however, remain cases where none of these qualifications apply, where an employer who is faced with a diminution of work still genuinely thinks (without misdirecting himself) that he is dismissing for a reason other than redundancy, and it is submitted that in

---

19 [1969] 1 All ER 836, [1969] 1 WLR 174, CA.

20 [1969] 1 All ER 836 at 842, [1969] 1 WLR 174 at 182, CA.

21 Approving the decision of the Court of Session in *MacLaughlan v Alexander Paterson Ltd* (1968) 3 ITR 251; see also his Lordship's judgment in *Mumford v Boulton and Paul (Steel Construction) Ltd* (1971) 6 ITR 76, CA.

22 [1969] 1 All ER 836 at 848, [1969] 1 WLR 174 at 188, CA.

23 Per Widgery LJ [1969] 1 All ER 836 at 847, [1969] 1 WLR 174 at 187.

24 On analogy with the unfair dismissal case of *Abernethy v Mott, Hay and Anderson* [1974] ICR 323, [1974] IRLR 213, CA, see p 464, above; this may be a particular danger in this area, since the word 'redundancy' in common usage in industry may mean much more than its restricted legal meaning.

25 *Johnson v Nottinghamshire Combined Police Authority* [1974] 1 All ER 1082, [1974] ICR 170, CA.

such a case the approach of the tribunal should remain subjective[26], particularly as the employer may now have to go further (where both redundancy and unfair dismissal are claimed) and show that that subjective reason is fair; it must be admitted though that *Hindle v Percival Boats Ltd*[27] is not clear authority for this view.

(ii) The definition of redundancy[28]

As stated above, the word 'redundancy' can mean different things to different people and in different contexts. For the purposes of the statutory scheme, however, it is defined in section 139, and this definition is exhaustive[29]. An employee is dismissed by reason of redundancy if the dismissal is attributable wholly or mainly:

'(a) the fact that his employer has ceased, or intends to cease (i) to carry on the business for the purposes of which the employee was employed by him, or (ii) to carry on that business in the place where the employee was so employed, or

(b) the fact that the requirements of that business (i) for employees to carry out work of a particular kind, or (ii) for employees to carry out work of a particular kind in the place where the employee was employed by the employer have ceased or diminished or are expected to cease to diminish.'

This definition applies in two principal cases – where the whole business closes down and where the business carries on (in some cases actually expanding) but its requirements for the services of people such as the applicant cease or diminish. In either case, this can happen either generally or just in the place where the applicant was employed to work. These major elements will now be considered.

(a) Closure of the business

This type of case is usually easy from the legal point (though it may be particularly appropriate for the compulsory consultation procedures which are discussed

---

26   Drawing an analogy with the requirements in unfair dismissal that the tribunal must look for the reason actually acting upon the employer's mind at the date of dismissal: *W Devis & Sons Ltd v Atkins* [1977] 3 All ER 40, [1977] ICR 662, HL.
27   See n 19 above.
28   See *Harvey* E [601].
29   *Hindle v Percival Boats Ltd* [1969] 1 All ER 836, [1969] 1 WLR 174, CA (Lord Denning MR dissenting). Per Widgery LJ at 847 and 187 respectively; 'It is not the policy of this Act to reward long service and good conduct as such, but only to compensate an employee who is dismissed for redundancy as defined in [s 139]'. The function of the tribunal is to apply the statutory definition to the facts, *not* to seek to look behind the facts and assess the rights and wrongs of the employer's decision to make the redundancy: *Moon v Homeworthy Furniture (Northern) Ltd* [1977] ICR 117, [1976] IRLR 298; *AUT v Newcastle-upon-Tyne University* [1987] ICR 317, [1988] IRLR 10; *James W Cook & Co (Wivenhoe) Ltd v Tipper* [1990] ICR 716, [1990] IRLR 386, CA; this is subject to the point made above, in the context of reorganisation, that the tribunal may look into the reasons at least to the extent of being satisfied that they are genuine and not just a sham.

in chapter 2 above). Some problems may arise, however, in defining the 'business' and the 'employer', although 'business' is widely defined in section 235 as including a trade or profession or any activity[30] carried on by a body of persons, whether corporate or unincorporate. Moreover, if the business is a company which has other associated companies[31] and the economic factors in question affect that group as a whole or some other part of it, that too can be taken into account to satisfy the definition. It is also established that it is not necessary to show that the employer was the legal owner of the 'business' in question, only that that person was generally in control of it prior to its closure. Thus, when a sub-postmistress gave up the business of the sub-post office upon her retirement it could not be argued that the 'business' was that carried on by the Post Office (which of course had not ceased), and so her ex-employee was able to claim a redundancy payment[32].

(b) Diminished requirements for employees to do work of a particular kind

Section 139 is designed to cover the case where the business remains (or even expands), but the employee's particular function disappears; the obvious case of this would occur when the function is automated or, on the same principle, if the work is given instead to independent contractors[33] or if work previously done by two employees is amalgamated and done by one, the other being dismissed[34].

The question whether there has been a diminution in the requirements for employees to do work of a particular kind has caused problems for years. To decide whether an individual employee comes within this wording, two tests evolved – the factual test (ie has the work he or she was actually doing gone?) and the contract test (has all the work that he or she *could* be required to do under the contract gone?). It was the latter that eventually gained ground[35], based on two decidedly ambiguous Court of Appeal decisions[36], which could have the effect of making it more difficult to establish redundancy where the contractual obligations were drafted to include a level of flexibility. However, on this point we have seen a major change of approach. This began with the

30 *Dallow Industrial Properties Ltd v Else* [1967] 2 QB 449, [1967] 2 All ER 30.
31 Defined in s 231: '... any two employers are to be treated as associated if one is a company of which the other (directly or indirectly) has control, or if both are companies of which a third person (directly or indirectly) has control ...'. See pp 30–32 above.
32 *Thomas v Jones* [1978] ICR 274, EAT.
33 *Bromby & Hoare Ltd v Evans* [1972] ICR 113, 12 KIR 160; *Amos v Max-Arc Ltd* [1973] ICR 46, [1973] IRLR 285. Contracting out of services or activities has been a dominant theme in modern employment relations: 'The 1998 Workplace Employee Relations Survey – First Findings' (DTI/ACAS/ESRC/PSI; URN/98/934) p 7. Where the employee takes a job knowing that the work is subject to steady decline so that his employment can only be temporary, there may still be a redundancy when he is eventually dismissed: *Nottinghamshire County Council v Lee* [1980] ICR 635, [1980] IRLR 284, CA; this case must cast doubt on the correctness of the EAT's decision in *O'Hare v Rotaprint Ltd* [1980] ICR 94, [1980] IRLR 47.
34 *Sutton v Revlon Overseas Corpn* [1973] IRLR 173; *Carry All Motors Ltd v Pennington* [1980] ICR 806, [1980] IRLR 455. The fact that the total amount of work to be done remains constant is irrelevant; there is a redundancy provided the number of employees required to do it has diminished: *McCrea v Cullen & Davison Ltd* [1988] IRLR 30, NICA.
35 *Cowen v Haden Ltd* [1983] ICR 1, [1982] IRLR 314, CA; *Pink v White* [1985] IRLR 489.
36 *Nelson v BBC* [1977] ICR 649, [1977] IRLR 148, CA and *Nelson v BBC (No 2)* [1980] ICR 110, [1979] IRLR 346, CA.

judgment of Judge Clark in *Safeway Stores plc v Burrell*[37] which went back to the pure wording of the section and held that both the factual and contractual tests are wrong, and unnecessary glosses on that wording. It was pointed out that the wording considers the need for employees (plural), not that particular employee, and so what matters is whether a redundancy situation has arisen and whether he or she has lost employment because of it. Shortly afterwards another division of the EAT in *Church v West Lancashire NHS Trust*[38] disagreed strongly, but when the matter went to the House of Lords in *Murray v Foyle Meats Ltd*[39] it was *Safeway Stores* that was unequivocally approved. Giving the principal speech, Lord Irvine LC said:

> '... the language of [section 139(1)(b)] is in my view simplicity itself. It asks two questions of fact. The first is whether one or other of various states of economic affairs exists. In this case the relevant one is whether the requirements of the business for employees to carry out work of a particular kind have diminished. The second question is whether the dismissal is attributable, wholly or mainly to that state of affairs. This is a question of causation. In the present case, the Tribunal found as a fact that the requirements of the business for employees to work in the slaughter house had diminished. Secondly, they found that that state of affairs had led to the appellants being dismissed. That, in my opinion, is the end of the matter. This conclusion is in accordance with the analysis of the statutory provisions by Judge Peter Clark in *Safeway Stores plc v Burrell* and I need to say no more than that I entirely agree with his admirably clear reasoning and conclusions.'

He went on to disapprove of the cases said to establish the contract test, and for good measure Lord Clyde giving the other speech castigated both previous tests as unnecessary.

This reinterpretation is very welcome and of great importance generally. However, it arose in the two EAT cases in a specialised and difficult area, known as a 'bumping' redundancy. This occurs where, for example, within a department employee A's job disappears, but A (thought to be a good worker) is retained and given B's job, with B being dismissed instead. Is B redundant? Under the old tests, B's job is still there, and so he is not redundant, but under the new approach there is a diminution in employees (plural) required by the employer and B's dismissal is causally linked ('attributable') to it, and so now B is indeed redundant. Given the curious agendas behind some of these cases this is in fact usually to the *employer's* advantage, redundancy often being the easier and cheaper option, whereas the employee may want *not* to be redundant, in order to open up an unfair dismissal action. Arguably, this is why the EAT in *Church* were so against this development especially when allied to what they saw as an objectionable *way* of bumping by the employer, namely sacking all employees and 'inviting' them to reapply for the jobs left (where, the EAT feared, there would be too much scope for subjective choice and favouritism by the

37 [1997] ICR 523, [1997] IRLR 200, EAT.
38 [1998] ICR 423, [1998] IRLR 4.
39 [1999] ICR 827, [1999] IRLR 562, HL. Arguably, the broader approach in this case brings the definition more into line with that now used in the Trade Union and Labour Relations (Consolidation) Act 1992, s 195 (on collective redundancies), ie 'dismissal for a reason not related to the individual concerned or for a number of reasons all of which are not so related'.

management). However, *Church* must now be considered wrong, and in a bumping case there now will normally be a redundancy. However, it may be that this will have the effect of increasing the importance of an unfair dismissal challenge based on the methods and procedures used to effect the eventual shedding of labour[40]. This may be the real answer to the problems faced in *Church*.

There remains, however, one further element of the definition of redundancy which is not affected by *Murray* (not being relevant on the facts of the case, and so are not addressed). This is the question of what is meant by 'work of a particular kind', a particularly crucial concept where for example, the numbers involved remain much the same (or indeed may even be increasing overall) but the *skills* required change. There is much case law on this, and the law clearly looks at the *work function* of the employee within the organisation, not necessarily at his particular job at the time, still less at any particular job title. Thus, the job may change over time in its organisation (and thereby, in some cases, in its suitability for, and attractiveness to, a particular employee) but, as long as the function remains, an employee who is dismissed for refusing to accept the changes (or who walks out because of them and then claims constructive dismissal under section 136(1)(c)) is *not* 'redundant'. In *Chapman v Goonvean and Rostowrack China Clay Co Ltd* [41] ten employees were provided with free transport to work; when three were made redundant during a trade recession the transport became uneconomic and the employer discontinued it for the remaining seven who, though offered continued employment with the employer, gave in their notice, left the employment and claimed redundancy payments. The Court of Appeal held that they were not redundant since the work that they performed had not ceased or diminished (the employer had shown that the seven were replaced by other employees taken on to do their work); the only change was in the organisation and attractiveness of the jobs for the time being. The facts of this case concern a relatively incidental aspect of employment, but the principle goes further and can apply to changes in the job structure itself, for there is no definite right to have employment continued indefinitely on the same terms and the courts and tribunals have ensured that an employer can take necessary steps to increase the efficiency of his enterprise without being liable to make redundancy payments unless there is a genuine diminution in the work function in question. In *Johnson v Nottinghamshire Combined Police Authority*[42] two clerks, whose work had been reorganised from a five-day week to a shift system operating over six days per week to increase overall efficiency, refused to accept this and claimed redundancy pay (in spite of the fact that they had been replaced by two new employees), but this was refused by the Court of Appeal on the ground that the kind of work remained the same and so the reorganisation was not due to redundancy:

'It is settled ... that an employer is entitled to reorganise his business so as to improve its efficiency and, in doing so, to propose to his staff a change in the terms and conditions of their employment; and to dispense with their

---

40   For unfair redundancy, see p 585 above.
41   [1973] 2 All ER 1063, [1973] ICR 310, CA, overruling *Dutton v CH Bailey Ltd* [1968] 2 Lloyd's Rep 122, 3 ITR 355; see also *Arnold v Thomas Harrington Ltd* [1969] 1 QB 312, [1967] 2 All ER 866.
42   [1974] 1 All ER 1082, [1974] ICR 170, CA.

services if they do not agree. Such a change does not automatically give the staff a right to redundancy payments. It only does so if the change in the terms and conditions is due to a redundancy situation.[43']

A similar result was achieved in *Lesney Products Ltd v Nolan*[44] where the work of machine setters was altered from a day shift and a night shift to a double day shift system, with a consequent decrease in overtime payments; when six of the setters refused to work the new system and claimed redundancy payments, the Court of Appeal held against them since the amount of work to be done remained constant, though reorganised on to a daytime basis (the undoubted overall 'redundancy situation' having been dealt with by the company by discontinuing the night shift worked by another class of employees who were not parties to the action). Moreover, this principle is not restricted to alterations in the structure or pattern of working hours and conditions, but may also apply to necessary changes in the discharging of the employee's function, for, as long as that function remains the same overall, the employer may introduce new methods and technology to increase the efficiency of the function and if the employee is either unwilling or unable to adapt to them, he may be dismissed without being redundant[45].

It can be seen from the above discussion that, under this head of redundancy, much will depend on the difficult question of fact – how radical does a change in the job, or the reorganisation of it, have to be before it can be said that the function itself has changed? To put it in the language of section 139 – what *is* work of that 'particular kind'? If the change is great enough to turn it into work of a different kind, then the employee who is unwilling or unable to perform the new function can claim that he is redundant since his old function has disappeared[46]. In the earlier cases, this was not easy since the courts and tribunals in general took a fairly wide view of what constitutes one type of work (thus allowing the employer more scope for reorganisation without having to make redundancy payments); thus, the function of 'barmaid' remained the same, even when an older style public house was transformed into a 'road house' requiring barmaids with certain attributes which no amount of retraining could possibly have produced in the original incumbent[47], and the function of 'boatbuilder' remained the same even though the boatyard went over to fibreglass boats instead of the wooden ones which the dismissed employee was

43   Per Lord Denning MR [1974] 1 All ER 1082 at 1084, [1974] ICR 170 at 176; the phrase 'redundancy situation' is clarified in his Lordship's judgment in *Lesney Products Ltd v Nolan* (n 44 below). The last two sentences in the dictum are important, for they make it clear that there *could* be a redundancy in certain circumstances; the EAT reaffirmed that there is no rule of law that a change of hours or shifts cannot produce a redundancy – it remains ultimately a question of fact for the tribunal: *MacFisheries Ltd v Findlay* [1985] ICR 160, EAT.
44   [1977] ICR 235, [1977] IRLR 77, CA.
45   *North Riding Garages Ltd v Butterwick* [1967] 2 QB 56, [1967] 1 All ER 644; *Hindle v Percival Boats Ltd* [1969] 1 All ER 836, [1969] 1 WLR 174, CA. It is argued above that the courts might be willing to apply in such cases an implied term of reasonable adaptation to new methods and techniques: see p 170 above and *Cresswell v Board of Inland Revenue* [1984] 2 All ER 713, [1984] ICR 508.
46   *Robinson v British Island Airways Ltd* [1978] ICR 304, [1977] IRLR 477, a case where the employee was arguing that he was *not* redundant, in order to claim the more generous remedies for unfair dismissal. A redundancy can arise from a change in specialisms within an overall job: *BBC v Farnworth* [1998] ICR 1116, EAT.

by long practice used to making[48]. Such questions may raise difficult borderline cases[49], and the approach in the later case of *Murphy v Epsom College*[50] shows a narrower approach to 'kind of work' and emphasises that if that changes there may be a redundancy even if the redundant employee is immediately replaced by someone else skilled in the new kind of work (ie where there is no net decrease in the workforce). In that case the college's heating system was modernised, calling for new skills to maintain it. One of the existing two plumbers said that he was unwilling/unable to perform all the necessary new functions; he was dismissed and replaced with a heating technician. The Court of Appeal upheld the tribunal's decision that the dismissed employee was redundant since the employer's need for *plumbers* was reduced from two to one on the reorganisation (with its corresponding requirement for a heating technician instead).

This whole problem flows from the emphasis in section 139 on the overall work function and not the particulars of the job as organised at the material time; it has been argued that this should not be so, as it puts the financial risk of a particular job becoming uneconomic upon the employee, rather than upon the employer[51]. However, the courts have consistently adopted the view that this legislation is not meant to be a brake upon necessary reorganisation, and it can be argued that the harsher result of this may be mitigated by two factors: first, it has been stated by the courts that a bogus reorganisation is not to be used by an employer as a cover for dismissals which are in fact due to redundancy[52]; secondly, since 1971 it has been possible for an employee dismissed because of changing work patterns (or resigning because of them and claiming constructive dismissal) to bring an action for unfair dismissal against the employer if he thinks he has been harshly treated over the change or reorganisation (or if he has grounds to doubt the bona fides of the employer's actions), and this action may lead to more generous remedies (especially since the major increase in the compensation limit in the Employment Relations Act 1999), so that in many cases it may be in the employee's favour *not* to be in law redundant, since that would prima facie be a *fair* ground for dismissal[53]. Therefore there can easily arise (especially in reorganisation cases) the topsy turvy situation of the employee (wanting more than the statutory redundancy payment) arguing that his dismissal was *not* for redundancy and the employer (happy to keep the labour-related cost of the reorganisation down to statutory redundancy payments) arguing that it was, as indeed was the case in *Murphy v Epsom College*[54]. Thus, the narrower approach to 'kind of work' in that case, with its easier

47   *Vaux and Associated Breweries Ltd v Ward* (1968) 3 ITR 385.
48   *Hindle v Percival Boats Ltd* [1969] 1 All ER 836, [1969] 1 WLR 174, CA.
49   See, eg, *European Chefs (Catering) Ltd v Currell* (1971) 6 ITR 37.
50   [1985] ICR 80, [1984] IRLR 271, CA.
51   See Freedland (1977) 6 ILJ 237.
52   *Johnson v Nottinghamshire Combined Police Authority* [1974] 1 All ER 1082 at 1087, [1974] ICR 170 at 179, per Stephenson LJ.
53   Employment Rights Act 1996, s 98(2)(c).
54   See n 50 above. This may blur the edge between a redundancy dismissal and a dismissal because of a business reorganisation; it is important for the employer to decide which route to go down, see eg *Shawkat v Nottingham City Hospital NHS Trust* [2001] EWCA Civ 954, [2001] IRLR 555, CA. This kind of perverted logic can also occur in TUPE cases (p 200 above) with the employees arguing that they have *no* TUPE protection, in order to cash in their redundancy rights against the transferor employers and start afresh with the transferee employer.

finding of redundancy, paradoxically may operate *against* the employee's wider interests[55].

(c) 'in the place where the employee was so employed'

Both of the above heads of redundancy envisage the relevant economic factors producing effects either generally or only in the place where the employee worked. It may therefore be vital to know what that 'place' is. It could cover the whole of the UK or be as small an area as one part of one city[56]. The problem often arises in cases where the employer orders the employee to move to a new workplace, for example if the company wishes to close down a factory in Ipswich, telling its employees there to work in its other factory in Norwich. The approach generally adopted here in the past has been that the question of law involved is whether the employer has *contractual* authority to give the order to move, so that 'in the place where the employee was so employed' means in the place where he could be obliged to work under the terms of his contract of employment, not simply where he had in fact been working prior to the order to move[57]. If the contract envisages working in the new location (for example, in the example used, a term that the employee would work anywhere in East Anglia), then the employee who refuses is dismissed for failure to comply (even if he had in fact been working solely in Ipswich for years); if the contract does not envisage this (ie Ipswich only), then the employee has prima facie a redundancy claim based upon the closure of the Ipswich factory.

Questions have therefore often arisen as to the construction of the individual's contract of employment. The contract may contain an express term[58] which will usually dispose of the matter as the traditional view is that a clear express term should not normally be subject to extension or restriction by any claimed implied term[59]. If there is no such express term the tribunal must consider whether a term should be implied in the contract[60] by looking at all the relevant evidence. In *O'Brien v Associated Fire Alarms Ltd*[61] two electricians worked for a company at its Liverpool office, working exclusively in that city (although the company operated

---

55 Though it is not necessarily so simple – even if the employee succeeds in showing (in an unfair dismissal case arising from a reorganisation) that he was *not* dismissed for redundancy, but rather for refusing to agree to changes insisted upon by the employer, contrary to his contractual rights, there is still the danger that the tribunal might hold the dismissal *fair*, as for 'some other substantial reason' (see p 599 above). In such a case he would receive *neither* a redundancy payment *nor* unfair dismissal compensation.

56 *Rowbotham v Arthur Lee & Sons Ltd* [1975] ICR 109, [1974] IRLR 377; *Air Canada v Lee* [1978] ICR 1202, [1978] IRLR 392, EAT.

57 *Sutcliffe v Hawker Siddeley Aviation Ltd* [1973] ICR 560, [1973] IRLR 304, NIRC; *Rank Xerox Ltd v Churchill* [1988] IRLR 280, EAT.

58 As eg in *Sutcliffe v Hawker Siddeley Aviation Ltd* (supra) and *United Kingdom Atomic Energy Authority v Claydon* [1974] ICR 128, [1974] IRLR 6. If the employer wishes to rely on a mobility clause, he should do so clearly, and not as an afterthought: *Curling v Securicor Ltd* [1992] IRLR 549, EAT.

59 *Nelson v BBC* [1977] ICR 649, [1977] IRLR 148, CA. However, modern cases have shown movement towards a concept of *overriding* implied terms (especially the term of trust and respect), see p 140 above; it is possible that this development (if it continues) could spread into redundancy law.

60 *GEC Telecommunications Ltd v McAllister* [1975] IRLR 346. For the implication of terms into contracts of employment, see p 138 above.

61 [1969] 1 All ER 93, [1968] 1 WLR 1916, CA; *Mumford v Boulton and Paul (Steel Construction) Ltd* (1970) 5 ITR 222; *Managers (Holborn) Ltd v Hohne* [1977] IRLR 230, EAT.

throughout the United Kingdom and the Liverpool office controlled the whole of the north west); when the company's business in Liverpool diminished and they were asked to work in Cumberland, they refused because it would have meant working away from home and they were dismissed. Their claims for redundancy payments were upheld by the Court of Appeal on the basis that, there being no relevant express term in their contracts, there was no implied term obliging them to work outside daily travelling distance from their homes, particularly as they had never been called upon to do so before and there was no clear evidence of any implied agreement to do so[62]. However, in *Stevenson v Teesside Bridge and Engineering Ltd*[63] a steel erector who refused to move to another site when work on the existing site (which was close to his home) finished was not entitled to a redundancy payment since travelling from site to site was found by the Divisional Court to be an integral part of that trade (which there was evidence he had accepted when interviewed for the post) and the contract of employment, though not containing an express mobility clause, was held to envisage such mobility through terms relating to travelling and subsistence allowances, and the transfer of contracts. However, this whole contractual approach had long been criticised in the leading practitioner work[64], which argued that a practical and geographical test (where was the employee *actually* working?) would fit better the purpose and intent of the legislation. The EAT in *Bass Leisure Ltd v Thomas*[65] agreed with that approach, held that the authority in favour of the contractual approach was only persuasive, and applied a geographical test. Thus, an employee whose work at a Coventry depot had ceased with its closure *was* redundant, even though the employers had a contractual right (which they had sought to exercise) to require her to work at another depot twenty miles away, where she did not wish to work. In this particular case, the geographical approach was in the employee's favour, but this is an area ripe for boomerang effects of decisions, and the overall result of this approach (if generally followed) is that it may make it easier for an employer to make an employee redundant (a prima facie fair ground of dismissal) at one location, even where there is a mobility clause in the contract. This could be significant where an employer wants to close down one whole location (where perhaps productivity and labour relations have not been good), dispense with the workforce there and build up production elsewhere by taking on new staff. Something of this sort occurred in *High Table Ltd v Horst*[66] where waitresses dismissed by a service company when the client no longer wanted their work were held to be redundant, in spite of a mobility clause in their contracts. The Court of Appeal approved *Bass Leisure*, on the basis that a factual approach to the actual place of work will normally resolve the question, subject to the caveat that if the employee has in fact been mobile it may well be necessary to consider the terms of the contract (as in the older case law considered above). Thus, their approach is an amalgam, though with a normal bias towards the factual/geographical test, applied by the good sense of the tribunal. Two points are

---

62 While each case must depend on its facts, it is likely that a term that an employee may be required to work *within* reasonable daily travel will be easy to imply where the contract is silent on the matter: *Courtaulds Northern Spinning Ltd v Sibson* [1988] ICR 451, [1988] IRLR 305, CA.
63 [1971] 1 All ER 296, 10 KIR 53.
64 *Harvey* E [657]ff.
65 [1994] IRLR 104.
66 [1998] ICR 409, [1997] IRLR 513, CA.

worth noting: (i) the court seemed to view this decision as pro-employee (ie redundancy rights are not to be prejudiced by the inclusion of a mobility clause), but as seen above it will often be in the employer's interests to establish a redundancy (and indeed, the end result of the case was to allow the *employers'* appeal); (ii) the employer may now have the best of both worlds with a mobility clause, in that if he tries to enforce it and the employee refuses to go, the latter is potentially subject to fair dismissal through disobedience to a lawful order, whereas if the work dries up in one area but the employer decides *not* to enforce the mobility clause and simply dismisses those working that, the result may well be a simple redundancy (which is *not* defeated by the existence of the clause).

There is, however, (whatever the test) one further factor that may cloud the issue; as will be seen below, a redundant employee may be under an obligation to accept suitable alternative work if it is offered by the employer[67] and it is possible that although an employee may have a right to refuse to transfer elsewhere (as in *O'Brien*'s case, or if the geographical test is widely applied), in certain cases where the distance is not great the offer to work at the new location may constitute an offer of suitable alternative work which the employee would be advised to accept.

(iii) The right to payment

(a) Qualification: transfer of business or undertaking

In order to qualify for a redundancy payment, the dismissed employee must have been continuously employed for at least two years on the 'relevant date'[68]. Continuity of employment is considered in detail in chapter 3 above; one particular point needs to be added to the general discussion there, relating to continuity through a transfer of business or undertaking. This is now covered by the general rules under (now) the 1996 Act and also by special rules under Regulations; as these unfortunately apply independently of each other, it is necessary to consider them separately.

A. Transfers of business under the 1996 Act

Continuity of employment through a transfer of business (where the employee in fact remains with that business) is preserved by section 218 of the 1996 Act[69], so that if the employee is later made redundant by the new employer he can count his time with the old employer for the purposes of qualification for and computation of a redundancy payment. These provisions related solely to questions of continuity of employment and did not prejudice the general common law rule that an employee could not be made to change employer without his consent[70]. Further, these longstanding provisions meant that if the transferor employer sold the business to the transferee who did not keep on the workforce, it was clear that the transferor employer, dismissing the workforce on the transfer, was liable for the redundancy payments.

---

67   Employment Rights Act 1996, s 141.
68   S 155, for the 'relevant date' see p 626 above.
69   Provided that there is a genuine transfer of business, and not just the sale of one of its assets – see p 198 above; *Melon v Hector Powe Ltd* [1981] ICR 43, [1980] IRLR 477, HL.
70   *Nokes v Doncaster Amalgamated Collieries Ltd* [1940] AC 1014, [1940] 3 All ER 549, HL.

B. Transfers of undertaking under the Regulations

The above position has however been materially complicated by the provisions of the Transfer of Undertakings (Protection of Employment) Regulations 1981[71] which apply where there has been a 'transfer of undertaking'. It is particularly unfortunate in this context that these changes were enacted by extraneous regulations, rather than by amendments to the existing provisions of the legislation, for the position is subject to a separate set of legislative provisions, on the assumption that there is a 'transfer of undertaking'[72]. On that assumption, the continuity of employment of those transferring to the employ of the transferee is preserved by regulation 5. To this extent, the regulation is in most cases otiose since (assuming it also to be a 'transfer of business') this will be the case anyway under section 218. However, regulation 5 goes considerably further, for it states that a relevant transfer automatically transfers the employee's contract of employment from the transferor employer to the transferee employer[73]. This means that the employee's previous right to claim a redundancy payment from the transferor is no longer applicable and, contrary to previous accepted practice, if the transferee does not take the workforce on he may still find that it is he, not the transferor, who has to pay the redundancy payments[74]. Regulation 5 applies wherever an employee is employed by the transferor employer 'immediately before' the transfer. It used to be the case that the regulation could be avoided relatively easily by the device of the transferee requiring the transferor to dismiss the workforce at some point before the transfer; this was possible because in *Secretary of State for Employment v Spence*[75] the Court of Appeal held that 'immediately before' meant 'at the time of' the transfer, so that an employee dismissed before that time (possibly by only a few hours) could not claim the protection of regulation 5, ie any gap was fatal (leaving the employee to pursue his remedies, including a redundancy payment, against the original employer who might well be insolvent). However, as pointed out at p 207 above, this position changed radically in the light of two decisions – that of the ECJ in *P Bork International A/S (in liquidation) v Foreningen of Arbejdsledere i Danmark*[76] on the meaning of Directive 77/187/EEC on which the regulations are based, and that of the House of

---

71 SI 1981/1794, see *Harvey* R [181]; McMullen *Business Transfers*. The effects of these Regulations are considered at pp 91–94 (union rights to consultation), pp 200–212 (continuity of employment) and p 593 (unfair dismissal). It is anticipated that the 1981 Regulations will be replace shortly into the currency of this edition (see p 212 above), but without making major changes to the points made here.

72 For the meaning of this phrase (and 'relevant transfer'), see p 201 above.

73 This was irrespective of the wishes of the parties (*Newns v British Airways plc* [1992] IRLR 575, CA) and meant that the old common law rule in *Nokes* (n 70 above) no longer applied to a case covered by the regulations. However, serious confusion was caused by the decision of the ECJ in *Katsikas v Konstantinidis* C-132/91 [1993] IRLR 179 that Directive 77/187/EEC does not *oblige* member states to legislate for automatic transfer against the employee's wishes. In the light of this, the Trade Union Reform and Employment Rights Act 1993 added a right to object to transfer, but for reasons given above (p 204) it appears that this may be an empty right for many employees, and so automatic transfer will continue to be the norm.

74 As in *Premier Motors (Medway) Ltd v Total Oil Great Britain Ltd* [1984] ICR 58, [1983] IRLR 471, in which Browne-Wilkinson P made it clear that the position now is the reverse of the old law, a fact that had not been realised when the parties negotiated the transfer deal.

75 [1986] ICR 651, [1986] IRLR 248, CA.

76 101/87: [1989] IRLR 41, ECJ.

Lords in *Litster v Forth Dry Dock and Engineering Co Ltd*[77], which followed and applied the decision of the ECJ. The end result is that if the transferor dismisses the employee because of the transfer (for example, at the transferee's request) and that dismissal is unfair under regulation 8 (which it will be unless it comes within the 'economic, technical or organisational reasons' defence in regulation 8(2))[78], then for the purposes of regulation 5 the employee will be deemed to have been still employed by the transferor immediately before the transfer, so that automatic transfer of his contract to the transferee will apply. Prior dismissal will therefore no longer be effective in itself in most cases.

C. The inapplicability of estoppel

Normally questions of continuity (for qualification and computation purposes) will be solved by applying the provisions of Part XIV of the 1996 Act or the Regulations but one judicial gloss was added in the case of a change from one employer to another where there has been no 'transfer of business' or 'transfer of undertaking' (so that the above provisions do not apply). In such a case, there is normally a break in continuity, but the Court of Appeal held in *Evenden v Guildford City AFC Ltd*[79] that where at the time of the change the new employer gave the employee an assurance that he would regard the employment as unbroken, so that time with the previous employer would count for redundancy purposes, the new employer should not be allowed to go back on that later and claim that continuity was in fact broken by the change. This meant that the presumption of continuity, now contained in section 210(5), was not rebutted and so the whole period could be counted; this principle was accepted by the whole court and Lord Denning MR (with the support of Browne LJ) added the further ground that such conduct by the new employer gives rise to a promissory estoppel[80] in the employee's favour. However, in the case of *Secretary of State for Employment v Globe Elastic Thread Co Ltd*[81], a case primarily concerned with the (now repealed) redundancy rebate aspect of this problem, the House of Lords overruled *Evenden*'s case and held that questions of continuity through a change of employment are governed by the statutory provisions alone; thus, if continuity is not preserved by a statutory provision such as that relating to a 'transfer of business' or the regulations on transfers of undertakings, it is broken by the change of employment and any agreement to the contrary between the parties at the time of the change can only be viewed, if at all, as a separate contract (with a view to which the transferred employee would be advised to demand a formal written agreement[82]).

(b) Exclusions

The following classes of employees are excluded from the redundancy payments scheme:

---

77   [1989] ICR 341, [1989] IRLR 161, HL.
78   See p 491, above.
79   [1975] 3 All ER 269, [1975] ICR 367; *Rastill v Automatic Refreshment Services Ltd* [1978] ICR 289, EAT.
80   *Central London Property Trust Ltd v High Trees House Ltd* [1947] KB 130, [1956] 1 All ER 256.
81   [1979] 2 All ER 1077, [1979] IRLR 327, HL.
82   Though even this would not help if, eg, the employee was dismissed by his new employer before serving the qualifying period for unfair dismissal.

(a) persons under 20^{83} or past normal retiring age (or, if there is no such age, 65)[84];

(b) employees with less than two years' continuous employment[85];

(c) employees dismissed for misconduct (see below);

(d) redundant employees refusing suitable alternative employment (see below);

(e) share fishermen[86], employees of foreign governments[87], civil servants and certain public officials[88];

(f) classes of employees specifically excluded by order of the Secretary of State, where a collective agreement covers the question of redundancy[89].

(c) Computation of a redundancy payment[90]

The procedure for calculating a payment is contained in section 162; it is calculated by reference to the period of whole years, ending with the relevant date, during which the employee has been continuously employed. He then receives (a) one and a half week's pay for each year in which the employee was over 41 years old; (b) one week's pay for each year not covered by (a) but in which he was over 22 years old; (c) half a week's pay for each other year (over the age of 18). The maximum number of years which may be counted is 20, and a 'week's pay' is calculated in accordance with Part XIV, Chapter II of the 1996 Act, subject to a statutory maximum figure for computation purposes[91].

It will be recalled that an employee who has reached the normal retiring age (if any) or 65 before the relevant date is not entitled to a redundancy payment. Where the relevant date falls in the last year of normal working life the payment will be reduced by the fraction $^x/_{12}$ where x is the number of months from the last birthday to the relevant date; the claimant keeps the remaining fraction, so that if he is made redundant at the end of the third month after the last birthday

---

83 Employment Rights Act 1996, s 211(2).

84 S 156. This provision had to be amended by the Employment Act 1989 to equalise the provision as between the sexes.

85 S 155. There used to be a further, frequently used, exclusion where, in a fixed-term contract of two years or more the employee signed away his or her redundancy rights (or, in practice, was obliged to do so by the employer as a condition of getting the job) but this was abolished by the Fixed-term Employees (Prevention of Less Favourable Treatment) Regulations 2002, SI 2002/2034 because it constituted institutional discrimination against fixed-termers.

86 S 199(2).

87 S 160.

88 S 159.

89 S 157.

90 See *Harvey* E [2201] and Department of Employment Booklet No 16 *Redundancy Payments*, which contains a 'ready reckoner'.

91 As from February 2003, £260 per week, yielding a maximum payment of £7,800. For the purpose of calculation, actual pay as at the 'relevant date' is used, even if there is a later pay rise back dated to before that date: *Leyland Vehicles Ltd v Reston* [1981] ICR 403, [1981] IRLR 19. Statutory redundancy payments are exempt from income tax: Income and Corporation Tax Act 1988, s 579; non-statutory (ie contractual) redundancy payments are treated in the same way up to the usual ceiling of £30,000, as a matter of concession, and this has been extended to payments made to buy out a contractual right to enhanced redundancy payments: *Mairs v Haughey* [1994] 1 AC 303, [1993] IRLR 551, HL; the Inland Revenue statement of practice on this matter was reissued (SP 1/94, see [1994] NLJ 599) to take *Mairs* into consideration.

before the normal retiring age (or 64) he is entitled to $^9/_{12}$ of the payment, at the end of the ninth month $^3/_{12}$ and so on[92].

(d) Procedure for claiming a redundancy payment

A claim for a payment is subject to a prima facie time limitation of six months from the relevant date, in that the employee will lose his entitlement unless during that period the payment has been agreed and paid or the employee has made a claim in writing to the employer, or has referred the question to an industrial tribunal (either directly, or indirectly through making a complaint of unfair dismissal)[93]. However, the employee is given a further six-month period in which to submit a claim, but in such a case the awarding of a payment is put into the discretion of the tribunal, which must have regard to whether an award would be 'just and equitable' in the light of the employee's reason for failure to claim during the first six months[94].

The claim in writing to the employer does not have to be in any particular form, the test being that it must be such that the employer could reasonably appreciate the employee's intention to claim[95]; however, it has been held that it must be submitted during the six month period *beginning with* the relevant date, so that a claim submitted earlier than the date of termination of employment is invalid[96], which seems to be an unnecessary complication capable of amounting to a trap for an unwary employee.

When an employer voluntarily gives the payment to which an employee is entitled, he must give a written statement to the employee showing how the amount has been calculated[97]; the consequences of failure are, first, that the employer may be fined and, second, that he may in fact have to pay the sum again in a proper manner, particularly if, for example, he just gives the employee one unspecified lump sum upon termination with a vague indication that it is meant to include something for redundancy[98].

Finally, two points should be noted about the potential role of the Secretary of State. The first is that he has a right to appear in any redundancy proceedings before a tribunal[99] (because of his interest as guardian of the National Insurance Fund). The second is that if the employer either refuses to pay after the employee has taken all reasonable steps (short of legal proceedings) to recover payment, or is insolvent, the employee may apply to the Secretary of State for payment of the amount directly out of the National Insurance Fund; when such a payment

---

92   Employment Rights Act 1996, s 162(4); *Slater v John Swain & Son Ltd* [1981] ICR 554, [1981] IRLR 303. For the position where the employee is entitled to a pension upon dismissal, see s 158 and the Redundancy Payments Pensions Regulations 1965, SI 1965/1932, *Harvey* R [15].

93   S 164(1). Semble provided the employee has taken one of these steps (and so safeguarded his entitlement) he may still dispute the amount of the payment even after the expiry of the six months: *Bentley Engineering Co Ltd v Miller* [1976] ICR 225, [1976] IRLR 146.

94   S 164(2).

95   *Price v Smithfield and Zwanenberg Group Ltd* [1978] ICR 93, [1978] IRLR 80, EAT.

96   *Watts v Rubery Owen Conveyancer Ltd* [1977] ICR 429, [1977] IRLR 112; *Pritchard-Rhodes Ltd v Boon and Milton* [1979] IRLR 19, EAT.

97   S 165. This can be done by using the final page of form RP 1.

98   It depends on the facts: *Barnsley Metropolitan Borough Council v Prest* [1996] ICR 85.

is made, the Secretary of State may exercise the employee's rights against the employer to attempt to recover the amount for the fund[100].

(iv) Special provisions

(a) Offers of alternative employment[101]

If the employer makes an offer to an employee before the termination of his contract of employment to renew the contract or re-engage him on suitable alternative work[102], two consequences may flow. The first is that if the employee accepts that renewal or re-engagement (and there is either no gap, or a gap of less than four weeks between the contracts), there is in law no 'dismissal' at the end of the first contract[103] (subject to the rules on trial periods, considered below). The second is that if the employee unreasonably refuses to accept the offer he is disqualified from claiming a redundancy payment[104].

Cases of 'renewal' are not likely to cause many problems, for the word means renewal on the *same* terms (including possibly cases where any differences are negligible)[105]. 'Re-engagement' may prove more difficult, for this envisages the new terms differing from the old ones, and raises two questions – first, was the alternative employment on offer suitable; second, was the employee's refusal of it reasonable? In theory, the tribunal should start with the first question which entails consideration of the nature of the new employment in relation to the employee's skills and abilities. In many cases the offer will be of a similar type of employment, and it has been said that the mere offer of the same salary may not be enough if the job is totally different[106]. However, this is not an invariable rule, and an offer of a completely different job may on the facts be suitable, even for a skilled employee, particularly if it is part of a larger, generally beneficial scheme, and particularly if it is of a temporary nature[107]. Naturally questions of pay may loom large, and difficulties may arise. Opportunities to earn overtime make a comparison of basic rates unreal, but on the other hand overtime may not be certain; the same problem applies to future prospects which might soon recoup and perhaps surpass an initial drop in earnings. Thus, the tribunal must take a realistic view of the question of pay[108], while at the same time accepting that the

---

99   Employment Tribunals (Constitution and Rules of Procedure) Regulations 2001, SI 2001/1171, reg 10(7).

100 Employment Rights Act 1996, s 166.

101 See *Harvey* E [1501].

102 In *SI (Systems and Instrumentation) Ltd v Grist* [1983] ICR 788, [1983] IRLR 391 the EAT stated obiter that on the strict wording of the subsection, there is a distinction between 'renewal' (which automatically operates to deem there to have been no dismissal) and 're-engagement' (which only so operates if in pursuance of a formal offer, whether in writing or not, made before the end of the first contract).

103 S 138(1).

104 S 141. In addition he may find himself disqualified for benefit for up to 26 weeks for neglecting, without good cause, to avail himself of a reasonable opportunity of employment: Jobseekers Act 1995, s 19(6).

105 *Devonald v J D Insulating Co Ltd* [1972] ICR 209, NIRC.

106 The judgment of Lord Parker CJ in *Taylor v Kent County Council* [1969] 2 QB 560, [1969] 2 All ER 1080 is often cited on this point, as to whether the offer is of 'employment which is substantially equivalent to the employment which has ceased'. However, this is not part of the statutory wording, and ultimately the question is one of fact for the tribunal: *Standard Telephones and Cables Ltd v Yates* [1981] IRLR 21, EAT.

107 *Dutton v Hawker Siddeley Aviation Ltd* [1978] ICR 1057, [1978] IRLR 390, EAT.

matter may be complicated by relevant changes in status and promotion prospects consequent upon acceptance of the new employment[109]. Two further matters which might be material are the expected duration of the new employment and its location. If the new employment is likely to last only for a short time, it has nevertheless been held that it may be suitable provided that it is full-time and regular during that time[110]. Once again, however, this is not a definite rule, for potential duration could be material in some cases, for example where the redundant employee, fearing a general recession in that particular industry if he stays in it, has found another job in another industry, particularly if he is approaching retirement age when employment for his last few years is not easy to find anywhere[111]. The fact that the employment on offer is in a different location, necessitating a move of home or increased travelling, does not necessarily render it unsuitable; obviously this is very much a question of fact, but it is an important qualification on the employee's right, discussed above, not to be required to move to a new locality not covered by his contract of employment – he can insist upon that right and refuse an *order* to move, but if in fact the *offer* of work elsewhere is considered 'suitable' by a tribunal, he may still lose his redundancy payment.

The second question, the reasonableness of a refusal, requires consideration of a wider range of different factors, looking at the matter more subjectively from the point of view of the employee who may have certain pressing reasons of a personal nature which make it reasonable to refuse what appears at first sight to be suitable alternative work (for example, health problems, family commitments); in addition, the employee may have personal objections to the job offered (for example, perceived lack of status), even though under the first test the job is objectively 'suitable'[112]. This produces a test that is a mixture of subjective and objective factors, as required by the legislation itself; it has been held that this is sufficient for that purpose and that it is *not* necessary to go further and import an equivalent of the 'range of reasonable responses test', on analogy with unfair dismissal law[113]. One effect of the test being partly subjective is that even where several employees of the same type are made redundant (where possibly one general offer of the same type of alternative work is made to them collectively by the employer)[114], a tribunal must look into the particular circumstances of each individual employee before disqualifying anyone for refusal[115]. The factors which may arise under this second question may be even more various than those under the first, so that the one overall point about the law relating to suitable alternative employment is that each case is heavily dependent upon its own facts, with the results that the tribunal has a wide

108 *Kennedy v Werneth Ring Mills Ltd* [1977] ICR 206, EAT.
109 *Harris v E Turner & Sons (Joinery) Ltd* [1973] ICR 31, NIRC; *Kane v Raine & Co Ltd* [1974] ICR 300, NIRC.
110 *Morganite Crucible Ltd v Street* [1972] 2 All ER 411, [1972] ICR 110, NIRC.
111 *Thomas Wragg & Sons v Wood* [1976] ICR 313, [1976] IRLR 145; *Paton Calvert & Co Ltd v Westerside* [1979] IRLR 108; cf *James and Jones v NCB* (1969) 4 ITR 70.
112 *Cambridge and District Co-operative Society Ltd v Ruse* [1993] IRLR 156, EAT.
113 *Hudson v George Harrison Ltd* (2003) Times, 15 January. For the range test in unfair dismissal law, see p 571 above.
114 *McCreadie v Thomson and MacIntyre (Patternmakers) Ltd* [1971] 2 All ER 1135, [1971] 1 WLR 1193, HL; cf *E & J Davis Transport Ltd v Chattaway* [1972] ICR 267, NIRC.

discretion to use its common sense, precedents from decided cases are of little use[116] and the EAT will only reverse a decision if it is clear that the tribunal completely misdirected itself[117]. Moreover, although the questions of suitability and reasonableness of refusal are in theory separate, they may often be run together in practice in the process of reaching a fair and common sense decision, particularly as it is well established that the employer bears the burden of proof on *both* questions[118].

The above discussion has tended to assume that the employee has either unequivocally accepted or refused the offer. However, it may be the case that he is unsure about the new employment because it differs from the old employment in material ways, but wishes to give it a try. To improve the position of such a person, there is now a statutory 'trial period' of four weeks from the end of the old employment[119]; if during that period the employee terminates the contract for any reason or the employer terminates it for a reason connected with the change of employment, the employee is treated as having been dismissed at the date of termination of the old contract, and for the reason or reasons prevalent at that date, and so may still bring redundancy proceedings on that basis. In the ordinary case where the employee is dismissed by the employer, but with the offer of other employment, this means that he has the next four weeks in which to make up his mind, without prejudice to his rights[120]. However, one problem has arisen in the case of 'constructive dismissal' within section 136(1)(c), ie where the employer, instead of dismissing the employee, says that he is not prepared to carry on employing him in his present capacity, but expects him to change to something different. In this case, the employee could leave and claim to have been constructively dismissed. What happens, however, if the employee is unsure whether to do so and in fact carries on with the employer, performing the new work on a trial basis and only resigns at a later date having decided that he does not like it? In such circumstances it was held (in cases decided before the Employment Protection Act 1975 introduced the statutory trial period) that mere continuance at work did not show acceptance of the new terms and that the employee dismissed under section 136(1)(c) had, in effect, a 'common law

115 *John Fowler (Don Foundry) Ltd v Parkin* [1975] IRLR 89.
116 In *Spencer and Griffin v Gloucestershire County Council* [1985] IRLR 393, CA, the EAT had stated as a principle that an employee could not reasonably object on the grounds that the quality of the work was not up to his or her standards, the setting of standards being a matter for the employer (the case concerned the dismissal of school cleaners and the offer to re-engage them on new, inferior contracts which would diminish the standard of cleaning). The Court of Appeal reversed this decision, holding that there is no room for any such principle and that reasonableness remains a question of fact for the tribunal.
117 *Collier v Smith's Dock Co Ltd* (1969) 4 ITR 338.
118 *Jones v Aston Cabinet Co Ltd* [1973] ICR 292. In an appeal against a benefit disqualification (n 104 above), however, the burden lies principally on the employee to show unsuitability and/or good cause for refusal: R(U) 26/52.
119 Employment Rights Act 1996, s 138(2); the trial period may be longer than four weeks if there is a written agreement to that effect, and there may be more than one trial period, in which case the same rules apply with necessary modifications. The four weeks of the trial period are to be applied on a simple calendar basis; the period cannot be extended merely because there was no work available for part of the time (eg because of a Christmas closure): *Benton v Sanderson Kayser Ltd* [1989] ICR 136, [1989] IRLR 19, CA.
120 If all that has happened is that the employee (already under notice) has agreed to work on temporarily, eg to finish a job, and is then dismissed, that remains an ordinary dismissal for redundancy, without the need to invoke those specialised provisions: *Mowlem Northern Ltd v Watson* [1990] ICR 751, [1990] IRLR 500, EAT.

trial period' of an agreed or reasonable length during which he would still decide that he did not like the new work, leave and still claim to have been constructively dismissed[121]. With the introduction of the statutory trial period, the question arose whether it replaced the common law period, or supplemented it (the practical point being that this period could be *longer* than the statutory four weeks – if a constructively dismissed employee left the new job more than four weeks after the change, could he still claim to be within the common law's 'reasonable period' instead?). The EAT have clearly held that the common law period is *not* abrogated and that the statutory period is in addition[122]. Thus, where the employee is dismissed in the ordinary way it is just a question of applying the statutory period, but where he claims to have been constructively dismissed he may claim to have a period at common law to decide whether to take on the new work (either an agreed period or, in the absence of agreement, a period which is 'reasonable' in all the circumstances), plus a further statutory four-week period (if he decides to try the new work) during which his right to leave and claim constructive dismissal is still protected:

> 'This is an improvement in the position of the employee who is dismissed in [ordinary dismissal] circumstances. It is also an improvement in the protection of the employee in [constructive dismissal] circumstances. He has a period X in which to make up his mind. If his decision is not to take the new job, he is treated as dismissed at the moment he brings period X to an end by leaving the new job. If his decision is to take the new job and he brings period X to an end by making a new contract or renewing the old one with variations he then has the further trial period created by [section 138] in which to make up his mind, before losing his right to say, "You dismissed me by repudiating the old contract" ... So he has his common law period X protection plus his statutory trial period protection.[123]'

In practice, the addition of four weeks may be of little significance; it is the fact that, in constructive dismissal cases, the common law trial period may be *longer* than four weeks which may be crucial in a particular case.

(b) The effects of misconduct and industrial action[124]

Although an employee may be prima facie redundant, it may be the case that he has also misconducted himself (whether by going on strike or otherwise) so that the employer would in fact be justified in dismissing him summarily because of that misconduct. In such a case, section 140 provides that he shall lose his entitlement to a redundancy payment *provided* that the employer dismisses him either (a) without notice, (b) with shorter notice than he is entitled to, or (c) with his full notice which must include a statement in writing that the employer would have been entitled, had he wished, to dismiss without notice (this last

---

121 *Marriott v Oxford and District Co-operative Society Ltd (No 2)* [1970] 1 QB 186, [1969] 3 All ER 1126, CA; *Shields Furniture Ltd v Goff* [1973] 2 All ER 653, [1973] ICR 187; *Sheet Metal Components Ltd v Plumridge* [1974] ICR 373, [1974] IRLR 86, NIRC.
122 *Air Canada v Lee* [1978] ICR 1202, [1978] IRLR 392; *Turvey v C W Cheyney & Son Ltd* [1979] ICR 341, [1979] IRLR 105.
123 *Turvey v C W Cheyney & Son Ltd* [1979] ICR 341 at 346, [1979] IRLR 105 at 108.
124 See *Harvey* E [1251], [1401].

possibility being referred to in the cases as 'special notice'). This subsection has caused problems in its interpretation, particularly as it is clear that, if the employer dismisses for cause, that is *not* a dismissal for redundancy anyway, so in theory there is no need in such a case for section 140 in order to disentitle the employee. Two principal interpretations have been put forward. The first, following on from this basic point, is that section 140 is meant to apply where the employee is dismissed for redundancy, but in circumstances where the employer could have dismissed for cause (and makes this known to the employee, either impliedly by giving no or short notice, or expressly by giving special notice). The second is that the subsection applies to dismissals for cause, in order to add the procedural rider that the employer must have given no, short or special notice if he is to rely on 'cause' to rebut the presumption of redundancy. There is still no clear decision as to which view is right; the most important case so far, *Sanders v Ernest A Neale Ltd* [125], clearly leans towards the first view, though at the same time stressing the importance of the procedural requirement of special notice:

> 'We agree ... that neither section [now section 140(1) and (3), discussed below] has any application if the dismissal is neither wholly nor mainly attributable to redundancy ... It seems therefore that, subject to [section 140(3)], a man who is dismissed solely on account of redundancy may lose his right to a redundancy payment if, by reason of the employee's conduct, his employer was actually entitled to dismiss him without notice.
>
> Sir Diarmid Conroy [in *Essen v Vanden Plas (England) Ltd* [126]] says he finds it difficult to understand why [section 140] provides for a special notice to be given to the employee if he is allowed to work out his notice and what sanction there is for not giving the notice. We suggest that the answer to the first question is that Parliament thought that an employer should not be allowed to resist a claim for a redundancy payment upon the ground that the employee could have been dismissed without notice, unless the employee was warned of the facts upon which this defence is based at the time of the dismissal ... The answer to the second question is that if the employee is dismissed wholly or mainly on account of redundancy and receives full notice of dismissal, the employer cannot rely on [section 140] unless he has given a notice complying with [section 140(1)(c)]. This is not an insignificant sanction.'

This dual approach can also be seen in the judgment of the EAT in *Simmons v Hoover Ltd* [127]:

> 'Certain matters can be stated with a fair amount of confidence:
>
> (1) [section 140] operates only by way of exclusion and, accordingly, has no effect in the case of an applicant who is not prima facie entitled to a redundancy payment, eg where, although there is a redundancy situation, his dismissal is not attributable wholly or mainly to redundancy but to some other cause such as misconduct; (2) the requirements of [section 140(1)(a), (b) or (c)] are presumably designed to ensure that the

---

125 [1974] 3 All ER 327 at 336, [1974] ICR 565 at 574.
126 (1966) 1 ITR 186.
127 [1977] ICR 61 at 79, [1977] 1 All ER 775 at 787.

employee is put on notice that he is being dismissed otherwise than in the ordinary course of the contract'; (3) a failure to serve such a notice under (a), (b) or (c) prevents the employer from relying on [section 140] ...'

Whichever is the preferable interpretation in theory, the practical point is that an employer is advised to safeguard his position by giving no short or special notice when dismissing an unsatisfactory employee for redundancy or, ex abundanti cautela, even when dismissing him for misconduct in circumstances where he may claim to have been redundant.

The exclusory effect of section 140, however it is construed, is subject to two main qualifications, found in that section. The first is that under subsection (2), where an employee under notice of dismissal for redundancy is in fact dismissed during the obligatory period[128] of that notice because of misconduct, the complete exclusion does not apply and a tribunal has discretion to award all or only part of the payment to which he would otherwise have been entitled. This is a wide discretion, not likely to be altered on appeal unless the tribunal has clearly made an error in principle in exercising it[129].

The second qualification applies where the misconduct in question is the participation in a strike. This is classed as misconduct, entitling the employer to dismiss without notice, and so the exclusion in section 140(1) is applicable[130]. However, subsection (2) provides that where the strike and dismissal take place during the obligatory period of an existing notice of dismissal for redundancy the exclusion does not apply, and so the employee may still seek a redundancy payment, subject to the employer's statutory right to serve a written notice of extension on the employee requiring him to work extra days after the expiry of the notice, equivalent to the number of days lost due to the strike[131]; if he fails to comply with such a notice, he loses his right to claim. Thus, the position of the redundant employee on strike during his notice period is safeguarded, but only if he is within the scheme of section 140(2). In *Simmons v Hoover Ltd*[132] the unusual situation arose where the employee was already on strike when he was dismissed for redundancy (ie the opposite of the facts envisaged by section 140(2)); the EAT held that this fell outside the wording of the section, so that the employee remained disqualified under subsection (1) and could not claim a redundancy payment. Finally on industrial action, it should be noted that there is no concept of 'self-induced redundancy' (operating to disqualify an employee); thus, even if the employee is a member of a group which has precipitated redundancies by continued industrial action, he will remain entitled to payment unless and until he is clearly disqualified in some way under the legislation:

'The court would like to take this opportunity of exorcising the ghost of self-induced redundancy. It can certainly occur, but as such it has no legal significance ... the mere fact that the employee's action created the redundancy situation does not disentitle them to a redundancy payment. The entitlement depends upon the words of the statute and there is no

128 Defined in s 136(4), see p 625 above.
129 *Lignacite Products Ltd v Krollman* [1979] IRLR 22.
130 *Simmons v Hoover Ltd* [1977] 1 All ER 775, [1977] ICR 61. Notice that the exclusion also applies, indirectly, to the case where an employee walks out because of a lock-out: s 143.
131 Employment Rights Act 1996, s 143.
132 N 130 above.

room for any general consideration of whether it is equitable that the employee should receive a payment[133].'

(c) Lay off and short time[134]

An ordinary claim for redundancy depends upon the existence of a 'dismissal'. In some cases of shortage of work, however, the employer may not dismiss, but instead may lay off the employee who has no work to do or put him on to short time. If he has no contractual right to do so, this may constitute constructive dismissal so that the employee may walk out and still claim his rights[135]. However, where the employer *has* such a contractual right this will not apply[136] and if the employee, short of money, walks out that will prima facie be a resignation not a dismissal, to the prejudice of his rights. To protect such a person, the legislation contains complicated provisions allowing the employee to claim a payment, though it is emphasised that to take advantage of these provisions the employee must qualify strictly under their wording – it is not necessarily enough to say that he was 'laid off' in common parlance. For statutory purposes, an employee is 'laid off' during any week when he receives no remuneration under this contract, and is on 'short time' if he receives during the week in question less than half his normal week's pay[137]; thus, if he receives more than half (for example, under a guaranteed minimum wage clause in his contract) he is not within the statutory scheme[138]. These definitions will be primarily applicable to piece-work employees, but are not restricted to this class[139]. The employee may claim a redundancy payment where he has been laid off or on short time (as defined) for a period of four consecutive weeks, or for a total of six weeks in a 13-week period; the procedure is that he must give written notice to the employer of his intention to claim a redundancy payment by virtue of the lay off or short time (within four weeks of the end of either of the specified periods) and must terminate his employment by giving the amount of notice required of him under his contract[140]. The employer may contest the claim by giving the employee a

---

133 *Sanders v Ernest A Neale Ltd* [1974] 3 All ER 327 at 335, [1974] ICR 565 at 573.
134 See Harvey E [1901].
135 *Powell Duffryn Wagon Co Ltd v House* [1974] ICR 123; *Jewell v Neptune Concrete Ltd* [1975] IRLR 147, IT; *Kenneth McRae & Co Ltd v Dawson* [1984] IRLR 5. This may be an important argument if for some reason the employee cannot rely on the statutory procedure about to be described (eg if he fails to comply with the detailed requirements); he can try to prove that there was *no* contractual right to lay off, so that he was constructively dismissed, on ordinary principles.
136 This conclusion was avoided in *A Dakri & Co Ltd v Tiffen* [1981] ICR 256, [1981] IRLR 57 by arguing that even an express lay-off term is subject to an implied term that any lay-off would only last for a reasonable period (so that if it lasted longer an employee could still leave and claim constructive dismissal). This reasoning was disapproved in *Kenneth McRae & Co Ltd v Dawson* (n 135 above) but surfaced again in *McClory v Post Office* [1992] ICR 758, [1993] IRLR 159 (in the context of a disciplinary suspension) and it can be seen to be consistent with other modern moves towards giving the implied term of trust and respect overriding effect: see p 140 above.
137 Employment Rights Act 1996, s 147. An employee is not on short time if he refuses work that is offered (eg because he thinks it too poorly paid): *Spinpress Ltd v Turner* [1986] ICR 433.
138 *Powell Duffryn Wagon Co Ltd v House*, n 135 above, at 126.
139 *Hulse v Perry* [1975] IRLR 181, IT; *Powell Duffryn Wagon Co Ltd v House*, n 135 above; cf *Hanson v Wood* (1967) 3 ITR 46.
140 Employment Rights Act 1996, s 148. Note the time limit on giving notice: s 150.

written counter-notice within seven days of receiving the employee's notice and by seeking to show that it could reasonably be expected (as the date of the employee's notice) that within four weeks the employee would enter a period of at least 13 weeks without any lay offs or short time[141]; this question is then decided by the employment tribunal. The period of work without lay offs or short time refers to work of the same type as that previously performed by the employee; this provision is not to be confused with the separate provisions on offers of alternative work of a different kind[142]. Finally, the legislation provides that if the lay off or short time in question is caused by a strike or lockout in *any* industry *anywhere*, these special provisions do not apply[143].

3 JOBSEEKER'S ALLOWANCE

(i) Background

Compulsory insurance against ill health and unemployment became law in this country for the first time in 1911 as a result of the National Insurance Act of that year[144]. That Act, limited in scope to certain specified industries, was enlarged and consolidated and eventually overtaken by the Beveridge reforms in the 1946 legislation setting up the modern Welfare State, as from 1948. Unemployment benefit became one of the central benefits. It was a contributory benefit, paid on flat rate scales for the first year of unemployment; if the claimant's needs (especially due to a family) were greater, it could be topped up with the means-tested income support. This system came under review by the Government in 1994, along with the question of benefits for the long-term sick and incapable. The latter resulted in the Social Security (Incapacity for Work) Act 1994 which sought to tighten entitlement to the (largely non-means-tested) benefits for sickness[145]. The second phase of these changes was the Jobseekers Act 1995. Like the 1994 Act which produced the unified incapacity benefit, this Act enacts a unified jobseeker's allowance in place of unemployment benefit and income support[146]. The Government said that it was necessary to produce a more 'modern' form of benefit, to do more to help people back into work, but it is clear that the opportunity was being taken to restrict expenditure on the benefit and also to tighten certain conditions of entitlement, especially the measures that a claimant must take to try to find work; the grafting on to this system of the

---

141 S 152; if the tribunal finds with hindsight that the employee was in fact laid off or on short time during the whole four weeks following the date of the notice, that is conclusively deemed to decide the case against the employer on this point: s 152(2).

142 *Neepsend Steel and Tool Corpn Ltd v Vaughan* [1972] 3 All ER 725, [1972] ICR 278.

143 S 154.

144 For the historical development, see Cornish and Clark *Law and Society in England 1750–1950* (1989), pp 447–472.

145 See p 842 below. The aim was to move substantial numbers off sickness-related benefit; if, however, those people (as was likely) were deemed capable of work but unable to find any, they would become claimants of unemployment benefit and/or income support, thus placing more strain on the system at that point, unless further economies could be made there too.

146 The changes were proposed in the White Paper 'Jobseeker's Allowance' (Cm 2687, 1994). On the policy behind the benefit, see Bryson 'The Jobseeker's Allowance: help or hindrance to the unemployed' (1995) 24 ILJ 204. Income Support remains a fall-back benefit for those not available for employment.

New Deal (for unemployed people aged 18–24, and for those over that age unemployed for two years) with its possibility of subsidised employment is a further example of this process. The fear of fraud and over-reliance on welfare has always been a strong political consideration in this area.

There is in fact a strong sense of déjà vu in this new benefit. Not only are many of the more justiciable rules (ie the ones most likely to produce appeals to appeal tribunals, which will be emphasised below) taken almost wholesale from the old unemployment benefit law, but also it was necessary to re-enact large parts of the complex income support rules. This is because the 1995 Act creates two forms of allowance – the contributions-based allowance (the equivalent of the old unemployment benefit *but* now payable only for six months) and the income-based allowance, which is income support under a new name. However, this should not be viewed merely as old wine in new bottles, since there were important changes in emphasis (along with incapacity benefit) to move from the old-style National Insurance benefits (based on contributions and entitlements) towards means-tested benefits; one version of this is that it concentrates help where it is needed, but another is simply that it cuts down on cost (especially for example, where the claimant has a working partner whose income must be taken into account where the benefit is means tested). Moreover, even the residue of the 'entitlement' benefit (the contributions-based allowance) was redefined in many ways on to the income support model, very deliberately. In some ways this was overdue. The old unemployment benefit was creaking in modern conditions because it was largely based on 1948 employment conditions, ie of full-time work or complete lack of work; it therefore caused problems with the modern tendency towards more diverse patterns of partial employment[147]. The replacement allowance addresses this, for example by setting hours limits for 'remunerative work' and allowing earning up to a limit (subject to deduction of those earnings from benefit), and by further trying to encourage claimants to ease themselves back into full work by taking on part-time employment by the new back-to-work bonus system. These ideas are more akin to the old income support system, but this in itself further emphasises the point made above about the movement towards means testing.

(ii) Entitlement to jobseeker's allowance

In order to qualify for the allowance a claimant must[148]:

(a) be available for employment[149];

---

147 Eg unemployment benefit was a daily benefit, still based on a six-day working week; it therefore needed special rules (very much the exception in 1948 but heavily relied on more recently) to deal with other patterns of work or temporary lay-offs. The notorious 'full extent normal' rules were examples of this and caused serious problems of application (see the fifth edition of this book, at p 433). Most such rules (on which there were large numbers of reported Commissioners' Decisions) have been abolished completely, and their complexity is not missed.

148 Jobseekers Act 1995, s 1.

149 The claimant must be willing and able to take up immediately any employed earner's employment, normally of at least 40 hours p.w.: s 6; Jobseeker's Allowance Regulations 1996, SI 1996/207, reg 6. A claimant can place restrictions on the work he will accept, but only where they mean he has a reasonable chance of employment; these restrictions may be to his normal occupation (on his previous terms) for up to 13 weeks; after six months, no restriction as to the acceptable level of pay is permitted: regs. 7, 8, 9, 16.

(b) have entered into a jobseeker's agreement;

(c) be actively seeking employment[150];

(d) satisfy either the contribution or income requirements;

(e) not be engaged in remunerative work[151];

(f) be capable of work[152];

(g) not be receiving relevant education;

(h) be under pensionable age;

(i) be in Great Britain.

If these eligibility tests are satisfied, the claimant may receive, first, the contributions-based allowance for up to twenty-six weeks (subject to the normal three waiting days) if he satisfied the normal contributions conditions[153]. The amount is fixed by regulations (with lower amounts for those under 25); unlike the old unemployment benefit, a person can remain eligible while doing part-time work (up to sixteen hours per week), but the amounts earned must be declared and deducted from the allowance (subject to a disregard of the first £5, or £10 for a couple, certain other miscellaneous disregards and the possibility of those earnings giving rise to a back-to-work bonus)[154]. Secondly, and quite independently, there is the income-based allowance. This is what the claimant is entitled to after twenty-six weeks, *and* can be claimed during that first period to top up the flat rate contributions-based allowance where the claimant has higher recognised needs (especially for a family and/or a mortgage). This part is income support under a new name, with the existing panoply of rules on the person's 'applicable amount' (for the claimant, spouse, children, and special premia for age or disability), the calculation of income, and the rules on capital stating that the claimant is ineligible if their capital exceeds £8,000, and that capital of between £3,000 and £8,000 is deemed to give 'notional income'[155]. Again any income from work (up to the permitted hours) is deducted from the applicable amount to give the entitlement.

Three innovations in the Jobseekers Act 1995 should be noted. The first was the introduction of the jobseeker's agreement which a claimant will be expected to enter with an employment officer. This will set out the claimant's availability

---

150 The claimant must take those reasonable steps which give him the best prospects of securing employment; following on from a general tightening of this requirement in 1989, the legislation sets out the details of what may be expected in any given case: s 8; regs. 18–22. These may of course link in to the jobseeker's agreement, the power to give the claimant directions (below), and to any special rules relating to persons under the New Deal programme.

151 'Remunerative work' for these purposes means work for not less than 16 hours per week (or, in the case of the claimant's partner, 24 hours p.w.): reg 51. Regs 52 and 53 have special rules covering those either deemed to be in remunerative work, or deemed not to be. This is a good example of the point made above about the adoption of the income support style of drafting.

152 Capability of work is now governed generally by the 'own work' and, more significantly, the 'all work' tests now applying to incapacity benefit: Jobseekers Act 1995, Sch 1, para 2; see p 842 below.

153 These are that the claimant has (a) actually paid contributions in one of the previous two tax years giving an 'earnings factor' of at least 25 times that year's lower earnings limit, and (b) actually paid, or been credited with, in the two previous tax years contributions yielding an earnings factor of at least 50 times those years' lower earnings factor: s 2.

154 S 4(1). In the case of a retired claimant, income from an occupational pension is deducted to the extent that it exceeds £50 pw: reg 81.

155 S 3. These rules are not set out here, being more purely social security provisions; they are covered in detail in the annual editions of Bonner et al. *Non-Means Tested Benefits* and Mesher and Wood *Income Related Benefits*.

and the steps to be taken in seeking work; failure to comply will result in a benefit sanction, though the claimant is given a right of appeal[156]. The second was the back-to-work bonus. As an incentive to take on part-time work (in order to keep a foothold in the employment market) it is provided that, although the income from that work is deducted from the benefit at the time, it can give rise to a stored 'credit' of half the amount earned, which can be paid to the claimant in a lump sum when he finds full-time work and goes off benefit, up to a maximum of £1,000[157]. The third innovation was an incentive (in the form of an National Insurance contributions reduction for a maximum of a year) for an employer to hire a person who has been in receipt of the allowance or its predecessor continuously for two years or more[158].

It is necessary now to look at the areas of the new allowance which are most justiciable, ie most likely to arise on an appeal to an appeal tribunal. These concern the important questions of disqualification of a claimant. Although much of the substance of the allowance (above) is taken from income support law, these next questions are taken almost entirely from the old unemployment benefit law, and so the existing case law on them continues to be applicable.

(iii) Disqualification

Even if a claimant is prima facie entitled to benefit, he might be disqualified in certain circumstances which must now be briefly considered. The trade dispute disqualification is 'permanent' in the sense that it lasts for as long as the dispute does; the other disqualifications are 'temporary', lasting for maximum periods of two, four or twenty-six weeks.

(a) The trade dispute disqualification

As this topic would be likely to be of some sensitivity, particularly if the rights and wrongs of a dispute had to be evaluated, the solution has been to disallow unemployment benefit altogether during the currency of the stoppage of work[159], this being analogous to the exclusion of claims for unfair dismissal when the termination arose out of a strike or lockout[160]. For the disqualification to apply, the loss of employment must arise out of a trade dispute at the claimant's place of work. 'Trade dispute' is defined as it used to be for the purpose of statutory immunity from tort liability in the Trade Disputes Act 1906, and as such it is capable of a wide definition which is ironic, for while a wide construction in the context of tort immunities is beneficial to the employee, in this context it can be

---

156 S 9; regs 31–45. Further, an employment officer may give a 'jobseeker's direction' to the claimant in writing, specifying further steps to be taken by him: s 19(5). The sanction is two week's loss of benefit, or four weeks if repeated: reg 69.

157 S 26; Social Security (Back to Work Bonus) (No 2) Regulations 1996, SI 1996/2570. This has been criticised on the basis that, although the lump sum bonus will be helpful, the time of greatest need is while still unemployed (at which time there is *no* provision for retention of part of the part-time income, other than the minimal £5/£10 disregard): Bryson, n 146 above, at p 207.

158 S 27; Employer's Contributions Reimbursement Regulations 1996, SI 1996/195.

159 Jobseekers Act 1995, s 14. For the history of the trade dispute disqualification; see the Donovan Report (Cmnd 3623, 1968) pp 246–256.

160 Trade Union and Labour Relations (Consolidation) Act 1992, ss 237, 238; see p 635, below.

most disadvantageous to him since it extends the ambit of the disqualification[161]. The disqualification lasts throughout the dispute, but it may cease even during the dispute in one of four ways:

(1) If the employee becomes bona fide employed elsewhere; if he then loses that other employment he may escape the disqualification even if the original dispute is still continuing. To come within this exception the employee must actually take up other employment – it is not enough that he has resigned his employment with the original employer without another job, no matter how genuine the resignation may be (though in such a case it now appears that the employee may seek to rely on the 'proviso', that he is no longer directly interested in the dispute, see (4), below). The phrase '*bona fide* employed' could be ambiguous, and could have ruled out the taking up of temporary employment, but it has been held[162] that bona fide means genuine employment not taken up merely to escape the section 14 disqualification; it could therefore cover temporary employment.

(2) If the employee's employment has been terminated by reason of redundancy[163]; this qualification was inserted by the Social Security Act 1986 in order to deal with the harshness of the decision in *Cartlidge v Chief Adjudication Officer*[164] where a miner who had already volunteered for redundancy before the miners' strike and who was made redundant during it was prevented from working because of the strike prior to his dismissal; this activated what is now section 14 and the Court of Appeal reluctantly upheld the Commissioners' decision that he was disqualified for the whole length of the strike, despite the bona fides of his dismissal for redundancy eight months before the end of it.

(3) If the employee has bona fide resumed employment with his employer but has subsequently left for a reason other than a trade dispute; again, this qualification was inserted by the Social Security Act 1986 in order to mitigate the effects of the disqualification on those genuinely losing employment for other reasons, especially during a protracted dispute.

(4) If the employee can prove that he is not directly interested in the dispute. This qualification (usually referred to as the 'proviso' to section 14, because of the way it used to be drafted) used to be more harsh in two ways, for the employee used to have to prove in addition (i) that he was not participating in the dispute, and (ii) that neither he nor others in his occupation were participating in or financing the dispute. The latter limb was repealed by the Employment Protection Act 1975 and the former disappeared when the section was redrafted by the Social Security Act 1986. However, the breadth of the remaining 'direct interest' limb should not be underestimated, for it makes clear that the disqualification applies not only to those taking an active part, but also to those who have lost their employment through the dispute but also stand to *gain* from the outcome. The crucial question therefore is how strict the nexus of gain must be between the dispute and the claimant. Clearly many people could be 'interested', in that a settlement concerning one group of workers could well have a ripple

---

161 R(U) 5/87.
162 R(U) 6/74, where the new work was to do a particular job of dismantling certain machinery, which was obviously finite.
163 This means redundancy as defined by the Employment Rights Act 1996, s 139; there is no requirement that a redundancy payment must actually be payable.
164 [1986] QB 360, [1986] ICR 256, CA.

effect throughout a plant or industry. The necessary restriction is to be found in the requirement of *direct* interest. In R(U) 13/71, the Commissioner said,

'I think that a claimant should not be regarded as having a direct interest in another's dispute ... unless there is a close association between the two occupations concerned, and the outcome of the dispute is likely to affect the claimant, not at a number of removes, but virtually automatically, without further intervening contingencies.'

This dictum, applied by the Court of Session in *Watt v Lord Advocate* [165], means that groups of workers other than those on strike, who are laid off, will only be disqualified if the settlement of the dispute would have a virtually automatic effect on their own terms and conditions [166] (for example, by some direct form of linkage); it is not enough that in practice the settlement may have an indirect effect through a further round of negotiations, however strong that effect might be [167]. At one end of the scale is the case of direct linkage of the wages of those on strike and those laid off (by contract or by collective agreement), in which case the disqualification will apply; at the other end is the case where a settlement in favour of those on strike will be used in further negotiations to attempt a similar settlement for those laid off, in which case the disqualification will not apply. The difficulty arises in the middle ground, where there is no formal direct linkage, but the employers' practice will almost inevitably mean that the settlement for those on strike will be applied to those laid off. This arose in *Presho v Insurance Officer* [168], where the Court of Appeal took a narrow approach and held that this was not direct interest, but this was reversed by the House of Lords, Lord Brandon stating that, in line with *Watt v Lord Advocate*, there are two conditions for the disqualification to apply:

'The first condition is that, whatever may be the outcome of the trade dispute, it will be applied by the common employers not only to the group of workers belonging to the one union participating in the dispute, but also the other groups of workers belonging to the other unions concerned. The second condition is that this application of the outcome of the dispute "across the board", as it has been aptly described, should come about automatically as a result of one or other of three things: first, a collective agreement which is legally binding; or, secondly, a collective agreement which is not legally binding; or, thirdly, established industrial custom and practice at the place of work concerned.'

It is the third of these that extends the disqualification to the middle ground in question, that explains why the House of Lords reversed the decision of the Court of Appeal, and that meant that the claimant was in fact disqualified.

---

165 1979 SC 120, 1979 SLT 137, on appeal from R(U) 6/78.
166 R(U) 8/80; this case also shows that the trade dispute does not have to be successful before the disqualification applies – it is enough if the employee would have benefited directly had the dispute led to a successful conclusion.
167 R(U) 5/79.
168 [1984] ICR 463, [1984] IRLR 74, HL; the passage cited is at 471 and 77 respectively. See Troup (1985) 14 ILJ 112.

As stated above, the disqualification lasts throughout the dispute; normally it will be obvious when the dispute (and so the disqualification) ends; but it could cause problems, particularly in a case where the employer in fact closed down the factory or subsidiary in question, or dispensed totally with the existing workforce (replacing some or all with new workers), never taking the employee back on – is that the end of the dispute, or could it be said that the dispute never ended and that the disqualification continues? This latter possibility would be highly disadvantageous to the employees concerned and was avoided in R(U) 15/80 by a finding that the eventual closure was primarily due to the financial collapse of the firm, not wholly due to the dispute; in such a case it can be said that, from the date of the closure, another cause operates and the disqualification ends. However, leaving the matter purely as one of causation would be unsatisfactory, for there would be still the possibility that a closure or widespread dismissal could be considered wholly due to the dispute, and so open-ended. Fortunately, this is now less likely since another approach is possible because of a change in the interpretation of the proviso (above). It had been held in R(U) 4/79 that the proviso could not apply once disqualification had been imposed – in other words, it could only be used to prevent disqualification arising in the first place and could not be relied on where the claimant argued that there had been a change of circumstances which meant that he was *no longer* (participating or) directly interested in the dispute[169]. However, that view was disapproved in R(U) 5/86[170], so that now the proviso *can* apply to end a disqualification because of a change of circumstances. Such a change could come about through the closure of the factory or the irrevocable dismissal of the workforce and so, as pointed out in the important decision in R(U) 1/87[171], the proviso applies *as from that date* to end the dispute, since the employees are no longer directly interested in the dispute. Further, it would appear from this decision that the same applies if, during the dispute, the employee resigns (even without having another job to go to), subject again to the qualification that the resignation must be intended to be a final termination of that employment relationship and not just a tactical move during the currency of the dispute.

The trade dispute disqualification applies to both the contributions-based allowance and the income-based allowance, but it is provided that the latter can be claimed in respect of the striker's family[172]. Moreover, the government has placed further restrictions on striking employees in two ways:

(i) there is to be deducted from the dependants' entitlement to the income-based allowance a 'prescribed sum' (set currently at £28)[173] which, though

---

169 The case concerned a fireman taking part in a dispute who resigned in December and took up other work in January; it was held that he was not entitled to benefit between December and January since he was already disqualified under the section and he did not cease to be so under the proviso when he resigned.

170 This was the decision that was appealed to the Court of Appeal in *Cartlidge v Chief Adjudication Officer*, in n 164 above, but this particular point was not in issue on the appeal.

171 28 employees withdrew their labour over rates of pay and were locked out and dismissed; three and a half months later, 13 (not including the claimant) were re-engaged and work restarted. *Held* as it was clear with hindsight that the dismissal of the claimant was not a manoeuvre in the dispute but was intended to be an irrevocable end to his employment, the proviso applied as from the date of dismissal, and so the claimant was *not* disqualified for the next three and a half months.

172 Jobseekers Act 1995, s 15.

173 S 15(2)(d); Jobseeker's Allowance Regulations 1996, SI 1996/207, reg 172.

not stating so expressly, was introduced to represent notional strike pay (the stated aim having been to encourage unions to make strike payments, at least to the extent of making up this shortfall)[174];

(ii) tax law has been altered to prevent the payment of tax rebates to persons on strike[175].

(b) Temporary disqualification

We have already seen that the new jobseeker's agreement and employment officer's power of direction are backed by disqualification sanctions of two or four weeks for failure to comply[176]. In addition, there are three other, principal grounds for disqualification which have existed for many years under the old unemployment benefit law and will continue to give rise to many of the appeals in this area; they each provide interesting parallels or comparisons with mainstream employment law. They are as follows:

(1) *Where the claimant lost his employment through misconduct*[177]. This is a potential area for controversy, for in effect the employment officer must evaluate the blameworthiness of the dismissed employee with a view to disqualifying him. The misconduct in question must be causally connected to the dismissal, but it could in an appropriate case arise from factors outside the actual employment, for example conviction of a criminal offence. Outside that principle, however, this is a wide question of fact. If the employee had just cause for leaving, for example through a breach of contract by his employer, that will not bring disqualification, and it has been held that misconduct in this context means 'conduct which is causally but not necessarily directly connected with employment, and having regard to the relationship of employer and employee and the rights and duties of both, can fairly be described as blameworthy, reprehensible and wrong'[178]. With the advent of the action for unfair dismissal, there is now far more likelihood of there being judicial consideration of the merits of any particular dismissal, and so, in order to avoid seemingly conflicting decisions, any decision by an employment tribunal on the fairness or otherwise of a dismissal is likely in practice to be followed by the Agency officer or appeal body on the question

---

174 The origin of this measure can be traced to the steel strike of 1979, but it assumed particular importance and prominence during the miners' strike of 1984/5 (see Mesher 'Social security in the coal dispute' (1985) 14 ILJ 191); an attempt was made by the NUM to circumvent it on the grounds that they were not able to make payments of strike pay but (not surprisingly given the clear wording of the statute) this failed: *R v Chief Adjudication Officer, ex p Bland* (1985) Times, 6 February, DC.

175 Finance Act 1981, s 29, SI 1982/66; see now the Income and Corporation Taxes Act 1988, s 204.

176 Jobseekers Act 1995, s 19(5). The subsection also covers failure to take up or attend a training scheme placement, or giving up such a placement, or losing it through misconduct. Each of these is subject to a 'good cause' defence. Factors to be taken into account in such a defence are set out in the Jobseeker's Allowance Regulations 1996, regs. 72 and 73.

177 S 19(6)(a). Use of the phrase 'lost his employment' means that this head can cover dismissal, voluntary leaving or resignation as an alternative to impending dismissal (R(U) 17/64; R(U) 2/76).

178 R(U) 2/77. Note, however, that if it is alleged that the misconduct consisted of refusing to obey an order, and the evidence shows that several employees did likewise because of a disagreement with the employer, that should probably be dealt with as a trade dispute case under s 14, *not* as individual misconduct under s 19.

of disqualification, provided the actual question of misconduct was considered, although it is not binding[179] and it must be remembered that in any given case the employment tribunal may have had to consider wider aspects of the case with no immediate relevance to unemployment benefit disqualification such as procedural unfairness and contributory fault.

(2) *Where the claimant voluntarily gives up his employment without just cause*[180]. Thus, the employee who resigns of his own accord will be disqualified unless he can show that he had just cause (a matter which might also be important if the employee is claiming to have been constructively dismissed for the purpose of an unfair dismissal claim), and unless there was some material deterioration in the job or some pressing personal factor operating this may be hard to show, particularly if he left without any job to go to; this can be seen from the following dictum from a Commissioner:

> 'An examination of the decisions on the topic leads me to think that in general it is only where circumstances are such that a person has virtually no alternative but to leave voluntarily that he will be found to have had just cause for doing so, rather as a person who throws his baggage overboard to make room in the lifeboat can claim on his baggage insurance[181].'

This is one further example of the premise that benefit is paid for involuntary unemployment, an approach clearly seen in the approach to this disqualification of the Court of Appeal in *Crewe v Social Security Comr*[182] where the test was said to be whether leaving the employment was right and reasonable from the point of view of the national insurance fund which has to bear the burden of the employee's decision, *not* whether it was reasonable or convenient as between employer and employee or generally in the interests of the community; this disqualification was thus seen as primarily a protection for the fund. While such an approach may be logical, it could have practical drawbacks in discouraging voluntary severance schemes (considered below). Faced with the large numbers of redundancies to be made in the mining industry on a voluntary basis, the previous government altered the position by the Social Security Act 1985, which inserted a new provision[183] which provides that a person who has been dismissed by his employer by reason of redundancy (within the meaning of section 139 of the Employment Rights Act 1996) after volunteering or agreeing so to be

---

179 R(U) 2/74; R(U) 4/78. This approach was reaffirmed in R(U) 3/79, though it was pointed out that for present purposes the state authorities are *not* concerned with dismissal as a matter between employer and employee, and so should be wary of using terms such as 'proper dismissal' or 'unfair dismissal'.

180 S 19(6)(b).

181 R(U) 4/87, para 9, per Commissioner Monroe.

182 [1982] 2 All ER 745, [1982] IRLR 295, CA, where a teacher who took early retirement in line with a local authority scheme to decrease the number of teachers (thus acting in accordance with the wishes of his employer and arguably in the wider interests of the community) was held to have left his employment without just cause and so was disqualified under s 19.

183 Now the Jobseeker's Allowance Regulations 1996, reg 71; this covers the case where employer and employee mutually agree severance, as well as where the employee is formally 'dismissed' for redundancy: R(U) 3/91.

dismissed or to leave without dismissal is not to be treated as having left his employment voluntarily.

Thus, provided the statutory definition of redundancy is satisfied[184], the decision in *Crewe* will no longer apply. One further practical problem now addressed specifically concerned the person who took a job, found it unsuitable and left. That person could be disqualified for benefit for voluntarily leaving, in spite of the fact that it was in the public interest for unemployed people to try to take up employment offers. As part of the general changes under the Social Security Act 1989, a 'trial period' was enacted; thus, a person who has been unemployed for over thirteen weeks may take a job on trial and, if he leaves between the beginning of the fifth week and the end of the twelfth week in that job, he is not to be disqualified for voluntarily leaving[185].

(3) *Where the claimant without good cause refuses or fails to apply for or avail himself of a suitable job*[186]. Once a vacancy has been notified to the unemployed claimant, he is expected to take reasonable steps to obtain it and, if offered it, should accept it. As seen above, this is closely tied in with the primary requirement that the claimant must be available for and actively seeking work. Just as those provisions were tightened up by the Social Security Act 1989, so there were also major amendments here, introducing a more complex scheme. Previously, there was a simple test as to whether the job offered was 'suitable', with questions such as the length of time a person could wait before lowering his sights and taking lesser work than before left as questions of fact and judgement. However, the drafting substituted in 1989 removes references to suitability and instead states that *any* failure to avail will trigger disqualification *unless* the claimant can prove 'good cause' for his failure. Criteria are then laid down[187] for deciding on good cause, including any condition or personal circumstances indicating serious harm to health or excessive physical and mental stress, any religious or conscientious belief, any responsibility for another member of the household, travelling time (more than an hour each way) and unreasonably high expenses in taking the job. The effect that taking up the employment may have on the claimant's income or that of his household is not a relevant factor[188]. On the crucial question of the time a newly unemployed person can spend looking only for a job of similar status, there is now a maximum 'permitted period' of thirteen weeks[189].

---

184 Note that it does not say that a redundancy payment has been made; there may be technical reasons why the employee is not eligible for a payment, but he may still be 'redundant' within s 139, and this is what matters.

185 S 20(3); reg 74.

186 S 19(6)(c),(d); this list covers not just failing to apply, but also refusal to accept or neglecting to avail himself of a reasonable opportunity.

187 Jobseeker's Allowance Regulations 1996, reg 72(2). Note that s 20(1) continues the old provision that a claimant does not have to accept a job which is vacant due to a trade dispute, ie he cannot be required to act as a strike breaker.

188 Reg 72(6); thus the claimant cannot argue that, overall, he was better off on benefit.

189 Regs 16, 72(5); it could be less than 13 weeks, in which case relevant factors are again laid down in reg 16. Once the period has expired, the claimant is subject to the rule that the level of pay is not good cause: s 19(9). There used to be a rule that the claimant could refuse a job in his trade but at below trade rates of pay (ie that he could not be used as cheap labour) but this was repealed.

If one of the above temporary disqualifications applies, how long is it to last? The maximum period stood for many years at six weeks, but then was raised by the previous government, first to thirteen weeks in 1986, and then to twenty-six weeks, in 1988. This radical increase has given greater importance to considering the appropriate length of disqualification, particularly as a person so disqualified is only eligible for a reduced version of the income-based allowance, and then only if certain tightly defined conditions of particular hardship apply to their case[190]. In the past, the standard practice has been for the Agency officer (having decided to apply one of the disqualifications) to apply the maximum period in many cases, leaving it for an aggrieved claimant to appeal to an Appeal Tribunal against such an award. Although officers have now been instructed not to do so and there is evidence of them using their discretion more often to give more consideration to length of disqualification when making their decisions, it remains the case that the increase of the maximum period to twenty-six weeks has increased the importance of the right of appeal in disqualification cases. On appeal, the tribunal may consider the length of disqualification imposed and alter it where appropriate; indeed, it has been held that failure to give such consideration (or to give reasons for the eventual decision) is an error of law, giving rise to further appeal to the Commissioner[191]. Within a figure as high as twenty-six weeks, there is therefore considerable scope for arguments in mitigation (even where the claimant/appellant accepts that *some* disqualification is merited). However, there is unfortunately little guidance as yet from the Commissioners as to how the adjudicating authorities are to exercise their powers; apart from stating that the discretion is to be exercised judicially, they have been content to leave it as a question of fact for the particular tribunal[192] (an approach that was easier to apply when the maximum period was only six weeks). In a misconduct case, this will mean considering how bad the misconduct was and any factors in mitigation[193]. In a case of voluntary leaving, it will mean considering *how much* cause the claimant had to leave (accepting that it was not sufficient to constitute 'just' cause) and how responsibly (or otherwise) he acted in giving up his existing job. An interesting, relatively liberal, example of this can be seen in R(U) 4/87 where a civil servant gave up his job to seek work as a social worker helping the mentally handicapped; because of the decision of the Court of Appeal in *Crewe v Social Security Comr*[194] this could not be considered just cause and so the voluntary leaving disqualification applied *but* in the light of the public interest involved in having people volunteer for such work the Commissioner held that a period of only one week's disqualification was appropriate.

---

190 Regs 140–146.
191 R(U) 4/87.
192 While this may be admirable from the point of view of flexibility and, dare one say it, anti-legalism, there may be certain areas where at least basic *principles* should be set out; for example, if the claimant was dismissed for taking home certain work items of minimal value (viewed as 'perks' by most of the workers there, ie a classic 'gleaning' case), should the tribunal take the view that 'theft is theft' and apply the maximum, or take into account that this was a very minor example of theft and apply only a few weeks' disqualification?
193 There may be a further overlap with unfair dismissal concepts here, eg whether the claimant had already been warned by his employer.
194 N 182 above.

(iv) Four overlaps with termination of employment

Although the law relating to jobseeker's allowance is contained in the social security legislation, it is important for an industrial lawyer to have a knowledge of it, because it may be an important background factor in certain areas of employment law, particularly termination of employment. Four particular points of overlap between the allowance and employment law might be borne in mind, the first two relating to major statutory rights and the last two to informal, ad hoc severance agreements.

The first point is that the relationship between benefits and compensation for unfair dismissal[195] is formalised in Regulations, so that the state may recover from the employer who unfairly dismissed the claimant the amount of allowance paid to the claimant in the period up to the tribunal hearing[196], and the claimant is disqualified from claiming benefit for the period in respect of which compensation is ordered by the tribunal to cover loss of future wages[197].

The second point is that it is well established that receipt of a statutory redundancy payment does not disentitle the redundant employee from claiming jobseeker's allowance, the point being that although in practice the receipt of the payment will help the ex-employee financially for a certain period into the future, it is calculated by reference to *past* service and so does not disentitle the claimant from future claims for benefit[198].

The third point is that, as seen above, the rules relating to employees volunteering for or accepting early severance of sorts were possibly a disincentive to such schemes before 1985, because of the decision of the Court of Appeal in *Crewe v Social Security Comr*[199] that such a volunteer could be disqualified on the ground of having left his employment without just cause. However, such schemes comprise a much-used form of shedding labour without the need to make compulsory redundancies, and the overruling of *Crewe* by the Social Security Act 1985 has already been considered.

Potentially more drastic is the fourth overlap which arises where the employee leaves employment with some form of lump sum (other than a statutory redundancy payment), once again a not-uncommon occurrence when firms are wishing to shed labour by agreement. Once again, there were major changes here in 1989. The old provision used to disqualify an employee leaving employment with a payment 'in lieu of notice or the remuneration which he would have received ... had his employment not been terminated'. Thus, someone leaving with wages in lieu of notice was ineligible for benefit for the notice period. However, it was held in *R v National Insurance Comr, ex p Stratton*[200] that it was necessary to look at the dominant nature of the payment and that if (as in that case) that nature was a reward for *past* services, it was analogous to a

---

195 For the relationship between a *finding* of fair and unfair dismissal and eligibility for benefit, see n 179 above.

196 Employment Protection (Recoupment of Jobseekers' Allowance and Income Support) Regulations 1996, SI 1996/2349; see p 617 above.

197 The amount ordered is considered to be 'earnings' for the period in question: Jobseeker's Allowance Regulations 1996, reg 98(1)(f).

198 Reg 98(2); R(U) 6/73, approved by the Court of Appeal in *Stratton*'s case (n 200 below). This is in line with Lord Denning's view in the early redundancy case of *Lloyd v Brassey* [1969] 2 QB 98, [1969] 1 All ER 382, CA (p 624 above) that a redundancy payment is not meant to be a glorified form of unemployment benefit.

199 [1982] 2 All ER 745, [1982] IRLR 295, CA.

200 [1979] 2 All ER 278, [1979] ICR 290, CA.

redundancy payment and so *not* caught by the provision. This gave considerable scope for avoidance of the regulation, either by the description given to the terminal payment, or by disguising it in some form of overall, unspecific 'severance pay', not uncommon in negotiated redundancies[201]. To counter this, the law was completely redrafted to produce a scheme which is far more difficult to avoid, and this was carried over into the Jobseeker's Allowance Regulations 1996. It is complicated, and works in four stages.

(1) Regulation 98(1) states that the claimant's earnings are deemed to include 'any compensation payment'.

(2) 'Compensation payment' is then defined in regulation 98(3) as *any* payment made *in respect of* the termination of the employment, *unless* it comes within one of several specific exceptions, the most important of which are (i) any remuneration or emolument which accrued in the period before the termination[202], (ii) holiday pay, (iii) a refund of pension contributions, (iv) maternity or sick pay, (v) employment expenses, (vi) an occupational pension or (vii) a statutory redundancy payment. If the payment cannot be shown to be under one of these exceptions (which concentrate primarily on money already earned or a *statutory* redundancy payment), it is likely to be caught, as it will be very difficult to show that a terminal payment (of whatever kind) was not made 'in respect of' the termination.

(3) Once the payment is caught, regulation 94(6) notionally spreads the payment over the period ending (a) where the employer represents that it (or part of it) was paid in lieu of notice of termination or on account of early termination of a fixed-term contract, on the 'expiry date'; (b) where it is paid in lieu of statutory consultation on collective redundancies[203], on the date that consultation period would have ended; (c) in any other case, on the 'standard date'.

(4) Regulation 94(8) then defines this verbiage. The 'expiry date' means the date on which the notice applicable to that person (by contract, statute or custom, whichever is the longer) would have expired, or the expiry date of a fixed-term contract. The (fall-back) 'standard date', if all else fails, means the earlier of (a) the expiry date (!) or (b) a period worked out mathematically by dividing the amount of the terminal payment by the maximum 'week's pay' for statutory purposes[204].

The end result of this tortured drafting is that in nearly all cases now where an employee leaves with a terminal payment which includes any element[205] of payment not falling within the above exemptions for already earned pay or statutory redundancy payments, that payment will be deemed to be their earnings for the period in question, which will normally disentitle them to the allowance. Moreover, the ineligibility will normally be for the contractual notice period,

---

201 See R(U) 1/80, R(U) 2/80 and R(U) 4/80, in each of which the element of past service avoided the regulation; cf R(U) 7/80 where the payment mentioned the obligatory consultation period for collective redundancies and payment in lieu thereof, and so that payment was caught.

202 This does not include a contractual or negotiated redundancy/severance payment, even though it is *calculated* by past service, because such a payment is not 'remuneration': R(U) 5/92 see below.

203 See p 84 above.

204 One saving grace is that no ineligible period, however calculated, can last for more than 52 weeks: reg 94(7).

205 R(U) 1/94.

whether the actual payment is the same as, more than or less than what would actually have been earned in that period[206].

A good example of this post-1989 regime is provided by R(U) 5/92, where a long-standing employee was made redundant, being given only two weeks' notice, though contractually entitled to twelve weeks. He received a terminal payment of £20,400, made up of a statutory redundancy payment, accrued wages, holiday pay and £14,229 'severance payment', calculated entirely by reference to past years of service. The first three were clearly exempt and the argument was over the severance payment. The Commissioner held that it was a payment 'in respect of the termination of the employment' and so constituted 'compensation' which was *not* within one of the exempt categories. The claimant was therefore disentitled for the 'ineligible period' which, on these facts, was until the 'expiry date', ie the end of ten weeks of notice that he had not had. Arguments by the claimant's representative that the overall nature of the payment should be considered were dismissed on the ground that these new provisions must be construed as they stand and that *ex p Stratton* and the other previous case law 'concerned the previous and very different version of [the Regulations] and do not seem to me to be of assistance in relation to the meaning of "compensation" in the new provisions'.

---

206 It may now be necessary to *sever* the payment into its component parts, rather than looking as its dominant characteristic: C(U)88/90. If *any* element is not exempt (as will usually be the case), it is 'compensation' and so is caught.

Chapter 10

The law on trade unions

I INTRODUCTION[1]

The legal history of trade unions is one of long periods of their treatment as illegal or potentially illegal either under particular statutes or by virtue of certain general common law tenets, particularly restraint of trade and criminal conspiracy. The removal of these threats and the repeal of the old master and servant legislation in the last quarter of the nineteenth century was a major step forward, but then the spectre was raised of unions being readily sued in the civil courts through the development of the industrial torts, until the granting of immunities to unions and their members by the Trade Disputes Act 1906. Even in the twentieth century, legislative intervention was necessary to reverse certain court decisions which could have had far-reaching consequences for what trade unionists see as their proper purposes. Legal regulation of the external activities of trade unions and the question of the proper limits of union-organised industrial action is considered in Chapter 11; in this chapter we examine the legal regulation of the internal workings of trade unions.

For much of the last hundred years the stance of the law towards union internal affairs was principally one of non-intervention, in line with the approach taken to the internal affairs of voluntary associations generally. The courts at common law assumed jurisdiction to interpret and enforce union rules, and the judges showed themselves vigilant in the protection of the rights of individual union members, particularly where livelihoods were at risk. However, with the exception of the Industrial Relations Act 1971, which proved to be a spectacular failure and a traumatic experience for all concerned, until the 1980s there had been no systematic attempt to regulate the internal workings of trade unions by legislation. The period since 1980 has seen a dramatic transformation in the legal regulation of internal union affairs, and as a result of the legislation of that period the internal workings of a trade union are now subjected to an unprecedented degree of

---

1   See Morris and Archer *Collective Labour Law* (2000); Thomas *The Trade Union Acts 1992 and 1993* (1994). For background reading, see Millward, Bryson and Forth *All Change at Work? British Employee Relations 1980–1998* (2000).

statutory control covering almost every aspect of union activity. This has come about largely through the enactment of new rights for union members in relation to matters such as expulsion, discipline and the use of union funds, and the imposition of legally enforceable balloting requirements. Some of these reforms did little more than extend the good practice of some trade unions to all unions, and over a period of time have come to be accepted by the union movement (for example the balloting requirements for union elections and the requirement of a ballot before industrial action); others (for example the controls on access to membership and the imposition of discipline) are widely seen as striking a lethal blow at the status of unions as voluntary associations, by undermining the very foundations of collective responsibility and self-determination upon which trade unions have traditionally been based.

At the root of the problem in applying the law to trade unions and their activities is the inherent conflict which exists between the individual and the collective interest[2], and the different natural standpoints of trade unionists and lawyers. The lawyer's natural sympathy often lies with an individual, particularly when opposed by a large body (of whatever sort) more powerful than him; when, however, that body is a trade union, the members may see nothing inherently sinister or dangerous about such an organisation – indeed, it is its very size and collective power that has historically been a worker's only protection against the infinitely greater economic power of the employer. The collective aspect can thus become dominant, and a certain (or even a large) amount of individualism may have to be sacrificed in order to maintain that collective power. Thus, for example, where a union member is improperly expelled (for example in breach of the rules, or in defiance of the rules of natural justice) and brings an action against the union, that one action may be seen entirely differently by the lawyer and the trade unionist; one man's persecuted individual is another man's threat to the collective security of the union. This divergence is most clearly seen in cases concerned with the rights of individuals (particularly members) vis-à-vis the union and in that context it may pose difficult questions as to how union rules are to be interpreted and applied (considered below). It has also been seen in other areas, for example the application of the TUC's internal rules and procedures for the resolution of inter-union disputes over membership. From the collective standpoint, such procedures may be considered necessary and desirable to avoid fragmentation of bargaining units and discourage competition between unions for members; but from the standpoint of an individual denied access to membership of a trade union, those procedures may appear to be an unwarranted interference with an individual's freedom to belong to the union of his or her choice.

Not surprisingly, where the courts have been faced with cases involving a clash between the collective interests of the union and the individual interests of a member, greater emphasis has tended to be placed upon the individual aspect, particularly in cases involving expulsion and discipline where the decision is likely to have a major impact on individual rights. However, in certain cases concerning more general questions as to the functioning and vires of unions, the courts have shown more appreciation of the collective side of the equation[3]. In *Goring v British Actors Equity Association*[4] one of the claimant's arguments was

---

2   See Kidner 'The individual and collective interest in trade union law' (1975) 5 ILJ 90.
3   See *Cheall v APEX* [1983] ICR 398, [1983] IRLR 215, HL (considered below at p 740), which provides a good example of this in a decision of the House of Lords.
4   [1987] IRLR 122 at 125, Ch D.

that a union instruction (that no member should work in South Africa) that he was challenging conflicted with the objects of the union which included the head 'to maintain the professional rights and liberties of its members individually and collectively', the point being that the instruction, in his submission, interfered with members' individual rights; dismissing this argument, Browne-Wilkinson V-C said:

> 'The essence of a trade union activity is that members are bound to act collectively to achieve the objects of the majority. Such collective action must necessarily impair the individual rights of some members ... [The objects clause in question] expresses objects. It enables the union to protect individuals as well as collective interests; it does not mean that the union can only do such things as are in the interests of all members both individually and collectively.'

In *Iwanuszezak v GMBATU*[5] the claimant union member had been adversely affected by an agreement negotiated by his union with his employer, which altered shift arrangements to the benefit of most employees, but to his detriment; he attempted to sue the union for breach of membership contract and negligence but his action was struck out at first instance and, in upholding that decision in the Court of Appeal, Lloyd LJ said:

> 'The judge put the matter well when he said that it is the primary function of a union to look after the collective interests of its members. Of course, it also looks after individual members in all sorts of different ways. But where the collective interests of the union conflict with the interests of an individual member, it only makes sense, as the judge said, that the collective interests of the members as a whole should prevail.'

While the courts at common law have therefore shown themselves able to recognise the collective interest, and even on occasion to uphold it at the expense of the interests of individuals, the stance of the Conservative government in its legislative stranglehold on internal union affairs during the 1980s and 1990s was increasingly one of almost total subordination of the collective interest and the adoption of a highly individualist model of trade unionism. Thus, for example, the restrictions on union expulsions and exclusions introduced by the Trade Union Reform and Employment Rights Act 1993 removed from a union the freedom to determine its own membership, and the tight controls on union discipline introduced by the Employment Act 1988 effectively allow the interests of individual members to override the interests of the membership as a whole in the observance of collective decisions reached in accordance with the rules. Given the historic tussles throughout much of the nineteenth century between the courts and Parliament over the legality of trade unions and their activities, there is a certain irony in the fact that in the latter years of the twentieth century the courts arguably showed a greater readiness to uphold the collective interest than did the legislature. The election of a Labour government in 1997 has not led to

---

5   [1988] IRLR 219, CA; the passage cited is at 220. See also, in an entirely different context, *Weaver v NATFHE* [1988] ICR 599, where the EAT upheld a union policy not to assist a member to make a complaint which might jeopardise the job of another member, even where that refusal of assistance might constitute racial discrimination.

any significant relaxation of the legislative stranglehold on internal trade union affairs, and if there is to be a resurgence of union autonomy and strengthening of union rights, it seems more likely at the time of writing that it will come about as a result of international standards, not least those established by Article 11 of the European Convention on Human Rights[6].

2 DEFINITION, LISTING AND LEGAL STATUS

(i) Definition

A trade union is defined in the Trade Union and Labour Relations (Consolidation) Act 1992, section 1 as an organisation which consists wholly or mainly of workers of one or more descriptions and whose principal purposes include the regulation of relations between workers of that description or those descriptions and employers or employers' associations[7] ; the definition also extends to organisations which consist of constituent or affiliated trade unions, or the representatives of such organisations. This definition contains three elements: first, there must be an 'organisation', whether temporary or permanent, which indicates that there must be some degree of formal structure as opposed to a casual grouping of workers[8]; secondly, the organisation must be composed wholly or mainly of workers[9] or their trade unions or federations[10]; and thirdly, the principal purposes of the organisation must include industrial relations with employers or their associations[11]. In *Midland Cold Storage v Turner*[12], a joint shop stewards' committee was held not to satisfy this requirement because it had not itself entered into negotiations with employers, but had merely acted as a pressure group, seeking to influence the decisions of the dock workers' unions on the taking of industrial action. In contrast, in *British Association of Advisers and Lecturers in Physical Education v National Union of Teachers*[13], a professional association whose objects clause stated that it 'shall be concerned with the professional interests of its members' was held to be a trade union, although

6   Discussed below at pp 669 and 712
7   An employers' association is similarly defined in s 122 as an organisation which consists wholly or mainly of employers or individual owners of undertakings and which has among its principal purposes the regulation of relations between employers and workers or trade unions: see eg *Greig v Insole* [1978] 3 All ER 449, [1978] 1 WLR 302; this definition also extends to federations of employers' associations.
8   *Frost v Clarke & Smith Manufacturing Co Ltd* [1973] IRLR 216; *Weeks v National Amalgamated Stevedores and Dockers' Union* (1940) 67 Ll L Rep 282; *Midland Cold Storage v Turner* [1972] ICR 230.
9   'Worker' is defined for these purposes as including those working or seeking to work under contracts of employment and those who contract personally to perform work or services for another, but excluding contracts with professional clients (see eg *Carter v Law Society* [1973] ICR 113): Trade Union and Labour Relations (Consolidation) Act 1992, s 296(1). There are specific exclusions for members of the armed forces (s 296(1)) and the police service (s 280).
10   Trade Union and Labour Relations (Consolidation) Act 1992, s 1(b). This covers union federations such as the International Transport Workers' Federation: see eg *Camellia Tanker Ltd SA v ITWF* [1976] ICR 274, [1976] IRLR 190, CA.
11   There is an exception in the case of union federations, where the definition is satisfied if the organisation's principal purposes include the regulation of relations between its constituent or affiliated organisations: Trade Union and Labour Relations (Consolidation) Act 1992, s 1(b).
12   [1972] ICR 230.
13   [1986] IRLR 497, CA.

to describe industrial relations as one of its principal purposes might seem on the facts to be stretching several points.

(ii) Listing

In practice, the simplest way to determine whether or not an organisation is a trade union is to see whether it is included in the list of trade unions maintained by the Certification Officer[14]. The procedure for listing trade unions is largely a formality, unlike the old requirement of registration under the Industrial Relations Act 1971. Under the 1971 Act, registration was the keystone to much of the rest of the legislation (which in turn meant that the TUC's tactic of non-registration was extremely effective). Now, however, listing is much more mechanical. The operation is carried out by the Certification Officer, who maintains a list (open to the public) of trade unions[15]. Any unlisted organisation may apply in prescribed form to be listed; if listing is refused, the organisation may appeal to the EAT (on both fact and law)[16]. An organisation also has a right to be removed from the list if it wishes. In deciding whether to list an organisation, the Certification Officer has two functions: (i) to decide whether it in fact qualifies as a trade union, under the definitions considered in head 1 above; (ii) to ensure that its name is not the same as that of an existing listed organisation, or misleadingly similar. Entry on the list is itself declared to be evidence that the organisation in fact is a trade union (and the organisation may request a certificate from the Certification Officer to the effect that it is on the list)[17]. There are two principal advantages for a trade union in being listed. The first is that it gains certain tax exemptions with regard to its provident benefits funds[18], the second is that listing is a precondition for the far more important step of gaining a certificate of independence[19], which is the key which unlocks the door to most of the statutory union rights contained in the modern legislation.

(iii) The legal status of a trade union

Except during the brief currency of the Industrial Relations Act 1971, trade unions have never been bodies corporate, and indeed under the present legislation are forbidden to be so[20]. In law, a trade union is an unincorporated association, a

---

14 See p 66.
15 Trade Union and Labour Relations (Consolidation) Act 1992, s 2. The Certification Officer also maintains a list of employers' associations, to which similar rules apply: see s 123. At the end of March 2002, there were 199 trade unions and 94 employers' associations on the list: *Annual Report of the Certification Officer 2001-2002.*
16 Trade Union and Labour Relations (Consolidation) Act 1992, ss 9 and 126.
17 Trade Union and Labour Relations (Consolidation) Act 1992, ss 2(4) and 123(4). The fact of being listed is not a necessary precondition of claiming to be a trade union or employers' association (see eg the attempt of the ICC and TCCB to claim the status of employers' associations in *Greig v Insole* [1978] 3 All ER 449, [1978] 1 WLR 302), but it may be useful evidence.
18 Income and Corporation Taxes Act 1988, s 467.
19 Trade Union and Labour Relations (Consolidation) Act 1992, s 6; see p 68 above.
20 Trade Union and Labour Relations (Consolidation) Act 1992, s 10; a professional organisation which is a 'special register body' as defined in s 117 (eg the British Medical Association) is permitted to have corporate status. An employers' association may be incorporated or unincorporated: s 127.

collection of individuals bound together by the contract of membership with no separate legal personality. However, trade unions are invested with some of the most important attributes of legal personality by statute, including the power to make contracts, to sue and be sued and to be prosecuted for criminal offences. A trade union can therefore be seen as a curious hybrid falling somewhere between an unincorporated association and a body corporate – a 'quasi-corporate' body. Until the landmark case of *Taff Vale Rly Co v ASRS* [21] it was thought that a trade union could not be sued because it had no legal personality. In that case the House of Lords held that, whatever the precise juristic basis, a union was a creature known to the law and could therefore be sued. The prospect of union funds (including benefit funds) being taken in satisfaction of judgment led to the enactment in 1906[22] of the blanket immunity for trade unions in tort, but this immunity was in turn removed by the Employment Act 1982[23]. The legal status of a trade union is now governed by section 10 of the Trade Union and Labour Relations (Consolidation) Act 1992, which provides that although a union is not a body corporate and is not to be treated as if it were a body corporate[24], it is capable of making contracts and of suing or being sued in its own name (in any cause of action), and furthermore that criminal proceedings may be brought against the union itself. All property belonging to the union must be vested in trustees[25] in trust for the union and that property may be attached for the satisfaction of any judgment, order or award in the same way as if the union were a body corporate. This vesting in trustees was important during the miners' strike of 1984/85, for when fines imposed on the National Union of Mineworkers for contempt of court were not paid and sequestration was ordered, an application was successfully made to the court to have the union's trustees removed and a receiver appointed in their place, who thus gained control of the union's property[26]. These steps were taken under the general law (though applying it to hitherto unchartered territory), but the position is now covered by statute[27].

Section 11 of the 1992 Act contains a provision which historically was of great significance when it was enacted[28], for it removed from unions the threat of being found to be illegal (directly or indirectly) on the basis of constituting a restraint

---

21 [1901] AC 426. Not all doubts were cleared away by the case; eg it was not established until the decision of the House of Lords in *Bonsor v Musicians' Union* [1956] AC 104, [1955] 3 All ER 518, HL, that a member could be awarded damages against the union.

22 Trade Disputes Act 1906, s 4.

23 S 15(1), repealing the Trade Union and Labour Relations Act 1974, s 14; see p 818 below.

24 On a literal interpretation of s 10 it has been held that a union cannot sue for libel in its own name, as it lacks sufficient legal personality: *EETPU v Times Newspapers Ltd* [1980] QB 585, [1980] 1 All ER 1097. This formulation also gives rise to the argument that the doctrine of ultra vires should not now apply to trade unions: Wedderburn (1985) 14 ILJ 127, commenting on the case of *Taylor v NUM (Derbyshire Area)* [1985] IRLR 99, in which the doctrine was applied; Clayton and Tomlinson 'Vicarious liability and trade unions' [1985] NLJ 361.

25 Trade Union and Labour Relations (Consolidation) Act 1992, s 12(1). S 129 applies similar provisions to an unincorporated employers' association.

26 *Clarke v Heathfield* [1985] ICR 203, CA; the action showed that the concentration of property-holding power in the hands of the trustees gave the union a vulnerability of which the Emperor Caligula would have been envious ('Would that the Roman people had but one neck').

27 See p 725 below.

28 Trade Union Act 1871, ss 2 and 3; s 128 of the 1992 Act gives similar protection to the purposes and rules of an unincorporated employers' association. For an example of the application of this section, see *Goring v British Actors Equity Association* [1987] IRLR 122, Ch D.

of trade. This provision states that the purposes of a trade union are not, by reason only that they are in restraint of trade, to be regarded as unlawful so as (a) to make any union member liable to criminal proceedings for conspiracy[29] or otherwise, or (b) to make any agreement or trust void or voidable. This protection also extends to the union's rules, which are not to be regarded as unlawful or unenforceable by reason only that they are in restraint of trade. The protection was extended to union rules as a direct result of certain views expressed in *Edwards v SOGAT*[30], where the Court of Appeal asserted a jurisdiction to supervise the content of union rules, not just to secure their proper enforcement. Sachs LJ based this power on the doctrine of restraint of trade, arguing that if a rule was capricious and oppressive it might not be made pursuant to the proper purposes of the union and so not be validated by the predecessor to section 11[31]. This view is no longer tenable in the light of the extended wording, though it should be noted that that does not necessarily mean the end of the possible legal development contained in *Edwards v SOGAT*, for Lord Denning MR's approach in that case was wider, being based on general public policy and a 'right to work', not tied to restraint of trade; if this approach is correct (which is respectfully doubted), it is not nullified by section 11.

Legal liabilities of unions markedly increased during the 1980s. As already stated, the general tort immunity was removed in 1982, with special statutory rules on when a union is to be liable for the acts of its officers and members (substantially modified in 1990), and statutory maximum amounts of damages recoverable; these matters are considered in chapter 11, below. Also, a union may now be made a party to unfair dismissal proceedings (either at the suit of the employee applicant or the employer respondent) where it is alleged that it put pressure on the employer to dismiss the employee because of non-membership, and may be ordered to pay some or all of the compensation (see p 688 below).

3 FREEDOM OF ASSOCIATION[32]

Trade unions can only exist where individuals are free to combine together in associations. This freedom to associate was granted in Britain as long ago as 1824 with the repeal of the Combination Acts[33], which had made it unlawful for workers to combine together in trade unions. At common law, therefore, individuals were free to form and join trade unions[34]. However, the common law did not grant positive *rights* of association, enforceable against others, so that at common law there was no protection against discriminatory action by an employer on grounds

---

29   Possible liability for conspiracy on more general grounds (where the object of the conspiracy is not itself unlawful) is excluded in the criminal context by the Criminal Law Act 1977, s 1(1) and in the tortious context by s 219 of the 1992 Act.

30   [1971] Ch 354, [1970] 3 All ER 689, CA; see head 4 below.

31   In spite of the rejection of this argument by the House of Lords in *Faramus v Film Artistes' Association* [1964] AC 925, [1964] 1 All ER 25, HL. For an interesting illustration of the effect of the restraint of trade doctrine in a case where s 11 did not apply, see *Boddington v Lawton* [1994] ICR 478, Ch D.

32   See, generally, Von Prondzynski *Freedom of Association and Industrial Relations* (1987); Wedderburn 'Freedom of association and philosophies of labour law' (1989) 18 ILJ 1.

33   Combination Laws Repeal Act 1824. Repeal of the legal restrictions on union activities did not come until much later – see ch 11.

34   With the exception of the police (Police Act 1996, s 64) and those working in the intelligence services, who are restricted from joining trade unions by contract.

of union membership, whether in the form of a refusal to hire, dismissal or some other action aimed at discouraging union membership or participation in union activities; neither did the common law give any enforceable right *not* to associate to non-union members seeking to work in a closed shop; and, with one possible exception[35], there was no common law right to insist on being admitted to a trade union of one's choice: admission to a union presupposed the willingness of that union to admit the applicant into membership. As Lord Diplock put it in *Cheall v APEX*[36] :

'My Lords, freedom of association can only be mutual; there can be no right of an individual to associate with other individuals who are not willing to associate with him ...'

Such positive rights to associate as there are in English law have been granted by statute, not in the form of a broad and general right to associate, but instead through the enactment of a complex set of measures (now contained in Part III of the Trade Union and Labour Relations (Consolidation) Act 1992), giving specific protection to those who are refused employment, discriminated against or dismissed for union reasons, and controlling admission to and expulsion from trade unions. The approach in English law has therefore been to build a collective right to associate 'out of the bricks of certain individual employment rights'[37]. These rights exist against the backdrop of an array of international treaties and conventions guaranteeing the principle of freedom of association (albeit in varying degrees), including Article 11 of the European Convention on Human Rights and Fundamental Freedoms, Article 5 of the European Social Charter, and ILO Conventions No 87 (on Freedom of Association and Protection of the Right to Organise) and No 98 (on the Right to Organise and Bargain Collectively)[38]. For many years there has been a lively debate over the extent to which the UK law on freedom of association complies with these international standards, fuelled by a number of cases in which the fragility of the right to associate has been graphically demonstrated, for example, the ban in 1984 on union membership at the government Communications Headquarters (GCHQ), on grounds of national security[39]. The debate took on an entirely new dimension in the UK as a result of the 'bringing home' to English law of the European Convention on Human Rights[40], Article 11 of which states:

'(1) Everyone has the right to freedom of peaceful assembly and to freedom of association with others, including the right to form and to join trade unions for the protection of his interests.

35 Lord Denning's 'right to work' principle: see p 710 below.
36 [1983] ICR 398, [1983] IRLR 215, HL.
37 Wedderburn (1976) 39 MLR 168.
38 See generally Ewing *Britain and the ILO* (2nd edn, 1994); Morris 'Freedom of Association and the Interests of the State' in Ewing, Gearty and Hepple (eds) *Human Rights and Labour Law: Essays for Paul O'Higgins* (1994).
39 *Council of Civil Service Unions v Minister for the Civil Service* [1985] ICR 14, [1985] IRLR 28, HL. See Morris [1985] PL 177. The ban was eventually lifted by the new Labour government in 1998.
40 See Ewing (ed) *Human Rights at Work* (2000); O'Dempsey et al *Employment Law and the Human Rights Act 1998* (2001); Hepple 'The Impact on Labour Law' in Markesinis (ed) *The Impact of the Human Rights Bill on English Law* (1998); Ewing 'The Human Rights Act and Labour Law' (1998) 27 ILJ 275; Palmer 'Human Rights: Implications for Labour Law' (2000) 59 CLJ 168. See p 42 above.

(2) No restrictions shall be placed on the exercise of these rights other than such as are prescribed by law and are necessary in a democratic society in the interests of national security or public safety, for the prevention of disorder or crime, for the protection of health or morals or for the protection of the rights and freedoms of others ...'

Until recently, the judgments of the European Court of Human Rights (and of the now defunct European Commission[41]) under Article 11 had given little cause for optimism that the incorporation of the Convention would lead to a strengthening of the right to associate[42]; indeed, individuals seeking to assert a right *not* to associate had had greater success under Article 11 than had trade unions and their members[43], hence Ewing's comment in 1998 that 'the contribution of Article 11 to date has been disappointing, failing to deliver any meaningful protection for trade union activities, while being used as an instrument for undermining trade union security'[44]. That gloomy assessment must now be reconsidered in the light of the landmark decision of the European Court of Human Rights in *Wilson and National Union of Journalists; Palmer, Wyeth and National Union of Rail, Maritime and Transport Workers v United Kingdom*[45], which has transformed the whole area and has necessitated a fundamental reappraisal of the protection of the right to associate under UK law.

The facts of the two cases were very similar; in both, the employers had offered a substantial pay increase to those employees who agreed to give up their right to have their terms and conditions negotiated through collective bargaining and sign individual contracts instead. Those who did not sign the new contracts did not get the pay increase. The main difference between the two was that in *Palmer*, the employees who refused to sign personal contracts had the option of continuing to be represented by their union, whereas in *Wilson* the employers had terminated the collective agreement and derecognised the union. The applicants complained that the withholding of pay increases from those who refused to sign individual contracts requiring them to forego the right to be represented by a union constituted a breach of their statutory right not to have 'action short of dismissal' taken against them for trade union reasons[46]. The House of Lords[47] ruled against the applicants on the grounds, first, that the statutory protection only applied to 'action', and that as the employers' failure to extend the pay increases to those who refused to sign individual contracts was technically an omission, it did not constitute 'action' within the meaning of the section[48]; and secondly, that the statutory protection only applied to action taken for the purpose of preventing or deterring union membership, and that on the facts there was no evidence that the employer's ultimate purpose was to deter union membership[49]. After the 1997 election, the new Labour government acted to

---

41   The Commission determined the admissibility of applications to the court until the procedures were streamlined by the 11th Protocol in 1998.
42   See eg *Council of Civil Service Unions v United Kingdom* (1987) 10 EHRR 269, EComHR.
43   *Young, James and Webster v United Kingdom* [1981] IRLR 408, ECtHR.
44   Ewing *Britain and the ILO* (2nd edn, 1994) p 279.
45   [2002] IRLR 568, ECtHR (hereinafter referred to as *Wilson and Palmer*).
46   Then contained in the Employment Protection (Consolidation) Act 1978, s 23; see now the Trade Union and Labour Relations (Consolidation) Act 1992, s 146, discussed below at p 676.
47   [1995] ICR 406, [1995] IRLR 258, HL.
48   See p 676 below.
49   See p 678 below.

overturn the first ground of the decision[50], but in all other respects the law remained as before[51]. Meanwhile, the applicants took their complaint to the European Court of Human Rights, which ruled in *Wilson and Palmer*[52] that UK law was in violation of Article 11 of the European Convention on Human Rights. In its decision, the Court stressed that the members of a trade union 'have a right, in order to protect their interests, that the trade union should be heard.[53]' According to the Court, 'it is of the essence of the right to join a trade union ... that employees should be free to instruct or permit the union to make representations to their employer or to take action in support of their interests on their behalf', and that 'it is the role of the State to ensure that trade union members are not prevented or restrained from using their union to represent them in attempts to regulate their relations with their employers.[54]' The Court considered that the UK had failed this test, because UK law had 'permitted employers to treat less favourably employees who were not prepared to renounce a freedom that was an essential feature of union membership[55]'. Furthermore, under UK law at the relevant time ' it was ... possible for an employer effectively to undermine or frustrate a trade union's ability to strive for the protection of its members' interests.[56]' The Court concluded that 'by permitting employers to use financial incentives to induce employees to surrender important union rights, the respondent State failed in its positive obligation to secure the enjoyment of the rights under Article 11 of the Convention.[57]'

As will be seen in the remainder of this chapter, the decision in *Wilson and Palmer* will necessitate some major changes to the UK law on freedom of association[58]. At the time of writing, the government had announced a series of proposed amendments to the 1992 Act[59], but it was unclear whether they satisfied all aspects of the European Court's decision. One issue in particular over which UK law may be vulnerable to further challenge is the way in which, as seen above, the *collective* right to associate is protected under UK law by a means of a series of *individual* rights. In *Wilson and Palmer*, the European Court held that the UK was in violation of Article 11 'as regards both the applicant unions and the individual applicants[60]', the clear implication being that 'trade unions have freedom of association rights in addition to and separate from the rights of their members'.[61] However, this begs the obvious question: what exactly do these collective rights

---

50 Employment Relations Act 1999, s 2, extending the statutory protection to omissions; see p 677 below. See Ewing 'Freedom of Association and the Employment Relations Act 1999' (1999) 28 ILJ 283.

51 Including the notorious 'Ullswater Amendment' (s 148(3) of the 1992 Act), which had been introduced by the previous government in 1993 to reverse the effect of the Court of Appeal decision in *Wilson and Palmer*, which had been in the employees' favour: see p 679 below.

52 See n 45 above.

53 *Wilson and Palmer* at para 42.

54 *Wilson and Palmer* at para 46.

55 *Wilson and Palmer* at para 47.

56 *Wilson and Palmer* at para 48.

57 *Wilson and Palmer* at para 48.

58 Including the law regulating internal trade union affairs (see p 713) and, arguably, the law on industrial action (see p 746).

59 DTI *Review of the Employment Relations Act 1999* (2003) paras 3.3–3.17.

60 See *Wilson and Palmer* at para 48. According to the court, a trade union 'must . . . be free to strive for the protection of its members interests': para 42

61 Ewing 'The Implications of *Wilson and Palmer*' (2003) 32 ILJ 1.

amount to, and how, if at all, can a union enforce them[62]? The Court stated that a union must be 'free to strive for the protection of its members' interests[63]', and free, 'in one way or another, to seek to persuade the employer to listen to what it has to say on behalf of its members[64]', but crucially the Court reasserted its consistently held view that the freedom of a union to make its voice heard does not extend to an obligation on an employer to recognise a union[65], and that contracting states 'enjoy a wide margin of appreciation as to how trade union freedom may be secured.[66]' The Court pointed instead to 'other measures' available to unions to further their members' interests, and in particular the protection conferred by domestic law on a trade union organising strike action[67]. In view of the inherently unreliable nature of that protection under UK law, based as it is on a set of legal immunities that are far from watertight, it seems reasonable to conclude that Article 11, as interpreted and applied by the European Court of Human Rights in *Wilson and Palmer*, offers more by way of protection to individuals than it does to trade unions[68]. Plus ça change . . .

The approach taken in this section will be, first, to examine the legal protection enjoyed by union members against dismissal or other discrimination by employers on the grounds of their union membership or activities, including the right not to be refused employment on grounds of trade union membership; secondly, to examine the circumstances where union officials and members may claim time off work for their trade union duties and activities; and, finally, to consider the legal protection of the right to dissociate, with particular reference to the closed shop. The controversial controls on union admissions and expulsions are considered below under head 5, in the context of the other statutory controls on internal union affairs.

(i) The right to associate

(a) Refusal of employment on grounds of union membership

Union members have for many years enjoyed protection within employment against dismissal and discriminatory action short of dismissal (for example demotion, blocking promotion, etc) for union reasons. However, until 1990 the law offered no redress to a union member who was refused employment on those

---

62   Ewing observes ((2003) 32 ILJ 1 at p 12) that this dimension of the case 'exposes an important omission in British labour law . . . namely that the rights of trade union membership are rights which vest only in the individual and not also in the union', and suggests that a new right enforceable by a trade union (possibly via the device of an 'unfair labour practice') may have to be created in order to secure trade union rights under Art 11.

63   *Wilson and Palmer* at para 42.

64   *Wilson and Palmer* at para 44.

65   'Although collective bargaining may be one of the ways by which trade unions may be enabled to protect their members' interests, it is not indispensable for the effective enjoyment of trade union freedom': *Wilson and Palmer* para 44.

66   *Wilson and Palmer* at para 44. 'Article 11 does not . . . secure any particular treatment of trade unions or their members and leaves each state a free choice of the means to be used to secure the right to be heard': para 42.

67   *Wilson and Palmer* at para 45. See p 761 below.

68   Although note the extent to which the Strasbourg Court in *Wilson and Palmer* drew on the broader, more pro-union European Social Charter and ILO Convention Nos 87 and 98 in interpreting Art 11.

grounds. That omission was rectified (at least in part) by the Employment Act 1990[69], which made it unlawful to refuse a person employment on grounds related to union membership[70]. It is generally accepted that the Conservative government's primary aim in introducing these measures was to attack the practice of the pre-entry closed shop, not to provide additional protection for union members (indeed, the Green Paper in which the proposals originally saw the light of day made no mention of extra protection for union members)[71], but in the event the protection was extended to union members and non-members alike. 'Refusal of employment' is defined very widely[72], and includes a refusal or 'deliberate omission' to entertain and process an application or to offer employment to the applicant (simple oversight will not be enough), causing the applicant to withdraw or cease to pursue his application, and making an offer of employment 'the terms of which are such as no reasonable employer who wished to fill the post would offer, and which is not accepted'. It will normally be for the applicant to prove that the refusal of employment was on grounds related to union membership and not for some other reason (for example inferior qualifications or experience), but in certain specific circumstances a refusal of employment will be deemed to be unlawful; in particular, where a job advertisement is published which indicates (or might reasonably be understood as indicating) that a particular job is only open to union members or to non-union members, a person who does not satisfy that requirement and who applies unsuccessfully for that job will be conclusively presumed to have been refused employment unlawfully, whatever the employer's reason for not appointing[73].

There is an important limitation on the protection afforded by this right, in that it only covers refusal of employment on grounds of union *membership*; it does not expressly cover an applicant who is refused employment because of his or her past union *activities*. It therefore compares unfavourably with the protection against discrimination within employment, where dismissal and detriment for taking part in union activities is specifically prohibited[74]. If membership of a union means no more than the mere possession of a union membership card, the statutory protection against refusal of employment on grounds of union membership would be narrow indeed. Significantly, however, in *Harrison v Kent County Council*[75], the first reported case on the new provisions, the EAT refused to draw a rigid distinction between membership of a trade union and taking part in union activities, holding that if a person was refused employment because he was a trade union activist or because of his union activities, it was open to a tribunal to conclude that he was refused employment because he was a member of a union. This broad, purposive interpretation of section 137 mirrors the approach taken

---

69 Employment Act 1990, s 1. The measures are now contained in the Trade Union and Labour Relations (Consolidation) Act 1992, s 137.
70 This includes a situation where a person is refused employment because he is unwilling to accept a requirement not to join or to cease to be a union member: s 137(1)(b).
71 *Removing Barriers to Employment* (Cm 655, 1989).
72 Trade Union and Labour Relations (Consolidation) Act 1992, s 137(5).
73 Trade Union and Labour Relations (Consolidation) Act 1992, s 137(3). A refusal of employment will also be deemed unlawful where it is in pursuance of a union-labour-supply arrangement and the applicant is not a member of the relevant union (s. 137(4)), and where the applicant rejects a job offer because he is unable or unwilling to accept or comply with conditions attached to it concerning union membership (s 137(6)).
74 See p 682ff, below.
75 [1995] ICR 434, EAT.

in an earlier case involving dismissal for union membership[76], where the EAT held that union membership must necessarily imply some degree of participation in union activities. In *Wilson and Palmer*[77] the House of Lords denied the existence of any general principle that a reference to union membership includes union activities , which seemed to place the correctness of the decision in *Harrison* in some doubt. However, in the wake of the European Court of Human Rights' decision in *Wilson and Palmer*, which made it plain that accessing the essential services of a union is intrinsic to exercising the right to belong to a union, the government acknowledged[78] that UK law would need to be changed so as to establish a clear positive right for members of independent unions to use their union's services. The precise extent of the proposed new right was uncertain at the time of writing, but it seems clear that the definition of 'membership' in section 137 will have to be amended to give individuals a right, within certain limits[79], not to be refused employment for accessing or using union services. Complaints of a breach of this right lie to an employment tribunal[80], which may make a declaration, order the employer to pay compensation (up to the limit of the compensatory award for unfair dismissal)[81] and/or recommend that the respondent take remedial action 'for the purpose of obviating or reducing the adverse effect on the complainant of any conduct to which the complaint relates'[82].

While the introduction in 1990 of the right not to be refused employment on grounds of union membership went some way towards plugging the gaps in the protection of the right to associate, it did not tackle the controversial practice of compiling 'blacklists' of union officials or members. The practice of blacklisting was well documented in the UK during the 1980s, when organisations such as the Economic League produced and sold blacklists to employers, and the failure of the UK government to prohibit the practice during that period was criticised on more than one occasion by the International Labour Organisation[83]. In recent years there has been no evidence of blacklisting activity, yet the government saw fit to enact section 3 of the Employment Relations Act 1999, which confers a power on the Secretary of State to make Regulations prohibiting the compilation, use, sale or supply of lists[84] which contain details of trade union members or persons

76 *Discount Tobacco and Confectionery Ltd v Armitage* [1995] ICR 431n, [1990] IRLR 15, EAT (a case involving dismissal for union membership under s 152; see p 681 below).

77 [1995] IRLR 258, HL. The case involved action short of dismissal under s 146. The House of Lords was prepared to accept that the decision in *Discount Tobacco* was correct on its facts. See also *Speciality Care plc v Pachela* [1996] IRLR 248, EAT, considered at p 681 below.

78 DTI *Review of the Employment Relations Act 1999* (2000) para 3.11.

79 The government has said it 'will ensure there is adequate protection for employers against excessive or inappropriate use of work time by workers when accessing union services.': *Review of the Employment Relations Act 1999* para 3.11.

80 Trade Union and Labour Relations (Consolidation) Act 1992, s 137(2). Complaints must be brought within three months of the conduct complained of, subject to the usual extension where not reasonably practicable: s 139(1).

81 At the time of writing, £53,500. Compensation is assessed on the same basis as an award of damages in tort for breach of statutory duty, and may include an amount for injury to feelings: s 140(2).

82 For the interpretation of this formula in the context of complaints of sex and race discrimination, see p 321, above. Failure to comply with such an order without reasonable justification may lead to an increased award of compensation, but still subject to the statutory maximum: s 140(3).

83 See eg ILO *287th Report of the Freedom of Association Committee* (1992) para 267.

84 'List' is defined widely to mean 'any index or other set of items whether recorded electronically or by any other means': Employment Relations Act 1999, s 3(5).

who have taken part in trade union activities, and which are compiled 'with a view to being used by employers or employment agencies for the purposes of discrimination in relation to recruitment or in relation to the treatment of workers'[85]. Enforcement of the anti-blacklisting provisions may be through the employment tribunals and EAT, with the possibility of criminal sanctions[86]. At the time of writing, the government had issued draft Regulations[87] on the prohibition of blacklists, modelled in part on the existing law governing dismissal and detriment on grounds of trade union membership and activities. The Regulations would make it unlawful to compile, use, sell or supply[88] a blacklist (referred to as a 'prohibited list') of trade union members or persons who have taken part in trade union activities, albeit with certain limited exceptions in the case of those who use a blacklist in order to expose its existence (for example investigative journalists), where there would be a public interest defence, and situations where significant trade union knowledge or experience is a necessary requirement of the job[89]. A person who suffers loss due to blacklisting would be entitled to seek damages from the county court, which (unlike an employment tribunal) could grant interim relief to prevent further damage from occurring. The Regulations would also make it unlawful for an employer to refuse a person employment, or to dismiss a worker or subject a worker to any detriment, because that person's name is, or is not, on a prohibited list. Complaint would lie to an employment tribunal, as under the existing provisions on refusal of employment, detriment and dismissal on trade union grounds.

It is by no means certain that the Prohibition of Blacklists Regulations will ever be brought into force. It seems that the government's intention is to leave the draft Regulations on the parliamentary shelf, ready for approval and implementation should there be evidence that blacklisting is returning to the UK[90], in order to 'minimise the risk of over-regulating'[91]. In truth, it is by no means obvious where the risk of over-regulation lies in this instance. The government's own Regulatory Impact Assessment acknowledges that 'many organisations will be completely unaffected by the Regulations because they would never consider using the services of a blacklister', and that in the majority of cases the work involved in checking to see that companies are complying with the legislation is 'likely to be minimal and will involve no more than an hour's work'[92]. It is tempting to draw the conclusion that the draft Regulations are merely an example of gesture politics, designed to mollify the trade union movement by appearing to respond to its historic concerns over blacklisting (possibly as a sop for not acceding to union pressure to make more far-reaching changes to other aspects of industrial relations law?) while in fact doing nothing of real legal significance.

---

85 Employment Relations Act 1999, s 3(1), (2).
86 Employment Relations Act 1999, s 3(3).
87 Draft Prohibition of Blacklists Regulations 2003.
88 The requirement in reg 3(4) for a person to sell or supply a prohibited list 'knowingly or recklessly' would clearly provide a defence for organisations such as the Royal Mail that distribute such lists unknowingly or accidentally.
89 Draft Prohibition of Blacklists Regulations, reg 3(5), (6).
90 'They will not be put before Parliament for approval or implemented until there is evidence that individuals or organisations are planning to draw up such lists, or if (sic) there is any evidence there is a demand from employers from them': DTI *Draft Regulations to Prohibit the Blacklisting of Trade Union Members - A Consultation Document* (2003), p 3.
91 See para 2(ii) of the DTI's Regulatory Impact Assessment.
92 DTI's Regulatory Impact Assessment, para 5(ii). The total cost of checks for all UK employers is estimated at a modest £305,000.

(b) Detriment short of dismissal on trade union grounds

Under section 146 of the Trade Union and Labour Relations (Consolidation) Act 1992[93], an employee has a right not to be subjected to any detriment as an individual by his employer, whether by an act or a deliberate failure to act, for the purpose of (a) preventing or deterring him from being or seeking to become a member of an independent trade union, or penalising him for doing so; (b) preventing or deterring him from taking part in the activities of an independent trade union at an appropriate time, or penalising him for doing so; or (c) compelling him to be or become a member of a trade union[94] Section 146 has been the subject of some exceptionally difficult and controversial case law, not least the landmark decision of the European Court of Human Rights in *Wilson and Palmer*[95] (discussed in the introduction to this Part), in which the Court ruled that UK law was in violation of Article 11 of the European Convention on Human Rights. The practical implications of the Court's ruling were still being considered by the government at the time of writing.

The first point to note about section 146 is that it now applies where an employee is 'subjected to any detriment' by the employer, whether by an act or a deliberate failure to act (ie an omission). Until 1999, the protection was stated to apply where an employer took '*action short of dismissal*' against an employee. It had long been thought to be established beyond doubt that 'action' in this context included an omission to act, such as a block on promotion or a refusal to extend a pay increase to the members of a particular union[96] (a view which appeared to be confirmed by the statute, which provides an extended definition of 'act' and 'action' as including an omission, 'unless the context otherwise requires'[97]). However, in *Associated Newspapers Ltd v Wilson; Associated British Ports v Palmer*[98], the House of Lords surprisingly held[99] that, for reasons of legislative history, the statutory definition of 'action' as including an omission did not apply in this context, and that as the conduct complained of (the employers' failure to extend pay increases to employees who refused to sign individual contracts) was an omission, it did not constitute 'action short of dismissal' on trade union grounds.

The effect of the House of Lords' decision (which has been described as 'a brilliant example of grammatical pedantry' and a 'singular triumph of the clever mind at the expense of the big picture'[100]) was to restrict the statutory protection

---

93 As amended by the Employment Relations Act 1999, s 2 and Sch 2. Note the analogous protection in Pt V of the Employment Rights Act 1996 for eg health and safety representatives and pension scheme trustees.

94 Before the Employment Act 1980 altered it, limb (c) was confined to action compelling the employee to join a *non-independent* trade union (such as the employer's 'house' union). The removal of this wording in 1980 altered its meaning completely, so that it now applies wherever there is managerial pressure to join any union; this aspect of s 146 is considered separately at p 695 below.

95 [2002] IRLR 568, ECtHR.

96 *National Coal Board v Ridgway* [1987] ICR 641, [1987] IRLR 80, CA. This was so even where the employer was under no obligation to do the act in question, as in *Ridgway*. See also *Carlson v Post Office* [1981] ICR 343, [1981] IRLR 158, EAT (refusal of a parking space).

97 Trade Union and Labour Relations (Consolidation) Act 1992, s 298; this definition was formerly located in the Employment Protection (Consolidation) Act 1978, s 153(1), with some minor differences in wording.

98 [1995] ICR 406, [1995] IRLR 258, HL, overruling the Court of Appeal in *National Coal Board v Ridgway*[1987] ICR 641, [1987] IRLR 80. See Simpson (1995) 24 ILJ 235.

99 By a 3:2 majority (reversing the Court of Appeal), Lord Keith and Lord Browne-Wilkinson agreeing with Lord Bridge on this point; Lord Lloyd and Lord Slynn dissented, preferring a more purposive interpretation of the provisions.

100 Ewing (1999) 28 ILJ 283 at p 287.

against victimisation on trade union grounds to positive acts, such as the imposition of a financial penalty. In view of the fact that the victimisation of union members is in practice very likely to involve the withholding of some benefit which is conferred on other employees, the effect of the decision was to render the statutory protection against action short of dismissal almost worthless. Indeed, Lord Browne-Wilkinson acknowledged that the conclusion 'leaves an undesirable lacuna in the legislation protecting employees against victimisation'[101]. The anomaly was subsequently corrected by the Employment Relations Act 1999, which amended section 146 so that it now applies where an employee is 'subjected to any detriment' by his employer, whether by an act or a deliberate failure to act (ie a deliberate omission).

Turning to the rest of section 146, to benefit from the statutory protection the employee must be subjected to a detriment 'as an individual', and the act or omission must take place 'for the purpose of' preventing or deterring union membership or participation in union activities, etc. The first of these requirements is designed to ensure that the protection cannot be used to claim what are essentially collective rights[102]. Action taken by the employer against a trade union (for example derecognition of the union, or the withdrawal of union facilities) may well have an indirect adverse effect on union members, but it is unlikely to constitute a detriment to them as individuals within the scope of the statutory protection unless it affects them personally, otherwise than merely as union members or officials (for example through their pay packets). A good example of action taken against a union which affected the members personally can be seen in *National Coal Board v Ridgway*[103], which arose in the aftermath of the 1984/85 miners' strike, and the breakaway of the Union of Democratic Mineworkers from the National Union of Mineworkers. A pay rise was negotiated with the UDM but rejected by the NUM, and at the colliery in question the rise was paid to UDM members but not to NUM members. The Court of Appeal held, inter alia[104], that this constituted action taken against the applicants (who were NUM members) as individuals, because the action against the union also affected them as individuals through their pay packets. It seems that derecognition of an individual shop steward (as opposed to derecognition of the union) can constitute action taken against that person as an individual, even though it may not directly affect him as an employee[105]. In the context of dismissal for union membership or activities, it has been held that the protection does not apply where action is taken by the employer in retaliation for activities by the union generally, unless those affected were singled out for attention because of their own trade union membership or activities[106]; it is unclear whether the same reasoning would be applied in a case involving detriment short of dismissal.

101 [1995] IRLR 258 at p 264.
102 As seen above at p 671, this may be an area where UK will have to change in order to comply with the ECtHR ruling in *Wilson and Palmer* (above, n 95), which confirmed that unions have a right to freedom of association separate from their members.
103 *National Coal Board v Ridgway* [1987] ICR 641, [1987] IRLR 80, CA. See also *Cheall v Vauxhall Motors Ltd* [1979] IRLR 253, where the employer's refusal to allow union representation in disciplinary proceedings was held to be action taken against individual employees. Although *Ridgway* was overruled by the House of Lords in *Associated Newspapers Ltd v Wilson; Associated British Ports v Palmer* (above, n 98) on other grounds, the reasoning of the Court of Appeal on this point still appears to be valid.
104 The other grounds of decision are discussed below at p 680.
105 *F W Farnsworth Ltd v McCoid* [1999] ICR 1047, CA, upholding the EAT decision on this point: [1998] IRLR 362.
106 *Carrington v Therm-A-Stor Ltd* [1983] ICR 208, [1983] IRLR 78, CA; the decision has been heavily criticised, and rightly so.

Once an employee has established that he was subjected to some detriment short of dismissal 'as an individual', it then falls to the employer to show the 'purpose' for which he acted or failed to act[107]. The courts have tended to take a narrow approach to this issue, and have refused to equate the employer's *purpose* with the *effect* of the action complained of. In *Gallacher v Department of Transport*[108], the employee, a civil servant who for several years had spent most of his time on trade union duties, was advised by his career development officer that in order to gain promotion he would need to acquire greater line management experience, which would necessitate a sharp reduction in his union activities. The tribunal held that this recommendation was intended to deter him from continuing with his union activities, and that the employers had therefore taken action short of dismissal against him for the purpose of deterring him from taking part in trade union activities. However, the Court of Appeal, upholding the EAT, held that the tribunal had misconstrued the meaning of the word 'purpose', by failing to distinguish between purpose and effect. According to Neill LJ, in this context the phrase 'for the purpose of' 'connotes an object which the employer desires or seeks to achieve'; on the facts, the employers' purpose was to ensure that only those with sufficient management experience were promoted, not to deter the employee from continuing with his union activities.

The same distinction was also drawn in *Associated Newspapers Ltd v Wilson*; *Associated British Ports v Palmer*[109], where one of the main issues was whether the purpose of the employers' actions in offering a pay rise only to those employees who agreed to sign personal contracts was to deter employees from continuing to be union members or to penalise them for doing so, or was instead to achieve a smooth transition from collective bargaining to individual contracting, and to achieve greater flexibility. The House of Lords held (reversing the Court of Appeal on this point[110]) that as the employers' purpose in *Wilson* was to smooth the transition from collective bargaining to individual contracting, and in *Palmer* to achieve greater flexibility, there was no unlawful purpose within the meaning of section 146. According to Lord Slynn, there was no evidence '... that the employers' purpose in paying a salary differential was to prevent or deter union membership, even if derecognition in itself might make the union less attractive to members or to potential members'[111]. This part of the House of Lords' decision was unaffected by the redrafting of section 146 in 1999 to include deliberate omissions, but their Lordships' reasoning has since been undermined by the decision of the European Court of Human Rights in *Wilson and Palmer*[112] that the law should not allow employers to offer financial inducements to workers on condition that they surrender their rights to union representation, or make it a

107 Trade Union and Labour Relations (Consolidation) Act 1992, s 148(1).
108 [1994] IRLR 231, CA.
109 [1995] ICR 406, [1995] IRLR 258, HL.
110 The Court of Appeal had held in *Wilson* that the purpose of the employers' actions in offering a 'douceur' (per Dillon LJ) to those who accepted personal contracts while withholding it from those who were not prepared to do so, was to persuade the employees to give up their right to union representation, and that this constituted action short of dismissal which deterred them from being union members and penalised them for their union membership if they refused to agree to the new arrangements: [1994] ICR 97, [1993] IRLR 336, CA (the appeal was heard together with the appeal in *Palmer*, which was also reversed).
111 Above, n 109 at 265. See also Lord Lloyd, at 266, on the importance of distinguishing between the *purposes* and the *consequences* of derecognition.
112 [2002] IRLR 568, ECtHR.

condition of entering individualised contracts that workers must relinquish those rights. At the time of writing, the government had accepted the need to amend UK law to specify that the entering of individualised contracts would not constitute unlawful union discrimination against those union members not offered them, 'as long as there was no inducement to relinquish union representation and no pre-condition in the contracts to relinquish it'.[113]

Potentially, one way in which the UK government might have sought to implement the *Wilson and Palmer* decision would have been to utilise section 17 of the Employment Relations Act 1999, which gives the Secretary of State a power to make Regulations about cases where a worker is subjected to a detriment by his employer or dismissed 'on the grounds that he refuses to enter into a contract which includes terms which differ from the terms of a collective agreement which applies to him'[114]. However, on closer examination it is clear that the regulation-making power in section 17 is not wide enough to achieve the desired effect, first, because it only covers one type of situation (detriment for refusing to enter a contract), and secondly, because it is expressly provided in section 17(4) that certain forms of conduct (including the payment of higher wages to other workers employed by the same employer) will *not* constitute a detriment so long as the workers receiving those enhanced payments or benefits are not contractually inhibited from being trade union members[115]. At the time of writing, the government had indicated that in the light of other changes which it proposes to make in order to comply with *Wilson and Palmer*, section 17 serves no obvious purpose and is therefore to be repealed.

There is one further change to the provisions on detriment short of dismissal which will be necessary in order to comply with the *Wilson and Palmer* decision – the repeal of the notorious 'Ullswater Amendment'. As seen above[116], the Court of Appeal in *Wilson and Palmer* had held that the employers *were* acting for an unlawful purpose, a decision which was widely seen at the time as threatening the trend towards individual contracting by preventing employers from offering a sweetener to those agreeing to give up collective bargaining. The Conservative government responded by rushing through an eleventh-hour amendment[117] to section 148 via the Trade Union Reform and Employment Rights Bill (then at Third Reading stage in the House of Lords) seeking to reverse the effect of the Court of Appeal's ruling[118]. By virtue of the Ullswater Amendment, a new section 148(3) was inserted into the 1992 Act which made it lawful for an employer to discriminate against union members where the purpose of the discriminatory action 'was to further a change in his relationship with all or any class[119] of his

---

113 DTI *Review of the Employment Relations Act 1999* (2003) para 3.13,
114 At the time of writing no Regulations had been made under s 17. In Committee, the minister suggested that a worker could be regarded as having been subjected to a detriment for refusing to give up the terms of a collective agreement where there was a block on promotion, the withholding of discretionary benefits or the allocation to less favourable duties or locations (*Hansard*, Standing Committee E, 18 March 1999, col 478).
115 Employment Relations Act 1999, s 17(4) (the subsection was an eleventh-hour Opposition amendment in the House of Lords).
116 At n 110 above.
117 Commonly referred to as the 'Ullswater Amendment' after the Peer who tabled it.
118 Trade Union Reform and Employment Rights Act 1993, s 13, inserting new ss (3)–(5) into the Trade Union and Labour Relations (Consolidation) Act 1992, s 148.
119 Defined as 'those employed at a particular place of work, those employees of a particular grade, category or description or those of a particular grade, category or description employed at a particular place of work': Trade Union and Labour Relations (Consolidation) Act 1992, s 148(5).

employees'[120] (for example to bring about derecognition of a union, or to restrict the coverage of collective bargaining or union representation rights). This amendment, heavily criticised upon its introduction for undermining the protection afforded to union members against attempts by employers to discourage union membership[121], was surprisingly left untouched by the Employment Relations Act 1999. At the time of writing, the government had conceded that in the light of the European Court of Human Rights' judgment in *Wilson and Palmer*, the Ullswater Amendment 'is no longer sustainable' because 'it enabled employers to induce union members to forego union representation, thereby interfering in the relationship between members and their union'[122], and had proposed the repeal of the Amendment.

Moving on to slightly firmer ground, as seen earlier, the statutory protection of union members arises where an employee is subjected to any detriment for the purpose of (a) preventing or deterring him from being or seeking to become a union member, or (b) preventing or deterring him from taking part in union activities, or penalising him for doing so. Under the first limb (preventing or deterring union membership), two particular issues have been especially problematic: the first concerns the possible application of section 146 to cases of inter-union rivalry, such as in *National Coal Board v Ridgway*[123]. As seen above[124], in that case a pay rise was paid by the employer to members of the UDM but not to those of the NUM, because the NUM had rejected a pay deal negotiated between the employer and the rival UDM. Two of the NUM members complained that this constituted a breach of section 146 because they were in effect being penalised for being members of the NUM rather than the UDM. The EAT ruled against the applicants on the grounds, inter alia, that section 146 only outlawed action to prevent an employee being a member of *any* trade union, not to prevent membership of a *particular* union (a finding which appeared to gain support from the fact that whereas limbs (a) and (b) of section 146 refer to preventing or deterring membership or activities 'of an independent trade union', limb (c) specifically refers to compelling membership 'of any trade union or of a particular trade union or of one of a number of trade unions'). However, the Court of Appeal allowed the applicants' appeal and held, inter alia[125], that on its proper construction, the protection in the section applied to penalising membership of a particular union as well as membership of unions generally[126]. The court therefore accepted the potential application of section 146 to inter-union disputes which lead to differential treatment by the employer.

The second issue arising from limb (a) concerns the scope of the protection of union membership, and in particular whether the right to be a trade union member means anything more than simply having a right to possess a union

---

120 This is so even if there is also evidence that the employer's purpose was an unlawful one of preventing or deterring union membership within section 146, unless the tribunal considers that no reasonable employer would have taken such action having regard to that former purpose: s 148(3).

121 See eg ILO *294th Report of the Freedom of Association Committee* para 162.

122 DTI *Review of the Employment Relations Act 1999* (2003) para 3.9.

123 [1987] ICR 641, [1987] IRLR 80, CA; rvsg [1986] IRLR 379, EAT; see Simpson (1987) 50 MLR 639.

124 At p 677.

125 The other issue in the case was whether the action was taken against them 'as individuals' rather than against their union: see p 677 above.

126 Although *Ridgway* was subsequently overruled on other grounds (see n 103), the reasoning of the Court of Appeal on this point would appear still to be valid.

membership card. In *Discount Tobacco and Confectionery Ltd v Armitage*[127] (a case on the parallel provisions concerning dismissal for union membership), the EAT declined to draw a sharp distinction between union membership and making use of the essential services of a union[128]. In that case, the employee was dismissed after invoking the assistance of a union representative in a matter concerning her terms of employment. The EAT upheld the tribunal's finding that she had been dismissed by reason of her union membership, Knox J stating that: 'In our judgment, the activities of a trade union officer in negotiating and elucidating terms of employment is, to use a prayer book expression, the outward and visible manifestation of trade union membership. It is an incident of union membership which is, if not the primary one, at any rate a very important one and we see no genuine distinction between membership of a union, on the one hand, and making use of the essential services of a union, on the other.' However, in *Associated Newspapers Ltd v Wilson; Associated British Ports v Palmer*[129], the House of Lords held[130] that while the decision in *Discount Tobacco* might have been correct on its facts, it did not establish any general principle that membership of a union was to be equated with making use of the union's services. The statutory protection was intended to protect union membership as such, and in their Lordships' opinion there was no justification for reading in the words 'or making use of the essential services of the union', still less for regarding trade union membership and the use of trade union services as the same thing[131]. This narrow interpretation of 'membership' would have reduced the protection of union membership under limb (a) almost to vanishing point[132], as in practice employers are far more likely to be concerned about the consequences of union membership than they are about the mere fact of membership. In *Specialty Care plc v Pachela*[133], the EAT made a bold attempt to salvage something from the wreckage of the House of Lords' decision in *Wilson* and *Palmer* by distinguishing *Discount Tobacco* on the facts, and holding that it was still open to a tribunal to find that an employee dismissed for engaging the assistance of a union in a dispute with the employer over working hours was dismissed on grounds of union membership[134]. In the light of the European Court of Human Rights' decision in *Wilson and Palmer*, it is clear that the broader interpretation of 'membership' is to be preferred, as the Court made

127 [1995] ICR 431n, [1990] IRLR 15, EAT.
128 *Discount Tobacco* was followed in *Harrison v Kent County Council* [1995] ICR 434, where the EAT held that it was open to a tribunal to conclude that a person who was refused employment because he was a trade union activist or because of his union activities was refused employment because he was a member of a union within the meaning of s 137(1); see p 673 above.
129 Above, n 109.
130 The comments of the House of Lords on this point were strictly speaking obiter, as the main ground of the decision was that the statutory protection only applies to actions, not to omissions.
131 See Lord Bridge at 264; Lord Lloyd at 266. Cf Lord Slynn at 265, taking a somewhat broader view.
132 Per Knox J in *Discount Tobacco and Confectionery Ltd v Armitage* [1995] ICR 431n, [1990] IRLR 15 at 16.
133 [1996] IRLR 248.
134 According to the EAT, in such a complaint the tribunal must find as a fact: '... whether or not the principal reason for dismissal related to the applicant's trade union membership not only by reference to whether he or she had simply joined a union, but also by reference to whether the introduction of union membership into the employment relationship had led the employer to dismiss the employee. Tribunals should answer that question robustly, based on their findings as to what really caused the dismissal in the mind of the employer.'

it plain that accessing the essential services of a union is intrinsic to exercising the Article 11 right to belong to a union, and at the time of writing the government had indicated its intention to change the law so as to confer on members of independent unions a clear positive right to use their union's services[135].

Turning to limb (b) (preventing or deterring union activities), it is clear that to be protected, the activities in question must be those of a trade union, in the sense of having a genuine trade union connection rather than just being the type of activity which one might expect a union to engage in. Thus, protected activities would include taking part in union meetings[136], consulting a shop steward or union official[137] and attempting to recruit new members or form a workplace union group[138] (particularly if the employee concerned is himself a shop steward or union officer). However, it would not include actions on an individual basis without any union involvement, as in *Chant v Aquaboats Ltd*[139] where the EAT held that the applicant's actions, in personally complaining about woodworking machinery which did not comply with safety standards and organising a petition of other employees to support the claim, did not qualify as trade union activities and so were not protected[140].

The section only protects activities which take place during the employment in question, not to previous activities in other employments, so that if the employer takes action against an individual (for example by transferring him to a non-sensitive area) on finding out about his record of union activity in a previous employment, that person may not complain under section 146. So, for example, in *City of Birmingham District Council v Beyer*[141], a case on the analogous provisions concerning dismissal for union activities, a well-known union activist gained employment with the council by using a false name, and was subsequently dismissed because of the deceit; the EAT held that the employee could not benefit from the statutory protection, because it did not extend to pre-employment activities. However, the protection does apply where action is taken to prevent or deter an employee from engaging in union activity within the current employment[142], and it may well be difficult for an employer in such a case to persuade the tribunal that he was entirely motivated by the employee's previous conduct and not by fears that it might be repeated in the present employment[143].

The principal limitation on limb (b), which attempts to hold a balance between the employee's rights and the employer's business interests, is that to be

---

135 DTI *Review of the Employment Relations Act 1999* (2000) para 3.11.
136 *Miller v Rafique* [1975] IRLR 70, IT; this may apply to attendance at a meeting which is critical of the union: *British Airways Engine Overhaul Ltd v Francis* [1981] ICR 278, [1981] IRLR 9, EAT.
137 *Marley Tile Co Ltd v Shaw* [1978] ICR 828, [1978] IRLR 238, EAT (rvsd on other grounds: [1980] ICR 72, [1980] IRLR 25, CA).
138 *Brennan v Ellward (Lancs) Ltd* [1976] IRLR 378, EAT; *Lyon and Scherk v St James Press Ltd* [1976] ICR 413, [1976] IRLR 215, EAT; *Dixon and Shaw v West Ella Developments Ltd* [1978] ICR 856, [1978] IRLR 151, EAT.
139 [1978] 3 All ER 102, [1978] ICR 643, EAT (an unfair dismissal case); *Gardner v Peeks Retail Ltd* [1975] IRLR 244, IT; *Drew v St Edmundsbury Borough Council* [1980] ICR 513, [1980] IRLR 459, EAT.
140 An employee raising health and safety concerns today may well be protected under the specific provisions concerning dismissal or other detriment for health and safety reasons in the Employment Rights Act 1996, ss 44 and 100: see p 595 above.
141 [1978] 1 All ER 910, [1977] IRLR 211, EAT. See Evans and Lewis 'Anti-union discrimination: practice, law and policy' (1987) 16 ILJ 88.
142 *Fitzpatrick v British Railways Board* [1992] ICR 221, [1991] IRLR 376, CA.
143 As seen above at p 673, a *refusal* of employment on grounds of previous union activity is unlikely to be covered by the Act (although the protection may need to be extended to comply with the ECtHR decision in *Wilson and Palmer*).

protected the union activities must take place at an 'appropriate time'. This is defined in section 146(2) as either outside the employee's working hours or during his working hours but with the agreement or consent of the employer. 'Working hours' are defined as time when the employee is contractually obliged to be at work, which has been construed as meaning when he is actually performing work, so that when an employee takes part in activities during a tea break or lunch break that will be an 'appropriate time', even if he is still on the premises and being paid by the employer during the break[144]. One potentially contentious area is whether the employer has in fact consented to an activity where it takes place during working hours. The case of *Robb v Leon Motor Services Ltd*[145] showed a fairly rigorous approach to the issue, in the employer's favour. The employee, a shop steward, was transferred to a department where he was no longer in contact with other employees (ie 'neutralised') because of his over-enthusiastic pursuit of union activities in working hours. The union was not recognised and there was no express agreement allowing union activities during working hours, but the employee's written statement of terms of employment stated that he would be permitted to take part in union activities 'at the appropriate time', though without defining it. The EAT dismissed the employee's claim under what is now section 146, holding that there was not the necessary agreement or consent to his union activities (the written term being too vague to be construed as such). In contrast, in *Bass Taverns Ltd v Burgess*[146], the employee, a pub manager who was also a shop steward of the National Association of Licensed House Managers, was regularly permitted by the company to make presentations on behalf of the union at induction courses for new employees. On one occasion he made some remarks which were highly critical of the company, and which led to his demotion; he resigned and claimed constructive dismissal, arguing that his dismissal was for taking part in union activities at an appropriate time, and was therefore automatically unfair under section 152. The Court of Appeal held that the employer's consent to his participation should not be considered as subject to an implied limitation that nothing critical of the company would be said, so that, despite his remarks, he was still taking part in trade union activities at an appropriate time, and his claim therefore succeeded.

It is, however, clear from other cases that consent does not have to be express (and also that recognition is not a prerequisite), though in practice an express agreement is more certain, and it may well be easier to imply consent from a course of conduct if the union is in fact recognised. This possibility of implied consent was accepted by the Court of Appeal in *Marley Tile Co Ltd v Shaw*[147], but the case also shows that consent will not be readily implied merely from the employer's silence (particularly on an ad hoc basis, where it is being argued that on one

---

144 *Post Office v UPOW* [1974] 1 All ER 229, [1974] ICR 378, HL; *Zucker v Astrid Jewels Ltd* [1978] ICR 1088, [1978] IRLR 385, EAT.

145 [1978] ICR 506, [1978] IRLR 26, EAT.

146 [1995] IRLR 596, CA. Cf the suggestion in the case that the activities might fall outside the protection of s 152 if the employee indulged in malicious, untruthful or irrelevant invective; see also *Shillito v Van Leer (UK) Ltd* [1997] IRLR 495, EAT (on the analogous provisions on victimisation for health and safety reasons).

147 [1980] ICR 72, [1980] IRLR 25, CA; *Zucker v Astrid Jewels Ltd* [1978] ICR 1088, [1978] IRLR 385, EAT. In *Marley's* case the Court of Appeal upheld the EAT on the possibility of implied consent, but reversed their decision on the facts, holding that no consent could be inferred in the circumstances.

particular occasion the employee proposed to do something during working hours and the employer did not strenuously object), and that implied consent is still not easy to establish where the union member is not accredited by the employer, or the union is not recognised. On the other hand, where the union presence is accepted by the employer it is possible that, even in the absence of express agreement, consent might be implied over a period of time on the basis of established workplace practice or good industrial relations practice. To this extent the onus is placed upon the employer, if he wishes to prevent extraneous activities during working hours (and so preserve his right to stop them), to state expressly that he does not agree or consent (either by notice or in contracts).

Three further points should be noticed on the question of appropriate time. The first is whether an employer can revoke his consent on any given occasion, especially if he has only given it indirectly, by implication; it is strongly arguable that the purpose of the section would be defeated if the employer was allowed to revoke on an ad hoc basis, though unfortunately the section does not contain provisions directly preventing it. Such revocation, if allowed, would certainly make the right in section 146(1)(b) highly uncertain and ultimately of little value. The second point is that if an activity is taking place at an appropriate time, the protection given to it by the section could be seen to presuppose some provision of material facilities by the employer (or, at least, no unreasonable withholding of them), if only to the extent of noticeboards or room for a meeting. However, once again the section is not specific on this question[148]. Finally, it seems clear that taking industrial action will rarely (if ever) constitute taking part in union activities at an appropriate time within the meaning of section 146, not least because it is unlikely to be an activity undertaken outside working hours or with the employer's consent; in *Brennan v Ellward (Lancs) Ltd*[149] Phillips J stated that the section: '... cannot extend to the activities of employees in suddenly downing tools and leaving the premises in order to consult their union officials elsewhere, and wherever they may happen to be.' The EAT has, however, held that the preliminary planning and organisation of industrial action can constitute taking part in union activities for the purposes of the protection against dismissal for union reasons[150].

An employee subjected to a detriment in contravention of section 146 may complain to a tribunal within three months of the act or failure to act (or within such further period as the tribunal thinks reasonable if it was not reasonably practicable for the complaint to be presented within three months)[151]. In such a complaint, the onus is upon the employer to show the purpose for which he acted or failed to act[152]. If the tribunal finds the complaint justified, it must make a

---

148 The statutory right to use the employer's premises for the purposes of a workplace ballot was repealed by the 1993 Act.

149 [1976] IRLR 378, EAT; see also *Drew v St Edmundsbury Borough Council* [1980] ICR 513, [1980] IRLR 459, EAT.

150 *Britool Ltd v Roberts* [1993] IRLR 481, EAT. See p 687 below.

151 Trade Union and Labour Relations (Consolidation) Act 1992, s 147. In *British Airways Board v Clark* [1982] IRLR 238 it was held by the EAT that where the disciplinary action complained of was only effective after exhaustion of the employer's disciplinary procedure (including an appeal), time only began to run (for computing the three-month period) from the date when the employee was finally informed of the failure of his appeal. Where the act or failure to act is part of a series of similar acts or failures, time runs from the last of them; where a single action has a continuing effect, time will run from the initial act: *Adlam v Salisbury and Wells Theological College* [1985] ICR 786, EAT.

152 Trade Union and Labour Relations (Consolidation) Act 1992, s 148(1).

declaration to that effect and may order such compensation as it thinks just and equitable[153]; the section states that the tribunal is to have regard to the infringement of the employee's rights under section 146 and to any loss sustained by the employee, in particular any expenses incurred by him and any loss of benefits which he might reasonably have expected but for the employer's act or failure to act. In *Brassington v Cauldon Wholesale Ltd*[154] the EAT held that, while the remedy is compensatory rather than penal, the tribunal is not restricted to the employee's pecuniary loss, and may award compensation over and above such pecuniary loss for any non-pecuniary injury such as stress and anxiety caused to the employee and deprivation of benefits which might have come from trade union membership; it is, however, for the employee to establish that he has suffered the type of injury for which he seeks compensation. Section 148(2) states that in determining a complaint the tribunal shall not take into account any pressure exerted upon the employer (by industrial action or the threat of it) by a union[155], which may mean that the employer is placed in a difficult position, particularly in the case of an inter-union dispute. However, if the pressure is exercised by the union in order to compel the employee to be or become a union member the union may be joined as a party to the action[156].

(c) Dismissal on trade union grounds[157]

In parallel with the previous provisions, section 152 of the Trade Union and Labour Relations (Consolidation) Act 1992 provides that a dismissal will be *automatically unfair* if the reason for it (or, if more than one, the principal reason) was that the employee (a) was, or proposed to become, a member of an independent trade union, or (b) had taken part, or proposed to take part, in the activities of an independent trade union at an appropriate time, or (c) was not a member of any trade union, or of a particular trade union, or of one of a number of particular trade unions, or had refused, or proposed to refuse, to become or remain a member. The section was subject to major amendment by the Employment Acts 1980, 1982 and 1988, and as it now stands it is a curious hybrid, for heads (a) and (b) are there to protect union members in their membership and activities, whereas head (c) serves the totally different purpose of protecting *non*-union members, and is therefore considered below in the context of the closed shop. A dismissal for redundancy will be deemed to be unfair under section 153 of the 1992 Act if it is shown that the circumstances producing the redundancy applied equally to other comparable employees in the same undertaking who were not dismissed[158], and the employee was selected for dismissal for any of the above reasons.

---

153 Trade Union and Labour Relations (Consolidation) Act 1992, s 149(2).
154 [1978] ICR 405, [1977] IRLR 479, EAT. In *Cleveland Ambulance NHS Trust v Blane* [1997] IRLR 332, the EAT confirmed that compensation for insult or injury to feelings may be awarded under this head.
155 A similar provision in the Employment Rights Act 1996, s 107 applies to unfair dismissal complaints; see p 566 above.
156 Trade Union and Labour Relations (Consolidation) Act 1992, s 150. Similar provisions apply in the case of dismissal for union reasons: see s 160. The joinder provisions are considered at p 688 below.
157 See *Harvey* N [5C].
158 In making the comparison with the position of other employees, anything that the employee did or had a right to do as a trade union official must be left out of account, lest the purpose of the section be defeated: *O'Dea v ISC Chemicals Ltd* [1995] IRLR 599, CA.

Apart from rendering a dismissal automatically unfair, the other significant difference (leaving aside for the moment the question of remedies, considered below) between a dismissal for union reasons and an ordinary unfair dismissal action is that the normal requirements as to the qualifying period of continuous employment and the restrictions on those who have reached retiring age do not apply in this context[159]. Establishing that a dismissal or a redundancy selection is on trade union grounds can give rise to considerable evidential problems, particularly where the employer claims that there was some other reason (for example misconduct) for the dismissal. As in other unfair dismissal cases, it will normally be for the employer to show what the reason for the dismissal was[160] ; however, where an employee lacks the necessary one year's continuous employment, the burden of proving that he was dismissed on trade union grounds (and can therefore bring his case) lies with him[161]. It is clear that an employer does not have to be motivated by malice or a deliberate desire to be rid of a trade union activist in order to fall foul of these provisions[162], and the EAT has emphasised that the scope of the factual enquiry into the reason for the dismissal should not be restricted[163].

The provisions in heads (a) and (b) are substantially the same as those in section 146 which protect the employee from detriment short of dismissal for trade union membership or activities, so that cases on the one section (for example on the meaning of 'activities of a trade union' and 'appropriate time') apply mutatis mutandis to the other. Two further points should be noted here. First, as in the case of detriment short of dismissal, the protection for those dismissed for taking part in union activities only applies to activities during the employment in question, and does not extend to an employee who is dismissed because of participation in union activities before the employment began[164]. However, in *Fitzpatrick v British Railways Board* [165], the Court of Appeal held that an employee with a reputation as a union activist in her previous employment who was dismissed not because of anything she had done in her present employment but because the employer feared that she might become a disruptive influence at some time in the future was still protected, because a dismissal will be unfair if the reason for it was that the employee was *proposing* to take part in trade union activities. Secondly, although one might be forgiven for thinking that participation in industrial action is a classic example of taking part in trade union activities, and therefore protected under section 152, the EAT has said, obiter, that taking part in industrial action does not count as taking part in the activities of a trade union

---

159 Trade Union and Labour Relations (Consolidation) Act 1992, s 154.
160 *Maund v Penwith District Council* [1984] ICR 143, [1994] IRLR 24, CA. The usual test applies, ie the reason for dismissal is the set of facts known to the employer or the set of beliefs held by him which causes him to dismiss; the 'but for' test which applies in sex and race discrimination cases does not apply in this context: *CGB Publishing v Killey* [1993] IRLR 520, EAT.
161 *Smith v Hayle Town Council* [1978] ICR 996, [1978] IRLR 413, CA; once he has done so, the burden of proof in the actual unfair dismissal hearing goes back to the employer: *Shannon v Michelin (Belfast) Ltd* [1981] IRLR 505, NICA.
162 *Dundon v GPT Ltd* [1995] IRLR 403, EAT.
163 See *Driver v Cleveland Structural Engineering Co Ltd* [1994] ICR 372, [1994] IRLR 636, EAT, where the employer's failure to select the applicant, a former shop steward, for alternative employment in a redundancy situation was held to be legally relevant in determining whether he was unfairly dismissed on account of his trade union activities under s 152.
164 *City of Birmingham District Council v Beyer* [1978] 1 All ER 910, [1977] IRLR 211, EAT (discussed at p 682 above).
165 [1991] IRLR 376, CA.

for present purposes, and that the two situations are mutually exclusive[166]. This was said to be because the legislation makes separate provision for those dismissed while taking part in industrial action[167], so that if an employee is dismissed while on strike, his complaint will be determined under the special rules which apply in such a case, and not under section 152. It is arguable that there are circumstances[168] where a tribunal might have to consider whether an employee dismissed during industrial action was dismissed for taking part in trade union activities within the meaning of section 152; however, the issue is of limited practical importance, because even if participation in industrial action could in principle constitute an activity of a trade union, it will rarely, if ever, be undertaken at an 'appropriate time', as it is unlikely to be an activity undertaken outside working hours or with the employer's consent[169]. Significantly, the EAT has held that participating in the preliminary planning and organisation of industrial action can amount to taking part in trade union activities within the meaning of section 152[170].

Turning to remedies, there are some significant differences between the remedies available in cases of dismissal for trade union reasons and in most other unfair dismissal cases. Where a dismissal is unfair by virtue of being for trade union reasons the amount of compensation is likely to be higher, because provision is made for a minimum basic award of £3,500 in such cases[171]. Until recently, an employee unfairly dismissed for trade union reasons was entitled to a 'special award' of compensation, on top of the normal basic and compensatory awards, where the employee requested the tribunal to make an order for reinstatement or re-engagement. The special award was however abolished by the Employment Relations Act 1999, and replaced by the additional award. Unlike the additional award, which can only be made where the employer fails to comply with an order of reinstatement or re-engagement, the special award was not conditional on the tribunal actually *making* such an order, and the amount of the special award was likely to be much higher than the additional award[172]. As in other unfair dismissal cases, compensation awarded in cases of dismissal for trade union reasons may be reduced where there is contributory fault, although it is specifically provided that failure on the part of the employee to comply with a requirement (whether

---

166 *Drew v St Edmundsbury Borough Council* [1980] ICR 513, [1980] IRLR 459, EAT.
167 Trade Union and Labour Relations (Consolidation) Act 1992, ss 237-238A; see p 751 below.
168 Eg where the employer has sacked or re-engaged some but not all of the strikers, and the dismissal is neither automatically unfair for taking protected industrial action, nor outside the jurisdiction of the tribunal because the industrial action is unofficial.
169 *Britool Ltd v Roberts* [1993] IRLR 481, EAT. One example of industrial action which could conceivably be held to be at an 'appropriate time' is a ban on voluntary (ie non-contractual) overtime.
170 *Britool Ltd v Roberts* [1993] IRLR 481, EAT.
171 Trade Union and Labour Relations (Consolidation) Act 1992, s 156. In common with most other statutory compensation limits, the minimum basic award is subject to indexation under the Employment Relations Act 1999, s 34. For the other special cases in which a minimum basic award will be made, see p 609.
172 At the time it was abolished, the amount of the special award where the tribunal did *not* order reinstatement or re-engagement was 104 weeks' pay (subject to a minimum of £14,500 and a maximum of £29,000); if such an order was made but not complied with, the special award was 152 weeks' pay (subject to a minimum of £21,800, but with no maximum). The maximum additional award is only £13,520: see p 606.

or not contractual) to join or not to join a union, or not to take part in union activities, is not to be regarded as 'fault' for these purposes[173].

The enhanced levels of compensation were originally introduced by the Employment Act 1982 as part of the attack on the closed shop[174] (the idea being to make an unfair dismissal because of a closed shop very expensive in order to have a deterrent effect), but the increased compensation was extended to *all* employees dismissed for union reasons, and not confined to those dismissed for *non-membership*. Clearly it was no part of the Conservative government's intention to put greater liabilities onto *employers* in closed shop cases, however much it wanted to improve the lot of those dismissed for refusing to become union members. The solution adopted[175] was to allow the employer or the dismissed employee to request the tribunal to join a trade union or other person as a party to the tribunal proceedings where it is claimed that (a) the employer was induced to dismiss the complainant by industrial pressure exercised by that third party (whether by strike or otherwise), and (b) that pressure was exercised because the complainant was not a union member[176]. Any award of compensation in those proceedings may then be made wholly or partly against the union or other person joined in the proceedings, as the tribunal considers just and equitable, instead of against the employer. Originally, the joinder provisions only allowed the *employer* to join the union, but the present position is that the *employee* can also join the union (as, in effect, a second defendant) and may be more likely to do so than the employer (who may be more inclined to pay up and hope to forget the whole matter). In practice today the joinder provisions are very rarely used, as complaints of dismissal for non-membership of a trade union are extremely uncommon.

Finally on remedies, sections 161–166 of the 1992 Act make special provision for 'interim relief' pending a hearing where an employee complains that he has been unfairly dismissed for trade union reasons[177]. The aim of interim relief is to secure the position of the employee pending the hearing by seeking to ensure that he remains in employment until the tribunal is able to hear the unfair dismissal complaint. An application for interim relief must be presented to a tribunal within seven days of the effective date of termination[178], and where the complaint is of dismissal for union membership or activities it must be backed by a certificate from an official of the union concerned[179] stating (a) that the applicant is a member of the union (or proposed to become one) and (b) that in

---

173 Trade Union and Labour Relations (Consolidation) Act 1992, s 155. In determining whether there has been contributory fault the tribunal is entitled to take into account the employee's conduct *leading up* to the dismissal, although clearly it must disregard the conduct which in fact led to the dismissal: *TGWU v Howard* [1992] ICR 106, [1992] IRLR 170, EAT.

174 See p 695 below.

175 See now the Trade Union and Labour Relations (Consolidation) Act 1992, s 160; similar provisions apply in the context of detriment short of dismissal: s 150.

176 Such a request must be granted if made before the hearing but thereafter the tribunal has a discretion to refuse it, save that no such request may be made after the tribunal has made a declaration that the complaint is well-founded: s 160(2).

177 Interim relief has subsequently been made available in certain other unfair dismissal complaints: see the Employment Rights Act 1996, s 128(1).

178 On which, see p 553 above.

179 The official must be authorised by the union to act for this purpose: s 161(4). If the authority of the official is challenged, it will be for the union to prove that the official was authorised to sign the certificate: *Sulemany v Habib Bank* [1983] ICR 60, EAT. For obvious reasons there is no requirement of a certificate where an application for interim relief is made in a case of dismissal for non-membership.

the official's opinion there are reasonable grounds for supposing that the dismissal was for union reasons. The tribunal must hear the application as soon as practicable, although the employer must be given at least seven days' notice of the hearing[180]. If the tribunal thinks it likely[181] that the employee's complaint will be upheld at the full hearing, it must ask the employer if he is willing to reinstate or re-engage the employee pending the hearing. If so, the tribunal will make an order to that effect; if not, the tribunal will make an order for the continuation of the employee's contract pending the full hearing[182]. This is an order that the contract shall continue until the hearing, but only for the stated purposes of pay or any other benefits, seniority, pension rights and other similar matters, and continuity of employment[183] ; the order must specify the amount to be paid, which will be the amount which the employee could reasonably have been expected to earn (had he not been dismissed) in the period between the date of the dismissal and the date of determination of the complaint[184]. Any payments received from the employer under the contract or by way of damages for breach of contract must be taken into account. The crucial point, however, is that other obligations under the contract, in particular the employee's duty to work, do not continue in force, which means that there is a very strong incentive for the employer to agree to re-employ the employee pending the hearing. If the employer fails to comply with the order, the applicant may complain to the tribunal which, in a case where the failure consists of non-payment of wages as specified in the order, will determine the amount owed under the order or, in the case of some other failure (for example failure to comply with an order for reinstatement or re-engagement), will order the employer to pay such compensation as it considers just and equitable[185].

(ii) Time off work

Since the Employment Protection Act 1975, trade union officials have had a statutory right to reasonable time off work to carry out trade union duties and to undertake trade union training, and union officials and members have had a statutory right to reasonable time off work to take part in trade union activities. The distinction between the two rights is crucial, as time off for union duties is with pay, whereas time off for union activities is unpaid (unless there is a contractual agreement to pay). In addition to these rights, the Employment Act 2002 introduced a new right for Union Learning Representatives (who need not be union officials) to take paid time off during working hours to undertake their duties and to undertake relevant training. The relevant provisions are contained in sections 168–173 of the Trade Union and Labour Relations (Consolidation)

---

180 Trade Union and Labour Relations (Consolidation) Act 1992, s 162.
181 Ie the applicant must have a 'pretty good' chance of success, per Slynn J, *Taplin v C Shippam Ltd* [1978] ICR 1068, [1978] IRLR 450, EAT.
182 Trade Union and Labour Relations (Consolidation) Act 1992, s 163. If the offer is one of re-engagement in another job, the tribunal must ask the employee whether he is willing to accept that job on the terms and conditions specified; if the employee unreasonably refuses the offer the tribunal will make no order: s 163(5).
183 Trade Union and Labour Relations (Consolidation) Act 1992, s 164(1).
184 Trade Union and Labour Relations (Consolidation) Act 1992, s 164(3).
185 Trade Union and Labour Relations (Consolidation) Act 1992, s 166. There is no statutory limit on the amount which may be awarded under this section.

Act 1992, and are supplemented by the ACAS Code of Practice No 3 on *Time Off for Trade Union Duties and Activities*[186], which recommends the negotiation of specific agreements on the question between employers and unions, to take into account the particular features of each industry, and to provide clear guidelines against which applications for time off can be determined, thereby avoiding misunderstanding, facilitating better planning and ensuring fair and reasonable treatment[187].

(a) Trade union duties

An employer is obliged by section 168 to allow an employee who is an official of an independent, recognised trade union to have a reasonable amount of paid time off during working hours[188] for the purposes of carrying on official duties concerned with (i) negotiations with the employer over matters falling within section 178(2) (which defines the subject matter of collective bargaining) in relation to which the union is recognised by the employer, or (ii) the performance of functions which the employer has agreed to the union performing on behalf of his employees; an official is also entitled to reasonable paid time off for undergoing training in aspects of industrial relations which is relevant to the above duties and approved by the TUC or his union[189]. 'Official' is defined as covering union officers and shop stewards elected or appointed under the union rules[190]. While the right to time off for trade union duties only applies to recognised unions, a union official also has a separate statutory right to a reasonable amount of paid time off to accompany a worker at a disciplinary or grievance hearing, regardless of whether the official belongs to a recognised union, so long as the worker being accompanied is employed by the same employer, and the official has been certified by the union as being capable of acting as a workers' companion[191].

Before 1989, the right to time off for trade union duties was much wider than it is today. A trade union official was entitled to reasonable paid time off for duties concerned with industrial relations between his employer (and any associated employer) and their employees, and for industrial relations training relevant to those duties, and the phrase 'concerned with industrial relations' was broadly interpreted[192]. The right was not restricted to actual negotiations with the

---

186 The Code is admissible in evidence and is to be taken into account when deciding what time off would be reasonable: s 168(3). The Code was revised in 2003 to take account of the new provisions on time off for Union Learning Representatives introduced by the Employment Act 2002.

187 COP No 3, para43. The Code is set out in *Harvey* S[101].

188 See n 201 below for a possible challenge to this restriction.

189 There are two stages in a claim to this right: (i) is the activity one envisaged by the Act and COP?; (ii) if it is, is it reasonable to give time off in all the circumstances? In *Ministry of Defence v Crook and Irving* [1982] IRLR 488, the EAT suggested that the question of reasonableness is to be approached by applying the 'range of reasonable responses' test evolved in the context of unfair dismissal (see p 571 above), but this view is not universally accepted. Note that employee trustees (who may well be union officials) also have a right to paid time off to perform their duties or undergo relevant training: Pensions Act 1995, s 42.

190 Trade Union and Labour Relations (Consolidation) Act 1992, s 119.

191 Employment Relations Act 1999, s 10. Alternatively, the worker can choose to be accompanied by an official who is employed by the union, or by a fellow worker.

192 See eg *Sood v GEC Elliott Process Automation Ltd* [1980] ICR 1, [1979] IRLR 416, EAT; *British Bakeries (Northern) Ltd v Adlington* [1989] ICR 438, [1989] IRLR 218, CA.

employer, or to matters in respect of which the employer recognised the union; it was enough if the duties for which time off was claimed were sufficiently proximate to industrial relations between the employees and their employer[193], and the union in question was recognised by the employer to any extent for the purposes of collective bargaining, even if the recognition was partial so that the union was not recognised in relation to the matters for which time off was claimed. However, the right to time off for union duties was significantly narrowed by the Employment Act 1989, which limited the proper subject matter for time off to duties 'concerned with negotiations'[194] with the employer, and to matters in respect of which the union is recognised by the employer (unless the employer has agreed to the union performing functions on behalf of his employees), and restricted time off for industrial relations training to training which is relevant to the above duties. Thus for the first time the scope of recognition became important in determining the *extent* of the right to time off, not just the eligibility of a particular union official to claim it[195].

The ACAS Code of Practice gives guidance on proper purposes for time off under the existing law, and offers a number of examples of trade union duties for which reasonable time off should be allowed, including duties concerned with terms and conditions of employment (for example pay or hours of work), recruitment and selection policies, redundancy and dismissal arrangements, job grading and job evaluation, flexible working practices, disciplinary procedures and arrangements, matters of trade union membership, facilities for union officials, collective bargaining machinery, grievance procedures and other procedures for consultation and communication (paragraph11). The Code also emphasises that the duties must be connected with or related to negotiations or the performance of agreed functions in time as well as in subject-matter, and suggests that reasonable time off may be sought to prepare for negotiations, inform members of progress, explain outcomes to members and prepare for meetings with the employer about matters for which the union has only representational rights (paragraph12). The Code is also concerned with the question of time off for relevant training, suggesting that employers should consider releasing employees for initial basic training in industrial relations duties as soon as possible after their election or appointment, and subsequently for further training covering special responsibilities and changing circumstances (paragraph 21). The Code makes two other general points which might be noted. The first is that it suggests that the management should consider making available to officials the facilities necessary for them to perform their duties efficiently and effectively, which might include (where resources permit) accommodation for meetings, telephones, use of noticeboards (which could include other forms of electronic communications such as email and Internet/intranet) and possibly even dedicated office space (paragraph 38), the irony here being that a small union should only claim such things after it has been certified as independent, since if

---

193 This was ultimately a question of fact for the tribunal: *British Bakeries (Northern) Ltd v Adlington* n 192 above.

194 The right is not necessarily restricted to actual negotiations with the employer: see *London Ambulance Service v Charlton* [1992] ICR 773, [1992] IRLR 510, EAT, where attendance at a union district co-ordinating committee to prepare for negotiations with the employer was held to fall within the scope of the section because on the facts there was sufficient nexus between the duty in question and negotiations with the employer.

195 As in the law relating to disclosure of bargaining information, where the extent of recognition is crucial in determining what information has to be disclosed. See p 80 above.

it obtains them beforehand, that might be a factor working against 'independence'[196]. The second point is that where an official is not himself engaged in industrial action being taken by his constituents, but he is still representing them, he should be allowed time off in the normal way to exercise that function (paragraph 49)[197].

Time off under this section is with pay[198]. According to the 1992 Act, the employee is entitled to be paid the amount which he would normally have received during the time off in question, as if he had worked his normal hours (or, where his remuneration varies with the amount of work done, on the basis of an average of his hourly earnings for that work)[199]. This causes few problems where paid time off is claimed for duties which take place at a time when the employee would normally have been at work; the position is, however, more problematic where the employee is a shift worker or part-time worker, and the duties in question are carried out at a time when the employee would not otherwise have been at work. In one case, the EAT held that as the right is to paid time off 'during his working hours', an employee who undertook trade union duties outside his working hours had no right under the 1992 Act to paid time off or to payment in lieu[200]. However, the ECJ has held[201] that it may be unlawful indirect sex discrimination not to pay a part-time female worker for the total number of hours spent on trade union duties (including those outside her normal working hours) in circumstances where a full-time male worker would have been paid for all the hours spent undertaking those duties. Such an outcome hinges upon whether the time off in question is for 'work' within the meaning of Article 141. It is clear from the ECJ decisions that time off to attend the employer's staff council, or to undergo training necessary for performing staff council functions, does constitute 'work' for the purposes of Article 141[202], and after some initial uncertainty[203] the EAT has confirmed[204] that attendance at a union-organised health and safety training course also constitutes 'work', because it is 'by reason of the existence of an employment relationship'[205] : 'Attending a training course organised by a

---

196 Trade Union and Labour Relations (Consolidation) Act 1992, s 5. See p 67 above.
197 The Code emphasises that there is no right to time off for trade union activities which themselves consist of industrial action.
198 It appeared to be self-evident from the section that once it was established that there was a 'duty' and that the time off requested was 'reasonable', the official was automatically entitled to be paid; this was accepted by the EAT in *Beecham Group Ltd v Beal (No 2)* [1983] IRLR 317, but in *Thomas Scott & Sons (Bakers) Ltd v Allen* [1983] IRLR 329, CA, May LJ seems to assume that there may be cases where it is reasonable to allow the time off, but not reasonable to pay the official for it; *sed quaere*. See Fitzpatrick (1983) 12 ILJ 258.
199 Trade Union and Labour Relations (Consolidation) Act 1992, s 169.
200 *Hairsine v Kingston upon Hull City Council* [1992] ICR 212, [1992] IRLR 211, EAT.
201 *Arbeiterwohlfahrt der Stadt Berlin v Botel* [1992] IRLR 423, ECJ. On equal pay generally, see p 325.
202 *Arbeiterwohlfahrt der Stadt Berlin v Botel* [1992] IRLR 423, ECJ. See also *Kuratorium fur Dialyse Und Nierentransplantation v Lewark* [1996] IRLR 637, where the ECJ considered the scope of the justification defence.
203 See *Manor Bakeries v Nazir* [1996] IRLR 604, where the EAT, distinguishing *Botel*, held that attendance at a trade union annual conference was not 'work'.
204 *Davies v Neath Port Talbot County Borough Council* [1999] ICR 1132, [1999] IRLR 769. The EAT acknowledged that the effect of their judgment was that s 169(2) 'is in conflict with Art 119' (now Art 141).
205 *Davies v Neath Port Talbot County Borough Council*, per Morison J. Arguably, it would have been open to the EAT in *Davies* to distinguish *Nazir* on the basis that while attendance at a union health and safety training course is 'work' because it is 'by reason of the existence of an employment relationship', attendance at a union's annual conference is not 'work' because it lacks sufficient nexus with the employment relationship; however, the EAT held that the decision in *Nazir* 'should not be followed'.

recognised trade union is still related to the employment relationship and is safeguarding staff interests which is ultimately beneficial to the employer.' Significantly, the EAT rejected the employer's argument that only paying part-time workers for their contractual working hours was not indirectly discriminatory because it was objectively justified: 'The issue is whether part-time workers (predominantly female) engaged on a full-time course should receive full-time pay. There cannot, it seems to us, be a justifiable policy or aim which maintains the inequality.' The position of part-timers in relation to time off has now been reinforced by the Part-time Workers (Prevention of Less Favourable Treatment) Regulations 2000[206], which give part-time workers the right not to be treated less favourably in relation to terms and conditions of employment than comparable full-time workers, unless the employer can show some objective justification for the less favourable treatment. The Regulations do not deal expressly with time off, but the DTI guidance on the Regulations recommends that training should be scheduled so that part-time workers can attend so far as possible, and the ACAS Code of Practice states that: 'There is no statutory requirement to pay for time off where the duty is carried out at a time when the official would not otherwise have been at work, but staff who work part time will be entitled to be paid if staff who work full time would be entitled to be paid' (paragraph 15).

It may be that, pursuant to the exhortation in the Code or otherwise, the employer has agreed to allow certain paid time off, in which case the employee may have a contractual right to his pay during the relevant times (in which case, the pay would be computed according to the contractual terms). Any such contractual remuneration which is received goes towards discharging (or extinguishing) the statutory liability, and vice versa[207].

(b) Trade union activities

An employee is entitled, under the Trade Union and Labour Relations (Consolidation) Act 1992, section 170, to reasonable time off during working hours to take part in any activities of an independent trade union to which the employee belongs and which is recognised by the employer in respect of such employees. In *Luce v Bexley London Borough Council*[208], the EAT interpreted this right narrowly, holding that time off may only be claimed for union activities that are in some way connected with the employment relationship between the employer, the employee and the union. In that case the employee, a member of the National Union of Teachers, was refused unpaid time off to attend a TUC lobby of Parliament in protest against the Education Reform Bill. The EAT held that the tribunal was entitled to take the view on the facts that as the lobby was intended to convey only political or ideological objections to the proposed legislation, attendance at it could not be regarded as a trade union activity within the meaning of the section. The ACAS Code of Practice suggests that the right should extend to activities such as attending workplace meetings to discuss and vote on the outcome of negotiations with the employer, meeting full-time officials to discuss issues relevant to the workplace, and voting in industrial action ballots and union elections (paragraph 30). Where the member is acting as a

---

206 SI 2000/1551. The Regulations implemented the Part Time Work Directive (97/81/EC).
207 Trade Union and Labour Relations (Consolidation) Act 1992, s 169(4).
208 [1990] ICR 591, [1990] IRLR 422, EAT.

representative of the union, the activities may also include taking part in branch, area or regional meetings of the union, attending meetings of official policy-making bodies such as the executive committee or annual conference, and attending meetings with full-time officials to discuss issues relevant to the workplace (paragraph 31). The section specifically excludes activities which themselves consist of industrial action, whether or not in contemplation or furtherance of a trade dispute. Time off for 'activities' under section 170 is without pay (in the absence of any contractual term to the contrary) and it has been held that what constitutes 'reasonable' time off may include a consideration of how much time off has already been given to the employee on previous occasions[209].

(c) Union Learning Representatives

The Employment Act 2002 introduced a new right for an employee to take paid time off during working hours to undertake the duties of a Union Learning Representative, and to undergo relevant training[210]. To qualify for this right, the employee must be a member of a recognised independent trade union, and have been appointed or elected as a Union Learning Representative, in accordance with the union's rules, to analyse learning or training needs, provide information and advice about learning or training matters, arrange learning or training or promote the value of learning and training[211]. A Union Learning Representative is entitled to reasonable paid time off for the above activities, and also for the purpose of consulting the employer about carrying on any of those activities, provided the union has notified the employer in writing that the employee is a Union Learning Representative, and the employee has undergone sufficient training to be capable of fulfilling the role (or will have undergone such training within six months)[212]. In addition, union members are entitled to reasonable unpaid time off during working hours to access the services of a Union Learning Representative[213].

These provisions are designed to help fill the learning and training gap, particularly in small and medium-sized organisations where employer-provided learning and training may be patchy, or even non-existent. The ACAS Code of Practice cautions that many employers will have in place well established training and development programmes for their employees, and that Union Learning Representatives should liaise with their employers to ensure that their respective training activities complement one another and that the scope for duplication is minimised (paragraph 14).

(d) Remedies for breach by the employer

Where an employer has failed to permit an employee to take time off in accordance with the statutory provisions, the employee may make a complaint to an employment tribunal within three months of the date when the failure occurred (or a longer period if the tribunal is satisfied that it was not reasonably practicable

---

209 *Wignall v British Gas Corpn* [1984] ICR 716, [1984] IRLR 493, EAT.
210 Trade Union and Labour Relations (Consolidation) Act 1992, s 168A.
211 Trade Union and Labour Relations (Consolidation) Act 1992, s 168A(2).
212 Trade Union and Labour Relations (Consolidation) Act 1992, s 168A(3), (4). The employee may be entitled to paid time off to undergo training relevant to the functions of a Union Learning Representative: s 168A(7).
213 Trade Union and Labour Relations (Consolidation) Act 1992, s 170(2B).

to complain within that period). Union officials and Union Learning Representatives may also complain if the employer has failed to pay them for the time necessary to perform their duties, in which case the tribunal may order payment of the amount due. The EAT has held that in order for a trade union official to show that the employer has failed to permit him to take time off in order to carry out union duties, the request for time off must have come to the notice of the employer's appropriate representative, and it must be established that they have either refused it, ignored it or, in some other way, knowing of it, simply failed to deal with it[214]. In the case of a complaint of failure to permit time off, the tribunal, if it finds it justified, must grant a declaration to that effect and may in addition award such compensation as it thinks just and equitable, having regard to the employer's default and any loss sustained by the employee attributable to the failure to permit time off[215]. If this is considered analogous to the similar provision on compensation for detriment short of dismissal on trade union grounds[216], it will mean that it will not be viewed as a penal fine on the employer, but at the same time the tribunal will not be limited to awarding compensation only for pecuniary loss and will be able to include an amount for non-pecuniary matters such as interference with the employee's rights and desires to participate in the activities in question. It has been decided by the EAT, however, that the tribunal's powers are only those of awarding a declaration and compensation, which are both essentially ex post facto; the tribunal cannot go further and lay down conditions upon which time off shall be allowed in future, and in particular it cannot rewrite any contractual terms which already exist on the question, even if it has decided that the operation of those terms in the past has not constituted 'reasonable' time off[217]. In *Ryford Ltd v Drinkwater*[218], the EAT confirmed that an employee does not lose the right to receive compensation by taking time off without permission.

(iii) The right to dissociate and the closed shop[219]

(a) Protection of individual non-members

While the right to associate has been protected since 1974 through the statutory controls on dismissal and action (now detriment) short of dismissal for trade union reasons, supplemented in 1990 by the statutory protection against refusal of employment, the protection afforded in English law to those not wishing to associate together with others is of more recent origin. When the Donovan Commission in 1968 examined the relationship between the right to associate and the right to dissociate it concluded that the one did not necessarily entail the other, since the latter was 'designed to frustrate the development of collective bargaining, which it is public policy to promote', whereas no such objection applied to the former[220]. For much of the following decade this reasoning was

---

214 *Ryford Ltd v Drinkwater* [1996] IRLR 16, EAT.
215 Trade Union and Labour Relations (Consolidation) Act 1992, s 172(2).
216 Trade Union and Labour Relations (Consolidation) Act 1992, s 149(2), as explained by the EAT in *Brassington v Cauldon Wholesale Ltd* [1978] ICR 405, [1977] IRLR 479; see p 685 above.
217 *Corner v Buckinghamshire County Council* [1978] ICR 836, [1978] IRLR 320, EAT.
218 [1996] IRLR 16, EAT.
219 See Davies and Freedland *Kahn-Freund's Labour and the Law* (3rd edn, 1983) pp 236–270; Millward, Bryson and Forth *All Change at Work? British Employee Relations 1980–1998* (2000).
220 *Royal Commission on Trade Unions and Employers' Associations* (Cmnd 3623, 1968) para 599.

applied to justify the greater protection afforded by the law to the positive right. The reason why this conceptual riddle has historically been so important is, of course, the long-standing tradition in British industrial relations of the closed shop, defined by McCarthy as 'a situation in which employees come to realise that a particular job is only to be obtained or retained if they become and remain members of one of a specified number of trade unions'[221]. Unlike in certain other jurisdictions where it has long been subject to detailed control or regulation, in Britain the law until comparatively recently adopted a studiously non-interventionist stance on the closed shop, a reflection perhaps of the philosophy of collective laissez-faire which dominated our labour law for much of the twentieth century. However, in the period after the 1979 General Election the political climate became increasingly hostile towards the closed shop, and this was reflected in legislation which, while not rendering the closed shop unlawful per se, made it increasingly difficult for employers and trade unions to enforce a closed shop agreement or arrangement within the law. As a consequence the importance of the closed shop as a social institution declined drastically during the 1980s[222], and there were many notable examples of employers terminating long-standing closed shop agreements (for example at British Gas, British Telecom and British Rail), without significant opposition from the unions. This startling turn-around came about in a series of stages, and in order to understand the present position it is necessary to trace those stages, starting with the highpoint of legal protection for the closed shop under the Labour governments of the 1970s.

Before the election of Margaret Thatcher's Conservative government in 1979 the principal legal significance of a closed shop (or 'union membership') agreement lay in the field of unfair dismissal; the relevant law supported the enforcement of the closed shop by providing that a dismissal for non-membership of an independent trade union would be automatically *fair* where there was a union membership agreement in operation which applied to the dismissed employee, unless the employee had a religious objection to union membership, or a genuine objection on reasonable grounds to being a member of a union, in which case the dismissal was deemed automatically *unfair*[223]. The second ground of objection was removed by the Trade Union and Labour Relations (Amendment) Act 1976, leaving religious objection as the only basis for exemption. The Trade Union and Labour Relations Act 1974 had also introduced a statutory right not to be excluded or expelled from trade union membership by way of arbitrary or unreasonable discrimination; however, this too was repealed in 1976, leaving any legal remedies back in the hands of the uncertain common law. As a quid pro quo for the retreat in the 1976 Act, the TUC set up an Independent Review Committee[224] (in consultation with ACAS and the Secretary of State for

---

221 *The Closed Shop in Britain* (1964).
222 In 1984, it was estimated that some 3.5 to 3.7 million employees were covered by closed shop arrangements: Millward and Stephens *British Workplace Industrial Relations 1980–1984* (1986); by the time of the follow-up survey, the estimated figure had fallen to somewhere between 0.3 and 0.5 million: Millward, Stephens, Smart and Hawes *Workplace Industrial Relations in Transition* (1992). The most dramatic fall was in the nationalised industries, from % of workplaces with manual closed shops in 1984 to less than 1% in 1990.
223 The same rules applied mutatis mutandis to the protection against action short of dismissal.
224 The Donovan Report (Cmnd 3623, 1968) had recommended the establishment of such a body, though not necessarily by the TUC: para 631. See Ewing and Rees 'The TUC Independent Review Committee and the closed shop' (1981) 10 ILJ 84.

Employment) to investigate complaints of improper or unreasonable expulsion and exclusion from unions, but the IRC only had jurisdiction (a) where the union was affiliated to the TUC and (b) where there was a closed shop in operation.

Thus, between 1974 and 1980 (and particularly after 1976) the closed shop was well established, with little legal protection for employees who did not wish to be union members, other than under the TUC's own voluntary procedure. The legislation of this period was subsequently challenged before the European Court of Human Rights in *Young, James and Webster v United Kingdom*[225] where the dismissal of three railway workers because of a closed shop was held to have violated Article 11 of the European Convention on Human Rights, which contains the right to freedom of association and to join a trade union[226]. The case was not a total denunciation of the closed shop – the latter was not declared illegal per se, and the court did not uphold the existence of a negative right to dissociate as strong as the positive right to associate contained in the wording of Article 11[227]. The case was decided on its facts, chief among which were that (a) the employees had already been in employment when the closed shop agreement came into force, and (b) there was already a very high level of union membership without invoking the full rigour of a closed shop; the Court considered that the threat of dismissal for non-membership, involving a loss of livelihood, was 'a most serious form of compulsion' which struck at 'the very substance of the freedom' guaranteed by Article 11. On the facts, interference with the employees' limited negative right was not 'necessary in a democratic society' and so the justification defence in Article 11 (2) did not apply[228]. If the legal effects of the ruling at that time were difficult to assess[229], the political effect was of course to give further backing to the incoming Conservative government, who had promised in their 1979 election manifesto to take steps to reform the closed shop.

The period between 1980 and 1990 saw a sustained legislative attack on the closed shop which meant that by the end of that period it was a spent force in British industrial relations. This transformation was achieved not by a frontal assault, by rather by a series of incremental reforms which steadily tightened the legal stranglehold on the closed shop. The starting point was the Employment Act 1980, which introduced a series of what were called 'crucial but limited reforms', with the aim of striking a balance between the collective interest of the union and its members in maintaining a closed shop, and the individual interests of those who did not wish to join. So, for example, dismissal for non-membership remained automatically fair where a closed shop agreement was in operation, but the 1980 Act extended the categories of employees exempted from membership to include, for example, those who had a genuine objection to union membership on the grounds of conscience or deeply held personal conviction, and those

---

225 [1981] IRLR 408, ECtHR; see Forde 'The "closed shop" case' (1982) 11 ILJ 1.
226 See p 670 above.
227 Although see *Sigurjonsson v Iceland* (1993) 16 EHRR 462, ECtHR.
228 Compare *Sibson v United Kingdom* (1993) 17 EHRR 193, ECtHR, where the court, distinguishing *Young, James and Webster*, held that the employer's actions in exercising his contractual right to relocate the employee because he had resigned from the union did not violate Art 11, because there was no question of the employee losing his job.
229 The Convention had not yet been incorporated into English law: see p 42.

already in employment before the closed shop agreement took effect[230]; the 1980 Act also introduced a balloting requirement for the establishment of a new closed shop, whereby dismissal for non-membership would be automatically unfair unless the closed shop had been approved in a secret ballot by not less than 80% of those entitled to vote[231].

The Employment Act 1982 took matters several stages further, by adding to the categories of exempted employees, and introducing a requirement for five-yearly review ballots of existing closed shops, again with a very high majority required for approval[232]. The 1982 Act also introduced significantly enhanced compensation levels (via a minimum basic award and a 'special' award) in cases of dismissal for trade union reasons, which could be awarded against the union which had pressurised the employer to dismiss, and introduced a scheme to compensate all those who had lost their employment without remedy during the period 1974–80[233].

After the Employment Act 1982, the law relating to dismissal for non-membership of a trade union was left in a state of considerable complexity. The combined effect of the 1980 and 1982 Acts was to make it difficult to establish a legally effective closed shop, and arguably even more difficult to enforce it (given the width of the individual exemptions, particularly that relating to conscientious objection), but a dismissal for non-membership could still be automatically fair if there was an approved closed shop agreement in operation, *unless* the employee was within one of the categories of exempted employees, in which case the dismissal would be unfair. However, in 1987 the Conservative government decided to take the further step of removing *all* legal protection from a closed shop[234], and most of this complexity was duly swept away by the Employment Act 1988, which removed all legal protection from action taken by an employer to enforce a closed shop against existing employees. This was achieved simply by providing that a dismissal for non-membership was automatically unfair in *all* cases if the reason (or principal reason) was that the employee 'was not a member of any trade union, or of a particular trade union, or of one of a number of particular trade unions, or had refused or proposed to refuse to become or remain a member'[235]. Similarly, all discriminatory action short of dismissal against non-members was made unlawful[236]. In short, the position, only reached after three bites of the legislative cherry, was that the protection against dismissal or detriment short of dismissal enjoyed by non-members became co-extensive with that enjoyed by union members.

---

230 The existence of this reform in the Employment Act 1980 allowed the Conservative government (defending the previous Labour government's legislation before the European Court of Human Rights in the *Young* case) to argue that even if that previous legislation had been contrary to Art 11, their new legislation met the most serious objection raised by the court on the facts of the case, ie that the employees had already been in employment with British Rail when the closed shop agreement was concluded.

231 See Lewis and Simpson 'Disorganising industrial relations' (1982) 11 ILJ at pp 239–244.

232 80% of those entitled to vote, or 85% of those actually voting.

233 Ewing and Rees 'Closed shop dismissals 1974–1980: a study of the retroactive compensation scheme' (1988) 12 ILJ 148.

234 Green Paper, *Trade Unions and Their Members* (February 1987).

235 See now the Trade Union and Labour Relations (Consolidation) Act 1992, s 152(1)(c). It will also be an automatically unfair dismissal to select an employee for redundancy because of his non-membership if other employees holding similar positions were equally affected and have not been dismissed: s 153.

236 See now the Trade Union and Labour Relations (Consolidation) Act 1992, s 146(1)(c).

While the 1988 Act removed the ability of an employer to enforce a closed shop against existing employees (the 'post-entry' closed shop), it remained lawful for an employer to discriminate against non-union members at the point of hiring, and thus to operate a pre-entry closed shop. That final loophole was, however, closed by the Employment Act 1990[237], which introduced the right not to be refused employment on grounds of union membership or non-membership[238]. It is still technically correct to say that the closed shop has not been 'outlawed', in that a closed shop agreement or arrangement is not illegal or proscribed as such. However, the reforms which were introduced during the period between 1980 and 1990 have made it legally very difficult for an employer to enforce a closed shop against existing or prospective employees. The current position in English law is therefore that, whether or not the right to dissociate is properly seen as the logical corollary of the right to associate, both rights are accorded equal respect.

(b) Other measures restricting the closed shop

In addition to the above measures restricting the enforcement of a closed shop by employers against individual employees, there are a series of further measures restricting its enforcement against employers and third parties through contract compliance or by industrial pressure. Thus, the Employment Act 1982 introduced measures designed to render illegal the practice of encouraging closed shops by making it a condition of contracts or tenders that the contractor or tenderer must use employees who are union members (whether generally, or of a particular trade union). Any such term in a contract is void and any person who refuses to contract or to accept tenders on such grounds may be liable in tort for breach of statutory duty to anyone adversely affected by his actions[239]. Moreover, that Act provided that if any other person (in practice a union) exerts industrial pressure in order to secure a union-labour-only clause in a contract or to induce an unlawful refusal to contract or tender on the ground of the employment of non-union labour, the usual immunities from suit in tort are expressly withdrawn from that industrial pressure[240], so that the union may be sued for an injunction or damages. The political impetus behind these complicated provisions appears to have come from the insistence on union-labour-only contracts by some Labour-controlled local authorities[241].

---

237 White Paper, *Employment for the 1990s* (Cm 540, 1988) para 2.23; Green Paper, *Removing Barriers to Employment* (Cm 655, 1989).
238 See now the Trade Union and Labour Relations (Consolidation) Act 1992, s 137.
239 See now the Trade Union and Labour Relations (Consolidation) Act 1992, ss 144, 145; s 145 also applies to refusals to contract or tender on the ground that the contractor or tenderer uses union labour. Ss 186 and 187 impose similar restrictions on such refusals where the aim is to oblige the contractor or tenderer to recognise or consult with a particular trade union (see p 79, above). It seems that only the term is void, not the whole contract, so that where such a contract has in fact been entered into the contractor may insist on performing (and being paid for) his part of the contract but ignore the void clause.
240 See now the Trade Union and Labour Relations (Consolidation) Act 1992, s 222(3). For the statutory immunities, see pp 761–780 below.
241 Lewis and Simpson 'Disorganising industrial relations' (1982) 11 ILJ at 227. One practical problem in a claim for wrongful refusal to contract on the ground of union membership would be in proving that that was in fact the real ground for the refusal, when the claimant's was only one of many tenders.

This process was taken an important stage further by the Employment Act 1988, which removed the immunity from suit in tort from any industrial action taken because a particular employer is employing, has employed or might employ a non-union member, or is failing, has failed or might fail to discriminate against such a non-union member[242]. This is aimed principally at the situation where an employer is unwilling to establish or (more likely) continue with a closed shop agreement and the union seeks to bring industrial pressure to bear to require him to do so; any person affected by that industrial action (directly or indirectly) may, if he has been injured tortiously by it, sue the union for an injunction and for damages without the union having its normal trade dispute immunity.

4 UNION RULES AND JUDICIAL INTERVENTION

Traditionally the main source of legal control of internal union affairs has been through the union's rule book, which is both the constitution of the union, defining and delimiting the powers enjoyed by the union, its officers and officials, and also the basis of the contract of membership which exists between the union and its members. In recent years the significance of union rules as a source of control of union activity has tended to be overshadowed by the legislative activity in this area, with a plethora of statutory provisions striking ever deeper into the structure and organisation of institutions which were previously regarded as autonomous. Those statutory provisions are considered below, but the common law on union rules and judicial intervention is still of importance, first, because common law actions may still have considerable impact (as was seen particularly in the miners' strike of 1984/85), and secondly, because the statutory provisions for the most part build upon the common law foundation rather than replacing it.

(i) Interpretation of union rules

The union's rule book is of crucial importance in the legal regulation of the relationship between the union and its members (and indeed the relationship between the constituent parts of the union). With very few exceptions, the drafting of the rules is left entirely to the union itself, and the statutory controls on union activity operate outside the rule book rather than through it[243]. The exceptions are (i) the implication into all contracts of trade union membership of a right to terminate membership on giving reasonable notice and complying with any reasonable conditions[244]; (ii) the compulsory provisions on the appointment and removal of auditors[245]; and (iii) the requirement that a union's political fund and political ballot rules comply with the relevant statutory provisions[246].

---

242 See now the Trade Union and Labour Relations (Consolidation) Act 1992, s 222(1), (2), discussed at p 785 below.
243 The Trade Union and Labour Relations Act 1974, s 6 laid down certain matters which had to be specified in the rules (eg eligibility for benefits, procedures for alteration of rules, election of officers and disciplinary procedures), but this was repealed in toto by the Trade Union and Labour Relations (Amendment) Act 1976.
244 Trade Union and Labour Relations (Consolidation) Act 1992, s 69.
245 Trade Union and Labour Relations (Consolidation) Act 1992, s 35; see p 727 below.
246 Trade Union and Labour Relations (Consolidation) Act 1992, s 71 (political fund rules) and s 74 (political ballot rules); see p 730 below.

While union rules have a vital role as the union's constitution, regulating the union's powers and duties towards its members, they may not in practice be drafted with the clarity of a legal or parliamentary document, particularly as many rules may be of long standing and may have been subject to periodic amendments[247]. As Lord Wilberforce observed in *Heatons Transpoort (St Helens) Ltd v TGWU*[248] : 'trade union rule books are not drafted by parliamentary draftsmen. Courts of law must resist the temptation to construe them as if they were, for that is not how they would be understood by the members who are the parties to the agreement of which the terms, or some of them, are set out in the rule book.' The approach of the courts to the construction of union rules has not, however, been consistent. On the one hand, primarily in the context of rules setting out the general running and constitution of the union, the courts have recognised that they should not expect legal precision and so may have to take a broad approach to construction, looking for the general intent and purpose of the provisions in question; this approach may allow a court to take into account the customs and practices of the union which have evolved to supplement the bare rules, as in *Heatons Transport*, where the question of the scope of the authority of a shop steward in a particular union was considered by the House of Lords in the light of customary arrangements, the union's rules being unclear on that point[249]. On the other hand, where the rules may have a direct effect on a member's individual rights (for example in cases of disciplining or expulsion), the courts have tended to take a much stricter view of the rule under which a union is acting, particularly in closed shop situations where the link between union membership and access to work enabled the union to exercise power over its members' livelihoods. So, for example, in *British Actors' Equity Association v Goring*[250] , Viscount Dilhorne considered that the same rules of construction should be applied to union rule books as to any written documents. Lord Denning MR in particular carried this proposition further and stated in several cases that, although the law had treated union rule books as a contract, that was a fiction: union rules were more like by-laws than a contract, and the denial or removal of a members' rights must therefore fall strictly within the powers contained in the rules:

'Trade unions are not above the law, but subject to it. Their rules are said to be a contract between the members and the union. So be it ... But the rules

---

247 See the confusion caused by failure specifically to include in union rules the terms of the Bridlington agreement (p 740 below): *Spring v NASDS* [1956] 2 All ER 221, [1956] 1 WLR 585 and *Rothwell v APEX* [1976] ICR 211, [1975] IRLR 375.
248 [1972] 3 All ER 101, [1972] ICR 308, HL.
249 The case concerned an action against a union under the Industrial Relations Act 1971. Where questions as to the vicarious liability of a union in tort arise, the position is now governed by statute (see p 818 below). Where the statutory test does not apply, however, the common law rules on vicarious liability as laid down by the House of Lords will still apply; see eg *Taylor v NUM (Derbyshire Area)* [1985] IRLR 99.
250 [1978] ICR 791, HL. The potential conflict between the two approaches was considered by Vinelott J in *Taylor v NUM (Derbyshire Area)* [1985] IRLR 99, Ch D and by Warner J in *Jacques v AUEW (Engineering Section)* [1987] 1 All ER 621, [1986] ICR 683, Ch D; in each case the judge, though purporting to synthesise the two approaches, in fact applied the wider approach in *Heatons Transport*. One caveat appears in *Burnley, Nelson, Rossendale and District Textile Workers' Union v Amalgamated Textile Workers' Union* [1987] ICR 69, [1986] IRLR 298, QBD, where it was held that a court may not invent missing union rules.

are in reality more than a contract. They are a legislative code laid down by the council of the union to be obeyed by the members. This code should be subject to control by the courts just as much as a code laid down by Parliament itself[251].'

In 1999, jurisdiction to hear complaints of breaches or threatened breaches of union rules was conferred on the Certification Officer[252], and it seems likely that in future the vast majority of such complaints will be dealt with by the Certification Officer rather than by the High Court[253]. It is therefore instructive to note that the Certification Officer's approach to the interpretation of union rules seems to owe rather more to Lord Wilberforce than to Lord Denning:

'Union rule books . . . are not statutes and the courts have consistently refused to interpret them as such. . . . In my view, union rule books set out the rules and principles governing the operation of a living, working organisation that has to respond to changing circumstances in the best way it can and in the interests of members whose organisation it is.'[254]

(ii) Grounds for judicial intervention

In general the courts seek to intervene as little as possible in the internal affairs of purely voluntary bodies[255], however, judges have taken the view, particularly since the decision of the Court of Appeal in *Lee v Showmen's Guild of Great Britain*[256], that the law has a significant role to play in protecting the rights of members of trade unions, particularly where denial of those rights could adversely affect individuals' livelihoods. As will be seen below, the greatly increased statutory protection for individual union members since 1980, particularly the enactment of the right not to be excluded or expelled from union membership and the right not to be unjustifiably disciplined, has meant that the common law has lost some of its practical significance. However, the common law will still be relevant in cases where the union member's complaint is not covered by the statutory provisions, for example where the complaint relates to a breach of the rules, or where the reason for the expulsion or other form of disciplining does not fall within the prohibited grounds set out in the 1992 Act; in such a case the member's rights will only lie, if at all, at common law. Moreover, there may be cases where

---

251 *Breen v AEU* [1971] 2 QB 175 at 190, [1971] 1 All ER 1148 at 1154, CA, per Lord Denning MR. See also *Bonsor v Musicians' Union* [1954] Ch 479, [1954] 1 All ER 822, CA; *Enderby Town Football Club Ltd v Football Association Ltd* [1971] Ch 591, [1971] 1 All ER 215, CA.
252 Trade Union and Labour Relations (Consolidation) Act 1992, ss 108A–108C. See p 66 above.
253 A person who has applied to the Certification Officer in relation to an alleged breach of the rules may not apply to the High Court in relation to that breach: s 108A(14); there is however, a right of appeal to the EAT on any question of law arising from a decision of the Certification Officer: s 108C.
254 *Cummings v Prison Officers' Association* (D/20/01), Certification Officer, at para 2.18.
255 *Edwards v Halliwell* [1950] 2 All ER 1064, CA.
256 [1952] 2 QB 329, [1952] 1 All ER 1175, CA.

the statutory actions are available, but some tactical advantage may be gained by bringing common law proceedings instead; such proceedings may be brought for speed[257], or in order to obtain declaratory or interim relief, particularly where what is at stake is not just the position of one individual member, but rather the government of the union itself. This was a particular feature of the unprecedented amount of litigation arising from the miners' strike of 1984/85, most of which was brought by groups of working miners using the long-established common law principles[258]. Some new principles were established and some reaffirmed (for example the clear decision that action taken by a union in defiance of a court order is ipso facto void[259]), but it could be argued that the principal significance of that litigation lay not so much in the establishment of new principles, but rather in the demonstration of a greater readiness on the part of union members to have recourse to the courts to enforce their rights under the union's rules and to restrain what they saw as abuses of power by the leadership. In recent years, and in particular since 1999, when the Certification Officer was given jurisdiction to deal with complaints of breaches or threatened breaches of union rules[260], there has been a marked increase in the numbers of such complaints by union members[261]. However, the Certification Officer's jurisdiction in this area is subject to two important restrictions; first, it only extends to breaches (or threatened breaches) of certain types of union rules[262], so that some complaints still lie only to the courts; and secondly, although the Certification Officer receives a considerable number of enquiries regarding inadequate representation of members by their union, he has no jurisdiction to consider such complaints[263].

Judicial intervention has principally been based on two grounds – the power of the courts to secure compliance with the union rules, and their insistence upon observation by the union of the rules of natural justice. The first ground, enforcement of the rules, rests upon the theory of the contract of membership,

257 Significantly, the Employment Relations Act 1999, s 29 conferred jurisdiction on the Certification Officer to hear complaints about certain alleged breaches of trade union rules, along with the power to make declarations and issue enforcement orders, as an alternative to the courts: Trade Union and Labour Relations (Consolidation) Act 1992, s 108A–108C. See p 66.
258 See Ewing 'The strike, the courts and the rule book' (1985) 14 ILJ 160.
259 See *Clarke v Chadburn* [1985] 1 All ER 211, [1984] IRLR 350, where a purported alteration to the NUM's disciplinary rules voted on in defiance of a court order was held to be void.
260 Trade Union and Labour Relations (Consolidation) Act 1992, ss 108A–108C. Members are still free to seek a remedy from the High Court for breach of the rules, but an application to the Certification Officer is likely to be quicker and cheaper. Note, however, that, unlike the High Court, the Certification Officer cannot order interim relief or award damages under this head.
261 In 2001/02 the Certification Officer issued 57 decisions in complaints of breach of the rules: *Annual Report of the Certification Officer, 2001-2002*, para 9.8. Ironically, the increase in complaints coincided with the abolition of the Commissioner for the Rights of Trade Union Members (CROTUM), an office established under the Employment Act 1988 to assist union members in bringing proceedings against their union: see p 67.
262 As set out in the Trade Union and Labour Relations (Consolidation) Act 1992, s 108A(2). The principal exclusions are complaints relating to industrial action ballots, and cases involving dismissal or disciplinary proceedings against an employee of the union.
263 In 2000/01, over 35% of the enquiries received related to inadequate representation: *Annual Report of the Certification Officer 2000-2001*, para 9.13. The reduction in the percentage of such enquiries (to 31%) in 2001/02 'is believed to have resulted from a wider public understanding of the role and areas of responsibility of the Certification Officer': *Annual Report of the Certification Officer, 2001-2002*, para 9.13

with every member having a contractual right to have the terms of that contract (ie the rules) observed[264], so that an aggrieved member may seek to restrain unlawful action by the union by declaration or injunction and may, in a suitable case, be awarded damages[265]. This power of intervention might be invoked in larger-scale internal disputes between different factions within a union, in which case the court may have to pronounce upon matters going to the very heart of the union's constitution[266]. More usually, the claimant will be an individual, or smaller group, claiming that certain material[267] irregularities are being committed by the union leadership, for example, in relation to the holding of meetings[268], the use of committees[269], rights of appeal from decisions[270], the treatment of union officers[271], the expenditure of funds[272], the alteration of union rules[273], the holding of union elections[274] and the calling and running of strike or other industrial action[275]. In the litigation arising out of the 1984/85 miners' strike, the court's rulings on the illegality under the NUM's rules of calling a national strike without a ballot were of crucial significance, for it meant that working miners did not have to join a strike called in breach of the rules, and the expenditure of union funds on the strike could be restrained[276]. However, the most vital area from the point of view of protection of the individual has been that of disciplining[277] and expulsion[278]; this was particularly important where there was a closed shop in operation, as loss of a union card could mean loss of a job, but a member may have important interests in remaining within the union even where his livelihood is

---

264 *Lee v Showmen's Guild*, n 256, above.
265 *Bonsor v Musicians' Union* [1956] AC 104, [1955] 3 All ER 518, HL. The Certification Officer is only empowered to make a declaration and an enforcement order requiring the union to take steps to remedy the breach and/or abstain from specified acts in the future: Trade Union and Labour Relations (Consolidation) Act 1992, s 108B(3). Any such order may be enforced in the same way as an order of the court: s 108B(8).
266 See eg *British Actors' Equity Association v Goring* [1978] ICR 791, HL and *Douglas v Graphical Paper and Media Union* [1995] IRLR 426.
267 *Brown v AUEW* [1976] ICR 147.
268 *MacLelland v NUJ* [1975] ICR 116.
269 *Abbott v Sullivan* [1952] 1 KB 189, [1952] 1 All ER 226, CA; *Leary v National Union of Vehicle Builders* [1971] Ch 34, [1970] 2 All ER 713.
270 *Hiles v Amalgamated Society of Woodworkers* [1968] Ch 440, [1967] 3 All ER 70; *Braithwaite v EETU* [1969] 2 All ER 859, CA; *Loosley v NUT* [1988] IRLR 157, CA.
271 *Taylor v NUS* [1967] 1 All ER 767, [1967] 1 WLR 532; *Stevenson v United Road Transport Union* [1977] 2 All ER 941, [1977] ICR 893, CA; see Kidner 'The right to be a candidate for union office' (1973) 2 ILJ 65.
272 *Drake v Morgan* [1978] ICR 56; *Thomas v NUM (South Wales Area)* [1985] 2 All ER 1, [1985] IRLR 136.
273 *Clarke v Chadburn* [1985] 1 All ER 211, [1984] IRLR 350; *Taylor and Foulstone v NUM (Yorkshire Area)* [1984] IRLR 445.
274 *Brown v AUEW*, n 267 above; *Douglas v Graphical Paper and Media Union*, n 266 above; *Warrington v MSF* (D/94/01), Certification Officer.
275 *Taylor v NUM (Derbyshire Area)* [1984] IRLR 440; *Taylor and Foulstone v NUM (Yorkshire Area)*, n 273 above.
276 *Taylor and Foulstone v NUM (Yorkshire Area)* n 273 above. That case was of great importance as it was defiance of its order not to call the strike official that led to a fine for contempt of court which, when not paid, led to sequestration and receivership (*Clarke v Heathfield* [1985] ICR 203, CA).
277 See eg *Ryan v Unison* (D/45-48/01), Certification Officer; *Beaumont v MSF* (D/1-9/02), Certification Officer.
278 *Porter v NUJ* [1980] IRLR 404, HL; *Hughes v Unison* (D/10-12/02), Certification Officer. On discipline and expulsion rules, see Gennard, Gregory and Dunn 'Throwing the book: trade union rules on admission, discipline and expulsion' [1980] Employment Gazette 591.

not at stake. Expulsion[279] will therefore be closely scrutinised by a court and must be fully in accordance with the relevant rules of the union. There is no inherent common law power to expel and the courts will not readily construe one from a vague rule[280], and thus there must normally be (a) an express power to expel and (b) strict adherence to any necessary procedure which is laid down by the rules[281]. Such adherence (or lack of it) is a question of fact, and in some cases it will be a simple matter to enquire whether the action taken by the union was within the ambit of the power conferred by the rules. In more complicated cases, however, the courts have extended their power to intervene by claiming jurisdiction, where necessary, to interpret the union's rules. Thus, if it is the construction put upon the rule in question by the union which has led to the expulsion of the member, he may challenge the correctness of that construction, for that is a matter of law within the jurisdiction of the court[282].

Traditionally, the courts have been very reluctant to imply terms into union rule books, especially in relation to discipline. However, in *McVitae v UNISON*[283] it was held that the courts can as a matter of principle imply a power by a union to discipline a member where there are compelling circumstances to justify it, although the power to imply a disciplinary power should be exercised with care in view of the potentially serious consequences for the reputation and livelihood of the union member. In that case, the claimants were former members of NALGO against whom disciplinary proceedings in relation to alleged sexist and racist acts were pending at the time when NALGO merged with NUPE and COHSE to form UNISON. Charges were subsequently brought against the claimants under the UNISON rules, but those rules did not contain any express power allowing UNISON to take disciplinary action against members in relation to conduct prior to the amalgamation. In a landmark decision, Harrison J held that UNISON did have the power to take disciplinary action against the claimants, notwithstanding that there was no express rule to that effect in its rule book. He considered that the circumstances warranted implying a term empowering UNISON to discipline its members for conduct prior to the amalgamation, where the conduct in question was contrary both to the rules of the former and the present union; there was no evidence that the parties had intended that there should be a complete amnesty for conduct before the inception of the new union, and common sense suggested that this would not have been the intention.

Four particular problems deserve special mention. The first arises if the rule in question is cast in subjective terms ('conduct prejudicial to the union in the opinion of the executive') for while the courts do have a wide jurisdiction, they should not simply act as appeal bodies on acts and matters properly left within the discretion of the domestic tribunal in question; in *Lee v Showmen's Guild of Great*

---

279 One class of case does not come under the normal rules on expulsion; this is where the member was improperly admitted in the first place, so that his membership is ultra vires and when his name is removed he is not 'expelled': *Faramus v Film Artistes' Association* [1964] AC 925, [1964] 1 All ER 25, HL; *Martin v Scottish TGWU* [1952] 1 All ER 691, 1952 SC 92, HL.

280 *Kelly v NATSOPA* (1915) 31 TLR 632, CA; *Luby v Warwickshire Miners' Association* [1912] 2 Ch 371; *Abbott v Sullivan* [1952] 1 KB 189, [1952] 1 All ER 226, CA.

281 See eg *Bonsor v Musicians' Union* [1954] Ch 479, [1954] 1 All ER 822, CA; *Hiles v Amalgamated Society of Woodworkers* [1968] Ch 440, [1967] 3 All ER 70.

282 *Lee v Showmen's Guild of Great Britain* [1952] 2 QB 329 at 344, 350, [1952] 1 All ER 1175 at 1182, 1185, CA, per Denning LJ and and Romer LJ, respectively. This power of interpretation applies to all rules, but may be particularly important in an expulsion case.

283 [1996] IRLR 33. See also *AB v CD* [2001] IRLR 808, ChD, where a tie-break provision was implied into the union's election rules in order to give efficacy to the contract.

Britain Romer LJ stated[284] that it would require clear language to establish that the rules meant that a question was to lie entirely within the discretion of the union or one of its organs, but even so subjective rules may be more difficult to challenge[285] and may require the claimant to show mala fides or that the decision is so wrong that no reasonable tribunal acting bona fides could have reached it[286].

The second problem is whether the claimant must have exhausted all possible internal remedies (particularly any appeals provided for in the rules) before resorting to the courts; in some cases, such internal measures may bring about a more effective settlement than escalation of the dispute by the service of claim forms, and in some of the older cases a definite requirement of exhaustion of internal remedies can be found[287]. However, the modern approach is that to be found in the judgment of Goff J in *Leigh v NUR*[288], where he said that even an express clause in the rules that the claimant must exhaust his internal remedies cannot oust the jurisdiction of the court[289], but in such a case the court will tend to apply the clause unless the claimant shows good cause why it should not (an approach which recognises the importance of resolving disputes through agreed procedures[290]); where there is no such express provision, the court will more readily hear the case without exhaustion, but still has a discretion to require exhaustion if that seems appropriate on the facts of the case[291]. One potential problem for a member pursuing internal procedures is that of delay, particularly where those procedures involve several stages. That issue is now addressed by statute, for the Trade Union and Labour Relations (Consolidation) Act 1992, section 63 provides that where a member applies to his union to have some matter determined and six months have elapsed since then without any such determination, a court is to ignore any union rule requiring the exhaustion of internal remedies (or indeed any court practice to that effect) when deciding whether to hear the case[292]. However, section 64(6) states that this six-month rule is without prejudice to any rule of law by which a court could ignore any such union rule already, and so a claimant could still try to invoke the principles of *Leigh v NUR* (above) in order to bring court proceedings before the expiration of

284 *Lee v Showmen's Guild of Great Britain* [1952] 2 QB 329 at 349, [1952] 1 All ER 1175 at 1185; a hostile judicial approach to such clauses may be supported by the principle that it is contrary to public policy to allow the jurisdiction of the courts to be ousted.

285 *Kelly v NATSOPA* (1915) 31 TLR 632, CA; *Wolstenholme v Amalgamated Musicians' Union* [1920] 2 Ch 388. If, however, Lord Denning's views in *Edwards v SOGAT* (p 710 below) were ever to be accepted, a vague and subjective rule might be in danger of being declared invalid.

286 *Lee v Showmen's Guild of Great Britain* [1952] 2 QB 329 at 339, [1952] 1 All ER 1175 at 1178, per Somervell LJ; *Esterman v NALGO* [1974] ICR 625.

287 *White v Kuzych* [1951] AC 585, [1951] 2 All ER 435, PC.

288 [1970] Ch 326, [1969] 3 All ER 1249; *Lawlor v UPOW* [1965] Ch 712, [1965] 1 All ER 353; *Radford v NATSOPA* [1972] ICR 484; *Partington v NALGO* [1981] IRLR 537, Ct of Sess.

289 *Scott v Avery* (1856) 5 HL Cas 811. This principle could invalidate other restrictions on legal action, such as a clause requiring union consent before such an action is brought: *Enderby Town Football Club Ltd v Football Association Ltd* [1971] Ch 591, [1971] 1 All ER 215, CA.

290 A point acknowledged by Ralph Gibson LJ in *Longley v NUJ* [1987] IRLR 109, CA.

291 The Certification Officer has the power to refuse to accept an application concerning a breach of the rules unless satisfied that all reasonable steps have been taken to use any internal complaints procedures to resolve the dispute: Trade Union and Labour Relations (Consolidation) Act 1992, s 108B(1).

292 If the court is satisfied that the delay is attributable to the claimant's unreasonable conduct, it may extend the six-month period: s 63(4). Rules on internal remedies include rules requiring or permitting some form of conciliation or arbitration machinery.

six months. One problem here is whether a claimant may bring an action to prevent impending proceedings by his union (for example disciplinary or expulsion proceedings); there have been cases where a court has been persuaded to intervene in advance, on the basis that no reasonable tribunal acting bona fides could possibly find against the claimant[293], but it is clear from the later decision of the Court of Appeal in *Longley v NUJ*[294] that such cases are highly exceptional. Normally, therefore, the court will expect the claimant to proceed at least with the original internal hearing against him, so that there is a substantive decision of sorts before the court on whose validity it can pronounce.

The third problem is one of terminology. The phrase 'ultra vires' is used frequently in these cases, but it appears to have two meanings – it is widely used to describe an act which is, quite simply, contrary to the union's rules (for example an act of the executive which is beyond their powers as defined by the rules), but it is also sometimes given a narrower meaning (more in line with company law) of an act which is outside the *objects* of the union itself. The use of 'ultra vires' as a synonym for breach of contract, while terminologically incorrect, is at least coherent in conceptual terms; however, the second meaning presents a greater difficulty, because it is doubtful whether the ultra vires doctrine (in this narrow sense) can be applied to trade unions *at all*. There are two main reasons for this view: first, under the present law a union does not have to have an objects clause, so any argument on this narrower ground would depend on being able to discern 'objects' from the rule book as it stands; secondly, the Trade Union and Labour Relations (Consolidation) Act 1992, section 10, states that a trade union is not and '*shall not be treated as if it were* a body corporate …', and so it can be argued that the application to a trade union, which is an unincorporated association, of a doctrine developed by the courts to restrict the activities of companies, which are artificial legal persons with limited capacity, is inappropriate[295]. Be that as it may, these two separate meanings can be seen in *Hopkins v National Union of Seamen*[296] in which a resolution by the union executive to raise a levy on members to support the NUM in the miners' strike was held to be 'ultra vires' (in the wider sense) since the executive did not, on a proper construction of the rules, have the right to raise such a levy; however, the expenditure by the executive of amounts from existing union funds on aid to the NUM was held not to be 'ultra vires' (in the narrow sense), since the union rules set out its objects as 'To improve the conditions and protect the interests of all members of the union' and it was quite arguable that giving aid to the NUM would help to achieve those objects (for example by ensuring a high supply of coal, to be transported in ships employing

---

293 *Esterman v NALGO* [1974] ICR 625 is the prime example; see also *Partington v NALGO*, n 288, above. Such actions were also seen during the miners' strike, restraining threatened disciplinary action against working miners either because the disciplinary rules had not been validly adopted (*Clarke v Chadburn* [1985] 1 All ER 211, [1984] IRLR 350; *Taylor and Foulstone v NUM (Yorkshire Area)* [1984] IRLR 445), or because the strike was not official because it had been called in defiance of the rules (*Taylor v NUM (Derbyshire Area)* [1984] IRLR 440).

294 [1987] IRLR 109, CA.

295 The case is put convincingly by Wedderburn (1985) 14 ILJ 127. Crucially, in the period between 1901 and 1971 unions were widely regarded as 'quasi-corporations', hence the argument that they were subject to the ultra vires doctrine: see for example *Cotter v NUS* [1929] 2 Ch 58, CA; however, the enactment in 1974 of the formula now contained in s 10 could be said to have closed off that particular line of reasoning.

296 [1985] ICR 268, [1985] IRLR 157.

NUS members)[297]. Thus, the levy was restrained by injunction but the expenditure was not.

The fourth problem concerns the possible application of the rule in *Foss v Harbottle* [298] to an action by a union member against his union and its executive. In company law, a member who wishes to bring an action to remedy an alleged wrong done to the company may be met with the rule in *Foss v Harbottle* that (a) the proper claimant in such a case is the company itself, not an individual member; and (b) that if the alleged wrong is something which might be ratified by a simple majority vote of the members, no individual member may maintain an action in respect of that matter, the logic being that if the majority decide to ratify the wrong, there is nothing left to complain of, whereas if the majority do not ratify the wrong, there is then no reason why the company itself should not sue. The company law rule is, however, subject to a number of exceptions; for example, it does not apply where the complainant's action is based on an infringement of his personal rights, nor to an ultra vires act, since such an act cannot lawfully be later ratified. The rule has in the past been applied to trade unions, on account of their quasi-corporate status[299], and the courts have declined to interfere in internal union affairs to remedy some minor or insignificant breach of the rules which causes no substantial injustice[300]. In practice, however, the court may readily be able to find that one of the exceptions to the rule applies; so, for example, in *Wise v Union of Shop, Distributive and Allied Workers*[301], a case involving a challenge by two union members to a decision of the union executive relating to the election of union officers, Chadwick J held that as the source of the union executive's powers was the contract between all of the members embodied in the rules of the union, each union member had a contractual right to complain of a breach of the rules which was individual to that member, and so the rule in *Foss v Harbottle* had no application; and in *Taylor v NUM (Derbyshire Area)*[302], Vinelott J granted an injunction restraining further expenditure on an improperly called strike[303], on the grounds that, being ultra vires, the misapplication of funds could not be ratified by a majority of the union's members. Ultimately, however, the practical point remains that an action by a member on behalf of the union may be less certain to produce results than an action based upon infringement of his personal rights since, at the end of the day, a judge might decide (as Vinelott J eventually did in *Taylor*[304]) that he will not interfere in the internal workings of the union if it appears that to do so would serve no useful purpose:

297   Similarly, it was held that the expenditure was not ultra vires merely because the miners' strike had been held by the courts to be unofficial; the legality of the expenditure was to be judged by references to the NUS's objects, not the NUM's rule book.
298   (1843) 2 Hare 461.
299   *Cotter v NUS* [1929] 2 Ch 58, CA; *Hodgson v NALGO* [1972] 1 All ER 15, [1972] 1 WLR 130. See n 295 above.
300   *See eg Brown v Amalgamated Union of Engineering Workers* [1976] ICR 147 (election irregularities).
301   [1996] ICR 691, [1996] IRLR 609, Ch D.
302   [1985] IRLR 99.
303   Applying *Howden v Yorkshire Miners' Association* [1903] 1 KB 308, CA; upheld [1905] AC 256, HL.
304   Vinelott J refused to make an order requiring the union officers to repay the £1.7m already spent in breach of their fiduciary duty to the union, on the grounds (at 108) that a majority of the members may have decided in the future not to seek repayment from the officers (who had acted throughout in good faith), so that the court order would have been unnecessary. However, this sits rather oddly alongside the holding that, as the officers' action was ultra vires, it could not be ratified; once again, this may beg the question of what is meant by 'ultra vires' in this context (above).

'... [I]t does not matter much whether the rule [in *Foss v Harbottle*] is held to apply to unions or not. The courts are in principle reluctant to intervene in the internal affairs of any association, corporate or unincorporate. If they do intervene, they take the view that the affairs of the association should generally be conducted in accordance with the will of the majority, and they will decline to interfere if the order sought can be overturned by a simple majority of the members. You can please yourself whether you call that the rule in *Foss v Harbottle* or not.[305]'

The second ground for judicial intervention at common law has been through enforcement of the procedural requirements of natural justice; the detailed requirements are fully discussed elsewhere[306], but may be summed up in brief as absence of bias (actual or potential), the right to a hearing and the maxim nemo judex in sua causa (ie no one person should act as both 'prosecutor' and 'judge'). In the nature of things, the rules against potential bias may have to be applied realistically in union cases, particularly in a dispute which has divided the union, making it difficult to find a tribunal which could not possibly be biased in any way[307]. However, there remains a clear rule against actual bias[308], and in an expulsion case the requirement of a genuine and unprejudiced hearing may be particularly strong[309], though once again the actual procedure need not follow a set legalistic pattern (other than that laid down in the rules), as long as it is fair; so, for example, there is no inalienable right to legal representation[310], though the member should be given proper notification of the charges against him and be given a proper opportunity to refute them[311]. It used to be a moot point whether the rules of natural justice could be expressly excluded in a union's rules (for example a rule specifically disentitling a member to a hearing), but the weight of modern authority is against any such power to exclude[312].

Thus it can be seen that, even before the legislative onslaught of the last two decades, the courts at common law had succeeded in evolving two considerable bases for their interventionist jurisdiction, in order to regulate to some extent the internal affairs of a union:

305 Perrins *Trade Union Law* (1985) p 97.
306 De Smith, Woolf and Jowell *Judicial Review of Administrative Action* (5th edn, 1998); Elias and Ewing *Trade Union Democracy, Members' Rights and the Law* (1987) pp 212–226.
307 *Maclean v Workers' Union* [1929] 1 Ch 602, per Maugham J. See also the decision in *Rowe v Radio Rentals Ltd* [1982] IRLR 177, EAT in the analogous context of dismissal from employment.
308 *Taylor v NUS* [1967] 1 All ER 767, [1967] 1 WLR 532; *Losinska v CPSA* [1976] ICR 473, CA; *Roebuck v NUM* [1977] ICR 573; *Roebuck v NUM (No 2)* [1978] ICR 676. Cf, however, the decision in *Hamlet v GMBATU* [1987] ICR 150, [1986] IRLR 293, Ch D that there is no immutable rule of natural justice that a person sitting on a union body at first instance cannot sit upon appeal, particularly where the rules allow for such double appearance (although note that this was not an expulsion case).
309 *Annamunthodo v Oilfield Workers' Trade Union* [1961] AC 945, [1961] 3 All ER 621, PC; *Losinksa v CPSA* [1976] ICR 473, CA.
310 *Enderby Town Football Club Ltd v Football Association Ltd* [1971] Ch 591, [1971] 1 All ER 215, CA. See also *Pett v Greyhound Racing Association* [1969] 1 QB 125, [1968] 2 All ER 545, CA; and *Maynard v Osmond* [1977] QB 240, [1977] 1 All ER 64, CA.
311 *Stevenson v United Road Transport Union* [1977] 2 All ER 941, [1977] ICR 893, CA.
312 *Faramus v Film Artistes' Association* [1964] AC 925, [1964] 1 All ER 25, HL, particularly per Lords Evershed and Pearce; *Enderby Town Football Club Ltd v Football Association Ltd* (n 289 above); *Breen v AEU* [1971] 2 QB 175, [1971] 1 All ER 1148, CA.

'It is through insisting on a strict observance of the union's own rules and of the elementary rules of decency which bear the ancient name of 'natural justice' that the courts can and do make up for the lack of a statutory guarantee of an equal opportunity to participate in the making of union decisions[313].'

However, in at least two respects the extent of this jurisdiction is uncertain. The first problem is whether the protective rules on expulsion can apply to refusal of membership in the first place. The second is whether the courts have jurisdiction over the substance of union rules, so as to be able to strike down harsh and oppressive rules. The first problem arises because, although the courts may enforce the contract of membership in an expulsion of someone already a member, that cannot apply to exclusion of an applicant for membership, for by definition there is at that stage no contract of membership to enforce. In the absence of legislation[314], there appeared to be little that the law could do about this. However, in *Nagle v Feilden*[315] Lord Denning MR put forward a legally recognised 'right to work' as a possible legal basis for protecting an applicant excluded from membership for arbitrary or capricious reasons; the extent of this development remains uncertain, partly because the case did not concern a trade union, a point which brings us on to the second problem. Can a court go beyond the simple interpretation of union rules as they stand, and actually strike down a rule which the court sees as causing an injustice to a member? The orthodox view was that the court could not query the substance of the rule[316] ; if any doctrine of law is capable of doing so, it is that of restraint of trade[317], and in a non-union case such as *Nagle v Feilden* that is feasible. However, the purposes of a trade union have been immune from the restraint of trade doctrine since the Trade Union Act 1871 and so a challenge to a restrictive union rule seemed to be impossible on that ground[318]. Nevertheless, in *Edwards v SOGAT*[319] the majority of the Court of Appeal considered that an automatic expulsion rule was invalid; Sachs LJ considered that it was in restraint of trade and not covered by the immunity in the 1871 Act (since it was not a 'proper' purpose for a union), but Lord Denning MR flew higher, striking it down on the basis that it was ultra vires and void since it interfered with the right to work. This approach, which is essentially one based upon concepts of public policy, can be seen again in his Lordship's judgment in *Enderby Town Football Club Ltd v Football Association Ltd*[320], where he asserted a wide

---

313 Kahn-Freund *Labour and the Law* (2nd edn, 1977) p 224.
314 Exclusion from a union is now covered by the Trade Union and Labour Relations (Consolidation) Act 1992, s 174; see p 713 below. Note also that the anti-discrimination legislation outlaws certain reasons for exclusion (see ch 5 above).
315 [1966] 2 QB 633, [1966] 1 All ER 689, CA; the case is discussed at p 267 above.
316 *Faramus v Film Artistes' Association* [1964] AC 925, [1964] 1 All ER 25, HL.
317 Which can be prayed in aid by a person not party to the actual agreement (*Eastham v Newcastle United Football Club Ltd* [1964] Ch 413, [1963] 3 All ER 139, HC; *Greig v Insole* [1978] 3 All ER 449, [1978] 1 WLR 302) and so could be used by a person not yet a member of an association, but wishing to join (as in *Nagle v Fielden*). For restraint of trade, see ch 3 above.
318 *Faramus v Film Artistes' Association*, n 316, above.
319 [1971] Ch 354, [1970] 3 All ER 689, CA; the case actually concerned the quantification of damages, the validity of the rule in question only arising indirectly; Megaw LJ came to the same decision as Lord Denning MR and Sachs LJ but without adopting their reasoning on this point.
320 [1971] Ch 591 at 606, [1971] 1 All ER 215 at 219, CA.

jurisdiction in the courts to control the rules of unions and other important associations on the basis that they form 'legislative codes' which must be subject to notions of public policy. The approach of Sachs LJ in *Edwards v SOGAT* is no longer tenable (if it ever was)[321] since the immunity from the restraint of trade doctrine now contained in section 11 of the Trade Union and Labour Relations (Consolidation) Act 1992, applies both to trade union purposes *and* rules. The approach of Lord Denning, however, is not so easily disposed of[322], and leads to considerable uncertainty as to the extent of a court's power to intervene.

5 STATUTORY CONTROL OF INTERNAL UNION AFFAIRS

The period between 1980 and 1997 saw a radical transformation in the law relating to internal union affairs, as a result of a series of legislative interventions of the profoundest significance. The statutory provisions were introduced in several stages, as part of the Conservative government's 'step-by-step' reform of trade union law. The Employment Acts 1980 and 1982 were largely concerned with external activities of trade unions rather than their internal workings, but the 1980 Act reintroduced a statutory right not to be unreasonably excluded or expelled from membership where a closed shop was in operation, and, in the days before balloting was compulsory, offered at least the carrot of state funding for union ballots by establishing a scheme (administered by the Certification Officer) whereby an independent trade union could apply for reimbursement of expenses incurred in holding a secret postal ballot for certain purposes; the 1982 Act laid down the circumstances where a union would be held liable in tort for the actions of its officers and members. The Trade Union Act 1984 represented a significant turning-point, for it was markedly more interventionist in the internal affairs of trade unions, the main theme of the Act being to 'give unions back to their members' by imposing minimum standards of democracy, including ballots for high union office, for political funds, and before industrial action (albeit indirectly, by removing the statutory immunities against liability in tort where such a ballot had not been held). Four years later, the Employment Act 1988 went considerably further, tightening up the rules on balloting for union office, giving members rights to be balloted before being called out on industrial action and to challenge certain perceived misuses of union funds, and introducing a new right not to be unjustifiably disciplined. That Act also established the office of the Commissioner for the Rights of Trade Union Members (CROTUM) to assist union members in taking legal action to enforce statutory rights against their union. The relentless pace continued with the Employment Act 1990, which although mainly concerned with external activities, greatly extended the range of circumstances where a union could be held responsible in tort for the actions of its officers and members[323], and extended the powers of the CROTUM to include action by union members to enforce union rules. Just when most commentators were beginning to think that this seemingly inexorable legislative steamroller had reached a halt, the Trade Union Reform and Employment Rights

---

321 It appeared directly to contradict the decision on this point by the House of Lords in *Faramus v Film Artistes' Association*, n 316 above.
322 It was applied to an automatic expulsion rule by Plowman J in *Radford v NATSOPA* [1972] ICR 484.
323 See p 818 below.

Act 1993 introduced a broad right not to be excluded or expelled from a trade union (no longer restricted to closed shop situations, unlike the provisions in the 1980 Act which it replaced), required periodic renewal of check-off arrangements for collecting union subscriptions, increased control over union financial affairs, and phased out the provisions entitling unions to claim state reimbursement of the cost of holding ballots[324].

Many of these reforms, while generating acute controversy upon their introduction, have over time gained a large measure of acceptance within the trade union movement (albeit a grudging acceptance in certain quarters); others, and in particular the controls over admission, discipline and expulsion, are still bitterly resented by many as undermining the status of trade unions as voluntary associations and as threatening the very principle of trade unionism itself. Any faint hopes there might have been within the union movement that the election of a Labour government in 1997 would lead to a widespread relaxation of the legislative stranglehold on internal union affairs were dashed by the publication of the White Paper, *Fairness at Work*[325], in 1998. There have, however, been a few modest reforms, in particular the relaxation of the strike ballot provisions (considered in chapter 11) and the abolition of the need to obtain periodic renewal of the employer's authorisation to deduct union subscriptions[326], and at the time of writing the government was consulting on a further modest series of proposed amendments to internal trade union law, including removing the requirement for union presidents to be elected by secret ballot where they are already elected members of the executive, widening the permitted range of balloting methods (for example to include electronic voting methods), and simplifying the law on political fund ballots and other statutory union ballots and elections[327].

Finally, it has been suggested that the extent of the statutory incursion into internal trade union affairs, particularly in relation to the control of membership and discipline, is so destructive of union autonomy that it constitutes a violation of Article 11 of the European Convention on Human Rights, the point being that freedom of association guarantees not only the right of individuals to associate together in organisations, but also the right of those organisations to draw up their own rules and administer their own affairs[328]. In *Cheall v United Kingdom*[329], the European Commission on Human Rights stated: 'In the exercise of their rights under Article 11(1), unions must remain free to decide, in accordance with union rules, questions concerning admission to and expulsion from the union.' Crucially, the Commission accepted that a trade union's right to choose its

---

324 Trade Union Reform and Employment Rights Act 1993, s 7. Take-up under the scheme was initially slow owing to a TUC boycott (only £72,496 was paid out in 1984), but at its peak in 1992 the scheme was costing the state in excess of £4.25m per year, hence the decision to phase it out, over a three-year period from April 1993; it ceased to operate altogether on 1 April 1996.
325 Cm 3968, 1998.
326 See p 726 below.
327 DTI *Review of the Employment Relations Act 1999* (2003), Annex C. The proposals were based on a suggestions from the Better Regulation Task Force of areas where regulation 'might impose unnecessary or burdensome restrictions on union behaviour'.
328 See Ewing 'Article 11 and the right to freedom of association' in Ewing (ed) *Human Rights at Work* (2000).
329 (1986) 8 EHRR 74; (1985) 42 DR 178, EComHR; see p 740 below.

members was not absolute, and that there might be circumstances where the state 'must protect the individual against any abuse of a dominant position by trade unions'[330], but it is arguable that the extent of the statutory control of internal union affairs at the present time goes well beyond what might be considered necessary to meet that particular need. The International Labour Organisation's Committee of Experts has denounced the provisions on discipline in the 1992 Act as incompatible with ILO Convention No 87 (Freedom of Association and Protection of the Right to Organise)[331], and there has been similar condemnation from the Social Rights Committee[332] in relation to infringements of the right to organise under Article 5 of the European Social Charter[333]. Unlike Article 11, these international standards have no direct legal force, and successive UK governments have seemingly been untroubled by the depressing regularity with which national law has been judged against them and found wanting. They are by no means without legal significance, however, because they may be used as a guide to the interpretation of Article 11[334], as the European Court of Human Rights has recently confirmed in *Wilson and Palmer v United Kingdom*[335]. As Ewing has observed: 'The fact that these statutory restraints [on union membership and discipline] violate the freedom of association guarantees of other relevant treaties strengthens the case that they also violate Article 11 of the ECHR, particularly in view of the importance accorded these treaties in the *Wilson and Palmer* case.[336]'

(i) Exclusion or expulsion

As seen above at head 4, the courts were able to develop a range of techniques at common law to protect the interests of individual union members in cases of discipline and expulsion, by requiring a rigid adherence to the rules and procedures laid down in the union's rule book, and by the imposition of standards of procedural fairness. However, these common law controls could be considered as deficient in certain respects, not least in the fact that they do not provide any

---

330 The Commission gave as examples the situation where exclusion or expulsion was not in accordance with the union's rules, or where the rules were wholly unreasonable or arbitrary, or where the consequences of exclusion or expulsion resulted in exceptional hardship such as job loss because of a closed shop.

331 Art 3 (1) states: 'Workers' and employers' organisations shall have the right to draw up their constitutions and rules, to elect their representatives in full freedom, to organise their administration and activities and to formulate their programmes.' Cf also Article 3(2): 'The public authorities shall refrain from any interference which would restrict this right or impede the lawful exercise thereof.'

332 Formerly known as the Committee of Independent Experts.

333 Art 5 states: 'With a view to ensuring or promoting the freedom of workers and employers to form local, national or international organisations for the protection of their economic or social interests and to join those organisations, the Contracting Parties undertake that national law shall not be such as to impair, nor shall it be so applied as to impair this freedom ...'

334 In *Cheall v United Kingdom* (n 329 above), the Commission stated that ILO Convention No 87 'must be taken into account' in construing Art 11. See also *Sigurjonsson v Iceland* (1993) 16 EHRR 462, where the ECtHR held that the Social Charter could be used as an aid to the construction of Article 11. The UK courts have to date shown a marked reluctance to have regard to ILO Conventions or the Social Charter: see Ewing, above n 328, p 102.

335 [2002] IRLR 568, ECtHR. The ILO Conventions and the Social Charter, together with the associated jurisprudence of the ILO's Committee of Experts and the Social Charter's Social Rights Committee, were described by the Court as 'relevant material' in the interpretation of Art 11.

336 Ewing 'The Implications of Wilson and Palmer' (2003) 32 ILJ 1 at p 17.

satisfactory mechanism for the control of exclusions. The Industrial Relations Act 1971 sought to impose statutory controls on admission to and expulsion from unions[337], with restrictions on the exclusion of appropriately qualified workers from membership by 'arbitrary or unreasonable discrimination', and on 'unfair or unreasonable disciplinary action'. These provisions were carried over into the Trade Union and Labour Relations Act 1974 by a reluctant minority Labour government, but were repealed in 1976 in a political compromise which involved the TUC in forming an Independent Review Committee to consider cases of expulsion and exclusion in a closed shop situation. The Employment Act 1980 reintroduced a statutory action against a union for a person expelled or refused membership, in the form of a right not to be unreasonably excluded or expelled from membership; it bore a resemblance to the action previously contained in the 1974 Act, but with the important difference that the protection only applied where a closed shop agreement was in operation. The justification for imposing *some* controls on union admissions and expulsions in a closed shop, where the possession of a union card may determine a worker's ability to pursue his trade, is self-evident, but rather than attempting to define the circumstances in which an exclusion or expulsion would be justifiable, the approach taken in the 1980 Act was to leave it to the tribunal (as the industrial jury) to decide whether or not the trade union had acted reasonably or unreasonably 'in accordance with equity and the substantial merits of the case'.

With the tightening of the statutory controls on the ability of employers to enforce a closed shop against both existing and prospective employees, the justification for the continued retention of measures controlling access to union membership could be said to have receded. However, the Conservative government's view, as expressed in the Green Paper, *Industrial Relations in the 1990s*[338], was that individuals should not only have the right to decide whether or not to belong to a trade union, but should also have the right to join the union of their choice. Accordingly, the Trade Union Reform and Employment Rights Act 1993 repealed the measures on unreasonable expulsion and exclusion dating from the 1980 Act, and replaced them with a new, more general right not to be excluded or expelled from a union[339]. Two highly significant features of the current provisions should be noted: first, unlike the pre-1993 laws, the statutory controls on expulsion and exclusion are not restricted to those seeking to work in closed shop employment, but apply generally; and secondly, the former approach whereby exclusions and expulsions fell to be judged by the tribunal against a broad test of reasonableness has been abandoned; instead, the present law provides for a limited number of circumstances where a union will be permitted to control access to or retention of membership. Thus, the exclusion or expulsion of an individual is permitted if (and only if):

(a) he does not satisfy, or no longer satisfies, an 'enforceable membership requirement' contained in the rules of the union;

(b) he does not qualify, or no longer qualifies, for membership of the union by reason of the union operating only in a particular geographical area;

---

337 Industrial Relations Act 1971, s 65.
338 Cm 1602, 1991.
339 Trade Union and Labour Relations (Consolidation) Act 1992, ss 174–177, as substituted by s 14 of the 1993 Act. 'Exclusion' from a union refers to a refusal to admit into membership, not to suspension of the privileges of membership: *NACODS v Gluchowski* [1996] IRLR 252, EAT.

(c) where the union is a single-employer union[340], he is not, or is no longer employed by that employer;

(d) the exclusion or expulsion is entirely[341] attributable to his conduct.

Paragraphs (a) and (d) are undoubtedly the key elements in the current provisions. An 'enforceable membership requirement' is defined[342] as one which restricts membership *solely* by reference to one or more of the following criteria: (a) employment in a specified trade, industry or profession; (b) occupational description (including grade, level or category of appointment); or (c) possession of specified trade, industrial or professional qualifications or work experience. Union membership rules which fall outside these categories (for example a union rule excluding fascists) will, it seems, be unenforceable, unless the union can show that the exclusion or expulsion is entirely attributable to that person's conduct. Certain types of conduct must be disregarded altogether, viz, being or ceasing to be (or having been or ceased to be) (i) a member of another trade union, (ii) employed by a particular employer or at a particular place, or (iii) a member of a political party; and conduct of the type which is protected from the imposition of discipline by virtue of the controls on unjustifiable discipline in section 65 (considered below). So, for example, it would appear that a union will be entitled to refuse membership to an applicant who is in arrears with subscriptions or under discipline with another union, but may not refuse membership simply because that person previously belonged to another union, or had failed to participate in industrial action while a member of that union or belonged to the BNP.

A person who claims to have been excluded or expelled in contravention of the section may present a complaint to an employment tribunal within six months of the expulsion or exclusion, or within a further reasonable period if the tribunal considers that it was not reasonably practicable to present the complaint within six months[343]. If the tribunal finds the complaint well-founded it must make a declaration to that effect[344], but no award of compensation will be made at that stage. A person who has obtained a declaration from a tribunal may claim compensation[345], but here the action becomes more complicated, for the procedure to be followed varies depending on whether the union has in fact admitted (or readmitted) the applicant pursuant to the declaration. The applicant must wait for at least four weeks after the date of the declaration (to give the union an opportunity to admit or readmit), but then has until six months after the date of the declaration to present a claim for an award of compensation. If the applicant has been admitted or readmitted by the time of the application, complaint lies to a tribunal (with appeal on law to the EAT); if not, complaint lies directly to the EAT, which becomes, in effect, a court of first instance for this purpose. In both cases the amount of compensation will be such as is considered just and equitable

---

340 This includes associated employers.

341 This may cause problems where there is arguably more than one reason for the expulsion or exclusion; in other contexts it is normally sufficient to show that the prohibited reason is the 'principal' reason (see eg s 152, p 685 above).

342 Trade Union and Labour Relations (Consolidation) Act 1992, s 174(3).

343 Trade Union and Labour Relations (Consolidation) Act 1992, s 175. The 'escape clause' in the limitation period is similar to that applying to an unfair dismissal claim, and so would be subject to the case law in that context: *GMB v Hamm* (15 November 2000, EAT); see p 512 above.

344 Trade Union and Labour Relations (Consolidation) Act 1992, s 176(1). There is an appeal to the EAT on a point of law: s 291. Under the pre-1993 provisions there was an appeal on law *and* fact.

345 Trade Union and Labour Relations (Consolidation) Act 1992, s 176(2).

in all the circumstances, subject to a maximum amount which is tied to the aggregate of the maximum basic and compensatory awards for unfair dismissal[346], and in the case of an award by the EAT, a minimum of £5,700.

These provisions add up to an extremely tight strait-jacket on union admissions and expulsions, particularly as there is no residual test of reasonableness where an exclusion or expulsion falls outside the permitted categories. The acknowledged target of the current provisions were the principles developed by the TUC to regulate inter-union disputes over membership (the Bridlington Principles, considered below), reflecting the previous government's view that the freedom of an individual worker to belong to the union of his choice should not be constrained by arrangements reached between unions over their respective spheres of influence. Under the pre-1993 provisions it was never clearly established whether an expulsion of a union member because of a decision of the TUC Disputes Committee under the Bridlington Principles would, in general, be held to be reasonable or unreasonable (although the Code of Practice on Closed Shop Agreements and Arrangements, revoked in 1991, stated that this might be a good reason not to admit). However, at common law the House of Lords in *Cheall v APEX*[347] held that the Bridlington Principles were not contrary to public policy, and that it was not unlawful for a union to expel a member pursuant to a rule allowing expulsion in order to comply with a decision of the TUC Disputes Committee. Lord Diplock in that case adopted a stance supportive of union autonomy over access to membership, stating that 'there can be no right of an individual to associate with other individuals who are not willing to associate with him'; the enactment of just such a right in the 1993 Act reflected a very different view of the meaning and dictates of freedom of association. The right of a majority of union members not to associate with another was also affirmed by the European Commission on Human Rights in *Cheall v United Kingdom*[348], but while the Commission decided that the right of association under Article 11 of the Convention does not create a right to join a trade union of one's choice in all circumstances, it also emphasised that a trade union's right to choose its members was not absolute, and that 'for the right to join a union to be effective the state must protect the individual against any abuse of a dominant position by trade unions'. As seen above, a challenge to the statutory provisions on exclusion and expulsion under the Human Rights Act 1998 remains a possibility, particularly in view of the expansive decision of the European Court of Human Rights in *Wilson and Palmer v United Kingdom*[349], but the emphasis in other cases decided under the Convention[350] on the individual rather than the collective aspect of freedom of association means that it remains doubtful whether such a challenge would succeed[351].

Finally, concern was expressed on the introduction of the present rules in 1993 that the undermining of the Bridlington Principles could lead to fragmentation

---

346 As from 1 February 2003, £61,300. Compensation may be reduced on account of contributory fault: s 176(5); on contributory fault under the pre-1993 provisions (which were identical on this point) see *Howard v NGA* [1985] ICR 101, [1984] IRLR 489, CA, and for an example of this procedure generally see *Day v SOGAT 1982* [1986] ICR 640, EAT. There is no express duty to mitigate loss, unlike under the pre-1993 provisions.

347 [1983] ICR 398, [1983] IRLR 215, HL; see p 740 below. The statutory action was not available in this case because there was no closed shop in operation.

348 (1986) 8 EHRR 74, 42 DR 178, EComHR.

349 [2002] IRLR 128; see p 670 above

350 See eg *Young, James and Webster v United Kingdom* (1981) 4 EHRR 38, ECtHR, discussed at p 697 above.

351 See generally Ewing, 'The Human Rights Act and Labour Law' (1998) 27 ILJ 275; Palmer 'Human Rights: Implications for Labour Law' (2000) 59 CLJ 168.

of union representation and have a destabilising effect on collective bargaining, particularly with regard to single-union deals. On one analysis there is no necessary reason why this should be so, since the law only gives workers a right to join a union of their choice: it places no obligation on an employer to recognise that union, as the statutory recognition procedure cannot be used by a union where the employer already recognises another trade union in respect of workers within the same bargaining unit[352]. However, it is not difficult to envisage circumstances where a disaffected group of union members might leave the recognised union to join a non-recognised union, which might itself then press hard for recognition, with potentially harmful consequences for industrial relations.

(ii) Unjustifiable disciplining

The Trade Union and Labour Relations (Consolidation) Act 1992, section 64[353] gives a trade union member a statutory right not to be unjustifiably disciplined by his union. This provision was introduced in the aftermath of the miners' strike of 1984/85, with the particular aim of protecting dissentient members who refused to go along with the majority view within the union (for example by refusing to comply with a strike call), and 'whistle-blowers' who allege wrongdoing by the union, or its officers or representatives. It is important to appreciate at the outset that while the generalised nature of the exposition of the right (in particular the use of the term 'unjustifiable') implies some evaluative process, the tribunal here has no wide discretion to determine whether the conduct in question is or is not unjustifiable; instead, subsection (2) lists the kinds of disciplining covered by the section and, crucially, section 65 lists exhaustively the circumstances in which any of those forms of disciplining will be considered 'unjustifiable' within the meaning of the Act. The question whether the imposition of discipline is or is not unjustifiable is therefore purely a matter of statutory interpretation[354].

Discipline is given a wide meaning in this context. Under subsection (2), the following forms of discipline are covered by the section: (a) expulsion from the union or a branch or section of the union; (b) a fine; (c) the treatment of sums paid by way of subscriptions or otherwise as not having been paid or paid for a different purpose; (d) deprivation of some or all of the benefits, services or facilities normally enjoyed by union members; (e) encouraging or advising another union not to accept the individual in question as a member; or (f) subjecting the individual to 'any other detriment'[355]. Any determination[356] by

---

352 See p 74 above.
353 As amended by the Trade Union Reform and Employment Rights Act 1993, s 16. The provisions derive from the Employment Act 1988, s 3.
354 On the prospects of a successful challenge to these provisions under the Human Rights Act 1998, see the text at n 349 above.
355 Detriment' is not defined; in *NALGO v Killorn and Simm* [1991] ICR 1, [1990] IRLR 464, the EAT held that suspension from membership necessarily implies deprivation of the benefits etc of membership, and that naming a member on a list of strike-breakers could constitute a detriment. For the interpretation of 'detriment' in discrimination cases, see p 283 above.
356 This means a final decision rather than a provisional or conditional recommendation: *TGWU v Webber* [1990] ICR 711, [1990] IRLR 462, EAT.

the union to impose such discipline will be 'unjustifiable' if the reason (or *one* of the reasons) for it being imposed is conduct falling within section 65; as originally enacted, the section listed the following as conduct for which the imposition of discipline would be unjustifiable: (a) failure to participate in or support any strike or other industrial action[357] (whether by his union or by others) or the expression of opposition or lack of support for such action; (b) failure to contravene (for purposes connected with a strike or other industrial action) any requirement of his contract of employment or any other agreement with his employer; (c) making any assertion that the union, its officers, representatives or trustees have broken the union's rules or the law[358]; (d) encouraging or assisting someone else to act as in (b) or (c) above; (e) contravening any requirement imposed by or in consequence of a determination by the union that is itself an infringement of individual rights under the section. As if this were not enough, the Trade Union Reform and Employment Rights Act 1993 added a further five categories to the list of conduct protected from discipline: (f) failure to agree to the deduction of membership subscriptions from wages; (g) resigning (or proposing to resign) from the union or from another union, or becoming, refusing to become or being a member of another union; (h) working (or proposing to work) with others who are not members of the union or who are or are not members of another union; (i) working (or proposing to work) for an employer who employs non-union labour; (j) requiring the union to fulfil any of its duties to its members under the 1992 Act (for example requesting a copy of the scrutineer's report on a ballot). A union member is also protected against being disciplined for consulting or seeking the advice or assistance of the Certification Officer, and for proposing to engage in any of the above conduct or doing anything preparatory or incidental to such conduct[359].

The specified conduct does not have to be the sole or even the main reason for the imposition of discipline by the union in order to be immune, and the only circumstance where conduct listed above falls outside the statutory protection is where the union can show that it would have disciplined the member for that conduct anyway, whether or not it fell within the section.

An individual member who considers that he has been unjustifiably disciplined may complain to an employment tribunal which, if it finds the complaint well-founded, must make a declaration to that effect[360]. The complaint must be made within three months of the date of the infringement; this is subject to the usual escape clause allowing a complaint to be made out of time where it was not reasonably practicable to bring it in time[361], but unusually the tribunal may also

---

357 This is undoubtedly the most controversial aspect of this right, since it gives a union member a right not to participate in industrial action even where a strike ballot has been properly held. It has therefore been dubbed (accurately, if rather predictably) a 'scabs' charter'. See *Knowles v Fire Brigades Union* [1996] IRLR 617, CA, where Neill LJ held that the question of what is 'industrial action' in this context is a mixed question of fact and law.

358 Protection under this head does not apply if the accusation was false to the individual's knowledge, or he was acting otherwise in bad faith, and he has been disciplined on that ground alone: s 65(6). There is no requirement that he has reasonable grounds for believing that the allegation is true.

359 Trade Union and Labour Relations (Consolidation) Act 1992, s 65(3), (4), as amended by the Employment Relations Act 1999, Sch 9.

360 Trade Union and Labour Relations (Consolidation) Act 1992, s 66(1), (3). Appeal lies to the EAT on a question of law: s 291(2).

361 Trade Union and Labour Relations (Consolidation) Act 1992, s 66(2). For the application of the escape clause in the context of unfair dismissal claims, see p 512 above.

allow a complaint out of time where the delay is wholly or partly attributable to the applicant's reasonable efforts to appeal against the disciplinary decision or to have it reconsidered or reviewed, for example by pursuing the union's internal grievance procedures. This is a welcome endorsement of the desirability of resolving disputes through domestic procedures, and avoids the risk of a tribunal holding that a delay occasioned by the pursuit of an internal appeal may not be a good reason for extending the statutory limitation period[362].

Adopting a similar (though not identical) procedure to that in a successful complaint of exclusion or expulsion (above), section 67 goes on to provide that an individual who has obtained a declaration that his complaint is well-founded may seek the further remedies of compensation from the union and/or the return of any fine, etc, paid by him. Such a further claim cannot be made until four weeks after the date of the tribunal declaration[363], thereby giving the union time to make amends. If by that time the union has rescinded the disciplinary decision in question and has taken all steps necessary[364] to reverse anything done in pursuance of it, complaint lies to the employment tribunal, but if not, it lies directly to the EAT (once again, as under section 176, giving that appellate body original jurisdiction)[365]. Compensation will be what the tribunal considers just and equitable in the circumstances[366], again subject to a maximum amount tied to the maximum sum of the basic and compensatory awards for unfair dismissal (at the time of writing, £61,300), and, in the case of an award by the EAT, a minimum of £5,700[367].

In enacting these provisions, the statute had to deal with two major overlaps. First, it is made clear in section 64(5) that the existence of the right not to be unjustifiably disciplined is without prejudice to any existing common law rights, and so there may still be cases where for some reason it is advantageous for a member to rely on such rights, based on the rules and the contract of membership described above. Secondly, given that the relevant forms of discipline set out above include expulsion, there is a potential overlap with the provisions on expulsion in section 174; before the changes to that section by the Trade Union Reform and Employment Rights Act 1993, the position was that in the event of an overlap the complaint lay under section 176, not under section 66, but if the exclusion or expulsion infringed the right not to be unjustifiably disciplined, it was deemed unreasonable under section 176. After that Act the position is simplified, in that once a complaint relating to an expulsion is declared to be well-founded under

---

362 Contrast *Palmer v Southend-on-Sea Borough Council* [1984] ICR 372, [1984] IRLR 119, CA (an unfair dismissal case): see p 514. In *NALGO v Killorn and Simm* [1991] ICR 1, [1990] IRLR 464, the EAT held that a letter to the union questioning the imposition of discipline may be sufficient for the limitation period to be extended.

363 Trade Union and Labour Relations (Consolidation) Act 1992, s 67(3); the claim must also be made within six months of the date of the declaration; the escape clause does not apply here.

364 This includes steps which the applicant could have taken himself, such as telling his employer to resume the check-off of his membership subscriptions: *NALGO v Courtney-Dunn* [1991] ICR 784, [1992] IRLR 114, EAT.

365 Trade Union and Labour Relations (Consolidation) Act 1992, s 67(2).

366 See *Bradley v NALGO* [1991] ICR 359, [1991] IRLR 159, where the EAT held that compensation for injury to feelings under this head may only be awarded where that injury is caused by the act of discipline itself.

367 Trade Union and Labour Relations (Consolidation) Act 1992, s 67(5), (8). By virtue of s 67(6), (7), the normal principles of mitigation and contributory fault apply.

either section, no complaint in respect of that expulsion may be brought under the other section.

(iii) Elections for union office[368]

It has always been possible for an individual union member to seek legal redress if he alleges that elections for union office have been conducted otherwise than in accordance with the rules of the union[369] ; this, however, restricted the role of the law to securing compliance with those rules as laid down through the internal constitutional workings of the union. Since the Trade Union Act 1984 there has been a separate statutory duty on a trade union to ensure that elections are held for certain major union offices, and that certain irreducible minimum requirements are observed in the conduct of those elections, irrespective of what a union's rules say on the matter[370]. While the mischief at which the election requirements were aimed was the spectre of the unrepresentative union 'baron' elected for life, it soon became clear that many of the prominent figures in the union movement to whom such a description was intended to apply were not affected by the original provisions, which only applied to *voting* members of the union's executive committee; hence the widening of the balloting requirement by the Employment Act 1988 to cover the president, general secretary and all members of the union executive, voting and non-voting.

Section 46 of the Trade Union and Labour Relations (Consolidation) Act 1992 imposes a duty on every trade union to ensure that certain officers are elected by a ballot which satisfies the Act[371], and that they stand for re-election at least once every five years. As seen above, the class of officers caught by the section was originally restricted to those who were voting members of the union's executive (defined as the 'principal committee of the union exercising executive functions, by whatever name it is called'). Whether any particular member of the union's executive was a voting member depended on the rules of the particular union in question, and it was not always the case that the major personalities associated with a union in fact had the necessary vote[372]. Even if he had, there was nothing to

---

368 See Kidner 'Trade union democracy: election of trade union officers' (1984) 13 ILJ 193; *Harvey* M[951]. The genesis of these provisions can be seen in the Green Paper *Democracy in Trade Unions* (Cmnd 8778, 1983).

369 A notable example (resolved by the union itself, to pre-empt any possible legal challenge) was the re-running of the election for the post of General Secretary of the TGWU in 1985, after allegations of irregularities in the original balloting. Complaint could also be made that an election has not been held at all (contrary to the rules), as in *Taylor and Foulstone v NUM (Yorkshire Area)* [1984] IRLR 445.

370 Thus, the Trade Union and Labour Relations (Consolidation) Act 1992, s 46(6) states that any term of employment in a union employee's contract (eg giving him permanent tenure of office under the rules) may be disregarded if to enforce it would prevent the union from complying with the Act. Curiously, however (as pointed out by Kidner (1984) 13 ILJ 193 at p 197) there is no general statement that the Act's provisions are to prevail over a union rule; in one sense this is obvious, but a difficult question could arise if a member sought to enforce a rule by a common law action which the union had breached in order to comply with the Act.

371 It is expressly provided that no ballot need be held at an uncontested election: Trade Union and Labour Relations (Consolidation) Act 1992, s 53.

372 Kidner (1984) 13 ILJ 193 at p 197 states that the general secretaries of the TGWU, NALGO, NUT, NUR, NGA, USDAW, ASTMS and NUM did not have the necessary vote.

373 Such a rule change was carried out, eg by the NUM in 1985 to remove their president's vote.

stop the union changing its rules (by the necessary constitutional means) to divest him of it and to avoid the application of the section to his office[373]. In the light of these points, the law was considerably tightened in the 'we'll-get-Scargill-this-time' amendments in the Employment Act 1988, whereby the election requirements were extended to all members of the executive (whether voting or not) and, in any event, to all union presidents and general secretaries[374]. 'Member of the executive' is broadly defined to include ex officio members and de facto members ('those who under the rules or practice of the union may attend and speak at some or all of the meetings of the executive'), although the net does not extend to those who attend the executive for the purpose of providing factual information or technical or professional advice (for example union legal officers, accountants, research officers, etc). Union presidents are usually members of the union's executive, which means that in practice they normally have to stand for election twice – once to join the executive, and a second time to become President - and the need to hold two ballots imposes a costly administrative burden on trade unions[375]. In 2002, the Better Regulation Task Force recommended that the law be changed to remove the need for union presidents to be elected by a secret postal ballot of the entire membership where they have already been elected to the union executive, on the grounds that the role of most union presidents is 'largely ceremonial' and that 'their influence over decision-taking within union can hardly be distinguished from that exercised by other executive members'. The government has indicated its intention to reform the 1992 Act accordingly[376].

There are a set of complex exemptions to the election requirements: thus, a 'federated trade union' (ie a union which is purely a federation of other unions and has no individual members) is exempt[377], as is a new union in the first year of its existence[378]. There is also a dispensation for a person holding the office of president or general secretary in an honorary capacity[379], and a 'pensioners' charter' allowing a long-standing union employee to continue in office without re-election (where that is permitted by the union rules) until his impending retirement[380]. Attempts were made during the passage of the 1988 Act to obtain an exemption for non-voting general secretaries appointed following public advertisement, who are in effect administrators responsible for implementing

---

374 Trade Union and Labour Relations (Consolidation) Act 1992, s 46(2)–(5). 'President' includes a person holding an office which is the nearest equivalent (s 119): see eg *Petters and Saunders v Musicians' Union* (D/88-90/01), where the Certification Officer upheld a complaint that the 'Chairperson' of the union held the position without having been elected at an election satisfying the requirements of the Act.

375 The cost for a medium-sized union of 60,000 members to elect its president is approximately £45,000–£60,000: *Review of the Employment Relations Act 1999* (2003) Annex C, para C5.

376 *Review of the Employment Relations Act 1999* (2003) Annex C, para C6.

377 Trade Union and Labour Relations (Consolidation) Act 1992, s 118(6). This is not such a statement of the blindingly obvious as it might appear, for the strike ballot provisions do not contain such an exemption, and it has been held that a purely federal union which took industrial action without a ballot (because it had no members to ballot) was still in breach of the Act and therefore lost its immunities: *Shipping Co Uniform Inc v ITWF* [1985] ICR 245, [1985] IRLR 71.

378 Trade Union and Labour Relations (Consolidation) Act 1992, s 57.

379 Trade Union and Labour Relations (Consolidation) Act 1992, s 46(4); this limited exception only applies to non-voting members who are not employees of the union and who cannot hold office for more than 13 months.

380 Trade Union and Labour Relations (Consolidation) Act 1992, s 58.

rather than determining policy (one analogy might be with a local authority chief executive), but no exemption was made.

The Act also provides that no member may be unreasonably excluded from standing as a candidate for office (although it is permissible to exclude all the members of a particular class from standing, as long as that class does not consist solely of those which the union chooses to exclude)[381], and no candidate may be required directly or indirectly to belong to a political party[382].

The procedural requirements to be satisfied in order for an election to be valid under the Act are extremely detailed: (a) all members of the union must have an equal entitlement to vote[383], except where entitlement to vote is restricted to a class of members under the rules (ie voting may be restricted to certain constituencies, whether defined by trade or occupation or geographical area, provided all members of those constituencies have a vote); (b) the voting must be by marking a numbered voting paper, sent and returned by post, and as far as reasonably practicable, without any direct cost to the voter[384]; (c) voting must be without any interference or constraint by the union or any of its members, officials or employees and, as far as reasonably practicable, in secret; (d) votes must be counted by one or more 'independent persons' appointed by the union[385]; and (e) the result of the election must be determined solely by counting the number of votes cast directly for each candidate. This final requirement is aimed at such practices as the block vote and voting through an electoral college; it is not infringed by an electoral rule which interprets the result of the ballot (for example a rule which provides that only a certain number of members from any one area may serve on the executive)[386].

Until 1988 a union could opt for a workplace election ballot where it was satisfied that such a ballot was equally capable of meeting the statutory requirements in relation to secrecy etc. However, the Conservative government became increasingly convinced that postal ballots provided the best security against manipulation and malpractice[387], and the Employment Act 1988 introduced a mandatory requirement of a fully postal ballot. To facilitate the

---

381 See *Ecclestone v National Union of Journalists* [1999] IRLR 166, where an attempt by the union to exclude from candidature those in whom the union's NEC had no confidence was held to infringe this proviso.

382 Trade Union and Labour Relations (Consolidation) Act 1992, s 47; there is nothing to prevent a union from *excluding* members of a particular political party from standing (eg the Communist party), but a positive requirement to *be* a member of a political party will be invalid.

383 Trade Union and Labour Relations (Consolidation) Act 1992, s 50; a union may validly exclude members out of work, those in arrears, apprentices (or trainees, students or new members) and any overseas members: ss 50(2), 60. By analogy with the strike ballot provisions, inadvertent failure to supply a ballot paper will probably not be regarded as a breach of the election requirements provided the union has done all that was reasonable in the circumstances: see p 791, below.

384 Trade Union and Labour Relations (Consolidation) Act 1992, s 51. The union can satisfy this requirement by supplying a pre-paid envelope: *Paul v NALGO* [1987] IRLR 43, CO.

385 Trade Union and Labour Relations (Consolidation) Act 1992, s 51A, inserted by the Trade Union Reform and Employment Rights Act 1993, s 2. This can either be the independent scrutineer, or some other competent person whose independence in relation to the union or the election cannot reasonably be called into question.

386 *R v Certification Officer, ex p EPEA* [1990] ICR 682, [1990] IRLR 398, HL.

387 See the Green Paper, *Trade Unions and their Members* (1987). Cf, however, the conclusions of Undy and Martin that 'no single system of voting maximises turn-out and secrecy and minimises the opportunity for malpractice': *Ballots and Trade Union Democracy* (1984).

balloting process, a union is required to compile, maintain and keep up to date a register of the names and addresses of its members, possibly by computer[388]. In addition, the Employment Act 1988 introduced two further requirements on elections for union office. The first is that each candidate must be given an opportunity to prepare an election address, and have it produced and distributed by the union[389]. The second is that the union must appoint an independent scrutineer to oversee the election, to supervise the production, distribution and return of ballot papers, and to prepare a report on the ballot, certifying that it was properly carried out[390] ; the union must not publish the result of the election until that report is received, and must then publicise the report to the members[391]. To ensure that members are left in no doubt as to the identity of the scrutineer, the union must take steps to notify them of his identity before he begins his duties (for example through a notice in the union newsletter) and the voting papers must state his name[392]. The legal requirement to hold a postal ballot currently prevents a union from adopting other, more modern (and no doubt less expensive) balloting methods, such as telephone or internet balloting. The Better Regulation Task Force has recommended that unions should be allowed to use a wider range of balloting methods (possibly at the discretion of the independent scrutineer), and the government has indicated that it intends to give the Secretary of State a power to change the balloting method via Regulations 'when there was evidence that the method was sufficiently developed to apply safely and economically to this type of ballot.[393] '

The remedy for failure on the part of a union to comply with the statutory election requirements is placed in the hands of a union member[394], who may complain either to the Certification Officer or to the High Court (or in Scotland, the Court of Session), seeking a declaration that the union is in breach of the

388 Trade Union and Labour Relations (Consolidation) Act 1992, s 24. A member can request in writing that an address other than his home address (eg his work address) be used. The register is to be kept open to inspection by individual members: s 24(3); and a copy must be made available to the election scrutineer: s 49. Complaint by a member of a breach of this duty lies to the Certification Officer or to the High Court, either of which may make a declaration and, where appropriate, an enforcement order: ss 25, 26, as amended by the Employment Relations Act 1999, Sch 6.

389 Trade Union and Labour Relations (Consolidation) Act 1992, s 48. The union may impose a word-limit of 100 words or more, and restrict the use of photographs, etc. Where a candidate's election address includes a link to a website which contains other material, the material on the website does not form part of the election address: *Beaumont v Amicus* (D/3-8/03), Certification Officer. The election address must be in the candidate's own words, but this does not prevent a candidate from choosing someone else's words written on his behalf: *Union of Shop Distributive and Allied Workers* (D/1-2/94), Certification Officer.

390 Trade Union and Labour Relations (Consolidation) Act 1992, s 49. To be qualified to act as an independent scrutineer a person must come within a list of approved persons designated by the Secretary of State: see the Trade Union Ballots and Elections (Independent Scrutineer Qualifications) Order 1993, SI 1993/1909, which specifies solicitors, chartered accountants, the Electoral Reform Society, the Industrial Society and Unity Security Balloting Services.

391 Trade Union and Labour Relations (Consolidation) Act 1992, s 52.

392 Trade Union and Labour Relations (Consolidation) Act 1992, ss 49(5), 51(2). These requirements were added by the Employment Act 1990 following accusations of ballot-rigging in the TGWU elections in early 1990, and apparent confusion over the identity of the independent scrutineer appointed to oversee that election.

393 *Review of the Employment Relations Act 1999* (2003) Annex C, para C12.

394 Trade Union and Labour Relations (Consolidation) Act 1992, s 54(2). This apparently includes retired members with no entitlement to vote: *Re SOGAT 1982* (D/3/90; D/2/91; D/3–4/94), Certification Officer. Where the complaint relates to an election that has been held, there is a limitation period of one year from the date of the election: s 54(3).

requirements. The member may choose which route to adopt; application to the Certification Officer will of course be cheaper and easier, and apparently highly effective[395]. Originally, the main difference between the two procedures was that the Certification Officer was unable to make an enforcement order requiring the union to take certain specified steps in order to remedy its failure to comply with the Act (for example ordering the union to hold an election). However, as part of the general enhancement of the Certification Officer's role by the Employment Relations Act 1999, he now has substantially the same powers to make an enforcement order as the court[396]. Under the pre-1999 provisions it was expressly stated that an application to the Certification Officer did not prevent the applicant from making a subsequent application to the court in respect of the same complaint[397], but the current provisions rule out any such possibility[398]. Where an enforcement order has been made, it can if necessary be enforced by any person who is a member of the union at the time the enforcement proceedings are begun and who was also a member at the time when the enforcement order was originally made[399]. As the Act does not lay down any special procedures in the case of breach of an enforcement order, the form of enforcement in question would be to bring proceedings against the union for contempt of court.

(iv) Ballots before industrial action

As will be seen in the next chapter, strike ballots have been a requirement of lawful industrial action since the enactment of the Trade Union Act 1984, but the peculiarity of that Act (which was otherwise concerned with 'giving unions back to their members') was that it contained no mechanism whereby an individual union member could take legal action to restrain the union from calling for industrial action without first holding a ballot. It merely rendered that industrial action actionable at the suit of an *employer*, by removing the statutory immunities from suit in tort from industrial action not supported by a ballot. That omission was subsequently remedied by the Employment Act 1988, which introduced a statutory cause of action for a union member aggrieved at being called out without a proper ballot[400]. Section 62 of the

---

395 The Certification Officer issued eight decisions under these provisions in 2001–02, a slightly smaller number than in recent years: *Annual Report of the Certification Officer, 2001-2002*, para 8.11ff. All decisions reached since 1 August 2001 are available on the Certification Officer's website at www.certoffice.org.

396 Trade Union and Labour Relations (Consolidation) Act 1992, s 55, as amended by the Employment Relations Act 1999, Sch 6. An enforcement order made by the Certification Officer may be enforced in the same way as an order of the court: s 55(9). There is a right of appeal to the EAT on any question of law arising in proceedings before or arising from any decision of the Certification Officer under this head: s 56A.

397 This was held to be so even if the original application had yet to be determined: *Lenahan v UCATT* [1991] ICR 378, [1991] IRLR 78.

398 Trade Union and Labour Relations (Consolidation) Act 1992, ss 55(10), 56(8). It is, however, possible for a *different* person to make an application to the Certification Officer in relation to an alleged failure which was previously the subject of a complaint to the court, and vice versa, and on any such application the Certification Officer or the court, as the case may be, is to have due regard to any declaration, order, observations or reasons made regarding that failure which are brought to its notice: ss 55(10), 56(8).

399 Trade Union and Labour Relations (Consolidation) Act 1992, ss 55(5C), 56(6). Note that the requirement of contemporary membership does not apply to enforcement by a person who was a candidate in the election.

400 The member may, of course, have a common law action based upon the union rules relating to strike ballots. The statutory right does not affect such an action, but it may be preferable since it applies standards for ballots across the board and operates independently of the union's rules.

Trade Union and Labour Relations (Consolidation) Act 1992 now states that a member who claims 'that members of the union, including himself, are likely to be or have been induced by the union to take part or to continue to take part in industrial action[401] which does not have the support of a ballot' may apply to the High Court[402] ; if that court is satisfied that the complaint is established, it may make such order as it considers appropriate to require the union to cease the inducement and stop the industrial action. The section only applies to industrial action which is official ('induced by the union'), in the sense that it is taken to have been authorised or endorsed by the union under the rules which determine the vicarious liability of a trade union in tort[403]. The balloting requirements are largely the same as those which apply for the purposes of tortious liability and the statutory immunities[404], and it is specifically provided that the same ballot may fulfil both requirements, so that there is no need for two ballots[405]. The Code of Practice on industrial action balloting, considered in the next chapter in the context of the tortious liability of a union, gives guidance on the statutory balloting requirements.

(v) Union funds

As seen at head 4 above, union members have the right at common law to ensure that their union's funds are applied in accordance with the rules, as was graphically demonstrated by the legal actions brought by union members during the miners' strike of 1984/85, where an application was successfully made to the court by union members to have the union's trustees removed and a receiver appointed in their place[406]. Those steps were taken under the general law (though applying it to hitherto uncharted territory), but the government of the day considered that the procedures for the removal of trustees were too slow and uncertain[407], and a statutory remedy against union trustees for the unlawful use of union property was therefore introduced in the Employment Act 1988. Now contained in the Trade Union and Labour Relations (Consolidation) Act 1992, section 16, this provides that where trustees have so carried out their functions (or propose to do so) as to 'cause or permit an unlawful application of the union's property' a member may apply to the High Court for relief[408]; if the complaint is well founded, the court may make such order as it considers appropriate, and in particular it

---

401 'Industrial action' is defined in s 62(6) as 'a strike or other industrial action by persons employed under contracts of employment'. 'Strike' and 'other industrial action' are not further defined in this context, although 'strike' is defined in s 246 as 'any concerted stoppage of work', for the purposes of Pt V of the 1992 Act (Industrial Action); for their interpretation in the context of the dismissal of those taking part in industrial action, see p 755 below.

402 But not, it should be noted, the Certification Officer; compare p 723.

403 Trade Union and Labour Relations (Consolidation) Act 1992, s 62(5). The rules governing vicarious liability of a union are contained in s 20. See p 818 below.

404 Trade Union and Labour Relations (Consolidation) Act 1992, ss 226–234A. These are considered at p 787 below. Note, however, that a failure to give notice of the ballot or a sample voting paper to the employer under s 226A, or to inform the employer of the result of the ballot under s 231A, will not be actionable by a union member under s 62.

405 Trade Union and Labour Relations (Consolidation) Act 1992, s 62(9).

406 *Clarke v Heathfield* [1985] ICR 203, CA.

407 Green Paper *Trade Unions and their Members* (1987), ch 3.

408 The existence of this statutory action is without prejudice to any other remedies available against the trustees in respect of breach of trust: s 16(6).

may (a) order the trustees to take action necessary to protect or recover the property, (b) appoint a receiver of the union's property and (c) remove one or more of the trustees[409]. The principal problem with this statutory action is that the word 'unlawful' is not defined (in particular, it is unclear whether it includes the use of union funds in support of industrial action unprotected by the statutory immunities), and so the section as it stands is open-ended, and in need of judicial interpretation.

The Employment Act 1988 introduced a further right in relation to union property, now contained in the Trade Union and Labour Relations (Consolidation) Act 1992, section 15, which applies where union property is applied for the purpose of paying any individual's fines (for an offence or for contempt of court), or indemnifying him for fines which have been or may be imposed on him. Such use of union property is declared to be unlawful[410] and the property is further declared to be recoverable from the individual by the union. The crucial provision is then section 15(3), which permits an aggrieved member, who considers the union's failure to recover the property to be unreasonable, to apply to the High Court which may make an order authorising the member to bring or continue proceedings for such recovery on the union's behalf and at the union's expense[411].

(vi) Union subscriptions

Traditionally, most trade union members paid their union subscription under a check-off system, whereby the amount of the subscription was deducted from their wages by the employer and passed on to the union. Since the Employment Act 1988, union members have had a right to require employers to stop deducting union subscriptions from wages immediately upon receiving notice that the individual has terminated his union membership[412]. However, the law concerning the operation of the check-off was controversially amended by the Trade Union Reform and Employment Rights Act 1993, which introduced a requirement for the employer to obtain a worker's renewed authorisation for the deduction of union subscriptions in writing at least every three years, and also required the employer to give at least one month's written advance notice to the worker of any increase in the amount of the subscription. On their introduction these requirements generated considerable controversy, particularly the need for periodic renewal of the authorisation, which was seen in certain quarters as a thinly veiled attempt to encourage workers to terminate their union membership. The incoming Labour government acted quickly to remove these two requirements

---

409 Trade Union and Labour Relations (Consolidation) Act 1992, s 16(3). In a case where the trustees have applied (or propose to apply) union property in contravention of a court order, the court *must* remove all the trustees, except any trustee who satisfies the court that there is a good reason for allowing him to remain a trustee: s 16(4).

410 This provision adds to the common law, for the position there was less certain; it appeared that an agreement by a union to indemnify members for any fines incurred *in future* was void but that a decision to indemnify for a fine already imposed was lawful, if within the rules: *Drake v Morgan* [1978] ICR 56; *Thomas v NUM (South Wales Area)* [1985] ICR 886, [1985] IRLR 136. Any such existing illegality (and any other actions against the trustees) is expressly preserved by s 15(6), but the blanket illegality under the section will normally be a better ground of challenge.

411 Thereby avoiding any problems under *Foss v Harbottle* (1843) 2 Hare 461, p 708 above.

412 A right which parallels the longer-standing right to require immediate discontinuance of deductions of the political levy: see p 735 below.

in 1998[413], but not before many trade unions had decided to abandon the check-off system and to collect subscriptions directly from their members by means of direct debit, the result being that many employers lost an extremely useful means of monitoring the level of union membership, and location of union members, within their organisation – information which can be particularly valuable in an industrial dispute. Needless to say, this was not a consequence which was intended (or, presumably, foreseen) by the authors of the 1993 Act. The current position, therefore, is that an employer must obtain a worker's written authorisation before making any subscription deductions, and that authorisation may be withdrawn by the worker at any time, but once given, the authorisation will remain valid unless and until it is withdrawn. It is expressly stated that a worker's authorisation of the making of subscription deductions does not give rise to any obligation on the part of the employer to continue the check-off arrangements[414].

A worker who believes that his employer has contravened these requirements has a right of complaint to an employment tribunal, which if it upholds the complaint must make an declaration to that effect and order the employer to repay any amount improperly deducted[415].

(vii) Union accounts

Every trade union (other than a federated trade union consisting wholly or mainly of representatives of constituent organisations) is subject to four principal requirements relating to financial matters under the Trade Union and Labour Relations (Consolidation) Act 1992, whether or not it is listed. First, under section 28, the union must keep proper accounting records with respect to its transactions, assets and liabilities (ie records which 'give a true and fair view of the state of the affairs of the trade union and explain its transactions'), and establish and maintain a satisfactory system of control of accounting records, cash holdings, and receipts and remittances. This may be done at either branch or union level. Following reforms introduced by the Employment Act 1988, these accounting records must be kept available for inspection for a period of six years after their preparation[416], and a union member has the right to inspect them, on request, provided he was a member for at least part of the period covered by the records he seeks to inspect[417]. If that qualification is met, he is entitled to inspect the records where they are normally kept, at a reasonable hour and paying only reasonable administrative expenses. Perhaps most importantly, the member is

---

413 Deregulation (Deduction from Pay of Union Subscriptions) Order 1998, SI 1998/1529, substituting the Trade Union and Labour Relations (Consolidation) Act 1992, s 68. There is a nice irony in the fact that this reform was achieved by the use of regulation-making powers contained in the Conservative government's Deregulation and Contracting Out Act 1994.

414 Trade Union and Labour Relations (Consolidation) Act 1992, s 68(4). This is, of course, significant in view of the practice of some employers to use the threat to end check-off arrangements as a means of bringing pressure to bear on a union in a trade dispute.

415 Trade Union and Labour Relations (Consolidation) Act 1992, s 68A, inserted by the Trade Union Reform and Employment Rights Act 1993, s 15.

416 Trade Union and Labour Relations (Consolidation) Act 1992, s 29.

417 Trade Union and Labour Relations (Consolidation) Act 1992, s 30.

entitled to be accompanied by an accountant[418] (provided the latter gives any assurance of confidentiality reasonably required by the union) and to take copies. Arrangements for inspection must be made within 28 days of the member's request. A person who claims that a union has failed to comply with his request may apply to the High Court or the Certification Officer[419] for an order to ensure compliance[420], and any order made by the Certification Officer may be enforced in the same way as an order of the court[421] ; it is an offence for a union to fail to keep its accounting records available for inspection[422].

Secondly, under section 32, the union must send to the Certification Officer an annual return relating to its affairs and containing audited accounts[423]. These returns are to be kept open to public inspection by the Certification Officer, and must also be provided by the union on request to any person free or on payment of a reasonable charge. The Trade Union Reform and Employment Rights Act 1993 introduced the additional requirement that the annual return must contain information about the salary and benefits paid to the union's president, general secretary and each member of the executive, and a statement of the number of names on the register and how many of those are not accompanied by an address[424].

Thirdly, under section 32A, inserted by the 1993 Act, a union must take all reasonable steps to secure that within eight weeks of sending its annual return to the Certification Officer, every member of the union is provided with a written statement giving details of the union's income and expenditure for the period in question, how much of that income came from membership subscriptions, the total income and expenditure on the political fund during that period, details of the salary and benefits of its leaders, and the full report of the auditors on the accounts contained in the annual return. The statement must also contain the lengthy statement set out in the Act which describes the steps which may be taken by any member concerned about possible irregularity in the conduct of the union's financial affairs.

Finally, under section 38, every trade union which maintains a members' superannuation scheme[425] must arrange to have it examined by an actuary at least once every five years, with a copy of the actuary's report sent to the Certification Officer.

---

418 Defined as a person who, at the time of inspection, is eligible for appointment as a company auditor under s 25 of the Companies Act 1989. The right to be accompanied by an accountant had, in fact, already been established at common law during the miners' strike (in *Taylor v NUM (Derbyshire Area)* [1985] IRLR 65, Ch D), but only where the member himself had a right of access under the rules: *Hughes v TGWU* [1985] IRLR 382.

419 Under the new powers introduced by the Employment Relations Act 1999, Sch 6; see p 66.

420 Trade Union and Labour Relations (Consolidation) Act 1992, s 31, as amended by the Employment Relations Act 1999, Sch 6. An application to the court precludes a subsequent application by the same person to the Certification Officer in relation to that failure, and vice versa: Trade Union and Labour Relations (Consolidation) Act 1992, s 31(6), (7).

421 Trade Union and Labour Relations (Consolidation) Act 1992, s 31(5). There is a right of appeal to the EAT on any question of law arising in proceedings before or arising from any decision of the Certification Officer under this head: s 45D.

422 Trade Union and Labour Relations (Consolidation) Act 1992, s 45(1).

423 There is a one-year exemption for newly formed unions: Trade Union and Labour Relations (Consolidation) Act 1992, s 43(1).

424 Trade Union and Labour Relations (Consolidation) Act 1992, s 32(3), as amended by the Trade Union Reform and Employment Rights Act 1993, s 8.

425 As at the end of March 2002, only eight unions maintained such schemes: *Annual Report of the Certification Officer, 2001–2002*, para 5.3.

If a union refuses or wilfully neglects to comply with any of these requirements, it renders itself and any officers charged with the relevant duties[426] liable to summary criminal proceedings under section 45. The Trade Union Reform and Employment Rights Act 1993 introduced sweeping (not to say draconian) new powers for the Certification Officer to investigate union financial affairs, including the power to require a union to produce documents relating to its financial affairs, and to appoint inspectors to conduct an investigation where there appears to have been some financial impropriety, backed up by criminal sanctions in the event of a failure to co-operate[427]. These new powers were introduced in the wake of the unsuccessful prosecution of the National Union of Mineworkers in 1990 over an alleged failure to keep proper accounting records and other alleged irregularities in the conduct of the union's financial affairs during and after the miners' strike of 1984/85[428]. The charges, brought by the Certification Officer, were dismissed following rulings by the stipendiary magistrate that certain 'crucial prosecution evidence'[429] was inadmissible, and the episode was cited by the government of the day[430] as an illustration of the limitations of the Certification Officer's powers in relation to trade union finances and the prosecution of offences under the Act, and the inadequacy of the existing legislative arrangements. The 1993 Act also extended the range of offences under section 45 to include, inter alia, the destruction, mutilation or falsification of a document relating to a union's financial affairs, or making or being privy to the making of a false entry in such a document, unless the official or agent concerned 'proves that he had no intention to conceal the financial affairs of the trade union or to defeat the law'[431]. It is also an offence if a person fraudulently parts with, alters or deletes anything in any such document, or is privy to such conduct, or knowingly or recklessly provides or makes an explanation or statement in purported compliance with the duty to co-operate which is false in a material particular. The penalties for the commission of certain of these offences include imprisonment for a term not exceeding six months[432]. Finally, any person convicted of an offence under section 45 is *automatically* disqualified from being the president or general secretary of a union, or a member of the union' executive, for a period of five or ten years, depending on the gravity of the offence[433]. Interestingly, under the Company Directors'

---

426 It is a defence for an officer to prove that he believed on reasonable grounds that some other person was discharging the relevant duty. The phrase 'wilfully neglects' is a curious one to a criminal lawyer; it presumably means 'knowingly fails' and does not include negligence or simple inadvertence.

427 Trade Union and Labour Relations (Consolidation) Act 1992, ss 37A–37E, inserted by the Trade Union Reform and Employment Rights Act 1993, s 10. The report of any such investigation is to be published by the Certification Officer and the expenses of an investigation may be recovered from a person convicted on a prosecution instigated as a result of the investigation.

428 See *The Lightman Report on the NUM* (1990); Lightman 'A trade union in chains: Scargill unbound – the legal constraints of receivership and sequestration' (1987) 40 CLP 25.

429 *Annual Report of the Certification Officer* (1991) p 8. The crucial evidence in question was the report by Gavin Lightman, n 428 above, which was commissioned by the NUM.

430 In the Green Paper *Industrial Relations in the 1990s* (Cm 1602, 1991).

431 Trade Union and Labour Relations (Consolidation) Act 1992, s 45(7).

432 Trade Union and Labour Relations (Consolidation) Act 1992, s 45A.

433 Trade Union and Labour Relations (Consolidation) Act 1992, s 45B. A member who claims that his union has failed to comply with the duty to disqualify offenders may apply to the Certification Officer or to the court for a declaration and, where appropriate, an order requiring the union to remedy its failure to comply: s 45C, as amended by the Employment Relations Act 1999, Sch 6.

Disqualification Act 1986, the court generally has a discretion whether or not to disqualify company directors (except in the case of unfit directors of insolvent companies, where there is a discretion over the length of the disqualification), whereas here the disqualification is automatic.

6 POLITICAL FUNDS[434]

The political activities of trade unions, particularly the giving of financial support to the nascent Labour party out of general union funds, received a major set-back in 1910 when the House of Lords held in *ASRS v Osborne* [435] that such activities were ultra vires the union's statutory objects[436]. Following this decision, the unions looked to Parliament to provide them with the means of lawfully carrying on such activities, while at the same time safeguarding the political independence of individual members. The solution was found in the Trade Union Act 1913, which permitted a union to spend money on political purposes ('political objects') where its members had voted to approve those objects and the establishment of a separate political fund into which the members could contribute through the political levy, and out of which any such expenditure could be made. Detailed rules were laid down safeguarding the position of those who wished to 'contract out' of the political levy. Those detailed rules were subject to major revision by the Trade Union Act 1984[437], which extended the definition of political objects (so that more payments now have to come out of the political fund), added further rules as to the running of political funds, strengthened the procedural requirements for ballots and, most important of all, provided that a political fund must be reballoted at least once every ten years to determine whether the membership wish to retain it. As the previous law only required an initial ballot, many funds had not been balloted on for many years, and not surprisingly, political differences over the introduction of political fund review ballots were intense. The Conservative government of the day argued that this move was simply part of its policy of returning decision-making in unions to the membership, that political funds were retained largely through apathy and that the frequently very high percentage of union members contributing (98% of the membership of the TGWU in 1983 was a figure often quoted) was unrepresentative of members' real political views. The Labour party view was that this was a partisan political move by the Conservative government to bankrupt the Labour party by cutting it off from its most important source of finance (particularly unfair as it was not accompanied by parallel restrictions on business financing of the Conservative party). This seemed to be a particularly potent threat to the Labour party, since in fact (contrary to much of the propaganda) the contribution rate in many of the

---

434 On political funds generally, see Ewing 'Trade union political fund rules' (1980) 9 ILJ 137. As at the end of March 2002, 33 unions maintained political funds; in 2002-2003 the total number of members contributing to political funds was 4.4m, the total income of political funds was £16.0m and the total expenditure was £16.4m; at the end of the period, total political fund assets stood at £14.3m: *Annual Report of the Certification Officer* (2001–02) Appendix 9.

435 [1910] AC 87, HL.

436 A strict view of ultra vires is not possible now, for the definition of a trade union in s 1 of the 1992 Act only lays down the principal objects, and so is not exhaustive.

437 Ewing 'Trade union political funds: the 1913 Act revised' (1984) 13 ILJ 227.

key unions at that time was quite low[438] – and if those who were already contracted out of the political levy took the further step of voting against having a fund at all, there was a serious risk that several of the major funds would disappear[439]. If, however, that was a major aim of the ten-year reballoting requirement, it failed spectacularly, because over the years since review ballots were introduced, the reballots have tended to go in favour of the retention of the political funds, even in unions where only a minority of members contribute. Review ballots are, however, a source of irritation to trade unions, not least because of the expense involved[440], and in 2002 the Better Regulation Task Force questioned whether, in view of the cost (both financially and in terms of resources), and the existence of other safeguards against abuse[441], it was still valid to require unions to hold review ballots every ten years. However, the government has indicated that it intends to retain review ballots (at least for the time being) because they 'serve an important democratic function and ensure that members can at regular intervals collectively authorise their union's involvement in political activities', although it seems that the balloting provisions themselves may be simplified[442].

One highly contentious facet of the law on political funds which has remained unaltered throughout all the legislative changes of the last 20 years is the old chestnut of whether those who wish to contribute should be required to 'contract in' or those who do not wish to contribute should be required to 'contract out' (the difference being, as has been said, where the burden of apathy lies). Contracting out remains the position, and in recent years attention has shifted away from the narrow debate over contracting-in versus contracting-out to the much more fundamental issue of the funding of political parties generally, and the need for transparency in relation to the sources of political donations.

Turning to the detailed rules on political funds, now contained in Part I of the Trade Union and Labour Relations (Consolidation) Act 1992, the basic position is that union funds may not be applied (directly or indirectly) in furtherance of 'political objects' unless those objects have been approved by a majority of the members voting in a ballot (ie the members must have passed a 'political resolution'), and the union must also have adopted certain rules (political fund rules) which have been approved by the Certification Officer[443]. A union member who claims that his union has applied funds in furtherance of political objects without having a valid political resolution in force, or without

---

438 Ewing (1984) 13 ILJ 227 at p 242, points out that in 1982, ten unions had political funds to which less than 50% of the membership contributed, including the Blastfurnacemen (48%), SOGAT (44%), NGA (42%), ASTMS (30%) and ACTT (7%).

439 This would have had wider implications than the loss of income to the Labour party, for if a union does not have (or loses in a reballot) a political fund, it may not spend money on anything defined as 'political' at all (since it has no fund out of which to finance it and, by definition, its general funds may not be used); thus eg if a union in the health service did not have a political fund it could still campaign on the basis of 'save the NHS', but not (even supposing it were minded to do so) on the basis of 'save the NHS by voting Labour'; see eg *Paul and Fraser v NALGO* [1987] IRLR 413, Ch D.

440 The Employment Act 1988 introduced a requirement that political fund ballots be conducted by post, and subject to independent scrutiny, which only served to increase the cost to unions of holding them. State funding for political fund review ballots ended in April 1996.

441 Eg the right of members to contract out (see below), the duty to include information about political expenditure in union annual returns, and the new legislation on the funding of political parties which identifies the political expenditure of individual unions.

442 *Review of the Employment Relations Act 1999* (2003) Annex C, para C8.

443 Trade Union and Labour Relations (Consolidation) Act 1992, s 71.

having adopted valid political fund rules, may apply to the Certification Officer, who may make a declaration and, if he thinks it just in the circumstances, an enforcement order requiring the union to remedy the breach[444].

This, of course, begs the fundamental question, what are 'political objects'? The definition of political objects was significantly altered and extended by the Trade Union Act 1984, and is now contained in the Trade Union and Labour Relations (Consolidation) Act 1992, section 72, which refers to the 'expenditure of money:

' (a) on any contribution[445] to the funds of, or on the payment of expenses incurred directly or indirectly by, a political party;

(b) on the provision of any service or property[446] for use by or on behalf of any political party;

(c) in connection with the registration of electors, the candidature of any person[447], the selection of any candidate or the holding of any ballot by the union in connection with any election to a political office[448] ;

(d) on the maintenance[449] of any holder of a political office;

(e) on the holding of any conference or meeting[450] by or on behalf of a political party or of any other meeting the main purpose of which is the transaction of business in connection with a political party;

(f) on the production, publication or distribution of any literature, documents, film, sound recording or advertisement the main purpose of which is to persuade people to vote for a political party or candidate or to persuade them not to vote for a political party or candidate.'

The post-1984 definition is considerably wider than the previous one[451], particularly in head (f) above, which now extends to negative persuasion. One direct consequence of the redefinition is that union campaigns critical of government policy are now likely to fall within the scope of political objects and

444 Trade Union and Labour Relations (Consolidation) Act 1992, s 72A, inserted by the Employment Relations Act 1999, Sch 6. An order made by the Certification Officer under this section may be enforced in the same way as an order of the court: s 72A(9). Such an order can be enforced by any person who is a member of the union and was a member at the time the enforcement order was originally made: s 72A(8). There is an appeal on a point of law from the Certification Officer to the EAT: s 95.

445 This includes affiliation fees to a political party and any loans made to it: Trade Union and Labour Relations (Consolidation) Act 1992, s 72(4).

446 One major subject of litigation under the pre-1984 definition of political objects was the provision by a consortium of unions of new London premises for the Labour party (the infamous Millbank); this was held to be of a political nature so that the large amounts concerned could not be taken from the unions' general funds: *Richards v NUM* [1981] IRLR 247, CO; *ASTMS v Parkin* [1984] ICR 127, [1983] IRLR 448, EAT. This is now expressly included as a 'political object'.

447 This includes the payment of expenses incurred by union employees assisting candidates for election to public office: Certification Officer, Decision CO/1913/13.

448 'Political office' is the key concept here; it means the office of MP, MEP, member of a local authority or any position within a political party: s 72(4). 'Candidate' includes a prospective candidate.

449 'Maintenance' here is to be construed widely. In *ASTMS v Parkin*, n 446 above, its use in the previous definition was held to cover money donated to provide research facilities for the Leader of the Opposition.

450 Including the payment of expenses incurred by delegates in attending any such conference or meeting: s 72(2). In *Richards v NUM* [1981] IRLR 247, it was even held to cover payment for a brass band at a political lobby.

451 See Ewing, above n 438, at pp 235–239. As the post-1984 definition involved such a comprehensive reformulation, it is submitted that the old case law on the previous definition is of little assistance, except to the limited extent already noted.

have to be financed out of the political fund, particularly where they take place in the run-up to national or local elections. In *Paul and Fraser v NALGO* [452], the union mounted a major campaign against government spending cuts and the effect of privatisation on the public services in the run-up to the 1987 election. The union had no political fund, and so the campaign was financed out of general funds. Browne-Wilkinson V-C held that this expenditure was caught by head (f), as the main purpose of the campaign was to persuade people not to vote for the Conservative party. He considered that a campaign to change government policy would not be caught by the section, whereas a campaign to change the government would be; however, this is clearly a very difficult distinction to draw, particularly at election time, and as a result of that decision a number of trade unions (including NALGO and the Association of University Teachers) voted to establish political funds for the first time to preserve their ability to campaign on policy issues affecting their members during election campaigns.

As seen above, before a political fund can be established the union must hold a ballot in which a political resolution is passed approving the furtherance of political objects, and since 1984 there has been a further requirement of periodic reballoting every ten years at least [453]. Such ballots must be in accordance with union rules approved for this purpose by the Certification Officer [454]. The rules must comply with a detailed set of requirements which are similar to those which apply in union elections. Thus, the union must appoint an independent scrutineer to oversee and report on the ballot (section 75 and 78); all members must be entitled to vote (section 76); and voting must be secret, by the marking of a numbered ballot paper (ie no ballots by show of hands), free from interference or constraint and without direct cost to the voter. As in the case of elections for union office, the balloting must be entirely postal, with ballot papers distributed and returned by post (section 77), the alternative of workplace ballots having been removed by the Employment Act 1988. A union member who claims that his union has held a ballot (or is proposing to do so) otherwise than in accordance with rules approved by the Certification Officer may apply either to the Certification Officer or to the High Court for a declaration to that effect [455] ; in such an application, similar rules (as to procedure and the power to make enforcement orders) apply here as apply to a complaint of failure to comply with the statutory requirements for elections to union office [456].

Where a union has passed a political resolution in a ballot of the membership, it must also adopt a set of political fund rules [457] providing (a) that payments in

452 [1987] IRLR 413, Ch D.
453 State funding was available until April 1996 in respect of political fund reballots but not in respect of a ballot on whether a political fund should be established in the first place: see p 712 above.
454 Trade Union and Labour Relations (Consolidation) Act 1992, s 74. Fresh approval is required before each ballot, even where the rules have been approved previously. The Certification Officer has model rules on balloting which may be adopted by a union. As seen above, at the time of writing the government was considering simplifying the burdens imposed by the balloting requirements.
455 Trade Union and Labour Relations (Consolidation) Act 1992, s 79; the application must be made within a year of the announcement of the result of the ballot: s 79(3).
456 Trade Union and Labour Relations (Consolidation) Act 1992, ss 80, 81, as amended by the Employment Relations Act 1999, Sch 6. For the similar procedures in complaints over elections, see p 723 above. There is an appeal on a point of law from the Certification Officer to the EAT: s 95.
457 Trade Union and Labour Relations (Consolidation) Act 1992, s 82(1). The Certification Officer will supply a set of 'model rules' on request.

furtherance of political objects shall be paid out of a separate 'political fund'; (b) that any member who does not wish to contribute to that fund shall be exempt if he gives notice in the prescribed form to 'contract out'[458] ; (c) that a member who is exempt from making contributions shall not be excluded from any benefits of the union or placed at a disadvantage as compared with other members of the union (except in relation to control or management of the political fund itself)[459] ; and (d) that contribution to the political fund shall not be made a condition of admission to the union. A member who claims that there has been a breach of the political fund rules (for example that the union has made payments in furtherance of political objects out of general funds instead of the political fund) may complain to the Certification Officer who may, after hearing the parties and making such enquiries as he thinks fit, make an order for remedying the breach which has the status of an order of the county court[460].

Administration of the assets and liabilities of a political fund (when a political resolution is in force) is governed by the Trade Union and Labour Relations (Consolidation) Act 1992, section 83[461]. The only moneys that may be added to the fund are those from members' contributions, donations from other persons (but not from the union itself from its general funds) and anything accruing from the administration of the fund itself (for example interest on investments). All political expenditure must come out of the fund; the union may not 'top up' its political fund by transferring money from its general funds or by adding income which results from the investment of those funds, nor may it borrow money to finance its political activities or secure an overdraft on its political fund by charging the deficit to its general property[462]. If a union ceases to have a valid political resolution (for example if the necessary periodic reballoting shows a majority against the fund's continuation), the fund is frozen and the union must take the necessary steps to cease collecting the political contributions[463]. The choices then available to the union are to leave the fund frozen (in the hope that a subsequent

---

458 The suggested form of notice is contained in s 84.

459 *Birch v NUR* [1950] Ch 602, [1950] 2 All ER 253.

460 Trade Union and Labour Relations (Consolidation) Act 1992, s 82(2); there is an appeal on a point of law to the EAT: s 95. Confusingly, this form of complaint is in addition to the specific rights of action given by s 72A (application of funds in breach of s 71), s 80 (failure to comply with ballot rules), s 87 (failure to discontinue deductions of the political levy), and s 90(4) (failure to discontinue collecting contributions after a resolution ceases to have effect). Complaints under these provisions are rare: in 2001–02 the Certification Officer heard only one complaint, and there were none in the previous year: *Annual Report of the Certification Officer* (2001–02), para 7.19. These statistics could be said to support the case for a lighter touch as regards the regulation of union political funds and the conduct of political fund ballots.

461 Note that a political fund constitutes 'protected property' in that as long as it cannot be used to finance industrial action, it cannot be seized in order to satisfy a judgment against the union: Trade Union and Labour Relations (Consolidation) Act 1992, s 23(2) (p 821 below). This does not apply, however, to sequestration for failure to pay a fine imposed for contempt of court.

462 It may even be questioned whether a union may run an overdraft on its political fund *at all,* as technically an overdraft represents the addition of money to the fund which is neither a contribution nor income from investments: see Elias and Ewing, above n 306, p 176.

463 Trade Union and Labour Relations (Consolidation) Act 1992, ss 89–91. If contributions have been collected after the resolution has lapsed, a member may apply to have them refunded: s 90(3). If the union does not discontinue collecting the contributions within a reasonable period, a member may complain to the High Court (but not, in this context, the Certification Officer) for a declaration and enforcement order: s 90(4), (5).

ballot may approve a political resolution again and so revive the fund)[464], to spend it on non-political objects (which could be done simply by transferring it into the general funds), or, where the resolution has ceased because of an adverse re-balloting, to spend the money left in the fund (but without incurring an overdraft) on political objects within six months of the lapse of the ballot[465].

Whenever a political resolution is adopted (or renewed in a review ballot) the members must be informed of their right to contract out of paying the political levy; this they may do at any time (either on the standard form or in any other form to like effect), though if the notice of objection is given more than one month after the members were notified of their right to contract out it does not take effect until the first day of January following[466]. There is no statutory obligation to inform new members of their right to contract out, although the TUC's *Statement of Guidance* (issued in 1984 to stave off further legislation) requires TUC unions to provide new members with an information sheet explaining how to contract out. Where the political levy is collected separately there is little difficulty in providing for the exemption of a contracted-out member. However, it may also be done by collecting one *combined* subscription and relieving the contracted-out members from that part of the subscription which is referable to the political levy[467]. The advantage for a union of the second method is that it may be operated through a 'check-off' system whereby the employer deducts the amount of the contribution from wages, on behalf of the union. One long-standing problem here is that an employer may be unwilling or unable to operate such a system on a differential basis for exempt members (ie Xp per week in the case of an ordinary member but X–Yp per week in the case of a contracted-out member). One widely adopted solution to this problem was for the whole sum to be deducted from all, with the amount of the political levy subsequently refunded to contracted-out members. This was approved by the EAT under the 1913 Act[468], but the idea of refunding was unpopular with the Conservative government and so the Trade Union Act 1984 made it unlawful for an employer to deduct the political levy where a contracted-out member has notified the employer in writing of his contracted-out status, in which case the employer must ensure that no amounts representing contributions to the political fund are deducted from his wages[469]; moreover, if the employer wishes to operate a check-off system he may not lawfully refuse to operate it in relation to contracted-out members while continuing to do so for other members[470], so that the employer must either be prepared to operate a differential system or no system at all. If this was all part of a cunning plan designed to make it more difficult for members to continue paying the political levy it seems to have failed, principally because of the move towards the collection of union subscriptions by direct debit rather than through the check-off[471].

---

464 The union may continue to administer a frozen fund: Trade Union and Labour Relations (Consolidation) Act 1992, s 91(1).
465 Union and Labour Relations (Consolidation) Act 1992, s 89(2).
466 Union and Labour Relations (Consolidation) Act 1992, s 84(4).
467 Union and Labour Relations (Consolidation) Act 1992, s 85(1).
468 *Reeves v TGWU* [1980] ICR 728, [1980] IRLR 307, EAT.
469 Trade Union and Labour Relations (Consolidation) Act 1992, s 86. Complaint of a breach of s 86 now lies to an employment tribunal which may make a declaration and, where appropriate, an order requiring the employer to pay any amount improperly deducted: s 87, as substituted by the Employment Rights (Dispute Resolution) Act 1998, s 15, Sch 2.
470 Trade Union and Labour Relations (Consolidation) Act 1992, s 86(3).
471 See p 726.

7 UNION AMALGAMATIONS AND INTER-UNION DISPUTES

(i) Union amalgamations

It has in the past been a frequent criticism of trade unions in England and Wales that they have been too numerous. However, rationalisation over several years has seen a marked decline in the number of unions[472], mainly as a result of union amalgamations, and in recent years the merger has come to be seen as an integral part of the modernisation process considered by many to be essential to the trade union movement, particularly in times of economic recession and falling membership[473]. At the end of March 2001 there were 16 trade unions with over 100,000 members, accounting for nearly 84% of the total union membership of 7.6 million, and nearly a half of all union members were concentrated in the largest four unions[474]. At the other end of the scale, however, nearly two-thirds of the total number of unions had less than 2,500 members, accounting for less than 1% of the total membership. At common law, there were difficulties in the way of mergers between unions, particularly the need to obtain the consent of every member of each of the merging organisations. For this reason, legislation was introduced at various times in the nineteenth century so as to mitigate the difficulties while still safeguarding to a reasonable extent the interests of individual members[475]. The current scheme was introduced by the Trade Union (Amalgamations, etc.) Act 1964, and is now contained in the Trade Union and Labour Relations (Consolidation) Act 1992, ss 97–106[476].

Under the 1992 Act, two forms of merger are provided: amalgamation (where two or more unions merge to form a new union); and transfer of engagements (where one union transfers its members and property to another, losing its identity in the process). In either case, detailed statutory procedures must be followed[477], including a ballot of the members on the resolution to merge. First, the instrument of amalgamation or transfer must be approved by the Certification Officer. Secondly, the union must take all reasonable steps to secure that every ballot paper supplied for voting on the resolution is accompanied by a notice (approved by the Certification Officer), either setting out the instrument of amalgamation or transfer in full or giving a reasonably full explanation of it[478].

---

472 The Certification Officer's figures show a total of 206 listed unions as at the end of March 2002, with a further 20 unlisted unions submitting annual returns: *Annual Report of the Certification Officer* (2001–02) Appendix 1; this is less than one sixth of the peak number of 1384 in 1920.

473 *ACAS Annual Report* (1992) p 19.

474 *Annual Report of the Certification Officer* (2001–02) Appendix 4. The largest UK trade union is UNISON, with 1.3m members. In January 2002, the Amalgamated Engineering and Electrical Union (AEEU) and the Manufacturing Science and Finance Union (MSF) merged to create Amicus, the country's second largest union, with nearly 1.1m members.

475 Trade Union Act Amendment Act 1876, s 12; Trade Union (Amalgamation) Act 1917; Societies (Miscellaneous Provisions) Act 1940, which introduced the idea of a transfer of engagements.

476 The statutory provisions are supported by the Trade Unions and Employers' Associations (Amalgamations, etc.) Regulations 1975, SI 1975/536, as amended; *Harvey* R[28]. The required procedure is set out in the *Certification Officer's Guide to Transfers of Engagements and Amalgamations*.

477 Trade Union and Labour Relations (Consolidation) Act 1992, ss 98–101.

478 Trade Union and Labour Relations (Consolidation) Act 1992, s 99; the notice must not contain any statement making a recommendation or expressing an opinion about the proposed merger: s 99(3A).

Thirdly, there must be a secret postal ballot of all the members[479] resulting in support for the proposed scheme[480]. Previous legislation had required special majorities or a minimum number of votes cast in order for a merger ballot to be effective, but now a simple majority suffices unless a union expressly adopts more restrictive rules. The requirements[481] for a valid merger ballot were significantly amended in 1993 to bring them into line with the rules on union elections and political fund ballots, in particular by introducing compulsory postal ballots and a requirement of independent scrutiny[482]. Finally, the instrument of amalgamation or transfer, once approved in the ballot, must be registered by the Certification Officer, who may not do so until six weeks have elapsed from the date of application for registration[483]. During that period, any member of the union may make a complaint of irregularities in the ballot to the Certification Officer, who will make such enquiries as he thinks fit[484]. If the Certification Officer finds the complaint justified he is required to make a declaration to that effect, and may also make an order specifying the steps which the union must take in order to rectify the irregularities in the ballot before registration is allowed[485]. Such complaints may only be brought before the Certification Officer, not before the courts, although there is an appeal on a point of law from his decision to the EAT[486].

Once the instrument is registered, the property of the original unions or the transferor union is automatically transferred 'without any conveyance, assignment or assignation' to the amalgamated union or transferee union, as the case may be (except for any property expressly excluded by the instrument, and any government stocks and securities)[487]. The question of the political fund should be dealt with in the instrument of amalgamation or transfer; in an amalgamation of two unions each of which has valid political fund rules, the newly amalgamated union will be deemed to have passed a valid political resolution[488], subject to the ordinary periodic reballoting rules (see head 6 above); if, however, there is an amalgamation in which one of the original unions did not have a political fund, then the new union will have to hold a ballot of its new membership in order to instigate a new political fund.

---

479 'Limited members' (eg former workers who have taken voluntary redundancy) are not necessarily 'members' for these purposes: *NUM (Yorkshire Area) v Millward* [1995] ICR 482, [1995] IRLR 411, EAT (overruling the Certification Officer on this point).

480 In the case of amalgamation this means a ballot of both unions; in the case of transfer, only a ballot of the transferor union is necessary.

481 Trade Union and Labour Relations (Consolidation) Act 1992, ss 100–100E, as substituted by the Trade Union Reform and Employment Rights Act 1993.

482 As seen above (at p 712), at the time of writing the government was considering simplifying the burdens imposed by the balloting requirements.

483 Trade Union and Labour Relations (Consolidation) Act 1992, s 101. The Certification Officer is required to ensure that the rules of the transferee organisation are not inconsistent with the instrument of transfer: *R v Certification Officer, ex p AUEW (Engineering Section)* [1983] ICR 125, [1983] IRLR 113, CA.

484 Trade Union and Labour Relations (Consolidation) Act 1992, s 103, as amended by the Employment Relations Act 1999, Sch 6. Complaints under these procedures are rare. There were several complaints in 1997 arising out of the merger of the Civil and Public Services Association with the Public Services Tax and Commerce Union, but only one abortive complaint since then.

485 Trade Union and Labour Relations (Consolidation) Act 1992, s 103(3).

486 Trade Union and Labour Relations (Consolidation) Act 1992, s 104.

487 Trade Union and Labour Relations (Consolidation) Act 1992, s 105.

488 Trade Union and Labour Relations (Consolidation) Act 1992, s 93(1).

Finally, it should be noted that the 1992 Act does not cover the question of de-amalgamation. This will only arise occasionally, but when it does it must be resolved under the relevant union rules, without recourse to statute; this may pose real difficulties if the unions on their amalgamation did not in fact provide for possible divorce in their rules, particularly as it has been held that the court's power to intervene does not extend to inventing a missing de-amalgamation rule[489].

(ii) Inter-union disputes

Inter-union disputes over membership could potentially be very damaging to the trade union movement, leading to poaching of members, fragmentation of bargaining units and floating memberships. To counter the undesirable effects of disputes over membership issues, the TUC drew up a set of principles in 1939 governing relations between TUC-affiliated unions, which have become known as the Bridlington Principles[490], after the 1939 Annual Congress at which they were adopted. The Principles are intended to minimise disputes between unions by providing clear guidance on a range of membership issues, together with a procedure to deal with complaints by one union against another. The preface to the Principles states that they are not intended to be a legally binding contract, but that they are 'accepted by all affiliated organisations as a binding commitment for their continued affiliation to the TUC.' The Principles are enforced by the TUC's Disputes Committee[491], which is empowered under TUC Rules to adjudicate on complaints that they have been breached. The Principles have been amended several times since 1939 to take account of changes to trade union law and practice. In recent times the most significant restructuring was in response to the Trade Union Reform and Employment Rights Act 1993, which enacted a right not to be excluded or expelled from a trade union[492], irrespective of any arrangements or understandings between unions over spheres of influence. The new right was foreshadowed in the Green Paper, *Industrial Relations in the 1990s*[493], which was critical of the impact of the Bridlington Principles in restricting competition between trade unions and denying individuals the right to join the union of their choice. The practical effect of the 1993 Act was to make it virtually impossible for a union lawfully to exclude or expel a member in order to comply with a ruling of the Disputes Committee[494], and the TUC was forced to revise the Principles accordingly[495]. More recently, the Principles were amended in 2000 to take account of the new statutory trade union recognition scheme and the new right for workers to be accompanied in disciplinary and grievance hearings, both of which could potentially give rise to inter-union disputes. There are currently four Principles, each of which is supplemented by more detailed explanatory notes which have equal status and validity with the main text of the Principles:

489 *Burnley, Nelson, Rossendale and District Textile Workers' Union v Amalgamated Textile Workers' Union* [1987] ICR 69, [1986] IRLR 298; compare the approach taken to the implication of union rules following a merger in *McVitae v UNISON* [1996] IRLR 33; see p 705 above.

490 *TUC Disputes Principles and Procedures* (2000).

491 On the working of the Disputes Committee, see Elgar and Simpson 'A Final Appraisal of "Bridlington"? An Evaluation of TUC Disputes Committee Decisions 1974–1991' (1994) BJIR 32.

492 See p 713 above.

493 Cm 1602, 1991.

494 It is specifically provided that being or ceasing to be a member of another trade union is not a sufficient ground for the expulsion or exclusion of an individual: see p 715 above.

495 On the Principles as revised in 1993, see Simpson 'Bridlington 2' (1994) 23 ILJ 170.

Principle 1 (*Co-operation and the Prevention of Disputes*) provides that affiliated unions must make every effort to establish joint working arrangements which prevent (and, where necessary, resolve by agreement) problems which arise between them, including for example procedures for resolving particular difficulties, arrangements concerning spheres of influence, agreed transfers of members and benefit rights, recognition of cards, and demarcation of work.

Principle 2 (*Membership*) provides that all unions affiliated to the TUC accept as a binding commitment that they will not knowingly[496] and actively seek to take into membership existing or recent[497] members of another union by making recruitment approaches, either directly or indirectly, without the agreement of that organisation[498]. Where a dispute over membership arises, the unions concerned must attempt to resolve it by agreement, and the respondent union has 'a moral obligation to offer compensation to the complainant union for any loss of income that it has suffered as a consequence of any knowing and active recruitment of its members'[499].

Principle 3 (*Organisation and Recognition*) provides that no union may commence organising activities at any company or undertaking in respect of any group of workers where another union has the majority of workers employed in membership and/or is recognised to negotiate terms and conditions, unless by arrangement with that union, nor may a union make approaches to an employer or respond to an employer initiative which would have the effect of undermining the position of the established union. Where a union considers that another affiliated union has low levels of membership, and no agreement or a moribund agreement, within any organisation in respect of any group of workers, the union must consult with the other affiliated union before commencing organising activities, and if agreement cannot be reached the matter must be referred to the TUC.

Special attention is given in the explanatory notes to single union deals. When making sole negotiating agreements or union membership agreements or arrangements, affiliated unions must have regard to the interests of other unions which may be affected and should consider their position in the drafting of such agreements; a union must not enter into or extend any such agreement where another union would be deprived of their existing recognition or negotiation rights, except by prior consultation and agreement; and where a union has been derecognised, no other affiliated union may attempt to recruit, organise or seek recognition at that company without prior consultation with the derecognised union[500].

---

496 Each union must include in its membership application form model questions about past or present membership of another union: *TUC Disputes Principles and Procedures* (2000) p 8.
497 'Recent' is normally understood as applying to applicants who have contributed to an affiliated union during the preceding 52 weeks: *TUC Disputes Principles and Procedures* (2000) p 8.
498 Where present or past union membership is indicated, the union must inform the other union, and if the other union objects to the recruitment of its present or former members, it should request a meeting to discuss the matter: *TUC Disputes Principles and Procedures* (2000) p 8.
499 *TUC Disputes Principles and Procedures* (2000) p 9.
500 *TUC Disputes Principles and Procedures* (2000) p 11. There is also a requirement to give early notification to the TUC General Secretary where a union is in the process of making a single union agreement: p 11.

Principle 4 (*Inter-Union Disputes and Industrial Action*) provides that in cases of inter-union dispute (whether relating to trade union membership, trade union recognition, negotiating rights, demarcation of work, or any other difficulty), no official or unauthorised stoppage of work or action short of a strike must take place before the TUC has had time to examine the issue, and the union or unions concerned have an obligation to take immediate and active steps to get their members to resume normal working.

In several respects the Bridlington Principles in their present form are a pale shadow of their previous incarnations. Until 1993, the Principles provided[501], inter alia, that no affiliated union should accept into membership a present or former member of another affiliated union without enquiring of that union whether the applicant had tendered his resignation, whether he was clear on the books, whether he was 'under discipline or penalty' and whether there were any other reasons why he should not be accepted. If the union objected to the transfer, or if the enquiries revealed that the applicant was under discipline, engaged in a trade dispute or in arrears with contributions, the enquiring union was not to admit the applicant into membership. If it considered the other union's objection to be unreasonable it could refer the matter to the TUC for adjudication by the Disputes Committee, which could order a union not to admit a person into membership, or to expel a member improperly recruited from another affiliated union. Affiliated unions were recommended to adopt a model rule which permitted the union's executive to expel members in order to comply with a ruling of the Disputes Committee[502], and in *Cheall v APEX*[503], the House of Lords upheld the validity of the model rule, and rejected the argument that the Bridlington principles were contrary to public policy because they restricted the right of an individual to join and remain a member of a trade union of his or her choice. Lord Diplock, in a strong affirmation of union autonomy over membership at common law, stated[504]:

> 'My Lords, freedom of association can only be mutual; there can be no right of an individual to associate with other individuals who are not willing to associate with him ... I know of no existing rule of public policy that would prevent trade unions from entering into arrangements with one another which they consider to be in the interests of their members in promoting order in industrial relations and enhancing their members' bargaining power with their employers; nor do I think it a permissible exercise of your Lordships' judicial power to create a new rule of public policy to that effect. If this is to be done at all it must be done by Parliament.'

While the decision in *Cheall v APEX* endorsed the legitimacy of the Bridlington Principles at common law, the reforms introduced by the Trade Union Reform and Employment Rights Act 1993 undermined them, because the practical effect of the 1993 Act was to make it impossible for a union lawfully to exclude or expel

---

501 For an analysis of the pre-1993 provisions, see Simpson 'Individualism versus Collectivism: an Evaluation of Section 14 of the Trade Union Reform and Employment Rights Act 1993' (1993) 22 ILJ 181.

502 This was essential after the decision in *Spring v NASDS* [1956] 2 All ER 221, [1956] 1 WLR 585, where the court refused to imply a power to expel in order to comply with such a ruling. See also *Rothwell v APEX* [1976] ICR 211, [1975] IRLR 375.

503 [1983] ICR 398, [1983] IRLR 215, HL, noted Simpson (1983) 46 MLR 635.

504 [1983] IRLR 215 at 218.

a member in order to comply with a ruling of the Disputes Committee – hence the reformulation of the Principles in 1993. Having said that, TUC-affiliated unions are still required under Principle 2 to make a binding commitment not to take the present or recent members of another union into membership by making recruitment approaches without agreement, and must continue to include questions about past or present membership of other unions in their membership application forms. Where a dispute arises, the unions concerned must try to reach a negotiated settlement, and if the attempt fails the matter may be referred by the TUC to the Disputes Committee, which may order the respondent union to pay financial compensation to the complainant union, subject to a maximum of two years' loss of contributions, and may also censure the respondent union[505]. However, the Disputes Committee no longer has the power to order a union to expel a member admitted in breach of the Principles[506]. It remains to be seen whether a purely financial disincentive is sufficient to dissuade unions from commencing recruitment campaigns targeted at the members of other unions.

505 The Disputes Committee may require the respondent union to publish the censure prominently in its journal.
506 This means that the model rule which was upheld in *Cheall v APEX* (see n 503 above) is in effect now a dead letter.

Chapter 11

Industrial action

1 INTRODUCTION[1]

Until the last quarter of the nineteenth century, important aspects of trade union aims and methods were in danger of being construed as criminal, either under certain statutes which outlawed certain forms of combination[2], or under the general law relating to conspiracy which was capable of rendering an agreement criminal even if the object of the agreement was in fact lawful. The Trade Union Act 1871 provided that the purposes of a union should not be deemed unlawful merely because they were in restraint of trade so as to render members liable to criminal prosecution for conspiracy or otherwise[3]. This, however, only covered one possible head of illegality, and the Criminal Law Amendment Act which was passed in the same year to liberalise the law relating to the use of non-violent means in a dispute was soon found to be ineffective. Thus, as late as 1872, servants of a gas company who had come out on strike as a protest against the dismissal of a fellow employee and who, in striking, had broken their contracts, could still be held guilty of criminal conspiracy[4]. The agitation which followed this decision led to the appointment of a Royal Commission, which in turn led to the passing of the Conspiracy and Protection of Property Act 1875, which repealed the Master and Servant legislation, codified the law relating to the use of intimidation and violence during industrial action and, most importantly in the present context, removed the possibility of a lawful combination of workmen constituting a criminal conspiracy by providing, in section 3, that an agreement or combination by two or

1   See generally, Ewing *The Right to Strike* (1991); Auerbach *Legislating for Conflict* (1992); Davies and Freedland *Labour Legislation and Public Policy* (1993); Millward, Bryson and Forth *All Change at Work? British Employee Relations 1980-1998* (2000); Morris and Archer, *Collective Labour Law* (2000), ch 6.
2   Combination Act 1800; Molestation of Workmen Act 1825. For the history of the intervention of criminal law, see Wedderburn *The Worker and the Law* (3rd edn, 1986) pp. 513–521. On the history of trade union law generally, see Orth *Combination and Conspiracy: A Legal History of Trade Unionism 1721–1906* (1991).
3   See now the Trade Union and Labour Relations (Consolidation) Act 1992, s 11.
4   *R v Bunn* (1872) 12 Cox CC 316. See generally Wallington, 'Criminal conspiracy and industrial conflict' (1975) 4 ILJ 69.

more persons to do or procure to be done any act in contemplation or furtherance of a trade dispute was not to be indictable as a conspiracy if such an act when committed by one person alone would not be punishable as a crime[5] . Thus, the mere fact of combination or agreement is not criminal[6] .

While the Conspiracy and Protection of Property Act 1875 had removed persons engaged in a trade dispute from the fear of prosecution for criminal conspiracy, it had no application to civil actions and so did not protect unions or their members from the payment of damages in a civil suit, and so, not unnaturally, it was to the civil remedy that aggrieved persons now turned. In *Allen v Flood*[7] , the House of Lords prevented the evolution of one general tort of intentionally causing harm to a person without justification, by holding that an act lawful in itself is not converted by a malicious or bad motive into an unlawful act leading to civil liability. However, in this same period the courts did create or approve the specific torts of conspiracy[8] and inducement of breach of contract[9] , so that if there was an element of combination (the 'magic of plurality') or contractual breach (both of which were missing in *Allen v Flood*), there could indeed be civil liability.

Moreover, in the famous *Taff Vale* case[10] the House of Lords held that a trade union could be sued in tort (in spite of not being a body corporate) and its assets could be taken in satisfaction of judgment. On one view this may have been no more than a refusal to put trade unions into a preferential position, but it created a genuine dilemma since all the funds of the union became attachable, including those to which members had subscribed for the receipt of benefits. A Royal Commission was set up under the chairmanship of Lord Dunedin which, in its report published in 1906, did not go as far as to recommend the reversal of the *Taff Vale* case, but instead made the more modest proposal that separate benefit funds should be established which would be protected from seizure. However, the government went further and passed the Trade Disputes Act 1906 which (a) gave complete immunity to unions in respect of actions in tort, (b) gave immunity from liability for conspiracy and inducement of breach of contract to officers and members of unions provided they acted in 'contemplation or furtherance of a trade dispute' (a phrase dubbed the 'golden formula' by Wedderburn in recognition of the crucial role which it plays in determining the existence of the statutory immunities) and (c) gave statutory backing to *Allen v Flood* by declaring, for the avoidance of doubt, that an act done in contemplation or furtherance of a trade dispute is not actionable in tort simply because it interferes with the legitimate interests of another person. This statutory protection was extended in the Trade Disputes Act 1965 to give immunity (within the golden formula) from liability for the tort of intimidation which was exhumed and applied by the House of Lords in *Rookes v Barnard*[11] .

---

5   This is still the criminal law position, though s 3 was repealed by the Criminal Law Act 1977 as being no longer necessary, for s 3 of that Act extends the principle to all conspiracies by restricting criminal conspiracies to agreements to commit crimes (with two exceptions, neither of which is relevant in industrial cases).

6   Agreements to commit acts which are themselves criminal are not protected, although summary offences may be disregarded in certain circumstances. See p 805.

7   [1898] AC 1, HL.

8   *Mogul Steamship Co v McGregor, Gow & Co* [1892] AC 25, HL; *Quinn v Leathem* [1901] AC 495, HL.

9   *South Wales Miners' Federation v Glamorgan Coal Co* [1905] AC 239, HL.

10   *Taff Vale Rly Co v ASRS* [1901] AC 426, HL.

11   [1964] AC 1129, [1964] 1 All ER 367, HL.

The whole scheme was then altered by the Industrial Relations Act 1971 which removed the union's complete immunity and introduced certain 'unfair industrial practices' based on the old heads of civil liability[12] . In 1974, however, the pre-Industrial Relations Act law was reinstated by the Trade Union and Labour Relations Act 1974 and the immunities were further extended by the Trade Union and Labour Relations (Amendment) Act 1976, which widened the immunity from the tort of inducement of breach of contract to cover commercial contracts as well as contracts of employment (thereby removing possible liability for secondary boycotts and 'blackings'), and extended the immunity to cover the development of a new head of tortious liability, that of interference with contract (ie short of an actual breach). By 1976, therefore, the immunities appeared almost watertight. For a time in the late 1970s it seemed that the Court of Appeal had succeeded in restricting the scope of the immunities, not by finding loopholes in the individual immunities themselves, but instead by taking a more stringent approach to what fell within the golden formula, upon which the immunities depend; however, his approach was subsequently disapproved by the House of Lords in three landmark cases[13] .

The incoming Conservative government, elected in 1979 in the wake of the notorious 'winter of discontent', embarked on a relentless 'step-by-step' reform of the law on industrial action which lasted for fourteen years and produced a remarkable transformation of industrial relations law. During that period there were no fewer than six Acts of Parliament affecting the law on industrial action, beginning with the Employment Act 1980, which contained complex provisions removing the immunities from most forms of secondary industrial action (ie action against employers not directly concerned in the dispute)[14]. This was accomplished by the notorious section 17 of the Employment Act 1980, which in effect reinstated much the same position as that reached by the Court of Appeal in the late 1970s. The Employment Act 1982 constituted a further stage in this process, with the narrowing of the definition of 'trade dispute' and the withdrawal of the immunities from union pressure to have union labour only and union recognition requirements inserted into commercial contracts and tenders. However, the most far-reaching reforms in that Act related to the position of a union itself. As stated above, the Trade Disputes Act 1906 made a union itself immune from an action in tort; any possible action by an employer lay against union officers and members (who themselves have specific immunities). However, the 1982 Act abolished that total immunity[15] , so that a union now only has the same immunity as its individual officers and members, and introduced special rules as to when a union can be liable for the acts of its officials and committees, how much for, and from what funds.

This process was taken a stage further by the Trade Union Act 1984, but unlike section 17 of the 1980 Act, which limited the scope of lawful industrial action, the 1984 Act concentrated on the machinery for calling the strike or other

---

12 For a discussion of the law under the 1971 Act, see Cooper's *Outlines of Industrial Law* (6th edn, 1972) ch XI.

13 *NWL Ltd v Nelson* [1979] ICR 867, [1979] IRLR 478, HL; *Express Newspapers Ltd v McShane* [1980] 1 All ER 65, [1980] IRLR 35, HL; *Duport Steels Ltd v Sirs* [1980] 1 All ER 529, [1980] IRLR 116, HL.

14 Crucially, the 1980 Act did permit secondary action in certain specified circumstances: see below.

15 Employment Act 1982, s 15. The immunity was previously contained in the Trade Union and Labour Relations Act 1974, s 14.

industrial action. It did this by making a strike ballot mandatory in the case of official action; industrial action without such a ballot was thus made litigable at the suit of any employer (or, semble, any person) adversely affected, by a simple device of withdrawing the statutory immunities altogether. This step, no less radical for its being so simple, has had a considerable effect, and in the years since the introduction of the 1984 Act a significant proportion of actions brought or threatened by employers against unions in relation to industrial action (actual or impending) have been under the strike ballot provisions rather than under the provisions of the earlier Acts[16] .

The next stage in this seemingly inexorable process was the Employment Act 1988 which, in addition to imposing extensive controls on internal union affairs (discussed in the previous chapter), removed the statutory immunities from industrial action taken to support or enforce union membership, thereby restricting a union's ability to defend a closed shop by means of industrial pressure. That Act also introduced a further refinement to the strike ballot provisions by requiring separate ballots to be held at each workplace unless certain stringent conditions were satisfied. Hard on the heels of the 1988 Act, the Employment Act 1990 contained a formidable series of measures designed to discourage secondary industrial action and unofficial industrial action. It removed the statutory immunities from virtually all forms of secondary action (repealing section 17 of the 1980 Act), significantly extended the range of circumstances where a union could be held responsible (and therefore potentially liable in tort) for the acts of its officials, committees and members, and completely removed the right to complain of unfair dismissal from those dismissed while taking part in unofficial industrial action.

To describe the state of the law on industrial action following the 1990 Act as confusing would be a considerable understatement. To gain a complete picture it was necessary to consult no fewer than nine statutes, stretching back as far as 1875, five of which had been enacted since 1980, all overlaid on a common law (ie the industrial torts) which was itself of great complexity. The decision to consolidate the whole of trade union law into one massive statute, the Trade Union and Labour Relations (Consolidation) Act 1992, was therefore greeted with relief by those toiling in the field, but in such a volatile area it was too much to hope that the consolidation would survive for long without further amendment. In fact, the Trade Union Reform and Employment Rights Act 1993 was introduced into the House of Commons within weeks of the 1992 Act coming into force; one can only wonder at the logic of proceeding with a major consolidation while further significant changes to the substantive law were in the pipeline. The 1993 Act contained several very significant and (needless to say) highly controversial reforms of the law on industrial action, some of which had been considered during the passage of earlier legislation and rejected as either unworkable or undesirable. Thus, there were major changes to the law on industrial action ballots, including compulsory postal ballots, independent scrutiny of the ballot process, and a requirement to give notice of a ballot, and of any subsequent industrial action, to the employers of those involved; furthermore, in a move influenced by the 'Citizen's Charter', the 1993 Act gave individuals a right (the Citizen's Right) to

---

16 It has been argued that the frequent use of the strike ballot provisions by employers may initially have been at least partly due to the perceived effectiveness of legal sanctions during the miners' strike (albeit at the suit of working miners rather than employers): Benedictus (1985) 14 ILJ 176.

seek an injunction restraining unlawful industrial action where that action affects the supply of goods or services to that person. The potential impact of this development cannot be overestimated, for its effect is to extend the range of potential claimants to embrace anyone adversely affected by unlawful industrial action, even those with no direct cause of action in tort (for example because the unlawful act was not directed at them). Having said that, to date very little use has been made of the Citizen's Right in practice, and it therefore remains something of an unexplored (unexploded?) weapon.

After 18 years of Conservative rule, any lingering hopes that a change of government might herald a return to the collective laissez-faire of the 1970s were dashed by the 1997 Labour general election manifesto, which made it clear that a new Labour government would not repeal the key elements of the Conservative trade union laws[17] . In his Foreword to the 1998 White Paper, *Fairness at Work*, the Prime Minister stated: 'There will be no going back. The days of strikes without ballots, mass picketing, closed shops and secondary action are over'[18] . However, in that document the government also signalled its intention to simplify the law on industrial action ballots and to extend unfair dismissal protection to those dismissed for taking part in lawfully organised official industrial action, and the Employment Relations Act 1999 duly enacted measures implementing those proposals. It soon became clear that the attempt to simplify the strike ballot provisions had backfired spectacularly as a result of restrictive judicial interpretation[19], and at the time of writing the government had signalled its intention to further revise the provisions in order to achieve the desired objective[20]. The measures protecting workers from dismissal for taking part in lawful, official industrial action were arguably of much greater significance, for while they cannot be said to guarantee a 'right to strike' as such (on account of the qualified nature of the protection against dismissal, and the absence of any protection against victimisation short of dismissal), they are undoubtedly the closest that UK law has ever come to such a right. There is one further dimension to this issue, and that is the impact of the Human Rights Act 1998 on the law on industrial action[21]. As seen in the previous chapter, Article 11 of the European Convention on Human Rights confers a right to freedom of association with others, including the right to form and join trade unions. Unlike the European Social Charter, Article 11 does not expressly include a right to strike, but the European Court of Human Rights has held that Article 11 safeguards the freedom of trade unions to protect the occupational interests of their members[22], and that '[t]he grant of a right to strike represents without any doubt one of the most important of [the] means' by which a State could seek to secure the protection of the Article

17 *New Labour: Because Britain Deserves Better* (1997) p 17.
18 Cm 3968, 1998.
19 See eg *London Underground Ltd v National Union of Rail, Maritime and Transport Workers* [2001] IRLR 228, CA (noted by Wedderburn (2001) 30 ILJ 206); *National Union of Rail, Maritime and Transport Workers v Midland Mainline* [2001] EWCA Civ 1206, [2001] IRLR 813. For a different and, it is submitted, more realistic approach, see *P v National Union of Schoolmasters/Union of Women Teachers* [2003] UKHL 8, [2003] 1 All ER 993.
20 *Review of the Employment Relations Act 1999* (DTI, February 2003).
21 See Hendy, 'Article 11 and the Right to Strike' in Ewing (ed) *Human Rights at Work* (2000); O'Dempsey et al *Employment Law and the Human Rights Act 1998* (2001) ch 4.
22 *UNISON v United Kingdom* [2002] IRLR 497, ECtHR; see also *Swedish Engine Drivers' Union v Sweden* (1976) 1 EHRR 617, ECtHR; *National Union of Belgian Police v Belgium* (1975) 1 EHRR 578.

11 rights[23]. Crucially, however, Article 11 leaves each state a free choice of the means to be used for safeguarding the freedom of unions to protect their members[24], and the court has acknowledged that a right to strike may be subject to restrictions under national laws[25]. It would seem therefore that any attempt to use Article 11 to challenge the restrictions on industrial action under national law is probably doomed to failure, although in a potentially significant shift in approach, the European Court of Human Rights held in *UNISON v United Kingdom*[26] that the prohibition of the strike in that case was a restriction on the union's power to protect the interests of its members, and therefore a restriction on the freedom of association guaranteed by Article 11(1). The court's ruling was not as significant as might at first appear, however, because on the facts the court dismissed the union's application as inadmissible, holding that the restriction under national law was justified under Article 11(2) as being 'necessary in a democratic society for the prevention of disorder or crime, for the protection of the health or morals or for the protection of the rights and freedoms of others' (in this case, the economic interests of the employer)[27]. The decision does, however, lend support to the argument that Article 11 may confer a right to strike as a weapon of last resort where a union has no other means of protecting the occupational interests of its members[28]. In addition to the right of association, Article 11 also gives a right to freedom of peaceful assembly, which could conceivably be used to challenge some of the existing legal restrictions on picketing (for example the common law of trespass, and the recommendation in the Code of Practice on Picketing that pickets be limited to six at each entrance), as could the right to freedom of expression in Article 10[29].

The complexity of the law on industrial action has in the past attracted adverse judicial comment on the basis that this is an area where it is particularly important that the players (the union leaders and managers) should know what the rules are and what is 'offside'[30]. The 1992 Consolidation Act helped to tidy up the structure of the legislation, but the law itself is still extremely difficult and

23 *Schmidt and Dahlström v Sweden* (1976) 1 EHRR 632, ECtHR.
24 In *Gustafsson v Sweden* (1996) 22 EHRR 409, the ECtHR emphasised that States enjoy 'a wide margin of appreciation' in the choice of means to be employed.
25 *Schmidt and Dahlström v Sweden* (1976) 1 EHRR 632. See eg *NATFHE v United Kingdom* (1998) 25 EHRR 122, where the Commission held that the then requirement under ss 226A and 234A of the 1992 Act to disclose to an employer the names of those to be balloted or to take part in industrial action was not 'a significant limitation on the right to take collective action'.
26 [2002] IRLR 497, ECtHR. The union had threatened industrial action against the employer, University College London Hospitals NHS Trust, because it refused to give an undertaking that the terms and conditions of staff to be transferred to a consortium which was to build and run a new PFI hospital would be maintained for a period of 30 years at an equivalent level to employees who were not transferred. The application to the ECtHR followed the issue of an injunction by the Court of Appeal ([1999] IRLR 31) restraining the industrial action on the grounds that the dispute was not a trade dispute: see p 777 below).
27 The Court noted that the union's members were not at any real or immediate risk of detriment, or of being left defenceless against future attempts to downgrade pay or conditions, and that the union remained able to take strike action if the employer took any step to dismiss employees or change their contracts prior to the transfer, or if the transferee in the future threatened the employment of its members or to derecognise the union.
28 Cf Hendy [1998] EHRLR 583.
29 See p 806 below. On human rights at work generally, see p 42 above.
30 *Merkur Island Shipping Corpn v Laughton* [1983] ICR 178, [1983] IRLR 26, CA, per Sir John Donaldson MR, echoed by Lord Diplock in the House of Lords, n 31 below.

complex. The approach adopted in this chapter is to look first at the effect of industrial action on the individual participants, and then to consider the position of the organisers of the industrial action, including the industrial torts that may be committed during a trade dispute, the statutory immunities which apply where those torts are committed within the 'golden formula', and (most importantly in practice) the restrictions on those immunities enacted by successive Conservative governments during the 1980s and early 1990s. We then turn to the potential criminal liability for industrial action, and the law on picketing, including the specific statutory immunity for 'peaceful picketing'; we assess the extent to which a union is vicariously liable for the acts of its officials and committees; and finally, we examine the use of injunctions in industrial disputes, including the controversial 'Citizen's Right' introduced in 1993.

While it is necessary for the sake of exposition to split the subject up in this way, it must be remembered that any particular case may depend on the effect and interaction of several of these factors. Indeed, the reforms introduced by the Employment Relations Act 1999 added to the complex interplay of issues by linking the protection against unfair dismissal to the legality of the industrial action. On the latter issue, it may help, when looking at the detail, to remember the three basic stages in an action in tort adopted by the House of Lords in *Merkur Island Shipping Corpn v Laughton*[31] : (i) does the industrial action in question give the claimant a cause of action in tort; (ii) if so, is that cause of action covered by the immunities in sections 219 or 220 of the Trade Union and Labour Relations (Consolidation) Act 1992; (iii) is the cause of action restored by anything in sections 222–234A of the Trade Union and Labour Relations (Consolidation) Act 1992?

2 THE EFFECT OF INDUSTRIAL ACTION ON THE INDIVIDUAL

As was seen in the introduction to this chapter, the approach traditionally taken in the law on industrial action has been to preserve the freedom to strike by providing immunities at the collective level (albeit within increasingly narrow boundaries) rather than by conferring any positive right to strike on the individual participants. At the collective level, the effect of industrial action on individual contracts of employment is of central importance because it may render the action 'unlawful' in the sense required by certain forms of the industrial torts, so opening the way to a successful civil action to stop the strike in any case where it can be argued that the statutory immunities do not apply[32]. Before turning to the collective dimension, however, it is necessary to examine more closely the effect of industrial action on the individual participants.

---

31   [1983] ICR 490, [1983] IRLR 218, HL.

32   Immunities are necessary because the very fact that a strike involves a breach of contract means that prima facie those organising it will be guilty of inducing a breach of contract, which may be tortious in itself and/or may provide the 'unlawful means' necessary for certain other torts (particularly indirect inducement of breach of commercial contracts or interference with the claimant's business); if the immunities are withheld (eg where there is no strike ballot), tortious liability will, in most cases, be easy to establish. One open question is whether the strikers' own breaches of contract can be 'unlawful means' in themselves, for the purposes of the economic torts; this is considered at p 772 below.

(i) The effect of industrial action on individual contracts of employment

As the most fundamental contractual obligation of an employee is to be ready and willing to serve the employer, the action of going on strike is likely to be regarded as constituting a breach of contract, giving the employer the right to dismiss summarily. In theory it may also entitle the employer to sue the employee for damages[33], although in practice the employer's common law power to withhold wages in respect of non-performance (or indeed partial performance) of contractual obligations is likely to be of far greater significance[34]. The orthodox view is that industrial action will be unlawful (as a breach of contract) however it is organised, and even if strike notice is given it will be construed merely as notice of an impending breach[35]. However, this orthodox view was challenged by Lord Denning MR in *Morgan v Fry*[36] where he suggested that where strike notice of adequate length (ie at least equal to the length required to terminate the contracts of employment) was given, the strike was not unlawful, since the notice had the effect of suspending the contracts, not breaking them:

> 'The truth is that neither employer nor workmen wish to take the drastic action of termination [of the contracts of employment] if it can be avoided. The men do not wish to leave their work for ever. The employers do not wish to scatter their labour force to the four winds. Each side is, therefore, content to accept a "strike notice" of proper length as lawful. It is an implication read into the modern law as to trade disputes. If a strike takes place, the contract of employment is not terminated. It is suspended during the strike and revives again when the strike is over[37].'

The Donovan Commission considered the possibility of introducing the concept of suspension through strike notice, but thought it surrounded by problems[38]; in spite of this, it was introduced by the Industrial Relations Act 1971, s 147, but disappeared with the repeal of that Act in 1974. The whole question arose (obliquely) for consideration by the EAT in *Simmons v Hoover Ltd*[39] where, in reaffirming that an employer has a right to dismiss a striking employee (who is thereby disentitled to a redundancy payment), Phillips J held that there is no common law doctrine of suspension by strike notice, and refused to apply Lord Denning's views in *Morgan v Fry*. He considered that those views were out of line with the modern statutory provisions relating to strikes (in contexts such as unfair

---

33 *National Coal Board v Galley* [1958] 1 All ER 91, [1958] 1 WLR 16, CA; *Neil v Strathclyde Regional Council* [1984] IRLR 14 (not an industrial dispute case).

34 See p 218 above.

35 See principally *Rookes v Barnard* [1964] AC 1129, [1964] 1 All ER 367, HL, at 1204 and 396 respectively, per Lord Devlin; *Stratford & Son Ltd v Lindley* [1965] AC 269 at 285, [1964] 2 All ER 209 at 217, CA, per Lord Denning MR.

36 [1968] 2 QB 710, [1968] 3 All ER 452, CA; Davies LJ supported Lord Denning's view, but Russell LJ did not and decided the case on other grounds. The case itself concerned an allegation of intimidation, though as the facts arose before the passage of the Trade Disputes Act 1965 the new immunity was not available.

37 [1968] 2 QB 710 at 728, [1968] 3 All ER 452 at 458.

38 (1968) Cmnd. 623, para 943.

39 [1977] ICR 61, [1976] IRLR 266, EAT; applied in *Wilkins v Cantrell and Cochrane (GB) Ltd* [1978] IRLR 483, EAT and *Haddow v ILEA* [1979] ICR 202, EAT.

dismissal, redundancy claims and continuity of employment), which operate on the assumption that participation in a strike is repudiatory conduct entitling the employer to dismiss, and then graft on special rules (depending on the context). *Simmons v Hoover Ltd* shows a clear move back to the original view of strikes as breaches of contract[40], and any mitigation of the potential harshness of this must be found in the legislation.

While it is clear that strike action will be a breach of contract, the position as regards industrial action short of a strike is less certain. Where the industrial action is inconsistent with contractual obligations, there is little doubt that it will be in breach of contract[41]. But what if the industrial action is question is a work to rule, or a ban on voluntary overtime? Will this constitute a breach of the contracts of employment of the participating employees? In *Secretary of State for Employment v ASLEF (No 2)*[42], the Court of Appeal held that concerted action by a group of workers which involved working strictly in accordance with their contracts of employment nevertheless amounted to a breach of contract where the object of the action was wilfully to disrupt the employer's business. This does not mean, however, that employees necessarily break their contracts whenever they withdraw their goodwill. In *Burgess v Stevedoring Services Ltd*[43], the Privy Council held that an overtime ban was not in breach of the contracts of the participants, Lord Hoffmann stating that employees are not in breach of their contracts 'for refusing to do things altogether outsider their contractual obligations (like going to work on Sunday) merely because they do not have a bona fide reason for refusal. They do not have to have any reason at all.'[44]

(ii) The effect of industrial action on statutory employment rights

Participation in a strike or other industrial action is likely to have a highly detrimental impact on an employee's statutory employment rights. The most serious consequence is likely to be the potential loss of the right to bring proceedings for unfair dismissal, discussed below; but other statutory rights of a striking employee will also be affected, in particular:

(a) the restrictions on deductions from pay do not apply to deductions in respect of a strike or other industrial action in which the employee took part[45];

(b) a striking employee's rights to a redundancy payment may be jeopardised[46];

---

40 This view could be said to be implicit in the Trade Union and Labour Relations (Consolidation) Act 1992, s 229(4), which requires a ballot paper to point out that a person who takes part in a strike or other industrial action may be in breach of his contract of employment. Note, however, the judgment of Saville J in *Boxfoldia Ltd v NGA (1982)* [1988] ICR 752, [1988] IRLR 383 to the effect that the question of whether a purported strike notice avoids a breach of contract is a matter of interpretation of the notice (which, in order to be effective, would have to be an unambiguous notice of termination of contracts by the strikers).

41 See eg *British Telecommunications plc v Ticehurst* [1992] ICR 383, [1992] IRLR 219, CA, discussed in ch 3, above.

42 [1972] 2 QB 455, CA.

43 [2002] UKPC 39, [2002] IRLR 810.

44 [2002] UKPC 39, [2002] IRLR 810 at 813. Their motive might have been relevant "if they had been assigned work and, as part of a concerted action, all claimed to be sick or have some other reason for declaring themselves not available."

45 Employment Rights Act 1996, s 14(5); see p 262 above. For the common law power to withhold wages in such circumstances, see p 218 above.

46 Employment Rights Act 1996, s 140; see p 644 above.

(c) a week during which an employee takes part in a strike will not count for the purposes of calculating that employee's continuity of employment[47];

(d) an employee is not entitled to a statutory guarantee payment where the failure to provide work is in consequence of a strike, lock-out or other industrial action involving his employer or an associated employer[48];

(e) an employee may be disqualified from receiving statutory sick pay where there is a stoppage of work due to a trade dispute at his place of work[49];

(f) rights to state benefits (for example Jobseeker's Allowance) will be materially affected[50].

(iii) Industrial action and unfair dismissal[51]

When employees strike, their employer has the contractual right to dismiss them[52], even if that right is infrequently exercised. However, while a dismissal in such circumstances is probably lawful at common law, it may still be unfair; indeed following the reforms introduced by the Employment Relations Act 1999, a dismissal may be *automatically* unfair where the employee is dismissed for taking 'protected industrial action'. This protection is however contingent on the industrial action in question being official (ie authorised or endorsed by the union), lawful (ie covered by the statutory immunities), and normally lasting for no longer than eight weeks[53]. Where these requirements are not satisfied, the pre-1999 law still applies, which means that in some circumstances an employment tribunal will have no jurisdiction to hear an unfair dismissal complaint, while in others the tribunal will only be able to consider the complaint on its merits if the employer has discriminated between the participants by selectively dismissing or re-engaging them. To gain a clear picture of the current position, it is necessary to explore how this highly intricate state of affairs has come about.

The approach of those responsible for drafting the original unfair dismissal legislation was to seek to protect the neutrality of the industrial (now employment) tribunals by relieving them of the necessity of investigating the rights and wrongs of an industrial dispute, while at the same time preserving the employer's ultimate freedom to dismiss the participants. This was achieved by providing that where, at the date of dismissal, the employee was taking part in a strike or other industrial action, or the employer was conducting or instituting a lock-out, the tribunal would have no jurisdiction to hear an unfair dismissal complaint by that employee unless the employer had discriminated between the participants, either by selectively dismissing only some of them, or by selectively offering re-engagement[54]. In *Heath v J F Longman (Meat Salesmen) Ltd*[55], Sir Hugh Griffiths expressed the policy behind this as follows:

47 Employment Rights Act 1996, s 216.
48 Employment Rights Act 1996, s 29(3). See p 228 above.
49 Social Security Contributions and Benefits Act 1992, Sch 11, paras 2(g) and 7.
50 Jobseekers Act 1995, s 14. See p 651 above.
51 See *Harvey* D 14; Ewing, n 1 above, ch 4.
52 *Simmons v Hoover Ltd* [1977] ICR 61, [1976] IRLR 266, EAT; *Wilkins v Cantrell and Cochrane (GB) Ltd* [1978] IRLR 483, EAT; *Haddow v ILEA* [1979] ICR 202, EAT.
53 Action lasting for longer than eight weeks may still be protected in certain circumstances: see below.
54 See *Gallagher v Wragg* [1977] ICR 174, EAT, per Phillips J; the neutrality explanation is arguably undermined by the fact that, where a dismissal or re-engagement is selective, the tribunal will have to decide whether the dismissal was fair or unfair.
55 [1973] ICR 407, [1973] IRLR 214, at 410 and 215 respectively.

'. . . the manifest overall purpose of [the section] is to give a measure of protection to an employer if his business is faced with ruin by a strike. It enables him in those circumstances, if he cannot carry on business without a labour force, to dismiss the labour force on strike; to take on another labour force without the stigma of its being an unfair dismissal.'

The Thatcher government considered the principle of non-selectivity to be too restrictive on employers faced with industrial action, and so the relevant provisions were modified to allow some selectivity in dismissals. Thus, the Employment Act 1982[56] confined the non-selectivity principle to those still taking part in the industrial action at the date of the complainant's dismissal (thereby allowing an employer faced with a strike to wait to see who in fact returns to work before dismissing all those still holding out), and introduced a time limit on the re-engagement of dismissed strikers (in effect permitting selective re-engagement after a three-month period); and the Employment Act 1990 took matters much further, by completely removing the right to complain of unfair dismissal from those dismissed while taking part in unofficial industrial action[57]. Taken together, these reforms significantly weakened the protection which the non-selectivity principle had given to those taking part in industrial action. In its 1998 White Paper, *Fairness at Work*, the incoming Labour government signalled a major policy shift in this area by proposing to give employees dismissed for taking part in lawfully organised official industrial action the right to complain of unfair dismissal to a tribunal[58], and the Employment Relations Act 1999 subsequently enacted the concept of protected industrial action (discussed below). The provisions on protected industrial action differ in several respects from the proposals contained in *Fairness at Work*; for example, the White Paper had not indicated any intention to restrict the protection temporally, whereas under the 1999 Act the protection normally only lasts for eight weeks. However, this temporal limit on the protection is offset by the fact that a dismissal during the protected period will be *automatically* unfair; in contrast, under the White Paper proposals, it would have been for a tribunal to decide whether the employer had acted fairly and reasonably in all the circumstances. On balance, the protection of an automatically unfair dismissal, albeit for a limited period, is likely in practice to be more advantageous to workers taking part in industrial action than protection for an unlimited period which is dependent on a tribunal finding on the facts that the dismissal was unfair. There are however some significant gaps in the protection. As previously mentioned, it is contingent on the industrial action in question being both official and, more controversially, lawful, which may make reliance on the protection something of a gamble, as an individual union member has no way of knowing whether the union has in fact complied with the Byzantine laws governing industrial action[59];

---

56   See Wallington 'The Employment Act 1982, s 9 – a recipe for victimisation?' (1983) 46 MLR 310; Ewing 'Industrial action: another step in the "right" direction' (1982) 11 ILJ 209; Townshend-Smith 'Taking part in a strike or other industrial action' [1984] NLJ 194, 240.

57   See now the Trade Union and Labour Relations (Consolidation) Act 1992, s 237

58   Cm 3968, 1998, paras 4.21-4.23. The White Paper confirmed that the government had no intention of changing the position in relation to those dismissed for taking unofficial action.

59   A satisfactory report on the ballot by the independent scrutineer (see p 798 below) may provide some reassurance that the union has safely navigated the legal minefield, but it will probably come too late to be of any help, and in any event it does not guarantee that the industrial action is lawful.

moreover, the protection does not extend to detriment *short* of dismissal, so that an employee who is victimised by the employer (for example by being denied promotion) for taking part in lawfully organised official industrial action remains unprotected under English law.

(a) Unofficial action

An employee has no right to bring an unfair dismissal complaint where at the time of the dismissal the employee was taking part in an unofficial strike or other unofficial industrial action[60]. The only exception is where it is shown that the dismissal was for family reasons, or because the employee has taken certain specified action in relation to health and safety, has acted as an employee representative, or has made a protected disclosure under the 'whistleblowing' provisions[61]. In such cases, the dismissal will be automatically unfair; in all other cases, the reason for the dismissal is wholly irrelevant. As seen above, the removal of unfair dismissal protection from unofficial strikers was introduced in 1990 as part of a series of measures designed to discourage unofficial industrial action[62]. The effect of the provisions is that an employer may selectively dismiss the ringleaders of unofficial action without fear of having to defend an unfair dismissal complaint[63].

(b) Official action

Where the industrial action is official, the present position is that the dismissal will be automatically unfair[64] if the reason (or, if more than one, the principal reason) for the dismissal is that the employee took 'protected industrial action'[65], and one of the following three conditions is satisfied: (i) the dismissal took place within eight weeks[66] of the day on which the employee started to take protected industrial action[67]; (ii) the dismissal took place after the end of that eight week

---

60 Trade Union and Labour Relations (Consolidation) Act 1992, s 237. In determining whether action is 'unofficial', the statutory test of vicarious liability in s 20 of the 1992 Act applies (see p 818 below), save that action will not be regarded as unofficial if none of those taking part are members of a trade union: s 237(2). The meaning of 'taking part', 'strike' and 'industrial action' are considered below in respect of s 238.

61 Trade Union and Labour Relations (Consolidation) Act 1992, s 237(1A). The health and safety exception was introduced to alleviate fears that employees dismissed for refusing to work in circumstances of danger might be held to be taking part in industrial action, and therefore excluded from the protection against unfair dismissal.

62 The measures were canvassed in the Green Paper, *Unofficial Action and the Law* (Cm 821, 1989), in which it was argued that the restrictions on selective dismissal impeded the employer's ability to take effective action against unofficial strikers (para 3.3). For the other restrictions on unofficial action, see p 787.

63 Green Paper, para 3.7. Where industrial action is repudiated by the union under s 21 of the 1992 Act, it does not become unofficial for present purposes before the end of the next working day after the day on which the repudiation takes place, in effect giving those involved a day's grace to decide whether to continue with the action.

64 The usual qualifying period and age restriction for unfair dismissal claims do not apply in complaints under s 238A: s 239(1). No reinstatement or re-engagement order may be made until after the end of the industrial action: s 239(4).

65 Trade Union and Labour Relations (Consolidation) Act 1992, s 238A.

66 Eight weeks was considered by the government to be 'a period that allows reasonable time for parties to resolve their dispute and so avoid dismissals' (Minister of State, Standing Committee E, 9 March 1999, col 289).

67 Note that the eight-week period runs from the day on which the dismissed employee started to take industrial action, not the day when the industrial action began; this has important implications where employees join in the action after it has already begun.

period, but the employee had stopped taking protected industrial action before the end of that period (thus protecting the participants against victimisation by the employer after they have returned to work); or (iii) the dismissal took place after the end of the eight week period and the employee had not stopped taking part in the industrial action before the end of that period, but the employer had failed to take reasonable procedural steps to resolve the dispute. Industrial action is 'protected' for those purposes if the employee is induced to take part in the industrial action 'by an act which by virtue of section 219 is not actionable in tort'[68]; in other words, the protection for the individual participants is contingent upon the union having complied with the complex legal requirements governing the organisation of industrial action, including the balloting requirements and the restrictions on certain forms of industrial action. As seen above, the unfair dismissal protection normally lasts for only eight weeks. However, a dismissal for taking protected industrial action will still be unfair where the industrial action has lasted for more than eight weeks, if the employer has failed to take 'such procedural steps as would have been reasonable for the purposes of resolving the dispute to which the protected industrial action relates'[69]. In deciding whether the employer has taken reasonable procedural steps, the tribunal must have regard to whether the employer or the union had complied with the procedures laid down in any applicable collective agreement, and whether, after the start of the protected industrial action, either party had offered or agreed to commence or resume negotiations, had unreasonably refused to a request that conciliation services be used, or had unreasonably refused a request to use mediation services in relation to the procedures to be used to resolve the dispute[70].

Where the industrial action is official but is *not* 'protected' within the meaning of the new provisions, a tribunal will not have jurisdiction to consider an unfair dismissal complaint[71] where, at the date of dismissal[72], the employer was conducting or instituting a lock-out or the complainant was taking part in a strike or other industrial action, unless the employee shows that either:

(a) one or more relevant employees have not been dismissed; or

(b) a relevant employee has, before the expiry of the period of three months beginning with that employee's date of dismissal, been offered re-engagement and the complainant has not been offered re-engagement[73].

---

68   Trade Union and Labour Relations (Consolidation) Act 1992, s 238A(1). On a strict interpretation, this could be taken to mean that if the industrial action is not tortious, or it involves the commission of a tort which is not covered by the s 219 immunities, the unfair dismissal protection does not apply! See Ewing (1999) 28 ILJ 283, at p 292.

69   Trade Union and Labour Relations (Consolidation) Act 1992, s 238A(5).

70   Trade Union and Labour Relations (Consolidation) Act 1992, s 238A(6). In determining whether the employer has taken reasonable procedural steps, the tribunal must disregard the merits of the dispute: s 238A(7).

71   The reason for the dismissal in such a situation is usually irrelevant, although again there is an exception where the dismissal was for family reasons, or because the employee has taken certain specified action in relation to health and safety, or has acted as an employee representative: s 238(2A).

72   This is defined in s 238(5). See *Heath v J F Longman (Meat Salesmen) Ltd* [1973] ICR 407, [1973] IRLR 214, where it was taken to mean that the employee must be taking part in industrial action at the time of dismissal, and not merely on the same date. A dismissal before the industrial action has started (*Midland Plastics v Till* [1983] ICR 118, [1983] IRLR 9, EAT) or after it has ended (*Seed v Crowther (Dyers)* [1973] IRLR 199) will not fall within the section.

73   Re-engagement means taking the employee back into the same job or in a different job which would be reasonably suitable in his case: s 238(4); the definition of 'job' (Employment Rights Act 1996, s 235(1)) allows the employer a certain leeway on the precise terms on which he takes the employee back: see *Williams v National Theatre Board Ltd* [1982] ICR 715, [1982]

If the dismissals are selective, or only some of the relevant employees are selected for re-engagement, the tribunal will then have jurisdiction to consider the case in the ordinary way, which means that they must consider the reason for the dismissal[74], and, if it is a prima facie fair one, the reasonableness of the decision to sack or not to re-engage that particular employee in those circumstances (unless the reason for selection concerned union membership or activities, in which case the dismissal may be automatically unfair[75]); a selective dismissal is therefore not automatically unfair as such (unlike a dismissal for taking protected industrial action), and the employer may be able to show that it was reasonable in all the circumstances to dismiss or not to re-engage some of the strikers. If the dismissal is held to be unfair the tribunal is not entitled to take into account the mere act of participating in industrial action in deciding whether to reduce the award of compensation on the grounds of contributory fault, but the award may be reduced where there is individual blameworthy conduct by the applicant, additional to or separate from the mere act of participation in the industrial action, which contributed to the dismissal and which was sufficiently blameworthy to make it just and equitable for the tribunal to reduce the compensation (for example, if the applicant is a strike leader who has contributed to his own dismissal by his over-zealous or inflammatory actions)[76].

The interpretation of the above provisions has proved to be especially problematic, not least because a number of key phrases are not defined. There is no definition of 'lock-out' or 'other industrial action', and until 1992 there was no definition of 'strike' either. However, as part of the consolidation process, the definition of 'strike' from the strike ballot provisions was extended to the whole of the law on industrial action, so that now 'strike' is defined in this context as 'any concerted stoppage of work[77].' There are definitions of 'strike' and 'lock-out' in section 235 of the Employment Rights Act 1996, but it has previously been held that those definitions are only for the purposes of continuity of employment and so are not to be applied under section 238[78], although they may provide some guidance to the tribunal in interpreting the section. However, at the end of the day the words should be given their ordinary and natural meaning, and their interpretation remains strictly a question of fact for the tribunal. This is entirely in line with the modern anti-legalism approach and, as stated above[79], the unpredictability and inconsistency that it can produce was commented on

IRLR 377, CA. An advertising campaign offering job vacancies is unlikely to be interpreted as an offer of re-engagement to a particular employee within the meaning of the section: *Crosville (Wales) Ltd v Tracey* [1993] IRLR 60, EAT.

74 See *Baxter v Limb Group of Companies* [1994] IRLR 572, CA.

75 Note however that the dismissal of a person while taking part in industrial action is unlikely to be automatically unfair under s.152 of the 1992 Act: see p 685 above.

76 *Tracey v Crosville Wales Ltd* [1997] ICR 862, [1997] IRLR 691, HL, overruling *TNT Express (UK) Ltd v Downes* [1994] ICR 1, [1993] IRLR 432, EAT. Contributory fault in unfair dismissal complaints is considered at p 618 above.

77 Trade Union and Labour Relations (Consolidation) Act 1992, s 246.

78 *McCormick v Horsepower Ltd* [1980] ICR 278, [1980] IRLR 182, EAT (upheld on other grounds on appeal) [1981] ICR 535, [1981] IRLR 217, CA and *Rasool v Hepworth Pipe Co Ltd* [1980] ICR 494, [1980] IRLR 88, EAT in relation to 'strike'; *Express and Star Ltd v Bunday* [1988] ICR 379, [1987] IRLR 422, CA in relation to 'lock-out'.

79 At p 503.

adversely by Browne-Wilkinson P in *Naylor v Orton and Smith Ltd*[80]; however, that approach was reaffirmed by the Court of Appeal in *Express and Star Ltd v Bunday*[81] where May LJ said:

> 'What are the necessary elements of a lock-out, or for that matter of a bicycle or an elephant, is not in my opinion a question of law. Nor I think is it necessarily a question of law whether a court or tribunal was correct in thinking that the presence of a particular element or ingredient in a given state of affairs is necessary before that can be, for instance, a "lock-out". This may be a mixed question of law and fact. Alternatively it may be solely a question of fact, which it is for the expert tribunal to determine[82].'

The dangers inherent in this strongly fact-based approach are graphically illustrated by *Lewis and Britton v E Mason & Sons*[83], where the EAT upheld the finding of the employment tribunal that one person acting alone was taking part in industrial action. In that case, the employee was dismissed after refusing to drive a heavy goods vehicle with no overnight heater from South Wales to Scotland in mid-December unless he was given an extra £5 for overnight bed and breakfast accommodation. The EAT held that whether the employee was taking part in industrial action was a question of fact for the tribunal alone, and that the tribunal's finding on that point was not perverse, as it was open to the tribunal to find that one person acting alone was taking part in industrial action where that person's conduct was designed to coerce the employer to improve the terms and conditions of employment in some way. Taken to its logical conclusion, this line of reasoning would appear to mean that any employee who refused to carry out a lawful instruction of his employer in order to gain an improvement in his terms and conditions of employment could be held to be taking part in industrial action, thus enabling his employer to dismiss him without fear of having to defend an unfair dismissal complaint. The EAT's ruling sits uneasily with earlier dicta to the effect that industrial action is a collective act which involves the concerted action of more than one person[84], and it is difficult to reconcile with the wording of the section, which requires a person to be *taking part* in industrial action (implying the involvement of others), rather than merely *taking* industrial action. It is to be hoped that the adoption in 1992 of the definition of 'strike' as a 'concerted stoppage of work' makes it unlikely that the decision in *Lewis and Britton* will be followed in the future[85].

80   [1983] ICR 665, [1983] IRLR 233, EAT.
81   N 78, above.
82   At 388 and 425 respectively; this view can perhaps best be summed up by saying that the law needs a definitive interpretation of 'lock-out' like an elephant needs a bicycle. Glidewell LJ thought that 'the proper construction of a word or words in a statute is a matter of *law*' (at 390 and 427), but was in a minority on this point.
83   [1994] IRLR 4, EAT. See Dolding (1994) 23 ILJ 243.
84   See *Tramp Shipping Corpn v Greenwich Marine Inc* [1975] ICR 261 at 266, CA, per Lord Denning: '... a strike is a concerted stoppage of work by men (sic) done with a view to improving their wages or conditions, or giving vent to a grievance or making a protest about something or other, or supporting or sympathising with other workmen in such endeavour'; see also *Coates v Modern Methods and Materials Ltd* [1982] ICR 763, [1982] IRLR 318, CA, per Eveleigh LJ: '... for a person to take part in a strike he must be acting jointly or in concert with others who withdraw their labour'; cf *London Underground Ltd v RMT* [1995] IRLR 636, CA, per Millet LJ (on the strike ballot provisions): 'Industrial action is collective action. An individual does not take collective action; he takes part in it.'
85   *Lewis and Britton* was heard by the tribunal before the enactment of the 1992 Consolidation Act.

In some cases, the dominant consideration for the tribunals in determining whether the circumstances amount to a strike or other industrial action within the meaning of the Act has been the purpose for which the action in question was taken, and in particular whether it involved the application of pressure on the employer[86] . So for example, in *Rasool v Hepworth Pipe Co (No 2)*[87], the EAT held that attendance at an unauthorised union meeting during working hours did not amount to industrial action because the purpose was to discuss wages and not to apply pressure on the employer, even though the meeting did in fact result in some disruption of production. However, while it is undoubtedly true that industrial action will usually be taken for the purpose of putting pressure on the employer, there may be circumstances where action is taken for a social or political rather than an industrial motive (for example in protest at government policy), and it is highly likely that such action would in practice be held to be industrial action. Greater emphasis is therefore likely to be placed on the nature and effect of the action, rather than on the reasons for it[88].

It is clear that the technical question of whether the action is in breach of contract is not conclusive, although once again it may be taken into account as a factor. Usually a strike will involve a breach of contract, but the lack of a need to show such a breach could be important in the case of a lock-out or, more especially, in cases of 'other industrial action' – a wide phrase which has been held to cover not just actions arguably in breach (such as a go-slow, partial refusal of work or a work-to-rule), but also actions clearly *not* in themselves in breach, such as a refusal to work voluntary overtime which, if done collectively and with a coercive purpose, may constitute industrial action even though individually each employee was perfectly entitled to refuse it[89].

The right to complain of unfair dismissal is only removed from employees who were 'taking part' in a strike or other industrial action at the date of the dismissal. Here again the Court of Appeal has emphasised that the question of whether or not an individual is 'taking part' is ultimately a question of fact for the tribunal[90] , but the cases nevertheless provide some guidance as to the correct approach. In *Coates v Modern Methods and Materials Ltd*[91], the employee had stayed away from work during the strike because she was frightened of crossing a picket line. The majority of the Court of Appeal held that the test to be applied is an objective one, focusing on what the employee in fact did, and not on her motivation; as

86   Cf Stephenson LJ in *Power Packing Casemakers Ltd v Faust* [1983] ICR 292, [1983] IRLR 117, CA: 'the continued application of pressure is industrial action in the commonsense of the words.' See also *Fire Brigades Union v Knowles* [1996] IRLR 337, EAT (under s 65(2)(a); see p 718).

87   [1980] IRLR 137, EAT. The case is a good illustration of the potentially fine dividing line between union activity and industrial action. The EAT has held that the two situations are mutually exclusive: *Drew v St Edmundsbury Borough Council* [1980] ICR 513, [1980] IRLR 459.

88   Cf *Rasool v Hepworth Pipe Co (No 2)*, supra, where the EAT acknowledged that it was 'probably incorrect to attempt to interpret [industrial action] narrowly in terms of specific intention and that the nature and effect of the concerted action are probably of greater importance.'

89   *Power Packing Casemakers Ltd v Faust* [1983] ICR 292, [1983] IRLR 117, CA. The decision has been heavily criticised.

90   *Coates v Modern Methods and Materials Ltd* [1982] ICR 763, [1982] IRLR 318, CA; *Naylor v Orton and Smith Ltd* [1983] ICR 665, [1983] IRLR 233, EAT.

91   Above, n 90. See also *Bolton Roadways Ltd v Edwards* [1987] IRLR 392, EAT; *Manifold Industries Ltd v Sims* [1991] ICR 504, [1991] IRLR 242, EAT.

Stephenson LJ put it: '. . . participation in a strike must be judged by what the employee does and not by what he thinks or why he does it[92].'

It follows that employees who are absent from work due to sickness or on holiday leave during the industrial action may still be held to be taking part in it, particularly if they associate themselves with the strike (for example by attending at the picket line)[93]. However, it seems that clear evidence of participation will be required before an employee who is off sick when the action begins will be found to be participating in it[94]. Just as the employee's subjective motivation is irrelevant, so also is subjective knowledge on the part of the employer, so that an employer's reasonable but mistaken belief that the employee is taking part in the industrial action will not be sufficient if the employee's actions and omissions do not justify the conclusion that he was in fact taking part in that action[95]. A threat to take industrial action does not of itself amount to taking part in industrial action within the meaning of the Act[96], but where an employee has stated his intention of joining in existing industrial action, he may be held to be taking part in that action before the time when he is contractually due to work in fact arrives[97]. In *Lewis and Britton v E Mason & Sons*[98], an employee was dismissed for refusing to drive a heavy goods vehicle which did not have an overnight heater unless he was given an allowance to cover the cost of overnight accommodation. On learning of the dismissal, one of his colleagues threatened the employer that there would be a strike the following day unless the dismissed employee was reinstated. The EAT controversially held that it was open to the tribunal to find that by making a definite threat not to come to work the following day, at a time when further negotiation could not have been expected to take place and where the work for the following day had been allocated by the employer, the employees were taking part in industrial action[99].

As seen above, where the industrial action is official but not 'protected' under the new provisions, the tribunal will have jurisdiction to determine the fairness of a dismissal where the employer has discriminated between 'relevant employees'

92 Kerr LJ expressed a similar view.
93 *Bolton Roadways Ltd v Edwards* [1987] IRLR 392, EAT, per Scott J. In *Hindle Gears Ltd v McGinty* [1985] ICR 111, [1984] IRLR 477, the EAT overturned as perverse the tribunal's decision that a sick employee who spent time talking to pickets while handing in his medical certificate was participating in the industrial action.
94 *Rogers v Chloride Systems Ltd* [1992] ICR 198, EAT.
95 *Bolton Roadways Ltd v Edwards*, supra; In *McKenzie v Crosville Motor Services Ltd* [1990] ICR 172, [1989] IRLR 516, the EAT held that the reasonable belief of the employer that the employee was participating would be sufficient, but this was rejected in favour of the approach in *Bolton* by the EAT in *Manifold Industries Ltd v Sims*, n 91 above (followed in *Jenkins v P&O European Ferries (Dover) Ltd* [1991] ICR 652).
96 *Midland Plastics v Till* [1983] ICR 118, [1983] IRLR 9, EAT.
97 See *Winnett v Seamarks Bros Ltd* [1978] ICR 1240, [1978] IRLR 387, EAT, where an employee who had made clear his intention to join a strike when his next shift began was held to be taking part in industrial action from the time when he made that intention clear.
98 [1994] IRLR 4, EAT. See Dolding (1994) 23 ILJ 243.
99 The decision goes considerably further than *Winnett v Seamarks Bros Ltd* [1978] ICR 1240, [1978] IRLR 387, because that case involved a threat to join an existing strike, rather than a threat to commence strike action. Cf Browne-Wilkinson J in *Midland Plastics v Till* [1983] ICR 118, [1983] IRLR 9 : 'The actual taking of industrial action is . . . quite distinct from the stage at which the threat of it is being used as a negotiating weapon.'

by selectively dismissing[100] or selectively re-engaging them. As defined in section 238(3), 'relevant employees' means:

(a) in relation to a lock-out, employees who were directly interested in the dispute in contemplation or furtherance of which the lock-out occurred; and

(b) in relation to a strike or other industrial action, those employees at the establishment of the employer at or from which the complainant works who at the date of his dismissal were taking part in the action.

In the case of strikes and other industrial action, the definition of 'relevant employees' is restricted to those taking part in the action at the date of the complainant's dismissal. Before 1982, the definition of relevant employees included all those who had taken part *at any stage* in the industrial action, so that an employee who had been on strike but had returned to work before the dismissal occurred was still a relevant employee. Accordingly, in *Stock v Frank Jones (Tipton) Ltd* [101], the House of Lords held that there had been selectivity where the employer had not sacked two employees who had returned to work before the date of the dismissals, so that the applicant could bring her case. The Employment Act 1982 reversed the decision in that case, thus enabling an employer to issue an ultimatum to those taking industrial action to return to work or face dismissal and then to dismiss all those who fail to comply, while still retaining the protection of the section against unfair dismissal proceedings brought by the dismissed employees[102].

A second significant amendment made by the 1982 Act was to introduce a time limit on the re-engagement of relevant employees, so that the anti-discrimination provisions only apply where a relevant employee is offered re-engagement within three months of his dismissal; thereafter the employer is free to re-engage strikers selectively without conferring jurisdiction on the tribunal[103] . Before 1982, any such re-engagement would lay the employer open to an unfair dismissal complaint, even if the taking on was at some time in the future[104] . The time limit also enables the employer to make an initial limited offer of re-engagement – in effect sanctioning a 'cooling-off' period and a phased return to work – provided that all those dismissed have been offered re-engagement within three months

---

100 The question of whether the dismissals are selective will be determined at the conclusion of the proceedings in which the tribunal determines whether or not it has jurisdiction: *P&O European Ferries (Dover) Ltd v Byrne* [1989] ICR 779, [1989] IRLR 254, CA; in that case the complainant was ordered to disclose the identity of an alleged relevant employee who had not been dismissed, thus enabling the employer to dismiss that employee before the conclusion of the hearing and so prevent the tribunal from acquiring jurisdiction to hear the complainant's case.

101 [1978] ICR 347, [1978] IRLR 87, HL.

102 The restrictions in the 1982 Act only applied to strikes etc., not to lock-outs, so that in the case of the latter the definition of relevant employees remains considerably wider, and an employee who was locked-out but has returned to work by the time of the dismissal will still be a relevant employee: *Fisher v York Trailer Co Ltd* [1979] ICR 834, [1979] IRLR 385, EAT; *H Campey & Sons Ltd v Bellwood* [1987] ICR 311, EAT.

103 This could cause limitation problems where the complainant and the relevant employee's dismissals took place at the same time, for the normal limitation period for the claimant to bring his action is also three months. Because of this, the limitation period is extended to six months in a case where the complainant is relying on the re-engagement of a relevant employee as a ground for arguing that the s 238 exclusion should not apply: Trade Union and Labour Relations (Consolidation) Act 1992, s 239(2). The six-month limit also applies to complaints under s 238A (protected industrial action).

104 See, eg, *Sealey v Avon Aluminium Co Ltd* [1978] IRLR 285, IT, where the taking back of a dismissed striker five months later was held to remove the exclusion.

of their dismissal[105] . The third amendment introduced by the 1982 Act dealt with the situation where there is industrial action at some or all of the plants of a multi-plant employer. Up to that time, if the industrial action all formed part of one dispute, the non-selectivity rule had to apply to all plants, so that an employer could not adopt a different response to the industrial action in different plants, for example by dismissing the workforce at one plant but not another. However, the 1982 Act restricted the definition of 'relevant employees' to those employed 'at the establishment of the employer at or from which the complainant works'[106] , so that any application of the selectivity principle has to be done on an establishment-by-establishment basis. One further potential difficulty for a large employer operating from several sites is that an employee dismissed for taking part in industrial action might be mistakenly re-engaged at another site within the three-month period, so opening up the employer to unfair dismissal complaints by those not re-engaged. However, the EAT has held that for there to be an effective offer of re-engagement, the employer must have actual or constructive knowledge (in the sense that he has the means of finding out) of the job from which the employee was dismissed and the reason why he was dismissed[107] .

The principle of non-selectivity was clearly weakened by the Employment Acts of 1982 and 1990, and further marginalised by the Employment Relations Act 1999, but where it still applies the basic concept remains that the employer must dismiss all or none if he is to rely on the exclusion. In most cases this narrows the scope of the exclusion in the employee's favour, but it has been argued that the whole concept of the exclusion is potentially too wide in a case where the employer is in fact willing to dispense with one whole group of employees, who may be deprived of their unfair dismissal rights in two ways – first, by the employer instituting a lock-out affecting them all, which is now treated in the same way as a strike[108] ; and secondly, because the employer might try to goad the employees in question into taking industrial action and then dismiss them all. In *Thompson v Eaton Ltd*[109], Phillips J suggested that this second possibility might be countered by the concept of an 'engineered' strike (ie one produced by 'gross provocation' by the employer) which would not fall within the exclusion. However, in *Marsden v Fairey Stainless Ltd*[110], the EAT disapproved of the idea of an engineered strike, pointing out that the wording of the section simply requires the employee to have

105 *Highland Fabricators Ltd v McLaughlin* [1985] ICR 183, [1984] IRLR 482, EAT.
106 There is no definition here of 'establishment'; it is used elsewhere (again without definition) in the context of redundancy consultation; for the case law there, which could by analogy apply here, see p 87 above; see also the Equal Pay Act 1970, s 1(6), and the Sex Discrimination Act 1975, s 6.
107 *Bigham and Keogh v GKN Kwikform* [1992] ICR 113, [1992] IRLR 4, EAT; the EAT also confirmed that a re-engagement resulting from fraud on the part of the employee will not deprive the employer of the protection of the section.
108 Compare the original drafting in the Trade Union and Labour Relations Act 1974, Sch 1, para 7. At the time of writing, the government was considering exempting lock-out days from the 8-week protected period, to prevent employers from sitting-out the protected period by preventing the strikers from returning to work during that period: *Review of the Employment Relations Act 1999*, para 3.39.
109 [1976] ICR 336 at 342, [1976] IRLR 308 at 311, EAT.
110 [1979] IRLR 103, EAT. See also *Wilkins v Cantrell and Cochrane (GB) Ltd* [1978] IRLR 483, EAT.

been dismissed *while* on strike[111] , so that the exclusion will apply even if the industrial action was provoked by the employer[112] .

3 LIABILITY IN TORT AND THE STATUTORY IMMUNITIES[113]

(i) Conspiracy

(a) *The cause of action*

That conspiracy is a head of civil, as well as criminal, liability was clearly established by the House of Lords at the end of the nineteenth century in the famous 'trilogy' of conspiracy cases[114] . The tort of conspiracy may take either of two forms. The first, 'conspiracy by lawful means'[115] , is committed where two or more persons combine together with intent to injure the claimant by the employment of means which are *lawful* in themselves, but with a predominant purpose to harm the claimant rather than to advance the legitimate interests of the combiners. The second, 'conspiracy to use unlawful means', is committed where two or more persons combine together with intent to injure the claimant by the employment of means which are *unlawful* in themselves. In the case of the latter, its scope is as wide as the scope of unlawful means, and so a conspiracy to injure by means that are criminal[116] or tortious[117] is actionable. Thus, the respondents in *Rookes v Barnard*[118] were liable on the basis of a conspiracy to intimidate, since intimidation was not at the time covered by a statutory immunity. Until recently it was thought[119]

---

111 Phillips J had been able to argue for the concept of an engineered strike because, as originally drafted, the section provided that the real reason for dismissal must be that the employee was on strike; however, the requirement of such a causal link was removed by the Employment Protection Act 1975, Sch 16, Part III, para 13.

112 A particularly controversial application of the exclusion was in the dispute between the printing unions and News International; see Ewing and Napier 'The Wapping dispute and labour law' (1986) 45 CLJ 285, at p 291. For an ingenious attempt to devise an argument avoiding this unfortunate state of affairs, see Elias 'The Strike and Breach of Contract: A Reassessment' in Ewing, Gearty and Hepple (eds.) *Human Rights and Labour Law: Essays for Paul O'Higgins* (1994).

113 See generally *Harvey*, N, para 2101 et seq; *Winfield and Jolowicz on Tort* (15th edn, 1998); *Clerk and Lindsell on Torts* (17th edn. 1995) ch 15; Elias and Ewing 'Economic torts and labour law: old principles and new liabilities' (1982) 41 CLJ 321; Carty 'Intentional Violation of Economic Interests: The Limits of Common Law Liability' (1988) 104 LQR 250.

114 *Mogul Steamship Co v McGregor, Gow & Co* [1892] AC 25, HL; *Allen v Flood* [1898] AC 1, HL: *Quinn v Leathem* [1901] AC 495, HL.

115 This version of the tort, sometimes referred to as 'conspiracy to injure' or 'simple' conspiracy or 'conspiracy to effect an unlawful purpose', was described as an 'anomalous tort' in *Lonrho Ltd v Shell Petroleum Co Ltd (No 2)* [1982] AC 173, [1981] 2 All ER 456, HL.

116 It has however been held in another context that a crime which is not also an actionable wrong at the suit of the claimant does not constitute unlawful means for the purposes of the tort of conspiracy: see *Crédit Lyonnais Bank Nederland NV (formerly known as Generale Bank Nederland NV) v Export Credits Guarantee Department* [1998] 1 Lloyds Rep 19, CA (affd on other grounds, [1999] 1 All ER 929, HL); *Yukong Lines Ltd of Korea v Rendsburg Investments Corpn of Liberia (No 2)* [1998] 4 All ER 82.

117 In *Rookes v Barnard*, Lord Devlin said that although a breach of contract was unlawful means for the purposes of intimidation, this did not necessarily mean that it was so for the purposes of conspiracy: [1964] AC at 1210, [1964] 1 All ER at 400. In *Barretts & Baird (Wholesale) Ltd v IPCS* [1987] IRLR 3, Henry J thought there was an arguable case that breach of contract was unlawful means for the purposes of conspiracy.

118 [1964] AC 1129, [1964] 1 All ER 367, HL.

119 Based on a dictum of Lord Diplock in *Lonrho Ltd v Shell Petroleum Co Ltd (No 2)* [1982] AC 173, [1981] 2 All ER 456, HL.

that for both forms of the tort it was necessary to show that the predominant purpose of the combiners must be to injure the claimant. However, the House of Lords in *Lonrho plc v Fayed* [120] has made it clear that under the second form there is no such requirement, and that it is sufficient to show that the defendants acted with intent to injure the claimant.

The emergence of the first form, that of conspiracy by lawful means, could have constituted a serious impediment to the lawfulness of industrial action, particularly after *Quinn v Leathem*, for almost any strike will require concerted action and will lead to loss to the employer. This consideration led to the immunity which was first granted in the Trade Disputes Act 1906 (see below), but in fact, as the tort was developed in subsequent cases (in particular by the House of Lords in *Sorrell v Smith*[121] and *Crofter Hand Woven Harris Tweed Co Ltd v Veitch*[122]), it is arguable that the immunity is in fact unnecessary, for the courts have taken a liberal approach to what constitutes the legitimate interests of organised labour. If the union can show a genuine trade union reason for the industrial action[123], then the conspiracy will not be actionable, in spite of the loss caused to the employer, because the employer will be unable to show that the union's predominant purpose was to harm him[124]; it is this element of the tort of conspiracy by lawful means which has become dominant, whether it be called lack of an improper purpose or, more commonly, a defence of 'justification'. In the light of this, this particular head of liability has played little part in the modern cases.

(b) The immunity

Section 219(2) of the Trade Union and Labour Relations (Consolidation) Act 1992 provides that an agreement or combination to do any act in contemplation or furtherance of a trade dispute is not actionable in tort if the act is one which, if done by one person alone, would not be actionable. This therefore gives protection from liability for conspiracy by lawful means (ie means which would not be actionable if done by only one person), but does *not* give immunity from suit for conspiracy by unlawful means (ie means which *would* be actionable if done by only one person), although in the latter case there may be an indirect immunity if the means are covered by one of the other immunities and are not therefore 'unlawful'. Thus, in most cases conspiracy will be a dead letter, but on the other hand it is not abolished, only held in abeyance while within the golden formula; if the act complained of is outside that formula, for example a personal vendetta

120 [1992] 1 AC 448, [1991] 3 All ER 303, HL, overruling *Metall und Rohstoff AG v Donaldson Lufkin & Jenrette Inc* [1990] 1 QB 391, [1989] 3 All ER 14, CA. cf also *Lonrho plc v Fayed (No 5)* [1994] 1 All ER 188, CA (the claimant must prove actual pecuniary or financial loss for both forms of the tort, as opposed eg to loss of reputation).
121 [1925] AC 700, HL.
122 [1942] AC 435, [1942] 1 All ER 142, HL.
123 See eg *Reynolds v Shipping Federation* [1924] 1 Ch 28 (action to enforce a closed shop); the *Crofters'* case [1942] AC 435, [1942] 1 All ER 142, HL (action to force up wages); *Scala Ballroom (Wolverhampton) Ltd v Ratcliffe* [1958] 3 All ER 220, [1958] 1 WLR 1057, CA (action to stamp out a colour bar operated by the employer).
124 *Quinn v Leathem* [1901] AC 495, above, is perhaps best explained as a rare case where the jury decided that the defendants' predominant purpose was vindictive; see also *Huntley v Thornton* [1957] 1 All ER 234, [1957] 1 WLR 321.

or clear misuse of union power for improper purpose, conspiracy could still be used as a cause of action[125].

(ii) Inducement of breach of contract

(a) The cause of action

In the light of the relatively innocuous nature of conspiracy, reliance in modern industrial tort cases has been placed principally upon inducement of breach of contract, a cause of action established in *Lumley v Gye*[126] where a theatre owner induced an opera singer to break her existing contract so that she could sing for him instead. There are two forms of inducement – direct and indirect. Direct inducement is where the defendant induces X, a third party, to break an existing contract which X has with the claimant, who thereby suffers loss. The necessary elements are that (i) the conduct must be intentional (ii) there must be clear evidence of actual inducement, in the sense of 'pressure, persuasion or procuration' directed at one of the parties to the contract[127] , and (iii) there must be actual knowledge on the part of the defendant of the contract which would be broken[128] or, according to later cases[129] , the means of having that knowledge (for example through the possibility of disclosure at an interim stage). This form of inducement may arise where a defendant union leader calls upon union members to strike in breach of their contracts of employment, or directly puts pressure on one of the employer's suppliers to cease deliveries of vital supplies in breach of their commercial supply contract with the claimant. However, in the latter scenario (an example of 'secondary action' or 'blacking'), the tort more likely to be committed is *indirect* inducement. This arises where the defendant induces X (typically a union member) to do an unlawful act to Y (typically X's employer), thereby making Y break a commercial supply contract with the claimant who thereby suffers loss. The requirements of intention, inducement and knowledge are the same as for direct inducement, but the crucial difference between the two forms of the tort is that while direct inducement is wrongful in itself, indirect

---

125 As in *Huntley v Thornton* [1957] 1 All ER 234, [1957] 1 WLR 321.

126 (1853) 2 E & B 216.

127 Lack of such evidence led to failure of the actions in *D C Thomson & Co Ltd v Deakin* [1952] Ch 646, [1952] 2 All ER 361, CA and *Camellia Tanker Ltd v ITWF* [1976] ICR 274, [1976] IRLR 190, CA. Pressure directed at *customers* of one of the parties will not suffice, although it may be actionable as an *indirect* inducement if unlawful means are used: *Middlebrook Mushrooms Ltd v TGWU* [1993] ICR 612, [1993] IRLR 232, CA (where the action failed as no unlawful means had been used).

128 *D C Thomson & Co Ltd v Deakin* [1952] Ch 646, [1952] 2 All ER 361, CA. See also *TimePlan Education Group Ltd v National Union of Teachers* [1997] IRLR 457, CA (union could not be held to have intended to interfere with a contract of which it was unaware). There is no need for knowledge that the conduct induced will in fact lead to a breach of contract; thus the tort is committed even where the defendant believes that there will be no breach: *Solihull Metropolitan Borough v NUT* [1985] IRLR 211 (teachers' union withdrawing functions such as lunchtime supervision which they considered voluntary).

129 *J T Stratford & Son Ltd v Lindley* [1965] AC 269, [1964] 3 All ER 102, HL, at 332 and 112 respectively, per Lord Pearce; *Emerald Construction Co v Lowthian* [1966] 1 All ER 1013, [1966] 1 WLR 691, CA. Where action is threatened against the claimant, his solicitors could ensure the necessary knowledge by formally serving notice of the relevant contracts on the defendants.

inducement must be by unlawful means (in order to keep it within any reasonable bounds) if it is to be actionable[130].

Questions of immunity aside, the tort of indirect inducement could arise where the union officials induce Y's employees to strike, or refuse to make deliveries to the claimant's factory, in breach of their contracts of employment, the inducement of the breach of those employment contracts prima facie being the unlawful means. In *J T Stratford & Son Ltd v Lindley*[131] the defendant union officials induced some of their members to break their contracts of employment, thus causing their employers (Y) to break their commercial hiring contracts with the claimant company (which was associated with another company that was the real target of the defendants' actions). The House of Lords held that the claimant was entitled to an injunction to restrain this indirect inducement of breach of the commercial contracts, the essential unlawful means being found in the direct inducement of breaches of the employment contracts. The facts (but not the decision) were similar in *Thomson & Co Ltd v Deakin*[132], where the defendant union officials were in dispute with the claimant company over union recognition. The claimant company, printers, were supplied with paper by Bowaters Ltd (Y) and the defendants sought help with unions who dealt with that firm. When Bowaters discovered that some of their employees objected to loading and delivering supplies to the claimant company, they decided not to ask their employees to effect such loading and delivering, and ceased to supply, thus being in breach of their commercial contract. The claimant company sought an injunction against the defendants, restraining them from procuring breaches of contract between the claimant and Bowaters. The union officials replied (a) that in approaching other unions they had only asked for help and (b) that Bowaters' employees had not been instructed by them not to load or deliver paper. The Court of Appeal found for the defendant union officials for, although it was clear that an action would have lain had the defendants, with the relevant knowledge of the commercial contract, contrived by wrongful acts a situation in which it was impossible for Bowaters to perform the contract, on the actual facts of the case the claimant had failed to show either sufficient 'inducement' or that the defendants had caused Bowaters' employees actually to break their contracts (the necessary element of unlawful means therefore being missing).

Two further points should be noted in relation to inducement. The first is that there is still uncertainty as to the 'intention to injure' requirement. The orthodox view[133] is that such a requirement is an essential ingredient of the tort.

---

130 *D C Thomson & Co Ltd v Deakin* [1952] Ch 646, [1952] 2 All ER 361, CA; *Torquay Hotel Co Ltd v Cousins* [1969] 2 Ch 106, [1969] 1 All ER 522, CA, per Lord Denning MR at 138 and 530 respectively, retracting his statement in *Daily Mirror Newspapers Ltd v Gardner* [1968] 2 QB 762, [1968] 2 All ER 163, CA that there was no difference between direct and indirect inducement.

131 [1965] AC 269, [1964] 3 All ER 102, HL. For other examples of indirect inducement, see the facts of *Associated Newspapers Group Ltd v Wade* [1979] ICR 664, [1979] IRLR 201, CA, or *Merkur Island Shipping Corpn v Laughton* [1983] ICR 490, [1983] IRLR 218, HL. *Dimbleby & Sons Ltd v NUJ* [1984] ICR 386, [1984] IRLR 161, HL is unusual in that the claimant was in fact in the position of Y, not in the usual position of the claimant as the one at the end of the line with whom the union is really in dispute.

132 [1952] Ch 646, [1952] 2 All ER 361, CA.

133 As expressed by Jenkins LJ in *Thomson & Co Ltd v Deakin* [1952] Ch 646, [1952] 2 All ER 361, CA.

However, in *Falconer v ASLEF and NUR*[134] inducement was found where the unions had taken action against British Rail in the course of an industrial dispute, thereby injuring the claimant who was unable to travel by train on the ticket that he had already bought; the union's argument that their intent was to harm British Rail, not the claimant, was rejected as 'naïve and divorced from reality'. This case therefore suggests that 'intent' is shown where the claimant (either individually or, as in this case, as one of a definable class) will foreseeably be injured even though the action is not actually aimed at him. This may be in line with concepts of intention elsewhere in the law[135], but it is inconsistent with other authority and is capable of extending liability very widely[136]. At the other extreme, Henry J in *Barretts & Baird (Wholesale) Ltd v IPCS*[137] stated that, to establish the tort of interference with business (below), it must be shown that intent to injure the claimant was the 'predominant purpose' of the action. This vital point awaits authoritative determination. The second point is that there is a defence of justification available, but its scope is uncertain, and it is not as wide as that for conspiracy by lawful means. Thus, in *South Wales Miners' Federation v Glamorgan Coal Co Ltd*[138] it was held that there was no defence of justification available on the facts, in spite of the fact that the workers involved were merely acting in genuine furtherance of their own interests and bore no ill will towards the employers. It appears that exercise of a 'duty' may amount to justification, but mere self-interest cannot[139]; in *Brimelow v Casson*[140] the justification defence succeeded in highly unusual circumstances, the defence in that case being that the union had a duty, as a representative association, to secure the payment of reasonable wages by a theatrical manager in order that chorus girls in his employ could live without having to resort to immoral earnings. The idea of a 'duty' to act as providing justification for the tort of inducement is a nebulous one; it is theoretically capable

---

134 [1986] IRLR 331, Co Ct; the case was not appealed by the union, in spite of (or because of?) the widespread publicity that it attracted. The question of intent to injure was vital because there had been no strike ballot, and as the immunities are withdrawn in toto in such a situation the union can only escape liability if it can show that no tort was committed in the first place.

135 Particularly in criminal law, where either 'wilful blindness' or the realisation that the consequence in question is almost certain to result from your action (*R v Hancock* [1986] AC 455, [1986] 1 All ER 641, CA) may justify an inference that you intended that consequence.

136 In some respects the argument in *Falconer* has been overtaken by events, in that the claimant in that case would now be able to apply for an injunction to restrain the unlawful industrial action under s 235A of the Trade Union and Labour Relations (Consolidation) Act 1992 (the 'Citizen's Right'), whether or not he could himself sue in tort; see p 826 below.

137 [1987] IRLR 3; note, however, that in *Lonrho plc v Fayed* [1990] 2 QB 479, [1989] 2 All ER 65, the Court of Appeal doubted whether for the tort of interference with business it is necessary to show that injury to the claimant was the predominant purpose; one explanation might simply be that the intent requirements for the two torts are different.

138 [1905] AC 239, HL; and see *British Motor Trade Association v Salvadori* [1949] Ch 556, [1949] 1 All ER 208.

139 See the *South Wales Miners'* case, in the Court of Appeal [1903] 2 KB 545, at 573 per Romer LJ and in the House of Lords [1905] AC 239 at 249 per Lord James; *Greig v Insole* [1978] 3 All ER 449, [1978] 1 WLR 302 at 491 and 340, respectively, per Slade J. See also *TimePlan Education Group Ltd v National Union of Teachers* [1997] IRLR 457, CA, per Peter Gibson LJ.

140 [1924] 1 Ch 302; *Camden Nominees Ltd v Forcey* [1940] Ch 352, [1940] 2 All ER 1. The suggestion in *British Industrial Plastics Ltd v Fergusson* [1938] 4 All ER 504, CA at 510 per Slesser LJ that a desire not to break the law might amount to justification must be doubtful.

of being extended to cover many union activities on the basis that a union officer may have certain legal and moral 'duties' towards the membership, but in practice the defence rarely succeeds[141].

(b) The immunity

Section 219(1)(a) of the Trade Union and Labour Relations (Consolidation) Act 1992 provides that an act done in contemplation or furtherance of a trade dispute is not actionable in tort on the ground only that it induces another person to break a contract. The immunity covers both direct and indirect inducement, and was significantly widened by the Trade Union and Labour Relations (Amendment) Act 1976, which extended the immunity to breach of *any* contract, not just a contract of employment, as had previously been the case; the effect of this was to extend the immunity to cover secondary boycotts and blackings aimed at breaking vital commercial contracts of the employer with whom the union is in dispute. Following this change in 1976 (and the inclusion within the immunity of the tort of interference, discussed below), it appeared that the immunity itself was almost watertight, *provided* that the acts in question remained within the golden formula. It should be stressed that in spite of the legislative changes since 1980, the actual immunity in section 219(1) has remained unchanged. The rules on secondary action, strike ballots, etc., operate not by altering the basic immunity, but instead by suspending its operation in certain defined circumstances.

(iii) Intimidation

(a) The cause of action

The tort of intimidation is committed when the claimant suffers damage as a result of an unlawful threat made by the defendant with the intention of causing harm to the claimant. Typically, intimidation arises where the claimant is harmed by action taken by a third party, X, in response to an unlawful[142] threat by the defendant which is directed at X[143], but which is in reality intended to harm the claimant[144]. The case of *Rookes v Barnard*[145] resurrected this old action and established that it embraced not only threats of criminal or tortious conduct, but also threats to break contracts. The appellant was lawfully[146] dismissed by his employer as a result of an ultimatum from the respondent union officers threatening industrial action which would have involved breaches of their

---

141 *Posluns v Toronto Stock Exchange* (1964) 46 DLR (2d) 210 at 270, per Gale J. cf *Pete's Towing Services Ltd v NIUW* [1970] NZLR 32 at 51 per Speight J.

142 Threats to take lawful action are not tortious: *Allen v Flood* [1898] AC 1, HL; *Hardie and Lane Ltd v Chilton* [1928] 2 KB 306, CA; *Thorne v Motor Trade Association* [1937] AC 797, HL.

143 Ie indirect intimidation. There may also be liability for direct (or 'two-party') intimidation, ie where D makes an unlawful threat to the claimant in order to make him act to his own detriment; in most instances, however, intimidation is unnecessary here as the claimant could sue upon the threatened unlawful act itself.

144 To succeed, the claimant must show that the threats, although directed at the third party, were in fact intended to harm him: *News Group Newspapers Ltd v SOGAT '82 (No 2)* [1987] ICR 181, [1986] IRLR 337.

145 [1964] AC 1129, [1964] 1 All ER 367, HL.

146 Hence no action on the facts for for inducing breach of contract.

employment contracts by the participants (primarily because those contracts contained a 'no-strike' clause). It was held by the House of Lords that the respondents had committed the tort of intimidation in that the appellant had suffered damage (loss of employment) as a result of action taken by his employer (lawful dismissal) in response to an unlawful threat (threat to break their employment contracts) directed against the employer by the respondents. This decision opened up a potentially large area of liability in respect of industrial action which was not covered by the statutory immunities then contained in the Trade Disputes Act 1906; this was hardly surprising, since the tort had seen no development since 1793, when it appeared to be confined to threats of physical violence[147].

(b) The immunity

In response to the threat posed by *Rookes v Barnard*, the Trade Disputes Act 1965 was passed creating a new immunity covering intimidation. This is now contained in section 219(1)(b) of the Trade Union and Labour Relations (Consolidation) Act 1992, which provides that an act done in contemplation or furtherance of a trade dispute is not actionable in tort on the ground only that it consists in his threatening that a contract (whether one to which he is a party or not) will be broken or its performance interfered with, or that he will induce another person to break a contract or to interfere with its performance. As with section 219(1)(a), this provision was widened in 1976 to cover *any* contract, not just a contract of employment. On the particular facts of *Rookes v Barnard*, further protection would today be given by section 180, for this provides that no-strike clauses in collective bargains are not to be incorporated into individual contracts of employment unless the collective bargain (which must be readily accessible to the individual worker and must have been negotiated by an independent trade union) expressly states that the clause shall or may be incorporated, and the individual contract does incorporate it expressly or impliedly[148]. Once again, however, the whole scheme of the immunities is dependent upon the act in question being within the golden formula.

(iv) Interference with contract, or with trade or business generally

(a) The cause of action

The tort of inducing a breach of contract has long been established, but more recent authority has held that there is a further head of liability, namely *interfering* with the performance of a contract (short of causing an actual breach). This was put forward in *Torquay Hotel Co Ltd v Cousins*[149] where a problem arose because the oil supply contract which was the target of the union's activities in fact contained a *force majeure* clause excepting liability for labour disputes, thus giving rise to the argument that by stopping supplies the union had not actually caused a breach of the contract. Whereas Russell and Winn LJJ held that there was still a breach in spite of the clause and so the defendants could be liable for ordinary inducement,

---

147 *Tarleton v M'Gawley* (1793) Peake 270.
148 On no-strike clauses generally, see Lewis 'Strike-free deals and pendulum arbitration' (1990) 28 BJIR 32.
149 [1969] 2 Ch 106, [1969] 1 All ER 522, CA.

Lord Denning MR stated that there could be liability even if there was no breach – 'interference' (in the sense of conduct which prevents or hinders one party from performing his contract) is enough, even though it does not actually procure a breach, provided that it is deliberate and done with knowledge of the contract (or, at any rate, turning a blind eye to it). His Lordship then went on to divide interference into direct and indirect interference (by analogy with inducement), saying that direct interference is unlawful in itself, but indirect interference requires unlawful means. This, however, was doubtful, for any liability for simple interference which could be committed by lawful means (even if direct) would arguably have outflanked the central principle established in *Allen v Flood*[150] that the intentional infliction of harm without justification is not in itself tortious. However, in the subsequent case of *Acrow (Automatic) Ltd v Rex Chainbelt Inc*[151], Lord Denning restated the law in a different way, which requires both direct and indirect interference to be by unlawful means:

> '... if one person, without just cause or excuse, deliberately interferes with the trade or business of another, and does so by unlawful means, that is, by an act which he is not at liberty to commit, then he is acting unlawfully. He is liable in damages and, in a proper case, an injunction can be granted against him[152].'

This extension of the tort to interference with contract was finally sanctioned by the House of Lords in *Merkur Island Shipping Corpn v Laughton*[153], where Lord Diplock drew a clear parallel with inducement of *breach* of contract and stated that when Jenkins LJ referred to breach of contract in his authoritative judgment in *D C Thomson & Co Ltd v Deakin*[154] that was only because the facts of the case disclosed a clear breach; according to Lord Diplock, the judgment in its true intent applies to any *interference* with contract (of which actual breach is but one form), and this is then made certain by his Lordship's approval of Lord Denning's judgment in *Torquay Hotel Co Ltd v Cousins*[155] and by his reference to Parliament's extension in 1976 of the relevant immunity to cover interference as well as breach.

However, the law has moved on yet further in this volatile area, for it now appears (as envisaged in the above dictum by Lord Denning) that there has evolved (almost *sub silentio*) a wider, more generalised, head of civil liability in the form of a tort of interference with the claimant's *trade or business*[156], the theory being that inducement of breach of contract, interference with contract and indeed intimidation are themselves, in turn, simply manifestations of this 'supertort'. So

150 [1898] AC 1, HL.
151 [1971] 3 All ER 1175, [1971] 1 WLR 1676, CA; *Esso Petroleum Ltd v Kingswood Motors (Addlestone) Ltd* [1974] QB 142, [1973] 3 All ER 1057; cf *Brekkes Ltd v Cattel* [1972] Ch 105, [1971] 1 All ER 1031.
152 [1971] 3 All ER 1175 at 1181, [1971] 1 WLR 1676 at 1682; the reference to 'unlawful means' meaning simply 'an act which he is not at liberty to commit' is probably too wide; the better view is that the unlawful means must themselves constitute an actionable wrong against the third party in question: *Lonrho Ltd v Shell Petroleum Co Ltd (No 2)* [1982] AC 173, [1981] 2 All ER 456, HL (a conspiracy case); see *Harvey* N 14 H (2).
153 [1983] ICR 490, [1983] IRLR 218, HL. The decision in the case is strongly criticised by Wedderburn (1983) 46 MLR 632.
154 [1952] Ch 646, [1952] 2 All ER 361, CA.
155 [1969] 2 Ch 106, [1969] 1 All ER 522, CA.
156 See, especially, Carty, 'Unlawful interference with trade' (1983) 3 LS 193.

far, it has not been a necessary part of the ratio of any of the cases to pronounce on the existence and extent of such a tort[157] , but in *Merkur Island Shipping Corpn v Laughton* Lord Diplock argued (from effect to cause) that its existence could be divined from the existence in the Trade Union and Labour Relations Act 1974, s 13(2), (3) of immunities apparently covering it[158]:

'. . . [T]he evidence also establishes a *prima facie* case of the common law tort, referred to in s 13(2) and (3) of the 1974 Act, of interfering with the trade or business of another person by doing unlawful acts. To fall within the genus of torts the unlawful act need not involve procuring another person to break a subsisting contract or to interfere with the performance of a subsisting contract. The immunity granted by s 13(2) and (3) I will call the "genus immunity". Where, however the procuring of another person to break a subsisting contract is the unlawful act involved, as it is in s 13(1), this is but one species of the wider genus of tort[159].'

The problems here are (a) that it is arguable that when Parliament originally enacted what became the section 13(2) immunity (in the Trade Disputes Act 1906) it only did so ex abundante cautela *in case* such a tort was ever propounded[160] , and (b) that in any event section 13(2) and (3) were repealed by the Employment Acts 1980 and 1982. Given, however, that the wider 'genus' tort does exist the most important points to notice about it are (i) that there is the essential element that the interference with trade or business must be by 'unlawful means' (were it otherwise, it would clearly be inconsistent with the fundamental rule in *Allen v Flood* [161]), and (ii) there appears to be a requirement of intent to injure the particular claimant in question[162].

---

157 It was pleaded as one of several causes of action in *Hadmor Productions Ltd v Hamilton* [1982] ICR 114, [1982] IRLR 102, HL, and likewise in *Shipping Co Uniform Inc v ITWF* [1985] ICR 245, [1985] IRLR 71, but in each case the eventual decision was largely on other grounds.

158 S 13(2) stated 'For the avoidance of doubt it is hereby declared that an act done by a person in contemplation or furtherance of a trade dispute is not actionable in tort on the ground only that it is an interference with the trade, business or employment of another person ...'.

159 [1983] ICR at 507, [1983] IRLR at 222. Lord Diplock considered that the tort of interference with contract is a different tort from interference with business, rather than just an example of it; sed quaere?

160 *Rookes v Barnard* [1964] AC 1129, [1964] 1 All ER 367, HL, at 1177 and 379, respectively, per Lord Reid.

161 [1898] AC 1, HL; see p 768 above. In *Barretts & Baird (Wholesale) Ltd v IPCS* [1987] IRLR 3, Henry J thought it was arguable that the employees' own breaches of contract could constitute the requisite unlawful means in this context, but this is respectfully doubted; see Simpson (1987) 50 MLR 506. The claimants in *Barretts* also argued that inducing breach of statutory duty (for which there is no immunity) constituted unlawful means, but failed on the facts; see below.

162 In *Barretts and Baird (Wholesale) Ltd v IPCS*, supra, Henry J imposed an 'intent' requirement as high as that in conspiracy, namely that the intent to injure the claimant must be the predominant purpose of the defendants' actions; however, in *Lonrho plc v Fayed* [1990] 2 QB 479, [1989] 2 All ER 65, the Court of Appeal held that it was not necessary to show that the defendant's predominant purpose was to injure the claimant rather than to pursue his own self-interest (or in the case of a trade union, its members' interests). See also *Associated British Ports v TGWU* [1989] 3 All ER 796, [1989] IRLR 305, CA (reversed on other grounds, [1989] 3 All ER 822, [1989] IRLR 399, HL).

(b) The immunity

Prior to 1976, the development of a possible tort of interference with contract was seen as a potential outflanking of the immunity then contained in section 13(1)(a) which only referred to *breach* of contract. However, the Trade Union and Labour Relations (Amendment) Act 1976 removed this possibility (in cases within the golden formula) by adding that an act is not to be actionable in tort on the ground only that it interferes or induces another person to interfere with the performance of a contract[163]. This covers both direct and indirect interference, and once again is dependent upon the acts in question falling within the golden formula and not falling within any of the circumstances in which the immunities are suspended by sections 222–234A of the Trade Union and Labour Relations (Consolidation) Act 1992. The wider 'genus' tort of interference with trade or business is not specifically covered by an immunity, either generally[164] or by virtue of the extension in 1976 (which only relates to interference with contract). However, as seen above, the essence of this new tort is the use of unlawful means; the result of this is that there may be *indirect* immunity if the means themselves are immune and therefore not 'unlawful'. This could arise where the means adopted consist of inducing the employees of someone in a business relationship (actual or potential) with the claimant to break their contracts of employment (for example by imposing a blacking); if that action itself is in contemplation or furtherance of a trade dispute and is immune, that means that any ensuing interference will be by lawful, not unlawful means[165]. As before, of course, any such (indirect) immunity is liable to be then removed if the action falls foul of sections 222–234A.

(v) Outflanking the immunities – three further possibilities

It is clear from the above that much of the stimulus for the development of the industrial torts during the twentieth century came from attempts to outflank the statutory immunities. The most significant development was undoubtedly the evolution of the 'genus' tort of interference with trade or business, discussed above, but there are three further possibilities, considered here in ascending order of importance. The first concerns the importation into industrial disputes of the contractual doctrine of 'economic duress', ie that if a party to a contract is obliged to enter into it, or to agree to certain terms, because of illegitimate coercion by the other party, he may claim that the contract is voidable for duress and so claim repayment of anything paid under it[166]. In *Universe Tankships Inc of*

163 See now the Trade Union and Labour Relations (Consolidation) Act 1992, s 219(1)(a).
164 The Trade Union and Labour Relations Act 1974, s 13(2), n 158 above, looked as though it provided an immunity, but the better view is that it was there in case an even more sweeping tort of interference by *lawful* means (but without justification) was developed. In any event, s 13(2) was repealed by the Employment Act 1982.
165 This is because if the inducement is within s 219(1) it is declared to be 'not actionable' and that means not actionable *by anyone*, ie lawful: *Hadmor Productions Ltd v Hamilton* [1982] ICR 114, [1982] IRLR 102, HL. Thus it cannot supply the unlawful means in an action by someone else; this used to be stated expressly by s 13(3)(a) of the Trade Union and Labour Relations Act 1974, but that was repealed by the Employment Act 1980, s 17(8).
166 Originally duress in contract law only covered threats of violence, but was widened to economic duress; see *North Ocean Shipping Co Ltd v Hyundai Construction Co Ltd* [1979] QB 705, [1978] 3 All ER 1170; *Pao On v Lau Yiu Long* [1980] AC 614, [1979] 3 All ER 65, PC; *Syros Shipping Co SA v Elaghill Trading Co* [1981] 3 All ER 189; *B & S Contracts and Design Ltd v Victor Green Publications Ltd* [1984] ICR 419, CA; *CTN Cash and Carry Ltd v Gallagher Ltd* [1994] 4 All ER 714, CA.

Monrovia v International Transport Workers' Federation[167] the ITWF, as part of its campaign against ships under flags of convenience, caused the blacking of the claimants' ship until certain demands were met, including the payment of $6,480 to a seamen's welfare fund. Once the ship was released, the claimants sought the return of this amount on the basis that it had been paid under duress. The House of Lords allowed recovery by a majority of three to two. The first point to note about this application of the doctrine of duress is that it does *not* constitute a new head of tort; rather, it gives rise to an action for restitution of moneys paid over, and given that such arrangements between unions and employers are not common, it is likely that in practice the occasions when such a claim will be brought will be few[168]. However, if a claim is brought, it raises an exceptionally difficult point – when does pressure by a union on an employer overstep the line between hard bargaining on the one hand and illegitimate coercion (giving rise to economic duress) on the other? The answer given by the House of Lords has at least the attribute of neatness – although the doctrine of duress does not give rise to an action in tort, so that the immunities in the Trade Union and Labour Relations (Consolidation) Act 1992, section 219 are not directly applicable, those immunities can be used *indirectly* to draw the line, the reasoning being that it would be contrary to Parliament's intention to hold voidable for duress actions which, had a suit been pleaded in tort, would have been covered by the statutory immunties. Thus, if an action would have been immune from a suit in tort, it will probably not be held to amount to economic duress. The majority went on to hold that the actions of the ITWF in fact would not have come within the statutory immunity, and so the claimants could recover the money paid over by them. One possible problem with this approach (which certainly seems logical, given that economic duress has to be applied to industrial relations at all) is that the scope of the immunities may itself be subject to change by legislation and case law, and when this happens it will presumably also lead to a redrawing of the line on economic duress, a doctrine whose full effect in this context remains to be worked out.

The second possible development is the extension of the tort of inducement of breach of contract to other situations which involve the violation of legal rights, and in particular to inducement of breach of statutory duty[169]. The basis for the new tort was laid by the Court of Appeal in *Meade v London Borough of Haringey*[170] a case concerning the legality (under the Education Act 1944) of a decision by a local authority to close its schools because of strike action by caretakers and ancillary staff. In the course of their judgments, both Lord Denning MR and Eveleigh LJ stated obiter that it was tortious for the union to induce the local authority to be in breach of its statutory duty, and moreover that such tortious action would not be covered by the statutory immunities. The existence of the tort was subsequently confirmed by the Court of Appeal in *Associated British Ports v TGWU*[171], but with the

---

167 [1982] 2 All ER 67, [1982] ICR 262, HL, noted (1982) 45 MLR 556; see Sterling 'Actions for duress, seafarers and industrial disputes' (1982) 11 ILJ 156.

168 Although cf *Dimskal Shipping Co SA v International Transport Workers' Federation, The Evia Luck (No 2)* [1992] ICR 37, [1992] IRLR 78, HL.

169 See also *Prudential Assurance Co Ltd v Lorenz* (1971) 11 KIR 78 (inducement of breach of equitable obligation).

170 [1979] 2 All ER 1016, [1979] ICR 494, CA. See also *Associated Newspapers Group Ltd v Wade* [1979] ICR 664, [1979] IRLR 201, CA and *Barretts & Baird (Wholesale) Ltd v IPCS* [1987] IRLR 3.

171 *Associated British Ports v TGWU* [1989] 3 All ER 796, [1989] IRLR 305, CA; revsd on other grounds [1989] 3 All ER 822, [1989] IRLR 399, HL.

important caveat that the statutory duty in question must be independently actionable[172]. The tort of inducement of breach of statutory duty could be of particular significance in the public sector, where employers are more likely to be under a statutory duty to provide and maintain goods or services, not least because there is no statutory immunity covering it.

The third possible development is of more general application, and concerns the central question of what amounts to unlawful means for present purposes. As seen above, while there is no specific immunity for the tort of interference with trade or business, in practice there may be an *indirect* immunity if the means adopted (for example inducing a breach of contract) are covered by an immunity and are therefore not unlawful[173]. An obvious way of outflanking this indirect immunity is by the development of types of unlawful means which are *not* themselves covered by an immunity. One such development was canvassed by Henry J in *Barretts & Baird (Wholesale) Ltd v IPCS*[174] , where fatstock officers staffing private abattoirs took industrial action in a dispute with their employers, the Meat and Livestock Commission. The abattoir owners brought proceedings for injunctions against the union and against an individual fatstock officer; as against the former, the case relied on inducement to breach of statutory duty (above), but against the latter the argument was that the officers had interfered with the claimant's business, the unlawful means being quite simply their own breaches of employment contracts with their employer. If such an action were accepted it would have the astonishing result that the union officials organising a strike would be immune[175] , but the individual employees could be sued by anyone affected by their action. The problem here is that it has never been authoritatively decided whether or not simple breach of contract could be unlawful means for the torts of inducement and interference[176] . Henry J was therefore driven to conclude that it was arguable that simple breach could constitute unlawful means[177] . In the event he avoided finding the fatstock officers individually liable, on the basis, first, that they lacked the necessary intention to injure the claimant[178] , and secondly, that

---

172 This is a matter of construction of the statute; to be independently actionable the claimant will usually need to show that the statute was passed for the benefit of a class which includes him, or that he has suffered some special damage: see *Cutler v Wandsworth Stadium Ltd* [1949] AC 398, HL; *Lonrho Ltd v Shell Petroleum Co Ltd (No 2)* [1982] AC 173, [1981] 2 All ER 465, HL. For an example of such an action being specifically written into a statute, see the Telecommunications Act 1984, s 18(6)(b), noted Carty (1984) 13 ILJ 165.

173 See n 770 above.

174 [1987] IRLR 3, noted Simpson (1987) 50 MLR 506, Napier (1987) 46 CLJ 222, Benedictus (1987) 16 ILJ 191.

175 Assuming there had been a ballot and that it remained primary action, the officials would have the protection of s 219(1) covering their inducement of the breaches of contract by the employees; that inducement would therefore not be actionable per se, nor would it constitute unlawful means, eg for the tort of interference on their part.

176 Breach of contract had been held to be unlawful means for the purposes of the tort of intimidation in *Rookes v Barnard* [1964] AC 1129, [1964] 1 All ER 367, HL, but it was not decided there that the same applied to the other economic torts, where the effect could be more drastic; s 13(3)(b) of the Trade Union and Labour Relations Act 1974 used to state 'for the avoidance of doubt' that such a breach in contemplation or furtherance of a trade dispute was not to be treated as unlawful means, but that subsection was repealed by the Employment Act 1980.

177 In so deciding (at p 9) the judge cites Wedderburn *The Worker and the Law* (3rd edn, 1986) at p 637 where the author pointed out this danger of the repeal of s 13(3)(b).

178 Henry J's view that the defendant's 'predominant purpose' must be to injure the claimant was however doubted by the Court of Appeal in *Lonrho plc v Fayed* [1990] 2 QB 479, [1989] 2 All ER 65. See above, p 769.

the remedy sought could not be granted against the individual employee defendant because of the statutory restrictions on the enforcement of contracts of employment against employees[179] . The result of the case therefore did not cause too much consternation, but the possibility of such an argument succeeding in the future cannot be discounted[180] . Another form of unlawful means which is of potentially great practical significance is the tort of inducement of breach of statutory duty. As seen above, this tort may provide a cause of action in its own right, but there its impact is restricted by the requirement that the breach of statutory duty be independently actionable at the suit of the claimant. However, in *Associated British Ports v TGWU*[181] , a majority of the Court of Appeal considered that it was 'strongly arguable' that for the purposes of the tort of interference with business, a breach of statutory duty could be relied upon as unlawful means even if not actionable at the suit of the claimant.

The fact that these major areas of uncertainty exist (along with the other unresolved questions relating to the nature and extent of the established economic torts, referred to earlier), and are at least capable of development, shows how deeply unsatisfactory and unpredictable our current law on industrial action is.

(vi) The golden formula

For the statutory immunities to apply, the industrial action in question must be within the 'golden formula', ie it must be 'in contemplation or furtherance of a trade dispute'; if it falls outside that, the immunities will not apply, and, in most cases, it will be easy for the claimant employer to show the elements of one or more of the above torts (particularly since the disapproval of the 'strike notice' theory in *Simmons v Hoover Ltd*[182]) and on that basis claim an interim injunction to stop the industrial action. Thus, a crucial first stage in an employer's action for an injunction is to consider whether the golden formula applies – if it does not, the employer will probably be successful; if it does, the immunities apply, unless they are disapplied (to use the extremely inelegant word commonly adopted in this context) by anything in sections 222–234A of the Trade Union and Labour Relations (Consolidation) Act 1992. Moreover, as will be seen later, the exemption from liability given to pickets by section 220 is also reliant upon the formula.

To be within the protection of the golden formula, two matters must be shown – there must be a 'trade dispute', and the acts in question must be 'in contemplation or furtherance' of it.

---

179 Now contained in the Trade Union and Labour Relations (Consolidation) Act 1992, s 236.
180 It has been referred to as 'a time-bomb in our labour law': Davies and Freedland *Labour Law Texts and Materials* (2nd edn, 1984) p 755. The restriction on the enforcement of contracts of employment would not, of course, apply to an action for damages (actual or threatened) against employees taking industrial action.
181 [1989] 3 All ER 796, [1989] IRLR 305, CA (reversed on other grounds, [1989] 3 All ER 822, [1989] IRLR 399, HL).
182 [1977] ICR 61, [1976] IRLR 266, EAT.

(a) Is there a trade dispute?

The statutory definition of a trade dispute is contained in section 244 of the Trade Union and Labour Relations (Consolidation) Act 1992[183]. It is defined as a dispute between 'workers[184] and their employer' which relates 'wholly or mainly to' one or more of the following[185] :

(a) terms and conditions of employment[186], or the physical conditions in which any workers are required to work;

(b) engagement or non-engagement, or termination or suspension of employment, or the duties of employment[187], of one or more workers;

(c) allocation of work or the duties of employment between workers or groups of workers[188];

(d) matters of discipline;

(e) the membership or non-membership of a trade union on the part of a worker[189];

(f) facilities for officials of trade unions; and

---

183 For the history of the definition, and a clear and detailed investigation of its pre-1982 form, see Simpson, ' "Trade dispute" and "industrial dispute" in British labour law' (1977) 40 MLR 16. On the alterations in the Employment Act 1982, see Simpson, 'A not so golden formula' (1983) 46 MLR 463 and Ewing 'Another step in the "right" direction' (1982) 11 ILJ 209. The wider pre-1982 definition is retained by s 218 for the purposes of Part IV of the 1992 Act, in particular for defining the powers of ACAS and Courts of Inquiry (see pp 58 and 64 above). Given that the trade dispute disqualification for the jobseeker's allowance uses yet another definition (taken from the Trade Disputes Act 1906; see p 651 above), we are now graced (or cursed?) with three definitions of trade dispute in our industrial law.

184 'Worker' is defined in s 296 and includes an independent contractor, provided he undertakes to perform work or services personally (other than in a professional capacity); *Broadbent v Crisp* [1974] ICR 248; cf *Writers' Guild of Great Britain v BBC* [1974] ICR 234.

185 A dispute which relates to matters occurring outside the UK qualifies as a trade dispute only if those taking action within the UK are likely to be affected by the outcome of the dispute in relation to one or more of the matters specified in section 244(1)(a)–(g): s 244(3).

186 The use of the composite expression 'terms and conditions of employment' shows that the phrase was intended to be given a broad meaning, as covering both the rules of employment and the application of those rules: *P v National Association of Schoolmasters/ Union of Women Teachers* [2003] UKHL 8, [2003] 1 All ER 993, per Lord Hoffmann; there must however be some limitation of it to terms which regulate the relationship between employer and employee, excluding any matters extraneous to that relationship: *Universe Tankships Inc of Monrovia v International Transport Workers' Federation* [1982] 2 All ER 67, [1982] ICR 262, HL.

187 A trade dispute arising out of fears for jobs in a period of high unemployment (involving, for example, a demand that what work there is should be done by existing employees, not by outside contractors) was said by Lord Diplock in *Hadmor Productions Ltd v Hamilton* [1982] 1 All ER 1042, [1982] ICR 114, HL to be a classic instance of a dispute covered by head (b); the Court of Appeal had held that there was no trade dispute in such a case.

188 This covers demarcation disputes, but note that the employer must be a party to such a dispute for it to qualify under head (c) because of the general requirement that the dispute be between 'workers and their employer'; moreover that requirement means that head (c) only applies to the allocation of work between the employer's own workers – it does not apply to a dispute over reallocation of work from the employer's own workers to an outside company: *Dimbleby & Sons Ltd v NUJ* [1984] ICR 386, [1984] IRLR 161, HL.

189 While the definition of trade dispute still includes disputes over non-membership, s 222 provides that the immunities will be withdrawn where industrial action is taken to enforce union membership; see p 785 below.

(g) machinery for negotiation or consultation, and other procedures, relating to any of the above matters, including recognition of a union by an employer or employer's association[190].

It is further provided in section 244(4) that there can still be a 'dispute' even if the employer in fact submits to the union's demands, so that the initial making of the demands can still be considered as within the golden formula[191].

'Trade dispute' is thus given a wide definition, capable of covering most disputes between employees and their employer about the job the employees are employed to do or the terms and conditions on which they are employed to do it, and therefore the actual definition will not normally be a significant legal restriction on a union's activities, provided it acts generally within an industrial relations context. If, however, it goes outside that and engages in what, for want of a better word, might be called 'political' action, then arguably it might be outside a trade dispute. Thus, industrial action taken *purely* as a protest against government action might be of dubious legality[192]. However, the mere fact that there is a 'political' aspect will not remove a dispute from the statutory definition, so that anti-government action might still be included if there is a genuine trade aspect as, for example, where the government is a significant employer of the union's members[193], or where those members may be directly affected by government policies in question (for example on questions of nationalisation or privatisation of the industry concerned[194]). Until 1982 it was possible for industrial action to qualify as a trade dispute even if the action was taken for predominantly political or more widely social reasons, as long as there was some genuine connection with terms and conditions of employment or any of the other matters in (a) to (g). This was because the wording of the trade dispute definition at that time merely required that the dispute be 'connected with' one of the listed matters, and it seemed that the connection might be relatively slight. Only if the industrial action was wholly unconnected with any of the matters would it fall outside the statutory definition. So, for example, in *BBC v Hearn*[195] a threat to disrupt the transmission of a television signal to South Africa during the Cup Final because of the union's anti-apartheid policy was restrained by the Court of Appeal since it did not constitute a trade dispute; it had nothing to do with the terms and conditions of

---

190 Recognition disputes also came within the original definition in the 1906 Act: *Beetham v Trinidad Cement Ltd* [1960] AC 132, [1960] 1 All ER 274, PC. However, the action must clearly be connected with the recognition issue, not just an aftermath: *J T Stratford & Son Ltd v Lindley* [1965] AC 269, [1964] 3 All ER 102, HL.

191 Nullifying statements to the contrary in *Cory Lighterage Ltd v TGWU* [1973] ICR 339, [1973] IRLR 152, CA.

192 *Associated Newspapers Group Ltd v Flynn* (1970) 10 KIR 17; in *National Sailors' and Firemen's Union v Reed* [1926] Ch 536, Astbury J held that the 1926 General Strike was illegal, sed quaere (see Goodhart, (1927) 36 Yale LJ 464). In *Sherard v AUEW* [1973] ICR 421, [1973] IRLR 188, CA, at 433 and 189 respectively, Lord Denning MR stated as his opinion that a dispute between the TUC and the government (simpliciter) would not be trade dispute. See also *Express Newspapers v Keys* [1980] IRLR 247, and *University College London Hospitals NHS Trust v UNISON* [1999] IRLR 31.

193 *Sherard v AUEW* [1973] ICR 421, [1973] IRLR 188, CA.

194 *General Aviation Services (UK) Ltd v TGWU* [1974] ICR 35, [1973] IRLR 355. Section 244(2) provides that a dispute between workers and a government Minister who is not their employer will be treated as a trade dispute with their employer where the dispute cannot be settled without the Minister's involvement or approval: see eg *Wandsworth London Borough Council v NASUWT* [1993] IRLR 344, CA.

195 [1977] ICR 685, [1977] IRLR 273, CA, approved by Lord Hoffmann in *P v National Association of Schoolmasters/Association of Women Teachers* [2003] UKHL 8, [2003] 1 All ER 993.

employment of the workers involved, and did not become a trade dispute merely because those workers were threatening to break their contracts; the union's argument that there should be read into the contracts of employment a term that employees would not be required to do anything to which they had a conscientious objection (thereby making it a trade dispute over terms and conditions) was not accepted. In contrast, Lord Diplock in *NWL Ltd v Nelson*[196] showed greater willingness to allow as a trade dispute a matter of basically a political nature, provided that it has some connection with terms and conditions of employment, and can be framed in such a way.

However, the Employment Act 1982 narrowed the trade dispute definition considerably by requiring that the dispute relate 'wholly or mainly to' one or more of the listed matters, rather than simply be 'connected with' them; this has made it far more difficult to alter the legal nature of a dispute by the way a demand is phrased, and its overall effect has been to throw the industrial/political distinction into much higher relief (rather than leaving it largely fudged, as was the case under the previous wording). The importance of this can clearly be seen in *Mercury Communications Ltd v Scott-Garner*[197]. The case concerned action taken by the union representing British Telecom workers to try to prevent the successful licensing of a private company by BT (a process referred to as 'liberalisation'). The company brought proceedings for an injunction to restrain this action. The union pleaded the immunity, on the basis that this was a trade dispute concerning possible job losses. However, the Court of Appeal granted the injunction on the basis that the facts did not show that fear of job losses was the major factor behind the action (particularly as there was in existence a job security agreement with BT), and that on the facts the dispute related wholly or mainly to the union's political objection to liberalisation, which was seen as a precursor to the entire privatisation of BT (that in the event followed). The case is a good illustration of the difficulties faced by the courts in attempting to determine what a particular dispute is *mainly* about, in circumstances where there are a range of factors and issues involved which are inextricably linked. In practice much is likely to turn upon the way in which the union presents the dispute to its members and to the public at large. In *Wandsworth London Borough Council v NASUWT*[198], the Court of Appeal had to decide whether industrial action by teachers which included a boycott of testing under the national curriculum was a 'trade dispute' and therefore covered by the statutory immunities. The local authority argued that the main impetus for the dispute was the objection of the union and its members to the principle of testing, so that it was not wholly or mainly related to terms and conditions, etc, but on the facts the Court of Appeal accepted the union's

---

196 [1979] ICR 867, [1979] IRLR 478, HL, at 878 and 483, respectively. In *Universe Tankships Inc of Monrovia v International Transport Workers' Federation* [1982] ICR 262, [1982] IRLR 200, HL, his Lordship stressed that there must still be some connection with one of the enumerated matters, even if it was not the predominant purpose of the defendant; Lord Cross was clearly against the idea of being able to turn a dispute into a trade dispute by insisting that the employer inserted certain terms into contracts of employment.

197 [1984] ICR 74, [1983] IRLR 494, CA; the judge at first instance had held that the dispute was mainly related to the BT workers' fears of redundancies, and had refused to grant the injunction. The decision of the Court of Appeal to grant it was seen as a significant factor in the moves towards privatisation, which could have been at risk if the union had lawfully managed to frustrate the process of liberalisation.

198 [1994] ICR 81, [1993] IRLR 344, CA. See also *University College London Hospitals NHS Trust v UNISON* [1999] IRLR 31, CA, and *Westminster City Council v UNISON* [2001] EWCA Civ 443, [2001] ICR 1046.

argument that the dispute related mainly to the increased workload on teachers in conducting the tests (a point stressed by union leaders at every turn and also emphasised in the wording of the strike ballot), and held that there was in fact a trade dispute. The Court attached 'considerable importance' to the fact that the wording of the question posed in the ballot paper referred to 'protest against the excessive workload and unreasonable imposition made upon teachers' as a result of the new national curriculum assessment and testing requirements.

The second major change to the trade dispute definition by the Employment Act 1982 was to require that the dispute be between 'workers and their employer'. Previously it was possible to have a trade dispute between workers and employers (whether or not their own employer), or workers and workers[199], and there was deemed to be a dispute involving workers if a union was a party to the dispute, even if the actual workers were not[200]. The definition was thus extremely wide on the question of parties. Since 1982, however, the wording of the definition has required the existence of a dispute 'between workers and their employer', ie a dispute between the employer and workers currently employed by him[201]. The aim of these changes was to reinforce the need for there to be, somewhere along the line, a genuine dispute between an employer and his employees[202]. One unfortunate consequence of the revised wording has been to throw into doubt the legality of industrial action aimed at securing the terms and conditions of employees following a business transfer. In *University College London Hospitals NHS Trust v UNISON*[203], the union threatened industrial action after the Trust refused to give an undertaking that the terms and conditions of staff to be transferred to a new consortium which was to build and run a PFI hospital would be maintained for a period of 30 years at an equivalent level to Trust employees who were not transferred. The Court of Appeal issued an injunction restraining the action, on the grounds that the trade dispute definition does not cover a dispute about the terms and conditions of employees of an as yet unidentified employer who have never been employed by the employer who is being threatened with industrial action. In so far as the decision relates to the as yet unidentified *future* employees of an as yet unidentified employer, it is perhaps unexceptionable, but the Court

199 Thus a demarcation dispute between two unions which did not involve the employer directly could be a trade dispute. Presumably such a dispute could still comply if one or both of the unions were to make demands on the employer relating to the performance of the work in question.

200 This was particularly important in a case where it was the union itself which had a grievance against the employer even if it did not have the backing (or, indeed, the membership) of his employees (as in the case of the ITWF in its campaign against shipowners who use flags of convenience; see *Star Sea Transport Corpn of Monrovia v Slater* [1978] IRLR 507, CA and *NWL Ltd v Nelson* [1979] ICR 867, [1979] IRLR 478, HL). The changes in the 1982 Act were particularly significant in that sort of case.

201 Trade Union and Labour Relations (Consolidation) Act 1992, s 244(5). A dispute between workers and their *former* employer will qualify as a trade dispute where their employment was terminated in connection with the dispute or the termination of employment was one of the factors which gave rise to the dispute: s 244(5).

202 The protection does not extend to disputes with an associated employer (eg another company in the corporate group), even where that employer is in reality making the decisions which are at the heart of the dispute. The effect of this limitation can be seen from *Dimbleby & Sons Ltd v NUJ* [1984] ICR 386, [1984] IRLR 161.

203 [1999] IRLR 31, CA. See also *UNISON v United Kingdom* [2002] IRLR 497, ECHR, discussed at p 747 above, where the ECHR rejected the union's claim that the Court of Appeal's interpretation was an unjustified restriction on the right to freedom of assembly and association in Article 11 of the European Convention on Human Rights.

of Appeal's suggestion that the trade dispute definition does not include industrial action to protect the terms and conditions of *existing* employees after they are transferred to a new employer is arguably an undesirably narrow interpretation of the trade dispute definition[204].

At first sight, the tightening up of the trade dispute definition to disputes between an employer and his employees might seem to outlaw all secondary action, by rendering any action other than that taken against the employer in dispute outside the definition of a trade dispute. However, this is not the case, for section 244 only defines when a trade dispute is in existence; the legality of any action away from the centre of that dispute will depend upon whether it is 'in contemplation or furtherance' of that initial dispute, and whether it is lawful under other statutory provisions, particularly the restrictions on secondary action in section 224. So, for example, if employees of employer A take action purely in support of employees of employer B who are in dispute with their own employer, the only trade dispute is that with B, but the actions of A's employees may well be in contemplation or furtherance of that dispute (see below), and therefore technically within the golden formula; however, their action is likely to fall foul of the restrictions on secondary action in section 224, and will therefore be unprotected[205]. The significance of the restricted trade dispute definition is that section 224 cannot be side-stepped by arguing that a fresh trade dispute has been created whenever and wherever industrial action is taken in support of the original dispute[206].

(b) Is the action 'in contemplation or furtherance'? Swings and roundabouts

It is not enough for there to be a trade dispute; to be within the golden formula, the action actually taken must be 'in contemplation or furtherance' of it. This phrase is a term of art, well known in industrial law, but at one crucially important time in the development of our modern law it was the subject of a major division of opinion between the Court of Appeal and the House of Lords as to its proper construction. Two preliminary points should be noted. First, it does *not* just mean 'connected with'; it has a more limited meaning than that. Second, it incorporates a time element, so that the trade dispute must either be about to or likely to happen ('contemplation'), or it must already be in existence ('furtherance'); thus, action could be too far in advance of any possible dispute to be in contemplation of it[207], and action taken after the conclusion of the dispute (for example to 'punish' certain participants in it or to regain prestige for the union)

---

204 A dispute over whether a proposed transfer should go ahead would clearly fall within the definition, as the identity of the employer is a term of the contract: see eg *Westminstrer City Council v UNISON* [2001] EWCA Civ 443, [2001] ICR 1046.

205 Until 1990, secondary action enjoyed the protection of the immunities if it was aimed at the first customers or first suppliers of the employer in dispute: Employment Act 1980, s 17. The restrictions on secondary action in s 224, introduced in 1990, remove the immunities in virtually all cases of secondary action. See p 781 below.

206 This is confirmed by s 224(4), which provides that an employer shall not be treated as party to a dispute between another employer and workers of that employer, and where more than one employer is in dispute with his workers, the dispute between each employer and his workers shall be treated as a separate dispute.

207 *Bents Brewery Co Ltd v Hogan* [1945] 2 All ER 570.

might be too late to be considered in furtherance of it[208] . In *Conway v Wade*[209] , Lord Shaw said:

'... the contemplation of such a dispute must be the contemplation of something impending or likely to occur and ... [it does] not cover the case of coercive interference in which the intervener may have in his own mind that if he does not get his own way he will thereupon take ways and means to bring a trade dispute into existence ... With regard to the term "furtherance" of a trade dispute, I think that must apply to a trade dispute in existence and that the act done must be in the course of it and for the purpose of promoting the interests of either party or both parties to it.'

Given that the timing was right and there was arguably a dispute in existence about industrial matters, it was thought at one time that the immunities were so widely drafted (especially after 1976) and the golden formula so widely construed that it was almost impossible for an employer to bring legal proceedings to stop industrial action. However, in a series of cases in the late 1970s (and particularly through the infamous 'winter of discontent' preceding the 1979 election)[210] the Court of Appeal sought to alter that (and, in so doing, alter the bounds of permissible union activity) by looking anew at the phrase 'in contemplation or furtherance of a trade dispute' and establishing three requirements for that phrase to apply to industrial action. These were that: (a) the action must be taken for the 'proper motive' of pursuing a legitimate trade object, not for some extraneous motive (such as, for example, a campaign against flags of convenience by a seamen's union; (b) the action must not be too 'remote' from the centre of the dispute; (c) the action must be capable of furthering the trade objectives of one party to the dispute (the 'objective test').

Had they been accepted by the House of Lords, these three requirements, taken together, would have substantially narrowed the meaning of the phrase 'in contemplation or furtherance of a trade dispute', and enabled the judges to take a more active role in deciding what was and what was not within the golden formula. However, the Court of Appeal's innovations were very quickly set at nought when appeals were taken to the House of Lords, and all three requirements were disapproved[211] , the House of Lords confirming in no uncertain terms that the question whether a person acts in contemplation or furtherance of a trade dispute is a subjective one which must be decided in the light of the intentions and beliefs of the actors; if a person has a genuine and honest belief that his actions will further the interests of one party to the dispute, the fact that those actions, considered objectively, are not reasonably capable of furthering the dispute will

---

208 *J T Stratford & Son Ltd v Lindley* [1965] AC 269, [1964] 3 All ER 102, HL; *Stewart v AUEW* [1973] ICR 128, [1973] IRLR 57, NIRC.

209 [1909] AC 506, HL at 522. The case remains good law on this point.

210 *Beaverbrook Newspapers Ltd v Keys* [1978] ICR 582, [1978] IRLR 34, CA; *Star Sea Transport Corpn of Monrovia v Slater, The Camilla M* [1978] IRLR 507, CA; *Associated Newspapers Group Ltd v Wade* [1979] ICR 664, [1979] IRLR 201, CA; *Express Newspapers Ltd v McShane* [1979] ICR 210, [1979] IRLR 79, CA.

211 *NWL Ltd v Nelson* [1979] ICR 867, [1979] IRLR 478, HL (disapproving the 'proper motive' requirement); *Express Newspapers Ltd v McShane* [1980] ICR 42, [1980] IRLR 35, HL (disapproving the objective test); *Duport Steels Ltd v Sirs* [1980] ICR 161, [1980] IRLR 116, HL (disapproving the 'remoteness' test).

be relevant only in so far as it casts doubt on the genuineness of that person's subjective belief. In the words of Lord Scarman in *Express Newspapers Ltd v McShane*:

> 'It follows therefore that, once it is shown that a trade dispute exists, the person who acts, but not the court, is the judge of whether his acts will further the dispute. If he is acting honestly, Parliament leaves to him the choice of what to do. I confess that I am relieved to find that this is the law. It would be a strange and embarrassing task for a judge to be called upon to review the tactics of a party to a trade dispute and to determine whether in the view of the court the tactic employed was likely to further or advance that party's side of the dispute … It would need very clear statutory language to persuade me that Parliament intended to allow the courts to act as some sort of backseat driver in trade disputes[212] .'

The result of these three House of Lords decisions was thus to negative completely the developments brought about by the activism of the Court of Appeal, and to establish clearly a subjective and pro-union interpretation of the phrase 'in contemplation or furtherance' of a trade dispute. That interpretation is still valid, and consequently this phrase is no longer a major limitation on the immunities; theoretically, it remains a stage in an action where it has to be established whether the immunities apply, but it is not normally an important hurdle for the defendant union or union official, except possibly in a rare case where the acts complained of bore no genuine relationship to a dispute whatsoever[213] or where there was no relationship in time between the acts and an existing dispute[214] .

The developments in the Court of Appeal had, however, been very much in line with the political approach to industrial disputes of the incoming Conservative government in 1979[215] , and not surprisingly the re-establishment and strengthening of the previous law by the House of Lords was not to the government's liking. The government's response was to introduce into the 1980 Employment Bill a complicated provision (the notorious section 17, discussed below), which sought to reinstate much the same position as had been reached by the Court of Appeal, using much the same devices – in effect a statutory 'remoteness' test. However, crucially that section operated by imposing *additional* requirements, not by amending the phrase 'in contemplation or furtherance', which remains as the House of Lords left it. Ironically, section 17 was itself repealed by the Employment Act 1990 and replaced with an even narrower provision[216] which takes the restrictions on secondary industrial action considerably further than the Court of Appeal had proposed in those controversial cases a decade earlier.

---

212 [1980] ICR 42 at 64, [1980] IRLR 35 at 78.
213 For example, where a defendant acted purely maliciously; *Express Newspapers Ltd v McShane* did retain a residual requirement that a defendant's purpose (whatever it might be in connection with the dispute) must be genuine and honest; if no reasonable person would have thought the acts in question capable of furthering the dispute, that may as a matter of evidence only call into question the defendant's bona fides.
214 See the dictum from *Conway v Wade* [1909] AC 506, HL, which appears to be still good law.
215 Indeed, in the light of them, the Employment Bill of 1980 (as originally published) did not propose to alter the law on the immunities as the Court of Appeal appeared to have achieved the government's objectives by its re-interpretation of the golden formula.
216 Now contained in s 224 of the Trade Union and Labour Relations (Consolidation) Act 1992.

4 RESTRICTIONS ON THE STATUTORY IMMUNITIES[217]

Even if industrial action passes the tests considered so far and thereby qualifies for protection under one of the statutory immunities, the final stage[218] in this involved progression is that it may still be rendered illegal and restrainable if it falls within one of the categories of industrial action from which the immunities have been removed by the legislation introduced since 1980. The picture is a particularly complicated one, as there are now no fewer than seven separate circumstances where the immunities will be withdrawn; in some cases this will be on the grounds of the *scope* of the industrial action, as in the case of unlawful secondary action (section 224) and (in part at least) unlawful picketing (section 220(3)); in others it will be because the industrial action is taken for what is declared to be an impermissible *reason*, for example action to enforce union membership (section 222), action taken because of the dismissal of unofficial strikers (section 223), and pressure to impose union recognition requirements (section 225); and, finally the immunities will be removed where the union has failed to comply with the mandatory *procedures* for official industrial action, for example where official action is taken without the support of a ballot (section 226), or the union fails to give the requisite strike notice to employers (section 234A). These are now considered.

(i) Secondary action

Since 1980, the statutory immunities have been severely curtailed in the case of 'secondary action', ie action which is taken against an employer other than the employer in dispute (sometimes referred to as 'sympathy' or 'solidarity' action), reflecting the previous Conservative government's belief that if trade unions must take industrial action at all, that action should be restricted to the employer in dispute, and not extended to other employers at one stage removed from the employer in dispute. The original restrictions on secondary action were contained in the notorious (and now repealed) section 17 of the Employment Act 1980[219], which attempted to strike a balance between, on the one hand, the interests of employers not party to the dispute to be protected from industrial action which does not directly concern them and, on the other, the desire of those taking industrial action to increase the pressure on the employer in dispute by widening their action to take in employers with a close relationship with that employer. Section 17 sought to achieve this by withdrawing the immunities in all cases of 'secondary action' as defined (see below), but then providing for three situations (the so-called 'gateways to freedom') in which secondary action was lawful, so that the immunities continued to apply. These were, first, where the purpose of the secondary action was to prevent or disrupt the supply of goods or services between the employer in dispute and his immediate customers or suppliers (the 'first customer/first supplier' exception); secondly, where the purpose of the secondary action was to prevent or disrupt the supply of goods or services during

---

217 See Auerbach *Legislating for Conflict* (Oxford, 1992).
218 This means the final stage in theory: in practice it may be obvious in a particular case that (a) the action is prima facie tortious and that (b) the statutory immunities are applicable, in which case arguments may be almost entirely upon this 'final' point.
219 On s 17 generally, see Bercusson (1980) 9 ILJ 215 and Wedderburn (1981) ILJ 113.

the dispute between an associated employer[220] of the employer in dispute and that associated employer's immediate customers or suppliers, where those goods or services were in substitution for those which would otherwise have been supplied to or by the employer in dispute (the 'associated employer' exception); and thirdly, where the secondary action was done in the course of peaceful picketing by a worker employed by the employer in dispute picketing his own place of work, or by a trade union official lawfully attending a picket line (the picketing exception).

The first of these, the 'first customer/first supplier' exception, can perhaps best be understood as an attempt to reintroduce in legislative form the remoteness test previously evolved by the Court of Appeal, and subsequently disapproved by the House of Lords. Its effect was to allow secondary action to be taken against a direct customer or supplier of the employer in dispute, but crucially, only where the supply of goods or services was *in pursuance of a contract between them subsisting at the time of the secondary action*. Thus it was the contractual link between the employer in dispute and the employer against whom the secondary action was taken that determined whether the action was protected by section 17. Action taken by a union against a supplier of a supplier, or a customer of a customer of the employer in dispute[221], or against a person or firm with no direct connection with the employer in dispute (as in the case of purely 'sympathy' action) was outside the protection of the section. The importance of the contractual link can be seen clearly from *Merkur Island Shipping Corpn v Laughton*[222] where a ship owned by A and sub-chartered to B was blacked while in port by the ITWF because of complaints of underpayment of the crew. The blacking was achieved by persuading tugmen to refuse to let the ship out, thereby breaking their contracts of employment with their employers, the tug company. The owners sought an injunction to restrain the blacking, which was granted, and upheld by the House of Lords. The point of the case was that the employer in dispute (the owner, A) and the employer subject to the secondary action (the tug company) were not in a direct contractual relationship, since when a chartered ship docks, the contract for the use of a facility such as tugs is between the tug company and the charterer (B); thus, the requirement of a subsisting contractual relationship between the employer in dispute and the employer subject to the secondary action was not satisfied, and the protection of section 17 was not available to the union officials.

The second exception, the 'associated employer' exception, was a narrow one, only covering the type of case where, because of a dispute, production is switched by the employer in dispute (employer A) to another employer within the same group (employer B); supplies relating to that switched production to or from employer B remained a valid target, even though the dispute was actually with employer A. However, for this exception to apply there was a clear requirement that the production must have been switched; it did not apply simply because the two employers were associated. This was illustrated by *Dimbleby & Sons Ltd v NUJ*[223] where the union was in (long-standing) dispute with T. Bailey Foreman

---

220 See p 30 above.
221 As, for example, on the facts of *Associated Newspapers Group Ltd v Wade* [1979] ICR 664, [1979] IRLR 201, CA and *Express Newspapers Ltd v McShane* [1980] 1 All ER 65, [1980] ICR 42, HL, itself.
222 [1983] ICR 490, [1983] IRLR 218, HL, approving the decision of the Court of Appeal in a case on almost identical facts: *Marina Shipping Ltd v Laughton, The Antama* [1982] ICR 215, [1982] IRLR 20, CA.
223 [1984] ICR 386, [1984] IRLR 161, HL.

Ltd and objected to the claimants (local newspaper publishers) contracting to have their printing done by that company; they therefore took industrial action against the claimants to prevent copy from being sent for printing. However, the problem then arose that in fact the printing contract was not with T. Bailey Foreman Ltd, but rather with TBF (Printers) Ltd, an associated company. As, however, there had been no switching of production, the associated employer exception did not apply and so, as the employer in dispute (T. Bailey Foreman Ltd) and the employer subject to the secondary action (the claimants) were not in direct contractual relations, the action was unlawful secondary action and so illegal[224].

The third exception, the 'picketing' exception, was necessary in order to prevent the immunity for peaceful picketing[225] being rendered worthless as a result of the secondary 'ripple' effect which picketing activity is likely to have on commercial contracts. So, for example, where pickets lawfully attending outside their place of work in pursuance of a dispute with their employer, employer A, turn away lorries carrying supplies from B (thereby inducing B's driver to break his contract of employment and interfering with B's commercial supply contracts), there would be an immunity under the *first* exception if there was an existing supply contract for those goods between A and B; but if there was no such contract, or if the lorry in fact belonged to C, a haulage contractor, so that the pickets could be said to have interfered with the haulage contract between B and C (to which A is *not* a party), that action would not be protected under the first exception. Provided the pickets were employed by the employer in dispute and remained within the scope of the immunity for peaceful picketing, the third exception prevented such action from being illegal.

The provisions in section 17 proved to be exceptionally difficult and controversial in practice[226]. As the *Merkur Island Shipping Corpn* case (above) showed, a union had to be careful about the exact contractual relations involved if it were to avoid liability under section 17; and the *Dimbleby* case showed that it had to be equally careful about the exact corporate organisation of the employers concerned. Indeed, it proved all too easy for an employer to render union action unlawful under section 17 by the device of creating a 'buffer' organisation (such as an associated employer) between itself and its customers or suppliers, thereby breaking the contractual nexus which was necessary for the first exception to operate[227]. On the other hand, there were those who argued that secondary action should never be protected, and that 'there is no good reason why employers who are not party to a dispute should be at risk of having industrial action organised against them'[228]. In the event the Conservative government were persuaded by

---

224 The union also argued that the court should lift the veil of incorporation unilaterally and declare the two companies to be in effect one and the same, but the House of Lords refused to do so.

225 Now contained in the Trade Union and Labour Relations (Consolidation) Act 1992, s 220. The immunity for picketing is discussed at p 814 below.

226 The section was described by Lord Denning in the Court of Appeal in *Hadmor Productions Ltd v Hamilton* [1981] ICR 690, [1981] IRLR 210, as 'the most tortuous section I have ever come across'; the discussion of s 17 in the Court of Appeal (whose decision was reversed by the House of Lords, [1982] ICR 114, [1982] IRLR 102, HL), is best tactfully forgotten as being, at best, completely wrong and, at worst, incomprehensible.

227 This happened in the dispute between News International and the print unions: Ewing and Napier 'The Wapping dispute and labour law' (1986) 45 CLJ 285.

228 See the Green Paper *Removing Barriers to Employment* (Cm. 655, 1989), para 3.10; ironically, the complexity of s 17 was one of the justifications advanced in the Green Paper for its repeal (para 3.10).

the latter view; the Employment Act 1990 repealed section 17 and replaced it with a far more restrictive provision (now contained in section 224 of the Trade Union and Labour Relations (Consolidation) Act 1992), which removes the statutory immunities in all cases of secondary action[229] other than that occurring in the course of 'lawful picketing'[230] (ie within what was formerly the third exception).

Section 224(2) provides that there is 'secondary action' in relation to a trade dispute when a person:

(a) induces another to break a contract of employment[231] or interferes or induces another to interfere with its performance; or

(b) threatens that a contract of employment under which he or another is employed will be broken or its performance interfered with, or that he will induce another to break a contract of employment or to interfere with its performance,

and the employer under the contract of employment is not the employer party to the dispute.

The gist of the definition is that to be secondary action the action must be directed against an employer *who is not a party to the trade dispute* and, moreover, must involve *interference with the contracts of employment* of that employer. Action which is in fact aimed at the employer in dispute, but which causes loss to that employer's customers or suppliers (ie 'primary action'[232] which has what might be termed secondary *effects*) is not 'secondary action' within the meaning of the section, and the legality of such action will be decided on ordinary principles[233] . One way of evading the restrictions on secondary action might have been for a union which was in dispute with employer A, but which wished to increase the pressure on employer A by taking action against employer B, to create a *fresh* trade dispute with B, and so avoid the potential application of the restrictions on secondary action. However, as seen above, the redrafting of the definition of 'trade dispute' by the Employment Act 1982 made this much more difficult, as the dispute with B would have to 'relate wholly or mainly' to the terms and conditions, etc., of the employees of B; simply acting in sympathy with, or promoting the cause of, A's employees would not be enough to generate a new trade dispute with B, so that the only dispute would be between the union and employer A, and any action against employer B would have to be judged according to section 224[234] .

229 Under s 17, the immunities were only removed where a person had induced a breach of or interfered with the performance of a *commercial* contract (or threatened to do so) by the use of secondary action; under the post-1990 provisions, the immunities are removed from the secondary action *itself*, whether or not that action results in breach or interference with commercial contracts.

230 Defined in s 224(3) as peaceful picketing within the meaning of s 220 by a worker employed (or last employed) by the employer in dispute or by a trade union official lawfully attending the picket line.

231 S. 224(6) adopts a wide definition of 'contract of employment' which includes self-employed and freelance workers, and others who personally do work or perform services for another.

232 As defined in s 224(5).

233 See, for example, *Hadmor Productions Ltd v Hamilton* [1982] ICR 114, [1982] IRLR 102, HL.

234 Note also s 224(4), which provides that for the purposes of the section an employer shall not be treated as party to a dispute between another employer and workers of that employer.

The result of the tightening of the restrictions on secondary action in 1990 is that, even more than before, the scope of lawful industrial action will be determined by the corporate structure of the employer in dispute[235] ; and the refusal of the courts to lift the corporate veil means that action taken against another employer, even one in the same group as (or otherwise closely related to) the employer in dispute will not be covered by the statutory immunities, unless it is possible to identify a separate trade dispute with that employer.

(ii) Unlawful picketing

The second removal of the immunities occurs under section 219(3) of the Trade Union and Labour Relations (Consolidation) Act 1992, which removes all the section 219 immunities from acts done in the course of picketing falling outside the scope of the picketing immunity conferred by section 220[236] . Those whose attendance is not lawful within section 220 enjoy no immunity whatsoever for acts done in the course of picketing. As will be seen, many of the potential liabilities of pickets attract no immunity anyway (for example liability for trespass or nuisance), but picketing activity is also very likely to involve the commission of torts such as inducement of breach of contract and interference with trade or business. Normally such liability would be covered by the immunities in section 219; however, one of the aims of the Employment Act 1980 was to curb secondary picketing and to allow employers affected by it to bring actions to stop it. Accordingly, section 219(3) limits the immunities (in relation to the tortious effects of the picketing) to attendance rendered lawful by the 'narrow but real' immunity in section 220, and section 220(1) confines that picketing immunity to attendance *at or near a picket's own place of work*. The combined effect is that any picketing activity other than at the picket's own place of work which has tortious effects is deprived of the immunities and may be restrained by injunction.

(iii) Action to enforce union membership

In an attempt to ensure that the stringent rules on the closed shop were not outflanked by practical measures designed to produce *de facto* requirements of union membership (in particular the use of 'contract compliance' by Labour-controlled local authorities to pressurise contractors into employing only union labour), the Conservative government introduced in the Employment Act 1982 a series of restrictions on union membership requirements in commercial contracts. Thus, any term or condition of a contract for the supply of goods or services which requires that some or all of the work to be done under that contract should be done only by members of a trade union (or of a particular trade union) is rendered void[237] , and it is unlawful to refuse to deal with a supplier of goods or services (for example, by the termination of a contract or the refusal to accept

---

235　Cf the obvious implications here of the break-up of the public utilities and the creation of NHS trusts.

236　See p 814 below.

237　Trade Union and Labour Relations (Consolidation) Act 1992, s 144. The restriction also applies to a requirement that the work be done by *non*-members of a trade union or of a particular trade union.

tenders or to enter a contract in the first place), on the grounds that the work under the contract would be done by non-union members[238] . Similar restrictions apply to contract terms requiring recognition of a trade union, and to a refusal to deal with a supplier of goods or services on the grounds of non-recognition of trade union[239] . The aim of these measures was to outlaw discrimination against employers employing non-union labour[240] . However, there remained the possibility that unions might seek to attain these goals by taking or threatening to take industrial action against unsympathetic employers, and so the 1982 Act[241] withdrew the statutory immunities from action aimed at inducing an employer to act in contravention of the above restrictions; thus, for example, not only could an excluded tenderer sue the employer for failure to permit him to tender because of his employment of non-union labour, but he could also sue a union that had induced the employer to exclude him[242] .

However, the relevant provisions then go considerably further, beyond issues of contract compliance, because section 222(1) of the Trade Union and Labour Relations (Consolidation) Act 1992 withdraws the immunities where the reason for the industrial action is the fact or belief that a particular employer (a) 'is employing, has employed or might employ a person' who is not a member of a trade union[243] , or (b) 'is failing, has failed or might fail to discriminate against such a person'. This sweeping provision was introduced by the Employment Act 1988 as part of the attack on the closed shop[244] , but while the main target of the 1988 Act was to outlaw industrial action taken in defence of a closed shop, in fact it went a great deal further by removing the immunities from *all* industrial action taken for reasons of non-union membership, irrespective of whether there is a closed shop in operation. By so doing it could be said to have fundamentally altered the boundaries of a lawful trade dispute, by outlawing industrial action on a matter which had previously been regarded as a legitimate basis for a dispute[245] .

---

238 Trade Union and Labour Relations (Consolidation) Act 1992, s 145. Failure to comply will be a breach of statutory duty, actionable at the suit of an aggrieved person.
239 Trade Union and Labour Relations (Consolidation) Act 1992, ss 186 and 187; see p 787 below.
240 Lewis and Simpson 'Disorganising industrial relations' (1982) 11 ILJ 227; Evans and Lewis 'Labour clauses: from voluntarism to regulation' (1988) 17 ILJ 209. Opposition to the use of 'contract compliance' is also reflected in the Local Government Act 1988, s 17, which bans the use of contract compliance by local authorities for the advancement of 'non-commercial' purposes, although s 18 allows a certain measure of contract compliance by authorities seeking to discharge their duties under the Race Relations Act 1976, s 71, to counteract racial discrimination.
241 See now the Trade Union and Labour Relations (Consolidation) Act 1992, s 222(3).
242 The torts of interference with contract or interference with trade or business might be particularly significant here.
243 Whether the person in question is not a member of any trade union or of a particular trade union or of one of a number of particular trade unions: s 222(5).
244 There used to be a similar provision in s 14 of the 1982 Act, but it only applied to action against employer A taken in order to impose a union-labour-only requirement on a *third party*, employer B (by disrupting commercial supplies between A and B). It did not apply to action in support of union membership taken *directly* against B. The provision introduced by the 1988 Act is stronger, in that it outlaws *all* industrial action aimed at establishing or preserving a closed shop, whether taken against A or B.
245 Cf the trade dispute definition in s 244, which still includes in subs. (1)(e) a dispute relating to 'a worker's membership *or non-membership* of a trade union'. See p 774 above.

(iv) Action taken because of the dismissal of unofficial strikers

As one of a series of measures designed to discourage unofficial industrial action, the Employment Act 1990 removed the right of those taking part in such action to complain of unfair dismissal[246]. In a related move, section 223 of the Trade Union and Labour Relations (Consolidation) Act 1992 aims to discourage a collective response to such dismissals by removing the statutory immunities where the reason (or *one* of the reasons) for the industrial action is the fact or belief that an employer has dismissed an employee taking part in unofficial industrial action. This will be the case even where the action in question has the support of a ballot. The result is that any industrial action taken by a union in support of members dismissed for taking part in unofficial action will be unprotected by the statutory immunities.

(v) Pressure to impose union recognition requirements

In parallel with the restrictions on union *membership* requirements discussed above, the Employment Act 1982 introduced a similar set of restrictions on union *recognition* requirements in contracts for the supply of goods or services, and made it unlawful to refuse to deal with a supplier of goods or services on the grounds that the supplier does not or is not likely to recognise, negotiate or consult with a trade union[247]. Section 225 of the Trade Union and Labour Relations (Consolidation) Act 1992[248] removes the statutory immunities from industrial action taken to impose a union recognition requirement, so that action aimed at inducing an employer to breach any of the above restrictions (for example, by inserting a term requiring union recognition in a commercial contract) will be unprotected. That section also withdraws the immunities from industrial action taken against employer A which interferes with the supply of goods or services between that employer and the supplier, employer B (or can reasonably be expected to do so), where the reason or one of the reasons for the action is the fact or belief that the employer B does not or might not recognise, negotiate with or consult with one or more trade unions. This is similar to the restriction in section 222 on industrial action to enforce union membership, but with the important difference that in that context the immunities are withdrawn from *all* action to enforce union membership, whereas here only action aimed at securing recognition, etc., by a *third party* employer is affected.

(vi) Action without the support of a ballot

Unquestionably the most impenetrable part of the labyrinth of legal requirements facing a union organising industrial action is the need to hold a secret ballot before taking official industrial action. Section 226 of the Trade Union and

---

246 See p 753 above, and the Green Paper, *Unofficial Action and the Law*, Cm 821, 1989.
247 See now the Trade Union and Labour Relations (Consolidation) Act 1992, ss 186 and 187.
248 Similar restrictions on the use of industrial pressure to enforce union membership are contained in s 222. See p 785 above.

Labour Relations (Consolidation) Act 1992 provides[249] that the immunities in section 219 do not apply where an act is 'done by a trade union'[250] to induce a person to take part (or continue to take part) in industrial action[251], unless the industrial action has the support of a ballot. Thus, the action could in all other respects be perfectly lawful (ie within the immunities and lawful under heads (i) to (v) above), but be rendered immediately unlawful if there is no ballot, or there is a ballot but it does not meet the detailed statutory requirements[252]. Where the immunities are removed the full weight of the common law liabilities will be restored, and so anyone suffering loss or damage through a tort committed by the union could sue, even ordinary customers or suppliers of the employer in dispute[253]; until 1993, the range of potential claimants was restricted by the (probable) requirement that the defendant must have intended to injure the claimant, but under the 'Citizen's Right' introduced by the Trade Union Reform and Employment Rights Act 1993, a person has the right to seek an injunction restraining unlawful official industrial action where that action affects, or is likely to affect, the supply of goods or services to that person, irrespective of whether that person could bring an action in tort in his or her own right[254].

The balloting provisions were originally introduced in the Trade Union Act 1984, and were further tightened up by the Employment Acts 1988 and 1990 and the Trade Union Reform and Employment Rights Act 1993. By the time of the 1997 General Election it had become clear that the balloting requirements were of such complexity that they presented a major hurdle to a trade union attempting to organise lawful industrial action. The legislation specified (often in byzantine detail) matters such as who was to be entitled to vote in the ballot, what was to be included on the ballot paper, how the ballot was to be conducted, and how the union was to instigate industrial action if the result of the ballot went the union's way. The complexity of the requirements was of particular significance because, as will be seen below, the primary objective of a claimant in an industrial dispute case is usually to secure an injunction to stop the industrial action, and it had become clear that the balloting requirements provided ample scope for the employer's lawyers to argue that there had been some technical infringement which justified the granting of an injunction[255] The incoming Labour government signalled its intention to clarify and simplify the law on industrial action ballots,

---

249 Section 62 of the 1992 Act gives a trade union member the right to a secret ballot before being induced by the union to take official industrial action; the same ballot is capable of satisfying both sets of requirements: see p 724 above.

250 Ie the immunities are removed only from *official* industrial action; see p 818 below. One very important consequence of the extension of the statutory vicarious liability test in 1990 to cover all officials and committees is that *most* industrial action will now be prima facie 'official', and will therefore need the support of a valid ballot if the immunities are to apply.

251 This is not defined for present purposes. For its interpretation in the context of dismissal of those taking part in industrial action, see p 755 above.

252 The mandatory nature of the balloting requirements means that they still apply even if the union physically cannot comply with them; this may be the case with a purely federal union which has no individual members to ballot – according to *Shipping Co Uniform Inc v ITWF* [1985] ICR 245, [1985] IRLR 71 that is irrelevant and the immunities are still removed for failure to ballot.

253 See for example *Falconer v ASLEF and NUR* [1986] IRLR 331 (p 765 above). Since the withdrawal of immunity is so immediate and so total, the only defence a union will have might be that no tort was committed in the first place.

254 Trade Union and Labour Relations (Consolidation) Act 1992, s 235A; see p 826 below.

255 The use of injunctions in industrial cases is considered below at p 822.

which it described as 'unnecessarily complex and rigid'[256], and the Employment Relations Act 1999 subsequently enacted a series of changes to the balloting provisions which appeared to relax the requirements in several important respects[257]. Of particular note was the introduction of an express provision allowing certain small[258] accidental failures in the conduct of the ballot to be disregarded[259], although crucially this dispensation was restricted to certain types of failure (for example in relation to entitlement to vote and the supply of ballot papers)[260]. Another highly significant change related to the information which the union was required to give to the employer. Case law under the pre-1999 provisions had established that in certain circumstances a union might have to supply the employer with the names of those members whom it intended to call upon to take industrial action[261], a controversial ruling which gave rise to understandable concern about the risk of threats and intimidation of the participants. The 1999 Act sought to avoid this possibility by making it clear that a union could not be forced to 'name names' in this way. However, far from of relaxing the requirements, the revised balloting provisions, as interpreted by the courts, appear to impose even greater burdens on unions than had previously been the case[262], and at the time of writing the government was consulting on a further round of revisions in order to redress the balance[263].

The Code of Practice on Industrial Action Ballots and Notice to Employers[264] gives guidance as to 'desirable practices' in relation to industrial action ballots. As with previous government-produced codes, it is a curious (and possibly objectionable) combination of (a) useful advice as to the application of the statutory rules on balloting, on such matters as defining the constituency, the content of voting papers, unlawful interference and accurate counting, and (b) an attempt at back-door legislation, adding requirements and practices which are not to be found in the statute. It is this second function that is open to criticism. Several recommendations of earlier versions of the Code have now found their way into law (for example, those relating to postal balloting and independent scrutiny), but there are still a number of areas in which the Code goes considerably further than the actual statutory requirements. So for example, the Code states that an industrial action ballot should not take place until any agreed procedures which might lead to the resolution of the dispute without the need for industrial action have been completed, or, where no such procedures are available or they have been exhausted, consideration has been given to resolving the dispute by

---

256 *Fairness at Work*, Cm. 3968 (1998), para 4.26.
257 Employment Relations Act 1999, Sch 3.
258 Ie on a scale which is unlikely to affect the result of the ballot.
259 Trade Union and Labour Relations (Consolidation) Act 1992, s 232B. The courts have always had a discretion not to grant an injunction where an infringement is very minor or technical (see eg *RJB Mining (UK) Ltd v National Union of Mineworkers*) [1997] IRLR 621; *British Railways Board v National Union of Railwaymen* [1989] ICR 678, [1989] IRLR 349, CA), but the introduction of an express provision should make the position more certain.
260 The precise extent of the disregard for small accidental failures has been the source of some controversy as a result of an apparent drafting error in s 232B of the 1999 Act: see *P v National Union of Schoolmasters/Union of Women Teachers* [2003] UKHL 8, [2003] 1 All ER 993.
261 *Blackpool and Fylde College v NATFHE* [1994] ICR 648, [1994] IRLR 227,CA; see p 799 below.
262 See eg *London Underground Ltd v National Union of Rail Maritime and Transport Workers* [2001] ICR 647, [2001] IRLR 228, CA (noted by Wedderburn (2001) 30 ILJ 206).
263 *Review of the Employment Relations Act 1999* (DTI, February 2003).
264 Revised in 2000 to reflect the changes made by the 1999 Act and to make the Code 'easier to understand and more concise'.

other means, including seeking assistance from ACAS[265] ; a union should only hold an industrial action ballot if it is contemplating authorising or endorsing industrial action (ie a ballot should not be used for purely tactical purposes), and only if the ballot (if properly conducted) would be capable of protecting the union against legal proceedings for organising the industrial action[266] ; even after a vote in favour of industrial action, the union 'should consider all options other than authorising or endorsing industrial action as a means of resolving the dispute or potential dispute which led to the ballot being held'[267]; and a union should consider delaying any call for industrial action following a ballot until it has obtained the scrutineer's report on the ballot[268] . The legal difficulty is to see how, if at all, these purported extensions to the balloting rules in the Code could have any legal effect, since (although the Code is of course admissible in legal proceedings) the relevant statutory provisions do not require ballots to be 'in accordance with good industrial relations practice', nor do they use phrases such as 'fairness' or 'equity or the substantial merits of the case' which could be used as a legislative peg upon which to hang the Code's suggestions. Instead, they simply lay down detailed requirements for a valid ballot. The result is that either the union satisfies the legal requirements or it does not; failure to comply with one of the Code's extensions (as opposed to its advice as to the interpretation of one of the Act's substantive provisions, for example on defining the constituency) seems to be neither here nor there. To take one example, there appears to be no way that a failure to exhaust agreed procedures (strongly suggested by the Code, but not required by the Act) could possibly render the ballot legally ineffective if it was otherwise properly conducted under the precise requirements of the statutory provisions. Furthermore, the exhortation not to use a ballot for tactical purposes flies in the face of industrial relations experience, which is that a positive ballot result has increasingly come to be seen by unions as an effective way of demonstrating collective strength, thereby improving a union's negotiating position .

(a) Entitlement to vote

Section 227(1) states that 'Entitlement to vote in the ballot must be accorded equally to all the members of the trade union who it is reasonable at the time of the ballot for the union to believe will be induced to take part ... in the industrial action in question, and to no others'[269] . The union must take great care when defining the balloting constituency, for if a member is not accorded entitlement to vote in the ballot and is subsequently induced to take part in the industrial

---

265 Para 8.
266 Para 9. The implication is that a ballot should not be used to determine the level of support among members for industrial action falling outside the statutory immunities (eg secondary action, or action to support an employee dismissed while taking part in industrial action). Sed quaere?
267 Para 58.
268 Para 62. This would be particularly onerous in view of the limited life-span of ballots, and the need to give the employer seven days' notice of the commencement of industrial action.
269 Trade Union and Labour Relations (Consolidation) Act 1992, s 227(1). A failure to comply will not be condoned simply because a union's complex structure makes full compliance difficult: *RJB Mining (UK) Ltd v National Union of Mineworkers* [1997] IRLR 621, QBD.

action, the whole ballot may be invalidated and the immunity lost (subject to the statutory dispensation permitting small accidental failures to be disregarded)[270]. There are two major problems with the interpretation of section 227(1), both of which have given rise to some exceptionally difficult case law: first, what is meant by 'entitlement to vote' and being 'accorded' entitlement to vote? and secondly, when will a union be regarded as having 'induced' a member to take part in the action? On the first issue, it is necessary to distinguish *entitlement* to vote from *opportunity* to vote. Section 227(1) is concerned with the former; it defines the class of members who must be accorded entitlement to vote – the balloting constituency - but it does not require that every member within that class must be given an opportunity of voting. This is of immense practical significance because, as has been judicially recognised, in the real world it will normally be impossible for a union to compile an accurate list of all its members within a particular balloting constituency: '... it is a fact of life that no trade union of any size can keep completely full and accurate records of the names and addresses of its ever-changing body of members, still less their current places of work, trade categories and pay grades.'[271] A union is required by law to maintain a register of members' names and addresses, and so far as is reasonably practicable to keep it accurate and up-to-date[272], but the union's record-keeping duty does not extend to the occupations, grades or workplaces of its members, nor is there any duty on members to inform the union when they change jobs or move house. In practice, therefore, it is very likely that some members who are within the balloting constituency may not be given an opportunity to vote - for example because the union's records are inaccurate, or because mistakes occur during the ballot process (such as ballot papers getting lost in the post), or because members change jobs or indeed join or leave the union during the balloting process. Such failures do not necessarily mean that those members were not accorded entitlement to vote within the meaning of section 227(1). As the House of Lords has confirmed, whether or not such failures invalidate the ballot must be determined by applying the other provisions of the Act, including section 230(2) (which states that 'so far as is reasonably practicable, every person who is entitled to vote in the ballot must ... be given a convenient opportunity to vote by post') and section 232B (which makes both sections 227(1) and 230(2) subject to a dispensation for small accidental errors): 'If failure to send a ballot paper to a person within the constituency falls within either of these exceptions, he is not by reason of that failure to be treated as having not been accorded entitlement to vote.'[273]

Even before the introduction of the dispensation for small accidental failures in 1999, it had been recognised that it would be unrealistic to expect a union to achieve total compliance by supplying a ballot paper to every single member of the balloting constituency. In one of the earliest cases on the strike ballot provisions, the Court of Appeal held that an inadvertent failure to give someone the opportunity of voting did not necessarily constitute an infringement of the

270 Trade Union and Labour Relations (Consolidation) Act 1992, s 232B.
271 *P v National Union of Schoolmasters/Union of Women Teachers* [2003] UKHL 8, [2003] 1 All ER 993, per Lord Walker at [65].
272 Trade Union and Labour Relations (Consolidation) Act 1992, s 24; see p 723 above.
273 *P v National Union of Schoolmasters/Union of Women Teachers* [2003] UKHL 8, [2003] 1 All ER 993, per Lord Hoffmann at [44].

balloting requirements[274], and the House of Lords has recently confirmed in *P v National Union of Schoolmasters/Union of Women Teachers*[275] that, despite the changes in the wording of the balloting provisions in 1999[276], the position remains the same. That case involved a point which has caused difficulty ever since the balloting provisions were first introduced: what is the position of new employees who did not start working for the employer, or working within the balloting constituency, until after the ballot? And what of new members who did not join the union until after the ballot? Can they be induced to take part in the industrial action? In *Post Office v Union of Communication Workers*[277], Lord Donaldson suggested obiter that, de minimis apart, any call for industrial action should be limited to those who were employed by the employer and given an opportunity of voting at the time of the ballot, but this dictum was disapproved by the Court of Appeal in *London Underground v RMT*[278], where the issue was whether the statutory immunities were lost because some 692 members who had joined the union since the date of the ballot were called upon to take part in the industrial action. The Court of Appeal held that the industrial action still had the support of a ballot: 'The union is required to ballot those, *and only those*, of *its members* who *at the time of the ballot* it is reasonable to believe will be called upon to take part in the industrial action. It cannot identify future members, but even if it could it must not ballot them, since the ballot is confined to persons who were members at the time of the ballot'[279]. But what of existing union members who were not working for the employer in dispute at the time of the ballot? Could they also be called upon to take part in the action? On one analysis, the logic of the decision in *London Underground v RMT* applied equally to such members, since it would not have been reasonable *at the time of the ballot* for the union to believe that those members would be called upon to take part in the action, in view of the fact that they were not employed by the employer in dispute at that time. Against that, however, section 227(2) used to state that section 227(1) was not satisfied 'if any person who was a member of the trade union at the time when the ballot was held was denied entitlement to vote in the ballot', which put the matter in doubt. In an attempt to clarify the position, the Employment Relations Act 1999 replaced section 227(2) with new section 232A, which was intended[280] to make clear that a union *can* in appropriate circumstances call upon a new employee who was a member of the union at the time of the ballot to take part in the industrial action. Section 232A states that

---

274 *British Railways Board v National Union of Railwaymen* [1989] ICR 678, [1989] IRLR 349, CA.

275 [2003] UKHL 8, [2003] 1 All ER 993.

276 Before 1999, s 227(2) stated that the balloting requirements were not satisfied if a member who was induced to take part in the action was 'denied' entitlement to vote. That provision was replaced by s 232A, which used the expression 'not accorded' in place of 'denied'. The House of Lords confirmed in *P v NASUWT* that the change in wording was not intended to mark a significant change of effect (a particularly significant finding in view of the fact that the dispensation for small accidental failures does not apply to s 232A: see p 793).

277 [1990] IRLR 143, CA.

278 [1995] IRLR 636, CA. Millett LJ also stated, obiter, that nothing in the statutory balloting provisions curtails a union's right to induce *non-members* to support industrial action called by the union, as those provisions are concerned exclusively with the relationship between the union and its members, and are intended for the protection of members, not the protection of the employer or the public.

279 [1995] IRLR 636 at 639. Millett LJ's emphasis.

280 See the Explanatory Notes to the Employment Relations Act 1999, para 137.

industrial action will not be regarded as having the support of the ballot if a person (a) was a member of the union at the time when the ballot was held; (b) it was reasonable at that time for the union to believe that he would be induced to take part in the industrial action; (c) he was not accorded entitlement to vote in the ballot; and (d) he was induced by the union to take part in the industrial action.

Unfortunately, section 232A gave rise to a whole new set of interpretative problems, as was shown in *P v National Union of Schoolmasters/Union of Women Teachers*[281]. In that case the union had organised a ballot of its members at a school in connection with a dispute over the expulsion and subsequent reinstatement of an allegedly disruptive pupil. One of the questions before the court was whether the ballot was invalidated because the union had failed to send ballot papers to two of its members who had recently moved to the school, and of whose existence the union only became aware after the ballot papers had been sent out but before the completion of the ballot process. At first blush this might seem like just the type of situation in which the union could expect to be exonerated by the dispensation for small accidental errors not affecting the result of the ballot in section 232B (not least because, of the thirty members balloted, twenty-six had voted in favour of industrial action, and none against), but crucially, section 232A is not one of the provisions listed in section 232B[282]. In a landmark ruling which shed some much-needed light on the complex relationship between the various statutory provisions, the House of Lords emphasised the importance of distinguishing between section 227(1), which defines who must be accorded entitlement to vote, and the other provisions of the Act, which define what counts as being accorded entitlement to vote[283]: 'In my opinion, compliance with [those] provisions in respect of the constituency identified by section 227(1) means that the members of that constituency have been accorded entitlement to vote. In the case of the distribution of ballot papers, section 230(2) makes those requirements subject to the proviso of reasonable practicability and section 232B makes both sections 227(1) and 230(2) subject to the disregard of small accidental errors. If failure to send a ballot paper to a person within the constituency falls within either of those exceptions, he is not by reason of that failure to be treated as having not been accorded entitlement to vote.'[284] Crucially, their Lordships rejected the argument that the use of the expression 'not accorded' in section 232A(c) in place of 'denied' was intended to mark a significant change of effect[285], even though this interpretation of section 232A seemed to mean that Parliament had enacted superfluous legislation, Lord Hoffmann remarking dryly that 'it would not be the first time. It is certainly more likely than that Parliament intended, at one and the same time, by section 232B to create a proviso for some accidental errors and by section 232A to deprive the union of protection from liability in the

---

281 [2003] UKHL 8, [2003] 1 All ER 993.
282 Morison J at first instance had inferred that the reference in s 232B to s 230(2A) (which makes no sense) was intended to be a reference to s 232A, because when spoken both sound the same, but the House of Lords agreed with the Court of Appeal that the reference in s 232B should have been, not to s 230(2A), but to s 230(2B) (voting by merchant seamen).
283 Or, as Lord Walker helpfully put it at [68], between entitlement to vote and opportunity to vote.
284 [2003] UKHL 8, [2003] 1 All ER 993, per Lord Hoffmann at [44].
285 'I do not think that the concept of being accorded entitlement to vote in section 232A(c) was intended to mean something different from what it meant in section 227 before the [1999 Act]': per Lord Hoffmann, at [45]; similarly Lord Walker at [72].

case of the accidental error most likely to occur, namely an omission to include a member in the ballot paper mailing list.'[286]

The second issue arising from section 227(1) is that the extent of the balloting constituency is defined in terms of the members who it is reasonable for the union to believe will be 'induced' to take part in the industrial action. The problem here is that, as interpreted by the courts, the concept of inducement is objective. The fact that the union did not subjectively intend to call upon a specific member to take part in the action is beside the point. The union may therefore have to extend the entitlement to vote to those of its members who may in fact be induced to take part in the action, even if the union did not intend them to take part. This controversial point was established in *National Union of Rail, Maritime and Transport Workers v Midland Mainline*[287], where the Court of Appeal held that the correct approach under section 227(1) is to ask, first, who did the union at the time of the ballot believe would be induced to take part in the industrial action; and secondly, was such a belief a reasonable one on the part of the union? In that case, the union had balloted 91 members of Midland Mainline's 'operational train crew' in connection with a dispute about their safety responsibilities. The ballot produced a small majority in favour of industrial action[288]. After the ballot it was discovered that twenty-five members employed as operational train crew had not received ballot papers. They included eleven members of whose employment the union was unaware because it had not received or recorded information about their joining those grades, ten members who were excluded from the ballot (in accordance with union policy) because they were believed to be in arrears with their union subscriptions, three members whose ballot papers were sent to the wrong addresses, and one member who was not sent a ballot paper due to an administrative error. The Court of Appeal held that while the latter two categories fell within the dispensation for small accidental failures, the first two categories did not, and that as the members in those categories were likely to be induced to take part in the industrial action, the ballot did not comply with the statutory requirements. Schiemann LJ, giving the judgment of the court, considered that the union's expectation that the operational train crew who it wished to take part in the industrial action would in fact take part when called upon to do so 'should in our judgment extend to at least some of those members of the designated class who have not received the ballot papers', because 'it is overwhelmingly probable that there will be some who are induced to take industrial action by their own feelings that this is appropriate'.[289] Moreover, even among those who would (given the chance) have voted against the strike, there would be some who would take industrial action because their colleagues would expect them to. In other words, the fact that the union did not intend to ask those members who had not received ballot papers to take part in the industrial action was beside the point; the test was whether the union reasonably believed that they would be induced to take part, and in the court's view it was not reasonable for the union to believe that all those unballoted members would not take part: 'the intention of the union is not

286 [2003] UKHL 8, [2003] 1 All ER 993 at [45].
287 [2001] EWCA Civ 1206, [2001] IRLR 813.
288 25 voted in favour of strike action, 17 against, and 49 did not vote.
289 [2001] EWCA Civ 1206, [2001] IRLR 813 at 816.

conclusive of who is entitled to vote in the ballot.'[290] As Simpson[291] has commented: 'Perhaps the most remarkable implication of this extraordinary piece of backwards reasoning is that a ballot will be defective[292] in any case where a union has members who have not been balloted but who will feel induced either by their own feelings or the expectations of their colleagues to join in any action that is called. How a union is expected to know precisely who these members are is not clear.'

The expansive approach to the balloting constituency taken in *Midland Mainline* places a heavy onus on a trade union to keep its membership records up-to-date. It was argued on behalf of the union in that case that the test of whether it was reasonably practicable for the union to supply ballot papers to members within the balloting constituency must be assessed in the light of the facts as they were on the day that the ballot papers were sent out, ie in the light of the information available to the union at that time. The Court of Appeal rejected that reading: 'It can not have been intended that a ballot will be regarded as having been properly conducted if the union does not properly record changes of address notified to it. Where, on the other hand, the union has a system for reminding members of the need to keep the union notified of any changes of addresses but a member fails to notify the union of such a change and the union is in fact ignorant of that change of address and sends a ballot paper to the old address then a court would probably find that the union will have done all that is reasonably practicable.'[293]

Finally, the Employment Act 1988 added a further refinement to the rules on the balloting constituency by introducing a requirement of separate workplace ballots[294] where a union wishes to organise industrial action at more than one place of work, the aim apparently being to prevent a union from manipulating the outcome of a ballot by creating 'artificial' balloting constituencies, combining different (and perhaps unrelated) groups of workers together so as to ensure an overall vote in favour of industrial action. As an insistence on separate workplace ballots in every case would have been a recipe for industrial relations chaos, the 1988 Act permitted a union to hold one aggregated ballot across several workplaces where those to be balloted had some particular factor in common. The separate workplace ballot provisions, heavily criticised at the outset for their complexity, were revised in 1999 in the interests of greater clarity and simplicity (although it must be said that at first sight the redrafted provisions do not appear to have achieved either objective). It is now provided that a union may hold an

---

290 At [44]. The notice instructing members to strike was sent only to those members who had previously been balloted, but according to Schiemann LJ (at [40]): 'it is clear that those who had not received the notice, being RMT members and operational train crew, would be likely to be induced to take part in the action.'

291 (2002) 31 ILJ 270.

292 Subject to the dispensation for small accidental failures, discussed above.

293 [2001] EWCA Civ 1206, [2001] IRLR 813, at para 21. The Court of Appeal suggested (at para 45) that a possible way forward for a union which is unable to identify all the members whom it wishes to take part in industrial action is to approach ACAS to carry out a confidential membership check, to confirm that all relevant members have in fact received ballot papers. This is a sensible suggestion, although there is no legal duty on the employer to co-operate in such a process.

294 See now the Trade Union and Labour Relations (Consolidation) Act 1992, ss 228 and 228A, as substituted by the Employment Relations Act 1999, Sch 3.

aggregated ballot across more than one workplace[295] if one of the following is satisfied: (a) where each workplace concerned is the workplace of at least one member of the union who is 'affected by the dispute'[296]; (b) where the union reasonably believes that it is balloting all its members of a particular occupational description (or descriptions) who are employed by an employer (or employers) with whom the union is in dispute; or (c) where the union reasonably believes that it is balloting all its members who are employed by an employer (or employers) with whom the union is in dispute.

(b) The voting paper

The content of the voting paper is specified in great detail. There are four requirements: first, the voting paper must contain at least one of the two 'statutory questions', asking the voter to say, by answering 'yes' or 'no', whether he is prepared to take part in a 'strike', or in 'industrial action short of a strike'[297]. If the union contemplates taking both types of action these two questions must be put separately, and separate approval must be obtained for each type of action[298]. In *West Midlands Travel Ltd v TGWU*[299], the employers argued that where separate questions are put, the union must obtain a majority approval of all those who had participated in the voting process, including those who had abstained, and not just a simple majority in respect of each individual question on the ballot paper[300]; however, the Court of Appeal sensibly held that where separate questions are posed, one relating to strike action and the other to industrial action short of a strike, each question must be regarded as a separate matter to be voted on individually, and the result of the ballot in respect of each question must be considered separately. There is no express requirement that the voting paper must identify the subject-matter of the dispute, or that the dispute so identified must fall within the trade dispute definition, but the courts have nevertheless been prepared to hold that a ballot is invalid if it covers a non-trade dispute

---

295 For these purposes, 'workplace' means, if the person works at or from a single set of premises, those premises, and in any other case, the premises with which the person's employment has the closest connection: s 228(4). On the original (narrower) definition, which defined the place of work in terms of the premises 'occupied' by the employer, see *InterCity West Coast Ltd v RMT* [1996] IRLR 583. Under the pre-1999 provisions, it was held that the freedom to hold an aggregate ballot was not confined to situations where the different workplaces all belonged to the same employer (see *University of Central England v NALGO* [1993] IRLR 81), and this is believed still to be the case.

296 A member will be 'affected by a dispute' if, eg, the dispute relates wholly or partly to a decision of the employer over a trade dispute matter, and the member is directly affected by that decision: s 228A(5).

297 Trade Union and Labour Relations (Consolidation) Act 1992, s 229(2). Overtime bans and call-out bans are to be treated as industrial action short of a strike for these purposes: Trade Union and Labour Relations (Consolidation) Act 1992, s 229(2A), inserted by the Employment Relations Act 1999, Sch 3 (reversing the effect of *Connex South Eastern Ltd v RMT* [1999] IRLR 249, CA).

298 *Post Office v Union of Communication Workers* [1990] ICR 258, [1990] IRLR 143, CA.

299 [1994] ICR 978, [1994] IRLR 578, CA.

300 The wording of the statute is certainly ambiguous, in that s 226(2) provides that 'the majority voting in [the] ballot' must have answered the relevant question affirmatively.

matter[301]. Secondly, the voting paper must contain a statement (a type of government health warning?) informing members that industrial action may be unlawful. The statement was amended in 1999 to include information about the new protection against unfair dismissal during the protected period; it now reads as follows: 'If you take part in a strike or other industrial action, you may be in breach of your contract of employment. However, if you are dismissed for taking part in strike or other industrial action which is called officially and is otherwise lawful, the dismissal will be unfair if it takes place fewer than eight weeks after you started taking part in the action, and depending on the circumstances may be unfair if it takes place later.' This statement may not be qualified or commented on by anything else on the ballot paper[302], even if it is clear that the action in question does not involve a breach of contract (as, for example, in the case of withdrawal from voluntary overtime[303]). Thirdly, the voting paper must identify the person or persons authorised by the union to call upon members to take part in industrial action in the event of a vote in favour (a requirement introduced by the Employment Act 1990 to prevent union officials from jumping the gun unauthorisedly by calling on members to take industrial action before the leadership has give the go-ahead to do so – see below). Finally, the voting paper must give the name of the independent scrutineer[304]. If any of these requirements is omitted the industrial action will not be regarded as having the support of a ballot, and the statutory immunities will be withdrawn. To facilitate a challenge on the ground of a defective ballot, a union is required to provide the employers of those entitled to vote in the ballot with a sample voting paper at least three days before the start of the ballot[305].

(c) Conduct of the ballot

Until 1993 the requirements of a valid industrial action ballot differed significantly from those which applied to union elections and political fund ballots[306], for while ballots for either of those purposes have, since the Employment Act 1988, been required to be fully postal (ie ballot papers delivered and returned by post) and subject to independent scrutiny, a strike ballot could be held at the workplace[307]

---

301 See eg *London Underground v National Union of Railwaymen* [1989] IRLR 341 (noted by Simpson (1989) 18 ILJ 234), where it was held that several issues may not be rolled up in one single question where there are doubts over whether some of those issues are in fact the subject of a trade dispute, and *University College London Hospitals NHS Trust v UNISON* [1999] ICR 204 (noted by Simpson (2002) 31 ILJ 270), where Lord Woolf held that the ballot failed to meet the statutory requirements because it referred to an issue which was not a trade dispute.
302 There does not appear to be anything to prevent a union from commenting on the statement in material enclosed with the voting paper, provided nothing appears on the voting paper itself.
303 *Power Packing Casemakers Ltd v Faust* [1983] ICR 292, [1983] IRLR 117, CA; see p 750 above.
304 A requirement added by the Trade Union Reform and Employment Rights Act 1993, s 20(2).
305 Trade Union and Labour Relations (Consolidation) Act 1992, s 226A(1). As a result of the 1999 Act, a union is now only required to send a sample of those voting papers which are to be sent to employees employed by that employer, not those which are to be sent only to the employees of other employers.
306 See pp 720 and 733 respectively.
307 Although until its revision in 1995, the Code of Practice on Trade Union Ballots on Industrial Action recommended that fully postal balloting 'should be the preferred choice' (para 20).

and was not subject to independent scrutiny. However, the requirements of postal balloting and independent scrutiny[308] were finally extended to industrial action ballots in 1993[309] . In retrospect it was perhaps surprising that workplace strike ballots survived for as long as they did, given the previous government's well-known antipathy towards that practice. One of the reasons for their retention was the recognition that postal ballots take time to organise, and so might be inappropriate in an industrial action ballot where speed of response is often of the essence. There is also evidence to suggest that workplace balloting achieves a higher rate of participation than postal balloting[310] . However, by 1993 the government had been persuaded that fully postal voting was less susceptible to malpractice than other forms of balloting and provided the best security against interference and intimidation, and the extension of postal balloting to industrial action ballots became inevitable. There was pressure for an exception to be made in the case of ballots involving relatively few employees (the Green Paper which proposed the extension of postal balloting would not have required a postal ballot where no more than 50 members were involved[311]), but the 1993 Act made no such exception[312] .

Members must be allowed to vote without interference from the union (although interference from other quarters will not invalidate the ballot), and, so far as reasonably practicable, the voting must be secret and at no direct cost to those voting[313]. Votes must be fairly and accurately counted (although accidental errors may be disregarded if incapable of affecting the result), and the detailed results must be made known both to those voting and to their employers as soon as reasonably practicable after the holding of the ballot[314].

One particularly controversial requirement, introduced in 1993, is the need for a union to give the employers of those entitled to vote in the ballot at least seven days' notice in writing of the date of the ballot[315] , the apparent aim being to give employers the opportunity to take action to minimise the disruptive effects of the industrial action, and to put the case against industrial action to their employees in advance of the ballot. As originally drafted, the ballot notice had to

---

308 Independent scrutiny is not required in the case of a ballot involving no more than 50 members: s 226(2)(c). On independent scrutiny generally, see p 723 above.

309 Trade Union Reform and Employment Rights Act 1993, ss 17 and 20 amending the Trade Union and Labour Relations (Consolidation) Act 1992, s 230 (postal ballots) and inserting new ss 226B and 231B (independent scrutiny). Significantly, the 1993 Act repealed the provisions whereby unions could claim government funding for postal ballots (see p 712 above).

310 See generally Undy and Martin *Ballots and Trade Union Democracy* (1984), and Leopold (1986) Ind Rels J 287.

311 *Industrial Relations in the 1990s* (Cm. 1602, 1991). See n 308 above.

312 The only exception is for merchant seamen at sea or at a foreign port for some or all of the balloting period, who are allowed to vote on board ship or at the place where the ship is, where it is convenient for them to vote in this way: s 230(2A), as amended by the Employment Relations Act 1999, Sch 3.

313 Trade Union and Labour Relations (Consolidation) Act 1992, s 230. This means that the union must pay the postage (eg by providing pre-paid envelopes).

314 Trade Union and Labour Relations (Consolidation) Act 1992, ss 231 and 231A. As a result of the 1999 Act, the failure to inform some employers of the result of the ballot will no longer invalidate the whole ballot, but will merely result in the removal of the statutory immunities in relation to those employers: s 226(3A), as amended by the Employment Relations Act 1999, Sch 3.

315 Trade Union and Labour Relations (Consolidation) Act 1992, s 226A, as amended by the Employment Relations Act 1999, Sch 3. Unions must also give notice to employers before taking industrial action: see p 802.

describe the employees to be balloted so that the employer could 'readily ascertain them'. In the first case on the notice provisions to come before the courts, *Blackpool and Fylde College v NATFHE*[316] , the Court of Appeal controversially held that the union had to supply the employer with the names of those to be balloted in order to satisfy its statutory duty (this despite an assurance from the Minister during the passage of the 1993 Act that he could 'envisage no circumstances' in which it would be necessary for the union to 'name names'[317]). The incoming Labour government gave notice of its intention to change the law to reverse the effect of this decision[318] , and the law as amended in 1999 requires the ballot notice to contain 'such information in the union's possession as would help the employer to make plans[319] and bring information to the attention of those of his employees who it is reasonable for the union to believe...will be entitled to vote in the ballot'[320] ; in particular, where the union has 'information as to the number, category or work-place of the employees concerned, a notice must contain that information (at least)'. The redrafted provisions expressly state that the fact that the notice does not contain the names of any of the employees to be balloted is not a ground for holding that the notice requirements have not been met[321].

Any hopes that these changes would remove controversy from this area of the law were dashed by the early case law on the redrafted provisions, which revealed that the 1999 reforms had, if anything, made the notice requirements even more difficult for unions to comply with. In *London Underground Ltd v National Union of Rail, Maritime and Transport Workers*[322], the union had written to the employer stating that it intended to ballot all its members employed by London Underground 'in all categories and at all workplaces', and giving the overall number of union members as 'approximately 4,938'. The Court of Appeal held that the union had not complied with the notice provisions as it had failed to include information which was in its possession as to the numbers, categories and workplaces of the workers concerned[323]. Crucially, the court held that membership information would be regarded as being in the possession of the union if it was held by union officials (including branch secretaries) who were concerned with maintaining

---

316 [1994] ICR 648, [1994] IRLR 227, CA. The union had notified the college that it intended to ballot 'all our members in your institution', but the Court of Appeal held that this was insufficiently precise to enable the employer readily to ascertain the employees involved, because they did not know which employees were in fact members of the union. The move away from the check-off of union subscriptions from pay has increased employer uncertainty over levels of union membership: see p 726 above.

317 *Hansard*, House of Commons, Standing Committee F, 15 December 1992, col. 247, thus allaying fears over the risk of employer interference with the ballot and possible intimidation of voters.

318 Cm. 3968 (1998), para 4.27.

319 E.g. 'to help the employer to minimise the adverse effects of possible industrial action on his organisation, on his customers and on the general public' (Minister of State, *Hansard*, House of Lords, 16 June 1999, col 299).

320 Trade Union and Labour Relations (Consolidation) Act 1992, s 226A(2)(c), as amended by the Employment Relations Act 1999, Sch 3.

321 Trade Union and Labour Relations (Consolidation) Act 1992, s 226(3A).

322 [2001] IRLR 228, CA. The only judgment was given by Robert Walker LJ. (Cf Wedderburn (2000) 30 ILJ 206).

323 This was said to be the "irreducible minimum of information" to be produced. There might be 'special circumstances' in which a union would have to do more, eg "cases where the employees were concerned with specialised and potentially dangerous infrastructure or plant, or with the care of humans or animals, or with matters of national security or commercial confidentiality." ([2001] IRLR 228 at para 49).

union records[324]. The fact that the information so held might be out-of-date, inaccurate, incomplete, or difficult to collate and produce is, it seems, beside the point: 'Unless the information which the union possesses is actually misinformation . . . then the union is obliged to include it, as an irreducible statutory minimum, in the notice.'[325] The Court of Appeal gave short shrift to the argument that the 1999 changes were intended to reduce the burdens on trade unions: 'Parliament altered the legislation by the 1999 Act so as to make plain that a union could not be compelled to provide a list of names . . . [b]ut there was not any significant change in the legislative policy or in the purpose for which information was to be given to the employer. The change was a change of means, not of objective, in order to meet the concerns of those members of a union who objected to being included in a list of names. It was not intended to make it easier for a union to prepare notices . . . and indeed it is clear from the facts of this case that it may make the task more onerous.'[326] The Court of Appeal's decision in *London Underground* shows that where a union does 'possess' such information, even if only in the hands of local officials, the union may have to collate that information and provide it to the employer if it is to maintain the right to organise lawful industrial action. When viewed together with some of the other decisions on the post-1999 provisions (for example *Midland Mainline*, discussed above), this decision shows that the 1999 changes, far from simplifying and clarifying the law in this area, in fact significantly increased the burdens on trade unions, particularly in relation to the maintenance of membership records[327]. At the time of writing, the government was consulting on further changes to the law on pre-ballot and pre-strike notices, aimed at reducing the administrative burdens on unions[328], including (i) simplifying the minimum informational requirement to avoid the need to supply detailed matrices, and replacing it with a requirement to identify the *total* number of employees involved and to list the categories and workplaces affected; (ii) defining the meaning of information 'in the union's possession' as only including information stored at national and regional union offices; (iii) redefining the purposes for which the information is provided by replacing the 'making plans' element with a more precise formulation; and (iv) introducing a dispensation for small accidental failures to follow the law where they are on a scale which would not significantly reduce the practical help provided through the notices to the employer.

(d) The calling of industrial action

Where there has been a vote in favour of industrial action, that action must commence before the ballot ceases to be effective (ie before it reaches its statutory

---

324 The Court of Appeal refused to rule out the possibility that there might be be 'exceptional' cases where the range of information possessed by the union might be held to include information known only to those who were not union officials (at para 58).

325 [2001] IRLR 228 at para 48. Unions have a duty under the Trade Union and Labour Relations (Consolidation) Act 1992, s 24, to maintain a register of members' names and addresses (see p 723 above), but this does not extend to information concerning the grades or workplaces of their members.

326 [2001] IRLR 228 at para 46.

327 If a union is still collecting subscriptions via employer check-off from salary, it may be sufficient for the union merely to state that it intends to ballot all those who are paying subscriptions via that method, as the employer will have access to the relevant information via the payroll: see eg *Westminster City Council v UNISON* [2001] EWCA Civ 443, [2001] ICR 1046.

328 *Review of the Employment Relations Act 1999* (DTI, February 2003).

'sell-by' date), otherwise the union will have to go through the whole process again[329] . An industrial action ballot normally ceases to be effective at the end of four weeks from the date of the ballot[330] , but sensibly the Employment Relations Act 1999 amended the law to enable the employer and the union to agree an extension of up to four more weeks, thereby reducing pressure on a union to commence industrial action simply to prevent the ballot from becoming ineffective in circumstances where further negotiations might enable the parties to reach an agreement[331] . In *Monsanto plc v TGWU*[332] , the Court of Appeal held that, provided the industrial action commences within the statutory time-limit, it may continue beyond that point, even if the union lifts the action during negotiations but then reimposes it if the negotiations prove unsuccessful, provided the dispute continues to be the same dispute as that in respect of which the original ballot was held.

Any strike call by the union in advance of the ballot will normally be fatal[333] ; however, in determining whether there has been a 'call' by the union, the statutory test of vicarious liability applies[334] . This means that an unauthorised and unballoted call by, for example, a shop steward, will now be regarded as a call *by the union*, and the resulting action will consequently be denied the protection of the statutory immunities. The only way in which the union might avoid liability in such a case would be to repudiate the unauthorised call[335], but by doing so it exposes those who continue to take part in the action to the risk of selective dismissal[336]. To add to the complication, the Employment Act 1990 introduced the requirement that industrial action be called by a 'specified person'[337] (ie a person specified by the union on the voting paper), to prevent local officials unauthorisedly 'jumping the gun' by calling on members to take industrial action without waiting for the union leadership to decide whether or not to implement the ballot decision. If action is called by someone *other* than a specified person, that action will not be regarded as having the support of a ballot, even where there is a clear vote in favour of the action and all the other statutory requirements are satisfied. There are, however, signs that this requirement will be interpreted flexibly, and that some limited degree of delegation may be acceptable; in *Tanks*

---

329 Trade Union and Labour Relations (Consolidation) Act 1992, s 233(3)(b); 234(1).

330 See *RJB Mining (UK) Ltd v National Union of Mineworkers* [1995] IRLR 556, CA.

331 Trade Union and Labour Relations (Consolidation) Act 1992, s 234(1), as amended by the Employment Relations Act 1999, Sch 3; there is also a discretion in the court to extend the time-limit up to a maximum of 12 weeks from the date of the ballot where the union has been prohibited from calling or organising industrial action by a court order or an undertaking given to the court, and that order or undertaking has subsequently lapsed: s 234(2).

332 [1987] ICR 269, [1986] IRLR 406, CA. But cf *Post Office v Union of Communication Workers* [1990] ICR 258, [1990] IRLR 143, CA, where it was stated, obiter, that the action must continue without substantial interruption, so that a gap of nine months was considered too long; see also *Secretary of State for Scotland v Scottish Prison Officers' Association* [1991] IRLR 371 Ct of Sess.

333 Trade Union and Labour Relations (Consolidation) Act 1992, s 233(3)(a). The prohibition on calling for industrial action before the date of the ballot is not infringed by a union recommendation to its members to vote in favour of industrial action: *Newham London Borough Council v NALGO* [1993] ICR 189, [1993] IRLR 83, CA.

334 Trade Union and Labour Relations (Consolidation) Act 1992, s 20. See p 818 below.

335 Trade Union and Labour Relations (Consolidation) Act 1992, s 21. See p 820 below.

336 Trade Union and Labour Relations (Consolidation) Act 1992, s 237. See p 753 above.

337 Trade Union and Labour Relations (Consolidation) Act 1992, s 233(1). The union can decide whom to specify, but the person (or description of persons) specified must come within the list of those for whom the union is deemed responsible under s 20 (see p 818 below).

and Drums Ltd v TGWU[338] , the Court of Appeal held that the section was satisfied where the specified person, the union's general secretary, authorised a district official to implement the industrial action if further negotiations with the employer the following day were not successful. Neill LJ stated that:

'in the field of industrial relations it would be impracticable to leave matters in such a way that there was no possibility for the exercise of judgment on the ground. Some matters must be left for the judgment of those on the ground who have to decide how and when as a matter of common sense the call for action is to be put into operation.'

However, Neill LJ also considered that a blanket delegation of authority to a local official would not be acceptable, and stressed the need for 'a close link in time between the call for the strike and the event, for example, an unsuccessful meeting which precipitates the final action'.

(vii) Notice of industrial action for employers

One of the most controversial of the reforms introduced by the Trade Union Reform and Employment Rights Act 1993 was the requirement for unions to give employers at least seven days' notice of official industrial action[339] . Apparently prompted by the disruption caused by random strikes in the public services (in particular a series of one-day strikes on the London Underground in 1989), the notice requirements apply to all types of industrial action, and across all sectors of employment. The notice must be in writing, must contain 'such information[340] in the union's possession as would help the employer to make plans and bring information to the attention of ...' the 'affected employees'[341] , and must state whether industrial action is intended to be continuous or discontinuous. If the action is to be continuous, the notice must state when it is to start; if intended to be discontinuous (ie if the union does not intend to take action on all the days on which it could do so), the notice must specify the particular *dates* on which it is to take place. The result is that unions are no longer able to use the threat of random, discontinuous action to bring pressure to bear on employers, although there is still some potential for disruption in that, having given notice of the dates on which it intends the discontinuous action to take place, the union does not then have to call for that action to take place on all (or indeed any) of those dates. One potentially unfortunate consequence of the notice requirements in their original form was that where continuous industrial action was suspended, for example to allow further negotiations to take place, the union was required to give a further seven days' notice before resuming the action, which could act as a disincentive to attempts at negotiation during the action. The provisions were therefore amended in 1999 so that where the industrial action has been suspended by joint agreement between the employer and the union, the action

338 [1992] ICR 1, [1991] IRLR 372, CA.
339 Trade Union and Labour Relations (Consolidation) Act 1992, s 234A, as amended by the Employment Relations Act 1999, Sch 3.
340 The same test applies here as in pre-ballot notices: see p 799 above.
341 Ie the employees of the employer whom the union intends to induce or has induced to take part, or continue to take part, in the industrial action: s 234A(3).

can be resumed after an agreed date ('the resumption date') without the need for the union to issue a fresh notice[342].

The earliest date that notice may be given is the day on which the employer is informed of the result of the ballot[343]. Given that a strike ballot normally only remains valid for four weeks *from the date of the ballot* (ie from the last day of voting), a further delay of seven days after disclosure of the results means that the 'window of opportunity' within which the ballot may be implemented is considerably shortened[344]. If the union fails to give the required notice the statutory immunities are withdrawn, but only as respects the employer of a person who is induced to take part in the action[345].

5 POTENTIAL CRIMINAL LIABILITY

As seen in the introduction to this chapter, criminal law does not play any significant role in the regulation of industrial action, outside the specialised law relating to picketing, and the application of the ordinary laws relating to violence and public order if a dispute gives rise to violence and disruption. Those matters are considered in the next section. Before turning to that, however, there are two contexts in which, in exceptional cases, there might be criminal liability. The first arises where employees occupy their employer's premises, for example by way of a sit-in or work-in. In civil law they become trespassers when they refuse to leave, and the employer may take civil action to regain possession of his factory[346]. However, English law has always been wary of imposing criminal sanctions for trespass, a position strengthened by the Criminal Law Act 1977, which provided that it could not be a criminal conspiracy for people to agree to commit an act which was merely tortious, such as trespass[347]. At the same time, Part II of that Act created several new trespass offences which could conceivably be committed by workers engaged in occupying the employer's premises, and in respect of which the police have powers of arrest and entry on to the property in question. Thus, it is an offence to use violence to secure entry when there is someone already on the premises[348], or to enter as a trespasser with a 'weapon of offence'[349]. In most sit-ins or work-ins, the former will not arise, as possession of the premises is usually

---

342 Trade Union and Labour Relations (Consolidation) Act 1992, s 234A(7B), as inserted by the Employment Relations Act 1999, Sch 3. The period of suspension may be extended by joint agreement.

343 Trade Union and Labour Relations (Consolidation) Act 1992, s 234A(4).

344 Indeed, the Code of Practice (at para 62) suggests that a call for industrial action following a ballot should be delayed until the union has received the scrutineer's report on the ballot, which would narrow the window of opportunity even further.

345 Trade Union and Labour Relations (Consolidation) Act 1992, s 234A(1). Note however that in such a case the industrial action will still be regarded as an unlawful act for the purposes of the 'Citizen's Right', discussed at p 826 below.

346 Under an expedited procedure: see RSC Ord 113.

347 Criminal Law Act 1977, s 1(1), overruling the decision of the House of Lords in *Kamara v DPP* [1974] AC 104, [1973] 2 All ER 1242, HL.

348 Criminal Law Act 1977, s 6, as amended by the Criminal Justice and Public Order Act 1994, s 72.

349 Criminal Law Act 1977, s 8.

gained by failing to leave (or, at least, by entry by stealth)[350] ; the occupiers may, however, be at risk under the latter, for many articles (even working tools) can constitute 'weapons of offence' if the person carrying them has the intention of using them to inflict injury on others. It is also an offence to resist bailiffs who are seeking to regain possession of the premises under a court order[351] . The other main trespass offence created by the 1977 Act, that of remaining in adverse possession after being requested to leave, is aimed essentially at squatting in residential property, and is therefore unlikely to be of any significance in an industrial context as it only applies where the person making the request is a 'displaced residential occupier' (or a 'protected intending occupier', as defined), which does not include a factory owner[352] .

The second area of possible criminal liability is under certain remaining (and in some cases anomalous) statutory provisions creating offences which limit the freedom to take industrial action. Thus, industrial action by postal workers may involve the commission of the offence of intentionally delaying a postal packet under the Postal Services Act 2000[353] , and telecommunications workers may commit an offence if they intentionally intercept a communication in the course of its transmission[354] ; likewise, there are punitive provisions in the merchant shipping legislation which may affect the legality of a strike by merchant seamen[355] , and there are statutory restrictions on union membership[356] and the organisation of strike action in the police force[357] , and on inducing prison officers to withhold their services or to commit breaches of discipline[358] . One further provision, dating from the Conspiracy and Protection of Property Act 1875[359] and now contained in the Trade Union and Labour Relations (Consolidation) Act 1992, section 240, makes it an offence for a person:

'... wilfully and maliciously [to break] a contract of service or hiring, knowing or having reasonable cause to believe that the probable consequences of his so doing, either alone or in combination with others, will be to endanger human life or cause serious bodily injury, or to expose valuable property, whether real or personal, to destruction or serious injury ...'

350 Indeed, once inside the occupiers could themselves be protected by s 6, which will render criminal any attempt by the factory owner to use violence to enter to evict them! Note, however, the decision of the Scottish High Court of Justiciary that a work-in can constitute 'watching or besetting' (under the Trade Union and Labour Relations (Consolidation) Act 1992, p 809 below) even though the people concerned are inside the premises: *Galt (Procurator Fiscal) v Philp* [1984] IRLR 156; this decision is potentially more damaging to occupations than the Criminal Law Act 1977.
351 Criminal Law Act 1977, s 10.
352 Criminal Law Act 1977, s 7, as substituted by the Criminal Justice and Public Order Act 1994, s 73.
353 Postal Services Act 2000, s 83. The offence is not committed where a postal packet is delayed as a result of industrial action in contemplation or furtherance of a trade dispute (a dispensation which did not apply under the previous provisions in the Post Office Act 1953, ss 58, 68; see *Gouriet v Union of Post Office Workers* [1978] AC 435, [1977] 3 All ER 70, HL).
354 Regulation of Investigatory Powers Act 2000, s 1.
355 Merchant Shipping Act 1995, s 59(1).
356 Police Act 1996, s 64. A person who belonged to a union before becoming a member of a police force may continue to be a union member: s 64(2).
357 Police Act 1996, s 91.
358 Criminal Justice and Public Order Act 1994, s 127; the section operates by imposing a statutory duty owed to the Home Secretary, not by imposing criminal liability.
359 The 1875 Act also created certain offences pertinent to picketing; see p 808 below.

This provision is potentially of great significance in industrial disputes, particularly in the context of industrial action by workers in the essential services such as nurses, doctors, firefighters and ambulance workers. The penalty is small, and there appears to be no record of any prosecution under it, but it is conceivable that the main significance of such a provision could lie in its use as the basis of an application for an injunction to restrain a threatened breach of it, rather than in the possibility of prosecution directly under it. In *Gouriet v UPOW*[360] the claimant sought an injunction to prevent a threatened boycott of mail to South Africa, on the basis that the action would contravene the Post Office Act 1953. This was ultimately refused by the House of Lords, which reaffirmed the traditional limitation on this use of a civil law remedy to prevent anticipated breaches of criminal law – ie that an action may only be brought by the Attorney-General or by an individual whose private rights were about to be infringed or who would suffer 'special damage'. As the claimant in *Gouriet* had failed to persuade the Attorney-General to bring the action, and had brought it himself merely qua member of the general public, he did not have the necessary locus standi. An action for an injunction to restrain a threatened breach of the criminal law would, however, be open to someone who did have the necessary legal interest, and this could conceivably arise in the circumstances envisaged by section 240, for example where someone stands to risk personal injury or property damage as a result of a strike.

Finally, while the possibility of a lawful combination of workers constituting a criminal conspiracy has long since been removed[361] , this protection does not extend to agreements to commit acts which are themselves criminal, and so if persons involved in industrial action agree among themselves to commit offences, for example to assault or intimidate people or destroy property, they may be prosecuted for those offences and also for criminal conspiracy[362] , as in *R v Jones*[363] (the 'Shrewsbury pickets' case). However, there is an exception to this where the offence in question is a summary offence not punishable by imprisonment, as section 242 of the Trade Union and Labour Relations (Consolidation) Act 1992 provides[364] that any such offence which is committed in contemplation or furtherance of a trade dispute shall be disregarded for the purposes of the law of criminal conspiracy. Moreover, the Criminal Law Act 1977 places two significant limitations on the use of criminal conspiracy – first, it ties the penalty for conspiracy to the maximum for the crime conspired at, thus removing the criticism that conspiracy could be used (or misused) to put the penalty at large[365] ; second, it requires the consent of the Director of Public Prosecutions before the prosecution may indict someone for conspiracy to commit an act which in itself is only a summary offence (for example intimidation)[366] . As a result of these limitations, criminal conspiracy is rarely of any relevance to industrial action in the present day.

360 [1978] AC 435, [1977] 3 All ER 70, HL; see Feldman (1979) 42 MLR 369.
361 Originally by the Conspiracy and Protection of Property Act 1875, s 3; see p 742 above.
362 And perhaps, on the facts, other 'group offences' under the Public Order Act 1986, see below.
363 [1974] ICR 310, 59 Cr App Rep 120, CA.
364 Re-enacting Criminal Law Act 1977, s 1(3).
365 Criminal Law Act 1977, s 3. In *R v Jones* [1974] ICR 310, 59 Cr App Rep 120, CA, the three defendants found guilty of conspiracy to intimidate received sentences of nine months', two years' and three years' imprisonment, even though intimidation itself (a summary offence under s 7 of the 1875 Act) then only carried three months. One of the defendants, Ricky Tomlinson, has since become better known as, *inter alia*, the recumbent paterfamilias in the BBC's *The Royle Family*.
366 Criminal Law Act 1977, s 4(1). Note, however, the Prosecution of Offences Act 1985, s 1(6) which allows an ordinary Crown Prosecutor to exercise the DPP's functions in this respect.

6 PICKETING[367]

The act of picketing the premises of another person may not be unlawful in itself[368], but in reality it can very easily become so, either as a tort, such as public or private nuisance or trespass to the highway, or under one of several specific or general criminal offences. This is recognised in the statutory immunity for peaceful picketing during a trade dispute, now contained in the Trade Union and Labour Relations (Consolidation) Act 1992, section 220. It is necessary, therefore, to consider first the ways in which a picket may prima facie fall foul of the law and then the extent to which he is protected.

Picketing is a form of public demonstration carried on in an industrial context, and the imposition of restrictions on picketing has important civil liberties implications, particularly for freedom of assembly and freedom of speech. As was seen in the introduction to this chapter, the 'bringing home' of the European Convention on Human Rights into English law by the Human Rights Act 1998 may well have important implications for the law affecting picketing, as the right to freedom of expression in Article 10 and the right to freedom of peaceful assembly in Article 11 could conceivably be used to challenge some of the existing legal restrictions on picketing[369]. Indeed, even before the coming into force of the Human Rights Act, there was evidence that the courts were increasingly aware of the need to preserve these fundamental freedoms. So, for example, in *Middlebrook Mushrooms Ltd v TGWU*[370], where the claimants, a firm of mushroom growers, sought an injunction restraining the union from distributing leaflets outside supermarkets supplied by the claimants asking customers not to buy their mushrooms, in support of members dismissed by the claimants for taking industrial action, the Court of Appeal emphasised the importance of keeping the civil law constraints on picketing within proper limits, Neill LJ stating that Article 10 should be taken into consideration 'in all cases which involve a proposed restriction on the right of free speech'[371]; similarly, in *DPP v Jones*[372], Lord Irvine LC expressed the view, obiter, that if English law did not give a right of peaceful assembly on the highway, Article 11 of the European Convention might in future require the common law to develop such a right. As in other areas of employment law potentially affected by human rights law, the key issue here will be the extent to which the guarantee of freedom of peaceful assembly in Article 11(1) is found to be qualified by Article 11(2), which permits restrictions on that freedom 'where

---

367 See Wallington 'Policing the miners' strike' (1985) 14 ILJ 145; Auerbach 'Legal restraint of picketing: new trends; new tensions' (1987) 16 ILJ 227; Auerbach 'Injunctions against picketing' (1989) 18 ILJ 166.

368 *Hubbard v Pitt* [1975] 3 All ER 1, [1975] ICR 308, CA, per Lord Denning MR (dissenting); the majority decided the case on procedural points relating to interlocutory injunctions, not primarily upon the substantive law on picketing. See Wallington 'Injunctions and the right to demonstrate' (1976) 35 CLJ 86.

369 See O'Dempsey et al, *Employment Law and the Human Rights Act 1998* (2001) pp 217–223. See also p 42 above

370 [1993] ICR 612, CA.

371 [1993] ICR 612 at 620. The Court of Appeal discharged the injunction granted by the judge at first instance on the grounds that as the leaflets were directed at *customers* of the supermarkets and not at the supermarkets themselves, any interference with business was *indirect* rather than direct, and therefore required the use of unlawful means (not established on the facts) in order to be actionable.

372 [1999] 2 All ER 257, HL; see n 415 below. The case demonstrates the difficulties in store for the courts in interpreting Article 11, for Lord Slynn and Lord Hope saw no necessary conflict between the common law and the Convention on this point.

necessary in a democratic society . . . for the prevention of disorder or crime ... or for the protection of rights and freedoms of others.'[373]

(i) Potential civil liability

Picketing is not tortious per se, but in common with other forms of industrial action it is likely to involve the commission of one or more of the industrial torts discussed above, and may therefore be restrainable at the suit of the employer or some other person involved. For example, a picket who persuades a delivery driver to turn around and not to cross a picket line probably induces that driver to break his contract of employment, and may also indirectly induce a breach of (or at least interfere with) the commercial supply contracts of the driver's employer[374] . The presence of pickets may also give rise to the tort of trespass to the highway[375] or nuisance[376] , and in *Thomas v NUM (South Wales Area)*[377] , Scott J granted an injunction against mass picketing on the grounds of a new common law tort of 'harassment' (a variant of private nuisance) at the suit of working miners who were being prevented from going to work, even though they were not the owners of the land being picketed. The case also illustrates that an action can lie at the suit of people other than the employer in dispute. Picketing could also conceivably involve the commission of the statutory tort of harassment under the Protection from Harassment Act 1997, although to date the civil remedy under that Act has not been used in the context of picketing[378]. An injunction to prevent the unlawful picketing may have the effect of stopping the picketing altogether, or may instead impose conditions on picketing activity (for example on the numbers of pickets and their location; see below).

---

373 There are similar restrictions in Article 10(2). In *Steel v United Kingdom* (1998) 28 EHRR 603, the ECtHR ruled that the detention for breach of the peace of protestors who were merely holding banners and distributing leaflets infringed Article 10, observing that while States have a margin of appreciation in deciding what restrictions are necessary, the overriding consideration was that the measures used should be proportionate to the end to be achieved. See Fenwick (1999) 62 MLR 491.

374 In *Union Traffic Ltd v TGWU* [1989] ICR 98, [1989] IRLR 127, the Court of Appeal held that the mere presence of pickets may constitute the tort of inducing breach of contract if it is clear that the presence of the pickets is intended to induce a breach of contract and it achieves its objective.

375 See *DPP v Jones* [1999] 2 All ER 257, a landmark case on the law on trespassory assemblies (p 813 below) arising from a protest at Stonehenge, where the House of Lords held that there is a public right of peaceful assembly on the highway for any reasonable purpose, provided the activity does not obstruct the highway by unreasonably impeding the rights of others to pass and repass, and does not amount to a public or private nuisance.

376 *Hubbard v Pitt* [1975] 3 All ER 1, [1975] ICR 308, CA.

377 [1985] 2 All ER 1, [1985] IRLR 136. See Benedictus 'The use of the law of tort in the miners' dispute' (1985) 14 ILJ 176. In *News Group Newspapers Ltd v SOGAT '82 (No 2)* [1987] ICR 181, [1986] IRLR 337 Stuart-Smith J expressed obiter reservations about the decision in *Thomas*. In *Khorasandjian v Bush* [1993] QB 727, [1993] 3 All ER 669 (a non-industrial case), the Court of Appeal accepted the existence of a common law tort of harassment as a form of private nuisance available to a person without an interest in land, but that case was overruled on that point in *Hunter v Canary Wharf Ltd* [1997] AC 655, HL.

378 Cf *Tuppen v Microsoft Corpn* (2000) Times, 15 November, where it was stated that the 1997 Act has a narrow ambit and breaches of it which give rise to a civil remedy are confined to cases of stalking, behaviour of an anti-social nature by neighbours and racial harassment.

(ii) Potential criminal liability

If picketing is violent, there will of course be criminal liability for (for example) assault, criminal damage and public order offences (see below), in the ordinary way, as seen most dramatically in the miners' strike of 1984/85[379]. Even if it is peaceful, however, picketing may constitute an obstruction of the highway[380], and any refusal to obey lawful police orders may constitute the offence of wilfully obstructing a police officer in the execution of his duty, contrary to the Police Act 1996, section 89. Picketing may also constitute the crime of harassment under the Protection from Harassment Act 1997[381], which makes it an offence for a person to pursue a 'course of conduct'[382] which amounts to harassment of another and which he knows or ought to know amounts to harassment of another[383]. Although primarily aimed at 'stalkers', the crime of harassment is clearly wide enough to apply to pickets; its significance in practice is likely to turn on the extent to which pickets are able to rely on the statutory defence 'that in the particular circumstances the pursuit of the course of conduct was reasonable.[384]'

In addition to the above, section 241 of the Trade Union and Labour Relations (Consolidation) Act 1992[385] makes it an offence for a person 'with a view to compelling[386] another person to abstain from doing or to do any act which that person has a legal right to do or abstain from doing, wrongfully and without legal authority' to:

(a) use violence to or intimidate[387] that person or his wife or children, or injure his property;

---

379 During the course of the strike, 10,372 criminal charges were brought, including 468 for assaults of sorts, 360 for assaulting a police officer, 137 for riot, 509 for unlawful assembly, 21 for affray, 4,107 for conduct conducive to breach of the peace (Public Order Act 1936, s 5), 1,019 for criminal damage, 352 for theft, 1,682 for obstructing a police officer, 640 for obstruction of the highway and 275 for intimidation. Subsequently, however, many of the major charges (especially those including riot) were not proceeded with.

380 Highways Act 1980, s 137; see eg *Broome v DPP* [1974] 1 All ER 314, [1974] ICR 84, HL. It seems that picketing will only be an offence under the Highways Act where it involves an unreasonable use of the highway: see *Hubbard v Pitt* [1975] 3 All ER 1, [1975] ICR 308.

381 See Mullender (1998) 61 MLR 236. Section 3 of the Act provides a civil remedy for a person who is harassed or threatened with harassment. Section 4 creates a more serious offence of putting people in fear of violence, which applies where a person's course of conduct causes another to fear, on at least two occasions, that violence will be used against him; there is a defence, inter alia, where the accused can show that the pursuit of his course of conduct was reasonable for the protection of himself or another or for the protection of his or another's property: s 4(3)(c).

382 This must involve conduct on at least two occasions: Protection from Harassment Act 1997, s 7(3); 'conduct' in this context includes speech: s 7(4).

383 Protection from Harassment Act 1997, ss 1(1), 2(1). 'Harassment' is not defined, save that references to harassing a person include alarming the person or causing the person distress: s 7(2). A person convicted of an offence under these provisions may be subjected to a restraining order for the purpose of protecting the victim (or any other person named in the order) from further harassment: s 5.

384 Protection from Harassment Act 1997, s 1(3)(c).

385 Re-enacting the Conspiracy and Protection of Property Act 1875, s 7. The offence is not necessarily restricted to industrial cases: see eg *DPP v Todd* [1996] Crim LR 344 (anti-road protesters)

386 The defendant must have acted with a view to *compelling* someone to do something he had a right not to do, or vice versa; an intention to persuade is not enough: *DPP v Fidler* [1992] 1 WLR 91 (another non-industrial case involving a picket outside an abortion clinic).

387 Actual violence or threats of immediate personal injury are not necessary, but there must be some definite element of causing someone to feel afraid: *Judge v Bennett* (1887) 36 WR 103; *Gibson v Lawson* [1891] 2 QB 545; *Curran v Treleaven* [1891] 2 QB 545; *R v Jones* [1974] ICR 310, 59 Cr App Rep 120, CA.

(b) persistently follow that person about from place to place[388] ;

(c) hide any tools, clothes or other property owned or used by that person, or deprive him of or hinder him in the use thereof[389] ;

(d) watch or beset[390] the house or other place where that person resides, works, carries on business or happens to be, or the approach to such house or place;

(e) follow that person with two or more other persons in a disorderly manner in or through any street or road.

The inclusion of the words 'wrongful and without legal authority' means that the acts complained of under 1–5 above must already be unlawful (ie either tortious[391] or criminal) – the aim of the section is to make them amenable to summary trial in addition to any other unlawfulness:

> '[Section 242] legalises nothing, and it renders nothing wrongful that was not so before. Its object is solely to visit certain selected classes of acts which were previously wrongful, ie were at least civil torts, with penal consequences capable of being summarily inflicted[392].'

The offence under section 241 was rarely used until revived during the 1984/85 miners' strike; subsequently, it was upgraded somewhat by the Public Order Act 1986, which made it an arrestable offence and increased the maximum penalty to six months' imprisonment or a level 5 fine, or both[393] .

(iii) The importance of an anticipated breach of the peace

The discussion so far has centred on substantive offences which might be committed by pickets. However, one concept which, in practice, has tended to be dominant in the physical control of picketing by the police is that of breach of the

---

388 *Smith v Thomasson* (1891) 16 Cox CC 740; *R v Wall* (1907) 21 Cox CC 401. For a rare example of a prosecution under this limb in Scotland, see *Elsey v Smith (Procurator Fiscal)* [1983] IRLR 292.

389 *Fowler v Kibble* [1922] 1 Ch 487, CA.

390 This limb is particularly relevant to picketing (see *R v Bonsall* [1985] Crim LR 150), and it is significant that the statutory immunity now contained in s 220 of the 1992 Act was originally a proviso to s 7 of the 1875 Act which deemed attendance for the purpose of obtaining or communicating information not to be watching or besetting. According to the Scottish High Court of Justiciary in *Galt (Procurator Fiscal) v Philp* [1984] IRLR 156 a person can be guilty of watching and besetting from inside the property, ie by occupying it, but this has been doubted.

391 The converse of this is that the fact that the conduct in question constitutes an offence under this section does not automatically mean that it is an actionable tort: *Thomas v NUM (South Wales Area)* [1985] 2 All ER 1, [1985] IRLR 136. Cf *Galt (Procurator Fiscal) v Philp* [1984] IRLR 156, where it was held that tortious acts protected by the statutory immunities remain 'wrongful' for the purposes of these provisions. If correct, the decision could have profound implications for the legality of picketing.

392 *Ward Lock & Co Ltd v Operative Printers' Assistants' Society* (1906) 22 TLR 327, CA, at 329 per Fletcher Moulton LJ; *Fowler v Kibble* [1922] 1 Ch 487, CA; cf *J Lyons & Sons v Wilkins* [1899] 1 Ch 255, where the Court of Appeal had previously held that the section created new offences complete in themselves. The approach in *Ward Lock* was preferred by Scott J in *Thomas v NUM (South Wales Area)* [1985] 2 All ER 1, [1985] IRLR 136.

393 The fact that the s 241 offence is punishable with imprisonment means that it is capable of founding a charge of criminal conspiracy under the Criminal Law Act 1977, s 1(1): Trade Union and Labour Relations (Consolidation) Act 1992, s 242.

peace[394] (either actual or reasonably apprehended), for it is a police officer's duty to prevent such a breach, if necessary by positive action to limit the numbers and placings of pickets. If a picket disregards an instruction from a police officer, and that officer can show grounds for reasonably anticipating[395] a breach of the peace at the time (for example through the imminent arrival of a lorry going into the picketed factory), then that picket is guilty of wilfully obstructing the police officer in the execution of his duty, contrary to section 89 of the Police Act 1996. Thus, breach of the peace acts as an umbrella head of liability which may justify the police in limiting numbers, as in *Piddington v Bates*[396], or holding back from the factory gates some, or even all, of the pickets[397] even if that means that there is little practical likelihood of the pickets (or their leaders) being able to converse with the lorry driver at all, provided that the drastic nature of any police action is justified by the magnitude of the risk of a breach of the peace. In the past, these powers have been used to control the activities of pickets at the premises being picketed. However, the miners' strike of 1984/5 saw a significant development when the police, faced with major disorders outside pits (particularly working pits in Nottinghamshire) began to close off areas altogether to would-be pickets, preventing them from reaching the premises in question at all, if necessary by the use of road blocks. Any pickets proceeding past such a barrier risked being arrested for obstruction of the police[398]. The legality of such drastic preventive tactics was questioned in *Moss v McLachlan*[399] in the case of four such would-be pickets charged with obstruction for trying to pass a police cordon. They were convicted by magistrates and their appeal was dismissed by the Divisional Court which held that, on the facts, the police had reasonably anticipated a breach of the peace and so their preventive action was justified. One important holding was that in forming their reasonable anticipation the police were entitled to take into account their common knowledge of the course of the dispute and the likelihood of further major violence. The problem with the case as a precedent is that in fact the police cordon was only between one-and-a-half and four miles from four working pits within one area served by that particular road. Thus, the physical nexus between the cordon and the premises was relatively close. It is perhaps unfortunate that the legality of certain more controversial actions taken by the police (such as the stopping of Kent miners on their way to the northern coalfields

---

394 See *R v Howell (Errol)* [1982] QB 416, [1981] 3 All ER 383, CA, per Watkins LJ: 'There is a breach of the peace whenever harm is actually done or is likely to be done to a person or in his presence to his property or a person is in fear of being so harmed through an assault, an affray, a riot, an unlawful assembly or other disturbance.' See also *Percy v DPP* [1995] 1 WLR 1382; *Nicol and Selvanayagam v DPP* (1995) 160 JP 155. The common law offence of breach of the peace was specifically retained by the Public Order Act 1986, s 40(4).

395 See *Foulkes v Chief Constable of the Merseyside Police* [1998] 3 All ER 705, CA, per Beldam LJ: 'There must ... be a sufficiently real and present threat to the peace to justify the extreme step of depriving of his liberty a citizen who is not at the time acting unlawfully.'

396 [1960] 3 All ER 660, [1961] 1 WLR 162.

397 *Kavanagh v Hiscock* [1974] 2 All ER 177, [1974] ICR 282.

398 Arrested pickets were routinely subjected to stringent bail conditions aimed at preventing them from returning; see eg *R v Mansfield Justices, ex p Sharkey* [1985] 1 All ER 193, [1984] IRLR 496, where the Divisional Court upheld the validity of what was then a common bail condition 'not to visit any premises or place for the purpose of picketing or demonstrating in connection with the current trade dispute between the NUM and the NCB other than peacefully to picket or demonstrate at his usual place of employment.'

399 [1985] IRLR 76. Police powers to use roadblocks are now codified: Police and Criminal Evidence Act 1984, s 4.

at the Dartford tunnel) was not properly tested in the courts. Were similar facts to arise today, the courts would have to give due weight to the exercise by the pickets of their Convention rights to freedom of expression and of peaceful assembly in deciding whether a police officer had reasonable grounds for apprehending a breach of the peace[400].

(iv) Public order offences[401]

As we have already seen, picketing which is not 'peaceful' may bring liability not only under specific criminal offences applying to industrial disputes, but also under the general laws relating to public order, which were subject to major amendment by the Public Order Act 1986. That Act had its origins in a review set up in 1979 to consider problems of public order generally, leading to a White Paper in 1985[402] ; although the remit was wide, it was given added impetus by certain newsworthy industrial disputes, particularly the events of the 1984/85 miners' strike, and so several of the provisions in the Act were intended to affect picketing. The law on public order was further amended by the Criminal Justice and Public Order Act 1994 and the Crime and Disorder Act 1998, as successive governments of (supposedly) different political persuasions have resorted to increasingly draconian measures in an attempt to assuage public concern over a perceived deterioration in law and order. The measures relevant to picketing lie principally in the following areas – (i) offences against public order, (ii) controls over public processions and assemblies.'

Considering first the applicable offences, the Public Order Act abolished the common law offences of riot, rout, unlawful assembly and affray, and repealed the well-known statutory offence of 'threatening behaviour', replacing them with five graduated offences, all carrying powers of arrest; a further offence, that of causing intentional harassment, alarm or distress, was added by the Criminal Justice and Public Order Act 1994, and the Crime and Disorder Act 1998 imposed more severe penalties for certain of the offences where racially aggravated. The offences are as follows:[403]

(a) Riot

Twelve or more persons present together using or threatening unlawful violence for a common purpose, their conduct being such as would cause a person of reasonable firmness present at the scene to fear for his personal safety[404] . Anyone using unlawful violence for the common purpose is liable on indictment to a maximum of ten years' imprisonment, a fine or both.

---

400 See Fenwick 'The Right to Protest, the Human Rights Act and the Margin of Appreciation' (1999) 62 MLR 491.
401 See Smith *Offences against Public Order* (1987); Wallington [1987] Crim LR 180; Carty 'The Public Order Act 1986: police powers and the picket line' (1987) 16 ILJ 146.
402 *Review of Public Order Law* (Cmnd 9510, 1985); also influential was the Law Commission's Report 'Offences relating to public order' (Law Com No. 123, 1983).
403 The following are condensed versions of the offences; for the full wording, see the text of the Act.
404 Public Order Act 1986, s 1.

(b) Violent disorder

Three or more persons present together using or threatening unlawful violence, their conduct being such as would cause a person of reasonable firmness present at the scene to fear for his personal safety[405]. Anyone using or threatening unlawful violence is liable on indictment to five years' imprisonment and/or a fine, or on summary conviction to six months' imprisonment and/or the maximum scale fine. This offence replaced the old common law offence of unlawful assembly, and is envisaged as being the major offence in practice in the case of serious disorder.

(c) Affray

Using or threatening unlawful violence towards another, such as would cause a person of reasonable firmness present at the scene to fear for his personal safety[406]. The maximum penalty here is three years' imprisonment and/or a fine on indictment, or six months' imprisonment and/or the maximum scale fine on summary conviction.

(d) Violent behaviour

Using threatening, abusive, or insulting words or behaviour (or distributing or displaying anything to like effect) to another person with intent to cause that person to fear immediate unlawful violence (to himself or another) or to provoke that person or another to use immediate unlawful violence[407]. This offence is triable summarily only and carries a maximum penalty of six months' imprisonment and/or a level 5 fine[408].

(e) Intentional harassment

This offence, which was added by the Criminal Justice and Public Order Act 1994, is based on the existing offence of disorderly behaviour (see below), but with the additional requirements that the person must intend to cause, and the victim must actually be caused, harassment, alarm or distress[409]. It carries a much stiffer penalty than the non-intentional version (reflecting the intentional element), being punishable on summary conviction by up to six months' imprisonment and/or a level 5 fine[410]. Although apparently aimed at serious, persistent racial harassment, it is clearly of great potential significance to picketing.

---

405 Public Order Act 1986, s 2.
406 Public Order Act 1986, s 3.
407 Public Order Act 1986, s 4. Violence includes violence to property; s 8.
408 The penalties are more severe in the case of a racially aggravated offence: Crime and Disorder Act 1998, s 31.
409 Public Order Act 1986, s 4A. Compare the offence of harassment under the Protection from Harassment Act 1997, where it is enough to show that the accused ought to have known that his course of conduct amounted to harassment: see p 808 above.
410 Again, the penalties are more severe in the case of a racially aggravated offence: see n 408.

(f) Disorderly behaviour

Using threatening, abusive or insulting words or behaviour, or disorderly behaviour (or displaying anything to like effect) within the hearing or sight of a person likely to be caused harassment, alarm or distress thereby, with the intention or the awareness that the words or behaviour may be threatening, abusive, insulting or disorderly[411] . This offence (perhaps best summed up colloquially as 'generally loutish behaviour') was particularly strongly criticised upon its introduction; it covers a multitude of sins, but is not of great importance in picketing cases since any such behaviour in that context is likely to lead to a breach of the peace (actual or reasonably apprehended), to which the present section probably adds little[412] . The offence is triable summarily only, with a maximum penalty of a level 3 fine[413] .

Turning to the imposition of controls on public processions and assemblies, sections 11–13 of the Public Order Act 1986 allow the police to be given advance notice of public processions, and to impose conditions on them or to prohibit them altogether in order to prevent disorderly or intimidatory conduct. These powers are considered in full elsewhere[414] and are not of immediate application to picketing (except in the case of, for example, marches in support of pickets). Of more obvious relevance to picketing is the power to regulate public assemblies in section 14[415] . This permits a senior police officer to impose conditions on a 'public assembly'[416] , either in advance or at the scene, where the officer reasonably believes that:

'(a) [the assembly] may result in serious public disorder, serious damage to property or serious disruption to the life of the community, or

(b) the purpose of the persons organising it is the intimidation of others with a view to compelling them not to do an act they have a right to do, or to do an act they have a right not to do ...'

The potential application of this provision to picketing is obvious. If the police officer has such a reasonable belief, he may:

'give directions imposing on the persons organising or taking part in the assembly such conditions as to the place at which the assembly may be (or continue to be) held, its maximum duration, or the maximum number of persons who may constitute it, as appear to him necessary to avoid disorder, damage, disruption or intimidation.'

411 Public Order Act 1986, s 5. The test of intention or awareness here is subjective: see *DPP v Clarke* (1991) 94 Cr App Rep 359.

412 Section 5 is principally aimed at conduct which is a social nuisance but which falls short of an actual breach of the peace because there is no actual or threatened harm to a person or his property; in that light, note the inclusion of mere 'disorderly behaviour'.

413 See n 408.

414 See n 401, above.

415 There is also a power to ban trespassory assemblies, introduced by the 1994 Act, which could conceivably be used where picketing (eg persistent mass picketing) results in 'serious disruption to the life of the community': Public Order Act 1986, s 14A; see *DPP v Jones* [1999] 2 All ER 257, HL.

416 This is defined as 'an assembly of 20 or more persons in a public place which is wholly or partly open to the air' (s 16), which clearly covers a picket line with that number of people (except in the unlikely event of it being entirely on private property). The requirement of advance notice and the power to ban (which apply to processions) do not apply to assemblies, although note the power to ban *trespassory* assemblies: see n 415 above.

As we have seen above, the concept of breach of the peace (which remains unaffected by the 1986 Act) already gives a police officer on the spot some of these directional powers, but section 14 puts them into a wider, clearer and more comprehensive statutory form[417] (backed by criminal sanctions on those organising or taking part in an assembly in breach of conditions), and of course allows conditions to be attached in advance. Particularly significant are possible conditions as to place, time (not at times of shift changes for working employees?) and, of course as to numbers, where a provision in the Code of Practice on Picketing suggesting a limit of six pickets per entrance (considered below) assumes great significance.

(v) The immunity

In view of the many and varied ways in which picketing can potentially fall foul of the law, the scope of the statutory immunity for picketing becomes of crucial significance, as it in effect defines the extent of the right to picket. Section 220 of the Trade Union and Labour Relations (Consolidation) Act 1992 provides that:

> 'It is lawful for a person in contemplation or furtherance of a trade dispute to attend –
> (a) at or near his own place of work, or
> (b) if he is an official of a trade union, at or near the place of work of a member of the union whom he is accompanying and whom he represents[418],
> for the purpose only of peacefully obtaining or communicating information, or peacefully persuading any person to work or abstain from working[419].'

It is important to appreciate that section 220 does not confer a 'right' to picket as such; it gives a limited right to *attend* for the stated purposes of peacefully obtaining or communicating information or peacefully persuading a person to work or abstain from working (ie 'peaceful picketing'), but it does not legitimise the *activities* of pickets. The section 220 immunity has therefore been described as 'narrow but real'[420] in that by protecting attendance for the purposes of peaceful picketing, it ensures that pickets will not incur either tortious liability (for example for nuisance) or criminal liability[421] (for example for obstruction of the highway or watching and besetting) from the mere fact of their attendance. Any

---

417 'The crucial difference is that reasons other than the need to preserve the peace may be relied upon, in particular the reasonable belief of the senior officer present that the picket organisers' purpose is to intimidate others' (Wallington [1987] Crim LR 180 p 190).

418 An official who is elected or appointed to represent some members of the union is to be regarded as representing only those members: s 220(4). This is to prevent the drafting in of large numbers of union officials, shop stewards, etc., from different parts of the country to do the picketing. A national officer, however, will be regarded as representing all members.

419 The 'persuasion' limb was introduced by the Trade Disputes Act 1906, s 2; it had not been included in the immunity given by the Conspiracy and Protection of Property Act 1875: *J Lyons & Sons v Wilkins* [1899] 1 Ch 255, CA.

420 *Broome v DPP* [1974] 1 All ER 314, [1974] ICR 84, HL at 325 and 96 respectively, per Lord Salmon.

421 The Code of Practice of Picketing, para 41, states that there is no immunity from the criminal law, but there are dicta in *Broome v DPP* to the contrary.

liability which arises from the activities of pickets is protected, if at all, under the general trade dispute immunities contained in section 219 of the 1992 Act; the two provisions are however inextricably linked, as picketing which falls outside the section 220 immunity loses any protection which it might otherwise have enjoyed under section 219, while picketing which is within section 220 retains the section 219 immunities, even if it constitutes secondary action which would normally not be immune. The interrelationship of the immunities is discussed further below.

As seen above, the section 220 immunity applies to attendance for the purposes of peaceful picketing. It follows that if some other purpose can be inferred from the actions of the pickets (for example intimidation of those seeking to enter the workplace, or blockading the entrance), the immunity does not apply. Thus, in *Tynan v Balmer*[422] where pickets walked in a circle around the factory gates in such a way as to seal off the entrance from traffic, the court was able to infer a purpose other than one of those in the section. Similarly, in *Broome v DPP*[423] the House of Lords held that the defendant's purpose in standing in front of a lorry to prevent its passage (having failed to persuade the driver not to enter the picketed premises) was to obstruct rather than to persuade or communicate; the justices had acquitted the defendant on a charge of obstruction because they thought that he had only spent a reasonable time in trying to exercise his 'statutory right' of peaceful persuasion, a right which they considered would be meaningless if he was not allowed actually to stop the vehicle. The House of Lords held that this was entirely misconceived – the section gives no 'right' to picket, and certainly does not allow a picket to compel someone to stop and listen if that person does not wish to do so (a point reaffirmed shortly afterwards by the Divisional Court in *Kavanagh v Hiscock*[424]). Lord Salmon put it thus,

'[The] words make it plain that it is nothing but the attendance of the pickets at the places specified which is protected; and then only if their attendance is for one of the specified purposes. The section gives no protection in relation to anything the pickets may say or do whilst they are attending if what they say or do is itself unlawful. But for the section, the mere attendance of pickets might constitute an offence under [section 241(1)(b) and (d) of the 1992 Act or under the Highways Act 1980] or constitute a tort, for example, nuisance. The section, therefore, gives a narrow but nevertheless real immunity to pickets. It clearly does no more.'

Before 1980, the statutory immunity for picketing applied so long as the attendance was for one of the stated purposes (ie peacefully obtaining or communicating information or peacefully persuading any person to work or abstain from working), and was within the golden formula. There were no restrictions on who could picket, or where, except that picketing a person's home was outside the immunity. This meant that those who engaged in so-called 'secondary picketing' enjoyed the full protection of the immunity. The phrase 'secondary picketing' is used to connote one of two things, either the attendance on picket lines of people who are not employed by the employer in dispute

---

422 [1967] 1 QB 91, [1966] 2 All ER 133. The case is a good example of a trespass committed by an unreasonable user of the highway: see p 807 above.
423 N 420 above.
424 [1974] 2 All ER 177, [1974] ICR 282.

(sometimes referred to as sympathy picketing), or the placing of picket lines elsewhere than at the premises of the employer in dispute (particularly the use of so-called 'flying pickets'). The incoming Conservative government in 1979 were determined to tackle secondary picketing, which was perceived as a major problem. The approach taken in the Employment Act 1980 was to restrict the scope of the immunity for peaceful picketing to a person picketing at or near[425] his *own* place of work[426] (and to a union representative accompanying such a person), so that the immunity no longer applies to secondary pickets engaged in sympathy picketing, or persons picketing a place other than their own place of work. As was mentioned above, crucially the 1980 Act also linked the immunity for *attendance* under section 220 with the immunities for the *activities* of pickets under section 219, by expressly removing the section 219 immunities from acts done in the course of picketing which falls outside the scope of section 220[427] (for example because it is not at that person's place of work, or is not peaceful). The effect of this is to allow an employer not a party to a dispute to obtain an injunction to stop employees of some other employer in dispute picketing his premises in the course of their dispute[428]. However, in one important respect the immunity for picketing is wider than the immunity for other forms of industrial action, because in certain circumstances pickets enjoy immunity for *secondary* action occurring during picketing[429]; indeed, following the tightening up of the law on secondary action by the Employment Act 1990, this is now the only form of secondary action which enjoys any statutory protection. This exception exists for the simple reason that without it the immunity for attendance conferred by section 220 would in practice be worthless. Workers peacefully picketing at their own place of work can very easily become involved in secondary action – for example, the actions of a picket who persuades a delivery driver not to cross a picket line (thereby probably inducing that driver to break his contract of employment and also indirectly interfering with the commercial supply contracts of the driver's employer) are likely to constitute secondary action if the driver is not employed by the employer in dispute. If there were no immunity for secondary action occurring during picketing, it would be virtually impossible for any lawful picketing to take place. Secondary action committed during peaceful picketing is therefore protected, but *only* as regards those employed (or last employed) by the employer in dispute, and union officials lawfully accompanying them. Those not employed by the

---

425   A realistic approach must be taken to the meaning of 'at or near': *Rayware Ltd v TGWU* [1989] ICR 457, [1989] IRLR 134, CA (pickets at the entrance to a private industrial estate which contained the employer's factory were held to be attending 'at or near' their place of work, even though 1,200 yards from their employer's premises).

426   Those with no fixed place of work, or whose workplace makes picketing impracticable (eg the proverbial lighthouse keeper), may picket 'any premises' from which they work or from which their work is administered: s 220(2); see *Union Traffic Ltd v Transport and General Workers' Union* [1989] IRLR 127, CA. Workers who have been dismissed because of the dispute (and so who technically have no place of work) may picket their former place of work: s 220(3), although note that if the employer moves production to a new plant, the dismissed workers may not lawfully picket that plant because it was never their place of work: *News Group Newspapers Ltd v SOGAT 1982 (No 2)* [1987] ICR 181, [1986] IRLR 337.

427   Trade Union and Labour Relations (Consolidation) Act 1992, s 219(3); see p 785 above.

428   As in *Mersey Docks and Harbour Co v Verrinder* [1982] IRLR 152. One problem for an employer may be to identify the pickets in order to bring civil proceedings against them; it is no part of the police function to do so (see the Code of Practice on Picketing, para 27).

429   Trade Union and Labour Relations (Consolidation) Act 1992, s 244(3). The protection is, of course, subject to the other restrictions on the statutory immunities, such as the need to hold a valid ballot.

employer in dispute (for example sympathy pickets who picket their own place of work in support of other workers) enjoy no protection against secondary action which occurs during picketing.

One other issue which in the past has been the cause of much controversy is mass picketing. Mass picketing is not in itself unlawful, and section 220 places no limits on the numbers of pickets who may lawfully attend. However, the section does require that the picketing be 'peaceful', ie for the stated purposes of obtaining or communicating information or peacefully persuading any person to work or abstain from working. Thus, while mass picketing is not unlawful in itself, it is in the nature of things easier to infer a purpose other than that of peaceful communication or persuasion as the numbers grow larger. In *Broome v DPP* [430] Lord Salmon said that each case would depend on its facts, with the number of pickets being just one of the factors in deciding whether the attendance was for statutory purposes, but Lord Reid said, perhaps more realistically, that in a case of mass picketing 'it would not be difficult to infer as a matter of fact that pickets who assemble in unreasonably large numbers do have the purpose of preventing free passage', ie a purpose outside those permitted in section 220, an approach echoed in the judgment of Scott J in *Thomas v NUM (South Wales Area)* [431]. When the 1980 Employment Bill was going through Parliament, there was some pressure to supplement this general position with a statutory provision limiting numbers of pickets. This was not done in the Act, but an attempt was made to achieve the same result indirectly in the Code of Practice on Picketing, issued later in the year and revised in 1992 [432]. Paragraph 47 states that 'the law does not impose a specific limit on the number of people who may picket at any one place; nor does this Code affect in any way the discretion of the police to limit the number of people on a particular picket line'. However, paragraph 51, after discussing the problems caused by large numbers, goes on to state that 'pickets and their organisers should ensure that in general the number of pickets does not exceed six at any entrance to, or exit from, a workplace; frequently a smaller number will be appropriate'. Although the Code itself is not legally binding it is expressly made admissible in tribunal or court proceedings [433], and this suggested maximum of six pickets per entrance has in the past been seized upon by the courts as a guide 'to a sensible number for a picket line in order that the weight of numbers should not intimidate those who wish to go to work' [434], the implication being that the presence of pickets in numbers greater than six may be taken to indicate a purpose outside those permitted by the section. It remains to be seen whether attempts to limit the numbers of pickets in this circuitous way can be reconciled with the greater weight which must now be given to the Convention rights of freedom of expression and of peaceful assembly.

---

430 [1974] 1 All ER 314, [1974] ICR 84, HL.
431 [1985] 2 All ER 1, [1985] IRLR 136.
432 The Code of Practice is discussed below.
433 Trade Union and Labour Relations (Consolidation) Act 1992, s 207.
434 *Thomas v NUM (South Wales Area)* [1985] ICR 886, [1985] IRLR 136, per Scott J; see also *News Group Newspapers Ltd v SOGAT 1982 (No 2)* [1987] ICR 181, [1986] IRLR 337, per Stuart-Smith J. In *Thomas v NUM*, the terms of the injunction were clearly drafted with the Code of Practice in mind, for they restrained the organising of picketing at the colliery in question in numbers greater than six for any purpose other than peaceful persuasion or communication.

(vi) The Code of Practice on Picketing

The Code was published in 1980 by the Secretary of State for Employment[435] , and revised in 1992. The Code is not legally binding, and much of it is concerned with explaining the relevant law. However, as seen above, one aspect of the Code, the suggested maximum number of six pickets per entrance[436] , has in the past been given indirect legal effect through being taken into account by the courts when deciding whether the picketing was 'peaceful' and so within the immunity. Other than that, the Code's general exhortations as to prior consultations with the police and proper organisation of picketing by officials[437] are of little legal significance. The revised Code includes the following new recommendations: (1) where an entrance or exit is used jointly by the workers of more than one employer, pickets should not interfere with those workers or call upon them to join in the dispute; (2) picketing should be confined to a location or locations as near as practicable to the place of work; (3) a picket should not be designated as official unless it is actually organised by a trade union and the union is prepared to accept responsibility for it. Finally, one part of the Code is open to serious objection as a misuse of the idea of codes of practice. This is Section G (Essential Supplies and Services) which states that pickets should ensure that such supplies and services are not impeded or prevented[438] . The problem is that it is difficult to see what legal effect this could have – it would be stretching several points to argue that picketing which did interfere with such services or supplies was thereby not 'peaceful', and it is the peaceful or other nature of it which is normally in issue in deciding whether or not the section 220 immunity can be relied upon. If it is correct that Section G has no legal effect, its inclusion can be seen either as merely pious hope or, more objectionably, an attempt to legislate by code of practice. If there are to be measures on something as important as the protection of essential supplies and services, it is surely not expecting too much that they should be properly enacted in a statute[439].

7 THE LIABILITY OF A UNION IN TORT

So far in this chapter we have been concerned with the legal gymnastics concerning the existence of a cause of action; the simplified position now is that industrial action by a union which has effects on commercial contracts or dealings is likely to be tortious, most of those torts are covered by immunities, but under

---

435 Under powers now contained in the Trade Union and Labour Relations (Consolidation) Act 1992, s 203, which allows him to promulgate codes of practice (with Parliamentary approval) after consultation with ACAS. The Code of Practice is set out in *Harvey* S [602].
436 Para 51.
437 One irony here is that, while the Code stresses the importance of good organisation and marshalling by officials, the law has never accepted that 'official pickets' should have any rights (other than the right of attendance) over and above ordinary pickets, eg a right to go through police cordons to talk to lorry drivers (see *Kavanagh v Hiscock* [1974] 2 All ER 177, [1974] ICR 282).
438 Para 62. Para 63 lists such supplies and services as including pharmaceutical and medical products; hospitals; fuel for institutions; supplies needed in a crisis for public health and safety; goods and services necessary to the maintenance of plant and machinery; livestock; food and animal feeding stuffs; the operation of essential public services and mortuaries, burial and cremation services.
439 On industrial action in the essential services generally, see Morris *Strikes in Essential Services* (1986), and 'Industrial Action in Essential Services: The New Law' (1991) 29 ILJ 89.

the present legislation there are several major inroads into those immunities. However, the next major question concerns enforcement, which (criminal law aside) operates entirely in the civil law domain. This means that while the government may legislate to create or permit causes of action, it is up to individuals to bring proceedings. Historically employers have been loath to do so. Perhaps one reason for this has been the nature of the defendant. Until 1982, unions enjoyed a blanket immunity under the Trade Disputes Act 1906, which meant that actions had to be brought, if at all, against named persons (usually senior union officials). If an injunction was obtained against a union official and the union failed to comply with it, the only remedy available to the employer lay against the individual union official for contempt of court, and continued failure to comply could lead ultimately to imprisonment and the creation of union 'martyrs', something which few employers were prepared to risk. The position was fundamentally changed by the Employment Act 1982, which abolished the blanket immunity of a trade union from liability in tort[440], leaving unions only with the same immunities (now contained in the Trade Union and Labour Relations (Consolidation) Act 1992, ss 219 and 220), as are enjoyed by individual union officers and members. If those immunities do not apply, the union itself may now be the defendant in an action brought by an employer[441]. This means that there is less chance of the spectre arising of imprisoned union leaders and that, in addition to the usual remedy of an injunction, the remedy of damages is now more than a mere technical possibility (being an action against the union funds, rather than against an individual). This raises three questions as to the legal effects: when is a union to be liable in tort for the acts of its officers and members; what remedies can be sought against it; and out of which union funds can an award of damages be satisfied?

Turning to the first of these points, before 1982 this problem had hardly ever arisen, for a union itself could not be sued. However, the immunity had been temporarily removed by the Industrial Relations Act 1971, and the difficulties that could be caused became apparent, particularly in the case of *Heatons Transport Ltd v TGWU*[442], where the House of Lords had to decide upon the scope of the implied authority of a shop steward where the union rules were unclear on the point. In an attempt to avoid the problem of applying ordinary common law rules of vicarious liability, the Employment Act 1982 enacted a statutory test of vicarious liability governing when a union is to be liable for one of the economic torts[443].

---

440 See Ewing 'Industrial action: another step in the "right" direction' (1982) 11 ILJ 209.

441 In a further twist, the Trade Union and Labour Relations (Consolidation) Act 1992, ss 235A–C (as inserted by the Trade Union Reform and Employment Rights Act 1993, s 22) gives an individual the right to apply for an injunction restraining unlawful industrial action where an effect (or a likely effect) of that action will be to (i) prevent or delay the supply of goods or services to that individual, or (ii) reduce the quality of goods or services supplied to him; see p 826 below.

442 [1972] 3 All ER 101, [1972] ICR 308, HL; see Hepple, 'Union responsibility for shop stewards' (1972) 1 ILJ 197. One problem is that, in ordinary tort cases, one tends to think of vicarious liability operating from the top downwards, whereas within a union power has traditionally tended tends to move upwards from the shop floor, particularly via the shop steward whose constitutional position may not be fully set out in the union's rules.

443 As originally enacted the statutory test applied to the economic torts but did not apply to contempt proceedings arising out of breach of an injunction granted on the basis of one of the economic torts: *Express and Star Ltd v NGA (1982)* [1986] ICR 589, [1986] IRLR 222, CA; however, the Employment Act 1990 applied the test to subsequent contempt proceedings. It still does not apply to any other form of liability, tortious or otherwise: *Thomas v NUM (South Wales Area)* [1985] ICR 886, [1985] IRLR 136 (nuisance). In such cases, the common law rules (as in *Heatons Transport v TGWU* [1972] 3 All ER 101, [1972] ICR 308, HL) continue to apply.

That test deemed a union to be responsible for acts which had been 'authorised or endorsed by a responsible person', viz.: (a) the union's principal executive committee, (b) any other person empowered by the union rules to authorise or endorse such acts, (c) the president or general secretary, (d) any other employed official, or (e) any committee of the union to whom an employed official reports. In the case of the last two categories the union was not to be held responsible where the official or committee in question was prevented under the rules from authorising or endorsing industrial action, or where the action had been repudiated by the principal executive committee, the president or the general secretary. However, in an attempt to force trade unions to carry more responsibility for unofficial industrial action, the Employment Act 1990[444] extended categories (d) and (e) so as to make a trade union liable for the actions of *all* its officials and committees, including lay officials such as shop stewards, irrespective of anything to the contrary in the rules of the union. The 1990 Act even went so far as to make a union responsible for the actions of a 'group of persons', or any individual member of such a group, where an official of the union was a member of the group at the material time and the purposes of the group included organising or co-ordinating industrial action (for example an ad hoc strike committee)[445].

In view of this immense extension of responsibility, the ability of a union to repudiate unauthorised actions by its officials and committees becomes of crucial importance. The requirements for a valid repudiation are of truly Byzantine complexity[446] : (i) the repudiation must take place as soon as reasonably practicable after the relevant act has come to the knowledge of the repudiator; (ii) written notice of the repudiation must be given to the committee or official in question without delay; (iii) the union must 'do its best'[447] to give individual written notice of the fact and date of the repudiation, without delay, to every member of the union who the union has reason to believe is taking part (or might otherwise take part) in industrial action as a result of the act which is being repudiated, and to the employer of every such member; (iv) the notice to union members must contain the following statement: 'Your union has repudiated the call (or calls) for industrial action to which this notice relates and will give no support to unofficial industrial action taken in response to it (or them). If you are dismissed while taking unofficial industrial action, you will have no right to complain of unfair dismissal'[448] ; (v) the repudiation will be deemed to be ineffective if the executive, president or general secretary subsequently behave

---

444 Employment Act 1990, s 6. See now the Trade Union and Labour Relations (Consolidation) Act 1992, s 20. The proposals were advanced in the Green Paper, *Unofficial Action and the Law* (Cm. 821, 1989).

445 Trade Union and Labour Relations (Consolidation) Act 1992, s 20(3)(b). As the section does not specify that the members of the group have to be members of the union, presumably this could render a union liable for the actions of a non-member in circumstances where the official who happens to belong to that group neither knows nor approves of that person's actions!

446 Trade Union and Labour Relations (Consolidation) Act 1992, s 21. The actions of the principal executive committee, president or general secretary may not be repudiated, nor may those of a person acting under the authority of the rules.

447 The 'boy scout' test?

448 The draftsman somehow managed to resist the temptation to include the words 'you have been warned' in large capitals at the end.

in a manner which is inconsistent with the purported repudiation[449] , or fail to confirm forthwith and in writing on request by a party to a commercial contract whose performance has been interfered with as a result of the act in question that it has been repudiated.

Given that a union may be liable under the above rules, what may it be liable for? Before the 1982 Act allowed an action in tort to be brought directly against a union, the aim of an action by an employer affected by industrial action was generally to obtain an injunction against named union leaders restraining them from organising the industrial action. To obtain such relief a full action for damages had in theory to be available, but in practice the prospect of an employer pursuing union leaders for damages was very remote. After the 1982 Act, an action in tort can now be brought against the union itself, which means that an action for damages (or, perhaps more to the point, the threat of an action for damages) is now a definite possibility, as the union is likely to have assets which could satisfy a judgment for damages. While the primary aim in most cases will still be an injunction, the possibility of unions having to pay damages raises one of the principal objections to laying unions open to actions in tort (ever since the *Taff Vale* decision[450] and the Trade Disputes Act 1906), namely that a strike or other industrial action could well cause vast losses by impeding production, losses which, if fully reflected in damages, could bankrupt the union. Section 22 of the Trade Union and Labour Relations (Consolidation) Act 1992 attempts to meet that argument by laying down maximum amounts of damages to be awarded against unions in tort actions (other than actions for personal injury or arising out of the ownership, occupation, possession, control or use of property, or product liability, where the statutory maxima do not apply). The limits are (a) £10,000 if the union has less than 5,000 members; (b) £50,000 if over 5,000 but less than 25,000 members; (c) £125,000 if over 25,000 but less than 100,000 members; (d) £250,000 if over 100,000 members[451] . These amounts may be varied by the Secretary of State by statutory instrument.

Given that an award of damages is made against the union, how is it to be satisfied? It may be remembered[452] that the Royal Commission set up after the *Taff Vale* case did not recommend the total immunity for a union that was later enacted by the Trade Disputes Act 1906, but rather recommended that certain types of union funds should not be liable to seizure to satisfy awards of damages. Section 23 of the Trade Union and Labour Relations (Consolidation) Act 1992 effects a similar compromise, in that it creates a class of 'protected property' which may not be

---

449 For a case where a purported repudiation was held on the facts to have been a sham, see *Express and Star Ltd v NGA (1982)* [1985] IRLR 455 ('nods, winks, turning of blind eyes and similar clandestine methods of approval', per Skinner J).

450 See p 743 above.

451 These are presumably the maximum amounts at the suit of one particular claimant, so that if there are several claimants, damages up to the maximum can be awarded in the case of each successful claimant, even if the actions arise from the same event. The section is not specific on this point, merely referring to 'any proceedings in tort'. It is unclear whether, if two or more actions are consolidated, or one claimant brings separate actions for damages based on separate events during the dispute, those are separate proceedings. Note that the restrictions on amount in s 22 only apply to damages; they do not apply to any interest awarded on damages (*Boxfoldia Ltd v National Graphical Association (1982)* [1988] IRLR 383) or to fines for contempt of court, and neither this section nor s 23 on protected property prevents the sequestration of the whole of a union's property if a fine is not paid.

452 See p 743 above.

taken to satisfy any award of damages, costs or expenses. This covers any property (a) belonging to trustees of the union in any other capacity (including personally); (b) belonging to any union member (otherwise than jointly or in common with the other members); (c) belonging to any union official who is neither a member nor a trustee; (d) comprised in a political fund[453] ; or (e) comprised in a provident benefits fund[454] .

8 THE USE OF INJUNCTIONS IN INDUSTRIAL CASES

Although the establishment of a viable cause of action in an industrial dispute case could, in theory, lead to an award of damages against the defendant union or its leaders or members[455] , the practical importance of such an action has always been that it permits the claimant to seek an injunction to *stop* the action. Moreover, as industrial disputes and stoppages may arise very quickly, the pattern has been for the claimant to apply for an interim injunction as quickly as possible. Such an injunction may stop the industrial action; in theory, it only does so in order to preserve the status quo pending the full trial of the substantive action, but in practice the claimant has achieved his aim and so the vast majority of these cases never proceed to trial; the granting of the injunction in effect decides the issue[456] . This raises two problems for a potential defendant. An interim injunction may be sought and granted at great speed[457], and indeed can be sought without notice[458] in the absence of the defendant, including before the issue of proceedings in cases of urgency[459] . The normal practice is for the claimant to show good reason why the court should proceed ie without giving notice to the defendant, and this is reinforced in industrial cases by the Trade Union and Labour Relations (Consolidation) Act 1992, section 221(1) which provides that a court shall not grant the injunction (in a case where the defendant is likely to claim that he acted in contemplation or furtherance of a trade dispute) unless it is 'satisfied that all steps which in the circumstances were reasonable have been taken with a view to securing that notice of the application and an opportunity of being heard with respect to the application have been given to [the defendant]'. It is probable that this provision does little other than repeat the normal procedure, for the avoidance of doubt.

The second problem is of more substance. In theory, an application for an interim injunction does not involve a trial of the issue, merely a decision whether to give certain temporary relief pending the action; if, however, the matter never

---

453 The political fund must be subject to rules of the union which prevent its contents from being used for financing strikes or other industrial action: s 23(2)(d). See p 734.

454 'Provident benefits' are defined in s 23(3) as including payments expressly authorised by the union rules, in respect of sickness, injury or unemployment; superannuation; accidents; loss of tools through fire or theft; funeral expenses; provision for the children of deceased members.

455 In *Huntley v Thornton* [1957] 1 All ER 234, [1957] 1 WLR 321 the claimant was awarded £500 damages for conspiracy.

456 See Anderman and Davies 'Injunction procedure in labour disputes' (1973) 2 ILJ 213 and (1974) 3 ILJ 30; Evans 'The use of injunctions in industrial disputes' (1987) 25 BJIR 419; Gall and McKay 'Injunctions as a legal weapon in industrial disputes' (1996) 34 BJIR 567.

457 See eg *Barretts & Baird* (p 765 above), where the injunction that Henry J discharged had originally been granted by another judge over the telephone on a Sunday afternoon.

458 Civil Procedure Rules 1998, r 25.3 (ex parte, in the pre-Woolf terminology).

459 CPR, 25.2. There is no right of appeal against a grant or refusal of an interim injunction without permission of a judge: CPR, 52.3.

goes any further (as in most industrial injunction cases) the interim stage is the only one at which the defendant can put forward his case. It used to be thought that, to be granted an interim injunction, the claimant had to show a 'prima facie' or 'strong prima facie' case that he would succeed at trial[460] ; while this fell short of proof of his case on a balance of probabilities, it still meant that there was some examination of the substantive merits of the case. However, in *American Cyanamid Co v Ethicon Ltd*[461] the House of Lords held that this was incorrect – all that has to be shown by the claimant is that there is a 'serious question to be tried' - in other words, an arguable case fit to go on trial; once that has been shown, the question whether to grant the injunction will be decided on the 'balance of convenience', ie whether the claimant will suffer more damage in the mean time if it is not granted than the defendant will suffer if it is. In ordinary commercial cases, this may make perfect sense and may be backed up by other devices such as an undertaking in damages by the successful claimant. In industrial cases, however, application of the ordinary principles on interim injunctions is likely to favour the employer[462], as the dominant feature is the balance of convenience test which is usually decided in the employer's favour, for he can usually point to definite pecuniary loss if the strike is allowed to continue, whereas the defendant union can only point to the intangible 'damage' of loss of a tactical advantage in the dispute if the strike is stopped. In an attempt to meet the potential problem, the Employment Protection Act 1975 added a new requirement, now contained in section 221 (2) of the Trade Union and Labour Relations (Consolidation) Act 1992, which provides that where an application is made to a court for an interim injunction pending the trial of an action, and the party against whom the injunction is sought claims that he acted in contemplation or furtherance of a trade dispute:

> 'the court shall, in exercising its discretion whether or not to grant the injunction, have regard to the likelihood of that party's succeeding at the trial of the action in establishing any matter which would afford a defence to the action.'

Section 221(2) was first considered by the House of Lords in *NWL Ltd v Nelson*[463], where Lord Diplock said that the section was enacted to enable judges to take into account the practical reality of industrial disputes when applying the 'balance of convenience' principle:

> '[Section 221(2)] ... appears to me to be intended as a reminder addressed to English judges that where industrial action is threatened that is prima facie tortious because it induces a breach of contract they should in exercising their discretion whether or not to grant an interim injunction, put into the balance of convenience in favour of the defendant those countervailing practical realities and, in particular, that the grant of an injunction is tantamount to giving final judgment against the defendant...

460 *J T Stratford & Son Ltd v Lindley* [1965] AC 269, [1964] 3 All ER 102, HL.
461 [1975] AC 396, [1975] 1 All ER 504, HL. See *Hubbard v Pitt* [1975] 3 All ER 1, [1975] ICR 308, CA, the judgment of Henry J in *Barretts & Baird (Wholesale) Ltd v IPCS* [1987] IRLR 3 and Gray 'Interlocutory injunctions since *Cyanamid*' (1981) 40 CLJ 307.
462 As was acknowledged by Lord Diplock in *NWL Ltd v Nelson* [1979] ICR 867, [1979] IRLR 478, HL.
463 [1979] ICR 867, [1979] IRLR 478, HL.

My Lords, when properly understood, there is in my view nothing in the decision of this House in *American Cyanamid Co v Ethicon Ltd* to suggest that in considering whether or not to grant an interim injunction the judge ought not to give full weight to all the practical realities of the situation to which the injunction will apply . . . Cases of this kind are exceptional, but when they do occur they bring into the balance of convenience an important additional element . . . it was clearly prudent of the draftsman of the section to state expressly that in considering whether or not to grant an interim injunction the court should have regard to the likelihood of the defendant's succeeding in establishing that what he did or threatened was done and threatened in contemplation or furtherance of a trade dispute[464] .'

In practice section 221(2) has placed little restraint upon the granting of interim injunctions in industrial disputes. It only exhorts the court to 'have regard to the likelihood' of an immunity defence, which in practice it will almost certainly do anyway: if there is little chance of the claimant employer succeeding, an injunction will not be granted, but otherwise the odds seem to be stacked in the employer's favour, particularly as it appears that the 'public interest' may in appropriate cases be taken into account at this stage[465] (a factor that could be particularly influential where the dispute may give rise to significant disruption to the public). A judge hearing an application for an interim injunction will usually give some (albeit often hurried) consideration to the points of law involved, particularly on the applicability or otherwise of the immunities, but the relevant law is so complex that it is usually not difficult for the employer's counsel to put together an arguable case that there may have been some (perhaps technical) infringement by the union that renders the immunities inapplicable[466], and that the balance of convenience favours the granting of an injunction.

Finally, four points should be noticed; the first is that an appeal against the granting or refusal of an interim injunction will only be allowed where the decision of the trial judge was wrong, or was unjust because of a serious procedural or other irregularity in the proceedings[467], or where there has been a change of circumstances since the order was made. The issue was considered in *Hadmor Productions Ltd v Hamilton*[468] where Lord Diplock emphasised that the appellate court's function is one of review only; an interim injunction is a discretionary remedy, lying essentially within the discretion of the trial judge, so that the appellate court should not on appeal treat the matter de novo and substitute its

464 [1979] ICR 867 at 879, [1979] IRLR 478 at 484.
465 *Beaverbrook Newspapers Ltd v Keys* [1978] ICR 582, [1978] IRLR 34, CA; *United Biscuits (UK) Ltd v Fall* [1979] IRLR 110; *Express Newspapers Ltd v McShane* [1980] 1 All ER 65, [1980] IRLR 35, HL; *Associated British Ports v TGWU* [1989] 3 All ER 822, [1989] ICR 557, HL.
466 This is much more likely as a result of the narrowing of the immunities since 1980, particularly with the introduction of the highly complex balloting and notice requirements; see head 4, above. The development of torts *not* covered by an immunity (eg inducing breach of statutory duty) is also highly significant here. See, eg, *Associated British Ports v TGWU* [1989] 3 All ER 796, [1989] IRLR 305, CA (reversed on other grounds, [1989] 3 All ER 822, [1989] IRLR 399, HL).
467 Civil Procedure Rules, r 52.11(3). There is no right of appeal against a grant or refusal of an interim injunction without the permission of a judge: CPR, r 52.3.
468 [1982] 1 All ER 1042, [1982] ICR 114, HL, applied in *Dimbleby & Sons Ltd v NUJ* [1984] ICR 386, [1984] IRLR 161 above.

own view on the facts[469]. Thus, not only is it likely that the initial application for an injunction will succeed, but also the trial judge's decision may be difficult to challenge on appeal[470].

The second point is that events during the miners' strike of 1984/5 showed how potent a weapon an injunction[471] can be when it is granted against a union itself, not a named individual, for breach of or failure to comply with it is a contempt of court[472] for which the union may be fined (the fine not being subject to the statutory maxima on damages); if the fine is not paid, the claimant may apply for sequestration of the union's assets, and the fact of sequestration could give rise to a claim by disaffected union members for the union to be placed in receivership. Indeed, it has been argued that sequestration and, to a lesser extent, receivership can be viewed as remedies in their own right (especially as sequestration is not merely an administrative means of gathering the fine, since even after the fine is recovered by the sequestrators the sequestration continues until the union purges its contempt).

The third point is that it must be remembered that an industrial dispute is an industrial relations problem, and at some stage the two sides will have to try to resume normal relations; this is unlikely to be helped by the service of claim forms, and a delicate balance may have to be preserved between the enforcement of legal rights in the short term, and the resolution of issues in the industrial relations context in the long term. ACAS have certainly found their collective conciliation efforts materially complicated in cases where there is the threat or actuality of legal proceedings, and at one point suggested that there should be some procedure whereby legal proceedings in industrial dispute cases could be temporarily stayed by the courts to allow at least an attempt at conciliation before final steps are taken[473], but the idea has not been taken up.

Finally, many employers faced with industrial action which is unlawful, and therefore potentially restrainable, choose not to pursue legal remedies for fear of inflaming an already difficult situation and reducing the chances of an early negotiated settlement. However, such a strategy on the part of an employer could in practice be frustrated by the Trade Union and Labour Relations (Consolidation) Act 1992, section 235A[474], which gives an individual who is deprived of goods or services[475] as a result of unlawful industrial action a right

---

469 Under the Civil Procedure Rules, the court can hold a re-hearing if it considers that it would be in the interests of justice to do so in the circumstances: CPR, r 52.11(1).

470 The terms of the injunction may give the defendant the right to apply to the court to discharge or vary the injunction, particularly where it was granted without notice, but there will usually be a delay, and the court may be reluctant to interfere with an injunction which has already been granted.

471 The principal injunctions during the strike were in fact granted to working miners, not employers, but the principles are the same. See Ewing (1985) 14 ILJ at 170; Lightman (1987) 40 CLP 25.

472 On contempt of court and its remedies, see *Harvey* N 19G and Kidner 'Sanctions for contempt by a trade union' (1986) 6 LS 18. Exactly which funds are subject to sequestration may have to be worked out with care in the case of a union with a diverse or decentralised constitution: *News Group Newspapers Ltd v SOGAT 82* [1986] ICR 716, [1986] IRLR 227, CA. For an example of a contempt fine for half-hearted and delayed compliance with a court order, see *Kent Free Press v NGA* [1987] IRLR 267.

473 *ACAS Annual Report 1983*, paras 1.16–1.18.

474 Introduced by the Trade Union Reform and Employment Rights Act 1993, s 22.

475 The original proposals in the Green Paper, *Industrial Relations in the 1990s* (Cm 1602, 1991), would have confined the right to customers of the public services within the scope of the Citizen's Charter, but as enacted the right goes considerably further.

(dubbed the 'Citizen's Right') to apply for an injunction restraining that action[476]. The right arises where 'an effect, or a likely effect, of the unlawful industrial action is or will be to (i) prevent or delay the supply of goods or services, or (ii) reduce the quality of goods or services supplied, to the individual making the claim'[477]. While the industrial action must be unlawful[478], it does not have to be actionable in tort on the part of the applicant, and it seems that he need not have suffered any quantifiable financial loss or damage as a result of it; moreover, it is immaterial whether or not the applicant is *entitled* to be supplied with the goods or services in question (this apparently designed to ensure that frustrated commuters stranded on station platforms are not denied the protection of the section by technical arguments over whether they have a contractual entitlement to travel on any particular train). The potential impact of this procedure was graphically illustrated in *P v National Association of Schoolmasters/Union of Women Teachers*[479], which arose out of the refusal of NASUWT members to accept the 'unreasonable direction' of the head teacher to teach a disruptive pupil who had been permanently excluded from school, only to be reinstated following a successful appeal to the school governors. The pupil sought an injunction restraining the industrial action on the grounds that it was unlawful, and that the separate tuition arrangements which had been made for him interfered with the provision of educational services to him and placed him at an disadvantage, but the application was rejected on the facts[480], and that decision was upheld on appeal by both the Court of Appeal and the House of Lords.

The Citizen's Right is significant on two levels: first, it represents a breathtaking extension of liability, and could be said to render much of the earlier discussion on the scope of the economic torts irrelevant, for as long as the industrial action is in theory actionable by at least one person, anyone else adversely affected by that action may seek an injunction to restrain it; secondly, it could have a damaging effect on attempts to reach negotiated settlements to industrial disputes. In explaining the rationale of the Citizen's Right, the then minister of state posed the question, 'Why should citizens be inconvenienced because a gutless and spineless employer fails to see a remedy for unlawful action which results in loss?'[481], a view which arguably fails to recognise the industrial relations realities of the situation.

---

476 The section does not give a right to damages. Until 1999 a claimant could seek financial assistance from the Commissioner for Protection Against Unlawful Industrial Action, but the Commissioner was abolished by the Employment Relations Act 1999 (see p 67). The White Paper *Fairness at Work* (Cm. 3968), recorded that the Commissioner assisted only one applicant under these provisions, which did not lead to a court case (para 4.31).
477 Trade Union and Labour Relations (Consolidation) Act 1992, s 235A(1)(b).
478 Trade Union and Labour Relations (Consolidation) Act 1992, s 235A(2), which provides that an act of inducement is unlawful if it is actionable in tort by any one or more persons (eg by the employer in dispute), or it could form the basis of an application by a member under s 62 of the 1992 Act (which gives union members a right to be balloted before industrial action). The effect of this is that any non-excusable failure to comply with the detailed statutory requirements (eg on balloting) will render the industrial action restrainable by anyone adversely affected by it.
479 [2003] UKHL 8, [2003] 1 All ER 993.
480 The claimant had alleged (i) that that the dispute was not a trade dispute because it did not relate wholly or mainly to terms and condition of employment; and (ii) that the statutory balloting requirements had not been complied with because two members of staff to whom ballot papers should have been sent did not receive them. Morison J at first instance found for the union on both points.
481 Minister of State, Mr Michael Forsyth, *Hansard*, HC (Standing Committee F).

Chapter 12

Industrial safety (1): compensation for industrial injury

1 INTRODUCTION – FORMS OF COMPENSATION

Compensation for injuries suffered at work has long been an important area of substantive law, which contains at its heart the potentially difficult problem of the relationship between private compensation through the law of tort and the role of the state in providing compensation through the social security system. The importance of the civil action for industrial injuries can be seen in the legal significance of the industrial safety legislation which on its face usually only imposes criminal liabilities on those in breach of a relevant provision, but which has been primarily of significance to the lawyer as a highly practicable head of civil liability upon the employer through the development by the courts of the independent tort of breach of statutory duty to such an extent that it is now of greater practical importance than the common law action for negligence. Indeed, this has given rise to the criticism of the present system (certainly prior to the reforms in the Health and Safety at Work etc. Act 1974 and the 'Six Pack' of EC-based Regulations in the early 1990s) that the lawyers' approach has been to regard the industrial safety legislation primarily in the negative sense as a way of compensating an employee once he is injured, rather than as a positive means of preventing accidents in the first place. The law on civil liability for industrial injuries has seen much development (particularly since freed from the harsher effects of three common law defences – common employment, contributory negligence and volenti non fit injuria[1]) and in the light of the large amount of statute and case law it is easy for the lawyer to overlook the fact that it is only one of *two* aspects, for in quantitative terms the state compensation scheme (primarily the provision of incapacity and disablement benefits) is the senior partner, particularly for all but the most serious of work injuries. It is therefore important for the industrial lawyer to have a knowledge of the state scheme as well as a knowledge of the more traditional law on industrial tort claims.

---

1   The doctrine of common employment was abolished in 1948, and contributory negligence ceased to be a complete defence in 1949; the modern approach to contributory negligence and volenti is discussed under head 3, below.

The present system of compensation is thus a mixed one of state insurance (financed by compulsory National Insurance contributions) and liability in tort (backed by widespread private insurance which, in the context of the liability of an employer to an injured employee, has been compulsory since 1969[2]); further, it is truly 'mixed' in that the injured employee does not have to elect to proceed under one scheme or the other – he may claim under both, though if eventually successful in the tort action, he can now be required to pay back the social security benefits he received in the meantime, out of the damages[3].

In the short term the practical remedy for the injured employee is to claim statutory sick pay while incapacitated from work; the state may also give compensation in the long term, through disablement benefit, but if his injuries are major or lasting, the employee may also wish to bring a civil action against his employer for damages[4]; in the case of the state scheme the question of fault is irrelevant but in the case of a civil action the claimant employee will normally have to prove fault of sorts. Over the years, the concept of fault liability has come under increasing criticism[5], and the principal arguments are well known – the fault-based tort action is slow, cumbersome and uncertain; it only compensates a small proportion of those in fact injured each year, and its method of compensating those few has always been in the past to give damages as a lump sum[6], often taking little or no account of future inflation; the risk of bringing an action is great, even with the substitution of no-win-no-fee arrangements to replace legal aid; proof of fault depends on the availability of evidence, and lack of such evidence may be fatal to the claimant's case, however badly injured he is; the system is extremely costly to run, certainly when compared with the low running costs of the state-run social security system. Such criticisms have been given impetus by the enactment of no-fault liability systems in other jurisdictions (either partial, for example in relation to motor accidents, or total); the obvious source for comparison has always been the New Zealand Accidents Compensation Scheme which provides comprehensive state insurance for all injuries (not just industrial ones) and bars any tort action for personal injuries caused by an accident[7]. With this background, the whole question of civil liability in this country

2   Employers' Liability (Compulsory Insurance) Act 1969. The area of motor vehicle accidents is also subject to compulsory insurance, which therefore covers the large majority of all tort actions, since the leading study on this area found that 47% of all tort claims concern work accidents and 41% concern motor vehicles accidents: Report of the Royal Commission on Civil Liability (Cmnd 7054, 1978), para 79.
3   Social Security (Recovery of Benefits) Act 1997.
4   In doing so, he may well receive assistance from his union if he is a member. For the union's liability in costs if the claim fails, see *Bourne v Colodense Ltd* [1985] ICR 291, [1985] IRLR 339, CA, noted Kidner (1985) 14 ILJ 124.
5   The literature is extensive. See Ison *The Forensic Lottery* (1967); Atiyah *Accidents, Compensation and the Law* (3rd edn, 1993); Jolowicz 'Liability for accidents' [1968] CLJ 50; Stoljar 'Accidents, costs and responsibility' (1973) 36 MLR 233; O'Connell 'No-fault insurance for Great Britain' (1973) 2 ILJ 187; Parsons 'A no-fault system?: not proven' (1974) 3 ILJ 129; the Industrial Law Society 'Compensation for industrial injury' (1975) 4 ILJ 195; Sugarman 'Personal injury law reform: a proposed first step' (1987) 16 ILJ 30.
6   There have, however, been some moves towards structured settlements, to meet the long-standing criticisms of lump sum damages.
7   Accident Compensation Act 1972, which came into force in 1974; it was based on the Report of the Royal Commission on Compensation for Personal Injury in New Zealand (1967), chaired by Woodhouse J, who also produced a similar report for the Australian government in 1974. On the content and operation of the original New Zealand scheme, see Harris 'Accident Compensation in New Zealand: a comprehensive insurance system' (1974) 37 MLR 361; Palmer 'Accident Compensation in New Zealand; the first two years' (1977) 25 Am J Comp L 1; Szakats 'The re-emergence of common law

(including industrial injury) was reviewed by the Royal Commission on Civil Liability, under the chairmanship of Lord Pearson[8], which did not recommend abolition of the action in tort for personal injuries, but instead recognised and emphasised the interrelationship of state insurance and the law of tort, envisaging that, although not abolished, the latter would increasingly become the 'junior partner'[9].

A detailed consideration of the Pearson Report is outside the scope of this book, but four particular suggested reforms should be mentioned and kept in mind when reading the rest of the chapter. The Report recommended, first, that the value of social security benefits should be deducted *in full* from subsequent tort damages, making it clear that the two systems are fully complementary[10]; second, that damages for non-pecuniary loss should not be recoverable for the first three months of injury[11] (emphasising the importance of the tort action in *serious* cases); third, that earnings related benefits under the industrial injuries scheme should be improved[12]; and fourth, that damages for future pecuniary loss should be through periodic payments (inflation-proofed, and subject to periodic review by the courts in the light of any changes in the claimant's medical condition) instead of the present lump sum, such a payment system to be obligatory in the case of death or lasting injury and discretionary in other cases[13]. However, the Report did not suggest alteration of the present basis of civil liability for industrial injuries and in particular did not recommend the imposition of strict liability as it did in the case of product liability and exceptionally hazardous operations[14]. Some cautious reforms were made in the Administration of Justice Act 1982, particularly in relation to the reassessment of damages at the suit of the claimant where an injury has worsened, but most of the other reforms were of a minor nature to deal with particular defects in the existing law (see head 3, below). Thus, the Report in fact produced little change in this area, which has remained curiously stable for many years (as to liability – procedure has been changed markedly by the Woolf reforms and the replacement of legal aid), as opposed to the frantic pace of change affecting most other areas of industrial law.

Bearing in mind the vital interrelationship of state insurance and tort liability we must now look at the law relating to state benefits for those injured at work and the actions that may be maintained in tort by the injured employee, with the

---

principles in the New Zealand Accident Compensation scheme' (1978) 7 ILJ 216. In recent years, however, the New Zealand scheme has run into financial difficulties and has had to be pruned since 1992 (especially in relation to medical injuries where an element of fault has been reintroduced) and so is no longer a 'pure' alternative: Miller 'An analysis and critique of the 1992 changes to New Zealand and New Zealand's Accident Compensation Scheme' (1992) 5 Canta LR 1.

8   *Report of the Royal Commission on Civil Liability* (Cmnd 7054, 1978). See Corfield, Harris and Ogus 'Pearson: principled reform or political compromise?' (1978) 7 ILJ 143; Fleming 'The Pearson Report: its "strategy" ' (1979) 42 MLR 249.

9   Pearson Report, para 1732.

10 Pearson Report, paras 467–483. This has now come about (see p 844 below), but for very different reasons, ie, simply to recoup the money.

11 Pearson Report, paras 382–389.

12 Pearson Report, paras 800–813. In fact, the earnings related supplement was abolished by the previous government (Social Security (No 2) Act 1980, s 4), as was the short-term industrial injury benefit (Social Security and Housing Benefits Act 1982, s 39).

13 Pearson Report, paras 550–614.

14 One of the major recommendations was that motor accidents should be covered by a no-fault state insurance scheme, closely modelled on that for industrial injuries.

caveat in the case of the latter that, as the subject of industrial law has now become so specialised and substantial in its own right, that part of the chapter has been confined to giving only an *outline* of an industrial tort action, and to pointing out what may be seen as the more specialised industrial aspects or applications of ordinary tort principles, with which it is assumed that the reader is already familiar.

2 STATE BENEFITS FOR THOSE INJURED AT WORK[15]

The present system of industrial injuries benefit grew out of the concept of workmen's compensation which, when first enacted in 1897, introduced the entirely new principle that in respect of certain employees and in relation to the risk of industrial injury, the employer became in effect the insurer of the employee's safety. The legislation provided for certain fixed benefits to be paid by the employer to an injured employee, either by periodic payments or a lump sum, whether or not the accident was the result of the employer's negligence. It thus provided the principal legal remedy for an injured employee, and the employer would cover his statutory liability by privately arranged insurance. While obviously much more available than redress through an ordinary tort action, the system was heavily criticised, primarily because of the huge amount of litigation that it caused, since the real parties to most claims were insurance companies and trade unions. The system of compensation was radically altered by the National Insurance (Industrial Injuries) Act 1946, which came into force in 1948 and changed the basis to one of state-run insurance, financed by compulsory contributions and administered by the relevant government department and not through the courts. The scheme as it existed prior to 1983 was that where an employed earner suffered personal injury caused by an accident arising out of and in the course of employment, he or she was eligible for weekly payments of industrial injury benefit for a maximum of six months, and for disablement benefit if there was some long-term loss of faculty.

The scheme thus drew two distinctions – between short term and longer term needs, and between those injured at work and those injured elsewhere or merely sick (who had to claim sickness benefit or, in the case of a lasting inability to work, invalidity benefit). The significance of the latter distinction was that, as a matter of policy, those injured at work were treated more generously than others. Thus, in 1948 injury benefit was 73% higher than sickness benefit. However, by 1981 that preference had steadily declined to only 12%, though the system still retained the complete separation of the two forms of benefit. Partly for that reason, and partly due to the then newly introduced administrative provisions requiring the employer to pay (initially for eight weeks per year, but now for a maximum of twenty-eight weeks per year) 'statutory sick pay'[16], the previous government decided upon what they saw as a rationalisation of the system. Thus, by virtue of the Social Security and Housing Benefits Act 1982, industrial injury benefit was abolished as from April 1983 and those injured at work are now subject to the same regime as those injured elsewhere or merely ill in relation to short-term

---

15   See Wikeley, Ogus and Barendt *The Law of Social Security* (5th edn, 2002) ch 7 for the basic structure and background; see also Lewis *Compensation for Industrial Injury* (1987).

16   See p 222 above. This administrative scheme applies to employees who would previously have claimed injury benefit, as well as to those claiming sickness benefit.

income maintenance, namely statutory sick pay for the first twenty-eight weeks if in employment and covered by that scheme, or the substituted incapacity benefit if not.

In the light of these changes it might have been thought that at last it would no longer be necessary to draw the often difficult distinction between an industrial injury and some other misfortune. Given that potential difficulty (and the enormous amount of case and statute law which has built up on it over the years), this would have been the greatest advantage of the supposed rationalisation and would have materially simplified this area of law. Unfortunately, however, that has not happened. The distinction has to continue because industrial disablement benefit has *not* been abolished – it was subject to major reforms in the Social Security Act 1986 which are considered below, but it remains payable to those who have suffered longer-term loss of faculty as a result of an *industrial* injury. Moreover, initial suggestions by the present government that the industrial disablement scheme should be in effect privatised met with very strong opposition, and at the time of writing have not been proceeded with. It is therefore still necessary to define industrial accidents and industrial diseases, and it is to these that we now turn.

(i) Industrial accidents

'Industrial accident' is a vital term which has produced a great volume of litigation, both under the old workmen's compensation legislation and the modern social security legislation, for both applied the same test, namely whether there was 'personal injury caused by an accident arising out of and in the course of employment'.

(a) Personal injury

This will normally be self-evident and has been construed widely, excluding only damage to an artificial aid such as false teeth or an artificial leg[17]. It can include mental or nervous shock[18]. A disease could well constitute personal injury, but the danger then is that its contraction might not be viewed as an accident; to counter this, certain more common diseases are covered separately, and this is considered below.

(b) Accident

There is no statutory definition of accident, even though as a concept it is essential in order to ensure that benefits are only payable in cases which are intended to be covered, not just in any case where there is some form of deterioration in health. The locus classicus has usually been said to be the dictum of Lord Macnaghten that an accident is 'an unlooked-for mishap or an untoward event which is not expected or designed'[19]. This must be applied from the viewpoint of the victim, so that even if injury is caused by an act, possibly criminal, which is

---

17   R(I) 7/56. However, damage to an artificial hip joint was held to be personal injury in R(I) 8/81 on the basis that it constituted an integral part of the body.
18   *Yates v South Kirby Collieries Ltd* [1910] 2 KB 538, CA; *Re Drake* [1945] 1 All ER 576.
19   *Fenton v J Thorley & Co Ltd* [1903] AC 443 at 448, HL.

entirely deliberate on the part of the perpetrator, that may still be an accident to the victim, as in *Trim Joint District School Board v Kelly* [20] where a master at an industrial school was killed by the deliberate acts of certain boys whom he had threatened to punish. This may also apply to acts of negligence by a third party or the victim:

> 'Speaking generally ... an accident means any unintended and unexpected occurrence which produces hurt or loss. But it is often used to denote any unintended or unexpected loss or hurt apart from its cause; and if the cause is not known the loss or hurt itself would certainly be called an accident ... The great majority of what are called accidents are occasioned by carelessness; but for legal purposes it is often unimportant to distinguish carelessness from other unintended and unexpected events.[21]'

It could indeed go as far as to cover suicide by the employee if there was a strong enough causal link between that and a work-related factor, for example producing depression or insanity leading to the death.

The personal injury must be caused by the accident in question. Questions of causation can cause much litigation, and principles well known to the law of tort (for example, 'breaking the chain of causation') may be applicable here in more difficult cases, for example where the original accident put the claimant in a position where he was subjected to a further, non-industrial happening. However, for most purposes a fairly relaxed approach to causation has been taken in this context, and it is sufficient if the accident in question was more than a background factor and was at least a contributory cause, even if not the sole one. The practical importance of this is that the claimant may still succeed even if the reason for his disability was that the accident aggravated a pre-existing condition, or only produced the injury in question because of such a condition[22].

The major problem with the term 'accident' is to distinguish it from what is called a 'process', ie some process of bodily or mental degeneration which is not ascribable to any particular event. While an accident may remain genuinely such, even though its result is a disease of sorts[23], it may be that in such a case there is more likelihood of a finding that there was no discernible accident and that the case merely concerns the sort of ordinary illness that this scheme is not designed to cover. Perhaps the classic kind of accident is where one definite event, external to the claimant, clearly causes physical injury:

> 'It must be something external which has some physiological or psychological effect on that part of the sufferer's anatomy which sustains the actual trauma, or some bodily activity of the sufferer which would be perceptible to an observer ...[24]'

20   [1914] AC 667, HL; see CI 63/49; R(I) 30/58.
21   *Fenton v J Thorley & Co Ltd* [1903] AC 443 at 453, HL, per Lord Lindley. See *Harris v Associated Portland Cement Manufacturers Ltd* [1939] AC 71, HL.. There must therefore be an 'accident', causative of injury; it is not enough that the individual suffered or contracted the condition in question 'accidentally': *Chief Adjudication Officer v Faulds* [2000] 2 All ER 961, [2000] 1 WLR 1035, HL.
22   R(I) 12/52; R(I) 19/63; cf R(I) 6/82.
23   *Brintons Ltd v Turvey* [1905] AC 230, at 233, HL per Lord Halsbury LC.
24   *Jones v Secretary of State for Social Services* [1972] AC 944 at 1009, [1972] 1 All ER 145 at 184, HL, per Lord Diplock.

However, many cases are not as clear as that (for example, where the claimant begins to feel internal pains after a period of time performing some particular operation at work), and in order that the concept of 'process' should not be applied too freely to disqualify too many people, the construction of accident has been broadened in two particular ways. The first is that, consistently with what was said above on causation, there can still be an accident where the event relied upon was merely the last in a chain of events or deteriorations, the proverbial last straw[25]. The second is that there may be no need to isolate one particular event, for a series of events may be sufficient to constitute an accident if they can reasonably be viewed together, as with constant minor burns or repeated loud noises suffered while at work[26]; obviously the nature of the 'series' will be important, but so also might the time over which it occurred, so that if a particular condition arose over a short period, it might be more readily construed overall as an 'accident'[27].

This may be an area where the borderline between accident and process is at its thinnest, for a series of factors taking place over anything other than a relatively short period may soon look like the sort of ordinary health hazard which, however unfortunate, is not meant to be covered by the scheme[28]. Thus, a trainee nurse at a day nursery who developed infantile paralysis after contact with a child suffering from it was held to have suffered an industrial accident, but a doctor who contracted TB as a result of a series of penetrations of the lung by bacilli at various times was held not entitled to benefit[29]. More topically, it has been accepted that lung injury, allegedly from inhaling a fellow employee's tobacco smoke ('passive smoking'), could be an accident where it happened on six specific, documented occasions, though the Commissioner pointed out that *simple* passive smoking over a period of time would remain a process[30]. Similarly, post-traumatic stress disorder suffered immediately after an abusive and aggressive incident with fellow workers who were on strike was held to be an 'accident'[31]. On the other hand, in the modern concept of stress injuries generally, it may be difficult to show the necessary accident and causation where that injury is the eventual result of exposure to a consistent level of stress in the occupation concerned (for example, as a firefighter or paramedic)[32]. These are obviously wide questions of fact, and it must be stressed that, in this context and throughout the whole area of injury benefit, each case must depend heavily upon its facts and so, while there are many decided cases, they do not constitute a consistent body of case law to which detailed reference must be made on every occasion; it is certainly easy to point to certain decisions which, when put side by side, seem distinctly odd.

---

25 R(I) 54/53.
26 R(I) 24/54; R(I) 43/55.
27 R(I) 4/62; R(I) 31/52.
28 There may of course be tortious liability, even if no injury benefit, if the 'process' was caused by the employer's neglect.
29 CI 159/50 and CI 83/50 respectively.
30 R(I) 6/91.
31 CI 2414/98.
32 *Chief Adjudication Officer v Faulds* [2000] 2 All ER 961, [2000] 1 WLR 1035, HL; there is a useful summary of the case law (from *Fenton v Thorley* onwards) in the speeches of Lord Hope and Lord Clyde.

(c) Arising out of and in the course of employment

This requirement has proved the most troublesome of all, and produced a disproportionate amount of litigation, both under the present state scheme and under the former workmen's compensation scheme. The usual approach has been that the phrase in fact contains two limbs; the requirement that the accident must arise 'in the course of employment' is a matter of the factual scope of the employment in question, while the requirement that it must arise 'out of' the employment is primarily a matter of causation. Thus, for example, in *Chief Adjudication Officer v Rhodes*[33] where a Benefits Agency officer was assaulted in her home by a neighbour whom she had reported for suspected benefit fraud, it was held that this 'accident' had arisen 'out of' her employment but *not* 'in the course of' it, and so her claim for benefit failed. Whether an accident is in the course of employment is a question of time, place and job content, and the Court of Appeal reaffirmed in *Nancollas v Insurance Officer*[34] that that question is largely one of fact for the adjudicating authorities. Sir John Donaldson MR stressed that there is no single test to be applied (particularly not a test of the contractual obligations of the employee simpliciter), and that the previous case law can only provide general guidance as to factors that may be thought important in a particular case.

Bearing this clear warning in mind, some of that guidance may now be considered, and the starting point is that the question may more easily be answered in the case of a person with definite hours and a set place of work. Outside that (as in the case of *Nancollas* itself) the problems that have arisen are legion. Thus, when a home help, employed by a local council to make certain defined calls at certain defined times, was injured on her way to her first call of the day, it was held that this did not arise in the course of her employment, for her journey was merely preparatory to her first place of work[35]. On the other hand when a civil servant, employed to work partly in his office and partly by visiting homes as the need arose, was injured in a street accident within his defined area when about to make his first visit of the day, it was held that that was in the course of his employment, for it was during his normal hours and in the proper exercise of his discretion in performing his functions[36]. On the question of the time of the accident, a claimant need not be injured in actual working time to be successful, for normal break times may count, and he may be allowed a reasonable period before and after actually working before he ceases to be in the course of employment, as where a successful claimant arrived, as she usually did, half an hour early in order to change into her working clothes and have a meal in the canteen, where she was injured[37]. In that case, Lord Widgery CJ approved this extract from one of the old works on workmen's compensation:

'The course of employment may be taken to have commenced although the hour for actual work has not struck, if the workman's arrival on the

---

33   [1999] IRLR 103, CA; the difficulty of drawing these distinctions is shown by the fact that the Court of Appeal split 2–1.
34   [1985] 1 All ER 833, CA; see eg R(I) 1/93. Note, however, that in *Smith v Stages* [1989] AC 928, [1989] 1 All ER 833, HL, Lord Lowry said that this does not mean a total lack of principles or, at the least, applicable guidelines.
35   R(I) 2/67; see also R(I) 12/75, R(I) 14/81 and R(I) 1/83.
36   R(I) 4/70.
37   *R v National Insurance Comr, ex p East* [1976] ICR 206; for the use of time after a shift, eg for bathing, see CI 22/49 and R(I) 22/51.

premises is either not unreasonably early, or is necessitated by the circumstances of the employment, or if, at the time of the accident, he is doing something on the employer's premises which is necessary to be done to equip himself for his work.'

The question of the place of employment has caused much litigation, particularly where the claimant was not tied to any particular machine, room, etc. Normally, the claimant may be successful if injured where he usually works in practice, or while using reasonable access to such a place; he may, however, fail if he was injured in a 'public zone', ie in a place to which in practice the public have general access (regardless of their strict legal rights)[38], on the basis that benefits are not payable for injuries which might have been suffered in the ordinary course of events by members of the public. Perhaps the most difficult aspect of the course of employment is the actual job content of the claimant, for it is clear that benefits are only payable for injuries sustained actually in the course of the claimant's work – it is not enough to show merely that at the material time he was legally engaged under a contract of employment. Thus if he was engaged in something outside the scope of his normal duties when injured, he may not be able to claim benefit. Even where a realistic view was taken of a claimant's duties, however, this test could work harshly, and one way to avoid that possibility was to look at the course of employment *and things reasonably incidental to it*[39]. Thus an employee may be doing something for his own purposes, such as having a break, taking a meal in the canteen or talking with other employees, but as long as it is something which he is not contractually disbarred from doing and may reasonably be said to be incidental to his actual work, he may still be in the course of his employment. This aspect was stressed by the Court of Appeal in *R v Industrial Injuries Comr, ex p AEU (No 2)*[40], but was subject to some restriction by that Court in the later case of *R v National Insurance Comr, ex p Michael*[41], where a policeman who was injured while representing his force in a football match was refused benefit, in spite of considerable support and encouragement being given to such sporting activities by the employing police authority. The Court of Appeal held that, while sports could in some cases be in the course of employment[42], that was not the case here, for it was not part of his ordinary work, nor was it 'reasonably incidental', for that was not part of the statutory test and, as a judicial gloss, should be restricted to cases where the injury occurred during some kind of interruption of the work which he was employed to do; it should not be used widely, to cover activities well outside the normal scope of the claimant's duties:

'This test of "reasonably incidental" is to be gathered from the speeches of Lord Sumner, Lord Parmoor and Lord Wrenbury in *Armstrong, Whitworth & Co Ltd v Redford* ... It was followed by this court in *R v Industrial Injuries Comr, ex p AEU* ... But in all these cases the workman was at the premises where he or she worked and was injured while on a visit to the canteen or other place,

38   R(I) 1/68; cf R(I) 3/72.
39   *Charles R Davidson & Co v M'Robb* [1918] AC 304, HL; *Armstrong, Whitworth & Co Ltd v Redford* [1920] AC 757, HL.
40   [1966] 2 QB 31, [1966] 1 All ER 97, CA.
41   [1977] 2 All ER 420, [1977] ICR 121, CA; R(I) 2/80; cf R(I) 3/81.
42   See [1977] 2 All ER 420 at 431, [1977] ICR 121 at 135, per Lawton LJ; see also R(I) 13/66 where a fireman injured playing volleyball during a recreation period of a duty watch, which was encouraged as a way of keeping fit, was able to claim benefit. Cf R(I) 3/81.

for a break. The words "reasonably incidental" should be read in that context, and limited to cases of that kind. They are not part of the statute and should not be extended to other cases without careful consideration.[43] '

This is particularly relevant on the question of breaks in the employment; normal coffee and tea breaks will probably remain within the course of employment, as will meal breaks taken in the works canteen, though not breaks taken elsewhere purely at the choice of the employee. The rule here is in theory beneficial to the employee, for it was said in *R v Industrial Injuries Comr, ex p AEU (No 2)* that the employee would only be taken out of the course of his employment if he was engaged in some *material* interruption of his work[44]. However, the actual result of that case showed a rather stringent application of this, for the employee who had been injured while still smoking in a corridor five minutes after the end of a ten minute tea break was held to have put himself outside the course of his employment and was not eligible for benefit.

Given that a particular injury happened in the course of employment, there is then the further requirement that it must have arisen out of that employment, for not every accident occurring during working time is actually referable to that work; it is a question of causation:

'Was it part of the injured man's employment to hazard, to suffer or to do that which caused his injury? … To ask if the cause of the accident was within the sphere of the employment, or was one of the ordinary risks of the employment, or reasonably incidental to the employment … are all different ways of asking whether it was a part of his employment that he should have acted as he was acting, or should have been in the position in which he was, whereby in the course of that employment he sustained injury.[45]'

Thus, if an employee while at work takes medicine which has an adverse effect, that will not be an industrial accident, for it was not an employment risk[46], but where an employee was injured by an explosion when he attempted to light a cigarette close to a gas leak in the factory where he worked, it was held that he was eligible for benefit:

'… there were two causes of this accident: the act of the claimant in operating his lighter and the presence of an explosive mixture of gas and air. The latter was dangerous, and the danger was clearly a risk of the claimant's employment. Prima facie therefore the accident arose out of the employment. The remaining question is whether the claimant's act, which

---

43 [1977] 2 All ER 420 at 423, [1977] ICR 121 at 126, per Lord Denning MR. In R(I) 10/80 a shop steward who was injured while attending a union course in pursuance of statutory time off work (see p 689 above) was held not eligible as the connection with her work was not sufficient. On the other hand, in R(I) 1/93 an employee injured while attending a meeting at work to consider her RSI claim against the employer succeeded.

44 [1966] 2 QB 31 at 51, [1966] 1 All ER 97 at 106, per Salmon LJ. In *R v National Insurance Comr, ex p Reed* (reported in the appendix to R(I) 7/80) a policeman injured whilst returning to the station from lunch at home was held eligible to claim by the Divisional Court, but the crucial factor was that while at home he was still on duty; this factor was missing in R(I) 5/81 in the case of a fireman killed whilst driving home who was merely on general call at any time in case of emergency.

45 *Lancashire and Yorkshire Rly Co v Highley* [1917] AC 352, at 372, HL per Lord Sumner.

46 R(I) 43/57.

was done for his own personal purposes, added a *different* risk which was the real cause of the accident. In our judgment, his act did not do so ... The claimant's act ... converted the danger of an explosion into an actual explosion. It did not make it a different danger or create a fresh one. In our judgment there was here an amply sufficient causal connection between the employment and its risks on the one hand and the accident on the other.[47],

Apart from the ordinary problems of causation, two particular points have arisen in this context. The first is that the injury concerned may in fact have befallen anyone in the position of the claimant, whether or not employed to do his kind of work, as where a lorry driver is struck by a flying piece of grit, which could easily have hit a private motorist instead. In theory, an employee injured by a common hazard such as this should not be eligible for benefit[48], but it appears that more lenient decisions have been reached in some cases, by holding that the employment was the reason for the employee being in the particular circumstances in which that risk operated upon him, though the distinction is hardly a satisfactory one. The second point is that the claimant's own conduct may have caused or contributed to his injuries, but here a relatively indulgent approach has been taken, for the claim will only fail on this ground if the claimant created by his conduct a risk different from that inherent in his employment, and it was that different risk which in fact caused the accident (see the passage cited above from R(I) 2/63); if the claimant's contribution was less dramatic than that, his claim may still succeed, and there are no provisions for reduction of benefit on analogy with contributory negligence in the law of tort or contributory fault in unfair dismissal.

Some of the practical importance of having the two requirements of 'out of' and 'in the course of' employment has been to some extent lessened by a statutory provision[49] that an accident arising in the course of employment is presumed to have arisen out of that employment, in the absence of evidence to the contrary. Given a broad interpretation, this presumption could place the burden of proof on the 'out of employment' limb on the Agency officer in most cases, and thus diminish the claimant's difficulties, but a narrow view has been taken by the Divisional Court, so that if *any* evidence points to a contrary conclusion the presumption is inoperative:

'The words of the sub-section are not "in the absence of proof to the contrary" or "unless the contrary is proved"; the words of the sub-section are "in the absence of evidence to the contrary". That has been held by commissioners quite rightly ... to mean no more than that, if there is evidence before the commissioner that the accident does not arise out of or in the course of employment, then there is no presumption at all and it is left to the parties to prove the case in the ordinary way.[50],

47 R(I) 2/63, para 29.
48 R(I) 62/53; R(I) 7/60; R(I) 6/82.
49 Social Security Contributions and Benefits Act 1992, s 94(3).
50 *R v National Insurance Comr, ex p Richardson* [1958] 2 All ER 689 at 690, [1958] 1 WLR 851 at 855, per Lord Goddard CJ. See, eg, the inapplicability of the presumption in R(I) 11/80.

If this is correct, the presumption will be of little effect, restricted in practice to those cases where no one knows how the accident happened, only that it arose in the course of employment. It would therefore be rash to state that the 'out of employment' limb is of waning importance, even though often criticised, and it certainly remains in principle as a device to ensure that only genuinely employment-linked accidents are covered by the industrial injuries scheme.

(d) Special statutory provisions

The general principles discussed above have been supplemented by four special statutory provisions, covering four potential problems:

(1) Where a claimant is injured whilst doing something in contravention of a relevant regulation or of any orders of the employer, that accident is still treated as arising out of and in the course of employment if (a) it would have been deemed so to have arisen if the claimant had not been in contravention, and (b) the 'illegal' act was done by the claimant for the purposes of and in connection with the employer's trade or business[51]. Thus, provided there remains a connection between the wrongful act and that which the claimant was employed to do, he may still succeed. In *Noble v Southern Rly Co*[52], Lord Maugham said that the approach should be to ask the following questions:

> 'First, looking at the facts proved as a whole, including any regulations or orders affecting the workman, was the accident one which arose out of and in the course of employment? Secondly, if the first question is answered in the negative, is the negative answer due to the fact that when the accident happened the workman was acting in contravention of some regulation or order? Thirdly, if the second question is answered in the affirmative, was the act which the workman was engaged in performing done by the workman for the purposes of and in connection with his employer's trade or business?'

The scope of this provision and the problems which arise can be seen by contrasting two cases. In R(I) 1/70 a dock labourer, employed in the loading of a ship, met with an accident while driving an electric truck to fetch two slings necessary for the loading. He was not authorised or permitted to drive the truck, which was owned by the port authorities and not by his employers. The Commissioner held that, by reason of the predecessor to section 98, the claimant could recover since in fetching the slings he was acting in the course of his employment, notwithstanding that he went about it in a prohibited manner. However, in an earlier case[53] a more restrictive view was taken. A dock labourer who, without authority or permission, decided to drive an unattended fork lift truck to remove an obstruction, and was injured whilst doing so, was held by the Commissioner to have taken himself outside the course of his employment, and beyond the scope of what is now section 98; this decision was affirmed by the Divisional Court. While it is true that section 98 will not avail someone who is injured while doing

51   Social Security Contributions and Benefits Act 1992, s 98.
52   [1940] AC 583, at 591, HL; adopted in CI 210/50.
53   *R v D'Albuquerque, ex p Bresnahan* [1966] 1 Lloyd's Rep 69.

something which was clearly not his job, the distinction between these two cases is a thin one, and it could be argued that the more liberal approach in the later case is more in line with the policy behind the section.

(2) An employee who is injured while travelling to work on transport operated by or for the employer (not being ordinary public transport) is eligible for benefit, even though he may have been under no obligation to use that particular transport[54]. This statutory provision covers the particular case of travelling on employer-provided transport; outside that provision, a case must be decided on general grounds. The question that arises here is the same as in the area of vicarious liability in tort (when is a travelling accident 'in the course of employment', so that the employer is liable?); in that context, valuable guidance has been given by Lord Lowry in *Smith v Stages*[55], which is set out at p 857 below in that context, and to which reference may also be made for statutory purposes.

The social security case law amply demonstrates the problems here, for one starts from the general premise that an employee will not be eligible if injured on a journey to or from work which is merely for the purpose of going to his work or back from it, using a route also used by the general public. If he is injured whilst using a private access to his place of work, or whilst crossing land owned by the employer, he may be eligible[56] but once on the public highway, or in an area open to the public, his chances of claiming benefit are slim, *unless* he can show that his journey was in the performance of a duty to his employer, not merely preparatory to the performance of a duty[57]. Thus if the employee was ordered to make a particular journey or the journey was part of, or incidental to, the content of his job (wholly or in part), the employee may be covered by the scheme, even if the accident happens while he is travelling from home to his first appointment[58]. However, this will be more easily established in the case of a person without fixed hours or place of work, or with a discretion in the exercise of his function; where a person has a fixed work pattern at places other than the employer's premises (for example, a home help), he or she may still be treated as an ordinary employee who is not eligible for benefit if injured when travelling to the first call[59].

(3) An accident befalling an employee on the employer's premises while he is trying to rescue or protect people or avert serious damage to property in an actual or supposed emergency at the premises is deemed to arise out of and in the course of employment[60].

(4) An accident arising in the course of employment which is caused by another person's 'misconduct, skylarking or negligence' or by steps taken in consequence of such matters is deemed to arise out of employment, and so give rise to a claim for benefit, provided the claimant did not 'directly or

---

54 Social Security Contributions and Benefits Act 1992, s 99. See Lewis 'Accidents on the way to work' [1981] NLJ 1218. The authority of the employer for the mode of transport is essential: R(I) 5/80.

55 [1989] AC 928, [1989] 1 All ER 833, HL, applied in R(I) 1/91.

56 *Weaver v Tredegar Iron and Coal Co Ltd* [1940] AC 955, at 983, HL, per Lord Romer; R(I) 5/67.

57 *R v National Industrial Injury Benefit Tribunal, ex p Fieldhouse* (1974) 17 KIR 63; R(I) 12/75; R(I) 5/77.

58 R(I) 18/55; *Nancollas v Insurance Officer* [1985] 1 All ER 833, CA.

59 Contrast R(I) 4/70 and R(I) 3/72 with R(I) 2/67 and R(I) 12/75.

60 Social Security Contributions and Benefits Act 1992, s 100.

indirectly induce or contribute to' the accident by his own conduct[61]. This provision is designed to include the case where, although the claimant suffered from the actions of another while doing his job, there might be doubt as to whether the injury arose 'out of' his employment, as in *R v National Insurance Comr, ex p Richardson*[62] where a bus conductor who was assaulted on his bus was denied benefit on the basis that the attack was made on him simply as a person who happened to be there, not *qua* conductor, and so the injury did not arise 'out of' the employment. The present provision was first introduced in 1961 and covers acts consequent upon misconduct, etc, as well as direct results of it. Thus, in R(I) 3/67 the claimant was hit by a snowball thrown by a fellow employee during a smoke break; when he went after the perpetrator with intent to remonstrate, his hand was injured by a slammed door and the Commissioner held that he was eligible for benefit under the predecessor of section 101. The section also covers injury in the course of employment caused by the behaviour or presence of an animal or by being struck by any object or by lightning.

(ii) Industrial diseases

While it is obvious that certain occupations may carry a risk of contracting certain diseases, these would in the main fall outside the basic industrial injury scheme which is reliant upon the physical injury in question being caused by an 'accident'; the gradual contraction of an industrial disease is prima facie a 'process' and so not covered. The answer to this has been to provide separate coverage for certain specified diseases which experience has shown to be often caused by certain employments. The machinery provided by the legislation is that the Secretary of State may by regulation (on the advice of the Industrial Injuries Advisory Council) prescribe a particular disease if he is satisfied that it ought to be treated as a risk of the occupation in question, not just as a risk common to all persons, and that it is such that there will be reasonable certainty in any given case that contraction of the disease can fairly be ascribed to the employment[63]. Regulations have been made under this power which specify approximately sixty diseases[64], and once a disease is specified in relation to an employment, the remedies of a person contracting it lie under these particular provisions, not under the general 'personal injury by accident' provisions. Schedule 1 to the Regulations contains a table of diseases and the occupations for which they are prescribed; a disease may be prescribed for one particular occupation, or for a general description of work, which may form part of a number of occupations. Thus, for example, ankylostomiasis is prescribed for 'work in or about a mine', whereas subcutaneous cellulitis of the hand is prescribed for any occupation involving 'manual labour causing severe or prolonged friction or pressure on the hand'. There are

---

61   S 101.
62   [1958] 2 All ER 689, [1958] 1 WLR 851.
63   Social Security Contributions and Benefits Act 1992, s 108(2). For the difficulties inherent in industrial disease cases, see Wikeley 'Social security adjudication and occupational lung diseases' (1988) 17 ILJ 92.
64   Social Security (Industrial Injuries) (Prescribed Diseases) Regulations 1985, SI 1985/ 967. See Wikeley 'Tinkering with tinpot legislation: reforms of the schedule of prescribed diseases' (1997) 26 ILJ 283.

particularly detailed provisions applying to pneumoconiosis, byssinosis, diffuse mesothelioma and occupational deafness[65].

To claim benefit, a person suffering from an industrial disease must show three things. The first is that he is in fact suffering from the disease; this is a medical question, with a general right of appeal to a Medical Board and then an Appeal Tribunal. The second is that the disease is prescribed for his particular occupation; where the Schedule prescribes it for a general activity, for example certain forms of manual labour, or contact with certain substances, he must show that his occupation included that activity to more than a purely minimal extent. The third is that contraction of the disease was caused by engaging in his particular occupation. Here the claimant is aided by a presumption that if the disease is prescribed for that occupation, it will be presumed to have been caused by it, unless the adjudication officer can prove the contrary, on a balance of probabilities[66]. This presumption will generally arise if the employee was in the relevant occupation on the date of development of the disease (as defined) or within one month previously.

(iii) Benefits

The state injuries scheme attempts to serve two different purposes in relation to injured employees – the provision of financial support while the employee is unable to work because of the injury or disease, and the provision of some form of compensation for a person who is left with a lasting disability after the accident, either total or partial. The short-term 'statutory sick pay' or 'incapacity benefit' covers the former, and the long-term 'disablement benefit' covers the latter.

(a) Income replacement benefits

Since the abolition of the special injury benefit for those suffering an accident or prescribed disease at work, the relevant claim became one for statutory sick pay for those still in work and short-term sickness benefit for those not. After twenty-eight weeks of either, if still incapable of work, the person could claim invalidity benefit, which was the principal benefit for the long-term sick. To claim such benefit, the claimant had to show that he was in fact incapable, by reason of some specific disease or bodily or mental impairment, of work which he could reasonably be expected to do. Once it became clear that he could no longer hope to resume his normal work (for example, because of heart or back problems), the question became whether there was other, usually lighter, work that he could be expected to do. Many of the appeals to appeal tribunals concerned exactly that point, ie in the jargon, whether the person was 'fit within limits' (a question

---

65 See R(I) 7/76, RI 2/85 and R(I) 8/85 on occupational deafness; see also the Pneumoconiosis etc. (Workers' Compensation) Act 1979 and the Pneumoconiosis etc (Workers' Compensation) (Payment of Claims) Regulations 1985, SI 1985/2035.

66 SI 1985/967, reg 4(1); longer time periods are prescribed for certain diseases (such as deafness and pneumoconiosis) before the presumption can apply.

akin to that of reasonable mitigation of damage in wrongful dismissal or personal injury cases).

Due to the previous government's concern over the increase in claims for invalidity benefit (from half a million in 1976 to one and a half million in 1992)[67], this whole system was subject to radical reform in 1995, with the abolition of sickness benefit and invalidity benefit and their replacement by the new incapacity benefit[68]. SSP is not affected, and so for the first twenty-eight weeks the employee still in work will claim that. If not so entitled, the person can claim lower-rate, short-term incapacity benefit for that period, provided incapable of his own, normal work. The major change comes if still sick after twenty-eight weeks. The person may then claim higher-rate, short-term incapacity benefit for the rest of the first year, and then long-term incapacity benefit for the future. However, after that initial twenty-eight weeks, the claimant becomes subject to the new 'All work' test for incapability. This deliberately abandons any link with *actual* inability to work, and instead concentrates on supposedly objective medical effects of the condition in question, with points attached to each. There are eighty-nine physical 'descriptors' under fourteen headings (from walking through to episodes of lost consciousness) and twenty-five mental descriptors under four headings (completion of tasks, daily living, coping with pressure and interaction with others)[69]. If the claimant (after a prescribed medical procedure involving self-assessment, his own GP and a Benefit Agency medical officer) scores fifteen points on the physical or ten on the mental descriptors, they get the benefit, in principle irrespective of whether they are actually capable of work. Clearly this is meant to be a tougher test, in order to stop the increased expenditure on what was invalidity benefit. Experience in the appeal tribunals suggested that it may not in fact have this effect, especially once the factor of pain and variability ('good days and bad') is fully taken into account[70]. The present government has stated its desire to amend the system yet again, with a view to putting more emphasis on what a claimant can do, not what they cannot do, and so we are likely to see further change here.

---

67   The reasons for this increase are complex, and certainly wider than the general fear of fraud and malingering that seems to have been behind the general political impetus for change. High unemployment probably had a background effect, even though it should not have done (the benefit being payable for inability to perform work, not inability to get a job), and the government's 'Care in the Community' policy has turned many from inmates into claimants. See generally Berthoud 'The medical assessment of incapacity' (1995) 2 JSSL 61.

68   Social Security (Incapacity for Work) Act 1994; Incapacity for Work (General) Regulations 1995, SI 1995/311. See Wikeley 'The Social Security (Incapacity for Work) Act 1994' (1995) 58 MLR 523; Bonner 'Incapacity for work: a new benefit and new tests' (1995) 2 JSSL 86.

69   Some descriptions qualify a person by themselves, eg inability to walk or not being able to stand unaided, each of which carries 15 points. Otherwise, the various lesser scores across several inabilities are aggregated.

70   The Act and Regulations are silent on pain and variability; in practice, such questions arise in the majority of the appeals coming to social security appeal tribunals, especially in relation to back and neck injuries. BA doctors were told informally that they must be taken into account, and it became common for tribunals to take them into account to a greater extent, in what has become a crucial gloss on the wording of the legislation, finally upheld by a Tribunal of Commissioners in CIB/14534/1996.

71   Social Security Contributions and Benefits Act 1992, s 103.

(b) Disablement benefit

This is payable for loss of physical or mental faculty resulting from the accident or disease in question[71]. Causal connection between the loss of faculty and the accident or disease must be shown and this will be primarily a matter for the statutory authorities (adjudication officer, SSAT or Commissioner). However, assessment of the disability is the province of a medical board or appeal tribunal who may, if necessary, reopen the question of the causal connection[72]. Disablement benefit may not be paid until a minimum of ninety days (disregarding Sundays) after the accident[73]. Where it is payable, it is calculated by reference to a tariff set out in Regulations[74], which lays down percentages for individual injuries (for example, 7% for loss of a little finger, 50% for amputation of a leg below the knee, 100% for loss of both legs); the relevant percentage for the claimant is established essentially by medical experts, and may be permanent or subject to a time limit if the disability is thought likely to end in that time; it is subject to review either upwards or downwards. Prior to 1986, the system for payment was that if the percentage of disability was less than 20%, the benefit was payable as a lump sum gratuity of an amount fixed by Regulations for that percentage; if 20% or over, the benefit was payable as a weekly pension, the amount again fixed by Regulations. However, by virtue of the amendments made by the Social Security Act 1986[75], benefit is only payable if the percentage disability is 20% or over (though a percentage of 14% to 19% is now rounded up to 20%)[76]. The effect is that injury of less than 14% is now not compensated, and the lump sum gratuity disappears, being replaced by weekly pension payments in all new cases[77]. The rationale behind the change was one that was claimed to be behind several of the major social security changes in the 1986 Act, namely better targetting of benefit on those in greatest need; however, it was highly criticised (particularly by the TUC), not just as a cost-cutting exercise but also as the removal of hard-won statutory rights for those involved in industrial accidents. Similar sentiments were again heard when the present government in their first term of office floated ideas of further changes to the benefit, in particular by making some version of it primarily the responsibility of the employer.

72 Social Security Administration Act 1992, ss 44, 45 and 60, reversing the decisions of the House of Lords in *Minister of Social Security v AEU* [1967] 1 AC 725, [1967] 1 All ER 210, HL and *Jones v Secretary of State for Social Services* [1972] AC 944, [1972] 1 All ER 145, HL.
73 Social Security Contributions and Benefits Act 1992, s 103(6).
74 Social Security (General Benefit) Regulations 1982, SI 1982/1408, Sch 2.
75 See Lewis 'The government's philosophy towards reform of social security: the case of industrial injuries benefit' (1986) 15 ILJ 256 for details of the amendments and likely impact in practice.
76 Social Security Contributions and Benefits Act 1992, s 103(3). The other principal changes were the abolition of (i) unemployability supplement (which had become superfluous in the light of other, earlier, changes), (ii) hospital treatment allowance, and (iii) industrial death benefit (industrial widows now being treated in the same way as those widowed by other causes).
77 Lewis (n 75 above) points out that one of the gravest effects of the minimum percentage of 14% may be in the area of certain industrial diseases where the link between the industrial process and the disease has been established (and incorporated into regulations) but the actual level of disability in many cases may be relatively small. Note, however, that certain chest diseases (pneumoconiosis, byssinosis and diffuse mesothelioma) are treated separately, and still attract compensation if the level of disability is 1% or more: Social Security (Industrial Injuries) (Prescribed Diseases) Regulations 1985, SI 1985/157, reg 20.

The amount of disablement benefit is thus linked to (a) the degree of disability and (b) a maximum fixed sum or sums; it is therefore not linked to any loss of income (so that, for example, it is unaffected by receipt of earnings or jobseeker's allowance). This could cause hardship where the accident has had an effect on the claimant's earning capabilities or ability to cope with life; the answer to this has been to provide certain further benefits. The old 'reduced earnings allowance' has been phased out (with no new claims permitted after 1990), but it remains the case that if a claimant suffers 100% disability and is in need of constant attendance, he is eligible for a further flat rate benefit on that basis[78], and in cases of permanent grave disability for a flat rate 'exceptionally severe disablement allowance'[79].

(iv) The overlap with damages

Receipt of state benefits for an industrial injury does not prejudice the claimant's rights to sue his employer for damages in the courts if he has a relevant cause of action. However, if he is successful in such an action the question arises whether the sums which he has already received in benefits should be taken into account in assessing his damages. Against deduction of state benefits, it could be argued that they were received under essentially an insurance scheme (albeit compulsory and state-run) which exists independently of the common law tort system, and so they should be treated as ordinary insurance moneys, which are not deducted[80]. On the other hand, a rule against deduction could be seen as sanctioning double compensation, and the insurance argument is heavily qualified by the fact that part of the contribution to the scheme comes from the employer (who then also has to pay the damages, through his premia to his insurer), so that it is not simply a question of the prudent employee benefiting from insurance moneys provided by his own premia, as is the case with private insurance. When the National Insurance system came into force in 1948 a compromise solution was enacted[81] whereby a court in assessing damages had to take into account one-half of the benefits received; this had the practical effect that the state paid the benefits, and the plaintiff and defendant shared the advantage, half each. The Royal Commission on Civil Liability, headed by Lord Pearson, recommended that benefits received should be deducted in full, as a matter of principle[82]. Total deductibility has now come about, by virtue of the Social Security Act 1989 (now the Social Security (Recovery of Benefits) Act 1997), however not as a matter of principle, but rather as a financial measure to allow the government to recoup

78 S 104.
79 S 105.
80 *Bradburn v Great Western Rly Co* (1874) LR 10 Exch 1; *Parry v Cleaver* [1970] AC 1, [1969] 1 All ER 555, HL; *Smoker v London Fire and Civil Defence Authority* [1991] 2 AC 502, [1991] 2 All ER 449, HL.
81 Law Reform (Personal Injuries) Act 1948, s 2.
82 Report (Cmnd 7054–1, 1978) vol 1, paras 277–280 and 467–483. The aim, as seen above, was to down-grade the tort action by making it less 'profitable', especially in smaller claims.
83 The government projection in 1989 was that it would apply to 120,000 compensation payments each year, recovering £55 million pa.
84 For the details of the scheme, see DSS Booklet Z1 'Deduction from Compensation'.

the amounts paid out[83]. The basis of the scheme[84] is that a final settlement of or award in a personal injury action is not to be made until the defendant (in practice, the insurer) has obtained from the DSS Compensation Recovery Unit a certificate of total benefits paid to the claimant; the defendant must then deduct that amount from the damages and account for it to that DSS department. The scheme has been subject to criticism; the power of recoupment is very broad[85], and the amount to be recouped may now be a significant factor in deciding on a settlement, especially where a considerable time has elapsed since the accident (ie where the amount of benefit received is substantial)[86]. One potentially unfair and highly criticised aspect of the original 1989 scheme was that benefit paid could be recouped for *any* damages awarded, if necessary biting into general damages for pain and suffering, etc. This was radically altered in the 1997 Act which splits damages into four – general damages, special damages for loss of earnings, compensation of cost of care and compensation for loss of mobility; the first head is *not* now subject to recoupment, and in relation to the other three it is provided that only benefits states to be relevant to them can be recouped from them (so that, for example, income support can only be recouped from damages for lost earnings and the care component of disability living allowance can only be recouped from compensation for care costs). This was an important reform, but there remains one other trap (not addressed by the 1997 Act), namely that if damages are reduced for contributory negligence, that fact does *not* affect the amount of benefit to be recouped, so that the recoupment requirement could weigh particularly heavily in such a case.

3 OUTLINE OF AN ACTION FOR DAMAGES

If an employee receives injuries from an industrial accident which are sufficiently serious and/or lasting, he may wish to consider bringing a civil action against his employer, in addition to receiving the essentially shorter-term remedy of incapacity benefit or disablement benefit. Such proceedings are brought in the normal way for an action in tort, for there is no special procedure and in most ways the form and substance of the action are governed by the ordinary rules of the law of tort[87]. Thus, questions of proof of fault, causation, remoteness, the quantum of damages[88]

---

85 One possible way to avoid recoupment is to argue that the benefit was not in fact paid because of the accident, but this will be difficult to prove; see, eg the appropriately named case of *Hassall v Secretary of State for Social Security* [1995] 3 All ER 909, [1995] 1 WLR 812, CA, applied in *Neal v Bingle* [1998] 2 All ER 58, CA.

86 One significant difference between this scheme and the long-established scheme for recouping benefit from unfair dismissal compensation (p 617 above), on which it was partly based, is that this scheme applies to *settlements* as well as awards, and so cannot be avoided by settling; this caught the parties out in *Rees v West Glamorgan County Council* [1994] PIQR P37, CA. The existence of the scheme may place emphasis on earlier settlement (to keep the amount of benefit down), which could put pressure on the plaintiff to settle for less earlier. For the overall effects of the scheme, see Milton 'Recoupment planning' [1995] NLJ 784.

87 The standard work on industrial injuries cases is Munkman *Employer's Liability* (13th edn, 2001). More detailed coverage of the legislation can be found in Redgrave, Fife and Machin *Health and Safety* (3rd edn, 1998).

88 A detailed discussion of the law on damages is outside the scope of this book. For authoritative treatment, see *McGregor on Damages* and *Kemp and Kemp on the Quantum of Damages* with its updating supplements and the regular 'Damages' heading in *Current Law*.

and the special rules applying in case of a fatality are dealt with in basically the same way as in any other tort action. In spite of that, there is a tendency to think of industrial injury cases as sui generis and there is some justification for this since they comprise such a high proportion of all tort actions brought in any particular year (as with motor accident cases) and, while the legal principles may be the same as elsewhere, they have evolved in certain particular ways which can make this type of action distinctive. The aim of this head of this chapter, therefore, is to set out the *form* of the typical action (and, where appropriate, to point out certain rules which either are rules of general application which have particular significance in this type of action, or have evolved as separate rules in the industrial context), while assuming a working knowledge on the part of the reader of the basics of the law of tort.

Perhaps the two most distinctive features of an industrial injury case are the distillation of the general common law duty of care into certain well-defined duties upon the employer (in contract as well as tort) and the importance in practice of the action for breach of statutory duty. These are considered below. First, the four principal heads of liability upon an employer will be outlined, then the possible defences which he may be able to raise, and finally the question of insurance.

(i) Liabilities upon the employer

(a) The common law liability as 'master'

It has long been established that an employer has a duty of reasonable care towards his employee while the latter is in the course of his employment. This duty can in theory be viewed as contractual as well as tortious, for it is one of the implied terms which will be read into a contract of employment[89]; normally, however, there will be no advantage in pleading the case in contract, and so the action will be brought as an ordinary tort action. Its principal significance is that it is 'personal' to both employer and employee. This means that the duty upon the employer is non-delegable, so that the employer will remain liable for injury caused by breach of the duty even if he purported to leave the matter in question to others (for example, to competent contractors); this was of great importance in the days when the employee's remedies were narrower than they are today (in particular, before the abolition of the doctrine of common employment in 1948), and remains of importance since it prevents the employer from claiming that he exercised due care simply by choosing competent people to whom to delegate his functions[90]. The personal nature of the duty further means that it is owed to each employee individually, not to the workforce as a whole, and so in applying

---

89   *Matthews v Kuwait Bechtel Corpn* [1959] 2 QB 57, [1959] 2 All ER 345, CA.
90   This also applies in a 'borrowed servant' case; if the employee is sent by his employer to work for Co X and is injured, his employer remains potentially liable, though able to seek a contribution or full indemnity from Co X: *Morris v Breaveglen Ltd* [1993] ICR 766, [1993] IRLR 350, CA; *Nelhams v Sandells Maintenance Ltd* (1995) Times, 15 June, CA.
91   *Paris v Stepney Borough Council* [1951] AC 367, [1951] 1 All ER 42, HL. If the claimant is to rely on any particular peculiarity or susceptibility, the employer must have known of it, or have had reasonable cause to know of it: *James v Hepworth and Grandage Ltd* [1968] 1 QB 94, [1967] 2 All ER 829, CA.

the ordinary rules of tortious liability (for example, the rules relating to the practicability of any precautions which could or should have been provided by the employer) the court is entitled to look at the individual circumstances of the injured employee, and what it was reasonable to expect of the employer in *his* case (which may differ from the *average* or *usual* case)[91]. Naturally, there is a large body of case law on the employer's common law liability[92] and, although it is clear that there is in theory only one general duty of reasonable care, the tendency has been to treat that duty in practice as imposing upon the employer the obligation to use reasonable care to provide:

(a) safe and adequate plant and equipment[93];
(b) safe premises and/or place of work[94];
(c) competent and safe fellow employees[95]; and
(d) a safe system of work, in all the circumstances.

The last heading is a wide, residual one which shows how extensive the common law duty upon the employer may be, for it can cover the overall aspects of the organisation and supervision of the work (possibly including precautions to protect the employee partly from his own actions)[96], and clearly demonstrates the continuing nature of the obligation. Its application will vary greatly with the type of work in question, and factors such as the physical lay-out of the job, the sequence in which work is to be carried out and the provision of warnings, notices and special instructions may all be relevant; it can be equally applicable to the long-term lay-out of the job and to a procedure adopted in the short term for one particular job. Moreover, it is arguable that this heading may now take on renewed

---

92 The leading authority is the decision of the House of Lords in *Wilsons and Clyde Coal Co Ltd v English* [1938] AC 57, [1937] 3 All ER 628 HL. It was reaffirmed in *McDermid v Nash Dredging and Reclamation Co Ltd* [1987] ICR 917, [1987] IRLR 334, HL. The duties can even apply where the employee was working abroad, but any question of *breach* must then be decided realistically: *Cook v Square D Ltd* [1992] ICR 262, [1992] IRLR 34, CA.

93 See Munkman, n 87 above, ch 5. In this area it is particularly important to note that the obligation upon the employer will usually be to provide *and maintain* the equipment. Much of the common law on this heading is now superseded by the Employer's Liability (Defective Equipment) Act 1969, considered below.

94 This duty applies to the employee's place of work when it is outside the employer's premises (eg in another factory, a customer's home or, in the case of a window cleaner, on a windowsill): *General Cleaning Contractors v Christmas* [1953] AC 180, [1952] 2 All ER 1110, HL; *Wilson v Tyneside Window Cleaning Co Ltd* [1958] 2 QB 110, [1958] 2 All ER 265, CA; *Smith v Austin Lifts Ltd* [1959] 1 All ER 81, [1959] 1 WLR 100, HL. However, the duty remains one of reasonable care (only), so the fact that the accident happened outside the employer's premises may be a relevant factor.

95 This will cover the competence of supervisors and persons in charge of safety precautions. It also covers fellow employees, so that reasonable care should be taken to protect the employee in question from incompetents, homicidal maniacs and practical jokers: *Hudson v Ridge Manufacturing Co Ltd* [1957] 2 QB 348, [1957] 2 All ER 229. This common law duty may be important in an unfair dismissal action if the employer decides that the only way to protect the other employees is to dismiss the practical joker.

96 It may cover a duty to *warn* employees of work dangers where the employer is in a better position to appreciate them: *Pape v Cumbria County Council* [1992] 3 All ER 211, [1992] ICR 132. One contentious point is whether there might be a common law duty *to dismiss* if this is the only way to protect the employee from the health danger in question (especially where the employee wants to continue in spite of the risk). Earlier case law discounted any such duty: *Withers v Perry Chain Co Ltd* [1961] 3 All ER 676, [1961] 1 WLR 1314, CA. However, in *Coxall v Goodyear GB Ltd* [2002] EWCA Civ 1010, [2002] IRLR 742 the only ground of negligence proved against the employer was in allowing the willing employee to continue in the work once the health risk was known, and Simon Brown LJ envisaged a case where dismissal might be a common law requirement.

vitality in the light of the Management of Health and Safety at Work Regulations 1999 (see p 889 below). These lay down important new legal duties on all employers, for example to undertake risk assessments. At a late stage a provision was inserted that these Regulations do not support civil liability; this means that, for example, a failure to undertake a risk assessment (leading to injury) could not be used in a breach of statutory duty action *but* there appears to be no reason why it could not be used in a *negligence* action, as failure to provide a safe system of work, using the obligations laid down in the Regulations as *evidence* of that failure[97].

In the light of these well-developed heads of liability, it is easy to imagine that compensation is fairly automatic once there is an industrial accident. However, that would be an over-simple view, for the above heads (wide as they are) only govern the sort of accident which *may* be the subject of compensation. Whether a particular accident *will* lead to a successful claim for damages depends on whether, on the facts of the case, the injured employee can clear the normal hurdles which must be cleared by the claimant in any tort action; the specialised *heads* of liability do not help him here. It must be remembered, therefore, that the burden of proof remains upon the employee, and that he must be able to prove fault.

The employee may discharge the burden of proof in the ordinary way by adducing the necessary evidence or, in a case where the precise details are unclear, by seeking to rely on the maxim res ipsa loquitur[98]. In an industrial accident case the claimant may in addition be able to rely on three special factors. The first is that if the employer can be shown to have acted contrary to the normal practice of the trade in question, that may raise an inference of negligence; this is not invariably so, for widespread adoption of a bad practice does not convert it into a good practice[99], but in the nature of things trade usages are likely to be of considerable evidential value, particularly in a trade or industry which is safety-conscious. Where the harm suffered is an industrial disease, rather than an accident, a difficulty may arise here in deciding from what date (the 'date of knowledge') it was reasonable for an employer to have realised the danger posed by the process or substance in question, especially where medical opinion on the matter gradually changed over a period of time[100]. The second is that the employee may be able to show that the employer has not complied with the recommendations of a relevant Code of Practice issued under the Health and Safety at Work etc. Act 1974. Section 17 of the Act expressly makes Codes of Practice admissible in

---

97 Smith, Goddard, Killalea and Randall *Health and Safety – the Modern Legal Framework* (2nd edn, 2000), ch 4. The point has not yet been decided judicially, but arguably the judgment of Lord Macfadyen in the Outer House of the Court of Session in *Cross v Highlands & Islands Enterprise* [2001] IRLR 336 is supportive – he ruled that *at the time in question* (1993, just as the Regulations were coming into force) it was not yet a breach of duty not to have a risk assessment, but declined to rule on what the position would now be (see at 354, 355).

98 The actual effect of the maxim upon the trial of the issue is still a matter for legal dispute – see *Winfield and Jolowicz on Tort* (16th edn, 2002), p 203.

99 This is equally important when applied in reverse, ie where the employer claims to have *complied* with standard practice and thereby to have discharged his duty of care.

100 One of the early cases was *Thompson v Smith Shiprepairers (North Shields) Ltd* [1984] QB 405 fixing the date of knowledge at 1963 (when government recommendations were first published) for occupational deafness. In *Barclays Bank plc v Fairclough Building Ltd (No 2)* [1995] IRLR 605, CA the date for asbestos-related processes was fixed at 1988, and in *Armstrong v British Coal Corpn* [1997] 8 Med LR 259, CA a claim by miners for vibration white finger was allowed back to 1975; See Munkman *Employer's Liability* (13th edn, 2001) pp 49–54 and ch 7.

criminal proceedings against the employer, but there is no reason why they should not be equally admissible in civil proceedings where relevant, though without the statutory presumption against the employer which applies in criminal proceedings by virtue of section 17(2). The third factor is that if the accident in question has been investigated by a health and safety inspector, information gathered by him may be released to a potential claimant for the purpose of bringing a civil action[101].

In these ways, the injured employee might be better placed than some other claimants on questions of proof, but he remains in the same position as any other claimant in a negligence action in that he must be able to prove *fault*. This means not only showing that there was a duty upon the employer (which in the light of the extensive case law may be easy), but also that the employer was in breach of that duty by not doing more to safeguard the employee, and that that breach of duty caused the injury which he suffered. In some cases this may raise difficult questions of the practicability of further safety precautions[102], and what knowledge the employer had or ought to have had of any defect which caused the injury. It is trite law to say that the duty upon the employer is only to take such care as is reasonable in the circumstances, not to *guarantee* the safety of the employee, but this can be a very real consideration in a common law action (explaining the preferability in many cases of the action for breach of statutory duty). This can be seen particularly from the cases on latent defects in tools and machinery used by the employee. As a 'latent defect' is one which could not be discovered by reasonable inspection, the employer is not in breach of his duty by not discovering it and, moreover, provided the employer used reasonable care in selecting the tool or machine (for example, by buying a well-known make from a reputable supplier) he will have discharged his duty and, if the tool later breaks or explodes causing injury to the employee, the employer will not be liable at common law[103]. It is true that the employee may have an action against the negligent manufacturer under the ordinary principles in *Donoghue v Stevenson*[104], but that is a less direct

---

101 Health and Safety at Work etc. Act 1974, s 28(9).
102 This point may be of particular significance in an industrial accident case for, although the safety of the employee is a vital factor, the law cannot expect total safety if the price would be a decrease or cessation of industrial output out of proportion to the potential danger. The classic example here is *Latimer v AEC Ltd* [1953] AC 643, [1953] 2 All ER 449, HL. The concept of causation may also occasionally pose problems; see, eg, *White v Holbrook Precision Castings Ltd* [1985] IRLR 215, CA where the plaintiff failed because the court took the view on the facts that even if the employer had given him a reasonable warning of the possible injurious effects of the work, the plaintiff would still have taken the job.
103 *Davie v New Merton Board Mills Ltd* [1959] AC 604, [1959] 1 All ER 346, HL. This does not jeopardise the principle that the duty upon the employer is non-delegable (*Wilsons and Clyde Coal Co Ltd v English* [1938] AC 57), for the manufacturer is not viewed as someone to whom the employer has delegated his functions; the obligation is still upon the employer to exercise care in selecting the equipment. The problem arises because no amount of reasonable care would have discovered the defect.
104 [1932] AC 562, HL. See, eg, *Hill v James Crowe (Cases) Ltd* [1978] 1 All ER 812, [1978] ICR 298. *Castree v E R Squibb & Sons Ltd* [1980] 2 All ER 589, [1980] 1 WLR 1248, CA, shows an application of the jurisdictional rules favourable to the claimant employee (or to a defendant employer wishing to issue third-party proceedings against the manufacturers of defective equipment) where the equipment was manufactured abroad.

action which may raise practical problems of bringing the action and of proof (for example, if the manufacturer is a foreign company). This particular problem in the common law led to the passage of the Employer's Liability (Defective Equipment) Act 1969 which provides that the employer is liable where the employee sustains personal injury in the course of his employment 'in consequence of a defect in equipment[105] provided by his employer for the purposes of the employer's business'. However, the liability is not strict, since the employee must be able to prove that 'the defect is attributable wholly or partly to the fault of a third party (whether identified or not)'; this will usually mean showing negligence on the part of the manufacturer, and if this can be shown the injured employee may proceed directly against his employer, leaving the employer to bring any further proceedings against the 'third party' for an indemnity for the damages which he has had to pay to the employee. This statute may provide valuable assistance to a claimant, particularly in a latent defect case, but it only applies to defective equipment and even then, as already stated, the claimant must be able to prove fault on the part of a third party, which may be particularly difficult where the nature of the 'defect' is not obvious[106]; outside the Act's ambit the ordinary common law rule continues to apply, requiring the employee to show negligence on the part of the employer.

The above discussion has tended to concentrate on the traditional form of damage in employers' liability cases, physical injury from a definable accident. However, as in health and safety law generally, increased emphasis in recent years has been on extending these principles to diseases or other medical conditions caused by work, or to psychiatric injuries; by their very nature these areas are more difficult to deal with, being more difficult to define and potentially raising questions of causation[107]. Asbestos and its related problems of mesothelioma have become a serious concern of probable long-term effect, which gave rise to extreme problems of causation. Given a possible onset period of up to forty years, this lies at the opposite end of the spectrum for the classic one-off (and wholly datable) physical accident. One particular problem is where the employee, now suffering a fatal asbestos-linked disease, worked for, say, four employers over the onset period, using asbestos with each. The causation problem is not what caused it, but who. When faced with this in the context of asbestosis,

---

105 Defined as including 'any plant and machinery, vehicle, aircraft and clothing'. It includes a ship (*Coltman v Bibby Tankers Ltd* [1988] AC 276, [1988] ICR 67, HL) and also may include material being worked on, as well as the equipment being used (*Knowles v Liverpool County Council* [1993] 4 All ER 321, [1993] IRLR 588, HL).

106 See Lang 'The Employer's Liability (Defective Equipment) Act – lion or mouse?' (1984) 47 MLR 48 for a review of the practical difficulties of the Act and a suggestion that a statutory reversal of the burden of proof is essential if it is to work in the way originally intended.

107 Barrett 'Work-induced stress' (1995) 24 ILJ 343. A good example of the swings-and-roundabouts effect sometimes seen here is litigation over repetitive strain injury (RSI). Much concern is health and safety circles is now expressed over 'upper limb disorders' but when RSI was first pleaded as a work-related injury per se its very existence was doubted: *Mughal v Reuters Ltd* [1993] IRLR 571. Pleading it more widely as wrist or forearm cramp led to acceptability in *Pickford v ICI plc* [1998] ICR 673, [1998] IRLR 435, HL though the plaintiff lost on foreseeability. In *Alexander v Midland Bank plc* [2000] ICR 464, [1999] IRLR 723, CA neck and upper limb pains from repetitive keyboard movements were found to be physical, not psychogenic, and foreseeable and the claimants succeeded.

the court could at least rely on the evidence that this disease is progressive over time (ie severity increases with exposure). On that basis the Court of Appeal felt able to *apportion* liability among all the employers based on the time the employee spent with each[108]. However, as has consistently been the case, mesothelioma caused the ultimate problem – it is *not* progressive, and can be caused by an individual inhalation of asbestos fibres at *some* time during the working life. When this finally arose in litigation in *Fairchild v Glenhaven Funeral Services Ltd*[109] the claimants failed in the Court of Appeal on the straightforward causation point that they had failed to prove breach of duty on the part of any particular employer. In a radical judgment the House of Lords allowed their appeals, holding that in these circumstances (where it is clear that *each* employer was in breach of duty by unreasonably exposing the employee to asbestos dust) an employee can recover damages against all the employers[110]. This was put wholly on policy grounds, on the basis that causation rules are not immutable, that in these circumstances it was enough that each employer had materially increased the risk of messthelioma,[111] that it was just and reasonable to accept a lower standard of causation here, and that any injustice to an individual employer (who may not have been the one during whose service the later-fatal inhalation took place) was outweighed by the injustice to the employee of recovering no damages at all. Outstanding though this case is, it can still be seen as merely the latest and best example of a process that we have seen since the early 1960s[112] of traditional tort principles (which were established to deal with accidents) being severely tested by, and having to evolve in the light of, the increased incidence of litigation over work-related diseases and conditions.

More recently, we have seen a similar picture with the emphasis moving beyond physical conditions to encompass *mental* conditions alleged to be work-related. Nervous shock or post traumatic stress disorder caused by events at work have

---

108 *Holtby v Brigham & Cowan (Hull) Ltd* [2000] 3 All ER 421, [2000] ICR 1086, CA.

109 [2002] 3 All ER 305, [2002] IRLR 533, HL.

110 One point of difficulty remains, in relation to what each defendant is liable *for*. At the end of his speech Lord Bingham stated that no argument had been put to the House as to apportionment, the assumption being that ordinary principles of joint tortfeasors should apply. Thus, with the example of 4 employers, the claimant could sue any one for the *whole* damage, leaving it to that employer to claim contributions from the others. However, *Holtby* (n 108 above) proceeded on the basis that, on a time apportionment, each employer could only be liable for his *own* share. The difference would be vital where, for example, two of the four employers had gone out of business years previously.

111 This picked up on the wider approach to causation first seen in *McGhee v NCB* [1972] 3 All ER 1008 [1973] 1 WLR 1, HL (another industrial injury case where pure causation could not be proved between the plaintiff's dermatitis and the defendant employer's failure to provide showers to wash off brick dust, but the plaintiff still won). However, this can only apply where it is clear what the causative agent was and who was responsible for it. *Fairchild* does not doubt *Wilsher v Essex Area Health Authority* [1988] AC 1074, [1988] 1 All ER 871, HL where it was held that the wider view in *McGhee* cannot apply where there remains doubt as to what the causative factor was. This problem might remain in an asbestos case where, say, one or two of the four employers concerned could *not* be shown to have negligently exposed the claimant employee to the dust.

112 This process can be seen as first seriously arising in the context of limitation. Early litigation over silicosis (with its long onset period) ran into severe problems with the simple three-year limitation period in *Cartledge v Jopling & Sons Ltd* [1963] AC 758, [1963] 1 All ER 341, HL, leading swiftly to the passage of the Limitation Act 1963 with its provision for the limitation period to run only from the 'date of knowledge' in such cases; see p 863 below.

caused increasing litigation[113]. However, perhaps the most important development has been in the area of mental stress from work causing psychiatric injury. In *Walker v Northumberland County Council*[114] social worker succeeded at first instance in a claim for damages for common law negligence against his employers, based on the second, debilitating nervous breakdown that he suffered, due to the ever-increasing workload placed on him and the failure of the employer to provide help which had been promised after the first breakdown. This widely reported decision (unfortunately not appealed) caused considerable consternation in personnel circles (especially with the ruling that the employer could not raise a defence that the increased workload was caused by externally imposed financial cutbacks), and raises the interesting prospect of the old common law rules on duties of care at work taking on a new role as possibly the only effective counterweight to what has seemed in recent years an irresistible movement in so many kinds of employment to demand more and more work of fewer and fewer employees and call it economic efficiency[115].

(b) Liability for breach of statutory duty

The action for breach of statutory duty may often be used to compensate for the defects and lack of certainty in the common law action against the employer. It is a device evolved by the courts to allow a claimant to sue for damages when the conduct of the defendant which caused the injury was in defiance of a duty cast upon him by statute, even though the statute itself will probably not even mention the question of civil liability, normally being concerned only to punish the transgression with criminal penalties (often in former times a fine of minute proportion). As the duty contained in the statute may be (a) stricter and (b) far more precise than the common law duty of reasonable care in all the circumstances, this action will tend in practice to be the primary one when pleading the injured employee's case, with the common law action in the past often little more than an afterthought or 'longstop' (a set of priorities which is not always reflected in tort texts). Although the result of this action may be more satisfactory for the claimant, its application is not automatic and so its constituent elements must be proved. To this extent, it can be a relatively technical action, and these elements must now be briefly summarised.

113 Employees have succeeded in actions against third parties who have put them in danger during their work, but the position against the employer is more uncertain. Ordinary nervous shock law, itself in a state of flux since the Hillsborough disaster litigation, makes a claim difficult where the employee was not himself in direct danger, even if he witnesses a horrifying work accident to others: *McFarlane v EE Caledonia Ltd* [1994] 2 All ER 1, CA; *Robertson v Forth Road Bridge Joint Board* [1995] IRLR 251, Ct of Sess. In a claim for nervous shock by police affected by the Hillsborough disaster, the House of Lords eventually held that there is *no* special duty owed to employees in this context, who therefore remain subject to the normal (restrictive) rules: *White v Chief Constable of South Yorkshire Police* [1999] 2 AC 455, [1999] 1 All ER 1, HL.

114 [1995] 1 All ER 737, [1995] IRLR 35. This area was then thoroughly reviewed by the Court of Appeal in *Sutherland v Hatton* [2002] IRLR 263, CA (see particularly the guidance given by Hale LJ at [43]); at the time of writing, further appeal to the House of Lords was awarded which could be crucial in delineating liability in this difficult case.

115 This could be particularly so because of the large amounts of damages possible – a broken leg from an accident heals; a nervous breakdown may make the sufferer incapable of ever working again. An interesting parallel is with *Johnstone v Bloomsbury Health Authority* [1991] ICR 269, [1991] IRLR 118, CA (p 142 above), where again there was a common law challenge (this time under the contract of employment and its implied obligations) to intolerable work requirements. These cases show the continuing vitality of the common law in areas not (yet) covered by protective legislation.

The first and most basic element is that the statutory provision upon which the claimant wishes to rely must be one which in law supports civil liability. This is not invariably so, and when a court has to consider the potential civil aspect of a section for the first time difficult questions may arise as to the presumed intention of Parliament, whether the statute was designed to give direct protection to people such as the claimant, what type of harm the statute was meant to prevent, and whether any criminal penalties which are provided are meant to give adequate protection on their own[116]. In most cases this exercise will now be unnecessary because of existing case law, and in industrial cases it has been well established (particularly after the decision of the Court of Appeal in *Groves v Lord Wimborne*[117]) that *safety* provisions in industrial legislation will usually support civil liability, though even this has exceptions, and moreover in the case of *health* or *welfare* provisions the position has been less certain. In the light of this uncertainty, the obvious point has been made that it would be preferable for the statutes in question to state whether they are intended to support civil liability[118]. In the past this has not usually been done[119], but this is in the process of changing. The Health and Safety at Work etc. Act 1974, section 47(2) states that Regulations made under the Act are to be construed as giving rise to civil liability unless the regulation in question expressly provides otherwise. This is of particular importance now, with the coming into force in 1993 of the six new sets of EC-inspired Regulations which largely replace the old factories legislation[120]. The 'head' Regulations, the Management of Health and Safety at Work Regulations 1992 (reissued in 1999), do exclude civil liability[121], but there is no such exclusion in the other five, more specific, sets (applying to the workplace, work equipment, personal protective equipment, manual handling and VDUs), and so breaches of these *will* give rise to an action for breach of statutory duty.

The second element is that the statutory duty in question must be owed to the claimant; this will depend upon the detailed wording of the section or regulation under which he wishes to sue. In the past, it was common to frame provisions as protecting 'persons employed' which clearly excludes independent contractors[122]. One of the main reasons for this was that many of the important detailed provisions were contained in Regulations rather than in the principal statutes, and under the Factories Act 1961, section 76 Regulations could only be made for the protection of 'persons employed' and so any regulation purporting to cover a wider class would have been ultra vires and void. Now, however, the

---

116 For two examples of this problem (in non-industrial cases) see *McCall v Abelesz* [1976] QB 585, [1976] 1 All ER 727, CA; *Ex p Island Records Ltd* [1978] Ch 122, [1978] 3 All ER 824, CA.

117 [1898] 2 QB 402; *Butler v Fife Coal Co Ltd* [1912] AC 149, HL.

118 See, eg, *Cutler v Wandsworth Stadium Ltd* [1949] AC 398 at 411, HL per Lord Du Parcq.

119 For rare examples, see the Resale Prices Act 1964, s 4(2) and the Mineral Workings (Offshore Installations) Act 1971, s 11.

120 See p 889 below.

121 This has become controversial. Although the only reported case to address the point held against the argument that this exclusion breached the general EC requirement of effective remedies in the transposition of the Framework Directive that lies behind the Management Regulations (*Cross v Highlands and Islands Enterprise* [2001] IRLR 336 Ct of Sess (OH)) there have been signs that the government may remove it by legislation.

122 Hence the importance of the distinction between employment and self-employment in a case such as *Ferguson v John Dawson & Partners (Contractors) Ltd* [1976] 3 All ER 817, [1976] IRLR 346, CA (see p 10 above). Such a restriction excludes not only independent contractors but also other non-employees lawfully on the premises, eg the fireman fighting a fire in *Hartley v Mayoh & Co* [1954] 1 QB 383, [1954] 1 All ER 375, CA. For an example in the context of the mines and quarries legislation, see *Thompson v National Coal Board* [1982] ICR 15, CA.

power to make Regulations is contained in the Health and Safety at Work etc. Act 1974, section 15 which is not so restricted, being a power to make Regulations for any of the general purposes of the first Part of the Act[123]. The modern Regulations under the Act (particularly the six that came into force in 1993) reflect this modern approach in full, not only applying to all employees across the board (subject to minor, specified exceptions), but also covering temporary workers[124] and placing duties on the self-employed to look after their own welfare. There should therefore be few problems in showing that a particular injured employee was within the scope of the new regulatory protection.

The third element is that the statutory duty must be imposed upon the defendant in the case. Under the old factory legislation, duties were normally cast on 'the occupier', which caused relatively few problems. Under the new Regulations there should be even fewer, since (a) duties are generally placed, without more ado, on 'the employer', and (b) key concepts such as 'workplace', 'work equipment', 'personal protective equipment' and (VDU) 'workstation' are given broad, general definitions.

The fourth element is that the defendant must be in breach of duty. If there is one central principle in the law relating to breach of statutory duty it is that each case will depend ultimately on the detailed wording of the statutory provision in question. Thus, it is that wording which will determine the *level* of the duty, which will have the major effect on whether the defendant has breached it. If the duty is strict (for example, that something 'shall be provided'), any failure to comply will constitute a breach and it will be no defence to say that the defendant acted reasonably, or could not have done otherwise, or even that the machine in question would be totally unusable if the statute were strictly applied[125]. A strict duty is thus clearly in the claimant's favour. However, a statutory duty may be cast in less mandatory terms, either by specifically providing the employer with a defence, or by specifying an alternative way to comply, or by imposing a lesser duty. In the last case, in the past the most common form of duty has been one to do or provide something as far as is 'practicable' or 'reasonably practicable', the former being essentially a matter of technical feasibility and the latter being a wider concept, introducing more factors (including the cost of provision of a safeguard, in relation to the magnitude of the risk). Although the latter (in particular) may impose a standard of duty prima facie akin to the ordinary duty of care in common law negligence, there may still be one advantage for the employee in relying on such a statutory provision, since it has been held that if a dispute arises as to whether something was or was not practicable or reasonably practicable within the statute, the burden of proof in a civil action lies upon the employer to prove that it was not[126]. Moreover, recent case law has tended to view references to 'reasonable practicability' as being in the nature only of a defence to otherwise absolute obligations on employers, and to construe those references more narrowly than

---

123 Sch 3 sets out certain particular purposes for which health and safety regulations may be made, without prejudice to the generality of the regulation-making power.

124 In order to comply with the Temporary Workers Directive (91/383/EEC) in relation to health and safety.

125 *John Summers & Sons Ltd v Frost* [1955] AC 740, [1955] 1 All ER 870, HL; the extreme effect of this case had to be lessened by the Abrasive Wheel Regulations 1970, SI 1970/535.

126 *Nimmo v Alexander Cowan & Sons Ltd* [1968] AC 107, [1967] 3 All ER 187, HL; *Larner v British Steel plc* [1993] ICR 551, [1993] IRLR 278, CA; in criminal proceedings under the Health and Safety at Work etc. Act 1974 there is an express, statutory reversal of the burden of proof on practicability or reasonable practicability: s 40.

in the past[127]. Under the new regime of health and safety Regulations, questions will arise as to the appropriate level of duty. This is because the drafting is a mixture of the older phrasing of practicability or reasonable practicability and new Euro-speak taken from the Directives on which the Regulations are based; the latter form of drafting tends to use phrases such as 'suitable and sufficient', 'suitable means' and 'adequate measures' which have not so far figured largely in domestic law and will need interpretation by the courts[128]. Clearly, the accompanying codes of practice and guidance notes will play a major role here, and in this context it is worth mentioning just how remarkably detailed the guidance contained therein is (including diagrams, flow charts, specific examples and cross-references to acceptable EC *product* standards, in relation particularly to work equipment and protective equipment).

The fifth element is that the damage done to the claimant must be the type of damage which the statute or regulation was designed to prevent[129]. Normally, in an industrial accident case this will be perfectly obvious, but the rule produced one particular anomaly under the old factory legislation, for it was held that the fencing requirements for dangerous machines were, to put it at its simplest, meant to keep the employee out of the machine, not to keep the machine and the material in, so that if part of the machine or material flew out of the machine and injured the employee, the fencing provisions would not provide him with a cause of action (if the fencing was defective), since the harm suffered was not the type of harm which those particular provisions were designed to prevent[130]. It is to be hoped that there will be considerably less scope under the present regime of health and safety Regulations for such fine distinctions, due to their wider approach and more general coverage, though it will still be important to sue under the right regulation (or combination of Regulations).

The final element is that the injury must be caused by the defendant's breach. Causation is always important in the law of tort and it has been reaffirmed by the House of Lords that the action for breach of statutory duty is no exception. The claimant must therefore be able to show the causal link between his injury and the defendant's breach; there is no presumption of causation once the breach is

127 *Larner v British Steel plc*, n 126 above; *R v British Steel plc* [1995] ICR 586 [1995] IRLR 311, CA; *Mains v Uniroyal Englebert Tyres Ltd* [1995] IRLR 544, Ct of Sess.

128 These phrases are often attached to obligations which are prima facie strict ('the employer *shall* provide *suitable and sufficient* means ...'). This may well be higher than reasonable practicability, since the *obligation* to provide is strict and the only argument is about what is suitable and sufficient, whereas under an old 'reasonably practicable' duty it could have been argued that it was not reasonably practicable to provide it *at all*. One problem in the opposite direction is whether a provision such as reg 11 of the Provision and Use of Work Equipment Regulations 1992, SI 1992/2932 (which replaces the famous s 14 of the Factories Act 1961 which imposed a strict duty to fence dangerous parts of machinery) in fact *lowers* the level of the duty because of the Euro-speak involved. Both of these points were addressed in *Stark v Post Office* [2000] ICR 1013 which held that: (a) a provision that the employer shall maintain equipment in an efficient state imposed an absolute obligation in its own terms; and anyway (b) the law pre-1993 would have imposed strict liability in such a case and the EC-based Regulations are not to be construed as lowering existing levels of duty.

129 *Gorris v Scott* (1874) LR 9 Exch 125.

130 *Nicholls v Austin (Leyton) Ltd* [1946] AC 493, [1946] 2 All ER 92, HL; *Close v Steel Co of Wales Ltd* [1962] AC 367, [1961] 2 All ER 953, HL; *Wearing v Pirelli Ltd* [1977] 1 All ER 339, [1977] 1 WLR 48, HL. For judicial criticism of this narrow approach, see *F E Callow (Engineers) Ltd v Johnson* [1971] AC 335, [1970] 3 All ER 639, HL.

shown[131]. The application of ideas of causation can lead to the employer being relieved of liability, in spite of a clear breach of statute, in two cases. The first is where the employer has failed to provide a safety precaution but it can be shown on a balance of probabilities that the employee would probably not have used it even if it had been available[132]. The second is where the defendant can show that he did everything in his power to comply with the statutory requirement (for example, by providing all the necessary equipment, instructing the employee in its use and ordering him to use it) and the only reason why he was placed in breach was the act or omission of the claimant himself (for example, in neglecting to use the equipment provided, in defiance of orders)[133]. In *Ross v Associated Portland Cement Manufacturers Ltd*[134] this was explained in terms of causation, whereas in the later case of *Boyle v Kodak Ltd*[135] the approach was to treat it as a specific defence to an action for breach of statutory duty:

> 'The plaintiff establishes a prima facie cause of action against his employer by proving the fact of non-compliance with a requirement of the regulation and that he suffered injury as a result. He need prove no more. No burden lies upon him to prove what steps should have been taken. But if the employer can prove that the only act or default of anyone which caused or contributed to the non-compliance was the act or default of the claimant himself, he establishes a good defence.[136]'

It must be emphasised, however, that the key word is 'only', for the effect of the defence upon the claimant's claim is total and it should not be found in any but the clearest cases; if there is *any* fault on the part of the employer (for example, failure to give proper orders, instruction or supervision) the defence will not be applicable and the case will be decided by the more sophisticated means of apportioning loss between the claimant and the defendant through the device of contributory negligence. It is interesting to note that the defence failed in both the *Ross* and the *Boyle* cases, and so the court went on to apportion the loss (the defendant employer bearing two-thirds and one-half of the loss respectively).

(c) Vicarious liability

The concept of vicarious liability means that if an employee injures someone in the course of his employment, that injured person may sue the employer for damages, a most useful action given the relative financial (and insurance) positions of the employee and employer. This action is normally thought of as giving redress to third parties (for example, passers-by or customers), but it can

---

131 *Bonnington Castings Ltd v Wardlaw* [1956] AC 613, [1956] 1 All ER 615, HL; *Qualcast (Wolverhampton) Ltd v Haynes* [1959] AC 743, [1959] 2 All ER 38, HL. Human intervention between the breach by the defendant and the injury to the plaintiff could break the chain of causation: *McGovern v British Steel Corpn* [1986] ICR 608, [1986] IRLR 411, CA.

132 *Cummings v Sir William Arrol & Co Ltd* [1962] 1 All ER 623, [1962] 1 WLR 295, HL; *Wigley v British Vinegars Ltd* [1964] AC 307, [1962] 3 All ER 161, HL. Even here, the employer may still be liable if the regulation imposes a duty to provide *and secure use* of the relevant safety device.

133 *Ginty v Belmont Building Supplies Ltd* [1959] 1 All ER 414.

134 [1964] 2 All ER 452, [1964] 1 WLR 768, HL.

135 [1969] 2 All ER 439, [1969] 1 WLR 661, HL.

136 [1969] 2 All ER 439 at 446, [1969] 1 WLR 661 at 672, HL, per Lord Diplock; *Lineker v Raleigh Industries Ltd* [1980] ICR 83, CA.

also apply where the injured person is a fellow employee. This was not always so, for under the doctrine of common employment[137] the courts held that an employee could not sue his employer when injured by a fellow employee, for he was deemed to have consented to the risk of such injury. This harsh doctrine excluded what could have been a wide head of liability (since (a) most employers are corporate and therefore have to do things through their employees, and (b) vicarious liability can apply widely to cover acts of the employee which at first sight may appear to be outside what he is really employed to do, including for example fraud by the employee and acts done in defiance of the employer's orders[138]). This led to pressure to find alternative causes of action for the injured employee, and in particular explains the significance of the personal, non-delegable common law liabilities upon the employer (discussed above)[139]. The doctrine of common employment was finally abolished in 1948[140], and so now the employee who is injured by the negligence of a fellow employee has this additional cause of action against his employer.

The law on vicarious liability contains some well-known difficulties, primarily on the question of what is in the course of employment; these are adequately covered in the tort texts[141]. Three specific points require mention here. The first is that one of the most difficult problems arises in relation to travelling time – is the employee in the course of his employment during it[142]? This matter arose in *Smith v Stages*[143] where a peripatetic worker travelling back from a particular job was held to be in the course of his employment (so that the employer was liable for the death of a fellow employee in a car accident caused by that worker's

137 *Priestley v Fowler* (1837) 3 M & W 1; *Hutchinson v York, Newcastle and Berwick Rly Co* (1850) 5 Exch 343.
138 See *Rose v Plenty* [1976] 1 All ER 97, [1976] 1 WLR 141, CA.
139 The duty to provide competent and safe fellow employees may still be particularly important, for if the fellow employee causes injury by a practical joke or an assault, that may take him outside the course of his employment, so that the employer will not be vicariously liable. If, however, the employer knew or ought to have known of the fellow employee's propensity for joking or violence, he may be liable for breach of his common law duty of care.
140 Law Reform (Personal Injuries) Act 1948, s 1.
141 In addition to the standard textbooks, see McKendrick 'Vicarious liability and independent contractors – a re-examination' (1990) 53 MLR 770; Collins 'Independent contractors and the challenge of vertical disintegration to employment protection laws' (1990) 10 OJLS 353; Kidner 'Vicarious liability: for whom should the employer be liable' (1995) 15 LS 47. The whole question of vicarious liability at common law was subject to major revision in *Lister v Hesley Hall Ltd* [2001] UKHL 33, [2002] 1 AC 215, [2001] IRLR 472 where, in holding a children's home liable for sexual abuse by its warden, the House of Lords went further than the previous orthodoxy (that the employee's acts must be authorised by the employer or an unauthorised way of doing what he was employed to do) and held that it may be enough that there is a close work connection, especially where the employee is performing a duty owed by the employer to the victim: see also *Fennelly v Connex South Eastern Ltd* [2001] IRLR 390, CA (railway company liable for assault by its ticket inspector); *Balfron Trustees Ltd v Peterson* [2001] IRLR 758 (solicitor's firm liable for misappropriation of pension fund assets aided by its employee); and Deakin 'Enterprise risk: the juridical nature of the firm revisited' (2003) 32 ILJ 97. Discrimination law, as a matter of legislative policy, already operated on a wider basis than common law vicarious liability: *Jones v Tower Boot Co Ltd* [1997] ICR 254, [1997] IRLR 168, CA; *ST v North Yorkshire County Council* [1999] IRLR 98, CA.
142 A similar problem arises under the social security rules relating to industrial accidents, see p 839 above.
143 [1989] AC 928, [1989] 1 All ER 833; the guidance from Lord Lowry is at 851, 956, respectively.

negligence). Although decisions in such cases are largely questions of fact, Lord Lowry gave the following guidance (which shows an interesting emphasis not only on job content but also on the payment system):

(1) an employee travelling from his ordinary residence to his ordinary place of work is not in the course of his employment (unless obliged to use the employer's transport);

(2) travelling in the employer's time between workplaces, or in the course of a peripatetic occupation, will be in the course of employment;

(3) receipt of wages (though *not* simply of a travelling allowance) will indicate that the employee is travelling in the employer's time and for his benefit;

(4) an employee travelling *in the employer's time* from his ordinary residence to a workplace *other* than his normal workplace, or on peripatetic work or to the scene of an emergency will be in the course of employment;

(5) a deviation from or interruption of a journey in the course of employment (other than a merely incidental one) will take the employee out of the course of his employment;

(6) return journeys are to be treated on the same footing as outward journeys.

The second point, as has already been made at p 17 above, is that the test for the existence of vicarious liability in tort is not necessarily identical to that for the existence of a longer-term employment relationship (for example, for the purpose of establishing a claim for unfair dismissal or some other employment protection right), even though ostensibly they are the same – is there a contract of employment? That the existence of an employment relationship and the incidence of vicarious liability may diverge is shown by the 'borrowed servant' cases[144], and the argument is advanced in chapter 1 that short-term factors such as control and supervision may be more important in the tort context, whereas longer-term factors may be more appropriate in the employment law context.

The third point is that the wider approach now taken to 'in the course of employment' in *Lister v Hesley Hall Ltd*[145] may have an indirect effect on the scope of the employer's power of discipline. Actions of the employee outside the employer's premises and after working hours may well previously have been considered that employee's own business, *not* legally appropriate for disciplinary action by the employer[146]. If, however, the new rules on vicarious liability now meant that the employer could be civilly liable for such actions, the other side of the coin would be that the employer would have a legitimate interest and a resulting power to discipline. This could be seen as the common law catching up with discrimination law where for some time now, especially in harassment cases, potential employer liability does not necessarily stop at the factory gate at 5 pm[147].

---

144 See *Mersey Docks and Harbour Board v Coggins and Griffiths Ltd* [1947] AC 1, [1946] 2 All ER 345, HL; *Donovan v Laing, Wharton and Down Construction Syndicate* [1893] 1 QB 629; *Denham v Midland Employers' Mutual Assurance* [1955] 2 QB 437, [1955] 2 All ER 561, CA; *Cross v Redpath Dorman Long (Contracting) Ltd* [1978] ICR 730. For the possible application of the Unfair Contract Terms Act 1977 to a clause apportioning liability as between the two employers, see Morris (1987) 16 ILJ 264.

145 See n 141 above.

146 There has always been a potential problem here with an employee's criminal activities outside employment, see p 583 above.

147 See p 316 above.

(d) Liability as occupier

The employer, where he is the 'occupier' of industrial premises, owes the common duty of care to all visitors lawfully on those premises, under the Occupier's Liability Act 1957[148]. In the ordinary case of the employee working on the employer's premises, this will add little to the existing common law duties, but it may be important (a) for an independent contractor working on those premises (to whom the employer does not owe those general duties) and (b) for an employee working on someone else's premises (for in a case of injury he may be able to sue that other 'occupier' as well as his employer). If a person is present on premises 'in the exercise of his calling', the occupier may expect that he will 'appreciate and guard against any special risks ordinarily incident to it', but this should only apply to such specialised risks and not to any overall conditions of the premises which may pose risks generally[149].

One aspect of occupiers' liability which has caused some difficulty in the past is the exclusion of liability for personal injury (by contractual term or by notice); this appeared to be effective when done properly[150] and, although factually unlikely to be applied to the occupier's own employees (who could still sue under the common law duties anyway), it was of significance to independent contractors coming on to the occupier's land. Now, however, such exclusion of liability for death or personal injury resulting from negligence (which includes the common duty of care under the 1957 Act) is ineffective, under the Unfair Contract Terms Act 1977, section 2 (whether by contract term or notice), provided the exclusion arises in a business context, which will of course be so where it relates to the occupier's business premises.

(ii) Defences for the employer

The most obvious 'defence' for the defendant employer is that one of the essential elements of the claimant's cause of action is missing; thus, for example, we have seen that causation must be proved and if for any reason it cannot be (for example, if, in a breach of statutory duty action, the employer successfully argues that the only act causing the employer to be in breach was that of the claimant himself), then the claimant's claim will fail. There are, however, three substantive defences which deserve mention (volenti, contributory negligence and limitation), though once again it is assumed that the reader is familiar with the basic law relating to each.

---

148 A person not lawfully on the land, ie a trespasser, used to be owed the lesser 'duty of common humanity' (*British Railways Board v Herrington* [1972] AC 877, [1972] 1 All ER 749, HL); but this was altered to a duty of reasonable care in *all* the circumstances (including the trespassory status) by the Occupiers' Liability Act 1984. For the circumstances in which such a duty is imposed by the statute, see s 1(3).

149 Occupiers' Liability Act 1957, s 2(3)(b); *Woollins v British Celanese Ltd* (1966) 1 KIR 438, CA. See also s 2(4)(b) which may exonerate an employer who has had work, maintenance, etc., done by a reputable independent contractor: *Ferguson v Welsh* [1987] 3 All ER 777, [1988] IRLR 112, HL.

150 *Ashdown v Samuel Williams & Sons Ltd* [1957] 1 QB 409, [1957] 1 All ER 35, CA; *White v Blackmore* [1972] 2 QB 651, [1972] 3 All ER 158, CA; Occupiers' Liability Act 1957, s 2(1).

(a) Volenti non fit injuria

Whatever may be the position in other branches of the law of tort, volenti will rarely ever succeed at common law in an industrial injury case, even though it is theoretically available[151]. Two particular rules relating to volenti are chiefly responsible for this, for they take on particular significance when applied to the employment context. The first is the rule that sciens is not volens (ie mere knowledge does not imply consent), so that it will not be enough for the employer simply to point to continuance at work by the employee with knowledge of the risk as establishing consent on his part[152]. The second is the rule that consent must be freely given; this will rarely be the case where the claimant is an employee, either because he will have been acting under orders, or because he was not in a position (economically or otherwise) to refuse to do the act in question, or because the act in question was one which in practice he had to do in order to discharge his work duties[153].

Turning from common law actions to that for breach of statutory duty the position is even clearer, for it has been held that volenti does not apply *at all* to an action for breach of a statutory duty laid upon the employer by the relevant legislation[154], the principal reason being that it would be contrary to public policy to allow an employee by agreement or consent to 'contract out' of his statutory protection (particularly as some of the legislation is designed to protect him from his own defaults as well as those of his employer). However, the House of Lords in *ICI Ltd v Shatwell*[155] held that this does not apply where the employer is not in breach of a statutory duty on himself[156], but is only liable vicariously for breach by another person. In that case, two shotfirers were injured when they agreed to test equipment in a manner that was contrary to statutory Regulations which applied to *them* (as well as contrary to the employer's express instructions). One of them sued the employer for damages (accepting 50% contributory negligence) on the basis that the employer was vicariously liable for the breach of statutory duty by the other shotfirer. The House of Lords held that in these circumstances, as there was no direct breach of statutory duty by the employer, the defence of volenti was available and indeed decided the case against the claimant.

Thus, volenti is of restricted application in employment cases; where, however, the claimant does run risks with full knowledge, that may still constitute contributory negligence (leading to a decrease in his damages against the employer), but that may be considered a more satisfactory approach to the problem

---

151 It is expressly retained in occupiers' liability actions (Occupiers' Liability Act 1957, s 2(5)). It is not to be used to circumvent the ban on clauses or notices excluding liability for death or personal injury: Unfair Contract Terms Act 1977, s 2(3).

152 *Smith v Baker & Sons* [1891] AC 325, HL.

153 *Bowater v Rowley Regis Corpn* [1944] KB 476, [1944] 1 All ER 465, CA; *Burnett v British Waterways Board* [1973] 2 All ER 631, [1973] 1 WLR 700, CA.

154 *Baddeley v Earl of Granville* (1887) 19 QBD 423; *Wheeler v New Merton Board Mills* [1933] 2 KB 669, CA.

155 [1965] AC 656, [1964] 2 All ER 999, HL; in this case the House approved the general principle laid down in *Baddeley* and *Wheeler*. For a rare example of the application of volenti to an industrial injury on this basis, see *McMullen v National Coal Board* [1982] ICR 148; cf *Storey v National Coal Board* [1983] 1 All ER 375, [1983] ICR 156; see Holgate (1983) 12 ILJ 185.

156 And, semble, provided he is not vicariously liable for a breach by someone placed upon the plaintiff (eg a foreman or manager), since in such a case the employee may not have been free to consent to the breach (per Lord Pearce).

for it is based upon the more modern approach of apportionment of blame and does not rule the claimant out altogether, unlike the more blunt instrument of volenti.

(b) Contributory negligence

Before the Law Reform (Contributory Negligence) Act 1945, contributory negligence by the claimant used to be a complete defence. Now it leads to a reduction of damages to 'such extent as the court thinks just and equitable having regard to the [claimant's] share in the responsibility for the damage'. This shows the modern approach to multiple causation of trying to reach an equitable apportionment instead of seeking to lay the blame wholly on one party or the other, and as such it is analogous to the modern rules on apportionment between joint tortfeasors, which proceed on similar principles[157].

In the industrial injury context, four particular points about the application of contributory negligence should be noticed. The first is that, unlike volenti, it applies to all cases of breach of statutory duty[158], as well as to common law actions. The second is that breach of a statutory duty by the *employee* (for example, failure to use a safety device, contrary to a duty to do so laid upon him by regulation) can constitute contributory negligence on his part if it contributes to the accident[159]. Under the modern law of health and safety, the following principal statutory obligations are placed on employees:

(1) to take reasonable care for the health and safety of himself and others, and to co-operate with his employers so far as is necessary to enable the employers to comply with their statutory duties[160];

(2) not, intentionally or recklessly, to interfere with or misuse anything provided in the interests of health, safety or welfare[161];

(3) to use anything provided by his employers (under their statutory duties) in accordance with training and instructions and to inform the employers of any work situation representing a serious and imminent danger to health and safety, and of any shortcomings in the employer's protection arrangements[162];

---

157 Civil Liability (Contribution) Act 1978, ss 1(1) and 2(1).
158 *Caswell v Powell Duffryn Associated Collieries Ltd* [1940] AC 152, [1939] 3 All ER 722, HL. It seemed established for some time that there could be 100% contributory negligence in an appropriate case where the accident was entirely the employee's fault: *Jayes v IMI (Kynoch) Ltd* [1985] ICR 155, CA. However, this was disapproved (and *Jayes* said to be no longer good law) in *Anderson v Newham College of Further Education* [2002] EWCA Civ 505, [2003] ICR 212 on the basis that contributory negligence can diminish an existing liability but cannot extinguish it completely. If the employee really was 100% to blame, the logical result is no liability in negligence in the first place (in a common law action) or (in a breach of statutory duty action) a finding of no statutory liability under the rule in *Boyle v Kodak Ltd* (p 856 above).
159 *Norris v Syndic Manufacturing Co* [1952] 2 QB 135, [1952] 1 All ER 935, CA.
160 Health and Safety at Work etc. Act 1974, s 7.
161 S 8.
162 Management of Health and Safety at Work Regulations 1999, reg 14; see generally ch 13, below. Note that an employee making such complaints is now protected from dismissal by the Employment Rights Act 1996, s 100 and from action short of dismissal by s 44, both originally enacted by the Trade Union Reform and Employment Rights Act 1993: see p 595 above.

(4) to use personal protective equipment provided, in accordance with training and instructions, to take all reasonable steps to return it, and to report forthwith any loss of or obvious defect in it[163];

(5) to make full and proper use of any system for manual handling provided by the employers[164].

Breach of these obligations, as well as potentially incurring criminal liability on the employee, could well give rise to a defence of contributory negligence (in spite of the fact that (1) to (3) come from statutory provisions which themselves do not support civil liability).

The third point is that, on general principles, to be held to have been contributorily negligent the claimant must have shown definite lack of care for his own safety. One ramification of this in the employment context is that disobedience of orders (for example, going into part of the premises declared by the employer to be out of bounds) will not necessarily constitute contributory negligence, unless the employee should have foreseen that the act of disobedience in question would place him in danger[165].

The fourth point is that the courts may be prepared to expect a lower standard of care by the claimant for his own safety in industrial accident cases, and so either find contributory negligence less easily or make a smaller deduction from damages. This is certainly so as regards breach of statutory duty. In *Caswell v Powell Duffryn Associated Collieries Ltd*[166] (the case which established that contributory negligence applies to breach of statutory duty actions), Lord Atkin said:

'I am of the opinion that the care to be expected of the plaintiff in the circumstances will vary with the circumstances; and that a different degree of care may well be expected from a workman in a factory or a mine from that which might be taken by an ordinary man not exposed continually to the noise, strain and manifold risks of factory or mine.'

Lord Wright said:

'What is all important is to adapt the standard of what is negligence to the facts, and to give due regard to the actual conditions under which men work in a factory or mine, to the long hours and the fatigue, to the slackening of attention which naturally comes from constant repetition of the same operation, to the noise and confusion in which the man works, to his preoccupation in what he is actually doing at the cost perhaps of some inattention to his own safety.'

However, doubt has been expressed whether this more lenient standard is to apply to the common law negligence action, particularly in *Staveley Iron and Chemical Co Ltd v Jones*[167] where Lord Reid declined to decide whether it applied outside actions for breach of statutory duty, and Lord Tucker said[168]:

---

163 Personal Protective Equipment at Work Regulations 1992, SI 1992/2966, regs 10 and 11.

164 Manual Handling Operations Regulations 1992, SI 1992/2793, reg 5.

165 *Westwood v Post Office* [1974] AC 1, [1973] 3 All ER 184, HL.

166 N 158 above; the following dicta are at 214 and 178, respectively. See Fagelson 'The last bastion of fault? Contributory negligence in actions for employers' liability' (1979) 42 MLR 646.

167 [1956] AC 627, [1956] 1 All ER 403, HL.

168 [1956] AC 627 at 647, [1956] 1 All ER 403 at 413.

'... while accepting without question this and other dicta to similar effect [ie in favour of the more lenient standard] which have been used in this House in relation to cases under the Factories Acts and other statutes imposing absolute obligations on employers or occupiers of premises, I doubt very much whether they were ever intended or could properly be applied to a simple case of common law negligence such as the present where there was no evidence of work-people performing repetitive work under strain or for long hours at dangerous machines.'

On its face, this is capable of two interpretations – that the lenient standard is never applicable to contributory negligence as a defence to a common law action, or that it is applicable *if* there is positive evidence of factors such as strain, long hours, noise, etc., which are capable of justifying it. It is submitted that the latter view is preferable, particularly as it would give greater uniformity between the common law and statutory actions which may, of course, be pleaded together.

(c) Limitation

The normal rule in actions for personal injury or death is that the action must be commenced within three years of the date of the accident. While a time limit is obviously necessary, a rigid one was seen to work injustice in certain cases where the damage did not manifest itself until a considerable time after it had been sustained; certain industrial diseases were prime examples of this. The Limitation Act 1963 attempted to alleviate this, allowing the limitation rule to be ignored in certain circumstances. The position was further improved by the Limitation Act 1975 which introduced new provisions which, with the consolidation of the limitation statutes in 1980, are now contained in the Limitation Act 1980, sections 11, 14 and 33. These new sections give to a claimant more scope to avoid the standard three-year period, in two ways. First, sections 11 and 14 provide that the three year period runs from either the date on which the cause of action accrued *or* the date (if later) of 'the plaintiff's knowledge'; this is defined as the date on which he first had knowledge of the following facts: (a) that the injury in question was significant; (b) that it was attributable in whole or in part to the act or omission relied upon; (c) the identity of the defendant and (d) the identity of any relevant third party (and the facts supporting the action against him). This includes not just facts within his actual knowledge, but also any facts which could have been ascertained by him with the help of expert advice (where it was reasonable for him to seek it). Second, section 33 gives the court a residual discretion, independently of sections 11 and 14, to allow an action to go ahead out of time where it is equitable to do so, having regard to factors such as the reasons for the delay, the effect it may have had on the cogency of the evidence, any dilatory conduct by the defendant, any period of disability suffered by the claimant after the accident, whether the claimant acted promptly once he realised he might have a cause of action against the defendant and whether the claimant took steps to obtain expert advice (and, if so, the nature of the advice which he received)[169].

---

169 This discretion under s 33 was construed widely by the Court of Appeal in *Firman v Ellis* [1978] QB 886, [1978] 2 All ER 851, CA, but doubt was cast on that construction by the decision of the House of Lords in *Walkley v Precision Forgings Ltd* [1979] 2 All ER 548, [1979] 1 WLR 606, HL which overruled the decision in *Firman v Ellis*. However, both of those cases were on a slightly different point and when the matter came directly before the House of Lords in *Thompson v Brown Construction (Ebbw Vale) Ltd* [1981] 2 All ER 296, [1981] 1 WLR 744, HL, they made it clear that the discretion is unfettered.

(iii) Insurance

It has always been the practice of the prudent employer to cover his 'employer's liability' with insurance under a policy covering at the least his potential liability to his own employees. However, not all employers were prudent and the result of a failure to insure might prejudice the ability of an injured employee to recover from a bankrupt employer.

Statutory provision was made to oblige an employer to insure against his liability for personal injury to his employees, in the Employer's Liability (Compulsory Insurance) Act 1969; the Act covers all employers except local authorities, statutory corporations, nationalised industries and certain others exempted by Regulations[170]. The duty is to maintain an approved policy with authorised insurers covering bodily injury or disease of an employee arising out of and in the course of employment[171] in Great Britain. The details defining such concepts as 'approved policy' and 'authorised insurers' are provided by Regulations made under the Act[172] (for example, they prohibit certain conditions of exemption of the insurers from liability).

Those to be covered by such insurance are defined by the Act as individuals working under a contract of service or apprenticeship 'whether by way of manual labour, clerical work or otherwise, whether such contract is expressed or implied, oral or in writing'[173]. Close relatives are excluded, as are those not ordinarily resident in Great Britain although Regulations make exceptions to the latter category[174]. The Act provides that certificates of insurance must be issued; the Regulations govern the form of the certificate and require that it shall be displayed at the employer's place of business[175]. Also, such certificates have to be produced to an inspector or to the Health and Safety Executive upon request, and failure to do so is a summary offence. Failure to insure is itself of course also backed by the criminal sanction of a summary offence of strict liability[176]; where the employer is a corporation, any officer who consented to, connived at, or facilitated by his negligence the failure to insure is also liable to be prosecuted.

Insurance against liability towards injured employees is thus made compulsory, and wider 'public liability' insurance (primarily covering vicarious liability towards third parties as a result of an employee's negligence) is also common, though not compulsory[177]. This means that when an action is brought by an injured person against the employer, it will in fact be an insurance company which will have control over negotiations for a settlement of the claim, and over any ensuing

---

170 Employers' Liability (Compulsory Insurance) Act 1969, s 3.
171 This is the same phrase as that used in the industrial injuries scheme – see head 2, above.
172 Employers' Liability (Compulsory Insurance) Regulations 1998, SI 1998/2573. The amount for which the employer must be insured is £5m in respect of claims relating to one or more employees arising out of any one occurrence: reg 3.
173 S 2(1).
174 S 2(2); see also the Offshore Installations and Pipeline Works (Management and Administration) Regulations 1995, SI 1995/738, reg 21.
175 Reg 5.
176 S 5. An attempt to interpret the Act as supporting civil liability as well (so that a claimant injured by the employer but prejudiced by the latter's failure to insure could sue for that breach of the Act) failed in *Richardson v Pitt-Stanley* [1995] QB 123, [1995] 1 All ER 460, CA.
177 If different policies with different insurance companies cover these matters, the exact legal status of the person injured can become a vital point in deciding which company is to indemnify the employer: *Denham v Midland Employers' Mutual Assurance Ltd* [1955] 2 QB 437, [1955] 2 All ER 561, CA.

litigation, even though such litigation will be defended in the name of the employer[178]. In the light of this modern emphasis on insurance[179] and its practical importance in the smooth running of our present system of recovery of damages for individual fault, it is perhaps permissible to wonder whether the insurance point in *Lister v Romford Ice and Cold Storage Co Ltd*[180] would have been decided the same way if the case had arisen today, or whether the courts would have held that there was indeed an implied term that the employer would 'look after the whole matter of insurance', and not just restrict himself to that which was legally obligatory, particularly in the light of the broader approach taken to possible obligations on an employer to inform and advise an employee (of matters not fully in the latter's knowledge) in *Scally v Southern Health and Social Services Board*[181].

For many years, however, the 1969 Act's requirements have not given rise to any such rethinking and have been a stable and unremarkable legal obligation on employers. However, true to form for employment law, they have suddenly become controversial at the time of writing, for two interlinked reasons. The first is that for years it has been argued that employer's liability insurance should be used more positively to improve safety standards, by varying premia with the individual employer's safety record (as in done with road insurance, but rarely has been here). The government and the Health and Safety Executive have shown interest in this[182] and there have been signs of it happening, with insurance companies becoming more actively involved in their insureds' safety policies and practice. Secondly, however, this has coincided in 2002/03 with problems within the insurance industry leading to some insurers pulling out of the employers' liability market and those left increasing premia suddenly and, in many cases, by astronomical amounts. This has been seen as capable of facing small employers with the choice in extreme cases of insolvency or operating without cover (in defiance of the 1969 Act), both to the potential disadvantages of employees. In late 2002 the Chancellor of the Exchequer announced a review of the whole employers' liability scheme, to be undertaken by the Department for Work and Pensions.

---

178 This is because of the doctrine of subrogation, on which see *Morris v Ford Motor Co Ltd* [1973] QB 792, [1973] 2 All ER 1084, CA. It will also normally be for the insurer to operate the civil recoupment system, p 844 above.
179 This is now to be seen in both of the major types of tort actions – those for industrial injuries and those for motor accidents.
180 [1957] AC 555, [1957] 1 All ER 125, HL; see p 139 above.
181 [1991] ICR 771, [1991] IRLR 52, HL; see p 163 above.
182 Revitalising Health & Safety (HSC/DETR, June 2000) p 23; Greenstreet Berman Ltd, Changing business behaviour – would bearing the true cost of poor health and safety performance make a difference? (HSE Contract Research Report, 2002).

Chapter 13

Industrial safety (2):
health and safety at work

1 INTRODUCTION

There is no aspect of industrial law more important than those rules, which are largely statutory, that attempt to ensure the health and safety of workers at their place of work[1]. Such legislation has a long history[2]; the first Factory Act, a substantial measure, was passed in 1802. Since that date the law to protect health and safety at work saw a steady flow of statute law. Later, particularly in the second half of the twentieth century concepts in the common law, especially the development of the torts of negligence and breach of statutory duty, have done much to help to protect the worker from injury. The possibility that the employer, or most usually his insurer, might have to pay large damages undoubtedly was a powerful pressure towards a safe working environment, but a pressure that was not as effective against the marginal employer as it might have been.

It has to be said, however, that despite this long history, there have been over the years relatively long periods with only slow development. There has been a strong tendency for legislation to lag behind developments in work practices, and the introduction and increasing use of increasingly dangerous processes and substances. So, while the old-fashioned factory was reasonably well covered by protective legislation, modern safeguards were slow to appear and statutes have tended to remain on the statute book while becoming increasingly outdated and ineffective.

The kernel of the law before the 1970s was a handful of major pieces of legislation. The first Factories Act of 1802 has already been mentioned. The last Act was the Factories Act 1961; a glance at its format shows clearly that it had as its backbone the nineteenth-century factory with boiler house, prime mover, transmission machinery and individual machines. This was long after the typical place of work was filled with newer dangers – dangers such as electricity, the

---

1 According to HSE figures, in 2000/01 there were 295 fatal injuries to employees (and 447 work-related fatalaties to members of the public), 27,303 major non-fatal injuries and 133,112 minor injuries (requiring more than three days off work); for comprehensive statistics, see www.hse.gov.uk/statistics/overpic.htm.
2 For an excellent exposition of the history, see Cornish and Clark *Law and Society in England 1750–1950* (1989) pp 301–308 and 483–541.

fumes from a host of newly introduced chemicals and mobile handling of materials with tractors and fork-lift trucks. Many of these dangers were at times covered, in part at least, by statutory Regulations but the law was fragmented and particular, lacking both general principles and catch-all duties of care.

Other similar major statutes must be noted. Perhaps the most comprehensive, and certainly the best respected and most carefully followed, was the Mines and Quarries Act 1954, itself the result of a long line of previous statutes stretching back into the nineteenth century. A relative latecomer was the equally comprehensive Offices, Shops and Railway Premises Act 1963. Indeed, those three statutes formed a formidable, if somewhat rigid code protecting safety and they were backed by a considerable weight of subsidiary legislation in the form of Regulations, made under the statutes.

The law was comprehensively reviewed by the Robens Committee on Safety and Health at Work[3] which recognised the importance of the existing law but was equally aware of the basic defects. The report itself led to the passing of the reforming Health and Safety at Work etc Act 1974, a major piece of modern legislation which is dealt with in the next section.

As far as the Committee was concerned it foresaw three levels of control – legislation, Regulations and statutory or approved Codes of Practice, supplemented by voluntary codes and rules within individual establishments. As far as the crucial legislation was concerned it indicated the need to deal with the issues in a general way, laying down basic principles of wide application. That was indeed the purpose of the Health and Safety at Work etc Act 1974 which followed. It supplemented and, in effect, overarched the major pieces of employment-type statutes mentioned in the preceding paragraph. Development was envisaged as both top down – Parliament insisting on basic standards; and bottom up – growing from individual experience leading employers and workers, through their trade unions, to develop from good practice voluntary codes which might themselves, as indication of good practice, give the impetus for new legally binding Regulations or approved Codes of Practice. This involved a shift of emphasis, which was not at the time universally popular, from particular types of places of work – mine, office or factory, to the idea of 'a workplace' for most of the general protections.

Important steps of reform almost always require appropriate administrative changes and new attitudes to the enforcement of law. The inspectorates under the major pieces of legislation had an excellent record and provided an ideal base for improvements. To ensure this, the Committee's Report led to the speedy establishment of the Health and Safety Commission and its Executive which have ensured that there has been a focal point for the development of the law, particularly Codes of Practice, and especially of good health and safety monitoring. It is in the area of legislation itself, however, as has been already indicated, where progress had until recently been disappointingly slow. The Health and Safety at Work etc Act 1974 was speedily put into place; an essential first step. Its expression of duties in general terms was unfamiliar and not particularly to the liking of many lawyers, but it was an important general basis for the law giving a clear indication that detailed control had to be matched by an overall duty to look generally at health and safety, and ensure that possible dangers were guarded against.

The following years did not continue the initial impetus in the form of legislation. Not only was there little attempt to revise the existing statute law,

3   Report of the Committee 1970–1972, Cmnd 5034.

admittedly a long and difficult exercise, even though the existing legislation was rapidly becoming both outdated and, more seriously, completely deficient in its control of the newer dangers that were arising. Such changes as there were came through the steady stream of statutory Regulations and Codes of Practice. But progress was very slow.

Health and safety was, not unnaturally, a subject that became of central concern to the EC. A social topic of importance to both employers and workers, it was an obvious area for major initiatives from the Community. It believes, with justification, that it 'is now recognised as the main force in the development of new safety and health legislation[4].' Directives on individual dangers have indeed had an influence on national legislation after a start which has to be described as somewhat slow[5]. In the last decade and a half, however, as a result of the Single European Act of 1987, which, in Article 118a, aimed at encouraging improvements, especially in the work environment, as regards the health and safety of workers, progress has accelerated. Following the 1987 Act a programme concerning safety, hygiene and health at work was instituted, and a group of directives was transmitted to the Council.

Those directives were adopted by the Community and at the beginning of 1993 became incorporated into English law by means of Regulations and Codes of Practice[6]. There seems every likelihood that this most important development represents the way forward for future reform and it is already leading to a comprehensive spring-cleaning of the English law in this area that is long overdue. Thus, for example, the Construction (Design and Management) Regulations 1994[7] (applying to one of our most dangerous industries) immediately took some of these EC-inspired ideas even further and have often been seen as a model for further developments. Major across-the-board provisions such as the Control of Substances Hazardous to Health Regulations ('COSHH') show strong similarities to the drafting of the Six Pack; they were updated again in 2002[8], when we also saw the reissuing in modern form of the Control of Lead at Work Regulations[9] and, of major topical concern, the Control of Asbestos at Work Regulations[10].

One peculiar aspect of this revolution in our health and safety law has been the time that elapsed before significant case law arose on the new Regulations. It was clear from the beginning that there would be a need for judicial interpretation (in both pure health and safety law and in cases of civil law claims by injured workers where the Regulations are now the basis for the claim for breach of statutory duty, considered in the previous chapter). This was because, although in places the Regulations use time-honoured phrases from UK common law and old statutes such as 'as far as reasonably practicable', for most purposes they adopt the new Euro-speak of the backing Directives. This tends

4   Social Europe – Health and Safety at work in the European Community, 2/90.
5   The years 1974–85 saw two Commission Action Programmes and a number of Directives and draft Directives.
6   See section 3 below. The principal Regulations are generally known as 'The Six Pack'.
7   SI 1994/3140; particularly notable are the provisions placing clear duties on the major parties to a construction project and the requirement of a health and safety plan, a planning supervisor, notification of the HSE, risk assessments and obligations on contractors to co-operate and comply with the safety plan.
8   SI 2002/2677. The original 1988 Regulations in fact pre-dated the Six Pack in adopting the new EC format.
9   SI 2002/2676.
10 SI 2002/2675.

to use new terminology such as 'suitable and sufficient' and 'efficient', which may well be linked with wording such as 'shall provide' or 'shall ensure', which to a common lawyer points to strict liability. Has the general level of liability been ratcheted up? This remained unclear for most of the 1990s. Case law is now finally appearing but it may take several years yet to establish a clear pattern. On the one hand, some case law points towards either strict or almost strict duties on employers. The first significant decision was in *Stark v Post Office*[11] where a postman was injured when the brake block on his bike broke and threw him off. The defect was unforeseeable but it was held that there had been a failure to 'ensure that work equipment is maintained in an efficient state, in efficient working order and in good repair'.[12] One important subsidiary point was that under the pre-1993 factories legislation there would have been strict liability in these circumstances and the coming into force of the Directives was not to have the effect of lowering any existing levels of duty. Similarly, in *Dugmore v Swansea NHS Trust*[13] a failure by a hospital to provide vinyl gloves to a nurse who unforeseeably had a sudden reaction to latex gloves was held to contravene a requirement to 'ensure that the exposure of his employees to a substance hazardous to health is either prevented or, where this is not reasonably practicable, adequately controlled'[14]. The reference to reasonable practicability was held to refer only to prevention and 'adequately' was held to have a partly objective meaning, not reliant on foreseeability. In cases like this, stress tends to be placed on the protective and preventative aims of the Regulations. On the other hand, many of the Regulations are of such wide drafting and application that cases may arise where such a strict and/or literal interpretation could produce results perceivable by courts as unrealistic or excessive. Here there may well be interpretations placed on the new wording to avoid such results. Particularly problematic here have been the Manual Handling Regulations (see below), potentially the widest of all. One interpretive technique has been to apply the relevant Regulations 'in context'. Thus, for example, in *Koonjul v Thameslink Healthcare Services NHS Trust*[15] which concerned a back injury to an experienced care assistant whose work required frequent lifting it was held that the reference in regulation 4 of the Manual Handling Regulations to the risk of injury meant that the assessment of that risk had to be context-based and looked at realistically. In the circumstances of the case, it was not possible to evaluate precisely the innumerable tasks of a care worker and the employer was not liable for failure to do so. Similarly, in *Palmer v Marks & Spencer plc*[16] the requirement that a floor be 'suitable for . . . the purpose for which it was used' was held to be strict as to the requirement to provide a suitable floor, but 'suitability' itself had to be considered in all the circumstances (so that there was no breach when an

---

11 [2000] ICR 1013, [2000] PIQR 105, CA.
12 Provision and Use of Work Equipment Regulations 1992, reg 6(1) (now the 1998 Regulations, see below).
13 [2002] EWCA Civ 1689, [2003] IRLR 164.
14 Control of Substances Hazardous to Health Regulations 1988, reg 7(1) (now the 2002 Regulations, see above).
15 [2000] PIQR 123, (2000) Times, 19 May, CA. This was applied in *O'Neill v DSE Retail Ltd* [2002] EWCA Civ 1139 (unreported) but here the claimant won because a training video covering the hazard that caused his back injury had not been shown to him; this constituted a failure to take 'appropriate steps' under reg 4(1)(b).
16 [2001] EWCA Civ 1528, [2001] All ER (D) 123 (Oct). The case concerned the Workplace (Health, Safety and Welfare) Regulations 1992, reg 12.

employee tripped over a slightly protruding weather strip on a door that was entirely normal and had caused no previous problems) and in *Horton v Taplin Contracts Ltd*[17] an employer was held not to have been in breach of an otherwise strict duty to provide 'suitable' scaffolding where it had been suitable for the reasonably foreseeable purposes of the work and the injury had been caused by the deliberate and malicious act of a fellow employee in toppling it. It therefore seems that the courts are still at a relatively early stage in the interpretation process of this vital new legislation; this is hardly surprising given the scale of the changes in 1993 and the historical precedent that the late nineteenth century perfection of the factories legislation led to massive litigation and decades' worth of explanatory case law, up to the highest level.

Two final points are offered by way of introduction. The first is that arguably we are seeing health and safety law becoming viewed (at last) as an integral part of employment or industrial law. There are increasing statutory overlaps, for example in relation to protection of health and safety complainants, the expanding law on whistleblowing and the requirements of consultation of the workforce; arguable the post-1993 regulatory framework fits into this development. We are also seeing it in the common law, with health and safety matters arising in contractual disputes and, of course, in the ubiquitous and Protean law on stress injuries suffered at work[18]. The second point is that, at the time of writing, there is the prospect of further major reform of health and safety law. For several years there has been controversy over how to charge in fatal accident cases (given the difficulties of applying common law manslaughter to corporations) and whether penalties generally should be increased. Specific legislation on these issues has been expected for some time. However, the Green Paper 'Revitalising Health and Safety'[19] went much further in setting out the present government's intentions (for example, in relation to corporate and directors' liabilities generally, alternative penalties, involvement of insurance companies, greater practical incentives for safety and the setting of government targets for accident reduction), to such an extent that proposals have been aired for much wider legislation in the form of a new Safety Bill, not just a Bill to amend the penalty provisions of the 1974 Act. This had a false start in 2001 and has failed to make it into the Queen's Speech since. However, it is possible that it may reappear during the currency of this edition; the question then will be whether it will be radical enough to be seen as a third revolution in this area, to rank alongside those in 1974 and 1993.

In the light of the above, the next section of this chapter deals in some detail with the Health and Safety at Work etc Act 1974 itself. The older subsidiary statutes mentioned already – the Mines and Quarries Act 1954, the Factories Act 1961 and the Offices, Shops and Railway Premises Act 1963 – have now finally disappeared (after a transitional period), and so the third section of the chapter will concentrate on the new EC-inspired Regulations.

17 [2002] EWCA Civ 1604, [2003] ICR 179.
18 One potential conflict here is with disability discrimination law where there may be a difficulty in deciding up to what point an employer can plead health and safety reasons as a defence under the Disability Discrimination Act 1995, eg in relation to justification or failure to make reasonable adjustments. See Davies and Davies 'Reconciling risk and the employment of disabled persons in a reformed welfare state' (2000) 29 ILJ 321.
19 Strategy Statement (HSC/DETR, June 2000); see particularly the list of action points in Annex C.

2 THE HEALTH AND SAFETY AT WORK ETC. ACT 1974

(i) The Robens Committee

The regulation of hours of work, health, safety and welfare in factories and workshops was one of the earliest statutory interventions for the regulation of industry[20]. The first statute was as early as 1802 and the process continued throughout the nineteenth century. The earliest Regulations applied to textile mills but the scope of the later provisions applied to a widening range of employment. The legislation was firmly based on types of work and upon premises. Parallel legislation on mines and quarries started in 1842. Other major areas followed: railways (1900), shop employees (1886). Agriculture lagged behind but it became similarly covered in 1956.

A great deal of the legislation sprang from the efforts of dedicated reformers. Some were the result of accidents which attracted publicity and wide concern. For example the regulation of fire precautions in factories only reached an acceptable level in the Factories Act 1959 which followed a tragic mill fire at Keighley. This important subject had never been looked at in a wide-ranging way until the Labour government, as almost one of its last acts in 1970, set up a Committee, chaired by Lord Robens, to review the whole field. Its report was published two years later and has formed the basis of renewed interest and activity in this important area.

It is important to summarise the principal findings of the Robens Committee before turning to the subsequent legislation. The initial criticism was of the existing state of the law. In paragraphs 24–26 the Committee identified eleven major statutes[21] and pointed out that there were nearly 500 supplementary statutory instruments. This body of law was continually increasing and in the view of the Committee it could be said that there was too much law[22]. Not only that, the law itself was found to be badly structured, largely because it had been assembled piecemeal with little regard to principle. Indeed the leading statute, the Factories Act 1961, reflected closely the needs of the typical nineteenth-century textile mill and bore little close relevance to, say, a modern chemical plant.

The responsibility for this legislation was split between a number of separate government departments with little or no co-ordination. Employment, Environment, Agriculture, Trade and Industry and the Home Office, all had a major responsibility. There were seven inspectorates – factories, mines and quarries, agriculture, explosives, radioactivity, chemical and alkali[23].

---

20 There is a useful summary of the history in Appendix 5 of the *Report of the Committee on Safety and Health at Work* (the Robens Committee) (Cmnd 5034, 1972). On the report generally, see Howells 'The Robens Report' (1972) 1 ILJ 185; Woolf 'The Robens Report – the wrong approach?' (1973) 2 ILJ 88.
21 Factories Act 1961, Offices, Shops and Railway Premises Act 1963, Mines and Quarries Act 1954, Agriculture (Poisonous Substances) Act 1952 and Agriculture (Safety, Health and Welfare Provisions) Act 1956 – all supported by extensive statutory regulations; Explosives Acts 1875 and 1923, Petroleum (Consolidation) Act 1928, Nuclear Installations Act 1965 and 1969 – those dealing with dangerous substances; and the Radioactive Substances Act 1960 and the Alkali, etc, Works Regulation Act 1906 – dealing with dangerous emissions.
22 Para 28.
23 See paras 32 and 33.

It was inevitable that the Committee would propose rationalisation of both the law and its administration. Before making its proposals the Committee looked at several general issues. The one which raised most controversy concerned the main line of approach to be adopted. Some felt that the best results could be achieved by more protective law and stricter enforcement. Although the Robens Committee accepted that there must be a legal code, properly enforced, it sought improvement by means of self-regulation[24]. In line with that approach, and also with the modern way of looking at industrial matters, the Committee felt that the basic relationship upon which to build the new safety and health code was that of employment. The previous bases, premises and substances for example, would remain as part of the code but the basic concept should be that of the employer's duty to his employee and the concomitant duty of the employee to look after himself[25].

The Committee made fairly specific proposals for a new statutory framework. The law was to be brought together into four broad categories. These differed largely in scope and stretched between the broad, wide-ranging provisions such as the Factories Act 1961 to statutes of much narrower scope dealing with special dangers, for example the Boiler Explosions Acts 1882 and 1890 and the Mines and Quarries (Tips) Act 1969[26]. Unified law was to be accompanied by a unified administration headed by a national body with overall responsibility[27].

The Committee commented upon the form and content of the new legislation. The major proposal was the enactment of a major statute setting out general principles. The Committee clearly had in mind the common law duties, developed in the law of negligence and outside the code of statutory regulation and enforcement[28]. It is this proposal that provided the principal provisions in the subsequent Health and Safety at Work etc Act 1974. The Committee had interesting views upon subordinate legislation. It felt that over the whole field there was an important place for statutory regulation. The hope was expressed that this would provide a flexible and responsive method of dealing with individual and detailed dangers[29]. Finally, encouragement was given to the development of non-statutory Codes of Practice. This process was said to be central to the proposals, as it built on the concept of self regulation[30].

The Committee, in looking at the law, saw the possibility of countervailing pressures. The importance of satisfactory compensation is obvious but there was said to be evidence that this tended to lessen the attention paid to prevention. Indeed the Committee, in Appendix 7, went further and suggested that the pressure in the field of compensation to narrow the application of the law was in contradiction of the clear need, in the interests of prevention, to adopt, wherever the matter is doubtful, the wider interpretation. The Committee did not feel able to do more than indicate its concern and suggest further consideration. In due course the matter was taken up by the Pearson Committee[31]. Its report

---

24 This approach underlies chs 2 and 3. It is an approach that met with criticism after the publication of the Report.
25 Chapter 4.
26 Paras 100–109. The last mentioned statute resulted from the tragic Aberfan disaster and illustrated the reactive nature of much of the legislation.
27 Paras 110–124.
28 See ch 12, head 3, above.
29 Paras 134–140.
30 Paras 148–154.
31 *Report of the Royal Commission on Civil Liability* (Cmnd 7054, 1978) ; see ch 12, head 1, above.

showed again the problem of reconciling the two facets of prevention and compensation and did not greatly assist those seeking greater concern for prevention.

The Robens Committee dealt with a wide range of additional matters. It proposed two relatively new methods of enforcement – improvement notices[32] and prohibition notices[33]. It looked at public safety[34], special topics such as fire and toxic substances[35], occupational medicine[36], training[37] and research[38].

The other major change recommended by the Committee, not surprisingly in view of the criticisms of the situation it found, was concerned with the administrative structure to supervise the whole fabric of health and safety legislation and its application[39]. Its approach has been followed in subsequent legislation and a discussion of the changes is best left until the reformed law is considered.

The Report ended, and this is very much the product of the Chairman's personality, with a Programme of Action[40]. This was not wishful thinking, for by 1973 the Conservative government had proposed and introduced a bill. That bill was lost as a result of the 1974 general election leading to a change of government early in 1974. However, an almost identical bill was immediately re-introduced and became the Health and Safety at Work etc Act 1974[41], which must now be considered.

(ii) The Health and Safety at Work etc. Act

(a) General

The Act, at the outset in section 2(1), lays down the basic general duty placed upon employers, and does so with simple clarity. 'It shall be the duty of every employer to ensure, so far as is reasonably practicable, the health, safety and welfare of all his employees.' This provision has a positive aspect which is comprehensive and wide to an extent that has given rise to criticism and fear. In its negative aspect, as far as is reasonably practicable, it has been criticised as imprecise and flawed. Both aspects need to be considered in turn.

The section continues, without detracting from the general duty of section 2(1) to particularise the duties, covered again in terms laying down areas of responsibility. These are the provision and maintenance of plant and systems of work so that they are safe and without risk to health[42]; the handling, storage and

---

32 Para 269.
33 Para 276.
34 Chapter 10.
35 Chapter 11.
36 Chapter 12 – a rather superficial treatment of an area of growing concern.
37 Chapter 13.
38 Chapter 14.
39 Chapters 4 and 7.
40 Chapter 19.
41 The odd, but not unprecedented 'etc' is present because the Act in Pt III covers 'Building Regulations and Amendments of Building (Scotland) Act 1959.' This was merely because the bill provided a suitable vehicle for these extraneous, but important and necessary matters. The oddities of Parliament's concept of a businesslike approach are not infrequent.
42 S 2(2)(a).

transport of articles and substances[43]; the provision of information, instructions, training and supervision[44]; the maintenance of places of work under the employer's control in a safe condition with safe and risk-free means of access and egress[45]; the provision and maintenance of a safe, risk-free working environment with adequate welfare facilities and arrangements[46]. Each of these provisions is qualified by the familiar phrase 'as far as is reasonably practicable'.

A detailed discussion of these responsibilities placed upon the employer would require a full discussion of the previous law on common law negligence and breach of statutory duty[47]. Only the most salient points can be considered here. The basis of the general duties is the relationship of employer and employee. Employee is defined as an individual who works under a contract of employment[48]. The legal rules as to scope and extent of employment will obviously be of importance. The restriction of the duty to the bounds of reasonable practicability raises again a concept well known in the law of tort and breach of statutory duty. The prime effect is to ensure that the duties are not absolute, as so many were historically under the various statutory codes such as the Factories Act 1961 or the Mines and Quarries Act 1954.

It must be emphasised that these duties fulfil two functions but not the third. Above all they ensure that employers have to think about their responsibilities in a wide range of areas, many of which, for example training, would be relatively new to many. This is in line with the Robens philosophy. Secondly the duties are enforceable by the inspectorate. The way this is done will be considered below but the ultimate sanction is criminal prosecution. That gives the duties a backing which ensures they receive close consideration. Finally, these statutory duties are *not* the basis for civil actions by those injured as a result of breach. Alternative grounds for action might be available, but the Health and Safety at Work Act duties are not such. This is specifically stated in section 47 of the Act which not only states that sections 2–8 do not confer rights of action but also makes the important provision that neither must those rights be construed as affecting other existing statutory provisions[49]. The other duties set out in section 2 concern matters involving participation between employers and trade unions and employees.

The structure of all the duties under the Act is complex and wide-ranging. For example the employer himself has an additional duty outside the field of employment. This is to conduct his undertaking so as to ensure as far as is reasonably practicable that persons, other than his employees, who might be affected are not exposed to risks to health and safety[50]. A precisely similar duty is placed upon self-employed persons[51]. A self-employed person is defined as anyone who works for gain or reward otherwise than under a contract of

43 S 2(2)(b).
44 S 2(2)(c).
45 S 2(2)(d).
46 S 2(2)(e).
47 For much of this see ch 12, head 3 above.
48 For a full discussion of the status of employment see p 9 above. The status of trainees under government work experience schemes had to be clarified by regulation.
49 S 47(1)(a), (b). Regulations made under the Act are similarly dealt with – they are to support civil liability unless they specifically provide otherwise: s 47(2).
50 S 3(1). See *R v Swan Hunter Shipbuilders Ltd* [1982] 1 All ER 264, [1981] ICR 831. He may be responsible for defective equipment, left by a contractor, but available for use by his employees: *R v Mara* [1987] ICR 165, [1987] IRLR 154, CA.
51 S 3(2).

employment and whether or not he himself employs others[52]. Power is given to make Regulations under the Act requiring both employers and the self-employed to provide information to others on the way the undertaking is conducted where their health and safety may be affected[53].

The previous statutory codes had often been based on premises. This approach was continued by provision of a general duty applying to those in control of premises to any extent. This duty covers non-employees and those who make use of non-domestic premises as a place of work or for using things available there[54]. One of the problems aimed at was premises such as launderettes where quite dangerous machines and processes (those involving dry cleaning fluids which produce noxious fumes for example) were left untended for unsupervised use by the general public. The duty laid down is to ensure as far as is reasonably practicable the safety of the premises and machines and processes and the absence of risks to health[55]. Control is widely drawn to cover those who, under a tenancy or by contract, have responsibility for the maintenance of the premises or access and egress to them, or for the safety and absence of risk concerning the plant or substances used on premises[56]. The section applies to those carrying on a business, whether for profit or not[57].

An even wider and more basic set of duties is laid down to cover the designer, manufacturer, importer or supplier of articles for use at work[58]. This section attempts to tackle safety at the earliest stage. It lays down, in the now familiar pattern of terminology, the duty to ensure that design and construction are safe and without risks to health. Information has also to be made available to indicate adequately the uses for which the article has been made and tested and setting out conditions necessary for safe and risk-free use. The designer and manufacturer are under a duty to undertake or arrange for necessary research aimed at discovering and eliminating or minimising dangers and risks[59]. The erector or installer is placed under a similar duty in relation to the way he carries out his task[60].

A similar pattern of duties is placed on the manufacturer, importer or supplier of substances used at work[61]. A substance for use at work is defined as any substance intended to be used by persons at work, which again is a definition noticeable for its breadth rather than its precision[62]. The duties laid down include testing, supplying adequate information upon use and conditions to be observed in use[63], and research to discover and eliminate or minimise danger and risk[64]. As far as research is concerned it is permissible to rely upon the work of others where such an approach is reasonable[65] and reliance may be placed upon the

52   S 53.
53   S 3(3).
54   S 4(1)(a), (b); *Westminster City Council v Select Management Ltd* [1985] 1 All ER 897, [1985] 1 WLR 576, CA.
55   S 4(2); *Austin Rover Group Ltd v HM Inspector of Factories* [1990] ICR 133, [1989] IRLR 404, HL.
56   S 4(3).
57   S 4(4).
58   S 6(1), strengthened by the Consumer Protection Act 1987.
59   S 6(2).
60   S 6(3).
61   S 6(4).
62   S 53(1).
63   S 6(4).
64   S 6(5).
65   S 6(6).

written undertaking that the recipient will himself take care of the various steps to be taken to fulfil these duties[66].

It will be observed that these duties comprise an overlapping structure. A solvent for use in a dry-cleaning machine, imported by a wholesaler and supplied to a laundry which also uses it in a launderette open to the public, will involve duties on very many people. The overlapping, although it might be said to complicate the question of liability in the common law sense, which of course has been stressed, is not affected by the Act. From the angle of safety the more people involved in a duty to avoid danger or risk, the less chance of an accident. In one particular case[67] it was held that a shipbuilder had a duty to inform workers of a sub-contractor of the dangers of the build up of oxygen. The argument that since the sub-contractor had a duty the shipbuilder need not act was firmly rejected.

This interlocking matrix is made even more secure by the provisions of section 7 which clearly place similar general duties upon the employee. Again the language is wide and important. It can usefully be quoted. The duty on every employee while at work is:

'(a) to take reasonable care for the health and safety of himself and of other persons who may be affected by his acts and omissions at work; and
(b) as regards any duty or requirement imposed on his employer or any other person by or under any of the relevant statutory provisions, to co-operate with him so far as is necessary to enable that duty or requirement to be performed or complied with.'

This section brings the employee's duty firmly within the group of duties enforceable by the inspectorate. That provision is of far less practical significance than the clear statement of the duty itself. It is within the context of works rules and disciplinary procedures that the real impact will lie. There is finally a duty on the employee not to interfere with or misuse anything provided in the interests of health, safety or welfare, under any of the relevant statutory provisions[68].

(b) Interpretation of the Act

After a relative dearth of case law on the interpretation of the 1974 Act, we have now seen some very important decisions of the higher courts, showing a willingness to interpret it on its own terms, and in order to achieve its overall protective aim. Two particular themes can be discerned, both important from the point of view of legal involvement in actually trying to avoid accidents.

The first is the emphasis on *risk* of harm, not just on proved damage or injury. Although many of the legislative provisions start from the common law duties (and in practice many prosecutions will arise from actual accidents), the Act is *not* concerned with compensation for injury. It goes much wider than that, which can be seen particularly in the wide duties to the public in section 3. In *R v Board of Trustees of the Science Museum*[69] an inspection showed that legionella bacteria in

---

66 S 6(8).
67 *R v Swan Hunter Shipbuilders Ltd* [1982] 1 All ER 264, [1981] ICR 831, CA.
68 S 8. The employer must not charge for such items: s 9.
69 [1993] ICR 876, [1993] IRLR 853, CA. A similar approach can be seen, under s 2, in *Bolton Metropolitan Borough Council v Malrod Insulations Ltd* [1993] ICR 358, [1993] IRLR 274, Div Ct.

the cooling system could be a danger to the public outside the building, due to faulty maintenance and monitoring. The museum, convicted on indictment under section 3 of failing to secure, as far as reasonably practicable, that persons not in their employment were not exposed to risks to their health and safety, appealed; they argued that the prosecution had failed to prove that any members of the public had *actually* been put at risk. Such an argument has strong common law foundations (where is the proved damage, caused by the defendant's default?), but was strongly disapproved by the Court of Appeal who held that the key to section 3 lies in the creation of a risk of *possible* harm; citing the Robens Report and the wide administrative powers granted to inspectors by the Act, they held that to restrict the section to cases of actual danger or injury would result in a substantial emasculation of a central part of the Act. It is argued that this purposive approach is particularly appropriate in the light of the new statutory duties in the Six Pack (see p 889), especially the requirements of risk assessments in the Management Regulations, the Personal Protective Equipment Regulations, the Manual Handling Regulations and the Display Screen Regulations. This emphasis on forward looking, pro-active measures against possible future risks is a feature of modern health and safety law, and failure to adopt such measures may well become central in civil claims too, with the Six Pack establishing the obligations on which the action for breach of statutory duty will be based. It also fits in with the reviewed emphasis (above) placed on the common law obligation to provide a safe *system* of work.

The second theme is the willingness of the courts to break free of interpretations of the Act based on the old common law concepts in this area. The old view that the Act merely adopted those civil law ideas and duties, and criminalised them (for the purposes of administrative enforcement) was a pervasive one for a long time[70]. The restrictive effects of this view could be seen as late as in the case of *RMC Roadstone Products Ltd v Jester*[71]. Independent sub-contractors working on the defendants' premises suggested a method of work that in the event killed one of them; it had been assented to by one of the defendants' managers. The defendants were convicted under section 3 but their appeal was allowed by the Divisional Court, on the basis that the section only applied to 'conducting his undertaking' and that, on a traditional view, the 'employer' was not liable for or to independent contractors, and so the only undertaking in question here was that of the subcontractors, who had been reasonably chosen by the defendants and were not subject to any exceptional powers of control[72]. However within six months there arose the seminal case of *R v Associated Octel Ltd*[73] which shows a very different approach indeed and overrules *Jester*. In this case, the defendants ran a chemical plant and each year hired a particular contractor to do repair work during the annual shut down. One of the contractor's employees was sent into a chemical tank to clean it; the lamp he took was not a safety lamp, there was no containment of the acetone cleaner being used and no forced ventilation provided. When the bulb broke the result was a flash fire in which the employee was badly injured. The

---

70 It could be seen, eg, in old editions of Munkman's *Employer's Liability*, and in dicta in *R v Swan Hunter Shipbuilders Ltd* [1982] 1 All ER 264, [1981] ICR 831, CA.
71 [1994] ICR 456, [1994] IRLR 330, DC.
72 The defendants' argument was accepted that this was a penal statute and there were no reasons of policy why the duties imposed should extend beyond the existing common law duties.
73 [1996] ICR 972, [1997] IRLR 123, HL.

defendants were convicted under section 3 and heavily fined. They appealed, relying on *Jester* (ie that liability under section 3 was co-terminous with common law liability, and that they were not liable for the acts of their contractors) but this time the appeal was dismissed. The Court of Appeal[74] stated that section 3 and its crucial phrasing of 'conducting his undertaking' is to be construed as it stands, and is wider than the old common law duties, being concerned with the creation of risks. The legislative intent is deliberately protective, and here the cleaning and repairing of the plant *was* part of the conducting of the undertaking, whether done by the defendant's own employees or a contractor. Thus, if a risk was created (and, a fortiori, if an accident actually happened) there was prima facie liability on the defendant, subject to the *defence* of reasonable practicability[75]. It is that defence, they said, that provides the counterweight to ensure that a defendant employer is not subject to unfair liability, especially where contractors are involved. On further appeal, the House of Lords strongly adopted the same approach to the meaning of conducting an undertaking. Emphasising the direct nature of the duty on an employer under the statute, and contrasting that with common law rules on vicarious liability, Lord Hoffmann said:

> '... section 3 is not concerned with vicarious liability. It imposes a duty on the employer himself. That duty is defined by reference to a certain kind of activity, namely the conduct by the employer of his undertaking. It is indifferent to the nature of the contractual relationships by which the employer chooses to conduct it.'

Given their decision, the House of Lords did not have to consider in detail the defence of reasonable practicability, and so it is still primarily the decision of the Court of Appeal that governs that point. Obviously, there will be cases where the contracted-out work is so specialised that it is not reasonably practicable for the employer to supervise it, and so the defence will be available[76]. However, that will be a question of fact in each case, and what is fundamental is that the employer is no longer simply *exonerated* by the involvement of contractors. This decision, and the emphasis it clearly shows on the protective intent of the legislation (which is not to be compromised by reliance on old common law doctrines), could be of great importance for the future and, again, it is very much in line with the modern approach in the Six Pack.

74 [1995] ICR 281, [1994] IRLR 540, CA.
75 The wide approach to 'undertaking' can also be seen in the earlier case of *R v Mara* [1987] 1 All ER 478, [1987] ICR 165, CA. The idea of the strict duty, subject *only* to a reasonable practicability defence (itself to be construed relatively narrowly) can also be seen in the contemporaneous decisions (on both the Act and civil liability) in the *Science Museum* case (n 69 above), *R v British Steel plc* [1995] ICR 586, [1995] IRLR 310, CA; *Larner v British Steel plc* [1993] 4 All ER 102, [1993] IRLR 278, CA; and *Mains v Uniroyal Engelbert Tyres Ltd* [1995] IRLR 544, Ct of Sess. The one exceptional case here so far has been s 4 (making non-domestic premises available as a place of work) which was held in *Austin-Rover Group plc v HM Inspector of Factories* [1990] 1 AC 619, [1989] 2 All ER 1087, HL not to impose strict liability. This can be distinguished on the basis that that section is drafted very differently (with two references to reasonable practicability); on the other hand, it is interesting to notice that the dissenting speech of Lord Goff is much more in line with the recent approach to ss 2 and 3.
76 There is an interesting analogy with the Occupiers Liability Act 1957, s 2(4)(b) (liability for repairs, etc, carried out by an independent contractor) and the case of *Heseldine v Daw & Son Ltd* [1941] 2 KB 343, [1941] 3 All ER 156, CA where it was reasonable to delegate entirely the maintenance of a lift.

(c) The Health and Safety Commission and Executive

The Act set up a Health and Safety Commission and an Executive. The Commission is appointed by the Secretary of State for Employment and consists of a Chairman and between six and nine members[77]. Before making the appointments various interest groups must be consulted – as to three, employers' organisations: as to three others, organisations representing employees and as to the rest a series of bodies such as local authorities and professional associations[78]. The Commission has been in existence since 1975 and its policies and actions can be followed in detail through the annual reports[79]. The Executive comprises three persons, one appointed as Director[80].

The functions of the Commission and the Executive are set out in section 11 and have been added to by accepted practices. The Commission is under a duty to assist and encourage all the purposes of the general provisions of the Act: to encourage research and its publication and safety training, to ensure wide dissemination of advice and information particularly to those practically concerned in this field and to prepare and propose Regulations[81]. The Commission has said that its basic strategy was based on three themes – the promotion of positive attitudes to health and safety at work, better information on the analysis of the cause and scale of hazards and the development of a better database and the review of the legislation[82].

The Commission is independent, though it receives its finances from government. The Secretary of State is given supervisory control and may give the Commission directions as to the discharge of its statutory functions[83]. The Commission itself is given the necessary wide legal powers for it to function efficiently. It may delegate its functions to government departments or in turn undertake work for them[84]. It may set up committees of advice and indeed its Reports show a considerable number[85]. It may order investigations or inquiries, one of the major ways in which understanding of problems is advanced[86]. The Act lays down outline powers and provides for Regulations to provide and govern the powers of those conducting an inquiry or investigation[87].

One of the important functions of the Secretary of State[88] in this field is the making of Regulations. The general statutory control of this power is set out in section 50 which also includes a duty upon the Commission, before submitting a proposed regulation, to consult government departments or other appropriate bodies[89]. The purposes for which Regulations can be made are set out in some

---

77 These are statutory requirements of Sch 2, para 15 of the Act. Sch 2 sets out the details regulating both the Commission and the Executive. The Annual Reports appear with a considerable and unfortunate delay.
78 S 10(2).
79 S 10(3).
80 S 10(5).
81 S 11(2).
82 Set out in the first Report.
83 S 12.
84 S 13(1)(b).
85 Eg on Major Hazards, on Arbitrations and a Medical Advisory Committee.
86 S 14.
87 S 14(2).
88 When the Department of Employment was abolished in 1995 the health and safety functions were transferred to the Secretary of State for the Environment; the sponsoring department is now the DETR.
89 S 50(3).

detail in section 15. Overall, the power lies within the purposes of Part I of the Act which are set out in section 1. This is a general statement in straightforward language covering securing health, safety and welfare; protection against danger and risks to health at work: controlling explosives and highly flammable or dangerous substances and controlling emissions into the atmosphere of noxious or offensive substances[90]. Regulations are intended as a continuing and important method of providing detailed legal regulation where it is felt that this is required. It means, in effect, continuation of previous practice.

A novel approach is set out in section 16 by means of the concept of approved Codes of Practice. The Robens Committee, within its philosophy of self-regulation, encouraged the idea of voluntary Codes of Practice. This provision enables these codes, where appropriate, to be integrated into the fabric of legal control. To supplement the provisions of duties laid down in sections 2–7 the Commission is empowered to approve and issue suitable Codes of Practice[91]. Consent of the Secretary of State is required as is the process of consultation with government departments or other appropriate bodies[92]. Such codes have to be formally dated and published but provision is made for their revision or withdrawal[93].

Of great interest are the provisions as to the use of those codes[94]. It is specifically stated that failure to observe the code will not make a person liable to either civil or criminal proceedings. This is to say the code itself cannot form the basis of legal action. However, where criminal proceedings for the enforcement of a duty are being taken reference may be made to any relevant provision in a Code of Practice. Proof of failure to meet the requirements of the code will be enough to establish a contravention unless the accused can show to the satisfaction of the court that the requirement was complied with in another way[95].

Enforcement is the responsibility of the Executive which has the duty to make adequate arrangements[96]. The Annual Reports of the Commission include a report from the Executive from which the current structuring of the inspectorates and the principles upon which they work can be seen. The Act empowers the Secretary of State to transfer the duty of enforcement to local authorities[97]. The appointment of inspectors is the duty of the enforcing authority[98].

The inspector has to be appointed in writing, setting out those of the statutory powers he is entitled to exercise[99]. The powers are detailed in section 20(2) of the Act and are aimed at ensuring that he can legally overcome obstruction to his lawful work. He is given, for example, power of entry at any reasonable time or at any time where there is danger. He may make examinations and investigations and may direct that matters be left undisturbed as long as is

90   S 1(1)(a)–(d).
91   S 16(1).
92   S 16(3).
93   S 16(4), (5).
94   There are, of course, important precedents eg the Highway Code in road traffic law and the Industrial Relations Codes. The use of codes in health and safety law is taken to new lengths in the six sets of EC-inspired provisions which came into force on 1 January 1993 (head 3 below), in which the regulations are short, but filled out extensively with practical advice in the Codes or guidance notes to each.
95   S 17(1), (2).
96   S 18(1).
97   S 18(2).
98   S 19(1).
99   S 19(2).

necessary for him to complete them. He can measure, take photographs, samples and so on. He has the power to ask for relevant information and to require the production of books and documents, both those required to be kept by statute and any other[100]. He has a duty to consult appropriate persons to ensure that nothing he proposes to do is, unknown to him, dangerous[101].

(d) Administrative and criminal enforcement

One of the fundamental dilemmas in the pursuit of health and safety is the balance achieved by the enforcement agencies between consultancy and advisory roles and use of enforcement powers. These powers fall into three categories. The improvement notice is established by section 21. An inspector who believes that one of the statutory provisions is being contravened and that this is likely to be continued or repeated can serve a notice on the person he regards as responsible. This improvement notice must specify the provisions in question and give reasons why the inspector thinks there is a breach. The notice requires the person upon whom it is served to remedy the contravention within a stated period[102]. Where an inspector is of the opinion that activities are being carried on, or are about to be, which are covered by statutory provision and which involve a risk of serious personal injury then he may issue a prohibition notice under section 22. The notice must specify the matters giving rise to the risk and set out the provisions which the inspector believes are being contravened. The notice directs that the activities specified should not be carried on until the matters specified have been remedied. Such a notice may be of immediate effect or take effect after a period set out. The Act indicates ways in which these two sorts of notice – improvement and prohibition – may be framed[103]. For example the inspector may refer to any approved Code of Practice. He may offer the person upon whom the notice is served alternative ways of dealing with the danger in question. Provision is made for an appeal where the person on whom the notice of either sort is served wishes to challenge it[104]. An appeal has the effect of suspending the operation of an improvement notice until the issue is determined. A prohibition notice remains effective unless the tribunal accepts an application that it should be suspended[105]. These issues are dealt with by the employment tribunals whose sole function is to determine the technical validity of the notice. In addition an inspector is given executive powers to deal with articles or substances in premises which he believes threaten imminent danger of serious personal injury[106].

It will be obvious that the use of notices is aimed at direct enforcement by the elimination of danger to health and safety. Considerable use is made of both

---

100 S 20(2). Safeguards upon disclosure of information so obtained are set out in s 28. The Commission and Executive are given powers of access to information: s 27.
101 S 20(5).
102 S 22(4).
103 S 23. Obviously the choice will depend upon the nature and imminence of the danger. In 2000/01 there were 6,673 improvement notices issued and 4,385 prohibition notices (148 being deferred notices). As a matter of policy, an inspector cannot be sued in negligence for exercising these notice-issuing powers, even if an appeal is successful: *Harris v Evans* [1998] 3 All ER 522, [1998] 1 WLR 1285, CA.
104 S 24. There are very few such appeals. Non-compliance is a strict offence: *Deary (HMI) v Mansion Hide Upholstery Ltd* [1983] ICR 610, [1983] IRLR 195.
105 S 24(3)(a) and (b).
106 S 25. He must if possible give a sample to a responsible person on the premises and he has to prepare a written report on his action.

types of action. They are plainly proving to be a useful bridge between exhortation and advice and actual prosecution. So far very few cases have occurred of challenge before the employment tribunals and especially of successful challenge.

The provisions for prosecution are based on the terms of section 33 which lay down a long list of offences under the Act. It should be remembered that the specific legislation also provides for large numbers of similar offences. In short it is only necessary to say that section 33 makes breach of the various duties laid down in sections 2–9 and of Regulations an offence. It protects the other methods of enforcement by making breach of the prohibition and improvement notices also an offence. There is a further series of offences aimed at protecting an inspector and ensuring that he is not obstructed or deceived. The usual pattern of procedure is provided for. An offence may be tried, depending upon its gravity, either summarily only or either summarily or on indictment.

This possibility of trial by judge and jury, with the attendant publicity and stigma if convicted, was very much in line with the Robens twin-track approach to criminal prosecution, namely that the aim is to use it only in serious cases (often where other means have failed) *but* to ensure that it is seen to be a serious matter if it has to be resorted to[107]. As seen above, at the time of writing the government are proposing a general increase in penalties by (a) making the majority of offences in section 33 triable either way and (b) where that is the case, increasing the maximum fine on summary conviction to £20,000. Most offences also carry six months' imprisonment on summary conviction. On conviction on indictment, the penalties are imprisonment for a term not exceeding two years, an unlimited fine, or both. Where a criminal prosecution is being brought, it is specifically provided that the onus of proof in relation to what was or was not reasonably practicable is reversed on to the defendant[108].

The penalties available are thus considerable (especially when defence costs are added), but a particularly live issue in recent years has been how these powers should be exercised, because prosecution *policy* plays a major role here. We have already seen that there will often be an emphasis on *not* prosecuting except as a last resort. Once a decision to prosecute is taken[109], however, three further questions of some sensitivity and topicality arise:

(i) *Who should be prosecuted?* The very existence of the punishment of imprisonment shows that the prosecution of individuals is envisaged, and in the early years of the 1974 Act it produced a considerable *in terrorem* effect among managers. However, such prosecutions in practice have proved to be relatively rare. The HSE have tended to take the view that, although an

---

107 This can cause problems when prosecuting a small firm, which could be severely affected by a large fine. In *R v Howe & Son (Engineers) Ltd* [1999] IRLR 434 the Court of Appeal laid down sentencing guidelines, saying that in the case of a small firm there has to be a balance between imposing a fine high enough to affect the owners/shareholders, but not so high as to risk bankrupting the firm and losing jobs.

108 Health and Safety at Work Act 1974, s 40. This statutory reversal of the burden of proof incorporates a vital issue of policy in this context and because of that does not infringe the Human Rights Act 1998: *Davies v Health and Safety Executive* [2002] EWCA Crim 2949, [2003] IRLR 170.

109 Factors taken into account will include the gravity of the offence, the general record and approach of the offender, public effect (including deterrence) and realistic prospect of conviction (adopting the CPS approach). The practice is adopted by the prosecuting authorities of preparing in advance for the court a statement of what the authorities believe are the relevant (aggravating) factors, and any mitigatory factors (eg steps taken to remedy the fault; good health and safety record) which may be significant on sentencing; this was suggested in *R v Friskies Petcare UK Ltd* [2000] 2 Cr App R (S) 401 and in the jargon they are known as 'Friskies statements'.

individual may be prosecuted if the facts are strong enough, that could be counter-productive because in many cases a health and safety breach will be the result of the negligence of a whole chain of people, rather than one named director, manager or employee. Indeed, simply to go for the individual in a case of managerial failure may be unfair[110]. Thus, the emphasis is on prosecuting the firm or organisation (where, for example, the stigma effect may be greatest), and this leads to the second question.

(ii) *For what is the company or organisation liable?* Vicarious liability is well developed in the law of tort, but has always raised real problems in criminal law. How do you establish corporate liability? Traditionally, this has been done by the 'identification doctrine', ie that the company acts through its 'guiding brains' only, usually meaning at board level. Thus, in the leading case of *Tesco Supermarkets Ltd v Nattrass*[111] a supermarket chain was not liable for breaches of the Trade Descriptions Act 1968 by the manager of one of its stores. Clearly, to apply that doctrine to health and safety cases could be disastrous because many dangerous practices evolve at shop floor level, so that at board level the company would often be able to deny knowledge and hence liability. In two important cases, the Court of Appeal have held that *Tesco Supermarkets* is *not* to apply under the Health and Safety at Work Act 1974. In *R v British Steel plc*[112] they stressed this as a matter of protective policy, based themselves on the *strict* liability (subject only to the defence of reasonable practicability) imposed by the Act, and said that to apply the identification doctrine would 'drive a juggernaut' through the Act.

Likewise, in *R v Gateway Foodmarkets Ltd*[113] (a case of a fatality through a dangerous practice growing up in a particular supermarket, of which the board had no knowledge) a similar result was achieved, stating that the policy in the recent case law on sections 2 and 3 was to impose liability on 'the employer', that there was no need to show that the company itself was to blame (hence the inapplicability of the identification doctrine) and that (although there might be further problems as to the eventual *depth* of a company's responsibility within its organisation) it was certainly the case that safety lapses at local managerial level *were* to be attributed to the company as employer. In both cases the company was convicted and its appeal rejected[114]. One glitch in this analysis occurred in *R v Nelson Group Services (Maintenance) Ltd*[115], an important test case for the HSE concerning the liability of post-privatisation gas maintenance organisations under both the Act and the relevant gas Regulations. One of the defendant company's fitters had failed to connect a domestic appliance properly, leaving a dangerous situation. The fitter had clearly not done everything reasonably practicable to ensure safety, but the company argued that at *its* level it had

---

110 Eg the only successful prosecution following the Zeebrugge ferry disaster was of the individual bosun who had left the bow doors open on that occasion; the organisation which had allowed that to happen was not convicted.
111 [1972] AC 153, [1971] 2 All ER 127, HL.
112 [1995] IRLR 310, CA.
113 [1997] IRLR 189, CA.
114 Note that the 1974 Act, s 37 adopts a very standard legislative provision that where a body corporate commits an offence with the consent or connivance of, as attributable to the neglect of, 'any director, manager, secretary or other similar officer', that individual may also be prosecuted. However, that only applies to senior, decision-making management: *R v Boal* [1992] QB 591, [1992] 3 All ER 177, CA.
115 [1999] IRLR 646, CA.

indeed done that which was reasonably practicable by training and instructing the fitter well – they were therefore not to be made liable by an individual failing by a fitter. The Court of Appeal agreed (drawing support from the fact that under the gas Regulations the fitter himself could also be liable). In a sense, this case only explored further the loose end in *Gateway Foodmarkets* (which was relied on) as to depth of responsibility, but in as much as it established that the reasonable practicability defence has to be operated at a relatively high level in the company (albeit not actually at board level, given that the court did not apply *Tesco Supermarkets*), it could be seen as contrary to the strict/protective intent of the Act. In the light of this, the case was effectively reversed when the Management of Health and Safety at Work Regulations were reissued in 1999, the new regulation 21 providing:

> 'Nothing in the relevant statutory provisions[116] shall operate so as to afford an employer a defence in any criminal proceedings for a contravention of those proceedings by reason of any act or default of ... an employee of his ... '

(iii) *Where does liability lie in a fatal accident case?* It is, however, when we turn to liability in industrial death cases that the most controversial problems have arisen. Clearly, there can be a prosecution under the Act in the normal way, but the controversy has been whether the law should go further and hold the company liable for manslaughter, on ordinary principles. The HSE have no power to prosecute for this common law crime, and so have to liaise with the CPS; to that end, they entered into a protocol with them in 1998 as to such liaison, modes of investigation and how prosecutions are to be co-ordinated (including the involvement of the police)[117]. In the past, however, a manslaughter charge has been rare, and the usual result of a death has been a health and safety offence conviction with (even on indictment) the perception that the company has evaded the full rigour of the law[118]. There are, on the other hand, two good reasons for this. The first is that, from the HSE's point of view, the mischief to be aimed at is the health and safety breach itself, not the fact that it has caused death. Without being heartless, the difference between a death and a near miss can be one of fortune and inches[119]. The principal health and safety aim is to ensure that the lapse itself does not recur; here, once again, health and safety law and the common

---

116 'Relevant statutory provisions' means (a) the provisions of Pt I (ie the general health and safety provisions) of the 1974 Act and any health and safety regulations and (b) the existing statutory provisions: s 53. In this context, it is the 'reasonable practicability' defences throughout the provisions that are particularly relevant.
117 [1998] NLJ 910, 1007.
118 An analogy may be drawn here with road traffic death cases; technically, in many of them there could be a manslaughter charge but in practice the likelihood is of the charge 'only' being the statutory offence of causing death by dangerous driving, with the public perception of light sentencing, a point often commented on in the media by relatives of the deceased.
119 A good example of this is the regulatory scheme on compulsory reporting to the HSE, which covers accidents, illnesses *or dangerous occurrences*, the point being that the latter are considered potentially just as serious, with a need to rectify the factors causing the danger. It all goes back to the emphasis (seen above) in modern health and safety law on *risk*, not actual harm. For an example of this, see Ecclestone (Solicitor to the HSE) 'Work related deaths' [1998] NLJ 910, and for a criticism based on traditional common law grounds, see the letter in reply by Professor Celia Wells [1998] NLJ 1007.

law (wanting punishment and perceived retribution) part company. The second reason is that the common law of manslaughter has been notoriously difficult to apply to a corporate defendant; when tried, it has usually failed. Thus, a health and safety charge as an alternative has always had the practical advantage that it may well actually *succeed*, and that in the longer term that will be the stronger deterrent to neglect by companies (which, after all, is the policy aim of the HSE). This second point has now been dramatically reaffirmed in *A-G's Reference (No 2 of 1999)*[120] which arose from the acquittal of a train operating company on multiple manslaughter charges after the Southall rail disaster in 1997. The company had pleaded guilty to health and safety offences, and had been fined £1.5m. However, on the manslaughter point the Court of Appeal held that 'a non-human defendant cannot be convicted of manslaughter by gross negligence in the absence of evidence establishing the guilt of an identified human being for the same crime'[121]. That was because at common law the identification doctrine (*Tesco Supermarkets*) applies in a manslaughter case; the relaxation of this rule under the 1974 Act in *British Steel* and *Gateway Foodmarkets* was only possible as a matter of statutory interpretation, and could not be translated into the common law. At the end of his judgment, Rose LJ pointed to what the court saw as the real way forward, namely (overdue) Parliamentary action on the Law Commission Report No 237 (1996) which suggests, as part of the overall reform of the law of manslaughter, a new statutory offence of corporate killing based on 'management failure', *not* involving the doctrine of identification. As seen above, at the time of writing, the present government have shown interest in this proposal, which could form the basis of a major change in this area during the currency of this edition, especially in the light of public concern over the recent rail disasters.

(e) Joint regulation

It cannot be said that the Act, despite the major impact it has had, introduced many new ways of regulating health and safety by law. So far, all that has been discussed has been basically a restructuring and development of the established approach. In one respect, however, there was a major shift in emphasis. This lay in the statutory provision for integration of the workforce in the machinery aimed at securing health and safety. This was sought to be done principally through the creation of statutory safety representatives and safety committees. Neither concept was new – the safety representative was familiar in mining and safety committees were a fairly common voluntary device, widely spread especially in manufacturing industry. The Act put these methods of ensuring practical concern with routine health and safety into a prominent place in the reformed structure. For reasons which will be explained, the significance of joint regulation seemed to be on the wane in recent years, but events and EC law have had the

---

120 [2000] IRLR 417, CA. The decision coincided with the publication of the report into the rail disaster in question, and was immediately said to mean that no manslaughter charges would be brought in relation to the Paddington rail disaster in 1999.
121 Again, the point is that many major accidents will be the result of a complex chain of events/neglects, not attributable to a particular individual, especially not one at 'guiding brain' level. A further result would be that convictions would only be likely against very small companies, run by one or two people, leaving large concerns immune.

effect of reviving interest in it. It is necessary first, however, to set out the scheme as originally set up in the Act.

The first provision in this respect, set out in section 2(3), is for the preparation by an employer of a notice. This has to cover two points. It must set out the employer's general policy on health and safety. It must also describe the organisation and arrangements set up by the employer in order to carry out his policy. The notice and any revisions of it must be made known to all the employees. In this way the Act seeks to ensure that the employer gives thought to his responsibilities and that the workforce is made aware of what is being done[122].

The detailed rules on safety representatives and safety committees have been laid down in Regulations. The Act in section 2 merely sets out the framework. This provides for the appointment by recognised trade unions[123] of safety representatives from amongst the employees concerned. These representatives have the right to represent the employees in consultation with the employer and the powers are set out by regulation. There is a corresponding duty on the employer to consult the representatives so appointed[124]. The purpose of such consultation is said to be co-operation in promoting and developing ways of ensuring health and safety and checking their effectiveness.

Safety committees have to be formed by an employer when he is asked to do so by the safety representatives. The function of the committee, set out in the Act, is said to be the monitoring of the measures taken to ensure health and safety. Other functions may be prescribed by Regulations and it is to these Regulations that attention must be turned.

Safety Representative and Safety Committees Regulations were promulgulated in 1976 and were accompanied by a Code of Practice[125]. These deal first with the appointment of safety representatives. Recognised trade unions are given the right to appoint safety representatives. The obvious basis for appointments is the bargaining unit but an indication is given that trade unions might jointly appoint a representative. The process is tied into the existing industrial relations structure[126]. Guidance notes on this area set out useful criteria, rather than lay down rules to be followed. Disputes are to be settled under the industrial relations machinery[127]. The emphasis is upon flexibility so

122 S 2(3) provides for exceptions to this duty to be prescribed by regulation. Employers with less than five employees are excepted by the Employers' Health and Safety Policy Statements (Exception) Regulations 1975, SI 1975/1584; see *Osborne v Bill Taylor of Huyton Ltd* [1982] ICR 168, [1982] IRLR 17. This requirement of writing is taken further in some of the Six Pack regulations, with their emphasis on risk assessment and information (see head 3).

123 See ch 2, head 3. The right of employees to *elect* such representatives, as well as the power of appointment by a recognised trade union, was originally provided for in s 2(5). This provision was repealed by s 125, of the Employment Protection Act 1975 – a rather sad example of the (then) aim of trade union growth taking precedence over another working aim. It is in this context that we have seen significant changes (below).

124 S 2(6).

125 The Health and Safety Commission publishes a useful booklet with both the regulations and the code conveniently set out in parallel. The Regulations and Code came into force in 1978 and were slightly amended by the Management of Health and Safety at Work Regulations 1992 in order to comply with the 'Framework Directive' (89/391/ EEC)..

126 Code, para 3. One legal limitation, however, is that the representative must be an 'employee'; any person not coming within that definition (eg an agency worker) is not validly appointed and would not have the special protection of the Employment Rights Act 1996, s 100(1)(b) (see p 595 below) if dismissed: *Costain Building & Engineering Ltd v Smith* [2000] ICR 215.

127 Eg reference to conciliation.

that adequate arrangements are made. This is particularly so in respect of numbers. Nowhere is specific guidance given. The Regulations do lay down one important qualification. A safety representative must, as far as reasonably practicable, have two years experience either with the employer or in similar employment[128].

The functions of the safety representatives are set out in some detail[129]. Generally there is the task of consulting with the employer on health and safety matters. To perform this detailed functions are set out[130]. These are to investigate potential hazards and the causes of accidents; to investigate employee complaints; to raise matters on health, safety and welfare with the employer; to carry out inspections; to consult with the various inspectors and enforcement authorities; to receive information and to attend meetings of safety committees. Provision is made that the representative should be given time off with pay to perform these functions[131] with the protection of recourse to an employment tribunal[132]. The Code emphasises the positive use of these functions and the need for the development of expertise[133].

Special powers are given to safety representatives in respect of inspections of the workplace, and conditions are set out[134]. Written notice must be given to the employer of the intention to inspect. Inspections at less than three-month intervals can only be made by agreement with the employer or where there has been a substantial change in conditions of work or where new information has been published by the Commission or Executive as to hazards. Inspections may be carried out in addition where there has been a notifiable accident or disease and inspection is safe and the represented employees' interests are involved[135]. The employer has to provide facilities and assistance where there is such an inspection. The guidance notes indicate some of the principal aims of inspections, for example general tours, sampling of dangerous processes, monitoring of dangerous activities. Similar powers are laid down in respect of inspection of documents and the right to information[136].

Safety committees have only brief mention in the Regulations. The employer must, if asked, establish such a committee in consultation with the safety representatives making the request, within three months, and he must post a notice drawing attention to the committee and the area of the workplace it covers[137]. The guidance notes take the matter little further, but express the view that a committee should evolve from the particular needs.

The original aim was to link these structures firmly into the existing industrial relations machinery. However, once that machinery itself came under attack in the 1980s and 1990s, and union membership and recognition declined substantially that original model in fact became a source of weakness. Of course it has always been open to an employing concern to have a safety representative or committee system even where there was no recognised union, but the evidence

128 Reg 2(4). For special employment, see reg 8.
129 Regs 4(1) and 4A.
130 Reg 4(1)(a)–(h).
131 Reg 4(2). The calculation of pay is laid down in the Schedule.
132 Reg 11.
133 Code, para 5. A great deal of effort has been made to train representatives – much under the auspices of the TUC.
134 Reg 5.
135 Reg 6.
136 Reg 7.
137 Reg 9.

showed another important move away from joint regulation – not only was there the decline in formal union recognition, but there was also a move in any event to view health and safety matters as an element of the increasingly dominant 'human resource management' philosophy, ie to reclaim it as an area of managerial prerogative[138]. This has, however, changed due to EC law. There was no challenge directly in this area, but the problem was the indirect effect of the decision in *EC Commission v United Kingdom*[139] by the ECJ that, in the areas of collective redundancies and transfers of undertakings the restriction of consultation rights to cases where there are recognised trade unions does not meet the requirements of the backing directives in those areas to consult with 'workers or their representatives'. The point was that similar requirements exist in the Framework Directive[140] which lies behind the Management of Health and Safety at Work Regulations 1992 (considered below). As a result, the previous government felt obliged to introduce the Health and Safety (Consultation with Employees) Regulations 1996[141] which broadens the obligation on an employer to consult on health and safety matters. Where there is a recognised trade union, the original 1977 Regulations continue to apply *but* where that is not the case the 1996 Regulations require consultation with elected 'representatives of employee safety'[142], and to give them such information as is 'necessary to enable them to participate fully and effectively in the consultation'[143]. The employer must provide reasonable training and facilities and an elected representative is allowed paid time off work to perform the functions; employment protection (against detriment or dismissal) is extended to representatives. While these provisions are not as extensive as those applying to safety representatives under the 1977 Regulations (for example, not giving positive powers of inspection or the right to require a safety committee), they have revitalised the question of *joint* regulation of health and safety in the workplace but, as with collective redundancies and transfers of undertakings, it is interesting to see that the proposed model for this is not the old one of trade unions as the sole conduit[144].

3 EUROPEAN INSPIRED REGULATIONS AND CODES

Statutory Regulations have long been an essential method of supplementing statutes that seek to protect health and safety at work. They enable detailed legislative rules to be prepared under the aegis of the basic statute, from time to time, as needs determine. By their nature such Regulations have tended to be precise and detailed, dealing with specific difficulties and dangers. They attract

---

138 Millward et al *Workplace Industrial Relations in Transition* (1992) pp 159–164. It remained the case that accident rates were higher in companies that did not have jointly appointed representatives or committees.
139 Cases C-382/92, 383/92 [1994] ICR 664, [1994] IRLR 392, ECJ. This led to the Collective Redundancies and Transfers of Undertakings (Protection of Employment) (Amendment) Regulations 1995, SI 1995/2587, which require consultation with recognised trade unions *or* directly elected employee representatives: see pp 85 and 95 above.
140 Directive 89/391/EEC.
141 SI 1996/1513.
142 Reg 4; the alternative is to consult the employees directly.
143 Reg 5.
144 James and Walters 'Non-union involvement: the case of health and safety at work' (1997) 26 ILJ 35.

little legal controversy as their requirements have generally been clearly drafted and disputes have normally concerned their application, rather than their meaning. Of recent years as the work environment has become more diverse and complicated, with many new dangers, the flow of Regulations has increased. The aim of the EC to establish common factors throughout the member states has, over the last decade, increased that flow. Health and safety is an obvious and important concern for the Community, and it is an area in which the setting of common standards, covering essential questions of health and safety, based on technical considerations and proved practice, was relative easy and fitted well into the overall aim of basing competition upon uniform conditions (the economic 'level playing field' argument).

After a relatively slow trickle of Regulations, the process has more recently changed into top gear. At the beginning of 1993 six major Regulations and their accompanying Codes of Practice came into effect[145]. The Health and Safety Executive has issued six booklets (the 'Six Pack') setting out provisions of the Regulations and approved Codes of Practice, along with a considerable amount of detailed guidance. Two of the sets of Regulations have since been reissued in slightly extended form.

These fall into two categories – three are very general and apply to most, if not all, places of work and cover very large numbers of employed persons. They are: the Management of Health and Safety at Work Regulations 1999[146]; the Workplace (Health, Safety and Welfare) Regulations 1992[147]; and the Provision and Use of Work Equipment Regulations 1998[148]. The titles indicate the width of these Regulations. The other three deal with slightly more specific issues. They are: the Personal Protective Equipment (EC Directive) Regulations 1992[149]; the Manual Handling Operations Regulations 1992[150]; and the Health and Safety (Display Screen Equipment) Regulations 1992[151].

The Management of Health and Safety at Work Regulations 1999 are backed by an Approved Code of Practice and guidance filling in details and giving helpful examples of what should be done. Since there are Regulations governing 'workplaces' these Regulations are important in their coverage of temporary and mobile sites. It is the pattern of the Regulations, rather than their detail, which is of crucial importance. Regulation 3, for example, makes it clear that these Regulations are the responsibility of the employer, in respect of his own employees and also of those not employed by him but involved arising out of the conduct of the undertaking. They also are the responsibility of a person who is self-employed in respect of his own position and that of those employed by him. It provides that the basic task is risk assessment, which must be repeated whenever there is reason to believe that the original is no longer valid, or where there have been significant changes. Moreover, these general duties were expanded in the 1999 reissuing of the Regulations to include the 'principles of prevention', taken from the Framework Directive. The steps to be taken to ensure the

145 Smith, Goddard, Killalea and Randall *Health and Safety – the Modern Legal Framework* (2nd edn, 2000); *Munkman on Employer's Liability* (13th edn, 2001); Eberlie 'The new health and safety legislation of the European Community' (1990) 19 ILJ 81.
146 SI 1999/3242 – derived from the European instruments 89/391/EEC, 'The Framework Directive', and 91/383/EEC.
147 SI 1992/3004 – derived from the European instrument 89/654/EEC.
148 SI 1998/2306 – derived from the European instrument 89/655/EEC.
149 SI 1992/3139 – derived from the European instrument 89/656/EEC.
150 SI 1992/2793 – derived from the European instrument 90/269/EEC.
151 SI 1992/2792 – derived from the European instrument 90/270/EEC.

protection of health and safety are expressed in very general terms in regulation 5 as such arrangements 'as are appropriate with particular reference to the size'. Where five or more are employed on site the arrangements have to be recorded. In the same way 'as is appropriate' there has to be health surveillance and the protection of health is further described in regulation 6 which provides for one or more competent person to be made responsible, with co-operation secured where there is more than one and with adequate time allowed for the duties to be discharged[152]. Those have to be provided with the necessary knowledge of the dangers and with proper training. Serious and imminent dangers, or areas of danger, are specially dealt with in a similar way with the additional duty to restrict access, and to deal with anyone who is exposed to danger who has to be told and allowed to stop work and go to a place of safety[153]. By the new regulation 9, necessary contact must be maintained with external agencies, particularly as regards first aid, emergency medical care and rescue work. Particular attention is given to ensuring that employees know of the risks, of the relevant preventive and protective measures and the procedures to be adopted. The same applies to outside employees or to the self-employed[154]. Where workplaces are shared, there has to be co-operation. There is an overall duty, in entrusting tasks to workers, to ensure that their capabilities, as regards matters of health and safety, are taken into account. Training has to be given on recruitment and repeated periodically. It has to be reinforced where there are new factors or increased risks[155]. Regulation 14 stresses that the employee has to use the workplace in accordance with the instructions and training, and to make known serious or immediate dangers[156]. Finally, regulation 22 makes the important point that breach of the Regulations does not, of itself, give rise to a civil action.[157]

The Workplace (Health, Safety and Welfare) Regulations 1992 and the accompanying Approved Code of Practice has a similar framework. Its scope is huge, applying as it does to every workplace with few exceptions[158]. Regulation 4 puts the duty to ensure compliance with these Regulations upon the employer. The basic duty, again in general terms, is to maintain the place of work, equipment, devices and systems. They have to be cleaned as appropriate, and maintained in an efficient state, working order and good repair[159]. The Regulations go on to cover matters such as ventilation, temperature in indoor workplaces – which must be reasonable and not involve the discharge of fumes that are injurious or offensive, lighting, cleanliness, working space, workstations, floor and traffic routes[160]. Regulation 13 deals with the prevention of falls and falling objects, and dangers likely to cause scalds, burns, and from substances

152 Reg 7.
153 Reg 8.
154 Regs 9 and 11.
155 Reg 13.
156 Reg 14(2); reg 15 covers temporary workers.
157 This provision, inserted at a late stage into the finalised form of the Regulations in 1992, has led to arguments that the Directive has not been fully transposed, due to the lack of full remedies. In *Cross v Highlands and Islands Enterprise* [2001] IRLR 336, Ct of Sess (OH) Lord Macfadyen held against this argument (and, for good measure, held that the Framework Directive does not have direct effect) but there have been suggestions that the government might remove reg 22 in future legislation.
158 Reg 3. It does not apply to a ship, building operations or any construction within s 176 of the Factories Act 1961. The regulations discussed in the previous paragraph will, of course, have to be taken into account.
159 Reg 5.
160 Regs 6–12, respectively.

that may scald, burn, or are poisonous or corrosive. The level of detail is best illustrated from the notes of guidance which cover well-known hazards such as ladders, roofwork, stacking, and the loading and unloading of vehicles. Attention is paid to windows, doors and skylights. Cleaning itself has to be done in a safe manner[161]. Regulation 17 deals with the organisation of traffic routes, so as to enable pedestrians and vehicles to circulate safely. The Approved Code of Practice and guidance notes go into greater detail on special dangers, for example drawings illustrating a safe loading bay are provided[162]. The remaining Regulations[163] deal with a variety of aspects – escalators, moving walkways, sanitary conveniences, drinking water, facilities for clothing and for eating meals. The fully comprehensive nature of these Regulations clearly indicates their importance and the width of protection they seek to ensure.

The same can be said of the Provision and Use of Work Equipment Regulations 1998. Their primary objective is to ensure, as their title indicates, the provision of safe work equipment and its safe usage. By now the structure will be obvious from the discussion in previous paragraphs of the other Regulations. Duties are placed both on the employer and employees, and apply also to the self-employed[164]. These duties form two groups: one covers selection of suitable equipment, its maintenance, information as to its use and appropriate training[165]; the other deals with equipment to deal with special dangers such as contact with dangerous parts, fires, explosions, contact with hot and cold surfaces, and instability of materials[166]. The purpose of these Regulations is to amplify the control and to make general duties more explicit. It is explained that most of the old law is replaced. Despite many repeals there is likely to remain some overlap, but it will be obvious that since the aim of the Regulations is protection that is not a matter of real concern. There is even an element of vagueness in that the guidance to the Regulations include a list of some thirty-eight articles, ranging from dumper trucks to hammers and meat cleavers, but expressly stated not to be an exhaustive list[167]. The duties cover suitability of equipment, its maintenance, specific risks, and the need to give information of risks and to train those likely to use the equipment[168]. Regulation 10 makes the important point that these general Regulations are said to be read as in conformity with other detailed Community directives, principally on product standards.

161 Regs 14–16. Doors and gates are reg 18.
162 Reg 17.
163 Regs 19–21.
164 Reg 4.
165 Regs 5–10. Significantly, in the first case in the Court of Appeal on the Work Equipment Regulations, the maintenance requirement in reg 6 was held to impose strict liability: *Stark v Post Office* [2000] ICR 1013, [200] PIQR 105, CA: see p 869 above.
166 Regs 11–24. Reg 11 ('Dangerous parts of machinery') is of particular interest for two reasons – (1) it is a good example of the 'hierarchy of measures' drafting technique sometimes used in the Six Pack (use fixed guards; if not possible, use other guards and protections; if not possible, use jigs, holders, etc; if not possible, inform, instruct, supervise and train) with the onus on the employer to get as high as possible; (2) it replaced the Factories Act 1961 s 14, one of the strongest provisions of the previous law, imposing strict liability for accidents at dangerous machines. One concern was whether reg 11 watered down this protection; this has not yet been specifically tested, but in *Stark v Post Office* (n 165 above) the general point was made that the Six Pack Regulations are not to be interpreted so as to lessen any existing protection.
167 Reg 2.
168 Regs 5–9.

The Personal Protective Equipment (EC Directive) Regulations 1992 covers its topic in a similar way, showing the basic intent very clearly and dealing with a most comprehensive range of matters. An interesting underlying general principle concerning the provision of protective equipment is made clear – that such provision is to be regarded as the 'last resort' to be used only where there is no practical way of obviating the danger itself [169]. That said, the now familiar approach is used to cover capability, assessment, maintenance and provision for storage. Information, instruction and training are equally provided for [170]. The employer has a duty to see that the equipment is properly used and the employee has a duty to report any defect in, or loss of, the equipment.

A rather different approach is adopted in the Manual Handling Operations Regulations 1992. These Regulations make it clear that they are put forward largely as guidance, since they, of necessity, cover an infinitely wide range of actions that a worker might be called upon to take in the course of his work. For this reason the Regulations take the form of a flow chart of questions that have to be asked and considered – does the work involve manual handling? Is there a risk of injury? Is it practicable to avoid the handling? Can the process be automated or mechanised? If these questions still leave manual handling then the obvious safety safeguards have to be put in place. In other words each task must be assessed and a way devised to perform it in a way that reduces the risk to a minimum. Measures to introduce this must then be considered to see if the risk that remains is acceptable. Once a system is devised, again one of the classic dangers has to be guarded against – any change in conditions must be the trigger for a review.

The Health and Safety (Display Screen Equipment) Regulations 1992 cover a modern development that is becoming an increasing feature of work. Their application basically is made to depend upon the intensity of use and the Regulations give careful guidance as to this, rather than a definitive definition. Some work is said to be clearly within scope – that involving word processing, or as a secretary, journalist or librarian, the categories mentioned as examples likely to have regular screen work. Another list indicates categories of work where the use may well cause the individual user to be covered by the Regulations if the time spent so dictates – client manager, scientist, building society manager, receptionist, airways clerk. Finally, others, such as a senior manager, may have access to a screen but will, because of infrequency of use, be basically a non-user. Again it is stressed that the possibility of a reduction of the risks has to be assessed. Daily exposure has to be monitored, care given to the health of eyes and eyesight, and training given and information that may be helpful given.

As indicated at the start of this chapter these Regulations show clearly both a pattern of regulation and above all an attitude as to what is expected. It will be difficult to resist breaches of Regulations if there has not been a considerable amount of forethought, careful consideration of risks and how to protect against them. There must be repeated inspection, information and training. Two final, general comments may be made. The first is that responsibilities here overlap so that both the employer and the employee may have a concurrent responsibility. If that gives a headache to the civil lawyers looking at compensation aspects, so be it; the Regulations are concerned at prevention which must be accorded undoubted priority. It is a very healthy development in the law. The second

169 Reg 4.
170 Reg 4.

comment is that this is law that is here to stay, with the EU as the prime mover. The previous government made some political capital out of taking to themselves in the Deregulation and Contracting Out Act 1994 a power to repeal (by an expedited procedure) health and safety legislation which, they said, was a burden on business. If anyone actually believed that large parts of the above, reformed legislation would be swept aside in a blaze of deregulatory zeal, they will have been sadly disappointed because one of the novel aspects of these Regulations is that they are of course entrenched by EU Directives. Thus, when in 1995 we finally had the one and only repealing order it swept aside a grand total of twelve pieces of legislation including (crucially) the Home Work (Lampshades) Order 1929 and the Horizontal Milling Machines (Amendment) Regulations 1934. Given that this whole subject of industrial law is an area in which substantial gaps between political invective and employment reality are not exactly unknown, that is perhaps not a bad note on which to conclude.

Index

Employee, duties of—*contd*
  inventions, 184-186. *See also*
    Employee's inventions
  misuse or disclosure of confidential
    information 176-184
    public interest, and 180-183
      common law 180-181
      statute 181-184
    Public Interest Disclosure Act
      1998, 181-183
    remedies 179-180
  obedience 168-169
    dismissal, and 169
    'lawful' order 168
    legality, and 169
    personal danger, and 169
Employee's inventions 184-186
  common law 184
  Patents Act 1977, 185-186
  Patents Act 1949, s56(2) 184
Employer, duties of 152-168
  confidentiality 164-166
  data protection, and 164-166
  deal promptly and properly with
    grievances 161-162
    grievance procedures, and 162
    significance of 162
  exercise of care 155-158
    competent and safe fellow
      employees 155
    generally 155
    health and safety 155
    indemnity against expenses 155
    loss of employee's goods 155
    references, 156-158. *See also* References
    safety complaints 155
  information as to pension rights 163
  pay wages 152
  permanent health insurance, and 166-
    168
    negation of rights 167
  provide reasonably suitable working
    environment 162-163
  provide work 152-155
    exceptional cases 153
    garden leave clause 154
    no express term, where 154
    stoppages of work, and 154-155
  treat employee with respect 158-161
    constructive dismissal, and 159
    disapplication of term 160-161
    fair dismissal procedures, and 158-
      159
    stigma damages 160
    termination, and 160-161
**Employer and employee, relationship of
  9-34**

**Employer and employee, relationship
  of**—*contd*
  agency workers 22-23
    EU intervention 29
  atypical workers 18-29
    EU intervention 24-29
    umbrella or global contract 20-21
  casual work 21-22
  company directors, and 17-18
  control test 11
  definition 10-16
  fixed-term employees
    EU intervention 26-29
  fundamental importance of 9-10
  government departments, approach
    of 13
  independent contractor, and 9-10
  'instinctive' approach 12-13
  integration test 11
  'irreducible minimum' 12
  labour-only sub-contracting, and 17
  multiple or pragmatic approach 11
  mutuality of obligations 12
  outworkers 18-23
  part-time workers, 18-22
    EU intervention 24-26
  particular applications 16-18
  statements and intentions of parties
    14-16
  temporary work 19
  tests 10-11
  vicarious liability, and 16-17
Employment
  wider definition 32-34
Employment Appeal Tribunal 497-500
  appeal from employment tribunal
    525-526
  appeal on point of law only 498-499
  composition 498
  fresh evidence 499
  precedent, and 499-500
  remitting case for further
    consideration 499
Employment tribunals 495-497
  administration 495-497
  appeal 525-526
  arbitration, and 508-509
  composition 496
  compromise agreements 520-521
  conciliation 518-521
    ACAS 518-520
  contract claims 528-529
  costs 497
  hearing 522-525
    decision 524-525
    informality 523-524
    preliminary issue 522